THE ECONOMICS OF
MONEY, BANKING, AND
FINANCIAL MARKETS

THE ECONOMICS OF
MONEY, BANKING, AND
FINANCIAL MARKETS

Thirteenth Edition

Frederic S. Mishkin
Columbia University

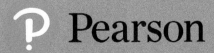
Pearson

Please contact https://support.pearson.com/getsupport/s/ with any queries on this content

Cover Images by Stuart Monk/Shutterstock, Sergiy Palamarchuk/Shutterstock, fstockfoto/Shutterstock, nobeastsofierce/Shutterstock, Treter/Shutterstock

Chapter Opener image: rsooll/Shutterstock

Cataloging-in-Publication Data is available on file at the Library of Congress.

3 2021

Rental
ISBN-10: 0-13-689435-6
ISBN-13: 978-0-13-689435-3

To Sally

About the Author

Frederic S. Mishkin is the Alfred Lerner Professor of Banking and Financial Institutions at the Graduate School of Business, Columbia University. He is also a Research Associate at the National Bureau of Economic Research, co-director of the U.S. Monetary Policy Forum, a member of the Squam Lake Working Group on Financial Reform, and past president of the Eastern Economics Association. Since receiving his Ph.D. from the Massachusetts Institute of Technology in 1976, he has taught at the University of Chicago, Northwestern University, Princeton University, and Columbia. He has also received an honorary professorship from the People's (Renmin) University of China. From 1994 to 1997, he was Executive Vice President and Director of Research at the Federal Reserve Bank of New York and an associate economist of the Federal Open Market Committee of the Federal Reserve System. From September 2006 to August 2008, he was a member (governor) of the Board of Governors of the Federal Reserve System.

Professor Mishkin's research focuses on monetary policy and its impact on financial markets and the aggregate economy. He is the author of more than twenty books, including *Macroeconomics: Policy and Practice,* Second Edition (Pearson, 2015); *Financial Markets and Institutions,* Ninth Edition (Pearson, 2018); *Monetary Policy Strategy* (MIT Press, 2007); *The Next Great Globalization: How Disadvantaged Nations Can Harness Their Financial Systems to Get Rich* (Princeton University Press, 2006); *Inflation Targeting: Lessons from the International Experience* (Princeton University Press, 1999); *Money, Interest Rates, and Inflation* (Edward Elgar, 1993); and *A Rational Expectations Approach to Macroeconometrics: Testing Policy Ineffectiveness and Efficient Markets Models* (University of Chicago Press, 1983). In addition, he has published more than 200 articles in such journals as *American Economic Review, Journal of Political Economy, Econometrica, Quarterly Journal of Economics, Journal of Finance,* and *Journal of Monetary Economics.*

Professor Mishkin has served on the editorial board of *American Economic Review* and has been an associate editor at *Journal of Business and Economic Statistics, Journal of Applied Econometrics, Journal of Economic Perspectives, Journal of International Money and Finance,* and *Journal of Money, Credit and Banking*; he also served as the editor of the Federal Reserve Bank of New York's *Economic Policy Review.* He is currently an associate editor (member of the editorial board) at six academic journals, including *International Finance; Finance India; Review of Development Finance; Borsa Economic Review; PSU Research Review* and *Emerging Markets;* and *Finance and Trade.* He has been a consultant to the Board of Governors of the Federal Reserve System, the World Bank, and the International Monetary Fund, as well as to many central banks throughout the world. He was also a member of the International Advisory Board to the Financial Supervisory Service of South Korea and an advisor to the Institute for Monetary and Economic Research at the Bank of Korea. Professor Mishkin was a Senior Fellow at the Federal Deposit Insurance Corporation's Center for Banking Research and was an academic consultant to and serves on the Economic Advisory Panel and Monetary Advisory Panel of the Federal Reserve Bank of New York.

Brief Contents

PART 1   Introduction   1

   1   Why Study Money, Banking, and Financial Markets? 2
   2   An Overview of the Financial System 22
   3   What Is Money? 49

PART 2   Financial Markets   63

   4   The Meaning of Interest Rates 64
   5   The Behavior of Interest Rates 86
   6   The Risk and Term Structure of Interest Rates 117
   7   The Stock Market, the Theory of Rational Expectations, and the Efficient Market Hypothesis 141

PART 3   Financial Institutions   163

   8   An Economic Analysis of Financial Structure 164
   9   Banking and the Management of Financial Institutions 188
  10   Economic Analysis of Financial Regulation 216
  11   Banking Industry: Structure and Competition 235
  12   Financial Crises 267

PART 4   Central Banking and the Conduct of Monetary Policy   293

  13   Central Banks and the Federal Reserve System 294
  14   The Money Supply Process 318
  15   Tools of Monetary Policy 343
  16   The Conduct of Monetary Policy: Strategy and Tactics 369

PART 5   International Finance and Monetary Policy   401

  17   The Foreign Exchange Market 402
  18   The International Financial System 425

PART 6   Monetary Theory   453

  19   Quantity Theory, Inflation, and the Demand for Money 454
  20   The *IS* Curve 472
  21   The Monetary Policy and Aggregate Demand Curves 491
  22   Aggregate Demand and Supply Analysis 506
  23   Monetary Policy Theory 549
  24   The Role of Expectations in Monetary Policy 576
  25   Transmission Mechanisms of Monetary Policy 595

Additional Chapters on MyLab Economics

1 Financial Crises in Emerging Market Economies
2 Nonbank Finance
3 Financial Derivatives
4 Conflicts of Interest in the Financial Services Industry

Contents in Detail

PART 1   Introduction   1

CHAPTER 1
Why Study Money, Banking, and Financial Markets?   2

1.1 Why Study Financial Markets? 2
   Debt Markets and Interest Rates 3
   The Stock Market 3

1.2 Why Study Financial Institutions and Banking? 5
   Structure of the Financial System 6
   Banks and Other Financial Institutions 6
   Financial Innovation 6
   Financial Crises 7

1.3 Why Study Money and Monetary Policy? 7
   Money and Business Cycles 7
   Money and Inflation 8
   Money and Interest Rates 10
   Conduct of Monetary Policy 10
   Fiscal Policy and Monetary Policy 11

1.4 Why Study International Finance? 12
   The Foreign Exchange Market 13
   The International Financial System 14

1.5 Money, Banking, and Financial Markets and Your Career 14

1.6 How We Will Study Money, Banking, and Financial Markets 15

Concluding Remarks 16

   Summary 16 • Key Terms 16 • Questions 16 • Applied Problems 17 •
   Data Analysis Problems 18

APPENDIX TO CHAPTER 1
**Defining Aggregate Output, Income, the Price Level,
and the Inflation Rate   19**

Aggregate Output and Income...19
Real Versus Nominal Magnitudes...19
Aggregate Price Level..20
Growth Rates and the Inflation Rate 21

CHAPTER 2
An Overview of the Financial System   22

2.1 Function of Financial Markets 22

2.2 Structure of Financial Markets 25
   Debt and Equity Markets 25
   Primary and Secondary Markets 25

Exchanges and Over-the-Counter Markets 26
Money and Capital Markets 27
2.3 Financial Market Instruments **27**
Money Market Instruments 27

Following the Financial News Money Market Rates   28

Capital Market Instruments 29

Following the Financial News Capital Market Interest Rates   30

2.4 Internationalization of Financial Markets **31**

Global Are U.S. Capital Markets Losing Their Edge?   32

International Bond Market, Eurobonds, and Eurocurrencies 32
World Stock Markets 33
2.5 Function of Financial Intermediaries: Indirect Finance **33**

Following the Financial News Foreign Stock Market Indexes   34

Transaction Costs 34

Global The Importance of Financial Intermediaries Relative to Securities Markets:
An International Comparison   35

Risk Sharing 36
Asymmetric Information: Adverse Selection and Moral Hazard 36
Economies of Scope and Conflicts of Interest 38
2.6 Types of Financial Intermediaries **38**
Depository Institutions 38
Contractual Savings Institutions 40
Investment Intermediaries 41
2.7 Regulation of the Financial System **42**
Increasing Information Available to Investors 42
Ensuring the Soundness of Financial Intermediaries 43
Financial Regulation Abroad 45

Summary 45 • Key Terms 46 • Questions 46 • Applied Problems 47 •
Data Analysis Problems 48

CHAPTER 3
What Is Money?   **49**
3.1 Meaning of Money **49**
3.2 Functions of Money **50**
Medium of Exchange 50
Unit of Account 51
Store of Value 52
3.3 Evolution of the Payments System **53**
Commodity Money 53
Fiat Money 53
Checks 53

Electronic Payment 54
E-Money 54

FYI Are We Headed for a Cashless Society? 55

APPLICATION Will Bitcoin or Other Cryptocurrencies Become
the Money of the Future? 55

3.4 Measuring Money 56
The Federal Reserve's Monetary Aggregates 57

Following the Financial News The Monetary Aggregates 57

FYI Where Are All the U.S. Dollars? 58

Summary 59 • Key Terms 60 • Questions 60 • Applied Problems 61 •
Data Analysis Problems 62

PART 2   Financial Markets   63

CHAPTER 4
The Meaning of Interest Rates **64**

4.1 Measuring Interest Rates 64
Present Value 65

APPLICATION Simple Present Value 66

APPLICATION How Much Is That Jackpot Worth? 67
Four Types of Credit Market Instruments 67
Yield to Maturity 68

APPLICATION Yield to Maturity on a Simple Loan 68

APPLICATION Yield to Maturity and the Yearly Payment on a
Fixed-Payment Loan 70

APPLICATION Yield to Maturity and Bond Price for a Coupon Bond 71

APPLICATION Yield to Maturity on a Perpetuity 73

APPLICATION Yield to Maturity on a Discount Bond 74

4.2 The Distinction Between Interest Rates and Returns 75

Global Negative Interest Rates? Japan First, Then the United States,
Then Europe 76

Maturity and the Volatility of Bond Returns: Interest-Rate Risk 78
Summary 79

4.3 The Distinction Between Real and Nominal Interest Rates 80

APPLICATION Calculating Real Interest Rates 81

Summary 83 • Key Terms 83 • Questions 83 • Applied Problems 84 •
Data Analysis Problems 85

CHAPTER 4 APPENDIX
Measuring Interest-Rate Risk: Duration
Go to MyLab Economics

CHAPTER 5
The Behavior of Interest Rates   **86**

5.1 Determinants of Asset Demand 86
    Wealth 87
    Expected Returns 87
    Risk 87
    Liquidity 88
    Theory of Portfolio Choice 88

5.2 Supply and Demand in the Bond Market 89
    Demand Curve 89
    Supply Curve 90
    Market Equilibrium 91
    Supply and Demand Analysis 92

5.3 Changes in Equilibrium Interest Rates 92
    Shifts in the Demand for Bonds 92
    Shifts in the Supply of Bonds 96

APPLICATION Changes in the Interest Rate Due to a Change in
    Expected Inflation: The Fisher Effect 98

APPLICATION Changes in the Interest Rate Due to a Business Cycle Expansion ... 100

APPLICATION Explaining Current Low Interest Rates in Europe, Japan,
    and the United States: Low Inflation and Secular Stagnation 101

5.4 Supply and Demand in the Market for Money:
    The Liquidity Preference Framework 102

5.5 Changes in Equilibrium Interest Rates in the Liquidity
    Preference Framework 105
    Shifts in the Demand for Money 105
    Shifts in the Supply of Money 105

APPLICATION Changes in the Equilibrium Interest Rate Due to
    Changes in Income, the Price Level, or the Money Supply 106
    Changes in Income 107
    Changes in the Price Level 107
    Changes in the Money Supply 107

5.6 Money and Interest Rates 108

APPLICATION Does a Higher Rate of Growth of the
    Money Supply Lower Interest Rates? 110

    Summary 113 • Key Terms 113 • Questions 113 • Applied Problems 114 •
    Data Analysis Problems 115

CHAPTER 5 APPENDIX
Loanable Funds Framework
Go to MyLab Economics

CHAPTER 6
The Risk and Term Structure of Interest Rates **117**

6.1 Risk Structure of Interest Rates 117
   Default Risk 118

FYI Conflicts of Interest at Credit-Rating Agencies and the Global Financial Crisis 121

APPLICATION The Coronavirus Pandemic and the Baa–Treasury Spread 122
   Liquidity 122
   Income Tax Considerations 123
   Summary 124

APPLICATION Effects of the Trump Tax Cuts on Bond Interest Rates 124

6.2 Term Structure of Interest Rates 125

Following the Financial News Yield Curves 125

   Expectations Theory 127
   Segmented Markets Theory 130
   Liquidity Premium and Preferred Habitat Theories 131
   Evidence on the Term Structure 134

FYI The Yield Curve as a Forecasting Tool for Inflation and the Business Cycle 135

   Summary 135

APPLICATION Interpreting Yield Curves, 1980–2020 135

   Summary 137 • Key Terms 137 • Questions 137 • Applied Problems 139 •
   Data Analysis Problems 139

CHAPTER 7
The Stock Market, the Theory of Rational Expectations,
and the Efficient Market Hypothesis **141**

7.1 Computing the Price of Common Stock 141
   The One-Period Valuation Model 142
   The Generalized Dividend Valuation Model 143
   The Gordon Growth Model 143

7.2 How the Market Sets Stock Prices 144

APPLICATION Monetary Policy and Stock Prices 146

APPLICATION The Coronavirus Stock Market Crash of 2020 146

7.3 The Theory of Rational Expectations 146
   Formal Statement of the Theory 148
   Rationale Behind the Theory 148
   Implications of the Theory 149

7.4 The Efficient Market Hypothesis: Rational Expectations in Financial Markets ..150
   Rationale Behind the Hypothesis 151
   Random-Walk Behavior of Stock Prices 152

Global Should Foreign Exchange Rates Follow a Random Walk? 153

APPLICATION Practical Guide to Investing in the Stock Market 153
   How Valuable Are Reports Published by Investment Advisers? 153

Should You Be Skeptical of Hot Tips? 154

FYI Should You Hire an Ape as Your Investment Adviser?   155
Do Stock Prices Always Rise When There Is Good News? 155
Efficient Market Prescription for the Investor 155

7.5 Why the Efficient Market Hypothesis Does Not Imply That
Financial Markets Are Efficient 156

APPLICATION What Do Stock Market Crashes Tell Us
About the Efficient Market Hypothesis and the Efficiency
of Financial Markets? 157

7.6 Behavioral Finance 157

Summary 158 • Key Terms 159 • Questions 159 • Applied Problems 160 •
Data Analysis Problems 161

PART 3   Financial Institutions   163

CHAPTER 8
An Economic Analysis of Financial Structure   164

8.1 Basic Facts About Financial Structure Throughout The World 164

8.2 Transaction Costs 167
How Transaction Costs Influence Financial Structure 167
How Financial Intermediaries Reduce Transaction Costs 168

8.3 Asymmetric Information: Adverse Selection and Moral Hazard 169

8.4 The Lemons Problem: How Adverse Selection Influences Financial Structure 169
Lemons in the Stock and Bond Markets 170
Tools to Help Solve Adverse Selection Problems 171

FYI The Enron Implosion   172

8.5 How Moral Hazard Affects the Choice Between Debt and Equity Contracts 175
Moral Hazard in Equity Contracts: The Principal–Agent Problem 175
Tools to Help Solve the Principal–Agent Problem 176

8.6 How Moral Hazard Influences Financial Structure in Debt Markets 178
Tools to Help Solve Moral Hazard in Debt Contracts 178
Summary 180

APPLICATION Financial Development and Economic Growth 181

FYI The Tyranny of Collateral   182

APPLICATION Is China a Counterexample to the Importance of Financial
Development? 183

Summary 184 • Key Terms 185 • Questions 185 • Applied Problems 186 •
Data Analysis Problems 187

CHAPTER 9
Banking and the Management of Financial Institutions   188

9.1 The Bank Balance Sheet 188
Liabilities 188
Assets 191

9.2 Basic Banking 192

9.3 General Principles of Bank Management 195
Liquidity Management and the Role of Reserves 195
Asset Management 198
Liability Management 199
Capital Adequacy Management 200

APPLICATION Strategies for Managing Bank Capital 202

APPLICATION How a Capital Crunch Caused a Credit Crunch During the
Global Financial Crisis 203

9.4 Managing Credit Risk 203
Screening and Monitoring 204
Long-Term Customer Relationships 205
Loan Commitments 206
Collateral and Compensating Balances 206
Credit Rationing 206

9.5 Managing Interest-Rate Risk 207
Gap and Duration Analysis 208

APPLICATION Strategies for Managing Interest-Rate Risk 209

9.6 Off-Balance-Sheet Activities 209
Loan Sales 210
Generation of Fee Income 210
Trading Activities and Risk Management Techniques 210

Global Barings, Daiwa, Sumitomo, Société Générale, and JP Morgan Chase:
Rogue Traders and the Principal–Agent Problem   211

Summary 212 • Key Terms 213 • Questions 213 • Applied Problems 214 •
Data Analysis Problem 215

CHAPTER 9 APPENDIX 1
Duration Gap Analysis
Go to MyLab Economics

CHAPTER 9 APPENDIX 2
Measuring Bank Performance
Go to MyLab Economics

CHAPTER 10
Economic Analysis of Financial Regulation   **216**

10.1 Asymmetric Information as a Rationale for Financial Regulation 216
Government Safety Net 216

Global The Spread of Government Deposit Insurance Throughout the World:
Is This a Good Thing?   218

Drawbacks of the Government Safety Net 219

10.2 Types of Financial Regulation 221
Restrictions on Asset Holdings 221
Capital Requirements 222

Global Where Is the Basel Accord Heading After the Global Financial Crisis? 223

Prompt Corrective Action 224
Financial Supervision: Chartering and Examination 224
Assessment of Risk Management 225
Disclosure Requirements 226
Consumer Protection 227
Restrictions on Competition 227
Summary 228

Global International Financial Regulation 229

Summary 231 • Key Terms 232 • Questions 232 • Applied Problems 233 •
Data Analysis Problems 233

CHAPTER 10 APPENDIX
Banking Crises Throughout the World
Go to MyLab Economics

CHAPTER 11
Banking Industry: Structure and Competition **235**
11.1 Historical Development of the Banking System 235
Multiple Regulatory Agencies 237
11.2 Financial Innovation and the Growth of the "Shadow Banking System" 238
Responses to Changes in Demand Conditions: Interest-Rate Volatility 239
Responses to Changes in Supply Conditions: Information Technology 240
Securitization and the Shadow Banking System 242
Avoidance of Existing Regulations 244

FYI Bruce Bent and the Money Market Mutual Fund Panic of 2008 246

Financial Innovation and the Decline of Traditional Banking 246
11.3 Structure of the U.S. Commercial Banking Industry 249
Restrictions on Branching 251
Response to Branching Restrictions 251
11.4 Bank Consolidation and Nationwide Banking 252
The Riegle-Neal Interstate Banking and Branching Efficiency Act of 1994 254
What Will the Structure of the U.S. Banking Industry Look Like in the Future? 254

Global Comparison of Banking Structure in the United States and Abroad 255

Are Bank Consolidation and Nationwide Banking Good Things? 255
11.5 Separation of Banking and Other Financial Service Industries 256
Erosion of Glass-Steagall 256
The Gramm-Leach-Bliley Financial Services Modernization Act of 1999: Repeal of
Glass-Steagall 257
Implications for Financial Consolidation 257
Separation of Banking and Other Financial Services Industries Throughout the World 257

FYI The Global Financial Crisis and the Demise of Large, Free-Standing
Investment Banks 258

11.6 Thrift Industry: Regulation and Structure 258
Savings and Loan Associations 259
Mutual Savings Banks 259
Credit Unions 259
11.7 International Banking 260
Eurodollar Market 260

Global Ironic Birth of the Eurodollar Market   265

Structure of U.S. Banking Overseas 261
Foreign Banks in the United States 262

Summary 263 • Key Terms 264 • Questions 264 • Data Analysis Problems 265

CHAPTER 12
Financial Crises   267

12.1 What is a Financial Crisis? 267
12.2 Dynamics of Financial Crises 268
Stage One: Initial Phase 268
Stage Two: Banking Crisis 270
Stage Three: Debt Deflation 271

APPLICATION The Mother of All Financial Crises: The Great Depression 272
Stock Market Crash 272
Bank Panics 272
Continuing Decline in Stock Prices 273
Debt Deflation 273
International Dimensions 274
12.3 The Global Financial Crisis of 2007–2009 274
Causes of the 2007–2009 Financial Crisis 274

FYI Collateralized Debt Obligations (CDOs)   275

Effects of the 2007–2009 Financial Crisis 276

Inside the Fed Was the Fed to Blame for the Housing Price Bubble?   277

Global The European Sovereign Debt Crisis   280

Height of the 2007–2009 Financial Crisis 281
Government Intervention and the Recovery 282

Global Worldwide Government Bailouts During the 2007–2009 Financial Crisis   282

APPLICATION Could the Coronavirus Pandemic Have Led to a Financial Crisis? 283
12.4 Response of Financial Regulation 284
Macroprudential Versus Microprudential Supervision 284
Dodd-Frank Wall Street Reform and Consumer Protection Act of 2010 285
12.5 Too-Big-to-Fail and Future Regulation 286
What Can Be Done About the Too-Big-to-Fail Problem? 287
Beyond Dodd-Frank: Where Might Regulation Head in the Future? 287

Summary 289 • Key Terms 290 • Questions 290 • Data Analysis Problems 291

PART 4   Central Banking and the Conduct of Monetary Policy   293

CHAPTER 13
Central Banks and the Federal Reserve System   294

13.1 Origins of the Federal Reserve System 294

Inside the Fed The Political Genius of the Founders of the
Federal Reserve System   295

13.2 Structure of the Federal Reserve System 295
Federal Reserve Banks 296

Inside the Fed The Special Role of the Federal Reserve Bank of New York   298
Member Banks 299
Board of Governors of the Federal Reserve System 300
Federal Open Market Committee (FOMC) 300

Inside the Fed The Role of the Research Staff   301

Inside the Fed The FOMC Meeting   302

Inside the Fed Green, Blue, Teal, and Beige: What Do These Colors
Mean at the Fed?   303
Why the Chair of the Board of Governors Really Runs the Show 303

Inside the Fed Styles of Federal Reserve Chairs: Bernanke,
Yellen, and Powell Versus Greenspan   304

13.3 How Independent is the Fed? 305

Inside the Fed Presidential Attacks on the Independence of the Fed   307

13.4 Should the Fed be Independent? 308
The Case for Independence 308
The Case Against Independence 309
Central Bank Independence and Macroeconomic Performance Throughout the World 310

13.5 Explaining Central Bank Behavior 310

Inside the Fed The Evolution of the Fed's Communication Strategy   311

13.6 Structure and Independence of the European Central Bank 312
Differences Between the European System of Central Banks and the Federal
Reserve System 312
Governing Council 312
How Independent Is the ECB? 313

13.7 Structure and Independence of Other Foreign Central Banks 314
Bank of Canada 314
Bank of England 314
Bank of Japan 315
The Trend Toward Greater Independence 315

Summary 316   •   Key Terms 316   •   Questions 316   •   Data Analysis Problems 317

CHAPTER 14
The Money Supply Process   318

14.1 Three Players in the Money Supply Process 318
14.2 The Fed's Balance Sheet 319
Liabilities 319
Assets 320

14.3 Control of the Monetary Base 321
Federal Reserve Open Market Operations 321
Shifts from Deposits into Currency 322
Loans to Financial Institutions 323
Other Factors That Affect the Monetary Base 324
Overview of the Fed's Ability to Control the Monetary Base 324

14.4 Multiple Deposit Creation: A Simple Model 325
Deposit Creation: The Single Bank 325
Deposit Creation: The Banking System 326
Deriving the Formula for Multiple Deposit Creation 329
Critique of the Simple Model 330

14.5 Factors that Determine the Money Supply 331
Changes in the Nonborrowed Monetary Base, MB_n 331
Changes in Borrowed Reserves, BR, from the Fed 331
Changes in the Required Reserve Ratio, rr 331
Changes in Excess Reserves 332
Changes in Currency Holdings 332

14.6 Overview of the Money Supply Process 332

14.7 The Money Multiplier 333
Deriving the Money Multiplier 333
Intuition Behind the Money Multiplier 335
Money Supply Response to Changes in the Factors 336

APPLICATION Quantitative Easing and the Money Supply During the
Global Financial and the Coronavirus Crises 337

Summary 339 • Key Terms 340 • Questions 340 • Applied Problems 341 •
Data Analysis Problems 342

CHAPTER 14 APPENDIX 1
The Fed's Balance Sheet and the Monetary Base
Go to MyLab Economics

CHAPTER 14 APPENDIX 2
The M2 Money Multiplier
Go to MyLab Economics

CHAPTER 14 APPENDIX 3
Explaining the Behavior of the Currency Ratio
Go to MyLab Economics

CHAPTER 14 APPENDIX 4
The Great Depression Bank Panics, 1930–1933, and the Money Supply
Go to MyLab Economics

CHAPTER 15
Tools of Monetary Policy   **343**

15.1 The Market for Reserves and the Federal Funds Rate 343
Demand and Supply in the Market for Reserves 344
How Changes in the Tools of Monetary Policy Affect the Federal Funds Rate 345

APPLICATION How the Federal Reserve's Operating Procedures Limit
Fluctuations in the Federal Funds Rate 349

15.2 Conventional Monetary Policy Tools 350

Open Market Operations 351

Inside the Fed A Day at the Trading Desk   352

Discount Policy and the Lender of Last Resort 353

Inside the Fed Using Discount Policy to Prevent a Financial Panic   355

Reserve Requirements 356

Interest on Excess Reserves 356

15.3 Nonconventional Monetary Policy Tools and Quantitative Easing in the
Wake of the Global Financial Crisis and the Coronavirus Pandemic 357

Liquidity Provision 357

Large-Scale Asset Purchases 358

Inside the Fed Fed Lending Facilities During the Global Financial and
Coronavirus Crises   359

Quantitative Easing Versus Credit Easing 360

Forward Guidance 362

Negative Interest Rates on Banks' Deposits 363

15.4 Monetary Policy Tools of the European Central Bank 364

Open Market Operations 364

Lending to Banks 365

Interest on Excess Reserves 365

Reserve Requirements 365

Summary 365   •   Key Terms 366   •   Questions 366   •   Applied Problems 367   •
Data Analysis Problems 368

CHAPTER 16
The Conduct of Monetary Policy: Strategy and Tactics   **369**

16.1 The Price Stability Goal and the Nominal Anchor 369

The Role of a Nominal Anchor 370

The Time-Inconsistency Problem 370

16.2 Other Goals of Monetary Policy 371

High Employment and Output Stability 371

Economic Growth 372

Stability of Financial Markets 372

Interest-Rate Stability 372

Stability in Foreign Exchange Markets 373

16.3 Should Price Stability be the Primary Goal of Monetary Policy? 373

Hierarchical Versus Dual Mandates 373

Price Stability as the Primary, Long-Run Goal of Monetary Policy 374

16.4 Inflation Targeting 374

Inflation Targeting in New Zealand, Canada, and the United Kingdom 375

Advantages of Inflation Targeting 377

Disadvantages of Inflation Targeting 379

16.5 The Evolution of the Federal Reserve's Monetary Policy Strategy 380

The Fed's "Just Do It" Monetary Policy Strategy 380

The Long Road to Inflation Targeting 382

Inside the Fed Ben Bernanke's Advocacy of Inflation Targeting   383

Global The European Central Bank's Monetary Policy Strategy   383

16.6 Lessons for Monetary Policy Strategy from the Global Financial Crisis 384
Implications for Inflation Targeting 385

Inside the Fed The Fed's New Monetary Policy Strategy: Average Inflation
Targeting 386

16.7 Should Central Banks Try to Stop Asset-Price Bubbles? 387
Two Types of Asset-Price Bubbles 387
The Debate over Whether Central Banks Should Try to Pop Bubbles 388

16.8 Tactics: Choosing the Policy Instrument 391
Criteria for Choosing the Policy Instrument 393

16.9 Tactics: The Taylor Rule 394

Inside the Fed The Fed's Use of the Taylor Rule 396

Summary 397 • Key Terms 398 • Questions 398 • Applied Problems 399 •
Data Analysis Problems 399

CHAPTER 16 APPENDIX 1
Monetary Targeting
Go to MyLab Economics

CHAPTER 16 APPENDIX 2
A Brief History of Federal Reserve Policymaking
Go to MyLab Economics

PART 5   International Finance and Monetary Policy   401

CHAPTER 17
The Foreign Exchange Market **402**

17.1 Foreign Exchange Market 402

Following the Financial News Foreign Exchange Rates   403

What Are Foreign Exchange Rates? 403
Why Are Exchange Rates Important? 403
How Is Foreign Exchange Traded? 404

17.2 Exchange Rates in the Long Run 405
Theory of Purchasing Power Parity 405

APPLICATION Burgernomics: Big Macs and PPP 407
Factors That Affect Exchange Rates in the Long Run 409

17.3 Exchange Rates in the Short Run: A Supply and Demand Analysis 411
Supply Curve for Domestic Assets 411
Demand Curve for Domestic Assets 412
Equilibrium in the Foreign Exchange Market 413

17.4 Explaining Changes in Exchange Rates 413
Shifts in the Demand for Domestic Assets 413
Recap: Factors That Change the Exchange Rate 416

APPLICATION Effects of Changes in Interest Rates on the Equilibrium
Exchange Rate 418

APPLICATION The Global Financial Crisis and the Dollar 420

APPLICATION Brexit and the British Pound 421

Summary 422 • Key Terms 423 • Questions 423 • Applied Problems 424 •
Data Analysis Problems 424

APPENDIX TO CHAPTER 17
The Interest Parity Condition
Go to MyLab Economics

CHAPTER 18
The International Financial System   425

18.1 Intervention in the Foreign Exchange Market 425
Foreign Exchange Intervention and the Money Supply 425

Inside the Fed A Day at the Federal Reserve Bank of New York's Foreign
Exchange Desk   426
Unsterilized Intervention 428
Sterilized Intervention 429

18.2 Balance of Payments 429
Current Account 430
Financial Account 430

Global Should We Worry About the Large U.S. Current Account Deficit?   431

18.3 Exchange Rate Regimes in the International Financial System 431
Gold Standard 432
The Bretton Woods System 432
How a Fixed Exchange Rate Regime Works 433
Speculative Attacks 435

APPLICATION The Foreign Exchange Crisis of September 1992 435
The Policy Trilemma 437

APPLICATION How Did China Accumulate $4 Trillion of International Reserves? 438
Monetary Unions 438
Managed Float 439

Global Will the Euro Survive?   439

18.4 Capital Controls 440
Controls on Capital Outflows 440
Controls on Capital Inflows 440

18.5 The Role of the IMF 441
Should the IMF Act as an International Lender of Last Resort? 441

18.6 International Considerations and Monetary Policy 442
Direct Effects of the Foreign Exchange Market on Monetary Policy 442
Exchange Rate Considerations 443

18.7 To PEG or Not to Peg: Exchange-Rate Targeting as an Alternative
Monetary Policy Strategy 443
Advantages of Exchange-Rate Targeting 443
Disadvantages of Exchange-Rate Targeting 444

When Is Exchange-Rate Targeting Desirable for Industrialized Countries? 446
When Is Exchange-Rate Targeting Desirable for Emerging Market Countries? 447
Currency Boards 447

Global Argentina's Currency Board   448

Dollarization 448

Summary 449 • Key Terms 450 • Questions 450 • Applied Problems 451 •
Data Analysis Problems 452

PART 6	Monetary Theory 453

CHAPTER 19
Quantity Theory, Inflation, and the Demand for Money   454

19.1 Quantity Theory of Money 454
Velocity of Money and Equation of Exchange 454
From the Equation of Exchange to the Quantity Theory of Money 456
Quantity Theory and the Price Level 456
Quantity Theory and Inflation 457

APPLICATION Testing the Quantity Theory of Money 458

19.2 Budget Deficits and Inflation 460
Government Budget Constraint 460

FYI Modern Monetary Theory   462

Hyperinflation 462

APPLICATION The Zimbabwean Hyperinflation 463

19.3 Keynesian Theories of Money Demand 463
Transactions Motive 464
Precautionary Motive 464
Speculative Motive 464
Putting the Three Motives Together 464

19.4 Portfolio Theories of Money Demand 465
Theory of Portfolio Choice and Keynesian Liquidity Preference 465
Other Factors That Affect the Demand for Money 466
Summary 466

19.5 Empirical Evidence on the Demand for Money 467
Interest Rates and Money Demand 467
Stability of Money Demand 468

Summary 468 • Key Terms 469 • Questions 469 • Applied Problems 470 •
Data Analysis Problems 471

CHAPTER 20
The *IS* Curve   472

20.1 Planned Expenditure and Aggregate Demand 472
20.2 The Components of Aggregate Demand 473
Consumption Expenditure 473

FYI Meaning of the Word *Investment*   474

Planned Investment Spending 474
Government Purchases and Taxes 476
Net Exports 477

20.3 Goods Market Equilibrium 478
Solving for Goods Market Equilibrium 478
Deriving the *IS* Curve 479

20.4 Understanding the *IS* Curve 479
What the *IS* Curve Tells Us: Intuition 479
What the *IS* Curve Tells Us: Numerical Example 479
Why the Economy Heads Toward Equilibrium 481

20.5 Factors that Shift the *IS* Curve 481
Changes in Government Purchases 481

APPLICATION The Vietnam War Buildup, 1964–1969 482
Changes in Taxes 483

APPLICATION The Fiscal Stimulus Package of 2009 484
Changes in Autonomous Spending 485
Changes in Financial Frictions 487
Summary of Factors That Shift the *IS* Curve 487

Summary 487 • Key Terms 487 • Questions 488 • Applied Problems 489 •
Data Analysis Problems 490

CHAPTER 21
The Monetary Policy and Aggregate Demand Curves   491

21.1 The Federal Reserve and Monetary Policy 491

21.2 The Monetary Policy Curve 492
Why the Monetary Policy Curve Has an Upward Slope 492
Shifts in the *MP* Curve 493
Movements Along Versus Shifts in the *MP* Curve 494

APPLICATION Movements Along the *MP* Curve: The Rise in the Federal
Funds Rate Target, 2004–2006 and 2015–2019 495

APPLICATION Shift in the *MP* Curve: Autonomous Monetary Easing During
the Global Financial and Coronavirus Crises 495

21.3 The Aggregate Demand Curve 496
Deriving the Aggregate Demand Curve Graphically 497

FYI Deriving the Aggregate Demand Curve Algebraically   497

Factors That Shift the Aggregate Demand Curve 499

Summary 502 • Key Terms 502 • Questions 502 • Applied Problems 503 •
Data Analysis Problems 504

CHAPTER 22
Aggregate Demand and Supply Analysis   506

22.1 Business Cycles and Inflation 506
Business Cycles 506
Inflation 509

22.2 Aggregate Demand 510
Components of Aggregate Demand 510

Following the Financial News Aggregate Output, Unemployment, and Inflation 510

Deriving the Aggregate Demand Curve 511
Factors That Shift the Aggregate Demand Curve 511

FYI What Does *Autonomous* Mean? 512

22.3 Aggregate Supply 515
Long-Run Aggregate Supply Curve 515
Short-Run Aggregate Supply Curve 516
Price Stickiness and the Short-Run Aggregate Supply Curve 518
22.4 Shifts in the Aggregate Supply Curves 518
Shifts in the Long-Run Aggregate Supply Curve 518
Shifts in the Short-Run Aggregate Supply Curve 519
22.5 Equilibrium in Aggregate Demand and Supply Analysis 522
Short-Run Equilibrium 523
Aggregate Demand and Supply Analysis Using an Aggregate Output Index 523
How the Short-Run Equilibrium Moves to the Long-Run Equilibrium over Time 524
Self-Correcting Mechanism 527
22.6 Changes in Equilibrium: Aggregate Demand Shocks 527

APPLICATION The Volcker Disinflation, 1980–1986 529
22.7 Changes in Equilibrium: Aggregate Supply (Inflation) Shocks 530

APPLICATION Negative Supply Shocks, 1973–1975 and 1978–1980 532
22.8 Conclusions from Aggregate Demand and Supply Analysis 533

APPLICATION *AD/AS* Analysis of the Great Recession of 2007–2009 534

APPLICATION An *AD/AS* Analysis of the Covid-19 Recession 535

Summary 538 • Key Terms 538 • Questions 539 • Applied Problems 539 •
Data Analysis Problems 540

APPENDIX TO CHAPTER 22
The Phillips Curve and the Short-Run Aggregate Supply Curve **541**
22.A1 The Phillips Curve..541
Phillips Curve Analysis in the 1960s 541
The Friedman-Phelps Phillips Curve Analysis 542

FYI The Phillips Curve Trade-Off and Macroeconomic Policy in the 1960s 543

The Phillips Curve After the 1960s...545
The Modern Phillips Curve 545
The Modern Phillips Curve with Adaptive (Backward-Looking) Expectations 546
22.A2 The Short-Run Aggregate Supply Curve...547

CHAPTER 22 APPENDIX 1
The Effects of Macroeconomic Shocks on Asset Prices
Go to MyLab Economics

CHAPTER 22 APPENDIX 2
Aggregate Demand and Supply: An Algebraic Example
Go to MyLab Economics

CHAPTER 23
Monetary Policy Theory   **549**

23.1 Response of Monetary Policy to Shocks 549
Response to an Aggregate Demand Shock 550
Response to a Supply Shock 551
The Bottom Line: The Relationship Between Stabilizing Inflation and
   Stabilizing Economic Activity 554

23.2 How Actively Should Policymakers Try to Stabilize Economic Activity? 555
Lags and Policy Implementation 556

FYI The Activist/Nonactivist Debate over the Obama Fiscal Stimulus Package   557

23.3 Inflation: Always and Everywhere a Monetary Phenomenon 557
23.4 Causes of Inflationary Monetary Policy 558
High Employment Targets and Inflation 559

APPLICATION The Great Inflation 562
23.5 Monetary Policy at the Effective Lower Bound 564
Deriving the Aggregate Demand Curve with the Effective Lower Bound 564
The Disappearance of the Self-Correcting Mechanism at the Effective Lower Bound 566

APPLICATION Nonconventional Monetary Policy and Quantitative Easing 567
Liquidity Provision 568
Asset Purchases and Quantitative Easing 569
Management of Expectations 570

APPLICATION Abenomics and the Shift in Japanese Monetary Policy in 2013 570

Summary 573 • Key Terms 573 • Questions 573 • Applied Problems 574 •
   Data Analysis Problems 575

CHAPTER 24
The Role of Expectations in Monetary Policy   **576**

24.1 Lucas Critique of Policy Evaluation 576
Econometric Policy Evaluation 577

APPLICATION The Term Structure of Interest Rates 577
24.2 Policy Conduct: Rules or Discretion? 578
Discretion and the Time-Inconsistency Problem 578
Types of Rules 579
The Case for Rules 579

FYI The Political Business Cycle and Richard Nixon   580

The Case for Discretion 580
Constrained Discretion 581

Global The Demise of Monetary Targeting in Switzerland   581

24.3 The Role of Credibility and a Nominal Anchor 582
Benefits of a Credible Nominal Anchor 582
Credibility and Aggregate Demand Shocks 583
Credibility and Aggregate Supply Shocks 585

APPLICATION A Tale of Three Oil Price Shocks 586
Credibility and Anti-Inflation Policy 588

Global Ending the Bolivian Hyperinflation: A Successful Anti-Inflation Program 589

24.4 Approaches to Establishing Central Bank Credibility 590
Nominal GDP Targeting 590
Appoint "Conservative" Central Bankers 591

Inside the Fed The Appointment of Paul Volcker, Anti-Inflation Hawk 591

Summary 592 • Key Terms 592 • Questions 593 • Applied Problems 594 •
Data Analysis Problems 594

CHAPTER 25
Transmission Mechanisms of Monetary Policy 595

25.1 Transmission Mechanisms of Monetary Policy 596
Traditional Interest-Rate Channels 596
Other Asset Price Channels 597
Credit View 600

FYI Consumers' Balance Sheets and the Great Depression 603

Why Are Credit Channels Likely to Be Important? 604

APPLICATION The Great Recession 604

25.2 Lessons for Monetary Policy 605

APPLICATION Applying the Monetary Policy Lessons to Japan's Two Lost Decades 606

Summary 607 • Key Terms 607 • Questions 608 • Applied Problems 609 •
Data Analysis Problems 609

CHAPTER 25 APPENDIX
Evaluating Empirical Evidence: The Debate Over the Importance of Money in Economic Fluctuations
Go to MyLab Economics

Glossary..G-1

Index I-1

Additional Contents on MyLab Economics

The following chapters and appendices are available on MyLab Economics

CHAPTER 1
Financial Crises in Emerging Market Economies **1**
Dynamics of Financial Crises in Emerging Market Economies... 1
   Stage One: Initial Phase 1
   Stage Two: Currency Crises 5
   Stage Three: Full-Fledged Financial Crisis 6

APPLICATION Crisis in South Korea, 1997–1998 7
   Financial Liberalization/Globalization Mismanaged 8
   Perversion of the Financial Liberalization/Globalization Process: Chaebols and the
     South Korean Crisis.. 9
   Stock Market Decline and Failure of Firms Increase Uncertainty 10
   Adverse Selection and Moral Hazard Problems Worsen and the Economy Contracts 11
   Currency Crisis Ensues 11
   Final Stage: Currency Crisis Triggers Full-Fledged Financial Crisis..................................... 11
   Recovery Commences.. 13

APPLICATION The Argentine Financial Crisis, 2001–2002 13
   Severe Fiscal Imbalances 13
   Adverse Selection and Moral Hazard Problems Worsen 14
   Bank Panic Begins 14
   Currency Crisis Ensues 14
   Currency Crisis Triggers Full-Fledged Financial Crisis 15
   Recovery Begins... 17

Global When an Advanced Economy Is Like an Emerging Market Economy:
The Icelandic Financial Crisis of 2008   18

Preventing Emerging Market Financial Crises 18
   Beef Up Prudential Regulation and Supervision of Banks............. 18
   Encourage Disclosure and Market-Based Discipline 19
   Limit Currency Mismatch... 19
   Sequence Financial Liberalization... 20

   Summary 20 • Key Terms 20 • Questions 21

CHAPTER 2
Nonbank Finance **1**
Insurance.. 1
   Life Insurance... 1
   Property and Casualty Insurance 2
   The Competitive Threat from the Banking Industry...................... 4
   Credit Insurance... 4

FYI The AIG Blowup   5

FYI The Global Financial Crisis and the Monoline Insurers   6

APPLICATION Insurance Management.. 6
    Screening 7
    Risk-Based Premiums 7
    Restrictive Provisions.. 7
    Prevention of Fraud... 8
    Cancellation of Insurance 8
    Deductibles 8
    Coinsurance 8
    Limits on the Amount of Insurance 8
    Summary.. 9
Pension Funds 9
    Private Pension Plans... 10
    Public Pension Plans... 10

FYI Should Social Security Be Privatized?   11

Finance Companies.. 12
Securities Market Operations.. 13
    Investment Banking... 13
    Securities Brokers and Dealers.. 14
    Organized Exchanges 14
Mutual Funds... 15

FYI Sovereign Wealth Funds: Are They a Danger?   16

    Money Market Mutual Funds 17
Hedge Funds... 17
Private Equity and Venture Capital Funds.. 18
Government Financial Intermediation 19
    Federal Credit Agencies.. 19

FYI The Global Financial Crisis and the Bailout of Fannie Mae and Freddie Mac   20

    Summary 21 • Key Terms 22 • Questions 22 • Applied Problems 23 •
    Data Analysis Problems 23

CHAPTER 3
Financial Derivatives   **1**
Hedging.. 1
Interest-Rate Forward Contracts 2

APPLICATION Hedging with Interest-Rate Forward Contracts 2
Pros and Cons of Forward Contracts.. 3
Financial Futures Contracts and Markets... 4

APPLICATION Hedging with Financial Futures 5
    Organization of Trading in Financial Futures Markets 7
    The Globalization of Financial Futures Markets...................................... 8
    Explaining the Success of Futures Markets 8

APPLICATION Hedging Foreign Exchange Risk...................................... 10
    Hedging Foreign Exchange Risk with Forward Contracts......................... 10
    Hedging Foreign Exchange Risk with Futures Contracts........................... 10

Options 11
   Options Contracts 12
   Profits and Losses on Option and Futures Contracts 12
APPLICATION Hedging with Future Options 15
   Factors Affecting Option Premiums 16
   Summary 17
Swaps 18
   Interest-Rate Swap Contracts 18
APPLICATION Hedging with Interest-Rate Swaps 19
   Advantages of Interest-Rate Swaps 19
   Disadvantages of Interest-Rate Swaps 20
   Financial Intermediaries in Interest-Rate Swaps 20
Credit Derivatives 20
   Credit Options 21
   Credit Swaps 21
   Credit-Linked Notes 22
APPLICATION Lessons from the Global Financial Crisis: When Are Financial
   Derivatives Likely to Be a Worldwide Time Bomb?   22

   Summary 24 • Key Terms 24 • Questions 25 • Applied Problems 25 •
   Data Analysis Problems 26

CHAPTER 4
Conflicts of Interest in the Financial Services Industry   1
What Are Conflicts of Interest, and Why Are They Important? 2
   Why Do We Care About Conflicts of Interest? 2
Ethics and Conflicts of Interest 2
Types of Conflicts of Interest 3
   Underwriting and Research in Investment Banking 3
   Auditing and Consulting in Accounting Firms 4
   Credit Assessment and Consulting in Credit-Rating Agencies 4
FYI The Collapse of Arthur Andersen   5
   Universal Banking 5
FYI Why Do Issuers of Securities Pay to Have Their Securities Rated?   6
FYI Banksters   7
Can the Market Limit Exploitations of Conflicts of Interest? 7
What Has Been Done to Remedy Conflicts of Interest? 9
   Sarbanes-Oxley Act of 2002 10
   Global Legal Settlement of 2002 10
   Dodd-Frank Bill of 2010 11
A Framework for Evaluating Policies to Remedy Conflicts of Interest 11
   Approaches to Remedying Conflicts of Interest 12
APPLICATION Evaluating Sarbanes-Oxley, the Global Legal Settlement,
   and the Dodd-Frank Bill 14

   Summary 16 • Key Terms 17 • Questions 17

CHAPTER APPENDICES IN MYLAB ECONOMICS

Chapter 4: Measuring Interest-Rate Risk: Duration
Chapter 5: Loanable Funds Framework
Chapter 9: Duration Gap Analysis
Chapter 9: Measuring Bank Performance
Chapter 10: Banking Crises Throughout the World
Chapter 14 The Fed's Balance Sheet and the Monetary Base
Chapter 14: The M2 Money Multiplier
Chapter 14: Explaining the Behavior of the Currency Ratio
Chapter 14: The Great Depression Bank Panics, 1930–1933,
      and the Money Supply
Chapter 16: Monetary Targeting
Chapter 16: A Brief History of Federal Reserve Policymaking
Chapter 17: The Interest Parity Condition
Chapter 22: The Effects of Macroeconomic Shocks on Asset Prices
Chapter 22: Aggregate Demand and Supply: An Algebraic Example
Chapter 25: Evaluating Empirical Evidence: The Debate Over the Importance of
      Money in Economic Fluctuations

Preface

There has never been a more exciting time to teach money and banking. The recent worldwide financial crisis and the coronavirus pandemic cast a spotlight on the importance of banks, financial markets, and monetary policy to the health of our economy. I experienced this firsthand when I served as a Governor of the Federal Reserve System from 2006 to 2008, and in this book, I emphasize the rich tapestry of recent economic events to enliven the study of money, banking, and financial markets.

NEW TO THIS EDITION

This text has undergone a major revision with new material in every part of the book, including updating of all data through 2020 whenever possible. However, it continues to retain the basic hallmarks that have made it the best-selling textbook on money and banking over the past twelve editions. As with past editions, this thirteenth edition uses basic economic principles to explain financial markets, financial institutions, and monetary policy with rigor and clarity. With each edition, I update content and features based on market feedback from economics professors and students using the book as well as the latest world financial episodes. For the past several editions, the digital assets for this book, which are available on MyLab Economics, have evolved and expanded.

Compelling New Material on the Coronavirus Pandemic

The coronavirus pandemic that spread throughout the world in 2020 is one of the signature events of the twenty-first century. This has required the addition of many timely new sections, applications, and boxes throughout the book.

- A new application which uses the analysis of the risk structure of interest rates to explain the effect of the coronavirus pandemic on the Baa-Treasury spread (Chapter 6).
- A new application on the coronavirus stock market crash of 2020 (Chapter 7), which illustrates how stock market prices are set.
- A new application on whether the coronavirus pandemic could have led to a financial crisis (Chapter 12) shows how to apply the analysis of the dynamics of financial crises to explain when financial crises might occur in the future.
- A new application on the effects of quantitative easing on the money supply during the coronavirus crisis (Chapter 14), which shows how to apply the model of the money supply process to recent data.
- An update to the section on nonconventional monetary policy tools and quantitative easing (Chapter 15) to discuss how they were used during the coronavirus pandemic.
- An updated Inside the Fed box on Fed lending facilities during the coronavirus crisis (Chapter 15).
- An update on the application discussing shifts in the *MP* curve (Chapter 21) to explain why the actions taken at the onset of the coronavirus pandemic were an autonomous monetary easing.
- A new application that shows how *AD/AS* analysis can explain what happened during the Coronavirus Recession (Chapter 22).

A More Real-World Approach to Monetary Theory

Part 6 of the text, Monetary Theory, has been substantially revised to make the analysis more real world by using actual data when conducting *AD/AS* analysis of business cycle episodes. Chapter 22 has been revised in two major ways. It now starts with an entirely new section, *Business Cycles*, that discusses what aggregate demand and supply analysis is trying to explain, that is, cyclical fluctuations in output, unemployment, and inflation. The *AD/AS* analysis is then developed using an aggregate output index (where 100 is potential GDP), which replaces aggregate output on the horizontal axis of the *AD/AS* diagram. This approach has two important advantages over the analysis in previous editions. First, it enables *AD/AS* diagrams to be a little simpler because the long-run aggregate supply curve does not have to be shown in the diagram because its position is always the same at an aggregate output index of 100. Second, and far more important, doing the analysis with an aggregate output index enables the *AD/AS* diagram to use actual data when it is used to describe what happened during particular business cycle episodes, such as the Great Recession and the Covid-19 recession. This change makes *AD/AS* analysis far more relevant to students because they now see that it can explain actual data and is not just a theoretical construct. This new approach is then used throughout the rest of the chapters in the monetary policy part of the book.

Additional New Material on Financial Markets and Money

Other new developments in the money and banking field have prompted me to add the following new boxes and applications that keep the text current.

- A revision of the application on whether bitcoin or other cryptocurrencies will become the money of the future (Chapter 3) enables students to better understand the attributes of money.
- A new application on the effects of the Trump tax cuts on bond interest rates (Chapter 6), which shows how supply and demand analysis of the bond market can be used to explain the effect of taxes on different interest rates.
- A new Inside the Fed box, which discusses presidential attacks on the independence of the Fed (Chapter 13) to illustrate how Federal Reserve independence can be threatened.
- A new Inside the Fed box on the Fed's new monetary policy strategy, announced in August of 2020, which involves a modification of inflation targeting.
- A new FYI box on Modern Monetary Theory (Chapter 19), which discusses this new theory that argues that the Green New Deal can be easily paid for by having the Federal Reserve buy government bonds to fund the resulting large budget deficits.
- An addition of another rationale for explaining why the monetary policy curve slopes upward (Chapter 21).

SOLVING TEACHING AND LEARNING CHALLENGES

It's important for students to understand the models, key terms, and equations in any economics textbook. However, students can get bogged down in this detail and miss the bigger picture. The content, structure, and features of this book were designed based on market feedback and many years of teaching experience to build students' skill in applying these elements—models, terms, and equations—to real-world events.

Students also learn to apply what they learn to decisions that are directly relevant to their lives, such as what might happen to interest rates on car loans or mortgages, and why events might affect the unemployment rate, which can have a major impact on how easy it is for them to get a job.

Hallmark Learning Features

Here is an overview of the hallmark features of the book that solve teaching problems and facilitate student learning.

- A **unifying, analytic framework** uses a few basic economic principles that enable students to develop a disciplined, logical way of analyzing the structure of financial markets and understanding foreign exchange changes, financial institution management, and the role of monetary policy in the economy.
- A **careful, step-by-step development of economic models** (the approach used in the best principles of economics textbooks), which makes it easier for students to learn.
- **Graphs and Mini-Lecture Videos** with detailed captions help students clearly understand the interrelationships among the plotted variables and the principles of analysis. For analytic figures, these mini-lectures build up each graph step-by-step and explain the intuition necessary to fully understand the theory behind the graph. The mini-lectures are an invaluable study tool for students who typically learn better when they see and hear economic analysis rather than read it.

Mini-lecture

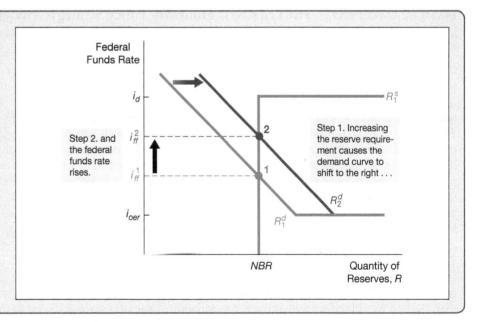

FIGURE 4
Response to a Change in Required Reserves
When the Fed raises reserve requirements, required reserves increase, which raises the demand for reserves. The demand curve shifts from R_1^d to R_2^d, the equilibrium moves from point 1 to point 2, and the federal funds rate rises from i_{ff}^1 to i_{ff}^2.

- The complete integration of an international perspective throughout the text through the use of **Global boxes.** These present interesting material with an international focus.

Global   Worldwide Government Bailouts During the 2007–2009 Financial Crisis

The spreading bank failures in Europe in the fall of 2008 led to massive bailouts of financial institutions: The Netherlands, Belgium, and Luxembourg injected $16 billion to prop up Fortis, a major European bank; the Netherlands injected $13 billion into ING, a banking and insurance giant; Germany provided a $50 billion rescue package for Hypo Real Estate Holdings; and Iceland took over its three largest banks after its banking system collapsed. Ireland's government guaranteed all the deposits of its commercial banks as well as interbank lending, as did Greece. Spain implemented a bailout package similar to that of the United States, in which it bought up to 50 billion euros ($70 billion) of assets in its banks in order to encourage

them to lend. The U.K. Treasury set up a bailout plan similar to that of the U.S. Treasury's plan with a price tag of 400 billion pounds ($699 billion). It guaranteed 250 billion pounds of bank liabilities, added 100 billion pounds to a facility that swaps these assets for government bonds, and allowed the U.K. government to buy up to 50 billion pounds of equity stakes in British banks. Bailout plans to the tune of over $100 billion in South Korea, $200 billion in Sweden, $400 billion in France, and $500 billion in Germany, all of which guaranteed the debt of their banks as well as the injection of capital into them, then followed. Both the scale of these bailout packages and the degree of international coordination was unprecedented.

- **Inside the Fed boxes** give students a feel for the operation and structure of the Federal Reserve.

Inside the Fed   The Fed's New Monetary Policy Strategy: Average Inflation Targeting

The Federal Reserve's original 2% point-target for inflation was one in which bygones are bygones: that is, it would continue to try to achieve a 2% annual inflation rate no matter what had happened to inflation in the past. The Fed announcement in August 2020 that it would now target an *average* inflation rate of 2% meant that bygones were no longer bygones because past inflation would affect its target in the short run. If inflation had been running below the 2% target level, as it had prior to 2020, then average inflation would fall below 2% and so to raise the average back to 2%, the Fed would seek to achieve an inflation rate above 2% for a short period of time. This would require the Fed to pursue easier monetary policy than it would have otherwise. If on the other hand, inflation had been running above 2%, then the Fed would temporarily shoot for an inflation rate below 2% and pursue a tighter monetary policy.

There are two major advantages to this new monetary policy strategy. First, it would make it less likely that inflation expectations would drift down below

the 2% level because past undershoots of the target would be made up over time by pursuing easier monetary policy. The second advantage of this new monetary policy strategy is that it would generate an automatic stabilizer for the economy. When a negative shock which caused inflation to fall below the 2% target occurs, average inflation targeting would commit the Fed to temporarily raise inflation to above 2%. Inflation expectations would then likely rise above the 2% level temporarily, thus lowering the real interest rate automatically even if the Fed did not or could not lower the federal funds rate.

There is one major objection to this new monetary policy strategy. If the Fed allowed inflation to temporarily rise above the 2% level, there might be concerns that the Fed is no longer committed to keep inflation at the 2% level in the long run. To avoid this problem, the Fed would need to convince the public that an overshoot of the 2% inflation objective would not weaken the Fed's commitment to stabilize inflation at the 2% level in the long run.

- **Applications,** numbering more than 50, which demonstrate how the analysis presented can be used to explain many important real-world situations.

APPLICATION ## Could the Coronavirus Pandemic Have Led to a Financial Crisis?

The coronavirus pandemic in 2020 had the potential to trigger a financial crisis as serious as the 2007–2009 global financial crisis. With the start of the lockdown of the U.S. economy in March 2020, the stock market crashed, falling by more than a third, unemployment skyrocketed, and many otherwise healthy firms now faced the prospect of being unable to pay their bills or pay back their loans. The framework we laid out in our discussion of Figure 1 can be used to analyze how the coronavirus pandemic provided the seeds for another financial crisis, 12 years after the previous one, and why it didn't become the next financial crisis.

- **FYI boxes** highlight dramatic historical episodes, interesting ideas, and intriguing facts related to the content of the chapter.

FYI Modern Monetary Theory

Modern Monetary Theory argues that the Green New Deal can be easily paid for by having the Federal Reserve buy government bonds to fund the resulting large budget deficits. As our analysis here suggests, Modern Monetary Theory is correct that the large budget deficit resulting from a large increase in government spending can be paid for by a central bank's purchases of government bonds. However, it ignores that this financing of a persistent budget deficit by a central bank's purchase of government bonds leads to an expansion in the money supply. The result of massive government spending financed by central bank purchases of government bonds can thus be very rapid growth of the money supply. As the quantity theory of money indicates, this very rapid growth of the money supply would then cause very high inflation.

Financing of the Green New Deal by the Fed's purchase of government bonds would thus not be "free" because it would likely result in very high inflation. Most mainstream economists, even those on the left, such as Paul Krugman, have rejected Modern Monetary Theory along the lines discussed above. Their criticisms are much in keeping with the economics adage "There is no such thing as a free lunch." A Green New Deal would need to be paid for by higher taxes at some point in the future if inflation is to be avoided, and so should be evaluated on whether it is productive spending that will pay for itself or have sufficient benefits for the society that make it worth the cost.

- **End-of-chapter questions and applied problems**, numbering more than 600, help students learn the subject matter by applying economic concepts.

QUESTIONS

1. For each of the following countries, identify the single most important (largest) and least important (smallest) source of external funding: United States; Germany; Japan; Canada. Comment on the similarities and differences among the countries' funding sources.

2. How can economies of scale help explain the existence of financial intermediaries?

3. Explain why dating can be considered a method to solve the adverse selection problem.

7. Suppose you have data about two groups of countries, one with efficient legal systems and the other with slow, costly, and inefficient legal systems. Which group of countries would you expect to exhibit higher living standards?

8. Which relationship would you expect to exist between measures of corruption and living standards at the country level? Explain by which channel corruption might affect living standards.

DEVELOPING CAREER SKILLS

The unifying, analytic framework and step-by-step development of economic models in this text enable students to develop the critical thinking skills they need to successfully pursue their careers. The study of money, banking, and financial markets is particularly valuable if a student wants a job in the financial sector. However, even if their interests lie elsewhere, students benefit by understanding why interest rates rise or fall, helping them to make decisions about whether to borrow now or to wait until later. Knowing how banks and other financial institutions are managed may help students get a better deal when they need to borrow or when they supply them with funds. Knowledge of how financial markets work can enable students to make better investment decisions, whether for themselves or for the companies they work for.

Career Skill Features

This text also has additional features, discussed below, which directly develop career skills.

- A special feature called "Following the Financial News," is included to encourage reading of a financial newspaper. **Following the Financial News boxes** introduce students to relevant news articles and data that are reported daily in the press and teach students how to interpret these data. Being able to think critically about what is reported in the financial press is a skill that can make students far more effective in their future jobs.

Following the Financial News Yield Curves

Many newspapers and Internet sites such as http://www.finance.yahoo.com publish a daily plot of the yield curves for Treasury securities. An example for May 22, 2020, is presented here. The numbers on the vertical axis indicate the interest rate for the Treasury security, with the maturity term given on the horizontal axis, with "m" denoting "month" and "y" denoting "year."

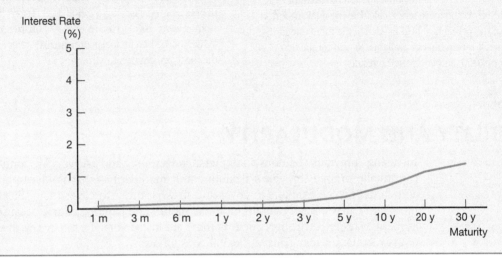

- **Real Time Data** in a high percentage of the in-text data figures are labeled *Real-Time Data*. For these figures, students can see the latest data in the enhanced Pearson e-text, using the Federal Reserve Bank of St. Louis's FRED database and learn where they can access this data when they need to throughout their career.
- **Real-Time Data Analysis Problems**, included in MyLab Economics, which ask students to apply up-to-the-minute data, taken from the St. Louis Federal Reserve Bank's FRED database, so that they can understand what is happening in the economy in real time. These problems, marked with **Real-time Data Analysis**, ask the student to download data from the Federal Reserve Bank of St. Louis FRED website and then use the data to answer questions about current issues in money and banking. In MyLab Economics, these easy-to-assign and automatically graded Real-Time Data Analysis exercises communicate directly with the FRED site, so that students see updated data every time new data is posted by FRED. Thus the Real-Time Data Analysis exercises offer a no-fuss solution for instructors who want to make the most current data a central part of their macroeconomics course. These exercises will give students practice manipulating data, a skill that employers value highly.

DATA ANALYSIS PROBLEMS

The Problems update with real-time data in **MyLab Economics** and are available for practice or instructor assignment.

1. **Real-time Data Analysis** Go to the St. Louis Federal Reserve FRED database, and find data on federal debt held by the Federal Reserve (FDHBFRBN), by private investors (FDHBPIN), and by international and foreign investors (FDHBFIN). Using these series, calculate the total amount held and the percentage held in each of the three categories for the most recent quarter available. Repeat for the first quarter of 2000, and compare the results.

2. **Real-time Data Analysis** Go to the St. Louis Federal Reserve FRED database, and find data on the total assets of all commercial banks (TLAACBM027SBOG) and the total assets of money market mutual funds (MMMFFAQ027S). Transform the commercial bank assets series to quarterly by adjusting the *Frequency* setting to "Quarterly." Calculate the percent increase in growth of assets for each series, from January 2000 to the most recent quarter available. Which of the two financial intermediaries has experienced the most percentage growth?

FLEXIBILITY AND MODULARITY

In using previous editions, adopters, reviewers, and survey respondents have continually praised this text's flexibility and modularity—that is, the option to pick and choose which chapters to cover and in what order to cover them. Flexibility and modularity are especially important in the money and banking course because there are as many ways to teach this course as there are instructors. To satisfy the diverse needs of instructors, the text achieves flexibility as follows:

- Core chapters provide the basic analysis used throughout the book, and other chapters or sections of chapters can be used or omitted according to instructor preferences. For example, Chapter 2 introduces the financial system and basic concepts such as transaction costs, adverse selection, and moral hazard. After covering Chapter 2, the instructor may decide to give more detailed coverage of financial structure by assigning Chapter 8 or may choose to skip Chapter 8 and take any of a number of different paths through the book.
- The text allows instructors to cover the most important issues in monetary theory even if they do not wish to present a detailed development of the *IS*, *MP*, and *AD* curves (provided in Chapters 20 and 21). Instructors who want to teach a more complete treatment of monetary theory can make use of these chapters.
- Part 6 on monetary theory can easily be taught before Part 4 of the text if the instructor wishes to give students a deeper understanding of the rationale behind monetary policy.
- Chapter 25 on the transmission mechanisms of monetary policy can be taught at many different points in the course—either with Part 4, when monetary policy is discussed, or with Chapter 20 or Chapter 22, when the concept of aggregate demand is developed. Transmission mechanisms of monetary policy can also be taught as a special topic at the end of the course.

- The international approach of the text, accomplished through marked international sections within chapters as well as separate chapters on the foreign exchange market and the international monetary system, is comprehensive yet flexible. Although many instructors will teach all the international material, others will not. Instructors who wish to put less emphasis on international topics can easily skip Chapter 17 on the foreign exchange market and Chapter 18 on the international financial system and monetary policy. The international sections within chapters are self-contained and can be omitted with little loss of continuity.

To illustrate how this book can be used for courses with varying emphases, several course outlines are suggested for a one-semester teaching schedule. More detailed information about how the text can be used flexibly in your course is available in the Instructor's Manual.

- *General Money and Banking Course:* Chapters 1–5, 9–13, 15, 16, 22–23, with a choice of 5 of the remaining 11 chapters
- *General Money and Banking Course with an International Emphasis:* Chapters 1–5, 9–13, 15–18, 22–23, with a choice of 3 of the remaining 9 chapters
- *Financial Markets and Institutions Course:* Chapters 1–12, with a choice of 7 of the remaining 13 chapters
- *Monetary Theory and Policy Course:* Chapters 1–5, 13–16, 19–24, with a choice of 4 of the remaining 10 chapters

A More Finance-Oriented Approach—the former Business School Edition

We are providing additional chapters in MyLab Economics that will serve instructors and students who previously used the Business School edition. In offering these chapters, we are offering all of the chapters that instructors would want to cover in a typical semester—regardless of where the course is offered. The additional chapters include nonbank finance, financial derivatives, and conflicts of interest in the financial industry.

Appendices and Additional Resources

Additional resources for the Thirteenth Edition of *The Economics of Money, Banking, and Financial Markets* include: (1) the three unique chapters that were previously found in the Business School Edition; (2) a chapter on financial crises in emerging market economies; and (3) fifteen appendices that cover additional topics and more technical material that instructors might want to include in their courses. This content can be accessed in MyLab Economics. Instructors can either use these chapters and appendices in class to supplement the material in the textbook or recommend them to students who want to expand their knowledge of the money and banking field.

INSTRUCTOR TEACHING RESOURCES

This program comes with the following teaching resources.

Supplements available to instructors at www. pearsonhighered.com	Features of the supplement
The Instructor's Resource Manual was prepared by the author and includes the following features:	• Sample course outlines • Chapter outlines • Answers to questions and problems in the text
The Test Bank includes the following features:	• More than 2,500 multiple-choice and essay test items, many with graphs • Questions are connected to the AACSB learning standards (Written and Oral Communication; Ethical Understanding and Reasoning; Analytical Thinking; Information Technology; Interpersonal Relations and Teamwork; Diverse and Multicultural Work; Reflective Thinking; Application of Knowledge)
The Testgen enables instructors to produce exams efficiently:	• This product consists of the multiple-choice and essay questions provided in the online Test Bank, and offers editing capabilities
The PowerPoint Presentation includes the following features:	• All of the tables and graphs presented in the text • Detailed lecture notes for all the course material • Instructors who prefer to teach with a blackboard can use these PowerPoint slides as their own class notes; for those who prefer to teach with visual aids, the PowerPoint slides afford them the flexibility to do so

ACKNOWLEDGMENTS

As always in so large a project, there are many people to thank. My gratitude goes especially to Chris DeJohn, my editor, and Samantha Lewis, my product manager. Also, I would like to thank Carolyn Philips and Kathy Smith for their contributions as well. From marketing, I want to thank Nayke Heine and Ashley DePace. I also have been assisted by comments from my colleagues at Columbia and from my students.

In addition, I have been guided by the thoughtful commentary of outside reviewers and correspondents, especially Jim Eaton and Aaron Jackson. Their feedback has made this a better book. In particular, I thank the following professors who reviewed the text in preparation for this edition and previous editions:

Burt Abrams, University of Delaware
Francis W. Ahking, University of Connecticut
Reena Ahuja, Flagler College
Mohammad Iqbal Ahmed, Texas State University
Mohammed Akacem, Metropolitan State College of Denver
Stefania Albanesi, Columbia University
Nancy Anderson, Mississippi College
Muhammad Anwar, University of Massachusetts
Harjit K. Arora, Le Moyne College

Bob Barnes, Northern Illinois University
Stacie Beck, University of Delaware
Larry Belcher, Stetson University
Thomas Bernardin, Smith College
Gerry Bialka, University of North Florida
Daniel K. Biederman, University of North Dakota
John Bishop, East Carolina University
Daniel Blake, California State University, Northridge
Robert Boatler, Texas Christian University
Henning Bohn, University of California, Santa Barbara
Michael W. Brandl, University of Texas at Austin
Oscar T. Brookins, Northeastern University
William Walter Brown, California State University, Northridge
James L. Butkiewicz, University of Delaware
Colleen M. Callahan, Lehigh University
Ray Canterbery, Florida State University
Mike Carew, Baruch University
Tina Carter, University of Florida
Sergio Castello, University of Mobile
Matthew S. Chambers, Towson University
Jen-Chi Cheng, Wichita State University
Chi-Young Choi, University of Texas, Arlington
Patrick Crowley, Middlebury College
Sarah E. Culver, University of Alabama, Birmingham
Julie Dahlquist, University of Texas, San Antonio
Maria Davis, San Antonio College
Michael DeDad, Indiana University
Ranjit S. Dighe, State University of New York, Oswego
Richard Douglas, Bowling Green University
Ram Sewak Dubey, Montclair State University
Donald H. Dutkowsky, Syracuse University
Richard Eichhorn, Colorado State University
Paul Emberton, Southwest Texas State University
Erick Eschker, Humboldt State University
Diego Escobari, The University of Texas–Pan American
Robert Eyler, Sonoma State University
L. S. Fan, Colorado State University
Imran Farooqi, University of Iowa
Sasan Fayazmanesh, California State University, Fresno
Dennis Fixler, George Washington University
Gary Fleming, Roanoke College
Grant D. Forsyth, Eastern Washington University
Layton W. Franko, Queens College
Timothy Fuerst, Bowling Green State University
Marc Fusaro, Arkansas Tech University
James Gale, Michigan Technological University
Shirley Gedeon, University of Vermont
Edgar Ghossoub, University of Texas, San Antonio
Mark Gibson, Washington State University

Lance Girton, University of Utah
Stuart M. Glosser, University of Wisconsin, Whitewater
Fred C. Graham, American University
Jo Anna Gray, University of Oregon
David Gulley, Bentley University
Ralph Gunderson, University of Wisconsin
Daniel Haak, Stanford University
Larbi Hammami, McGill University
Bassan Harik, Western Michigan University
J. C. Hartline, Rutgers University
Scott Hein, Texas Tech
Robert Stanley Herren, North Dakota State University
Jane Himarios, University of Texas, Arlington
Chad Hogan, University of Michigan
Linda Hooks, Washington and Lee University
James Hueng, Western Michigan University
Dar-Yeh Hwang, National Taiwan University
Jayvanth Ishwaran, Stephen F. Austin State University
Aaron Jackson, Bentley University
Jonatan Jelen, Queens College and City College of CUNY
U Jin Jhun, State University of New York, Oswego
Jingze Jiang, Edinboro University
Frederick L. Joutz, George Washington University
Ahmed Kalifa, Colorado State University
Bryce Kanago, University of Northern Iowa
Magda Kandil, International Monetary Fund
Theodore Kariotis, Towson University
George G. Kaufman, Loyola University Chicago
Richard H. Keehn, University of Wisconsin, Parkside
Elizabeth Sawyer Kelly, University of Wisconsin, Madison
Kathy Kelly, University of Texas, Arlington
Michael Kelsay, University of Missouri, Kansas City
Hyeongwoo Kim, Auburn University
Paul Kubik, DePaul University
Sungkyu Kwak, Washburn University
Fritz Laux, Northeastern State University
Jim Lee, Fort Hays State University
Robert Leeson, University of Western Ontario
Mary H. Lesser, Lenoir–Rhyne University
Ting Levy, Florida Atlantic University
Tony Lima, California State University, Hayward
Fiona Maclachlan, Manhattan College
Elham Mafi-Kreft, Indiana University
Bernard Malamud, University of Nevada, Las Vegas
James Maloy, University of Pittsburgh
James Marchand, Mercer University
Marvin Margolis, Millersville University
Elaine McBeth, College of William and Mary
Stephen McCafferty, Ohio State University

James McCown, Ohio State University
Robin McCutcheon, Marshall University
Cheryl McGaughey, Angelo State University
William McLean, Oklahoma State University
W. Douglas McMillin, Louisiana State University
William Merrill, Iowa State University
Carrie Meyer, George Mason University
Stephen M. Miller, University of Connecticut
Masoud Moghaddam, Saint Cloud State University
Thomas S. Mondschean, DePaul University
George Monokroussos, University of Albany
Shahriar Mostashari, Campbell University
Clair Morris, U.S. Naval Academy
Jon Nadenichek, California State University, Northridge
John Nader, Grand Valley State University
Andrew Nahlik, Illinois College
Hiranya K. Nath, Sam Houston State University
Leonce Ndikumana, University of Massachusetts, Amherst
Ray Nelson, Brigham Young University
Inder P. Nijhawan, Fayetteville State University
Nick Noble, Miami University of Ohio
Dennis O'Toole, Virginia Commonwealth University
Miyoung Oh, Iowa State University
William R. Parke, University of North Carolina, Chapel Hill
Mark J. Perry, University of Michigan, Flint
Chung Pham, University of New Mexico
Marvin M. Phaup, George Washington University
Andy Prevost, Ohio University
Ganga P. Ramdas, Lincoln University
Ronald A. Ratti, University of Missouri, Columbia
Hans Rau, Ball State University
Prosper Raynold, Miami University
Javier Reyes, Texas A&M University
Stefan Ruediger, Arizona State University
Jack Russ, San Diego State University
Steve Russell, IUPUI
Robert S. Rycroft, Mary Washington College
Joe Santos, South Dakota State University
Lynn Schneider, Auburn University, Montgomery
Walter Schwarm, Colorado State University
John Shea, University of Maryland
Wei Simi, Baruch College – CUNY
Harinder Singh, Grand Valley State University
Rajesh Singh, Iowa State University
Richard Stahl, Louisiana State University
Burak Sungu, Miami University
Larry Taylor, Lehigh University
Leigh Tesfatsion, Iowa State University
Aditi Thapar, New York University

Frederick D. Thum, University of Texas, Austin
Robert Tokle, Idaho State University
Demetri Tsanacas, Ferrum College and Hollins University
C. Van Marrewijk, Erasmus University
Rubina Vohra, New Jersey City University
Christopher J. Waller, Indiana University
Yongsheng Wang, Washington and Jefferson College
Chao Wei, George Washington University
Maurice Weinrobe, Clark University
James R. Wible, University of New Hampshire
Philip R. Wiest, George Mason University
William Wilkes, Athens State University
Thomas Williams, William Paterson University
Elliot Willman, New Mexico State University
Donald Wills, University of Washington, Tacoma
Laura Wolff, Southern Illinois University, Edwardsville
JaeJoon Woo, DePaul University
Robert Wright, University of Virginia
Ben T. Yu, California State University, Northridge
Ky H. Yuhn, Florida Atlantic University
Ed Zajicek, Winston-Salem State University
David Zalewski, Providence College
Liping Zheng, Drake University
Jeffrey Zimmerman, Methodist College

Finally, I want to thank my wife, Sally; my son, Matthew; my daughter, Laura; my three god-daughters, Glenda, Alba, and Norma; and my seven grandchildren, Roby, Sofia, Sammy, Sarita, Adrian, Olivia, and Ellis, all of whom provide me with a warm and happy environment that enables me to do my work, and also my father, Sidney, now deceased, who a long time ago put me on the path that led to this book.

FREDERIC S. MISHKIN

Introduction

Crisis and Response: The Global Financial and the Covid-19 Crises

In August 2007, financial markets began to seize up, and over the next two years the world economy experienced a global financial crisis that was the most severe since the Great Depression years of the 1930s. Housing prices plummeted, the stock market crashed, unemployment skyrocketed, and both businesses and households found they couldn't get credit. Not only did the central bank of the United States, the Federal Reserve, respond by sharply lowering interest rates and intervening in credit markets to provide them with massive amounts of liquidity but the federal government also entered into the act with a $700 billion bailout of weakened financial institutions and huge fiscal stimulus packages totaling over $1 trillion. However, even with these aggressive actions aimed at stabilizing the financial system and boosting the economy, it took ten years before the U.S. economy returned to full employment. The financial systems and economies of many governments throughout the world were also in tatters.

In 2020, the world economy was hit by another crisis, but this time the source was not man-made, but from a strain of coronavirus that originated in Wuhan, China. On March 11, 2020, the World Health Organization (WHO) declared a world pandemic, and economies all over the world began to lock down and the stock market crashed. The Federal Reserve stepped in by again lowering interest rates and by providing massive amounts of liquidity to shore up the financial system and stimulate lending by banks and other institutions. The U.S. Congress then passed a series of fiscal stimulus packages exceeding $3 trillion, the largest ones in U.S. history. Despite these efforts, by April 2020, the unemployment rate had risen to 14.7%, the highest level since the Great Depression of the 1930s.

The aftermath of the global financial and the coronavirus crises demonstrates the importance of banks and financial systems to economic well-being, as well as the major role of money in the economy. Part 1 of this book provides an introduction to the study of money, banking, and financial markets. Chapter 1 outlines a road map of the book and discusses why it is so worthwhile to study money, banking, and financial markets. Chapter 2 provides a general overview of the financial system. Chapter 3 then explains what money is and how it is measured.

1 Why Study Money, Banking, and Financial Markets?

Learning Objectives

1.1 Recognize the importance of financial markets in the economy.

1.2 Describe how financial intermediation and financial innovation affect banking and the economy.

1.3 Identify the basic links among monetary policy, the business cycle, and economic variables.

1.4 Explain the importance of exchange rates in a global economy.

1.5 Explain how the study of money, banking, and financial markets may advance your career.

1.6 Describe how the text approaches the teaching of money, banking, and financial markets.

Preview

You have just heard on the evening news that the Federal Reserve is raising the federal funds rate by $\frac{1}{2}$ of a percentage point. What effect might this have on the interest rate of an automobile loan when you finance your purchase of a sleek new sports car? Does it mean that a house will be more or less affordable in the future? Will it make it easier or harder for you to get a job next year?

This book provides answers to these and other questions by examining how financial markets (such as those for bonds, stocks, and foreign exchange) and financial institutions (banks, insurance companies, mutual funds, and other institutions) work and by exploring the role of money in the economy. Financial markets and institutions affect not only your everyday life but also the flow of trillions of dollars of funds throughout our economy, which in turn affects business profits, the production of goods and services, and even the economic well-being of countries other than the United States. What happens to financial markets, financial institutions, and money is of great concern to politicians and can have a major impact on elections. The study of money, banking, and financial markets will reward you with an understanding of many exciting issues. In this chapter, we provide a road map of this book by outlining these issues and exploring why they are worth studying.

1.1 WHY STUDY FINANCIAL MARKETS?

LO 1.1 Recognize the importance of financial markets in the economy.

Part 2 of this book focuses on **financial markets**—markets in which funds are transferred from people who have an excess of available funds to people who have a shortage. Financial markets, such as bond and stock markets, are crucial to promoting greater economic efficiency by channeling funds from people who do not have a productive use for them to those who do. Indeed, well-functioning financial markets are a key factor in producing high economic growth, and poorly performing financial markets are one reason that many countries in the world remain desperately poor. Activities in financial markets also have a direct effect on personal wealth, the behavior of businesses and consumers, and the cyclical performance of the economy.

Debt Markets and Interest Rates

A **security** (also called a *financial instrument*) is a claim on the issuer's future income or **assets** (any financial claim or piece of property that is subject to ownership). A **bond** is a debt security that promises to make periodic payments for a specified period of time.[1] Debt markets, also often generically referred to as *bond markets*, are especially important to economic activity because they enable corporations and governments to borrow money to finance their activities, and because it is where interest rates are determined. An **interest rate** is the cost of borrowing or the price paid for the rental of funds (usually expressed as a percentage of the rental of $100 per year). Many types of interest rates are found in the economy—mortgage interest rates, car loan rates, and interest rates on many different types of bonds.

Interest rates are important on a number of levels. On a personal level, high interest rates might deter you from buying a house or a car because the cost of financing would be high. Conversely, high interest rates might encourage you to save because you can earn more interest income by putting aside some of your earnings as savings. On a more general level, interest rates have an impact on the overall health of the economy because they affect not only consumers' willingness to spend or save but also businesses' investment decisions. High interest rates, for example, might cause a corporation to postpone building a new plant that would provide more jobs.

Because changes in interest rates affect individuals, financial institutions, businesses, and the overall economy, it is important to explain substantial fluctuations in interest rates over the past 40 years. For example, the interest rate on three-month Treasury bills peaked at over 16% in 1981. This interest rate fell to below 1% in 2004 and rose to 5% by 2007. It then fell to near zero from 2009 to 2015, then rose to above 2% in 2018, only to fall back to near zero again when the coronavirus pandemic led to the Covid-19 recession in March 2020.

Because different interest rates have a tendency to move in unison, economists frequently lump interest rates together and refer to "the" interest rate. As Figure 1 shows, however, interest rates on several types of bonds can differ substantially. The interest rate on three-month Treasury bills, for example, fluctuates more than the other interest rates and is lower on average. The interest rate on Baa (medium-quality) corporate bonds is higher, on average, than the other interest rates, and the spread between it and the other rates became larger in the 1970s, narrowed in the 1990s, rose briefly in the early 2000s, narrowed again, and then rose sharply starting in the summer of 2007. It then began to decline toward the end of 2009, returning to low levels by 2018, and then rose again during the Covid-19 recession in 2020.

In Chapter 2 we study the role of bond markets in the economy, and in Chapters 4 through 6 we examine what an interest rate is, how the common movements in interest rates come about, and why the interest rates on different bonds vary.

The Stock Market

A **common stock** (typically called simply a **stock**) represents a share of ownership in a corporation. It is a security that is a claim on the earnings and assets of the corporation. Issuing stock and selling it to the public is a way for corporations to raise funds

---

[1]The definition of *bond* used throughout this book is the broad one commonly used in academic settings, which covers both short- and long-term debt instruments. However, some practitioners in financial markets use the word *bond* to describe only specific long-term debt instruments such as corporate bonds or U.S. Treasury bonds.

Real-time data

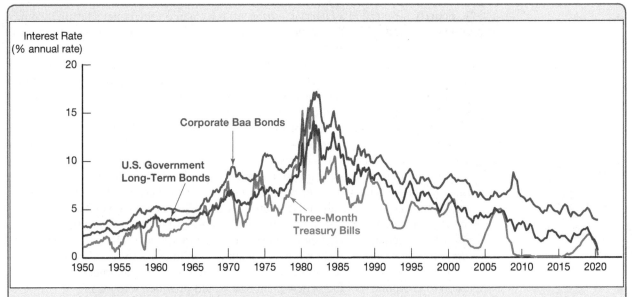

FIGURE 1   Interest Rates on Selected Bonds, 1950–2020

Although different interest rates have a tendency to move in unison, they often differ substantially, and the spreads between them fluctuate.

Source: Federal Reserve Bank of St. Louis, FRED database: https://fred.stlouisfed.org/series/TB3MS; https://fred.stlouisfed.org/series/GS10; https://fred.stlouisfed.org/series/BAA

to finance their activities. The stock market, in which claims on the earnings of corporations (shares of stock) are traded, is the most widely followed financial market in almost every country that has one; that's why it's often called simply "the market." A big swing in the prices of shares in the stock market is always a major story on the evening news. People often speculate on where the market is heading and get very excited when they can brag about their latest "big killing," but they become depressed when they suffer a big loss. The attention the market receives can probably be best explained by one simple fact: It is a place where people can get rich—or poor—very quickly.

As Figure 2 indicates, stock prices are extremely volatile. After rising steadily during the 1980s, the market experienced the worst one-day drop in its entire history on October 19, 1987—"Black Monday"—with the Dow Jones Industrial Average (DJIA) falling by 22%. From then until 2000, the stock market experienced one of the greatest rises (often referred to as a "bull market") in its history, with the Dow climbing to a peak of over 11,000. With the collapse of the high-tech bubble in 2000, the stock market fell sharply, dropping by over 30% by late 2002. It then rose to an all-time high above the 14,000 level in 2007, only to fall by over 50% of its value to a low below 7,000 in 2009. Another bull market then began, with the Dow reaching a peak just short of 30,000 in February 2020. The stock market then crashed in the wake of the coronavirus pandemic, falling by over 25% in the space of a month. These considerable fluctuations in stock prices affect the size of people's wealth and, as a result, their willingness to spend.

The stock market is also an important factor in business investment decisions, because the price of shares affects the amount of funds that can be raised by selling newly issued stock to finance investment spending. A higher price for a firm's shares

Real-time data

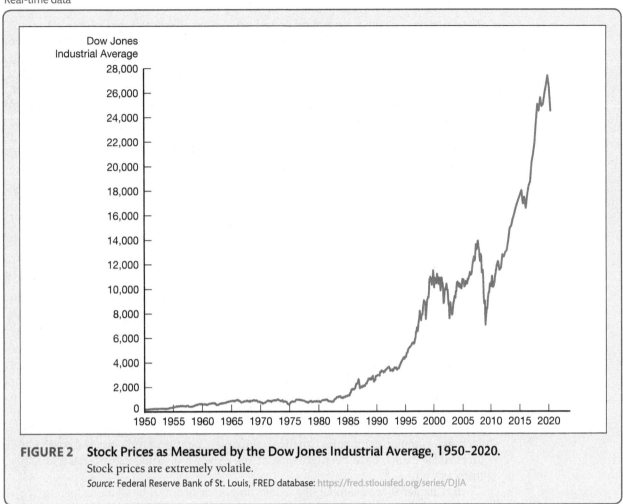

FIGURE 2 **Stock Prices as Measured by the Dow Jones Industrial Average, 1950–2020.**
Stock prices are extremely volatile.
Source: Federal Reserve Bank of St. Louis, FRED database: https://fred.stlouisfed.org/series/DJIA

means that the firm can raise a larger amount of funds, which it can then use to buy production facilities and equipment.

In Chapter 2 we examine the role the stock market plays in the financial system, and in Chapter 7 we return to the issue of how stock prices behave and respond to information in the marketplace.

1.2 WHY STUDY FINANCIAL INSTITUTIONS AND BANKING?

LO 1.2 Describe how financial intermediation and financial innovation affect banking and the economy.

Part 3 of this book focuses on financial institutions and the business of banking. Banks and other financial institutions are what make financial markets work. Without them, financial markets would not be able to move funds from people who save to people who have productive investment opportunities. Thus financial institutions play a crucial role in the economy.

Structure of the Financial System

The financial system is complex, comprising many different types of private sector financial institutions, including banks, insurance companies, mutual funds, finance companies, and investment banks, all of which are heavily regulated by the government. If an individual wanted to make a loan to IBM or General Motors, for example, he or she would not go directly to the president of the company and offer a loan. Instead, the individual would lend to such a company indirectly through **financial intermediaries**, which are institutions that borrow funds from people who have saved and in turn make loans to people who need funds.

Why are financial intermediaries so crucial to well-functioning financial markets? Why do they extend credit to one party but not to another? Why do they usually write complicated legal documents when they extend loans? Why are they the most heavily regulated businesses in the economy?

We answer these questions in Chapter 8 by developing a coherent framework for analyzing financial structure in the United States and in the rest of the world.

Banks and Other Financial Institutions

Banks are financial institutions that accept deposits and make loans. The term *banks* includes firms such as commercial banks, savings and loan associations, mutual savings banks, and credit unions. Banks are the financial intermediaries that the average person interacts with most frequently. A person who needs a loan to buy a house or a car usually obtains it from a local bank. Most Americans keep a large portion of their financial wealth in banks in the form of checking accounts, savings accounts, or other types of bank deposits. Because banks are the largest financial intermediaries in our economy, they deserve the most careful study. However, banks are not the only important financial institutions. Indeed, in recent years, other financial institutions, such as insurance companies, finance companies, pension funds, mutual funds, and investment banks, have been growing at the expense of banks, so we need to study them as well.

In Chapter 9, we examine how banks and other financial institutions manage their assets and liabilities to make profits. In Chapter 10, we extend the economic analysis in Chapter 8 to understand why financial regulation takes the form it does and what can go wrong in the regulatory process. In Chapter 11, we look at the banking industry and examine how the competitive environment has changed this industry. We also learn why some financial institutions have been growing at the expense of others.

Financial Innovation

In Chapter 11, we also study **financial innovation**, the development of new financial products and services. We will see why and how financial innovation takes place, with particular emphasis on how the dramatic improvements in information technology have led to new financial products and the ability to deliver financial services electronically through what has become known as **e-finance**. We also study financial innovation because it shows us how creative thinking on the part of financial institutions can lead to higher profits but can also sometimes result in financial disasters. By studying how financial institutions have been creative in the past, we obtain a better grasp of how they may be creative in the future. This knowledge provides us with useful clues about how the financial system may change over time.

Financial Crises

At times, the financial system seizes up and produces **financial crises**, which are major disruptions in financial markets that are characterized by sharp declines in asset prices and the failures of many financial and nonfinancial firms. Financial crises have been a feature of capitalist economies for hundreds of years and are typically followed by severe business cycle downturns. Starting in August 2007, the U.S. economy was hit by the worst financial crisis since the Great Depression. Defaults in subprime residential mortgages led to major losses in financial institutions, producing not only numerous bank failures but also the demise of Bear Stearns and Lehman Brothers, two of the largest investment banks in the United States. The crisis produced the worst economic downturn since the Great Depression, and as a result, it is now referred to as the "Great Recession."

We discuss why these crises occur and why they do so much damage to the economy in Chapter 12.

1.3 WHY STUDY MONEY AND MONETARY POLICY?

LO 1.3 Identify the basic links among monetary policy, the business cycle, and economic variables.

Money, also referred to as the **money supply**, is defined as anything that is generally accepted as payment for goods or services or in the repayment of debts. Money is linked to changes in economic variables that affect all of us and are important to the health of the economy. The final two parts of this book examine the role of money in the economy.

Money and Business Cycles

During 1981–1982, the total production of goods and services (called **aggregate output**) in the U.S. economy fell and the **unemployment rate** (the percentage of the available labor force unemployed) rose to over 10%. After 1982, the economy began to expand rapidly, and by 1989, the unemployment rate had declined to 5%. In 1990, the eight-year expansion came to an end, with the unemployment rate rising to above 7%. The economy bottomed out in 1991, and the subsequent recovery was the longest in U.S. history up to that time, with the unemployment rate falling to around 4%. A mild economic downturn began in March 2001, with unemployment rising to 6%; the economy began to recover in November 2001, with unemployment eventually declining to a low of 4.4%. Starting in December 2007, the economy went into a steep economic downturn and unemployment rose to over 10% before the economy slowly began to recover in June 2009. By early 2020, the unemployment rate had fallen to 3.5%, only to rise sharply starting in March 2020, with the onset of the Covid-19 recession.

Why did the economy undergo such pronounced fluctuations? Evidence suggests that money plays an important role in generating **business cycles**, the upward and downward movement of aggregate output produced in the economy. Business cycles affect all of us in immediate and important ways. When output is rising, for example, it is easier to find a good job; when output is falling, finding a good job might be difficult. Figure 3 shows the movements of the rate of growth of the money supply over the 1950–2020 period, with the shaded areas representing **recessions**, or periods of declining aggregate output. We see that the rate of money growth declined before most recessions, indicating that changes in money growth might be a driving force behind

Real-time data

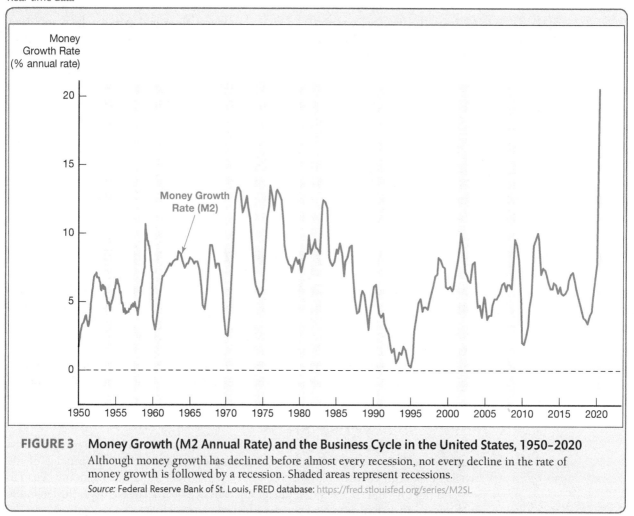

FIGURE 3   **Money Growth (M2 Annual Rate) and the Business Cycle in the United States, 1950–2020**

Although money growth has declined before almost every recession, not every decline in the rate of money growth is followed by a recession. Shaded areas represent recessions.

Source: Federal Reserve Bank of St. Louis, FRED database: https://fred.stlouisfed.org/series/M2SL

business cycle fluctuations. However, declines in the rate of money growth are often not followed by a recession.

We explore how money and monetary policy might affect aggregate output in Chapters 19 through 25 (Part 6) of this book, where we study **monetary theory**, the theory that relates the quantity of money and monetary policy to changes in aggregate economic activity and inflation.

Money and Inflation

The movie you paid $10 to see last week would have set you back only a dollar or two 30 years ago. In fact, for $10, you probably could have had dinner, seen the movie, and bought yourself a big bucket of hot buttered popcorn. As shown in Figure 4, which illustrates the movement of average prices in the U.S. economy from 1950 to 2020, the prices of most items are quite a bit higher now than they were then. The average price of goods and services in an economy is called the **aggregate price level** or, more simply, the *price level* (a more precise definition is found in the appendix to this chapter). From 1960 to 2020, the price level has increased more than sevenfold. **Inflation**, a continual increase in

Real-time data

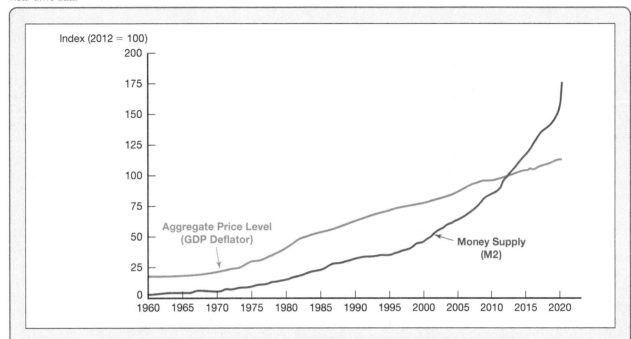

FIGURE 4 Aggregate Price Level and the Money Supply in the United States, 1960–2020
From 1960 to 2020, the price level has increased more than sevenfold.
Source: Federal Reserve Bank of St. Louis, FRED database: https://fred.stlouisfed.org/series/M2SL; https://fred.stlouisfed.org/series/GDPDEF

the price level, affects individuals, businesses, and the government. It is generally regarded as an important problem to be solved and is often at the top of political and policymaking agendas. To solve the inflation problem, we need to know something about its causes.

What explains inflation? One clue to answering this question is found in Figure 4, which plots the money supply versus the price level. As we can see, the price level and the money supply generally rise together. These data seem to indicate that a continuing increase in the money supply might be an important factor in causing the continuing increase in the price level that we call inflation.

Further evidence that inflation may be tied to continuing increases in the money supply is found in Figure 5, which plots the average **inflation rate** (the rate of change of the price level, usually measured as a percentage change per year) for a number of countries over the ten-year period 2009–2019 against the average rate of money growth over the same period. As you can see, a positive association exists between inflation and the growth rate of the money supply: The countries with high money growth rates, such as Russia and Turkey, tend to have higher inflation rates. By contrast, Japan and the Euro area experienced low inflation rates over the same period, and their rates of money growth were low. Such evidence led Milton Friedman, a Nobel laureate in economics, to make the famous statement, "Inflation is always and everywhere a monetary phenomenon."[2] We look at the quantity of money and monetary policy's role in creating inflation in Chapters 19 and 23.

[2]Milton Friedman, *Dollars and Deficits* (Upper Saddle River, NJ: Prentice Hall, 1968), 39.

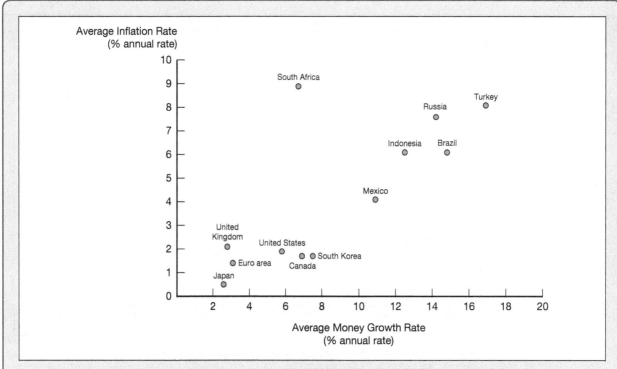

FIGURE 5   **Average Inflation Rate Versus Average Rate of Money Growth for Selected Countries, 2009–2019**

A positive association can be seen between the ten-year averages of inflation and the growth rate of the money supply: Countries with high money growth rates tend to have higher inflation rates.

Source: Federal Reserve Bank of St. Louis, FRED database: https://fred.stlouisfed.org/

Money and Interest Rates

In addition to other factors, money plays an important role in interest-rate fluctuations, which are of great concern to businesses and consumers. Figure 6 shows changes in the interest rate on long-term Treasury bonds and the rate of money growth from 1950 to 2020. As the money growth rate rose in the 1960s and 1970s, the long-term bond rate rose with it. However, the relationship between money growth and interest rates has been less clear-cut since 1980. We analyze the relationship between money growth and interest rates when we examine the behavior of interest rates in Chapter 5.

Conduct of Monetary Policy

Because money affects many economic variables that are important to the well-being of our economy, politicians and policymakers throughout the world care about the conduct of **monetary policy**, the management of money and interest rates. The organization responsible for the conduct of a nation's monetary policy is the **central bank**. The United States' central bank is the **Federal Reserve System** (also called simply "**the Fed**"). In Chapters 13 through 16 (Part 4), we study how central banks such as the Federal Reserve System can affect the quantity of money and interest rates in the economy, and then we look at how monetary policy is actually conducted in the United States and elsewhere.

Real-time data

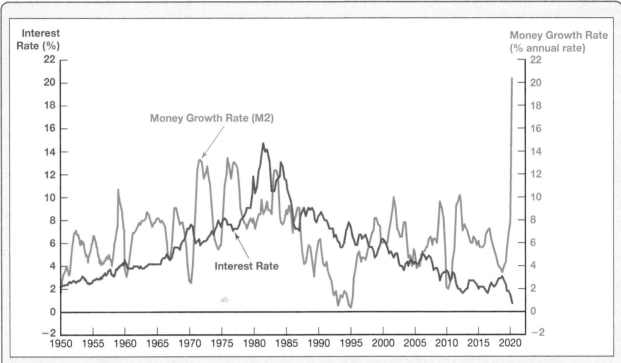

FIGURE 6   **Money Growth (M2 Annual Rate) and Interest Rates (Long-Term U.S. Treasury Bonds), 1950–2020**

As the money growth rate rose in the 1960s and 1970s, the long-term bond rate rose with it. However, the relationship between money growth and interest rates has been less clear-cut since 1980.

Source: Federal Reserve Bank of St. Louis, FRED database: https://fred.stlouisfed.org/series/M2SL; https://fred.stlouisfed.org/series/GS10

Fiscal Policy and Monetary Policy

Fiscal policy involves decisions about government spending and taxation. A **budget deficit** is an excess of government expenditures with respect to tax revenues for a particular time period, typically a year, while a **budget surplus** arises when tax revenues exceed government expenditures. The government must finance any budget deficit by borrowing, whereas a budget surplus leads to a lower government debt burden. As Figure 7 shows, the budget deficit, relative to the size of the U.S. economy, peaked in 1983 at 6% of national output (as calculated by the **gross domestic product**, or **GDP**, a measure of aggregate output described in the appendix to this chapter). Since then, the budget deficit at first declined to less than 3% of GDP, rose again to 5% of GDP by the early 1990s, and fell subsequently, leading to budget surpluses from 1999 to 2001. In the aftermath of the terrorist attacks of September 11, 2001, the war in Iraq that began in March 2003, and the 2007–2009 financial crisis, the budget swung back into deficit, with deficits at one point exceeding 10% of GDP and then falling substantially thereafter. The budget deficit then rose starting in 2016 and shot up sharply when the coronavirus pandemic hit the economy in 2020. What to do about budget deficits has been the subject of legislation and the source of bitter battles between the president and Congress in recent years.

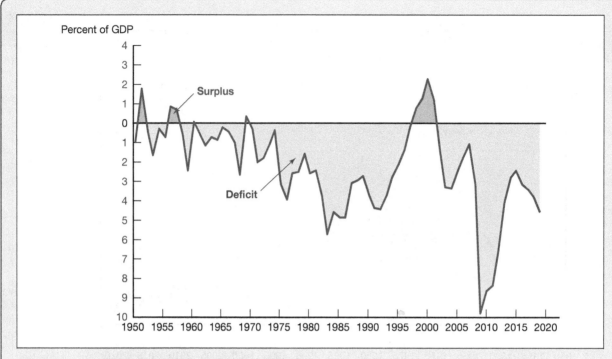

FIGURE 7   **Government Budget Surplus or Deficit as a Percentage of Gross Domestic Product, 1950–2019**

The budget deficit, relative to the size of the U.S. economy, has fluctuated substantially over the years. It rose to 6% of GDP in 1983 and then fell, eventually leading to budget surpluses from 1999 to 2001. Subsequently, budget deficits climbed, peaking at nearly 10% of GDP in 2009, fell substantially thereafter, and then rose starting in 2016.

Source: Federal Reserve Bank of St. Louis, FRED database: https://fred.stlouisfed.org/series/FYFSGDA188S

You may have read statements in newspapers or heard on TV that budget surpluses are a good thing, while deficits are undesirable. In Chapter 19, we examine why deficits might result in a higher rate of money growth, a higher rate of inflation, and higher interest rates.

1.4 WHY STUDY INTERNATIONAL FINANCE?

LO 1.4 Explain the importance of exchange rates in a global economy.

The globalization of financial markets has accelerated at a rapid pace in recent years. Financial markets have become increasingly integrated throughout the world. American companies often borrow in foreign financial markets, and foreign companies borrow in U.S. financial markets. Banks and other financial institutions, such as JPMorgan Chase, Citigroup, UBS, and Deutsche Bank, have become increasingly international, with operations in many countries throughout the world. Part 5 of this book explores the foreign exchange market and the international financial system.

The Foreign Exchange Market

For funds to be transferred from one country to another, they have to be converted from the currency of the country of origin (say, dollars) into the currency of the country they are going to (say, euros). The **foreign exchange market** is where this conversion takes place, so it is instrumental in moving funds between countries. It is also important because it is where the **foreign exchange rate**, or the price of one country's currency in terms of another's, is determined.

Figure 8 shows the exchange rate for the U.S. dollar from 1973 to 2020 (measured as the value of the U.S. dollar in terms of a basket of major foreign currencies). The fluctuations in prices in this market have been substantial: The dollar's value rose slightly until 1976 and then reached a low point in the 1978–1980 period. From 1980 to early 1985, the dollar's value appreciated dramatically and then declined again, reaching another low in 1995. The dollar subsequently appreciated until 2002 and then depreciated substantially from 2002 until 2011, with only a temporary upturn in 2008 and 2009. From 2011 until 2020, the dollar appreciated again to values near its previous peak in 2002.

What have these fluctuations in the exchange rate meant to the American public and businesses? A change in the exchange rate has a direct effect on American consumers because it affects the cost of imports. In 2001, when the euro was worth around 85 cents, 100 euros of European goods (say, French wine) cost $85. When the dollar subsequently weakened, raising the cost of one euro to a peak of nearly $1.50, the same 100 euros of wine now cost $150. Thus a weaker dollar leads to more expensive foreign goods, makes vacationing abroad more expensive, and raises the cost of indulging your desire for imported delicacies. When the value of the dollar drops, Americans decrease their purchases of foreign goods and increase their consumption of domestic goods (such as travel within the United States or American-made wine).

Real-time data

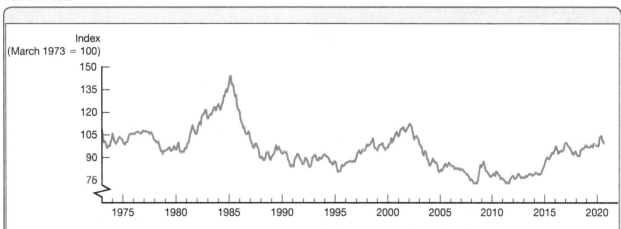

FIGURE 8   **Exchange Rate of the U.S. Dollar, 1973–2020**

The value of the U.S. dollar relative to other currencies has fluctuated substantially over the years.

Source: Federal Reserve Bank of St. Louis, FRED database: https://fred.stlouisfed.org/series/TWEXM and https://fred.stlouisfed.org/series/DTWEXBGS

Conversely, a strong dollar means that U.S. goods exported abroad will cost more in foreign countries, and hence foreigners will buy fewer of them. Exports of steel, for example, declined when the dollar strengthened during the 1980–1985, 1995–2002, and 2011–2020 periods. A strong dollar benefited American consumers by making foreign goods cheaper but hurt American businesses and eliminated some jobs by cutting both domestic and foreign sales of the businesses' products. The decline in the value of the dollar from 1985 to 1995 and from 2002 to 2011 had the opposite effect: It made foreign goods more expensive but made American businesses more competitive. Fluctuations in the foreign exchange markets have major consequences for the American economy.

In Chapter 17, we study how exchange rates are determined in the foreign exchange market, in which dollars are bought and sold for foreign currencies.

The International Financial System

The tremendous increase in capital flows among countries has heightened the international financial system's impact on domestic economies. Issues we will explore in Chapter 18 include:

- How does a country's decision to fix its exchange rate to that of another nation shape the conduct of monetary policy?
- What is the impact of capital controls that restrict mobility of capital across national borders on domestic financial systems and the performance of the economy?
- What role should international financial institutions, such as the International Monetary Fund, play in the international financial system?

1.5 MONEY, BANKING, AND FINANCIAL MARKETS AND YOUR CAREER

LO 1.5 Explain how the study of money, banking, and financial markets may advance your career.

Before taking this class, you might have asked yourself the practical question, "How will the study of money, banking, and financial markets help my career?" For some of you, the answer is straightforward. Financial institutions are among the largest employers in the country, and studying money, banking, and financial markets can help you get a good job in the financial sector.

Even if your interests lie elsewhere, the study of money, banking, and financial institutions can help advance your career because at many times in your life, as an employee or the owner of a business, the critical thinking skills learned in this study will improve your performance. For example, understanding monetary policy may help you predict when interest rates will rise or fall, helping you to make decisions about whether it is better to borrow now or to wait until later. Knowing how banks and other financial institutions are managed may help you get a better deal when you need to borrow from them or if you decide to supply them with funds. Knowledge of how financial markets work may enable you to make better investment decisions, whether for yourself or for the company you work for.

1.6 HOW WE WILL STUDY MONEY, BANKING, AND FINANCIAL MARKETS

LO 1.6 Describe how the text approaches the teaching of money, banking, and financial markets.

This textbook stresses the "economic way of thinking" by developing a unifying framework in which you will study money, banking, and financial markets. This analytic framework uses a few basic economic concepts to organize your thinking about the determination of asset prices, the structure of financial markets, bank management, and the role of money in the economy. It encompasses the following basic concepts:

- A simplified approach to the demand for assets
- The concept of equilibrium
- Basic supply and demand analysis to explain behavior of financial markets
- The search for profits
- An approach to financial structure based on transaction costs and asymmetric information
- Aggregate supply and demand analysis

The unifying framework used in this book will keep your knowledge from becoming obsolete and make the material more interesting. It will enable you to learn what *really* matters without having to memorize a mass of dull facts that you will forget soon after the final exam. This framework will also provide you with the tools you need to understand trends in the financial marketplace and in variables such as interest rates, exchange rates, inflation, and aggregate output.

To help you understand and apply the unifying analytic framework, simple models are constructed in which the variables held constant are carefully delineated. Each step in the derivation of the model is clearly and carefully laid out, and the models are then used to explain various phenomena by focusing on changes in one variable at a time, holding all other variables constant.

To reinforce the models' usefulness, this text uses case studies, applications, and special-interest boxes to present evidence that supports or casts doubts on the theories being discussed. This exposure to real-life events and empirical data should dissuade you from thinking that all economists do is make abstract assumptions and develop theories that have little to do with actual behavior.

To function better financially in the real world outside the classroom, you must have the tools with which to follow the financial news that is reported in leading financial publications and on the Web. To help and encourage you to read the financial news, this book contains special boxed inserts titled "Following the Financial News" that provide detailed information and definitions to help you evaluate data that are discussed frequently in the media. This text also allows you to view the most current data for a high percentage of the in-text data figures using the Federal Reserve Bank of St. Louis's FRED database. Figures for which you can do this are labeled *Real-Time Data*.

To master any field, you need to practice, practice, practice. To help you in this endeavor, this book contains over 700 end-of-chapter questions and applied problems that ask you to apply the analytic concepts you have learned to real-world issues. In addition, at the end of almost every chapter there are several real-time data analysis problems, which ask you to download the most recent data from the Federal Reserve Bank of St. Louis's FRED database and then use these data to answer interesting questions.

CONCLUDING REMARKS

The study of money, banking, and financial markets is an exciting field that directly affects your life and career. Interest rates influence the earnings you make on your savings and the payments on loans you may seek for a car or a house, and monetary policy may affect your job prospects and the prices you will pay for goods in the future. Your study of money, banking, and financial markets will introduce you to many of the controversies related to economic policy that are hotly debated in the political arena and will help you gain a clearer understanding of the economic phenomena you hear about in the news media. The knowledge you gain will stay with you and benefit you long after this course is over.

SUMMARY

1. Activities in financial markets directly affect individuals' wealth, the behavior of businesses, and the efficiency of our economy. Three financial markets deserve particular attention: the bond market (where interest rates are determined), the stock market (which has a major effect on people's wealth and on firms' investment decisions), and the foreign exchange market (because fluctuations in the foreign exchange rate have major consequences for the U.S. economy).

2. Banks and other financial institutions channel funds from people who might not put them to productive use to people who can do so and thus play a crucial role in improving the efficiency of the economy. When the financial system seizes up and produces a financial crisis, financial firms fail, which causes severe damage to the economy.

3. Money and monetary policy appear to have a major influence on inflation, business cycles, and interest rates.

Because these economic variables are so important to the health of the economy, we need to understand how monetary policy is and should be conducted. We also need to study government fiscal policy because it can be an influential factor in the conduct of monetary policy.

4. The study of money, banking, and financial markets can help advance your career by helping you get a high-paying job in the financial sector, decide when you or your firm should borrow, get a better deal from financial institutions, or make better investment decisions.

5. This textbook stresses the "economic way of thinking" by developing a unifying analytic framework in which to study money, banking, and financial markets, using a few basic economic principles. The textbook also emphasizes the interaction of theoretical analysis and empirical data.

KEY TERMS

aggregate income, p. 19
aggregate output, p. 7
aggregate price level, p. 8
asset, p. 3
banks, p. 6
bond, p. 3
budget deficit, p. 11
budget surplus, p. 11
business cycles, p. 7
central bank, p. 10
common stock, p. 3

e-finance, p. 6
Federal Reserve System (the Fed), p. 10
financial crises, p. 7
financial innovation, p. 6
financial intermediaries, p. 6
financial markets, p. 2
fiscal policy, p. 11
foreign exchange market, p. 13
foreign exchange rate, p. 13
gross domestic product (GDP), p. 19
inflation, p. 8

inflation rate, p. 9
interest rate, p. 3
monetary policy, p. 10
monetary theory, p. 8
money (money supply), p. 7
recession, p. 7
security, p. 3
stock, p. 3
unemployment rate, p. 7

QUESTIONS

1. What is the typical relationship among interest rates on three-month Treasury bills, long-term Treasury bonds, and Baa corporate bonds?

2. What effect might a fall in stock prices have on business investment?

3. Explain the main difference between a bond and a common stock.

4. Explain the link between well-performing financial markets and economic growth. Name one channel through which financial markets might affect economic growth and poverty.

5. What was the main cause of the recession that began in 2007?

6. Can you think of a reason why people in general do not lend money to one another to buy a house or a car? How would your answer explain the existence of banks?

7. What are the other important financial intermediaries in the economy, besides banks?

8. Can you date the latest financial crisis in the United States or in Europe? Are there reasons to think that these crises might have been related? Why?

9. Has the inflation rate in the United States increased or decreased in the past few years? What about interest rates?

10. If history repeats itself and we see a decline in the rate of money growth, what might you expect to happen to
    a. real output?
    b. the inflation rate?
    c. interest rates?

11. When interest rates decrease, how might businesses and consumers change their economic behavior?

12. Is everybody worse off when interest rates rise?

13. Why do managers of financial institutions care so much about the activities of the Federal Reserve System?

14. How does the current size of the U.S. budget deficit compare to the historical budget deficit or surplus for the time period since 1950?

15. How would a fall in the value of the pound sterling affect British consumers?

16. How would an increase in the value of the pound sterling affect American businesses?

17. How can changes in foreign exchange rates affect the profitability of financial institutions?

18. According to Figure 8, in which years would you have chosen to visit the Grand Canyon in Arizona rather than the Tower of London?

19. When the dollar is worth more in relation to currencies of other countries, are you more likely to buy American-made or foreign-made jeans? Are U.S. companies that manufacture jeans happier when the dollar is strong or when it is weak? What about an American company that is in the business of importing jeans into the United States?

20. Much of the U.S. government debt is held by foreign investors as Treasury bonds and bills. How do fluctuations in the dollar exchange rate affect the value of that debt held by foreigners?

APPLIED PROBLEMS

21. The following table lists the foreign exchange rate between U.S. dollars and British pounds (GBP) during May 2020. Which day would have been the best for converting $200 into British pounds? Which day would have been the worst? What would be the difference in pounds?

Date	$/£	Date	$/£
05-01	1.2509	05-18	1.2211
05-04	1.2430	05-19	1.2255
05 05	1.2449	05-20	1.2257
05-06	1.2347	05 21	1.2227
05-07	1.2349	05-22	1.2178
05-08	1.2436	05-25	NA
05-11	1.2330	05-26	1.2337
05-12	1.2299	05-27	1.2231
05-13	1.2225	05-28	1.2325
05-14	1.2194	05-29	1.2320
05-15	1.2129		

DATA ANALYSIS PROBLEMS

The Problems update with real-time data in **MyLab Economics** and are available for practice or instructor assignment.

1. **Real-time Data Analysis** Go to the St. Louis Federal Reserve FRED database, and find data on the three-month Treasury bill rate (TB3MS), the three-month AA nonfinancial commercial paper rate (CPN3M), the 30-year Treasury bond rate (GS30), the 30-year conventional mortgage rate (MORTGAGE30US), and the NBER recession indicators (USREC). For the mortgage rate indicator, set the frequency to "monthly."

   a. In general, how do these interest rates behave during recessions and during expansionary periods?

   b. In general, how do the three-month rates compare to the 30-year rates? How do the Treasury rates compare to the respective commercial paper and mortgage rates?

   c. For the most recent available month of data, take the average of each of the three-month rates and compare it to the average of the three-month rates from January 2000. How do the averages compare?

   d. For the most recent available month of data, take the average of each of the 30-year rates and compare it to the average of the 30-year rates from January 2000. How do the averages compare?

2. **Real-time Data Analysis** Go to the St. Louis Federal Reserve FRED database, and find data on the M1 money supply (M1SL) and the 10-year Treasury bond rate (GS10). Add the two series into a single graph by using the "Add Data Series" feature. Transform the M1 money supply variable into the M1 growth rate by adjusting the *units* for the M1 money supply to "Percent Change from Year Ago."

   a. In general, how have the growth rate of the M1 money supply and the 10-year Treasury bond rate behaved during recessions and during expansionary periods since the year 2000?

   b. In general, is there an obvious, stable relationship between money growth and the 10-year interest rate since the year 2000?

   c. Compare the money growth rate and the 10-year interest rate for the most recent month available to the rates for January 2000. How do the rates compare?

1

Defining Aggregate Output, Income, the Price Level, and the Inflation Rate

Because these terms are used so frequently throughout the text, we need to have a clear understanding of the definitions of *aggregate output*, *income*, the *price level*, and the *inflation rate*.

AGGREGATE OUTPUT AND INCOME

The most commonly reported measure of aggregate output, the **gross domestic product (GDP)**, is the market value of all final goods and services produced in a country during the course of a year. This measure excludes two sets of items that at first glance you might think it would include. Purchases of goods that have been produced in the past, whether a Rembrandt painting or a house built 20 years ago, are not counted as part of GDP; nor are purchases of stocks or bonds. Neither of these categories enters into the GDP because these categories do not include goods and services produced during the course of the year. Intermediate goods, which are used up in producing final goods and services, such as the sugar in a candy bar or the energy used to produce steel, are also not counted separately as part of the GDP. Because the value of the final goods already includes the value of the intermediate goods, to count them separately would be to count them twice.

Aggregate income, the total income of *factors of production* (land, labor, and capital) from producing goods and services in the economy during the course of the year, is best thought of as being equal to aggregate output. Because the payments for final goods and services must eventually flow back to the owners of the factors of production as income, income payments must equal payments for final goods and services. For example, if the economy has an aggregate output of $10 trillion, total income payments in the economy (aggregate income) are also $10 trillion.

REAL VERSUS NOMINAL MAGNITUDES

When the total value of final goods and services is calculated using current prices, the resulting GDP measure is referred to as *nominal GDP*. The word *nominal* indicates that values are measured using current prices. If all prices doubled but actual production of goods and services remained the same, nominal GDP would double, even though people would not enjoy the benefits of twice as many goods and services. As a result, nominal variables can be misleading measures of economic well-being.

A more reliable measure of economic production expresses values in terms of prices for an arbitrary base year, currently 2009. GDP measured with constant prices is referred to as *real GDP*, the word *real* indicating that values are measured in terms of fixed prices. Real variables thus measure the quantities of goods and services and do not change because prices have changed, but rather only if actual quantities have changed.

A brief example will make the distinction clearer. Suppose that you have a nominal income of $30,000 in 2022 and that your nominal income was $15,000 in 2012. If all prices doubled between 2012 and 2022, are you better off? The answer is no: Although your income has doubled, your $30,000 buys you only the same amount of goods because prices have also doubled. A *real* income measure indicates that your income in terms of the goods it can buy is the same. Measured in 2012 prices, the $30,000 of nominal income in 2022 turns out to be only $15,000 of real income. Because your real income is actually the same for the two years, you are no better or worse off in 2022 than you were in 2012.

Because real variables measure quantities in terms of real goods and services, they are typically of more interest than nominal variables. In this text, discussion of aggregate output or aggregate income always refers to real measures (such as real GDP).

AGGREGATE PRICE LEVEL

In this chapter, we defined the aggregate price level as a measure of average prices in the economy. Three measures of the aggregate price level are commonly encountered in economic data. The first is the *GDP deflator*, which is defined as nominal GDP divided by real GDP. Thus, if 2022 nominal GDP is $10 trillion but 2022 real GDP in 2012 prices is $9 trillion,

$$\text{GDP deflator} = \frac{\$10 \text{ trillion}}{\$9 \text{ trillion}} = 1.11$$

The GDP deflator equation indicates that, on average, prices have risen 11% since 2012. Typically, measures of the price level are presented in the form of a price index, which expresses the price level for the base year (in our example, 2012) as 100. Thus the GDP deflator for 2022 would be 111.

Another popular measure of the aggregate price level (which officials in the Fed frequently focus on) is the *PCE deflator*, which is similar to the GDP deflator and is defined as nominal personal consumption expenditures (PCE) divided by real PCE.

The measure of the aggregate price level that is most frequently reported in the press is the *consumer price index (CPI)*. The CPI is measured by pricing a "basket" of goods and services bought by a typical urban household. If, over the course of the year, the cost of this basket of goods and services rises from $500 to $600, the CPI has risen by 20%. The CPI is also expressed as a price index with the base year equal to 100.

The CPI, the PCE deflator, and the GDP deflator measures of the price level can be used to convert or deflate a nominal magnitude into a real magnitude. This is accomplished by dividing the nominal magnitude by the price index. In our example, in which the GDP deflator for 2022 is 1.11 (expressed as an index value of 111), real GDP for 2022 equals

$$\frac{\$10 \text{ trillion}}{1.11} = \$9 \text{ trillion in 2012 prices}$$

which corresponds to the real GDP figure for 2022 assumed earlier.

GROWTH RATES AND THE INFLATION RATE

The media often talk about the economy's growth rate, and particularly the growth rate of real GDP. A growth rate is defined as the percentage change in a variable, that is,

$$\text{growth rate of } x = \frac{x_t - x_{t-1}}{x_{t-1}} \times 100$$

where t indicates today and $t - 1$ indicates a year earlier.

For example, if real GDP grew from $9 trillion in 2022 to $9.5 trillion in 2023, then the GDP growth rate for 2023 would be 5.6%:

$$\text{GDP growth rate} = \frac{\$9.5 \text{ trillion} - \$9 \text{ trillion}}{\$9 \text{ trillion}} \times 100 = 5.6\%$$

The inflation rate is defined as the growth rate of the aggregate price level. Thus, if the GDP deflator rose from 111 in 2022 to 113 in 2023, the inflation rate using the GDP deflator would be 1.8%:

$$\text{inflation rate} = \frac{113 - 111}{111} \times 100 = 1.8\%$$

If the growth rate is for a period of less than one year, it is usually reported on an annualized basis; that is, it is converted to the growth rate over a year's time, assuming that the growth rate remains constant. For GDP, which is reported quarterly, the annualized growth rate would be approximately four times the percentage change in GDP from the previous quarter. For example, if GDP rose $\frac{1}{2}$% from the first quarter of 2022 to the second quarter of 2022, then the annualized GDP growth rate for the second quarter of 2022 would be reported as 2%($= 4 \times \frac{1}{2}$%). (A more accurate calculation would be 2.02%, because a precise quarterly growth rate should be compounded on a quarterly basis.)

2 An Overview of the Financial System

Learning Objectives

2.1 Compare and contrast direct and indirect finance.

2.2 Identify the structure and components of financial markets.

2.3 List and describe the different types of financial market instruments.

2.4 Recognize the international dimensions of financial markets.

2.5 Summarize the roles of transaction costs, risk sharing, and information costs as they relate to financial intermediaries.

2.6 List and describe the different types of financial intermediaries.

2.7 Identify the reasons for and list the types of financial market regulations.

Preview

Inez the Inventor has designed a low-cost robot that cleans the house (even does the windows!), washes the car, and mows the lawn, but she has no funds to put her wonderful invention into production. Walter the Widower has plenty of savings, which he and his wife accumulated over the years. If Inez and Walter could get together so that Walter could provide funds to Inez, Inez's robot would see the light of day, and the economy would be better off: We would have cleaner houses, shinier cars, and more beautiful lawns.

Financial markets (bond and stock markets) and financial intermediaries (such as banks, insurance companies, and pension funds) serve the basic function of getting people like Inez and Walter together so that funds can move from those who have a surplus of funds (Walter) to those who have a shortage of funds (Inez). More realistically, when Apple invents a better iPad, it may need funds to bring its new product to market. Similarly, when a local government needs to build a road or a school, it may require more funds than local property taxes provide. Well-functioning financial markets and financial intermediaries are crucial to economic health.

To study the effects of financial markets and financial intermediaries on the economy, we need to acquire an understanding of their general structure and operation. In this chapter, we learn about the major financial intermediaries and the instruments that are traded in financial markets, as well as how these markets are regulated.

This chapter presents an overview of the fascinating study of financial markets and institutions. We return to a more detailed treatment of the regulation, structure, and evolution of the financial system in Chapters 8 through 12.

2.1 FUNCTION OF FINANCIAL MARKETS

LO 2.1 Compare and contrast direct and indirect finance.

Financial markets perform the essential economic function of channeling funds from households, firms, and governments that have saved surplus funds by spending less than their income to those that have a shortage of funds because they wish to spend more than their income. This function is shown schematically in Figure 1. Those who have saved and are lending funds, the lender-savers, are at the left, and those who must

Mini-lecture

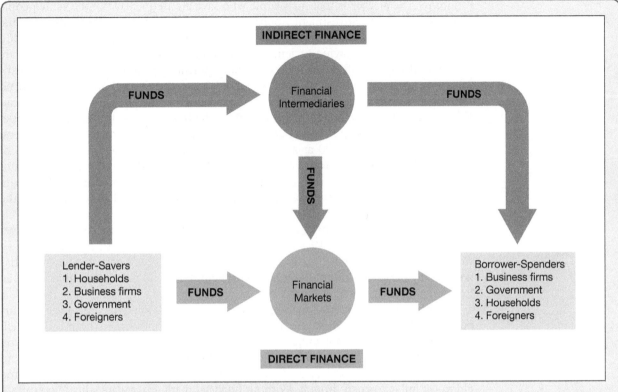

FIGURE 1 **Flows of Funds Through the Financial System**
The arrows show that funds flow from lender-savers to borrower-spenders via two routes: *direct finance,* in which borrowers borrow funds directly from financial markets by selling securities, and *indirect finance,* in which a financial intermediary borrows funds from lender-savers and then uses these funds to make loans to borrower-spenders.

borrow funds to finance their spending, the borrower-spenders, are at the right. The principal lender-savers are households, but business enterprises and the government (particularly state and local government), as well as foreigners and their governments, sometimes also find themselves with excess funds and so lend them out. The most important borrower-spenders are businesses and the government (particularly the federal government), but households and foreigners also borrow to finance their purchases of cars, furniture, and houses. The arrows show that funds flow from lender-savers to borrower-spenders via two routes.

In *direct finance* (the route at the bottom of Figure 1), borrowers borrow funds directly from lenders in financial markets by selling the lenders *securities* (also called *financial instruments*), which are claims on the borrower's future income or assets. Securities are assets for the person who buys them but **liabilities** (IOUs or debts) for the individual or firm that sells (issues) them. For example, if Ford needs to borrow funds to pay for a new factory to manufacture electric cars, it might borrow the funds from savers by selling them a *bond*, a debt security that promises to make periodic payments for a specified period of time, or a *stock*, a security that entitles the owner to a share of the company's profits and assets.

Why is this channeling of funds from savers to spenders so important to the economy? The answer is that the people who save are frequently not the same people who have profitable investment opportunities available to them, the entrepreneurs. Let's first think about this on a personal level. Suppose that you have saved $1,000 this year, but no borrowing or lending is possible because no financial markets are available. If you do not have an investment opportunity that will permit you to earn income with your savings, you will just hold on to the $1,000 and it will earn no interest. However, Carl the Carpenter has a productive use for your $1,000: He can use it to purchase a new tool that will shorten the time it takes him to build a house, thereby earning an extra $200 per year. If you could get in touch with Carl, you could lend him the $1,000 at a rental fee (interest) of $100 per year, and both of you would be better off. You would earn $100 per year on your $1,000, instead of the zero amount that you would earn otherwise, while Carl would earn $100 more income per year (the $200 extra earnings per year minus the $100 rental fee for the use of the funds).

In the absence of financial markets, you and Carl the Carpenter might never get together. You would both be stuck with the status quo, and both of you would be worse off. Without financial markets, it is hard to transfer funds from a person who has no investment opportunities to one who has them. Financial markets are thus essential to promoting economic efficiency.

The existence of financial markets is beneficial even if someone borrows for a purpose other than increasing production in a business. Say that you are recently married, have a good job, and want to buy a house. You earn a good salary, but because you have just started to work, you have not saved much. Over time, you would have no problem saving enough to buy the house of your dreams, but by then you would be too old to get full enjoyment from it. Without financial markets, you are stuck; you cannot buy the house and must continue to live in your tiny apartment.

If a financial market were set up so that people who had built up savings could lend you the funds to buy the house, you would be more than happy to pay them some interest so that you could own a home while you are still young enough to enjoy it. Then, over time, you would pay back your loan. If this loan could occur, you would be better off, as would the persons who made you the loan. They would now earn some interest, whereas they would not if the financial market did not exist.

Now we can see why financial markets have such an important function in the economy. They allow funds to move from people who lack productive investment opportunities to people who have such opportunities. Financial markets are critical for producing an efficient allocation of **capital** (wealth, either financial or physical, that is employed to produce more wealth), which contributes to higher production and efficiency for the overall economy. Indeed, as we will explore in Chapter 12, when financial markets break down during financial crises, as they did during the recent global financial crisis from 2007–2009, severe economic hardship results, which can sometimes lead to dangerous political instability.

Well-functioning financial markets also directly improve the well-being of consumers by allowing them to time their purchases better. They provide funds to young people to buy what they need (and will eventually be able to afford) without forcing them to wait until they have saved up the entire purchase price. Financial markets that are operating efficiently improve the economic welfare of everyone in the society.

2.2 STRUCTURE OF FINANCIAL MARKETS

LO 2.2 Identify the structure and components of financial markets.

Now that we understand the basic function of financial markets, let's look at their structure. The following descriptions of several categories of financial markets illustrate essential features of these markets.

Debt and Equity Markets

A firm or an individual can obtain funds in a financial market in two ways. The most common method is through the issuance of a debt instrument, such as a bond or a mortgage, which is a contractual agreement by the borrower to pay the holder of the instrument fixed dollar amounts at regular intervals (interest and principal payments) until a specified date (the maturity date), when a final payment is made. The **maturity** of a debt instrument is the number of years (term) until that instrument's expiration date. A debt instrument is **short-term** if its maturity term is less than a year and **long-term** if its maturity term is ten years or longer. Debt instruments with a maturity term between one and ten years are said to be **intermediate-term**.

The second method of raising funds is through the issuance of **equities**, such as common stock, which are claims to share in the *net income* (income after expenses and taxes) and the assets of a business. If you own one share of common stock in a company that has issued one million shares, you are entitled to 1 one-millionth of the firm's net income and 1 one-millionth of the firm's assets. Equities often make periodic payments (**dividends**) to their holders and are considered long-term securities because they have no maturity date. In addition, owning stock means that you own a portion of the firm and thus have the right to vote on issues important to the firm and to elect its directors.

The main disadvantage of owning a corporation's equities rather than its debt is that an equity holder is a *residual claimant*; that is, the corporation must pay all its debt holders before it pays its equity holders. The advantage of holding equities is that equity holders benefit directly from any increases in the corporation's profitability or asset value because equities confer ownership rights on the equity holders. Debt holders do not share in this benefit, because their dollar payments are fixed. We examine the pros and cons of debt versus equity instruments in more detail in Chapter 8, which provides an economic analysis of financial structure.

The total value of equities in the United States has fluctuated between $3 and $55 trillion since 1990, depending on the prices of shares. Although the average person is more aware of the stock market than of any other financial market, the size of the debt market is often substantially larger than the size of the equities market: At the end of 2019, the value of debt instruments was $47 trillion, while the value of equities was $55 trillion.

Primary and Secondary Markets

A **primary market** is a financial market in which new issues of a security, such as a bond or a stock, are sold to initial buyers by the corporation or government agency borrowing the funds. A **secondary market** is a financial market in which securities that have been previously issued can be resold.

The primary markets for securities are not well known to the public because the selling of securities to initial buyers often takes place behind closed doors. An important financial institution that assists in the initial sale of securities in the primary market is the **investment bank**. The investment bank does this by **underwriting** securities: It guarantees a price for a corporation's securities and then sells them to the public.

The New York Stock Exchange and NASDAQ (National Association of Securities Dealers Automated Quotation System), in which previously issued stocks are traded, are the best-known examples of secondary markets, although the bond markets, in which previously issued bonds of major corporations and the U.S. government are bought and sold, actually have a larger trading volume. Other examples of secondary markets are foreign exchange markets, futures markets, and options markets. Securities brokers and dealers are crucial to a well-functioning secondary market. **Brokers** are agents of investors who match buyers with sellers of securities; **dealers** link buyers and sellers by buying and selling securities at stated prices.

When an individual buys a security in the secondary market, the person who has sold the security receives money in exchange for the security, but the corporation that issued the security acquires no new funds. A corporation acquires new funds only when its securities are first sold in the primary market. Nonetheless, secondary markets serve two important functions. First, they make it easier and quicker to sell these financial instruments to raise cash; that is, they make the financial instruments more **liquid**. The increased liquidity of these instruments then makes them more desirable and thus easier for the issuing firm to sell in the primary market. Second, secondary markets determine the price of the security that the issuing firm sells in the primary market. The investors who buy securities in the primary market will pay the issuing corporation no more than the price they think the secondary market will set for this security. The higher the security's price in the secondary market, the higher the price the issuing firm will receive for a new security in the primary market, and hence the greater the amount of financial capital it can raise. Conditions in the secondary market are therefore the most relevant to corporations issuing securities. For this reason, books like this one, which deal with financial markets, focus on the behavior of secondary markets rather than that of primary markets.

Exchanges and Over-the-Counter Markets

Secondary markets can be organized in two ways. One method is through **exchanges**, where buyers and sellers of securities (or their agents or brokers) meet in one central location to conduct trades. The New York Stock Exchange for stocks and the Chicago Board of Trade for commodities (wheat, corn, silver, and other raw materials) are examples of organized exchanges.

The other forum for a secondary market is an **over-the-counter (OTC) market**, in which dealers at different locations who have an inventory of securities stand ready to buy and sell securities "over the counter" to anyone who comes to them and is willing to accept their prices. Because over-the-counter dealers are in contact via computers and know the prices set by one another, the OTC market is very competitive and not very different from a market with an organized exchange.

Many common stocks are traded over-the-counter, although a majority of the largest corporations have their shares traded at organized stock exchanges. The U.S. government bond market, with a larger trading volume than the New York Stock Exchange, by contrast, is set up as an over-the-counter market. Forty or so dealers establish a "market" in these securities by standing ready to buy and sell U.S. government bonds. Other over-the-counter markets include those that trade other types of financial instruments, such as negotiable certificates of deposit, federal funds, and foreign exchange instruments.

Money and Capital Markets

Another way of distinguishing between markets is on the basis of the maturity of the securities traded in each market. The **money market** is a financial market in which only short-term debt instruments (generally those with original maturity terms of less than one year) are traded; the **capital market** is the market in which longer-term debt instruments (generally those with original maturity terms of one year or greater) and equity instruments are traded. Money market securities are usually more widely traded than longer-term securities and so tend to be more liquid. In addition, as we will see in Chapter 4, short-term securities have smaller fluctuations in prices than long-term securities, making them safer investments. As a result, corporations and banks actively use the money market to earn interest on surplus funds that they expect to have only temporarily. Capital market securities, such as stocks and long-term bonds, are often held by financial intermediaries such as insurance companies and pension funds, which have little uncertainty about the amount of funds they will have available in the future.

2.3 FINANCIAL MARKET INSTRUMENTS

LO 2.3 List and describe the different types of financial market instruments.

To complete our understanding of how financial markets perform the important role of channeling funds from lender-savers to borrower-spenders, we need to examine the securities (instruments) traded in financial markets. We first focus on the instruments traded in the money market and then turn to those traded in the capital market.

Money Market Instruments

Because of their short terms to maturity, the debt instruments traded in the money market undergo the least price fluctuations and so are the least risky investments. The money market has undergone great changes in the past three decades, with the amounts of some financial instruments growing at a far more rapid rate than others.

The principal money market instruments are listed in Table 1, along with the amount at the end of 1990, 2000, 2010, and 2019. The Following the Financial News box discusses the money market interest rates most frequently reported in the media.

TABLE 1 Principal Money Market Instruments				
	Amount **($ billions, end of year)**			
Type of Instrument	**1990**	**2000**	**2010**	**2019**
U.S. Treasury bills	527	617	1,767	2,416
Negotiable bank certificates of deposit (large denominations)	547	1,053	1,923	1,859
Commercial paper	558	1,602	1,058	1,045
Federal funds and security repurchase agreements	372	1,197	3,598	4,356

Source: Federal Reserve Financial Accounts of the United States: https://www.federalreserve.gov/releases/Z1

Following the Financial News   Money Market Rates

The four money market interest rates discussed most frequently in the media are as follows:

Prime rate: The base interest rate on corporate bank loans, an indicator of the cost of businesses borrowing from banks

Federal funds rate: The interest rate charged on overnight loans in the federal funds market, a sensitive indicator of the cost to banks of borrowing funds from other banks and the stance of monetary policy

Treasury bill rate: The interest rate on U.S. Treasury bills, an indicator of general interest-rate movements

Libor rate: The British Banker's Association average of interbank rates for dollar deposits in the London market

The data for these interest rates are reported daily in newspapers and on Internet sites such as http:// www.bankrate.com.

U.S. Treasury Bills   These short-term debt instruments of the U.S. government are issued in one-, three-, and six-month maturities to finance the federal government. They pay a set amount at maturity and have no interest payments, but they effectively pay interest by initially selling at a discount—that is, at a price lower than the set amount paid at maturity. For instance, in May 2022, you might buy a six-month Treasury bill for $9,000 that can be redeemed in November 2022 for $10,000.

U.S. Treasury bills are the most liquid of all money market instruments because they are the most actively traded. They are also the safest money market instrument because there is a low probability of **default**, a situation in which the party issuing the debt instrument (the federal government, in this case) is unable to make interest payments or pay off the amount owed when the instrument matures. The federal government can always meet its debt obligations because it can raise taxes or issue **currency** (paper money or coins) to pay off its debts. Treasury bills are held mainly by banks, although small amounts are held by households, corporations, and other financial intermediaries.

Negotiable Bank Certificates of Deposit   A *certificate of deposit* (CD) is a debt instrument sold by a bank to depositors that pays annual interest of a given amount and at maturity pays back the original purchase price. Negotiable CDs are sold in secondary markets, with the amount outstanding in 2019 equal to $1.9 trillion. Negotiable CDs are an extremely important source of funds for commercial banks from corporations, money market mutual funds, charitable institutions, and government agencies.

Commercial Paper   *Commercial paper* is a short-term debt instrument issued by large banks and well-known corporations, such as Microsoft and General Motors, and the amount outstanding is around $1 trillion.

Repurchase Agreements   *Repurchase agreements* (*repos*) are effectively short-term loans (usually with a maturity term of less than two weeks) for which Treasury bills serve as *collateral*, an asset that the lender receives if the borrower does not pay back the loan. Repos are made as follows: A large corporation, such as Microsoft, may have some idle funds in its bank account, say $1 million, which it would like to lend for a week. Microsoft uses this excess $1 million to buy Treasury bills from a bank, which agrees to repurchase them the next week at a price slightly above Microsoft's purchase price. The net effect of this agreement is that Microsoft makes a loan of $1 million to the bank and holds $1 million of the bank's Treasury bills until the bank repurchases the bills to pay off the loan. Repurchase agreements are now an important source of bank funds (over $100 billion). The most important lenders in this market are large corporations.

Federal (Fed) Funds These instruments are typically overnight loans between banks of their deposits at the Federal Reserve. The *federal funds* designation is somewhat confusing because these loans are not made by the federal government or by the Federal Reserve but rather by banks to other banks. One reason why a bank might borrow in the federal funds market is that it might find it does not have enough funds in its deposit accounts at the Fed to meet the amount required by regulators. It can then borrow these funds from another bank, which transfers them to the borrowing bank using the Fed's wire transfer system. This market is very sensitive to the credit needs of the banks, so the interest rate on these loans, called the **federal funds rate**, is a closely watched barometer of the tightness of credit market conditions in the banking system and the stance of monetary policy. When high, the federal funds rate indicates that banks are strapped for funds; when low, it indicates that banks' credit needs are low.

Capital Market Instruments

Capital market instruments are debt and equity instruments with maturities of greater than one year. They have far wider price fluctuations than money market instruments and are considered to be fairly risky investments. The principal capital market instruments are listed in Table 2, which shows the amount at the end of 1990, 2000, 2010,

TABLE 2 Principal Capital Market Instruments				
	Amount **($ billions, end of year)**			
Type of Instrument	**1990**	**2000**	**2010**	**2019**
Corporate stocks (market value)	3,530	17,628	23,567	54,624
Residential mortgages	2,676	5,205	10,446	11,159
Corporate bonds	1,703	4,991	10,337	14,033
U.S. government securities (marketable long-term)	2,340	3,171	7,405	14,204
U.S. government agency securities	1,446	4,345	7,598	9,431
State and local government bonds	957	1,139	2,961	3,068
Bank commercial loans	818	1,497	2,001	3,818
Consumer loans	811	1,728	2,647	4,181
Commercial and farm mortgages	838	1,276	2,450	3,230

Source: Federal Reserve Financial Accounts of the United States: https://www.federalreserve.gov/releases/Z1

Following the Financial News　Capital Market Interest Rates

The five interest rates on capital market instruments discussed most frequently in the media are as follows:

30-year mortgage rate: The interest rate on a 30-year, fixed-rate residential mortgage that is less than $510,400 ($765,600 in high-cost areas) in amount and is guaranteed by the Federal Housing Administration (FHA).

Jumbo mortgage rate: The interest rate on a 30-year, fixed-rate residential mortgage for prime customers that is in excess of $510,400 ($765,600 in high-cost areas) in amount.

Five-year adjustable rate mortgage (ARM) rate: The interest rate for the first five years on a residential mortgage that adjusts after five years for prime customers.

New-car loan rate: The interest rate on a four-year, fixed-rate new-car loan.

10-year Treasury rate: The interest rate on U.S. Treasury bonds maturing in ten years.

The data for these interest rates are reported daily in newspapers and on Internet sites such as http://www.bankrate.com and http://www.finance.yahoo.com.

and 2019. The Following the Financial News box discusses the capital market interest rates most frequently reported in the media.

Stocks　*Stocks* are equity claims on the net income and assets of a corporation. Their value of $55 trillion at the end of 2019 exceeds that of any other type of security in the capital market. However, the amount of new stock issues in any given year is typically quite small, less than 1% of the total value of shares outstanding. Individuals hold around half of the value of stocks; the rest is held by pension funds, mutual funds, and insurance companies.

Mortgages and Mortgage-Backed Securities　**Mortgages** are loans to households or firms to purchase land, housing, or other real structures, in which the structure or land itself serves as collateral for the loans. The mortgage market is the third largest debt market in the United States, with the amount of residential mortgages (used to purchase residential housing) outstanding almost four times the amount of commercial and farm mortgages. Mortgages are provided by financial institutions such as savings and loan associations, mutual savings banks, commercial banks, and insurance companies. However, in recent years a growing amount of the funds for mortgages have been provided by **mortgage-backed securities**, bond-like debt instruments backed by a bundle of individual mortgages, whose interest and principal payments are collectively paid to the holders of the security. As we will see in Chapter 12, mortgage-backed securities and more complicated variants (CDOs) have become notorious because they played a key role in promoting the 2007–2009 global financial crisis. The federal government plays an active role in the mortgage market via the three government agencies—the Federal National Mortgage Association (FNMA, "Fannie Mae"), the Government National Mortgage Association (GNMA, "Ginnie Mae"), and the Federal Home Loan Mortgage Corporation (FHLMC, "Freddie Mac")—that provide funds to the mortgage market by selling bonds and using the proceeds to buy mortgages.

Corporate Bonds   These long-term bonds are issued by corporations with very strong credit ratings. The typical *corporate bond* sends the holder an interest payment twice a year and pays off the face value when the bond matures. Some corporate bonds, called *convertible bonds,* have the additional feature of allowing the holder to convert them into a specified number of shares of stock at any time up to the maturity date. This feature makes these convertible bonds more desirable to prospective purchasers than bonds without it, and it allows the corporation to reduce its interest payments because the bonds can increase in value if the price of the stock appreciates sufficiently. Because the outstanding amount of both convertible and nonconvertible bonds for any given corporation is small, corporate bonds are not nearly as liquid as other securities such as U.S. government bonds.

Although the size of the corporate bond market is substantially smaller than that of the stock market, with the amount of corporate bonds outstanding less than one-third that of stocks, the volume of new corporate bonds issued each year is substantially greater than the volume of new stock issues. Thus the behavior of the corporate bond market is probably far more important to a firm's financing decisions than is the behavior of the stock market. The principal buyers of corporate bonds are life insurance companies; pension funds and households are other large holders.

U.S. Government Securities   These long-term debt instruments are issued by the U.S. Treasury to finance the deficits of the federal government. Because they are the most widely traded bonds in the United States (the volume of transactions on average is over $500 billion daily), they are the most liquid security traded in the capital market. They are held by the Federal Reserve, banks, households, and foreigners.

U.S. Government Agency Securities   These long-term bonds are issued by various government agencies such as Ginnie Mae, the Federal Farm Credit Bank, and the Tennessee Valley Authority to finance such items as mortgages, farm loans, or power-generating equipment. Many of these securities are guaranteed by the federal government. They function much like U.S. government bonds and are held by similar parties.

State and Local Government Bonds   State and local bonds, also called *municipal bonds,* are long-term debt instruments issued by state and local governments to finance expenditures on schools, roads, and other large programs. An important feature of these bonds is that their interest payments are exempt from federal income tax and generally from state taxes in the issuing state. Commercial banks, with their high income tax rates, are the biggest buyers of these securities, owning over half the total amount outstanding. The next biggest group of holders consists of wealthy individuals in high income-tax brackets, followed by insurance companies.

Consumer and Bank Commercial Loans   These loans to consumers and businesses are made principally by banks but, in the case of consumer loans, also by finance companies.

2.4 INTERNATIONALIZATION OF FINANCIAL MARKETS

LO 2.4 Recognize the international dimensions of financial markets.

The growing internationalization of financial markets has become an important trend. Before the 1980s, U.S. financial markets were much larger than those outside the United States, but in recent years the dominance of U.S. markets has been weakening. (See the Global box "Are U.S. Capital Markets Losing Their Edge?") The extraordinary growth of

Global   Are U.S. Capital Markets Losing Their Edge?

Over the past few decades, the United States lost its international dominance in a number of manufacturing industries, including automobiles and consumer electronics, as other countries became more competitive in global markets. Recent evidence suggests that financial markets now are undergoing a similar trend: Just as Ford and General Motors have lost global market share to Toyota and Honda, U.S. stock and bond markets recently have seen their share of sales of newly issued corporate securities slip. The London and Hong Kong stock exchanges now handle a larger share of initial public offerings (IPOs) of stock than does the New York Stock Exchange, which had been by far the dominant exchange in terms of IPO value before 2000. Furthermore, the number of stocks listed on U.S. exchanges has been falling, while stock listings abroad have been growing rapidly: Listings outside the United States are now about ten times greater than those in the United States. Likewise, the portion of new corporate bonds issued worldwide that are initially sold in U.S. capital markets has fallen below the share sold in European debt markets.

Why do corporations that issue new securities to raise capital now conduct more of this business in financial markets in Europe and Asia? Among the factors contributing to this trend are quicker adoption of technological innovation by foreign financial markets, tighter immigration controls in the United States following the terrorist attacks of 2001, and perceptions that listing on American exchanges will expose foreign securities issuers to greater risks of lawsuits.

Many people see burdensome financial regulation as the main cause, however, and point specifically to the Sarbanes-Oxley Act of 2002. Congress passed this act after a number of accounting scandals involving U.S. corporations and the accounting firms that audited them came to light. Sarbanes-Oxley aims to strengthen the integrity of the auditing process and the quality of information provided in corporate financial statements. The costs to corporations of complying with the new rules and procedures are high, especially for smaller firms, but largely avoidable if firms choose to issue their securities in financial markets outside the United States. For this reason, there is much support for revising Sarbanes-Oxley to lessen its allegedly harmful effects and induce more securities issuers to return to U.S. financial markets. However, evidence is not conclusive to support the view that Sarbanes-Oxley is the main cause of the relative decline of U.S. financial markets and therefore in need of reform.

Discussion of the relative decline of U.S. financial markets and debate about the factors that are contributing to it likely will continue. Chapter 8 provides more detail on the Sarbanes-Oxley Act and its effects on the U.S. financial system.

foreign financial markets has been the result of both large increases in the pool of savings in foreign countries such as Japan and the deregulation of foreign financial markets, which has enabled foreign markets to expand their activities. American corporations and banks are now more likely to tap international capital markets to raise needed funds, and American investors often seek investment opportunities abroad. Similarly, foreign corporations and banks raise funds from Americans, and foreigners have become important investors in the United States. A look at international bond markets and world stock markets will give us a picture of how this globalization of financial markets is taking place.

International Bond Market, Eurobonds, and Eurocurrencies

The traditional instruments in the international bond market are known as **foreign bonds**. Foreign bonds are sold in a foreign country and are denominated in that country's currency. For example, if the German automaker Porsche sells a bond in the United States denominated in U.S. dollars, it is classified as a foreign bond. Foreign bonds have been an important instrument in the international capital market for centuries. In fact, a large percentage of U.S. railroads built in the nineteenth century were financed by sales of foreign bonds in Britain.

A more recent innovation in the international bond market is the **Eurobond**, a bond denominated in a currency other than that of the country in which it is sold—for example, a bond denominated in U.S. dollars sold in London. Currently, over 80% of the new issues in the international bond market are Eurobonds, and the market for these securities has grown very rapidly. As a result, the Eurobond market is now larger than the U.S. corporate bond market.

A variant of the Eurobond is **Eurocurrencies**, which are foreign currencies deposited in banks outside the home country. The most important of the Eurocurrencies are **Eurodollars**, which are U.S. dollars deposited in foreign banks outside the United States or in foreign branches of U.S. banks. Because these short-term deposits earn interest, they are similar to short-term Eurobonds. American banks borrow Eurodollar deposits from other banks or from their own foreign branches, and Eurodollars are now an important source of funds for American banks.

Note that the currency, the euro, can create some confusion about the terms *Eurobond*, *Eurocurrencies*, and *Eurodollars*. A bond denominated in euros is called a Eurobond *only if it is sold outside the countries that have adopted the euro.* In fact, most Eurobonds are not denominated in euros but are instead denominated in U.S. dollars. Similarly, Eurodollars have nothing to do with euros, but are instead U.S. dollars deposited in banks outside the United States.

World Stock Markets

Until recently, the U.S. stock market was by far the largest in the world, but foreign stock markets have been growing in importance, with the United States not always number one. The increased interest in foreign stocks has prompted the development in the United States of mutual funds that specialize in trading in foreign stock markets. As the Following the Financial News box indicates, American investors now pay attention not only to the Dow Jones Industrial Average but also to stock price indexes for foreign stock markets, such as the Nikkei 300 Average (Tokyo) and the Financial Times Stock Exchange (FTSE) 100-Share Index (London).

The internationalization of financial markets is having profound effects on the United States. Foreigners, particularly Japanese investors, are not only providing funds to corporations in the United States but are also helping finance the federal government. Without these foreign funds, the U.S. economy would have grown far less rapidly in the past 20 years. The internationalization of financial markets is also leading the way to a more integrated world economy in which flows of goods and technology between countries are more commonplace. In later chapters, we will encounter many examples of the important roles that international factors play in our economy.

2.5 FUNCTION OF FINANCIAL INTERMEDIARIES: INDIRECT FINANCE

LO 2.5 Summarize the roles of transaction costs, risk sharing, and information costs as they relate to financial intermediaries.

As shown in Figure 1 (p. 23), funds can move from lenders to borrowers by a second route, called *indirect finance* because it involves a financial intermediary that stands between the lender-savers and the borrower-spenders and helps transfer funds from

Following the Financial News   Foreign Stock Market Indexes

Foreign stock market indexes are published daily in newspapers and on Internet sites such as finance .yahoo.com.

The most important of these stock market indexes are as follows:

Dow Jones Industrial Average (DJIA): An index of the 30 largest publicly traded corporations in the United States, maintained by the Dow Jones Corporation

S&P 500: An index of 500 of the largest companies traded in the United States, maintained by Standard & Poor's

NASDAQ Composite: An index for all the stocks that trade on the NASDAQ stock market, where most of the technology stocks in the United States are traded

FTSE 100: An index of the 100 most highly capitalized UK companies listed on the London Stock Exchange

DAX: An index of the 30 largest German companies trading on the Frankfurt Stock Exchange

CAC 40: An index of the 40 largest French companies trading on Euronext Paris

Hang Seng: An index of the largest companies trading on the Hong Kong stock markets

Strait Times: An index of the 30 largest companies trading on the Singapore Exchange

These indexes are reported daily in newspapers and on Internet sites such as http://www.finance.yahoo.com.

---

one to the other. A financial intermediary does this by borrowing funds from lender-savers and then using these funds to make loans to borrower-spenders. For example, a bank might acquire funds by issuing a liability to the public in the form of savings deposits (an asset for the public). It might then use the funds to acquire an asset by making a loan to General Motors or by buying a U.S. Treasury bond in the financial market. The ultimate result is that funds have been transferred from the public (the lender-savers) to General Motors or the U.S. Treasury (the borrower-spender) with the help of the financial intermediary (the bank).

The process of indirect financing using financial intermediaries, called **financial intermediation**, is the primary route for moving funds from lenders to borrowers. Indeed, although the media focus much of their attention on securities markets, particularly the stock market, financial intermediaries are a far more important source of financing for corporations than securities markets are. This is true not only for the United States but for other industrialized countries as well (see the Global box, "The Importance of Financial Intermediaries Relative to Securities Markets: An International Comparison"). Why are financial intermediaries and indirect finance so important in financial markets? To answer this question, we need to understand the roles of transaction costs, risk sharing, and information costs in financial markets.

Transaction Costs

Transaction costs, the time and money spent in carrying out financial transactions, are a major problem for people who have excess funds to lend. As we have seen, Carl the Carpenter needs $1,000 for his new tool, and you know that it is an excellent investment opportunity. You have the cash and would like to lend him the money, but to protect your investment, you have to hire a lawyer to write up the loan contract that specifies how much interest Carl will pay you, when he will make these interest payments, and when he will repay you the $1,000. Obtaining the contract will cost

Global The Importance of Financial Intermediaries Relative to Securities Markets: An International Comparison

Patterns of financing corporations differ across countries, but one key fact emerges: Studies of the major developed countries, including the United States, Canada, the United Kingdom, Japan, Italy, Germany, and France, show that when businesses go looking for funds to finance their activities, they usually obtain them indirectly through financial intermediaries and not directly from securities markets.* Even in the United States and Canada, which have the most developed securities markets in the world, loans from financial intermediaries are far more important for corporate finance than securities markets are. The countries that have made the least use of securities markets are Germany and Japan; in these two countries, financing from financial intermediaries has been almost ten times greater than that from securities markets. However, after the deregulation of Japanese securities markets in recent years, the share of corporate financing by financial intermediaries has been declining relative to the use of securities markets.

Although the dominance of financial intermediaries over securities markets is clear in all countries, the relative importance of bond versus stock markets differs widely across countries. In the United States, the bond market is far more important as a source of corporate finance: On average, the amount of new financing raised using bonds is ten times the amount raised using stocks. By contrast, countries such as France and Italy make more use of equities markets than of the bond market to raise capital.

*See, for example, Colin Mayer, "Financial Systems, Corporate Finance, and Economic Development," in *Asymmetric Information, Corporate Finance, and Investment,* ed. R. Glenn Hubbard (Chicago: University of Chicago Press, 1990), 307–332.

you $500. When you figure in this transaction cost for making the loan, you realize that you can't earn enough from the deal (you spend $500 to make perhaps $100) and reluctantly tell Carl that he will have to look elsewhere.

This example illustrates that small savers like you or potential borrowers like Carl might be frozen out of financial markets and thus be unable to benefit from them. Can anyone come to the rescue? Financial intermediaries can.

Financial intermediaries can substantially reduce transaction costs because they have developed expertise in lowering them and because their large size allows them to take advantage of **economies of scale**, the reduction in transaction costs per dollar of transactions as the size (scale) of transactions increases. For example, a bank knows how to find a good lawyer to produce an airtight loan contract, and this contract can be used over and over again in its loan transactions, thus lowering the legal cost per transaction. Instead of a loan contract (which may not be all that well written) costing $500, a bank can hire a top-flight lawyer for $5,000 to draw up an airtight loan contract that can be used for 2,000 loans at a cost of $2.50 per loan. At a cost of $2.50 per loan, it now becomes profitable for the financial intermediary to lend Carl the $1,000.

Because financial intermediaries are able to reduce transaction costs substantially, they make it possible for you to provide funds indirectly to people like Carl with productive investment opportunities. In addition, a financial intermediary's low transaction costs mean that it can provide its customers with **liquidity services**, services that make it easier for customers to conduct transactions. For example, banks provide depositors with checking accounts that enable them to pay their bills easily. In addition, depositors can earn interest on checking and savings accounts and yet still convert them into goods and services whenever necessary.

Risk Sharing

Another benefit made possible by the low transaction costs of financial institutions is that these institutions can help reduce the exposure of investors to **risk**—that is, uncertainty about the returns investors will earn on assets. Financial intermediaries do this through the process known as **risk sharing**: They create and sell assets with risk characteristics that people are comfortable with, and the intermediaries then use the funds they acquire by selling these assets to purchase other assets that may have far more risk. Low transaction costs allow financial intermediaries to share risk at low cost, enabling them to earn a profit on the spread between the returns they earn on risky assets and the payments they make on the assets they have sold. This process of risk sharing is also sometimes referred to as **asset transformation**, because in a sense, risky assets are turned into safer assets for investors.

Financial intermediaries also promote risk sharing by helping individuals to diversify and thereby lower the amount of risk to which they are exposed. **Diversification** entails investing in a collection (**portfolio**) of assets whose returns do not always move together, with the result that overall risk is lower than for individual assets. (Diversification is just another name for the old adage "You shouldn't put all your eggs in one basket.") Low transaction costs allow financial intermediaries to pool a collection of assets into a new asset and then sell it to individuals.

Asymmetric Information: Adverse Selection and Moral Hazard

The presence of transaction costs in financial markets explains, in part, why financial intermediaries and indirect finance play such an important role in financial markets. An additional reason is that in financial markets, one party often does not know enough about the other party to make accurate decisions. This inequality is called **asymmetric information**. For example, a borrower who takes out a loan usually has better information about the potential returns and risks associated with the investment projects for which the funds are earmarked than the lender does. Lack of information creates problems in the financial system on two fronts: before the transaction is entered into, and afterward.[1]

Adverse selection is the problem created by asymmetric information *before* the transaction occurs. Adverse selection occurs when one party to a transaction has information about a hidden characteristic and takes economic advantage of this information by making an agreement (transaction) with less informed parties. In financial markets, adverse selection occurs when the potential borrowers who are the most likely to produce an undesirable (*adverse*) outcome—the bad credit risks—actively seek out a loan and are thus more likely to be selected. Because adverse selection makes it more likely that loans might be made to bad credit risks, lenders may decide not to make any loans, even though good credit risks exist in the marketplace.

To understand why adverse selection occurs, suppose you have two aunts to whom you might make a loan—Aunt Louise and Aunt Sheila. Aunt Louise is a conservative type who borrows only when she has an investment she is quite sure will pay off. Aunt Sheila, by contrast, is an inveterate gambler who has just come across a get-rich-quick scheme that will make her a millionaire if she can just borrow $1,000 to invest in it. Unfortunately, as with most get-rich-quick schemes, the probability is high that the investment won't pay off and that Aunt Sheila will lose the $1,000.

---

[1]Asymmetric information and the adverse selection and moral hazard concepts are also crucial problems for the insurance industry.

Which of your aunts is more likely to call you to ask for a loan? Aunt Sheila, of course, because she has so much to gain if the investment pays off. You, however, would not want to make a loan to her because the probability is high that her investment will turn sour and she will be unable to pay you back.

If you know both your aunts very well—that is, if your information is not asymmetric—you won't have a problem, because you will know that Aunt Sheila is a bad risk and so you will not lend to her. Suppose, though, that you don't know your aunts well. You will be more likely to lend to Aunt Sheila than to Aunt Louise because Aunt Sheila will be hounding you for the loan. Because of the possibility of adverse selection, you might decide not to lend to either of your aunts, even though there are times when Aunt Louise, who is an excellent credit risk, might need a loan for a worthwhile investment.

Moral hazard is the problem created by asymmetric information *after* the transaction occurs. Moral hazard occurs when an informed party takes a hidden (unobserved) action that harms the less informed party. In financial markets, moral hazard is the risk (*hazard*) that the borrower might engage in hidden actions that are undesirable (*immoral*) from the lender's point of view, because they make it less likely that the loan will be paid back. Because moral hazard lowers the probability that the loan will be repaid, lenders may decide that they would rather not make a loan.

As an example of moral hazard, suppose that you made a $1,000 loan to another relative, Uncle Melvin, who tells you he needs the money to purchase a computer so that he can set up a business typing students' term papers. Once you have made the loan, however, Uncle Melvin is more likely to secretly slip off to the track and play the horses than to purchase the computer. If he bets on a 20-to-1 long shot and wins with your money, he is able to pay back your $1,000 and live high-off-the-hog with the remaining $19,000. But if he loses, as is likely, you won't get paid back, and all he has lost is his reputation as a reliable, upstanding uncle. Uncle Melvin therefore has an incentive to go to the track because his gains ($19,000) if he bets correctly are much greater than the cost to him (his reputation) if he bets incorrectly. If you knew what Uncle Melvin was up to, you would prevent him from going to the track, and he would not be able to increase the moral hazard. However, because it is hard for you to keep informed of his whereabouts—that is, because information is asymmetric—there is a good chance that Uncle Melvin will go to the track and you will not get paid back. The risk of moral hazard might therefore discourage you from making the $1,000 loan to Uncle Melvin, even if you are sure that you will be paid back if he uses it to set up his business.

The problems created by adverse selection and moral hazard are a major impediment to well-functioning financial markets. Again, financial intermediaries can alleviate these problems.

With financial intermediaries in the economy, small savers can provide their funds to the financial markets by lending these funds to a trustworthy intermediary—say, the Honest John Bank—which in turn lends the funds out either by making loans or by buying securities such as stocks or bonds. Successful financial intermediaries have higher earnings on their investments than do small savers because they are better equipped than individuals to screen out bad credit risks from good ones, thereby reducing losses due to adverse selection. In addition, financial intermediaries have high earnings because they develop expertise in monitoring the parties they lend to, thus reducing losses due to moral hazard. The result is that financial intermediaries can afford to pay lender-savers interest or provide substantial services and still earn a profit.

As we have seen, financial intermediaries play an important role in the economy because they provide liquidity services, promote risk sharing, and solve information problems, thereby allowing small savers and borrowers to benefit from the existence of financial markets. The success of financial intermediaries in performing this role is evidenced by the fact that most Americans invest their savings with them and obtain loans from them. Financial intermediaries play a key role in improving economic efficiency because they help financial markets channel funds from lender-savers to people with productive investment opportunities. Without a well-functioning set of financial intermediaries, it is very hard for an economy to reach its full potential. We will explore further the role of financial intermediaries in the economy in Part 3.

Economies of Scope and Conflicts of Interest

Another reason why financial intermediaries play such an important part in the economy is that by providing multiple financial services to their customers, such as offering them bank loans or selling their bonds for them, they can also achieve **economies of scope**; that is, they can lower the cost of information production for each service by applying one information resource to many different services. A bank, for example, when making a loan to a corporation, can evaluate how good a credit risk the firm is, which then helps the bank decide whether it would be easy to sell the bonds of this corporation to the public.

Although economies of scope may substantially benefit financial institutions, they also create potential costs in terms of **conflicts of interest**. Conflicts of interest, a type of moral hazard problem, arise when a person or institution has multiple objectives (interests), some of which conflict with each other. Conflicts of interest are especially likely to occur when a financial institution provides multiple services. The potentially competing interests of those services may lead an individual or firm to conceal information or disseminate misleading information. We care about conflicts of interest because a substantial reduction in the quality of information in financial markets increases asymmetric information problems and prevents financial markets from channeling funds into the most productive investment opportunities. Consequently, the financial markets and the economy become less efficient.

2.6 TYPES OF FINANCIAL INTERMEDIARIES

LO 2.6 List and describe the different types of financial intermediaries.

We have seen why financial intermediaries have such an important function in the economy. Now we take a look at the principal financial intermediaries and how they perform the intermediation function. Financial intermediaries fall into three categories: depository institutions (banks), contractual savings institutions, and investment intermediaries. Table 3 describes the primary liabilities (sources of funds) and assets (uses of funds) of the financial intermediaries in each category. The relative sizes of these intermediaries in the United States are indicated in Table 4, which lists the amounts of their assets at the end of 1990, 2000, 2010, and 2019.

Depository Institutions

Depository institutions (for simplicity, we refer to these as *banks* throughout this text) are financial intermediaries that accept deposits from individuals and institutions and make loans. The study of money and banking focuses special attention on this group of financial institutions because they are involved in the creation of deposits, an important component of the money supply. These institutions include commercial banks and the so-called **thrift institutions (thrifts)**: savings and loan associations, mutual savings banks, and credit unions.

TABLE 3	Primary Assets and Liabilities of Financial Intermediaries	
Type of Intermediary	**Primary Liabilities (Sources of Funds)**	**Primary Assets (Uses of Funds)**
Depository institutions (banks)		
Commercial banks	Deposits	Business and consumer loans, mortgages, U.S. government securities, and municipal bonds
Savings and loan associations	Deposits	Mortgages
Mutual savings banks	Deposits	Mortgages
Credit unions	Deposits	Consumer loans
Contractual savings institutions		
Life insurance companies	Premiums from policies	Corporate bonds and mortgages
Fire and casualty insurance companies	Premiums from policies	Municipal bonds, corporate bonds and stock, and U.S. government securities
Pension funds, government retirement funds	Employer and employee contributions	Corporate bonds and stock
Investment intermediaries		
Finance companies	Commercial paper, stocks, bonds	Consumer and business loans
Mutual funds	Shares	Stocks, bonds
Money market mutual funds	Shares	Money market instruments
Hedge funds	Partnership participation	Stocks, bonds, loans, foreign currencies, and many other assets

Commercial Banks   These financial intermediaries raise funds primarily by issuing checkable deposits (deposits on which checks can be written), savings deposits (deposits that are payable on demand but do not allow their owners to write checks), and time deposits (deposits with fixed terms to maturity). They then use these funds to make commercial, consumer, and mortgage loans and to buy U.S. government securities and municipal bonds. Around 4,500 commercial banks are found in the United States and, as a group, they are the largest financial intermediary and have the most diversified portfolios (collections) of assets.

Savings and Loan Associations (S&Ls) and Mutual Savings Banks   These depository institutions, which number approximately 700 in the United States, obtain funds primarily through savings deposits (often called *shares*) and time and checkable deposits. In the past, these institutions were constrained in their activities and mostly made mortgage loans for residential housing. Over time, these restrictions have been loosened, so the distinction between these depository institutions and commercial banks has blurred. These intermediaries have become more alike and are now more competitive with each other.

TABLE 4	Primary Financial Intermediaries and Value of Their Assets			
	Value of Assets ($ billions, end of year)			
Type of Intermediary	**1990**	**2000**	**2010**	**2019**
Depository institutions (banks)				
Commercial banks, savings and loans, and mutual savings banks	4,744	7,687	12,821	18,518
Credit unions	217	441	876	1,534
Contractual savings institutions				
Life insurance companies	1,367	3,136	5,168	8,508
Fire and casualty insurance companies	533	866	1,361	2,650
Pension funds (private)	1,619	4,423	6,614	10,919
State and local government retirement funds	820	2,290	4,779	9,335
Investment intermediaries				
Finance companies	612	1,140	1,589	1,528
Mutual funds	608	4,435	7,873	17,660
Money market mutual funds	493	1,812	2,755	3,634

Source: Federal Reserve Financial Accounts of the United States: https://www.federalreserve.gov/releases/Z1, Tables L110, L114, L115, L116, L118, L120, L121, L122, L127.

Credit Unions　These financial institutions, numbering a little over 5,000 in the United States, are typically very small cooperative lending institutions organized around a particular group: union members, employees of a particular firm, and so forth. They acquire funds from deposits called *shares* and primarily make consumer loans.

Contractual Savings Institutions

Contractual savings institutions, such as insurance companies and pension funds, are financial intermediaries that acquire funds at periodic intervals on a contractual basis. Because they can predict with reasonable accuracy how much they will have to pay out in benefits in the coming years, they do not have to worry as much as depository institutions about losing funds quickly. As a result, the liquidity of assets is not as important a consideration for them as it is for depository institutions, and they tend to invest their funds primarily in long-term securities such as corporate bonds, stocks, and mortgages.

Life Insurance Companies　Life insurance companies insure people against financial hazards following a death and sell annuities (annual income payments upon retirement). They acquire funds from the premiums that people pay to keep their policies in force and use them mainly to buy corporate bonds and mortgages. They also purchase stocks but are restricted in the amount that they can hold. Currently, with over $8 trillion in assets, they are among the largest of the contractual savings institutions.

Fire and Casualty Insurance Companies   These companies insure their policyholders against loss from theft, fire, and accidents. They are very much like life insurance companies, receiving funds through premiums for their policies, but they have a greater possibility of losing funds if major disasters occur. For this reason, they use their funds to buy more liquid assets than life insurance companies do. Their largest holding of assets consists of municipal bonds; they also hold corporate bonds and stocks and U.S. government securities.

Pension Funds and Government Retirement Funds   Private pension funds and state and local retirement funds provide retirement income in the form of annuities to employees who are covered by a pension plan. Funds are acquired by contributions from employers and from employees, who either have a contribution automatically deducted from their paychecks or contribute voluntarily. The largest asset holdings of pension funds are corporate bonds and stocks. The establishment of pension funds has been actively encouraged by the federal government, both through legislation requiring pension plans and through tax incentives to encourage contributions.

Investment Intermediaries

This category of financial intermediary includes finance companies, mutual funds, money market mutual funds, and hedge funds.

Finance Companies   Finance companies raise funds by selling commercial paper (a short-term debt instrument) and by issuing stocks and bonds. They lend these funds to consumers, who use them to purchase such items as furniture, automobiles, and home improvements, and to small businesses. Some finance companies are organized by a parent corporation to help sell its product. For example, Ford Motor Credit Company makes loans to consumers who purchase Ford automobiles.

Mutual Funds   These financial intermediaries acquire funds by selling shares to many individuals and then using the proceeds to purchase diversified portfolios of stocks and bonds. Mutual funds allow shareholders to pool their resources so that they can take advantage of lower transaction costs when buying large blocks of stocks or bonds. In addition, mutual funds allow shareholders to hold more diversified portfolios than they otherwise would. Shareholders can sell (redeem) shares at any time, but the value of these shares will be determined by the value of the mutual fund's holdings of securities. Because these fluctuate greatly, the value of mutual fund shares does, too; therefore, investments in mutual funds can be risky.

Money Market Mutual Funds   These financial institutions are similar to mutual funds but also function to some extent as depository institutions because they offer deposit-type accounts. Like most mutual funds, they sell shares to acquire funds. These funds are then used to buy money market instruments that are both safe and very liquid. The interest on these assets is paid out to the shareholders.

A key feature of these funds is that shareholders can write checks against the value of their shareholdings. In effect, shares in a money market mutual fund function like checking account deposits that pay interest. Money market mutual funds have experienced extraordinary growth since 1971, when they first appeared. In 2019, their assets had climbed to $3.6 trillion.

Hedge Funds   Hedge funds are a type of mutual fund with special characteristics. Hedge funds are organized as limited partnerships with minimum investments ranging from $100,000 to, more typically, $1 million or more. These limitations mean that hedge funds are subject to much weaker regulation than other mutual funds. Hedge funds invest in many types of assets, with some specializing in stocks, others in bonds, others in foreign currencies, and still others in far more exotic assets.

Investment Banks   Despite its name, an investment bank is not a bank or a financial intermediary in the ordinary sense; that is, it does not take in funds and then lend them out. Instead, an investment bank is a different type of intermediary that helps a corporation issue securities. First it advises the corporation on which type of securities to issue (stocks or bonds); then it helps sell (**underwrite**) the securities by purchasing them from the corporation at a predetermined price and reselling them in the market. Investment banks also act as deal makers and earn enormous fees by helping corporations acquire other companies through mergers or acquisitions.

2.7 REGULATION OF THE FINANCIAL SYSTEM

LO 2.7 Identify the reasons for and list the types of financial market regulations.

The financial system is among the most heavily regulated sectors of the American economy. The government regulates financial markets for two main reasons: to increase the information available to investors and to ensure the soundness of the financial system. We will examine how these two goals have led to the present regulatory environment. As a study aid, the principal regulatory agencies of the U.S. financial system are listed in Table 5.

Increasing Information Available to Investors

Asymmetric information in financial markets means that investors may be subject to adverse selection and moral hazard problems that may hinder the efficient operation of financial markets. Risky firms or outright crooks may be the most eager to sell securities to unwary investors, and the resulting adverse selection problem may keep investors out of financial markets. Furthermore, once an investor has bought a security, thereby lending money to a firm, the borrower may have incentives to engage in risky activities or to commit outright fraud. The presence of this moral hazard problem may also keep investors away from financial markets. Government regulation can reduce adverse selection and moral hazard problems in financial markets and enhance the efficiency of the markets by increasing the amount of information available to investors.

As a result of the stock market crash of 1929 and revelations of widespread fraud in the aftermath, political demands for regulation culminated in the Securities Act of 1933 and the establishment of the Securities and Exchange Commission (SEC) in 1934. The SEC requires corporations issuing securities to disclose certain information about their sales, assets, and earnings to the public and restricts trading by the largest stockholders (known as *insiders*) in the corporation. By requiring disclosure and by discouraging insider trading, which could be used to manipulate security prices, the SEC hopes that investors will be better informed and protected from the types of abuses that occurred in financial markets before 1933. Indeed, in recent years, the SEC has been particularly active in prosecuting people involved in insider trading.

TABLE 5	Principal Regulatory Agencies of the U.S. Financial System	
Regulatory Agency	**Subject of Regulation**	**Nature of Regulations**
Securities and Exchange Commission (SEC)	Organized exchanges and financial markets	Requires disclosure of information; restricts insider trading
Commodities Futures Trading Commission (CFTC)	Futures market exchanges	Regulates procedures for trading in futures markets
Office of the Comptroller of the Currency	Federally chartered commercial banks and thrift institutions	Charters and examines the books of federally chartered commercial banks and thrift institutions; imposes restrictions on assets they can hold
National Credit Union Administration (NCUA)	Federally chartered credit unions	Charters and examines the books of federally chartered credit unions and imposes restrictions on assets they can hold
State banking and insurance commissions	State-chartered depository institutions and insurance companies	Charter and examine the books of state-chartered banks and insurance companies, impose restrictions on assets they can hold, and impose restrictions on branching
Federal Deposit Insurance Corporation (FDIC)	Commercial banks, mutual savings banks, savings and loan associations	Provides insurance of up to $250,000 for each depositor at a bank, examines the books of insured banks, and imposes restrictions on assets they can hold
Federal Reserve System	All depository institutions	Examines the books of commercial banks and systemically important financial institutions; sets reserve requirements for all banks

Ensuring the Soundness of Financial Intermediaries

Asymmetric information can lead to the widespread collapse of financial intermediaries, referred to as a **financial panic**. Because providers of funds to financial intermediaries may not be able to assess whether the institutions holding their funds are sound, if they have doubts about the overall health of financial intermediaries, they may want to pull their funds out of both sound and unsound institutions. The possible outcome is a financial panic that produces large losses for the public and causes serious damage to the economy. To protect the public and the economy from financial panics, the government has implemented six types of regulations.

Restrictions on Entry   State banking and insurance commissions, as well as the Office of the Comptroller of the Currency (an agency of the federal government), have created tight regulations governing who is allowed to set up a financial intermediary. Individuals or groups that want to establish a financial intermediary, such as a bank or an insurance company, must obtain a charter from the state or the federal government. Only upstanding citizens with impeccable credentials and a large amount of initial funds will be given a charter.

Disclosure

Reporting requirements for financial intermediaries are stringent. Their bookkeeping must follow certain strict principles, their books are subject to periodic inspection, and they must make certain information available to the public.

Restrictions on Assets and Activities

Financial intermediaries are restricted in what they are allowed to do and what assets they can hold. Before you put funds into a bank or similar institution, you will want to know that your funds are safe and that the bank or other financial intermediary will be able to meet its obligations to you. One way of ensuring the trustworthiness of financial intermediaries is to restrict them from engaging in certain risky activities. Legislation passed in 1933 (and repealed in 1999) separated commercial banking from the securities industry so that banks could not engage in risky ventures associated with this industry. Another way to limit a financial intermediary's behavior is to restrict it from holding certain risky assets, or at least from holding a greater quantity of these risky assets than is prudent. For example, commercial banks and other depository institutions are not allowed to hold common stock because stock prices experience substantial fluctuations. Insurance companies are allowed to hold common stock, but their holdings cannot exceed a certain fraction of their total assets.

Deposit Insurance

The government can insure people's deposits so that they do not suffer great financial loss if the financial intermediary that holds these deposits should fail. The most important government agency that provides this type of insurance is the Federal Deposit Insurance Corporation (FDIC), which insures each depositor at a commercial bank or mutual savings bank up to a loss of $250,000 per account. Premiums paid by these financial institutions go into the FDIC's Deposit Insurance Fund, which is used to pay off depositors if an institution fails. The FDIC was created in 1934 after the massive bank failures of 1930–1933, in which the savings of many depositors at commercial banks were wiped out. The National Credit Union Share Insurance Fund (NCUSIF) does the same for credit unions.

Limits on Competition

Politicians have often declared that unbridled competition among financial intermediaries promotes failures that harm the public. Although the evidence that competition does indeed have this effect is extremely weak, state and federal governments at times have imposed restrictions on the opening of additional locations (branches). In the past, banks were not allowed to open branches in other states, and in some states banks were restricted from opening branches in additional locations.

Restrictions on Interest Rates

Competition has also been inhibited by regulations that impose restrictions on interest rates that can be paid on deposits. For decades after 1933, banks were prohibited from paying interest on checking accounts. In addition, until 1986, the Federal Reserve System had the power under *Regulation Q* to set maximum interest rates that banks could pay on savings deposits. These regulations were instituted because of the widespread belief that unrestricted interest-rate competition helped encourage bank failures during the Great Depression. Later evidence does not seem to support this view, and Regulation Q has been abolished (although there are still restrictions on paying interest on checking accounts held by businesses).

In later chapters, we will look more closely at government regulation of financial markets and explore whether it has improved their functioning.

Financial Regulation Abroad

Not surprisingly, given the similarity of the economic systems here and in Japan, Canada, and the nations of Western Europe, financial regulation in these countries is similar to that in the United States. Provision of information is improved by requiring corporations issuing securities to report details about assets and liabilities, earnings, and sales of stock, and by prohibiting insider trading. The soundness of intermediaries is ensured by licensing, periodic inspection of financial intermediaries' books, and provision of deposit insurance (although its coverage is smaller than that in the United States and its existence is often intentionally not advertised).

The major differences between financial regulation in the United States and abroad relate to bank regulation. In the past, the United States was the only industrialized country that subjected banks to restrictions on branching, which limited their size and confined them to certain geographic regions. (These restrictions were abolished by legislation in 1994.) U.S. banks are also the most restricted in the range of assets they may hold. Banks abroad frequently hold shares in commercial firms; in Japan and Germany, those stakes can be sizable.

SUMMARY

1. The basic function of financial markets is to channel funds from savers who have an excess of funds to spenders who have a shortage of funds. Financial markets can do this either through direct finance, in which borrowers borrow funds directly from lenders by selling them securities, or through indirect finance, which involves a financial intermediary that stands between the lender-savers and the borrower-spenders and helps transfer funds from one to the other. This channeling of funds improves the economic welfare of everyone in society. Because they allow funds to move from people who have no productive investment opportunities to those who have such opportunities, financial markets contribute to economic efficiency. In addition, channeling of funds directly benefits consumers by allowing them to make purchases when they need them most.

2. Financial markets can be classified as debt and equity markets, primary and secondary markets, exchanges and over-the-counter markets, and money and capital markets.

3. The principal money market instruments (debt instruments with maturities of less than one year) are U.S. Treasury bills, negotiable bank certificates of deposit, commercial paper, repurchase agreements, and federal funds. The principal capital market instruments (debt and equity instruments with maturities greater than one year) are stocks, mortgages, corporate bonds, U.S. government securities, U.S. government agency securities, state and local government bonds, and consumer and bank commercial loans.

4. An important trend in recent years is the growing internationalization of financial markets. Eurobonds, which are denominated in a currency other than that of the country in which they are sold, are now the dominant security in the international bond market and have surpassed U.S. corporate bonds as a source of new funds. Eurodollars, which are U.S. dollars deposited in foreign banks, are an important source of funds for American banks.

5. Financial intermediaries are financial institutions that acquire funds by issuing liabilities and, in turn, use those funds to acquire assets by purchasing securities or making loans. Financial intermediaries play an important role in the financial system because they reduce transaction costs, allow risk sharing, and solve problems created by adverse selection and moral hazard. As a result, financial intermediaries allow small savers and borrowers to benefit from the existence of

financial markets, thereby increasing the efficiency of the economy. However, the economies of scope that help make financial intermediaries successful can lead to conflicts of interest that make the financial system less efficient.

6. The principal financial intermediaries fall into three categories: (a) banks—commercial banks, savings and loan associations, mutual savings banks, and credit unions; (b) contractual savings institutions—life insurance companies, fire and casualty insurance companies, and pension funds; and (c) investment intermediaries—finance

companies, mutual funds, money market mutual funds, hedge funds, and investment banks.

7. The government regulates financial markets and financial intermediaries for two main reasons: to increase the information available to investors and to ensure the soundness of the financial system. Regulations include requiring disclosure of information to the public, restrictions on who can set up a financial intermediary, restrictions on what assets financial intermediaries can hold, the provision of deposit insurance, limits on competition, and restrictions on interest rates.

KEY TERMS

adverse selection, p. 36
asset transformation, p. 36
asymmetric information, p. 36
brokers, p. 26
capital, p. 24
capital market, p. 27
conflicts of interest, p. 38
currency, p. 28
dealers, p. 26
default, p. 28
diversification, p. 36
dividends, p. 25
economies of scale, p. 35
economies of scope, p. 38
equities, p. 25

Eurobond, p. 33
Eurocurrencies, p. 33
Eurodollars, p. 33
exchanges, p. 26
federal funds rate, p. 29
financial intermediation, p. 34
financial panic, p. 43
foreign bonds, p. 32
intermediate-term, p. 25
investment bank, p. 26
liabilities, p. 23
liquid, p. 26
liquidity services, p. 35
long-term, p. 25
maturity, p. 25

money market, p. 27
moral hazard, p. 37
mortgage-backed securities, p. 30
mortgages, p. 30
over-the-counter (OTC) market, p. 26
portfolio, p. 36
primary market, p. 25
risk, p. 36
risk sharing, p. 36
secondary market, p. 25
short-term, p. 25
thrift institutions (thrifts), p. 38
transaction costs, p. 34
underwrite, p. 42
underwriting, p. 26

QUESTIONS

1. If I can buy a car today for $5,000 and it is worth $10,000 in extra income to me next year because it enables me to get a job as a traveling salesman, should I take out a loan from Larry the Loan Shark at a 90% interest rate if no one else will give me a loan? Will I be better or worse off as a result of taking out this loan? Can you make a case for legalizing loan sharking?

2. Some economists suspect that one of the reasons economies in developing countries grow so slowly is that they do not have well-developed financial markets. Does this argument make sense?

3. Give at least three examples of a situation in which financial markets allow consumers to better time their purchases.

4. If you suspect that a company will go bankrupt next year, which would you rather hold—bonds issued by the company or equities issued by the company? Why?

5. Suppose that Toyota sells yen-denominated bonds in Tokyo. Is this debt instrument considered a Eurobond? How would your answer change if the bond were sold in New York?

6. Describe who issues each of the following money market instruments:
   a. Treasury bills
   b. Certificates of deposit
   c. Commercial paper
   d. Repurchase agreement
   e. Fed funds

7. What is the difference between a *mortgage* and a *mortgage-backed security*?

8. The U.S. economy borrowed heavily from the British in the nineteenth century to build a railroad system. Why did this make both countries better off?

9. A significant number of European banks held large amounts of assets as mortgage-backed securities derived from the U.S. housing market, which crashed after 2006. How does this demonstrate both a benefit and a cost to the internationalization of financial markets?

10. How does risk sharing benefit both financial intermediaries and private investors?

11. How can the adverse selection problem explain why you are more likely to make a loan to a family member than to a stranger?

12. One of the factors contributing to the financial crisis of 2007–2009 was the widespread issuance of subprime mortgages. How does this demonstrate adverse selection?

13. Why do loan sharks worry less about moral hazard in connection with their borrowers than some other lenders do?

14. If you are an employer, what kinds of moral hazard problems might you worry about with regard to your employees?

15. If there were no asymmetry in the information that a borrower and a lender had, could a moral hazard problem still exist?

16. "In a world without information costs and transaction costs, financial intermediaries would not exist." Is this statement true, false, or uncertain? Explain your answer.

17. Why might you be willing to make a loan to your neighbor by putting funds in a savings account earning a 5% interest rate at the bank and having the bank lend her the funds at a 10% interest rate, rather than lend her the funds yourself?

18. How do conflicts of interest make the asymmetric information problem worse?

19. How can the provision of several types of financial services by one firm be both beneficial and problematic?

20. If you were going to get a loan to purchase a new car, which financial intermediary would you use: a credit union, a pension fund, or an investment bank?

21. Why would a life insurance company be concerned about the financial stability of major corporations or the health of the housing market?

22. In 2008, as a financial crisis began to unfold in the United States, the FDIC raised the limit on insured losses to bank depositors from $100,000 per account to $250,000 per account. How would this help stabilize the financial system?

23. Financial regulation is similar, but not exactly the same, in industrialized countries. Discuss why it might be desirable—or undesirable—to have the same financial regulation across industrialized countries.

APPLIED PROBLEMS

24. Suppose you have just inherited $10,000 and are considering the following options for investing the money to maximize your return:

    Option 1: Put the money in an interest-bearing checking account that earns 2%. The FDIC insures the account against bank failure.

    Option 2: Invest the money in a corporate bond with a stated return of 5%, although there is a 10% chance the company could go bankrupt.

    Option 3: Loan the money to one of your friend's roommates, Mike, at an agreed-upon interest rate of 8%, even though you believe there is a 7% chance that Mike will leave town without repaying you.

    Option 4: Hold the money in cash and earn zero return.

    a. If you are risk-neutral (that is, neither seek out nor shy away from risk), which of the four options should you choose to maximize your expected return? (*Hint:* To calculate the *expected return* of an outcome, multiply the probability that an event will occur by the outcome of that event and then add them up.)

    b. Suppose Option 3 and Option 4 are your only choices. If you could pay your friend $100 to find out extra information about Mike that would indicate with certainty whether he will leave town without paying, would you pay the $100? What does this say about the value of better information regarding risk?

DATA ANALYSIS PROBLEMS

The Problems update with real-time data in **MyLab Economics** and are available for practice or instructor assignment.

1. **Real-time Data Analysis** Go to the St. Louis Federal Reserve FRED database, and find data on federal debt held by the Federal Reserve (FDHBFRBN), by private investors (FDHBPIN), and by international and foreign investors (FDHBFIN). Using these series, calculate the total amount held and the percentage held in each of the three categories for the most recent quarter available. Repeat for the first quarter of 2000, and compare the results.

2. **Real-time Data Analysis** Go to the St. Louis Federal Reserve FRED database, and find data on the total assets of all commercial banks (TLAACBM027SBOG) and the total assets of money market mutual funds (MMMFFAQ027S). Transform the commercial bank assets series to quarterly by adjusting the *Frequency* setting to "Quarterly." Calculate the percent increase in growth of assets for each series, from January 2000 to the most recent quarter available. Which of the two financial intermediaries has experienced the most percentage growth?

3

What Is Money?

Learning Objectives

3.1 Describe what money is.

3.2 List and summarize the functions of money.

3.3 Identify different types of payment systems.

3.4 Compare and contrast the M1 and M2 money supplies.

Preview

If you had lived in America before the Revolutionary War, your money might have consisted primarily of Spanish doubloons (silver coins that were also called *pieces of eight*). Before the Civil War, the principal forms of money in the United States were gold and silver coins and paper notes, called *banknotes*, issued by private banks. Today, you use as money not only coins and paper bills issued by the government but also debit cards and checks written on accounts held at banks. Money has taken different forms at different times, but it has **always** been important to people and to the economy.

To understand the effects of money on the economy, we must understand exactly what money is. In this chapter, we develop precise definitions by exploring the functions of money, looking at why and how it promotes economic efficiency, tracing how its forms have evolved over time, and examining how money is currently measured.

3.1 MEANING OF MONEY

LO 3.1 Describe what money is.

As used in everyday conversation, the word *money* can mean many things, but to economists it has a very specific meaning. To avoid confusion, we must clarify how economists' use of the word *money* differs from conventional usage.

Economists define *money* (also referred to as the *money supply*) as anything that is generally accepted as payment for goods or services or in the repayment of debts. **Currency**, consisting of paper bills and coins, clearly fits this definition and is one type of money. When most people talk about money, they're talking about currency. If, for example, someone comes up to you and says, "Your money or your life," you should quickly hand over all of your currency rather than ask, "What exactly do you mean by 'money'?"

To define money merely as currency is much too narrow a definition for economists. Because checks are also accepted as payment for purchases, checking account deposits are considered money as well. An even broader definition of money is needed because other items, such as savings deposits, can, in effect, function as money if they can be quickly and easily converted into currency or checking account deposits. As you can see, no single, precise definition of money or the money supply is possible, even for economists.

To complicate matters further, the word *money* is frequently used synonymously with *wealth*. When people say, "Joe is rich—he has an awful lot of money," they probably mean that Joe not only has a lot of currency and a high balance in his checking account but also has stocks, bonds, four cars, three houses, and a yacht. Thus, while "currency" is too narrow a definition of money, this other popular usage is much too broad. Economists make a distinction between money in the form of currency, demand deposits, and other items that are used to make purchases, and **wealth**, the total collection of pieces of property that serve to store value. Wealth includes not only money but also other assets such as bonds, common stock, art, land, furniture, cars, and houses.

People also use the word *money* to describe what economists call *income*, as in the sentence "Sheila would be a wonderful catch; she has a good job and earns a lot of money." **Income** is a *flow* of earnings per unit of time. Money, by contrast, is a *stock*: It is a certain amount at a given point in time. If someone tells you that he has an income of $1,000, you cannot tell whether he earns a lot or a little without knowing whether this $1,000 is earned per year, per month, or even per day. But if someone tells you that she has $1,000 in her pocket, you know exactly how much this is.

Keep in mind that the money discussed in this book refers to anything that is generally accepted as payment for goods and services or in the repayment of debts and is distinct from income and wealth.

3.2 FUNCTIONS OF MONEY

LO 3.2 List and summarize the functions of money.

Whether money is shells or rocks or gold or paper, it has three primary functions in any economy: as a medium of exchange, as a unit of account, and as a store of value. Of the three functions, its function as a medium of exchange is what distinguishes money from other assets such as stocks, bonds, and houses.

Medium of Exchange

In almost all market transactions in our economy, money in the form of currency or checks is a **medium of exchange**; it is used to pay for goods and services. The use of money as a medium of exchange promotes economic efficiency by minimizing the time spent in exchanging goods and services. To see why, let's look at a *barter economy*, one without money, in which goods and services are exchanged directly for other goods and services.

Take the case of Ellen the Economics Professor, who can do just one thing well: give brilliant economics lectures. In a barter economy, if Ellen wants to eat, she must find a farmer who not only produces the food she likes but also wants to learn economics. As you might expect, this search will be difficult and time-consuming, and Ellen might spend more time looking for such an economics-hungry farmer than she will teaching. It is even possible that she will have to quit lecturing and go into farming herself. Even so, she may still starve to death.

The time spent trying to exchange goods or services is called a *transaction cost*. In a barter economy, transaction costs are high because people have to satisfy a "double coincidence of wants"—they have to find someone who has a good or service they want and who also wants the good or service they have to offer.

Let's see what happens if we introduce money into Ellen the Economics Professor's world. Ellen can teach anyone who is willing to pay money to hear her lecture. She can then go to any farmer (or his representative at the supermarket) and buy the food she needs with the money she has been paid. The problem of the double coincidence of wants is avoided, and Ellen saves a lot of time, which she may spend doing what she does best: teaching.

As this example shows, money promotes economic efficiency by eliminating much of the time spent exchanging goods and services. It also promotes efficiency by allowing people to specialize in what they do best. Money is therefore essential in an economy: It is a lubricant that allows the economy to run more smoothly by lowering transaction costs, thereby encouraging specialization and division of labor.

The need for money is so strong that almost every society beyond the most primitive invents it. For a commodity to function effectively as money, it has to meet several criteria: (1) It must be easily standardized, making it simple to ascertain its value; (2) it must be widely accepted; (3) it must be divisible, so that it is easy to "make change"; (4) it must be easy to carry; and (5) it must not deteriorate quickly. Objects that have satisfied these criteria have taken many unusual forms throughout human history, ranging from wampum (strings of beads) used by Native Americans; to tobacco and whiskey, used by the early American colonists; to cigarettes, used in prisoner-of-war camps during World War II.[1] The diverse forms of money that have been developed over the years are as much a testament to the inventiveness of the human race as are the developments of tools and language.

Unit of Account

The second role of money is to provide a **unit of account**; that is, money is used to measure value in an economy. We measure the value of goods and services in terms of money, just as we measure weight in terms of pounds or distance in terms of miles. To see why this function is important, let's look again at a barter economy, in which money does not perform this function. If the economy has only three goods—say, peaches, economics lectures, and movies—then we need to know only three prices to tell us how to exchange one for another: the price of peaches in terms of economics lectures (that is, how many economics lectures you have to pay for a peach), the price of peaches in terms of movies, and the price of economics lectures in terms of movies. If there were 10 goods, we would need to know 45 prices in order to exchange one good for another; with 100 goods, we would need 4,950 prices; and with 1,000 goods, we would need 499,500 prices.[2]

Imagine how hard it would be in a barter economy to shop at a supermarket with 1,000 different items on its shelves and be faced with deciding whether chicken or fish is a better buy if the price of a pound of chicken were quoted as 4 pounds of butter and the price of a pound of fish as 8 pounds of tomatoes. To make it possible to compare prices, the tag on each item would have to list up to 999 different prices, and the time spent reading them would result in very high transaction costs.

---

[1]An extremely entertaining article on the development of money in a prisoner of war camp during World War II is R. A. Radford, "The Economic Organization of a P.O.W. Camp," *Economica* 12 (November 1945): 189–201.

[2]The formula for telling us the number of prices we need when we have N goods is the same formula that tells us the number of pairs when there are N items. It is

$$\frac{N(N-1)}{2}$$

In the case of ten goods, for example, we would need

$$\frac{10(10-1)}{2} = \frac{90}{2} = 45 \text{ prices}$$

The solution to the problem is to introduce money into the economy and have all prices quoted in terms of units of that money, enabling us to quote the price of economics lectures, peaches, and movies in terms of, say, dollars. If there were only three goods in the economy, this would not be a great advantage over the barter system, because we would still need three prices to conduct transactions. But for 10 goods we would need only 10 prices; for 100 goods, 100 prices; and so on. At the 1,000-goods supermarket, now only 1,000 prices need to be considered, not 499,500!

We can see that using money as a unit of account lowers transaction costs in an economy by reducing the number of prices that need to be considered. The benefits of this function of money grow as the economy becomes more complex.

Store of Value

Money also functions as a **store of value**; it is a repository of purchasing power available over time. A store of value is used to save purchasing power from the time income is received until the time it is spent. This function of money is useful because most of us do not want to spend our income immediately upon receiving it, but rather prefer to wait until we have the time or the desire to shop.

Money is not unique as a store of value; any asset—whether money, stocks, bonds, land, houses, art, or jewelry—can be used to store wealth. Many such assets have advantages over money as a store of value: They often pay the owner a higher interest rate than money, experience price appreciation, and deliver services such as providing a roof over one's head. If these assets are a more desirable store of value than money, why do people hold money at all?

The answer to this question relates to the important economic concept of **liquidity**, the relative ease and speed with which an asset can be converted into a medium of exchange. Liquidity is highly desirable. Money is the most liquid asset of all because it is the medium of exchange; it does not have to be converted into anything else to make purchases. Other assets involve transaction costs when they are converted into money. When you sell your house, for example, you have to pay a brokerage commission (usually 4%–6% of the sales price), and if you need cash immediately to pay some pressing bills, you might have to settle for a lower price if you want to sell the house quickly. Because money is the most liquid asset, people are willing to hold it even if it is not the most attractive store of value.

How good a store of value money is depends on the price level. A doubling of all prices, for example, means that the value of money has dropped by half; conversely, a halving of all prices means that the value of money has doubled. During times of inflation, when the price level is increasing rapidly, money loses value rapidly, and people become more reluctant to hold their wealth in this form. This is especially true during periods of extreme inflation, known as **hyperinflation**, in which the inflation rate exceeds 50% per month.

Hyperinflation occurred in Germany after World War I, with inflation rates sometimes exceeding 1,000% per month. By the end of the hyperinflation of 1923, the price level had risen to more than 30 billion times what it had been just two years before. The quantity of money needed to purchase even the most basic items became excessive. There are stories, for example, that near the end of the hyperinflation, a wheelbarrow of cash would be required to pay for a loaf of bread. Money was losing its value so rapidly that workers were paid and then given time off on several occasions during the day to spend their wages before the money became worthless. No one wanted to hold on to money, so the use of money to carry out transactions declined, and barter became more and more dominant. Transaction costs skyrocketed and, as we would expect, output in the economy fell sharply.

3.3 EVOLUTION OF THE PAYMENTS SYSTEM

LO 3.3 Identify different types of payment systems.

We can obtain a better picture of the functions of money and the forms it has taken over time by looking at the evolution of the **payments system**, the method of conducting transactions in the economy. The payments system has been evolving over centuries, and with it the form of money. At one point, precious metals such as gold were used as the principal means of payment and were the main form of money. Later, paper assets such as checks and currency began to be used in the payments system and viewed as money. Where the payments system is heading has an important bearing on how money will be defined in the future.

Commodity Money

To obtain perspective on where the payments system is heading, it's worth exploring how it has evolved. For any object to function as money, it must be universally acceptable; everyone must be willing to take it in payment for goods and services. An object that clearly has value to everyone is a likely candidate to serve as money, and a natural choice is a precious metal such as gold or silver. Money made up of precious metals or another valuable commodity is called **commodity money**, and from ancient times until several hundred years ago, commodity money functioned as the medium of exchange in all but the most primitive societies. The problem with a payments system based exclusively on precious metals is that such a form of money is very heavy and is hard to transport from one place to another. Imagine the holes you'd wear in your pockets if you had to buy things only with coins! Indeed, for a large purchase such as a house, you'd have to rent a truck to transport the money payment.

Fiat Money

The next development in the payments system was *paper currency* (pieces of paper that function as a medium of exchange). Initially, paper currency carried a guarantee that it was convertible into coins or into a fixed quantity of precious metal. However, currency has evolved into **fiat money**, paper currency decreed by governments as legal tender (meaning that it must be accepted as legal payment for debts) but not convertible into coins or precious metal. Paper currency has the advantage of being much lighter than coins or precious metal, but it can be accepted as a medium of exchange only if there is some trust in the authorities who issue it and if printing has reached a sufficiently advanced stage that counterfeiting is extremely difficult. Because paper currency has evolved into a legal arrangement, countries can change the currency they use at will. Indeed, this is what many European countries did when they abandoned their currencies for euro bills and coins in 2002.

Major drawbacks of paper currency and coins are that they are easily stolen and can be expensive to transport in large amounts because of their bulk. To combat this problem, another step in the evolution of the payments system occurred with the development of modern banking: the invention of *checks*.

Checks

A check is an instruction from you to your bank to transfer money from your account to someone else's account when she deposits the check. Checks allow transactions to take place without the need to carry around large amounts of currency. The introduction of checks was a major innovation that improved the efficiency of the payments system. Frequently, payments made back and forth cancel each other; without checks, this would involve the movement of a lot of currency. With checks, payments that cancel each other can be settled by canceling the checks, and no currency need be moved. The use of checks thus reduces the transportation costs associated with the payments system and improves economic efficiency. Another advantage of checks is that they can be written for any amount up to the balance in the account, making transactions for large amounts much easier. Checks are also advantageous in that loss from theft is greatly reduced and because they provide convenient receipts for purchases.

Two problems arise, however, with a payments system based on checks. First, it takes time to get checks from one place to another, a particularly serious problem if you are paying someone in a different location who needs to be paid quickly. In addition, if you have a checking account, you know that it often takes several business days before a bank will allow you to make use of the funds from a check you have deposited. If your need for cash is urgent, this feature of paying by check can be frustrating. Second, the paper shuffling required to process checks is costly; currently, the cost of processing all checks written in the United States is estimated at over $5 billion per year.

Electronic Payment

The development of inexpensive computers and the spread of the Internet now make it cheap to pay bills electronically. In the past, you had to pay a bill by mailing a check, but now banks provide websites at which you just log on, make a few clicks, and thereby transmit your payment electronically. Not only do you save the cost of the stamp, but paying bills becomes (almost) a pleasure, requiring little effort. Electronic payment systems provided by banks now even spare you the step of logging on to pay the bill. Instead, recurring bills can be automatically deducted from your bank account. Estimated cost savings when a bill is paid electronically rather than by a check exceed one dollar per transaction. Electronic payment is thus becoming more and more common in the United States.

E-Money

Electronic payments technology can substitute not only for checks but also for cash, in the form of **electronic money** (or **e-money**)—money that exists only in electronic form. The first form of e-money was the *debit card*. Debit cards, which look like credit cards, enable consumers to purchase goods and services by electronically transferring funds directly from their bank accounts to a merchant's account. Debit cards are used in almost all of the same places that accept credit cards and are now often faster to use than cash. At most supermarkets, for example, you can swipe your debit card through the card reader at the checkout station, press a button, and the amount of your purchase is deducted from your bank account. Most banks, as well as companies such as Visa and MasterCard, issue debit cards, and your ATM card typically can function as a debit card.

A more advanced form of e-money is the *stored-value card*. The simplest form of stored-value card is purchased for a preset dollar amount that the consumer pays up front, like a prepaid phone card. The more sophisticated stored-value card is known as a **smart card**. It contains a computer chip that allows it to be loaded with digital cash from the owner's bank account whenever needed. In Asian countries, such as Japan and Korea, cell phones now have a smart card feature that raises the expression "pay by phone" to a new level. Smart cards can be loaded from ATM machines, personal computers with a smart card reader, or specially equipped telephones.

A third form of electronic money, often referred to as **e-cash**, is used on the Internet to purchase goods or services. A consumer gets e-cash by transferring cash from her

---

FYI   **Are We Headed for a Cashless Society?**

Predictions of a cashless society have been around for decades, but they have not come to fruition. For example, *Business Week* predicted in 1975 that electronic means of payment "would soon revolutionize the very concept of money itself," only to reverse its view several years later. Despite wider use of e-money, people still make use of a lot of cash. Why has the movement to a cashless society been so slow in coming?

Although e-money might be more convenient and efficient than a payments system based on paper, several factors work against the disappearance of the paper system. First, it is very expensive to set up the computer, card reader, and telecommunications networks necessary to make electronic money the dominant form of payment. Second, electronic means of payment raise security and privacy concerns. We often hear media reports of an unauthorized hacker who has been able to access a computer database and alter the information stored there. Because this is not an uncommon occurrence, unscrupulous persons might be able to access bank accounts in electronic payments systems and steal funds by moving them from someone else's accounts into their own. The prevention of this type of fraud is no easy task, and a whole new field of computer science has developed to cope with such security issues. A further concern is that the use of electronic means of payment leaves an electronic trail that contains a large amount of personal data on buying habits. There are worries that government agencies, employers, and marketers might be able to access these data, thereby enabling them to encroach on our privacy if they choose to do so.

In conclusion, although the use of e-money will surely increase in the future, to paraphrase Mark Twain, "the reports of cash's death are greatly exaggerated."

---

bank to an account with an online payment provider such as PayPal. When she wants to buy something with e-cash, she uses her computer, tablet, or smartphone to click the "buy" option for a particular item from a store, whereupon the e-cash is automatically transferred from her account to the merchant's account. Given the convenience of e-money, you might think that we would move quickly to a cashless society in which all payments are made electronically. However, this hasn't happened, as discussed in the FYI box, "Are We Headed for a Cashless Society?"

APPLICATION   # Will Bitcoin or Other Cryptocurrencies Become the Money of the Future?

Cryptocurrencies are a form of e-cash that uses cryptography to make financial transactions secure. Bitcoin is considered the first successful cryptocurrency and was created by pseudonymous software developer Satoshi Nakamoto in 2009. Cryptocurrencies, such as Bitcoin, are not controlled by a single entity like a central bank, but rather are created in a decentralized fashion by users who generate new units of the cryptocurrency when they use their computing power to verify and process transactions, a process referred to as "mining." Bitcoin is currently the cryptocurrency with the largest amount outstanding, but other cryptocurrencies, such as Ethereum, Ripple, Bitcoin Cash, and EOS are widely used.

Some tech enthusiasts have characterized Bitcoin and other cryptocurrencies as the money of the future. But do these cryptocurrencies satisfy the three key functions of money that we discussed earlier? That is, do they function as a medium of exchange, a unit of account, and a store of value?

Cryptocurrencies certainly function well as a medium of exchange. They have two features that make them attractive for conducting transactions. First, the transaction fees are substantially lower than those associated with credit cards and debit cards. Second, transactions made with cryptocurrencies can be made anonymously, which is very attractive to those who want to preserve their privacy.

However, the value of cryptocurrencies undergoes huge fluctuations. For example, the price of Bitcoin has been extremely volatile, with its volatility estimated to be over seven times that of the price of gold and over eight times that of stock market indexes such as the S&P 500. In 2011, the price of a Bitcoin fluctuated between 30 cents and $32. It then rose to a peak of $255 on April 10, 2013, only to fall back down to $55 on April 17. On November 30, 2013, the price of a Bitcoin peaked at $1,125, but it fell to around $200 by June 2015, and then took off to a peak value of nearly $20,000 in December 2017. By 2020, it had fallen to a value below $7,000.

The high volatility of the value of the cryptocurrencies means that they do not function well as a store of value; they are just too risky. In addition, the large changes in their prices in terms of dollars from day to day mean that they cannot function as a unit of account because the prices of goods and services in terms of the cryptocurrency would also have massive fluctuations day to day. Not surprisingly, no cryptocurrency has become a unit of account: Almost no one quotes the prices of their products in terms of bitcoins or any other cryptocurrency.

Furthermore, Bitcoin and other cryptocurrencies, which are hard to trace, are used by criminal enterprises operating on the so-called dark web, websites that are hard to find by browsing. Governments may therefore restrict the use of these cryptocurrencies in the future. China has already outlawed the use of Bitcoin as a currency.

Bitcoin and other cryptocurrencies do not satisfy two of the three key functions of money. Despite the hype, our understanding of the functions of money strongly suggests that cryptocurrencies will not be the money of the future. However, some of cryptocurrencies technology, which enables users to conduct electronic transactions cheaply, may become a feature of future electronic payments systems. Indeed, central banks are contemplating issuing their own forms of digital currencies that will have many features of cryptocurrencies but will be fixed in value to a unit of account, such as the U.S. dollar. ◆

3.4 MEASURING MONEY

LO 3.4 Compare and contrast the M1 and M2 money supplies.

The definition of money as anything that is generally accepted as payment for goods and services tells us that money is defined by people's behavior. An asset is considered money only if people believe it will be accepted by others when making payment. As we have seen, many different assets have performed this role over the centuries, ranging from gold to paper currency to checking accounts. For this reason, a behavioral definition does not tell us which assets in our economy should be considered money. To measure money, we need a precise definition that tells us exactly which assets should be included.

TABLE 1	Measures of the Monetary Aggregates	
		Value as of August 31, 2020 ($ billions)
M1	= Currency	1,920.4
	+ Demand deposits	2,317.0
	+ Other checkable deposits	1,176.4
Total M1		5,413.8
M2	= M1	
	+ Small-denomination time deposits	351.9
	+ Savings deposits and money market deposit accounts	11,593.4
	+ Money market mutual fund shares (retail)	1,105.2
Total M2		18,464.3

Source: Federal Reserve Statistical Release, H.6, Money Stock Measures: https://www.federalreserve.gov/releases/H6/current.

The Federal Reserve's Monetary Aggregates

The Federal Reserve System (the Fed), the central banking authority responsible for monetary policy in the United States, has conducted many studies on how to measure money. The problem of measuring money has recently become especially crucial because extensive financial innovation has produced new types of assets that might properly belong in a measure of money. Since 1980, the Fed has modified its measures of money several times and has settled on the following measures of the money supply, which are also referred to as **monetary aggregates** (see Table 1 and the Following the Financial News box).

The narrowest measure of money reported by the Fed is **M1**, which includes the most liquid assets: currency, checking account deposits, and traveler's checks. The components of M1 are shown in Table 1. The *currency* component of M1 includes only paper money and coins in the hands of the nonbank public and does not include cash held in ATMs or bank vaults. Surprisingly, more than $5,000 of cash is in circulation for each person in the United States (see the FYI box). The *demand deposits* component includes business checking accounts that do not pay interest. The *other checkable deposits* item includes all other checkable deposits, particularly interest-bearing

Following the Financial News   The Monetary Aggregates

Every week on Thursday, the Federal Reserve publishes the data for M1 and M2 in its H.6 release. These numbers are often reported on in the media.

The H.6 release can be found at http://www.federalreserve.gov/releases/h6/current/h6.htm.

FYI   Where Are All the U.S. Dollars?

The more than $5,000 of U.S. currency held per person in the United States is a surprisingly large number. U.S. currency is bulky, can be easily stolen, and pays no interest, so it doesn't make sense for most of us to keep a lot of it. Do you know anyone who carries $5,000 in his or her pockets? We have a puzzle: Where are all these dollars, and who is holding them?

Criminals are one group that holds a lot of dollars. If you were engaged in illegal activity, you would not conduct your transactions with checks because they are traceable and therefore a potentially powerful piece of evidence against you. That explains why gangsters and drug dealers conduct most of their transactions in cash. Some businesses like to retain a lot of cash because, if they operate as a cash business, it makes their transactions less traceable; thus they can avoid declaring income on which they would otherwise have to pay taxes.

Foreigners are the other group that routinely holds U.S. dollars. In many countries, people do not trust their own currency because their country often experiences high inflation, which erodes the value of that currency; these people hold U.S. dollars as a hedge against this inflation risk. Lack of trust in the ruble, for example, has led Russians to hoard enormous amounts of U.S. dollars. More than half of U.S. dollars are held abroad.

checking accounts held by households. These assets are clearly money because they can be used directly as a medium of exchange.

Until the mid-1970s, only commercial banks were permitted to establish checking accounts, and they were not allowed to pay interest on them. With the advent of financial innovation (discussed more extensively in Chapter 11), regulations have changed so that other types of banks, such as savings and loan associations, mutual savings banks, and credit unions, can also offer checking accounts. In addition, banking institutions can offer other checkable deposits, such as NOW (negotiated order of withdrawal) accounts and ATS (automatic transfer from savings) accounts, that do pay interest on their balances.

The **M2** monetary aggregate adds to M1 other assets that are not quite as liquid as those included in M1: assets that have check-writing features (money market deposit accounts and money market mutual fund shares) and other assets (savings deposits and small-denomination time deposits) that can be turned into cash quickly and at very little cost. *Small-denomination time deposits* are certificates of deposit with a denomination of less than $100,000 that can be redeemed without a penalty only at a fixed maturity date. *Savings deposits* are nontransaction deposits that can be added to or taken out at any time. *Money market deposit accounts* are similar to money market mutual funds but are issued by banks. The *money market mutual fund shares* are retail accounts on which households can write checks.

Because economists and policymakers cannot be sure which of the monetary aggregates is the best measure of money, it is logical to wonder if the movements of M1 and M2 closely parallel one another. If they do, then using one monetary aggregate to predict future economic performance and to conduct policy will be the same as using the other, and it does not much matter that we are not sure of the appropriate definition of money for a given policy decision. However, if the monetary aggregates do *not* move together, then what one monetary aggregate tells us is happening to the money supply might be quite different from what the other monetary aggregate would tell us. Conflicting information would present a confusing picture, making it hard for policymakers to decide on the right course of action.

Figure 1 plots the growth rates of M1 and M2 from 1960 to 2020. The growth rates of these two monetary aggregates do tend to move together; the timing of their rise and fall is roughly similar until the 1990s, and they both show a higher growth rate, on average, in the 1970s than in the 1960s.

Real-time data

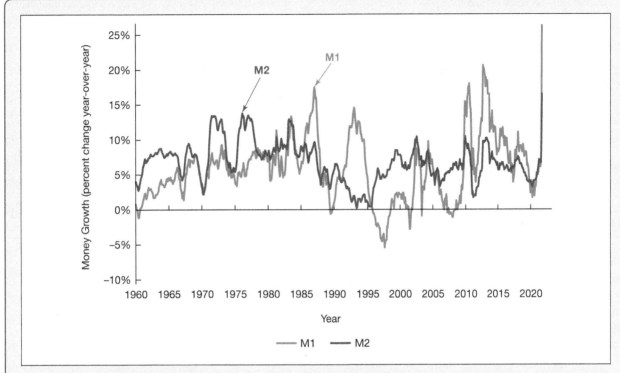

FIGURE 1   Growth Rates of the M1 and M2 Aggregates, 1960–2020

The timing of the rise and fall of growth rates is roughly similar for both M1 and M2. There were periods, however, such as 1990–1994 and 2005–2007, during which M1 and M2 moved in opposite directions, leading to conflicting recommendations about the best course of monetary policy.

Source: Federal Reserve Bank of St. Louis, FRED Database: https://fred.stlouisfed.org/series/M1SL

Yet some glaring discrepancies exist between the movements of these aggregates. Contrast M1's high rates of growth from 1992 to 1994 with the much lower growth rates of M2. Also notice that from 2004 to 2007, M2's growth rate increased slightly, while M1's growth rate decelerated sharply and became negative. In 2009 and 2011, M1 growth surged to over 15% from near zero the year before, while M2 growth rose less dramatically. Thus, the different measures of money tell a very different story about the results of monetary policy in recent years.

From the data in Figure 1, you can see that obtaining a single, precise, and correct measure of money does seem to matter, and that it does make a difference which monetary aggregate policymakers and economists choose as the best measure of money.

SUMMARY

1. To economists, the word *money* has a different meaning than *income* or *wealth*. Money is anything that is generally accepted as payment for goods or services or in the repayment of debts.

2. Money serves three primary functions: as a medium of exchange, as a unit of account, and as a store of value. Money as a medium of exchange helps an economy avoid the problem of double coincidence of wants that arises in a barter economy and thus lowers transaction costs and encourages specialization and the division of labor. Money as a unit of account reduces the number of prices needed in an economy, which also reduces transaction costs. Money also functions as a store of value but performs this role poorly if it is rapidly losing value due to inflation.

3. The payments system has evolved over time. Until several hundred years ago, the payments systems in all but the most primitive societies were based primarily on precious metals. The introduction of paper currency lowered the cost of transporting money. The next major advance was the introduction of checks, which lowered transaction

costs still further. We are currently moving toward an electronic payments system in which paper is eliminated and all transactions are handled by computers. Despite the potential efficiency of such a system, obstacles are slowing the movement to a checkless society and the development of new forms of electronic money.

4. The Federal Reserve System has defined two different measures of the money supply—M1 and M2. These measures are not equivalent and do not always move together, so they cannot be used interchangeably by policymakers. Obtaining the precise, correct measure of money does seem to matter and has implications for the conduct of monetary policy.

KEY TERMS

commodity money, p. 53
currency, p. 49
e-cash, p. 54
electronic money (e-money), p. 54
fiat money, p. 53
hyperinflation, p. 52

income, p. 50
liquidity, p. 52
M1, p. 57
M2, p. 58
medium of exchange, p. 50
monetary aggregates, p. 57

payments system, p. 53
smart card, p. 54
store of value, p. 52
unit of account, p. 51
wealth, p. 50

QUESTIONS

1. Why is simply counting currency an inadequate measure of money?

2. In prison, cigarettes are sometimes used among inmates as a form of payment. How is it possible for cigarettes to solve the "double coincidence of wants" problem, even if a prisoner does not smoke?

3. Three goods are produced in an economy by three individuals:

Good	**Producer**
Apples	Orchard owner
Bananas	Banana grower
Chocolate	Chocolatier

If the orchard owner likes only bananas, the banana grower likes only chocolate, and the chocolatier likes only apples, will any trade between these three persons take place in a barter economy? How will introducing money into the economy benefit these three producers?

4. Why did cavemen and women not need money?

5. Most of the time it is quite difficult to separate the three functions of money. Money performs its three functions at all times, but sometimes we can stress one in particular. For each of the following situations, identify which function of money is emphasized.

a. Brooke accepts money in exchange for performing her daily tasks at her office, since she knows she can use that money to buy goods and services.

b. Tim wants to calculate the relative value of oranges and apples and therefore checks the price per pound of each of these goods as quoted in currency units.

c. Maria is currently pregnant. She expects her expenditures to increase in the future and decides to increase the balance in her savings account.

6. In Brazil, a country that underwent a rapid inflation before 1994, many transactions were conducted in dollars rather than in reals, the domestic currency. Why?

7. Was money a better store of value in the United States in the 1950s than in the 1970s? Why or why not? In which period would you have been more willing to hold money?

8. Why have some economists described money during a hyperinflation as a "hot potato" that is quickly passed from one person to another?

9. Why were people in the United States in the nineteenth century sometimes willing to be paid by check rather than with gold, even though they knew there was a possibility that the check might bounce?

10. In ancient Greece, why was gold a more likely candidate for use as money than wine?

11. If you use an online payment system such as PayPal to purchase goods or services on the Internet, does this affect the M1 money supply, the M2 money supply, both, or neither? Explain.

12. Rank the following assets from most liquid to least liquid:
    a. Checking account deposits
    b. Houses
    c. Currency
    d. Automobiles
    e. Savings deposits
    f. Common stock

13. Which of the Federal Reserve's measures of the monetary aggregates—M1 or M2—is composed of the most liquid assets? Which is the larger measure?

14. It is not unusual to find a business that displays a sign saying "no personal checks, please." On the basis of this observation, comment on the relative degree of liquidity of a checking account versus currency.

15. For each of the following assets, indicate which of the monetary aggregates (M1 and M2) includes them:
    a. Currency
    b. Money market mutual funds
    c. Small-denomination time deposits
    d. Checkable deposits

16. Assume that you are interested in earning some return on the idle balances you usually keep in your checking account and decide to buy some money market mutual funds shares by writing a check. Comment on the effect of your action (with everything else the same) on M1 and M2.

17. In April 2009, year-over-year the growth rate of M1 fell to 6.1%, while the growth rate of M2 rose to 10.3%. In September 2013, the growth rate of the M1 money supply was 6.5%, while the growth rate of the M2 money supply was about 8.3%. How should Federal Reserve policymakers interpret these changes in the growth rates of M1 and M2?

18. Suppose a researcher discovers that a measure of the total amount of debt in the U.S. economy over the past 20 years was a better predictor of inflation and the business cycle than M1 or M2. Does this discovery mean that we should define money as equal to the total amount of debt in the economy?

APPLIED PROBLEMS

19. The table below shows hypothetical values, in billions of dollars, of different forms of money.
    a. Use the table to calculate the M1 and M2 money supplies for each year, as well as the growth rates of the M1 and M2 money supplies from the previous year.
    b. Why are the growth rates of M1 and M2 so different? Explain.

		2021	2022	2023	2024
A.	Currency	900	920	925	931
B.	Money market mutual fund shares	680	681	679	688
C.	Savings account deposits	5,500	5,780	5,968	6,105
D.	Money market deposit accounts	1,214	1,245	1,274	1,329
E.	Demand and checkable deposits	1,000	972	980	993
F.	Small-denomination time deposits	830	861	1,123	1,566
G.	3-month Treasury bills	1,986	2,374	2,436	2,502

DATA ANALYSIS PROBLEMS

The Problems update with real-time data in **MyLab Economics** and are available for practice or instructor assignment.

1. **Real-time Data Analysis** Go to the St. Louis Federal Reserve FRED database, and find data on currency (CURRSL), demand deposits (DEMDEPSL), and other checkable deposits (OCDSL). Calculate the M1 money supply, and calculate the percentage change in M1 and in each of the three components of M1 from the most recent month of data available to the same time one year prior. Which component has the highest growth rate? The lowest growth rate? Repeat the calculations using the data from January 2000 to the most recent month of data available, and compare your results.

2. **Real-time Data Analysis** Go to the St. Louis Federal Reserve FRED database, and find data on small-denomination time deposits (STDSL), savings deposits and money market deposit accounts (SAVINGSL), and retail money market funds (RMFSL). Calculate the percentage change of each of these three components of M2 (not included in M1) from the most recent month of data available to the same time one year prior. Which component has the highest growth rate? The lowest growth rate? Repeat the calculations using the data from January 2000 to the most recent month of data available, and compare your results. Use your answers from question 1 to determine which grew faster: the non-M1 components of M2, or the M1 money supply.

Financial Markets

Crisis and Response: Credit Market Turmoil and the Stock Market Crashes of October 2008 and March 2020

The financial crisis that started during the summer of 2007 began to snowball as the value of mortgage-backed securities on financial institutions' balance sheets plummeted. When the House of Representatives, fearing the wrath of constituents who were angry about proposals to bail out Wall Street, voted down a $700 billion bailout package proposed by the Bush administration on Monday, September 29, 2008, the financial crisis took an even more virulent turn, despite the bailout package that was passed four days later.

A "flight to quality" drove three-month Treasury bill rates down to almost zero, rates not seen since the Great Depression of the 1930s. Credit spreads—an indicator of risk—shot through the roof, with the gap between Eurodollar and Treasury bill rates (the TED spread) going from around 40 basis points (0.40 percentage point) before the financial crisis began to over 450 basis points in mid-October, the highest value in its history. After earlier sharp declines, the stock market crashed further, with the week beginning on October 6, 2008, showing the worst weekly decline in U.S. history.

When Covid-19 became a worldwide pandemic, the three-month Treasury bill rate again fell to near zero; the stock market crashed, falling by more than 35% from February 19, 2020, to March 23, 2020; and the TED spread rose from around 10 basis points in February to over 140 basis points by the end of March.

The recent financial crisis and impact of the coronavirus pandemic illustrate how volatile financial markets can be. This volatility can hit financial consumers directly, leading to difficulty in getting loans, falling home values, and declining retirement account values and putting jobs in jeopardy. How can policy respond to disruptions in financial markets? We begin addressing this question by examining the inner workings of financial markets, particularly interest rate dynamics. Chapter 4 explains what an interest rate is, as well as the relationships among interest rates, bond prices, and returns. Chapter 5 examines how the overall level of interest rates is determined. In Chapter 6, we extend the analysis of the bond market to explain changes in credit spreads and the relationship of long-term to short-term interest rates. Chapter 7 looks at the role of expectations in the stock market and explores what drives stock prices.

4

The Meaning of Interest Rates

Learning Objectives

4.1 Calculate the present value of future cash flows and the yield to maturity on the four types of credit market instruments.

4.2 Recognize the distinctions among yield to maturity, current yield, rate of return, and rate of capital gain.

4.3 Interpret the distinction between real and nominal interest rates.

Preview

Interest rates are among the most closely watched variables in the economy. Their movements are reported almost daily by the news media because they directly affect our everyday lives and have important consequences for the health of the economy. They influence personal decisions such as whether to consume or save, whether to buy a house, and whether to purchase bonds or put funds into a savings account. Interest rates also affect the economic decisions of businesses and households, such as whether to use their funds to invest in new equipment for factories or to save rather than spend their money.

Before we can go on with the study of money, banking, and financial markets, we must understand exactly what the phrase *interest rates* means. In this chapter, we see that a concept known as the *yield to maturity* is the most accurate measure of interest rates; the yield to maturity is what economists mean when they use the term *interest rate*. We'll discuss how the yield to maturity is measured. We'll also see that a bond's interest rate does not necessarily indicate how good an investment the bond is, because what the bond earns (its rate of return) does not necessarily equal its interest rate. Finally, we'll explore the distinction between real interest rates, which are adjusted for inflation, and nominal interest rates, which are not.

Although learning definitions is not always the most exciting of pursuits, it is important to read carefully and understand the concepts presented in this chapter. Not only are they used continually throughout the remainder of this text, but a firm grasp of these terms will give you a clearer understanding of the role that interest rates play in your life as well as in the general economy.

4.1 MEASURING INTEREST RATES

LO 4.1 Calculate the present value of future cash flows and the yield to maturity on the four types of credit market instruments.

Different debt instruments have very different streams of cash payments (known as **cash flows**) to the holder, with very different timing. Thus we first need to understand how we can compare the value of one kind of debt instrument with the value of another before we see how interest rates are measured. To do this, we make use of the concept of *present value*.

Present Value

The concept of **present value** (or **present discounted value**) is based on the commonsense notion that a dollar paid to you one year from now is less valuable than a dollar paid to you today. This notion is true because you can deposit a dollar today in a savings account that earns interest and have more than a dollar in one year. Economists use a more formal definition, as explained in this section.

Let's look at the simplest kind of debt instrument, which we will call a **simple loan**. In this loan, the lender provides the borrower with an amount of funds (called the *principal*) that must be repaid to the lender at the *maturity date*, along with an additional payment for the interest. For example, if you made your friend, Jane, a simple loan of $100 for one year, you would require her to repay the principal of $100 in one year's time, along with an additional payment for interest—say, $10. In the case of a simple loan like this one, the interest payment divided by the amount of the loan is a natural and sensible way to measure the interest rate. This measure of the so-called *simple interest rate*, i, is

$$i = \frac{\$10}{\$100} = 0.10 = 10\%$$

If you make this $100 loan, at the end of the year you will have $110, which can be rewritten as

$$\$100 \times (1 + 0.10) = \$110$$

If you then lent out the $110 at the same interest rate, at the end of the second year you would have

$$\$110 \times (1 + 0.10) = \$121$$

or, equivalently,

$$\$100 \times (1 + 0.10) \times (1 + 0.10) = \$100 \times (1 + 0.10)^2 = \$121$$

Continuing with the loan again, at the end of the third year you would have

$$\$121 \times (1 + 0.10) = \$100 \times (1 + 0.10)^3 = \$133$$

Generalizing, we can see that at the end of n years, your $100 would turn into

$$\$100 \times (1 + i)^n$$

The amounts you would have at the end of each year by making the $100 loan today can be seen in the following timeline:

This timeline clearly indicates that you are just as happy having $100 today as you will be having $110 a year from now (of course, as long as you are sure that Jane will pay you back). You are also just as happy having $100 today as you will be having $121 two years from now, or $133 three years from now, or $100 \times (1 + 0.10)^n$ dollars n years from now. The timeline indicates that we can also work backward from future amounts to the present. For example, $\$133 = \$100 \times (1 + 0.10)^3$ three years from now is worth $\$100$ today, so

$$\$100 = \frac{\$133}{(1 + 0.10)^3}$$

The process of calculating today's value of dollars received in the future, as we have done above, is called *discounting the future*. This is why the concept of present value is also referred to as *present discounted value*. We can generalize this process by writing today's (present) value of $\$100$ as *PV* and the future cash flow (payment) of $\$133$ as *CF*, and then replacing 0.10 (the 10% interest rate) by *i*. This leads to the following formula:

$$PV = \frac{CF}{(1 + i)^n} \tag{1}$$

Intuitively, Equation 1 tells us that if you are promised $\$1$ of cash flow, for certain, ten years from now, this dollar would not be as valuable to you as $\$1$ is today because, if you had the $\$1$ today, you could invest it and end up with more than $\$1$ in ten years.

The concept of present value is extremely useful, because it allows us to figure out today's value (price) of a credit (debt) market instrument at a given simple interest rate *i* by just adding up the individual present values of all the future payments received. This information enables us to compare the values of two or more instruments that have very different timing of their payments.

APPLICATION Simple Present Value

What is the present value of $\$250$ to be paid in two years if the interest rate is 15%?

Solution

The present value would be $\$189.04$. We find this value by using Equation 1,

$$PV = \frac{CF}{(1 + i)^n}$$

where

$$\begin{aligned} CF &= \text{cash flow in two years} = 250 \\ i &= \text{annual interest rate} \quad = 0.15 \\ n &= \text{number of years} \quad = 2 \end{aligned}$$

Thus

$$PV = \frac{\$250}{(1 + 0.15)^2} = \frac{\$250}{1.3225} = \$189.04$$

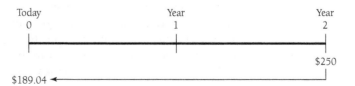

APPLICATION   How Much Is That Jackpot Worth?

Assume that you just hit the $20 million jackpot in the New York State Lottery, which promises you a payment of $1 million every year for the next 20 years. You are clearly excited, but have you really won $20 million?

Solution

No, not in the present value sense. In today's dollars, that $20 million is worth a lot less. If we assume an interest rate of 10% as in the earlier examples, the first payment of $1 million is clearly worth $1 million today, but the second payment next year is worth only $1 million/$(1 + 0.10)$ = $909,090, a lot less than $1 million. The following year, the payment is worth $1 million/$(1 + 0.10)^2$ = $826,446 in today's dollars, and so on. When you add up all these amounts, they total $9.4 million. You are still pretty excited (who wouldn't be?), but because you understand the concept of present value, you recognize that you are the victim of false advertising. In present-value terms, you didn't really win $20 million, but instead won less than half that amount. (And that's before taxes!) ◆

Four Types of Credit Market Instruments

In terms of the timing of their cash flow payments, there are four basic types of credit market instruments.

1. A simple loan, which we have already discussed, in which the lender provides the borrower with an amount of funds that must be repaid to the lender at the maturity date, along with an additional payment for the interest. Many money market instruments are of this type—for example, short-term commercial loans to businesses.

2. A **fixed-payment loan** (also called a **fully amortized loan**) in which the lender provides the borrower with an amount of funds that the borrower must repay by making the same payment, consisting of part of the principal and interest, every period (such as a month) for a set number of years. For example, if you borrow $1,000, a fixed-payment loan might require you to pay $126 every year for 25 years. Installment loans (such as auto loans) and mortgages are frequently of the fixed-payment type.

3. A **coupon bond** pays the owner of the bond a fixed interest payment (coupon payment) every year until the maturity date, when a specified final amount (**face value** or **par value**) is repaid. (The coupon payment is so named because in the past, the bondholder obtained payment by clipping a coupon off the bond and sending it to the bond issuer, who then sent the payment to the holder. Today, it is no longer necessary to send in coupons to receive payments.) A coupon bond with $1,000 face value, for example, might pay you a coupon payment of $100 per year for ten years, and then repay you the face value amount of $1,000 at the maturity date. (The face value of a bond is usually in $1,000 increments.)

   A coupon bond is identified by four pieces of information: First is the bond's face value; second is the corporation or government agency that issues the bond; third is the maturity date of the bond; and fourth is the bond's **coupon rate**, which is the dollar amount of the yearly coupon payment expressed as a percentage of the face value of the bond. In our example, the coupon bond has a yearly coupon payment of $100 and a face value of $1,000. The coupon rate is then $100/$1,000 = 0.10, or 10%. Capital market instruments such as U.S. Treasury bonds and notes and corporate bonds are examples of coupon bonds.

4. A **discount bond** (also called a **zero-coupon bond**) is bought at a price below its face value (at a discount), and the face value is repaid at the maturity date. Unlike a coupon bond, a discount bond does not make any interest payments; it just pays off the face value. For example, a one-year discount bond with a face value of $1,000 might be bought for $900; in a year's time, the owner would be repaid the face value of $1,000. U.S. Treasury bills, U.S. savings bonds, and long-term zero-coupon bonds are examples of discount bonds.

These four types of instruments make payments at different times: Simple loans and discount bonds make payments only at their maturity dates, whereas fixed-payment loans and coupon bonds make payments periodically until maturity. How can you decide which of these instruments will provide you with the most income? They all seem so different because they make payments at different times. To solve this problem, we use the concept of present value, explained earlier, to provide us with a procedure for measuring interest rates on these different types of instruments.

Yield to Maturity

Of the several common ways of calculating interest rates, the most important is the **yield to maturity**, which is the interest rate that equates the present value of cash flow payments received from a debt instrument with its value today.[1] Because the concept behind the calculation of the yield to maturity makes good economic sense, economists consider it the most accurate measure of interest rates.

To better understand the yield to maturity, we now look at how it is calculated for the four types of credit market instruments. In all of these examples, the key to understanding the calculation of the yield to maturity is realizing that we are equating today's value of the debt instrument with the present value of all of its future cash flow payments.

Simple Loan   Using the concept of present value, the yield to maturity on a simple loan is easy to calculate. For the one-year loan we discussed, today's value is $100, and the payments in one year's time would be $110 (the repayment of $100 plus the interest payment of $10). We can use this information to solve for the yield to maturity *i* by recognizing that the present value of the future payments must equal today's value of the loan.

APPLICATION ## Yield to Maturity on a Simple Loan

If Pete borrows $100 from his sister and next year she wants $110 back from him, what is the yield to maturity on this loan?

Solution
The yield to maturity on the loan is 10%.

$$PV = \frac{CF}{(1 + i)^n}$$

where

$$PV = \text{amount borrowed} = \$100$$
$$CF = \text{cash flow in one year} = \$110$$
$$n = \text{number of years} = 1$$

---

[1]In other contexts, the yield to maturity is also called the *internal rate of return*.

Thus

$$\$100 = \frac{\$110}{(1 + i)}$$

$$(1 + i)\$100 = \$110$$

$$(1 + i) = \frac{\$110}{\$100}$$

$$i = 1.10 - 1 = 0.10 = 10\%$$

```
      Today                          Year
        0                             1
        |─────────────────────────────|
      $100                          $110
        ──────────→ i = 10% ←──────────
```

This calculation of the yield to maturity should look familiar because it equals the interest payment of $10 divided by the loan amount of $100; that is, it equals the simple interest rate on the loan. An important point to recognize is that *for simple loans, the simple interest rate equals the yield to maturity*. Hence the same term i is used to denote both the yield to maturity and the simple interest rate.

Fixed-Payment Loan   Recall that this type of loan has the same cash flow payment every period throughout the life of the loan. On a fixed-rate mortgage, for example, the borrower makes the same payment to the bank every month until the maturity date, at which time the loan will be completely paid off. To calculate the yield to maturity for a fixed-payment loan, we follow the same strategy that we used for the simple loan—we equate today's value of the loan with its present value. Because the fixed-payment loan involves more than one cash flow payment, the present value of the fixed-payment loan is calculated (using Equation 1) as the sum of the present values of all cash flow payments.

In the case of our earlier example, the loan is $1,000 and the yearly payment is $126 for the next 25 years. The present value (*PV*) is calculated as follows: At the end of one year, there is a $126 payment with a *PV* of $126/(1 + i)$; at the end of two years, there is another $126 payment with a *PV* of $\$126/(1 + i)^2$; and so on until, at the end of the twenty-fifth year, the last payment of $126 with a *PV* of $\$126/(1 + i)^{25}$ is made. Setting today's value of the loan ($1,000) equal to the sum of the present values of all the yearly payments gives us

$$\$1,000 = \frac{\$126}{1 + i} + \frac{\$126}{(1 + i)^2} + \frac{\$126}{(1 + i)^3} + \ldots + \frac{\$126}{(1 + i)^{25}}$$

More generally, for any fixed-payment loan,

$$LV = \frac{FP}{(1 + i)} + \frac{FP}{(1 + i)^2} + \frac{FP}{(1 + i)^3} + \ldots + \frac{FP}{(1 + i)^n} \qquad (2)$$

where

$$LV = \text{loan value}$$
$$FP = \text{fixed yearly payment}$$
$$n = \text{number of years until maturity}$$

For a fixed-payment loan, the loan value, the fixed yearly payment, and the number of years until maturity are known quantities, and only the yield to maturity is not. So we can solve this equation for the yield to maturity i. Because this calculation is not easy, many financial calculators have programs that enable you to find i given the loan's numbers for LV, FP, and n. For example, in the case of a 25-year $1,000 loan with yearly payments of $85.81, the yield to maturity that results from solving Equation 2 is 7%. Real estate brokers always have handy a financial calculator that can solve such equations so that they can immediately tell the prospective house buyer exactly what the yearly (or monthly) payments will be if the house purchase is financed by a mortgage.

APPLICATION   # Yield to Maturity and the Yearly Payment on a Fixed-Payment Loan

You decide to purchase a new home and need a $100,000 mortgage. You take out a loan from the bank that has an interest rate of 7%. What is the yearly payment to the bank if you wish to pay off the loan in 20 years?

Solution
The yearly payment to the bank is $9,439.29.

$$LV = \frac{FP}{(1 + i)} + \frac{FP}{(1 + i)^2} + \frac{FP}{(1 + i)^3} + \cdots + \frac{FP}{(1 + i)^n}$$

where

$$LV = \text{loan value amount} = 100,000$$
$$i = \text{annual interest rate} = 0.07$$
$$n = \text{number of years} = 20$$

Thus

$$\$100,000 = \frac{FP}{(1 + 0.07)} + \frac{FP}{(1 + 0.07)^2} + \frac{FP}{(1 + 0.07)^3} + \cdots + \frac{FP}{(1 + 0.07)^{20}}$$

To find the monthly payment for the loan using a financial calculator:

$$n = \text{number of years} = 20$$
$$PV = \text{amount of the loan } (LV) = 100,000$$
$$FV = \text{amount of the loan after 20 years} = 0$$
$$i = \text{annual interest rate} = 0.07$$

Then push the *PMT* button to get the fixed yearly payment $(FP) = \$9,439.29.$ ◆

Coupon Bond To calculate the yield to maturity for a coupon bond, follow the same strategy used for the fixed-payment loan: Equate today's value of the bond with its present value. Because coupon bonds also have more than one cash flow payment, the present value of the bond is calculated as the sum of the present values of all the coupon payments plus the present value of the final payment of the face value of the bond.

The present value of a $1,000-face-value bond with ten years to maturity and yearly coupon payments of $100 (a 10% coupon rate) can be calculated as follows: At the end of one year, there is a $100 coupon payment with a *PV* of $100/(1 + i)$; at the end of the second year, there is another $100 coupon payment with a *PV* of $100/(1 + i)^2$; and so on until, at maturity, there is a $100 coupon payment with a *PV* of $100/(1 + i)^{10}$ plus the repayment of the $1,000 face value with a *PV* of $1,000/(1 + i)^{10}$. Setting today's value of the bond (its current price, denoted by *P*) equal to the sum of the present values of all the cash flow payments for the bond gives

$$P = \frac{\$100}{1 + i} + \frac{\$100}{(1 + i)^2} + \frac{\$100}{(1 + i)^3} + \cdots + \frac{\$100}{(1 + i)^{10}} + \frac{\$1,000}{(1 + i)^{10}}$$

More generally, for any coupon bond,[2]

$$P = \frac{C}{1 + i} + \frac{C}{(1 + i)^2} + \frac{C}{(1 + i)^3} + \cdots + \frac{C}{(1 + i)^n} + \frac{F}{(1 + i)^n} \quad (3)$$

where

P = price of the coupon bond
C = yearly coupon payment
F = face value of the bond
n = years to maturity date

In Equation 3, the coupon payment, the face value, the years to maturity, and the price of the bond are known quantities, and only the yield to maturity is not. Hence we can solve this equation for the yield to maturity *i*. As in the case of the fixed-payment loan, this calculation is not easy, so business-oriented software and financial calculators have built-in programs that solve the equation for you.

APPLICATION   Yield to Maturity and Bond Price for a Coupon Bond

Find the price of a 10% coupon bond with a face value of $1,000, a 12.25% yield to maturity, and eight years to maturity.

Solution
The price of the bond is $889.20. To solve using a financial calculator:

$$\begin{aligned} n &= \text{years to maturity} & &= 8 \\ FV &= \text{face value of the bond } (F) & &= 1,000 \\ i &= \text{yield to maturity} & &= 12.25\% \\ PMT &= \text{yearly coupon payments } (C) & &= 100 \end{aligned}$$

Then push the *PV* button to get the price of the bond = $889.20.

[2]Most coupon bonds actually make coupon payments on a semiannual basis rather than once a year, as we assumed here. The effect on the calculations is very slight and will be ignored here.

Alternatively, you could solve for the yield to maturity given the bond price by entering $889.20 for *PV* and pushing the *i* button to get a yield to maturity of 12.25%. ◆

Table 1 shows the yields to maturity calculated for several bond prices. Three interesting facts emerge:

1. When the coupon bond is priced at its face value, the yield to maturity equals the coupon rate.
2. The price of a coupon bond and the yield to maturity are negatively related; that is, as the yield to maturity rises, the price of the bond falls. As the yield to maturity falls, the price of the bond rises.
3. The yield to maturity is greater than the coupon rate when the bond price is below its face value and is less than the coupon rate when the bond price is above its face value.

These three facts are true for any coupon bond and are really not surprising if you think about the reasoning behind the calculation of the yield to maturity. When you put $1,000 in a bank account with an interest rate of 10%, you can take out $100 every year and you will be left with the $1,000 at the end of ten years. This process is similar to buying the $1,000 bond with a 10% coupon rate analyzed in Table 1, which pays a $100 coupon payment every year and then repays $1,000 at the end of ten years. If the bond is purchased at the par value of $1,000, its yield to maturity must equal 10%, which is also equal to the coupon rate of 10%. The same reasoning applied to any coupon bond demonstrates that if the coupon bond is purchased at its par value, the yield to maturity and the coupon rate must be equal.

It is a straightforward process to show that the bond price and the yield to maturity are negatively correlated. As *i*, the yield to maturity, increases, all denominators in the bond price formula (Equation 3) must necessarily increase, because the rise in *i* lowers the present value of all future cash flow payments for this bond. Hence a rise in the interest rate, as measured by the yield to maturity, means that the price of the bond must fall. Another way to explain why the bond price falls when the interest rate rises is to consider that a higher interest rate implies that the future coupon payments and final payment are worth less when discounted back to the present; hence the price of the bond must be lower.

The third fact, that the yield to maturity is greater than the coupon rate when the bond price is below its par value, follows directly from facts 1 and 2. When the yield to maturity equals the coupon rate, then the bond price is at the face value; when the yield

TABLE 1	Yields to Maturity on a 10%-Coupon-Rate Bond Maturing in Ten Years (Face Value = $1,000)
Price of Bond ($)	**Yield to Maturity (%)**
1,200	7.13
1,100	8.48
1,000	10.00
900	11.75
800	13.81

to maturity rises above the coupon rate, the bond price necessarily falls and so must be below the face value of the bond.

One special case of a coupon bond is worth discussing here because its yield to maturity is particularly easy to calculate. This bond is called a **consol** or a **perpetuity**; it is a perpetual bond with no maturity date and no repayment of principal that makes fixed coupon payments of C forever. Consols were first sold by the British Treasury during the Napoleonic wars and are still traded today; they are quite rare, however, in American capital markets. The formula in Equation 3 for the price of the consol P_c simplifies to the following:[3]

$$P_c = \frac{C}{i_c} \qquad (4)$$

where

P_c = Price of the perpetuity (consol)
C = yearly payment
i_c = yield to maturity of the perpetuity (consol)

One nice feature of perpetuities is that you can immediately see that as i_c increases, the price of the bond falls. For example, if a perpetuity pays $100 per year forever and the interest rate is 10%, its price will be $1,000 = $100/0.10. If the interest rate rises to 20%, its price will fall to $500 = $100/0.20. We can rewrite this formula as

$$i_c = \frac{C}{P_c} \qquad (5)$$

APPLICATION ## Yield to Maturity on a Perpetuity

What is the yield to maturity on a bond that has a price of $2,000 and pays $100 of interest annually, forever?

Solution
The yield to maturity is 5%.

$$i_c = \frac{C}{P_c}$$

[3]The bond price formula for a consol is

$$P = \frac{C}{1+i} + \frac{C}{(1+i)^2} + \frac{C}{(1+i)^3} + \dots$$

which can be written as

$$P = C(x + x^2 + x^3 + \dots)$$

in which $x = 1/(1+i)$. The formula for an infinite sum is

$$1 + x + x^2 + x^3 + \dots = \frac{1}{1-x} \text{ for } x < 1$$

and so

$$P = C\left(\frac{1}{1-x} - 1\right) = C\left[\frac{1}{1 - 1/(1+i)} - 1\right]$$

which by suitable algebraic manipulation becomes

$$P = C\left(\frac{1+i}{i} - \frac{i}{i}\right) = \frac{C}{i}$$

where

$$C = \text{yearly payment} = \$100$$
$$P_c = \text{price of perpetuity (consol)} = \$2,000$$

Thus

$$i_c = \frac{\$100}{\$2,000}$$

$$i_c = 0.05 = 5\%$$ ♦

The formula given in Equation 5, which describes the calculation of the yield to maturity for a perpetuity, also provides a useful approximation for the yield to maturity on coupon bonds. When a coupon bond has a long term to maturity (say, 20 years or more), it is very much like a perpetuity, which pays coupon payments forever. This is because the cash flows more than 20 years in the future have such small present discounted values that the value of a long-term coupon bond is very close to the value of a perpetuity with the same coupon rate. Thus i_c in Equation 5 will be very close to the yield to maturity for any long-term bond. For this reason, i_c, the yearly coupon payment divided by the price of the security, has been given the name **current yield** and is frequently used as an approximation to describe interest rates on long-term bonds.

Discount Bond   The yield-to-maturity calculation for a discount bond is similar to that for a simple loan. Let's consider a discount bond such as a one-year U.S. Treasury bill that pays a face value of $1,000 in one year's time but today has a price of $900.

APPLICATION   Yield to Maturity on a Discount Bond

What is the yield to maturity on a one-year, $1,000 Treasury bill with a current price of $900?

Solution
The yield to maturity is 11.1%.
Using the present value formula,

$$PV = \frac{CF}{(1 + i)^n}$$

and recognizing that the present value (*PV*) is the current price of $900, the cash flow in one year is $1,000, and the number of years is 1, we can write:

$$\$900 = \frac{\$1,000}{1 + i}$$

Solving for *i*, we get

$$(1 + i) \times \$900 = \$1,000$$

$$\$900 + \$900i = \$1,000$$

$$\$900i = \$1,000 - \$900$$

$$i = \frac{\$1,000 - \$900}{\$900} = 0.111 = 11.1\%$$ ♦

As we just saw in the preceding application, the yield to maturity for a one-year discount bond equals the increase in price over the year, $1,000 − $900, divided by the initial price, $900. Hence, more generally, for any one-year discount bond, the yield to maturity can be written as

$$i = \frac{F - P}{P} \tag{6}$$

where
$$F = \text{face value of the discount bond}$$
$$P = \text{current price of the discount bond}$$

In other words, the yield to maturity equals the increase in price over the year $F - P$ divided by the initial price P. In normal circumstances, investors earn positive returns from holding these securities and so they sell at a discount, meaning that the current price of the bond is below the face value. Therefore, $F - P$ should be positive, and the yield to maturity should be positive as well. However, this is not always the case, as extraordinary events in Japan and elsewhere have indicated (see the Global box).

An important feature of this equation is that it indicates that, for a discount bond, the yield to maturity is negatively related to the current bond price. This is the same conclusion that we reached for a coupon bond. Equation 6 shows that a rise in the bond price—say, from $900 to $950—means that the bond will have a smaller increase in its price at maturity and so the yield to maturity will fall, from 11.1% to 5.3% in our example. Similarly, a fall in the yield to maturity means that the current price of the discount bond has risen.

Summary   The concept of present value tells you that a dollar in the future is not as valuable to you as a dollar today because you can earn interest on a dollar you have today. Specifically, a dollar received n years from now is worth only $\$1/(1 + i)^n$ today. The present value of a set of future cash flow payments on a debt instrument equals the sum of the present values of each of the future payments. The yield to maturity for an instrument is the interest rate that equates the present value of the future payments on that instrument to its value today. Because the procedure for calculating the yield to maturity is based on sound economic principles, the yield to maturity is the measure that economists think most accurately describes the interest rate.

Our calculations of the yield to maturity for a variety of bonds reveal the important fact that **current bond prices and interest rates are negatively related: When the interest rate rises, the price of the bond falls, and vice versa**.

4.2 THE DISTINCTION BETWEEN INTEREST RATES AND RETURNS

LO 4.2 Recognize the distinctions among yield to maturity, current yield, rate of return, and rate of capital gain.

Many people think that the interest rate on a bond tells them all they need to know about how well off they are as a result of owning it. If Irving the Investor thinks he is well off when he owns a long-term bond yielding a 10% interest rate, and the interest rate then rises to 20%, he will have a rude awakening: As we will shortly see, if he has to sell the bond, Irving will lose his shirt! How well a person does financially by holding a bond or any other security over a particular time period is accurately measured by the security's **return**, or, in more precise terminology, the **rate of return**. We will

---

Global   Negative Interest Rates? Japan First, Then the United States, Then Europe

We normally assume that the yield to maturity must always be positive. A negative yield to maturity would imply that you are willing to pay more for a bond today than you will receive for it in the future (as our formula for yield to maturity on a discount bond demonstrates). A negative yield to maturity therefore seems like an impossibility because you would do better by holding cash that has the same value in the future as it does today.

Events in Japan in the late 1990s and then in the United States during the 2008 global financial crisis and finally in Europe in recent years have demonstrated that this reasoning is not quite correct. In November 1998, the yield to maturity on Japanese six-month Treasury bills became negative, at −0.004%. In September 2008, the yield to maturity on three-month U.S. T-bills fell very slightly below zero for a very brief period. Interest rates that banks

are paid on deposits they keep at their central banks became negative first in Sweden in July 2009, followed by Denmark in July 2012, the Eurozone in June 2014, Switzerland in December 2014, and Japan in January 2016. Negative interest rates have rarely occurred in the past. How could this happen in recent years?

As we will see in Chapter 5, a dearth of investment opportunities and very low inflation can drive interest rates to low levels, but these two factors can't explain the negative yield to maturity. The answer is that despite negative interest rates, large investors and banks found it more convenient to hold Treasury bills or keep their funds as deposits at the central bank because they are stored electronically. For that reason, investors and banks were willing to accept negative interest rates, even though in pure monetary terms the investors would be better off holding cash.

---

use the concept of *return* continually throughout this book: Understanding this concept will make the material presented later in the book easier to follow.

For any security, the rate of return is defined as the amount of each payment to the owner plus the change in the security's value, expressed as a fraction of its purchase price. To make this definition clearer, let us see what the return would look like for a $1,000-face-value coupon bond with a coupon rate of 10% that is bought for $1,000, held for one year, and then sold for $1,200. The payments to the owner are the yearly coupon payments of $100, and the change in the bond's value is $1,200 − $1,000 = $200. Adding these values together and expressing them as a fraction of the purchase price of $1,000 gives us the one-year holding-period return for this bond:

$$\frac{\$100 + \$200}{\$1,000} = \frac{\$300}{\$1,000} = 0.30 = 30\%$$

You may have noticed something quite surprising about the return that we just calculated: It equals 30%, yet as Table 1 indicates, initially the yield to maturity was only 10%. This discrepancy demonstrates that **the return on a bond will not necessarily equal the yield to maturity on that bond**. We now see that the distinction between interest rate and return can be important, although for many securities the two may be closely related.

More generally, the return on a bond held from time t to time $t + 1$ can be written as

$$R = \frac{C + P_{t+1} - P_t}{P_t} \tag{7}$$

where R = return from holding the bond from time t to time $t + 1$
               C = coupon payment
               P_t = price of the bond at time t
               P_{t+1} = price of the bond at time $t + 1$

A convenient way to rewrite the return formula in Equation 7 is to recognize that it can be split into two separate terms:

$$R = \frac{C}{P_t} + \frac{P_{t+1} - P_t}{P_t}$$

The first term is the current yield i_c (the coupon payment over the purchase price):

$$\frac{C}{P_t} = i_c$$

The second term is the **rate of capital gain**, or the change in the bond's price relative to the initial price:

$$\frac{P_{t+1} - P_t}{P_t} = g$$

where g is the rate of capital gain. Equation 7 can then be rewritten as

$$R = i_c + g \tag{8}$$

which shows that the return on a bond is the current yield i_c plus the rate of capital gain g. This rewritten formula illustrates the point we just discovered: Even for a bond for which the current yield i_c is an accurate measure of the yield to maturity, the return can differ substantially from the interest rate. Returns will differ substantially from the interest rate if the price of the bond experiences sizable fluctuations that produce substantial capital gains or losses.

To explore this point even further, let's look at what happens to the returns on bonds of different maturities when interest rates rise. Table 2 calculates the one-year returns, using Equation 8 above, on several 10%-coupon-rate bonds, all purchased at par, when interest rates on all these bonds rise from 10% to 20%. Several key findings from this table are generally true of all bonds:

- The only bonds whose returns will equal their initial yields to maturity are those whose times to maturity are the same as their holding periods (see, for example, the last bond in Table 2).
- A rise in interest rates is associated with a fall in bond prices, resulting in capital losses on bonds whose terms to maturity are longer than their holding periods.
- The more distant a bond's maturity date, the greater the size of the percentage price change associated with an interest rate change.
- The more distant a bond's maturity date, the lower the rate of return that occurs as a result of an increase in the interest rate.
- Even though a bond may have a substantial initial interest rate, its return can turn out to be negative if interest rates rise.

TABLE 2	One-Year Returns on Different-Maturity 10%-Coupon-Rate Bonds When Interest Rates Rise from 10% to 20%				
(1) Years to Maturity When Bond Is Purchased	**(2)** Initial Current Yield (%)	**(3)** Initial Price ($)	**(4)** Price Next Year* ($)	**(5)** Rate of Capital Gain (%)	**(6)** Rate of Return [col (2) + col (5)] (%)
30	10	1,000	503	−49.7	−39.7
20	10	1,000	516	−48.4	−38.4
10	10	1,000	597	−40.3	−30.3
5	10	1,000	741	−25.9	−15.9
2	10	1,000	917	−8.3	+1.7
1	10	1,000	1,000	0.0	+10.0

*Calculated with a financial calculator, using Equation 3.

At first, students are frequently puzzled (as was poor Irving the Investor) that a rise in interest rates can mean that a bond has been a poor investment. The trick to understanding this fact is to recognize Irving has already purchased the bond, so that a rise in the interest rate means that the price of the bond Irving is holding falls and he experiences a capital loss. If this loss is large enough, the bond can be a poor investment indeed. For example, we see in Table 2 that the bond that has 30 years to maturity when purchased has a capital loss of 49.7% when the interest rate rises from 10% to 20%. This loss is so large that it exceeds the current yield of 10%, resulting in a negative return (loss) of –39.7%. If Irving does not sell the bond, his capital loss is often referred to as a "paper loss." This is a loss nonetheless because if Irving had not bought this bond and had instead put his money in the bank, he would now be able to buy more bonds at their lower price than he presently owns.

Maturity and the Volatility of Bond Returns: Interest-Rate Risk

The finding that the prices of longer-maturity bonds respond more dramatically to changes in interest rates helps explain an important fact about the behavior of bond markets: *Prices and returns for long-term bonds are more volatile than those for shorter-term bonds.* Price changes of +20% and −20% within a year, with corresponding variations in returns, are common for bonds that are more than 20 years away from maturity.

We now see that changes in interest rates make investments in long-term bonds quite risky. Indeed, the risk level associated with an asset's return that results from interest-rate changes is so important that it has been given a special name, **interest-rate risk**.[4] Dealing with interest-rate risk is a major concern of managers of financial institutions and of investors, as we will see in later chapters.

[4]Interest-rate risk can be quantitatively measured using the concept of *duration*. This concept and its calculation are discussed in an appendix to this chapter, which can be found in **MyLab Economics**.

Although long-term debt instruments have substantial interest-rate risk, short-term debt instruments do not. Indeed, bonds with a maturity term that is as short as the holding period have no interest-rate risk.[5] We see this for the coupon bond at the bottom of Table 2, which has no uncertainty about the rate of return because it equals the yield to maturity, which is known at the time the bond is purchased. The key to understanding why there is no interest-rate risk for *any* bond whose time to maturity matches the holding period is to recognize that (in this case) the price at the end of the holding period is already fixed at the face value. A change in interest rates can then have no effect on the price at the end of the holding period for these bonds, and the return will therefore be equal to the yield to maturity, which is known at the time the bond is purchased.[6]

Summary

The return on a bond, which tells you how good an investment it has been over the holding period, is equal to the yield to maturity in only one special case—when the holding period and the term to maturity of the bond are identical. Bonds whose terms to maturity are longer than their holding periods are subject to interest-rate risk: Changes in interest rates lead to capital gains and losses that produce substantial differences between the return and the yield to maturity known at the time the bond is purchased. Interest-rate risk is especially important

---

[5]The statement that there is no interest-rate risk for any bond whose time to maturity matches the holding period is literally true only for discount (zero-coupon) bonds that make no intermediate cash payments before the holding period is over. A coupon bond that makes an intermediate cash payment before the holding period is over requires this payment to be reinvested. Because the interest rate at which this payment can be reinvested is uncertain, some uncertainty exists about the return on this coupon bond even when the time to maturity equals the holding period. However, the riskiness of the return on a coupon bond from reinvesting the coupon payments is typically quite small, so a coupon bond with a time to maturity equal to its holding period still has very little risk.

[6]In this text we assume that holding periods on all short-term bonds are equal to the term to maturity, and thus the bonds are not subject to interest-rate risk. However, if the term to maturity of the bond is shorter than an investor's holding period, the investor is exposed to a type of interest-rate risk called *reinvestment risk*. Reinvestment risk occurs because the proceeds from the short-term bond need to be reinvested at a future interest rate that is uncertain.

To understand reinvestment risk, suppose that Irving the Investor has a holding period of two years and decides to purchase a $1,000, one-year bond at face value and then another one at the end of the first year. If the initial interest rate is 10%, Irving will have $1,100 at the end of the first year. If the interest rate rises to 20%, as in Table 2, Irving will find that buying $1,100 worth of another one-year bond will leave him at the end of the second year with $1,100 × (1 + 0.20) = $1,320. Thus Irving's two-year return will be ($1,320 − $1,000)/$1,000 = 0.32 = 32%, which equals 14.9% at an annual rate. In this case, Irving has earned more by buying the one-year bonds than he would have if he had initially purchased a two-year bond with an interest rate of 10%. Thus, when Irving has a holding period that is longer than the term to maturity of the bonds he purchases, he benefits from a rise in interest rates. Conversely, if interest rates fall to 5%, Irving will have only $1,155 at the end of two years: $1,100 × (1 + 0.05). His two-year return will be ($1,555 − $1,000)/$1,000 = 0.155 = 15.5%, which is 7.2% at an annual rate. With a holding period greater than the term to maturity of the bond, Irving now loses from a decline in interest rates.

We have seen that when the holding period is longer than the term to maturity of a bond, the return is uncertain because the future interest rate when reinvestment occurs is also uncertain—in short, there is reinvestment risk. We also see that if the holding period is longer than the term to maturity of the bond, the investor benefits from a rise in interest rates and is hurt by a fall in interest rates.

for long-term bonds, on which capital gains and losses can be substantial. This is why long-term bonds are not considered safe assets with a sure return over short holding periods.

4.3 THE DISTINCTION BETWEEN REAL AND NOMINAL INTEREST RATES

LO 4.3 Interpret the distinction between real and nominal interest rates.

So far in our discussion of interest rates, we have ignored the effects of inflation on the cost of borrowing. What we up to this point have been calling the interest rate makes no allowance for inflation, and it is more precisely referred to as the **nominal interest rate**. We must distinguish the nominal interest rate from the **real interest rate**, which is the interest rate that is adjusted by subtracting expected changes in the price level (inflation) so that it more accurately reflects the true cost of borrowing. This interest rate is more precisely referred to as the *ex ante real interest rate* because it is adjusted for *expected* changes in the price level. The ex ante real interest rate is very important to economic decisions, and typically it is what economists mean when they make reference to the "real" interest rate. The interest rate that is adjusted for actual changes in the price level is called the *ex post real interest rate*. It describes how well a lender has done in real terms *after the fact*.

The real interest rate is more accurately defined from the *Fisher equation*, named for Irving Fisher, one of the great monetary economists of the twentieth century. The Fisher equation states that the nominal interest rate i equals the real interest rate r plus the expected rate of inflation π^e:[7]

$$i = r + \pi^e \tag{9}$$

Rearranging terms, we find that the real interest rate equals the nominal interest rate minus the expected inflation rate:

$$r = i - \pi^e \tag{10}$$

To see why this definition makes sense, let's first consider a situation in which you have made a simple one-year loan with a 5% interest rate ($i = 5\%$), and you expect the price level to rise by 3% over the course of the year ($\pi^e = 3\%$). As a result of making the loan, at the end of the year you expect to have 2% more in **real terms**—that

---

[7]A more precise formulation of the Fisher equation is

$$i = r + \pi^e + (r \times \pi^e)$$

because

$$1 + i = (1 + r)(1 + \pi^e) = 1 + r + \pi^e + (r \times \pi^e)$$

and subtracting 1 from both sides gives us the first equation. For small values of r and π^e, the term $r \times \pi^e$ is so small that we ignore it, as in the text.

is, in terms of real goods and services you can buy. In this case, the interest rate you expect to earn in terms of real goods and services is 2%:

$$r = 5\% - 3\% = 2\%$$

as indicated by Equation 10.[8]

APPLICATION   Calculating Real Interest Rates

What is the real interest rate if the nominal interest rate is 8% and the expected inflation rate is 10% over the course of a year?

Solution

The real interest rate is −2%. Although you will be receiving 8% more dollars at the end of the year, you will be paying 10% more for goods. The result is that you will be able to buy 2% fewer goods at the end of the year, and you will be 2% worse off in real terms. Mathematically,

$$r = i - \pi^e$$

where

$$i = \text{nominal interest rate} \ = 0.08$$
$$\pi^e = \text{expected inflation rate} = 0.10$$

Thus

$$r = 0.08 - 0.10 = -0.02 = -2\% \qquad \blacklozenge$$

As a lender, you are clearly less eager to make a loan in this case, because in terms of real goods and services you have actually earned a negative interest rate of 2%. By contrast, as a borrower, you fare quite well because at the end of the year, the amounts you will have to pay back will be worth 2% less in terms of goods and services—you

---

[8]Because most interest income in the United States is subject to federal income taxes, the true earnings in real terms from holding a debt instrument are not reflected by the real interest rate defined by the Fisher equation but rather by the *after-tax real interest rate*, which equals the nominal interest rate *after income tax payments have been subtracted*, minus the expected inflation rate. For a person facing a 30% tax rate, the after-tax interest rate earned on a bond yielding 10% is only 7% because 30% of the interest income must be paid to the Internal Revenue Service. Thus the after-tax real interest rate on this bond when expected inflation is 5% equals 2% (= 7% − 5%).

More generally, the after-tax real interest rate can be expressed as

$$i(1 - \tau) - \pi^e$$

where τ = the income tax rate.

This formula for the after-tax real interest rate also provides a better measure of the effective cost of borrowing for many corporations and homeowners in the United States because, in calculating income taxes, they can deduct interest payments on loans from their income. Thus, if you face a 30% tax rate and take out a mortgage loan with a 10% interest rate, you are able to deduct the 10% interest payment and lower your taxes by 30% of this amount. Your after-tax nominal cost of borrowing is then 7% (10% minus 30% of the 10% interest payment), and when the expected inflation rate is 5%, the effective cost of borrowing in real terms is again 2% (= 7% − 5%).

As the example (and the formula) indicates, after-tax real interest rates are always below the real interest rate defined by the Fisher equation. For a further discussion of measures of after-tax real interest rates, see Frederic S. Mishkin, "The Real Interest Rate: An Empirical Investigation," *Carnegie-Rochester Conference Series on Public Policy* 15 (1981): 151–200.

Real-time data

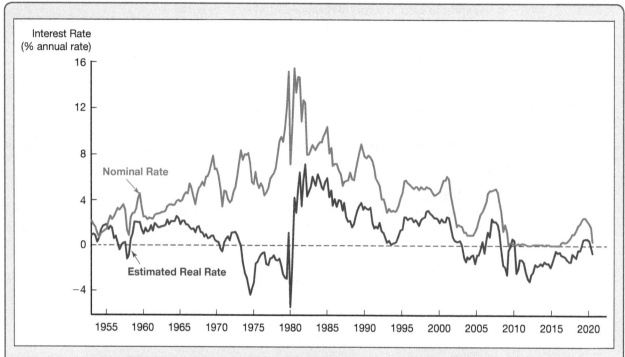

Interest Rate
(% annual rate)

Nominal Rate

Estimated Real Rate

FIGURE 1   Real and Nominal Interest Rates (Three-Month Treasury Bill), 1953–2020
Nominal and real interest rates often do not move together. When U.S. nominal rates were high in the 1970s, real rates were actually extremely low—often negative.
Sources: Nominal rates from Federal Reserve Bank of St. Louis FRED database: https://fred.stlouisfed.org/series/TB3MS and https://fred.stlouisfed.org/series/CPIAUCSL. The real rate is constructed using the procedure outlined in Frederic S. Mishkin, "The Real Interest Rate: An Empirical Investigation," *Carnegie-Rochester Conference Series on Public Policy* 15 (1981): 151–200. This procedure involves estimating expected inflation as a function of past interest rates, inflation, and time trends, and then subtracting the expected inflation measure from the nominal interest rate.

as the borrower will be ahead by 2% in real terms. **When the real interest rate is low, there are greater incentives to borrow and fewer incentives to lend.**

A similar distinction can be made between nominal returns and real returns. Nominal returns, which do not allow for inflation, are what we have been referring to as simply "returns." When inflation is subtracted from a nominal return, we have the real return, which indicates the amount of extra goods and services that we can purchase as a result of holding the security.

The distinction between real and nominal interest rates is important because the real interest rate, which reflects the real cost of borrowing, is likely to be a better indicator of the incentives to borrow and lend. It appears to be a better guide to how people will respond to what is happening in credit markets. Figure 1, which presents estimates from 1953 to 2020 of the real and nominal interest rates on three-month U.S. Treasury bills, shows us that nominal and real rates usually move together but do not always do so. (This is also true for nominal and real interest rates in the rest of the world.) In particular, when nominal rates in the United States were high in the 1970s, real rates were actually extremely low—often negative. By the standard of nominal interest rates, you would have thought that credit market conditions were tight during this period because it was expensive to borrow. However, the estimates of the real rates indicate that you would have been mistaken. In real terms, the cost of borrowing was actually quite low.

SUMMARY

1. The yield to maturity, which is the measure that most accurately reflects the interest rate, is the interest rate that equates the present value of future payments of a debt instrument with the instrument's value today. Application of this principle reveals that bond prices and interest rates are negatively correlated: When the interest rate rises, the price of the bond must fall, and vice versa.

2. The return on a security, which tells you how well you have done by holding the security over a stated period of time, can differ substantially from the interest rate

as measured by the yield to maturity. Long-term bond prices experience substantial fluctuations when interest rates change and thus bear interest-rate risk. The resulting capital gains and losses can be large, which is why long-term bonds are not considered safe assets with a sure return.

3. The real interest rate is defined as the nominal interest rate minus the expected rate of inflation. It is both a better measure of the incentives to borrow and lend and a more accurate indicator of the tightness of credit market conditions than is the nominal interest rate.

KEY TERMS

cash flows, p. 64
consol or perpetuity, p. 73
coupon bond, p. 67
coupon rate, p. 67
current yield, p. 74
discount bond (zero-coupon bond), p. 68

face value (par value), p. 67
fixed-payment loan (fully amortized loan), p. 67
interest-rate risk, p. 78
nominal interest rate, p. 80
present value (present discounted value), p. 65

rate of capital gain, p. 77
real interest rate, p. 80
real terms, p. 80
return (rate of return), p. 75
simple loan, p. 65
yield to maturity, p. 68

QUESTIONS

1. Would a dollar tomorrow be worth more to you today when the interest rate is 20% or when it is 10%?

2. Explain which information you would need to take into consideration when deciding to receive $5,000 today or $5,500 one year from today.

3. To help pay for college, you have just taken out a $1,000 government loan that makes you pay $126 per year for 25 years. However, you don't have to start making these payments until you graduate from college two years from now. Why is the yield to maturity necessarily less than 12%? (This is the yield to maturity on a normal $1,000 fixed-payment loan on which you pay $126 per year for 25 years.)

4. Do bondholders fare better when the yield to maturity increases or when it decreases? Why?

5. Suppose today you buy a coupon bond that you plan to sell one year later. Which part of the rate of return formula incorporates future changes into the bond's price? *Note:* Check Equations 7 and 8 in this chapter.

6. If mortgage rates rise from 5% to 10%, but the expected rate of increase in housing prices rises from 2% to 9%, are people more or less likely to buy houses?

7. When is the current yield a good approximation of the yield to maturity?

8. Why would a government choose to issue a perpetuity, which requires payments forever, instead of a terminal loan, such as a fixed-payment loan, discount bond, or coupon bond?

9. Under what conditions will a discount bond have a negative nominal interest rate? Is it possible for a coupon bond or a perpetuity to have a negative nominal interest rate?

10. True or False: With a discount bond, the return on the bond is equal to the rate of capital gain.

11. If interest rates decline, which would you rather be holding, long-term bonds or short-term bonds? Why? Which type of bond has the greater interest-rate risk?

12. Interest rates were lower in the mid-1980s than in the late 1970s, yet many economists have commented that real interest rates were actually much higher in the mid-1980s than in the late 1970s. Does this make sense? Do you think that these economists are right?

13. Retired persons often have much of their wealth placed in savings accounts and other interest-bearing investments and complain whenever interest rates are low. Do they have a valid complaint?

APPLIED PROBLEMS

14. If the interest rate is 10%, what is the present value of a security that pays you $1,100 next year, $1,210 the year after, and $1,331 the year after that?

15. Calculate the present value of a $1,000 discount bond with five years to maturity if the yield to maturity is 6%.

16. A lottery claims its grand prize is $10 million, payable over five years at $2,000,000 per year. If the first payment is made immediately, what is this grand prize really worth? Use an interest rate of 6%.

17. Suppose that a commercial bank wants to buy Treasury bills. These instruments pay $5,000 in one year and are currently selling for $5,012. What is the yield to maturity of these bonds? Is this a typical situation? Why?

18. What is the yield to maturity on a simple loan for $1 million that requires a repayment of $2 million in five years' time?

19. Which $1,000 bond has the higher yield to maturity, a 20-year bond selling for $800 with a current yield of 15% or a 1-year bond selling for $800 with a current yield of 5%?

20. Consider a bond with a 4% annual coupon and a face value of $1,000. Complete the following table. What relationships do you observe between years to maturity, yield to maturity, and the current price?

Years to Maturity	Yield to Maturity	Current Price
2	2%	
2	4%	
3	4%	
5	2%	
5	6%	

21. Consider a coupon bond that has a $1,000 par value and a coupon rate of 10%. The bond is currently selling for $1,044.89 and has two years to maturity. What is the bond's yield to maturity?

22. What is the price of a perpetuity that has a coupon of $50 per year and a yield to maturity of 2.5%? If the yield to maturity doubles, what will happen to the perpetuity's price?

23. Property taxes in a particular district are 4% of the purchase price of a home every year. If you just purchased a $250,000 home, what is the present value of all the future property tax payments? Assume that the house remains worth $250,000 forever, property tax rates never change, and a 6% interest rate is used for discounting.

24. A $1,000-face-value bond has a 10% coupon rate, its current price is $960, and its price is expected to increase to $980 next year. Calculate the current yield, the expected rate of capital gain, and the expected rate of return.

25. Suppose that you want to take out a loan and that your local bank wants to charge you an annual real interest rate equal to 3%. Assuming that the annualized expected rate of inflation over the life of the bond is 1%, determine the nominal interest rate that the bank will charge you. What happens if, over the life of the loan, actual inflation is 0.5%?

DATA ANALYSIS PROBLEMS

The Problems update with real-time data in **MyLab Economics** and are available for practice or instructor assignment.

1. **Real-time Data Analysis** Go to the St. Louis Federal Reserve FRED database, and find data on the interest rate on a four-year auto loan (TERMCBAUTO48NS). Assume that you borrow $20,000 to purchase a new automobile and that you finance it with a four-year loan at the most recent interest rate given in the database. If you make one payment per year for four years, what will the yearly payment be? What is the total amount that will be paid out on the $20,000 loan?

2. **Real-time Data Analysis** The U.S. Treasury issues some bonds as *Treasury Inflation Indexed Securities, or TIIS*, which are bonds adjusted for inflation; hence the yields can be roughly interpreted as real interest rates. Go to the St. Louis Federal Reserve FRED database, and find data on the following TIIS bonds and their nominal counterparts. Then answer the questions below.

   - 5-year U.S. Treasury (DGS5) and 5-year TIIS (DFII5)
   - 7-year U.S. Treasury (DGS7) and 7-year TIIS (DFII7)
   - 10-year U.S. Treasury (DGS10) and 10-year TIIS (DFII10)
   - 20-year U.S. Treasury (DGS20) and 20-year TIIS (DFII20)
   - 30-year U.S. Treasury (DGS30) and 30-year TIIS (DFII30)

     a. Following the Great Recession of 2008–2009, the 5-, 7-, 10-, and even the 20-year TIIS yields became negative for a period of time. How is this possible?

     b. Using the most recent data available, calculate the difference between the yields for each pair of bonds (DGS5 – DFII5 etc.) listed above. What does this difference represent?

     c. Based on your answer to part (b), are there significant variations among the differences in the bond-pair yields? Interpret the magnitude of the variation in differences among the pairs.

5

The Behavior of Interest Rates

Learning Objectives

5.1 Identify the factors that affect the demand for assets.

5.2 Draw the demand and supply curves for the bond market, and identify the equilibrium interest rate.

5.3 List and describe the factors that affect the equilibrium interest rate in the bond market.

5.4 Describe the connection between the bond market and the money market through the liquidity preference framework.

5.5 List and describe the factors that affect the money market and the equilibrium interest rate.

5.6 Identify and illustrate the effects on the interest rate of changes in money growth over time.

Preview

In the early 1950s, nominal interest rates on three-month Treasury bills were about 1% at an annual rate; by 1981, they had reached over 15%. They fell below 1% in 2003, rose to 5% in 2007, and then fell to close to zero in 2008 and for many years afterward. They rose to above 2% in 2019, falling back to zero during the Covid-19 recession in 2020. What explains these substantial fluctuations in interest rates? One reason why we study money, banking, and financial markets is to provide some answers to this question.

In this chapter, we examine how the overall level of *nominal* interest rates (which we refer to simply as "interest rates") is determined and which factors influence their behavior. We learned in Chapter 4 that interest rates are negatively related to the price of bonds, so if we can explain why bond prices change, we can also explain why interest rates fluctuate. We make use of supply and demand analysis for bond markets and markets for money to examine how interest rates change.

To derive a demand curve for assets such as money or bonds, the first step in our analysis, we must first understand what determines the demand for these assets. We do this by examining *portfolio theory*, an economic theory that outlines criteria that are important when deciding how much of an asset to buy. Armed with this theory, we can then go on to derive the demand curve for bonds or money. After deriving supply curves for these assets, we develop the concept of *market equilibrium*, which is defined as the point at which the quantity supplied equals the quantity demanded. Then we use this model to explain changes in equilibrium interest rates.

Because interest rates on different securities tend to move together, in this chapter we will proceed as if there were only one type of security and one interest rate in the entire economy. In the following chapter, we expand our analysis to look at why interest rates on different types of securities differ.

5.1 DETERMINANTS OF ASSET DEMAND

LO 5.1 Identify the factors that affect the demand for assets.

Before going on to our supply and demand analysis of the bond market and the market for money, we must first understand what determines the quantity demanded of an asset. Recall that an asset is a piece of property that is a store of value. Items such as money, bonds, stocks, art, land, houses, farm equipment, and manufacturing machinery are all assets. Faced with the question of whether to buy and hold an asset or whether to buy one asset rather than another, an individual must consider the following factors:

1. **Wealth**, the total resources owned by the individual, including all assets
2. **Expected return** (the return expected over the next period) on one asset relative to alternative assets
3. **Risk** (the degree of uncertainty associated with the return) on one asset relative to alternative assets
4. **Liquidity** (the ease and speed with which an asset can be turned into cash) relative to alternative assets

Wealth

When we find that our wealth has increased, we have more resources available with which to purchase assets, and so, not surprisingly, the quantity of assets we demand increases. Therefore, the effect of changes in wealth on the quantity demanded of an asset can be summarized as follows: *Holding everything else constant, an increase in wealth raises the quantity demanded of an asset.*

Expected Returns

In Chapter 4, we saw that the return on an asset (such as a bond) measures how much we gain from holding that asset. When we make a decision to buy an asset, we are influenced by what we expect the return on that asset to be. If an ExxonMobil bond, for example, has a return of 15% half the time and 5% the other half, its expected return (which you can think of as the average return) is 10% ($= 0.5 \times 15\% + 0.5 \times 5\%$). If the expected return on the ExxonMobil bond rises relative to expected returns on alternative assets, then, holding everything else constant, it becomes more desirable to purchase the ExxonMobil bond, and the quantity demanded increases. This can occur in either of two ways: (1) when the expected return on the ExxonMobil bond rises while the return on an alternative asset—say, stock in Facebook—remains unchanged or (2) when the return on the alternative asset, the Facebook stock, falls while the return on the ExxonMobil bond remains unchanged. To summarize, *an increase in an asset's expected return relative to that of an alternative asset, holding everything else unchanged, raises the quantity demanded of the asset.*

Risk

The degree of risk or uncertainty of an asset's returns also affects demand for the asset. Consider two assets, stock in Fly-by-Night Airlines and stock in Feet-on-the-Ground Bus Company. Suppose that Fly-by-Night stock has a return of 15% half the time and 5% the other half, making its expected return 10%, while Feet-on-the-Ground stock has a fixed return of 10%. Fly-by-Night stock has uncertainty associated with its returns and so has greater risk than Feet-on-the-Ground stock, whose return is a sure thing.

A *risk-averse* person prefers stock in Feet-on-the-Ground (the sure thing) to Fly-by-Night stock (the riskier asset), even though the stocks have the same expected return, 10%. By contrast, a person who prefers risk is a *risk preferrer* or *risk lover*. Most people are risk-averse, especially in their financial decisions: Everything else being equal, they prefer to hold the less risky asset. Hence, *holding everything else constant, if an asset's risk rises relative to that of alternative assets, its quantity demanded will fall.*

Liquidity

Another factor that affects the demand for an asset is how quickly it can be converted into cash at low costs—its liquidity. An asset is liquid if the market in which it is traded has depth and breadth, that is, if the market has many buyers and sellers. A house is not a very liquid asset because it may be hard to find a buyer quickly; if a house must be sold to pay off bills, it might have to be sold for a much lower price. And the transaction costs associated with selling a house (broker's commissions, lawyer's fees, and so on) are substantial. A U.S. Treasury bill, by contrast, is a highly liquid asset. It can be sold in a well-organized market with many buyers, and so it can be sold quickly at low cost. *The more liquid an asset is relative to alternative assets, holding everything else unchanged, the more desirable it is and the greater the quantity demanded will be.*

Theory of Portfolio Choice

All the determining factors we have just discussed can be assembled into the **theory of portfolio choice**, which tells us how much of an asset people will want to hold in their portfolios. It states that, holding all other factors constant:

1. The quantity demanded of an asset is positively related to wealth.
2. The quantity demanded of an asset is positively related to its expected return relative to alternative assets.
3. The quantity demanded of an asset is negatively related to the risk of its returns relative to alternative assets.
4. The quantity demanded of an asset is positively related to its liquidity relative to alternative assets.

These results are summarized in Table 1.

SUMMARY TABLE 1

Response of the Quantity of an Asset Demanded to Changes in Wealth, Expected Returns, Risk, and Liquidity

Variable	Change in Variable	Change in Quantity Demanded
Wealth	↑	↑
Expected return relative to other assets	↑	↑
Risk relative to other assets	↑	↓
Liquidity relative to other assets	↑	↑

Note: Only increases in the variables are shown. The effects of decreases in the variables on the quantity demanded would be the opposite of those indicated in the rightmost column.

5.2 SUPPLY AND DEMAND IN THE BOND MARKET

LO 5.2 Draw the demand and supply curves for the bond market, and identify the equilibrium interest rate.

Our first approach to the analysis of interest-rate determination looks at supply and demand in the bond market so that we can better understand how the prices of bonds are determined. Thanks to our knowledge from Chapter 4 of how interest rates are measured, we know that each bond price is associated with a particular level of the interest rate. Specifically, the negative relationship between bond prices and interest rates means that when a bond's price rises, its interest rate falls, and vice versa.

The first step in our analysis is to obtain a bond **demand curve**, which shows the relationship between the quantity demanded and the price when all other economic variables are held constant (that is, values of other variables are taken as given). You may recall from previous economics courses that the assumption that all other economic variables are held constant is called *ceteris paribus*, which means "other things being equal" in Latin.

Demand Curve

To clarify and simplify our analysis, let's consider the demand for one-year discount bonds, which make no coupon payments but pay the owner the $1,000 face value in a year. If the holding period is one year, then, as we saw in Chapter 4, the return on the bonds is known absolutely and is equal to the interest rate as measured by the yield to maturity. This means that the expected return on this bond is equal to the interest rate i, which, using Equation 6 in Chapter 4, is

$$i = R^e = \frac{F - P}{P}$$

where
$$\begin{aligned} i &= \text{interest rate } = \text{yield to maturity} \\ R^e &= \text{expected return} \\ F &= \text{face value of the discount bond} \\ P &= \text{initial purchase price of the discount bond} \end{aligned}$$

This formula shows that a particular value of the interest rate corresponds to each bond price. If the bond sells for $950, the interest rate and expected return are

$$\frac{\$1,000 - \$950}{\$950} = 0.053 = 5.3\%$$

At this 5.3% interest rate and expected return corresponding to a bond price of $950, let us assume that the quantity of bonds demanded is $100 billion, which is plotted as point A in Figure 1.

At a price of $900, the interest rate and expected return are

$$\frac{\$1,000 - \$900}{\$900} = 0.111 = 11.1\%$$

Because the expected return is higher, with all other economic variables (such as wealth, expected returns on other assets, risk, and liquidity) held constant, the quantity demanded of these bonds will be higher, as predicted by portfolio theory. Point B in Figure 1 shows that the quantity of bonds demanded at the price of $900 has risen to $200 billion. Continuing with this reasoning, we see that if the bond price is $850 (interest rate and expected return = 17.6%), the quantity of bonds demanded (point C)

Mini-lecture

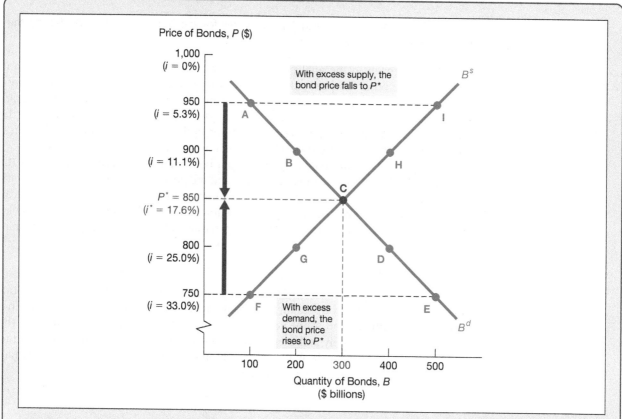

FIGURE 1 **Supply and Demand for Bonds**

Equilibrium in the bond market occurs at point C, the intersection of the demand curve B^d and the bond supply curve B^s. The equilibrium price is $P^* = \$850$, and the equilibrium interest rate is $i^* = 17.6\%$.

will be greater than at point B. Similarly, at the even lower prices of $800 (interest rate = 25%) and $750 (interest rate = 33.3%), the quantity of bonds demanded will be even higher (points D and E). The curve B^d, which connects these points, is the demand curve for bonds. It has the usual downward slope, indicating that at lower prices of the bond (everything else being equal), the quantity demanded is higher.[1]

Supply Curve

An important assumption behind the demand curve for bonds in Figure 1 is that all other economic variables besides the bond's price and interest rate are held constant. We use the same assumption in deriving a **supply curve**, which shows the relationship between the quantity supplied and the price when all other economic variables are held constant.

In Figure 1, when the price of the bonds is $750 (interest rate = 33.3%), point F shows that the quantity of bonds supplied is $100 billion for the example we are considering. If the price is $800, the interest rate is the lower rate of 25%. Because at this interest rate it is now less costly to borrow by issuing bonds, firms will be willing to borrow

---

[1]Although our analysis indicates that the demand curve is downward-sloping, it does not imply that the curve is a straight line. For ease of exposition, however, we will draw demand curves and supply curves as straight lines.

more through bond issues, and the quantity of bonds supplied is at the higher level of $200 billion (point G). An even higher price of $850, corresponding to a lower interest rate of 17.6%, results in a larger quantity of bonds supplied of $300 billion (point C). Higher prices of $900 and $950 result in even lower interest rates and even greater quantities of bonds supplied (points H and I). The B^s curve, which connects these points, is the supply curve for bonds. It has the usual upward slope found in supply curves, indicating that as the price increases (everything else being equal), the quantity supplied increases.

Market Equilibrium

In economics, **market equilibrium** occurs when the amount that people are willing to buy (*demand*) equals the amount that people are willing to sell (*supply*) at a given price. In the bond market, this is achieved when the quantity of bonds demanded equals the quantity of bonds supplied:

$$B^d = B^s \tag{1}$$

In Figure 1, equilibrium occurs at point C, where the demand and supply curves intersect at a bond price of $850 (interest rate of 17.6%) and a quantity of bonds of $300 billion. The price of $P^* = 850$, where the quantity demanded equals the quantity supplied, is called the *equilibrium* or *market-clearing* price. Similarly, the interest rate of $i^* = 17.6\%$ that corresponds to this price is called the equilibrium or market-clearing interest rate.

The concepts of market equilibrium and equilibrium price or interest rate are useful because the market tends to head toward them. We can see this in Figure 1 by first looking at what happens when we have a bond price that is above the equilibrium price. When the price of bonds is set too high, at, say, $950, the quantity of bonds supplied at point I is greater than the quantity of bonds demanded at point A. A situation like this, in which the quantity of bonds supplied exceeds the quantity of bonds demanded, is called a condition of **excess supply**. Because people (borrowers) want to sell more bonds than others (lender-savers) want to buy, the price of the bonds will fall, as shown by the downward arrow in the figure at the bond price of $950. As long as the bond price remains above the equilibrium price, an excess supply of bonds will continue to be available, and the price of bonds will continue to fall. This decline will stop only when the price has reached the equilibrium price of $850, the price at which the excess supply of bonds has been eliminated.

Now let's look at what happens when the price of bonds is below the equilibrium price. If the price of the bonds is set too low, at, say, $750, the quantity demanded at point E is greater than the quantity supplied at point F. This is called a condition of **excess demand**. People (lender-savers) now want to buy more bonds than others (borrowers) are willing to sell, so the price of bonds will be driven up, as illustrated by the upward arrow in the figure at the bond price of $750. Only when the excess demand for bonds is eliminated by the bond price rising to the equilibrium level of $850 is there no further tendency for the price to rise.

We can see that the concept of equilibrium price is a useful one because it indicates where the market will settle. Because each price on the vertical axis of Figure 1 corresponds to a particular value of the interest rate, the same diagram also shows that the interest rate will head toward the equilibrium interest rate of 17.6%. When the interest rate is below the equilibrium interest rate, as it is when it is at 5.3%, the price of the bond is above the equilibrium price, and an excess supply of bonds results. The price of the bond then falls, leading to a rise in the interest rate toward the equilibrium level. Similarly, when the interest rate is above the equilibrium level, as it is when it is at

33.3%, an excess demand for bonds occurs, and the bond price rises, driving the interest rate back down to the equilibrium level of 17.6%.

Supply and Demand Analysis

Our Figure 1 is a conventional supply and demand diagram with price on the vertical axis and quantity on the horizontal axis. Because the interest rate that corresponds to each bond price is also marked on the vertical axis, this diagram allows us to read the equilibrium interest rate, giving us a model that describes the determination of interest rates. It is important to recognize that a supply and demand diagram like Figure 1 can be drawn for *any* type of bond because the interest rate and price of a bond are *always* negatively related for all kinds of bonds, whether a discount bond or a coupon bond.

An important feature of the analysis here is that supply and demand are always described in terms of *stocks* (amounts at a given point in time) of assets, not in terms of *flows*. The **asset market approach** for understanding behavior in financial markets—which emphasizes stocks of assets, rather than flows, in determining asset prices—is the dominant methodology used by economists, because correctly conducting analyses in terms of flows is very tricky, especially when we encounter inflation.[2]

5.3 CHANGES IN EQUILIBRIUM INTEREST RATES

LO 5.3 List and describe the factors that affect the equilibrium interest rate in the bond market.

We will now use the supply and demand framework for bonds to analyze why interest rates change. To avoid confusion, it is important to make the distinction between *movements along* a demand (or supply) curve and *shifts in* a demand (or supply) curve. When quantity demanded (or supplied) changes as a result of a change in the price of the bond (or, equivalently, a change in the interest rate), we have a *movement along* the demand (or supply) curve. The change in the quantity demanded when we move from points A to B to C in Figure 1, for example, is a movement along a demand curve. A *shift in* the demand (or supply) curve, by contrast, occurs when the quantity demanded (or supplied) changes *at each given price (or interest rate)* of the bond in response to a change in some other factor besides the bond's price or interest rate. When one of these factors changes, causing a shift in the demand or supply curve, there will be a new equilibrium value for the interest rate.

In the following pages, we will look at how the supply and demand curves shift in response to changes in variables, such as expected inflation and wealth, and what effects these changes have on the equilibrium value of interest rates.

Shifts in the Demand for Bonds

The theory of portfolio choice, which we developed at the beginning of the chapter, provides a framework for deciding which factors will cause the demand curve for bonds to shift. These factors include changes in the following four parameters:

---

[2]The analysis of the bond market that we have developed here has another interpretation that uses a different terminology and framework involving the supply and demand for loanable funds. This loanable funds framework is discussed in appendix to this chapter that is available in **MyLab Economics**.

1. Wealth
2. Expected returns on bonds relative to alternative assets
3. Risk of bonds relative to alternative assets
4. Liquidity of bonds relative to alternative assets

To see how a change in each of these factors (holding all other factors constant) can shift the demand curve, let's look at some examples. (As a study aid, Table 2 summarizes the effects of changes in these factors on the bond demand curve.)

Wealth   When the economy is growing rapidly in a business cycle expansion and wealth is increasing, the quantity of bonds demanded at each bond price (or interest rate) increases, as shown in Figure 2. To see how this works, consider point B on the initial demand curve for bonds, B_1^d. With higher wealth, the quantity of bonds demanded at the same price must rise, to point B'. Similarly, for point D, the higher wealth causes the quantity demanded at the same bond price to rise to point D'. Continuing with this reasoning for every point on the initial demand curve B_1^d, we can see that the demand curve shifts to the right from B_1^d to B_2^d, as indicated by the arrows.

We can conclude that *in a business cycle expansion with growing income and wealth, the demand for bonds rises and the demand curve for bonds shifts to the right.* Applying the same reasoning, *in a recession, when income and wealth are falling, the demand for bonds falls, and the demand curve shifts to the left.*

Another factor that affects wealth is the public's propensity to save. If households save more, wealth increases and, as we have seen, the demand for bonds rises and the

Mini-lecture

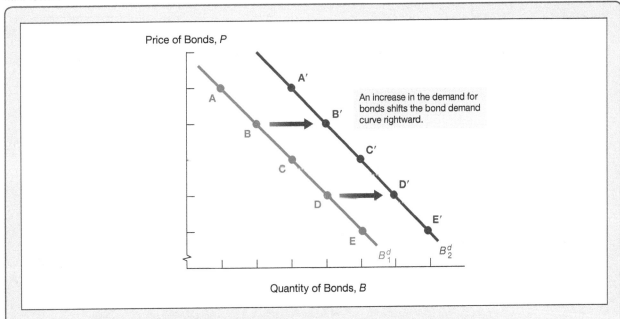

FIGURE 2   Shift in the Demand Curve for Bonds
When the demand for bonds increases, the demand curve shifts to the right as shown.

SUMMARY TABLE 2

Factors That Shift the Demand Curve for Bonds

Variable	Change in Variable	Change in Quantity Demanded at Each Bond Price	Shift in Demand Curve
Wealth	↑	↑	
Expected interest rate	↑	↓	
Expected inflation	↑	↓	
Riskiness of bonds relative to other assets	↑	↓	
Liquidity of bonds relative to other assets	↑	↑	

Note: Only increases in the variables are shown. The effects of decreases in the variables on demand would be the opposite of those indicated in the remaining columns.

demand curve for bonds shifts to the right. Conversely, if people save less, wealth and the demand for bonds fall, and the demand curve shifts to the left.

Expected Returns   For a one-year discount bond and a one-year holding period, the expected return and the interest rate are identical, so nothing other than today's interest rate affects the expected return.

For bonds with maturities of greater than one year, the expected return may differ from the interest rate. For example, we saw in Chapter 4, Table 2, that a rise in the interest rate on a long-term bond from 10% to 20% would lead to a sharp decline in price and a very large negative return. Hence, if people began to think that interest rates would be higher next year than they had originally anticipated, the expected return today on long-term bonds would fall, and the quantity demanded would fall at each interest rate. *Higher expected future interest rates lower the expected return for long-term bonds, decrease the demand, and shift the demand curve to the left.*

By contrast, an expectation of lower future interest rates would mean that long-term bond prices would be expected to rise more than originally anticipated, and the resulting higher expected return today would raise the quantity demanded at each bond price and interest rate. *Lower expected future interest rates increase the demand for long-term bonds and shift the demand curve to the right* (as in Figure 2).

Changes in expected returns on other assets can also shift the demand curve for bonds. If people suddenly become more optimistic about the stock market and begin to expect higher stock prices in the future, both expected capital gains and expected returns on stocks will rise. With the expected return on bonds held constant, the expected return on bonds today relative to stocks will fall, lowering the demand for bonds and shifting the demand curve to the left. *An increase in expected return on alternative assets lowers the demand for bonds and shifts the demand curve to the left.*

A change in expected inflation is likely to alter expected returns on physical assets (also called *real assets*), such as automobiles and houses, which affect the demand for bonds. An increase in expected inflation from, say, 5% to 10% will lead to higher prices on cars and houses in the future and hence higher nominal capital gains. The resulting rise in the expected returns today on these real assets will lead to a fall in the expected return on bonds relative to the expected return on real assets today and thus cause the demand for bonds to fall. Alternatively, we can think of the rise in expected inflation as lowering the real interest rate on bonds, and thus the resulting decline in the relative expected return on bonds will cause the demand for bonds to fall. *An increase in the expected rate of inflation lowers the expected return on bonds, causing their demand to decline and the demand curve to shift to the left.*

Risk   If prices in the bond market become more volatile, the risk associated with bonds increases, and bonds become a less attractive asset. *An increase in the riskiness of bonds causes the demand for bonds to fall and the demand curve to shift to the left.*

Conversely, an increase in the volatility of prices in another asset market, such as the stock market, would make bonds more attractive. *An increase in the riskiness of alternative assets causes the demand for bonds to rise and the demand curve to shift to the right* (as in Figure 2).

Liquidity   If more people started trading in the bond market, and as a result it became easier to sell bonds quickly, the increase in their liquidity would cause the quantity of bonds demanded at each interest rate to rise. *Increased liquidity of bonds results in an increased demand for bonds, and the demand curve shifts to the right* (see Figure 2). *Similarly, increased liquidity of alternative assets lowers the demand* *for bonds and shifts the demand curve to the left.* The reduction of brokerage commissions for trading common stocks that occurred when the fixed-rate commission structure was abolished in 1975, for example, increased the liquidity of stocks relative to bonds, and the resulting lower demand for bonds shifted the demand curve to the left.

Shifts in the Supply of Bonds

Certain factors can cause the supply curve for bonds to shift. Among these factors are the following:

1. Expected profitability of investment opportunities
2. Expected inflation
3. Government budget deficits

We will look at how the supply curve shifts when each of these factors changes (all others remaining constant). (As a study aid, Table 3 summarizes the effects of changes in these factors on the bond supply curve.)

SUMMARY TABLE 3

Factors That Shift the Supply of Bonds

Variable	Change in Variable	Change in Quantity Supplied at Each Bond Price	Shift in Supply Curve
Profitability of investments	↑	↑	
Expected inflation	↑	↑	
Government deficit	↑	↑	

Note: Only increases in the variables are shown. The effects of decreases in the variables on the supply would be the opposite of those indicated in the remaining columns.

Mini-lecture

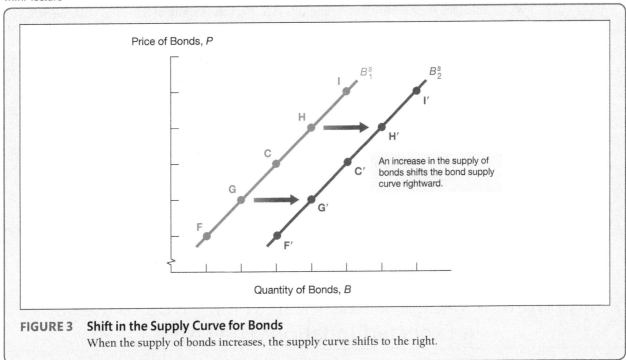

FIGURE 3   Shift in the Supply Curve for Bonds
When the supply of bonds increases, the supply curve shifts to the right.

Expected Profitability of Investment Opportunities   When opportunities for profitable plant and equipment investments are plentiful, firms are more willing to borrow to finance these investments. When the economy is growing rapidly, as in a business cycle expansion, investment opportunities that are expected to be profitable abound, and the quantity of bonds supplied at any given bond price increases (for example, from G to G′ or H to H′ in Figure 3). *Therefore, in a business cycle expansion, the supply of bonds increases and the supply curve shifts to the right. Likewise, in a recession, when far fewer profitable investment opportunities are expected, the supply of bonds falls and the supply curve shifts to the left.*

Expected Inflation   As we saw in Chapter 4, the real cost of borrowing is most accurately measured by the real interest rate, which equals the (nominal) interest rate minus the expected inflation rate. For a given interest rate (and bond price), when expected inflation increases, the real cost of borrowing falls; hence, the quantity of bonds supplied increases at any given bond price. *An increase in expected inflation causes the supply of bonds to increase and the supply curve to shift to the right* (see Figure 3), *and a decrease in expected inflation causes the supply of bonds to decrease and the supply curve to shift to the left.*

Government Budget Deficits   The activities of the government can influence the supply of bonds in several ways. The U.S. Treasury issues bonds to finance government deficits, caused by gaps between the government's expenditures and its revenues. When these deficits are large, the Treasury sells more bonds, and the quantity of bonds supplied at each bond price increases. *Higher government deficits increase the supply of bonds and shift the supply curve to the right* (see Figure 3). *On the other hand, government surpluses, as occurred in the late 1990s, decrease the supply of bonds and shift the supply curve to the left.*

State and local governments and other government agencies also issue bonds to finance their expenditures, and this can affect the supply of bonds as well. We will see in later chapters that the conduct of monetary policy involves the purchase and sale of bonds, which in turn influences the supply of bonds.

We now can use our knowledge of how supply and demand curves shift to analyze how the equilibrium interest rate can change. The best way to do this is to pursue several applications that are particularly relevant to our understanding of how monetary policy affects interest rates. In studying these applications, keep two things in mind:

1. When we examine the effect of a variable change, remember we are assuming that all other variables are unchanged; that is, we are making use of the *ceteris paribus* assumption.
2. Remember that the interest rate is negatively related to the bond price, so when the equilibrium bond price rises, the equilibrium interest rate falls. Conversely, if the equilibrium bond price moves downward, the equilibrium interest rate rises.

APPLICATION   ## Changes in the Interest Rate Due to a Change in Expected Inflation: The Fisher Effect

We have already done most of the work necessary to evaluate how a change in expected inflation affects the nominal interest rate, in that we have already analyzed how a change in expected inflation shifts the supply and demand curves for bonds. Figure 4 shows the effect on the equilibrium interest rate of an increase in expected inflation.

Mini-lecture

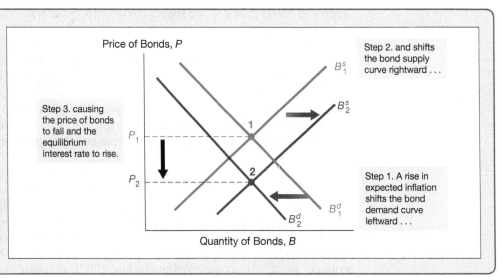

FIGURE 4
Response to a Change in Expected Inflation

When expected inflation rises, the supply curve shifts from B_1^s to B_2^s, and the demand curve shifts from B_1^d to B_2^d. The equilibrium moves from point 1 to point 2, causing the equilibrium bond price to fall from P_1 to P_2 and the equilibrium interest rate to rise.

Price of Bonds, P

Step 2. and shifts the bond supply curve rightward . . .

Step 3. causing the price of bonds to fall and the equilibrium interest rate to rise.

Step 1. A rise in expected inflation shifts the bond demand curve leftward . . .

Quantity of Bonds, B

Suppose that expected inflation is initially 5% and the initial supply and demand curves B_1^s and B_1^d intersect at point 1, where the equilibrium bond price is P_1. If expected inflation rises to 10%, the expected return on bonds relative to real assets falls for any given bond price and interest rate. As a result, the demand for bonds falls, and the demand curve shifts to the left from B_1^d to B_2^d. The rise in expected inflation also shifts the supply curve. At any given bond price and interest rate, the real cost of borrowing declines, causing the quantity of bonds supplied to increase and the supply curve to shift to the right, from B_1^s to B_2^s.

When the demand and supply curves shift in response to the rise in expected inflation, the equilibrium moves from point 1 to point 2, at the intersection of B_2^d and B_2^s. The equilibrium bond price falls from P_1 to P_2 and, because the bond price is negatively related to the interest rate, this means that the equilibrium interest rate rises. Note that Figure 4 has been drawn so that the equilibrium quantity of bonds remains the same at both point 1 and point 2. However, depending on the size of the shifts in the supply and demand curves, the equilibrium quantity of bonds can either rise or fall when expected inflation rises.

Our supply and demand analysis has led us to an important observation: **When expected inflation rises, interest rates will rise.** This result has been named the **Fisher effect**, after Irving Fisher, the economist who first pointed out the relationship of expected inflation to interest rates. The accuracy of this prediction is shown in Figure 5. The interest rate on three-month Treasury bills has usually moved along with the expected inflation rate. Consequently, many economists recommend that inflation must be kept low if we want to keep nominal interest rates low. ◆

Real-time data

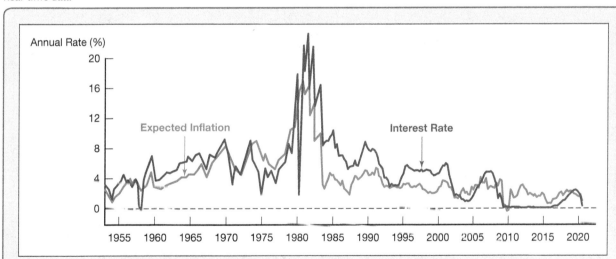

FIGURE 5   Expected Inflation and Interest Rates (Three-Month Treasury Bills), 1953–2020

The interest rate on three-month Treasury bills and the expected inflation rate generally move together, as the Fisher effect predicts.

Sources: Federal Reserve Bank of St. Louis FRED database: https://fred.stlouisfed.org/series/TB3MS; https://fred.stlouisfed.org/series/CPIAUCSL/.

Expected inflation calculated using procedures outlined in Frederic S. Mishkin, "The Real Interest Rate: An Empirical Investigation," *Carnegie-Rochester Conference Series on Public Policy* 15 (1981): 151–200. These procedures involve estimating expected inflation as a function of past interest rates, inflation, and time trends.

APPLICATION   Changes in the Interest Rate Due to a Business Cycle Expansion

Figure 6 analyzes the effects of a business cycle expansion on interest rates. In a business cycle expansion, the amounts of goods and services being produced in the economy increase, so national income rises. When this occurs, businesses are more willing to borrow because they are likely to have many profitable investment opportunities for which they need financing. Hence, at a given bond price, the quantity of bonds that firms want to sell (that is, the supply of bonds) will increase. This means that during a business cycle expansion, the supply curve for bonds shifts to the right (see Figure 6) from B_1^s to B_2^s.

Expansion in the economy also affects the demand for bonds. As the economy expands, wealth is likely to increase, and the theory of portfolio choice tells us that the demand for bonds will rise as well. We see this in Figure 6, where the demand curve has shifted to the right, from B_1^d to B_2^d.

Given that both the supply and demand curves have shifted to the right, we know that the new equilibrium reached at the intersection of B_2^d and B_2^s must also move to the right. However, depending on whether the supply curve shifts more than the demand curve or vice versa, the new equilibrium interest rate can either rise or fall.

The supply and demand analysis used here gives us an ambiguous answer to the question of what happens to interest rates in a business cycle expansion. Figure 6 has been drawn so that the shift in the supply curve is greater than the shift in the demand curve,

Mini-lecture

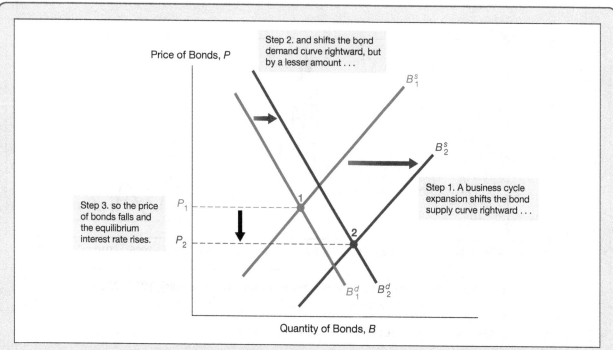

FIGURE 6   Response to a Business Cycle Expansion

In a business cycle expansion, when income and wealth are rising, the demand curve shifts rightward from B_1^d to B_2^d. If the supply curve shifts to the right more than the demand curve, as in this figure, the equilibrium bond price moves down from P_1 to P_2 and the equilibrium interest rate rises.

Real-time data

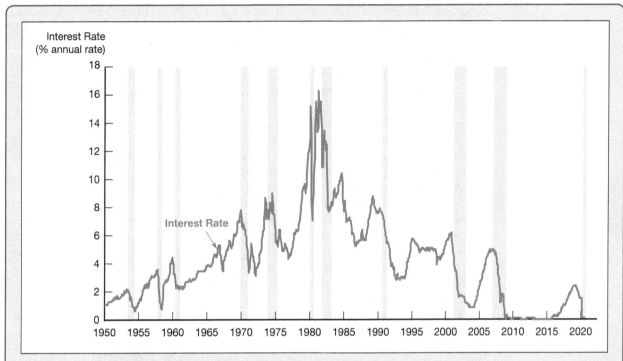

FIGURE 7   **Business Cycle and Interest Rates (Three-Month Treasury Bills), 1951–2020**

Shaded areas indicate periods of recession. The interest rate tends to rise during business cycle expansions and fall during recessions.

Source: Federal Reserve Bank of St. Louis FRED database: https://fred.stlouisfed.org/series/TB3MS.

causing the equilibrium bond price to fall to P_2 and the equilibrium interest rate to rise. The reason the figure has been drawn such that a business cycle expansion and a rise in income lead to a higher interest rate is that this is the outcome we actually see in the data. Figure 7 plots the movement of the interest rate on three-month U.S. Treasury bills from 1951 to 2020 and indicates when the business cycle went through recessions (shaded areas). As you can see, the interest rate tends to rise during business cycle expansions and fall during recessions, as indicated by the supply and demand diagram in Figure 6. ◆

APPLICATION   Explaining Current Low Interest Rates in Europe, Japan, and the United States: Low Inflation and Secular Stagnation

In the aftermath of the global financial crisis, interest rates in Europe and the United States, as well as in Japan, have fallen to extremely low levels. They fell even lower during the Covid-19 recession in 2020. Indeed, as discussed in Chapter 4, we have seen that interest rates have even sometimes turned negative. Why are interest rates in these countries at such low levels?

The answer is that inflation has fallen to very low levels in all these countries, sometimes even going negative, while at the same time there has been a dearth of attractive investment opportunities. Using these facts, analysis similar to that used in the preceding applications explains why interest rates have become so low.

Very low and even negative inflation causes the demand for bonds to rise because the expected return on real assets falls, thereby raising the relative expected return on bonds and in turn causing the demand curve to shift to the right. Low and even negative inflation also raises the real interest rate and therefore the real cost of borrowing for any given nominal rate, thereby causing the supply of bonds to contract and the supply curve to shift to the left. The outcome is then exactly the opposite of that graphed in Figure 4: The rightward shift of the demand curve and leftward shift of the supply curve lead to a rise in the bond price and a fall in interest rates.

All of these countries have also been experiencing very low economic growth rates and a lack of profitable investment opportunities. The former president of Harvard University and former U.S. Treasury Secretary, Lawrence Summers, has described this phenomenon with the phrase "secular stagnation." As a result of secular stagnation, firms have cut back on their investment spending, with the result that they supply fewer bonds, shifting the supply curve to the left. The leftward shift of the supply curve for bonds leads to a further rise in the bond price and interest rates fall (the opposite outcome to that in Figure 6).

Usually we think that low interest rates are a good thing because they make it cheap to borrow. But the recent episodes of low interest rates in the United States, Europe, and Japan show that just as a fallacy is present in the adage "You can never be too rich or too thin" (maybe you can't be too rich, but you can certainly be too thin and thereby damage your health), a fallacy is present in always thinking that lower interest rates are better. In the United States, Europe, and Japan, the low and even negative interest rates are a sign that these economies are not doing all that well, with slow growth and inflation that is too low. ◆

5.4 SUPPLY AND DEMAND IN THE MARKET FOR MONEY: THE LIQUIDITY PREFERENCE FRAMEWORK

LO 5.4 Describe the connection between the bond market and the money market through the liquidity preference framework.

An alternative model for determining the equilibrium interest rate, developed by John Maynard Keynes, is known as the **liquidity preference framework**. This framework determines the equilibrium interest rate in terms of the supply of and demand for money rather than the supply of and demand for bonds. Although the two frameworks look different, the liquidity preference analysis of the market for money is closely related to the supply and demand framework of the bond market.[3]

The starting point of Keynes's analysis is his assumption that people use two main categories of assets to store their wealth: money and bonds. Therefore, total wealth in the economy must equal the total quantity of bonds plus money in the economy,

---

[3]Note that the term *market for money* refers to the market for the medium of exchange, money. This market differs from the *money market* referred to by finance practitioners, which, as discussed in Chapter 2, is the financial market in which short-term debt instruments are traded.

which equals the quantity of bonds supplied (B^s) plus the quantity of money supplied (M^s). The quantity of bonds demanded (B^d) plus the quantity of money demanded (M^d) must also equal the total amount of wealth, because people cannot purchase more assets than their available resources allow. Thus the quantity of bonds and money supplied must equal the quantity of bonds and money demanded:

$$B^s + M^s = B^d + M^d \tag{2}$$

Collecting the bond terms on one side of the equation and the money terms on the other, this equation can be rewritten as

$$B^s - B^d = M^d - M^s \tag{3}$$

Equation 3 tells us that if the market for money is in equilibrium $(M^s = M^d)$, then the right-hand side of the equation equals zero, implying that $B^s = B^d$, which in turn means the bond market is also in equilibrium.

Thus we arrive at the same result whether we determine the equilibrium interest rate by equating the supply and demand for bonds or by equating the supply and demand for money. In this sense, the liquidity preference framework, which analyzes the market for money, is equivalent to a framework analyzing supply and demand in the bond market. In practice, the approaches differ because, by assuming there are only two kinds of assets, money and bonds, the liquidity preference approach implicitly ignores any effects on interest rates that arise from changes in the expected returns on real assets such as automobiles and houses. In most instances, however, both frameworks yield the same predictions.

The reason we approach the determination of interest rates using both frameworks is that the bond supply and demand framework is easier to use when analyzing the effects caused by changes in expected inflation, whereas the liquidity preference framework is easier to use when analyzing the effects caused by changes in income, the price level, and the supply of money.

Because the definition of money used by Keynes includes currency (which earns no interest) and checking account deposits (which in his time typically earned little or no interest), he assumed that money has a zero rate of return. Bonds, the only alternative asset to money in Keynes's framework, have an expected return equal to the interest rate i.[4] As this interest rate rises (holding everything else unchanged), the expected return on money falls relative to the expected return on bonds, causing a fall in the quantity of money demanded, as predicted by the theory of portfolio choice.

We can also see that the quantity of money demanded and the interest rate should be negatively related by using the concept of **opportunity cost**, which is the amount of interest (expected return) sacrificed by not holding the alternative asset—in this case, a bond. As the interest rate on bonds, i, rises, the opportunity cost of holding money rises; thus money is less desirable and the quantity of money demanded falls.

Figure 8 shows the quantity of money demanded at a number of interest rates, with all other economic variables, such as income and the price level, held constant. At an interest rate of 25%, point A shows that the quantity of money demanded is $100 billion. If the interest rate is at the lower rate of 20%, the opportunity cost of

---

[4]Keynes did not actually assume that the expected returns on bonds equaled the interest rate but rather argued that they were closely related. This distinction makes no appreciable difference in our analysis.

Mini-lecture

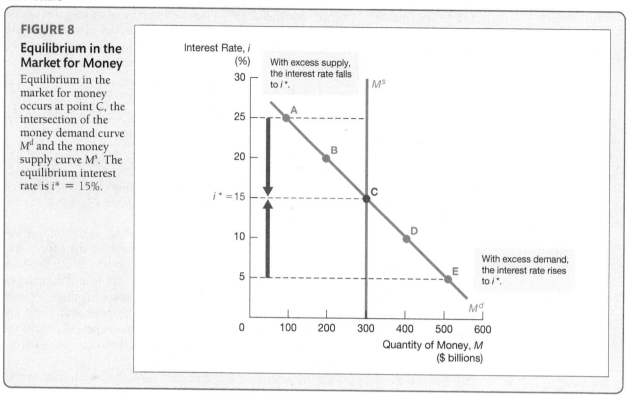

FIGURE 8

Equilibrium in the Market for Money

Equilibrium in the market for money occurs at point C, the intersection of the money demand curve M^d and the money supply curve M^s. The equilibrium interest rate is $i^* = 15\%$.

holding money is lower, and the quantity of money demanded rises to $200 billion, as indicated by the move from point A to point B. If the interest rate is even lower, the quantity of money demanded is even higher, as is indicated by points C, D, and E. The curve M^d connecting these points is the demand curve for money, and it slopes downward.

At this point in our analysis, we will assume that a central bank controls the amount of money supplied at a fixed quantity of $300 billion, so that the supply curve for money M^s in the figure is a vertical line at $300 billion. The equilibrium at which the quantity of money demanded equals the quantity of money supplied occurs at the intersection of the supply and demand curves at point C, where

$$M^d = M^s \tag{4}$$

The resulting equilibrium interest rate is $i^* = 15\%$.

We can again see that there is a tendency to approach this equilibrium rate by first looking at the relationship of money demand and supply when the interest rate is above the equilibrium interest rate. When the interest rate is 25%, the quantity of money demanded at point A is $100 billion, yet the quantity of money supplied is $300 billion. The excess supply of money means that people are holding more money than they desire, so they will try to get rid of their excess money balances by trying to buy bonds. Accordingly, they will bid up the price of bonds. As the bond price rises, the interest rate will fall toward the equilibrium interest rate of 15%. This tendency is shown by the downward arrow drawn at the interest rate of 25%.

Likewise, if the interest rate is 5%, the quantity of money demanded at p~~~ is $500 billion, but the quantity of money supplied is only $300 billion. An e~~~ demand for money now exists because people want to hold more money than t~~~ currently have. To try to obtain more money, they will sell their only other asset—bonds—and the price will fall. As the price of bonds falls, the interest rate will ris~ toward the equilibrium rate of 15%. Only when the interest rate is at its equilibrium value will there be no tendency for it to move further, and so the interest rate will settle at this value.

5.5 CHANGES IN EQUILIBRIUM INTEREST RATES IN THE LIQUIDITY PREFERENCE FRAMEWORK

LO 5.5 List and describe the factors that affect the money market and the equilibrium interest rate.

To use the liquidity preference framework to analyze how the equilibrium interest rate changes, we must understand what causes the demand and supply curves for money to shift.

Shifts in the Demand for Money

In Keynes's liquidity preference analysis, two factors cause the demand curve for money to shift: income and the price level.

Income Effect   In Keynes's view, there were two reasons why income would affect the demand for money. First, as an economy expands and income rises, wealth increases and people want to hold more money as a store of value. Second, as the economy expands and income rises, people want to carry out more transactions using money as a medium of exchange, and so they also want to hold more money. The conclusion is that *a higher level of income causes the demand for money at each interest rate to increase and the demand curve to shift to the right.*

Price-Level Effect   Keynes took the view that people care about the amount of money they hold in real terms—that is, in terms of the goods and services it can buy. When the price level rises, the same nominal quantity of money is no longer as valuable; it cannot be used to purchase as many real goods or services. To restore their holdings of money in real terms to the former level, people will want to hold a greater nominal quantity of money, so *a rise in the price level causes the demand for money at each interest rate to increase and the demand curve to shift to the right.*

Shifts in the Supply of Money

We will assume that the supply of money is completely controlled by the central bank, which in the United States is the Federal Reserve. (Actually, the process that determines the money supply is substantially more complicated, involving banks, depositors, and borrowers from banks. We will study it in more detail later in the book.) For now, all we need to know is that *an increase in the money supply engineered by the Federal Reserve will shift the supply curve for money to the right.*

Changes in the Equilibrium Interest Rate Due to Changes in Income, the Price Level, or the Money Supply

To see how we can use the liquidity preference framework to analyze the movement of interest rates, we will again look at several applications that will help us evaluate the effect of monetary policy on interest rates. In going through these applications, remember to use the *ceteris paribus* assumption: When examining the effect of a change in one variable, hold all other variables constant. (As a study aid, Table 4 summarizes the shifts in the demand and supply curves for money.)

SUMMARY TABLE 4

Factors That Shift the Demand for and Supply of Money

Variable	Change in Variable	Change in Money Demand (M^d) or Supply (M^s) at Each Interest Rate	Change in Interest Rate	
Income	↑	M^d↑	↑	
Price level	↑	M^d↑	↑	
Money supply	↑	M^s↑	↓	

Note: Only increases in the variables are shown. The effects of decreases in the variables on demand and supply would be the opposite of those indicated in the remaining columns.

Mini-lecture

FIGURE 9

Response to a Change in Income or the Price Level

In a business cycle expansion, when income is rising, or when the price level rises, the demand curve shifts from M_1^d to M_2^d. The supply curve is fixed at $M^s = \overline{M}$. The equilibrium interest rate rises from i_1 to i_2.

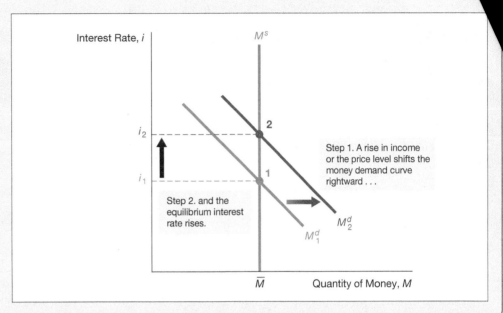

Step 1. A rise in income or the price level shifts the money demand curve rightward . . .

Step 2. and the equilibrium interest rate rises.

Changes in Income

We have seen that when income is rising during a business cycle expansion, the demand for money will rise, shown in Figure 9 by the rightward shift in the demand curve from M_1^d to M_2^d. The new equilibrium is reached at point 2, at the intersection of the M_2^d curve with the money supply curve M^s. As you can see, the equilibrium interest rate rises from i_1 to i_2. The liquidity preference framework thus generates the conclusion that **when income is rising during a business cycle expansion (holding other economic variables constant), interest rates will rise.** This conclusion is unambiguous, unlike the conclusion we reached using the bond demand and supply framework.

Changes in the Price Level

When the price level rises, the value of money in terms of its purchasing power is lower. To restore their money's purchasing power in real terms to its former level, people will want to hold a greater nominal quantity of money. A higher price level shifts the demand curve for money to the right from M_1^d to M_2^d (see Figure 9). The equilibrium moves from point 1 to point 2, where the equilibrium interest rate has risen from i_1 to i_2, illustrating that **when the price level increases, with the supply of money and other economic variables held constant, interest rates will rise.**

Changes in the Money Supply

An increase in the money supply due to expansionary monetary policy by the Federal Reserve implies that the supply curve for money will shift to the right. As shown in Figure 10 by the movement of the supply curve from M_1^s to M_2^s, the equilibrium moves

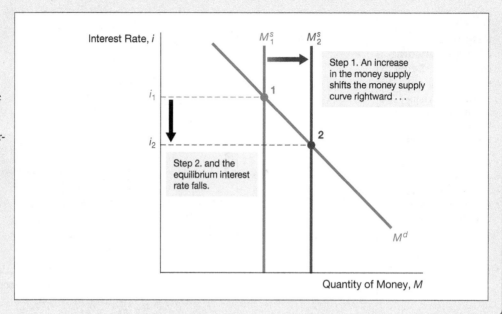

…e to a
…ge in the
…oney Supply

When the money supply increases, the supply curve shifts from M_1^s to M_2^s and the equilibrium interest rate falls from i_1 to i_2.

from point 1 down to point 2, where the M_2^s supply curve intersects with the demand curve M^d and the equilibrium interest rate has fallen from i_1 to i_2. **When the money supply increases (everything else remaining equal), interest rates will decline.**[5] ◆

5.6 MONEY AND INTEREST RATES

LO 5.6 Identify and illustrate the effects on the interest rate of changes in money growth over time.

The liquidity preference analysis in Figure 10 seems to suggest that an increase in the money supply will lower interest rates. This conclusion has important policy implications because it has frequently caused politicians to call for a more rapid growth of the money supply in an effort to drive down interest rates.

But is it correct to conclude that money and interest rates should be negatively related? Might other important factors have been left out of the liquidity preference analysis in Figure 10, factors that would reverse this conclusion? We will provide answers to these questions by applying the supply and demand analysis we used in this chapter to obtain a deeper understanding of the relationship between money and interest rates.

An important criticism of the idea that an increase in the money supply lowers interest rates was raised by Milton Friedman, a Nobel laureate in economics. He acknowledged that the liquidity preference analysis was correct and called the

---

[5]This same result can be generated using the bond supply and demand framework. As we will see in Chapter 14, a central bank increases the money supply primarily by buying bonds and thereby decreasing the supply of bonds available to the public. The resulting shift to the left of the supply curve for bonds leads to an increase in the equilibrium price of bonds and a decline in the equilibrium interest rate.

result—that an increase in the money supply (*everything else remaining equal*) low
interest rates—the *liquidity effect*. However, he viewed the liquidity effect as merely pa
of the story: An increase in the money supply might not leave "everything else equal
and will have other effects on the economy that may make interest rates rise. If these
effects are substantial, it is entirely possible that when the money supply increases,
interest rates might also increase.

We have already laid the groundwork for our discussion of these other effects,
because we have shown how changes in income, the price level, and expected inflation
influence the equilibrium interest rate.

1. *Income Effect.* An increasing money supply can cause national income and wealth to
   rise. Both the liquidity preference and bond supply and demand frameworks indicate that interest rates will then rise (see Figures 6 and 9). Thus **the income effect
   of an increase in the money supply is a rise in interest rates in response to the
   higher level of income.**

2. *Price-Level Effect.* An increase in the money supply can also cause the overall price
   level in the economy to rise. The liquidity preference framework predicts that this
   will lead to a rise in interest rates. Thus **the price-level effect from an increase in
   the money supply is a rise in interest rates in response to the rise in price level.**

3. *Expected-Inflation Effect.* The higher inflation rate that can result from an increase
   in the money supply can also affect interest rates by influencing the expected inflation rate. Specifically, an increase in the money supply may lead people to expect
   a higher price level in the future—and hence the expected inflation rate will be
   higher. The bond supply and demand framework has shown us that this increase
   in expected inflation will lead to a higher level of interest rates. Therefore, **the
   expected-inflation effect of an increase in the money supply is a rise in interest
   rates in response to the rise in the expected inflation rate.**

At first glance it might appear that the price-level effect and the expected-inflation
effect are the same thing. They both indicate that increases in the price level induced
by an increase in the money supply will raise interest rates. However, there is a subtle
difference between the two, and this is why they are discussed as two separate effects.

Suppose that a one-time increase in the money supply today leads to a rise in prices
to a permanently higher level by next year. As the price level rises over the course of
this year, the interest rate will rise via the price-level effect. Only at the end of the year,
when the price level has risen to its peak, will the price-level effect be at a maximum.

The rising price level will also raise interest rates via the expected-inflation effect,
because people will expect that inflation will be higher over the course of the year.
However, when the price level stops rising next year, inflation and the expected inflation rate will return to zero. Any rise in interest rates as a result of the earlier rise in
expected inflation will then be reversed. We thus see that in contrast to the price-level
effect, which reaches its greatest impact next year, the expected-inflation effect will
have its smallest impact (zero impact) next year. The basic difference between the two
effects, then, is that the price-level effect remains even after prices have stopped rising,
whereas the expected-inflation effect disappears.

An important point is that the expected-inflation effect will persist only as long as
the price level continues to rise. As we will see in our discussion of monetary theory
in subsequent chapters, a one-time increase in the money supply will not produce a
continually rising price level; only a higher rate of money supply growth will. Thus
a higher rate of money supply growth is needed if the expected-inflation effect is to
persist.

Does a Higher Rate of Growth of the Money Supply Lower Interest Rates?

We can now put together all the effects we have discussed to help us decide whether our analysis supports the politicians who advocate a greater rate of growth of the money supply when they feel that interest rates are too high. Of all the effects, only the liquidity effect indicates that a higher rate of money growth will cause a decline in interest rates. In contrast, the income, price-level, and expected-inflation effects indicate that interest rates will rise when money growth is higher. Which of these effects is largest, and how quickly does each take effect? The answers are critical in determining whether interest rates will rise or fall when money supply growth is increased.

Generally, the liquidity effect from greater money growth takes effect immediately, because the rising money supply leads to an immediate decline in the equilibrium interest rate. The income and price-level effects take longer to work because time is needed for the increasing money supply to raise the price level and income, which in turn raise interest rates. The expected-inflation effect, which also raises interest rates, can be slow or fast, depending on whether people adjust their expectations of inflation slowly or quickly when the money growth rate is increased.

Three possibilities are outlined in Figure 11; each shows how interest rates respond over time to an increased rate of money supply growth, starting at time T. Panel (a) shows a case in which the liquidity effect dominates the other effects so that the interest rate falls from i_1 at time T to a final level of i_2. The liquidity effect operates quickly to lower the interest rate, but as time goes by, the other effects start to reverse some of the decline. Because the liquidity effect is larger than the others, however, the interest rate never rises back to its initial level.

In panel (b), the liquidity effect is smaller than the other effects, with the expected-inflation effect operating slowly because expectations of inflation are slow to adjust upward. Initially, the liquidity effect drives down the interest rate. Then the income, price-level, and expected-inflation effects begin to raise it. Because these effects are dominant, the interest rate eventually rises above its initial level to i_2. In the short run, lower interest rates result from increased money growth, but eventually they end up climbing above the initial level.

In panel (c), the expected-inflation effect dominates and operates rapidly because people quickly raise their expectations of inflation when the rate of money growth increases. The expected-inflation effect begins immediately to overpower the liquidity effect, and the interest rate immediately starts to climb. Over time, as the income and price-level effects start to take hold, the interest rate rises even higher, and the eventual outcome is an interest rate that is substantially higher than the initial interest rate. The result shows clearly that increasing money supply growth is not the answer to reducing interest rates; rather, money growth should be *reduced* to lower interest rates!

An important issue for economic policymakers is deciding which of these three scenarios is closest to reality. If a decline in interest rates is desired, then an increase in money supply growth is called for when the liquidity effect dominates the other effects, as in panel (a). A decrease in money growth is appropriate when the other effects dominate the liquidity effect and expectations of inflation adjust rapidly, as in panel (c). If the other effects dominate the liquidity effect but expectations of inflation adjust only slowly, as in panel (b), then the decision to increase or decrease money growth depends on whether policymakers care more about what happens in the short run or in the long run.

Mini-lecture

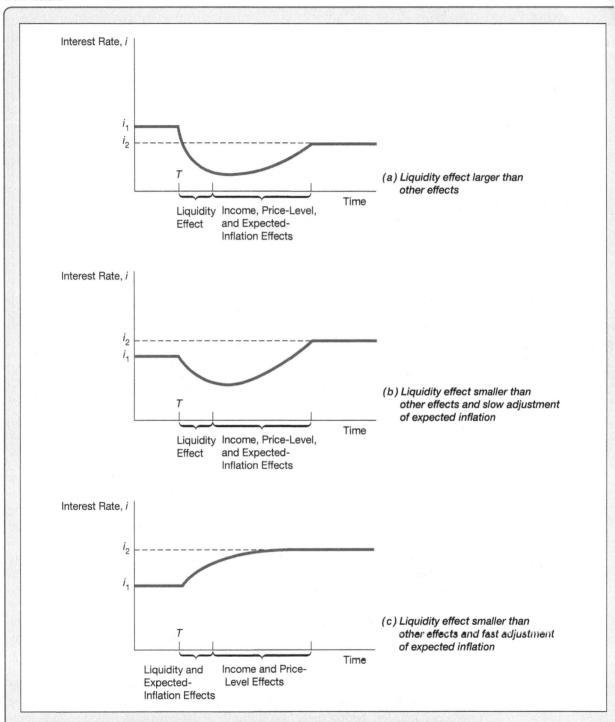

FIGURE 11   Response over Time to an Increase in Money Supply Growth
Each panel shows how interest rates respond over time to an increased rate of money supply growth, starting at time *T*.

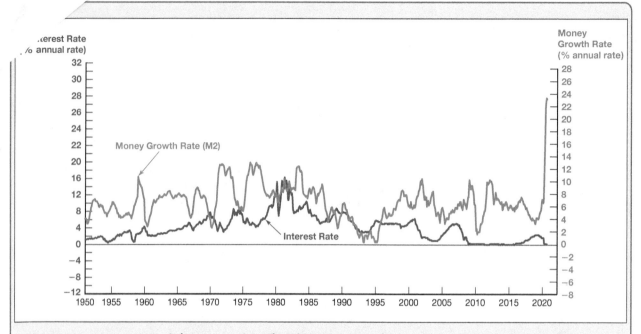

FIGURE 12 Money Growth (M2, Annual Rate) and Interest Rates (Three-Month Treasury Bills), 1950–2020

When the rate of money supply growth began to climb in the mid-1960s, interest rates rose, indicating that the liquidity effect was dominated by the price-level, income, and expected-inflation effects. By the 1970s, both interest rates and money growth reached levels unprecedented in the post–World War II period.

Source: Federal Reserve Bank of St. Louis FRED database: https://fred.stlouisfed.org/series/M2SL; https://fred.stlouisfed.org/series/TB3MS.

Which scenario is supported by the evidence? The relationship between interest rates and money growth from 1950 to 2020 is plotted in Figure 12. When the rate of money supply growth began to climb in the mid-1960s, interest rates rose, indicating that the liquidity effect was dominated by the price-level, income, and expected-inflation effects. By the 1970s, interest rates reached levels unprecedented in the post–World War II period, as did the rate of money supply growth. The decline in money supply growth from the early 1980s until the early 1990s was associated with a decline in interest rates. However, since 1995 when the inflation rate has been pretty stable, there has been no clear-cut relationship between money supply growth and interest rates.

The scenario depicted in panel (a) of Figure 11 seems doubtful, and the case for lowering interest rates by raising the rate of money growth is much weakened. Looking back at Figure 5, which shows the relationship between interest rates and expected inflation, you should not find this too surprising. The rise in the rate of money supply growth in the 1960s and 1970s is matched by a large rise in expected inflation, while the fall in money growth from the early 1980s until the early 1990s is also associated with a decline in expected inflation. Both of these facts suggest that the expected inflation effect is dominant. It is the most plausible explanation for why interest rates rose in the face of higher money growth and then fell with the decline in money growth. However, Figure 12 does not really tell us which one of the two scenarios depicted in panels (b) and (c) of Figure 11 is more accurate. It depends critically on how fast people's expectations about inflation adjust. Research done using more sophisticated methods than just looking a graph like Figure 12 indicates that increased money growth temporarily lowers short term interest rates and thus conforms to the scenario in panel (b). ◆

SUMMARY

1. The theory of portfolio choice tells us that the quantity demanded of an asset is (a) positively related to wealth, (b) positively related to the expected return on the asset relative to alternative assets, (c) negatively related to the riskiness of the asset relative to alternative assets, and (d) positively related to the liquidity of the asset relative to alternative assets.

2. The supply and demand analysis for bonds provides one theory of how interest rates are determined. It predicts that interest rates will change when there is a change in demand caused by changes in income (or wealth), expected returns, risk, or liquidity, or when there is a change in supply caused by changes in the attractiveness of investment opportunities, the real cost of borrowing, or the government budget.

3. An alternative theory of how interest rates are determined is provided by the liquidity preference framework, which analyzes the supply of and demand for money. It shows that interest rates will change when the demand for money changes because of alterations in income or the price level, or when the supply of money changes.

4. An increase in the money supply has four possible effects on interest rates: the liquidity effect, the income effect, the price-level effect, and the expected-inflation effect. The liquidity effect indicates that a rise in money supply growth will lead to a decline in interest rates; the other effects work in the opposite direction. The evidence seems to indicate that the income, price-level, and expected-inflation effects dominate the liquidity effect such that an increase in money supply growth leads to higher—rather than lower—interest rates.

KEY TERMS

asset market approach, p. 92
demand curve, p. 89
excess demand, p. 91
excess supply, p. 91
expected return, p. 87

Fisher effect, p. 99
liquidity, p. 87
liquidity preference framework, p. 102
market equilibrium, p. 91
opportunity cost, p. 103

risk, p. 87
supply curve, p. 90
theory of portfolio choice, p. 88
wealth, p. 87

QUESTIONS

1. Explain why you would be more or less willing to buy a share of Microsoft stock in the following situations:
   a. Your wealth falls.
   b. You expect the stock to appreciate in value.
   c. The bond market becomes more liquid.
   d. You expect gold to appreciate in value.
   e. Prices in the bond market become more volatile.

2. Explain why you would be more or less willing to buy a house under the following circumstances:
   a. You just inherited $100,000.
   b. Real estate commissions fall from 6% of the sales price to 5% of the sales price.

   c. You expect Microsoft stock to double in value next year.
   d. Prices in the stock market become more volatile.
   e. You expect housing prices to fall.

3. Explain why you would be more or less willing to buy gold under the following circumstances:
   a. Gold again becomes acceptable as a medium of exchange.
   b. Prices in the gold market become more volatile.
   c. You expect inflation to rise, and gold prices tend to move with the aggregate price level.
   d. You expect interest rates to rise.

at

, you would be more or less willing to buy
.n AT&T bonds under the following circum-
.ces:

a. Trading in these bonds increases, making them easier to sell.

b. You expect a bear market in stocks (stock prices are expected to decline).

c. Brokerage commissions on stocks fall.

d. You expect interest rates to rise.

e. Brokerage commissions on bonds fall.

5. What will happen to the demand for Rembrandt paintings if the stock market undergoes a boom? Why?

6. Raphael observes that at the current level of interest rates there is an excess supply of bonds, and therefore he anticipates an increase in the price of bonds. Is Raphael correct?

7. Suppose Maria prefers to buy a bond with a 7% expected return and 2% standard deviation of its expected return, while Jennifer prefers to buy a bond with a 4% expected return and 1% standard deviation of its expected return. Can you tell if Maria is more or less risk-averse than Jennifer?

8. What will happen in the bond market if the government imposes a limit on the amount of daily transactions? Which characteristic of an asset would be affected?

9. How might a sudden increase in people's expectations of future real estate prices affect interest rates?

10. Suppose that many big corporations decide not to issue bonds, since it is now too costly to comply with new financial market regulations. Can you describe the expected effect on interest rates?

11. In the aftermath of the global economic crisis that started to take hold in 2008, U.S. government budget deficits increased dramatically, yet interest rates on U.S. Treasury debt fell sharply and stayed low for quite some time. Does this make sense? Why or why not?

12. Will there be an effect on interest rates if brokerage commissions on stocks fall? Explain your answer.

13. The president of the United States announces in a press conference that he will fight the higher inflation rate with a new anti-inflation program. Predict what will happen to interest rates if the public believes him.

14. Suppose that people in France decide to permanently increase their savings rate. Predict what will happen to the French bond market in the future. Can France expect higher or lower domestic interest rates?

15. Suppose you are in charge of the financial department of your company and you have to decide whether to borrow short or long term. Checking the news, you realize that the government is about to engage in a major infrastructure plan in the near future. Predict what will happen to interest rates. Will you advise borrowing short or long term?

16. Would fiscal policymakers ever have reason to worry about potentially inflationary conditions? Why or why not?

17. Why should a rise in the price level (but not in expected inflation) cause interest rates to rise when the nominal money supply is fixed?

18. If the next chair of the Federal Reserve Board has a reputation for advocating an even slower rate of money growth than the current chair, what will happen to interest rates? Discuss the possible resulting situations.

19. M1 money growth in the United States was about 15% in 2011 and 2012, and 10% in 2013. Over the same time period, the yield on three-month Treasury bills was close to 0%. Given these high rates of money growth, why did interest rates stay so low, rather than increase? What does this say about the income, price-level, and expected-inflation effects?

APPLIED PROBLEMS

20. Suppose you visit with a financial adviser, and you are considering investing some of your wealth in one of three investment portfolios: stocks, bonds, or commodities. Your financial adviser provides you with the following table, which gives the probabilities of possible returns from each investment:

a. Which investment should you choose to maximize your expected return: stocks, bonds, or commodities?

b. If you are risk-averse and have to choose between the stock and the bond investments, which should you choose? Why?

Stocks		Bonds		Commodities	
Probability	Return	Probability	Return	Probability	Return
0.25	12%	0.6	10%	0.2	20%
0.25	10%	0.4	7.50%	0.25	12%
0.25	8%			0.25	6%
0.25	6%			0.25	4%
				0.05	0%

21. An important way in which the Federal Reserve decreases the money supply is by selling bonds to the public. Using a supply and demand analysis for bonds, show what effect this action has on interest rates. Is your answer consistent with what you would expect to find with the liquidity preference framework?

22. Using both the liquidity preference framework and the supply and demand for bonds framework, show why interest rates are procyclical (rising when the economy is expanding and falling during recessions).

23. Using both the supply and demand for bonds and liquidity preference frameworks, show how interest rates are affected when the riskiness of bonds rises. Are the results the same in the two frameworks?

24. The demand curve and supply curve for one-year discount bonds with a face value of $1,000 are represented by the following equations:

B^d: Price $= -0.6 \times$ Quantity $+ 1140$

B^s: Price $=$ Quantity $+ 700$

a. What is the expected equilibrium price and quantity of bonds in this market?

b. Given your answer to part (a), what is the expected interest rate in this market?

25. The demand curve and supply curve for one-year discount bonds with a face value of $1,000 are represented by the following equations:

B^d: Price $= -0.6 \times$ Quantity $+ 1140$

B^s: Price $=$ Quantity $+ 700$

Suppose that, as a result of monetary policy actions, the Federal Reserve sells 80 bonds that it holds. Assume that bond demand and money demand are held constant.

a. How does the Federal Reserve policy affect the bond supply equation?

b. Calculate the effect of the Federal Reserve's action on the equilibrium interest rate in this market.

DATA ANALYSIS PROBLEMS

The Problems update with real-time data in **MyLab Economics** and are available for practice or instructor assignment.

1. Real-time Data Analysis Go to the St. Louis Federal Reserve FRED database, and find data on net worth of households (BOGZ1FL192090005Q) and the 10-year U.S. Treasury bond (GS10). For the net worth indicator, adjust the *units* setting to "Percent Change from Year Ago," and for the 10-year bond, adjust the *frequency* setting to "Quarterly."

    a. What is the percent change in net worth over the most recent year of data available? All else being equal, what do you expect should happen to the price and yield on the 10-year Treasury bond? Why?

    b. What is the change in yield on the 10-year Treasury bond over the past year of data available? Is this result consistent with your answer to part (a)? Briefly explain.

2. Real-time Data Analysis Go to the St. Louis Federal Reserve FRED database, and find data on the M1 money supply (M1SL) and the 10-year U.S. Treasury bond rate (GS10). For the M1 money supply indicator, adjust the *units* setting to "Percent Change from Year Ago," and for both variables, adjust the *frequency* setting to "Quarterly." Download the data into a spreadsheet.

    a. Create a scatter plot, with money growth on the horizontal axis and the 10-year Treasury rate on the vertical axis, from 2000:Q1 to the most recent quarter of data available. On the scatter plot, graph a fitted (regression) line of the data (there are several ways to do this; however, one particular chart layout has this option built in). Based on the fitted line, are the data consistent with the liquidity effect? Briefly explain.

b. Repeat part (a), but this time compare the contemporaneous money growth rate with the interest rate four quarters later. For example, create a scatter plot comparing money growth from 2000:Q1 with the interest rate from 2001:Q1, and so on, up to the most recent pairwise data available. Compare your results to those obtained in part (a), and interpret the liquidity effect as it relates to the income, price-level, and expected-inflation effects.

c. Repeat part (a) again, except this time compare the contemporaneous money growth rate with the interest rate eight quarters later. For example, create a scatter plot comparing money growth from 2000:Q1 with the interest rate from 2002:Q1, and so on, up to the most recent pairwise data available. Assuming the liquidity and other effects are fully incorporated into the bond market after two years, what do your results imply about the overall effect of money growth on interest rates?

d. Based on your answers to parts (a) through (c), how do the actual data on money growth and interest rates compare to the three scenarios presented in Figure 11 of this chapter?

6

The Risk and Term Structure of Interest Rates

Learning Objectives

6.1 Identify and explain the three factors affecting the risk structure of interest rates.

6.2 List and explain the three theories of why interest rates vary across different maturities.

Preview

In our supply and demand analysis of interest-rate behavior in Chapter 5, we examined the determination of just one interest rate. Yet we saw earlier that there are enormous numbers of bonds on which the interest rates can and do differ. In this chapter, we complete the interest-rate picture by examining the relationships of the various interest rates to one another. Understanding why interest rates differ from bond to bond can help businesses, banks, insurance companies, and private investors decide which bonds to purchase as investments and which ones to sell.

We first look at why bonds with the same term to maturity have different interest rates. The relationship among these interest rates is called the **risk structure of interest rates**, although risk, liquidity, and income tax rules all play a role in determining the risk structure. A bond's term to maturity also affects its interest rate, and the relationship among interest rates on bonds with different terms to maturity is called the **term structure of interest rates**. In this chapter, we examine the sources and causes of fluctuations in interest rates relative to one another and look at a number of theories that explain these fluctuations.

6.1 RISK STRUCTURE OF INTEREST RATES

LO 6.1 Identify and explain the three factors affecting the risk structure of interest rates.

Figure 1 shows the yields to maturity for several categories of long-term bonds from 1919 to 2020. It shows us two important features of interest-rate behavior for bonds of the same maturity: Interest rates on different categories of bonds, although they generally move together, differ from one another in any given year, and the spread (or difference) between the interest rates varies over time. The interest rates on municipal bonds, for example, were higher than those on U.S. government (Treasury) bonds in the late 1930s but lower thereafter. In addition, the spread between the interest rates on Baa corporate bonds (riskier than Aaa corporate bonds) and U.S. government bonds was very large during the Great Depression years from 1930 to 1933, was smaller during the 1940s–1960s, and then widened again afterward, particularly during the global financial crisis from 2007 to 2009. Which factors are responsible for these phenomena?

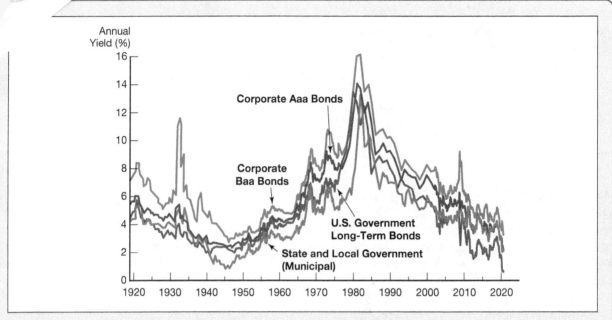

FIGURE 1 **Long-Term Bond Yields, 1919–2020**

Interest rates on different categories of bonds differ from one another in any given year, and the spread (or difference) between the interest rates varies over time.

Sources: Board of Governors of the Federal Reserve System, *Banking and Monetary Statistics, 1941–1970*; Federal Reserve Bank of St. Louis FRED database: https://fred.stlouisfed.org/series/GS10; https://fred.stlouisfed.org/series/DAAA; https://fred.stlouisfed.org/series/DBAA and https://fred.stlouisfed.org/series/WSLB20

Default Risk

One attribute of a bond that influences its interest rate is its risk of **default**. Default occurs when the issuer of the bond is unable or unwilling to make interest payments when promised or pay off the face value when the bond matures. Corporations suffering big losses, such as airline and car rental companies during the coronavirus pandemic in 2020, might be more likely to suspend interest payments on their bonds. The default risk on their bonds would therefore be quite high. By contrast, U.S. Treasury bonds have usually been considered to have no default risk because the federal government can always increase taxes or print money to pay off its obligations. Bonds like these with no default risk are called **default-free bonds**. (However, during the budget negotiations in Congress in 2013, which led to a government shutdown, the Republicans threatened to let Treasury bonds default, and this threat had an adverse impact on the bond market.) The spread between interest rates on bonds with default risk and interest rates on default-free bonds, both of the same maturity, is called the **risk premium**. The risk premium indicates how much additional interest people must earn to be willing to hold the risky bond. Our supply and demand analysis of the bond market in Chapter 5 can be used to explain why a bond with default risk always has a positive risk premium, and why a higher default risk means a larger risk premium.

To examine the effect of default risk on interest rates, let's look at the supply and demand diagrams for the default-free (U.S. Treasury) and corporate long-term bond

Mini-lecture

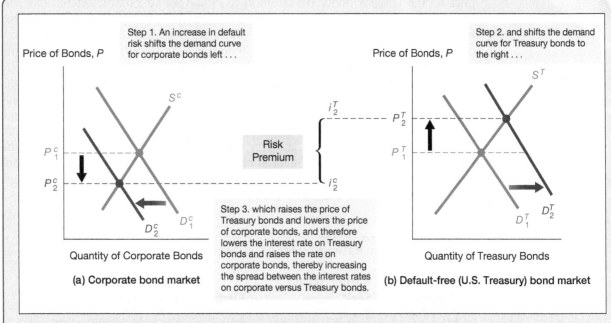

FIGURE 2   Response to an Increase in Default Risk on Corporate Bonds

Initially, $P_1^c = P_1^T$, $i_1^c = i_1^T$, and the risk premium is zero. An increase in default risk on corporate bonds shifts the demand curve from D_1^c to D_2^c; simultaneously, it shifts the demand curve for Treasury bonds from D_1^T to D_2^T. The equilibrium price for corporate bonds falls from P_1^c to P_2^c, and the equilibrium interest rate on corporate bonds rises to i_2^c. In the Treasury market, the equilibrium bond price rises from P_1^T to P_2^T, and the equilibrium interest rate falls to i_2^T. The brace indicates the difference between i_2^c and i_2^T, the risk premium on corporate bonds. (Note that because P_2^c is lower than P_2^T, i_2^c is greater than i_2^T.)

markets in Figure 2. To make the diagrams somewhat easier to read, let's assume that initially corporate bonds have the same default risk as U.S. Treasury bonds. In this case, these two bonds have the same attributes (identical risk and maturity); their equilibrium prices and interest rates will initially be equal $(P_1^c = P_1^T$ and $i_1^c = i_1^T)$, and the risk premium on corporate bonds $(i_1^c - i_1^T)$ will be zero.

If the possibility of a default increases because a corporation begins to suffer large losses, the default risk on corporate bonds will increase and the expected return on these bonds will decrease. In addition, the corporate bond's return will be more uncertain. The theory of portfolio choice predicts that because the expected return on the corporate bond falls relative to the expected return on the default-free Treasury bond while its relative riskiness rises, the corporate bond is less desirable (holding everything else equal), and demand for it will fall. Another way of thinking about this is that if you were an investor, you would want to hold (demand) a smaller amount of corporate bonds. The demand curve for corporate bonds in panel (a) of Figure 2 then shifts to the left, from D_1^c to D_2^c.

At the same time, the expected return on default-free Treasury bonds increases relative to the expected return on corporate bonds, while their relative riskiness declines. The Treasury bonds thus become more desirable, and demand rises, as shown in panel (b) by the rightward shift in the demand curve for these bonds from D_1^T to D_2^T.

As we can see in Figure 2, the equilibrium price for corporate bonds falls from P_1^c to P_2^c, and since the bond price is negatively correlated to the interest rate, the equilibrium interest rate on corporate bonds rises to i_2^c. At the same time, however, the equilibrium price for the Treasury bonds rises from P_1^T to P_2^T and the equilibrium interest rate falls to i_2^T. The spread between the interest rates on corporate and default-free bonds—that is, the risk premium on corporate bonds—has risen from zero to $i_2^c - i_2^T$. We can now conclude that *a bond with default risk will always have a positive risk premium, and an increase in its default risk will raise the risk premium.*

Because default risk is so important to the size of the risk premium, purchasers of bonds need to know whether a corporation is likely to default on its bonds. This information is provided by **credit-rating agencies**, investment advisory firms that rate the quality of corporate and municipal bonds in terms of their probability of default. Credit-rating agencies have become very controversial in recent years because of the role they played in the global financial crisis of 2007–2009 (see the FYI box, "Conflicts of Interest at Credit-Rating Agencies and the Global Financial Crisis"). Table 1

TABLE 1	Bond Ratings by Moody's, Standard and Poor's, and Fitch		
Moody's	**Rating Agency** **S&P**	**Fitch**	**Definitions**
Aaa	AAA	AAA	Prime Maximum Safety
Aa1	AA+	AA+	High Grade High Quality
Aa2	AA	AA	
Aa3	AA–	AA–	
A1	A+	A+	Upper Medium Grade
A2	A	A	
A3	A–	A–	
Baa1	BBB+	BBB+	Lower Medium Grade
Baa2	BBB	BBB	
Baa3	BBB–	BBB–	
Ba1	BB+	BB+	Noninvestment Grade
Ba2	BB	BB	Speculative
Ba3	BB–	BB–	
B1	B+	B+	Highly Speculative
B2	B	B	
B3	B–	B–	
Caa1	CCC+	CCC	Substantial Risk
Caa2	CCC	—	In Poor Standing
Caa3	CCC–	—	
Ca	—	—	Extremely Speculative
C	—	—	May Be in Default
—	—	D	Default

FYI   **Conflicts of Interest at Credit-Rating Agencies and the Global Financial Crisis**

Debt ratings play a major role in the pricing of debt securities and in the regulatory process. Conflicts of interest arose for credit-rating agencies in the years leading up to the global financial crisis when these agencies advised clients on how to structure complex financial instruments that paid out cash flows from subprime mortgages. At the same time, the agencies were rating these identical products, leading to the potential for severe conflicts of interest. Specifically, the large fees they earned from advising clients on how to structure products that the agencies themselves were rating meant they did not have sufficient incentives to make sure their ratings were accurate.

When housing prices began to fall and subprime mortgages began to default, it became crystal clear that the ratings agencies had done a terrible job of assessing the risk in the subprime products they had helped to structure. Many AAA-rated products had to be downgraded over and over again until they reached junk status. The resulting massive losses on these assets were one reason why so many financial institutions that were holding them got into trouble. Indeed, some commentators have cited credit-rating agencies as among the chief villains that should be blamed for the global financial crisis.

---

provides the bond ratings and their descriptions as defined by the three largest credit-rating agencies, Moody's Investor Service, Standard and Poor's Corporation, and Fitch Ratings. Bonds with relatively low risk of default are called *investment-grade* securities and have a rating of Baa (or BBB) and above. Bonds with ratings below Baa (or BBB) have higher default risk and have been aptly dubbed speculative-grade or **junk bonds**. Because these bonds always have higher interest rates than investment-grade securities, they are also referred to as high-yield bonds.

Next let's look at Figure 1 at the beginning of the chapter and see if we can explain the relationship between interest rates on corporate and those on U.S. Treasury bonds. Corporate bonds always have higher interest rates than U.S. Treasury bonds because they always have some risk of default, whereas U.S. Treasury bonds do not. Because Baa-rated corporate bonds have a greater default risk than the higher-rated Aaa bonds, their risk premium is greater, and the Baa rate therefore always exceeds the Aaa rate. We can use the same analysis to explain the huge jump in the risk premium on Baa corporate bond rates during the Great Depression years of 1930–1933, as well as the rise in the risk premium after 1970 (see Figure 1). The Depression period saw a very high rate of business failures and defaults. As we would expect, these factors led to a substantial increase in the default risk for bonds issued by vulnerable corporations, and the risk premium for Baa bonds reached unprecedentedly high levels. Since 1970, we have again seen higher levels of business failures and defaults, although they have been well below Great Depression levels. Again, as expected, both default risks and risk premiums for corporate bonds rose, widening the spread between interest rates on corporate bonds and those on Treasury bonds.

TION ## The Coronavirus Pandemic and the Baa–Treasury Spread

When the coronavirus officially became a pandemic in March 2020, the resulting lockdowns and social distancing dealt a knockout blow to the world economy. Many investors began to doubt the financial health of corporations with low credit ratings such as Baa. The perceived increase in default risk for Baa bonds made them less desirable at any given price, decreased the quantity demanded, and shifted the demand curve for Baa bonds to the left. As shown in panel (a) of Figure 2, the interest rate on Baa bonds should have risen, which is indeed what happened. Interest rates on Baa bonds jumped by 70 basis points (0.70 percentage point), from 3.6% in February 2020 to 4.3% in March 2020. At the same time, the increase in perceived default risk for Baa bonds made default-free U.S. Treasury bonds relatively more attractive and shifted the demand curve for these securities to the right—an outcome described by some analysts as a "flight to quality." Just as our analysis in Figure 2 predicts, interest rates on Treasury bonds fell by 60 basis points, from 1.50% in February 2020 to 0.9% in March 2020. In just one month, the spread between interest rates on Baa and Treasury bonds rose by 140 basis points, from 2.1% before the pandemic to 3.40% in March 2020, when the pandemic spread worldwide. ◆

Liquidity

Another attribute of a bond that influences its interest rate is its liquidity. As we learned in Chapter 4, a liquid asset is one that can be quickly and cheaply converted into cash if the need arises. The more liquid an asset is, the more desirable it is (holding everything else constant). U.S. Treasury bonds are the most liquid of all long-term bonds; because they are so widely traded, they are the easiest to sell quickly, and the cost of selling them is low. Corporate bonds are not as liquid because fewer bonds for any one corporation are traded; thus it can be costly to sell these bonds in an emergency because it might be hard to find buyers quickly.

How does the reduced liquidity of the corporate bonds affect their interest rates relative to the interest rate on Treasury bonds? We can use supply and demand analysis with the same figure that was used to analyze the effect of default risk, Figure 2, to show that the lower liquidity of corporate bonds relative to Treasury bonds increases the spread between the interest rates on these two bonds.

Let's start the analysis by assuming that, initially, corporate and Treasury bonds are equally liquid and all their other attributes are the same. As shown in Figure 2, their equilibrium prices and interest rates will initially be equal: $P_1^c = P_1^T$ and $i_1^c = i_1^T$. If the corporate bond becomes less liquid than the Treasury bond because it is less widely traded, then (as the theory of portfolio choice indicates) demand for it will fall, shifting its demand curve leftward from D_1^c to D_2^c, as in panel (a). The Treasury bond now becomes relatively more liquid in comparison with the corporate bond, so its demand curve shifts rightward from D_1^T to D_2^T, as in panel (b). The shifts in the curves in Figure 2 show that the price of the less liquid corporate bond falls and its interest rate rises, while the price of the more liquid Treasury bond rises and its interest rate falls.

The result is that the spread between the interest rates on the two bond types ri
Therefore, the differences between interest rates on corporate bonds and Treasu
bonds (that is, the risk premiums) reflect not only the corporate bonds' default risk bu
also their lesser liquidity. This is why a risk premium should more accurately be called
a "risk and liquidity premium," but convention dictates the label *risk premium*.

Income Tax Considerations

Returning to Figure 1, we are still left with one puzzle—the behavior of municipal
bond rates. Municipal bonds are certainly not default-free: State and local governments
have defaulted on municipal bonds in the past, particularly during the Great Depression, and even more recently in the cases of Detroit, Michigan; San Bernadino, Mam-
moth Lakes, and Stockton, all in California; Jefferson County, Alabama; Harrisburg,
Pennsylvania; Central Falls, Rhode Island; and Boise County, Idaho. Also, municipal
bonds are not as liquid as U.S. Treasury bonds.

Why is it, then, that these bonds have had lower interest rates than U.S. Treasury bonds for most of the past 100 years, as indicated in Figure 1? The explanation
lies in the fact that interest payments on municipal bonds are exempt from federal
income taxes, a factor that has the same effect on the demand for municipal bonds as
an increase in their expected return.

Let's imagine that your income is high enough to put you in a 40% income tax
bracket, where for every extra dollar of income you earn you have to pay 40 cents to the
government. If you own a $1,000-face-value U.S. Treasury bond that sells for $1,000
and has a coupon payment of $100, you get to keep only $60 of the payment after taxes.
Although the bond has a 10% interest rate, you actually earn only 6.0% after taxes.

Suppose, however, that you put your savings into a $1,000-face-value municipal
bond that sells for $1,000 and pays only $80 in coupon payments. Its interest rate is
only 8%, but because it is a tax-exempt security, you pay no taxes on the $80 coupon
payment, so you earn 8% after taxes. Clearly, you earn more on the municipal bond
after taxes, so you are willing to hold the riskier and less liquid municipal bond even
though it has a lower interest rate than the U.S. Treasury bond. (This was not true
before World War II, when the tax-exempt status of municipal bonds did not convey
much of an advantage because income tax rates were extremely low.)

Another way of understanding why municipal bonds have lower interest rates than
Treasury bonds is to use the supply and demand analysis depicted in Figure 3. We initially assume that municipal and Treasury bonds have identical attributes and so have
the same bond prices as drawn in the figure, $P_1^m = P_1^T$, and the same interest rates. Once
the municipal bonds are given a tax advantage that raises their after-tax expected return
relative to Treasury bonds and makes them more desirable, demand for them rises, and
their demand curve shifts to the right, from D_1^m to D_2^m. Their equilibrium bond price
then rises from P_1^m to P_2^m, and their equilibrium interest rate falls. By contrast, Treasury
bonds have now become less desirable relative to municipal bonds; demand for Treasury bonds decreases, and D_1^T shifts to the left to D_2^T. The Treasury bond price falls from
P_1^T to P_2^T, and the interest rate rises. The federal income tax exemption, which leads to
a higher expected return for municipal bonds relative to Treasury bonds, explains why
municipal bonds can have interest rates below those of Treasury bonds.[1]

---

[1]In contrast to corporate bonds, Treasury bonds are exempt from state and local income taxes. Using the analysis
in the text, you should be able to show that this feature of Treasury bonds provides an additional reason why interest rates on corporate bonds are higher than those on Treasury bonds.

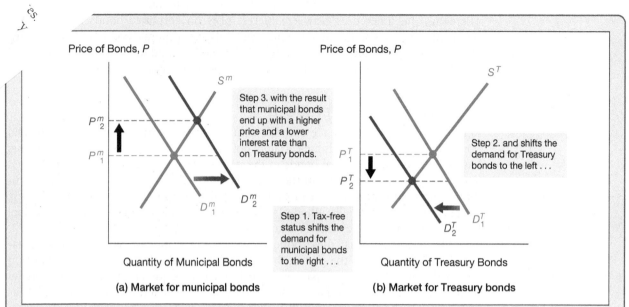

FIGURE 3 **Interest Rates on Municipal and Treasury Bonds**

When a municipal bond is given tax-free status, demand for the municipal bond shifts rightward from D_1^m to D_2^m and demand for the Treasury bond shifts leftward from D_1^T to D_2^T. The equilibrium price of the municipal bond rises from P_1^m to P_2^m, so its interest rate falls, while the equilibrium price of the Treasury bond falls from P_1^T to P_2^T and its interest rate rises. The result is that municipal bonds end up with lower interest rates than Treasury bonds.

Summary

The risk structure of interest rates (the relationships among interest rates on bonds with the same maturity) is explained by three factors: default risk, liquidity, and the income tax treatment of a bond's interest payments. As a bond's default risk increases, the risk premium on that bond (the spread between its interest rate and the interest rate on a default-free Treasury bond) rises. The greater liquidity of Treasury bonds also explains why their interest rates are lower than those on less liquid bonds. If a bond has a favorable tax treatment, as do municipal bonds, whose interest payments are exempt from federal income taxes, its interest rate will be lower.

APPLICATION ## Effects of the Trump Tax Cuts on Bond Interest Rates

In 2017, Congress approved legislation proposed by the Trump administration to decrease the income tax rate on high-income taxpayers from 39.6% to 37% when it repealed the tax increases implemented under the Obama administration. What was the effect of this income tax decrease on interest rates in the municipal bond market relative to those in the Treasury bond market?

Our supply and demand analysis provides the answer. A lower income tax rate for wealthy people means that the after-tax expected return on tax-free municipal bonds relative to that on Treasury bonds is lower, because the interest on Treasury bonds is now taxed at a lower rate. Because municipal bonds now become less desirable, their demand decreases, shifting the demand curve to the left, which lowers their price and raises their interest rate. Conversely, the lower income tax rate makes Treasury bonds more desirable; this change shifts their demand curve to the right, raises their price, and lowers their interest rates.

Our analysis thus shows that the cut in income tax rates for wealthy people helped to raise the interest rates on municipal bonds relative to the interest rate on Treasury bonds. ◆

6.2 TERM STRUCTURE OF INTEREST RATES

LO 6.2 List and explain the three theories of why interest rates vary across different maturities.

We have seen how risk, liquidity, and tax considerations (collectively embedded in the risk structure) can influence interest rates. Another factor that influences the interest rate on a bond is its term to maturity: Bonds with identical risk, liquidity, and tax characteristics may have different interest rates because their times remaining to maturity are different. A plot of the yields on bonds with differing terms to maturity but the same risk, liquidity, and tax considerations is called a **yield curve**, and it describes the term structure of interest rates for particular types of bonds, such as government bonds. The Following

Following the Financial News   Yield Curves

Many newspapers and Internet sites such as http://www.finance.yahoo.com publish a daily plot of the yield curves for Treasury securities. An example for May 22, 2020, is presented here. The numbers on the vertical axis indicate the interest rate for the Treasury security, with the maturity term given on the horizontal axis, with "m" denoting "month" and "y" denoting "year."

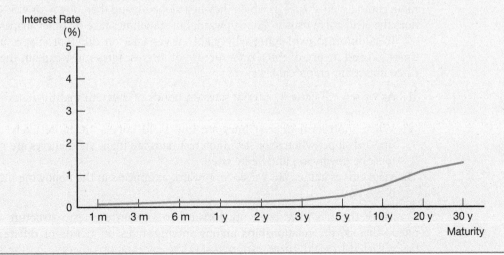

Real-time data

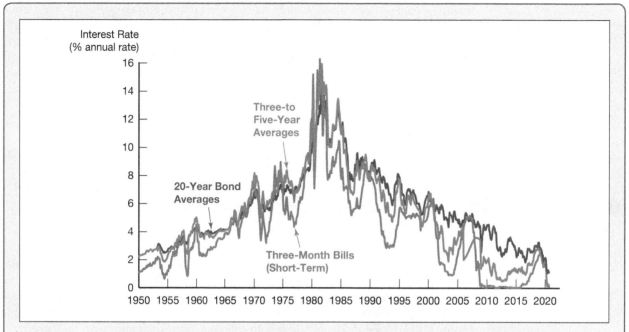

FIGURE 4   Movements over Time of Interest Rates on U.S. Government Bonds with Different Maturities

Interest rates on bonds of different maturities move together over time.

Source: Federal Reserve Bank of St. Louis FRED database: https://fred.stlouisfed.org/series/TB3MS; https://fred.stlouisfed.org/series/GS3; https://fred.stlouisfed.org/series/GS5; https://fred.stlouisfed.org/series/GS20.

the Financial News box shows a yield curve for Treasury securities. Yield curves can be classified as upward-sloping, flat, or downward-sloping (the last sort is often referred to as an **inverted yield curve**). When yield curves slope upward, which is the most common case, long-term interest rates are above short-term interest rates; when yield curves are flat, short- and long-term interest rates are the same; and when yield curves are inverted, long-term interest rates are below short-term interest rates. Yield curves can also have more complicated shapes in which they first slope up and then down, or vice versa. Why does the yield curve usually slope upward, but sometimes take on other shapes?

In addition to explaining why yield curves take on different shapes at different times, a good theory of the term structure of interest rates must explain the following three important empirical facts:

1. As we see in Figure 4, interest rates on bonds of different maturities move together over time.
2. When short-term interest rates are low, yield curves are more likely to have an upward slope; when short-term interest rates are high, yield curves are more likely to slope downward and be inverted.
3. Yield curves almost always slope upward, as appears in the Following the Financial News box.

Three theories have been put forward to explain the term structure of interest rates—that is, the relationships among interest rates on bonds of different maturities reflected in yield curve patterns—(1) the expectations theory, (2) the segmented markets theory, and (3) the liquidity premium theory. Each of these theories is described in the following sections. The expectations theory does a good job of explaining the first two facts on our list, but not the third. The segmented markets theory can account for fact 3 but not the other two facts, which are well explained by the expectations theory. Because each theory explains facts that the other cannot, a natural way of seeking a better understanding of the term structure is to combine the features of both theories, which leads us to the liquidity premium theory, a theory that explains all three facts.

If the liquidity premium theory does a better job of explaining the facts and is hence the most widely accepted theory, why do we spend time discussing the other two theories? There are two reasons. First, the ideas in these two theories lay the groundwork for the liquidity premium theory. Second, it is important to see how economists modify theories to improve them when they find that the predicted results are inconsistent with the empirical evidence.

Expectations Theory

The **expectations theory** of the term structure states the following commonsense proposition: The interest rate on a long-term bond will equal the average of the short-term interest rates that people expect to occur over the life of the long-term bond. For example, if people expect that short-term interest rates will be 10%, on average, over the coming five years, the expectations theory predicts that the interest rate on bonds with five years to maturity will be 10%, too. If short-term interest rates are expected to rise even higher after this five-year period, so that the average short-term interest rate over the coming 20 years is 11%, then the interest rate on 20-year bonds will equal 11% and will be higher than the interest rate on five-year bonds. Thus the expectations theory predicts that interest rates on bonds of different maturities differ because short-term interest rates are expected to have different values at future dates.

The key assumption behind this theory is that buyers of bonds do not prefer bonds of one maturity over another, so they will not hold any quantity of a bond if its expected return is less than that of another bond with a different maturity. Bonds that have this characteristic are said to be *perfect substitutes*. In practice, this means that if bonds with different maturities are perfect substitutes, then the expected returns on those bonds must be equal.

To see how the assumption that bonds with different maturities are perfect substitutes leads to the expectations theory, let us consider the following two investment strategies:

1. Purchase a one-year bond, and when it matures in one year, purchase another one-year bond.
2. Purchase a two-year bond and hold it until maturity.

Because both strategies must have the same expected return, the interest rate on the two-year bond must equal the average of the two one-year interest rates. For example, let's say that the current interest rate on the one-year bond is 9%, and you expect the interest rate on the one-year bond next year to be 11%. If you pursue the first strategy of buying the two one-year bonds, the expected return over the two years will average out to be (9% + 11%)/2 = 10% per year. You will be willing to hold both the one- and two-year bonds only if the expected return per year on the two-year bond equals this return. Therefore, the interest rate on the two-year bond must equal 10%, the average interest rate on the two one-year bonds.

We can make this argument more general. For an investment of $1, consider the choice of holding, for two periods, a two-period bond or two one-period bonds. Using the definitions

i_t = today's (time t) interest rate on a one-period bond
i^e_{t+1} = interest rate on a one-period bond expected for next period (time $t + 1$)
i_{2t} = today's (time t) interest rate on the two-period bond

the expected return from investing $1 in the two-period bond and holding it for the two periods can be calculated as

$$(1 + i_{2t})(1 + i_{2t}) - 1 = 1 + 2i_{2t} + (i_{2t})^2 - 1 = 2i_{2t} + (i_{2t})^2$$

After the second period, the $1 investment is worth $(1 + i_{2t})(1 + i_{2t})$. Subtracting the $1 initial investment from this amount and dividing by the initial $1 investment gives the rate of return calculated in the previous equation. Because $(i_{2t})^2$ is extremely small—if $i_{2t} = 10\% = 0.10$, then $(i_{2t})^2 = 0.01$—we can simplify the expected return for holding the two-period bond for the two periods to

$$2i_{2t}$$

With the other strategy, in which one-period bonds are bought, the expected return on the $1 investment over the two periods is

$$(1 + i_t)(1 + i^e_{t+1}) - 1 = 1 + i_t + i^e_{t+1} + i_t(i^e_{t+1}) - 1 = i_t + i^e_{t+1} + i_t(i^e_{t+1})$$

This calculation is derived by recognizing that, after the first period, the $1 investment becomes $1 + i_t$, and this is reinvested in the one-period bond for the next period, yielding an amount $(1 + i_t)(1 + i^e_{t+1})$. Then, subtracting the $1 initial investment from this amount and dividing by the initial investment of $1 gives the expected return for the strategy of holding one-period bonds for the two periods. Because $i_t(i^e_{t+1})$ is also extremely small—if $i_t = i^e_{t+1} = 0.10$, then $i_t(i^e_{t+1}) = 0.01$—we can simplify this to

$$i_t + i^e_{t+1}$$

Both bonds will be held only if these expected returns are equal—that is, when

$$2i_{2t} = i_t + i^e_{t+1}$$

Solving for i_{2t} in terms of the one-period rates, we have

$$i_{2t} = \frac{i_t + i^e_{t+1}}{2} \tag{1}$$

which tells us that the two-period rate must equal the average of the two one-period rates. Graphically, this can be shown as

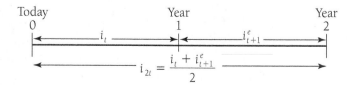

We can conduct the same steps for bonds with longer maturities so that we can examine the whole term structure of interest rates. By doing so, we find that the interest rate *int* on an *n*-period bond must be

$$i_{\mathrm{nt}} = \frac{i_t + i_{t+1}^e + i_{t+2}^e + \ldots + i_{t+(n-1)}^e}{n} \tag{2}$$

Equation 2 states that the *n*-period interest rate equals the average of the one-period interest rates expected to occur over the *n*-period life of the bond. This is a restatement of the expectations theory, in more precise terms.[2]

A simple numerical example might help clarify the expectations theory presented in Equation 2. If the one-year interest rates over the next five years are expected to be 5%, 6%, 7%, 8%, and 9%, Equation 2 indicates that the interest rate on the two-year bond will be

$$\frac{5\% + 6\%}{2} = 5.5\%$$

On the five-year bond, it will be

$$\frac{5\% + 6\% + 7\% + 8\% + 9\%}{5} = 7\%$$

By doing similar calculations for the one-, three-, and four-year interest rates, you should be able to verify that the one- to five-year interest rates are 5.0%, 5.5%, 6.0%, 6.5%, and 7.0%, respectively. Thus we see that the rising trend in expected short-term interest rates produces an upward-sloping yield curve along which interest rates rise as maturity lengthens.

The expectations theory is an elegant theory that explains why the term structure of interest rates (as represented by yield curves) changes at different times. When the yield curve is upward-sloping, the expectations theory suggests that short-term interest rates are expected to rise in the future, as we have seen in our numerical example. In this situation, in which the long-term rate is currently higher than the short-term rate, the average of future short-term rates is expected to be higher than the current short-term rate, which can occur only if short-term interest rates are expected to rise. This result is depicted in our numerical example. When the yield curve is inverted (slopes downward), the average of future short-term interest rates is expected to be lower than the current short-term rate, implying that short-term interest rates are expected to fall, on average, in the future. Only when the yield curve is flat does the expectations theory suggest that short-term interest rates are not expected to change, on average, in the future.

The expectations theory also explains fact 1, which states that interest rates on bonds with different maturities move together over time. Historically, short-term interest rates have shown the following trend: If they increase today, they will tend to be higher in the future. Hence a rise in short-term rates will raise people's expectations of future higher short-term rates. Because long-term rates are the average of expected future short-term rates, a rise in short-term rates will also raise long-term rates, causing short- and long-term rates to move together.

---

[2]The analysis here has been conducted for discount bonds. Formulas for interest rates on coupon bonds would differ slightly from those used here but would convey the same principle.

The expectations theory also explains fact 2, which states that yield curves tend to have an upward slope when short-term interest rates are low and be inverted when short-term rates are high. When short-term rates are low, people generally expect them to rise to some normal level in the future, and the average of future expected short-term rates is high relative to the current short-term rate. Therefore, long-term interest rates will be substantially higher than current short-term rates, and the yield curve will have an upward slope. Conversely, if short-term rates are high, people usually expect them to come back down. Long-term rates will then drop below short-term rates because the average of expected future short-term rates will be lower than current short-term rates, and the yield curve will slope downward and become inverted.[3]

The expectations theory is an attractive theory because it provides a simple explanation of the behavior of the term structure, but unfortunately it has a major shortcoming: It cannot explain fact 3, which states that yield curves usually slope upward. The typical upward slope of yield curves implies that short-term interest rates are usually expected to rise in the future. In practice, short-term interest rates are just as likely to fall as they are to rise, and so the expectations theory suggests that the typical yield curve should be flat rather than upward-sloping.

Segmented Markets Theory

As the name suggests, the **segmented markets theory** of the term structure sees markets for different-maturity bonds as completely separate and segmented. The interest rate on a bond of a particular maturity is then determined by the supply of and demand for that bond and is not affected by expected returns on other bonds with other maturities.

The key assumption of the segmented markets theory is that bonds of different maturities are not substitutes at all, and so the expected return from holding a bond of one maturity has no effect on the demand for a bond of another maturity. This theory of the term structure is the opposite extreme of the expectations theory, which assumes that bonds of different maturities are perfect substitutes.

The argument for why bonds of different maturities are not substitutes is that investors have very strong preferences for bonds of one maturity as opposed to another, so they are concerned only with the expected returns on bonds of the maturity they prefer. This might be because they have a particular holding period in mind, and if they match the maturity of the bond to the desired holding period, they can obtain a certain return with no risk at all.[4] (We saw in Chapter 4 that if the term to maturity equals the holding period, then the return is known for certain because it equals the yield exactly, and no interest-rate risk exists.) For example, people who are limited by a short holding

---

[3]The expectations theory explains another important fact about the relationship between short-term and long-term interest rates. As you can see in Figure 4, short-term interest rates are more volatile than long-term rates. If interest rates are *mean-reverting*—that is, if they tend to head back down after they reach unusually high levels or go back up after they fall to unusually low levels—then an average of these short-term rates must necessarily have less volatility than the short-term rates themselves. Because the expectations theory suggests that the long-term rate will be equal to an average of future short-term rates, it implies that the long-term rate will have less volatility than short-term rates.

[4]The statement that there is no uncertainty about the return if the term to maturity equals the holding period is literally true only for a discount bond. For a coupon bond with a long holding period, some risk exists because coupon payments must be reinvested before the bond matures. Our analysis here is thus being conducted for discount bonds. However, the gist of the analysis remains the same for coupon bonds because the amount of risk from reinvestment is small when coupon bonds have the same term to maturity as the holding period.

period will prefer to hold short-term bonds. Conversely, if you are putting away funds for your young child to go to college in the future, your desired holding period will be much longer, and you will want to hold longer-term bonds.

In the segmented markets theory, differing yield curve patterns are accounted for by supply and demand differences associated with bonds of different maturities. If, as seems sensible, risk-averse investors have short desired holding periods and generally prefer bonds with shorter maturities that have less interest-rate risk, the segmented markets theory can explain fact 3, which states that yield curves typically slope upward. Because the demand for long-term bonds is typically relatively lower than that for short-term bonds, long-term bonds will have lower prices and higher interest rates, and hence the yield curve will typically slope upward.

Although the segmented markets theory can explain why yield curves usually tend to slope upward, it has a major flaw in that it cannot explain facts 1 and 2. First, because it views the market for bonds of different maturities as completely segmented, there is no reason that a rise in the interest rate on a bond of one maturity would affect the interest rate on a bond of another maturity. Therefore, the segmented markets theory cannot explain why interest rates on bonds of different maturities tend to move together (fact 1). Second, because it is not clear how the demand for and supply of short- versus long-term bonds change with the level of short-term interest rates, the theory does not explain why yield curves tend to slope upward when short-term interest rates are low and to be inverted when short-term interest rates are high (fact 2).

Because each of our two theories explains empirical facts that the other cannot, a logical step is to combine the theories, which leads us to the liquidity premium theory.

Liquidity Premium and Preferred Habitat Theories

The **liquidity premium theory** of the term structure states that the interest rate on a long-term bond will equal an average of short-term interest rates expected to occur over the life of the long-term bond plus a liquidity premium (also referred to as a term premium) that responds to supply and demand conditions for that bond.

The liquidity premium theory's key assumption is that bonds of different maturities are substitutes, which means that the expected return on one bond *does* influence the expected return on a bond of a different maturity. However, the theory allows investors to prefer one bond maturity over another. In other words, bonds of different maturities are assumed to be substitutes, but not *perfect* substitutes. Investors tend to prefer shorter-term bonds because these bonds bear less interest-rate risk. For this reason, investors must be offered a positive liquidity premium to induce them to hold longer-term bonds. Thus the expectations theory is modified by adding a positive liquidity premium to the equation that describes the relationship between long- and short-term interest rates. The liquidity premium theory is written as

$$i_{nt} = \frac{i_t + i_{t+1}^e + i_{t+2}^e + \cdots + i_{t+(n-1)}^e}{n} + l_{nt} \tag{3}$$

where l_{nt} is the liquidity (term) premium for the n-period bond at time t, which is always positive and rises with the term to maturity of the bond, n.

Closely related to the liquidity premium theory is the **preferred habitat theory**, which takes a somewhat less direct approach to modifying the expectations hypothesis but comes to a similar conclusion. It assumes that investors have a preference for bonds of one maturity over bonds of another—a particular bond maturity ("preferred

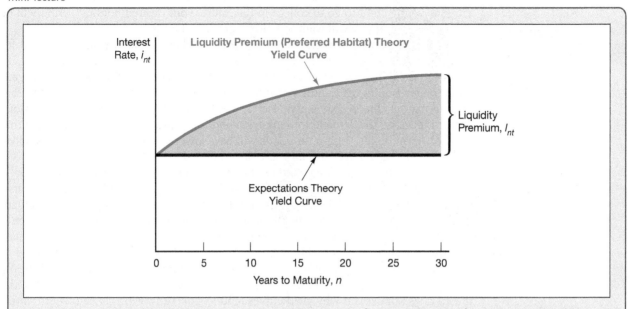

FIGURE 5 **The Relationship Between the Liquidity Premium (Preferred Habitat) and Expectations Theory**
Because the liquidity premium is always positive and grows as the term to maturity increases, the yield curve implied by the liquidity premium and preferred habitat theories is always above the yield curve implied by the expectations theory and has a steeper slope. For simplicity, the yield curve implied by the expectations theory shown here assumes unchanging future one-year interest rates.

habitat") in which they prefer to invest. Because they prefer bonds of one maturity over bonds of another, they are willing to buy bonds that do not have the preferred maturity (habitat) only if those bonds earn a somewhat higher expected return. Because risk-averse investors are likely to prefer the habitat of short-term bonds over that of longer-term bonds, they are willing to hold long-term bonds only if they have higher expected returns. This reasoning leads to the same Equation 3 implied by the liquidity premium theory, with a term premium that typically rises with maturity.

The relationship between the expectations theory and the liquidity premium and preferred habitat theories is shown in Figure 5. There we see that because the liquidity premium is always positive and typically grows as the term to maturity increases, the yield curve implied by the liquidity premium theory is always above the yield curve implied by the expectations theory and generally has a steeper slope. (For simplicity, we are assuming that the expectations theory yield curve is flat.)

A simple numerical example, similar to the one we used for the expectations hypothesis, further clarifies the liquidity premium and preferred habitat theories given in Equation 3. Again suppose that the one-year interest rates over the next five years are expected to be 5%, 6%, 7%, 8%, and 9%, while investors' preferences for holding short-term bonds means that the liquidity premiums for one- to five-year bonds are 0%, 0.25%, 0.5%, 0.75%, and 1.0%, respectively. Equation 3 then indicates that the interest rate on the two-year bond would be

$$\frac{5\% + 6\%}{2} + 0.25\% = 5.75\%$$

For the five-year bond, it would be

$$\frac{5\% + 6\% + 7\% + 8\% + 9\%}{5} + 1\% = 8\%$$

By doing similar calculations for the one-, three-, and four-year interest rates, you should be able to verify that the one- to five-year interest rates are 5.0%, 5.75%, 6.5%, 7.25%, and 8.0%, respectively. Comparing these findings with those for the expectations theory, we see that the liquidity premium and preferred habitat theories produce yield curves that slope more steeply upward because of investors' preferences for short-term bonds.

Let's see if the liquidity premium and preferred habitat theories are consistent with all three empirical facts we have discussed. They explain fact 1, which states that interest rates on different-maturity bonds move together over time: A rise in short-term interest rates indicates that short-term interest rates will, on average, be higher in the future, and the first term in Equation 3 then implies that long-term interest rates will rise along with them.

The liquidity and preferred habitat theories also explain why yield curves tend to have an especially steep upward slope when short-term interest rates are low and to be inverted when short-term rates are high (fact 2). Because investors generally expect short-term interest rates to rise to some normal level when they are low, the average of future expected short-term rates will be high relative to the current short-term rate. With the additional boost of a positive liquidity premium, long-term interest rates will be substantially higher than current short-term rates, and the yield curve will have a steep upward slope. Conversely, if short-term rates are high, people usually expect them to come back down. Long-term rates will then drop below short-term rates because the average of expected future short-term rates will be far below current short-term rates, despite positive liquidity premiums, and so the yield curve will slope downward.

The liquidity premium and preferred habitat theories explain fact 3, which states that yield curves typically slope upward, by recognizing that the liquidity premium rises with a bond's maturity because of investors' preferences for short-term bonds. Even if short-term interest rates are expected to stay the same, on average, in the future, long-term interest rates will be above short-term interest rates, and yield curves will typically slope upward.

How can the liquidity premium and preferred habitat theories explain the occasional appearance of inverted yield curves if the liquidity premium is positive? It must be that, at times, short-term interest rates are expected to fall so much in the future that the average of the expected short-term rates is well below the current short-term rate. Even when the positive liquidity premium is added to this average, the resulting long-term rate is still lower than the current short-term interest rate.

As our discussion indicates, a particularly attractive feature of the liquidity premium and preferred habitat theories is that you can see what the market is predicting about future short-term interest rates just from the slope of the yield curve. A steeply rising yield curve, as in panel (a) of Figure 6, indicates that short-term interest rates are expected to rise in the future. A moderately steep yield curve, as in panel (b), indicates that short-term interest rates are not expected to rise or fall much in the future. A flat yield curve, as in panel (c), indicates that short-term rates are expected to fall moderately in the future. Finally, an inverted yield curve, as in panel (d), indicates that short-term interest rates are expected to fall sharply in the future.

Mini-lecture

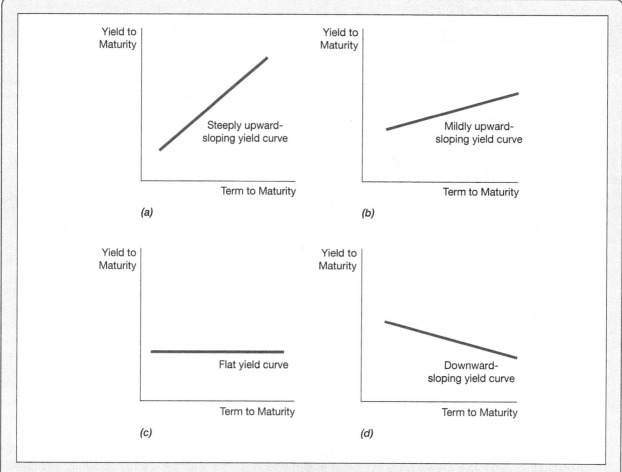

FIGURE 6   Yield Curves and the Market's Expectations of Future Short-Term Interest Rates According to the Liquidity Premium (Preferred Habitat) Theory

A steeply rising yield curve, as in panel (a), indicates that short-term interest rates are expected to rise in the future. A moderately steep yield curve, as in panel (b), indicates that short-term interest rates are not expected to rise or fall much in the future. A flat yield curve, as in panel (c), indicates that short-term rates are expected to fall moderately in the future. Finally, an inverted yield curve, as in panel (d), indicates that short-term interest rates are expected to fall sharply in the future.

Evidence on the Term Structure

In the 1980s, researchers examining the term structure of interest rates questioned whether the slope of the yield curve provides information about movements of future short-term interest rates. They found that the spread between long- and short-term interest rates does not always help predict future short-term interest rates, a finding that may stem from substantial fluctuations in the liquidity (term) premium for long-term bonds. More recent research using more discriminating tests now favors a different view. It shows that the term structure contains quite a bit of information for the very short run (over the next several months) and the long run (over several years) but

FYI   The Yield Curve as a Forecasting Tool for Inflation and the Business Cycle

Because the yield curve contains information about future expected interest rates, it should have the capacity to help forecast inflation and real output fluctuations. To see why, recall from Chapter 5 that rising interest rates are associated with economic booms and falling interest rates with recessions. When the yield curve is either flat or downward-sloping, it suggests that future short-term interest rates are expected to fall because the economy is more likely to enter a recession. Indeed, the yield curve is found to be an accurate predictor of the business cycle.

In Chapter 4, we learned that a nominal interest rate is composed of a real interest rate and expected inflation, implying that the yield curve contains information about both the future path of nominal interest rates and future inflation. A steep yield curve predicts a future increase in inflation, while a flat or downward-sloping yield curve forecasts a future decline in inflation.

Because the yield curve can be used to forecast business cycles and inflation, the slope of the yield curve is part of the tool kit of many economic forecasters and is often viewed as a useful indicator of the stance of monetary policy, with a steep yield curve indicating loose policy and a flat or downward-sloping yield curve indicating tight policy.

is unreliable at predicting movements in interest rates over the intermediate term (the time in between). Research also has found that the yield curve can be used to help forecast future inflation and business cycles (see the FYI box).

Summary

The liquidity premium and preferred habitat theories are the most widely accepted theories of the term structure of interest rates because they explain the major empirical facts about the term structure so well. They combine the features of both the expectations theory and the segmented markets theory by asserting that a long-term interest rate will be the sum of a liquidity (term) premium and the average of the short-term interest rates that are expected to occur over the life of the bond.

The liquidity premium and preferred habitat theories explain the following facts: (1) Interest rates on bonds of different maturities tend to move together over time; (2) when short-term interest rates are low, yield curves are more likely to have a steep upward slope; (3) yield curves usually slope upward, but when short-term interest rates are high, yield curves are more likely to be inverted.

The theories also help us predict the movement of short-term interest rates in the future. A steep upward slope of the yield curve means that short-term rates are expected to rise, a mild upward slope means that short-term rates are expected to remain the same, a flat slope means that short-term rates are expected to fall moderately, and an inverted yield curve means that short-term rates are expected to fall sharply.

APPLICATION   Interpreting Yield Curves, 1980–2020

Figure 7 illustrates several yield curves for U.S. government bonds, for selected dates from 1981 to 2020. What do these yield curves tell us about the public's expectations of future movements of short-term interest rates?

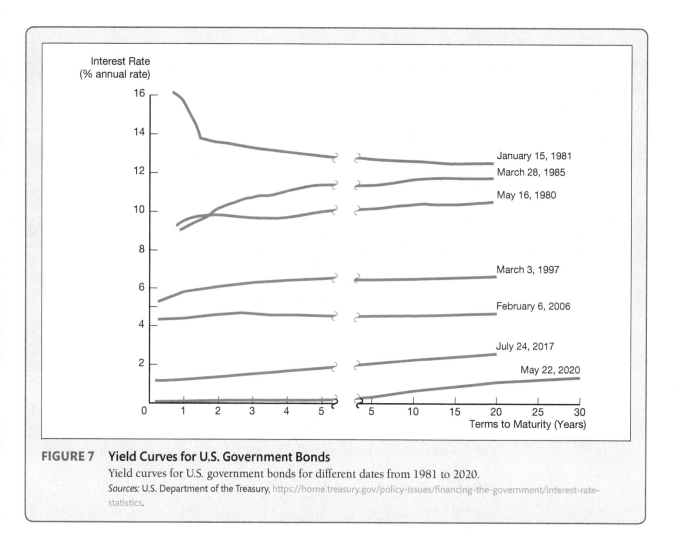

FIGURE 7 **Yield Curves for U.S. Government Bonds**
Yield curves for U.S. government bonds for different dates from 1981 to 2020.
Sources: U.S. Department of the Treasury, https://home.treasury.gov/policy-issues/financing-the-government/interest-rate-statistics.

The steep inverted yield curve that occurred on January 15, 1981, indicated that short-term interest rates were expected to decline sharply in the future. For longer-term interest rates, along with their positive liquidity premiums, to be well below short-term interest rates, short-term interest rates must be expected to decline so sharply that their average would be far below the current short-term rate. Indeed, the public's expectations of sharply lower short-term interest rates evident in the yield curve were realized soon after January 15; by March, three-month Treasury bill rates had declined from the 16% level to 13%.

The steep, upward-sloping yield curves that occurred on March 28, 1985, and July 24, 2017, indicated that short-term interest rates were expected to climb in the future. Long-term interest rates are higher than short-term interest rates when short-term interest rates are expected to rise because their average plus the liquidity premium will be higher than the current short-term rate. The moderately upward-sloping yield curves on May 16, 1980, March 3, 1997, and May 22, 2020, indicated that short-term interest rates were expected neither to rise nor to fall in the near future. In this case, their average remains the same as the current short-term rate, and the positive liquidity premium for longer-term bonds explains the moderate upward slope of the yield curve. The flat yield curve of February 6, 2006, indicated that short-term interest rates were expected to fall slightly. ◆

SUMMARY

1. Bonds with the same maturity will have different interest rates because of three factors: default risk, liquidity, and tax considerations. The greater a bond's default risk, the higher its interest rate relative to the interest rates of other bonds; the greater a bond's liquidity, the lower its interest rate; and bonds with tax-exempt status will have lower interest rates than they otherwise would. The relationship among interest rates on bonds with the same maturity that arises because of these three factors is known as the *risk structure of interest rates*.

2. Three theories of the term structure provide explanations of how interest rates on bonds with different terms to maturity are related. The expectations theory views long-term interest rates as equaling the average of future short-term interest rates expected to occur over the life of the bond. By contrast, the segmented markets theory treats the determination of interest rates for each bond's maturity as the outcome of supply and demand in that market only. Neither of these theories by itself can explain the fact that interest rates on bonds of different maturities move together over time and that yield curves usually slope upward.

3. The liquidity premium (preferred habitat) theory combines the features of the other two theories, and by so doing is able to explain the facts just mentioned. The liquidity premium (preferred habitat) theory views long-term interest rates as equaling the average of future short-term interest rates expected to occur over the life of the bond plus a liquidity premium. The liquidity premium (preferred habitat) theory allows us to infer the market's expectations about the movement of future short-term interest rates from the yield curve. A steeply upward-sloping curve indicates that future short-term rates are expected to rise; a mildly upward-sloping curve, that short-term rates are expected to stay the same; a flat curve, that short-term rates are expected to decline slightly; and an inverted yield curve, that a substantial decline in short-term rates is expected in the future.

KEY TERMS

credit-rating agencies, p. 120
default, p. 118
default-free bonds, p. 118
expectations theory, p. 127
inverted yield curve, p. 126

junk bonds, p. 121
liquidity premium theory, p. 131
preferred habitat theory, p. 131
risk premium, p. 118
risk structure of interest rates, p. 117

segmented markets theory, p. 130
term structure of interest rates, p. 117
yield curve, p. 125

QUESTIONS

1. If junk bonds are "junk," then why do investors buy them?

2. Which should have the higher risk premium on its interest rates, a corporate bond with a Moody's Baa rating or a corporate bond with a C rating? Why?

3. Do you think that a U.S. Treasury bill will have a risk premium that is higher than, lower than, or the same as that of a similar security (in terms of maturity and liquidity) issued by the government of Colombia?

4. In the fall of 2008, AIG, the largest insurance company in the world at the time, was at risk of defaulting due to the severity of the global financial crisis. As a result, the U.S. government stepped in to support AIG with large capital injections and an ownership stake. How would this affect, if at all, the yield and risk premium on AIG corporate debt?

5. Risk premiums on corporate bonds are usually *anticyclical*; that is, they decrease during business cycle expansions and increase during recessions. Why is this so?

6. Just before the collapse of the subprime mortgage market in 2007, the most important credit-rating agencies rated mortgage-backed securities with Aaa and AAA ratings. Explain how it was possible that a few months into 2008, the same securities had the lowest possible ratings. Should we always trust credit-rating agencies?

7. The U.S. Treasury offers some of its debt as Treasury Inflation Indexed Securities, or TIIS (more commonly known as TIPS, an acronym for Treasury Inflation Protected Securities), in which the price of bonds is adjusted for inflation over the life of the debt instrument. TIPS bonds are traded on a much smaller scale than nominal U.S. Treasury bonds of equivalent maturity. What can you conclude about the liquidity premiums of TIPS versus nominal U.S. bonds?

8. Predict what will happen to interest rates on a corporation's bonds if the federal government guarantees today that it will pay creditors if the corporation goes bankrupt in the future. What will happen to the interest rates on Treasury securities?

9. Predict what would happen to the risk premiums of municipal bonds if the federal government guarantees today that it will pay creditors if municipal governments default on their payments. Do you think that it will then make sense for municipal bonds to be exempt from income taxes?

10. During 2008, the difference in yield (the *yield spread*) between three-month AA-rated financial commercial paper and three-month AA-rated nonfinancial commercial paper steadily increased from its usual level of close to zero, spiking to over a full percentage point at its peak in October 2008. What explains this sudden increase?

11. If the income tax exemption on municipal bonds were abolished, what would happen to the interest rates on these bonds? What effect would the change have on interest rates on U.S. Treasury securities?

12. Prior to 2008, mortgage lenders required a house inspection to assess a home's value and often used the same one or two inspection companies in the same geographic market. Following the collapse of the housing market in 2008, mortgage lenders required a house inspection, but this inspection was arranged through a third party. How does the pre-2008 scenario illustrate a conflict of interest similar to the role that credit-rating agencies played in the global financial crisis?

13. "According to the expectations theory of the term structure, it is better to invest in one-year bonds, reinvested over two years, than to invest in a two-year bond if interest rates on one-year bonds are expected to be the same in both years." Is this statement true, false, or uncertain?

14. If bond investors decide that 30-year bonds are no longer as desirable an investment as they were previously, predict what will happen to the yield curve, assuming (a) the expectations theory of the term structure holds; and (b) the segmented markets theory of the term structure holds.

15. Suppose the interest rates on one-, five-, and ten-year U.S. Treasury bonds are currently 3%, 6%, and 6%, respectively. Investor A chooses to hold only one-year bonds, and Investor B is indifferent with regard to holding five- and ten-year bonds. How can you explain the behavior of Investors A and B?

16. If a yield curve looks like the one shown in the figure below, what is the market predicting about the movement of future short-term interest rates? What might the yield curve indicate about the market's predictions for the inflation rate in the future?

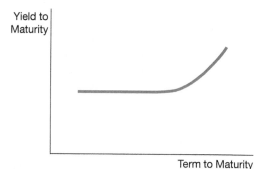

17. If a yield curve looks like the one shown in the figure below, what is the market predicting about the movement of future short-term interest rates? What might the yield curve indicate about the market's predictions for the inflation rate in the future?

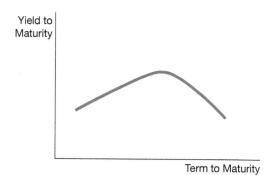

18. If yield curves, on average, were flat, what would this say about the liquidity (term) premiums in the term structure? Would you be more or less willing to accept the expectations theory?

19. If the yield curve suddenly became steeper, how would you revise your predictions of interest rates in the future?

20. If expectations of future short-term interest rates suddenly fell, what would happen to the slope of the yield curve?

21. Following a policy meeting on March 19, 2009, the Federal Reserve made an announcement that it would purchase up to $300 billion of longer-term Treasury securities over the following six months. What effect might this policy have on the yield curve?

APPLIED PROBLEMS

22. In 2010 and 2011, the government of Greece risked defaulting on its debt due to a severe budget crisis. Using bond market graphs, compare the effects on the risk premium between U.S. Treasury debt and comparable-maturity Greek debt.

23. Assuming the expectations theory is the correct theory of the term structure, calculate the interest rates in the term structure for maturities of one to five years, and plot the resulting yield curves for the following paths of one-year interest rates over the next five years:

    a. 5%, 7%, 7%, 7%, 7%

    b. 5%, 4%, 4%, 4%, 4%

    How would your yield curves change if people preferred shorter-term bonds to longer-term bonds?

24. Assuming the expectations theory is the correct theory of the term structure, calculate the interest rates in the term structure for maturities of one to five years, and plot the resulting yield curves for the following paths of one-year interest rates over the next five years:

    a. 5%, 6%, 7%, 6%, 5%

    b. 5%, 4%, 3%, 4%, 5%

    How would your yield curves change if people preferred shorter-term bonds over longer-term bonds?

25. The table below shows current and expected future one-year interest rates, as well as current interest rates on multiyear bonds. Use the table to calculate the liquidity premium for each multiyear bond.

Year	One-Year Bond Rate	Multiyear Bond Rate
1	2%	2%
2	3%	3%
3	4%	5%
4	6%	6%
5	7%	8%

DATA ANALYSIS PROBLEMS

The Problems update with real-time data in **MyLab Economics** and are available for practice or instructor assignment.

1. **Real-time Data Analysis** Go to the St. Louis Federal Reserve FRED database, and find data on Moody's Aaa corporate bond yield (AAA) and Moody's Baa corporate bond yield (BAA). Download the data into a spreadsheet.

    a. Calculate the spread (difference) between the Baa and Aaa corporate bond yields for the most recent month of data available. What does this difference represent?

    b. Calculate the spread again, for the same month but one year prior, and compare the result to your answer to part (a). What do your answers say about how the risk premium has changed over the past year?

    c. Identify the month of highest and lowest spreads since the beginning of the year 2000. How do these spreads compare to the most current spread data available? Interpret the results.

2. **Real-time Data Analysis** Go to the St. Louis Federal Reserve FRED database, and find daily yield data on the following U.S. treasuries securities: one-month (DGS1MO), three-month (DGS3MO), six-month (DGS6MO), one-year (DGS1), two-year (DGS2), three-year (DGS3), five-year (DGS5), seven-year (DGS7), 10-year (DGS10), 20-year (DGS20), and 30-year (DGS30). Download the last full year of data available into a spreadsheet.

   a. Construct a yield curve by creating a line graph for the most recent day of data available, and for the same day (or as close to the same day as possible) one year prior, across all the maturities. How do the yield curves compare? What does the changing slope say about potential changes in economic conditions?

   b. Determine the date of the most recent Federal Open Market Committee policy statement. Construct yield curves for both the day before the policy statement was released and the day on which the policy statement was released. Was there any significant change in the yield curve as a result of the policy statement? How might this be explained?

7

The Stock Market, the Theory of Rational Expectations, and the Efficient Market Hypothesis

Learning Objectives

7.1 Calculate the price of common stock.

7.2 Recognize the impact of new information on stock prices.

7.3 Compare and contrast adaptive expectations and rational expectations.

7.4 Explain why arbitrage opportunities imply that the efficient market hypothesis holds.

7.5 Identify and explain the implications of the efficient market hypothesis for financial markets.

7.6 Summarize the reasons why behavioral finance suggests that the efficient market hypothesis may not hold.

Preview

Rarely does a day go by that the stock market isn't a major news item. We have witnessed huge swings in the stock market in recent years. The 1990s were an extraordinary decade for stocks: The Dow Jones and S&P 500 indexes increased by more than 400%, while the tech-laden NASDAQ index rose by more than 1,000%. By early 2000, all three indexes had reached record highs. Unfortunately, the good times did not last. Starting in early 2000, the stock market began to decline and many investors lost their shirts. The NASDAQ crashed, falling by more than 50%, while the Dow Jones and S&P 500 indexes fell by 30% through January 2003. After subsequently rising by over 30%, the stock market crashed again during the global financial crisis, falling by over 50% from its peak in the fall of 2007. Starting in 2009, the stock market recovered quickly, more than quadrupling by February 2020, only to crash with the onset of the coronavirus pandemic.

Because so many people invest in the stock market and the prices of stocks affect the ability of people to retire comfortably, the market for stocks is undoubtedly the financial market that receives the most attention and scrutiny. In this chapter, we look first at how this important market works.

We begin by discussing the fundamental theories that underlie the valuation of stocks. These theories are critical to understanding the forces that cause the value of stocks to rise and fall minute by minute and day by day. Once we have learned the methods for stock valuation, we need to explore how expectations about the market affect its behavior. We do so by examining the *theory of rational expectations*. When this theory is applied to financial markets, the outcome is the *efficient market hypothesis*, which has some general implications for how markets in other securities besides stocks operate. The theory of rational expectations is also central to debates about the conduct of monetary policy, to be discussed in Chapter 24.

7.1 COMPUTING THE PRICE OF COMMON STOCK

LO 7.1 Calculate the price of common stock.

Common stock is the principal medium through which corporations raise equity capital. **Stockholders**—those who hold stock in a corporation—own an interest in the corporation equal to the percentage of outstanding shares they own. This ownership interest gives them a bundle of rights. The most important are the right to vote and to be a

141

residual claimant of all funds flowing into the firm (known as **cash flows**), meaning that the stockholder receives whatever remains after all other claims against the firm's assets have been satisfied. Stockholders may receive dividends from the net earnings of the corporation. **Dividends** are payments made periodically, usually every quarter, to stockholders. The board of directors of the firm sets the level of the dividend, usually based on the recommendation of management. In addition, the stockholder has the right to sell the stock.

One basic principle of finance is that the value of any investment is calculated by computing the present value of all cash flows the investment will generate over its life. For example, a commercial building will sell for a price that reflects the net cash flows (rents minus expenses) it is projected to have over its useful life. Similarly, we value common stock as the value in today's dollars of all future cash flows. The cash flows that a stockholder might earn from stock are dividends, the sales price, or both.

To develop the theory of stock valuation, we begin with the simplest possible scenario: You buy the stock, hold it for one period to get a dividend, then sell the stock. We call this the *one-period valuation model*.

The One-Period Valuation Model

Suppose that you have some extra money to invest for one year. After a year, you will need to sell your investment to pay tuition. After watching CNBC or *Nightly Business Report* on TV, you decide that you want to buy Intel Corp. stock. You call your broker and find that Intel is currently selling for $50 per share and pays $0.16 per year in dividends. The analyst on CNBC predicts that the stock will be selling for $60 in one year. Should you buy this stock?

To answer this question, you need to determine whether the current price accurately reflects the analyst's forecast. To value the stock today, you need to find the present discounted value of the expected cash flows (future payments) using the formula in Equation 1 of Chapter 4. In this equation, the discount factor used to discount the cash flows is the required return on investments in equity rather than the interest rate. The cash flows consist of one dividend payment plus a final sales price. When these cash flows are discounted back to the present, the following equation computes the current price of the stock:

$$P_0 = \frac{D_1}{(1 + k_e)} + \frac{P_1}{(1 + k_e)} \tag{1}$$

where

P_0 = the current price of the stock. The zero subscript refers to time period zero, or the present.

D_1 = the dividend paid at the end of year 1

k_e = the required return on investments in equity

P_1 = the price at the end of year 1; the predicted sales price of the stock

To see how Equation 1 works, let's compute the price of the Intel stock if, after careful consideration, you decide that you would be satisfied to earn a 12% return on the investment. If you have decided that $k_e = 0.12$, are told that Intel pays $0.16 per year in dividends ($D_1 = 0.16$), and forecast the share price of $60 at the end of year 1 ($P_1 = \$60$), you get the following result from Equation 1:

$$P_0 = \frac{0.16}{1 + 0.12} + \frac{\$60}{1 + 0.12} = \$0.14 + \$53.57 = \$53.71$$

On the basis of your analysis, you find that the present value of all cash flows from the stock is $53.71. Because the stock is currently priced at $50 per share, you would choose to buy it. However, you should be aware that the stock may be selling for less than $53.71, because other investors have placed a greater risk on the cash flows or estimated the cash flows to be less than you did.

The Generalized Dividend Valuation Model

Using the present value concept, we can extend the one-period dividend valuation model to any number of periods: The value of a stock today is the present value of all future cash flows. The only cash flows that an investor will receive are dividends and a final sales price when the stock is ultimately sold in period n. The generalized multiperiod formula for stock valuation can be written as

$$P_0 = \frac{D_1}{(1 + k_e)^1} + \frac{D_2}{(1 + k_e)^2} + \cdots + \frac{D_n}{(1 + k_e)^n} + \frac{P_n}{(1 + k_e)^n} \qquad (2)$$

where
P_n = the price of the stock at the end of period n
D_i = the dividend paid at the end of year i

If you tried to use Equation 2 to find the value of a share of stock, you would soon realize that you must first estimate the value the stock will have at some point in the future before you can estimate its value today. In other words, you must find P_n before you can find P_0. However, if P_n is far in the future, it will not affect P_0. For example, the present value of a share of stock that sells for $50 seventy-five years from now, using a 12% discount rate, is just one cent $[\$50/(1.12^{75}) = \$0.01]$. This reasoning implies that the current value of a share of stock can be calculated as simply the present value of the future dividend stream. The **generalized dividend model** is given in Equation 3. Note that it is the same formula as Equation 2, but without the final sales price:

$$P_0 = \sum_{t=1}^{\infty} \frac{D_t}{(1 + k_e)^t} \qquad (3)$$

Consider the implications of Equation 3 for a moment. The generalized dividend model states that the price of a stock is determined only by the present value of the dividends and that nothing else matters. Many stocks do not pay dividends, so how is it that these stocks have value? *Buyers of the stock expect that the firm will pay dividends someday.* Most of the time a firm institutes dividends as soon as it has completed the rapid growth phase of its life cycle.

The generalized dividend valuation model requires that we compute the present value of an infinite stream of dividends, a process that could be difficult, to say the least. Therefore, simplified models have been developed to make the calculations easier. One such model is the **Gordon growth model**, which assumes constant dividend growth.

The Gordon Growth Model

Many firms strive to increase their dividends at a constant rate each year. Equation 4 is derived from Equation 3 to reflect this constant growth in dividends:

$$P_0 = \frac{D_0 \times (1 + g)^1}{(1 + k_e)^1} + \frac{D_0 \times (1 + g)^2}{(1 + k_e)^2} + \cdots + \frac{D_0 \times (1 + g)^\infty}{(1 + k_e)^\infty} \qquad (4)$$

where D_0 = the most recent dividend paid
                 g = the expected constant growth rate in dividends
                 k_e = the required return on an investment in equity

Equation 4 can be simplified to obtain Equation 5:[1]

$$P_0 = \frac{D_0 \times (1 + g)}{(k_e - g)} = \frac{D_1}{(k_e - g)} \tag{5}$$

This model is useful for finding the value of a stock, given a few assumptions:

1. *Dividends are assumed to continue growing at a constant rate forever.* Actually, as long as the dividends are expected to grow at a constant rate for an extended period of time, the model should yield reasonable results. This is because errors about distant cash flows become small when discounted to the present.
2. *The growth rate is assumed to be less than the required return on equity, k_e.* Myron Gordon, in his development of the model, demonstrated that this is a reasonable assumption. In theory, if the growth rate were faster than the rate demanded by holders of the firm's equity, then in the long run the firm would grow impossibly large.

7.2 HOW THE MARKET SETS STOCK PRICES

LO 7.2 Recognize the impact of new information on stock prices.

Suppose you go to an auto auction. The cars are available for inspection before the auction begins, and you find a little pre-owned, Tesla Model 3 that you like. You test-drive it in the parking lot and notice that it makes a few strange noises, but you decide that you still like the car. You decide that $20,000 is a fair price that will allow you to pay some repair bills, should the noises turn out to be serious. You see that the auction is ready to begin, so you go in and wait for the pre-owned, Tesla Model 3 to be auctioned.

Suppose another buyer also spots the pre-owned, Tesla Model 3. He test-drives the car and recognizes that the noises are simply the result of worn brake pads that he can fix himself at a nominal cost. He decides that the car is worth $22,000. He also goes in and waits for the pre-owned, Tesla Model 3 to come up for auction.

---

[1]To generate Equation 5 from Equation 4, first multiply both sides of Equation 4 by $(1 + k_e)/(1 + g)$, and then subtract Equation 4 from the result. This yields

$$\frac{P_0 \times (1 + k_e)}{(1 + g)} - P_0 = D_0 - \frac{D_0 \times (1 + g)^\infty}{(1 + k_e)^\infty}$$

Assuming that k_e is greater than g, the term on the far right will approach zero and so can be dropped. Thus, after factoring P_0 out of the left-hand side,

$$P_0 \times \left[\frac{1 + k_e}{1 + g} - 1 \right] = D_0$$

Next, simplify by combining terms:

$$P_0 \times \frac{(1 + k_e) - (1 + g)}{1 + g} = D_0$$

$$P_0 = \frac{D_0 \times (1 + g)}{k_e - g} = \frac{D_1}{k_e - g}$$

Who will buy the car, and for how much? Suppose only the two of you are interested in the pre-owned Tesla Model 3. You begin the bidding at $18,000. Your competitor ups your bid to $19,000. You bid your top price of $20,000. He counters with $21,000. The price is now higher than you are willing to pay, so you stop bidding. The car is sold to the more informed buyer for $21,000.

This simple example raises a number of important points. First, the price is set by the buyer who is willing to pay the highest price. This price is not necessarily the highest price the asset could fetch, but it is incrementally greater than what any other buyer is willing to pay.

Second, the market price will be set by the buyer who can take best advantage of the asset. The buyer who purchased the car knew that he could fix the noise easily and cheaply. As a consequence, he was willing to pay more for the car than you were. The same concept holds for other assets. For example, a piece of property or a building will sell to the buyer who can put the asset to the most productive use.

Finally, the example shows the role played by information in asset pricing. Superior information about an asset can increase its value by reducing its risk. When you consider buying a stock, the future cash flows are subject to many unknowns. The buyer who has the best information about these cash flows will discount them at a lower interest rate than will a buyer who is very uncertain.

Now let's apply these ideas to stock valuation. Suppose you are considering the purchase of stock expected to pay a $2 dividend next year. Market analysts expect the firm to grow at 3% indefinitely. You are *uncertain* about both the constancy of the dividend stream and the accuracy of the estimated growth rate. To compensate yourself for this uncertainty (risk), you require a return of 15%.

Now suppose Jennifer, another investor, has spoken with industry insiders and feels more confident about the projected cash flows. Jennifer requires only a 12% return because her perceived risk is lower than yours. Bud, however, is dating the CEO of the company. He knows with more certainty what the future of the firm actually looks like, and thus requires only a 10% return.

What value will each investor give to the stock? Applying the Gordon growth model yields the following stock prices:

Investor	Discount Rate	Stock Price
You	15%	$16.67
Jennifer	12%	$22.22
Bud	10%	$28.57

You are willing to pay $16.67 for the stock. Jennifer will pay up to $22.22, and Bud will pay $28.57. The investor with the lowest perceived risk is willing to pay the most for the stock. If there were no other traders but these three, the market price would be between $22.22 and $28.57. If you already held the stock, you would sell it to Bud.

We thus see that the players in the market, bidding against one another, establish the market price. When new information is released about a firm, expectations change, and with them, prices change. New information can cause changes in expectations about the level of future dividends or the risk of those dividends. Because market participants are constantly receiving new information and revising their expectations, it is reasonable that stock prices are constantly changing as well.

APPLICATION   Monetary Policy and Stock Prices

Stock market analysts tend to hang on every word uttered by the chair of the Federal Reserve because they know that an important determinant of stock prices is monetary policy. But how does monetary policy affect stock prices?

The Gordon growth model in Equation 5 explains this relationship. Monetary policy can affect stock prices in two ways. First, when the Fed lowers interest rates, the return on bonds (an alternative asset to stocks) declines, and investors are likely to accept a lower required rate of return on an investment in equity (k_e). The resulting decline in k_e lowers the denominator in the Gordon growth model (Equation 5), leads to a higher value of P_0, and raises stock prices. Furthermore, a lowering of interest rates is likely to stimulate the economy, so the growth rate in dividends, g, is likely to be somewhat higher. This rise in g also causes the denominator in Equation 5 to decrease, which also leads to a higher P_0 and a rise in stock prices.

As we will see in Chapter 25, the impact of monetary policy on stock prices is one of the key ways in which monetary policy affects the economy. ◆

APPLICATION   The Coronavirus Stock Market Crash of 2020

The spread of the coronavirus in February 2020 triggered a stock market crash in which the Dow Jones Industrial Average fell from a peak of 29,551 on February 12 to 18,561 on March 20, a decline of 37%. Our analysis of stock price valuation, again using the Gordon growth model, can help us understand how the coronavirus pandemic affected stock prices.

The coronavirus pandemic led to a major lockdown of the economy, resulting in a sharp downward revision of the growth prospects for U.S. companies, thus lowering the dividend growth rate (g) in the Gordon model. In terms of Equation 5, the resulting increase in the numerator would lead to a decline in P_0 and hence a decline in stock prices.

The coronavirus pandemic also increased uncertainty about the U.S. economy and led to a widening of credit spreads. As a result, the required return on investment in equity rose. In terms of Equation 5, a higher k_e produces an increase in the denominator, a decline in P_0, and a general fall in stock prices.

The combination of expectations of a lower dividend growth rate (g) and a higher required return on investment in equity (k_e) led to one of the steepest stock market declines in U.S. history. ◆

7.3 THE THEORY OF RATIONAL EXPECTATIONS

LO 7.3 Compare and contrast adaptive expectations and rational expectations.

The analysis of stock price evaluation we outlined in the previous section depends on people's expectations—especially expectations of cash flows. Indeed, it is difficult to think of any sector of the economy in which expectations are not crucial; this is why it is important to examine how expectations are formed. We do so by outlining the *theory of rational expectations*, currently the most widely used theory to describe the formation of business and consumer expectations.

In the 1950s and 1960s, economists regularly viewed expectations as formed from past experience only. Expectations of inflation, for example, were typically viewed as being an average of past inflation rates. This view of expectation formation, called **adaptive expectations**, suggests that changes in expectations will occur slowly over time, as data for a variable evolve.[2] So, if inflation had formerly been steady at a 5% rate, expectations of future inflation would be 5%, too. If inflation rose to a steady rate of 10%, expectations of future inflation would rise toward 10%, but slowly: In the first year, expected inflation might rise only to 6%; in the second year, to 7%; and so on.

The adaptive expectations hypothesis has been faulted on the grounds that people use more information than just past data on a single variable to form their expectations of that variable. Their expectations of inflation will almost surely be affected by their predictions of future monetary policy, as well as by current and past monetary policy. In addition, people often change their expectations quickly in the light of new information. To address these objections to the validity of adaptive expectations, John Muth developed an alternative theory of expectations, called **rational expectations**, which can be stated as follows: *Expectations will be identical to optimal forecasts (the best guess of the future) using all available information.*[3]

What exactly does this mean? To explain it more clearly, let's use the theory of rational expectations to examine how expectations are formed in a situation that most of us will encounter at some point in our lifetime: our drive to work. Suppose that if Joe Commuter travels when it is not rush hour, his trip takes an average of 30 minutes. Sometimes his trip takes 35 minutes; other times, 25 minutes; but the average, non-rush-hour driving time is 30 minutes. If, however, Joe leaves for work during the rush hour, it takes him, on average, an additional 10 minutes to get to work. Given that he leaves for work during the rush hour, the best guess of his driving time—the **optimal forecast**—is 40 minutes.

If the only information available to Joe before he leaves for work related to his driving time is that he is leaving during the rush hour, what does rational expectations theory allow you to predict about Joe's expectations of his driving time? Since the best guess of his driving time, using all available information, is 40 minutes, Joe's expectation should be the same. Clearly, an expectation of 35 minutes would not be rational, because it is not equal to the optimal forecast, or the best guess of the driving time.

Suppose that the next day, given the same conditions and expectations, it takes Joe 45 minutes to drive to work because he hits an abnormally large number of red lights. The day after that, Joe hits all the lights right and it takes him only 35 minutes to drive to work. Do these variations mean that Joe's 40-minute expectation is irrational? No; an expectation of 40 minutes' driving time is still a rational expectation. In both cases, the forecast is off by 5 minutes, so the expectation has not been perfectly accurate each

---

[2]More specifically, adaptive expectations—say, of inflation—are written as a weighted average of past inflation rates:

$$\pi_t^e = (1 - \lambda) \sum_{j=0}^{\infty} \lambda^j \pi_{t-j}$$

where

$$\pi_t^e = \text{adaptive expectation of inflation at time } t$$
$$\pi_{t-j} = \text{inflation at time } t - j$$
$$\lambda = \text{a constant between the values of 0 and 1}$$

[3]John Muth, "Rational Expectations and the Theory of Price Movements," *Econometrica* 29 (1961): 315–335.

time. However, the forecast does not have to be perfectly accurate to be rational—it need only be the *best possible* forecast given the available information; that is, it has to be correct *on average*, and the 40-minute expectation meets this requirement. As there is bound to be some randomness in Joe's driving time regardless of driving conditions, an optimal forecast will never be completely accurate.

The example makes the following important point about rational expectations: ***Even though a rational expectation equals the optimal forecast using all available information, a prediction based on it may not always be perfectly accurate.***

What if an item of information relevant to predicting driving time is unavailable or ignored? Suppose that on Joe's usual route to work, an accident occurs and causes a 2-hour traffic jam. If Joe has no way of ascertaining this information, his rush-hour expectation of 40 minutes' driving time is still rational, because the accident information is not available to him for incorporation into his optimal forecast. However, if there was a radio or TV traffic report about the accident that Joe did not bother to listen to, or heard but ignored, his 40-minute expectation is no longer rational. In light of the availability of this information, Joe's optimal forecast should have been 2 hours and 40 minutes.

Accordingly, an expectation may fail to be rational for two reasons:

1. People might be aware of all available information but find it takes too much effort to make their expectation the best guess possible.
2. People might be unaware of some available relevant information, so their best guess of the future will not be accurate.

Nonetheless, it is important to recognize that if an additional factor is important but information about it is not available, an expectation that does not take that factor into account can still be rational.

Formal Statement of the Theory

We can state the theory of rational expectations somewhat more formally. If X stands for the variable that is being forecast (in our example, Joe Commuter's driving time), X^e for the expectation of this variable (Joe's expectation of his driving time), and X^{of} for the optimal forecast of X using all available information (the best guess possible of Joe's driving time), the theory of rational expectations then simply states

$$X^e = X^{of} \tag{6}$$

That is, the expectation of X equals the optimal forecast using all available information.

Rationale Behind the Theory

Why do people try to make their expectations match their best possible guess of future results, using all available information? The simplest explanation is that it is costly for people not to do so. Joe Commuter has a strong incentive to make his expectation of the time it takes him to drive to work as accurate as possible. If he underpredicts his driving time, he will often be late to work and risk being fired. If he overpredicts, he will, on average, get to work too early and will have given up sleep or leisure time unnecessarily. Accurate expectations are desirable, and therefore people have a strong incentive to try to make expectations equal to optimal forecasts by using all available information.

The same principle applies to businesses. Suppose an appliance manufacturer—say, General Electric—knows that interest-rate movements are important to the sales of appliances. If GE makes poor forecasts of interest rates, it will earn less profit, because it will produce either too many or too few appliances. The incentives are strong for GE to acquire all available information to help it forecast interest rates and make the best possible guess of future interest-rate movements.

Implications of the Theory

Rational expectations theory leads to two commonsense implications regarding the formation of expectations. These implications are important in the analysis of both the stock market and the aggregate economy:

1. *If there is a change in the way a variable moves, the way in which expectations of this variable are formed will change as well.* This tenet of rational expectations theory can be most easily understood through a concrete example. Suppose interest rates move in such a way that they tend to return to a "normal" level over time. If today's interest rate is high relative to the normal level, an optimal forecast of the interest rate in the future is that it will decline to the normal level. Rational expectations theory would imply that when today's interest rate is high, the expectation is that it will fall in the future.

   Suppose now that the way in which the interest rate moves changes so that when the interest rate is high, it stays high. In this case, when today's interest rate is high, the optimal forecast of the future interest rate, and hence the rational expectation, is that it will stay high. Expectations of the future interest rate will no longer indicate that the interest rate will fall. The change in the way the interest-rate variable moves has therefore led to a change in the way that expectations of future interest rates are formed. The rational expectations analysis here is generalizable to expectations of any variable. Hence, when a change occurs in the way any variable moves, the way in which expectations of this variable are formed will change, too.

2. *The forecast errors of expectations will, on average, be zero and cannot be predicted ahead of time.* The forecast error of an expectation is $X - X^e$, the difference between the realization of a variable X and the expectation of the variable. That is, if Joe Commuter's driving time on a particular day is 45 minutes and his expectation of the driving time is 40 minutes, the forecast error is 5 minutes.

   Suppose that in violation of the rational expectations tenet, Joe's forecast error is not, on average, equal to zero; instead, it equals 5 minutes. The forecast error is now predictable ahead of time because Joe will soon notice that he is, on average, 5 minutes late for work and can improve his forecast by increasing it by 5 minutes. Rational expectations theory implies that this is exactly what Joe will do because he will want his forecast to be the best guess possible. When Joe has revised his forecast upward by 5 minutes, on average, the forecast error will equal zero, so it cannot be predicted ahead of time. Rational expectations theory implies that forecast errors of expectations cannot be predicted.

The incentives for equating expectations with optimal forecasts are especially strong in financial markets. In these markets, people with better forecasts of the future get rich. The application of the theory of rational expectations to financial markets (where it is called the **efficient market hypothesis** or the **theory of efficient capital markets**) is thus particularly useful.

7.4 THE EFFICIENT MARKET HYPOTHESIS: RATIONAL EXPECTATIONS IN FINANCIAL MARKETS

LO 7.4 Explain why arbitrage opportunities imply that the efficient market hypothesis holds.

While monetary economists were developing the theory of rational expectations, financial economists were developing a parallel theory of expectations formation for financial markets. It led them to the same conclusion as that of the rational expectations theorists: Expectations in financial markets are equal to optimal forecasts using all available information.[4] Although financial economists, such as Eugene Fama, later a winner of the Nobel Prize in economics, gave their theory another name, calling it the *efficient market hypothesis,* in fact their theory is just an application of rational expectations to the pricing of stocks and other securities.

The efficient market hypothesis is based on the assumption that prices of securities in financial markets fully reflect all available information. You may recall from Chapter 4 that the rate of return from holding a security equals the sum of the capital gain on the security (the change in the price), plus any cash payments, divided by the initial purchase price of the security:

$$R = \frac{P_{t+1} - P_t + C}{P_t} \tag{7}$$

where
R = rate of return on the security held from time t to time $t + 1$ (say, the end of 2021 to the end of 2022)
P_{t+1} = price of the security at time $t + 1$, the end of the holding period
P_t = price of the security at time t, the beginning of the holding period
C = cash payment (coupon or dividend payments) made in the period t to $t + 1$

Let's look at the expectation of this return at time t, the beginning of the holding period. Because the current price P_t and the cash payment C are known at the outset, the only variable in the definition of the return that is uncertain is the price next period, P_{t+1}.[5] Denoting expectation of the security's price at the end of the holding period as P_{t+1}^e, the expected return R^e is

$$R^e = \frac{P_{t+1}^e - P_t + C}{P_t}$$

The efficient market hypothesis views expectations of future prices as equal to optimal forecasts using all currently available information. In other words, the market's expectations of future securities prices are rational, so that

$$P_{t+1}^e = P_{t+1}^{of}$$

which in turn implies that the expected return on the security will equal the optimal forecast of the return:

$$R^e = R^{of} \tag{8}$$

---

[4]The development of the efficient market hypothesis was not wholly independent of the development of rational expectations theory in that financial economists were aware of Muth's work.

[5]There are cases in which C might not be known at the beginning of the period, but that does not make a substantial difference to the analysis. We would in that case assume that not only price expectations but also the expectations of C are optimal forecasts using all available information.

Unfortunately, we cannot observe either R^e or P^e_{t+1}, so the rational expectations equations by themselves do not tell us much about how the financial market behaves. However, if we can devise some way to measure the value of R^e, these equations will have important implications for how prices of securities change in financial markets.

The supply and demand analysis of the bond market that we developed in Chapter 5 showed us that the expected return on a security (the interest rate, in the case of the one-year discount bond) will have a tendency to move toward the equilibrium return that equates the quantity demanded to the quantity supplied. Supply and demand analysis enables us to determine the expected return on a security with the following equilibrium condition:

The expected return on a security R^e equals the equilibrium return R^*, which equates the quantity of the security demanded to the quantity supplied; that is,

$$R^e = R^* \tag{9}$$

The academic field of finance explores the factors (risk and liquidity, for example) that influence the equilibrium returns on securities. For our purposes, it is sufficient to know that we can determine the equilibrium return and thus determine the expected return with the equilibrium condition.

We can derive an equation to describe pricing behavior in an efficient market by using the equilibrium condition to replace R^e with R^* in the rational expectations equation (Equation 8). In this way, we obtain

$$R^{of} = R^* \tag{10}$$

This equation tells us that *current prices in a financial market will be set so that the optimal forecast of a security's return using all available information equals the security's equilibrium return*. Financial economists state it more simply: In an efficient market, a security's price fully reflects all available information.

Rationale Behind the Hypothesis

To see why the efficient market hypothesis makes sense, we make use of the concept of **arbitrage**, in which market participants (*arbitrageurs*) eliminate **unexploited profit opportunities**, that is, returns on a security that are larger than what is justified by the characteristics of that security. Arbitrage is of two types: *pure arbitrage*, in which the elimination of unexploited profit opportunities involves no risk, and the type of arbitrage we discuss here, in which the arbitrageur takes on some risk when eliminating the unexploited profit opportunities. To see how arbitrage leads to the efficient market hypothesis given a security's risk characteristics, let's look at an example. Suppose the normal return on ExxonMobil common stock is 10% at an annual rate, and its current price P_t is lower than the optimal forecast of tomorrow's price P^{of}_{t+1}, so that the optimal forecast of the return at an annual rate is 50%, which is greater than the equilibrium return of 10%. We are now able to predict that, on average, ExxonMobil's return will be abnormally high, so there is an unexploited profit opportunity. Knowing that, on average, you can earn an abnormally high rate of return on ExxonMobil stock (because $R^{of} > R^*$), you will buy more, which will in turn drive up the stock's current price P_t relative to its expected future price P^{of}_{t+1}, thereby lowering R^{of}. When the current price has risen sufficiently so that R^{of} equals R^* and the efficient market condition (Equation 10) is satisfied, the buying of ExxonMobil stock will stop, and the unexploited profit opportunity will disappear.

Similarly, a security for which the optimal forecast of the return is -5% and the equilibrium return is 10% $(R^{of} < R^*)$ would be a poor investment because, on average, the security earns less than the equilibrium return. In such a case, you would sell the security and drive down its current price relative to the expected future price until R^{of} rose to the level of R^* and the efficient market condition was again satisfied. Our discussion can be summarized as follows:

$$R^{of} > R^* \rightarrow P_t\uparrow \rightarrow R^{of}\downarrow$$

$$R^{of} < R^* \rightarrow P_t\downarrow \rightarrow R^{of}\uparrow$$

until

$$R^{of} = R^*$$

Another way to state the efficient market condition is this: **In an efficient market, all unexploited profit opportunities will be eliminated.**

An extremely important factor in this reasoning is that *not everyone in a financial market must be well informed about a security or have rational expectations for its price to be driven to the point at which the efficient market condition holds.* Financial markets are structured so that many participants can play. As long as a few people (often referred to as the "smart money") keep their eyes open for unexploited profit opportunities, they will eliminate the profit opportunities that appear, because in doing so they make a profit. The efficient market hypothesis makes sense because it does not require that everyone in a market be cognizant of what is happening to every security.

Random-Walk Behavior of Stock Prices

The term **random walk** describes the movements of a variable whose future values cannot be predicted (are random) because, given today's value, the value of the variable is just as likely to fall as it is to rise. An important implication of the efficient market hypothesis is that stock prices should approximately follow a random walk; that is, *future changes in stock prices should, for all practical purposes, be unpredictable.* The random-walk implication of the efficient market hypothesis is the one most commonly mentioned in the press because it is the most readily comprehensible to the public. In fact, when people mention the "random-walk theory of stock prices," they are in reality referring to the efficient market hypothesis.

The case for random-walk stock prices can be demonstrated. Suppose people could predict that the price of Happy Feet Corporation (HFC) stock would rise 1% in the coming week. The predicted rate of capital gains and rate of return on HFC stock would then exceed 50% at an annual rate. Since this is very likely to be far higher than the equilibrium rate of return on HFC stock $(R^{of} > R^*)$, the efficient market hypothesis indicates that people would immediately buy this stock and bid up its current price. The action would stop only when the predictable change in the price dropped to near zero, so that $R^{of} = R^*$.

Similarly, if people could predict that the price of HFC stock would fall by 1%, the predicted rate of return would be negative $(R^{of} < R^*)$, and people would immediately sell the stock. The current price would fall until the predictable change in the price rose back to near zero, where the efficient market condition again would hold. The efficient market hypothesis suggests that the predictable change in stock prices will be near

Global   **Should Foreign Exchange Rates Follow a Random Walk?**

Although the efficient market hypothesis is usually applied to the stock market, it can also be used to show that foreign exchange rates, like stock prices, should generally follow a random walk. To see why this is the case, consider what would happen if investors could predict that a currency would rise in value by 1% in the coming week. By buying this currency, they could earn a greater than 50% return at an annual rate, which is likely to be far above the equilibrium return for holding a currency. As a result, investors would immediately buy the currency and bid up its current price, thereby reducing the expected return. The process would only stop when the predictable change in the exchange rate dropped to near zero so that the optimal forecast of the return no longer differed from the equilibrium return. Likewise, if investors could predict that the currency would fall in value by 1% in the coming week, they would sell it until the predictable change in the exchange rate was again near zero. The efficient market hypothesis therefore implies that future changes in exchange rates should, for all practical purposes, be unpredictable; in other words, exchange rates should follow random walks. Indeed, the random-walk behavior of exchange rates is exactly what is found in the data.

zero, leading to the conclusion that stock prices will generally follow a random walk.[6] As the Global Box "Should Foreign Exchange Rates Follow a Random Walk?" indicates, the efficient market hypothesis suggests that foreign exchange rates should also follow a random walk.

APPLICATION   Practical Guide to Investing in the Stock Market

The efficient market hypothesis has numerous applications to the real world. It is especially valuable because it can be applied directly to an issue that concerns many of us: how to get rich (or at least not get poor) by investing in the stock market. A practical guide to investing in the stock market, which we develop here, provides a better understanding of the use and implications of the efficient market hypothesis.

How Valuable Are Reports Published by Investment Advisers?

Suppose you have just read in the "Heard on the Street" column of the *Wall Street Journal* that investment advisers are predicting a boom in oil stocks because an oil shortage is developing. Should you proceed to withdraw all of your hard-earned savings from the bank and invest them in oil stocks?

[6]Note that the random-walk behavior of stock prices is only an *approximation* derived from the efficient market hypothesis. Random-walk behavior would hold *exactly* only for a stock for which an unchanged price leads to its having the equilibrium return. Then, when the predictable change in the stock price is exactly zero, $R^{of} = R^*$.

The efficient market hypothesis tells us that when purchasing a security, we cannot expect to earn an abnormally high return, or a return greater than the equilibrium return. Information in newspapers and in the published reports of investment advisers is readily available to many market participants and is already reflected in market prices. So acting on this information will not yield abnormally high returns, on average. The empirical evidence for the most part confirms that recommendations from investment advisers cannot help us outperform the general market. Indeed, as the FYI box, "Should You Hire an Ape as Your Investment Adviser?" suggests, human investment advisers in San Francisco do not, on average, even outperform an orangutan!

Probably no other conclusion is met with more skepticism by students than this one when they first hear it. We all know, or have heard of, someone who has been successful in the stock market for a period of many years. We wonder, "How could someone be so consistently successful if he or she did not really know how to predict when returns would be abnormally high?" The following story, reported in the press, illustrates why such anecdotal evidence is not reliable.

A get-rich-quick artist invented a clever scam. Every week, he wrote two letters. In letter A, he would pick team A to win a particular football game; in letter B, he would pick the opponent, team B. He would then separate a mailing list into two groups, and he would send letter A to the people in one group and letter B to the people in the other. The following week he would do the same thing, but this time he would send these letters only to the group who had received the first letters containing the correct prediction. After doing this for ten games, he had a small cluster of people who had received letters predicting the correct winning team for every game. He then mailed a final letter to this group, declaring that since he was obviously an expert predictor of the outcome of football games (he had picked the winning teams ten weeks in a row), and since his predictions were profitable for the recipients who bet on the games, he would continue to send his predictions only if he were paid a substantial amount of money. When one of his clients figured out what he was up to, the con man was prosecuted and thrown in jail!

What is the lesson of the story? Even if no forecaster can always accurately predict the market, there always will be some who appear to be consistent winners. A person who has done well regularly in the past cannot guarantee that he or she will do well in the future. Note that there will also be a group of persistent losers, but you rarely hear about them because no one brags about a poor forecasting record.

Should You Be Skeptical of Hot Tips?

Suppose your broker phones you with a hot tip to buy stock in the Happy Feet Corporation (HFC) because it has just developed a product that is completely effective in curing athlete's foot. The stock price is sure to go up. Should you follow this advice and buy HFC stock?

The efficient market hypothesis indicates that you should be skeptical of such news. If the stock market is efficient, it has already priced HFC stock so that its expected return will equal the equilibrium return. The hot tip is not particularly valuable and will not enable you to earn an abnormally high return.

You might wonder, though, if the hot tip is based on new information and would give you an edge on the rest of the market. If other market participants have gotten this information before you, the answer again is no. As soon as the information hits the street, the unexploited profit opportunity it creates will be quickly eliminated. The stock's price will already reflect the information, and you should expect to realize only

---

FYI   **Should You Hire an Ape as Your Investment Adviser?**

The *San Francisco Chronicle* came up with an amusing way of evaluating how successful investment advisers are at picking stocks. They asked eight analysts to pick five stocks at the beginning of the year and then compared the performance of their stock picks to those chosen by Jolyn, an orangutan living at Marine World/Africa USA in Vallejo, California. Jolyn beat the investment advisers as often as they beat her. Given this result, you might be just as well off hiring an orangutan as your investment adviser as you would be hiring a human being!

---

the equilibrium return. But if you are one of the first to gain the new information, it *can* do you some good. Only then can you be one of the lucky ones who, on average, will earn an abnormally high return by helping eliminate the profit opportunity by buying HFC stock.

Do Stock Prices Always Rise When There Is Good News?

If you follow the stock market, you might have noticed a puzzling phenomenon: When good news about a corporation, such as a particularly favorable earnings report, is announced, the price of the corporation's stock frequently does not rise. The efficient market hypothesis explains this phenomenon.

Because changes in stock prices are unpredictable, when information is announced that has already been expected by the market, stock prices will remain unchanged. The announcement does not contain any new information that would lead to a change in stock prices. If this were not the case, and the announcement led to a change in stock prices, it would mean that the change was predictable. Because such a scenario is ruled out in an efficient market, **stock prices will respond to announcements only when the information being announced is new and unexpected**. If the news is expected, no stock price response will occur. This is exactly what the evidence shows: Stock prices do reflect publicly available information.

Sometimes an individual stock price declines when good news is announced. Although this seems somewhat peculiar, it is completely consistent with the workings of an efficient market. Suppose that although the announced news is good, it is not as good as expected. HFC's earnings may have risen by 15%, but if the market expected earnings to rise by 20%, the new information is actually unfavorable, and the stock price declines.

Efficient Market Prescription for the Investor

What does the efficient market hypothesis recommend for investing in the stock market? It tells us that hot tips and investment advisers' published recommendations—all of which make use of publicly available information—cannot help an investor outperform the market. Indeed, it indicates that anyone without better information than other market participants cannot expect to beat the market. So what is an investor to do?

The efficient market hypothesis leads to the conclusion that such an investor (and almost all of us fit into this category) should not try to outguess the market by constantly buying and selling securities. This process does nothing but boost the income of brokers, who earn commissions on each trade.[7] Instead, the investor should pursue a "buy-and-hold" strategy—purchase stocks and hold them for long periods of time. This will lead to the same returns, on average, but the investor's net profits will be higher because fewer brokerage commissions will have to be paid.

A sensible strategy for a small investor, whose costs of managing a portfolio may be high relative to its size, is to buy into a mutual fund rather than to buy individual stocks. Because the efficient market hypothesis indicates that no mutual fund can consistently outperform the market, an investor should not buy into a fund that has high management fees or pays sales commissions to brokers, but rather should purchase a no-load (commission-free) mutual fund that has low management fees. ◆

7.5 WHY THE EFFICIENT MARKET HYPOTHESIS DOES NOT IMPLY THAT FINANCIAL MARKETS ARE EFFICIENT

LO 7.5 Identify and explain the implications of the efficient market hypothesis for financial markets.

Many financial economists take the efficient market hypothesis one step further in their analysis of financial markets. Not only do they believe that expectations in financial markets are rational—that is, equal to optimal forecasts using all available information—but they also add the condition that prices in financial markets reflect the true fundamental (intrinsic) value of the securities. In other words, all prices are always correct and reflect **market fundamentals** (items that have a direct impact on future income streams of the securities), and so financial markets are efficient.

This stronger view of market efficiency has several important implications in the academic field of finance. First, it implies that in an efficient capital market, one investment is as good as any other because the securities' prices are correct. Second, it implies that a security's price reflects all available information about the intrinsic value of the security. Third, it implies that security prices can be used by managers of both financial and nonfinancial firms to assess their costs of capital (costs of financing their investments) accurately and hence that security prices can be used to help these managers make correct decisions about whether a specific investment is worth making. This stronger version of market efficiency is a basic tenet of much analysis in the finance field.

The efficient market hypothesis may be misnamed, however. It does not imply the stronger view of market efficiency, but rather just that prices in markets like the stock market are unpredictable. Indeed, as the following application suggests, the existence of market crashes and **bubbles**, in which the prices of assets rise well above their fundamental values, casts serious doubt on the stronger view that financial markets are efficient. However, market crashes and bubbles do not necessarily provide strong evidence against the basic tenets of the efficient market hypothesis.

---

[7]The investor may also have to pay Uncle Sam capital gains taxes on any profits that are realized when a security is sold—an additional reason why continual buying and selling does not make sense.

APPLICATION   What Do Stock Market Crashes Tell Us About the Efficient Market Hypothesis and the Efficiency of Financial Markets?

On October 19, 1987, dubbed "Black Monday," the Dow Jones Industrial Average declined by more than 20%, the largest one-day decline in U.S. history. The collapse of the high-tech companies' share prices from their peaks in March 2000 caused the heavily tech-laden NASDAQ index to fall from about 5,000 in March 2000 to about 1,500 in 2001 and 2002, a decline of well over 60%. These stock market crashes caused many economists to question the validity of the efficient market hypothesis. These economists do not believe that a rational marketplace could have produced such a massive swing in share prices. To what degree should these stock market crashes make us doubt the validity of the efficient market hypothesis?

Nothing in efficient markets theory rules out large changes in stock prices. A large change in stock prices can result from new information that produces a dramatic decline in optimal forecasts of the future valuation of firms. However, economists are hard pressed to find fundamental changes in the economy that would have caused the Black Monday and tech crashes. One lesson from these crashes is that factors other than market fundamentals probably have an effect on asset prices. Indeed, as we will explore in Chapters 8 and 12, there are good reasons to believe that impediments to the proper functioning of financial markets do exist. Hence these crashes have convinced many economists that the stronger version of market efficiency, which states that asset prices reflect the true fundamental (intrinsic) value of securities, is incorrect. These economists attribute a large role in determination of stock and other asset prices to market psychology and to the institutional structure of the marketplace. However, nothing in this view contradicts the basic reasoning behind rational expectations or the efficient market hypothesis—that market participants eliminate unexploited profit opportunities. Even though stock market prices may not always solely reflect market fundamentals, as long as market crashes are unpredictable, the basic premises of efficient markets theory hold.

However, other economists believe that market crashes and bubbles suggest that unexploited profit opportunities may exist and that the efficient market hypothesis might be fundamentally flawed. The controversy over the efficient market hypothesis continues. ◆

7.6 BEHAVIORAL FINANCE

LO 7.6 Summarize the reasons why behavioral finance suggests that the efficient market hypothesis may not hold.

Doubts about the efficiency of financial markets, triggered by the stock market crash of 1987, led economists such as Nobel Prize winner Robert Shiller to develop a new field of study called **behavioral finance**. It applies concepts from other social sciences, such as anthropology, sociology, and particularly psychology, to explain the behavior of securities prices.[8]

[8]Surveys of this field can be found in Hersh Shefrin, *Beyond Greed and Fear: Understanding of Behavioral Finance and the Psychology of Investing* (Boston: Harvard Business School Press, 2000); Andrei Shleifer, *Inefficient Markets* (Oxford, UK: Oxford University Press, 2000); and Robert J. Shiller, "From Efficient Market Theory to Behavioral Finance," Cowles Foundation Discussion Paper No. 1385 (October 2002).

As we have seen, the efficient market hypothesis assumes that unexploited profit opportunities are eliminated by "smart money" market participants. But can smart money dominate ordinary investors so that financial markets are efficient? Specifically, the efficient market hypothesis suggests that smart money participants will sell when a stock price goes up irrationally, with the result that the stock price falls back down to a level that is justified by fundamentals. For this to occur, smart money investors must be able to engage in **short sales**; that is, they must borrow stock from brokers and then sell it in the market, with the aim of earning a profit by buying the stock back again ("covering the short") after it has fallen in price. Work by psychologists, however, suggests that people are subject to loss aversion: They are more unhappy when they suffer losses than they are happy when they achieve gains. Short sales can result in losses far in excess of an investor's initial investment if the stock price climbs sharply higher than the price at which the short sale is made (and losses might be unlimited if the stock price climbs to astronomical heights).

Loss aversion can thus explain an important phenomenon: Very little short selling actually takes place. Short selling may also be constrained by rules restricting it, because it seems unsavory for someone to make money from another person's misfortune. The existence of so little short selling can explain why stock prices are sometimes overvalued. That is, the lack of enough short selling means that smart money does not drive stock prices back down to their fundamental value.

Psychologists have also found that people tend to be overconfident in their own judgments. As a result, investors tend to believe that they are smarter than other investors. Because investors are willing to assume that the market typically doesn't get it right, they trade on their beliefs rather than on pure facts. This theory may explain why securities markets have such a large trading volume—something that the efficient market hypothesis does not predict.

Overconfidence and social contagion (fads) provide an explanation for stock market bubbles. When stock prices go up, investors attribute their profits to their intelligence and talk up the stock market. This word-of-mouth enthusiasm and glowing media reports then can produce an environment in which even more investors think stock prices will rise in the future. The result is a positive feedback loop in which prices continue to rise, producing a speculative bubble, which finally crashes when prices get too far out of line with fundamentals.[9]

The field of behavioral finance is a young one, but it holds out hope that we might be able to explain some features of securities markets' behavior that are not well explained by the efficient market hypothesis.

[9]See Robert J. Shiller, *Irrational Exuberance* (New York: Broadway Books, 2001).

SUMMARY

1. Stocks are valued as the present value of future dividends. Unfortunately, we do not know very precisely what these dividends will be. This uncertainty introduces a great deal of error into the valuation process. The Gordon growth model is a simplified method of computing stock value that depends on the assumption that the dividends are growing at a constant rate forever. Given our uncertainty regarding future dividends, this assumption is often the best we can do.

2. The interaction among traders in the market is what actually sets prices on a day-to-day basis. The trader who values the security the most (either because of less uncertainty about cash flows or because of greater estimated cash flows) will be willing to pay the most. As new information is released, investors will revise their estimates of the true value of the security and will either buy or sell it, depending on how the market price compares with their estimated valuation. Because small

changes in estimated growth rates or required returns result in large changes in price, it is not surprising that the markets are often volatile.

3. The efficient market hypothesis states that current security prices will fully reflect all available information, because in an efficient market, all unexploited profit opportunities are eliminated. The elimination of unexploited profit opportunities necessary for a financial market to be efficient does not require that all market participants be well informed. The efficient markets hypothesis implies that stock prices generally follow a random walk.

4. The efficient market hypothesis indicates that hot tips and investment advisers' published recommendations cannot help an investor outperform the market. The best prescription for investors is to pursue a buy-and-hold strategy—purchase stocks and hold them for long periods of time. Empirical evidence generally supports these implications of the efficient market hypothesis in the stock market.

5. The existence of market crashes and bubbles has convinced many economists that the stronger version of market efficiency, which states that asset prices reflect the true fundamental (intrinsic) value of securities, is not correct. There is, however, less evidence that these crashes prove that the efficient market hypothesis is wrong. Even if the stock market were driven by factors other than fundamentals, these crashes do not clearly demonstrate that many basic tenets of the efficient market hypothesis are no longer valid, as long as the crashes could not have been predicted.

6. The new field of behavioral finance applies concepts from other social sciences, such as anthropology, sociology, and psychology, to our understanding of the behavior of securities prices. Loss aversion, overconfidence, and social contagion can explain why trading volume is so high, why stock prices become overvalued, and why speculative bubbles occur.

KEY TERMS

adaptive expectations, p. 147
arbitrage, p. 151
behavioral finance, p. 157
bubbles, p. 156
cash flows, p. 142
dividends, p. 142

efficient market hypothesis, p. 149
generalized dividend model, p. 143
Gordon growth model, p. 143
market fundamentals, p. 156
optimal forecast, p. 147
random walk, p. 152

rational expectations, p. 147
residual claimant, p. 142
short sales, p. 158
stockholders, p. 141
theory of efficient capital markets, p. 149
unexploited profit opportunity, p. 151

QUESTIONS

1. What basic principle of finance can be applied to the valuation of any investment asset?

2. What are the two main sources of cash flows for a stockholder? How reliably can these cash flows be estimated? Compare the problem of estimating stock cash flows to the problem of estimating bond cash flows. Which security would you predict to be more volatile?

3. Some economists think that central banks should try to prick bubbles in the stock market before they get out of hand and cause later damage when they burst. How can monetary policy be used to prick a market bubble? Explain using the Gordon growth model.

4. If monetary policy becomes more transparent about the future course of interest rates, how will stock prices be affected, if at all?

5. Suppose that you are asked to forecast future stock prices of ABC Corporation, so you proceed to collect all available information. The day you announce your forecast, competitors of ABC Corporation announce a brand new plan to merge and reshape the structure of the industry. Would your forecast still be considered optimal?

6. "Anytime it is snowing when Joe Commuter gets up in the morning, he misjudges how long it will take him to drive to work. When it is not snowing, his expectations of the driving time are perfectly accurate. Considering that it snows only once every ten years where Joe lives, Joe's expectations are almost always perfectly accurate." Are Joe's expectations rational? Why or why not?

7. Suppose that you decide to play a game. You buy stock by throwing a die a few times, using that method to select which stock to buy. After ten months you calculate the

return on your investment and the return earned by someone who followed "expert" advice during the same period. If both returns are similar, would this constitute evidence in favor of or against the efficient market hypothesis?

8. "If stock prices did not follow a random walk, there would be unexploited profit opportunities in the market." Is this statement true, false, or uncertain? Explain your answer.

9. Suppose that increases in the money supply lead to a rise in stock prices. Does this mean that when you see that the money supply has sharply increased in the past week, you should go out and buy stocks? Why or why not?

10. If the public expects a corporation to lose $5 per share this quarter and it actually loses $4, which is still the largest loss in the history of the company, what does the efficient market hypothesis predict will happen to the price of the stock when the $4 loss is announced?

11. If you read in the *Wall Street Journal* that the "smart money" on Wall Street expects stock prices to fall, should you follow that lead and sell all your stocks?

12. If your broker has been right in her five previous buy and sell recommendations, should you continue listening to her advice?

13. Can a person with rational expectations expect the price of a share of Google to rise by 10% in the next month?

14. Suppose that in every last week of November stock prices go up by an average of 3%. Would this constitute evidence in favor of or against the efficient market hypothesis?

15. "An efficient market is one in which no one ever profits from having better information than the rest of the market participants." Is this statement true, false, or uncertain? Explain your answer.

16. If higher money growth is associated with higher future inflation, and if announced money growth turns out to be extremely high but is still less than the market expected, what do you think will happen to long-term bond prices?

17. "Foreign exchange rates, like stock prices, should follow a random walk." Is this statement true, false, or uncertain? Explain your answer.

18. Assume that the efficient market hypothesis holds. Marcos has been recently hired by a brokerage firm and claims that he now has access to the best market information. However, he is the "new guy," and no one at the firm tells him much about the business. Would you expect Marcos's clients to be better or worse off than the rest of the firm's clients?

19. Suppose that you work as a forecaster of future monthly inflation rates and that your last six forecasts have been off by minus 1%. Is it likely that your expectations are optimal?

20. In the late 1990s, as information technology advanced rapidly and the Internet was widely developed, U.S. stock markets soared, peaking in early 2001. Later that year, these markets began to unwind and then crashed, with many commentators identifying the previous few years as a "stock market bubble." How might it be possible for this episode to be a bubble but still adhere to the efficient market hypothesis?

21. Why might the efficient market hypothesis be less likely to hold when fundamentals suggest stocks should be at a lower level?

APPLIED PROBLEMS

22. Compute the price of a share of stock that pays a $1 per year dividend and that you expect to be able to sell in one year for $20, assuming you require a 15% return.

23. After careful analysis, you have determined that a firm's dividends should grow at 7%, on average, in the foreseeable future. The firm's last dividend was $3. Compute the current price of this stock, assuming the required return is 18%.

24. The current price of a stock is $65.88. If dividends are expected to be $1 per share for the next five years, and the required return is 10%, what should the price of the stock be in five years when you plan to sell it? If the dividend and required return remain the same, and the stock price is expected to increase by $1 five years from now, does the current stock price also increase by $1? Why or why not?

25. A company has just announced a 3-for-1 stock split, effective immediately. Prior to the split, the company had a market value of $5 billion with 100 million shares outstanding. Assuming the split conveys no new information about the company, what are the value of the company, the number of shares outstanding, and the price per share after the split? If the actual market price immediately following the split is $17.00 per share, what does this tell us about market efficiency?

DATA ANALYSIS PROBLEMS

The Problems update with real-time data in **MyLab Economics** and are available for practice or instructor assignment.

1. **Real-time Data Analysis** Go to the St. Louis Federal Reserve FRED database, and find data on the Dow Jones Industrial Average (DJIA). Assume the DJIA is a stock that pays no dividends. Apply the one-period valuation model, using the data from one year prior up to the most current date available, to determine the required return on equity investment. In other words, assume the most recent stock price of DJIA is known one year prior. What rate of return would be required to "buy" a share of DJIA? Suppose that a 100 points dividend is paid out instead. How does this change the required rate of return?

2. **Real-time Data Analysis** Go to the St. Louis Federal Reserve FRED database, and find data on net corporate dividend payments (B056RC1A027NBEA). Adjust the *units* setting to "Percent Change from Year Ago," and download the data into a spreadsheet.

   a. Calculate the average annual growth rate of dividends from 1960 to the most recent year of data available.

   b. Find data on the Dow Jones Industrial Average (DJIA) for the most recent day of data available. Suppose that a 100 points dividend is paid out at the end of next year. Use the Gordon growth model and your answer to part (a) to calculate the rate of return that would be required for equity investment over the next year, assuming you could buy a share of DJIA.

Financial Institutions

Crisis and Response: The $700 Billion Bailout Package

After a heated national debate, the U.S. House of Representatives passed the Emergency Economic Stabilization Act on October 3, 2008. This stunning $700 billion bailout package sought to promote economic recovery from the global financial crisis by authorizing the Treasury to purchase troubled mortgage assets from struggling financial institutions or to inject capital into banking institutions. To calm fears further, the Act raised the federal deposit insurance limit from $100,000 to $250,000.

The initial bill was voted down on September 29, when constituents flooded their representatives with complaints about bailing out the greedy Wall Street executives behind the crisis. The national debate pitted Wall Street against Main Street: Many people who sided with struggling homeowners saw the proposed federal bailout of financial institutions as government hypocrisy. How could injecting capital into the financial system help those fearful of losing their jobs or, worse yet, those who found themselves suddenly without work?

The central role of financial institutions in the workings of the economy—the focus of Part 3—was being overlooked. Banks and other financial institutions make financial markets work by moving funds from people who save to people who have productive investment opportunities. That bank branch on Main Street was not going to be able to lend freely to a small business owner or recent college graduate looking to fund a new car purchase until capital once again flowed.

The global financial crisis highlights how financial systems change over time, be it from financial innovations or through hard lessons learned from such crises. Chapter 8 analyzes financial structure in the United States and in the rest of the world. In Chapter 9, we look at the business and process of banking. In Chapter 10, we extend the economic analysis developed in Chapter 8 to understand the motivations for bank regulation, and we examine the pitfalls of the regulatory process. Chapter 11 examines the development of the American banking system over time and the growing internationalization of banking. In Chapter 12, we develop a framework for understanding the dynamics of financial crises, which is then used to explain what happened during the global financial crisis of 2007–2009 and whether the coronavirus pandemic could have led to another financial crisis.

8

An Economic Analysis of Financial Structure

Learning Objectives

8.1 Identify eight basic facts about the global financial system.

8.2 Summarize how transaction costs affect financial intermediaries.

8.3 Describe why asymmetric information leads to adverse selection and moral hazard.

8.4 Recognize adverse selection and summarize the ways in which it can be reduced.

8.5 Recognize the principal–agent problem arising from moral hazard in equity contracts and summarize the methods for reducing it.

8.6 Summarize the methods used to reduce moral hazard in debt contracts.

Preview

A healthy and vibrant economy requires a financial system that moves funds from people who save to people who have productive investment opportunities. But how does the financial system make sure that your hard-earned savings get channeled to Paula the Productive Investor rather than to Benny the Bum?

This chapter answers that question by providing an economic analysis of how our financial structure is designed to promote economic efficiency. The analysis focuses on a few simple but powerful economic concepts that enable us to explain features of our financial system, such as why financial contracts are written as they are and why financial intermediaries are more important than securities markets for getting funds to borrowers. The analysis also demonstrates the important link between the financial system and the performance of the aggregate economy, which is the subject of Part 6 of this book.

8.1 BASIC FACTS ABOUT FINANCIAL STRUCTURE THROUGHOUT THE WORLD

LO 8.1 Identify eight basic facts about the global financial system.

The financial system is complex in structure and function throughout the world. It includes many different types of institutions: banks, insurance companies, mutual funds, stock and bond markets, and so on—all of which are regulated by government. The financial system channels trillions of dollars per year from savers to people with productive investment opportunities. If we take a close look at financial structure all over the world, we find eight basic facts, some of which are quite surprising, that we must explain if we are to understand how the financial system works.

The bar chart in Figure 1 shows how American businesses financed their activities using external funds (those obtained from outside the business itself) in the period 1970–2000 and compares U.S. data with data for Germany, Japan, and Canada. The conclusions drawn from this period still hold true today. The *Bank Loans* category is made up primarily of loans from depository institutions; *Nonbank Loans* are primarily loans by other financial intermediaries; the *Bonds* category includes marketable debt securities, such as corporate bonds and commercial paper; and *Stock* consists of new issues of equity (stock market shares).

Mini-lecture

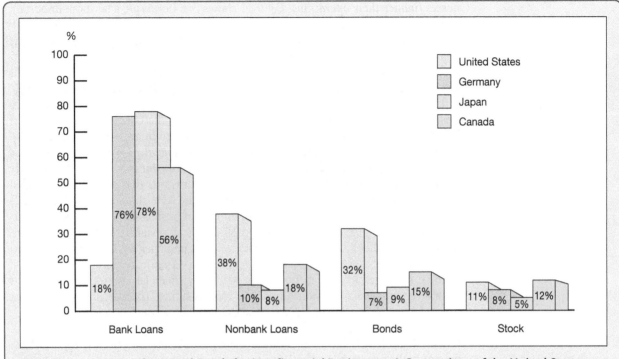

FIGURE 1   **Sources of External Funds for Nonfinancial Businesses: A Comparison of the United States with Germany, Japan, and Canada**

The *Bank Loans* category is made up primarily of loans from depository institutions; the *Nonbank Loans* are primarily loans by other financial intermediaries; the *Bonds* category includes marketable debt securities, such as corporate bonds and commercial paper; and *Stock* consists of new issues of new equity (stock market shares).

Source: Andreas Hackethal and Reinhard H. Schmidt, "Financing Patterns: Measurement Concepts and Empirical Results," Johann Wolfgang Goethe-Universitat Working Paper No. 125, January 2004. The data are for 1970–2000 and are gross flows as percentages of the total, not including trade and other credit data, which are not available.

Now let's explore the eight facts.

1. ***Stocks are not the most important source of external financing for businesses.*** Because so much attention in the media is focused on the stock market, many people have the impression that stocks are the most important source of financing for American corporations. However, as we can see from the bar chart in Figure 1, the stock market accounted for only a small fraction of the external financing of American businesses in the 1970–2000 period: 11%.[1] Similarly low figures apply for the other countries presented in Figure 1. Why is the stock market less important than other sources of financing in the United States and other countries?

[1] The 11% figure for the percentage of external financing provided by stocks is based on the flows of external funds to corporations. However, this flow figure is somewhat misleading because when a share of stock is issued, it raises funds permanently, whereas when a bond is issued, it raises funds only temporarily until it is paid back at maturity. To see this, suppose a firm raises $1,000 by selling a share of stock and another $1,000 by selling a $1,000 one-year bond. In the case of the stock issue, the firm can hold on to the $1,000 it raised by selling the stock. However, to hold on to the $1,000 it raised through debt, the firm has to issue a new $1,000 bond every year. If we look at the flow of funds to corporations over a 30-year period, as shown in Figure 1, the firm will have raised $1,000 through a stock issue only once in the 30-year period, while it will have raised $1,000 through debt 30 times, once in each of the 30 years. Thus it looks as though debt is 30 times more important than stocks in raising funds, even though our example indicates that the two methods are actually equally important for the firm.

2. *Issuing marketable debt and equity securities is not the primary way in which businesses finance their operations.* Figure 1 shows that bonds are a far more important source of financing in the United States than stocks are (32% versus 11%). However, stocks and bonds combined (43%), which make up the total share of marketable securities, still supply less than one-half of the external funds needed by U.S. corporations to finance their activities. The fact that issuing marketable securities is not the most important source of financing is true elsewhere in the world as well. Indeed, as we see in Figure 1, other countries have a much smaller share of external financing supplied by marketable securities than does the United States. Why don't businesses use marketable securities more extensively to finance their activities?

3. *Indirect finance, which involves the activities of financial intermediaries, is many times more important than direct finance, in which businesses raise funds directly from lenders in financial markets.* Direct finance involves the sale to households of marketable securities, such as stocks and bonds. The 43% share of stocks and bonds used as a source of external financing for American businesses actually greatly overstates the importance of direct finance in our financial system. Since 1970, less than 5% of newly issued corporate bonds and commercial paper, and less than one-third of new issues of stocks, have been sold directly to American households. The rest of these securities have been bought primarily by financial intermediaries such as insurance companies, pension funds, and mutual funds. These figures indicate that direct finance is used in less than 10% of the external funding of American business. Because in most countries marketable securities are an even less important source of finance than in the United States, direct finance is also far less important than indirect finance in the rest of the world. Why are financial intermediaries and indirect finance so important in financial markets? In recent years, however, indirect finance has been declining in importance. Why is this happening?

4. *Financial intermediaries, particularly banks, are the most important source of external funds used to finance businesses.* As we can see in Figure 1, the primary source of external funds for businesses throughout the world is loans made by banks and other nonbank financial intermediaries, such as insurance companies, pension funds, and finance companies (56% in the United States, but more than 70% in Germany, Japan, and Canada). In other industrialized countries, bank loans are the largest category of sources of external finance (more than 70% in Germany and Japan, and more than 50% in Canada). Thus the data suggest that banks in these countries have the most important role in financing business activities. In developing countries, banks play an even more important role in the financial system than they do in industrialized countries. What makes banks so important to the workings of the financial system? Although banks remain important, their contributions to external funds for businesses have been declining in recent years. What is driving this decline?

5. *The financial system is among the most heavily regulated sectors of the economy.* The financial system is heavily regulated in the United States and in all other developed countries. Governments regulate financial markets primarily to promote the provision of information and to ensure the soundness (stability) of the financial system. Why are financial markets so extensively regulated throughout the world?

6. *Only large, well-established corporations have easy access to securities markets to finance their activities.* Individuals and smaller businesses that are not well established are less likely to raise funds by issuing marketable securities. Instead, they most often obtain their financing from banks. Why do only large, well-known corporations find it easier to raise funds in securities markets?

7. *Collateral is a prevalent feature of debt contracts for both households and businesses.* **Collateral** is property that is pledged to a lender to guarantee payment in the event that the borrower is unable to make debt payments. Collateralized debt (also known as **secured debt** to contrast it with **unsecured debt**, such as credit card debt, which is not collateralized) is the predominant form of household debt and is widely used in business borrowing as well. The majority of household debt in the United States consists of collateralized loans: Your automobile is collateral for your auto loan, and your house is collateral for your mortgage. Commercial and farm mortgages, for which property is pledged as collateral, make up one-quarter of borrowing by nonfinancial businesses; corporate bonds and other bank loans also often involve pledges of collateral. Why is collateral such an important feature of debt contracts?

8. *Debt contracts typically are extremely complicated legal documents that place substantial restrictions on the behavior of the borrower.* Many students think of a debt contract as a simple IOU that can be written on a single piece of paper. The reality of debt contracts is far different, however. In all countries, bond or loan contracts typically are long legal documents with provisions (called **restrictive covenants**) that restrict and specify certain activities that the borrower can engage in. Restrictive covenants are not just a feature of debt contracts for businesses; for example, personal automobile loan and home mortgage contracts include covenants that require the borrower to maintain sufficient insurance on the automobile or house purchased with the loan. Why are debt contracts so complex and restrictive?

As you may recall from Chapter 2, an important feature of financial markets is their substantial transaction and information costs. An economic analysis of how these costs affect financial markets will help us understand the eight facts, which will in turn give us a much deeper understanding of how our financial system works. In the next section, we examine the impact of transaction costs on the structure of our financial system. Then we turn to the effects of information costs on financial structure.

8.2 TRANSACTION COSTS

LO 8.2 Summarize how transaction costs affect financial intermediaries.

Transaction costs are a major problem in financial markets. An example will make this clear.

How Transaction Costs Influence Financial Structure

Say you have $5,000 that you would like to invest, and you are thinking about investing in the stock market. Because you have only $5,000, you can buy only a small number of shares. Even if you use online trading, your purchase is so small that the brokerage commission for buying the stock you pick will be a large percentage of the purchase price of the shares. If, instead, you decide to buy a bond, the problem becomes even worse; the smallest denomination offered on some bonds that you might want to buy is as large as $10,000, and you do not have that much money to invest. You are disappointed and realize that you will not be able to use financial markets to earn a return on your hard-earned savings. You can take some consolation, however, in the fact that you are not alone in being stymied by high transaction costs. This is a fact of life for many of us: About one-half of American households own any securities.

You also face another problem related to transaction costs. Because you have only a small amount of funds available, you can make only a restricted number of investments, because a large number of small transactions would result in very high transaction costs. That is, you have to put all your eggs in one basket, and your inability to diversify will subject you to a lot of risk.

How Financial Intermediaries Reduce Transaction Costs

This example of the problems posed by transaction costs, along with the example outlined in Chapter 2, in which legal costs kept you from making a loan to Carl the Carpenter, illustrates that small savers like you are frozen out of financial markets and are unable to benefit from them. Fortunately, financial intermediaries, an important part of the financial structure, have evolved to reduce transaction costs and allow small savers and borrowers to benefit from the existence of financial markets.

Economies of Scale

One solution to the problem of high transaction costs is to bundle the funds of many investors together so that they can take advantage of *economies of scale*, the reduction in transaction costs per dollar of investment as the size (scale) of transactions increases. Bundling investors' funds together reduces transaction costs for each individual investor. Economies of scale exist because the total cost of carrying out a transaction in financial markets increases only a little as the size of the transaction grows. For example, the cost of arranging a purchase of 10,000 shares of stock is not much greater than the cost of arranging a purchase of 50 shares of stock.

The presence of economies of scale in financial markets helps explain the development of financial intermediaries and why financial intermediaries have become such an important part of our financial structure. The clearest example of a financial intermediary that arose because of economies of scale is a mutual fund. A *mutual fund* is a financial intermediary that sells shares to individuals and then invests the proceeds in bonds or stocks. Because it buys large blocks of stocks or bonds, a mutual fund can take advantage of lower transaction costs. These cost savings are then passed on to individual investors after the mutual fund has taken its cut in the form of management fees for administering their accounts. An additional benefit for individual investors is that a mutual fund is large enough to purchase a widely diversified portfolio of securities. The increased diversification for individual investors reduces their risk, making them better off.

Economies of scale are also important in lowering the costs of resources that financial institutions need to accomplish their tasks, such as computer technology. Once a large mutual fund has invested a lot of money in setting up a telecommunications system, for example, the system can be used for a huge number of transactions at a low cost per transaction.

Expertise

Financial intermediaries are also better able to develop expertise that can be used to lower transaction costs. Their expertise in computer technology, for example, enables them to offer their customers convenient services such as check-writing privileges on their accounts and toll-free numbers that customers can call for information on how well their investments are doing.

Low transaction costs enable financial intermediaries to provide their customers with *liquidity services*, which are services that make it easier for customers to conduct transactions. Money market mutual funds, for example, not only pay shareholders relatively high interest rates but also allow them to write checks for convenient bill paying.

8.3 ASYMMETRIC INFORMATION: ADVERSE SELECTION AND MORAL HAZARD

LO 8.3 Describe why asymmetric information leads to adverse selection and moral hazard.

The presence of transaction costs in financial markets partly explains why financial intermediaries and indirect finance play such an important role in financial markets (fact 3). To understand financial structure more fully, however, we turn to the role of information in financial markets.

Asymmetric information—a situation that arises when one party's insufficient knowledge about the other party involved in a transaction makes it impossible for the first party to make accurate decisions when conducting the transaction—is an important aspect of financial markets. For example, managers of a corporation know whether they are honest and usually have better information about how well their business is doing than stockholders do. The presence of asymmetric information leads to adverse selection and moral hazard problems, which were introduced in Chapter 2.

Adverse selection is an asymmetric information problem that occurs *before* a transaction occurs. Adverse selection occurs when one party to a transaction has information about a hidden characteristic and takes economic advantage of this information by engaging in a transaction with less informed parties. Specifically, potential bad credit risks are the ones who most actively seek out loans. Thus the parties who are most likely to produce an undesirable outcome are also the ones most likely to want to engage in the transaction. For example, big risk takers or outright crooks are often the most eager to take out a loan because they know they are unlikely to pay it back. Because adverse selection increases the chances that a loan might be made to a bad credit risk, lenders might decide not to make any loans, even though good credit risks can be found in the marketplace.

Moral hazard arises *after* the transaction occurs. Moral hazard occurs when an informed party takes a hidden (unobserved) action that harms the less informed party. A lender runs the risk that the borrower will engage in activities that are undesirable from the lender's point of view, because such activities make it less likely that the loan will be paid back. For example, once borrowers have obtained a loan, they may take on big risks (which have possible high returns but also run a greater risk of default) because they are playing with someone else's money. Because moral hazard lowers the probability that the loan will be repaid, lenders may decide that they would rather not make a loan.

The analysis of how asymmetric information problems affect economic behavior is called **agency theory**. We will apply this theory here to explain why financial structure takes the form it does, thereby explaining the facts outlined at the beginning of the chapter.

8.4 THE LEMONS PROBLEM: HOW ADVERSE SELECTION INFLUENCES FINANCIAL STRUCTURE

LO 8.4 Recognize adverse selection and summarize the ways in which it can be reduced.

A particular aspect of the way the adverse selection problem interferes with the efficient functioning of a market was outlined in a famous article by Nobel Prize winner George Akerlof. It is called the "lemons problem" because it resembles the problem created by "lemons," that is, bad cars, in the used-car market.[2] Potential buyers of used cars are frequently unable to assess the quality of a car; that is, they can't tell whether a particular used car is one that will run well or a lemon that will continually give them grief. The price that a buyer pays must therefore reflect the *average* quality of the cars in the market, somewhere between the low value of a lemon and the high value of a good car.

The owner of a used car, by contrast, is more likely to know whether the car is a peach or a lemon. If the car is a lemon, the owner is more than happy to sell it at the price the buyer is willing to pay, which, being somewhere between the value of a lemon and that of a good car, is greater than the lemon's value. However, if the car is a peach, that is, a good car, the owner knows that the car is undervalued at the price the buyer is willing to pay, and so the owner may not want to sell it. As a result of this adverse selection problem, fewer good used cars will come to the market. Because the average quality of a used car available in the market will be low, and because very few people want to buy a lemon, there will be few sales. The used-car market will function poorly, if at all.

Lemons in the Stock and Bond Markets

A similar lemons problem arises in securities markets—that is, the debt (bond) and equity (stock) markets. Suppose that our friend Irving the Investor, a potential buyer of securities such as common stock, can't distinguish between good firms with high expected profits and low risk and bad firms with low expected profits and high risk. In this situation, Irving will be willing to pay only a price that reflects the *average* quality of firms issuing securities—a price that lies between the value of securities from bad firms and the value of those from good firms. If the owners or managers of a good firm have better information than Irving and *know* that they have a good firm, then they know that their securities are undervalued and will not want to sell them to Irving at the price he is willing to pay. The only firms willing to sell Irving securities will be bad firms (because his price is higher than the securities are worth). Our friend Irving is not stupid; he does not want to hold securities in bad firms, and hence he will decide not to purchase securities in the market. In an outcome similar to that in the used-car market, this securities market will not work very well because few firms will sell securities in it to raise capital.

The analysis is similar if Irving considers purchasing a corporate debt instrument in the bond market rather than an equity share. Irving will buy a bond only if its interest rate is high enough to compensate him for the average default risk of the good and bad firms trying to sell the debt. The knowledgeable owners of a good firm realize that they will be paying a higher interest rate than they should, so they are unlikely to want to borrow in this market. Only the bad firms will be willing to borrow, and because investors like Irving are not eager to buy bonds issued by bad firms, they will probably not buy any bonds at all. Few bonds are likely to sell in this market, so it will not be a good source of financing.

The analysis we have just conducted explains fact 2—why marketable securities are not the primary source of financing for businesses in any country in the world. It also partly explains fact 1—why stocks are not the most important source of financing for American businesses. The presence of the lemons problem keeps securities markets such as the stock and bond markets from being effective in channeling funds from savers to borrowers.

---

[2]George Akerlof, "The Market for 'Lemons': Quality, Uncertainty and the Market Mechanism," *Quarterly Journal of Economics* 84 (1970): 488–500. Two important papers that have applied the lemons problem analysis to financial markets are Stewart Myers and N. S. Majluf, "Corporate Financing and Investment Decisions: When Firms Have Information That Investors Do Not Have," *Journal of Financial Economics* 13 (1984): 187–221; and Bruce Greenwald, Joseph E. Stiglitz, and Andrew Weiss, "Information Imperfections in the Capital Market and Macroeconomic Fluctuations," *American Economic Review* 74 (1984): 194–199.

Tools to Help Solve Adverse Selection Problems

In the absence of asymmetric information, the lemons problem goes away. If buyers know as much about the quality of used cars as sellers, so that all involved can tell a good car from a bad one, buyers will be willing to pay full value for good used cars. Because the owners of good used cars can now get a fair price, they will be willing to sell them in the market. The market will have many transactions and will perform its intended job of channeling good cars to people who want them.

Similarly, if purchasers of securities can distinguish good firms from bad, they will pay the full value of securities issued by good firms, and good firms will sell their securities in the market. The securities market will then be able to move funds to the good firms that have the most productive investment opportunities.

Private Production and Sale of Information

The solution to the adverse selection problem in financial markets is to reduce asymmetric information by furnishing the people supplying funds with more details about the individuals or firms seeking to finance their investment activities. One way for saver-lenders to get this information is through private companies that collect and produce information distinguishing good firms from bad firms and then sell it to the saver-lenders. In the United States, companies such as Standard & Poor's, Moody's, and Value Line gather information on firms' balance sheet positions and investment activities, publish these data, and sell them to subscribers (individuals, libraries, and financial intermediaries involved in purchasing securities).

The system of private production and sale of information does not completely solve the adverse selection problem in securities markets, however, because of the **free-rider problem**. The free-rider problem occurs when people who do not pay for information take advantage of the information that other people have paid for. The free-rider problem suggests that the private sale of information is only a partial solution to the lemons problem. To see why, suppose you have just purchased information that tells you which firms are good and which are bad. You believe that this purchase is worthwhile because you can make up the cost of acquiring this information, and then some, by purchasing the securities of good firms that are undervalued. However, when our savvy (free-riding) investor Irving sees you buying certain securities, he buys right along with you, even though he has not paid for any information. If many other investors act as Irving does, the increased demand for the undervalued good securities causes their low price to be bid up immediately to reflect the securities' true value. Because of all these free riders, you can no longer buy the securities for less than their true value. Now, because you will not gain any profit from purchasing the information, you realize that you never should have paid for the information in the first place. If other investors come to the same realization, private firms and individuals may not be able to sell enough of this information to make it worth their while to gather and produce it. The weakened ability of private firms to profit from selling information will mean that less information is produced in the marketplace, so adverse selection (the lemons problem) will still interfere with the efficient functioning of securities markets.

Government Regulation to Increase Information

The free-rider problem prevents the private market from producing enough information to eliminate all the asymmetric information that leads to adverse selection. Could financial markets benefit from government intervention? The government could, for instance, produce information to help investors distinguish good from bad firms and provide it to the public free of charge. This solution, however, would involve the government releasing negative information about firms, a practice that might be politically difficult. A second possibility (and one followed by the United States and most governments throughout the world) is for the

---

FYI   The Enron Implosion

Until 2001, Enron Corporation, a firm that specialized in trading in the energy market, appeared to be spectacularly successful. It controlled a quarter of the energy-trading market and was valued as high as $77 billion in August 2000 (just a little over a year before its collapse), making it the seventh largest corporation in the United States at that time. However, toward the end of 2001, Enron came crashing down. In October 2001, Enron announced a third-quarter loss of $618 million and disclosed accounting "mistakes." The SEC then engaged in a formal investigation of Enron's financial dealings with partnerships led by its former finance chief. It became clear that Enron was engaged in a complex set of transactions by which it was keeping substantial amounts of debt and financial contracts off its balance sheet. These transactions enabled Enron to hide its financial difficulties. Despite securing as much as $1.5 billion of new financing from J. P. Morgan Chase and Citigroup, the company was forced to declare bankruptcy in December 2001, up to that point the largest bankruptcy declaration in U.S. history.

The Enron collapse illustrates that government regulation can lessen asymmetric information problems but cannot eliminate them. Managers have tremendous incentives to hide their companies' problems, making it hard for investors to know the true value of firms.

The Enron bankruptcy not only increased concerns in financial markets about the quality of accounting information supplied by corporations but also led to hardship for many of the firm's former employees, who found that their pensions had become worthless. Outrage against the duplicity of executives at Enron was high, and several of them were convicted and sent to jail.

---

government to regulate securities markets in a way that encourages firms to reveal honest information about themselves so that investors can determine how good or bad the firms are. In the United States, the Securities and Exchange Commission (SEC) is the government agency that requires firms selling their securities to undergo independent audits, in which accounting firms certify that the firm is adhering to standard accounting principles and disclosing accurate information about sales, assets, and earnings. Similar regulations are found in other countries. However, disclosure requirements do not always work well, as the collapse of Enron and accounting scandals at other corporations, such as World-Com and Parmalat (an Italian company), suggest (see the FYI box "The Enron Implosion").

The asymmetric information problem of adverse selection in financial markets helps explain why financial markets are among the most heavily regulated sectors of the economy (fact 5). Government regulation aimed at increasing the information available to investors is necessary to reduce the adverse selection problem, which interferes with the efficient functioning of securities (stock and bond) markets.

Although government regulation lessens the adverse selection problem, it does not eliminate it entirely. Even when firms provide information to the public about their sales, assets, or earnings, they still have more information than investors: A lot more is involved in knowing the quality of a firm than statistics alone can provide. Furthermore, bad firms have an incentive to make themselves look like good firms because this enables them to fetch a higher price for their securities. Bad firms will slant the information they are required to transmit to the public, thus making it harder for investors to sort out the good firms from the bad.

Financial Intermediation   So far we have seen that private production of information and government regulation to encourage provision of information lessen, but do not eliminate, the adverse selection problem in financial markets. How, then, can the financial structure help promote the flow of funds to people with productive investment opportunities when asymmetric information exists? A clue is provided by the structure of the used-car market.

An important feature of the used-car market is that most used cars are not sold directly by one individual to another. An individual who considers buying a used car might pay for privately produced information by subscribing to a magazine like *Consumer Reports* to find out if a particular make of car has a good repair record. Nevertheless, reading *Consumer Reports* does not solve the adverse selection problem, because even if a particular make of car has a good reputation, the specific car someone is trying to sell could be a lemon. The prospective buyer might also bring the used car to a mechanic for a once-over. But what if the prospective buyer doesn't know a mechanic who can be trusted or the mechanic charges a high fee to evaluate the car?

Because these roadblocks make it hard for individuals to acquire enough information about used cars, most used cars are not sold directly by one individual to another. Instead, they are sold by an intermediary, a used-car dealer who purchases used cars from individuals and resells them to other individuals. Used-car dealers produce information in the market by becoming experts in determining whether a car is a peach or a lemon. Once a dealer knows that a car is good, the dealer can sell it with some form of a guarantee: either an explicit guarantee such as a warranty or an implicit guarantee in which the dealer stands by its reputation for honesty. People are more likely to purchase a used car because of a dealer guarantee, and the dealer is able to sell the used car at a higher price than he or she paid for it. Thus the dealer profits from the production of information about automobile quality. If dealers purchase and then resell cars on which they have produced information, they avoid the problem of other people free-riding on the information they produced.

Just as used-car dealers help solve adverse selection problems in the automobile market, financial intermediaries play a similar role in financial markets. A financial intermediary, such as a bank, becomes an expert in producing information about firms so that it can sort out good credit risks from bad ones. It then can acquire funds from depositors and lend them to the good firms. Because the bank is able to lend mostly to good firms, it is able to earn a higher return on its loans than the interest it has to pay to its depositors. The resulting profit that the bank earns gives it the incentive to engage in this information production activity.

An important element of the bank's ability to profit from the information it produces is that it avoids the free-rider problem by primarily making private loans, rather than by purchasing securities that are traded in the open market. Because a private loan is not traded, other investors cannot watch what the bank is doing and bid down the loan's interest rate to the point that the bank receives no compensation for the information it has produced. The bank's role as an intermediary that holds mostly nontraded loans is the key to its success in reducing asymmetric information in financial markets.

Our analysis of adverse selection indicates that financial intermediaries in general—and banks in particular, because they hold a large fraction of nontraded loans—should play a greater role in moving funds to corporations than securities markets do. Our analysis thus explains facts 3 and 4: why indirect finance is so much more important than direct finance and why banks are the most important source of external funds for financing businesses.

Our analysis also explains the greater importance of banks, as opposed to securities markets, in the financial systems of developing countries. As we have seen, better information about the quality of firms lessens asymmetric information problems, making it easier for firms to issue securities. Information about private firms is harder to collect in developing countries than in industrialized countries; therefore, the smaller role played by securities markets leads to a greater role for financial intermediaries such as banks. As a corollary to our analysis, as information about firms becomes easier to acquire, the role of banks should decline. A major development in the past 30 years in the United States has been huge improvements in information technology. Thus our analysis suggests that the lending role of financial institutions such as banks in the United States should have declined, and this is exactly what has occurred (see Chapter 11).

Our analysis of adverse selection also explains fact 6, which questions why large firms are more likely to obtain funds from securities markets, a direct route, rather than from banks and financial intermediaries, an indirect route. The better known a corporation is, the more information about its activities is available in the marketplace. Thus it is easier for investors to evaluate the quality of the corporation and determine whether it is a good firm or a bad one. Because investors have fewer worries about adverse selection when dealing with well-known corporations, they are more willing to invest directly in their securities. Thus, in accordance with adverse selection, a pecking order for firms that can issue securities should exist. Hence we have an explanation for fact 6: The larger and more established a corporation is, the more likely it will be to issue securities to raise funds.

Collateral and Net Worth   Adverse selection interferes with the functioning of financial markets only if a lender suffers a loss when a borrower is unable to make loan payments and thereby defaults on the loan. *Collateral*, property promised to the lender if the borrower defaults, reduces the consequences of adverse selection because it reduces the lender's losses in the event of a default. If a borrower defaults on a loan, the lender can sell the collateral and use the proceeds to make up for the losses on the loan. For example, if you fail to make your mortgage payments, the lender can take the title to your house, auction it off, and use the receipts to pay off the loan. Lenders are thus more willing to make loans secured by collateral, and borrowers are willing to supply collateral because the reduced risk for the lender makes it more likely that the loan will be made, perhaps even at a better loan rate. The presence of adverse selection in credit markets thus explains why collateral is an important feature of debt contracts (fact 7).

Net worth (also called **equity capital**), the difference between a firm's assets (what it owns or is owed) and its liabilities (what it owes), can perform a similar role to that of collateral. If a firm has a high net worth, then even if it engages in investments that lead to negative profits and so defaults on its debt payments, the lender can take title to the firm's net worth, sell it off, and use the proceeds to recoup some of the losses from the loan. In addition, the more net worth a firm has in the first place, the less likely it is to default, because the firm has a cushion of assets that it can use to pay off its loans. Hence, when firms seeking credit have high net worth, the consequences of adverse selection are less important and lenders are more willing to make loans. This concept lies behind the often-heard lament, "Only the people who don't need money can borrow it!"

Summary   So far we have used the concept of adverse selection to explain seven of the eight facts about financial structure introduced earlier: The first four facts emphasize the importance of financial intermediaries and the relative unimportance of securities markets with regard to the financing of corporations; the fifth, that financial markets are among the most heavily regulated sectors of the economy; the sixth, that only large, well-established corporations have access to securities markets; and the seventh, that collateral is an important feature of debt contracts. In the next section, we will see that the other asymmetric information concept, moral hazard, provides additional reasons for the importance of financial intermediaries and the relative unimportance of securities markets as related to the financing of corporations, the prevalence of government regulation, and the importance of collateral in debt contracts. In addition, the concept of moral hazard can be used to explain our final fact (fact 8): why debt contracts are complicated legal documents that place substantial restrictions on the behavior of the borrower.

8.5 HOW MORAL HAZARD AFFECTS THE CHOICE BETWEEN DEBT AND EQUITY CONTRACTS

LO 8.5 Recognize the principal-agent problem arising from moral hazard in equity contracts and summarize the methods for reducing it.

Moral hazard is the asymmetric information problem that occurs after a financial transaction takes place, when the seller of a security may have incentives to hide information and engage in activities that are undesirable for the purchaser of the security. Moral hazard has important consequences for whether a firm finds it easier to raise funds with debt than with equity contracts.

Moral Hazard in Equity Contracts: The Principal–Agent Problem

Equity contracts, such as common stock, are claims to a share in the profits and assets of a business. Equity contracts are subject to a particular type of moral hazard called the **principal–agent problem**. When managers own only a small fraction of the firm they work for, the stockholders who own most of the firm's equity (called the *principals*) are not the same people as the managers of the firm. Thus the managers are the *agents* of the owners. This separation of ownership and control involves moral hazard, in that the managers in control (the agents) may act in their own interest rather than in the interest of the stockholder-owners (the principals) because the managers have less incentive to maximize profits than the stockholder-owners do.

To understand the principal–agent problem more fully, suppose that your friend Steve asks you to become a silent partner in his ice-cream store. The store setup requires an initial investment of $10,000, and Steve has only $1,000. So you purchase an equity stake (stock shares) for $9,000, which entitles you to 90% of the ownership of the firm, while Steve owns only 10%. If Steve works hard to make tasty ice cream, keeps the store clean, smiles at all the customers, and hustles to wait on tables quickly, after all expenses (including Steve's salary) have been paid, the store will make $50,000 in profits per year, of which Steve will receive 10% ($5,000) and you will receive 90% ($45,000).

But if Steve doesn't provide quick and friendly service to his customers, uses the $50,000 in income to buy artwork for his office, and even sneaks off to the beach while he should be at the store, the store will not earn any profit. Steve can earn the additional $5,000 (his 10% share of the profits) over his salary only if he works hard and forgoes unproductive investments (such as art for his office). Steve might decide that the extra $5,000 just isn't enough to make him expend the effort to be a good manager. If Steve feels this way, he does not have enough incentive to be a good manager and will end up with a beautiful office, a good tan, and a store that doesn't show any profits. Because the store won't show any profits, Steve's decision not to act in your interest will cost you $45,000 (your 90% of the profits had he chosen to be a good manager instead).

The moral hazard arising from the principal–agent problem might be even worse if Steve is not totally honest. Because his ice-cream store is a cash business, Steve has the incentive to pocket $50,000 in cash and tell you that the profits were zero. He now gets a return of $50,000, and you get nothing.

Further proof that the principal–agent problem created by equity contracts can be severe is provided by past scandals involving corporations such as Enron and Tyco International, in which managers were found to have diverted corporate funds for their own personal use. In addition to pursuing personal benefits, managers might also pursue corporate strategies (such as the acquisition of other firms) that enhance their personal power but do not increase the corporation's profitability.

The principal–agent problem would not arise if the owners of a firm had complete information about what the managers were up to and could prevent wasteful expenditures or fraud. The principal–agent problem, which is an example of moral hazard, arises only because a manager, such as Steve, has more information about his activities than the stockholder does—that is, information is asymmetric. The principal–agent problem also would not occur if Steve alone owned the store, and ownership and control were not separate. If this were the case, Steve's hard work and avoidance of unproductive investments would yield him a profit (and extra income) of $50,000, an amount that would make it worth his while to be a good manager.

Tools to Help Solve the Principal–Agent Problem

Production of Information: Monitoring   You have seen that the principal–agent problem arises because managers have more information about their activities and actual profits than stockholders do. One way for stockholders to reduce this moral hazard problem is for them to engage in a particular type of information production: monitoring the firm's activities by auditing the firm frequently and checking on what the management is doing. The problem is that the monitoring process can be expensive in terms of time and money, as reflected in the name economists give it: **costly state verification**. Costly state verification makes the equity contract less desirable and explains in part why equity is not a more important element in our financial structure.

As with adverse selection, the free-rider problem decreases the amount of private information production that would reduce the moral hazard (principal–agent) problem. In this example, the free-rider problem decreases monitoring. If you know that other stockholders are paying to monitor the activities of the company you hold shares in, you can take a free ride on their activities. Then you can use the money you save by not engaging in monitoring to vacation on a Caribbean island. If you can do this, though, so can other stockholders. Perhaps all the stockholders will go to the islands, and no one will spend any resources on monitoring the firm. The moral hazard problem for shares of common stock will then be severe, making it hard for firms to issue them to raise capital (providing an additional explanation for fact 1).

Government Regulation to Increase Information   As with adverse selection, the government has an incentive to try to reduce the moral hazard problem created by asymmetric information, which provides another reason why the financial system is so heavily regulated (fact 5). Governments everywhere have laws to force firms to adhere to standard accounting principles that make profit verification easier. They also pass laws to impose stiff criminal penalties on people who commit the fraud of hiding and stealing profits. However, these measures can be only partly effective.

Catching this kind of fraud is not easy; fraudulent managers have the incentive to make it very hard for government agencies to find or prove fraud.

Financial Intermediation   Financial intermediaries have the ability to avoid the free-rider problem in the face of moral hazard, and this is another reason why indirect finance is so important (fact 3). Two types of financial intermediaries are specifically designed to reduce the moral hazard arising from the principal–agent problem: venture-capital firms and private-equity firms. The **venture-capital firm** pools the resources of its partners and uses the funds to help budding entrepreneurs start *new* businesses. The **private-equity firm** has a similar structure to that of a venture-capital firm, but instead of investing in new businesses, it buys the shares of *existing* corporations. In exchange for supplying capital, venture-capital and private-equity firms receive an equity share in the business. Because verification of earnings and profits is so important in eliminating moral hazard, venture-capital and private-equity firms usually insist on having several of their own people participate as members of the managing body—the board of directors—of the new business so that they can keep a close watch on the new firm's activities. A key feature of venture-capital and private-equity firms is that the equity in the business they have bought is private—that is, not marketable to anyone *except* the venture-capital and private-equity firms. Thus other investors are unable to take a free ride on these firm's verification activities. As a result of this arrangement, venture-capital and private-equity firms are able to garner the full benefits of their verification activities and are given the appropriate incentives to reduce the moral hazard problem. Private-equity firms have played an important role in improving the efficiency of many corporations, while venture-capital firms have been important in the development of the high-tech sector in the United States. Both of these financial intermediaries have promoted economic growth and increased international competitiveness.

Debt Contracts   Moral hazard arises with an equity contract, which is a claim on profits in all situations, whether the firm is making or losing money. If a contract could be structured so that moral hazard would exist only in certain situations, the need to monitor managers would be reduced, and the contract would be more attractive than the equity contract. The debt contract has exactly these attributes because it is a contractual agreement by the borrower to pay the lender *fixed* dollar amounts at periodic intervals. When a firm has high profits, the lender receives the contractual payments and does not need to know the exact profits of the firm. If the managers are hiding profits or pursuing activities that are personally beneficial but don't increase the firm's profitability, the lender doesn't care, as long as these activities do not interfere with the ability of the firm to make its debt payments on time. Only when the firm cannot meet its debt payments, thereby putting itself in a state of default, does the lender need to verify the state of the firm's profits. Only in this situation do lenders involved in debt contracts need to act more like equity holders; to get their fair share, they now must know how much income the firm has.

The less frequent need to monitor the firm, and thus the lower cost of state verification, helps explain why debt contracts are used more frequently than equity contracts to raise capital. The concept of moral hazard therefore helps explain fact 1, which states that stocks are not the most important source of financing for businesses.[3]

---

[3]Another factor that encourages the use of debt contracts rather than equity contracts in the United States is our tax code. Debt interest payments are a deductible expense for American firms, whereas dividend payments to equity shareholders are not.

8.6 HOW MORAL HAZARD INFLUENCES FINANCIAL STRUCTURE IN DEBT MARKETS

LO 8.6 Summarize the methods used to reduce moral hazard in debt contracts.

Even with the advantages just described, debt contracts are still subject to moral hazard. Because a debt contract requires the borrowers to pay out a fixed amount and lets them keep any profits above this amount, the borrowers have an incentive to take on investment projects that are riskier than the lenders would like.

For example, suppose you are concerned about the problem of verifying the profits of Steve's ice-cream store, and so you decide not to become an equity partner. Instead, you lend Steve the $9,000 he needs to set up his business, and you and he sign a debt contract that pays you an interest rate of 10%. As far as you are concerned, this is a surefire investment, because the demand for ice cream is strong and steady in your neighborhood. However, once you give Steve the funds, he might use them for purposes other than what he proposed to you. Instead of opening up the ice-cream store, Steve might use your $9,000 loan to invest in chemical research equipment because he thinks he has a 1-in-10 chance of inventing a diet ice cream that tastes every bit as good as the premium brands but has no fat or calories.

Obviously, this is a very risky investment, but if Steve is successful, he will become a multimillionaire. He has a strong incentive to undertake the riskier investment with your money because the gains to him would be so large if he succeeded. You would clearly be very unhappy if Steve used your loan for the riskier investment, because if he were unsuccessful, which is highly likely, you would lose most, if not all, of the money you gave him. And if he were successful, you wouldn't share in his success—you would still get only a 10% return on the loan because the principal and interest payments are fixed. Because of the potential moral hazard (that Steve might use your money to finance a very risky venture), you would probably not make the loan to Steve, even though an ice-cream store in the neighborhood is a good investment that would provide benefits to everyone.

Tools to Help Solve Moral Hazard in Debt Contracts

Net Worth and Collateral When borrowers have more at stake because their net worth (the difference between their assets and their liabilities) is high or the collateral they have pledged to the lender is valuable, the risk of moral hazard—the temptation to act in a manner that lenders find objectionable—is greatly reduced because the borrowers themselves have a lot to lose. In other words, if borrowers have more "skin in the game" because they have higher net worth or pledge collateral, they are likely to take less risk at the lender's expense. Let's return to Steve and his ice-cream business. Suppose that the cost of setting up either the ice-cream store or the research equipment is $100,000 instead of $10,000. Now Steve needs to invest $91,000 (instead of $1,000) of his own money in the business, in addition to the $9,000 supplied by your loan. If Steve is unsuccessful in inventing the no-calorie, nonfat ice cream, he has a lot to lose—the $91,000 of net worth (the $100,000 in assets minus the $9,000 loan from you). He will think twice about undertaking the riskier investment and is more likely to invest in the ice-cream store, which is more of a sure thing. Thus, when Steve has more of his own money (net worth) invested in the business, and hence more skin in the game, you are more likely to make him the loan. Similarly, if you have pledged your house as collateral, you are less likely to go to Las Vegas and gamble away your earnings that month, because you might not be able to make your mortgage payments and therefore might lose your house.

One way of describing the solution that high net worth and collateral provide to the moral hazard problem is to say that it makes the debt contract **incentive-compatible**; that is, it aligns the incentives of the borrower with those of the lender. The greater the borrower's net worth and collateral pledged, then the greater the borrower's incentive to behave in the way that the lender expects and desires, the smaller the moral hazard problem in the debt contract, and the easier it is for the firm or household to borrow. Conversely, when the borrower's net worth and collateral are lower, the moral hazard problem is greater, making it harder to borrow.

Monitoring and Enforcement of Restrictive Covenants

As the example of Steve and his ice-cream store shows, if you could make sure that Steve doesn't invest in anything riskier than the ice-cream store, it would be worth your while to make him the loan. You can ensure that Steve uses your money for the purpose *you* expect by writing provisions (restrictive covenants) into the debt contract that restrict his firm's activities. By monitoring Steve's activities to check whether he is complying with the restrictive covenants and by enforcing the covenants if he is not, you can make sure that he will not take on risks at your expense. Restrictive covenants are directed at reducing moral hazard either by ruling out undesirable behavior or by encouraging desirable behavior. Four types of restrictive covenants achieve this objective:

1. *Covenants to discourage undesirable behavior.* Covenants can be designed to lower moral hazard by keeping the borrower from engaging in the undesirable behavior of undertaking risky investment projects. Some covenants mandate that a loan be used only to finance specific activities, such as the purchase of particular equipment or inventories. Others restrict the borrowing firm from engaging in certain risky business activities, such as purchasing other businesses.
2. *Covenants to encourage desirable behavior.* Restrictive covenants can encourage the borrower to engage in desirable activities that make it more likely that the loan will be paid off. One such restrictive covenant requires the breadwinner in a household to carry life insurance that will pay off the mortgage upon that person's death. For businesses, restrictive covenants of this type focus on encouraging the borrowing firm to keep its net worth high because higher borrower net worth reduces moral hazard and makes it less likely that the lender will suffer losses. These restrictive covenants typically specify that the borrowing firm must maintain minimum holdings of certain assets relative to the firm's size.
3. *Covenants to keep collateral valuable.* Because collateral is an important protection for the lender, restrictive covenants can encourage the borrower to keep the collateral in good condition and make sure that it stays in the possession of the borrower. This is the type of covenant ordinary people encounter most often. Automobile loan contracts, for example, require the car owner to maintain a minimum amount of collision and theft insurance and prevent the sale of the car unless the loan is paid off. Similarly, the recipient of a home mortgage must have adequate insurance on the home and must pay off the mortgage when the property is sold.
4. *Covenants to provide information.* Restrictive covenants also require a borrowing firm to provide information about its activities periodically, in the form of quarterly accounting and income reports, thereby making it easier for the lender to monitor

the firm and reduce moral hazard. This type of covenant may also stipulate that the lender has the right to audit and inspect the firm's books at any time.

We now see why debt contracts are often complicated legal documents with numerous restrictions on the borrower's behavior (fact 8): Debt contracts require complicated restrictive covenants to lower moral hazard.

Financial Intermediation   Although restrictive covenants help reduce the moral hazard problem, they do not eliminate it completely. It is almost impossible to write covenants that rule out *every* risky activity. Furthermore, borrowers may be clever enough to find loopholes in restrictive covenants that make them ineffective.

Another problem with restrictive covenants is that they must be monitored and enforced. A restrictive covenant is meaningless if the borrower can violate it knowing that the lender won't check up or is unwilling to pay for legal recourse. Because monitoring and enforcement of restrictive covenants are costly, the free-rider problem arises in the debt securities (bond) market just as it does in the stock market. If you know that other bondholders are monitoring and enforcing the restrictive covenants, you can free-ride on their monitoring and enforcement. But other bondholders can do the same thing, so the likely outcome is that not enough resources will be devoted to monitoring and enforcing the restrictive covenants. Moral hazard therefore continues to be a severe problem for marketable debt.

As we have seen before, financial intermediaries—particularly banks—can avoid the free-rider problem by primarily making *private* loans. Private loans are not traded, so no one else can free-ride on the intermediary's monitoring and enforcement of the restrictive covenants. The intermediary making private loans thus receives the full benefits of monitoring and enforcement and will work to shrink the moral hazard problem inherent in debt contracts. The concept of moral hazard has provided us with additional reasons why financial intermediaries play a more important role in channeling funds from savers to borrowers than marketable securities do, as described in facts 3 and 4.

Summary

Asymmetric information in financial markets leads to adverse selection and moral hazard problems that interfere with the efficient functioning of those markets. Tools to help solve these problems involve the private production and sale of information, government regulation to increase information in financial markets, the importance of collateral and net worth to debt contracts, and the use of monitoring and restrictive covenants. Our analysis suggests that the existence of the free-rider problem for traded securities such as stocks and bonds indicates that financial intermediaries—particularly banks—should play a greater role than securities markets in financing the activities of businesses. Economic analysis of the consequences of adverse selection and moral hazard has helped explain the basic features of our financial system, including the eight facts about our financial structure outlined at the beginning of this chapter.

As a study aid, Table 1 summarizes the asymmetric information problems and tools that help solve them. In addition, it notes how these tools and asymmetric information problems explain the eight facts of financial structure described at the beginning of the chapter.

SUMMARY TABLE 1

Asymmetric Information Problems and Tools to Solve Them

Asymmetric Information Problem	Tools to Solve It	Explains Fact Number
Adverse selection	Private production and sale of information	1, 2
	Government regulation to increase information	5
	Financial intermediation	3, 4, 6
	Collateral and net worth	7
Moral hazard in equity contracts	Production of information: monitoring	1
(principal–agent problem)	Government regulation to increase information	5
	Financial intermediation	3
	Debt contracts	1
Moral hazard in debt contracts	Collateral and net worth	6, 7
	Monitoring and enforcement of restrictive covenants	8
	Financial intermediation	3, 4

Note: List of facts:
1. Stocks are not the most important source of external financing.
2. Marketable securities are not the primary source of financing.
3. Indirect finance is more important than direct finance.
4. Banks are the most important source of external funds.
5. The financial system is heavily regulated.
6. Only large, well-established firms have access to securities markets.
7. Collateral is prevalent in debt contracts.
8. Debt contracts have numerous restrictive covenants.

APPLICATION Financial Development and Economic Growth

Recent research has found that an important reason why many developing countries and ex-communist countries like Russia (which are referred to as *transition countries*) experience very low rates of economic growth is that their financial systems are underdeveloped (a situation referred to as *financial repression*).[4] The economic analysis of financial structure helps explain how an underdeveloped financial system leads to a low state of economic development and economic growth.

The financial systems of developing and transition countries face several difficulties that keep them from operating efficiently. As we have seen, two important tools used to

---

[4]See World Bank, *Finance for Growth: Policy Choices in a Volatile World* (World Bank and Oxford University Press, 2001), and Frederic S. Mishkin, *The Next Great Globalization: How Disadvantaged Nations Can Harness Their Financial Systems to Get Rich* (Princeton University Press, 2006) for a survey of the literature linking economic growth with financial development and a list of additional references.

FYI   The Tyranny of Collateral

To use property, such as land or capital, as collateral, a person must legally own it. Unfortunately, as Hernando De Soto documents in his book *The Mystery of Capital*, it is extremely expensive and time-consuming for the poor in developing countries to make their ownership of property legal. Obtaining legal title to a dwelling on urban land in the Philippines, for example, involved 168 bureaucratic steps and 53 public and private agencies, and the process took anywhere from 13 to 25 years. Obtaining legal title to desert land in Egypt took 77 steps, 31 public and private agencies, and anywhere from 5 to 14 years. To legally buy government land in Haiti, an ordinary citizen had to go through 176 steps over 19 years. These legal barriers do not mean that the poor do not invest: They still build houses and buy equipment, even if they don't have legal title to these assets. By De Soto's calculations, the "total value of the real estate held but not legally owned by the poor of the Third World and former communist nations is at least $9.3 trillion."*

Without legal title, however, none of this property can be used as collateral to borrow funds, a requirement for most lenders. Even when people have legal title to their property, the legal system in most developing countries is so inefficient that collateral does not mean much. Typically, creditors must first sue the defaulting debtor for payment, which takes several years, and then, upon obtaining a favorable judgment, the creditor has to sue again to obtain title to

the collateral. This process often takes in excess of five years. By the time the lender acquires the collateral, it is likely to have been neglected or stolen and thus has little value. In addition, governments often block lenders from foreclosing on borrowers in politically powerful sectors of a society, such as agriculture.

When the financial system is unable to use collateral effectively, the adverse selection problem worsens because the lender needs even more information about the quality of the borrower in order to distinguish a good loan from a bad one. Little lending will take place, especially in transactions that involve collateral, such as mortgages. In Peru, for example, the value of mortgage loans relative to the size of the economy is less than 1/20 that in the United States.

The poor in developing countries have an even harder time obtaining loans because it is too costly for them to get title to their property, and therefore they have no collateral to offer, resulting in what Raghuram Rajan, the governor of India's central bank, and Luigi Zingales of the University of Chicago refer to as the "tyranny of collateral."** Even when poor people have a good idea for a business and are willing to work hard, they cannot get the funds to finance the business, making it difficult for them to escape poverty.

* Hernando De Soto, *The Mystery of Capital: Why Capitalism Triumphs in the West and Fails Everywhere Else* (New York: Basic Books, 2000), 35.

** Raghuram Rajan and Luigi Zingales, *Saving Capitalism from the Capitalists: Unleashing the Power of Financial Markets to Create Wealth and Spread Opportunity* (New York: Crown Business, 2003).

help solve adverse selection and moral hazard problems in credit markets are collateral and restrictive covenants. In many developing countries, the system of property rights (the rule of law, constraints on government expropriation, and the absence of corruption) functions poorly, making it hard for these two tools to function effectively.

As discussed in the FYI box "The Tyranny of Collateral," the weak systems of property rights common in developing and transition countries impede the use of collateral, making adverse selection problems worse because the lender will need even more information about the quality of the borrower in order to screen out a good loan from a bad one. As a result, it is harder for lenders to channel funds to the borrowers with the most productive investment opportunities, ultimately leading to less productive investment and hence a slower-growing economy.

Similarly, a poorly developed or corrupt legal system makes it extremely difficult for lenders to enforce restrictive covenants. Thus their ability to reduce moral hazard on the part of borrowers is severely limited, and so they are less willing to lend. Again, the outcome is less productive investment and a lower growth rate for the economy. The importance of an effective legal system in promoting economic growth suggests that lawyers play a more positive role in the economy than we give them credit for.

Governments in developing and transition countries often use their financial systems to direct credit to themselves or to favored sectors of the economy by setting interest rates at artificially low levels for certain types of loans, by creating development finance institutions to make specific types of loans, or by directing existing institutions to lend to certain entities. As we have seen, private institutions have an incentive to solve adverse selection and moral hazard problems and to lend to borrowers with the most productive investment opportunities. Governments have less incentive to do so because they are not driven by the profit motive and thus their directed credit programs may not channel funds to sectors that will produce high growth for the economy. The likely outcome is, again, less efficient investment and slower economic growth.

In addition, banks in many developing and transition countries are owned by their governments. Again, because of the absence of the profit motive, these **state-owned banks** have little incentive to allocate their capital to the most productive uses. Not surprisingly, the primary loan customer of these state-owned banks is often the government itself, which does not always use the funds wisely.

We have seen that government regulation can increase the amount of information available in financial markets and thus help them work more efficiently. Many developing and transition countries have an underdeveloped regulatory apparatus that retards the provision of adequate information to the marketplace. For example, these countries often have weak accounting standards, making it very hard to ascertain the quality of a borrower's balance sheet. As a result, asymmetric information problems are more severe, and the financial system is severely hampered in channeling funds to the most productive uses.

The institutional environment of a poor legal system, weak accounting standards, inadequate government regulation, and government intervention through directed credit programs and state ownership of banks all help explain why many countries stay poor while others grow rich. ◆

APPLICATION ## Is China a Counterexample to the Importance of Financial Development?

Although China appears to be on its way to becoming an economic powerhouse, its financial development remains in the early stages. The country's legal system is weak, so that financial contracts are difficult to enforce, and accounting standards are lax, making high-quality information about creditors hard to obtain. Regulation of the banking system is still in its formative stages, and the banking sector is dominated by large, state-owned banks. Yet the Chinese economy has enjoyed one of the highest growth rates in the world over the past 30 years. How has China been able to grow so rapidly, given its low level of financial development?

As noted above, China is in an early state of financial development, with a per capita income that is around $20,000, less than a third of per capita income in the

United States. With an extremely high savings rate, averaging around 40% over the past three decades, the country has been able to rapidly build up its capital stock and shift a massive pool of underutilized labor from the subsistence-agriculture sector into higher-productivity activities that use capital. Even though available savings have not always been allocated to their most productive uses, the huge increase in capital, combined with the gains in productivity achieved by moving labor out of low-productivity, subsistence agriculture, have been enough to produce high growth.

As China gets richer, however, this strategy is unlikely to continue to work. The Soviet Union provides a graphic example. In the 1950s and 1960s, the Soviet Union shared many characteristics with modern-day China: high growth fueled by a high savings rate, a massive buildup of capital, and shifts of a large pool of underutilized labor from subsistence agriculture to manufacturing. During this high-growth phase, however, the Soviet Union was unable to develop the institutions needed to allocate capital efficiently. As a result, once the pool of subsistence laborers was used up, the Soviet Union's growth slowed dramatically and it was unable to keep up with the Western economies. Today, no one considers the Soviet Union an economic success story, and its inability to develop the institutions necessary to sustain financial development and growth is an important reason for the demise of this superpower.

To move into the next stage of development, China will need to allocate its capital more efficiently, which requires that it improve its financial system. The Chinese leadership is well aware of this challenge; the government has announced that state-owned banks are being put on the path to privatization. In addition, the government is engaged in legal reform aimed at making financial contracts more enforceable. New bankruptcy law is being developed so that lenders will have the ability to take over the assets of firms that default on their loan contracts. Whether the Chinese government will succeed in developing a first-rate financial system, thereby enabling China to join the ranks of developed countries, is a big question mark. ◆

SUMMARY

1. Eight basic facts summarize the U.S. financial structure. The first four emphasize the importance of financial intermediaries and the relative unimportance of securities markets with regard to the financing of corporations; the fifth recognizes that financial markets are among the most heavily regulated sectors of the economy; the sixth states that only large, well-established corporations have access to securities markets; the seventh indicates that collateral is an important feature of debt contracts; and the eighth presents debt contracts as complicated legal documents that place substantial restrictions on the behavior of the borrower.

2. Transaction costs freeze many small savers and borrowers out of direct involvement with financial markets. Financial intermediaries can take advantage of economies of scale and are better able to develop expertise, leading to lower transaction costs and thus enabling their savers and borrowers to benefit from the existence of financial markets.

3. Asymmetric information results in two problems: adverse selection, which occurs before the transaction takes place, and moral hazard, which occurs after the transaction has taken place. Adverse selection refers to the fact that bad credit risks are the ones most likely to seek loans, and moral hazard refers to the risk of the borrower engaging in activities that are undesirable from the lender's point of view.

4. Adverse selection interferes with the efficient functioning of financial markets. Tools that help reduce the adverse selection problem include private production and sale of information, government regulation to increase information, financial intermediation, and

collateral and net worth. The free-rider problem occurs when people who do not pay for information take advantage of information that other people have paid for. This problem explains why financial intermediaries, particularly banks, play a more important role in financing the activities of businesses than do securities markets.

5. Moral hazard in equity contracts, known as the principal–agent problem, occurs because managers (the agents) have less incentive to maximize profits than

stockholders (the principals). The principal–agent problem explains why debt contracts are so much more prevalent in financial markets than equity contracts. Tools that help reduce the principal–agent problem include monitoring, government regulation to increase information, and financial intermediation.

6. Tools that are used to reduce the moral hazard problem in debt contracts include net worth, monitoring and enforcement of restrictive covenants, and financial intermediaries.

KEY TERMS

agency theory, p. 169
collateral, p. 167
costly state verification, p. 176
free-rider problem, p. 171
incentive-compatible, p. 179

net worth (equity capital), p. 174
principal–agent problem, p. 175
private-equity firm, p. 177
restrictive covenants, p. 167
secured debt, p. 167

state-owned banks, p. 183
unsecured debt, p. 167
venture capital firm, p. 177

QUESTIONS

1. For each of the following countries, identify the single most important (largest) and least important (smallest) source of external funding: United States; Germany; Japan; Canada. Comment on the similarities and differences among the countries' funding sources.

2. How can economies of scale help explain the existence of financial intermediaries?

3. Explain why dating can be considered a method to solve the adverse selection problem.

4. Why are financial intermediaries willing to engage in information collection activities when investors in financial instruments may be unwilling to do so?

5. Suppose you go to your local bank, intending to buy a certificate of deposit with your savings. Explain why you would prefer this to offering a loan, at an interest rate that is higher than the rate the bank pays on certificates of deposit (but lower than the rate the bank charges for car loans), to the next individual who enters the bank and applies for a car loan.

6. Suppose you are applying for a mortgage loan. The loan officer tells you that if you get the loan, the bank will keep the house title until you pay back the loan. Which problem of asymmetric information is the bank trying to solve?

7. Suppose you have data about two groups of countries, one with efficient legal systems and the other with slow, costly, and inefficient legal systems. Which group of countries would you expect to exhibit higher living standards?

8. Which relationship would you expect to exist between measures of corruption and living standards at the country level? Explain by which channel corruption might affect living standards.

9. Would you be more willing to lend to a friend if she had put all of her life savings into her business than you would be if she had not done so? Why?

10. What steps can the government take to reduce asymmetric information problems and help the financial system function more smoothly and efficiently?

11. How can asymmetric information problems lead to a bank panic?

12. In December 2001, Argentina announced it would not honor its sovereign (government-issued) debt. Many investors were left holding Argentinean bonds priced at a fraction of their previous value. A few years later, Argentina announced it would pay back 25% of the face value of its debt. Comment on the effects of information asymmetries on government bond markets. Do

you think investors are currently willing to buy bonds issued by the government of Argentina?

13. How does the free-rider problem aggravate adverse selection and moral hazard problems in financial markets?

14. Suppose that in a given bond market, there is currently no information that can help potential bond buyers to distinguish between bonds. Which bond issuers have an incentive to disclose information about their companies? Explain why.

15. How do standardized accounting principles help financial markets work more efficiently?

16. Which problem of asymmetric information are prospective employers trying to solve when they ask applicants to go through a job interview? Is that the end of the information asymmetry?

17. How can the existence of asymmetric information provide a rationale for government regulation of financial markets?

18. "The more collateral there is backing a loan, the less the lender has to worry about adverse selection." Is this statement true, false, or uncertain? Explain your answer.

19. Explain how the separation of ownership and control in American corporations might lead to poor management.

20. Many policymakers in developing countries have proposed the implementation of a system of deposit insurance similar to the system that exists in the United States. Explain why this might create more problems than solutions in the financial system of a developing country.

21. Gustavo is a young doctor who lives in a country with a relatively inefficient legal and financial system. When Gustavo applied for a mortgage, he found that banks usually required collateral for up to 300% of the amount of the loan. Explain why banks might require that much collateral in such a financial system. Comment on the consequences of such a system for economic growth.

APPLIED PROBLEMS

For Problems 22–25, use the fact that the expected value of an event is a probability weighted average, the sum of each possible outcome multiplied by the probability of the event occurring.

22. You are in the market for a used car and decide to visit a used-car dealership. You know that the Blue Book value of the car you are looking at is between $20,000 and $24,000. If you believe the dealer knows *as much* about the car as you do, how much are you willing to pay? Why? Assume that you care about only the expected value of the car you will buy and that the car values are symmetrically distributed.

23. Refer to Problem 22. Now you believe the dealer knows *more* about the car than you do. How much are you willing to pay? Why? How can this asymmetric information problem be resolved in a competitive market?

24. You wish to hire Ron to manage your Dallas operations. The profits from the operations depend partially on how hard Ron works, as follows.

	Profit Probabilities	
	Profit = $10,000	Profit = $50,000
Lazy	60%	40%
Hard worker	20%	80%

If Ron is lazy, he will surf the Internet all day, and he views this as a zero-cost opportunity. However, Ron views working hard as a "personal cost" valued at $1,000. What fixed percentage of the profits should you offer Ron? Assume Ron cares only about his expected payment less any "personal cost."

25. You own a house worth $400,000 that is located on a river. If the river floods moderately, the house will be completely destroyed. Moderate flooding happens about once every 50 years. If you build a seawall, the river would have to flood heavily to destroy your house, and such heavy flooding happens only about once every 200 years. What would be the annual premium for a flood insurance policy that offers full insurance? For a policy that pays only 75% of the home value, what are your expected costs with and without a seawall? Do the different policies provide an incentive to be safer (i.e., to build the seawall)?

DATA ANALYSIS PROBLEMS

The Problems update with real-time data in **MyLab Economics** and are available for practice or instructor assignment.

1. **Real-time Data Analysis** Go to the St. Louis Federal Reserve FRED database, and find data on net worth of households (BOGZ1FL192090005Q) and the net percentage of domestic banks tightening standards for auto loans (STDSAUTO). Adjust the *units* setting for the net worth indicator to "Percent Change from Year Ago," and download the data into a spreadsheet.

   a. Calculate the average, over the most recent four quarters and the four quarters prior to that, for the bank standards indicator and the "percent change in net worth" indicator. Do these averages behave as you would expect?

   b. Use the Data Analysis tool in Excel to calculate the correlation coefficient for the two data series from 2011:Q2 to the most recent quarter of data available. What can you conclude about the relationship between the net worth of households and bank auto lending standards? Is this result consistent with efforts to reduce asymmetric information?

Banking and the Management of Financial Institutions

Learning Objectives

9.1 Summarize the features of a bank balance sheet.

9.2 Apply changes to a bank's assets and liabilities on a T-account.

9.3 Identify the ways in which banks can manage their assets and liabilities to maximize profit.

9.4 List the ways in which banks deal with credit risk.

9.5 Apply gap analysis and duration analysis, and identify interest-rate risk.

9.6 Summarize the types of off-balance-sheet activities.

Preview

Because banking plays such a major role in channeling funds to borrowers with productive investment opportunities, this financial activity is important in ensuring that the financial system and the economy run smoothly and efficiently. In the United States, banks (depository institutions) supply on the order of $20 trillion in credit annually. They provide loans to businesses, help us finance our college educations and our purchases of new cars and homes, and provide us with services such as checking and savings accounts, debit cards, and ATMs.

In this chapter, we examine how banking is conducted to earn the highest profits possible: how and why banks make loans, how they acquire funds and manage their assets and liabilities (debts), and how they earn income. Although we focus on commercial banks, because they are the most important financial intermediary, many of the same principles are applicable to other types of financial intermediaries.

9.1 THE BANK BALANCE SHEET

LO 9.1 Summarize the features of a bank balance sheet.

To understand how banking works, we start by looking at the bank **balance sheet**, a list of the bank's assets and liabilities. As the name implies, this list balances; that is, it has the characteristic that

$$\text{total assets} = \text{total liabilities} + \text{capital}$$

A bank's balance sheet is also a list of its *sources* of bank funds (liabilities and capital) and *uses* to which the funds are put (assets). Banks obtain funds by borrowing and by issuing other liabilities, such as deposits. They then use these funds to acquire assets such as securities and loans. Banks make profits by earning interest on their asset holdings of securities and loans that is higher than the interest and other expenses on their liabilities. The balance sheet of all U.S. commercial banks as of June 2020 is shown in Table 1.

Liabilities

A bank acquires funds by issuing (selling) liabilities, which are the *sources of funds* the bank uses. The funds obtained from issuing liabilities are used to purchase income-earning assets.

TABLE 1	Balance Sheet of All Commercial Banks (items as a percentage of the total, June 2020)			

Assets (Uses of Funds)*		**Liabilities (Sources of Funds)**	
Reserves and cash items	15%	Checkable deposits	14%
Securities		Nontransaction deposits	
U.S. government and agency	16	Savings deposits	52
State and local government and	4	Small-denomination time deposits	2
other securities		Large-denomination time deposits	9
		Borrowings	10
Loans		Bank capital	13
Commercial and industrial	14		
Real estate	23		
Consumer	7		
Other	8		
Other assets (for example,	13		
physical capital)			
Total	100	Total	100

*In order of decreasing liquidity.
Source: Federal Reserve Bank of St. Louis, FRED database: http://www.federalreserve.gov/releases/h8/current/ and https://www.federalreserve.gov/releases/H6/current.

Checkable Deposits   Checkable deposits are bank accounts that allow the owner of the account to write checks to third parties. Checkable deposits include all accounts on which checks can be drawn. Table 1 shows that the category of checkable deposits accounts for 14% of bank liabilities. Checkable deposits were once the most important source of bank funds (more than 60% of bank liabilities in 1960), but with the advent of new, more attractive financial instruments, such as money market deposit accounts, the share of checkable deposits in total bank liabilities has shrunk over time.

Checkable deposits are payable on demand; that is, if a depositor shows up at the bank and requests payment by making a withdrawal, the bank must pay the depositor immediately. Similarly, if a person who receives a check written on an account from a bank presents that check at the bank, the bank must pay the funds out immediately (or credit them to that person's account).

A checkable deposit is an asset for the depositor because it is part of his or her wealth. Because the depositor can withdraw funds and the bank is obligated to pay, checkable deposits are a liability for the bank. They are usually the lowest-cost source of bank funds, because depositors are willing to forgo some interest in exchange for access to a liquid asset that they can use to make purchases immediately. The bank's costs of maintaining checkable deposits include interest payments and the costs incurred in servicing these accounts—processing, preparing, and sending out monthly statements; providing efficient tellers (human or otherwise); maintaining an impressive building and conveniently located branches; and advertising and marketing aimed at enticing customers to deposit their funds in the bank. In recent years, interest paid on deposits (checkable and nontransaction) has accounted for around 20% of total bank operating expenses, whereas the costs involved in servicing accounts (employee salaries, building rent, and so on) have been approximately 70% of operating expenses.

Nontransaction Deposits

Nontransaction deposits are the primary source of bank funds (63% of bank liabilities in Table 1). Owners cannot write checks on nontransaction deposits, but the interest rates paid on these deposits are usually higher than those on checkable deposits. There are two basic types of nontransaction deposits: savings accounts and time deposits (also called certificates of deposit, or CDs).

Savings accounts were once the most common type of nontransaction deposit. Funds can be added to or withdrawn from savings accounts at any time. For these accounts, transactions and interest payments are recorded in a monthly statement or in a passbook held by the owner of the account.

Time deposits have a fixed maturity length, ranging from several months to over five years, and assess substantial penalties (the forfeiture of several months' interest) for early withdrawal of funds. Small-denomination time deposits (deposits of less than $100,000) are less liquid for the depositor than passbook savings, earn higher interest rates, and are a more costly source of funds for the banks.

Large-denomination time deposits (CDs) are available in denominations of $100,000 or more and are typically bought by corporations or other banks. Large-denomination CDs are negotiable; like bonds, they can be resold in a secondary market before they mature. For this reason, negotiable CDs are held by corporations, money market mutual funds, and other financial institutions as alternative assets to Treasury bills and other short-term bonds. Since 1961, when they first appeared, negotiable CDs have become an important source of bank funds (10% in Table 1).

Borrowings

Banks also obtain funds by borrowing from the Federal Reserve System, the Federal Home Loan banks, other banks, and corporations. Borrowings from the Fed are called **discount loans** (also known as *advances*). Banks also borrow reserves overnight in the federal (fed) funds market from other U.S. banks and financial institutions. Banks borrow funds overnight in order to have enough deposits at the Federal Reserve to meet the amount required by the Fed. (The *federal funds* designation is somewhat confusing, because these loans are not made by the federal government or by the Federal Reserve, but rather by banks to other banks.) Other sources of borrowed funds are loans made to banks by their parent companies (bank holding companies), loan arrangements with corporations (such as repurchase agreements), and borrowings of Eurodollars (deposits denominated in U.S. dollars residing in foreign banks or foreign branches of U.S. banks). Borrowings have become a more important source of bank funds over time: In 1960, they made up only 2% of bank liabilities; currently, they account for 10% of bank liabilities.

Bank Capital

The final category on the right-hand side of the balance sheet is bank capital, or the bank's net worth, which equals the difference between total assets and liabilities (13% of total bank assets in Table 1). Bank capital is raised by selling new equity (stock) or from retained earnings. A bank's capital is its cushion against a drop in the value of its assets, which could force the bank into insolvency, which occurs when a bank has liabilities in excess of assets, meaning that the bank can be forced into liquidation.

Assets

A bank uses the funds that it has acquired by issuing liabilities to purchase income-earning assets. Bank assets are thus naturally referred to as *uses of funds*, and the interest payments earned on them are what enable banks to make profits.

Reserves   All banks hold some of the funds they acquire as deposits in an account at the Fed. **Reserves** consist of these deposits plus currency that is physically held by banks (called **vault cash** because it is stored in bank vaults overnight). Although reserves earn a low interest rate, banks hold them for two reasons. First, some reserves, called **required reserves**, are held because of **reserve requirements**, the regulation that for every dollar of checkable deposits at a bank, a certain fraction (10 cents, for example) must be kept as reserves. This fraction (10% in our example) is called the **required reserve ratio**. Banks hold additional reserves, called **excess reserves**, because they are the most liquid of all bank assets and a bank can use them to meet its obligations when funds are withdrawn, either directly by a depositor or indirectly when a check is written on an account.

Cash Items in Process of Collection   Suppose that a check written on an account at another bank is deposited in your bank, and the funds for this check have not yet been received (collected) from the other bank. The check is classified as a "cash item in process of collection," and it is an asset for your bank because it is a claim on another bank for funds that will be paid within a few days.

Deposits at Other Banks   Many small banks hold deposits in larger banks in exchange for a variety of services, including check collection, foreign exchange transactions, and help with securities purchases. This is one aspect of a system called *correspondent banking*.

Collectively, cash items in process of collection and deposits at other banks are referred to as *cash items*. As can be seen in Table 1, in June 2020, reserves and cash items made up 15% of total assets.

Securities   A bank's holdings of securities are an important income-earning asset: Securities (made up entirely of debt instruments for commercial banks, because U.S. banks are not allowed to hold stock) account for 20% of bank assets in Table 1, and they provide commercial banks with about 10% of their revenue. These securities can be classified into three categories: U.S. government and agency securities, state and local government securities, and other securities. The U.S. government and agency securities are the most liquid because they can be easily traded and converted into cash with low transaction costs. Because of their high liquidity, short-term U.S. government securities are called **secondary reserves**.

Banks hold state and local government securities because state and local governments are more likely to do business with banks that hold their securities. State and local government and other securities are both less marketable (less liquid) and riskier than U.S. government securities, primarily because of default risk: Some possibility exists that the issuer of the securities may not be able to make its interest payments or pay back the face value of the securities when they mature.

Loans   Banks make their profits primarily by issuing loans. In Table 1, some 52% of bank assets are in the form of loans, and in recent years loans have generally produced more than half of bank revenues. A loan is a liability for the individual or corporation receiving it but an asset for a bank, because it provides income to the bank. Loans are typically less liquid than other assets because they cannot be turned into cash until the loan matures. If a bank makes a one-year loan, for example, it cannot get its funds back until the loan comes due in one year. Loans also have a higher probability of default than other assets. Because of their lack of liquidity and their higher default risk, the bank earns its highest return on loans.

As indicated in Table 1, the largest categories of loans for commercial banks are commercial and industrial loans made to businesses and real estate loans. Commercial banks also make consumer loans and lend to each other. The bulk of these interbank loans are overnight loans lent in the federal funds market. The major difference in the balance sheets of the various categories of depository institutions is primarily in the type of loan in which they specialize. Savings and loans and mutual savings banks, for example, specialize in residential mortgages, while credit unions tend to make consumer loans.

Other Assets   The physical capital (bank buildings, computers, and other equipment) owned by banks is included in the other assets category.

9.2 BASIC BANKING

LO 9.2 Apply changes to a bank's assets and liabilities on a T-account.

Before proceeding to a more detailed study of how a bank manages its assets and liabilities to make the highest profit, you should understand the basic operation of a bank.

In general terms, banks make profits by selling liabilities with one set of characteristics (a particular combination of liquidity, risk, size, and return) and using the proceeds to buy assets with a different set of characteristics. This process is often referred to as **asset transformation**. For example, a savings deposit held by one person can provide the funds that enable the bank to make a mortgage loan to another person. The bank has, in effect, transformed the savings deposit (an asset held by the depositor) into a mortgage loan (an asset held by the bank). Another way of describing this process of asset transformation is to say that the bank "borrows short and lends long" because it makes long-term loans and funds them by issuing short-term deposits.

The process of transforming assets and providing a set of services (check clearing, record keeping, credit analysis, and so forth) is like any other production process in a firm. If the bank produces desirable services at low cost and earns substantial income on its assets, it earns profits; if not, the bank suffers losses.

To make our analysis of the operation of a bank more concrete, we use a tool called a **T-account**. A T-account is a simplified balance sheet, with lines in the form of a T, that lists only the changes that occur in balance sheet items starting from some initial balance sheet position. Let's say that Jane Brown has heard that the First National Bank provides excellent service, so she opens a checking account with a $100 bill. She now has a $100 checkable deposit at the bank, which shows up as a $100 liability on the bank's balance sheet. The bank now puts her $100 bill into its vault so that the bank's assets rise by the $100 increase in vault cash. The T-account for the bank looks like this:

First National Bank			
Assets		**Liabilities**	
Vault cash	+$100	Checkable deposits	+$100

Because vault cash is also part of the bank's reserves, we can rewrite the T-account as follows:

Assets		Liabilities	
Reserves	+$100	Checkable deposits	+$100

Note that Jane Brown's opening of a checking account leads to *an increase in the bank's reserves equal to the increase in checkable deposits*.

If Jane had opened her account with a $100 check written on an account at another bank, say, the Second National Bank, we would get the same result. The initial effect on the T-account of the First National Bank would be as follows:

Assets		Liabilities	
Cash items in process of collection	+$100	Checkable deposits	+$100

Checkable deposits increase by $100 as before, but now the First National Bank is owed $100 by the Second National Bank. This asset for the First National Bank is entered in the T-account as $100 of cash items in process of collection because the First National Bank will now try to collect the funds that it is owed. It could go directly to the Second National Bank and ask for payment of the funds, but if the two banks are in separate states, that would be a time-consuming and costly process. Instead, the First National Bank deposits the check in its account at the Fed, and the Fed collects the funds from the Second National Bank. The net result is that the Fed transfers $100 of reserves from the Second National Bank to the First National Bank, and the final balance sheet positions of the two banks are as follows:

First National Bank				Second National Bank			
Assets		Liabilities		Assets		Liabilities	
Reserves	+$100	Checkable deposits	+$100	Reserves	−$100	Checkable deposits	−$100

The process initiated by Jane Brown can be summarized as follows: When a check written on an account at one bank is deposited in another, the bank receiving the deposit gains reserves equal to the amount of the check, while the bank on which the check is written sees its reserves fall by the same amount. Therefore, *when a bank receives additional deposits, it gains an equal amount of reserves; when it loses deposits, it loses an equal amount of reserves.*

Now that you understand how banks gain and lose reserves, we can examine how a bank rearranges its balance sheet to make a profit when it experiences a change in its deposits. Let's return to the situation in which the First National Bank has just received the extra $100 of checkable deposits. As you know, the bank is obliged to keep a certain fraction of its checkable deposits as required reserves. If the fraction (the required reserve ratio) is 10%, the First National Bank's required reserves have increased by $10, and we can rewrite its T-account as follows:

Assets		Liabilities	
Required reserves	+$10	Checkable deposits	+$100
Excess reserves	+$90		

Let's see how well the bank is doing as a result of the additional checkable deposits. Servicing the extra $100 of checkable deposits is costly, because the bank must keep records, pay tellers, pay for check clearing, and so forth. Because reserves earn little interest, the bank is taking a loss! The situation is even worse if the bank makes interest payments on the deposits. To make a profit, the bank must put to productive use all or part of the $90 of excess reserves it has available. One way to do this is to invest in securities. The other is to make loans; as we have seen, loans account for approximately 50% of the total value of bank assets (uses of funds). Because lenders are subject to the asymmetric information problems of adverse selection and moral hazard (discussed in Chapter 8), banks take steps to reduce the incidence and severity of these problems. Bank loan officers evaluate potential borrowers using what are called the "five C's"—character, capacity (ability to repay), collateral, conditions (in the local and national economies), and capital (net worth)—before they agree to lend. (A more detailed discussion of the methods banks use to reduce the risk involved in lending is given later in this chapter.)

Let's assume that the First National Bank chooses not to hold any excess reserves but to make loans instead. The T-account then looks like this:

First National Bank			
Assets		Liabilities	
Required reserves	+$10	Checkable deposits	+$100
Loans	+$90		

The bank is now making a profit because it holds short-term liabilities, such as checkable deposits, and uses the proceeds to fund longer-term assets, such as loans with higher interest rates. As mentioned earlier, this process of asset transformation is frequently described by saying that banks are in the business of "borrowing short and lending long." For example, if the loans have an interest rate of 10% per year, the bank earns $9 in income from its loans over the year. If the $100 of checkable deposits is in a NOW account with a 5% interest rate and it costs another $3 per year to service the account, the cost per year of these deposits is $8. The bank's profit on the new deposits is then $1 per year, plus any interest that it earns on required reserves.

9.3 GENERAL PRINCIPLES OF BANK MANAGEMENT

LO 9.3 Identify the ways in which banks can manage their assets and liabilities to maximize profit.

Now that you have some idea of how a bank operates, let's look at how a bank manages its assets and liabilities to earn the highest possible profit. The bank manager has four primary concerns. The first is to make sure that the bank has enough ready cash to pay its depositors when there are **deposit outflows**—that is, when deposits are lost because depositors make withdrawals and demand payment. To keep enough cash on hand, the bank must engage in **liquidity management**, the acquisition of assets that are liquid enough to meet the bank's obligations to depositors. Second, the bank manager must pursue an acceptably low level of risk by acquiring assets that have a low rate of default and by diversifying asset holdings (**asset management**). The manager's third concern is acquiring funds at low cost (**liability management**). Finally, the manager must decide the amount of capital the bank should maintain and then acquire the needed capital (**capital adequacy management**).

To understand bank (and other financial institution) management fully, we must go beyond the general principles of bank asset and liability management described next and look in more detail at how a financial institution manages its assets. The two sections following this one provide an in-depth discussion of how a financial institution manages **credit risk**, the risk arising because borrowers may default, and how it manages **interest-rate risk**, the riskiness of earnings and returns on bank assets caused by interest-rate changes.

Liquidity Management and the Role of Reserves

Let's see how a typical bank, the First National Bank, can deal with deposit outflows that occur when its depositors withdraw cash from checking or savings accounts or write checks that are deposited in other banks. In the example that follows, we assume that the bank has ample excess reserves and that all deposits have the same required reserve ratio of 10% (the bank is required to keep 10% of deposits as reserves). Suppose that the First National Bank's initial balance sheet is as follows:

Assets		Liabilities	
Reserves	$20 million	Deposits	$100 million
Loans	$80 million	Bank capital	$ 10 million
Securities	$10 million		

The bank's required reserves are 10% of $100 million, or $10 million. Given that it holds $20 million of reserves, the First National Bank has excess reserves of $10 million.

If a deposit outflow of $10 million occurs, the bank's balance sheet becomes

Assets		Liabilities	
Reserves	$10 million	Deposits	$90 million
Loans	$80 million	Bank capital	$10 million
Securities	$10 million		

The bank loses $10 million of deposits *and* $10 million of reserves, but because its required reserves are now 10% of only $90 million (that is, $9 million), its reserves still exceed this amount by $1 million. In short, *if a bank has ample excess reserves, a deposit outflow does not necessitate changes in other parts of its balance sheet.*

The situation is quite different when a bank holds insufficient excess reserves. Let's assume that instead of initially holding $10 million in excess reserves, the First National Bank makes additional loans of $10 million, so that it holds no excess reserves. Its initial balance sheet would then be

Assets		Liabilities	
Reserves	$10 million	Deposits	$100 million
Loans	$90 million	Bank capital	$ 10 million
Securities	$10 million		

When it suffers the $10 million deposit outflow, its balance sheet becomes

Assets		Liabilities	
Reserves	$ 0	Deposits	$90 million
Loans	$90 million	Bank capital	$10 million
Securities	$10 million		

After $10 million has been withdrawn from deposits and hence reserves, the bank has a problem: It has a reserve requirement of 10% of $90 million, or $9 million, but it has no reserves! To eliminate this shortfall, the bank has four basic options. One option is to acquire the reserves needed to meet a deposit outflow by borrowing them from other banks in the federal funds market, or by borrowing from corporations.[1] If the First National Bank acquires the $9 million shortfall in reserves by borrowing it from other banks or corporations, its balance sheet becomes

Assets		Liabilities	
Reserves	$ 9 million	Deposits	$90 million
Loans	$90 million	Borrowings from other banks or corporations	$ 9 million
Securities	$10 million	Bank capital	$10 million

---

[1] One way in which the First National Bank can borrow from other banks and corporations is by selling negotiable certificates of deposit. This method for obtaining funds is discussed in the section on liability management.

The cost of this activity is the interest rate on these borrowings, such as the federal funds rate.

A second alternative is for the bank to sell some of its securities to help cover the deposit outflow. For example, it might sell $9 million of its securities and deposit the proceeds with the Fed, resulting in the following balance sheet:

Assets		Liabilities	
Reserves	$ 9 million	Deposits	$90 million
Loans	$90 million	Bank capital	$10 million
Securities	$ 1 million		

The bank incurs some brokerage and other transaction costs when it sells these securities. The U.S. government securities that are classified as secondary reserves are very liquid, so the transaction costs of selling them are quite modest. However, the other securities the bank holds are less liquid, and the transaction costs can be appreciably higher.

The bank has a third option for meeting a deposit outflow: It can acquire reserves by borrowing from the Fed. In our example, the First National Bank could leave its security and loan holdings the same, and borrow $9 million in discount loans from the Fed. Its balance sheet would then be

Assets		Liabilities	
Reserves	$ 9 million	Deposits	$90 million
Loans	$90 million	Borrowings from the Fed $ 9 million	
Securities	$10 million	Bank capital	$10 million

The cost associated with discount loans is the interest rate that must be paid to the Fed (called the **discount rate**).

As a last option, a bank can acquire the $9 million of reserves to meet the deposit outflow by reducing its loans by this amount and depositing the $9 million it then receives with the Fed, thereby increasing its reserves by $9 million. This transaction changes the balance sheet as follows:

Assets		Liabilities	
Reserves	$ 9 million	Deposits	$90 million
Loans	$81 million	Bank capital	$10 million
Securities	$10 million		

The First National Bank is once again in good shape because its $9 million of reserves satisfies the reserve requirement.

However, this process of reducing its loans is the bank's costliest way of acquiring reserves when a deposit outflow exists. If the First National Bank has numerous short-term loans renewed at fairly short intervals, it can reduce its total amount of loans outstanding fairly quickly by *calling in* loans—that is, by not renewing some loans when they come due. Unfortunately for the bank, this is likely to antagonize the customers whose loans are not being renewed because they have not done anything to deserve such treatment. Indeed, they are likely to take their business elsewhere in the future, a very costly consequence for the bank.

A second method of reducing its loans is for the bank to sell them off to other banks. Again, this is very costly because other banks do not know how risky these loans are and so may not be willing to buy the loans at their full value. (This is an example of the lemons adverse selection problem described in Chapter 8.)

The foregoing discussion explains why banks hold excess reserves even though loans or securities earn a higher return. When a deposit outflow occurs, excess reserves enable the bank to escape the costs of (1) borrowing from other banks or corporations, (2) selling securities, (3) borrowing from the Fed, or (4) calling in or selling off loans. **Excess reserves are insurance against the costs associated with deposit outflows. The higher the costs associated with deposit outflows, the more excess reserves a bank will want to hold.**

Just as you and I would be willing to pay an insurance company to insure us against a casualty loss such as the theft of a car, a bank is willing to pay the cost of holding excess reserves (the opportunity cost—that is, the earnings forgone by not holding income-earning assets such as loans or securities) to insure against losses due to deposit outflows. Because excess reserves, like insurance, have a cost, banks also take other steps to protect themselves; for example, they might shift their holdings of assets to more liquid securities (secondary reserves).

Asset Management

Now that you understand a bank's need for liquidity, we can examine the basic strategy a bank pursues in managing its assets. To maximize its profits, a bank must simultaneously seek the highest returns possible on loans and securities, reduce risk, and make adequate provisions for liquidity by holding liquid assets. Banks try to accomplish these three goals in four basic ways.

First, banks try to find borrowers who will pay high interest rates and are unlikely to default on their loans. They seek out loan business by advertising their borrowing rates and by approaching corporations directly to solicit loans. It is up to the bank's loan officer to decide if potential borrowers are good credit risks who will make interest and principal payments on time (i.e., banks engage in screening to reduce the adverse selection problem). Typically, banks are conservative in their loan policies; the default rate is usually less than 1%. It is important, however, that banks not be so conservative that they miss out on attractive lending opportunities that earn high interest rates.

Second, banks try to purchase securities with high returns and low risk.

Third, in managing their assets, banks must attempt to lower risk by diversifying. They accomplish this by purchasing many different types of assets (short- and long-term, U.S. Treasury, and municipal bonds) and approving many types of loans to a variety of customers. Banks that have not sufficiently sought the benefits of diversification often come to regret it later. For example, banks that had overspecialized in making loans to energy companies, real estate developers, or farmers suffered huge losses in the 1980s with the slump in energy, property, and farm prices. Indeed, many of these banks went broke because they had "put too many eggs in one basket."

Finally, the bank must manage the liquidity of its assets so that it can meet deposit outflows and still satisfy its reserve requirements without bearing huge costs. This means that it will hold liquid securities even if they earn a somewhat lower return than other assets. The bank must decide, for example, how much it should hold in excess reserves to avoid the costs associated with a deposit outflow. In addition, it will want to hold U.S. government securities as secondary reserves so that even if a deposit outflow forces some costs on the bank, these will not be terribly high. Again, it is not wise for a bank to be too conservative. If it avoids all costs associated with deposit outflows by holding only excess reserves, the bank suffers losses, because reserves earn low interest, while the bank's liabilities are costly to maintain. The bank must balance its desire for liquidity against the benefits of the increased earnings that can be obtained from less liquid assets, such as loans.

Liability Management

Before the 1960s, liability management was a staid affair: For the most part, banks took their liabilities as fixed and spent their time trying to achieve an optimal mix of assets. There were two main reasons for the emphasis on asset management. First, more than 60% of bank funds were obtained through checkable (demand) deposits that by law could not pay any interest. Thus banks could not actively compete with one another for these deposits by paying interest on them, and so their amount was effectively a given for an individual bank. Second, because the markets for making overnight loans between banks were not well developed, banks rarely borrowed from other banks to meet their reserve needs.

Starting in the 1960s, however, large banks (called **money center banks**) in key financial centers, such as New York, Chicago, and San Francisco, began to explore ways in which the liabilities on their balance sheets could provide them with reserves and liquidity. This move led to an expansion of overnight loan markets, such as the federal funds market, and the development of new financial instruments, such as negotiable CDs (first developed in 1961), which enabled money center banks to acquire funds quickly.[2]

This new flexibility in liability management meant that banks could take a different approach to bank management. They no longer needed to depend on checkable deposits as the primary source of bank funds and as a result no longer treated their sources of funds (liabilities) as given. Instead, they aggressively set target goals for their asset growth and tried to acquire funds (by issuing liabilities) as they were needed.

For example, today, when a money center bank finds an attractive loan opportunity, it can acquire funds by selling a negotiable CD. Or, if it has a reserve shortfall, it can borrow funds from another bank in the federal funds market without incurring high transaction costs. The federal funds market can also be used to finance loans. Because of the increased importance of liability management, most banks now manage both sides of the balance sheet together in an *asset–liability management (ALM) committee.*

The greater emphasis on liability management explains some of the important changes over the past three decades in the composition of banks' balance sheets. While negotiable CDs and bank borrowings have greatly increased in importance as a source of bank funds in recent years (rising from 2% of bank liabilities in 1960 to 27% by mid-2020), checkable deposits have decreased in importance (from 61% of bank liabilities in 1960 to 14% by mid-2020). Newfound flexibility in liability management and the search for higher profits have also stimulated banks to increase the proportion of their assets held in loans, which earn higher income (from 46% of bank assets in 1960 to 52% by mid-2020) than other assets.

---

[2]Because small banks are not as well known as money center banks and so might be a higher credit risk, they find it harder to raise funds in the negotiable CD market. Hence they do not engage nearly as actively in liability management.

Capital Adequacy Management

Banks have to make decisions about the amount of capital they need to hold for three reasons. First, bank capital helps prevent *bank failure*, a situation in which the bank cannot satisfy its obligations to pay its depositors and other creditors and so goes out of business. Second, the amount of capital held affects returns for the owners (equity holders) of the bank. Third, a minimum amount of bank capital (bank capital requirements) is required by regulatory authorities.

How Bank Capital Helps Prevent Bank Failure   Let's consider two banks with identical balance sheets, except that High Capital Bank has a ratio of capital to assets of 10%, while Low Capital Bank has a ratio of 4%.

High Capital Bank				Low Capital Bank			
Assets		**Liabilities**		**Assets**		**Liabilities**	
Reserves	$10 million	Deposits	$90 million	Reserves	$10 million	Deposits	$96 million
Loans	$90 million	Bank capital	$10 million	Loans	$90 million	Bank capital	$ 4 million

Suppose both banks get caught up in the euphoria of the housing market, only to find later that $5 million of their housing loans have become worthless. When these bad loans are written off (valued at zero), the total value of assets declines by $5 million. As a consequence, bank capital, which equals total assets minus liabilities, also declines by $5 million. The balance sheets of the two banks now look like this:

High Capital Bank				Low Capital Bank			
Assets		**Liabilities**		**Assets**		**Liabilities**	
Reserves	$10 million	Deposits	$90 million	Reserves	$10 million	Deposits	$96 million
Loans	$85 million	Bank capital	$ 5 million	Loans	$85 million	Bank capital	–$ 1 million

High Capital Bank takes the $5 million loss in stride because its initial cushion of $10 million in capital means that it still has a positive net worth (bank capital) of $5 million after the loss. Low Capital Bank, however, is in big trouble. The value of its assets has fallen below that of its liabilities, and its net worth is now –$1 million. Because the bank has a negative net worth, it is insolvent: It does not have sufficient assets to pay off all holders of its liabilities. When a bank becomes insolvent, government regulators close the bank, its assets are sold off, and its managers are fired. Because the owners of Low Capital Bank will find their investment wiped out, they clearly would have preferred the bank to have had a large enough cushion of bank capital to absorb the losses, as was the case for High Capital Bank. We therefore see an important rationale for a bank to maintain a sufficient level of capital: *A bank maintains bank capital to lessen the chance that it will become insolvent.*

How the Amount of Bank Capital Affects Returns to Equity Holders

Because owners of a bank must know whether their bank is being managed well, they need good measures of bank profitability. A basic measure of bank profitability is the **return on assets (ROA)**, the net profit after taxes per dollar of assets:

$$\text{ROA} = \frac{\text{net profit after taxes}}{\text{assets}}$$

The return on assets provides information on how efficiently a bank is being run because it indicates how much profit is generated, on average, by each dollar of assets.

However, what the bank's owners (equity holders) care about most is how much the bank is earning on their equity investment. This information is provided by the other basic measure of bank profitability, the **return on equity (ROE)**, which is defined as the net profit after taxes per dollar of equity (bank) capital:

$$\text{ROE} = \frac{\text{net profit after taxes}}{\text{equity capital}}$$

There is a direct relationship between the return on assets (which measures how efficiently the bank is run) and the return on equity (which measures how well the owners are doing on their investment). This relationship is determined by the **equity multiplier (EM)**, or the amount of assets per dollar of equity capital:

$$\text{EM} = \frac{\text{assets}}{\text{equity capital}}$$

To see this, we note that

$$\frac{\text{net profit after taxes}}{\text{equity capital}} = \frac{\text{net profit after taxes}}{\text{assets}} \times \frac{\text{assets}}{\text{equity capital}}$$

which, using our definitions, yields

$$\text{ROE} = \text{ROA} \times \text{EM} \tag{1}$$

The formula in Equation 1 tells us what happens to the return on equity when a bank holds a smaller amount of capital (equity) for a given amount of assets. As we have seen, High Capital Bank initially has $100 million of assets and $10 million of equity, which gives it an equity multiplier of 10 (= $100 million/$10 million). Low Capital Bank, by contrast, has only $4 million of equity, so its equity multiplier is higher, equaling 25 (= $100 million/$4 million). Suppose these banks have been equally well run, so that they both have the same return on assets, 1%. The return on equity for High Capital Bank equals 1% × 10 = 10%, whereas the return on equity for Low Capital Bank equals 1% × 25 = 25%. The equity holders in Low Capital Bank are clearly a lot happier than the equity holders in High Capital Bank because they are earning more than twice as high a return. We now see why the owners of a bank may not want it to hold too much capital. *Given the return on assets, the lower the bank capital, the higher the return for the owners of the bank.*

Trade-Off Between Safety and Returns to Equity Holders

We now see that bank capital has both benefits and costs. Bank capital benefits the owners of a bank in that it makes their investment safer by reducing the likelihood of bankruptcy. But bank capital is costly because the higher it is, the lower will be the return on equity for a given return on assets. In determining the optimal amount of bank capital, managers must compare the benefit of maintaining higher capital (increased safety) with the cost of higher capital (the lower return on equity for bank owners).

In more uncertain times, when the possibility of large losses on loans increases, bank managers might want to hold more capital to protect the equity holders. Conversely, if the managers have confidence that loan losses won't occur, they might want to reduce the amount of bank capital, have a high equity multiplier, and thereby increase the return on equity.

Bank Capital Requirements Banks also hold capital because they are required to do so by regulatory authorities. Because of the high costs of holding capital (for the reasons just described), bank managers often want to hold less bank capital relative to assets than is required by the regulatory authorities. In this case, the amount of bank capital is determined by the bank capital requirements. We discuss the details of bank capital requirements and their important role in bank regulation in Chapter 10.

APPLICATION Strategies for Managing Bank Capital

Suppose that, as the manager of the First National Bank, you have to make decisions about the appropriate amount of bank capital to hold in your bank. Looking at the balance sheet of the bank, which, like that of High Capital Bank, has a ratio of bank capital to assets of 10% ($10 million of capital and $100 million of assets), you are concerned that the large amount of bank capital is causing the return on equity to be too low. You conclude that the bank has a capital surplus and should increase the equity multiplier to raise the return on equity. What should you do next?

To lower the amount of capital relative to assets and raise the equity multiplier, you can do any of three things: (1) You can reduce the amount of bank capital by buying back some of the bank's stock; (2) you can reduce the bank's capital by paying out higher dividends to its stockholders, thereby reducing the bank's retained earnings; or (3) you can keep bank capital constant but increase the bank's assets by acquiring new funds—say, by issuing CDs—and then seeking out loan business or purchasing more securities with these new funds. Because you think it will enhance your position with the stockholders, you decide to pursue the second alternative and raise the dividend on the First National Bank stock.

Now suppose that the First National Bank is in a situation similar to that of Low Capital Bank and has a ratio of bank capital to assets of 4%. You now worry that the bank is short on capital relative to assets because it does not have a sufficient cushion to prevent bank failure. To raise the amount of capital relative to assets, you now have the following three choices: (1) You can raise capital for the bank by having it issue equity (common stock); (2) you can raise capital by reducing the bank's dividends to shareholders, thereby increasing retained earnings that it can put into its capital account; or (3) you can keep capital at the same level but reduce the bank's assets by making fewer loans or by selling off securities and then using the proceeds to reduce the bank's liabilities. Suppose that raising bank capital is not easy to do at the current time because bank stock is selling at low prices or because shareholders will protest if their dividends are cut. Then you might have to choose the third alternative and shrink the size of the bank.

Our discussion of the strategies for managing bank capital at the First National Bank leads to the following conclusion, which deserves particular emphasis: *A shortfall of bank capital is likely to lead a bank to reduce its assets and therefore is likely to cause a contraction in lending.* In past years, many banks experienced capital shortfalls and had to restrict asset and lending growth. The important consequences of this decision for the credit markets are illustrated by the application that follows. ◆

APPLICATION ## How a Capital Crunch Caused a Credit Crunch During the Global Financial Crisis

The dramatic slowdown in the growth of credit in the wake of the financial crisis that began in 2007 triggered a "credit crunch" during which credit was hard to get. As a result, the performance of the economy in 2008 and 2009 was very poor. What caused the credit crunch?

Our analysis of how a bank manages its capital indicates that the 2008–2009 credit crunch was caused, at least in part, by the capital crunch, in which shortfalls of bank capital led to slower credit growth.

A major boom and bust in the housing market led to huge losses for banks from their holdings of securities backed by residential mortgages. These losses reduced bank capital, which led to capital shortfalls: Banks had to either raise new capital or restrict asset growth by cutting back on lending. Banks did raise some capital, but with the growing weakness of the economy, raising new capital was extremely difficult, so banks also chose to tighten their lending standards and reduce lending. Both of these reactions to capital shortfalls helped produce a weak economy in 2008 and 2009. ◆

9.4 MANAGING CREDIT RISK

LO 9.4 List the ways in which banks deal with credit risk.

As noted in our earlier discussion of the general principles of asset management, banks and other financial institutions must make successful loans that are paid back in full (and so subject the institution to little credit risk) if they are to earn high profits. The economic concepts of adverse selection and moral hazard (discussed in Chapters 2 and 8) provide a framework for understanding the principles that financial institutions must follow if they are to reduce credit risk and make successful loans.[3]

Adverse selection in loan markets occurs because bad credit risks (those most likely to default on their loans) are the ones who usually line up for loans; in other words, those who are most likely to produce an *adverse* outcome are also the most likely to be *selected*. Borrowers with very risky investment projects have much to gain if their projects are successful, so they are the most eager to obtain loans. Clearly, however, they are the least desirable borrowers because of the greater possibility that they will be unable to pay back their loans.

Moral hazard exists in loan markets because borrowers may have incentives to engage in activities that are undesirable from the lender's point of view. In such situations, it is more likely that the lender will be subjected to the *hazard* of default. Once borrowers have obtained a loan, they are more likely to invest in high-risk investment projects—projects that pay high returns to the borrower if successful. The high risk associated with these investments, however, makes it less likely that these borrowers will be able to pay back their loans.

To be profitable, financial institutions must overcome the adverse selection and moral hazard problems that make loan defaults more likely. Financial institutions attempt to solve these problems by using a number of principles for managing credit

[3]Other financial intermediaries, such as insurance companies, pension funds, and finance companies, also make private loans, and the credit risk management principles we outline here apply to them as well.

risk: screening and monitoring, establishment of long-term customer relationships, loan commitments, collateral and compensating balance requirements, and credit rationing.

Screening and Monitoring

Asymmetric information is present in loan markets because lenders have less information about the investment opportunities and activities of borrowers than borrowers do. This situation leads banks and other financial institutions to perform two information-producing activities: screening and monitoring. Indeed, Walter Wriston, a former head of Citicorp, one of the largest bank corporations in the United States, was often quoted as stating that the business of banking is the production of information.

Screening   Adverse selection in loan markets requires lenders to screen out the bad credit risks from the good ones, so that loans are profitable to them. To accomplish effective screening, lenders must collect reliable information from prospective borrowers. Effective screening and information collection together form an important principle of credit risk management.

When you apply for a consumer loan (such as a car loan or a mortgage to purchase a house), the first thing you are asked to do is fill out forms that elicit a great deal of information about your personal finances. You are asked about your salary, your bank accounts and other assets (such as cars, insurance policies, and furnishings), and your outstanding loans; your record of loan, credit card, and charge account repayments; and the number of years you've worked and the names of your employers. You also are asked personal questions such as your age, marital status, and number of children. The lender uses this information to evaluate how good a credit risk you are by calculating your credit score, a statistical measure derived from your answers that is used to predict whether you are likely to have trouble making your loan payments. Deciding how good a risk you are cannot be entirely scientific, so the lender must also use judgment. The loan officer, whose job it is to decide whether you should be given the loan, might call your employer or talk to some of the personal references you have supplied. The officer might even make a judgment based on your demeanor or your appearance. (This is why most people dress neatly and conservatively when they go to a bank to apply for a loan.)

The process of screening and collecting information is similar when a financial institution makes a business loan. It collects information about the company's profits and losses (income) along with information about its assets and liabilities. The lender also has to evaluate the likely future success of the business. So, in addition to obtaining information such as sales figures, a loan officer might ask questions about the company's future plans, the purpose of the loan, and competition within the industry. The officer may even visit the company to obtain a firsthand look at its operations. The bottom line is that, whether they are considering making personal loans or business loans, bankers and other financial institutions need to be nosy.

Specialization in Lending   One puzzling feature of bank lending is that a bank often specializes in lending to local firms or to firms in particular industries, such as energy. In one sense, this behavior seems surprising because it means that the bank is not diversifying its portfolio of loans and thus is exposing itself to more risk. But from another perspective, such specialization makes perfect sense. The adverse selection problem requires the bank to screen out bad credit risks. It is easier for the bank to collect information about local firms and determine their creditworthiness than to collect comparable information on firms that are farther away. Similarly, by concentrating its lending on firms in specific industries, the bank becomes more knowledgeable about these industries and is therefore better able to predict which firms will be able to make timely payments on their debt.

Monitoring and Enforcement of Restrictive Covenants Once a loan has been made, the borrower has an incentive to engage in risky activities that make it less likely that the loan will be paid off. To reduce this moral hazard, financial institutions must write provisions (restrictive covenants) into loan contracts that restrict borrowers from engaging in risky activities. By monitoring borrowers' activities to see whether they are complying with the restrictive covenants and by enforcing the covenants if they are not, lenders can make sure that borrowers are not taking on risks at their expense. The need for banks and other financial institutions to engage in screening and monitoring explains why they spend so much money on auditing and information-collecting activities.

Long-Term Customer Relationships

An additional way for banks and other financial institutions to obtain information about their borrowers is through long-term customer relationships, another important principle of credit risk management.

If a prospective borrower has had a checking account, a savings account, or a loan with a bank over a long period of time, a loan officer can look at past activity on the accounts and learn quite a bit about the borrower. The balances in the checking and savings accounts tell the banker how liquid the potential borrower is and at what time of year the borrower has a strong need for cash. A review of the checks the borrower has written reveals the borrower's suppliers. If the borrower has borrowed previously from the bank, the bank has a record of the loan payments. Thus long-term customer relationships reduce the costs of information collection and make it easier to screen out bad credit risks.

The need for monitoring by lenders adds to the importance of long-term customer relationships. If the borrower has borrowed from the bank before, the bank has already established procedures for monitoring that customer. Therefore, the costs of monitoring long-term customers are lower than the costs of monitoring new customers.

Long-term relationships benefit customers as well as banks. A firm that has had a previous relationship with a bank will find it easier to obtain a loan from the bank at a low interest rate because the bank has an easier time determining if the prospective borrower is a good credit risk and therefore incurs fewer costs in monitoring the borrower.

A long-term customer relationship has another advantage for the bank. No bank can think of every contingency when it writes a restrictive covenant into a loan contract; there will always be risky borrower activities that are not ruled out. However, what if a borrower wants to preserve a long-term relationship with a bank because it will be easier to get future loans from the bank, at low interest rates? The borrower then has the incentive to avoid risky activities that would upset the bank, even if restrictions on these risky activities are not specified in the loan contract. Indeed, if a bank doesn't like what a borrower is doing even when the borrower isn't violating any restrictive covenants, it has some power to discourage the borrower from such activity: The bank can threaten not to give the borrower new loans in the future. Long-term customer relationships therefore enable banks to deal with even unanticipated moral hazard contingencies.

Loan Commitments

Banks also create long-term relationships and gather information by issuing **loan commitments** to commercial customers. A loan commitment is a bank's commitment (for a specified future period of time) to provide a firm with loans up to a given amount at an interest rate that is tied to some market interest rate. The majority of commercial and industrial loans are made under the loan commitment arrangement. The advantage for the firm is that it has a source of credit when it needs it. The advantage for the bank is that the loan commitment promotes a long-term relationship, which in turn facilitates information collection. In addition, provisions in the loan commitment agreement require the firm to continually supply the bank with information about the firm's income, asset and liability position, business activities, and so on. A loan commitment arrangement is a powerful method for reducing the bank's costs of screening and information collection.

Collateral and Compensating Balances

Collateral requirements for loans are important credit risk management tools. Collateral, which is property promised to the lender as compensation if the borrower defaults, lessens the consequences of adverse selection because it reduces the lender's losses in the case of a loan default. It also reduces moral hazard because the borrower has more to lose from a default. If a borrower defaults on a loan, the lender can sell the collateral and use the proceeds to make up for its losses on the loan. One particular form of collateral required when a bank makes commercial loans is called **compensating balances**: A firm receiving a loan must keep a required minimum amount of funds in a checking account at the bank. For example, a business getting a $10 million loan may be required to keep compensating balances of at least $1 million in its checking account at the bank. This $1 million in compensating balances can then be taken by the bank to make up some of the losses on the loan if the borrower defaults.

In addition to serving as collateral, compensating balances increase the likelihood that a loan will be paid off. They do this by helping the bank monitor the borrower and consequently reduce moral hazard. Specifically, by requiring the borrower to use a checking account at the bank, the bank can observe the firm's check payment practices, which may yield a great deal of information about the borrower's financial condition. For example, a sustained drop in the borrower's checking account balance may signal that the borrower is having financial trouble, or account activity may suggest that the borrower is engaging in risky activities; perhaps a change in suppliers means the borrower is pursuing a new line of business. Any significant change in the borrower's payment procedures is a signal to the bank that it should make inquiries. Compensating balances therefore make it easier for banks to monitor borrowers more effectively and are an important credit risk management tool.

Credit Rationing

Another way in which financial institutions deal with adverse selection and moral hazard is through **credit rationing**: refusing to make loans even though borrowers are willing to pay the stated interest rate, or even a higher rate. Credit rationing takes two forms. The first occurs when a lender refuses to make a loan *of any amount* to a borrower, even if the borrower is willing to pay a higher interest rate. The second occurs when a lender is willing to make a loan but restricts the size of the loan to less than the borrower would like.

Initially, you might be puzzled by the first type of credit rationing. After all, even if the potential borrower is a credit risk, why doesn't the lender just extend the loan, but at a higher interest rate? The answer is that adverse selection prevents this from being a wise course of action. Individuals and firms with the riskiest investment projects are exactly those that are willing to pay the highest interest rates. If a borrower took on a high-risk investment and succeeded, the borrower would become extremely rich. But a lender wouldn't want to make such a loan precisely because the credit risk is high; the likely outcome is that the borrower will *not* succeed and the lender will not be paid back. Charging a higher interest rate just makes adverse selection worse for the lender; that is, it increases the likelihood that the lender is lending to a bad credit risk. The lender would therefore rather not make any loans at a higher interest rate; instead, it would engage in the first type of credit rationing and would turn down loans.

Financial institutions engage in the second type of credit rationing to guard against moral hazard: They grant loans to borrowers, but loans that are not as large as the borrowers want. Such credit rationing is necessary because the larger the loan, the greater the benefits from moral hazard. If a bank gives you a $1,000 loan, for example, you are likely to take actions that enable you to pay it back because you don't want to hurt your credit rating for the future. However, if the bank lends you $10 million, you are more likely to fly down to Rio to celebrate. The larger your loan, the greater your incentives to engage in activities that make it less likely that you will repay the loan. Because more borrowers repay their loans if the loan amounts are small, financial institutions ration credit by providing borrowers with smaller loans than they seek.

9.5 MANAGING INTEREST-RATE RISK

LO 9.5 Apply gap analysis and duration analysis, and identify interest-rate risk.

With the increased volatility of interest rates that occurred in the 1980s, banks and other financial institutions became more concerned about their exposure to interest-rate risk, the riskiness of earnings and returns that is associated with changes in interest rates. To see what interest-rate risk is all about, let's again take a look at the First National Bank, which has the following balance sheet:

First National Bank			
Assets		**Liabilities**	
Rate-sensitive assets	$20 million	Rate-sensitive liabilities	$50 million
Variable-rate and		Variable-rate CDs	
short-term loans		Money market deposit	
Short-term securities		accounts	
Fixed-rate assets	$80 million	Fixed-rate liabilities	$50 million
Reserves		Checkable deposits	
Long-term loans		Savings deposits	
Long-term securities		Long-term CDs	
		Equity capital	

A total of $20 million of First National Bank's assets are rate-sensitive, with interest rates that change frequently (at least once a year), and $80 million of its assets are fixed-rate, with interest rates that remain unchanged for a long period (over a year). On the liabilities side, the First National Bank has $50 million of rate-sensitive liabilities and $50 million of fixed-rate liabilities. Suppose that interest rates rise by 5 percentage points on average, from 10% to 15%. The income on the assets increases by $1 million (= 5% × $20 million of rate-sensitive assets), while the payments on the liabilities increase by $2.5 million (= 5% × $50 million of rate-sensitive liabilities). The First National Bank's profits now decline by $1.5 million (= $1 million − $2.5 million). Conversely, if interest rates fall by 5 percentage points, similar reasoning tells us that the First National Bank's profits increase by $1.5 million. This example illustrates the following point: *If a bank has more rate-sensitive liabilities than assets, a rise in interest rates will reduce bank profits, and a decline in interest rates will raise bank profits.*

Gap and Duration Analysis

The sensitivity of bank profits to changes in interest rates can be measured more directly using **gap analysis**, in which the amount of rate-sensitive liabilities is subtracted from the amount of rate-sensitive assets. In our example, this calculation (called the "gap") is −$30 million (= $20 million − $50 million). By multiplying the gap times the change in the interest rate, we can immediately obtain the effect on bank profits. For example, when interest rates rise by 5 percentage points, the change in profits is 5% × −$30 million, which equals −$1.5 million, as we saw.

The analysis we just conducted is known as *basic gap analysis*, and it can be refined in two ways. Clearly, not all assets and liabilities in the fixed-rate category have the same maturity. One refinement, the *maturity bucket approach*, is to measure the gap for several maturity subintervals, called *maturity buckets*, so that effects of interest-rate changes over a multiyear period can be calculated. The second refinement, called *standardized gap analysis*, accounts for the differing degrees of rate sensitivity among rate-sensitive assets and liabilities.

An alternative method for measuring interest-rate risk, called **duration analysis**, examines the sensitivity of the market value of the bank's total assets and liabilities to changes in interest rates. Duration analysis is based on what is known as Macaulay's concept of *duration*, which measures the average lifetime of a security's stream of payments.[4] Duration is a useful concept because it provides a good approximation of the sensitivity of a security's market value to a change in its interest rate:

$$\text{percent change in market value of security} \approx$$
$$-\text{percentage-point change in interest rate} \times \text{duration in years}$$

where $\approx$ denotes "approximately equals."

Duration analysis involves using the average (weighted) duration of a financial institution's assets and of its liabilities to see how its net worth responds to a change in interest rates. Going back to our example of the First National Bank, suppose the average duration of the bank's assets is three years (that is, the average lifetime of the stream of payments is three years), whereas the average duration of its liabilities is two years.

---

[4]Algebraically, Macaulay's duration, D, is defined as

$$D = \sum_{\tau=1}^{N} \tau \frac{CP_\tau}{(1 + i^\tau)} \Big/ \sum_{\tau=1}^{N} \frac{CP_\tau}{(1 + i^\tau)}$$

where $\tau =$ time until cash payment is made
  $CP_\tau =$ cash payment (interest plus principal) at time τ
   $i =$ interest rate
  $N =$ time to maturity of the security

For a more detailed discussion of duration gap analysis using the concept of Macaulay's duration, see the appendix to this chapter in MyLab Economics.

In addition, the First National Bank has $100 million of assets and, say, $90 million of liabilities, so its bank capital is 10% of assets. With a 5-percentage-point increase in interest rates, the market value of the bank's assets falls by 15% ($= -5\% \times 3$ years), a decline of $15 million on the $100 million of assets. However, the market value of the liabilities falls by 10% ($= -5\% \times 2$ years), a decline of $9 million on the $90 million of liabilities. The net result is that the net worth (the market value of the assets minus the liabilities) has declined by $6 million, or 6% of the total original asset value. Similarly, a 5-percentage-point decline in interest rates increases the net worth of the First National Bank by 6% of the total asset value.

As our example makes clear, both duration analysis and gap analysis indicate that the First National Bank will suffer if interest rates rise but will gain if they fall. Duration analysis and gap analysis are thus useful tools for a manager of a financial institution who is concerned about its degree of exposure to interest-rate risk.

APPLICATION   Strategies for Managing Interest-Rate Risk

Suppose that as manager of the First National Bank, you have done a duration and gap analysis for the bank. Now you need to decide which alternative strategies you should pursue to manage the interest-rate risk.

If you firmly believe that interest rates will fall in the future, you may be willing to forgo action because you know that the bank has more rate-sensitive liabilities than rate-sensitive assets and so will benefit from the expected interest-rate decline. However, you also realize that the First National Bank is subject to substantial interest-rate risk because there is always a possibility that interest rates will rise rather than fall. What should you do to eliminate this interest-rate risk? One thing you could do is to shorten the duration of the bank's assets to increase their rate sensitivity. Alternatively, you could lengthen the duration of the liabilities. By this adjustment of the bank's assets or liabilities, the bank's income will be less affected by interest-rate swings.

One problem with eliminating the First National Bank's interest-rate risk by altering the balance sheet is that doing so might be very costly in the short run. The bank may be locked into assets and liabilities of particular durations because of where its expertise lies. Fortunately, recently developed financial instruments known as financial derivatives—financial forwards and futures, options, and swaps—can help the bank reduce its interest-rate risk exposure but do not require the bank to rearrange its balance sheet. ◆

9.6 OFF-BALANCE-SHEET ACTIVITIES

LO 9.6 Summarize the types of off-balance-sheet activities.

Although asset and liability management has traditionally been the primary concern of banks, in the more competitive environment of recent years banks have been aggressively seeking out profits by engaging in off-balance-sheet activities.[5] **Off-balance-sheet activities** involve trading financial instruments and generating income from fees and loan

---

[5]Managers of financial institutions also need to know how well their banks are doing at any point in time. A second appendix to this chapter, which can be found in MyLab Economics, discusses how bank performance is measured.

sales, activities that affect bank profits but do not appear on bank balance sheets. Indeed, off-balance-sheet activities have been growing in importance for banks: The income from these activities as a percentage of assets has increased more than fivefold since 1980.

Loan Sales

One type of off-balance-sheet activity that has grown in importance in recent years involves income generated by loan sales. A **loan sale**, also called a *secondary loan participation*, involves a contract that sells all or part of the cash stream from a specific loan and thereby removes the loan so that it is no longer an asset on the bank's balance sheet. Banks earn profits by selling loans for amounts that are slightly greater than the amounts of the original loans. Because the high interest rate on these loans makes them attractive, institutions are willing to buy them, even though the higher price means that they earn a slightly lower interest rate than the original interest rate on the loan, usually on the order of 0.15 percentage point.

Generation of Fee Income

Another type of off-balance-sheet activity involves the generation of income from fees that banks receive for providing specialized services to their customers, such as making foreign exchange trades on a customer's behalf, servicing a mortgage-backed security by collecting interest and principal payments and then paying them out, guaranteeing debt securities such as banker's acceptances (by which the bank promises to make interest and principal payments if the party issuing the security cannot), and providing backup lines of credit. There are several types of backup lines of credit. We have already mentioned the most important, the loan commitment, under which, for a fee, the bank agrees to provide a loan at the customer's request, up to a given dollar amount, over a specified period of time. Credit lines with "overdraft privileges" are also now available to bank depositors—these bank customers can write checks in excess of their deposit balances and, in effect, write themselves a loan. Other lines of credit for which banks get fees include standby letters of credit to back up issues of commercial paper and other securities, and credit lines (called *note issuance facilities*, NIFs, and *revolving underwriting facilities*, RUFs) for underwriting Euronotes, which are medium-term Eurobonds.

Off-balance-sheet activities involving guarantees of securities and backup credit lines increase the risk a bank faces. Even though a guaranteed security does not appear on a bank's balance sheet, it still exposes the bank to default risk: If the issuer of the security defaults, the bank is left holding the bag and must pay off the security's owner. Backup credit lines also expose the bank to risk because the bank may be forced to provide loans when it does not have sufficient liquidity or when the borrower is a very poor credit risk.

Trading Activities and Risk Management Techniques

We have already mentioned that banks' attempts to manage interest-rate risk have led them to trading in financial futures, options for debt instruments, and interest-rate swaps. Banks engaged in international banking also conduct transactions in the foreign exchange market. All transactions in these markets are off-balance-sheet activities because they do not have a direct effect on the bank's balance sheet. Although bank trading in these markets is often directed toward reducing risk or facilitating other bank business, banks also try to outguess the markets and engage in speculation. This speculation can be a very risky business and has led to bank insolvencies, the most dramatic being the failure of Barings, a British bank, in 1995.

Global   Barings, Daiwa, Sumitomo, Société Générale, and JP Morgan Chase: Rogue Traders and the Principal–Agent Problem

The demise of Barings, a venerable British bank more than a century old, is a sad morality tale of how the principal–agent problem operating through a rogue trader can take a financial institution that has a healthy balance sheet one month and turn it into an insolvent tragedy the next.

In July 1992, Nick Leeson, Barings's new head clerk at its Singapore branch, began to speculate on the Nikkei, the Japanese version of the Dow Jones stock index. By late 1992, Leeson had suffered losses of $3 million, which he hid from his superiors by stashing the losses in a secret account. He even fooled his superiors into thinking he was generating large profits, thanks to a failure of internal controls at his firm, which allowed him to execute trades on the Singapore exchange *and* oversee the bookkeeping of those trades. (As anyone who runs a cash business, such as a bar, knows, there is always a lower likelihood of fraud if more than one person handles the cash. Similarly, in trading operations, you never mix management of the back room with management of the front room; this principle was grossly violated by Barings management.)

Things didn't get better for Leeson, who by late 1994 had suffered losses exceeding $250 million. In January and February 1995, Leeson bet the bank. On January 17, 1995, the day of the earthquake in Kobe, Japan, he lost $75 million, and by the end of the week he had lost more than $150 million. When the stock market declined on February 23, leaving him with a further loss of $250 million, he called it quits and fled Singapore. Three days later, he turned himself in at the Frankfurt airport. By the end of his wild ride, Leeson's losses, $1.3 billion in all, ate up Barings's capital and caused the bank to fail. Leeson was subsequently convicted and sent to jail in Singapore for his activities. He was released in 1999 and apologized for his actions.

Our asymmetric information analysis of the principal–agent problem explains Leeson's behavior and highlights the danger of a management lapse like Barings's. Letting Leeson control both his own trades and the back room increased asymmetric information, because it reduced the principal's (Barings's) knowledge about Leeson's trading activities. This lapse increased the moral hazard incentive for him to take risks at the bank's expense, as he was now less likely to be caught. Furthermore, once he had experienced large losses, he had even greater incentives to take on even higher risk because, if his bets worked out, he could reverse his losses and keep in good standing with the company; whereas if his bets soured, he had little to lose because he was out of a job anyway. Indeed, the bigger his losses, the more he had to gain by bigger bets, which explains the escalation of the amount of his trades as his losses mounted. If Barings's managers had understood the principal–agent problem, they would have been more vigilant at finding out what Leeson was up to, and the bank might still be here today.

Unfortunately, Nick Leeson is no longer a rarity in the rogue traders' billionaires club, made up of those who have lost more than $1 billion. Over 11 years, Toshihide Iguchi, an officer in the New York branch of Daiwa Bank, also had control of both the bond trading operation and the back room bookkeeping activities, and he racked up $1.1 billion in losses over the period. In July 1995, Iguchi disclosed his losses to his superiors, but the management of the bank did not disclose them to its regulators. The result was that Daiwa was slapped with a $340 million fine and the bank was thrown out of the country by U.S. bank regulators.

Yasuo Hamanaka is another member of the billionaires club. In July 1996, he topped Leeson's and Iguchi's record, losing $2.6 billion for his employer, the Sumitomo Corporation, one of Japan's top trading companies. In January 2008, Jerome Kerviel's loss for his bank, Société Générale, set the all-time record for a rogue trader: His unauthorized trades cost the French bank $7.2 billion. In 2012, even the highly successful JP Morgan Chase bank experienced a trading loss of over $2 billion, caused by rogue trader Bruno Iksill, who was colorfully nicknamed "the London Whale."

The moral of these stories is that management of firms engaged in trading activities must reduce the principal–agent problem by closely monitoring their traders' activities, or the rogues' gallery will continue to grow.

Trading activities, although often highly profitable, are also highly risky because they make it easy for financial institutions and their employees to make huge bets quickly. The principal–agent problem, discussed in Chapter 8, is an especially severe problem for management of trading activities. Because a trader (the agent) has the opportunity to place large bets, whether she trades in bond markets, foreign exchange markets, or financial derivatives, she has an incentive to take on excessive risks: If her trading strategy leads to large profits, she is likely to receive a high salary and bonuses, but if she takes large losses, the financial institution (the principal) will have to cover them. As the Barings Bank failure of 1995 so forcefully demonstrated, a trader subject to the principal–agent problem can take an institution that is quite healthy and drive it into insolvency very rapidly (see the Global box on the preceding page).

To reduce the principal–agent problem, managers of financial institutions must set up internal controls to prevent debacles like the one at Barings. Such controls include the complete separation of the people in charge of trading activities from those in charge of the bookkeeping for trades. In addition, managers must set limits on the total amount of traders' transactions and on the institution's risk exposure. Managers must also scrutinize risk assessment procedures using the latest computer technology.

One such method involves the value-at-risk approach. In this approach, the institution develops a statistical model with which it can calculate the maximum loss that its portfolio is likely to sustain over a given time interval, dubbed the value at risk, or VaR. For example, a bank might estimate that the maximum loss it would be likely to sustain over one day with a probability of 1 in 100 is $1 million; the $1 million figure is the bank's calculated value at risk. Another approach is called "stress testing." In this approach, a manager uses a computer model to project what would happen if a doomsday scenario occurred; that is, she looks at the losses the institution would sustain in the event of an unusual combination of bad events. With the value-at-risk approach and stress testing, a financial institution can assess its risk exposure and take steps to reduce it.

U.S. bank regulators have become concerned about the increased risk that banks are facing from their off-balance-sheet activities and, as we will see in Chapter 10, are encouraging banks to pay increased attention to risk management. In addition, the Bank for International Settlements is developing additional bank capital requirements based on value-at-risk calculations for a bank's trading activities.

SUMMARY

1. The balance sheet of a commercial bank can be thought of as a list of the sources and uses of bank funds. A bank's liabilities are its sources of funds, which include checkable deposits, savings and time deposits, discount loans from the Fed, borrowings from other banks and corporations, and bank capital. A bank's assets are its uses of funds, which include reserves, cash items in process of collection, deposits at other banks, securities, loans, and other assets (mostly physical capital).

2. Banks make profits through the process of asset transformation: They borrow short (accept short-term deposits) and lend long (make long-term loans). When a bank takes in additional deposits, it gains an equal amount of reserves; when it pays out deposits, it loses an equal amount of reserves.

3. Although more-liquid assets tend to earn lower returns, banks still desire to hold them. Specifically, banks hold excess and secondary reserves because they provide insurance against the costs of a deposit outflow. Banks manage their assets to maximize profits by seeking the highest returns possible on loans and securities while at the same time trying to lower risk and make adequate provisions for liquidity. Although liability management was once a staid affair, large (money center) banks now

actively seek out sources of funds by issuing liabilities such as negotiable CDs or by actively borrowing from other banks and corporations. Banks manage the amount of capital they hold with the goals of preventing bank failure and meeting bank capital requirements set by the regulatory authorities. However, banks do not want to hold too much capital because by so doing they will lower the returns to equity holders.

4. The concepts of adverse selection and moral hazard explain many credit risk management principles involving loan activities: screening and monitoring, establishment of long-term customer relationships and loan commitments, collateral and compensating balances, and credit rationing.

5. With the increased volatility of interest rates that occurred in the 1980s, financial institutions became more concerned about their exposure to interest-rate risk. Gap and duration analyses tell a financial institution if it has more rate-sensitive liabilities than assets (in which case a rise in interest rates will reduce profits, and a fall in interest rates will raise profits). Financial institutions manage their interest-rate risk by modifying their balance sheets but can also use strategies involving financial derivatives.

6. Off-balance-sheet activities consist of trading financial instruments and generating income from fees and loan sales, all of which affect bank profits but are not visible on bank balance sheets. Because these off-balance-sheet activities expose banks to increased risk, bank management must pay particular attention to risk assessment procedures and internal controls to restrict employees from taking on too much risk.

KEY TERMS

asset management, p. 195
asset transformation, p. 192
balance sheet, p. 188
capital adequacy management, p. 195
compensating balances, p. 206
credit rationing, p. 206
credit risk, p. 195
deposit outflows, p. 195
discount loans, p. 190
discount rate, p. 197

duration analysis, p. 208
equity multiplier (EM), p. 201
excess reserves, p. 191
gap analysis, p. 208
interest-rate risk, p. 195
liability management, p. 195
liquidity management, p. 195
loan commitment, p. 206
loan sale, p. 210
money center banks, p. 199

off-balance-sheet activities, p. 209
required reserve ratio, p. 191
required reserves, p. 191
reserve requirements, p. 191
reserves, p. 191
return on assets (ROA), p. 201
return on equity (ROE), p. 201
secondary reserves, p. 191
T-account, p. 192
vault cash, p. 191

QUESTIONS

1. Why might a bank be willing to borrow funds from other banks at a higher rate than the rate at which it can borrow from the Fed?

2. Rank the following bank assets from most to least liquid:
   a. Commercial loans
   b. Securities
   c. Reserves
   d. Physical capital

3. The bank you own has the following balance sheet:

Assets		Liabilities	
Reserves	$ 75 million	Deposits	$500 million
Loans	$525 million	Bank capital	$100 million

If the bank suffers a deposit outflow of $50 million with a required reserve ratio on deposits of 10%, what actions should you take?

4. If a deposit outflow of $50 million occurs, which balance sheet would a bank rather have initially, the balance sheet in Question 3 or the following balance sheet? Why?

Assets		Liabilities	
Reserves	$100 million	Deposits	$500 million
Loans	$500 million	Bank capital	$100 million

5. If no decent lending opportunity arises in the economy, and the central bank pays an interest rate on reserves that is similar to other low-risk investments, do you think banks will be willing to hold large amounts of excess reserves?

6. If the bank you own has no excess reserves and a sound customer comes in asking for a loan, should you automatically turn the customer down, explaining that you don't have any excess reserves to lend out? Why or why not? What options are available that will enable you to provide the funds your customer needs?

7. If a bank finds that its ROE is too low because it has too much bank capital, what can it do to raise its ROE?

8. If a bank is falling short of meeting its capital requirements by $1 million, what three things can it do to rectify the situation?

9. Why do equity holders care more about ROE than about ROA?

10. If a bank doubles the amount of its capital and ROA stays constant, what will happen to ROE?

11. What are the benefits and costs for a bank when it decides to increase the amount of its bank capital?

12. Why is being nosy a desirable trait for a banker?

13. A bank almost always insists that the firms it lends to keep compensating balances at the bank. Why?

14. If the president of a bank told you that the bank was so well run that it has never had to call in loans, sell securities, or borrow as a result of a deposit outflow, would you be willing to buy stock in that bank? Why or why not?

15. "Because diversification is a desirable strategy for avoiding risk, it never makes sense for a bank to specialize in making specific types of loans." Is this statement true, false, or uncertain? Explain your answer.

16. If you are a banker and expect interest rates to rise in the future, would you prefer to make short-term loans or long-term loans?

17. "Bank managers should always seek the highest return possible on their assets." Is this statement true, false, or uncertain? Explain your answer.

18. After July 2010, bank customers using a debit card had to specifically opt-in to the bank's overdraft protection plan. Explain the effect of this regulation on a bank's noninterest income.

APPLIED PROBLEMS

19. Using the T-accounts of the First National Bank and the Second National Bank given in this chapter, describe what happens when Jane Brown writes a $50 check on her account at the First National Bank to pay her friend Joe Green, who in turn deposits the check in his account at the Second National Bank.

20. What happens to reserves at the First National Bank if one person withdraws $1,000 of cash and another person deposits $500 of cash? Use T-accounts to explain your answer.

21. Angus Bank holds no excess reserves but complies with the reserve requirement. The required reserves ratio is 9%, and reserves are currently $27 million. Determine the amount of deposits, the reserve shortage created by a deposit outflow of $5 million, and the cost of the reserve shortage if Angus Bank borrows in the federal funds market (assume the federal funds rate is 0.25%).

22. Excess reserves act as insurance against deposit outflows. Suppose that on a yearly basis Malcom Bank holds $12 million in excess reserves and $88 million in required reserves. Suppose that Malcom Bank can earn 3.5% on its loans and that the interest paid on (total) reserves is 0.2%. What would be the cost of this insurance policy?

23. Victory Bank reports an EM of 25, while Batovi Bank reports an EM equal to 14. Which bank is better prepared to respond against large losses on loans?

24. Suppose you are the manager of a bank whose $100 billion of assets have an average duration of four years and whose $90 billion of liabilities have an average duration of six years. Conduct a duration analysis for the bank, and show what will happen to the net worth of the bank if interest rates rise by 2 percentage points. What actions could you take to reduce the bank's interest-rate risk?

25. Suppose you are the manager of a bank that has $15 million of fixed-rate assets, $30 million of rate-sensitive assets, $25 million of fixed-rate liabilities, and $20 million of rate-sensitive liabilities. Conduct a gap analysis for the bank, and show what will happen to bank profits if interest rates rise by 5 percentage points. What actions could you take to reduce the bank's interest-rate risk?

DATA ANALYSIS PROBLEM

The Problem updates with real-time data in **MyLab Economics** and is available for practice or instructor assignment.

1. **Real-time Data Analysis** Go to the St. Louis Federal Reserve FRED database, and find data for all commercial banks on total liabilities (TLBACBM027SBOG), total deposits (DPSACBM027SBOG), and residual of assets less liabilities (RALACBM027SBOG).

   a. What is the balance sheet interpretation of the residual of assets less liabilities?
   b. For the most recent month of data available, use the three indicators listed in the problem introduction to calculate the total amount of borrowings by banks.

10 Economic Analysis of Financial Regulation

Learning Objectives

10.1 Identify the reasons for and forms of a government safety net in financial markets.

10.2 List and summarize the types of financial regulation and how each reduces asymmetric information problems.

Preview

As we have seen in previous chapters, the financial system is among the most heavily regulated sectors of the economy, and banks are among the most heavily regulated of financial institutions. In this chapter, we develop an economic analysis of why regulation of the financial system takes the form it does.

Unfortunately, the regulatory process may not always work very well, as evidenced by the recent global financial crisis. Here we also use our economic analysis of financial regulation to explain the worldwide crises in banking and to consider how the regulatory system can be reformed to prevent future such disasters.

10.1 ASYMMETRIC INFORMATION AS A RATIONALE FOR FINANCIAL REGULATION

LO 10.1 Identify the reasons for and forms of a government safety net in financial markets.

In earlier chapters, we saw how asymmetric information—the fact that different parties in a financial contract do not have the same information—leads to adverse selection and moral hazard problems, which have an important impact on our financial system. The concepts of asymmetric information, adverse selection, and moral hazard are especially useful in understanding why governments pursue financial regulation.

Government Safety Net

As we saw in Chapter 8, financial intermediaries, like banks, are particularly well suited to solving adverse selection and moral hazard problems because they make private loans that help avoid the free-rider problem. However, this solution to the free-rider problem creates another asymmetric information problem, because depositors lack information about the quality of these private loans. This asymmetric information problem leads to other problems that interfere with the proper functioning of the financial system.

Bank Panics and the Need for Deposit Insurance Before the FDIC (Federal Deposit Insurance Corporation) started operations in 1934, a **bank failure** (in which a bank is unable to meet its obligations to pay its depositors and other creditors, and so must go out of business) meant that depositors would have to wait until the bank was liquidated (until its assets had been turned into cash) to get their deposit funds; at that time, they would be paid only a fraction of the value of their deposits. Because they couldn't know if bank managers were taking on too much risk or were outright crooks, depositors would be reluctant to put money in banks, thus making banking institutions less viable. Second, depositors' lack of information about the quality of bank assets can lead to a **bank panic**, in which many banks fail simultaneously. Because the simultaneous failure of many banks leads to a sharp decline in bank lending, bank panics have serious, harmful consequences for the economy.

To understand why bank panics occur, consider the following situation. Deposit insurance does not exist, and an adverse shock hits the economy. As a result of the shock, 5% of banks have such large losses on loans that they become insolvent (have a negative net worth and so are bankrupt). Because of asymmetric information, depositors are unable to tell whether their bank is a "good" bank or one of the 5% that are insolvent. Depositors at bad *and* good banks recognize that they may not get back 100 cents on the dollar for their deposits and therefore are inclined to withdraw them. Indeed, because banks operate on a "sequential service constraint" (a first-come, first-served basis), depositors have a very strong incentive to be the first to show up at the bank, because if they are last in line, the bank may have paid out all its funds and they will get nothing. The incentive to "run" to the bank to be first is why withdrawals when there is fear about the health of a bank is described as a "bank run." Uncertainty about the health of the banking system in general can lead to runs on both good and bad banks, and the failure of one bank can hasten the failure of others (referred to as the *contagion effect*). If nothing is done to restore the public's confidence, a bank panic can ensue.

Indeed, bank panics were a fact of American life in the nineteenth and early twentieth centuries, with major panics occurring every 20 years or so, in 1819, 1837, 1857, 1873, 1884, 1893, 1907, and 1930–1933. Bank failures were a serious problem even during the boom years of the 1920s, when the number of bank failures averaged around 600 per year.

A government safety net for depositors can short-circuit runs on banks and bank panics, and by providing protection for the depositor, it can overcome depositors' reluctance to put funds into the banking system. One form of safety net is deposit insurance, such as that provided by the Federal Deposit Insurance Corporation (FDIC) of the United States. The FDIC guarantees that current depositors will be paid off in full on the first $250,000 they have deposited in a bank if the bank fails. (In 1934, deposits were insured up to $2,500.) With fully insured deposits, depositors don't need to run to the bank to make withdrawals—even if they are worried about the bank's health—because their deposits will be worth 100 cents on the dollar no matter what. From 1930 to 1933, the years immediately preceding the creation of the FDIC, the number of bank failures averaged more than 2,000 per year. After the establishment of the FDIC in 1934, bank failures averaged fewer than 15 per year until 1981.

The FDIC uses two primary methods to handle a failed bank. In the first, called the *payoff method*, the FDIC allows the bank to fail and pays off depositors up to the $250,000 insurance limit (with funds acquired from the insurance premiums paid by the banks who have bought FDIC insurance). After the bank has been liquidated, the FDIC lines up with other creditors of the bank and is paid its share of the proceeds from the liquidated assets. Typically, when the payoff method is used, account holders with deposits in excess of the $250,000 limit get back more than 90 cents on the dollar, although the process can take several years to complete.

In the second method, called the *purchase and assumption method*, the FDIC reorganizes the bank, typically by finding a willing merger partner who assumes (takes over) all of the failed bank's liabilities so that no depositor or other creditor loses a penny. The FDIC often sweetens the pot for the merger partner by providing it with subsidized loans or by buying some of the failed bank's weaker loans. The net effect of the purchase and assumption method is that the FDIC has guaranteed *all* liabilities and deposits, not just deposits under the $250,000 limit. The purchase and assumption method is typically more costly for the FDIC than the payoff method but nevertheless was the FDIC's more common procedure for dealing with a failed bank before new banking legislation was introduced in 1991.

In recent years, government deposit insurance has been growing in popularity and has spread to many countries throughout the world. Whether this trend is desirable is discussed in the Global box "The Spread of Government Deposit Insurance Throughout the World: Is This a Good Thing?"

Other Forms of the Government Safety Net　Deposit insurance is not the only form of government safety net. In other countries, governments have often stood ready to provide support to domestic banks facing runs even in the absence of explicit deposit insurance. Furthermore, banks are not the only financial intermediaries that can pose a systemic threat to the financial system. When financial institutions are very large or highly interconnected with other financial institutions or markets, their failure has the potential to bring down the entire financial system. This is exactly what happened with Bear Stearns and Lehman Brothers, two investment banks, and AIG, an insurance company, during the global financial crisis in 2008.

One way in which governments provide support is through lending from the central bank to troubled institutions, as the Federal Reserve did during the global financial

---

Global　The Spread of Government Deposit Insurance Throughout the World: Is This a Good Thing?

For the first 30 years after federal deposit insurance was established in the United States, only six countries emulated the United States and adopted deposit insurance. However, this began to change in the late 1960s, with the trend accelerating in the 1990s, when the number of countries adopting deposit insurance topped 70. Government deposit insurance has taken off throughout the world because of growing concern about the health of banking systems, particularly after the increasing number of banking crises in recent years (documented in the appendix to this chapter, available on MyLab). Has this spread of deposit insurance been a good thing? Has it helped improve the performance of the financial system and prevent banking crises?

The answer seems to be "no" under many circumstances. Research at the World Bank has found that, on average, the adoption of explicit government deposit insurance is associated with less banking sector stability and a higher incidence of banking crises.* Furthermore, on average, deposit insurance seems to retard financial development. However, these negative effects of deposit insurance occur only in countries with weak institutional environments: an absence of rule of law, ineffective regulation and supervision of the financial sector, and high corruption. This situation is exactly what might be expected because, as we will see later in this chapter, a strong institutional environment is needed to limit the moral hazard incentives for banks to engage in the excessively risky behavior encouraged by deposit insurance. The problem is that development of a strong institutional environment may be very difficult to achieve in many emerging market countries. We are left with the following conclusion: Adoption of deposit insurance may be exactly the wrong medicine for promoting stability and efficiency of banking systems in emerging market countries.

*See World Bank, *Finance for Growth: Policy Choices in a Volatile World* (Oxford: World Bank and Oxford University Press, 2001).

crisis (more on this in Chapter 15). This form of support is often referred to as the "lender of last resort" role of the central bank. In other cases, funds are provided directly to troubled institutions, as was done by the U.S. Treasury and by other governments in 2008 during a particularly virulent phase of the global financial crisis (see Chapter 12). Governments can also take over (nationalize) troubled institutions and guarantee that all creditors' loans will be paid in full.

Drawbacks of the Government Safety Net

Although a government safety net can help protect depositors and other creditors and prevent, or ameliorate, financial crises, it is a mixed blessing.

Moral Hazard and the Government Safety Net

The most serious drawback of the government safety net stems from moral hazard, the incentives of one party in a transaction to engage in activities detrimental to the other party. Moral hazard is an important concern in insurance arrangements in general because the existence of insurance provides increased incentives for taking risks that might result in an insurance payoff. For example, some drivers with automobile collision insurance that has a low deductible might be more likely to drive recklessly, because if they get into an accident, the insurance company pays most of the costs for damage and repairs.

Moral hazard is a prominent concern associated with government safety nets. With a safety net, depositors and creditors know they will not suffer losses if a financial institution fails, so they do not impose the discipline of the marketplace on these institutions by withdrawing funds when they suspect that the financial institution is taking on too much risk. Consequently, financial institutions with a government safety net have an incentive to take on greater risks than they otherwise would, because taxpayers will foot the bill if the bank subsequently goes belly up. Financial institutions can place the following bet: "Heads, I win; tails, the taxpayer loses."

Adverse Selection and the Government Safety Net

A further problem with a government safety net like deposit insurance is adverse selection. Just as bad drivers are more likely than good drivers to take out automobile collision insurance with a low deductible, the people who are most likely to produce the adverse outcome a bank is insured against—bank failure—are the same people who most want to take advantage of the insurance. Because depositors and creditors protected by a government safety net have little reason to impose discipline on financial institutions, risk-loving entrepreneurs might find the financial industry a particularly attractive one—they know they will be able to engage in highly risky activities. Even worse, because protected depositors and creditors have so little reason to monitor the financial institution's activities, without government intervention outright crooks might also find finance an attractive industry for their activities because it is easy for them to get away with fraud and embezzlement.

"Too Big to Fail"

The moral hazard created by a government safety net and the desire to prevent financial institution failures have presented financial regulators with a particular quandary, the **too-big-to-fail problem**, in which regulators are reluctant to close down large financial institutions and impose losses on the institution's depositors and creditors because doing so might precipitate a financial crisis. The too-big-to-fail problem first arose when Continental Illinois, one of the ten largest banks in the United States, became insolvent in May 1984. Not only did the FDIC guarantee depositors up to the $100,000 insurance limit (the maximum at that time) but it also guaranteed accounts exceeding $100,000 and even prevented losses for Continental Illinois bond-holders. Shortly thereafter, the comptroller of the currency (the regulator of national banks) testified to Congress that 11 of the largest banks would receive treatment similar to that received by Continental Illinois.

Although the comptroller did not use the term "too big to fail" (it was actually used by Congressman Stewart McKinney in those congressional hearings), this term is now applied to a policy in which the government provides guarantees of repayment of large, uninsured creditors of the largest banks, so that no depositor or creditor suffers a loss, even when these depositors and creditors are not automatically entitled to this guarantee. The FDIC does this by using the purchase and assumption method, giving the insolvent bank a large infusion of capital and then finding a willing merger partner to take over the bank and its deposits. The too-big-to-fail policy was extended to big banks that were not even among the 11 largest. (Note that "too big to fail" is a some-what misleading term, because when a financial institution is closed or merged into another financial institution, the managers are usually fired and the stockholders in the financial institution lose their investment.)

One problem with the too-big-to-fail policy is that it increases the moral hazard incentives for big banks. If the FDIC were willing to close a bank using the payoff method, paying depositors only up to the current $250,000 limit, large depositors with more than $250,000 would suffer losses if the bank failed. Thus they would have an incentive to monitor the bank by examining the bank's activities closely and pulling their money out if the bank was taking on too much risk. To prevent such a loss of deposits, the bank would be more likely to engage in less risky activities. However, once large depositors know that a bank is too big to fail, they have no incentive to monitor the bank and pull out their deposits when it takes on too much risk: No matter what the bank does, large depositors will not suffer any losses. The result of the too-big-to-fail policy is that big financial insti-tutions might take on even greater risks, thereby making bank failures more likely.

Similarly, the too-big-to-fail policy increases the moral hazard incentives for non-bank financial institutions that are extended a government safety net. Knowing that the financial institution will be bailed out, creditors have little incentive to monitor the institution and pull their money out when the institution is taking on excessive risk. As a result, large or interconnected financial institutions are more likely to engage in highly risky activities, making a financial crisis more likely.

Indeed, financial institutions that were considered too big to fail—including Bear Stearns, Lehman Brothers, and AIG—did take on excessive risk in the period leading to the global financial crisis, and their subsequent collapse helped trigger the worst finan-cial crisis (discussed in Chapter 12) since the Great Depression.

Financial Consolidation and the Government Safety Net   With financial innovation and the passage of the Riegle-Neal Interstate Banking and Branching Effi-ciency Act of 1994 and the Gramm-Leach-Bliley Financial Services Modernization Act in 1999, financial consolidation has been proceeding at a rapid pace, leading to both larger and more complex financial organizations. Financial consolidation poses two challenges to financial regulation because of the existence of the government safety net.

First, the increased size of financial institutions resulting from financial consolida-tion increases the too-big-to-fail problem, because there are now more large institutions whose failure would expose the financial system to systemic (system-wide) risk. Thus, more financial institutions are likely to be treated as too big to fail, and the increased moral hazard incentives for these large institutions to take on greater risk increase the fragility of the financial system.

Second, financial consolidation of banks with other financial services firms means that the government safety net may be extended to new activities, such as securities underwriting, insurance, or real estate activities, as occurred during the global financial crisis. This situation increases incentives for greater risk taking in these activities, which can also weaken the fabric of the financial system. Limiting the moral hazard incentives for the larger, more complex financial organizations that have arisen as a result of recent changes in legislation is one of the key issues facing banking regulators in the aftermath of the global financial crisis.

10.2 TYPES OF FINANCIAL REGULATION

LO 10.2 List and summarize the types of financial regulation and how each reduces asymmetric information problems.

There are eight basic types of financial regulation aimed at lessening asymmetric information problems and excessive risk taking in the financial system: (1) restrictions on asset holdings, (2) capital requirements, (3) prompt corrective action, (4) chartering and examination, (5) assessment of risk management, (6) disclosure requirements, (7) consumer protection, and (8) restrictions on competition.

Restrictions on Asset Holdings

As we have seen, the moral hazard associated with a government safety net encourages too much risk taking on the part of financial institutions. Bank regulations that restrict asset holdings are directed at minimizing this moral hazard, which can cost taxpayers dearly.

Even in the absence of a government safety net, financial institutions still have the incentive to take on too much risk. Risky assets may provide the financial institution with higher earnings when they pay off, but if they do not pay off and the institution fails, depositors and creditors are left holding the bag. If depositors and creditors were able to monitor the bank easily by acquiring information on its risk-taking activities, they would be able to withdraw their funds immediately if the institution was taking on too much risk. To prevent such a loss of funds, the institution would be more likely to reduce its risk-taking activities. Unfortunately, acquiring information on an institution's activities to learn how much risk it is taking on can be a difficult task. Hence most depositors and many creditors are incapable of imposing the discipline that might prevent financial institutions from engaging in risky activities. A strong rationale for government regulation aimed at reducing risk taking on the part of financial institutions therefore existed even before the establishment of government safety nets like federal deposit insurance.

Because banks are the financial institutions most prone to panics, they are subjected to strict regulations that restrict their holdings of risky assets, such as common stocks. Bank regulations also promote diversification, which reduces risk by limiting the dollar amounts of loans in particular categories or to individual borrowers. With the extension of the government safety net during the global financial crisis, and the calls for regulatory reform in its aftermath, it is likely that nonbank financial institutions may face greater restrictions on their holdings of risky assets in the future. The danger exists, however, that these restrictions may become so onerous that the efficiency of the financial system will be impaired.

Capital Requirements

Government-imposed capital requirements are another way of minimizing moral hazard at financial institutions. When a financial institution is forced to hold a large amount of equity capital, the institution has more to lose if it fails and is thus more likely to pursue less risky activities. In addition, as was illustrated in Chapter 9, capital functions as a cushion when bad shocks occur, making it less likely that a financial institution will fail, thereby directly adding to the safety and soundness of financial institutions.

Capital requirements for banks take two forms. The first type is based on the **leverage ratio**, the amount of capital divided by the bank's total assets. To be classified as well capitalized, a bank's leverage ratio must exceed 5%; a lower leverage ratio, especially one below 3%, triggers increased regulatory restrictions on the bank. Through most of the 1980s, minimum bank capital in the United States was set solely by specifying a minimum leverage ratio.

In the wake of the Continental Illinois and savings and loans bailouts of the 1980s, regulators in the United States and the rest of the world have become increasingly worried about banks' holdings of risky assets and about the increase in banks' **off-balance-sheet activities**. Off-balance-sheet activities, which do not appear on bank balance sheets but nevertheless expose banks to risk, involve trading financial instruments and generating income from fees.

To help combat the problems of risky assets and off-balance-sheet activities, banking officials from industrialized nations agreed to set up the **Basel Committee on Banking Supervision** (so named because it meets under the auspices of the Bank for International Settlements in Basel, Switzerland), which implemented the **Basel Accord**, which deals with a second type of capital requirements, risk-based capital requirements. The Basel Accord, which requires that banks hold as capital at least 8% of their risk-weighted assets, has been adopted by more than 100 countries, including the United States. Assets are allocated into four categories, each with a different weight to reflect the degree of credit risk. The first category carries a zero weight and includes items that have little default risk, such as reserves and government securities issued by the Organization for Economic Cooperation and Development (OECD—industrialized) countries. The second category has a 20% weight and includes claims on banks in OECD countries. The third category has a weight of 50% and includes municipal bonds and residential mortgages. The fourth category has the maximum weight of 100% and includes loans to consumers and corporations. Off-balance-sheet activities are treated in a similar manner. They are assigned a credit-equivalent percentage that converts them to on-balance-sheet items to which the appropriate risk weight applies, and there are minimum capital requirements for risks in banks' trading accounts.

Over time, the limitations of the Basel Accord have become apparent, because the regulatory measure of bank risk, as stipulated by the risk weights, can differ substantially from the actual risk the bank faces. This discrepancy has resulted in **regulatory arbitrage**, a practice in which banks keep on their books assets that have the same risk-based capital requirement but are relatively risky, such as a loan to a company with a very low credit rating, while taking off their books low-risk assets, such as a loan to a company with a very high credit rating. The Basel Accord thus might lead to increased risk taking, the opposite of its intent. To address these limitations, the Basel Committee on Bank Supervision came up with a new capital accord, often referred to as Basel 2. However, in the aftermath of the global financial crisis, the committee developed an even newer accord, which the media has dubbed "Basel 3." These accords are described in the Global box "Where Is the Basel Accord Heading After the Global Financial Crisis?"

Global Where Is the Basel Accord Heading After the Global Financial Crisis?

Starting in June 1999, the Basel Committee on Banking Supervision released several proposals to reform the original 1988 Basel Accord. These efforts have culminated in what bank supervisors refer to as Basel 2, which is based on three pillars.

1. Pillar 1 links capital requirements for large, internationally active banks more closely to actual risk of three types: market risk, credit risk, and operational risk. It does so by specifying many more categories of assets, with different risk weights, in its standardized approach. Alternatively, it allows sophisticated banks to pursue an internal ratings-based approach that permits these banks to use their own models of credit risk.

2. Pillar 2 focuses on strengthening the supervisory process, particularly in assessing the quality of risk management in banking institutions and evaluating whether these institutions have adequate procedures in place for determining how much capital they need.

3. Pillar 3 focuses on improving market discipline through increased disclosure of details about a bank's credit exposures, its amount of reserves and capital, the officials who control the bank, and the effectiveness of its internal rating system.

Although Basel 2 made great strides toward limiting excessive risk taking by internationally active banking institutions, it greatly increased the complexity of the accord. The document describing the original Basel Accord was 26 pages long, whereas the final draft of Basel 2 exceeded 500 pages. The original timetable called for the completion of the final round of consultation by the end of 2001, with the new rules taking effect by 2004. However, criticism from banks, trade associations, and national regulators led to several postponements. The final draft of Basel 2 was not published until June 2004, and European banks began to implement the new accord at the start of 2008. U.S. banks submitted plans for compliance with Basel 2 in 2008, but full implementation did not occur until 2009. Only the dozen or so largest U.S. banks are subject to Basel 2; all others are allowed to use a simplified version of the standards it imposes.

The global financial crisis, however, revealed many limitations of the new accord. First, Basel 2 did not require banks to have sufficient capital to weather the financial disruption that occurred during this period. Second, risk weights in the standardized approach are heavily reliant on credit ratings, which proved to be extremely unreliable in the run-up to the financial crisis. Third, Basel 2 is very procyclical—that is, it demands that banks hold less capital when times are good but more when times are bad, thereby exacerbating credit cycles. Because the probability of default and expected losses on different classes of assets rises during bad times, Basel 2 may require more capital at exactly the time when capital is most short. This has been a particularly serious concern in the aftermath of the global financial crisis. As a result of this crisis, banks' capital balances eroded, leading to a cutback on lending that was a big drag on the economy. Basel 2 made this cutback in lending even worse, doing yet more harm to the economy. Fourth, Basel 2 did not focus sufficiently on the dangers of a possible drying up of liquidity, a problem that brought down financial institutions during the financial crisis.

As a result of these limitations, in 2010 the Basel Committee developed a new accord, Basel 3. It beefs up capital standards not only by raising them substantially but also by improving the quality of the capital, makes capital standards less procyclical by raising capital requirements in good times and lowering them in bad, makes new rules on the use of credit ratings, and requires financial institutions to have more stable funding so that they are better able to withstand liquidity shocks. Measures to achieve these objectives are highly controversial because of concerns that tightening up capital standards might cause banks to restrict their lending, which would make it harder for economies throughout the world to recover from the recent deep recession. Basel 3 was originally scheduled to be fully implemented by 2015, but its implementation has been extended repeatedly and now is slated for completion in January 2022. However, whether Basel 3 will be fully in place by that time, and whether it will be successful in restraining risk taking, is highly uncertain.

Prompt Corrective Action

If the amount of a financial institution's capital falls to low levels, two serious problems result. First, the bank is more likely to fail because it has a smaller capital cushion if it suffers loan losses or other asset write-downs. Second, with less capital, a financial institution has less "skin in the game" and is therefore more likely to take on excessive risks. In other words, the moral hazard problem becomes more severe, making it more likely that the institution will fail and the taxpayer will be left holding the bag. To prevent this, the Federal Deposit Insurance Corporation Improvement Act of 1991 adopted prompt corrective action provisions that require the FDIC to intervene earlier and more vigorously when a bank gets into trouble.

Banks are now classified into five groups based on bank capital. Group 1, classified as "well capitalized," comprises banks that significantly exceed minimum capital requirements and are allowed privileges such as the ability to do some securities underwriting. Banks in group 2, classified as "adequately capitalized," meet minimum capital requirements and are not subject to corrective actions but are not allowed the privileges of the well-capitalized banks. Banks in group 3, "undercapitalized," fail to meet capital requirements. Banks in groups 4 and 5 are "significantly undercapitalized" and "critically undercapitalized," respectively, and are not allowed to pay interest on their deposits at rates that are higher than average. In addition, for group 4 and 5 banks, the FDIC is required to take prompt corrective actions, such as requiring these banks to submit capital restoration plans, restrict their asset growth, and seek regulatory approval to open new branches or develop new lines of business. Banks that are so undercapitalized as to have equity capital that amounts to less than 2% of assets fall into group 5, and the FDIC must take steps to close them down.

Financial Supervision: Chartering and Examination

Overseeing who operates financial institutions and how they are operated, referred to as **financial supervision** or **prudential supervision**, is an important method for reducing adverse selection and moral hazard in the financial industry. Because financial institutions can be used by crooks or overambitious entrepreneurs to engage in highly speculative activities, such undesirable people are often eager to run a financial institution. Chartering financial institutions is one method of preventing this adverse selection problem; through chartering, proposals for new institutions are screened to prevent undesirable people from controlling them.

A commercial bank obtains a charter either from the comptroller of the currency (in the case of a national bank) or from a state banking authority (in the case of a state bank). To obtain a charter, the people planning to organize the bank must submit an application that shows how they plan to operate the bank. In evaluating the application, the regulatory authority looks at whether the bank is likely to be sound by examining the quality of the bank's intended management, the likely earnings of the bank, and the amount of the bank's initial capital. Before 1980, the chartering agency typically explored the issue of whether the community needed a new bank. Often a new bank charter would not be granted if existing banks in a community would be hurt by its presence. Today this anticompetitive stance (justified by the desire to prevent failures of existing banks) is no longer as strong in the chartering agencies.

Once a bank has been chartered, it is required to file periodic (usually quarterly) *call reports* that reveal the bank's assets and liabilities, income and dividends, ownership, foreign exchange operations, and other details. The bank is also subject to examination by the bank regulatory agencies to ascertain its financial condition at least once a year. To avoid duplication of effort, the three federal agencies work together and usually accept each other's examinations. This means that, typically, national banks are examined by the Office of the Comptroller of the Currency, state banks that are members of the Federal Reserve System are examined by the Fed, and insured nonmember state banks are examined by the FDIC.

Regular on-site examinations, which allow regulators to monitor whether the institution is complying with capital requirements and restrictions on asset holdings, function to limit moral hazard. Bank examiners give banks a *CAMELS rating*. The acronym is based on the six areas assessed: capital adequacy, asset quality, management, earnings, liquidity, and sensitivity to market risk. With this information about a bank's activities, regulators can enforce regulations by taking formal actions such as issuing *cease and desist orders* to alter the bank's behavior, or even closing a bank if its CAMELS rating is sufficiently low. Actions taken to reduce moral hazard by restricting banks from taking on too much risk also help reduce the adverse selection problem further, because with less opportunity for risk taking, risk-loving entrepreneurs are less likely to be attracted to the banking industry.

Note that the methods used by regulators to cope with adverse selection and moral hazard have their counterparts in private financial markets (see Chapters 8 and 9). Chartering is similar to the screening of potential borrowers; regulations that restrict risky asset holdings are similar to restrictive covenants that prevent borrowing firms from engaging in risky investment activities; capital requirements act like restrictive covenants that require minimum amounts of net worth for borrowing firms; and regular examinations are similar to the monitoring of borrowers by lending institutions.

Bank examinations are conducted by bank examiners, who sometimes make unannounced visits to the bank (so that nothing can be "swept under the rug" in anticipation of their examination). The examiners study a bank's books to see whether it is complying with the rules and regulations that apply to its holdings of assets. If a bank is holding securities or loans that are too risky, the bank examiner can force the bank to get rid of them. If a bank examiner decides that a loan is unlikely to be repaid, the examiner can force the bank to declare the loan worthless (to write off the loan, which reduces the bank's capital). If, after examining the bank, the examiner feels that it does not have sufficient capital or has engaged in dishonest practices, the bank can be declared a "problem bank" and will be subject to more frequent examinations.

Assessment of Risk Management

Traditionally, on-site examinations have focused primarily on assessment of the quality of a financial institution's balance sheet at a point in time and whether it complies with capital requirements and restrictions on asset holdings. Although the traditional focus is still important in reducing excessive risk taking by financial institutions, it is no longer thought to be adequate in today's world, in which financial innovation has produced new markets and instruments that make it easy for financial institutions and their employees to make huge bets easily and quickly. In this new financial environment, a financial institution that is healthy at a particular point in time can be driven into insolvency extremely rapidly by trading losses, as forcefully demonstrated by the failure of Barings in 1995 (discussed in Chapter 9). Thus an examination that focuses only on a financial institution's position at a point in time may not be effective in indicating whether it will, in fact, be taking on excessive risk in the near future.

This change in the financial environment resulted in a major shift in thinking about the prudential supervisory process throughout the world. Bank examiners, for example, now place far greater emphasis on evaluating the soundness of a bank's management processes with regard to controlling risk. This shift in thinking was reflected in a new focus on risk management by the Federal Reserve System, starting with 1993 guidelines for examiners regarding trading and derivatives activities. The focus was expanded and formalized in the *Trading Activities Manual* issued early in 1994, which provided bank examiners with tools to evaluate risk management systems. In late 1995, the Federal Reserve and the comptroller of the currency announced that they would be assessing risk management processes at the banks they supervised. Now, bank examiners give a separate risk management rating, from 1 to 5, that feeds into the overall management rating as part of the CAMELS system. Four elements of sound risk management are assessed to arrive at the risk management rating: (1) the quality of oversight provided by the board of directors and senior management; (2) the adequacy of policies and limits for all activities that present significant risks; (3) the quality of the risk measurement and monitoring systems; and (4) the adequacy of internal controls to prevent fraud or unauthorized activities on the part of employees.

This shift toward focusing on management processes is also reflected in recent guidelines adopted by the U.S. bank regulatory authorities to deal with interest-rate risk. These guidelines require the bank's board of directors to establish interest-rate risk limits, appoint officials of the bank to manage this risk, and monitor the bank's risk exposure. The guidelines also require that senior management of a bank develop formal risk management policies and procedures to ensure that the board of directors' risk limits are not violated and to implement internal controls to monitor interest-rate risk and compliance with the board's directives. Particularly important is the implementation of **stress tests**, which calculate potential losses and the need for more capital under fictional dire scenarios, and **value-at-risk (VaR)** calculations, which measure the size of the loss on a trading portfolio—say, over a two-week period—that might happen 1% of the time. In addition to these guidelines, bank examiners will continue to consider interest-rate risk in deciding the bank's capital requirements.

Disclosure Requirements

The free-rider problem described in Chapter 8 indicates that individual depositors and creditors do not have enough incentive to produce private information about the quality of a financial institution's assets. To ensure that better information is available in the marketplace, regulators can require that financial institutions adhere to certain standard accounting principles and disclose a wide range of information that helps the market assess the quality of an institution's portfolio and the amount of its exposure to risk. More public information about the risks incurred by financial institutions and the quality of their portfolios can better enable stockholders, creditors, and depositors to evaluate and monitor financial institutions and so act as a deterrent to excessive risk taking.

Disclosure requirements are a key element of financial regulation. Basel 2 puts a particular emphasis on disclosure requirements, with one of its three pillars focusing on increasing market discipline by mandating increased disclosure by banking institutions of their credit exposure, amount of reserves, and capital. The Securities Act of 1933 and the Securities and Exchange Commission (SEC), which was established in 1934, also impose disclosure requirements on any corporation, including financial institutions, that issues publicly traded securities. In addition, the SEC has required financial institutions to provide additional disclosure regarding their off-balance-sheet positions and more information about how they value their portfolios.

Regulation to increase disclosure is needed to limit incentives to take on excessive risk and to upgrade the quality of information in the marketplace so that investors can make informed decisions, thereby improving the ability of financial markets to allocate capital to its most productive uses. The efficiency of markets is assisted by the SEC's disclosure requirements mentioned above, as well as its regulation of brokerage firms, mutual funds, exchanges, and credit-rating agencies to ensure that they produce reliable information and protect investors. The Sarbanes-Oxley Act of 2002 took disclosure of information even further by increasing the incentives to produce accurate audits of corporate income statements and balance sheets, establishing the Public Company Accounting Oversight Board (PCAOB) to oversee the audit industry, and putting in place regulations to limit conflicts of interest in the financial services industry.

Consumer Protection

The existence of asymmetric information suggests that consumers may not have enough information to protect themselves fully in financial dealings. Consumer protection regulation has taken several forms. The Consumer Protection Act of 1969 (more commonly referred to as the Truth in Lending Act) requires all lenders, not just banks, to provide information to consumers about the cost of borrowing, including the disclosure of a standardized interest rate (called the *annual percentage rate*, or *APR*) and the total finance charges on the loan. The Fair Credit Billing Act of 1974 requires creditors, especially credit card issuers, to provide information on the method of assessing finance charges, and requires that billing complaints be handled quickly.

Congress also passed legislation to reduce discrimination in credit markets. The Equal Credit Opportunity Act of 1974 and its extension in 1976 forbid discrimination by lenders based on race, gender, marital status, age, or national origin. The act is administered by the Federal Reserve under Regulation B. The Community Reinvestment Act (CRA) of 1977 was enacted to prevent "redlining," a lender's refusal to lend in a particular area (marked off by a hypothetical red line on a map). The Community Reinvestment Act requires banks to show that they lend in all areas in which they take deposits, and if banks are found to be in noncompliance with the act, regulators can reject their applications for mergers, branching, or other new activities.

The global financial crisis has illustrated the need for greater consumer protection, because so many borrowers took out loans with terms they did not understand and that were well beyond their means to repay. (Most infamous were so-called NINJA loans, which were issued to borrowers with No Income, No Job, and No Assets.) The result was millions of foreclosures, with many households losing their homes. As we will see in Chapter 12, Congress responded by creating a new consumer protection agency to prevent this type of lending from happening again.

Restrictions on Competition

Increased competition can also increase moral hazard incentives for financial institutions to take on more risk. Declining profitability resulting from increased competition could tip the incentives of financial institutions toward assuming greater risk in an effort to maintain former profit levels. Thus governments in many countries have instituted regulations to protect financial institutions from competition. These regulations took two forms in the United States in the past. First were restrictions on branching, described in Chapter 11, which reduced competition between banks. These restrictions were eliminated, however, in 1994. The second form involved preventing nonbank institutions from competing with banks by preventing them from engaging in banking business, as embodied in the Glass-Steagall Act, which was repealed in 1999.

Although restrictions on competition propped up the health of banks, they had some serious disadvantages: They led to higher charges to consumers and decreased the efficiency of banking institutions, which now did not have to compete as vigorously. Thus, although the existence of asymmetric information provided a rationale for anticompetitive regulations, it did not mean they would be beneficial. Indeed, in recent years, the impulse of governments in industrialized countries to restrict competition has been waning.

Summary

Asymmetric information analysis explains the types of financial regulations that are needed to reduce moral hazard and adverse selection problems in the financial system. However, understanding the theory behind regulation does not mean that regulation and supervision of the financial system are easy in practice. Getting regulators and supervisors to do their job properly is difficult for several reasons. First, as we will see in our discussion of financial innovation in Chapter 11, financial institutions, in their search for profits, have strong incentives to avoid existing regulations by loophole mining. Thus regulation applies to a moving target. Regulators are continually playing cat-and-mouse with financial institutions—financial institutions think up clever ways to avoid regulations, which then leads regulators to modify their regulation activities. Regulators continually face new challenges in a dynamically changing financial system, and unless they can respond rapidly, they may not be able to keep financial institutions from taking on excessive risk. This problem can be exacerbated if regulators and supervisors do not have the resources or expertise necessary to keep up with clever people seeking to circumvent the existing regulations.

Financial regulation and supervision are difficult for two other reasons. In the regulation and supervision game, the devil is in the details. Subtle differences in the details may have unintended consequences; unless regulators get the regulation and supervision just right, they may be unable to prevent excessive risk taking. In addition, regulated firms may lobby politicians to lean on regulators and supervisors to go easy on them.

For all these reasons, there is no guarantee that regulators and supervisors will be successful in promoting a healthy financial system. These same problems bedevil financial regulators in other countries as well, as indicated in the Global box "International Financial Regulation." Indeed, financial regulation and supervision have not always worked well, leading to banking crises in the United States and throughout the world.[1]

Because so many laws regulating the financial system have been passed in the United States, it is hard to keep track of them all. As a study aid, Table 1 lists the major financial legislation passed since the beginning of the twentieth century and outlines the key provisions of each act.

---

[1]For more detail on these foreign banking crises, see the appendix to this chapter, "Banking Crises Throughout the World," which can be found in **MyLab Economics**.

Global International Financial Regulation

Because asymmetric information problems in the banking industry are a fact of life throughout the world, financial regulation in other countries is similar to that in the United States. Financial institutions are chartered and supervised by government regulators, just as they are in the United States. Disclosure requirements for financial institutions and corporations issuing securities are similar in other developed countries. Deposit insurance is also a feature of the regulatory systems of most other countries, although its coverage is often smaller than that in the United States, and it is intentionally not advertised. We have also seen that capital requirements are in the process of being standardized across countries in compliance with agreements like the Basel Accord.

Particular problems in financial regulation occur when financial institutions operate in many countries and thus can shift their business readily from one country to another. Financial regulators closely examine the domestic operations of financial institutions in their own country, but they often do not have the knowledge or ability to keep a close watch on operations in other countries, operations run either by domestic institutions' foreign affiliates or by foreign institutions with domestic branches. In addition, when a financial institution operates in many countries, it is not always clear which national regulatory authority should have primary responsibility for keeping the institution from engaging in overly risky activities.

The difficulties inherent in international financial regulation were highlighted by the collapse of the Bank of Credit and Commerce International (BCCI) in 1991. BCCI, although it operated in more than 70 countries, including the United States and the United Kingdom, was supervised by Luxembourg, a tiny country unlikely to be up to the task. When massive fraud was discovered, the Bank of England closed BCCI down, but not before depositors and stockholders were exposed to huge losses. Cooperation among regulators in different countries and standardization of regulatory requirements provide potential solutions to the problems of international financial regulation. The world has moved in this direction through agreements like the Basel Accord and oversight procedures announced by the Basel Committee in July 1992, which require a bank's worldwide operations to be under the scrutiny of a single home-country regulator with enhanced powers to acquire information on the bank's activities. The Basel Committee also ruled that regulators in other countries can restrict the operations of a foreign bank if they believe it lacks effective oversight. Whether agreements of this type will solve the problem of international financial regulation in the future is an open question.

TABLE 1	Major Financial Legislation in the United States

Federal Reserve Act (1913)

　Created the Federal Reserve System

McFadden Act of 1927

　Effectively prohibited banks from branching across state lines

　Put national and state banks on equal footing regarding branching

Banking Acts of 1933 (Glass-Steagall) and 1935

　Created the FDIC

　Separated commercial banking from the securities industry

　Prohibited interest on checkable deposits and restricted such deposits to commercial banks

　Put interest-rate ceilings on other deposits

TABLE 1   (continued)

Securities Act of 1933 and Securities Exchange Act of 1934
Required that investors receive financial information on securities offered for public sale
Prohibited misrepresentations and fraud in the sale of securities
Created the Securities and Exchange Commission (SEC)

Investment Company Act of 1940 and Investment Advisers Act of 1940
Regulated investment companies, including mutual funds
Regulated investment advisers

Bank Holding Company Act and Douglas Amendment (1956)
Clarified the status of bank holding companies (BHCs)
Gave the Federal Reserve regulatory responsibility for BHCs

Depository Institutions Deregulation and Monetary Control Act (DIDMCA) of 1980
Gave thrift institutions wider latitude in activities
Approved NOW and sweep accounts nationwide
Phased out interest-rate ceilings on deposits
Imposed uniform reserve requirements on depository institutions
Eliminated usury ceilings on loans
Increased deposit insurance to $100,000 per account

Depository Institutions Act of 1982 (Garn-St. Germain)
Gave the FDIC and the Federal Savings and Loan Insurance Corporation (FSLIC) emergency powers to
    merge banks and thrifts across state lines
Allowed depository institutions to offer money market deposit accounts (MMDAs)
Granted thrifts wider latitude in commercial and consumer lending

Competitive Equality in Banking Act (CEBA) of 1987
Provided $10.8 billion to shore up the FSLIC
Made provisions for regulatory forbearance in depressed areas

Financial Institutions Reform, Recovery, and Enforcement Act (FIRREA) of 1989
Provided funds to resolve savings and loan (S&L) failures
Eliminated FSLIC and the Federal Home Loan Bank Board
Created the Office of Thrift Supervision to regulate thrifts
Created the Resolution Trust Corporation to resolve insolvent thrifts
Raised deposit insurance premiums
Reimposed restrictions on S&L activities

Federal Deposit Insurance Corporation Improvement Act (FDICIA) of 1991
Recapitalized the FDIC
Limited brokered deposits and the too-big-to-fail policy

TABLE 1	(continued)

Set provisions for prompt corrective action

Instructed the FDIC to establish risk-based premiums

Increased examinations, capital requirements, and reporting requirements

Included the Foreign Bank Supervision Enhancement Act (FBSEA), which strengthened the Fed's authority to supervise foreign banks

Riegle-Neal Interstate Banking and Branching Efficiency Act of 1994

Overturned prohibition of interstate banking

Allowed branching across state lines

Gramm-Leach-Bliley Financial Services Modernization Act of 1999

Repealed Glass-Steagall and removed the separation of banking and securities industries

Sarbanes-Oxley Act of 2002

Created Public Company Accounting Oversight Board (PCAOB)

Prohibited certain conflicts of interest

Required certification by CEO and CFO of financial statements and independence of audit committee

Federal Deposit Insurance Reform Act of 2005

Merged the Bank Insurance Fund and the Savings Association Insurance Fund

Increased deposit insurance on individual retirement accounts to $250,000 per account

Dodd-Frank Wall Street Reform and Consumer Protection Act of 2010

Created Consumer Financial Protection Bureau to regulate mortgages and other financial products

Required routine derivatives to be cleared through central clearinghouses and exchanges

Required annual bank stress tests

Limits Federal Reserve lending to individual firms

Authorized government takeovers of financial holding companies

Created Financial Stability Oversight Council to regulate systemically important financial institutions

Banned banks from proprietary trading and from owning large percentages of hedge funds

SUMMARY

1. The concepts of asymmetric information, adverse selection, and moral hazard help explain why governments pursue financial regulation.

2. There are eight basic types of financial regulation aimed at lessening asymmetric information problems and excessive risk taking in the financial system:

(1) restrictions on asset holdings; (2) capital requirements; (3) prompt corrective action; (4) chartering and examination; (5) assessment of risk management; (6) disclosure requirements; (7) consumer protection; and (8) restrictions on competition.

KEY TERMS

bank failure, p. 216
bank panic, p. 217
Basel Accord, p. 222
Basel Committee on Banking
   Supervision, p. 222

financial supervision (prudential
   supervision), p. 224
leverage ratio, p. 222
off-balance-sheet activities, p. 222

regulatory arbitrage, p. 222
stress tests, p. 226
too-big-to-fail problem, p. 219
value-at-risk (VaR), p. 226

QUESTIONS

1. Why are deposit insurance and other types of government safety nets important to the health of the economy?

2. If casualty insurance companies provided fire insurance without any restrictions, what kind of adverse selection and moral hazard problems might result?

3. Do you think that eliminating or limiting the amount of deposit insurance would be a good idea? Explain your answer.

4. How could higher deposit insurance premiums for banks with riskier assets benefit the economy?

5. What are the costs and benefits of a too-big-to-fail policy?

6. Suppose that you have $300,000 in deposits at a bank. After careful consideration, the FDIC decides that this bank is now insolvent. Which method would you like to see the FDIC apply? What if your deposit were $200,000?

7. Would you recommend the adoption of a system of deposit insurance, like the FDIC in the United States, in a country with weak institutions, prevalent corruption, and ineffective regulation of the financial sector?

8. At the height of the global financial crisis in October 2008, the U.S. Treasury forced nine of the largest U.S. banks to accept capital injections in exchange for nonvoting ownership stock, even though some of the banks did not need the capital and did not want to participate. What could have been the Treasury's rationale for doing this?

9. What special problem do off-balance-sheet activities present to bank regulators, and what have they done about it?

10. What are some of the limitations to the Basel and Basel 2 Accords? How does the Basel 3 Accord attempt to address these limitations?

11. How does bank chartering reduce adverse selection problems? Does it always work?

12. Why has the trend in bank supervision moved away from a focus on capital requirements to a focus on risk management?

13. Suppose that after a few mergers and acquisitions, only one bank holds 70% of all deposits in the United States. Would you say that this bank would be considered too big to fail? What does this tell you about the ongoing process of financial consolidation and the government safety net?

14. Suppose Universal Bank holds $100 million in assets, which are composed of the following:

Required reserves:	$10 million
Excess reserves:	$ 5 million
Mortgage loans:	$20 million
Corporate bonds:	$15 million
Stocks:	$25 million
Commodities:	$25 million

Do you think it is a good idea for Universal Bank to hold stocks, corporate bonds, and commodities as assets? Why or why not?

15. Why might more competition in financial markets be a bad idea? Would restrictions on competition be a better idea? Why or why not?

16. In what way might consumer protection regulations negatively affect a financial intermediary's profits? Can you think of a positive effect of such regulations on profits?

APPLIED PROBLEMS

17. Consider a failing bank. A deposit of $350,000 is worth how much to the depositor if the FDIC uses the *payoff* method given the typical recovery rate? How much is the same deposit worth to the depositor if the *purchase-and-assumption* method is used? Which is more costly to taxpayers?

18. Consider a bank with the following balance sheet:

Assets		Liabilities	
Required reserves	$17 million	Checkable deposits	$205 million
Excess reserves	$ 3 million	Bank capital	$ 10 million
Municipal bonds	$65 million		
Residential mortgages	$70 million		
Commercial loans	$60 million		

Under the original Basel Accord, calculate the bank's risk-weighted assets.

Problems 19–21 relate to a sequence of transactions at Oldhat Financial.

19. Oldhat Financial starts its first day of operations with $9 million in capital. A total of $130 million in checkable deposits is received. The bank makes a $25 million commercial loan and another $50 million in mortgages with the following terms: 200 standard, 30-year, fixed-rate mortgages with a nominal annual rate of 5.25%, each for $250,000.

    Assume that required reserves are 8%.

    a. What does the bank balance sheet look like?

    b. How well capitalized is the bank?

    c. Calculate the risk-weighted assets and risk-weighted capital ratio after Oldhat's first day.

20. Early the next day, the bank invests $50 million of its excess reserves in commercial loans. Later that day, terrible news hits the mortgage markets, and mortgage rates jump to 13%, implying a present value of Oldhat's current mortgage holdings of $124,798 per mortgage. Bank regulators force Oldhat to sell its mortgages to recognize the fair market value. What does Oldhat's balance sheet look like? How do these events affect its capital position?

21. To avoid insolvency, regulators decide to provide the bank with $25 million in bank capital. However, the bad news about the mortgages is featured in the local newspaper, causing a bank run. As a result, $30 million in deposits is withdrawn. Show the effects of the capital injection and the bank run on the balance sheet. Was the capital injection enough to stabilize the bank? If the bank regulators decide that the bank needs a capital ratio of 10% to prevent further runs on the bank, how much of an additional capital injection is required to reach a 10% capital ratio?

DATA ANALYSIS PROBLEMS

The Problems update with real-time data in **MyLab Economics** and are available for practice or instructor assignment.

1. **Real-time Data Analysis** Go to the St. Louis Federal Reserve FRED database, and find data on the number of commercial banks in the United States in each of the following categories: average assets less than $100 million (US100NUM), average assets between $100 million and $300 million (US13NUM), average assets between $300 million and $1 billion (US31NUM), average assets between $1 billion and $15 billion (US115NUM), and average assets greater than $15 billion (USG15NUM). Download the data into a spreadsheet. Calculate the percentage of banks in the smallest (less than $100 million) and largest (greater than $15 billion) categories, as a percentage of the total number of banks, for the most recent quarter of data available and for 1990:Q1. What has happened to the proportion of very large banks? What has happened to the proportion of very small banks? What does this say about the "too-big-to-fail" problem and moral hazard?

2. **Real-time Data Analysis** Go to the St. Louis Federal Reserve FRED database, and find data on the residual of assets less liabilities, or bank capital (RALACBM027SBOG), and total assets of commercial banks (TLAACBM027SBOG). Download the data from January 1990 through the most recent month available into a spreadsheet. For each monthly observation, calculate the bank leverage ratio as the ratio of bank capital to total assets. Create a line graph of the leverage ratio over time. All else being equal, what can you conclude about leverage and moral hazard in commercial banks over time?

11 Banking Industry: Structure and Competition

Learning Objectives

11.1 Recognize the key features of the banking system and the historical context of the implementation of these features.

11.2 Explain how financial innovation led to the growth of the shadow banking system.

11.3 Identify the key structural changes in the commercial banking industry.

11.4 Summarize the factors that led to consolidation in the commercial banking industry.

11.5 Assess the reasons for separating banking from other financial services through legislation.

11.6 Summarize the distinctions between thrift institutions and commercial banks.

11.7 Identify the reasons for U.S. banks to operate in foreign countries and for foreign banks to operate in the United States.

Preview

The operations of individual banks (how they acquire, use, and manage funds to make a profit) are roughly similar throughout the world. In all countries, banks are financial intermediaries in the business of earning profits. When you consider the structure and operation of the banking industry as a whole, however, the United States is in a class by itself. In most countries, four or five large banks typically dominate the banking industry, but in the United States there are on the order of 4,500 commercial banks, 700 savings institutions (savings and loan associations and mutual savings banks), and 5,000 credit unions.

Is more necessarily better? Does this diversity mean that the American banking system is more competitive and therefore more economically efficient and sound than banking systems in other countries? What in the American economic and political system explains this large number of banking institutions? In this chapter, we try to answer these questions by examining the historical trends in the banking industry and its overall structure.

We start by examining the historical development of the banking system and how financial innovation has increased the competitive environment for the banking industry and is causing fundamental changes in it. We go on to look at the commercial banking industry in detail and then discuss the thrift industry, which includes savings and loan associations, mutual savings banks, and credit unions. We spend more time on commercial banks because they are by far the largest depository institutions, accounting for more than two-thirds of the deposits in the banking system. In addition to looking at our domestic banking system, we examine the forces behind the growth of international banking to see how it has affected us in the United States.

11.1 HISTORICAL DEVELOPMENT OF THE BANKING SYSTEM

LO 11.1 Recognize the key features of the banking system and the historical context of the implementation of these features.

The modern commercial banking industry in the United States began when the Bank of North America was chartered in Philadelphia in 1782. With the success of this bank, other banks opened for business, and the American banking industry was off and running. (As a study aid, Figure 1 provides a timeline of the most important dates in the history of American banking before World War II.)

Mini-lecture

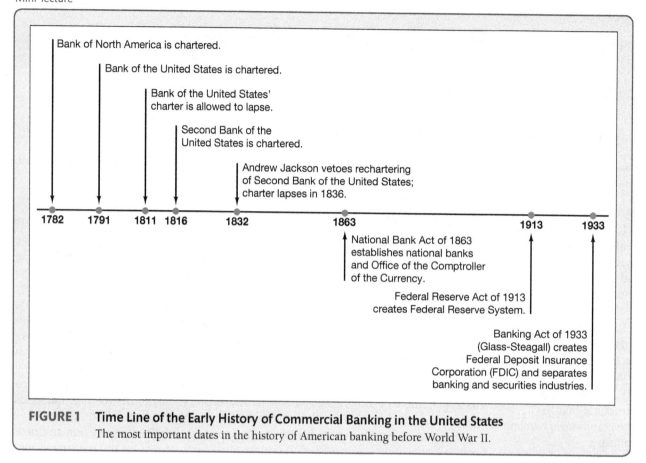

Bank of North America is chartered.

Bank of the United States is chartered.

Bank of the United States' charter is allowed to lapse.

Second Bank of the United States is chartered.

Andrew Jackson vetoes rechartering of Second Bank of the United States; charter lapses in 1836.

1782   1791   1811 1816   1832   1863   1913   1933

National Bank Act of 1863 establishes national banks and Office of the Comptroller of the Currency.

Federal Reserve Act of 1913 creates Federal Reserve System.

Banking Act of 1933 (Glass-Steagall) creates Federal Deposit Insurance Corporation (FDIC) and separates banking and securities industries.

FIGURE 1   Time Line of the Early History of Commercial Banking in the United States
The most important dates in the history of American banking before World War II.

A major controversy involving the industry in its early years was whether the federal government or the states should charter banks. The Federalists, particularly Alexander Hamilton, advocated greater centralized control of banking and federal chartering of banks. Their efforts led to the creation in 1791 of the Bank of the United States, which had elements of both a private bank and a **central bank**, a government institution that has responsibility for the amount of money and credit supplied in the economy as a whole. Agricultural and other interests, however, were quite suspicious of centralized power and hence advocated chartering by the states. Furthermore, their distrust of moneyed interests in the big cities led them to exert political pressure in an effort to eliminate the Bank of the United States, and in 1811 their efforts met with success when its charter was not renewed. Because of abuses by state banks and the clear need for a central bank to help the federal government raise funds during the War of 1812, Congress was stimulated to create the Second Bank of the United States in 1816. Tensions between advocates and opponents of centralized banking power were a recurrent theme during the operation of this second attempt at central banking in the United States, and with the election of Andrew Jackson, a strong advocate of states' rights, the fate of the Second Bank was sealed. After the election in 1832, Jackson vetoed the rechartering of the Second Bank of the United States as a national bank, and its charter lapsed in 1836.

Until 1863, all commercial banks in the United States were chartered by the banking commission of the state in which each operated. No national currency existed, and banks obtained funds primarily by issuing *banknotes* (currency circulated by the banks that could be redeemed for gold). Because banking regulations were extremely lax in many states, banks regularly failed due to fraud or lack of sufficient bank capital; their banknotes became worthless.

To eliminate the abuses of the state-chartered banks (called **state banks**), the National Bank Act of 1863 (and subsequent amendments to it) created a new banking system of federally chartered banks (called **national banks**), supervised by the Office of the Comptroller of the Currency, a department of the U.S. Treasury. This legislation was originally intended to dry up sources of funds to state banks by imposing a prohibitive tax on their banknotes while leaving the banknotes of the federally chartered banks untaxed. The state banks cleverly escaped extinction by acquiring funds through deposits. As a result, today the United States has a **dual banking system** in which banks chartered by the federal government and banks chartered by the states operate side by side.

Central banking did not reappear in this country until the Federal Reserve System (the Fed) was created in 1913 to promote an even safer banking system. All national banks were required to become members of the Federal Reserve System and became subject to a new set of regulations issued by the Fed. State banks could choose (but were not required) to become members of the system, and most did not because of the high costs of membership stemming from the Fed's regulations.

During the Great Depression years 1930–1933, some 9,000 bank failures wiped out the savings of many depositors at commercial banks. To prevent future depositor losses from such failures, banking legislation in 1933 established the Federal Deposit Insurance Corporation (FDIC), which provided federal insurance on bank deposits. Member banks of the Federal Reserve System were required to purchase FDIC insurance for their depositors, and non–Federal Reserve commercial banks could choose to buy this insurance (almost all of them did). The purchase of FDIC insurance made banks subject to another set of regulations imposed by the FDIC.

Because the investment banking activities of the commercial banks were blamed for many bank failures, provisions in the banking legislation in 1933 (also known as the Glass-Steagall Act) prohibited commercial banks from underwriting or dealing in corporate securities (though allowing them to sell new issues of government securities) and limited banks to the purchase of debt securities approved by the bank regulatory agencies. Likewise, this legislation prohibited investment banks from engaging in commercial banking activities. In effect, the Glass-Steagall Act separated the activities of commercial banks from those of the securities industry.

Under the conditions of the Glass-Steagall Act, which was repealed in 1999, commercial banks had to sell off their investment banking operations. The First National Bank of Boston, for example, spun off its investment banking operations into the First Boston Corporation, now part of one of the most important investment banking firms in America, Credit Suisse First Boston. Investment banking firms typically discontinued their deposit business, although J.P. Morgan discontinued its investment banking business and reorganized as a commercial bank; however, some senior officers of J.P. Morgan went on to organize Morgan Stanley, another one of the largest investment banking firms today.

Multiple Regulatory Agencies

Commercial bank regulation in the United States has developed into a crazy quilt of multiple regulatory agencies with overlapping jurisdictions. The Office of the Comptroller of the Currency has the primary supervisory responsibility for national banks that own more than half of the assets in the commercial banking system. The Federal

Reserve and the state banking authorities have joint primary responsibility for state banks that are members of the Federal Reserve System. The Fed also has regulatory responsibility over companies that own one or more banks (called **bank holding companies**) and secondary responsibility for the national banks. The FDIC and the state banking authorities jointly supervise state banks that have FDIC insurance but are not members of the Federal Reserve System. The state banking authorities have sole jurisdiction over state banks without FDIC insurance. (Such banks hold less than 0.2% of the deposits in the commercial banking system.)

If you find the U.S. bank regulatory system confusing, imagine how confusing it is for the banks, which have to deal with multiple regulatory agencies. Several proposals have been raised by the U.S. Treasury to rectify this situation by centralizing the regulation of all depository institutions under one independent agency. However, none of these proposals has been successful in Congress, and whether there will be regulatory consolidation in the future is highly uncertain.

11.2 FINANCIAL INNOVATION AND THE GROWTH OF THE "SHADOW BANKING SYSTEM"

LO 11.2 Explain how financial innovation led to the growth of the shadow banking system.

Although banking institutions are still the most important financial institutions in the U.S. economy, in recent years the traditional banking business of making loans that are funded by deposits has been in decline. Some of this business has been replaced by the **shadow banking system**, in which bank lending has been replaced by lending via the securities markets, with the involvement of a number of different financial institutions.

To understand how the banking industry has evolved over time, we must first understand the process of financial innovation, which has transformed the entire financial system. Like other industries, the financial industry is in business to earn profits by selling its products. If a soap company perceives that a need exists in the marketplace for a laundry detergent with fabric softener, it develops a product to fit that need. Similarly, to maximize their profits, financial institutions develop new products to satisfy their own needs as well as those of their customers; in other words, innovation—which can be extremely beneficial to the economy—is driven by the desire to get (or stay) rich. This view of the innovation process leads to the following simple analysis: *A change in the financial environment will stimulate a search by financial institutions for innovations that are likely to be profitable.*

Starting in the 1960s, individuals and financial institutions operating in financial markets were confronted with drastic changes in the economic environment: Inflation and interest rates climbed sharply and became harder to predict, a situation that changed demand conditions in financial markets. The rapid advances in computer technology changed supply conditions. In addition, financial regulations became more burdensome. Financial institutions found that many of the old ways of doing business were no longer profitable; the financial services and products they had been offering to the public were not selling. Many financial intermediaries found that they were no longer able to acquire funds with their traditional financial instruments, and without these funds they would soon be out of business. To survive in the new economic environment, financial institutions had to research and develop new products and services that would meet customer needs and prove profitable, a process referred to as **financial engineering**. In their case, necessity was the mother of innovation.

Our discussion of the factors that drive financial innovation suggests that there are three basic types of financial innovation: responses to changes in demand conditions, responses to changes in supply conditions, and avoidance of existing regulations. These three motivations often interact to produce particular financial innovations. Now that we have a framework for understanding why financial institutions produce innovations, let's look at examples of how financial institutions, in their search for profits, have produced financial innovations of the three basic types.

Responses to Changes in Demand Conditions: Interest-Rate Volatility

The most significant change in the economic environment that altered the demand for financial products in recent years has been the dramatic increase in the volatility of interest rates. In the 1950s, the interest rate on three-month Treasury bills fluctuated between 1.0% and 3.5%; in the 1970s, it fluctuated between 4.0% and 11.5%; in the 1980s, it ranged from 5% to more than 15%. Large fluctuations in interest rates lead to substantial capital gains or losses and greater uncertainty about returns on investments. Recall that the risk related to the uncertainty about interest-rate movements and returns is called *interest-rate risk*, and high volatility of interest rates, such as we saw in the 1970s and 1980s, leads to a higher level of interest-rate risk.

We would expect the increase in interest-rate risk to increase the demand for financial products and services that could reduce that risk. This change in the economic environment would thus stimulate a search by financial institutions for profitable innovations that meet this new demand and would spur the creation of new financial instruments that help lower interest-rate risk. Two financial innovations that were developed in the 1970s confirm this prediction: adjustable-rate mortgages and financial derivatives.

Adjustable-Rate Mortgages   Like other investors, financial institutions find that lending is more attractive if interest-rate risk is lower. They would not want to make a mortgage loan at a 10% interest rate and two months later find that they could obtain 12% in interest on the same mortgage. To reduce interest-rate risk, in 1975 savings and loans (S&Ls) in California began to issue adjustable-rate mortgages, that is, mortgage loans on which the interest rate changes when a market interest rate (usually the Treasury bill rate) changes. Initially, an adjustable-rate mortgage might have a 5% interest rate. In six months, this interest rate might increase or decrease by the amount of the increase or decrease in, say, the six-month Treasury bill rate, and the mortgage payment would then change. Because adjustable-rate mortgages allow mortgage-issuing institutions to earn higher interest rates on existing mortgages when market rates rise, profits remain high during these periods.

This attractive feature of adjustable-rate mortgages has encouraged mortgage-issuing institutions to issue adjustable-rate mortgages with lower initial interest rates than those on conventional fixed-rate mortgages, making them popular with many households. However, because the mortgage payment on a variable-rate mortgage can increase, many households continue to prefer fixed-rate mortgages. Hence both types of mortgages are widespread.

Financial Derivatives   Given the greater demand for the reduction of interest-rate risk, commodity exchanges such as the Chicago Board of Trade recognized that if they could develop a product that would help investors and financial institutions protect themselves from, or **hedge**, interest-rate risk, then they could make profits by selling this new instrument. **Futures contracts**, in which the seller agrees to provide a certain standardized commodity to the buyer on a specific future date at an agreed-on price, had been around for a long time. Officials at the Chicago Board of Trade realized that if they created futures contracts in financial instruments, which are called **financial derivatives** because their payoffs are linked to (i.e., derived from) previously issued securities, they could be used to hedge risk. Thus, in 1975, financial derivatives were born.

Responses to Changes in Supply Conditions: Information Technology

The most important source of the changes in supply conditions that stimulated financial innovation has been the improvement in computer and telecommunications technology. This technology, called *information technology,* has had two effects. First, it has lowered the cost of processing financial transactions, making it profitable for financial institutions to create new financial products and services for the public. Second, it has made it easier for investors to acquire information, thereby making it easier for firms to issue securities. The rapid developments in information technology have resulted in many new financial products and services, which we examine here.

Bank Credit and Debit Cards

Credit cards have been around since well before World War II. Many individual stores (Sears, Macy's) institutionalized charge accounts by providing customers with credit cards that allowed them to make purchases at these stores without cash. Nationwide credit cards were not established until after World War II, when Diners Club developed a card to be used in restaurants all over the country (and abroad). Similar credit card programs were started by American Express and Carte Blanche, but because of the high cost of operating these programs, cards were issued only to select persons and businesses that could afford expensive purchases.

A firm issuing credit cards earns income from loans it makes to credit card holders and from payments made by stores on credit card purchases (a percentage of the purchase price, say, 3%). A credit card program's costs arise from loan defaults, stolen cards, and the expense involved in processing credit card transactions.

Seeing the success of Diners Club, American Express, and Carte Blanche, bankers wanted to share in the profitable credit card business. Several commercial banks attempted to expand the credit card business to a wider market in the 1950s, but the cost per transaction of running these programs was so high that their early attempts failed.

In the late 1960s, improved computer technology, which lowered the transaction costs for providing credit card services, made it more likely that bank credit card programs would be profitable. The banks tried to enter this business again, and this time their efforts led to the creation of two successful bank credit card programs: Bank Americard (originally started by Bank of America but now an independent organization called Visa) and MasterCharge (now MasterCard, run by the Interbank Card Association). These programs have become phenomenally successful; over 500 million of their cards are in use in the United States and over a billion more in the rest of the world. Indeed, bank credit cards have been so profitable that nonfinancial institutions such as Sears (which launched the Discover card), General Motors, and AT&T have also entered the credit card business. Consumers have benefited because credit cards are more widely accepted than checks as a method of paying for purchases (particularly abroad), and they allow consumers to take out loans more easily.

The success of bank credit cards led these institutions to come up with another financial innovation, *debit cards*. Debit cards often look just like credit cards and can be used to make purchases in an identical fashion. However, in contrast to credit cards, which extend the purchaser a loan that does not have to be paid off immediately, a debit card purchase is immediately deducted from the card holder's bank account. Debit cards depend even more on low costs of processing transactions, because their profits are generated entirely from the fees paid by merchants on debit card purchases at their stores. Debit cards have grown extremely popular in recent years.

Electronic Banking   The wonders of modern computer technology have also enabled banks to lower the cost of bank transactions by having the customer interact with an electronic banking (e-banking) facility rather than with a human being. One important form of an e-banking facility is the **automated teller machine (ATM)**, an electronic machine that allows customers to get cash, make deposits, transfer funds from one account to another, and check balances. ATM machines do not have to be paid overtime and never sleep and thus are available for use 24 hours a day. Not only does this result in cheaper transactions for the bank but it also provides more convenience for the customer. Because of their low cost, ATMs can be put at locations other than a bank or its **branches** (additional offices for the conduct of bank operations), further increasing customer convenience. The low cost of ATMs has encouraged banks to install them everywhere, and ATMs now number close to 500,000 in the United States alone. Furthermore, it is now just as easy to get foreign currency from an ATM when you are traveling in Europe as it is to get cash from your local bank.

With the drop in the cost of telecommunications, banks have developed another financial innovation, *home banking*. It is now cost-effective for banks to set up an electronic banking facility in which the bank's customer is linked up with the bank's computer and allowed to carry out transactions by using a smartphone, tablet, or personal computer. Now a bank's customers can conduct many of their bank transactions without ever leaving the comfort of home. The advantage for the customer is the convenience of home banking, while banks find that the cost of transactions is substantially less than the cost associated with brick-and-mortar banking.

With the decline in the price of personal computers and their increasing presence in the home, we have seen a further innovation in the home banking area, the creation of a new type of banking institution, the **virtual bank**, a bank that has no physical location but rather exists only in cyberspace. In 1995, Security First Network Bank, based in Atlanta but now owned by Royal Bank of Canada, became the first virtual bank, offering an array of banking services on the Internet—accepting checking account and savings deposits, selling certificates of deposits, issuing ATM cards, providing bill-paying facilities, and so on. The virtual bank thus takes home banking one step further, enabling the customer to have a full set of banking services at home, 24 hours a day. In 1996, Bank of America and Wells Fargo entered the virtual banking market, to be followed by many others, with Bank of America now being the largest Internet bank in the United States.

Junk Bonds   Before the advent of computers and advanced telecommunications, it was difficult to acquire information about the financial situations of firms that might want to sell securities. Because of the difficulty in screening out bad from good credit risks, the only firms that were able to sell bonds were very well-established corporations that had high credit ratings.[1] Before the 1980s, then, only corporations that could issue bonds with ratings of Baa or above could raise funds by selling newly issued

---

[1]The discussion of adverse selection problems in Chapter 8 provides a more detailed analysis of why only well-established firms with high credit ratings were able to sell securities.

bonds. Some firms that had fallen on bad times, known as *fallen angels*, had previously issued long-term corporate bonds with ratings that had now fallen below Baa, bonds that were pejoratively dubbed "junk bonds."

With the improvement in information technology in the 1970s, it became easier for investors to acquire financial information about corporations, making it easier to screen out bad from good credit risks. With easier screening, investors were more willing to buy long-term debt securities from less-well-known corporations with lower credit ratings. With this change in supply conditions, we would expect that some smart individual would pioneer the concept of selling new public issues of junk bonds, not for fallen angels but for companies that had not yet achieved investment-grade status. This is exactly what Michael Milken of Drexel Burnham Lambert, an investment banking firm, started to do in 1977. Junk bonds became an important factor in the corporate bond market, with the amount outstanding exceeding $200 billion by the late 1980s. Although there was a sharp slowdown in activity in the junk bond market after Milken was indicted for securities law violations in 1989, the junk bond market heated up again in the 1990s and 2000s, with the amount outstanding now exceeding $1 trillion.

Commercial Paper Market   *Commercial paper* is a short-term debt security issued by large banks and corporations. The commercial paper market underwent tremendous growth in the 1970s and 1980s, rising from $33 billion in 1970 to over $550 billion by 1990, an increase of over 1,500%. Commercial paper became one of the most important money market instruments.

Improvements in information technology also help explain the rapid rise of the commercial paper market. We have seen that improvements in information technology made it easier for investors to screen out bad from good credit risks, thus making it easier for corporations to issue debt securities. Not only did this make it simpler for corporations to issue long-term debt securities, as in the junk bond market, but it also meant they could raise funds by issuing short-term debt securities, such as commercial paper, with greater ease. Many corporations that used to do their short-term borrowing from banks now frequently raise short-term funds in the commercial paper market instead.

The development of money market mutual funds has been another factor in the rapid growth of the commercial paper market. Because money market mutual funds need to hold liquid, high-quality, short-term assets such as commercial paper, the growth of assets in these funds to around $3.6 trillion has created a ready market in commercial paper. The growth of pension and other large funds that invest in commercial paper has also stimulated the growth of this market.

Securitization and the Shadow Banking System

One of the most important financial innovations of the past two decades, arising from improvements in information technology, is securitization. **Securitization** is the process of bundling small and otherwise illiquid financial assets (such as residential mortgages, auto loans, and credit card receivables), which have typically been the bread and butter of banking institutions, into marketable capital market securities. Securitization is the fundamental building block of the shadow banking system.

How the Shadow Banking System Works   In traditional banking, one entity engages in the process of asset transformation—that is, it issues liabilities with one set of desirable characteristics (say, deposits with high liquidity and low risk) to fund the purchase of assets with a different set of characteristics (say, loans with low liquidity and high returns). Securitization, in contrast, is a process of asset transformation that involves a number of different financial institutions working together. These institutions constitute the shadow banking system. In other words, asset transformation accomplished through securitization and the shadow banking system is not done "under one roof," as is traditional banking.

For example, a mortgage broker (more generally referred to as a *loan originator*) will arrange for a residential mortgage loan to be made by a financial institution that will then service the loan (that is, collect the interest and principal payments). This *servicer* then sells the mortgage to another financial institution, which bundles the mortgage with a large number of other residential mortgages. The *bundler* takes the interest and principal payments on the portfolio of mortgages and "passes them through" (pays them out) to third parties. The bundler goes to a *distributor* (typically an investment bank), which designs a security that divides the portfolio of loans into standardized amounts. The distributor then sells the claims to these interest and principal payments as securities, mostly to other financial intermediaries that are also part of the shadow banking system—for example, a money market mutual fund or a pension fund. Schematically, the securitization process is described by the following sequence:

$$\text{loan origination} \Rightarrow \text{servicing} \Rightarrow \text{bundling} \Rightarrow \text{distribution}$$

Because the securitization process involves the origination of loans and then finally the distribution of securities, securitization is also characterized as an **originate-to-distribute** business model.

At each step of the securitization process, the loan originator, servicer, bundler, and distributor earn a fee. Each of these four institutions has specialized in a particular element of the financial intermediation process. The shadow banking system, which comprises all of the financial institutions involved in the securitization process, can thus be very profitable if transaction costs and the costs of collecting information are low. Advances in information technology have therefore been critical to the growth of securitization and the shadow banking system. Lower costs of acquiring information make it far easier to sell capital market securities, while lower transaction costs make it cheaper for financial institutions to collect interest and principal payments on bundled loans and then pay them out to the securities holders.

Subprime Mortgage Market   A particularly important financial innovation that developed in the 2000s as a result of securitization and the shadow banking system was the **subprime mortgage**, a new class of residential mortgages offered to borrowers with less-than-stellar credit records. Before 2000, only the most creditworthy (prime) borrowers could obtain residential mortgages. Advances in computer technology and new statistical techniques, known as data mining, led to enhanced, quantitative evaluation of the credit risk for residential mortgages. Households with credit records could now be assigned a numerical credit score, known as a FICO score (named after the Fair Isaac Corporation that developed it), that predicted how likely the household would be to default on its loan payments. Because it now became easier to assess the risk associated with a pool of subprime mortgages, it became possible to bundle them into a mortgage-backed security, providing a new source of funding for these mortgages. The result was an explosion of subprime mortgage lending, which, as we will see in Chapter 12, was a key factor that led to the global financial crisis of 2007–2009.

Avoidance of Existing Regulations

The process of financial innovation, as we have discussed it so far, is much like innovation in other areas of the economy: It occurs in response to changes in demand and supply conditions. However, because the financial industry is more heavily regulated than other industries, government regulation is a much greater spur to innovation in this industry. Government regulation leads to financial innovation by creating incentives for firms to skirt regulations that restrict their ability to earn profits. Edward Kane, an economist at Boston College, describes this process of avoiding regulations as "loophole mining." The economic analysis of innovation suggests that when the economic environment changes such that regulatory constraints are so burdensome that large profits can be made by avoiding them, loophole mining and innovation are more likely to occur.

Because banking is one of the most heavily regulated industries in America, loophole mining is especially likely to occur. The rise in inflation and interest rates from the late 1960s to 1980 made the regulatory constraints imposed on this industry even more burdensome, leading to financial innovation.

Two sets of regulations have seriously restricted the ability of banks to make profits: reserve requirements that force banks to keep a certain fraction of their deposits as reserves (vault cash and deposits in the Federal Reserve System) and restrictions on the interest rates that can be paid on deposits. For the following reasons, these regulations have been major forces behind financial innovation.

1. *Reserve requirements.* The key to understanding why reserve requirements led to financial innovation is to recognize that they act, in effect, as a tax on deposits. Because up until 2008 the Fed did not pay interest on reserves, the opportunity cost of holding them was the interest that a bank could otherwise earn by lending the reserves out. For each dollar of deposits, reserve requirements therefore imposed a cost on the bank equal to the interest rate, i, that could be earned if the reserves could be lent out times the fraction of deposits required as reserves, r. The cost of $i \times r$ imposed on the bank was just like a tax on bank deposits of $i \times r$ per dollar of deposits. This "tax" on deposits rises as interest rates rise.

   It is a great tradition to avoid taxes if possible, and banks also play this game. Just as taxpayers look for loopholes to lower their tax bills, banks seek to increase their profits by mining loopholes and by producing financial innovations that enable them to escape the tax on deposits imposed by reserve requirements.

2. *Restrictions on interest paid on deposits.* Until 1980, legislation prohibited banks in most states from paying interest on checking account deposits, and through Regulation Q, the Fed set maximum limits on the interest rate that could be paid on savings and time deposits. To this day, banks are not allowed to pay interest on corporate checking accounts. The desire of banks to avoid these **deposit rate ceilings** also led to financial innovations.

   If market interest rates rose above the maximum rates that banks paid on savings and time deposits under Regulation Q, depositors withdrew funds from banks to put them into higher-yielding securities. This loss of deposits from the banking system restricted the amount of funds that banks could lend (called **disintermediation**) and thus limited bank profits. Banks had an incentive to get around deposit rate ceilings, because by so doing, they could acquire more funds to make loans and earn higher profits.

We can now look at how the desire to avoid restrictions on interest payments and the tax effect of reserve requirements led to two important financial innovations.

Money Market Mutual Funds

Money market mutual funds issue shares that are redeemable at a fixed price (usually $1) by writing checks. For example, if you buy 5,000 shares for $5,000, the money market fund uses these funds to invest in short-term money market securities (Treasury bills, negotiable certificates of deposit, commercial paper) that provide you with interest payments. In addition, you are able to write checks up to the $5,000 held as shares in the money market fund. Although money market fund shares effectively function as checking account deposits that earn interest, they are not legally deposits and so are not subject to reserve requirements or prohibitions on interest payments. For this reason, they can pay higher interest rates than deposits at banks.

The first money market mutual fund was created by two Wall Street mavericks, Bruce Bent and Henry Brown, in 1970. However, the low market interest rates from 1970 to 1977 (which were just slightly above Regulation Q ceilings of 5.25% to 5.5%) kept money market mutual funds from being particularly advantageous relative to bank deposits. In early 1978, the situation changed rapidly as inflation rose and market interest rates began to climb over 10%, well above the 5.5% maximum interest rates payable on savings accounts and time deposits under Regulation Q. In 1977, money market mutual funds had assets of less than $4 billion; in 1978, their assets climbed to close to $10 billion; in 1979, to more than $40 billion; and in 1982, to $230 billion. Currently, their assets are around $2.7 trillion. To say the least, money market mutual funds have been a successful financial innovation, which is exactly what we would have predicted given the financial climate of the late 1970s and early 1980s, in which interest rates soared beyond Regulation Q ceilings.

In a supreme irony, risky investments by a money market mutual fund founded by Bruce Brent almost brought down the money market mutual fund industry during the global financial crisis in 2008 (see the FYI box "Bruce Bent and the Money Market Mutual Fund Panic of 2008").

Sweep Accounts

Another innovation that enables banks to avoid the "tax" from reserve requirements is the **sweep account**. In this arrangement, any balances above a certain amount in a corporation's checking account at the end of a business day are "swept out" of the account and invested in overnight securities that pay interest. Because the "swept out" funds are no longer classified as checkable deposits, they are not subject to reserve requirements and thus are not "taxed." They also have the advantage that they allow banks, in effect, to pay interest on these checking accounts, which otherwise is not allowed under existing regulations. Because sweep accounts have become so popular, they have lowered the amount of required reserves to the degree that most banking institutions do not find reserve requirements binding: In other words, they voluntarily hold more reserves than they are required to.

The financial innovations of sweep accounts and money market mutual funds are particularly interesting because they were stimulated not only by the desire to avoid a costly regulation but also by a change in supply conditions—in this case, information technology. Without low-cost computers to process inexpensively the additional transactions required by these innovations, they would not have been profitable and therefore would not have been developed. Technological factors often combine with other incentives, such as the desire to get around a regulation, to produce innovation.

Bruce Bent, one of the originators of money market mutual funds, almost brought down the industry during the global financial crisis in the fall of 2008. Mr. Bent told his shareholders in a letter written in July 2008 that the fund was managed on a basis of "unwavering discipline focused on protecting your principal." He also wrote to the Securities and Exchange Commission in September 2007, stating, "When I first created the money market fund back in 1970, it was designed with the tenets of safety and liquidity." He added that these principles had "fallen by the wayside as portfolio managers chased the highest yield and compromised the integrity of the money fund." Alas, Bent did not follow his own advice, and his fund, the Reserve Primary Fund, bought risky assets that made its yield higher than the industry average.

When Lehman Brothers went into bankruptcy on September 15, 2008, the Reserve Primary Fund, with assets of over $60 billion, was caught holding the bag on $785 million of Lehman's debt, which then had to be marked down to zero. The resulting losses meant that on September 16, Bent's fund could no longer afford to redeem its shares at the par value of $1, a situation known as "breaking the buck." Bent's shareholders began to pull their money out of the fund, causing it to lose 90% of its assets.

The fear that this could happen to other money market mutual funds led to a classic panic in which shareholders began to withdraw their funds at an alarming rate. The whole money market mutual fund industry looked as though it would come crashing down. To prevent this, the Federal Reserve and the U.S. Treasury rode to the rescue on September 19. The Fed set up a facility, discussed in Chapter 15, to make loans to be used to purchase commercial paper from money market mutual funds so that they could meet the demands for redemptions from their investors. The Treasury then put in a temporary guarantee for all money market mutual fund redemptions, and the panic subsided.

Not surprisingly, given the extension of a government safety net to the money market mutual fund industry, there are calls to regulate this industry more heavily. The money market mutual fund industry will never be the same.

Financial Innovation and the Decline of Traditional Banking

The traditional financial intermediation role of banking has been to make long-term loans and to fund them by issuing short-term deposits, a process of asset transformation commonly referred to as "borrowing short and lending long." Here we examine how financial innovations have created a more competitive environment for the banking industry, causing the industry to change dramatically, with its traditional banking business going into decline.

In the United States, the importance of commercial banks as a source of funds for nonfinancial borrowers has shrunk dramatically. As we can see in Figure 2, in 1974, banks provided over 40% of these funds; by 2020 their market share was down to slightly above 20%.

To understand why the traditional banking business has declined in size, we need to look at how the financial innovations described earlier have caused banks to suffer declines in their cost advantages in acquiring funds—that is, on the liabilities side of their balance sheet—while at the same time losing income advantages on the assets side of their balance sheet. The simultaneous decline of cost and income advantages has resulted in reduced profitability of traditional banking and an effort by banks to leave this business and engage in new and more profitable activities.

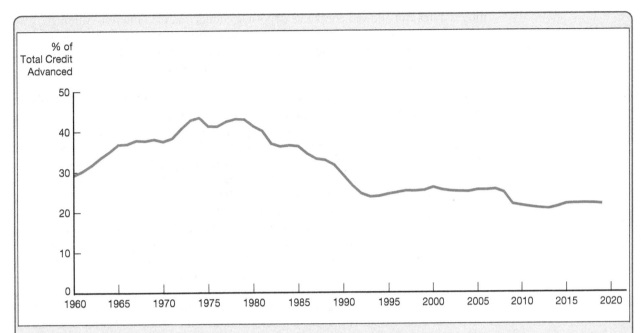

FIGURE 2   **Bank Share of Total Nonfinancial Borrowing, 1960–2020**

In 1974, banks provided over 40% of these funds; by 2020 their market share was down to slightly above 20%.

Source: Federal Reserve Bank of St. Louis, FRED database: https://fred.stlouisfed.org/series/TODNS and https://www .federalreserve.gov/releases/z1/current/data.htm, Table L110.

Decline in Cost Advantages in Acquiring Funds (Liabilities)   Until 1980, banks were subject to deposit rate ceilings that restricted them from paying any interest on checkable deposits and (under Regulation Q) limited them to paying a maximum interest rate of a little more than 5% on savings and time deposits. Until the 1960s, these restrictions worked to the banks' advantage because their major source of funds (in excess of 60%) was checkable deposits, and the zero interest cost on these deposits meant that the banks had a very low cost of funds. Unfortunately, this cost advantage for banks did not last.

The rise in inflation beginning in the late 1960s led to higher interest rates, which made investors more sensitive to yield differentials on different assets. The result was the *disintermediation* process, in which people began to take their money out of banks, with their low interest rates on both checkable, savings and time deposits, and began to seek out higher-yielding investments. At the same time, as we have seen, attempts to get around deposit rate ceilings and reserve requirements led to the financial innovation of money market mutual funds, which put the banks at an even further disadvantage because depositors could now obtain checking account–like services while earning high interest on their money market mutual fund accounts. One manifestation of these changes in the financial system was that the low-cost source of funds, checkable deposits, declined dramatically in importance for banks, falling from more than 60% of bank liabilities to 14% today.

The growing difficulty for banks in raising funds led them to support legislation in the 1980s that eliminated Regulation Q ceilings on time and savings deposit interest rates and allowed checkable deposit accounts that paid interest. Although these changes in regulation helped make banks more competitive in their quest for funds, it also meant that their cost of acquiring funds had risen substantially, thereby reducing their earlier cost advantage over other financial institutions.

Decline in Income Advantages on Uses of Funds (Assets)

The loss of cost advantages on the liabilities side of the balance sheet for American banks is one reason they have become less competitive, but they have also been hit by a decline in income advantages on the assets side from the financial innovations we discussed earlier—junk bonds, securitization, and the rise of the commercial paper market. The resulting loss of income advantages for banks relative to these innovations has resulted in a loss of market share and has led to the growth of the shadow banking system, which has made use of these innovations to enable borrowers to bypass the traditional banking system.

We have seen that improvements in information technology have made it easier for firms to issue securities directly to the public. This change means that instead of going to banks to finance short-term credit needs, many of the banks' best business customers now find it cheaper to go instead to the commercial paper market for funds. The emergence of the junk bond market has also eaten into banks' loan business. Improvements in information technology have made it easier for corporations to sell their bonds to the public directly, thereby bypassing banks. Although Fortune 500 companies started taking this route in the 1970s, now lower-quality and less well-known corporate borrowers are using banks less often because they have access to the junk bond market.

We have also seen that improvements in computer technology have led to the growth of the shadow banking system and securitization, whereby illiquid financial assets such as bank loans and mortgages are transformed into marketable securities. Computers enable other financial institutions to originate loans because these institutions can now accurately evaluate credit risk with statistical methods. Computers also have lowered transaction costs, making it possible to bundle these loans and sell them as securities. When default risk can be easily evaluated using computers, banks no longer have an advantage in making loans. Without their former advantages, banks have lost loan business to other financial institutions even though the banks themselves are involved in the process of securitization. Securitization has been a particular problem for mortgage-issuing institutions such as S&Ls, because most residential mortgages are now securitized.

Banks' Responses

In any industry, a decline in profitability usually results in an exit from the industry (often due to widespread bankruptcies) and a shrinkage of market share. This occurred in the U.S. banking industry during the 1980s via consolidations and bank failures.

In an attempt to survive and maintain adequate profit levels, many U.S. banks faced two alternatives. First, they could attempt to maintain their traditional lending activity by expanding into new and riskier areas of lending. For example, U.S. banks increased their risk taking by placing a greater percentage of their total funds in commercial real estate loans, traditionally a riskier type of loan. In addition, they increased lending for corporate takeovers and leveraged buyouts, which are highly leveraged transactions. The decline in the profitability of banks' traditional business may thus have helped lead to the global financial crisis of 2007–2009.

The second way in which banks have sought to maintain their former profit levels is by pursuing new off-balance-sheet activities that are more profitable and in effect embrace the shadow banking system. U.S. commercial banks did this during the early 1980s, more than doubling the share of their income coming from off-balance-sheet, non–interest-income activities. Nontraditional bank activities can be riskier and, therefore, result in excessive risk taking by banks. Indeed, they led to a substantial weakening of bank balance sheets during the global financial crisis.

The decline of banks' traditional business has driven the banking industry to seek out new lines of business. This search for business opportunities may be beneficial because it may ultimately keep banks vibrant and healthy. Indeed, bank profitability was high up until 2007, and nontraditional, off-balance-sheet activities played an important role in the high bank profits. However, the new directions in banking led to increased risk taking, and thus the decline in traditional banking has required regulators to be more vigilant. Nontraditional bank activities pose new challenges for bank regulators, who, as we saw in Chapter 10, must now be far more concerned about banks' off-balance-sheet activities.

Decline of Traditional Banking in Other Industrialized Countries Forces similar to those in the United States have led to the decline of traditional banking in other industrialized countries. The loss of banks' monopoly power over depositors has occurred outside the United States as well. Financial innovation and deregulation are occurring worldwide and have created attractive alternatives for both depositors and borrowers. In Japan, for example, deregulation opened a wide array of new financial instruments to the public, causing a disintermediation process similar to that in the United States. In European countries, innovations have steadily eroded the barriers that have traditionally protected banks from competition.

Banks in other countries also faced increased competition from the expansion of securities markets and the growth of the shadow banking system. Both financial deregulation and advances in information technology in other countries have improved the availability of information in securities markets, making it easier and less costly for firms to finance their activities by issuing securities rather than going to banks. Further, even in countries where securities markets have not grown, banks have still lost loan business because their best corporate customers have had increasing access to foreign and offshore capital markets, such as the Eurobond market. In smaller economies, like that of Australia, which still do not have as well-developed corporate bond or commercial paper markets, banks have lost loan business to international securities markets. In addition, the same forces that drove the securitization process in the United States have been at work in other countries and have undercut the profitability of traditional banking in these countries as well. The United States has not been unique in seeing its banks face a more difficult competitive environment. Thus, although the decline of traditional banking occurred earlier in the United States than in other countries, the same forces have caused a decline in traditional banking abroad.

11.3 STRUCTURE OF THE U.S. COMMERCIAL BANKING INDUSTRY

LO 11.3 Identify the key structural changes in the commercial banking industry.

There are approximately 6,000 banks in the United States, far more than in any other country in the world. As Table 1 indicates, we have an extraordinary number of small banks. Over 22% of the banks have less than $100 million in assets. Far more typical is the size distribution in Canada or the United Kingdom, where five or fewer banks

TABLE 1	Size Distribution of FDIC-Insured Banks, March 31, 2020		
Assets	**Number of Banks**	**Share of Banks (%)**	**Share of Assets Held (%)**
Less than $100 million	1,124	22.0	0.5
$100 million–$1 billion	3,168	61.9	6.7
$1 billion–$10 billion	680	13.3	10.0
$10 billion–$250 billion	131	2.6	32.3
More than $250 billion	13	0.3	50.4
Total	5,116	100.00	100.00

Source: FDIC Quarterly Banking Profile, https://www.fdic.gov/bank/analytical/qbp/index.html.

dominate the industry. In contrast, the ten largest commercial banks in the United States (listed in Table 2) together hold under 70% of the assets in their industry.

Most industries in the United States have far fewer firms than the commercial banking industry; typically, large firms tend to dominate these industries to a greater extent than in the commercial banking industry. (Consider the computer software industry, which is dominated by Microsoft, or the automobile industry, which is dominated by General Motors, Ford, Daimler-Chrysler, Toyota, and Honda.) Does the large number of banks in the commercial banking industry and the absence of a few dominant firms suggest that commercial banking is more competitive than other industries?

TABLE 2	Ten Largest U.S. Banks, 2020	
Bank	**Assets ($ trillions)**	**Share of All Commercial Bank Assets (%)**
1. J.P. Morgan Chase & Co.	2.74	15.4
2. Bank of America Corp.	2.38	13.4
3. Citigroup Inc.	1.96	11.0
4. Wells Fargo & Co.	1.89	10.6
5. Goldman Sachs Group	0.93	5.2
6. Morgan Stanley	0.88	4.9
7. U.S. Bankcorp	0.48	2.7
8. PNC Financial Services Group	0.39	2.2
9. TD Group US	0.38	2.1
10. Capital One Financial Corp.	0.37	2.1
Total	12.40	69.6

Source: From Bankrate.com—Compare mortgage, refinance, insurance, CD rates: http://www.bankrate.com/banking/americas-top-10-biggest-banks/#slide=1.

Restrictions on Branching

The presence of so many commercial banks in the United States actually reflects past regulations that restricted the ability of these financial institutions to open branches. Each state had its own regulations on the type and number of branches that a bank could open. Regulations on both coasts, for example, tended to allow banks to open branches throughout a state; in the middle part of the country, regulations on branching were more restrictive, in some cases allowing no branches at all. The McFadden Act of 1927, which was designed to put national banks and state banks on equal footing (and the Douglas Amendment of 1956, which closed a loophole in the McFadden Act), effectively prohibited banks from branching across state lines and forced all national banks to conform to the branching regulations of the state in which their headquarters were located.

The McFadden Act and state branching regulations constituted strong anticompetitive forces in the commercial banking industry, allowing many small banks to stay in existence because larger banks were prevented from opening branches nearby. If competition is beneficial to society, why did regulations restricting branching arise in America? The simplest explanation is that the American public has historically been hostile to large banks. States with the most restrictive branching regulations were typically ones in which populist antibank sentiment was strongest in the nineteenth century. (These states usually had large farming populations whose relations with banks periodically became tempestuous when banks would foreclose on farmers who couldn't pay their debts.) The legacy of nineteenth-century politics was a banking system with restrictive branching regulations and hence an inordinate number of small banks. However, as we will see later in this chapter, branching restrictions have been eliminated, and we have moved toward nationwide banking.

Response to Branching Restrictions

An important feature of the U.S. banking industry is that competition can be repressed by regulation but not completely quashed. As we saw earlier in this chapter, the existence of restrictive regulation stimulates financial innovations that get around these regulations, in the banks' search for profits. Regulations restricting branching have stimulated similar economic forces and have promoted the development of two financial innovations: bank holding companies and automated teller machines.

Bank Holding Companies   A holding company is a corporation that owns several different companies. This form of corporate ownership has important advantages for banks. It has allowed them to circumvent restrictive branching regulations, because the holding company can own a controlling interest in several banks even if branching is not permitted. Furthermore, a bank holding company can engage in other activities related to banking, such as the provision of investment advice, data processing and transmission services, leasing, credit card services, and servicing of loans in other states.

The growth of bank holding companies has been dramatic over the past three decades. Today bank holding companies own almost all large banks, and more than 90% of all commercial bank deposits are held in banks owned by holding companies.

Automated Teller Machines   Another financial innovation that resulted from the desire to avoid restrictions on branching is the automated teller machine (ATM). Banks quickly realized that if they did not own or rent an ATM, but instead let it be owned by someone else and paid a fee for each transaction, the ATM would probably not be considered a branch of the bank and thus would not be subject to branching regulations. This is exactly what the regulatory agencies and courts in most states concluded. Because they enable banks to widen their markets, a number of these shared facilities (such as Cirrus and NYCE) have been established nationwide. Furthermore, even when an ATM is owned by a bank, states typically have special provisions that allow wider establishment of ATMs than is permissible for traditional "brick-and-mortar" branches.

As we saw earlier in this chapter, avoiding regulation was not the only reason for the development of the ATM. The advent of cheaper computer and telecommunications technology enabled banks to provide ATMs at low cost, making them a profitable innovation. This example further illustrates that technological factors often combine with incentives, such as the desire to avoid restrictive regulations, to produce financial innovation.

11.4 BANK CONSOLIDATION AND NATIONWIDE BANKING

LO 11.4 Summarize the factors that led to consolidation in the commercial banking industry.

As we can see in Figure 3, after a remarkable period of stability from 1934 to the mid-1980s, the number of commercial banks in the United States began to fall dramatically. Why did this sudden decline take place?

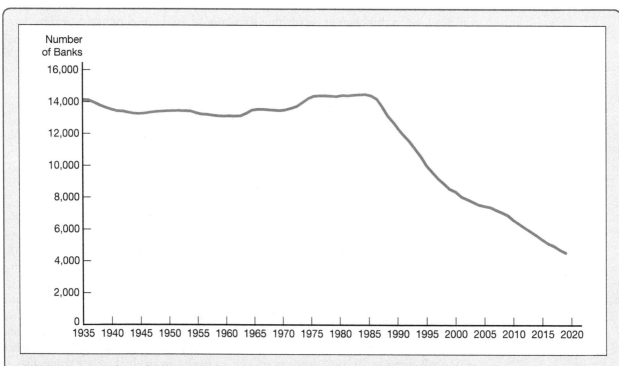

FIGURE 3   **Number of Commercial Banks in the United States, 1934–2019**

After a period of stability from 1934 to the mid-1980s, the number of commercial banks began to fall dramatically.

Source: Federal Reserve Bank of St. Louis, FRED database: https://fred.stlouisfed.org/series/USNUM.

The banking industry hit some hard times in the 1980s and early 1990s, with bank failures running at a rate of over 100 per year from 1985 to 1992 (more on this later in the chapter). But bank failures are only part of the story. In the years 1985–1992, the number of banks declined by 3,000—more than double the number of failures. And in the period 1992–2007, when the banking industry returned to health, the number of commercial banks decreased by a little over 3,800, less than 5% of which were bank failures, and most of these were of small banks. Thus we see that bank failures played an important, though not predominant, role in reducing the number of banks in the 1985–1992 period and an almost negligible role through 2007. The global financial crisis, however, led to additional declines in the number of banks because of bank failures.

So what explains the rest of the story? The answer is bank consolidation. Banks have been merging to create larger entities or have been buying up other banks. This gives rise to a new question: Why has bank consolidation been taking place in recent years?

As we have seen, loophole mining by banks reduced the effectiveness of branching restrictions, with the result that many states recognized it would be in their best interest if they allowed ownership of banks across state lines. The result was the formation of reciprocal regional compacts in which banks in one state were allowed to own banks in other states in the region. In 1975, Maine enacted the first interstate banking legislation that allowed out-of-state bank holding companies to purchase banks in that state. In 1982, Massachusetts enacted a regional compact with other New England states to allow interstate banking, and many other regional compacts were adopted thereafter until, by the early 1990s, almost all states allowed some form of interstate banking.

With the barriers to interstate banking breaking down in the early 1980s, banks recognized that they could gain the benefits of diversification because they would now be able to make loans in many states rather than just one. This gave them an advantage: If one state's economy was weak, another state in which they operated might have a strong economy, thus decreasing the likelihood that loans in different states would default at the same time. In addition, allowing banks to own banks in other states meant that they could increase their size through out-of-state acquisition of banks or by merging with banks in other states. Mergers and acquisitions explain the first phase of banking consolidation, which has played such an important role in the decline in the number of banks since 1985. Another result of the loosening of restrictions on interstate branching is the development of a new class of banks, called **superregional banks**, which are bank holding companies that have begun to rival the money center banks in size but whose headquarters are not in one of the money center cities (New York, Chicago, and San Francisco). Examples of these superregional banks are Bank of America of Charlotte, North Carolina, and Banc One of Columbus, Ohio.

Not surprisingly, the advent of the Web and improved computer technology is another factor driving bank consolidation. Economies of scale have increased because large, upfront investments are required to set up information technology platforms for financial institutions. To take advantage of these economies of scale, banks have needed to get bigger, and this development has led to additional consolidation. Information technology has also been increasing **economies of scope**, the ability to use one resource to provide many different products and services. For example, details about the quality and creditworthiness of firms not only inform decisions about whether to make loans to them but also can be useful in determining at what price their shares should trade. Similarly, once you have marketed one financial product to an investor, you probably know how to market another. Businesspeople describe economies of scope by saying there are "synergies" between different lines of business, and information technology is making these synergies more likely. The result is that consolidation is taking place not only to make financial institutions bigger but also to increase the combination of products and services they can provide.

This consolidation has had two consequences. First, different types of financial intermediaries are encroaching on each other's territory, making them more alike. Second, consolidation has led to the development of large, complex banking organizations. This development has been facilitated by the repeal of the Glass-Steagall restrictions on combinations of banking and other financial service industries, as discussed in the next section.

The Riegle-Neal Interstate Banking and Branching Efficiency Act of 1994

Banking consolidation was given further stimulus by the passage in 1994 of the Riegle-Neal Interstate Banking and Branching Efficiency Act. This legislation expanded the regional compacts to the entire nation and overturned the McFadden Act and Douglas Amendment's prohibition of interstate banking. Not only did this act allow bank holding companies to acquire banks in any other state, notwithstanding any state laws to the contrary, but bank holding companies could also merge the banks they owned into one bank with branches in different states. States were, however, given the option of opting out of interstate branching, but only Texas did so, although it later reversed its position and now allows it.

The Riegle-Neal Act finally established the basis for a true nationwide banking system. Although interstate banking was accomplished previously by out-of-state purchase of banks by bank holding companies, until 1994 it was virtually nonexistent because very few states had enacted interstate branching legislation. Allowing banks to conduct interstate banking through branching is especially important because many bankers feel that economies of scale cannot be fully exploited through the bank holding company structure, but only through branching networks in which all of the bank's operations are fully coordinated.

Nationwide banks have now emerged. Starting with the merger in 1998 of Bank of America and NationsBank, which created the first bank with branches on both coasts, consolidation in the banking industry has created some banking organizations with operations in all 50 states.

What Will the Structure of the U.S. Banking Industry Look Like in the Future?

Now that true nationwide banking in the United States is a reality, the benefits of bank consolidation for the banking industry have increased substantially, driving the next phase of mergers and acquisitions and accelerating the decline in the number of commercial banks. With great changes occurring in the structure of this industry, the question naturally arises: What will the industry look like in ten years?

One view is that the industry will become more like that in many other countries (see the Global box "Comparison of Banking Structure in the United States and Abroad"), and we will end up with only a couple of hundred banks. A more extreme view is that the industry will look like that of Canada or the United Kingdom, with a few large banks dominating the industry. Most experts come up with a different answer:

Global   Comparison of Banking Structure in the United States and Abroad

The structure of the commercial banking industry in the United States is radically different from that in other industrialized nations. The United States came late to developing a true national banking system in which banks have branches throughout the country. One result is that many more banks are found in the United States than in other industrialized countries. In contrast to the United States, which has on the order of 5,000 banks, every other industrialized country has far fewer than 1,000. Japan, for example, has fewer than 100 commercial banks—a mere fraction of the number in the United States, even though its economy and population are half the size of those of the United States. Another result of past restrictions on branching in the United States is that our banks tend to be much smaller than those in other countries.

The structure of the U.S. banking industry will still be unique, but not to the degree it once was. The consolidation surge is likely to settle down as the U.S. banking industry approaches several thousand, rather than several hundred, banks. Banking consolidation will result not only in a smaller number of banks but also in a shift in assets from smaller banks to larger banks.

Are Bank Consolidation and Nationwide Banking Good Things?

Advocates of nationwide banking believe that consolidation will produce more efficient banks and a healthier banking system that is less prone to bank failures. However, critics of bank consolidation fear that it will eliminate small banks, referred to as **community banks**, and that this will result in less lending to small businesses. In addition, they worry that a few banks will come to dominate the industry, making the banking business less competitive.

Most economists are skeptical of these criticisms of bank consolidation. As we have seen, research indicates that even after bank consolidation is completed, the United States will still have plenty of banks. The banking industry will thus remain highly competitive, probably even more so than it is now, considering that banks that had been protected from competition from out-of-state banks now have to compete with them vigorously to stay in business.

It also does not look as though community banks will disappear. When New York State liberalized its branching laws in 1962, there were fears that community banks upstate would be driven from the market by the big New York City banks. Not only did this not happen, but some of the big boys found that the small banks were able to run rings around them in the local markets. Similarly, California, which has allowed unrestricted statewide branching for a long time, continues to have a thriving population of community banks.

Economists see some important benefits from bank consolidation and nationwide banking. The elimination of geographic restrictions on banking increases competition and drives inefficient banks out of business, increasing the efficiency of the banking sector. The move to larger banking organizations also means that there is some increase in efficiency because these organizations can take advantage of economies of scale and scope. The increased diversification of banks' loan portfolios may lower the probability of a banking crisis in the future.

In the 1980s and early 1990s, bank failures were often concentrated in states with weak economies. For example, after the decline in oil prices in 1986, all of the major commercial banks in Texas, which had been very profitable, found themselves in trouble. At that time, banks in New England were doing fine. However, when the 1990–1991 recession hit New England hard, some New England banks started failing. With nationwide banking, a bank could make loans in both New England and Texas and would thus be less likely to fail because when loans went sour in one location, they probably still would be doing well in the other. Thus nationwide banking is seen as a major step toward creating a banking system that is less vulnerable to banking crises.

Two concerns remain about the effects of bank consolidation—that it may lead to a reduction in lending to small businesses and that banks rushing to expand into new geographic markets may take increased risks leading to bank failures. The jury is still out on these concerns, but most economists see the benefits of bank consolidation and nationwide banking as outweighing the costs.

11.5 SEPARATION OF BANKING AND OTHER FINANCIAL SERVICE INDUSTRIES

LO 11.5 Assess the reasons for separating banking from other financial services through legislation.

Until recently, an important feature of the structure of the banking industry in the United States was the separation of the banking and other financial services industries—such as securities, insurance, and real estate—mandated by the Glass-Steagall Act of 1933. As pointed out earlier in the chapter, Glass-Steagall allowed commercial banks to sell new offerings of government securities but prohibited them from underwriting corporate securities or from engaging in brokerage activities. It also prevented banks from engaging in insurance and real estate activities. In turn, it prevented investment banks and insurance companies from engaging in commercial banking activities and thus protected banks from competition.

Erosion of Glass-Steagall

Despite the Glass-Steagall prohibitions, the pursuit of profits and financial innovation stimulated both banks and other financial institutions to bypass the intent of the Glass-Steagall Act and encroach on each other's traditional territory. With the development of money market mutual funds and cash management accounts, brokerage firms began to engage in the traditional banking business of issuing deposit instruments. After the Federal Reserve used a loophole in Section 20 of the Glass-Steagall Act in 1987 to allow bank holding companies to underwrite previously prohibited classes of securities, banks began to enter this business. The loophole allowed affiliates of approved commercial banks to engage in underwriting activities as long as the revenue didn't exceed a specified amount, which started at 10% but was raised to 25% of the affiliates' total revenue. After the U.S. Supreme Court validated the Fed's action in July 1988, the Federal Reserve allowed J.P. Morgan, a commercial bank holding company, to underwrite corporate debt securities (in January 1989) and to underwrite stocks (in September 1990), with the privilege later extended to other bank holding companies. The regulatory agencies also allowed banks to engage in some real estate and insurance activities.

The Gramm-Leach-Bliley Financial Services Modernization Act of 1999: Repeal of Glass-Steagall

Because restrictions on commercial banks' securities and insurance activities put American banks at a competitive disadvantage relative to foreign banks, bills to overturn Glass-Steagall appeared in almost every session of Congress in the 1990s. With the merger in 1998 of Citicorp, the second largest bank in the United States, and Travelers Group, an insurance company that also owned the third largest securities firm in the country (Salomon Smith Barney), the pressure to abolish Glass-Steagall became overwhelming. Legislation to eliminate Glass-Steagall finally came to fruition in 1999.

This legislation, the Gramm-Leach-Bliley Financial Services Modernization Act of 1999, allows securities firms and insurance companies to purchase banks, and allows banks to underwrite insurance and securities and engage in real estate activities. Under this legislation, states retain regulatory authority over insurance activities, while the Securities and Exchange Commission continues to have oversight of securities activities. The Office of the Comptroller of the Currency has the authority to regulate bank subsidiaries engaged in securities underwriting, but the Federal Reserve continues to have the authority to oversee the bank holding companies under which all real estate and insurance activities and large securities operations will be housed.

Implications for Financial Consolidation

As we have seen, the Riegle-Neal Interstate Banking and Branching Efficiency Act of 1994 stimulated consolidation of the banking industry. The financial consolidation process was further hastened by the Gramm-Leach-Bliley Act of 1999, because the way is now open to consolidation not only in terms of the number of banking institutions but also across financial service activities. Given that information technology is increasing economies of scope, mergers of banks with other financial service firms like that of Citicorp and Travelers have become increasingly common, and more mega-mergers are likely to be on the way. Banking institutions are becoming not only larger but also increasingly complex organizations, engaging in the full gamut of financial service activities. The trend toward larger and more complex banking organizations has been accelerated by the global financial crisis of 2007–2009 (see the FYI box "The Global Financial Crisis and the Demise of Large, Free-Standing Investment Banks").

Separation of Banking and Other Financial Services Industries Throughout the World

In the aftermath of the Great Depression, not many other countries followed the lead of the United States in separating the banking and other financial services industries. In fact, in the past this separation was the most prominent difference between banking regulation in the United States and that in other countries. Around the world, there are three basic frameworks for the banking and securities industries.

The first framework is *universal banking,* which exists in Germany, the Netherlands, and Switzerland. It provides no separation at all between the banking and securities industries. In a universal banking system, commercial banks provide a full range of banking, securities, real estate, and insurance services, all within a single legal entity. Banks are allowed to own sizable equity shares in commercial firms, and often they do.

The *British-style universal banking system,* the second framework, is found in the United Kingdom and countries with close ties to it, such as Canada and Australia, and now the United States and Japan. The British-style universal bank engages in securities underwriting, but it differs from the German-style universal bank in three ways: Separate legal subsidiaries are more common, bank equity holdings of commercial firms are less common, and combinations of banking and insurance firms are less common.

The third framework, which existed in Japan, featured some legal separation of the banking and other financial services industries. A major difference between the U.S. and Japanese banking systems is that Japanese banks are allowed to hold substantial equity stakes in commercial firms, whereas American banks are not. Although the banking and securities industries were legally separated in Japan until 2006, Japanese commercial banks are now allowed to engage in securities activities and, like U.S. banks, have become more like British-style universal banks.

11.6 THRIFT INDUSTRY: REGULATION AND STRUCTURE

LO 11.6 Summarize the distinctions between thrift institutions and commercial banks.

Not surprisingly, the regulation and structure of the thrift industry (savings and loan associations, mutual savings banks, and credit unions) closely parallel the regulation and structure of the commercial banking industry.

Savings and Loan Associations

Just as there is a dual banking system for commercial banks, savings and loan associations (S&Ls) can be chartered either by the federal government or by the states. Most S&Ls, whether state or federally chartered, are members of the Federal Home Loan Bank System (FHLBS). Established in 1932, the FHLBS was styled after the Federal Reserve System. It has 11 district Federal Home Loan banks, which are supervised by the Federal Housing Finance Agency.

Federal deposit insurance up to $250,000 per account for S&Ls is provided by the FDIC. The Office of the Comptroller of the Currency regulates federally insured S&Ls by setting minimum capital requirements, requiring periodic reports, and examining the S&Ls. It is also the chartering agency for federally chartered S&Ls, and for these S&Ls it approves mergers and sets the rules for branching.

The FHLBS, like the Fed, makes loans to the members of the system (obtaining funds for this purpose by issuing bonds). However, in contrast to the Fed's discount loans, which are expected to be repaid quickly, loans from the FHLBS often need not be repaid for long periods of time. In addition, the rates charged to S&Ls for these loans are often below the rates that the S&Ls must pay when they borrow in the open market. In this way, the FHLBS loan program provides a subsidy to the savings and loan industry (and implicitly to the housing industry, since most S&L loans are for residential mortgages).

The savings and loans industry experienced serious difficulties in the 1980s. Because savings and loans now engage in many of the same activities as commercial banks, many experts view the existence of a separate charter and regulatory apparatus for S&Ls as an anachronism that no longer makes sense.

Mutual Savings Banks

Mutual savings banks are similar to S&Ls, but are jointly owned by the depositors; approximately half are chartered by states. Although the mutual savings banks are primarily regulated by the states in which they are located, the majority have their deposits insured by the FDIC up to the limit of $250,000 per account; these banks are also subject to many of the FDIC's regulations for state-chartered banks. As a rule, the mutual savings banks whose deposits are not insured by the FDIC have their deposits insured by state insurance funds.

Credit Unions

Credit unions are small cooperative lending institutions organized around a particular group of individuals with a common bond (e.g., union members or employees of a particular firm). They are the only depository institutions that are tax-exempt and can be chartered either by the states or by the federal government; more than half are federally chartered. The National Credit Union Administration (NCUA) issues federal charters and regulates federally chartered credit unions by setting minimum capital requirements, requiring periodic reports, and examining the credit unions. Federal deposit insurance (up to the $250,000-per-account limit) is provided to both federally chartered and state-chartered credit unions by a subsidiary of the NCUA, the National Credit Union Share Insurance Fund (NCUSIF). Because the majority of credit union lending is for consumer loans with fairly short terms to maturity, these institutions did not suffer the financial difficulties of the S&Ls and mutual savings banks in the 1980s.

Because their members share a common bond, credit unions are typically quite small; most hold less than $10 million of assets. In addition, their ties to a particular industry or company make them more likely to fail when large numbers of workers in that industry or company are laid off and have trouble making loan payments. Recent regulatory changes allow individual credit unions to cater to a more diverse group of people by interpreting the common bond requirement less strictly, and this has encouraged an expansion in the size of credit unions that may help reduce credit union failures in the future.

11.7 INTERNATIONAL BANKING

LO 11.7 Identify the reasons for U.S. banks to operate in foreign countries and for foreign banks to operate in the United States.

In 1960, only eight U.S. banks operated branches in foreign countries, and their total assets were less than $4 billion. Currently, around 100 American banks have branches abroad, with assets totaling more than $2.9 trillion. The spectacular growth in international banking can be explained by three factors.

First is the rapid growth in international trade and multinational corporations that has occurred since 1960. When American firms operate abroad, they need banking services in foreign countries to help finance international trade. For example, they might need a loan in a foreign currency to operate a factory abroad. And when they sell goods abroad, they need to have a bank exchange the foreign currency they have received for their goods into dollars. Although these firms could use foreign banks to provide them with these international banking services, many of them prefer to do business with the U.S. banks with which they have established long-term relationships and which understand American business customs and practices. As international trade has grown, international banking has grown with it.

Second, American banks have been able to earn substantial profits by being very active in global investment banking, in which they underwrite foreign securities. They also sell insurance abroad, and they derive substantial profits from these investment banking and insurance activities.

Third, American banks have wanted to tap into the large pool of dollar-denominated deposits in foreign countries known as Eurodollars. To understand the structure of U.S. banking overseas, let's first look at the Eurodollar market, an important source of growth for international banking.

Eurodollar Market

Eurodollars are created when deposits in accounts in the United States are transferred to a bank outside the country and are kept in the form of dollars. (For a discussion of the birth of the Eurodollar, see the Global box "Ironic Birth of the Eurodollar Market.") For example, if Rolls-Royce PLC deposits a $1 million check, written on an account at an American bank, in its bank in London—specifying that the deposit is payable in dollars—$1 million in Eurodollars is created.[2] More than 90% of Eurodollar deposits are time deposits, more than half of them certificates of deposit with maturities of 30 days or more. The Eurodollar market is massive, over $10 trillion, making it one of the most important financial markets in the world economy.

[2]Note that the London bank keeps the $1 million on deposit at the American bank, so the creation of Eurodollars has not caused a reduction in the amount of bank deposits in the United States.

Global   **Ironic Birth of the Eurodollar Market**

One of capitalism's great ironies is that the Eurodollar market, one of the most important financial markets used by capitalists, was fathered by the Soviet Union. In the early 1950s, during the height of the Cold War, the Soviets had accumulated a substantial amount of dollar balances held by banks in the United States. Because the Russians feared that the U.S. government might freeze these assets in the United States, they wanted to move the deposits to Europe, where they would be safe from expropriation. (This fear was not unjustified—consider the U.S. freeze on Iranian assets in 1979 and on Iraqi assets in 1990.) However, they also wanted to keep the deposits in dollars so that they could be used in their international transactions. The solution to the problem was to transfer the deposits to European banks but to keep the deposits denominated in dollars. When the Soviets did this, the Eurodollar was born.

Why would companies such as Rolls-Royce want to hold dollar deposits outside the United States? First, the dollar is the most widely used currency in international trade, so Rolls-Royce might want to hold deposits in dollars to conduct its international transactions. Second, Eurodollars are "offshore" deposits—they are held in countries that will not subject them to regulations such as reserve requirements or restrictions (called *capital controls*) on taking the deposits outside the country.[3]

The main center of the Eurodollar market is London, a major international financial center for hundreds of years. Eurodollars are also held outside Europe in locations that provide offshore status to these deposits—for example, Singapore, the Bahamas, and the Cayman Islands.

The minimum transaction in the Eurodollar market is typically $1 million, and approximately 75% of Eurodollar deposits are held by banks. Plainly, you and I are unlikely to come into direct contact with Eurodollars. Rather than using an intermediary and borrowing all the deposits from foreign banks, American banks decided that they could earn higher profits by opening their own branches abroad to attract these deposits. Consequently, the Eurodollar market has been an important stimulus to U.S. banking overseas.

Structure of U.S. Banking Overseas

U.S. banks have most of their foreign branches in Latin America, the Far East, the Caribbean, and London. The largest volume of assets is held by branches in London, because it is a major international financial center and the central location for the Eurodollar market. Latin America and the Far East have many branches because of the importance of U.S. trade with these regions. Parts of the Caribbean (especially the Bahamas and the Cayman Islands) have become important as tax havens, with minimal taxation and few restrictive regulations. In actuality, the bank branches in the Bahamas and the Cayman Islands are "shell operations" because they function primarily as bookkeeping centers and do not provide normal banking services.

---

[3]Although most offshore deposits are denominated in dollars, some are denominated in other currencies. Collectively, these offshore deposits are referred to as Eurocurrencies. A Japanese yen-denominated deposit held in London, for example, is called a Euroyen.

An alternative corporate structure for U.S. banks that operate overseas is the **Edge Act corporation**, a special subsidiary engaged primarily in international banking. U.S. banks (through their holding companies) can also own a controlling interest in foreign banks and in foreign companies that provide financial services, such as finance companies. The international activities of U.S. banking organizations are governed primarily by the Federal Reserve's Regulation K.

In late 1981, the Federal Reserve approved the creation of **international banking facilities (IBFs)** within the United States that can accept time deposits from foreigners but are not subject to either reserve requirements or restrictions on interest payments. IBFs are also allowed to make loans to foreigners, but they are not allowed to make loans to domestic residents. States have encouraged the establishment of IBFs by exempting them from state and local taxes. In essence, IBFs are treated like foreign branches of U.S. banks and are not subject to domestic regulations and taxes. The purpose of establishing IBFs is to encourage American and foreign banks to do more banking business in the United States rather than abroad. From this point of view, IBFs are a success: Their assets climbed to nearly $200 billion in the first two years, and are in excess of $1 trillion currently.

Foreign Banks in the United States

The growth in international trade has not only encouraged U.S. banks to open offices overseas but has also encouraged foreign banks to establish offices in the United States. Foreign banks have been extremely successful in the United States. Currently, they hold around 20% of total U.S. domestic bank assets and do a similar share of all U.S. bank lending to U.S. corporations.

Foreign banks engage in banking activities in the United States by operating an agency office of the foreign bank, a subsidiary U.S. bank, or a branch of the foreign bank. An agency office can lend and transfer funds in the United States, but it cannot accept deposits from domestic residents. Agency offices have the advantage of not being subject to regulations that apply to full-service banking offices (such as requirements for FDIC insurance). A subsidiary U.S. bank is just like any other U.S. bank (it may even have an American-sounding name) and is subject to the same regulations, but it is owned by the foreign bank. A branch of a foreign bank bears the foreign bank's name and is usually a full-service office. Foreign banks may also form Edge Act corporations and IBFs.

Before 1978, foreign banks were not subject to many of the regulations that applied to domestic banks: They could open branches across state lines and were not expected to meet reserve requirements, for example. The passage of the International Banking Act of 1978, however, put foreign and domestic banks on more equal footing. Limited-service branches and agency offices in any other state were permitted, and foreign banks were allowed to retain any full-service branches opened before the act was ratified.

The internationalization of banking, both by U.S. banks going abroad and by foreign banks entering the United States, has meant that financial markets throughout the world have become more integrated. As a result, there is a growing trend toward international coordination of bank regulation, one example of which is the Basel Accords, discussed in Chapter 10, which were established to standardize minimum bank capital requirements in industrialized countries. Financial market integration has also encouraged bank consolidation abroad, culminating in the creation of the first trillion-dollar bank with the merger of the Industrial Bank of Japan, Dai-Ichi Kangyo Bank, and Fuji

TABLE 3	Ten Largest Banks in the World, 2020
Bank	**Assets (U.S. $ trillions)**
1. Industrial and Commercial Bank of China, China	4.32
2. China Construction Bank Corp., China	3.82
3. Agricultural Bank of China, China	3.70
4. Bank of China, China	3.39
5. JPMorgan Chase, US	3.14
6. HSBC Holdings plc, United Kingdom	2.92
7. Mistubishi UFJ Financial Group, Japan	2.89
8. Bank of America, US	2.62
9. BNP Paribas	2.43
10. Credit Agricole Group, France	1.98

Source: FXSSI: https://fxssi.com/top-20-largest-world-banks-in-current-year.

Bank, in 2002. Another development has been the importance of foreign banks in international banking. As is shown in Table 3, in 2020, eight out of ten of the largest banking groups in the world were foreign. The implications of this financial market integration for the operation of our economy are examined further in Chapter 18, where we discuss the international financial system in more detail.

SUMMARY

1. The history of banking in the United States has left us with a dual banking system, with commercial banks chartered by the states and the federal government. Multiple agencies regulate commercial banks: the Office of the Comptroller, the Federal Reserve, the FDIC, and the state banking authorities.

2. A change in the economic environment will stimulate financial institutions to search for financial innovations. Changes in demand conditions, especially an increase in interest-rate risk; changes in supply conditions, especially improvements in information technology; and the desire to avoid costly regulations have been major driving forces behind financial innovation. Financial innovation has caused banks to suffer declines in cost advantages in acquiring funds and in income advantages on their assets. The resulting squeeze has hurt profitability in banks' traditional lines of business and has led to a decline in traditional banking and to the rise of shadow banking.

3. Restrictive state branching regulations and the McFadden Act, which prohibited branching across state lines, led to a large number of small commercial banks. The large number of commercial banks in the United States reflects the past *lack* of competition, not the presence of vigorous competition. Bank holding companies and ATMs were important responses to branching restrictions that weakened the restrictions' anticompetitive effect.

4. Since the mid-1980s, bank consolidation has been occurring at a rapid pace. The first phase of bank consolidation was the result of bank failures and the reduced effectiveness of branching restrictions. The second phase was stimulated by enhanced information technology and the Riegle-Neal Interstate Banking and Branching Efficiency Act of 1994, which establishes the basis for a nationwide banking system. Once banking consolidation has settled down, we are likely to be left with a banking system with several thousand banks.

Most economists believe that the benefits of bank consolidation and nationwide banking will outweigh the costs.

5. The Glass-Steagall Act separated commercial banking from the securities industry. Legislation in 1999, however, repealed the Glass-Steagall Act, removing the separation of these industries.

6. The regulation and structure of the thrift industry (savings and loan associations, mutual savings banks, and credit unions) parallel closely the regulation and structure of the commercial banking industry. Savings and loans are primarily regulated by the Office of Thrift Supervision, and deposit insurance is administered by the FDIC. Mutual savings banks are regulated by the

states, and federal deposit insurance is provided by the FDIC. Credit unions are regulated by the National Credit Union Administration, and deposit insurance is provided by the National Credit Union Share Insurance Fund.

7. With the rapid growth of world trade since 1960, international banking has grown dramatically. U.S. banks engage in international banking activities by opening branches abroad, owning controlling interests in foreign banks, forming Edge Act corporations, and operating international banking facilities (IBFs) located in the United States. Foreign banks operate in the United States by owning a subsidiary American bank or by operating branches or agency offices in the United States.

KEY TERMS

automated teller machine (ATM), p. 241
bank holding companies, p. 238
branches, p. 241
central bank, p. 236
community banks, p. 255
deposit rate ceilings, p. 244
disintermediation, p. 244
dual banking system, p. 237
economies of scope, p. 253

Edge Act corporation, p. 262
financial derivatives, p. 240
financial engineering, p. 238
futures contracts, p. 240
hedge, p. 239
international banking facilities
   (IBFs), p. 262
national banks, p. 237

originate-to-distribute, p. 243
securitization, p. 242
shadow banking system, p. 238
state banks, p. 237
subprime mortgage, p. 243
superregional banks, p. 253
sweep account, p. 246
virtual bank, p. 241

QUESTIONS

1. Do you think that before the National Bank Act of 1863 the prevailing conditions in the banking industry fostered or hindered trade across states in the United States?

2. Why does the United States operate under a dual banking system?

3. In light of the recent financial crisis of 2007–2009, do you think that the firewall created by the Glass-Steagall Act of 1933 between commercial banking and the securities industry proved to be a good thing or not?

4. Which regulatory agency has the primary responsibility for supervising the following categories of commercial banks?

a. National banks
b. Bank holding companies
c. Non–Federal Reserve member state banks
d. Federal Reserve member state banks
e. Federally chartered savings and loan associations
f. Federally chartered credit unions

5. How does the emergence of interest-rate risk help explain financial innovation?

6. Why did new technology make it harder to enforce limitations on bank branching?

7. "The invention of the computer is the major factor behind the decline of the banking industry." Is

this statement true, false, or uncertain? Explain your answer.

8. "If inflation had not risen in the 1960s and 1970s, the banking industry might be healthier today." Is this statement true, false, or uncertain? Explain your answer.

9. How do sweep accounts and money market mutual funds allow banks to avoid reserve requirements?

10. If reserve requirements were eliminated in the future, as some economists advocate, what effects would this have on the size of money market mutual funds?

11. Why is loophole mining so prevalent in the banking industry in the United States?

12. Why have banks been losing cost advantages in acquiring funds in recent years?

13. Why have banks been losing income advantages on their assets in recent years?

14. "The commercial banking industry in Canada is less competitive than the commercial banking industry in the United States because in Canada only a few large banks dominate the industry, while in the United States there are around 4,500 banks." Is this statement true, false, or uncertain? Explain your answer.

15. Why is there a higher percentage of banks with less than $25 million of assets among commercial banks than among savings and loans and mutual savings banks?

16. Unlike commercial banks, savings and loans, and mutual savings banks, credit unions did not have restrictions on setting up branches in other states. Why,

then, are credit unions typically smaller than the other depository institutions?

17. Why has the number of bank holding companies dramatically increased?

18. Given the role of the loan originator in the securitization process of a mortgage loan described in the text, do you think the loan originator will be worried about the ability of a household to meet its monthly mortgage payments?

19. How did competitive forces lead to the repeal of the Glass-Steagall Act's separation of the banking and securities industries?

20. What has been the likely effect of the Gramm-Leach-Bliley Act on financial consolidation?

21. What factors explain the rapid growth of international banking?

22. What incentives have regulatory agencies created to encourage international banking? Why have they done this?

23. How could the approval of international banking facilities (IBFs) by the Fed in 1981 have reduced employment in the banking industry in Europe?

24. If the bank at which you keep your checking account is owned by foreigners, should you worry that your deposits are less safe than if the bank were owned by Americans?

25. Why are there only two U.S. banks among the ten largest banks in the world?

DATA ANALYSIS PROBLEMS

The Problems update with real-time data in **MyLab Economics** and are available for practice or instructor assignment.

1. **Real-time Data Analysis** Go to the St. Louis Federal Reserve FRED database, and find data on the 30-year fixed rate average mortgage rate (MORTGAGE30US) and the 5/1-year adjustable-rate mortgage (MORTGAGE5US).

   a. What are the mortgage rates reported for the most recent week of data available?

   b. If the principal payment for a given month were $2,000, then what would be the inter-

est payment per month (using simple interest) for each of the mortgage types, using the most recent week of data?

   c. Over a one-year period, how much would the difference in interest payments between the two mortgage types amount to?

2. **Real-time Data Analysis** Go to the St. Louis Federal Reserve FRED database, and find data on the level of

money market mutual fund assets (MMMFFAQ027S). Download the data into a spreadsheet.

    a. When did assets start entering money market mutual funds? What was the total worth of assets in money market mutual funds at the end of 1970?

    b. For each decade period, calculate the total percentage change in assets from the beginning of the decade to the end of the decade: 1980:Q1–1990:Q1; 1990:Q1–2000:Q1; 2000:Q1–2010:Q1; 2010:Q1–2020:Q1.

For each decade period, divide the total percentage change by 10 to get the average yearly percentage increase. Which decade had the largest average yearly growth in money market mutual funds?

    c. Calculate the growth rate from the most recent quarter of data available to the same quarter a year prior. How does this growth rate compare to the highest average yearly growth rate for the decades from part (b)?

12 Financial Crises

Learning Objectives

12.1 Define the term *financial crisis.*

12.2 Identify the key features of the three stages of a financial crisis.

12.3 Describe the causes and consequences of the global financial crisis of 2007–2009.

12.4 Summarize the changes to financial regulation that occurred in response to the global financial crisis of 2007–2009.

12.5 Identify the gaps in current financial regulation and how those gaps may be addressed with future regulatory changes.

Preview

Financial crises are major disruptions in financial markets characterized by sharp declines in asset prices and firm failures. Beginning in August 2007, defaults in the subprime mortgage market (by borrowers with weak credit records) sent a shudder through the financial markets, leading to the worst financial crisis since the Great Depression. In congressional testimony, Alan Greenspan, former chairman of the Fed, described the financial crisis as a "once-in-a-century credit tsunami." Wall Street firms and commercial banks suffered hundreds of billions of dollars of losses. Households and businesses found they had to pay higher rates on their borrowings—and it was much harder to get credit. All over the world, stock markets crashed, with the U.S market falling by over 50% from its peak. Many financial firms, including commercial banks, investment banks, and insurance companies, went belly up. A recession began in December 2007, and by the fall of 2008, the economy was in a tailspin. The recession, which ended in June 2009, was the most severe since World War II and is now known as the "Great Recession."

Why did this global financial crisis occur? Why have financial crises been so prevalent throughout U.S. history, as well as in so many other countries, and what insights do they provide on the financial crisis from 2007 to 2009? Why are financial crises almost always followed by severe contractions in economic activity, as occurred during the Great Recession? We will examine these questions in this chapter by developing a framework with which to understand the dynamics of financial crises. Building on Chapter 8, we make use of agency theory, the economic analysis of the effects of asymmetric information (adverse selection and moral hazard) on financial markets, to see why financial crises occur and why they have such devastating effects on the economy. We then apply our analysis to explain the course of events that led to a number of past financial crises, including the global financial crisis from 2007 to 2009.[1]

12.1 WHAT IS A FINANCIAL CRISIS?

LO 12.1 Define the term *financial crisis.*

In Chapter 8, we saw that a well-functioning financial system solves asymmetric information problems (moral hazard and adverse selection) so that capital is allocated to its most productive uses. These asymmetric information problems, which act as a barrier

[1]An additional chapter, "Financial Crises in Emerging Market Economies," available in **MyLab Economics**, extends the analysis to financial crises in *emerging market economies*, economies in an early stage of market development that have opened up to the flow of goods, services, and capital from the rest of the world.

to efficient allocation of capital, are often described by economists as **financial frictions**. When financial frictions increase, financial markets are less capable of channeling funds efficiently from savers to households and firms with productive investment opportunities, with the result that economic activity declines. A **financial crisis** occurs when information flows in financial markets experience a particularly large disruption, with the result that financial frictions increase sharply and financial markets stop functioning. Then economic activity collapses.

12.2 DYNAMICS OF FINANCIAL CRISES

LO 12.2 Identify the key features of the three stages of a financial crisis.

As earth-shaking and headline-grabbing as the 2007–2009 financial crisis was, it was only one of a number of financial crises that have hit industrialized countries like the United States over the years. These experiences have helped economists uncover insights into present-day economic turmoil.

Financial crises in advanced economies have progressed in two and sometimes three stages. To understand how these crises have unfolded, refer to Figure 1, which traces the stages and sequence of events in financial crises in advanced economies.

Stage One: Initial Phase

Financial crises can begin in two ways: credit boom and bust, or a general increase in uncertainty caused by failures of major financial institutions.

Credit Boom and Bust The seeds of a financial crisis are often sown when an economy introduces new types of loans or other financial products, known as **financial innovation**, or when countries engage in **financial liberalization**, the elimination of restrictions on financial markets and institutions. In the long run, financial liberalization promotes financial development and encourages a well-run financial system that allocates capital efficiently. However, financial liberalization has a dark side: In the short run, it can prompt financial institutions to go on a lending spree, called a **credit boom**. Unfortunately, lenders may not have the expertise, or the incentives, to manage risk appropriately in these new lines of business. Even with proper management, credit booms eventually outstrip the ability of institutions—and government regulators—to screen and monitor credit risks, leading to overly risky lending.

As we learned in Chapter 10, government safety nets, such as deposit insurance, weaken market discipline and increase the moral hazard incentive for banks to take on greater risk than they otherwise would. Because lender-savers know that government-guaranteed insurance protects them from losses, they will supply even undisciplined banks with funds. Without proper monitoring, risk taking grows unchecked.

Eventually, losses on loans begin to mount, and the value of the loans (on the asset side of the balance sheet) falls relative to liabilities, thereby driving down the net worth (capital) of banks and other financial institutions. With less capital, these financial institutions cut back on their lending to borrower-spenders, a process called **deleveraging**. Furthermore, with less capital, banks and other financial institutions become riskier, causing lender-savers and other potential lenders to these institutions to pull out their funds. Fewer funds mean fewer loans to fund productive investments and a credit freeze: The lending boom turns into a lending crash.

Mini-lecture

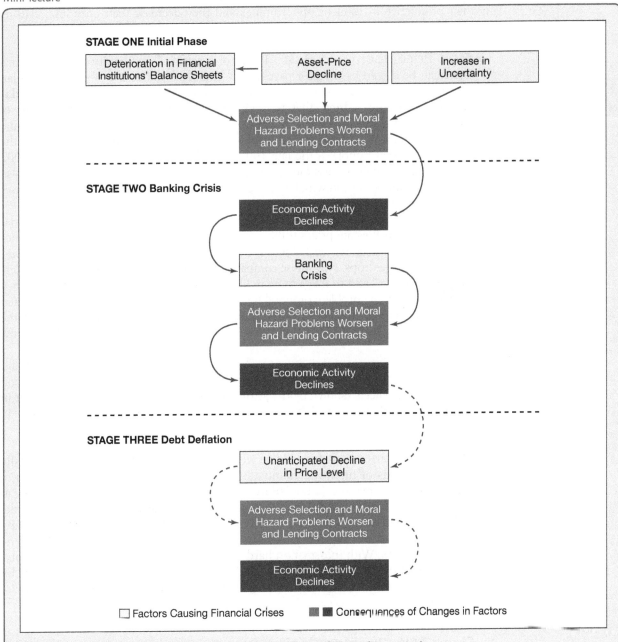

STAGE ONE Initial Phase

| Deterioration in Financial Institutions' Balance Sheets | ← | Asset-Price Decline | | Increase in Uncertainty |

Adverse Selection and Moral Hazard Problems Worsen and Lending Contracts

STAGE TWO Banking Crisis

Economic Activity Declines

Banking Crisis

Adverse Selection and Moral Hazard Problems Worsen and Lending Contracts

Economic Activity Declines

STAGE THREE Debt Deflation

Unanticipated Decline in Price Level

Adverse Selection and Moral Hazard Problems Worsen and Lending Contracts

Economic Activity Declines

☐ Factors Causing Financial Crises   ■ ■ Consequences of Changes in Factors

FIGURE 1 Sequence of Events in Financial Crises in Advanced Economies

The solid arrows trace the sequence of events during a typical financial crisis; the dotted arrows show the additional set of events that occurs if the crisis develops into a debt deflation. The sections separated by the dashed horizontal lines show the different stages of a financial crisis.

When financial institutions stop collecting information and making loans, financial frictions rise, limiting the financial system's ability to address the asymmetric information problems of adverse selection and moral hazard (as shown in the arrow pointing from the first factor, "Deterioration in Financial Institutions' Balance Sheets," in the top row of Figure 1). As loans become scarce, borrower-spenders are no longer able to fund their productive investment opportunities and they decrease their spending, causing economic activity to contract.

Asset-Price Boom and Bust

Prices of assets such as equity shares and real estate can be driven by investor psychology (dubbed "irrational exuberance" by Alan Greenspan when he was chairman of the Federal Reserve) well above their **fundamental economic values**, that is, their values based on realistic expectations of the assets' future income streams. The rise of asset prices above their fundamental economic values is an **asset-price bubble**. Examples of asset-price bubbles are the tech stock market bubble of the late 1990s and the housing price bubble from 2002 to 2006 that we will discuss later in this chapter. Asset-price bubbles are often also driven by credit booms, in which the large increase in credit is used to fund purchases of assets, thereby driving up their price.

When the bubble bursts and asset prices realign with fundamental economic values, stock and real estate prices tumble, companies see their net worth (the difference between their assets and their liabilities) decline, and the value of collateral these companies can pledge drops. Now these companies have less at stake because they have less "skin in the game," and so they are more likely to make risky investments because they have less to lose, the problem of moral hazard. As a result, financial institutions tighten lending standards for these borrower-spenders and lending contracts (as shown by the downward arrow pointing from the second factor, "Asset-Price Decline," in the top row of Figure 1).

The asset-price bust also causes a decline in the value of financial institutions' assets, thereby causing a decline in the institutions' net worth and hence a deterioration in their balance sheets (shown by the arrow from the second factor to the first factor in the top row of Figure 1), which causes them to deleverage, steepening the decline in economic activity.

Increase in Uncertainty

Financial crises in the United States have usually begun in periods of high uncertainty, such as just after the start of a recession, a crash in the stock market, or the failure of a major financial institution. Crises began after the failure of Ohio Life Insurance and Trust Company in 1857; the Jay Cooke and Company in 1873; Grant and Ward in 1884; the Knickerbocker Trust Company in 1907; the Bank of the United States in 1930; and Bear Stearns, Lehman Brothers, and AIG in 2008. With information hard to come by in a period of high uncertainty, financial frictions increase, reducing lending and economic activity (as shown by the arrow pointing from the last factor, "Increase in Uncertainty," in the top row of Figure 1).

Stage Two: Banking Crisis

Deteriorating balance sheets and tougher business conditions lead some financial institutions into insolvency, which happens when their net worth becomes negative. Unable to pay off depositors or other creditors, some banks go out of business. If severe enough, these factors can lead to a bank panic in which multiple banks fail simultaneously. The source of the contagion is asymmetric information. In a panic, depositors, fearing for the safety of their deposits (in the absence of or with limited amounts of deposit insurance) and not knowing the quality of banks' loan portfolios, withdraw their deposits to the point that the banks fail. Uncertainty about the health of the banking system in general can lead to runs on banks, both good and bad, which forces banks to sell off assets quickly to raise the necessary funds. These **fire sales** of assets may cause their prices to decline so much that more banks become insolvent and the resulting contagion can then lead to multiple bank failures and a full-fledged bank panic.

With fewer banks operating, information about the creditworthiness of borrower-spenders disappears. Increasingly severe adverse selection and moral hazard problems in financial markets deepen the financial crisis, causing declines in asset prices and the failure of firms throughout the economy that lack funds for productive investment opportunities. Figure 1 represents this progression in the stage two portion. Bank panics were a feature of all U.S. financial crises during the nineteenth and twentieth centuries, occurring every 20 years or so until World War II—1819, 1837, 1857, 1873, 1884, 1893, 1907, and 1930–1933. (The 1933 establishment of federal deposit insurance, which protects depositors from losses, has prevented subsequent bank panics in the United States.)

Eventually, public and private authorities shut down insolvent firms and sell them off or liquidate them. Uncertainty in financial markets declines, the stock market recovers, and balance sheets improve. Financial frictions diminish and the financial crisis subsides. With the financial markets able to operate well again, the stage is set for an economic recovery.

Stage Three: Debt Deflation

If, however, the economic downturn leads to a sharp decline in the price level, the recovery process can be short-circuited. In stage three of Figure 1, **debt deflation** occurs when a substantial unanticipated decline in the price level sets in, leading to a further deterioration in firms' net worth because of the increased burden of indebtedness.

In economies with moderate inflation, which characterizes most advanced countries, many debt contracts with fixed interest rates are typically of fairly long maturity, ten years or more. Because debt payments are contractually fixed in nominal terms, an unanticipated decline in the price level raises the value of borrowing firms' and households' liabilities in real terms (increases the burden of the debt) but does not raise the real value of their assets. The borrowers' net worth in real terms (the difference between assets and liabilities in real terms) thus declines.

To better understand how this decline in net worth occurs, consider what happens if a firm in 2022 has assets of $100 million (in 2022 dollars) and $90 million of long term liabilities, so that it has $10 million in net worth (the difference between the values of assets and liabilities). If the price level falls by 10% in 2023, the real value of the liabilities would rise to $99 million in 2022 dollars, while the real value of the assets would remain unchanged at $100 million. The result would be that real net worth in 2022 dollars would fall from $10 million to $1 million ($100 million minus $99 million).

The substantial decline in the real net worth of borrowers caused by a sharp drop in the price level creates an increase in adverse selection and moral hazard problems for lenders. Lending and economic activity decline for a long time. The most significant financial crisis that displayed debt deflation was the Great Depression, the worst economic contraction in U.S. history.

APPLICATION # The Mother of All Financial Crises: The Great Depression

With our framework for understanding financial crises in place, we are prepared to analyze how a financial crisis unfolded during the Great Depression and how it led to the worst economic downturn in U.S. history.

Stock Market Crash

In 1928 and 1929, U.S. stock prices doubled. Federal Reserve officials viewed the stock market boom as caused by excessive speculation. To curb it, they pursued a tightening of monetary policy to raise interest rates in an effort to limit the rise in stock prices. The Fed got more than it bargained for when the stock market crashed in October 1929, falling by 40% by the end of 1929, as shown in Figure 2.

Bank Panics

By the middle of 1930, stocks had recovered almost half of their losses and credit market conditions had stabilized. What might have been a normal recession turned into something far worse, however, when severe droughts in the Midwest led to a sharp decline in agricultural production, with the result that farmers could not pay back their bank loans. The resulting defaults on farm mortgages led to large loan losses on bank balance sheets in agricultural regions. The general weakness of the economy, and of the banks in agricultural regions in particular, prompted substantial withdrawals from banks, building to a full-fledged panic in November and December of 1930, with the stock market falling sharply. For more than two years, the Fed sat idly by through one bank panic after another, the most severe spate of panics in U.S. history. After what would be the era's final panic in March 1933, President Franklin Delano Roosevelt declared a bank

FIGURE 2

Stock Prices During the Great Depression Period

Stock prices crashed in 1929, falling by 40% by the end of 1929, and then continued to fall to only 10% of their peak value by 1932.
Source: Federal Reserve Bank of St. Louis FRED database: https://fred. stlouisfed.org/series/ M1109BUSM293NNBR.

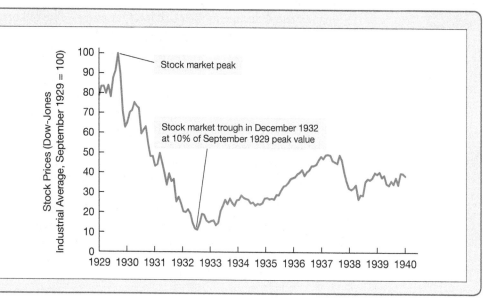

holiday, a temporary closing of all banks. "The only thing we have to fear is fear itself," Roosevelt told the nation. The damage was done, however, and more than one-third of U.S. commercial banks had failed.

Continuing Decline in Stock Prices

Stock prices kept falling. By mid-1932, stocks had declined to 10% of their value at the 1929 peak (as shown in Figure 2), and the increase in uncertainty from the unsettled business conditions created by the economic contraction worsened adverse selection and moral hazard problems in financial markets. With a greatly reduced number of financial intermediaries still in business, adverse selection and moral hazard problems intensified even further. Financial markets struggled to channel funds to borrower-spenders with productive investment opportunities. The amount of outstanding commercial loans fell by half from 1929 to 1933, and investment spending collapsed, declining by 90% from its 1929 level.

A manifestation of the rise in financial frictions is that lenders began charging businesses much higher interest rates to protect themselves from credit losses. The resulting rise in the **credit spread**—the difference between the interest rate on loans to households and businesses and the interest rate on completely safe assets that are sure to be paid back, such as U.S. Treasury securities—is shown in Figure 3, which displays the difference between interest rates on corporate bonds with a Baa (medium-quality) credit rating and rates on similar-maturity Treasury bonds. (Note the credit spread is closely related to the risk premium discussed in Chapter 6.)

Debt Deflation

The ongoing deflation that accompanied declining economic activity eventually led to a 25% decline in the price level. This deflation short-circuited the normal recovery process that occurs in most recessions. The huge decline in prices triggered a debt deflation in which real net worth fell because of the increased burden of indebtedness borne by firms and households. The decline in net worth and the resulting increase in adverse selection

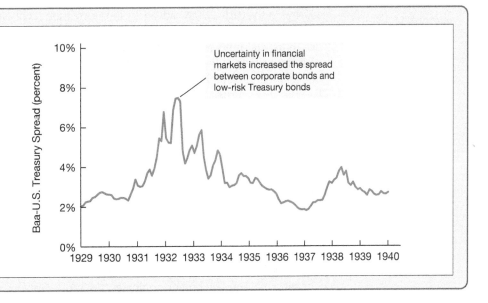

FIGURE 3

Credit Spreads During the Great Depression

Credit spreads (the difference between rates on Baa corporate bonds and U.S. Treasury bonds) rose sharply during the Great Depression.

Source: Banking and Monetary Statistics 1914-1941 (Board of Governors of the Federal Reserve, 1943)

and moral hazard problems in the credit markets led to a prolonged economic contraction in which unemployment rose to 25% of the labor force. The financial crisis of the Great Depression was the worst ever experienced in the United States, which explains why the economic contraction was also the most severe ever experienced by the nation.

International Dimensions

Although the Great Depression started in the United States, it was not just a U.S. phenomenon. Bank panics in the United States also spread to the rest of the world, and the contraction of the U.S. economy sharply decreased the demand for foreign goods. The worldwide depression caused great hardship, with millions upon millions of people out of work, and the resulting discontent led to the rise of fascism and World War II. The consequences of the Great Depression financial crisis were disastrous. ◆

12.3 THE GLOBAL FINANCIAL CRISIS OF 2007–2009

LO 12.3 Describe the causes and consequences of the global financial crisis of 2007–2009.

For many years, most economists thought that financial crises of the type experienced during the Great Depression were a thing of the past for advanced countries like the United States. Unfortunately, the financial crisis that engulfed the world in 2007–2009 proved them wrong.

Causes of the 2007–2009 Financial Crisis

We begin our look at the 2007–2009 financial crisis by examining three central factors: financial innovation in mortgage markets, agency problems in mortgage markets, and the role of asymmetric information in the credit-rating process.

Financial Innovation in the Mortgage Markets   As we saw in Chapter 11, starting in the early 2000s, advances in information technology made it easier to securitize subprime mortgages, leading to an explosion in subprime mortgage-backed securities. Financial innovation didn't stop there. Financial engineering, the development of new, sophisticated financial instruments, led to **structured credit products** that paid out income streams from a collection of underlying assets, designed to have particular risk characteristics that appealed to investors with differing preferences. The most notorious of these products were collateralized debt obligations (CDOs) (discussed in the FYI box "Collateralized Debt Obligations (CDOs)").

Agency Problems in the Mortgage Markets   The mortgage brokers who originated the mortgage loans often did not make a strong effort to evaluate whether a borrower could pay off the mortgage, since they planned to quickly sell (distribute) the loans to investors in the form of mortgage-backed securities. This originate-to-distribute business model was exposed to the principal–agent problem of the type discussed in Chapter 8, in which the mortgage brokers acted as agents for investors (the principals) but did not have the investors' best interests at heart. Once the mortgage broker earns his or her fee, why should the broker care if the borrower makes good on the payment? The more volume the broker originates, the more money the broker makes.

FYI Collateralized Debt Obligations (CDOs)

The creation of a collateralized debt obligation involves a corporate entity called a *special purpose vehicle (SPV)*, which buys a collection of assets such as corporate bonds and loans, commercial real estate bonds, and mortgage-backed securities. The SPV then separates the payment streams (cash flows) from these assets into a number of buckets that are referred to as *tranches*. The highest-rated tranches, called *super senior tranches*, are the ones that are paid off first and so have the least risk. The super senior CDO is a bond that pays out these cash flows to investors, and because it has the least risk, it also has the lowest interest rate. The next bucket of cash flows, known as the *senior tranche*, is paid out next; the senior CDO has a little more risk and pays a higher interest rate. The next tranche of payment streams, the *mezzanine tranche* of the CDO, is paid out after the super senior and senior tranches and so it bears more risk and has an even higher interest rate. The lowest tranche of the CDO is the *equity tranche*; this is the first set of cash flows that are not paid out if the underlying assets go

into default and stop making payments. This tranche has the highest risk and is often not traded.

If all of this sounds complicated, it is. Tranches also included CDO^2s and CDO^3s that sliced and diced risk even further, paying out the cash flows from CDOs to CDO^2s and from CDO^2s to CDO^3s. Although financial engineering carries the potential benefit of creating products and services that match investors' risk appetites, it also has a dark side. Structured products like CDOs, CDO^2s, and CDO^3s can get so complicated that it becomes hard to value the cash flows of the underlying assets for a security or to determine who actually owns these assets. Indeed, in October 2007, Ben Bernanke, then chairman of the Federal Reserve, joked that he "would like to know what those damn things are worth." In other words, the increased complexity of structured products can actually reduce the amount of information in financial markets, thereby worsening asymmetric information in the financial system and increasing the severity of adverse selection and moral hazard problems.

Not surprisingly, adverse selection became a major problem. Risk-loving real-estate investors lined up to obtain loans to acquire houses that would be very profitable if housing prices went up, knowing they could "walk away" if housing prices went down. The principal–agent problem also created incentives for mortgage brokers to encourage households to take on mortgages they could not afford or to commit fraud by falsifying information on borrowers' mortgage applications in order to qualify them for mortgages. Compounding this problem was lax regulation of originators, who were not required to disclose information to borrowers that would have helped them assess whether they could afford the loans.

The agency problems went even deeper. Commercial and investment banks, which were earning large fees by underwriting mortgage-backed securities and structured credit products like CDOs, also had weak incentives to make sure that the ultimate holders of the securities would be paid off. **Financial derivatives**, financial instruments whose payoffs are linked to (i.e., derived from) previously issued securities, also were an important source of excessive risk taking. Large fees from writing a type of financial insurance contract called a **credit default swap**, a financial derivative that provides payments to holders of bonds if they default, also drove units of insurance companies like AIG to write hundreds of billions of dollars' worth of these risky contracts.

Asymmetric Information and Credit-Rating Agencies   Credit-rating agencies, who rate the quality of debt securities in terms of the probability of default, were another contributor to asymmetric information in financial markets. The rating agencies advised clients on how to structure complex financial instruments, like CDOs, while at the same time they were rating these identical products. The rating agencies were thus subject to conflicts of interest because the large fees they earned from advising clients on how to structure products that they themselves were rating meant that they did not have sufficient incentives to make sure their ratings were accurate. The result was wildly inflated ratings that enabled the sale of complex financial products that were far riskier than investors recognized.

Effects of the 2007–2009 Financial Crisis

Consumers and businesses alike suffered as a result of the 2007–2009 financial crisis. The impact of the crisis was most evident in five key areas: the U.S. residential housing market, financial institutions' balance sheets, the shadow banking system, global financial markets, and the headline-grabbing failures of major firms in the financial industry.

Residential Housing Prices: Boom and Bust   The subprime mortgage market took off after the recession ended in 2001. By 2007, it had become over a trillion-dollar market. The development of the subprime mortgage market was encouraged by economists and politicians alike because it led to a "democratization of credit" and helped raise U.S. homeownership rates to the highest levels in history. The asset-price boom in housing (see Figure 4), which took off after the 2000–2001 recession was over, also

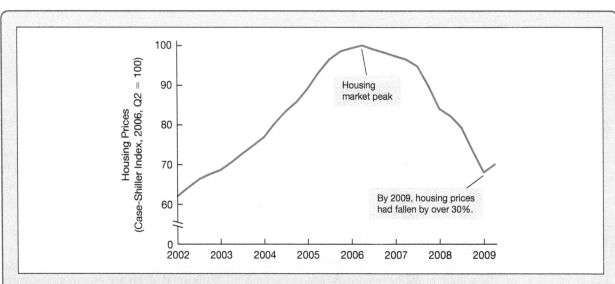

FIGURE 4   **Housing Prices and the Financial Crisis of 2007–2009**

Housing prices boomed from 2002 to 2006, fueling the market for subprime mortgages and forming an asset-price bubble. Housing prices began declining in 2006, falling by more than 30% subsequently, which led to defaults by subprime mortgage holders.

Source: Case-Shiller U.S. National Composite House Price Index from Federal Reserve Bank of St. Louis FRED database: https://fred.stlouisfed.org/series/SPCS20RSA.

Inside the Fed   Was the Fed to Blame for the Housing Price Bubble?

Some economists—most prominently, John Taylor of Stanford University—have argued that the low interest rate policy of the Federal Reserve in the 2003–2006 period caused the housing price bubble.[*] Taylor argues that the low federal funds rate led to low mortgage rates that stimulated housing demand and encouraged the issuance of subprime mortgages, both of which led to rising housing prices and a bubble.

In a speech given in January 2010, then-Federal Reserve Chairman Ben Bernanke countered this argument.[†] He concluded that monetary policy was not to blame for the housing price bubble. First, he said, it is not at all clear that the federal funds rate was too low during the 2003–2006 period. Rather,

the culprits were the proliferation of new mortgage products that lowered mortgage payments, a relaxation of lending standards that brought more buyers into the housing market, and capital inflows from countries such as China and India. Bernanke's speech was very controversial, and the debate over whether monetary policy was to blame for the housing price bubble continues to this day.

[*]John Taylor, "Housing and Monetary Policy," in Federal Reserve Bank of Kansas City, *Housing, Housing Finance and Monetary Policy* (Kansas City: Federal Reserve Bank of Kansas City, 2007), 463–476.

[†]Ben S. Bernanke, "Monetary Policy and the Housing Bubble," speech given at the annual meeting of the American Economic Association, Atlanta, Georgia, January 3, 2010; http://www.federalreserve.gov/newsevents/speech/bernanke20100103a.htm.

helped stimulate the growth of the subprime mortgage market. High housing prices meant that subprime borrowers could refinance their houses with even larger loans when their homes appreciated in value. With housing prices rising, subprime borrowers were also unlikely to default because they could always sell their house to pay off the loan, making investors happy because the securities backed by cash flows from subprime mortgages had high returns. The growth of the subprime mortgage market, in turn, increased the demand for houses and so fueled the boom in housing prices, resulting in a housing-price bubble.

Further stimulus for the inflated housing market came from low interest rates on residential mortgages, which were the result of several different forces. First were the huge capital inflows into the United States from countries like China and India. Second was congressional legislation that encouraged Fannie Mae and Freddie Mac to purchase trillions of dollars of mortgage-backed securities.[2] Third was Federal Reserve monetary policy that made it easy to lower interest rates. The low cost of financing for housing purchases that resulted from these forces further stimulated the demand for housing, pushing up housing prices. (A highly controversial issue is whether the Federal Reserve was to blame for the housing price bubble, and this is discussed in the Inside the Fed box.)

As housing prices rose and profitability for mortgage originators and lenders grew higher, the underwriting standards for subprime mortgages fell lower and lower. High-risk borrowers were able to obtain mortgages, and the amount of the mortgage relative to the value of the house, the loan-to-value ratio (LTV), rose. Borrowers were often able to get piggyback, second, and third mortgages on top of their original 80% loan-to-value mortgage so that they had to put almost no money down. When asset prices rise too far

[2]For a discussion of the government's role in encouraging the housing boom, which led to a subsequent bust in the housing market, see Thomas Sowell, *The Housing Boom and Bust*, rev. ed. (New York: Basic Books, 2010).

out of line with fundamentals—in the case of housing, the cost of purchasing a home relative to the cost of renting it, or the cost of houses relative to households' median income—they must come down. Eventually, the housing price bubble burst. With housing prices falling after their peak in 2006 (see Figure 4), the rot in the financial system began to reveal itself. The decline in housing prices led many subprime borrowers to find that their mortgages were "underwater"—that is, the value of the house was below the amount of the mortgage. When this happened, struggling homeowners had tremendous incentives to walk away from their homes and just send the keys back to the lender. Defaults on mortgages shot up sharply, eventually leading to foreclosures on millions of mortgages.

Deterioration of Financial Institutions' Balance Sheets
The decline in U.S. housing prices led to rising defaults on mortgages. As a result, the values of mortgage-backed securities and CDOs collapsed, leaving banks and other financial institutions holding those securities with a lower value of assets and thus a lower net worth. With weakened balance sheets, these banks and other financial institutions began to deleverage, selling off assets and restricting the availability of credit to both households and businesses. With no one else able to step in to collect information and make loans, the reduction in bank lending meant that financial frictions increased in financial markets.

Run on the Shadow Banking System
The sharp decline in the values of mortgages and other financial assets triggered a run on the shadow banking system, composed of hedge funds, investment banks, and other nondepository financial firms, which are not as tightly regulated as banks. Funds from shadow banks flowed through the financial system and for many years supported the issuance of low-interest-rate mortgages and auto loans.

These securities were funded primarily by **repurchase agreements (repos)**, short-term borrowing that, in effect, uses assets like mortgage-backed securities as collateral. Rising concern about the quality of a financial institution's balance sheet led lenders to require larger amounts of collateral, known as **haircuts**. For example, if a borrower took out a $100 million loan in a repo agreement, the borrower might have to post $105 million of mortgage-backed securities as collateral, for a haircut of 5%.

Rising defaults on mortgages caused the values of mortgage-backed securities to fall, which then led to a rise in haircuts. At the start of the crisis, haircuts were close to zero, but eventually they rose to nearly 50%.[3] The result was that financial institutions could borrow only half as much with the same amount of collateral. Thus, to raise funds, financial institutions had to engage in fire sales and sell off their assets very rapidly. Because selling assets quickly requires lowering their price, the fire sales led to a further decline in financial institutions' asset values. This decline lowered the value of collateral further, raising haircuts and thereby forcing financial institutions to scramble even more for liquidity. The result was similar to the run on the banking system that occurred during the Great Depression, causing massive deleveraging that resulted in a restriction of lending and a decline in economic activity.

The decline in asset prices in the stock market (which fell by over 50% from October 2007 to March 2009, as shown in Figure 5) and the more than 30% drop in residential house prices (shown in Figure 4), along with the fire sales resulting from the run on the shadow banking system, weakened both firms' and households' balance sheets. This worsening of financial frictions manifested itself in widening credit spreads, causing higher costs of credit for households and businesses and tighter lending standards.

---

[3]See Gary Gorton and Andrew Metrick, "Securitized Banking and the Run on Repo," *Journal of Financial Economics* 104, no. 3 (2012): 425–51.

FIGURE 5

Stock Prices and the Financial Crisis of 2007–2009

Stock prices fell by 50% from October 2007 to March 2009. *Source:* Federal Reserve Bank of St. Louis FRED database, https://fred. stlouisfed.org/series/DJIA.

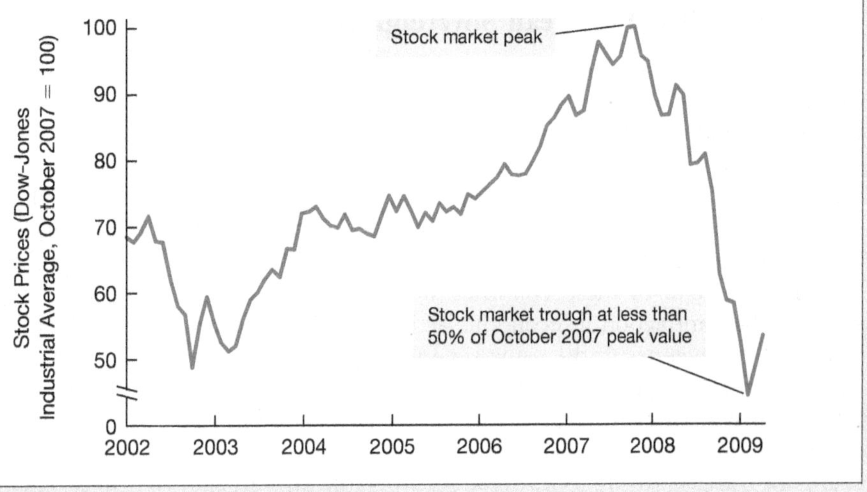

The resulting decline in lending meant that both consumption expenditure and investment fell, causing the economy to contract.[4]

Global Financial Markets   Although the problem originated in the United States, the wake-up call for the financial crisis came from Europe, a sign of how extensive the globalization of financial markets had become. After Fitch and Standard & Poor's announced ratings downgrades on mortgage-backed securities and CDOs totaling more than $10 billion, on August 7, 2007, a French investment house, BNP Paribas, suspended redemption of shares held in some of its money market funds, which had sustained large losses. The run on the shadow banking system began, only to become worse and worse over time. Despite huge injections of liquidity into the financial system by the European Central Bank and the Federal Reserve, banks began to horde cash and were unwilling to lend to each other. The drying up of credit led to the first major bank failure in the United Kingdom in over 100 years when Northern Rock, which had relied on short-term borrowing in the repo market rather than deposits for its funding, collapsed in September 2007. A string of other European financial institutions then failed as well. Particularly hard hit were countries like Greece, Ireland, Portugal, and Spain. The resulting crisis in markets for government-issued (sovereign) debt in Europe is described in the Global box, "The European Sovereign Debt Crisis."

Failure of High-Profile Firms   The impact of the financial crisis on firms' balance sheets forced major players in the financial markets to take drastic action. In March 2008, Bear Stearns, the fifth-largest investment bank in the United States, which had invested heavily in subprime-related securities, had a run on its repo funding and was forced to sell itself to J.P. Morgan for less than one-tenth of its worth just a year earlier. To broker the deal, the Federal Reserve had to take over $30 billion of Bear Stearns's

---

[4]This period was also characterized by a substantial supply shock that occurred when oil and other commodity prices rose sharply until the summer of 2008, but then fell precipitously thereafter. We discuss the aggregate demand and supply analysis of the impact of this supply shock in Chapter 22.

Global The European Sovereign Debt Crisis

The global financial crisis of 2007–2009 led not only to a worldwide recession but also to a sovereign debt crisis that still threatens to destabilize Europe today. Up until 2007, all of the countries that had adopted the euro found their interest rates converging to very low levels, but with the onset of the global financial crisis, several of these countries were hit very hard by the contraction in economic activity, which reduced tax revenues at the same time that government bailouts of failed financial institutions required additional government outlays. The resulting surge in budget deficits then led to fears that the governments of these hard-hit countries would default on their debt. The result was a surge in interest rates that threatened to spiral out of control.*

Greece was the first domino to fall in Europe. In September 2009, with an economy weakened by reduced tax revenues and increased spending demands, the Greek government was projecting a budget deficit for the year of 6% and a debt-to-GDP ratio near 100%. However, when a new government was elected in October, it revealed that the budget situation was far worse than anyone had imagined, because the previous government had provided misleading numbers about both the budget deficit, which was at least double the 6% number, and the amount of government debt, which was 10 percentage points higher than previously reported. Despite

austerity measures aimed at dramatically cutting government spending and raising taxes, interest rates on Greek debt soared, eventually rising to nearly 40%, and the debt-to-GDP ratio climbed to 160% of GDP in 2012. Even with bailouts from other European countries and liquidity support from the European Central Bank, Greece was forced to write down the value of its debt held in private hands by more than half, and the country was subject to civil unrest, with massive strikes and the resignation of the prime minister.

The sovereign debt crisis spread from Greece to Ireland, Portugal, Spain, and Italy. The governments of these countries were forced to embrace austerity measures to shore up their public finances while interest rates climbed to double-digit levels. Only with a speech in July 2012 by Mario Draghi, the president of the European Central Bank, in which he stated that the ECB was ready to do "whatever it takes" to save the euro, did the markets begin to calm down. Nonetheless, despite a sharp decline in interest rates in these countries, they experienced severe recessions, with unemployment rates rising to double-digit levels and Spain's unemployment rate exceeding 25%. The stresses that the European sovereign debt crisis produced for the euro zone, the countries that have adopted the euro, has raised doubts about whether the euro will survive.

*For a discussion of the dynamics of sovereign debt crises and case studies of the European debt crisis, see David Greenlaw, James D. Hamilton, Frederic S. Mishkin, and Peter Hooper, "Crunch Time: Fiscal Crises and the Role of Monetary Policy," *U.S. Monetary Policy Forum* (Chicago: Chicago Booth Initiative on Global Markets, 2013).

hard-to-value assets. In July, Fannie Mae and Freddie Mac, the two privately owned, government-sponsored enterprises that together insured over $5 trillion of mortgages or mortgage-backed assets, were propped up by the U.S. Treasury and the Federal Reserve after suffering substantial losses from their holdings of subprime securities. In early September 2008, Fannie Mae and Freddy Mac were put into conservatorship (in effect, run by the government).

On Monday, September 15, 2008, after suffering losses in the subprime market, Lehman Brothers, the fourth-largest investment bank by asset size with over $600 billion in assets and 25,000 employees, filed for bankruptcy, making it the largest bankruptcy filing in U.S. history. The day before, Merrill Lynch, the third largest investment bank, which had also suffered large losses on its holdings of subprime securities, announced its sale to Bank of America for a price 60% below its value a year earlier. On

Tuesday, September 16, AIG, an insurance giant with assets of over $1 trillion, suffered an extreme liquidity crisis when its credit rating was downgraded. It had written over $400 billion of insurance contracts (credit default swaps) that had to make payouts on possible losses from subprime mortgage securities. The Federal Reserve then stepped in with an $85 billion loan to keep AIG afloat (with total government loans later increased to $173 billion).

Height of the 2007–2009 Financial Crisis

The financial crisis reached its peak in September 2008 after the House of Representatives, fearing the wrath of constituents who were angry about the Wall Street bailout, voted down a $700 billion dollar bailout package proposed by the Bush administration. The Emergency Economic Stabilization Act was finally passed nearly a week later. The stock market crash accelerated, with the week beginning October 6, 2008, showing the worst weekly decline in U.S. history. Credit spreads went through the roof over the next three weeks, with the spread between Baa corporate bonds (just above investment grade) and U.S. Treasury bonds going to over 5.5 percentage points (550 basis points), as illustrated by Figure 6.

The impaired financial markets and surging interest rates faced by borrower-spenders led to sharp declines in consumer spending and investment. Real GDP declined sharply, falling at a −1.3% annual rate in the third quarter of 2008 and then at a −5.4% and −6.4% annual rate in the next two quarters. The unemployment rate shot up, going over the 10% level in late 2009. The recession that started in December 2007 became the worst economic contraction in the United States since World War II and, as a result, is now referred to as the "Great Recession."

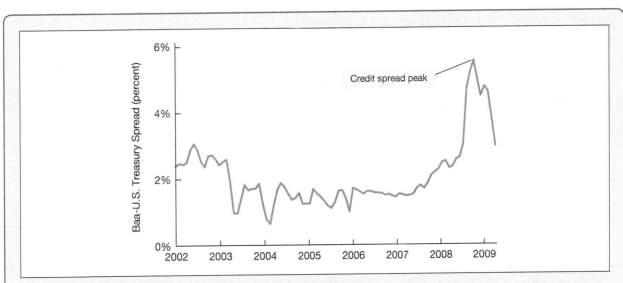

FIGURE 6   **Credit Spreads and the 2007–2009 Financial Crisis**

Credit spreads (the difference between rates on Baa corporate bonds and U.S. Treasury bonds) rose by more than 4 percentage points (400 basis points) during the crisis. Debate over the bailout package and the stock market crash caused credit spreads to peak in December 2008.

Source: Federal Reserve Bank of St. Louis FRED database: https://fred.stlouisfed.org/series/BAA10Y.

Government Intervention and the Recovery

Although the recession produced by the global financial crisis was very severe, the economic contraction was far smaller in magnitude than during the Great Depression because of massive interventions by governments to prop up financial markets and stimulate the economy.

As we will see in Chapter 15, the Federal Reserve took extraordinary actions to contain the crisis, actions involving both monetary policy to stimulate the economy and liquidity provision to support orderly functioning of financial markets. In addition, the U.S. government engaged in massive bailouts, with over $150 billion of loans to AIG and the **Troubled Asset Relief Program (TARP)**, the most important provision of the Bush administration's Emergency Economic Stabilization Act passed in October 2008, which authorized the Treasury to spend $700 billion purchasing subprime mortgage assets from troubled financial institutions or to inject capital into these institutions—the route actually followed. In addition, the act raised the federal deposit insurance limit temporarily from $100,000 to $250,000 in order to limit withdrawals from banks. Shortly thereafter, the FDIC put in place a guarantee for certain debt newly issued by banks, and the Treasury guaranteed for a year money market mutual fund shares at par value. Similarly, European governments conducted massive bailouts, in excess of $10 trillion, to prop up their banking systems (see the Global box "Worldwide Government Bailouts During the 2007–2009 Financial Crisis").

Fiscal policy aimed at stimulating the economy was another key piece of the U.S. government's response to the crisis. In February 2008, Congress passed the Bush administration's Economic Stimulus Act of 2008, whereby the government gave out one-time tax rebates totaling $78 billion by sending $600 checks to individual taxpayers. Shortly after coming to office, the Obama administration proposed the American Recovery and Reinvestment Act of 2009, a much bigger, $787 billion fiscal stimulus package passed by Congress that to this day is highly controversial. This stimulus package is discussed more extensively in Part 6 of the book.

Global   Worldwide Government Bailouts During the 2007–2009 Financial Crisis

The spreading bank failures in Europe in the fall of 2008 led to massive bailouts of financial institutions: The Netherlands, Belgium, and Luxembourg injected $16 billion to prop up Fortis, a major European bank; the Netherlands injected $13 billion into ING, a banking and insurance giant; Germany provided a $50 billion rescue package for Hypo Real Estate Holdings; and Iceland took over its three largest banks after its banking system collapsed. Ireland's government guaranteed all the deposits of its commercial banks as well as interbank lending, as did Greece. Spain implemented a bailout package similar to that of the United States, in which it bought up to 50 billion euros ($70 billion) of assets in its banks in order to encourage them to lend. The U.K. Treasury set up a bailout plan similar to that of the U.S. Treasury's plan with a price tag of 400 billion pounds ($699 billion). It guaranteed 250 billion pounds of bank liabilities, added 100 billion pounds to a facility that swaps these assets for government bonds, and allowed the U.K. government to buy up to 50 billion pounds of equity stakes in British banks. Bailout plans to the tune of over $100 billion in South Korea, $200 billion in Sweden, $400 billion in France, and $500 billion in Germany, all of which guaranteed the debt of their banks as well as the injection of capital into them, then followed. Both the scale of these bailout packages and the degree of international coordination was unprecedented.

With the government bailouts, the Fed's extraordinary actions, and fiscal stimulus, a bull market in stocks got under way starting in March 2009 (see Figure 5), and credit spreads began to fall (Figure 6). With the recovery of financial markets, the economy also started to recover, but unfortunately the pace of recovery has been slow.

APPLICATION   ## Could the Coronavirus Pandemic Have Led to a Financial Crisis?

The coronavirus pandemic in 2020 had the potential to trigger a financial crisis as serious as the 2007–2009 global financial crisis. With the start of the lockdown of the U.S. economy in March 2020, the stock market crashed, falling by more than a third, unemployment skyrocketed, and many otherwise healthy firms now faced the prospect of being unable to pay their bills or pay back their loans. The framework we laid out in our discussion of Figure 1 can be used to analyze how the coronavirus pandemic provided the seeds for another financial crisis, 12 years after the previous one, and why it didn't become the next financial crisis.

All the factors that potentially lead to a financial crisis, shown in the first row of Figure 1, came into play when the pandemic became severe in March 2020. The lockdown dealt a serious blow to the income of both businesses and households, making it more likely that they would be unable to pay back their loans. A severe deterioration in financial institutions balance sheets thus became a real possibility, which could have led to severe restrictions on lending. The stock market crash resulted in more than a 35% decline in stock prices, and the sharp decline in income of a multitude of businesses produced a sharp drop in the net worth of firms, which would increase both adverse selection and moral hazard. The high degree of uncertainty about the spread of the virus and how long it would disrupt the economy increased the asymmetry of information, making it harder to assess credit risks.

The seeds of a financial crisis were then planted, and indeed, credit spreads, such as the Baa-Treasury spread doubled, shooting up from 2 percentage points in February to a peak of 4.3 percentage points on March 23, 2020. Although the coronavirus pandemic had the potential to trigger a full-fledged financial crisis in the United States, this did not occur. The reason was the massive response by both the U.S. federal government and the Federal Reserve. Both the Federal Reserve and the federal government reacted with unprecedented speed once the World Health Organization (WHO) announced that the spread of the coronavirus could now be classified as a pandemic on March 11, 2020. On March 15, the Federal Reserve not only slashed its policy rate (federal funds rate) to zero but also embarked on large-scale programs to stabilize the financial markets (see Chapter 15). After earlier legislation to provide money for public health measures, on March 27, the Congress passed the largest rescue package in U.S. history, the CARES (Coronavirus Aid, Relief, and Economic Security) Act. This massive $2 trillion package provided loans and grants to small businesses and large corporations, aid to state governments, increases in unemployment insurance, and direct payments of $1,200 to most taxpayers, with an additional $500 per child.

The coronavirus pandemic had the potential to unleash another financial crisis, with disastrous effects on the U.S. economy. However, the combination of Federal Reserve and U.S. government policies helped shore up businesses, and the Baa-Treasury spread began to decline. As of this writing, the impact of the coronavirus pandemic on the U.S. economy is still uncertain, but the likelihood of a financial crisis has decreased substantially. ◆

12.4 RESPONSE OF FINANCIAL REGULATION

LO 12.4 Summarize the changes to financial regulation that occurred in response to the global financial crisis of 2007–2009.

Given the cost to the economy of the 2007–2009 financial crisis, the size of the bailouts, and the nationalization of so many financial institutions, the system of financial regulation is currently undergoing dramatic changes.

Macroprudential Versus Microprudential Supervision

Before the global financial crisis, regulatory authorities engaged in **microprudential supervision**, which focuses on the safety and soundness of *individual* financial institutions. Microprudential supervision looks at each individual institution separately and assesses the riskiness of its activities and whether it complies with disclosure requirements. Most importantly, microprudential supervision checks whether a particular institution satisfies capital *ratios* and, if it does not, either engages in prompt corrective action to force the institution to raise its capital ratios or the supervisor closes it down, along the lines we have discussed in Chapter 10.

A focus on microprudential supervision is not enough to prevent financial crises. The run on the shadow banking system illustrates how the problems of one financial institution can harm other financial institutions that are otherwise healthy. When the troubled financial institution is forced to engage in fire sales and sell off assets in order to meet target capital ratios or haircut requirements, this leads to a decline in asset values. The decline in asset values then causes other institutions to engage in fire sales, leading to a rapid deleveraging process and a systemic crisis. In situations like this, even institutions that have high capital ratios and would normally be healthy may find themselves in trouble.

The global financial crisis has therefore made it clear that there is a need for **macroprudential supervision**, which focuses on the safety and soundness of the financial system *in the aggregate*. Rather than focusing on the safety and soundness of individual institutions, macroprudential supervision seeks to mitigate systemwide fire sales and deleveraging by assessing the overall capacity of the financial system to avoid them. In addition, because many institutions that were well capitalized faced liquidity shortages and found that their access to short-term funding was cut off, macroprudential supervision focuses not only on capital adequacy as a whole but also on whether the financial system has sufficient liquidity.

Macroprudential policies can take several forms. The run-up to the global financial crisis included a so-called **leverage cycle**, in which a feedback loop resulted from a boom in issuing credit, which led to higher asset prices, which resulted in higher capital buffers at financial institutions, which supported further lending in the context of unchanging capital requirements, which then raised asset prices further, and so on; in the bust, the opposite occurs, with the value of the capital dropping precipitously, leading to a cut in lending. To short-circuit this leverage cycle, macroprudential policies make capital requirements countercyclical; that is, they are adjusted upward during a boom and downward during a bust.

In addition, during the upward swing in the leverage cycle, macroprudential policies might involve forcing financial institutions to tighten credit standards or even direct limits on the growth of credit. In the downward swing, macroprudential supervision might be needed to force the banking system as a whole to raise an aggregate amount of new capital so that banks will not curtail lending in order to reduce the level of their assets and raise capital ratios. To ensure that financial institutions have enough liquidity, macroprudential policies could require that financial institutions have a sufficiently low *net stable funding ratio* (NSFR), which is the percentage of the institution's short-term funding in relation to total funding. Macroprudential policies of the type discussed here are being considered as part of the Basel 3 framework but have not yet been completely worked out.

Dodd-Frank Wall Street Reform and Consumer Protection Act of 2010

The global financial crisis raised calls for a new regulatory structure that would make a repeat of the crisis less likely. The result was the Dodd-Frank bill, which was passed in July 2010 after more than a year of discussion. It is the most comprehensive financial reform legislation since the Great Depression. The bill addresses seven different categories of regulation, which are discussed next.

Consumer Protection   Dodd-Frank created a new Consumer Financial Protection Bureau that is funded and housed within the Federal Reserve, although it is a completely independent agency. It has the authority to examine and enforce regulations on all businesses with more than $10 billion in assets that are engaged in issuing residential mortgage products, as well as on issuers of other financial products marketed to low-income people. The legislation requires lenders to make sure borrowers can repay residential mortgages by requiring verification of their income, credit history, and job status. It also bans payments to brokers for pushing borrowers into higher-priced loans. It allows states to impose stricter consumer protection laws on national banks and gives state attorneys general the power to enforce certain rules issued by the new bureau. It also permanently increased the level of federal deposit insurance to $250,000.

Annual Stress Tests   Dodd-Frank requires that banks with assets of more than $10 billion be subject every year to **stress tests**, a supervisory assessment of whether banks have sufficient bank capital if they are faced with a scenario of bad macroeconomic outcomes, such as a collapse in housing prices or a severe recession. Not only are the results of these stress tests published every year but if a bank "fails" the stress test and is found to have insufficient capital, it also has to restrict the amount of dividends it pays out and come up with a plan to raise new capital to eliminate this deficiency.

Stress tests were first conducted for 19 banks at the height of the financial crisis in the first half of 2009. When the results were announced in May 2009, they were well received by market participants, enabling these banks to raise substantial amounts of capital from private capital markets. The stress tests were a key factor that helped increase the amount of information in the marketplace, thereby reducing asymmetric information and adverse selection and moral hazard problems. Their success led to Dodd-Frank making them a regular exercise on an annual basis.

Resolution Authority   Before the new legislation was passed, the FDIC had the authority to seize failing banks and wind them down, but it did not have such resolution authority over the largest financial institutions—those structured as holding companies. Indeed, the U.S. Treasury and the Federal Reserve argued that one reason they were unable to rescue Lehman Brothers, and instead had to let it go into bankruptcy, was that they did not have the legal means with which to take over Lehman and break it up. The Dodd-Frank bill now provides the U.S. government this resolution authority, called the Orderly Liquidation Authority, for financial firms that are deemed systemic—that is, firms that pose a risk to the overall health of the financial system because their failure would cause widespread economic damage. It also gives regulators the right to levy fees on financial institutions with more than $50 billion in assets to recoup any losses.

Limits on Federal Reserve Lending   As we have seen, during the financial crisis, the Federal Reserve made loans to individual firms such as Bear Stearns and AIG under an emergency lending authority. Because of concerns that this Fed lending to individual firms entailed a bailout that would encourage firms to take on excessive risk in the future, the Dodd-Frank bill directed the Federal Reserve to limit emergency lending to "broad-based" programs rather than to individual firms, and also required the Fed to get approval from the U.S. Treasury Department to make use of its emergency lending authority.

Systemic Risk Regulation   The Dodd-Frank bill created a Financial Stability Oversight Council, chaired by the Treasury secretary, that monitors markets for asset-price bubbles and the buildup of systemic risk. In addition, it designates which financial firms are systemically important and so receive the official designation of **systemically important financial institutions (SIFIs)**. These firms are subject to additional regulation by the Federal Reserve, which includes higher capital standards and stricter liquidity requirements, along with the requirement that such firms draw up a "living will," that is, a plan for orderly liquidation if the firm gets into financial difficulties.

Volcker Rule   Under the new legislation, banks are limited in the extent of their proprietary trading—that is, trading with their own money—and are allowed to own only a small percentage of hedge and private equity funds. These provisions are named after Paul Volcker, a former chairman of the Board of Governors of the Federal Reserve, who argued that banks should not be allowed to take large trading risks when they receive the benefits of federal deposit insurance.

Derivatives   As discussed in Chapter 11, derivatives such as credit default swaps ended up being "weapons of mass destruction" that helped lead to a financial meltdown when AIG had to be rescued after making overly extensive use of them. To prevent this from happening again, the Dodd-Frank bill requires that many standardized derivative products be traded on exchanges to make their trading more transparent and also requires that they be cleared through clearinghouses to reduce the risk of losses if one counterparty in the derivative transaction goes bankrupt. More customized derivative products are subject to higher capital requirements. Banks are banned from some of their derivative-dealing operations, such as those involving riskier swaps. In addition, the bill imposes capital and margin requirements on firms dealing in derivatives and forces them to disclose more information about their activities.

12.5 TOO-BIG-TO-FAIL AND FUTURE REGULATION

LO 12.5 Identify the gaps in current financial regulation and how those gaps may be addressed with future regulatory changes.

The Dodd-Frank bill leaves out many of the details of future regulation, and there are doubts as to whether it has dealt sufficiently with the too-big-to-fail problem, which, as we have seen, was an important factor that contributed to the global financial crisis. Here we discuss some possible measures to reduce the too-big-to-fail problem and explore several areas in which regulation might be heading in the future.

What Can Be Done About the Too-Big-to-Fail Problem?

Three approaches to solving the too-big-to-fail problem have been actively debated.

Break Up Large, Systemically Important Financial Institutions One way to eliminate the too-big-to-fail problem is to make sure that no financial institution is so large that it can bring down the financial system. Then, regulators will no longer see the need to bail out these institutions if they fail, thereby subjecting them to market discipline. One way to shrink overly large institutions is to reimpose the restrictions that were in place before Glass-Steagall was repealed, thereby forcing these large SIFIs to break up their different activities into smaller, cohesive companies. Alternatively, regulations could specify that no financial institution can have assets over a specified maximum limit, forcing SIFIs to break up into smaller pieces.

Not surprisingly, both of these approaches have been vehemently opposed by the largest financial institutions. Although breaking up SIFIs would eliminate the too-big-to-fail problem, if there are synergies available that might enable large institutions to manage risk better or to provide financial services at a lower cost, then breaking up SIFIs might decrease the efficiency of the financial system rather than increase it.

Higher Capital Requirements Because institutions that are "too big to fail" have incentives to take on excessive risk, another way to reduce their risk taking is to impose higher capital requirements on them. With higher capital, not only will these institutions have a larger buffer with which to withstand losses if they occur but they will also have more to lose and hence have more "skin in the game," thereby reducing moral hazard and giving them less incentive to take on excessive risk. Another way of describing this approach is to say that higher capital requirements reduce the subsidy to risk taking for institutions that are too big to fail. In addition, because risk taking by SIFIs is far greater during booms, capital requirements could be increased when credit is expanding rapidly and reduced when credit is contracting. Such measures would cause capital requirements to become more countercyclical and could help restrain the boom-bust credit cycle.

The Swiss central bank has been a leader in this kind of approach: It has the highest capital requirements among advanced countries for its largest banks, and it raises them when credit markets become particularly frothy. Legislation has been proposed in the U.S. Congress to double capital requirements for large financial institutions, legislation that these institutions vigorously oppose.

Leave It to Dodd-Frank Another view is that Dodd-Frank has effectively eliminated the too-big-to-fail problem by making it harder for the Federal Reserve to bail out financial institutions, by imposing stricter regulations on SIFIs, and through application of the Volcker rule. Indeed, the authors of the bill have declared that Dodd-Frank will "end too-big-to-fail as we know it." Although the provisions of Dodd-Frank do take away some of the incentives for excessive risk taking by large, systemically important financial institutions, there are doubts that this bill completely removes the too-big-to-fail problem.

Beyond Dodd-Frank: Where Might Regulation Head in the Future?

In February 2017, the new president, Donald Trump, signed an executive order directing the Secretary of the Treasury to review the financial regulations in the Dodd-Frank bill. Critics of Dodd-Frank, such as the Trump administration, have argued that many of its regulations have restricted banks from lending, especially to households, making it harder for them to borrow. Supporters of Dodd-Frank argue that it has made the financial system sounder, reducing the likelihood of a financial crisis. Here we examine debates about where regulation should head in the future in several areas.

Consumer Protection   Congressional critics of the Consumer Financial Protection Bureau argue that its regulations, such as those requiring lenders to make sure that borrowers have the ability to repay loans and mortgages, have led banks to be overly conservative in extending credit to consumers. Some of these critics would even go beyond restraining the Consumer Financial Protection Bureau and would like to see it abolished, arguing that this would promote more lending to households. Advocates for consumer protection have vowed to fight to retain these regulations and the Consumer Financial Protection Bureau because they argue that not only will these regulations and the Consumer Financial Protection Bureau protect consumers from fraud and deception but they will also make the financial system safer because fraudulent practices helped promote the subprime lending boom and the global financial crisis.

Resolution Authority   There are proposals in the U.S. Congress to abolish the Orderly Liquidation Authority. Advocates for these proposals argue that the Orderly Liquidation Authority legitimizes federal bailouts of large financial firms and therefore increases the too-big-to-fail problem. Instead, they propose an enhanced bankruptcy procedure for failing financial firms that would be determined by the courts. Defenders of a federal resolution authority argue that although the Orderly Liquidation Authority can be improved, it is still needed because bankruptcy, even an enhanced procedure, is a messy legal process that makes orderly resolutions of failing financial institutions in a crisis extremely difficult. Without an Orderly Liquidation Authority, the failure of a major financial institution is more likely to cause a financial crisis to spin out of control.

Volcker Rule   The Volcker rule to limit banks from proprietary trading with their own money, which has the advantage of limiting excessive risk taking by banks, has come under attack for several reasons. First, regulators have found it very difficult to differentiate proprietary trading from banks trading for their customers, so the Volcker rule has resulted in very complex regulations that might be very difficult and costly to enforce. Second, it limits banks from engaging in a profitable activity that could offset possible losses from lending. Third, critics of the Volcker rule argue that by limiting trading, it has reduced liquidity in many financial markets. In 2018, the Federal Reserve loosened some of the restrictions imposed by the Volcker rule.

Derivatives Trading   Proposals in Congress seek to roll back the Dodd-Frank rules on derivatives trading. Their proponents argue that these rules have hurt the ability of financial institutions in the United States to make these trades, with the result that derivatives trading, particularly in credit default swaps, has moved overseas, making it harder for American financial firms to make profits and reducing the ability of U.S. nonfinancial firms to insure against risk. Supporters of the Dodd-Frank rules on derivatives trading argue that they make derivatives trading more transparent and safer, thereby reducing the likelihood of future financial crises.

Government-Sponsored Enterprises (GSEs)   A major gap in the Dodd-Frank bill is that it does not address privately owned, government-sponsored enterprises, such as Fannie Mae and Freddie Mac. During the global financial crisis, both of these firms got into serious financial trouble and had to be taken over by the government, with massive loans and government guarantees needed to prop them up. To prevent this from occurring again, there are proposals to reform the GSEs by four different routes:

1. Fully privatize GSEs by taking away their government sponsorship, thereby removing the implicit backing for their debt
2. Completely nationalize them by taking away their private status and making them government agencies
3. Leave them as privately owned GSEs, but strengthen regulations to restrict the amount of risk they take and to impose higher capital standards
4. Leave them as privately owned GSEs, but force them to shrink dramatically so that they no longer expose the taxpayer to huge losses or pose a systemic risk to the financial system when they fail

However, supporters of the current status of the GSEs argue against these reforms because they would limit GSE activity, thereby making it harder for households to get credit.

SUMMARY

1. A financial crisis occurs when a particularly large disruption to information flows occurs in financial markets, with the result that financial frictions increase sharply, thereby rendering financial markets incapable of channeling funds to households and firms with productive investment opportunities and causing a sharp contraction in economic activity.

2. Financial crises start in advanced countries like the United States in two ways: credit booms and busts, or a general increase in uncertainty when major financial institutions fail. The result is a substantial increase in adverse selection and moral hazard problems, which leads to a contraction of lending and a decline in economic activity. The worsening business conditions and deterioration in bank balance sheets then trigger the second stage of the crisis, the simultaneous failure of many banking institutions, a banking crisis. The resulting decrease in the number of banks causes a loss of their information capital, leading to a further decline of lending and a spiraling down of the economy. In some instances, the resulting economic downturn leads to a sharp slide in prices, which increases the real liabilities of firms and households and therefore lowers their net worth, leading to a debt deflation. The further decline in borrowers' net worth worsens adverse selection and moral hazard problems, so that lending, investment spending, and aggregate economic activity remain depressed for a long time.

3. The most significant financial crisis in U.S. history, that which led to the Great Depression, involved several stages: a stock market crash, bank panics, worsening of asymmetric information problems, and finally a debt deflation.

4. The global financial crisis of 2007–2009 was triggered by mismanagement of financial innovations involving subprime residential mortgages and the bursting of a housing price bubble. The crisis spread globally, with substantial deterioration in banks' and other financial institutions' balance sheets, a run on the shadow banking system, and the failure of many high-profile firms.

5. Financial regulation has undergone many changes in the wake of the global financial crisis. First is the shift from microprudential supervision, which focuses on the safety and soundness of individual institutions, to macroprudential supervision, which focuses on the safety and soundness of the financial system in the aggregate. Second is the Dodd-Frank Act of 2010, which is the most comprehensive financial reform legislation since the Great Depression. It makes provisions in seven areas: (1) consumer protection, (2) annual stress tests, (3) resolution authority, (4) limits on Federal Reserve lending, (5) systemic risk regulation, (6) the Volcker rule, and (7) derivatives trading.

6. Future regulation needs to address several issues: (1) the too-big-to-fail problem, which can be at least

partially addressed either by breaking up large financial institutions or by imposing higher capital requirements on them; (2) many of the provisions of the Dodd-Frank legislation; and (3) reform of the GSEs to make it less likely that they will require government bailouts in the future.

KEY TERMS

asset-price bubble, p. 270
credit boom, p. 268
credit default swaps, p. 275
credit spread, p. 273
debt deflation, p. 271
deleveraging, p. 268
financial crisis, p. 268
financial derivatives, p. 275

financial frictions, p. 268
financial innovation, p. 268
financial liberalization, p. 268
fire sales, p. 271
fundamental economic values, p. 270
haircuts, p. 278
leverage cycle, p. 284
macroprudential supervision, p. 284

microprudential supervision, p. 284
repurchase agreements (repos), p. 278
stress tests, p. 285
structured credit products, p. 274
systemically important financial institutions (SIFIs), p. 286
Troubled Asset Relief Program (TARP), p. 282

QUESTIONS

1. How does the concept of asymmetric information help to define a financial crisis?

2. How can the bursting of an asset-price bubble in the stock market help trigger a financial crisis?

3. How does an unanticipated decline in the price level cause a drop in lending?

4. Define "financial frictions" in your own terms and explain why an increase in financial frictions is a key element in financial crises.

5. How does a deterioration in balance sheets of financial institutions and the simultaneous failures of these institutions cause a decline in economic activity?

6. How does a general increase in uncertainty as a result of the failure of a major financial institution lead to an increase in adverse selection and moral hazard problems?

7. What is a credit spread? Why do credit spreads rise significantly during a financial crisis?

8. Some countries do not advertise that a system of deposit insurance like the FDIC in the United States exists in their banking system. Explain why some countries would want to do that.

9. Describe the process of "securitization" in your own words. Was this process solely responsible for the Great Recession financial crisis of 2007–2009?

10. Provide one argument in favor of and one against the idea that the Fed was responsible for the housing price bubble of the mid-2000s.

11. What role does weak financial regulation and supervision play in causing financial crises?

12. Describe two similarities and two differences between the United States' experiences during the Great Depression and the Great Recession financial crisis of 2007–2009.

13. What do you think prevented the financial crisis of 2007–2009 from becoming a depression?

14. What technological innovations led to the development of the subprime mortgage market?

15. Why is the originate-to-distribute business model subject to the principal–agent problem?

16. True, false, or uncertain: Deposit insurance always and everywhere prevents financial crises.

17. How did a decline in housing prices help trigger the subprime financial crisis that began in 2007?

18. What role did the shadow banking system play in the 2007–2009 financial crisis?

19. Why would haircuts on collateral increase sharply during a financial crisis? How would this lead to fire sales on assets?

20. How did the global financial crisis promote a sovereign debt crisis in Europe?

21. Why is it a good idea for macroprudential policies to require countercyclical capital requirements?

22. How does the process of financial innovation affect the effectiveness of macroprudential regulation?

23. What are the three approaches to limiting the too-big-to-fail problem? Briefly describe the advantages and disadvantages of each approach.

24. Why were consumer protection provisions included in the Dodd-Frank bill, a bill designed to strengthen the financial system? What are some of the problems with these regulations?

25. Why is it important for the U.S. government to have resolution authority?

DATA ANALYSIS PROBLEMS

The Problems update with real-time data in **MyLab Economics** and are available for practice or instructor assignment.

1. Real-time Data Analysis Go to the St. Louis Federal Reserve FRED database, and find data on house prices (SPCS20RSA), stock prices (NASDAQCOM), a measure of the net wealth of households (BOGZ1FL192090005Q), and personal consumption expenditures (PCE). For all four measures, be sure to convert the *frequency* setting to "Quarterly." Download the data into a spreadsheet, and make sure the data align correctly with the appropriate dates. For all four series, for each quarter, calculate the annualized growth rate from quarter to quarter. To do this, take the current-period data minus the previous-quarter data, and then divide by the previous-quarter data. Multiply by 100 to change each result to a percentage, and multiply by 4 to annualize the data.

   a. For the four series, calculate the average growth rates over the most recent four quarters of data available. Comment on the relationships among house prices, stock prices, net wealth of households, and consumption as they relate to your results.

   b. Repeat part (a) for the four quarters of 2005, and again for the period from 2008:Q3 to 2009:Q2. Comment on the relationships among house prices, stock prices, net wealth of households, and consumption as they relate to your results, before and during the crisis.

   c. How do the current household data compare to the data from the period prior to the financial crisis, and during the crisis? Do you think the current data are indicative of a bubble?

2. Real-time Data Analysis Go to the St. Louis Federal Reserve FRED database, and find data on corporate net worth of nonfinancial businesses (TNWMVBSNNCB), private domestic investment (GPDIC1), and a measure of financial frictions, the St. Louis Fed financial stress index (STLFSI2). For all three measures, be sure to convert the *frequency* setting to "Quarterly." Download the data into a spreadsheet, and make sure the data align correctly with the appropriate dates. For corporate net worth and private domestic investment, calculate the annualized growth rates from quarter to quarter. To do this, take the current-period data minus the previous-quarter data, then divide by the previous-quarter data. Multiply by 100 to change the results to percentage form, and then multiply by 4 to annualize the data.

   a. Calculate the average growth rates over the most recent four quarters of data available for the corporate net worth and private domestic investment variables. Calculate the difference between the value of the stress index during the most recent quarter and the value of the stress index one year earlier. Comment on the relationships among financial stress, net wealth of corporate businesses, and private domestic investment.

   b. Repeat part (a) for the four quarters of 2005 and for the period from 2008:Q3 to 2009:Q2. Comment on the relationships among financial stress, net wealth of corporate businesses, and private domestic investment before and during the crisis as they relate to your results. Assuming the financial stress measure is indicative of heightened asymmetric information problems, comment on how the crisis-period data relate to the typical dynamics of a financial crisis.

   c. How do the current investment data compare to the data for the period prior to the financial crisis and during the crisis? Do you think the current data are indicative of a bubble?

Central Banking and the Conduct of Monetary Policy

Crisis and Response: The Federal Reserve Response to the Global Financial Crisis and the Coronavirus Pandemic

When the Federal Reserve was confronted with what former Chair Alan Greenspan described as a "once-in-a-century credit tsunami," it resolved to come to the rescue. Starting in September 2007, the Federal Reserve lowered the federal funds rate target, bringing it down to zero by the end of 2008. At the same time, the Fed implemented large liquidity injections into the credit markets to encourage them to lend again. In mid-August 2007, the Fed lowered the discount rate at which it lent to banks to just 50 basis points above the federal funds rate target, from the normal 100 basis points. Over the course of the crisis, the Fed broadened its provision of liquidity to the financial system well outside its traditional lending to depository institutions. Indeed, after the Fed made loans to assist in the takeover of Bear Stearns by JPMorgan Chase in March 2008, Paul Volcker, a former chair of the Federal Reserve, described the Fed's actions as going to the "very edge of its lawful and implied powers." The number of new Fed lending programs over the course of the crisis spawned a whole new set of acronyms—TAF, TSLF, PDCF, AMLF, CPFF, and MMIFF—making the Fed sound like the Pentagon with code-named initiatives and weapons. Like the Pentagon, the Fed was fighting a war, although its weapons were financial rather than guns, tanks, or aircraft.

Once the severity of the coronavirus pandemic became clear, the Federal Reserve again went to war. In March 2020, it again lowered the federal funds rate to zero and reestablished many of the lending programs it had set up during the global financial crisis. Furthermore, it dramatically expanded these programs to lend to new sectors of the economy, including small businesses, corporations, and state and local governments. The result was a new set of Federal Reserve acronyms—MMLF, PMCCF, PPPLF, MLF, MSNLF, and MSELF.

The recent global financial crisis and the coronavirus pandemic demonstrate the importance of central banks like the Federal Reserve to the health of the financial system and the economy. Chapter 13 outlines what central banks are trying to achieve, what motivates them, and how they are set up. Chapter 14 describes how the money supply is determined. In Chapter 15, we look at the tools that central banks like the Fed have at their disposal and how they use them. Chapter 16 extends the discussion of the conduct of monetary policy to focus on the broader picture of central banks' strategies and tactics.

13 Central Banks and the Federal Reserve System

Learning Objectives

13.1 Recognize the historical context of the development of the Federal Reserve System.

13.2 Describe the key features and functions of the Federal Reserve System.

13.3 Assess the degree of independence of the Federal Reserve.

13.4 Summarize the arguments for and against the independence of the Federal Reserve.

13.5 Identify the ways in which the theory of bureaucratic behavior can help explain Federal Reserve actions.

13.6 Identify the similarities and distinctions in structure and independence between the European Central Bank and the Federal Reserve.

13.7 Assess the degree of independence of other major central banks around the world.

Preview

Among the most important players in financial markets throughout the world are central banks, the government authorities in charge of monetary policy. Central banks' actions affect interest rates, the amount of credit available, and the money supply, all of which have direct impacts not only on financial markets but also on aggregate output and inflation. To understand the role that central banks play in financial markets and the overall economy, we need to understand how these organizations work. Who controls central banks and determines their actions? What motivates their behavior? Who holds the reins of power?

In this chapter, we look at the institutional structure of major central banks and focus particularly on the Federal Reserve System, one of the most important central banks in the world. We start by examining the elements of the Fed's institutional structure that determine where the true power within the Federal Reserve System lies. By understanding who makes the decisions, we will have a better idea of how they are made. We then examine the reasons behind central bank behavior and whether it is a good idea to make central banks independent by insulating them from politicians. Finally, we look at the structure and independence of other major central banks, particularly the European Central Bank. With this context in place, we will be prepared to comprehend the actual conduct of monetary policy described in the following chapters.

13.1 ORIGINS OF THE FEDERAL RESERVE SYSTEM

LO 13.1 Recognize the historical context of the development of the Federal Reserve System.

Of all the central banks in the world, the Federal Reserve System probably has the most unusual structure. To understand how this structure arose, we must go back to before 1913, when the Federal Reserve System was created.

Before the twentieth century, a major characteristic of American politics was the fear of centralized power, as seen in the checks and balances provisions of the Constitution and the preservation of states' rights. This fear of centralized power was one source of American resistance to the establishment of a central bank. Another source was the traditional American distrust of moneyed interests, the most prominent symbol of which was a central bank. The open hostility of the American public to the existence of a central bank resulted in the demise of the first two experiments in central banking, whose function it was to police the banking system: The First Bank of the United States was disbanded in 1811, and the national charter of the Second Bank of the United States expired in 1836 after its renewal was vetoed in 1832 by President Andrew Jackson.

Inside the Fed   The Political Genius of the Founders of the Federal Reserve System

The history of the United States has been one of public hostility to banks and especially to a central bank. How were the politicians who founded the Federal Reserve able to design a system that has become one of the most prestigious institutions in the United States?

The answer is that the founders recognized that if power was too concentrated in either Washington, DC, or New York, two cities that many Americans loved to hate, an American central bank might not have enough public support to operate effectively. They thus decided to set up a decentralized system with 12 Federal Reserve Banks spread throughout the country, to make sure that all regions of the country were represented in monetary policy deliberations. In addition, they made the Federal Reserve Banks quasi-private institutions overseen by directors from the private sector living in each district. These directors would represent the views of their individual regions and would be in close contact with the president of their Federal Reserve Bank. The unusual structure of the Federal Reserve System ensured that regional issues would be addressed, as is evident in Federal Reserve Bank publications. Without this unusual structure, the Federal Reserve System might have been far less popular with the public, making the institution far less effective.

The termination of the Second Bank's national charter in 1836 created a severe problem for American financial markets because there was no lender of last resort that could provide reserves to the banking system in order to avert a bank panic. Hence, in the nineteenth and early twentieth centuries, nationwide bank panics became a regular event, occurring every 20 years or so, culminating in the panic of 1907. The 1907 panic resulted in such widespread bank failures and such substantial losses to depositors that the public was finally convinced that a central bank was needed to prevent future panics.

The hostility of the American public to banks and centralized authority meant great opposition to the establishment of a single central bank like the Bank of England. Fear was rampant that the moneyed interests on Wall Street (including the largest corporations and banks) would be able to manipulate such an institution to gain control over the economy, and that federal operation of the central bank might result in too much government intervention in the affairs of private banks. Serious disagreements existed over whether the central bank should be a private bank or a government institution. Because of the heated debates on these issues, a compromise was struck. In the great American tradition, Congress wrote an elaborate system of checks and balances into the Federal Reserve Act of 1913, which created the Federal Reserve System with its 12 regional Federal Reserve Banks (see the Inside the Fed box "The Political Genius of the Founders of the Federal Reserve System").

13.2 STRUCTURE OF THE FEDERAL RESERVE SYSTEM

LO 13.2 Describe the key features and functions of the Federal Reserve System.

The writers of the Federal Reserve Act wanted to diffuse power along regional lines, between the private sector and the government, and among bankers, business people, and the public. This initial diffusion of power resulted in the evolution of the Federal Reserve System to include the following entities: the **Federal Reserve Banks**, the **Board of Governors of the Federal Reserve System**, the **Federal Open Market Committee (FOMC)**, the Federal Advisory Council, and around 3,000 member commercial

Mini-lecture

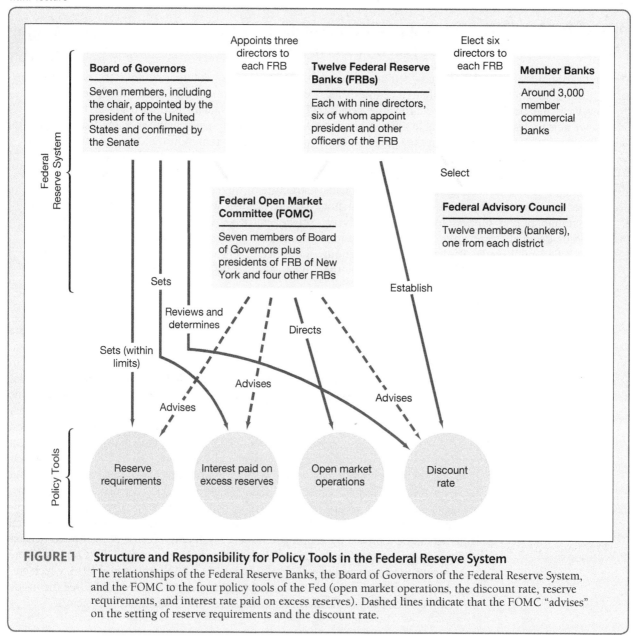

FIGURE 1   Structure and Responsibility for Policy Tools in the Federal Reserve System

The relationships of the Federal Reserve Banks, the Board of Governors of the Federal Reserve System, and the FOMC to the four policy tools of the Fed (open market operations, the discount rate, reserve requirements, and interest rate paid on excess reserves). Dashed lines indicate that the FOMC "advises" on the setting of reserve requirements and the discount rate.

banks. Figure 1 outlines the relationships of these entities to one another and to the four policy tools of the Fed (open market operations, the discount rate, reserve requirements, and interest paid on excess reserves), discussed in Chapters 14 and 15.

Federal Reserve Banks

Each of the 12 Federal Reserve districts defined by the Federal Reserve Act of 1913 has one main Federal Reserve Bank, which may have branches in other cities in the district. The locations of these districts, the Federal Reserve Banks, and the Federal Reserve

Mini-lecture

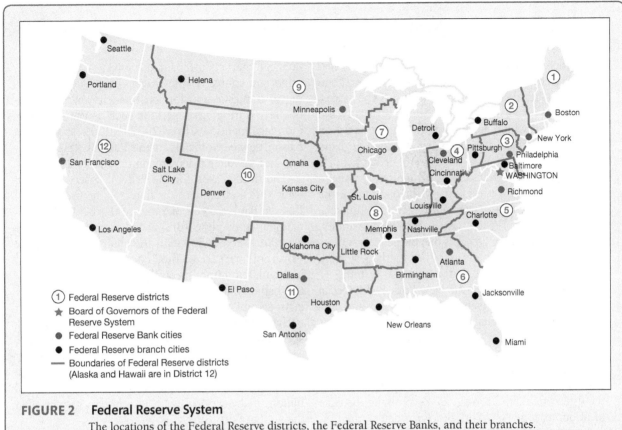

FIGURE 2   Federal Reserve System

The locations of the Federal Reserve districts, the Federal Reserve Banks, and their branches.

Source: Federal Reserve Bulletin.

Bank branches are shown in Figure 2. The three largest Federal Reserve Banks in terms of assets are those of New York, Chicago, and San Francisco—combined, they hold more than 50% of the assets (discount loans, securities, and other holdings) of the Federal Reserve System. The New York bank, with around one-quarter of the assets, is the most important of the Federal Reserve Banks (see the Inside the Fed box "The Special Role of the Federal Reserve Bank of New York").

Each of the Federal Reserve Banks is a quasi-public (part private, part government) institution owned by the private commercial banks in its district that are members of the Federal Reserve System. These member banks have purchased stock in their district Federal Reserve Bank (a requirement of membership), and the dividends paid by that stock are limited by law to 6% annually. The member banks elect six directors for each district bank; three more are appointed by the Board of Governors.

The directors of a district bank are classified into three categories: A, B, and C. The three A directors (elected by the member banks) are professional bankers, and the three B directors (also elected by the member banks) are prominent leaders from industry, labor, agriculture, or the consumer sector. The three C directors, who are appointed by the Board of Governors to represent the public interest, are not allowed to be officers, employees, or stockholders of banks.

Inside the Fed — The Special Role of the Federal Reserve Bank of New York

The Federal Reserve Bank of New York plays a special role in the Federal Reserve System for several reasons. First, its district contains many of the largest commercial banks in the United States, the safety and soundness of which are paramount to the health of the U.S. financial system. The Federal Reserve Bank of New York conducts examinations of bank holding companies and state-chartered member banks in its district, making it the supervisor of some of the most important financial institutions in our financial system. Not surprisingly, given this responsibility, the bank supervision group is one of the largest units of the New York Fed and is by far the largest bank supervision group in the Federal Reserve System.

The second reason for the New York Fed's special role is its active involvement in the bond and foreign exchange markets. The New York Fed houses the open market desk, which conducts open market operations—the purchase and sale of bonds—that determine the amount of reserves in the banking system. Because of this involvement in the Treasury securities market, as well as its walking-distance location near the New York Stock Exchange, the officials at the Federal Reserve Bank of New York are in constant contact with the major domestic financial markets in the United States. In addition, the Federal Reserve Bank of New York houses the foreign exchange desk, which conducts foreign exchange interventions on behalf of the Federal Reserve System and the U.S. Treasury. Its involvement in these financial markets means that the New York Fed is an important source of information on what is happening in domestic and foreign financial markets, particularly during crisis periods such as the subprime mortgage meltdown from 2007 to 2009, as well as a liaison between officials in the Federal Reserve System and private participants in the markets.

The third reason for the Federal Reserve Bank of New York's prominence is that it is the only Federal Reserve Bank to be a member of the Bank for International Settlements (BIS). Thus the president of the New York Fed, along with the chair of the Board of Governors, represents the Federal Reserve System in its regular monthly meetings with other major central bankers at the BIS. This close contact with foreign central bankers and interaction with foreign exchange markets means that the New York Fed has a special role in international relations, both with other central bankers and with private market participants. Adding to its prominence in international circles, the New York Fed is the repository for more than $100 billion of the world's gold, an amount greater than the gold at Fort Knox.

Finally, the president of the Federal Reserve Bank of New York is the only permanent voting member of the FOMC among the Federal Reserve Bank presidents, serving as the vice-chair of the committee. Therefore, he or she and the chair and vice-chair of the Board of Governors are the three most important officials in the Federal Reserve System.

The directors oversee the activities of the district bank, but their most important job is to appoint the president of the bank (subject to the approval of the Board of Governors). Up until 2010, all nine directors participated in this decision, but the Dodd-Frank legislation passed in July 2010 excluded the three class A directors from involvement in choosing the president of the bank. Congress viewed it as inappropriate for bankers to be involved in choosing the president of the Federal Reserve Bank that would have supervisory oversight of these same banks.

The 12 Federal Reserve Banks are involved in monetary policy in several ways:

- Their directors legally "establish" the discount rate (although the discount rate is in practice set at a fixed amount over the federal funds rate target).
- They decide which banks, member and nonmember alike, can obtain discount loans from the Federal Reserve Bank.

- Their directors select one commercial banker from each bank's district to serve on the Federal Advisory Council, which consults with the Board of Governors and provides information that helps in the conduct of monetary policy.
- Five of the 12 bank presidents each have a vote on the Federal Open Market Committee, which directs **open market operations** (the purchase and sale of government securities that affect both interest rates and the amount of reserves in the banking system). As explained in the Inside the Fed box "The Special Role of the Federal Reserve Bank of New York," because the president of the New York Fed is a permanent member of the FOMC, he or she always has a vote on the FOMC, making the New York Fed the most important of all the banks; the other four votes allocated to the district banks rotate annually among the remaining 11 presidents.

The 12 Federal Reserve Banks also perform the following functions:

- Clear checks
- Issue new currency and withdraw damaged currency from circulation
- Administer and make discount loans to banks in their districts
- Evaluate proposed mergers and applications for banks to expand their activities
- Act as liaisons between the business community and the Federal Reserve System
- Examine bank holding companies and state-chartered member banks
- Collect data on local business conditions
- Use their staffs of professional economists to research topics related to the conduct of monetary policy

Member Banks

All *national banks* (commercial banks chartered by the Office of the Comptroller of the Currency) are required to be members of the Federal Reserve System. Commercial banks chartered by the states are not required to be members, but they can choose to join. Currently, 40% of the commercial banks in the United States are members of the Federal Reserve System, having declined from a peak figure of 49% in 1947.

Before 1980, only member banks were required to keep reserves as deposits at the Federal Reserve Banks. Nonmember banks were subject to reserve requirements determined by their states, which typically allowed them to hold much of their reserves in interest-bearing securities. Because at the time no interest was paid on reserves deposited at the Federal Reserve Banks, it was costly to be a member of the system, and as interest rates rose, the relative cost of membership rose, and more and more banks left the system.

This decline in Fed membership was a major concern of the Board of Governors; one reason was that it lessened the Fed's control over the money supply, making it more difficult for the Fed to conduct monetary policy. The chair of the Board of Governors repeatedly called for new legislation requiring all commercial banks to be members of the Federal Reserve System. One result of the Fed's pressure on Congress was a provision in the Depository Institutions Deregulation and Monetary Control Act of 1980: All depository institutions became subject (by 1987) to the same requirements to keep deposits at the Fed, so member and nonmember banks would be on equal footing in terms of reserve requirements. In addition, all depository institutions were given equal access to the Federal Reserve facilities, such as the discount window (discussed in Chapter 15) and Fed check clearing. These provisions ended the decline in Fed membership and reduced the distinction between member and nonmember banks.

Board of Governors of the Federal Reserve System

At the head of the Federal Reserve System is the seven-member Board of Governors, headquartered in Washington, DC. Each governor is appointed by the president of the United States and confirmed by the Senate. To limit the president's control over the Fed and insulate the Fed from other political pressures, the governors can each serve one full, nonrenewable, 14-year term plus part of another term, with one governor's term expiring every other January.[1] The governors (many are professional economists) are required to come from different Federal Reserve districts so that the interests of one particular region of the country are not overrepresented. The chair of the Board of Governors is chosen from among the seven governors and serves a four-year, renewable term. It is expected that once a new chair is chosen, the old chair will resign from the Board of Governors, even if many years are left in his or her term as a governor.

The Board of Governors is actively involved in the conduct of monetary policy in the following ways:

- All seven governors are members of the FOMC and vote on the conduct of open market operations. Because only 12 voting members are on this committee (seven governors and five presidents of the district banks), the Board has the majority of the votes.
- It sets reserve requirements (within limits imposed by legislation).
- It sets the interest rate paid on excess reserves.
- It effectively controls the fixed amount by which the discount rate exceeds the federal funds rate target by means of the "review and determination" process, whereby it approves or disapproves the discount rate "established" by the Federal Reserve Banks.
- The chair of the Board advises the president of the United States on economic policy, testifies in Congress, and speaks on behalf of the Federal Reserve System to the media.

Through legislation, the Board of Governors has often been given duties not directly related to the conduct of monetary policy, which are as follows:

- Sets margin requirements, the fraction of the purchase price of securities that must be paid for with cash rather than borrowed funds
- Sets the salary of the president and all officers of each Federal Reserve Bank, and reviews each bank's budget
- Approves bank mergers and applications for new activities, specifies the permissible activities of bank holding companies and nonbank systemically important financial institutions, and supervises the activities of foreign banks in the United States
- Hires a staff of professional economists (larger than the staffs of individual Federal Reserve Banks) who provide economic analysis that the Board of Governors then uses in making its decisions (see the Inside the Fed box "The Role of the Research Staff")

Federal Open Market Committee (FOMC)

The FOMC usually meets eight times a year (about every six weeks) and makes decisions regarding the conduct of open market operations; the setting of the policy interest rate; the **federal funds rate**, which is the interest rate on overnight loans from one

---

[1]Although technically the governor's term is nonrenewable, a governor can resign just before his or her term expires and then be reappointed by the president. This explains how one governor, William McChesney Martin, Jr., served for 28 years. Since Martin, the chair from 1951 to 1970, retired from the board in 1970, the practice of allowing a governor to, in effect, serve a second full term has been eliminated, and this is why Alan Greenspan had to retire from the Board after his 14-year term expired in 2006.

Inside the Fed   The Role of the Research Staff

The Federal Reserve System is the largest employer of economists not just in the United States, but in the world. The system's research staff has approximately 1,000 people, about half of whom are economists. Of these 500 economists, about 250 are at the Board of Governors, 100 are at the Federal Reserve Bank of New York, and the remainder are at the other Federal Reserve Banks. What do all these economists do?

The most important task of the Fed's economists is to follow the incoming economic data from government agencies and private sector organizations and provide guidance to the policymakers on the direction in which the economy might be headed and the potential impact of monetary policy actions on the economy. Before each FOMC meeting, the research staff of each Federal Reserve Bank briefs its president and the senior management of the bank on the staff's forecast for the U.S. economy and the issues that are likely to be discussed at the meeting. The research staff also provides briefing materials or a formal briefing on the economic outlook for the bank's region, something that each president discusses at the FOMC meeting. Meanwhile, at the Board of Governors, economists maintain a large econometric model (a model whose equations are estimated using statistical procedures) that helps them produce their forecasts of the national economy, and they, too, brief the governors on the national economic outlook.

The research staffers at the banks and the Board also provide support to the bank supervisory staff by tracking developments in the banking sector and other financial markets and institutions, and by supplying bank examiners with the technical advice they might need in the course of their examinations. Because the Board of Governors has to decide whether to approve bank mergers, the research staffs at both the Board and the bank in whose district the merger is to take place prepare information on the possible effects of the proposed merger on the competitive environment. To ensure compliance with the Community Reinvestment Act, economists also analyze a bank's performance regarding its lending activities in different communities.

Because of the increased influence of developments in foreign countries on the U.S. economy, members of the research staff, particularly those at the New York Fed and the Board, produce reports on the major foreign economies. They also conduct research on developments in the foreign exchange market because of its growing importance in the monetary policy process and to support the activities of the foreign exchange desk. Economists help support the operation of the open market desk by projecting reserve growth and the growth of monetary aggregates.

Staff economists also engage in basic research on the effects of monetary policy on output and inflation, developments in the labor markets, international trade, international capital markets, banking and other financial institutions, financial markets, and the regional economy, among other topics. This research is published widely in academic journals and in Reserve Bank publications. (Federal Reserve Bank reviews are a good source of supplemental material for money and banking students.) Another important activity of the research staff, primarily at the Reserve Banks, is public education. Staff economists are called on frequently to make presentations to the boards of directors at their banks or to make speeches to the public in their districts.

bank to another; and the setting of the interest rate paid on excess reserves. (Details on how the FOMC meeting is conducted are discussed in the Inside the Fed box "The FOMC Meeting," and the documents produced for the meeting are described in the second Inside the Fed box, "Green, Blue, Teal, and Beige: What Do These Colors Mean at the Fed?") Indeed, the FOMC is often referred to as the "Fed" in the press. For example, when the media report that the Fed is meeting, they actually mean that the FOMC is meeting. The committee consists of the seven members of the Board of Governors, the president of the Federal Reserve Bank of New York, and the presidents of four other

Inside the Fed The FOMC Meeting

The FOMC meeting takes place over a two-day period in the boardroom on the second floor of the main building of the Board of Governors in Washington, DC. The seven governors and the 12 Reserve Bank presidents, along with the secretary of the FOMC, the Board's director of the Research and Statistics Division and his or her deputy, and the directors of the Monetary Affairs and International Finance Divisions, sit around a massive conference table. Although only five of the Reserve Bank presidents have voting rights on the FOMC at any given time, all actively participate in the deliberations. Seated around the sides of the room are the directors of research for each of the Reserve Banks and other senior board and Reserve Bank officials, who, by tradition, do not speak at the meeting.

The meeting starts with a quick approval of the minutes of the previous meeting of the FOMC. The first substantive agenda item is the report by the manager of system open market operations on foreign currency and domestic open market operations and other issues related to these topics. After the governors and Reserve Bank presidents finish asking questions and discussing these reports, a vote is taken to ratify them.

The next stage of the meeting is a presentation of the Board staff's national economic forecast by the director of the Research and Statistics Division of the Board. After the governors and Reserve Bank presidents have queried the division director about the forecast, the *go-round* occurs: Each bank president presents an overview of economic conditions in his or her district and the bank's assessment of the national outlook, and each governor, including the chair, gives a view of the national outlook. By tradition, remarks avoid the topic of monetary policy at this time.

The agenda then turns to current monetary policy and the domestic policy directive. The Board's director of the Monetary Affairs Division leads off the discussion by outlining the different scenarios for monetary policy actions and may describe an issue relating to how monetary policy should be conducted. After a question-and-answer period, each of the FOMC members, as well as the nonvoting bank presidents, expresses his or her views on monetary policy and on the monetary policy statement. The chair then summarizes the discussion and proposes specific wording for the monetary policy statement and the directive on the federal funds rate target transmitted to the open market desk, indicating whether the federal funds rate target is to be raised or lowered, say, by 1/4 of a percentage point, or to be left unchanged. The secretary of the FOMC formally reads the proposed statement, and the members of the FOMC vote.*

At 2:15 p.m. on the final day of the meeting, a public announcement is made about the outcome of the meeting: whether the federal funds rate target and discount rate have been raised, lowered, or left unchanged; and an assessment of the "balance of risks" in the future, whether toward higher inflation or a weaker economy. The postmeeting announcement is an innovation initiated in 1994. Before that year, no such announcement was ever made, and the markets had to guess what policy action had been taken. The decision to announce this information was a step in the direction of greater openness by the Fed. A further step in this direction started in April 2011: After the FOMC meetings in March, June, September, and December, the chair of the Federal Reserve gives a press conference in which he or she briefs the press about the FOMC decisions.

*The decisions expressed in the directive may not be unanimous, and the dissenting views are made public. However, except in extremely rare cases, the chair's vote is always on the winning side.

Federal Reserve Banks. The chair of the Board of Governors also presides as the chair of the FOMC. Even though only the presidents of five of the Federal Reserve Banks are voting members of the FOMC, the other seven presidents of the district banks attend FOMC meetings and participate in discussions. Hence they have some input into the committee's decisions.

Inside the Fed   Green, Blue, Teal, and Beige: What Do These Colors Mean at the Fed?

Three research documents play an important role in the monetary policy process and at Federal Open Market Committee meetings. Up until 2010, a detailed national forecast for the next three years, generated by the Federal Reserve Board of Governors' Research and Statistics Division, was placed between green covers and was thus known as the "green book." Projections for the monetary aggregates prepared by the Monetary Affairs Division of the Board of Governors, along with typically three alternative scenarios for the stance of monetary policy (labeled A, B, and C), were contained in the "blue book" in blue covers. Both books were distributed to all participants in FOMC meetings. Starting in 2010, the green and blue books were combined into the "teal book" with teal covers: Teal is a combination of green and blue.* The "beige book," with beige covers, is produced by the Reserve Banks and details evidence gleaned either from surveys or from talks with key businesses and financial institutions on the state of the economy in each of the Federal Reserve districts. This is the only one of the three books that is distributed publicly, and it often receives a lot of attention in the press.

*These FOMC documents are made public after five years, and their contents can be found at https://www.federalreserve.gov/monetarypolicy/fomc_historical.htm.

Because, prior to 2008, open market operations were the most important policy tool the Fed had for controlling the money supply, and because it is where decisions about **tightening of monetary policy** (a rise in the federal funds rate) or **easing of monetary policy** (a lowering of the federal funds rate) are made, the FOMC is necessarily the focal point for policymaking in the Federal Reserve System. Although reserve requirements, the discount rate, and the interest rate paid on excess reserves are not actually set by the FOMC, decisions in regard to these policy tools are effectively made there, and this is why Figure 1 includes dashed lines indicating that the FOMC "advises" on the setting of reserve requirements and the discount rate. The FOMC does not actually carry out securities purchases or sales. Instead, it issues directives to the trading desk at the Federal Reserve Bank of New York, where the manager for domestic open market operations supervises a roomful of people who execute the purchases and sales of the government or agency securities. The manager communicates daily with the FOMC members and their staffs concerning the activities of the trading desk.

Why the Chair of the Board of Governors Really Runs the Show

At first glance, the chair of the Board of Governors is just 1 of 12 voting members of the FOMC and has no legal authority to exercise control over this body. So why does the media pay so much attention to every word the chair speaks? Does the chair really call the shots at the Fed? If so, why does the chair have so much power?

The chair does indeed run the show. He or she is the spokesperson for the Fed and negotiates with Congress and the president of the United States. The chair also exercises control by setting the agenda of Board and FOMC meetings and by influencing the Board through the forces of stature and personality. Chairs of the Board of Governors (including Marriner S. Eccles, William McChesney Martin Jr., Arthur Burns, Paul A. Volcker, Alan Greenspan, Ben Bernanke, Janet Yellen, and Jay Powell) have typically had strong personalities and have wielded great power.

The chair also exercises power by supervising the Board's staff of professional economists and advisers. Because the staff gathers information for the Board and conducts the analyses the Board uses in its decisions, it has some influence over monetary policy. In addition, in the past, several appointments to the Board itself have come from within the ranks of its professional staff, making the chair's influence even farther-reaching and longer-lasting than a four-year term. The chair's style also matters, as suggested by the Inside the Fed box "Styles of Federal Reserve Chairs: Bernanke, Yellen, and Powell Versus Greenspan."

Inside the Fed   Styles of Federal Reserve Chairs: Bernanke, Yellen, and Powell Versus Greenspan

Every Federal Reserve chair has a different style, and these styles affect how policy decisions are made at the Fed. There has been much discussion of how three recent chairs of the Fed, former chairs Ben Bernanke and Janet Yellen, and current chair Jay Powell, differ from Alan Greenspan, who was the chair of the Federal Reserve Board for 19 years, from 1987 until 2006.

Alan Greenspan dominated the Fed like no other prior Federal Reserve chair. His background was very different from that of Bernanke and Yellen, who spent most of the early parts of their careers in academia, and Jay Powell, a lawyer who worked in the financial sector. Greenspan, a disciple of Ayn Rand, was a strong advocate for laissez-faire capitalism and headed a very successful economic consulting firm, Townsend-Greenspan. Greenspan was never an economic theorist, but rather was famous for immersing himself in the data—literally so, because he was known to review data in his bathtub at the beginning of the day—and often focused on rather obscure data series to come up with his forecasts. As a result, Greenspan did not rely exclusively on the Federal Reserve Board staff's forecast in making his policy decisions. A prominent example occurred during 1997, when the Board staff was forecasting a surge in inflation, which would have required a tightening of monetary policy. Yet Greenspan believed that inflation would not rise and convinced the FOMC not to tighten monetary policy. Greenspan proved to be right and was dubbed the "maestro" by the media.

Bernanke, in contrast, before going to Washington as a governor of the Fed in 2002, and before becoming the chair of the Council of Economic Advisors in 2005 and the Fed chair in 2006, spent his entire career as a professor, first at Stanford University's Graduate School of Business and then in the Economics Department at Princeton University, where he became chair of the department. Similarly, Janet Yellen was a professor for 20 years, first at Harvard University and then at the University of California, before working for the Federal Reserve System as a member of the Board of Governors from 1994 to 1997. She served as president of the Federal Reserve Bank of San Francisco from 2004 to 2010, and then as vice-chair of the Federal Reserve from 2010 to 2014. Jay Powell started his career as a lawyer, but then in 1984 moved to work in the financial industry, with a stint in the U.S. Treasury from 1990 to 1993. He became a member of the Board of Governors of the Federal Reserve in 2012, and then chair in 2018. Because Bernanke, Yellen, and Powell did not make their names as economic forecasters, the Board staff's forecast now plays a much greater role in decision making at the FOMC.

The style of policy discussions also has changed with the more recent chairs. Greenspan exercised extensive control over the discussion at the FOMC. During the Greenspan era, the discussion was formal, with each participant speaking after being put on a list by the secretary of the FOMC. Under Bernanke, Yellen, and Powell, there has been more give and take. These chairs have encouraged so-called two-handed interventions. When a participant wants to go out of turn to ask a question or make a point about something another participant has just said, he or she raises two hands and is then acknowledged by the chair and called on to speak.

The order of the discussion at the FOMC has also changed, in a very subtle but extremely important way. Under Greenspan, after the other FOMC participants had expressed their views on the economy, Greenspan would present his views on the state of the economy and then make a recommendation regarding the course of monetary policy action. This protocol required the other participants to just agree or disagree with Greenspan's recommendation during the following round of discussion about monetary policy. In contrast, Bernanke, Yellen, and Powell usually have not made a recommendation for the course of monetary policy immediately after the other FOMC participants have expressed their views on the economy. Instead, they would summarize what they had heard from the other participants, make some comments of their own, and then wait until after

they had heard the views of all the other participants before making a monetary policy recommendation. Under Greenspan's process, the chair was pretty much making the decision about policy, whereas Bernanke, Yellen, and Powell have favored procedures that are more democratic and enable participants to have greater influence over the chair's vote.

Another big difference in the chairs' styles is in terms of transparency. On the one hand, Greenspan was famous for being obscure, and even quipped at a congressional hearing, "I guess I should warn you, if I turn out to be particularly clear, you've probably misunderstood what I've said." Bernanke, Yellen, and Powell, on the other hand, have tried to be clear speakers. Although advances in transparency were made under Greenspan, he adopted more transparent communication only reluctantly. His successor, Ben Bernanke, was a much stronger supporter of transparency, and he moved the Fed to announce its inflation objective (see Chapter 16) and launched major initiatives in an effort to increase Fed transparency (as discussed in the Inside the Fed box "The Evolution of the Fed's Communication Strategy," on page 311).

13.3 HOW INDEPENDENT IS THE FED?

LO 13.3 Assess the degree of independence of the Federal Reserve.

When we look, in the next three chapters, at how the Federal Reserve conducts monetary policy, we will want to know why the Fed decides to take certain policy actions but not others. To understand its actions, we must understand the incentives that motivate the Fed's behavior. How free is the Fed from presidential and congressional pressures? Do economic, bureaucratic, or political considerations guide it? Is the Fed truly independent of outside pressures?

Stanley Fischer, who was a professor at MIT and much later a vice-chair of the Federal Reserve, has defined two different types of independence of central banks: **instrument independence**, the ability of the central bank to set monetary policy instruments, and **goal independence**, the ability of the central bank to set the goals of monetary policy. The Federal Reserve has both types of independence and is remarkably free of the political pressures that influence other government agencies. Not only are the members of the Board of Governors appointed for a 14-year term (and so cannot be ousted from office) but also the term is technically not renewable, eliminating some of the incentive for the governors to curry favor with the president and Congress.

Probably even more important to its freedom from the whims of Congress is the Fed's independent and substantial source of revenue from its holdings of securities and, to a lesser extent, from its loans to banks. In 2019, for example, the Fed had net earnings after expenses of $55 billion—not a bad living if you can find it! Because it returns the bulk of these earnings to the Treasury, it does not get rich from its activities, but this income gives the Fed an important advantage over other government agencies: It is not subject to the appropriations process usually controlled by Congress. Indeed, the General Accounting Office, the auditing agency of the federal government, cannot audit the monetary policy or foreign exchange market functions of the Federal Reserve. Because the power to control the purse strings is usually synonymous with the power of overall control, this feature of the Federal Reserve System contributes to its independence more than any other factor.

Yet the Federal Reserve is still subject to the influence of Congress, because the legislation that structures it is written by Congress and is subject to change at any time. When legislators are upset with the Fed's conduct of monetary policy, they frequently threaten to weaken its independence. An example was a bill sponsored by Representative Ron Paul in 2009. The bill advocated subjecting the Fed's monetary policy actions to audits by the General Accounting Office (GAO). Threats like this are a powerful club to wield, and they certainly have some effect in keeping the Fed from straying too far from congressional wishes.

Congress also has passed legislation to make the Federal Reserve more accountable for its actions. Under the Humphrey-Hawkins Act of 1978 and later legislation, the Federal Reserve is required to issue a *Monetary Policy Report to the Congress* semiannually, with accompanying testimony by the chair of the Board of Governors, to explain how the conduct of monetary policy is consistent with the objectives outlined by the Federal Reserve Act.

The president can also influence the Federal Reserve. Because Congressional legislation can affect the Fed directly or affect its ability to conduct monetary policy, the president can be a powerful ally through his influence on Congress. Second, although ostensibly a president might be able to appoint only one or two members to the Board of Governors during each presidential term, in actual practice the president appoints members far more often. One reason is that most governors do not serve out a full 14-year term. (Governors' salaries are substantially below the salaries they could earn in the private sector or even at universities, thus providing an incentive for them to return to academia or take private sector jobs before their term expires.) In addition, the president is able to appoint a new chair of the Board of Governors every four years, and a chair who is not reappointed is expected to resign from the board so that a new member can be appointed. Presidents have attacked Federal Reserve independence, although it is not clear how successful they have been (see the Inside the Fed box "Presidential Attacks on the Independence of the Fed").

The power enjoyed by the president through his appointments to the Board of Governors is limited, however. Because the term of the chair is not necessarily concurrent with that of the president, a president may have to deal with a chair of the Board of Governors who was appointed by a previous administration. Alan Greenspan, for example, was appointed chair in 1987 by President Ronald Reagan and was reappointed to another term by a Republican president, George H. W. Bush, in 1992. When Bill Clinton, a Democrat, became president in 1993, Greenspan had several years left to his term. Clinton was put under tremendous pressure to reappoint Greenspan when his term expired and did so in 1996 and again in 2000, even though Greenspan is a Republican.[2] George W. Bush, a Republican, then reappointed Greenspan in 2004, while Barack Obama, a Democrat, reappointed Ben Bernanke, a Republican, in 2010.

You can see that the Federal Reserve has extraordinary independence for a government agency. Nonetheless, the Fed is not free from political pressures. Indeed, to

---

[2]Similarly, William McChesney Martin Jr., the chair from 1951 to 1970, was appointed by President Truman (Dem.) but was reappointed by Presidents Eisenhower (Rep.), Kennedy (Dem.), Johnson (Dem.), and Nixon (Rep.). Also, Paul Volcker, the chair from 1979 to 1987, was appointed by President Carter (Dem.) but was reappointed by President Reagan (Rep.). Ben Bernanke was appointed by President Bush (Rep.) but was reappointed by President Obama (Dem.).

Inside the Fed   Presidential Attacks on the Independence of the Fed

U.S. presidents have often tried to influence Federal Reserve policies by attacking Fed independence. Lyndon Johnson privately made appeals to the then-chair of the Federal Reserve, William McChesney Martin, to not raise interest rates at the December 1965 FOMC meeting and considered trying to fire Martin, but was informed that he could not legally fire a Fed chair for just disagreeing with a presidential administration's policies. After the FOMC raised rates at the December FOMC meeting, Johnson was livid and summoned Martin to fly down to the Johnson Ranch in Texas for what Johnson referred to as "a trip to the woodshed." Johnson was not above physical force to intimidate Martin: The 6-foot 4-inch Johnson actually shoved the shorter Martin up against a wall. Martin stood his ground and told Johnson that the Federal Reserve Act gave the Fed, not the president or Congress, the responsibility for setting interest rates.

Richard Nixon also leaned on his appointed chair of the Federal Reserve, Arthur Burns, to keep interest rates low in the run-up to the 1972 election. Arthur Burns was very close to Nixon, and many economists have argued that Burns gave into Nixon, dealing a blow to Federal Reserve independence. Subsequently, inflation rose sharply, leading to a period that economists have referred to as the Great Inflation. Ronald Reagan and George H. W. Bush also expressed their unhappiness with Paul Volcker's push to raise the federal funds rate to extremely high levels (20%) in Volcker's successful attempt to control inflation (see Chapter 22). However, neither of them took overt steps to weaken the independence of the Fed.

When President Clinton came into office, Robert Rubin, who initially had a position in the White House, and subsequently became Treasury Secretary, convinced Clinton that he should respect the independence of the Fed and not publicly comment on Fed policies. This so-called Rubin doctrine—that the independence of the Fed should be respected by having the president not comment on Fed policies—was then adopted by George W. Bush and later by Barack Obama.

With the presidency of Donald Trump, the Rubin doctrine has been totally abandoned. The virulence of the public attacks by Trump on the Fed starting in 2018 have been unprecedented. Beginning in July 2018, Trump complained publicly that he was "not thrilled" with the Fed's raising interest rates. At a campaign rally in October 2018, he escalated his attacks on the Fed by saying that the Fed's monetary policy was too tight and that the "Fed has gone crazy." Shortly afterward he gave a telephone interview on Fox News in which he expressed that the Fed was "going loco" when it raised interest rates. Starting in 2019, Trump began to attack Jay Powell personally by telling numerous media outlets that he was unhappy with his selection of Jay Powell and "maybe" regretted appointing Powell to the chair of the Federal Reserve Board. In addition, he accused Powell of being "clueless" and of having "a horrendous lack of vision." The White House also leaked to the press that Trump was discussing firing Powell, but Trump was then advised that he did not have the legal right to do so. Trump also tweeted that the economy would soar "like a rocket" if the Fed would just lower the federal funds rate and engage in large-scale purchases of bonds. When the Fed did not accede to his requests, he tweeted that the Fed was behaving like a "stubborn child" and that its officials were "boneheads."

Chair Powell has vociferously defended the independence of the Federal Reserve and has stated that the Fed has not acceded to pressure from the White House. However, when the Fed started to lower interest rates at the end of July 2019, many economic commentators took the opposite view that the Federal Reserve was giving in to presidential pressure, which would compromise the independence of the Federal Reserve.

understand the Fed's behavior, we must recognize that public support for the actions of the Federal Reserve plays a very important role in its decisions.[3]

[3]To get a further inside view of how the Fed has interacted with the public and politicians, see Bob Woodward, *Maestro: Greenspan's Fed and the American Boom* (New York: Simon and Schuster, 2000) and David Wessel, *In Fed We Trust* (New York: Random House, 2009).

13.4 SHOULD THE FED BE INDEPENDENT?

LO 13.4 Summarize the arguments for and against the independence of the Federal Reserve.

As we have seen, the Federal Reserve is probably the most independent government agency in the United States; central banks in most other countries are similarly independent. Every few years, the question arises in Congress of whether the independence given the Fed should be curtailed. Politicians who strongly oppose a specific Fed policy often want to bring the Fed under their supervision to impose a policy more to their liking. Should the Fed be independent, or would we be better off with a central bank under the control of the president or Congress?

The Case for Independence

The strongest argument for an independent central bank rests on the view that subjecting it to more political pressures would impart an inflationary bias to monetary policy. In the view of many observers, politicians in a democratic society are shortsighted because they are driven by the need to win their next election. With this as their primary goal, they are unlikely to focus on long-run objectives such as promoting a stable price level. Instead, they will seek short-run solutions to problems such as high unemployment and high interest rates, even if the short-run solutions have undesirable long-run consequences. For example, we saw in Chapter 5 that high money growth can lead initially to a drop in interest rates but might cause an increase later, as inflation heats up. Would a Federal Reserve under the control of Congress or the president be more likely to pursue a policy of excessive money growth when interest rates are high, even though such a policy would eventually lead to inflation and even higher interest rates in the future? The advocates of an independent Federal Reserve say yes. They believe that a politically insulated Fed is more likely to be concerned with long-run objectives and thus more likely to defend a sound dollar and a stable price level.

A variation on the preceding argument is that the political process in America could lead to a **political business cycle**, in which just before an election, expansionary policies are pursued to lower unemployment and interest rates. After the election, the bad effects of these policies—high inflation and high interest rates—come home to roost, requiring contractionary policies that politicians hope the public will forget before the next election. There is some evidence that such a political business cycle exists in the United States, and a Federal Reserve under the control of Congress or the president might make the cycle even more pronounced.

Putting the Fed under the control of the Treasury (and thus making it more subject to influence by the president) is also considered dangerous because the Fed can be used to facilitate Treasury financing of large budget deficits by its purchases of Treasury bonds.[4] Treasury pressure on the Fed to "help out" might lead to more inflation in the economy. An independent Fed is better able to resist this pressure from the Treasury.

---

[4]The Federal Reserve Act prohibited the Fed from buying Treasury bonds directly from the Treasury (except to roll over maturing securities); instead, the Fed buys Treasury bonds on the open market. One possible reason for this prohibition is consistent with the foregoing argument: The Fed would find it harder to facilitate Treasury financing of large budget deficits.

Another argument for central bank independence is that control of monetary policy is too important to be left to politicians, a group that has repeatedly demonstrated a lack of expertise at making hard decisions on issues of great economic importance, such as reducing the budget deficit or reforming the banking system. This argument can also be stated in terms of the principal–agent problem discussed in Chapters 8, 10, and 12. Both the Federal Reserve and politicians are agents of the public (the principals), and both politicians and the Fed have incentives to act in their own interest rather than in the interest of the public. The argument supporting Federal Reserve independence is that the principal–agent problem is worse for politicians than for the Fed because politicians have fewer incentives to act in the public interest.

Indeed, some politicians prefer an independent Fed because it can be used as a public "whipping boy" to take some of the heat off their backs. It is possible that a politician who in private opposes an inflationary monetary policy will be forced to support such a policy in public for fear of not being reelected. An independent Fed can pursue policies that are politically unpopular yet ultimately in the public interest.

The Case Against Independence

Proponents of a Fed under the control of the president or Congress argue that it is undemocratic to have monetary policy (which affects almost everyone in the economy) controlled by an elite group responsible to no one. The current lack of accountability of the Federal Reserve has serious consequences: If the Fed performs badly, no provision is in place for replacing members (as there is with politicians). True, the Fed needs to pursue long-run objectives, but elected officials of Congress vote on long-run issues also (foreign policy, for example). If we push the argument further that policy is always performed better by elite groups like the Fed, we end up with such conclusions as "the Joint Chiefs of Staff should determine military budgets" or "the IRS should set tax policies with no oversight by the president or Congress." Would you advocate this degree of independence for the Joint Chiefs or the IRS?

The public holds the president and Congress responsible for the economic well-being of the country, yet it lacks control over the government agency that may well be the most important factor in determining the health of the economy. In addition, to achieve a cohesive program that will promote economic stability, monetary policy must be coordinated with fiscal policy (the management of government spending and taxation). Only by placing monetary policy under the control of the politicians who also control fiscal policy can these two policies be prevented from working at cross-purposes.

Another argument against Federal Reserve independence is that, historically, an independent Fed has not always used its freedom successfully. The Fed failed miserably in its stated role as lender of last resort during the Great Depression, and its independence certainly didn't prevent it from pursuing an overly expansionary monetary policy in the 1960s and 1970s that contributed to rapid inflation in this period.

Our earlier discussion also suggests that the Federal Reserve is not immune from political pressures. Its independence may encourage it to pursue a course of narrow self-interest rather than actions that are in the public interest.

No consensus has yet been reached on whether central bank independence is a good thing, although public support for independence of the central bank seems to have been growing in both the United States and abroad. As you might expect, people who like the Fed's policies are more likely to support its independence, whereas those who dislike its policies advocate a less independent Fed.

Central Bank Independence and Macroeconomic Performance Throughout the World

We have seen that advocates of an independent central bank believe that macroeconomic performance will be improved by making the central bank more independent. Empirical evidence seems to support this conjecture: When central banks are ranked from least independent to most independent, inflation performance is found to be the best for countries with the most independent central banks. Although a more independent central bank appears to lead to a lower inflation rate, this is not achieved at the expense of poorer real economic performance. Countries with independent central banks are no more likely to have high unemployment or greater output fluctuations than countries with less independent central banks.

13.5 EXPLAINING CENTRAL BANK BEHAVIOR

LO 13.5 Identify the ways in which the theory of bureaucratic behavior can help explain Federal Reserve actions.

One view of government bureaucratic behavior is that bureaucracies serve the public interest (this is called the *public interest view*). Yet some economists have developed a theory of bureaucratic behavior that emphasizes other factors that influence the operation of bureaucracies. The *theory of bureaucratic behavior* suggests that the objective of a bureaucracy is to maximize its own welfare, just as a consumer's behavior is motivated by the desire to maximize personal welfare and a firm's behavior is motivated by the desire to maximize profits. The welfare of a bureaucracy is related to its power and prestige. Thus this theory suggests that an important factor affecting a central bank's behavior is its wish to increase its power and prestige.

What predictions stem from this particular view of a central bank such as the Fed? One is that the Federal Reserve will fight vigorously to preserve its autonomy, a prediction verified time and time again as the Fed has continually counterattacked congressional attempts to control its budget. In fact, it is extraordinary how effectively the Fed has been able to mobilize a lobby of bankers and business people to preserve its independence when threatened.

Another prediction is that the Federal Reserve will try to avoid conflict with powerful groups that might threaten to curtail its power and reduce its autonomy. Under this scenario, the Fed's behavior may take several forms. The Fed may be slow to increase interest rates and thus smooth out their fluctuations because it wishes to avoid a conflict with the president and Congress over increases in interest rates. The desire to avoid conflict with Congress and the president may also explain why, in the past, the Fed has not embraced transparency (see the Inside the Fed box "The Evolution of the Fed's Communication Strategy").

The Fed's desire to hold as much power as possible also explains why it vigorously pursued a campaign to gain control over more banks. The campaign culminated in legislation that expanded jurisdiction of the Fed's reserve requirements to *all* banks (not just the member commercial banks) by 1987.

The theory of bureaucratic behavior seems applicable to the Federal Reserve's actions, but we must recognize that this view of the Fed as being solely concerned with its own self-interest is too extreme. Maximizing one's own welfare does not rule out altruism. (You might give generously to a charity because it makes you feel good about yourself, but in the process you are helping a worthy cause.) The Fed is surely concerned

Inside the Fed   The Evolution of the Fed's Communication Strategy

As the theory of bureaucratic behavior predicts, the Fed has incentives to hide its actions from the public and from politicians in order to avoid conflicts with them. In the past, this motivation led to a penchant for secrecy in the Fed. As one former Fed official remarked, "a lot of staffers would concede that [secrecy] is designed to shield the Fed from political oversight."* For example, the Fed once actively defended its delay in releasing FOMC directives to Congress and the public. However, as we learned, in 1994 it began to reveal the FOMC directive immediately after each FOMC meeting. In 1999, it also began to immediately announce the "bias" toward the direction in which monetary policy was likely to go, later expressed as the balance of risks in the economy. In 2002, the Fed started to report the roll call vote on the federal funds rate target taken at the FOMC meeting. In December 2004, it moved up the release date of the minutes of FOMC meetings from six weeks after the meeting (its previous policy) to three weeks after the meeting.

The Fed has dramatically increased its transparency in recent years but was slower to do so than many other central banks. One important trend toward greater transparency is the announcement by a central bank of a specific numerical objective for inflation, often referred to as an inflation target, which will be discussed in Chapter 16. Alan Greenspan was strongly opposed to the Fed's moving in this direction, but former chairs Ben Bernanke and Janet Yellen, who previously had been the chair of an internal Federal Reserve subcommittee that proposed new communication policies, were much more favorably disposed, having advocated the announcement of a specific numerical inflation objective in their writings and speeches.

In November 2007, the Federal Reserve announced major enhancements to its communication strategy. First, the forecast horizon for the FOMC's projections under "appropriate policy" for inflation, unemployment, and GDP growth, which were mandated by the Humphrey-Hawkins legislation in 1978, was extended from two calendar years to three, with long-run projections added in 2009. In 2011, the Fed announced a further move toward increased transparency: After the FOMC meetings in March, June, September, and December, the chair of the Federal Reserve would give a press conference outlining the FOMC's decisions. The goal of the press conference would be to enhance the clarity and timeliness of the Federal Reserve's monetary policy communications.

Starting in August 2011, the Fed provided forward guidance on the target for the federal funds rate with FOMC statements that often specified levels of the federal funds rate that would be likely to occur at specific calendar dates. Beginning in January 2012, the FOMC provided even more information about the future path of its policy interest rate by adding to its projections the FOMC participants' forecasts of the appropriate level of the target for the federal funds rate. At the same meeting, the FOMC adopted a numerical inflation objective of 2% to improve the control of inflation by anchoring inflation expectations more firmly.

*Quoted in "Monetary Zeal: How the Federal Reserve Under Volcker Finally Slowed Down Inflation," *Wall Street Journal*, December 7, 1984, 23.

with conducting monetary policy that is in the public interest. However, much uncertainty and disagreement often exist over what that monetary policy should be.[5] When it is unclear what policy will best serve the public interest, other motives may influence the Fed's behavior. In these situations, the theory of bureaucratic behavior can be a useful guide in predicting the motivation behind the actions of the Fed and other central banks.

[5]As an example of the uncertainty over how best to conduct monetary policy, economists are not sure how to measure money (discussed in Chapter 3). So even if economists agree that controlling the quantity of money is the appropriate way to conduct monetary policy (a controversial position, as we will see in later chapters), the Fed cannot be sure which monetary aggregate it should control.

13.6 STRUCTURE AND INDEPENDENCE OF THE EUROPEAN CENTRAL BANK

LO 13.6 Identify the similarities and distinctions in structure and independence between the European Central Bank and the Federal Reserve.

Until recently, the Federal Reserve had no rivals in terms of its importance in the central banking world. However, this situation changed in January 1999 with the full operational start-up of the European Central Bank (ECB) and European System of Central Banks (ESCB), which now conduct monetary policy for countries that are members of the European Monetary Union. These countries, taken together, have a population that exceeds that of the United States and a GDP comparable to that of the United States. The Maastricht Treaty, which established the ECB and ESCB, patterned these institutions after the Federal Reserve in that the central bank of each member country (referred to as *National Central Banks*, or *NCBs*) has a role similar to that of the Federal Reserve Banks. The European Central Bank, which is housed in Frankfurt, Germany, has an Executive Board that is similar in structure to the Board of Governors of the Federal Reserve; it is made up of the president, the vice president, and four other members, who are appointed to eight-year, nonrenewable terms. The Governing Council, which comprises the Executive Board and the presidents of the National Central Banks, is similar to the FOMC and makes the decisions on monetary policy. While the presidents of the National Central Banks are appointed by their countries' governments, the members of the Executive Board are appointed by a committee consisting of the heads of state of all of the countries that are part of the European Monetary Union.

Differences Between the European System of Central Banks and the Federal Reserve System

In the popular press, the European System of Central Banks is usually referred to as the European Central Bank (ECB), even though it would be more accurate to refer to it as the *Eurosystem*, just as it would be more accurate to refer to the Fed as the Federal Reserve System. Although the structure of the Eurosystem is similar to that of the Federal Reserve System, some important differences distinguish the two. First, the budgets of the Federal Reserve Banks are controlled by the Board of Governors, whereas the National Central Banks control their own budgets *and* the budget of the ECB in Frankfurt. The ECB in the Eurosystem therefore has less power than does the Board of Governors in the Federal Reserve System. Second, the monetary operations of the Eurosystem are conducted by the National Central Banks in each country, so monetary operations are not centralized as they are in the Federal Reserve System.

Governing Council

Just as there is a focus on meetings of the FOMC in the United States, there is a similar focus in Europe on meetings of the Governing Council, which gathers monthly at the ECB in Frankfurt to make decisions on monetary policy. Currently, 19 countries are members of the European Monetary Union, and the heads of the 19 National Central Banks share 15 votes on the Governing Council; each of the 6 Executive Board Members has 1 vote. In contrast to FOMC meetings, which are attended by staff from both the Board of Governors and the individual Federal Reserve Banks, only the 25 members of the Governing Council attend its meetings, with no staff present.

The Governing Council has decided that although its members have the legal right to vote, no formal vote will actually be taken; instead, the Council operates by consensus. One reason the Governing Council has decided not to take votes is because of worries that the casting of individual votes might lead the heads of National Central Banks to support a monetary policy that would be appropriate for their individual countries, but not necessarily for the countries of the European Monetary Union as a whole. This problem is less severe for the Federal Reserve: Although Federal Reserve Bank presidents do live in different regions of the country, all have the same nationality and are more likely to take a national view in monetary policy decisions rather than a regional view.

Just as the Federal Reserve releases the FOMC's decision on the setting of the policy interest rate (the federal funds rate) immediately after the meeting is over, the ECB does the same after the conclusion of the monthly Governing Council meeting (by announcing the target for a similar short-term interest rate for interbank loans). In addition, immediately after every monetary policy meeting of the Governing Council, the president and vice president of the ECB hold a press conference in which they take questions from the news media. (A similar press conference is held by the Federal Reserve chair, but it is less frequent, held only four times a year.) The large number of voters in the Governing Council presents a particular dilemma. The current size of the Governing Council (25 members, with 21 voting members) is substantially larger than that of the FOMC (19 participants, with 12 voting members). Many commentators have wondered whether the Governing Council is already too unwieldy—a situation that will get considerably worse as more countries join the European Monetary Union. To deal with this potential problem, the Governing Council decided on a complex system of rotation, somewhat like that of the FOMC, in which National Central Banks from the larger countries will vote more often than National Central Banks from the smaller countries.

How Independent Is the ECB?

Although the Federal Reserve is a highly independent central bank, the Maastricht Treaty, which established the Eurosystem, has made the latter the most independent central bank in the world. Like the Board of Governors, the members of the Executive Board have long terms (eight years), while heads of National Central Banks are required to serve for at least five years. Like the Fed, the Eurosystem determines its own budget, and the governments of the member countries are not allowed to issue instructions to the ECB. These elements of the Maastricht Treaty make the ECB highly independent.

The Maastricht Treaty specifies that the overriding, long-term goal of the ECB is price stability, which means that the goal of the Eurosystem is more clearly specified than it is for the Federal Reserve System. However, the Maastricht Treaty did not specify exactly what "price stability" means. The Eurosystem has defined the quantitative goal of monetary policy to be an inflation rate slightly less than 2%, so from this perspective, the ECB is slightly less goal-independent than the Fed. The Eurosystem is, however, much more goal-independent than the Federal Reserve System in one way: The Eurosystem's charter cannot be changed by legislation; it can be changed only by revision of the Maastricht Treaty—a difficult process because *all* signatories to the treaty must agree to accept any proposed change.

13.7 STRUCTURE AND INDEPENDENCE OF OTHER FOREIGN CENTRAL BANKS

LO 13.7 Assess the degree of independence of other major central banks around the world.

Here we examine the structure and degree of independence of three other important foreign central banks: the Bank of Canada, the Bank of England, and the Bank of Japan.

Bank of Canada

Canada was late in establishing a central bank: The Bank of Canada was founded in 1934. Its directors are appointed by the government to three-year terms, and they appoint the governor, who serves a seven-year term. A governing council, consisting of the four deputy governors and the governor, is the policymaking body comparable to the FOMC that makes decisions about monetary policy.

The Bank Act was amended in 1967 to give the ultimate responsibility for monetary policy to the government. So, on paper, the Bank of Canada is not as instrument-independent as the Federal Reserve. In practice, however, the Bank of Canada does essentially control monetary policy. In the event of a disagreement between the bank and the government, the minister of finance can issue a directive that the bank must follow. However, because the directive must be in writing, and must be specific and applicable for a specified period, it would be subject to intense public scrutiny. As a result, it is unlikely that such a directive would be issued, and none has been to date. The goal for monetary policy, a target for inflation, is set jointly by the Bank of Canada and the government, so the Bank of Canada has less goal independence than the Fed.

Bank of England

Founded in 1694, the Bank of England is the second-oldest central bank (the Riksbank of Sweden is the oldest). The Bank Act of 1946 gave the government statutory authority over the Bank of England. The Court (equivalent to a board of directors) of the Bank of England is made up of the governor and two deputy governors, who are appointed for five-year terms, and sixteen nonexecutive directors, who are appointed for three-year terms.

Until 1997, the Bank of England was the least independent of the central banks examined in this chapter because the decision to raise or lower interest rates resided not within the Bank of England but with the Chancellor of the Exchequer (the equivalent of the U.S. Secretary of the Treasury). All of this changed when a new Labour government came to power in May 1997 and the Chancellor of the Exchequer, Gordon Brown, made a surprise announcement that the Bank of England would henceforth have the power to set interest rates. However, the Bank was not granted total instrument independence: The government can overrule the Bank and set rates "in extreme economic circumstances" and "for a limited period." Nonetheless, as in Canada, overruling the Bank is likely to be a rare occurrence, because doing so would be highly public and is meant to occur only in highly unusual circumstances and for a limited time.

Because the United Kingdom is not a member of the European Monetary Union, the Bank of England makes its monetary policy decisions independently from the European Central Bank. The power to set interest rates resides with the Monetary Policy Committee, made up of the governor, two deputy governors, two members (normally central bank officials) appointed by the governor after consultation with the chancellor, plus four outside economic experts appointed by the chancellor. (Surprisingly, two of the four outside experts initially appointed to this committee were not British citizens—one was Dutch and the other American. Even more remarkably, the governor of the Bank of England from 2013 to 2020, Mark Carney, was a Canadian.) The inflation target for the Bank of England is set by the Chancellor of the Exchequer, so the Bank of England is also less goal-independent than the Fed.

Bank of Japan

The Bank of Japan (Nippon Ginko) was founded in 1882 during the Meiji Restoration. Monetary policy is determined by the Bank's Policy Board, which is composed of the governor; two vice-governors; and six outside members appointed by the cabinet and approved by the parliament, all of whom serve for five-year terms.

Until recently, the Bank of Japan was not formally independent of the government, with the ultimate power residing with the Ministry of Finance. However, the Bank of Japan Law, which took effect in April 1998 and was the first major change in the relative power of the Bank of Japan in 55 years, changed this situation. In addition to stipulating that the objective of monetary policy is to attain price stability, the law granted greater instrument and goal independence to the Bank of Japan. Before this, the government had two voting members on the Policy Board, one from the Ministry of Finance and the other from the Economic Planning Agency. Now the government may send two representatives from these agencies to board meetings, but they no longer have voting rights, although they are allowed to request delays in monetary policy decisions. In addition, the Ministry of Finance lost its authority to oversee many operations of the Bank of Japan, particularly the right to dismiss senior officials. However, the Ministry of Finance continues to have control over the part of the Bank's budget that is unrelated to monetary policy. The 2013 episode in which the recently elected Abe government put pressure on the Bank of Japan to adopt a 2% inflation target, against the wishes of the Bank's current governor, who then resigned, suggests that the Bank of Japan's independence is limited.

The Trend Toward Greater Independence

As our survey of the structure and independence of the major central banks indicates, in recent years we have been seeing a remarkable trend toward increasing independence of central banks. It used to be that the Federal Reserve was substantially more independent than almost all other central banks, with the exception of those in Germany and Switzerland. Now, the newly established European Central Bank is far more independent than the Fed, and greater independence has been granted to central banks like the Bank of England and the Bank of Japan, putting them more on a par with the Fed, as well as to central banks in such diverse countries as New Zealand, Sweden, and the euro nations. Both theory and experience suggest that more independent central banks produce better monetary policy, thus providing an impetus for this trend.

SUMMARY

1. The Federal Reserve System was created in 1913 to lessen the frequency of bank panics. Because of public hostility to central banks and to the centralization of power in general, the Federal Reserve System was created with many checks and balances aimed at diffusing power.

2. The Federal Reserve System consists of 12 regional Federal Reserve Banks, around 3,000 member commercial banks, the Board of Governors of the Federal Reserve System, the Federal Open Market Committee (FOMC), and the Federal Advisory Council. Although on paper the Federal Reserve System appears to be decentralized, in practice it has come to function as a unified central bank controlled by the Board of Governors, especially the board's chair.

3. The Federal Reserve is more independent than most agencies of the U.S. government, but it is still subject to political pressures because the legislation that structures the Fed is written by Congress and can be changed at any time.

4. The case for an independent Federal Reserve rests on the view that curtailing the Fed's independence and subjecting it to more political pressures would impart an inflationary bias to monetary policy. An independent Fed can afford to take the long view and not respond to short-run problems, which would result in expansionary monetary policy and a political business cycle. The case against an independent Fed holds that it is undemocratic for monetary policy (so important to the public) to be controlled by an elite group that is not accountable

to the public. An independent Fed also makes the coordination of monetary and fiscal policy difficult.

5. The theory of bureaucratic behavior suggests that one factor driving central banks' behavior might be their attempt to increase their power and prestige. This view explains many central bank actions, although central banks may also act in the public interest.

6. The European System of Central Banks has a similar structure to that of the Federal Reserve System, with each member country having a National Central Bank, and an Executive Board of the European Central Bank (located in Frankfurt, Germany). The Governing Council, which is made up of the six members of the Executive Board (which includes the president of the European Central Bank) and the presidents of the National Central Banks, makes the decisions on monetary policy. The Eurosystem, which was established under the terms of the Maastricht Treaty, is even more independent than the Federal Reserve System because its charter cannot be changed by legislation. Indeed, it is the most independent central bank in the world.

7. There has been a remarkable trend toward increasing independence of central banks throughout the world. Greater independence has been granted to central banks such as the Bank of England and the Bank of Japan in recent years, as well as to other central banks in such diverse countries as New Zealand and Sweden. Both theory and experience suggest that more independent central banks produce better monetary policy.

KEY TERMS

Board of Governors of the Federal
  Reserve System, p. 295
easing of monetary policy, p. 303
federal funds rate, p. 300

Federal Open Market Committee
  (FOMC), p. 295
Federal Reserve Banks, p. 295
goal independence, p. 305

instrument independence, p. 305
open market operations, p. 299
political business cycle, p. 308
tightening of monetary policy, p. 303

QUESTIONS

1. Why was the Federal Reserve System set up with 12 regional Federal Reserve Banks, rather than one central bank, as in other countries?

2. Why is the Twelfth Federal Reserve district (San Francisco) so geographically large, while the Second Federal Reserve district (New York) is so small by comparison?

3. Should the Federal Reserve redraw its district boundaries, similar to the manner in which congressional districts are periodically realigned? Why or why not?

4. "The Federal Reserve System resembles the U.S. Constitution in that it was designed with many checks and balances." Is this statement true, false, or uncertain? Explain your answer.

5. Which entities in the Federal Reserve System control the discount rate? Reserve requirements? Open market operations? Interest rate paid on excess reserves?

6. In what ways can the regional Federal Reserve Banks influence the conduct of monetary policy?

7. Why is it important for the regional Federal Reserve Bank presidents to attend the FOMC meetings, even if they are nonvoting members?

8. Why is the New York Federal Reserve always a voting member of the FOMC?

9. The presidents of each of the district Federal Reserve Banks (including the New York Federal Reserve Bank) are currently not required to undergo a formal political appointment and approval process. Do you think this is appropriate? Why or why not?

10. Do you think that the 14-year, nonrenewable terms for governors effectively insulate the Board of Governors from political pressure?

11. Despite the important role played by the Board of Governors in setting monetary policy, seats to serve on the Board of Governors can sometimes be empty for several years. How might this happen?

12. How is the president of the United States able to exert influence over the Federal Reserve?

13. Why is it unlikely that the policy recommendation put forth by the chair of the Board of Governors would ever be voted down by the rest of the FOMC?

14. In what way does the Federal Reserve have a high degree of instrument independence? If it has a specific mandate from Congress to achieve "maximum employment and low, stable prices," then how does the Fed have goal independence?

15. The Fed is the most independent of all U.S. government agencies. What is the main difference between it and other government agencies that explains the Fed's greater independence?

16. What is the primary tool that Congress uses to exercise some control over the Fed?

17. Should the Federal Reserve be subject to periodic auditing of its policies, procedures, and finances? Why or why not?

18. In the 1960s and 1970s, the Federal Reserve System lost member banks at a rapid rate. How can the theory of bureaucratic behavior explain the Fed's campaign for legislation to require all commercial banks to become members? Was the Fed successful in this campaign?

19. "The theory of bureaucratic behavior indicates that the Fed never operates in the public interest." Is this statement true, false, or uncertain? Explain your answer.

20. Why might eliminating the Fed's independence lead to a more pronounced political business cycle?

21. "The independence of the Fed leaves it completely unaccountable for its actions." Is this statement true, false, or uncertain? Explain your answer.

22. "The independence of the Fed means that it takes the long view and not the short view." Is this statement true, false, or uncertain? Explain your answer.

23. The Fed promotes secrecy by not releasing the minutes of FOMC meetings to Congress or the public immediately. Discuss the arguments for and against this policy.

24. Which is more independent, the Federal Reserve or the European Central Bank? Why?

25. Why did the Bank of England up until 1997 have a low degree of independence?

DATA ANALYSIS PROBLEMS

The Problems update with real-time data in **MyLab Economics** and are available for practice or instructor assignment.

1. **Real-time Data Analysis** Go to the St. Louis Federal Reserve FRED database, and find data on the unemployment rate in the following states: Kentucky (KYUR), North Dakota (NDUR), Alaska (AKUR), New York (NYUR), Alabama (ALUR), Texas (TXUR), and the national unemployment rate (UNRATE).
   a. For the most recent month of data available, determine which of those states had the highest, and which had the lowest, unemployment rate; how do these compare to the national average?

   b. Given your answer to part (a), what does this say about the need for all 12 Federal Reserve district presidents to participate in the FOMC meetings?

2. **Real-time Data Analysis** Go to the St. Louis Federal Reserve FRED database, and find data on the federal funds rate target (DFEDTARU, and DFEDTARL) and the discount, or primary credit rate (DPCREDIT). When was the last time the federal funds rate target was changed? When was the last time the primary credit rate was changed? Did the rates increase or decrease?

14 The Money Supply Process

Learning Objectives

14.1 List and describe the "three players" that influence the money supply.

14.2 Classify the factors affecting the Federal Reserve's assets and liabilities.

14.3 Identify the factors that affect the monetary base and discuss their effects on the Federal Reserve's balance sheet.

14.4 Explain and illustrate the deposit creation process through T-accounts.

14.5 List the factors that affect the money supply.

14.6 Summarize how the "three players" can influence the money supply.

14.7 Calculate and interpret changes in the money multiplier.

Preview

As we saw in Chapter 5 and will see in later chapters on monetary theory, movements in the money supply affect interest rates and inflation and thus affect us all. Because of its far-reaching effects on economic activity, it is important to understand how the money supply is determined. Who controls it? What causes it to change? How might control of it be improved? In this chapter, we start to answer these questions by providing a detailed description of the *money supply process*, the mechanism that determines the level of the money supply.

Because deposits at banks are by far the largest component of the money supply, learning how these deposits are created is the first step in understanding the money supply process. This chapter provides an overview of how the banking system creates deposits and describes the basic principles of the money supply, concepts that will form the foundation for the material presented in later chapters.

14.1 THREE PLAYERS IN THE MONEY SUPPLY PROCESS

LO 14.1 List and describe the "three players" that influence the money supply.

The "cast of characters" in the money supply story is as follows:

1. The *central bank*—the government agency that oversees the banking system and is responsible for the conduct of monetary policy; in the United States, the Federal Reserve System
2. *Banks* (depository institutions)—the financial intermediaries that accept deposits from individuals and institutions and make loans: commercial banks, savings and loan associations, mutual savings banks, and credit unions
3. *Depositors*—individuals and institutions that hold deposits in banks

Of the three players, the central bank—the Federal Reserve System—is the most important. The Fed's conduct of monetary policy involves actions that affect its balance sheet (holdings of assets and liabilities), to which we turn now.

14.2 THE FED'S BALANCE SHEET

LO 14.2 Classify the factors affecting the Federal Reserve's assets and liabilities.

The operation of the Fed and its monetary policy involve actions that affect its balance sheet, or its holdings of assets and liabilities. Here we discuss a simplified balance sheet that includes just four items that are essential to our understanding of the money supply process.[1]

Federal Reserve System	
Assets	**Liabilities**
Securities	Currency in circulation
Loans to financial institutions	Reserves

Liabilities

The two liabilities on the balance sheet, currency in circulation and reserves, are often referred to as the *monetary liabilities* of the Fed. They are an important part of the money supply story, because increases in either or both will lead to an increase in the money supply (everything else held constant). The sum of the Fed's monetary liabilities (currency in circulation and reserves) and the U.S. Treasury's monetary liabilities (Treasury currency in circulation, primarily coins) is called the **monetary base** (also called **high-powered money**). When discussing the monetary base, we will focus only on the monetary liabilities of the Fed, because those of the Treasury account for less than 10% of the base.[2]

1. *Currency in circulation.* The Fed issues currency (those green-and-gray pieces of paper in your wallet that say "Federal Reserve Note" at the top). Currency in circulation is the amount of currency in the hands of the public. Currency held by depository institutions is also a liability of the Fed, but is counted as part of the reserves.

    Federal Reserve notes are IOUs from the Fed to the bearer and are also liabilities, but unlike most liabilities, they promise to pay back the bearer solely with Federal Reserve notes; that is, they pay off IOUs with other IOUs. Accordingly, if you bring a $100 bill to the Federal Reserve and demand payment, you will receive two $50s, five $20s, ten $10s, one hundred $1 bills, or some other combination of bills that adds to $100.

    People are more willing to accept IOUs from the Fed than from you or me because Federal Reserve notes are a recognized medium of exchange; that is, they are accepted as a means of payment and so function as money. Unfortunately,

---

[1]A detailed discussion of the Fed's balance sheet and the factors that affect the monetary base can be found in the first appendix to this chapter found in **MyLab Economics**.

[2]It is also safe to ignore the Treasury's monetary liabilities when discussing the monetary base because legal restrictions prevent the Treasury from actively supplying its monetary liabilities to the economy.

neither you nor I can convince people that our IOUs are worth anything more than the paper they are written on.[3]

2. *Reserves.* All banks have an account at the Fed in which they hold deposits. **Reserves** consist of deposits at the Fed plus currency that is physically held by banks (called *vault cash* because it is stored in bank vaults). Reserves are assets for the banks but liabilities for the Fed, because the banks can demand payment on them at any time and the Fed is required to satisfy its obligation by paying Federal Reserve notes. As you will see, an increase in reserves leads to an increase in the level of deposits and hence in the money supply.

Total reserves can be divided into two categories: reserves that the Fed requires banks to hold (**required reserves**) and any additional reserves the banks choose to hold (**excess reserves**). For example, the Fed might require that for every dollar of deposits at a depository institution, a certain fraction (say, 10 cents) must be held as reserves. This fraction (10%) is called the **required reserve ratio**.

Assets

The two assets on the Fed's balance sheet are important for two reasons. First, changes in the asset items lead to changes in reserves and the monetary base, and consequently to changes in the money supply. Second, because these assets (government securities and Fed loans) earn higher interest rates than the liabilities (currency in circulation, which pays no interest, and reserves), the Fed makes billions of dollars every year—its assets earn income, and its liabilities cost practically nothing. Although it returns most of its earnings to the federal government, the Fed does spend some of it on "worthy causes," such as supporting economic research.

1. *Securities.* This category of assets covers the Fed's holdings of securities issued by the U.S. Treasury and, in unusual circumstances (as will be discussed in Chapter 15), other securities. As we will see, the primary way in which the Fed provides reserves to the banking system is by purchasing securities, thereby increasing its holdings of these assets. An increase in government or other securities held by the Fed leads to an increase in the money supply.

2. *Loans to financial institutions.* The second way in which the Fed can provide reserves to the banking system is by making loans to banks and other financial institutions. The loans taken out by these institutions are referred to as *discount loans*, or alternatively as *borrowings from the Fed* or as *borrowed reserves*. These loans appear as a liability on financial institutions' balance sheets. An increase in loans to financial institutions can also be the source of an increase in the money supply. During normal times, the Fed makes loans only to banking institutions, and the interest rate charged to banks for these loans is called the **discount rate**. (As we will discuss in Chapter 15, however, during the 2007–2009 financial crisis, the Fed made loans to other financial institutions.)

---

[3]The currency item on our balance sheet refers only to currency *in circulation*—that is, the amount in the hands of the public. Currency that has been printed by the U.S. Bureau of Engraving and Printing is not automatically a liability of the Fed. For example, consider the importance of having $1 million of your own IOUs printed. You give out $100 worth to other people and keep the other $999,900 in your pocket. The $999,900 of IOUs does not make you richer or poorer and does not affect your indebtedness. You care only about the $100 of liabilities from the $100 of circulated IOUs. The same reasoning applies to the Fed in regard to its Federal Reserve notes.

For similar reasons, the currency component of the money supply, no matter how it is defined, includes only currency in circulation. It does not include any additional currency that is not yet in the hands of the public. The fact that currency has been printed but is not circulating means that it is not anyone's asset or liability and thus cannot affect anyone's behavior. Therefore, it makes sense not to include it in the money supply.

14.3 CONTROL OF THE MONETARY BASE

LO 14.3 Identify the factors that affect the monetary base and discuss their effects on the Federal Reserve's balance sheet.

The monetary base equals currency in circulation C plus the total reserves in banking system R.[4] The monetary base MB can be expressed as

$$MB = C + R$$

The Federal Reserve exercises control over the monetary base through its purchases or sales of securities in the open market, called **open market operations**, and through its extension of discount loans to banks.

Federal Reserve Open Market Operations

The primary way in which the Fed causes changes in the monetary base is through its open market operations. A purchase of bonds by the Fed is called an **open market purchase**, and a sale of bonds by the Fed is called an **open market sale**. Federal Reserve purchases and sales of bonds are always done through **primary dealers**, government securities dealers who operate out of private banking institutions.

Open Market Purchase   Suppose the Fed purchases $100 million of bonds from a primary dealer. To understand the consequences of this transaction, we look at *T-accounts*, which list only the changes that occur in balance sheet items, starting from the initial balance sheet position.

When the primary dealer sells the $100 million of bonds to the Fed, the Fed adds $100 million to the dealer's deposit account at the Fed, so that reserves in the banking system go up by $100 million. The banking system's T-account after this transaction is

Banking System		
Assets		**Liabilities**
Securities	−$100 m	
Reserves	+$100 m	

The effects on the Fed's balance sheet are shown next. The balance sheet shows an increase of $100 million of securities in its assets column, along with an increase of $100 million of reserves in its liabilities column:

Federal Reserve System		
Assets		**Liabilities**
Securities	+$100 m	Reserves +$100 m

---

[4]Here, currency in circulation includes both Federal Reserve currency (Federal Reserve notes) and Treasury currency (primarily coins).

As you can see, the Fed's open market purchase of $100 million causes an expansion of reserves in the banking system by an equal amount. Another way of seeing this is to recognize that open market purchases of bonds expand reserves because the central bank pays for the bonds with reserves. Because the monetary base equals currency plus reserves, an open market purchase increases the monetary base by an amount equal to the amount of the purchase.

Open Market Sale   Similar reasoning indicates that if the Fed conducts an open market sale of $100 million of bonds to a primary dealer, the Fed deducts $100 million from the dealer's deposit account, so the Fed's reserves (liabilities) fall by $100 million (and the monetary base falls by the same amount). The T-account is now

Federal Reserve System			
Assets		**Liabilities**	
Securities	−$100 m	Reserves	−$100 m

Shifts from Deposits into Currency

Even when the Fed does not conduct open market operations, a shift from deposits to currency will affect the reserves in the banking system. However, such a shift will have no effect on the monetary base. This tells us that the Fed has more control over the monetary base than over reserves.

Let's suppose that during the Christmas season, the public wants to hold more currency to buy gifts and so withdraws $100 million in cash. The effect on the T-account of the nonbank public is

Nonbank Public			
Assets		**Liabilities**	
Checkable deposits	−$100 m		
Currency	+$100 m		

The banking system loses $100 million of deposits and hence $100 million of reserves:

Banking System			
Assets		**Liabilities**	
Reserves	−$100 m	Checkable deposits	−$100 m

For the Fed, the public's action means that $100 million of additional currency is circulating in the hands of the public, while reserves in the banking system have fallen by $100 million. The Fed's T-account is

Federal Reserve System	
Assets	**Liabilities**
	Currency in circulation +$100 m
	Reserves −$100 m

The net effect on the monetary liabilities of the Fed is a wash; the monetary base is unaffected by the public's increased desire for cash. But reserves *are* affected. Random fluctuations of reserves can occur as a result of random shifts into currency and out of deposits, and vice versa. The same is not true for the monetary base, making it a more stable variable and more controllable by the Fed.

Loans to Financial Institutions

In this chapter so far, we have seen how changes in the monetary base occur as a result of open market operations. However, the monetary base is also affected when the Fed makes a loan to a financial institution. When the Fed makes a $100 million loan to the First National Bank, the bank is credited with $100 million of reserves from the proceeds of the loan. The effects on the balance sheets of the banking system and the Fed are illustrated by the following T-accounts:

Banking System		Federal Reserve System	
Assets	**Liabilities**	**Assets**	**Liabilities**
Reserves +$100 m	Loans +$100 m (borrowings from the Fed)	Loans +$100 m (borrowings from the Fed)	Reserves +$100 m

The monetary liabilities of the Fed have now increased by $100 million, and the monetary base, too, has increased by this amount. However, if a bank pays off a loan from the Fed, thereby reducing its borrowings from the Fed by $100 million, the T-accounts of the banking system and the Fed are as follows:

Banking System		Federal Reserve System	
Assets	**Liabilities**	**Assets**	**Liabilities**
Reserves −$100 m	Loans −$100 m (borrowings from the Fed)	Loans −$100 m (borrowings from the Fed)	Reserves −$100 m

The net effect on the monetary liabilities of the Fed, and hence on the monetary base, is a reduction of $100 million. We see that the monetary base changes in a one-to-one ratio with the change in the borrowings from the Fed.

Other Factors That Affect the Monetary Base

So far in this chapter, it seems as though the Fed has complete control of the monetary base through its open market operations and loans to financial institutions. However, the world is a little bit more complicated for the Fed. Two important items that affect the monetary base, but are not controlled by the Fed, are *float* and *Treasury deposits at the Fed*. When the Fed clears checks for banks, it often credits the amount of the check to a bank that has deposited it (increases the bank's reserves) before it debits (decreases the reserves of) the bank on which the check is drawn. The resulting temporary net increase in the total amount of reserves in the banking system (and hence in the monetary base) caused by the Fed's check-clearing process is called **float**. When the U.S. Treasury moves deposits from commercial banks to its account at the Fed, leading to an increase in *Treasury deposits at the Fed*, it causes a deposit outflow at these banks such as that shown in Chapter 9, and thus causes reserves in the banking system and the monetary base to decrease. Thus *float* (affected by random events such as the weather, which influences how quickly checks are presented for payment) and *Treasury deposits at the Fed* (determined by the U.S. Treasury's actions) both affect the monetary base but are not controlled by the Fed at all. Decisions by the U.S. Treasury to have the Fed intervene in the foreign exchange market also affect the monetary base.

Overview of the Fed's Ability to Control the Monetary Base

Our discussion above indicates that two primary features determine the monetary base: open market operations and lending to financial institutions. Whereas the amount of open market purchases or sales is completely controlled by the Fed's placing orders with dealers in bond markets, the central bank cannot unilaterally determine, and therefore cannot perfectly predict, the amount of borrowings from the Fed. The Federal Reserve sets the discount rate (interest rate on loans to banks), and then banks make decisions about whether to borrow. The amount of lending, though influenced by the Fed's setting of the discount rate, is not completely controlled by the Fed; banks' decisions play a role, too.

Therefore, we might want to split the monetary base into two components: one that the Fed can control completely and another that is less tightly controlled. The less tightly controlled component is the amount of the base that is created by loans from the Fed. The remainder of the base (called the **nonborrowed monetary base**) is under the Fed's control because it results primarily from open market operations.[5] The nonborrowed monetary base is formally defined as the monetary base minus borrowings from the Fed, which are referred to as **borrowed reserves**:

$$MB_n = MB - BR$$

where MB_n = nonborrowed monetary base
             MB = monetary base
             BR = borrowed reserves from the Fed

Factors not controlled at all by the Fed (for example, float and Treasury deposits with the Fed) undergo substantial short-run variations and can be important sources of fluctuations in the monetary base over time periods as short as a week. However, these

---

[5]Actually, other items on the Fed's balance sheet (discussed in the first appendix to Chapter 14 located in **MyLab Economics**) affect the magnitude of the nonborrowed monetary base. Because their effects on the nonborrowed base relative to open market operations are both small and predictable, these other items do not present the Fed with difficulties in controlling the nonborrowed base.

fluctuations are usually predictable and so can be offset through open market operations. *Although float and Treasury deposits with the Fed undergo substantial short-run fluctuations, which complicate control of the monetary base, they do not prevent the Fed from accurately controlling it.*

14.4 MULTIPLE DEPOSIT CREATION: A SIMPLE MODEL

LO 14.4 Explain and illustrate the deposit creation process through T-accounts.

With our understanding of how the Federal Reserve controls the monetary base and how banks operate (Chapter 9), we now have the tools necessary to explain how deposits are created. When the Fed supplies the banking system with $1 of additional reserves, deposits increase by a multiple of this amount—a process called **multiple deposit creation**.

Deposit Creation: The Single Bank

Suppose the $100 million open market purchase described earlier was conducted with the First National Bank. After the Fed has bought the $100 million in bonds from the First National Bank, the bank finds that it has an increase in reserves of $100 million. To analyze what the bank will do with these additional reserves, assume that the bank does not want to hold excess reserves because it earns little interest on them. We begin the analysis with the following T-account:

First National Bank			
Assets		**Liabilities**	
Securities	−$100 m		
Reserves	+$100 m		

Because the bank has no increase in its checkable deposits, required reserves remain the same, and the bank finds that its additional $100 million of reserves means that its excess reserves have risen by $100 million. Let's say the bank decides to make a loan equal in amount to the $100 million rise in excess reserves. When the bank makes the loan, it sets up a checking account for the borrower and puts the proceeds of the loan into this account. In this way, the bank alters its balance sheet by increasing its liabilities with $100 million of checkable deposits and at the same time increasing its assets with the $100 million loan. The resulting T-account looks like this:

First National Bank			
Assets		**Liabilities**	
Securities	−$100 m	Checkable deposits	+$100 m
Reserves	+$100 m		
Loans	+$100 m		

The bank has created checkable deposits by its act of lending. Because checkable deposits are part of the money supply, the bank's act of lending has, in fact, created money.

In its current balance sheet position, the First National Bank still has excess reserves and so might want to make additional loans. However, these reserves will not stay at the bank for very long. The borrowers took out loans not to leave $100 million sitting idle in a checking account at the First National Bank but to purchase goods and services from other individuals and corporations. When the borrowers make these purchases by writing checks, the checks will be deposited at other banks, and the $100 million of reserves will leave the First National Bank. *As a result, a bank cannot safely make a loan for an amount greater than the excess reserves that it has before it makes the loan.*

The final T-account of the First National Bank is

First National Bank			
Assets		**Liabilities**	
Securities	−$100 m		
Loans	+$100 m		

The increase in reserves of $100 million has been converted into additional loans of $100 million at the First National Bank, plus an additional $100 million of deposits that have made their way to other banks. (All the checks written on accounts at the First National Bank are deposited in banks rather than converted into cash, because we are assuming that the public does not want to hold any additional currency.) Now let's see what happens to these deposits at the other banks.

Deposit Creation: The Banking System

To simplify the analysis, let's assume that the $100 million of deposits created by First National Bank's loan is deposited at Bank A and that this bank and all other banks hold no excess reserves. Bank A's T-account becomes

Bank A			
Assets		**Liabilities**	
Reserves	+$100 m	Checkable deposits	+$100 m

If the required reserve ratio is 10%, this bank will now find itself with a $10 million increase in required reserves, leaving it $90 million of excess reserves. Because Bank A (like the First National Bank) does not want to hold on to excess reserves, it will make loans for the entire amount. Its loans and checkable deposits will then increase by $90 million, but when the borrowers spend the $90 million of checkable deposits, they and the reserves at Bank A will fall back down by this same amount. The net result is that Bank A's T-account will look like this:

Bank A				
Assets			**Liabilities**	
Reserves	+$10 m		Checkable deposits	+$100 m
Loans	+$90 m			

If the money spent by the borrowers to whom Bank A lent the $90 million is deposited in another bank, such as Bank B, the T-account for Bank B will be

Bank B				
Assets			**Liabilities**	
Reserves	+$90 m		Checkable deposits	+$90 m

The checkable deposits in the banking system have risen by another $90 million, for a total increase of $190 million ($100 million at Bank A plus $90 million at Bank B). In fact, the distinction between Bank A and Bank B is not necessary to obtain the same result on the overall expansion of deposits. If the borrowers from Bank A write checks to someone who deposits them at Bank A, the same change in deposits occurs. The T-accounts for Bank B would just apply to Bank A, and its checkable deposits would increase by the total amount of $190 million.

Bank B will want to modify its balance sheet further. It must keep 10% of $90 million ($9 million) as required reserves and has 90% of $90 million ($81 million) in excess reserves and so can make loans of this amount. Bank B will make loans totaling $81 million to borrowers, who spend the proceeds from the loans. Bank B's T-account will be

Bank B				
Assets			**Liabilities**	
Reserves	+$ 9 m		Checkable deposits	+$90 m
Loans	+$81 m			

The $81 million spent by the borrowers from Bank B will be deposited in another bank (Bank C). Consequently, from the initial $100 million increase of reserves in the banking system, the total increase of checkable deposits in the system so far is $271 million ($= \$100 \,\mathrm{m} + \$90 \,\mathrm{m} + \$81 \,\mathrm{m}$).

Following the same reasoning, if all banks make loans for the full amount of their excess reserves, further increments in checkable deposits will continue (at Banks C, D, E, and so on), as depicted in Table 1. Therefore, the total increase in deposits from the initial $100 increase in reserves will be $1,000 million: The increase is tenfold, the reciprocal of the 10% (0.10) reserve requirement.

TABLE 1	Creation of Deposits (assuming a 10% reserve requirement and a $100 million increase in reserves)		
Bank	**Increase in Deposits ($)**	**Increase in Loans ($)**	**Increase in Reserves ($)**
First National	0.00	100.00 m	0.00
A	100.00 m	90.00 m	10.00 m
B	90.00 m	81.00 m	9.00 m
C	81.00 m	72.90 m	8.10 m
D	72.90 m	65.61 m	7.29 m
E	65.61 m	59.05 m	6.56 m
F	59.05 m	53.14 m	5.91 m
.	.	.	.
.	.	.	.
.	.	.	.
.	.	.	.
Total for all banks	1,000.00 m	1,000.00 m	100.00 m

If the banks choose to invest their excess reserves in securities, the result is the same. If Bank A had taken its excess reserves and purchased securities instead of making loans, its T-account would have looked like this:

Bank A		
Assets		**Liabilities**
Reserves	+$10 m	Checkable deposits +$100 m
Securities	+$90 m	

When the bank buys $90 million of securities, it writes $90 million in checks to the sellers of the securities, who in turn deposit the $90 million at a bank such as Bank B. Bank B's checkable deposits increase by $90 million, and the deposit expansion process is the same as before. *Whether a bank chooses to use its excess reserves to make loans or to purchase securities, the effect on deposit expansion is the same.*

You can now see the difference in deposit creation for a single bank versus the banking system as a whole. Because a single bank can create deposits equal only to the amount of its excess reserves, it cannot by itself generate multiple deposit expansion. A single bank cannot make loans greater in amount than its excess reserves, because the bank will lose these reserves as the deposits created by the loan find their way to other banks. However, the banking system as a whole can generate a multiple expansion of deposits, because when a bank loses its excess reserves, these reserves do not leave the banking system, even though they are lost to the individual bank. So as each bank makes a loan and creates deposits, the reserves find their way to another bank, which uses them to make additional loans and create additional deposits. As you have seen, this process continues until the initial increase in reserves results in a multiple increase in deposits.

The multiple increase in deposits generated from an increase in the banking system's reserves is called the **simple deposit multiplier**.[6] In our example, with a 10% required reserve ratio, the simple deposit multiplier is 10. More generally, the simple deposit multiplier equals the reciprocal of the required reserve ratio, expressed as a fraction (for example, 10 = 1/0.10). So the formula for the multiple expansion of deposits can be written as follows:

$$\Delta D = \frac{1}{rr} \times \Delta R \qquad (1)$$

where ΔD = change in total checkable deposits in the banking system
      rr = required reserve ratio (0.10 in the example)
      ΔR = change in reserves for the banking system ($100 million in the example)

Deriving the Formula for Multiple Deposit Creation

The formula for the multiple creation of deposits can be derived directly using algebra. We obtain the same result for the relationship between a change in deposits and a change in reserves.

Our assumption that banks do not hold on to any excess reserves means that the total amount of required reserves in the banking system RR will equal the total reserves in the banking system R:

$$RR = R$$

The total amount of required reserves equals the required reserve ratio rr times the total amount of checkable deposits D:

$$RR = rr \times D$$

Substituting $rr \times D$ for RR in the first equation,

$$rr \times D = R$$

and dividing both sides of the preceding equation by rr gives

$$D = \frac{1}{rr} \times R$$

Taking the change in both sides of this equation and using delta to indicate a change gives

$$\Delta D = \frac{1}{rr} \times \Delta R$$

which is the same formula for deposit creation given in Equation 1.[7]

---

[6]This multiplier should not be confused with the Keynesian multiplier, which is derived through a similar step-by-step analysis. That multiplier relates an increase in income to an increase in investment, whereas the simple deposit multiplier relates an increase in deposits to an increase in reserves.

[7]A formal derivation of this formula follows. Using the reasoning in the text, the change in checkable deposits is $100(= \Delta R \times 1$) plus $90 $[= \Delta R \times (1 - rr)]$ plus $81 $[= \Delta R \times (1 - rr)^2]$ and so on, which can be rewritten as

$$\Delta D = \Delta R \times [1 + (1 - rr) + (1 - rr)^2 + (1 - rr)^3 + \cdots]$$

Using the formula for the sum of an infinite series found in footnote 3 of Chapter 4, this equation can be rewritten as

$$\Delta D = \Delta R \times \frac{1}{1 - (1 - rr)} = \frac{1}{rr} \times \Delta R$$

This derivation provides us with another way of looking at the multiple creation of deposits, because it forces us to examine the banking system as a whole rather than one bank at a time. For the banking system as a whole, deposit creation (or contraction) will stop only when excess reserves in the banking system are zero; that is, the banking system will be in equilibrium when the total amount of required reserves equals the total amount of reserves, as seen in the equation $RR = R$. When $rr \times D$ is substituted for RR, the resulting equation $rr \times D = R$ tells us how high checkable deposits must be for required reserves to equal total reserves. Accordingly, a given level of reserves in the banking system determines the level of checkable deposits when the banking system is in equilibrium (when $ER = 0$); put another way, the given level of reserves supports a given level of checkable deposits.

In our example, the required reserve ratio is 10%. If reserves increase by $100 million, checkable deposits must rise by $1,000 million for total required reserves also to increase by $100 million. If the increase in checkable deposits is less than this—say, $900 million—then the increase in required reserves of $90 million remains below the $100 million increase in reserves, so excess reserves still exist somewhere in the banking system. The banks holding the excess reserves will now make additional loans, thereby creating new deposits; this process will continue until all reserves in the system are used up, which occurs when checkable deposits rise by $1,000 million.

We can also see this by looking at the resulting T-account of the banking system as a whole (including the First National Bank):

Banking System			
Assets		**Liabilities**	
Securities	$-\$\ \ \ 100\ m$	Checkable deposits	$+\$1,000\ m$
Reserves	$+\$\ \ \ 100\ m$		
Loans	$+\$1,000\ m$		

The procedure of eliminating excess reserves by loaning them out continues until the banking system (First National Bank and Banks A, B, C, D, and so on) has made $1,000 million of loans and created $1,000 million of deposits. In this way, $100 million of reserves supports $1,000 million (ten times the quantity) of deposits.

Critique of the Simple Model

Our model of multiple deposit creation seems to indicate that the Federal Reserve is able to exercise complete control over the level of checkable deposits by setting the required reserve ratio and the level of reserves. The actual creation of deposits is much less mechanical than the simple model indicates. If proceeds from Bank A's $90 million loan are not deposited but are kept in currency, nothing is deposited in Bank B and the deposit creation process ceases. The total increase in the money supply is now the $90 million increase in currency plus the initial $100 million of deposits created by First National Bank's loans, which were deposited at Bank A, for a total of only $190 million—considerably less than the $1,000 million we calculated using the simple model above. In other words, currency does not lead to multiple deposit expansion, whereas deposits do. Thus, if some proceeds from loans are not deposited in banks but instead are used to raise the holdings of currency, less multiple expansion occurs overall, and the money supply does not increase by the amount predicted by our simple model of multiple deposit creation.

Another situation ignored in our model is one in which banks do not make loans or buy securities in the full amount of their excess reserves. If Bank A decides to hold on to all $90 million of its excess reserves, no deposits will be made in Bank B, and this will stop the deposit creation process. The total increase in deposits will be only $100 million, not the $1,000 million increase in our example. Hence, if banks choose to hold on to all or some of their excess reserves, the full expansion of deposits predicted by the simple model of multiple deposit creation again does not occur.

Our examples indicate that the Fed is not the only player whose behavior influences the level of deposits and therefore the money supply. Depositors' decisions regarding how much currency to hold and banks' decisions regarding the amount of excess reserves to hold also can cause the money supply to change.

14.5 FACTORS THAT DETERMINE THE MONEY SUPPLY

LO 14.5 List the factors that affect the money supply.

Our critique of the simple model shows how we can expand on it to discuss all the factors that affect the money supply. Let's look at changes in each factor in turn, holding all other factors constant.

Changes in the Nonborrowed Monetary Base, MB_n

As shown earlier in the chapter, the Fed's open market purchases increase the nonborrowed monetary base, and its open market sales decrease it. Holding all other variables constant, an increase in MB_n arising from an open market purchase raises the amount of the monetary base and reserves so that multiple deposit creation occurs and the money supply increases. Similarly, an open market sale that reduces MB_n shrinks the amount of the monetary base and reserves, thereby causing a multiple contraction of deposits and a decrease in the money supply. We have the following result: ***The money supply is positively related to the nonborrowed monetary base MB_n.***

Changes in Borrowed Reserves, *BR*, from the Fed

An increase in loans from the Fed provides additional borrowed reserves and thereby increases the amount of the monetary base and reserves so that multiple deposit creation occurs and the money supply expands. If banks reduce the level of their discount loans, all other variables held constant, the monetary base and amount of reserves fall, and the money supply decreases. The result is this: ***The money supply is positively related to the level of borrowed reserves, BR, from the Fed.***

Changes in the Required Reserve Ratio, *rr*

If the required reserve ratio on checkable deposits increases while all other variables, such as the monetary base, stay the same, we have seen that multiple deposit expansion is reduced and hence the money supply falls. If, in contrast, the required reserve ratio falls, multiple deposit expansion is higher and the money supply rises.

We now have the following result: *The money supply is negatively related to the required reserve ratio rr.* In the past, the Fed sometimes used reserve requirements to affect the size of the money supply. In recent years, however, reserve requirements have become a less important factor in the determination of the money multiplier and the money supply, as we shall see in the next chapter.

Changes in Excess Reserves

When banks increase their holdings of excess reserves, those reserves are no longer being used to make loans, causing multiple deposit creation to stop dead in its tracks, resulting in less expansion of the money supply. If, however, banks choose to hold fewer excess reserves, loans and multiple deposit creation increase, and the money supply rises. *The money supply is negatively related to the amount of excess reserves.*

Recall from Chapter 9 that the primary benefit to a bank of holding excess reserves is that they provide insurance against losses due to deposit outflows; that is, they enable the bank experiencing deposit outflows to escape the costs of calling in loans, selling securities, borrowing from the Fed or other corporations, or bank failure. If banks fear that deposit outflows are likely to increase (that is, if expected deposit outflows increase), they will seek more insurance against this possibility, and excess reserves will rise.

Changes in Currency Holdings

As shown before, checkable deposits undergo multiple expansion, whereas currency does not. Hence, when checkable deposits are converted into currency, as long as the amount of excess reserves is held constant, a switch is made from a component of the money supply that undergoes multiple expansion to one that does not. The overall level of multiple expansion declines, and the money supply falls. However, if currency holdings fall, a switch is made into checkable deposits that undergo multiple deposit expansion, so the money supply rises. This analysis suggests the following result: *Holding excess reserves constant, the money supply is negatively related to currency holdings.*

14.6 OVERVIEW OF THE MONEY SUPPLY PROCESS

LO 14.6 Summarize how the "three players" can influence the money supply.

We now have a model of the money supply process in which all three of the players—the Federal Reserve System, depositors, and banks—directly influence the money supply. As a study aid, Summary Table 1 charts the money supply responses to the five factors discussed above and gives a brief synopsis of the reasoning behind them.

The variables are grouped by the player who is the primary influence behind the variable. The Federal Reserve, for example, influences the money supply by controlling the first two variables. Depositors influence the money supply through their decisions about holdings of currency, while banks influence the money supply with their decisions about borrowings from the Fed and excess reserves.

SUMMARY TABLE 1

Money Supply Response

Player	Variable	Change in Variable	Money Supply Response	Reason
Federal Reserve System	Nonborrowed monetary base, MB_n	↑	↑	More MB for deposit creation
	Required reserve ratio, rr	↑	↓	Less multiple deposit expansion
Banks	Borrowed reserves, BR	↑	↑	More MB for deposit creation
	Excess reserves	↑	↓	Less loans and deposit creation
Depositors	Currency holdings	↑	↓	Less multiple deposit expansion

Note: Only increases (↑) in the variables are shown. The effects of decreases on the money supply would be the opposite of those indicated in the "Money Supply Response" column.

14.7 THE MONEY MULTIPLIER

LO 14.7 Calculate and interpret changes in the money multiplier.

The intuition inherent in the preceding section is sufficient for you to understand how the money supply process works. For those of you who are more mathematically inclined, we can derive all of the above results using a concept called the **money multiplier**, denoted by m, which tells us how much the money supply changes for a given change in the monetary base. The relationship between the money supply M, the money multiplier, and the monetary base is described by the following equation:

$$M = m \times MB \tag{2}$$

The money multiplier m tells us what multiple of the monetary base is transformed into the money supply. Because the money multiplier is typically larger than 1, the alternative name for the monetary base, *high-powered money*, is logical: A \$1 change in the monetary base typically leads to more than a \$1 change in the money supply.

Deriving the Money Multiplier

Let's assume that the desired holdings of currency C and excess reserves ER grow proportionally with checkable deposits D; in other words, we assume that the ratios of these items to checkable deposits are constants in equilibrium, as the braces in the following expressions indicate:

$$c = \{C/D\} = \text{currency ratio}$$
$$e = \{ER/D\} = \text{excess reserves ratio}$$

We will now derive a formula that describes how the currency ratio desired by depositors, the excess reserves ratio desired by banks, and the required reserve ratio set by the Fed affect the multiplier m. We begin the derivation of the model of the money supply with the following equation:

$$R = RR + ER$$

which states that the total amount of reserves in the banking system R equals the sum of required reserves RR and excess reserves ER. (Note that this equation corresponds to the equilibrium condition $RR = R$ given earlier in the chapter, where excess reserves were assumed to be zero.)

The total amount of required reserves equals the required reserve ratio rr times the amount of checkable deposits D:

$$RR = rr \times D$$

Substituting $rr \times D$ for RR in the first equation yields an equation that links reserves in the banking system to the amount of checkable deposits and excess reserves they can support:

$$R = (rr \times D) + ER$$

A key point here is that the Fed sets the required reserve ratio rr to less than 1. Thus $1 of reserves can support more than $1 of deposits, and the multiple expansion of deposits can occur.

Let's see how this works in practice. If excess reserves are held at zero $(ER = 0)$, the required reserve ratio is set at $rr = 0.10$, and the level of checkable deposits in the banking system is $1,600 billion, then the amount of reserves needed to support these deposits is $160 billion $(= 0.10 \times \$1,600$ billion$)$. The $160 billion of reserves can support ten times this amount in checkable deposits because multiple deposit creation will occur.

Because the monetary base MB equals currency C plus reserves R, we can generate an equation that links the amount of the monetary base to the levels of checkable deposits and currency by adding currency to both sides of the preceding equation:

$$MB = R + C = (rr \times D) + ER + C$$

Notice that this equation reveals the amount of the monetary base needed to support the existing amounts of checkable deposits, currency, and excess reserves.

To derive the money multiplier formula in terms of the currency ratio $c = \{C/D\}$ and the excess reserves ratio $e = \{ER/D\}$, we rewrite the last equation, specifying C as $c \times D$ and ER as $e \times D$:

$$MB = (rr \times D) + (e \times D) + (c \times D) = (rr + e + c) \times D$$

We next divide both sides of the equation by the term inside the parentheses to get an expression linking checkable deposits D to the monetary base MB:

$$D = \frac{1}{rr + e + c} \times MB \tag{3}$$

Using the M1 definition of the money supply as currency plus checkable deposits $(M = D + C)$ and again specifying C as $c \times D$, we get

$$M = D + (c \times D) = (1 + c) \times D$$

Substituting in this equation the expression for D from Equation 3 yields

$$M = \frac{1 + c}{rr + e + c} \times MB \tag{4}$$

We have derived an expression in the form of our earlier Equation 2. As you can see, the ratio that multiplies MB is the money multiplier, which tells how much the money supply changes in response to a given change in the monetary base (high-powered money). The money multiplier m is thus

$$m = \frac{1 + c}{rr + e + c} \tag{5}$$

It is a function of the currency ratio set by depositors c, the excess reserves ratio set by banks e, and the required reserve ratio set by the Fed rr.

Intuition Behind the Money Multiplier

To get a feel for what the money multiplier means, let's construct a numerical example with realistic numbers for the following variables:

$$rr = \text{required reserve ratio} = 0.10$$
$$C = \text{currency in circulation} = \$1,200 \text{ billion}$$
$$D = \text{checkable deposits} = \$1,600 \text{ billion}$$
$$ER = \text{excess reserves} = \$2,500 \text{ billion}$$
$$M = \text{money supply (M1)} = C + D = \$2,800 \text{ billion}$$

From these numbers we can calculate the values for the currency ratio c and the excess reserves ratio e:

$$c = \frac{\$1,200 \text{ billion}}{\$1,600 \text{ billion}} = 0.75$$

$$e = \frac{\$2,500 \text{ billion}}{\$1,600 \text{ billion}} = 1.56$$

The resulting value of the money multiplier is

$$m = \frac{1 + 0.75}{0.1 + 1.56 + 0.75} = \frac{1.75}{2.41} = 0.73$$

The money multiplier of 0.73 tells us that, given the required reserve ratio of 10% on checkable deposits and the behavior of depositors, as represented by $c = 0.75$, and banks, as represented by $e = 1.56$, a \$1 increase in the monetary base leads to a \$0.73 increase in the money supply (M1).

An important characteristic of the money multiplier is that it is far less than the simple deposit multiplier of 10 found earlier in the chapter. There are two reasons for this result. First, *although deposits undergo multiple expansion, currency does not.* Thus, if some portion of the increase in high-powered money finds its way into currency, this portion does not undergo multiple deposit expansion. In our simple model earlier in the chapter, we did not allow for this possibility, and so the increase in reserves led to the maximum amount of multiple deposit creation. However, in our current model of the money multiplier, the level of currency does rise when the monetary base MB and checkable deposits D increase, because c is greater than zero. As previously stated, any increase in MB that goes into an increase in currency is not multiplied, so only part of the increase in MB is available to support checkable deposits that undergo multiple expansion. The overall level of multiple deposit expansion must be lower, meaning that the increase in M, given an increase in MB, is smaller than indicated by the simple model earlier in the chapter.

Second, since e is positive, ***any increase in the monetary base and deposits leads to higher excess reserves.*** When there is an increase in MB and D, the resulting increase in excess reserves means that the amount of reserves used to support checkable deposits does not increase as much as it otherwise would. Hence the increase in checkable deposits and the money supply are lower, and the money multiplier is smaller.

Prior to 2008, the excess reserves ratio e was almost always very close to zero (less than 0.001), and so its impact on the money multiplier (Equation 5) was essentially irrelevant. When e is close to zero, the money multiplier is always greater than 1, and it was around 1.6 during that period. However, as we will see in the next chapter, nonconventional monetary policy during the global financial crisis, and again during the coronavirus pandemic, caused excess reserves to skyrocket to over $2 trillion. Such an extraordinarily large value of e caused the excess reserves factor in the money multiplier equation to become dominant, and so the money multiplier fell to below 1, as discussed above.

Money Supply Response to Changes in the Factors

By recognizing that the monetary base is $MB = MB_n + BR$, we can rewrite Equation 2 as

$$M = m \times (MB_n + BR) \tag{6}$$

Now we can demonstrate algebraically all the results given in Summary Table 1, which shows how the money supply responds to the changes in the factors.

As you can see from Equation 6, a rise in MB_n or BR raises the money supply M because the money multiplier m is always greater than zero. We can see that a rise in the required reserve ratio rr lowers the money supply by calculating the value of the money multiplier (using Equation 5) in our numerical example when rr increases from 10% to 15% (leaving all other variables unchanged). The money multiplier then becomes

$$m = \frac{1 + 0.75}{0.15 + 1.56 + 0.75} = \frac{1.75}{2.46} = 0.71$$

which, as we would expect, is less than 0.73.

Similarly, we can see that a rise in excess reserves lowers the money supply by calculating the money multiplier when e is increased from 1.56 to 3.0. The money multiplier decreases from 0.73 to

$$m = \frac{1 + 0.75}{0.1 + 3.00 + 0.75} = \frac{1.75}{3.85} = 0.45$$

We can also analyze what happens in our numerical example when there is a rise in the currency ratio c from 0.75 to 1.50. In this case, something peculiar happens. Instead of falling, the money multiplier rises from 0.73 to

$$m = \frac{1 + 1.50}{0.1 + 1.56 + 1.50} = \frac{2.50}{3.20} = 0.78$$

At first glance, this result might seem counterintuitive. After all, a dollar of monetary base that goes into currency only increases the money supply by one dollar, whereas a dollar of monetary base that goes into deposits leads to multiple deposit expansion that increases the money supply by a factor of 10. Thus it seems as though the shift from deposits to currency should lower the overall amount of multiple expansion and hence the money supply. This reasoning is correct, but it assumes a small value of the excess reserves ratio. Indeed, that is the case during normal times, when the excess reserves ratio is near zero. However, in our current situation, in which the excess reserves ratio e is abnormally high, when a dollar moves from deposits into currency, the amount of excess reserves falls by a large amount, which releases reserves to support more deposits, causing the money multiplier to rise.[8]

APPLICATION Quantitative Easing and the Money Supply During the Global Financial and the Coronavirus Crises

When the global financial crisis became virulent in September 2008, the Fed initiated lending programs and large-scale asset-purchase programs in an attempt to bolster the economy. By the end of 2014, these lending programs and purchases of securities had led to a 350% increase in the Fed's balance sheet and the monetary base. Because these lending and asset-purchase programs, discussed further in Chapter 15, resulted in a huge expansion of the monetary base, they have been given the name "quantitative easing." As our analysis in this chapter indicates, such a massive expansion of the monetary base could potentially lead to a large expansion of the money supply. However, as shown in Figure 1, when the monetary base increased by 350%, the M1 money supply rose by only 100%. How can we explain this result using our money supply model?[9]

The answer is that despite the huge increase in the monetary base, the money supply rose by much less because the money multiplier fell by over 50%. To explain this decline in the money multiplier, let's look at Figure 2, which shows the currency ratio c and the excess reserves ratio e for 2007–2020. We see that the currency ratio had a slight downward trend, which would have raised, not lowered, the money multiplier. Instead, we have to look to the extraordinary rise in the excess reserves ratio e, which climbed 30-fold from September 2008 to December 2014.

What explains this substantial increase in the excess reserves ratio e from September 2008 to December 2014? When the Federal Reserve began to pay interest on excess reserves in October 2008, the interest rate on these reserves was either equal to or slightly greater than the rate at which the banks could lend them out in the federal

---

[8]All the above results can be derived more generally from the Equation 5 formula for m as follows. When rr or e increases, the denominator of the money multiplier increases, and therefore the money multiplier must decrease. As long as $rr + e$ is less than 1 (as is usually the case), an increase in c raises the denominator of the money multiplier proportionally by more than it raises the numerator. The increase in c causes the money multiplier to fall. However, when $rr + e$ is greater than 1 (the current situation), an increase in c raises the numerator of the money multiplier proportionally by more than it raises the denominator, so the money multiplier rises. Recall that the money multiplier in Equation 5 is for the M1 definition of money. The second appendix to Chapter 14 in **MyLab Economics** discusses how the multiplier for M2 is determined. For more background on the currency ratio c, consult the third appendix to this chapter at **MyLab Economics.**

[9]If you would like to see a similar application of the money supply model to what happened to the money supply during the Great Depression period from 1930 to 1933, go to the fourth appendix to Chapter 14 found in **MyLab Economics**.

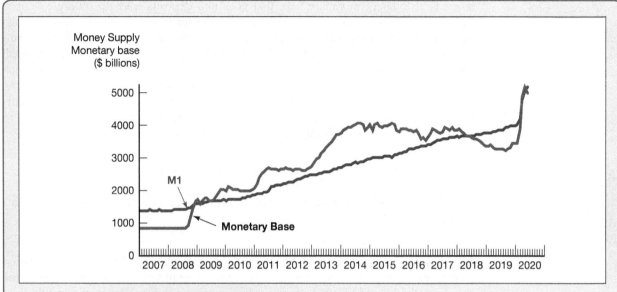

FIGURE 1 **M1 and the Monetary Base, 2007–2020**

In percentage terms the money supply rose by substantially less than the monetary base during the two quantitative easing episodes, the global financial crisis and the coronavirus pandemic.

Source: Federal Reserve Bank of St. Louis FRED database: https://fred.stlouisfed.org/series/BOGMBASE; https://fred.stlouisfed.org/series/M1SL.

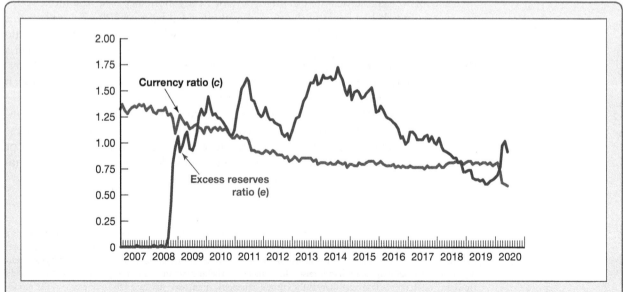

FIGURE 2 **Excess Reserves and Currency Ratio, 2007–2020**

The currency ratio *c* was relatively steady during this period, whereas the excess reserves ratio *e* rose sharply after quantitative easing during the global financial and coronavirus crises.

Source: Federal Reserve Bank of St. Louis FRED database: https://fred.stlouisfed.org/series/EXCSRESNS; https://fred.stlouisfed.org/series/CURRCIR; https://fred.stlouisfed.org/series/TCDNS.

funds market. Because excess reserves now had an opportunity cost close to zero, when the Fed's actions created far more reserves than were needed for banks to meet their reserve requirements, banks were willing to hold any amount of these excess reserves. Therefore, the increase in reserves from quantitative easing led to a large increase in the excess reserves ratio e. As predicted by our money supply model, the huge increase in e sharply lowered the money multiplier, and so the money supply did not undergo that large an expansion from August 2008 to December 2014, despite the huge increase in the monetary base.

When the coronavirus pandemic struck in March 2020, the Federal Reserve again engaged in massive quantitative easing programs to prevent a collapse of the economy. The effects on the monetary base and the money supply displayed a similar pattern to that which occurred when the global financial crisis struck. From February 2020 to June 2020, the monetary base increased by 45%, while the money supply only increased by a much smaller 29%. Just as in the aftermath of the global financial crisis, the increase in excess reserves led to the excess reserves ratio rising sharply: From February 2020 to June 2020, the excess reserves ratio climbed by 33%. As predicted by our money supply model, this increase in e led to a decline in the money multiplier, so the increase in the monetary base again did not lead to as large an increase in the money supply. ◆

SUMMARY

1. The three players in the money supply process are the central bank, banks (depository institutions), and depositors.

2. Four items in the Fed's balance sheet are essential to our understanding of the money supply process: the two liability items, currency in circulation and reserves, which together make up the monetary base; and the two asset items, securities and loans to financial institutions.

3. The Federal Reserve controls the monetary base through open market operations and extensions of loans to financial institutions and has better control over the monetary base than over reserves. Although float and Treasury deposits with the Fed undergo substantial short-run fluctuations, which complicate control of the monetary base, they do not prevent the Fed from accurately controlling it.

4. A single bank can make loans up to the amount of its excess reserves, thereby creating an equal amount of deposits. The banking system can create a multiple expansion of deposits, because as each bank makes a loan and creates deposits, the reserves find their way to another bank, which uses them to make loans and create additional deposits. In the simple model of multiple deposit creation, in which banks do not hold on to excess reserves and the public holds no currency, the multiple increase in checkable deposits (simple deposit multiplier) equals the reciprocal of the required reserve ratio.

5. The simple model of multiple deposit creation has serious deficiencies. Decisions by depositors to increase their holdings of currency or by banks to hold excess reserves will result in a smaller expansion of deposits than is predicted by the simple model. All three players—the Fed, banks, and depositors—are important in the determination of the money supply.

6. The money supply is positively related to the nonborrowed monetary base MB_n, which is determined by open market operations, and the level of borrowed reserves (lending) from the Fed, BR. The money supply is negatively related to the required reserve ratio, rr, and excess reserves. The money supply is also negatively related to holdings of currency but only if excess reserves do not vary much when there is a shift between deposits and currency. The model of the money supply process takes into account the behavior of all three players in the money supply process: the Fed through open market operations and setting of the

required reserve ratio; banks through their decisions to borrow from the Federal Reserve and hold excess reserves; and depositors through their decisions about the holding of currency.

7. The monetary base is linked to the money supply using the concept of the money multiplier, which tells us how much the money supply changes when the monetary base changes.

KEY TERMS

borrowed reserves, p. 324
discount rate, p. 320
excess reserves, p. 320
float, p. 324
high-powered money, p. 319

monetary base, p. 319
money multiplier, p. 333
multiple deposit creation, p. 325
nonborrowed monetary base, p. 324
open market operations, p. 321
open market purchase, p. 321

open market sale, p. 321
primary dealers, p. 321
required reserve ratio, p. 320
required reserves, p. 320
reserves, p. 320
simple deposit multiplier, p. 329

QUESTIONS

Unless otherwise noted, the following assumptions are made in all questions: The required reserve ratio on checkable deposits is 10%, banks do not hold any excess reserves, and the public's holdings of currency do not change.

1. Classify each of these transactions as an asset, a liability, or neither for each of the "players" in the money supply process—the Federal Reserve, banks, and depositors.

   a. You get a $10,000 loan from the bank to buy an automobile.

   b. You deposit $400 into your checking account at the local bank.

   c. The Fed provides an emergency loan to a bank for $1,000,000.

   d. A bank borrows $500,000 in overnight loans from another bank.

   e. You use your debit card to purchase a meal at a restaurant for $100.

2. The First National Bank receives an extra $100 of reserves but decides not to lend out any of these reserves. How much deposit creation takes place for the entire banking system?

3. Suppose the Fed buys $1 million of bonds from the First National Bank. If the First National Bank and all other banks use the resulting increase in reserves to purchase securities only and not to make loans, what will happen to checkable deposits?

4. If a bank depositor withdraws $1,000 of currency from an account, what happens to reserves, checkable deposits, and the monetary base?

5. If a bank sells $10 million of bonds to the Fed to pay back $10 million on the loan it owes, what is the effect on the level of checkable deposits?

6. If you decide to hold $100 less cash than usual and therefore deposit $100 more cash in the bank, what effect will this have on checkable deposits in the banking system if the rest of the public keeps its holdings of currency constant?

7. "The Fed can perfectly control the amount of reserves in the system." Is this statement true, false, or uncertain? Explain.

8. "The Fed can perfectly control the amount of the monetary base, but has less control over the composition of the monetary base." Is this statement true, false, or uncertain? Explain.

9. The Fed buys $100 million of bonds from the public and also lowers the required reserve ratio. What will happen to the money supply?

10. Describe how each of the following can affect the money supply: (a) the central bank; (b) banks; and (c) depositors.

11. "The money multiplier is necessarily greater than 1." Is this statement true, false, or uncertain? Explain your answer.

12. What effect might a financial panic have on the money multiplier and the money supply? Why?

13. During the Great Depression years from 1930 to 1933, both the currency ratio c and the excess reserves ratio e rose dramatically. What effect did these factors have on the money multiplier?

14. In October 2008, the Federal Reserve began paying interest on the amount of excess reserves held by banks. How, if at all, might this affect the multiplier process and the money supply?

15. The money multiplier declined significantly during the period 1930–1933 and also during the recent financial crisis of 2008–2010. Yet the M1 money supply *decreased* by 25% in the Depression period but *increased* by more than 20% during the recent financial crisis. What explains the difference in outcomes?

APPLIED PROBLEMS

Unless otherwise noted, the following assumptions are made in all of the applied problems: The required reserve ratio on checkable deposits is 10%, banks do not hold any excess reserves, and the public's holdings of currency do not change.

16. If the Fed sells $2 million of bonds to the First National Bank, what happens to reserves and the monetary base? Use T-accounts to explain your answer.

17. If the Fed sells $2 million of bonds to Irving the Investor, who pays for the bonds with a briefcase filled with currency, what happens to reserves and the monetary base? Use T-accounts to explain your answer.

18. If the Fed lends five banks a total of $100 million but depositors withdraw $50 million and hold it as currency, what happens to reserves and the monetary base? Use T-accounts to explain your answer.

19. Using T-accounts, show what happens to checkable deposits in the banking system when the Fed lends $1 million to the First National Bank.

20. Using T-accounts, show what happens to checkable deposits in the banking system when the Fed sells $2 million of bonds to the First National Bank.

21. If the Fed buys $1 million of bonds from the First National Bank, but an additional 10% of any deposit is held as excess reserves, what is the total increase in checkable deposits? (*Hint:* Use T-accounts to show what happens at each step of the multiple expansion process.)

22. If reserves in the banking system increase by $1 billion because the Fed lends $1 billion to financial institutions, and checkable deposits increase by $9 billion, why isn't the banking system in equilibrium? What will continue to happen in the banking system until equilibrium is reached? Show the T-account for the banking system in equilibrium.

23. If the Fed reduces reserves by selling $5 million worth of bonds to the banks, what will the T-account of the banking system look like when the banking system is in equilibrium? What will have happened to the level of checkable deposits?

24. If the Fed sells $1 million of bonds and banks reduce their borrowings from the Fed by $1 million, predict what will happen to the money supply.

25. Suppose that currency in circulation is $600 billion, the amount of checkable deposits is $900 billion, and excess reserves are $15 billion.

   a. Calculate the money supply, the currency deposit ratio, the excess reserve ratio, and the money multiplier.

   b. Suppose the central bank conducts an unusually large open market purchase of bonds held by banks of $1,400 billion due to a sharp contraction in the economy. Assuming the ratios you calculated in part (a) remain the same, predict the effect on the money supply.

   c. Suppose the central bank conducts the same open market purchase as in part (b), except that banks choose to hold all of these proceeds as excess reserves rather than loan them out, due to fear of a financial crisis. Assuming that currency and deposits remain the same, what happens to the amount of excess reserves, the excess reserve ratio, the money supply, and the money multiplier?

   d. During the financial crisis in 2008, the Federal Reserve began injecting the banking system with massive amounts of liquidity, and at the same time, very little lending occurred. As a result, the M1 money multiplier was below 1 for most of the time from October 2008 through 2011. How does this scenario relate to your answer to part (c)?

DATA ANALYSIS PROBLEMS

The Problems update with real-time data in **MyLab Economics** and are available for practice or instructor assignment.

1. **Real-time Data Analysis** Go to the St. Louis Federal Reserve FRED database, and find the most current data available on Currency (CURRNS), Total Checkable Deposits (TCDNS), and Excess Reserves (EXCSRESNS).
   a. Calculate the value of the currency deposit ratio c.
   b. Calculate the value of the excess reserve ratio, e.
   c. Assuming a required reserve ratio rr of 11%, calculate the value of the money multiplier m.

2. **Real-time Data Analysis** Go to the St. Louis Federal Reserve FRED database, and find data on the M1 Money Stock (M1SL) and the Monetary Base (BOGMBASE).
   a. Calculate the value of the money multiplier using the most recent data available and the data from five years prior.
   b. Based on your answer to part (a), how much would a $100 million open market purchase of securities affect the M1 money supply today and five years ago?

15

Tools of Monetary Policy

Learning Objectives

15.1 Illustrate the market for reserves, and demonstrate how changes in monetary policy can affect the equilibrium federal funds rate.

15.2 Summarize how conventional monetary policy tools are implemented and the relative advantages and limitations of each tool.

15.3 Explain the key monetary policy tools that are used when conventional policy is no longer effective.

15.4 Identify the distinctions and similarities between the monetary policy tools of the Federal Reserve and those of the European Central Bank.

Preview

In this chapter, we examine the tools of monetary policy used by the Fed to control the money supply and interest rates. Because the Fed's use of these policy tools has such an important impact on interest rates and economic activity, it is vital to understand how the Fed wields them in practice and how relatively useful each tool is.

In recent years, the Federal Reserve has increasingly focused on the **federal funds rate** (the interest rate on overnight loans of reserves from one bank to another) as the primary instrument of monetary policy. Since February 1994, the Fed has announced a federal funds rate target at each Federal Open Market Committee (FOMC) meeting, an announcement that is watched closely by market participants because it affects interest rates throughout the economy. Thus, to fully comprehend how the Fed uses its tools in the conduct of monetary policy, we must understand not only their effect on the money supply but also their direct effect on the federal funds rate and how they can be used to help achieve a federal funds rate that is close to the target. The chapter therefore begins with a supply and demand analysis of the market for reserves to explain how the Fed's settings for the four tools of monetary policy—open market operations, discount policy, reserve requirements, and the interest paid on excess reserves—determine the federal funds rate. We next go on to look in more detail at each of these tools of monetary policy to see how they are used in practice and to gain a sense of their relative advantages. We then examine the nonconventional tools of monetary policy that the Federal Reserve was forced to use during the extraordinary circumstances of the 2007–2009 financial crisis and the coronavirus pandemic in 2020. The chapter ends with a discussion of the tools of monetary policy used by other central banks besides the Federal Reserve.

15.1 THE MARKET FOR RESERVES AND THE FEDERAL FUNDS RATE

LO 15.1 Illustrate the market for reserves, and demonstrate how changes in monetary policy can affect the equilibrium federal funds rate.

In Chapter 14, we saw how open market operations (changes in nonborrowed reserves) and Federal Reserve lending (changes in borrowed reserves) affect the balance sheet of the Fed and the amount of reserves. The market for reserves is where the federal funds rate is determined, and this is why we turn to a supply and demand analysis of this market to analyze how the tools of monetary policy affect the federal funds rate.

Demand and Supply in the Market for Reserves

The analysis of the market for reserves proceeds in a similar fashion to the analysis of the bond market that we conducted in Chapter 5. First, we derive demand and supply curves for reserves. Then, the market equilibrium in which the quantity of reserves demanded equals the quantity of reserves supplied determines the level of the federal funds rate, the interest rate charged on the loans of these reserves.

Demand Curve   To derive the demand curve for reserves, we need to ask what happens to the quantity of reserves demanded by banks, holding everything else constant, as the federal funds rate changes. Recall from Chapter 14 that the amount of reserves can be split up into two components: (1) required reserves, which are equal to the required reserve ratio times the amount of deposits on which reserves are required; and (2) excess reserves, the additional reserves banks choose to hold. Therefore, the quantity of reserves demanded by banks equals required reserves plus the quantity of excess reserves demanded. Excess reserves are insurance against deposit outflows, and the cost of holding these excess reserves is their *opportunity cost*—the interest rate that could have been earned on lending these reserves out minus the interest rate that is earned on these reserves, i_{oer}.

Before the fall of 2008, the Federal Reserve did not pay interest on reserves, but since then it has paid interest on excess reserves at a level that is typically set near the federal funds rate target and therefore changes when the target changes. When the federal funds rate is above the rate paid on excess reserves, i_{oer}, then as the federal funds rate decreases, the opportunity cost of holding excess reserves falls. Holding everything else constant, including the quantity of required reserves, the quantity of reserves demanded rises. Consequently, the demand curve for reserves, R^d, slopes downward in Figure 1 when the federal funds rate is above i_{oer}. If, however, the federal funds rate begins to fall below the interest rate paid on excess reserves i_{oer}, banks do not lend in the overnight market at a lower interest rate. Instead, they just keep on adding to their holdings of excess reserves indefinitely. The result is that the demand curve for reserves, R^d, becomes flat (infinitely elastic) at i_{oer} in Figure 1.

Mini-lecture

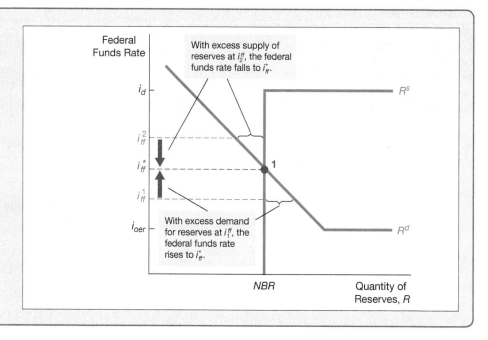

FIGURE 1

Equilibrium in the Market for Reserves

Equilibrium occurs at the intersection of the supply curve R^s and the demand curve R^d, at point 1 and an interest rate of i_{ff}^*.

Supply Curve   The supply of reserves, R^s, can be broken up into two components: the amount of reserves that are supplied by the Fed's open market operations, called *nonborrowed reserves* (NBR), and the amount of reserves borrowed from the Fed, called *borrowed reserves* (BR). The primary cost of borrowing from the Fed is the interest rate charged by the Fed on these loans—the discount rate, i_d, which is set at a fixed amount above the federal funds target rate and thus changes when the target changes. Because borrowing federal funds from other banks is a substitute for borrowing (taking out discount loans) from the Fed, if the federal funds rate i_{ff} is below the discount rate i_d, then banks will not borrow from the Fed. Borrowed reserves will be zero because borrowing in the federal funds market is cheaper. Thus, as long as i_{ff} remains below i_d, the supply of reserves will just equal the amount of nonborrowed reserves supplied by the Fed, NBR, and so the supply curve will be vertical, as shown in Figure 1. If, however, the federal funds rate begins to rise above the discount rate, then banks will not borrow in the federal funds market at all but rather will borrow from the Fed at the discount rate, and so the federal funds rate cannot rise above the discount rate. The result is that the supply curve becomes flat (infinitely elastic) at i_d, as shown in Figure 1.

Market Equilibrium   Market equilibrium occurs when the quantity of reserves demanded equals the quantity supplied, $R^s = R^d$. Equilibrium therefore occurs at the intersection of the demand curve R^d and the supply curve R^s at point 1, with an equilibrium federal funds rate of i_{ff}^*. When the federal funds rate is above the equilibrium rate at i_{ff}^2, more reserves are supplied than are demanded (excess supply), and so the federal funds rate falls to i_{ff}^*, as shown by the downward arrow. When the federal funds rate is below the equilibrium rate at i_{ff}^1, more reserves are demanded than are supplied (excess demand), and so the federal funds rate rises, as shown by the upward arrow. (Note that Figure 1 is drawn so that i_d is above i_{ff}^* because the Federal Reserve typically keeps the discount rate substantially above the target for the federal funds rate.)

How Changes in the Tools of Monetary Policy Affect the Federal Funds Rate

Now that we understand how the federal funds rate is determined, we can examine how changes in the four tools of monetary policy—open market operations, discount lending, reserve requirements, and the interest rate paid on excess reserves—affect the market for reserves and the equilibrium federal funds rate.

Open Market Operations   The effect of an open market operation depends on whether the supply curve initially intersects the demand curve in its downward-sloped section or in its flat section. Panel (a) of Figure 2 shows what happens if the intersection initially occurs on the downward-sloped section of the demand curve. We have already seen that an open market purchase leads to a greater quantity of reserves supplied; this is true at any given federal funds rate because of the higher amount of nonborrowed reserves, which rises from NBR_1 to NBR_2. An open market purchase therefore shifts the supply curve to the right from R_1^s to R_2^s and moves the equilibrium from point 1 to point 2, lowering the federal funds rate from i_{ff}^1 to i_{ff}^2.[1] The same reasoning implies that an open market sale decreases the quantity of nonborrowed reserves supplied, shifts the supply

---

[1]We come to the same conclusion if we use the money supply framework outlined in Chapter 14, along with the liquidity preference framework outlined in Chapter 5. An open market purchase raises reserves and the money supply, and then the liquidity preference framework shows that interest rates fall as a result.

Mini-lecture

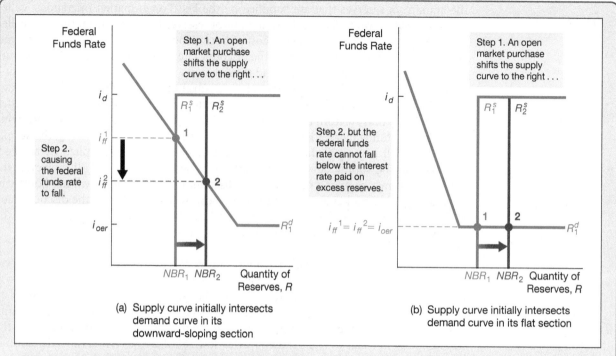

FIGURE 2 **Response to an Open Market Operation**

An open market purchase increases nonborrowed reserves and hence the reserves supplied, and shifts the supply curve from R_1^s to R_2^s. In panel (a), the equilibrium moves from point 1 to point 2, lowering the federal funds rate from i_{ff}^1 to i_{ff}^2. In panel (b), the equilibrium moves from point 1 to point 2, but the federal funds rate remains unchanged, $i_{ff}^1 = i_{ff}^2 = i_{oer}$.

curve to the left, and causes the federal funds rate to rise. Because this is the typical situation—since the Fed usually keeps the federal funds rate target above the interest rate paid on excess reserves—the conclusion is that **an open market purchase causes the federal funds rate to fall, whereas an open market sale causes the federal funds rate to rise.**

However, if the supply curve initially intersects the demand curve on its flat section, as in panel (b) of Figure 2, open market operations have no effect on the federal funds rate. To see this, let's again look at an open market purchase that raises the quantity of reserves supplied, which shifts the supply curve from R_1^s to R_2^s. However, this time we consider the case in which $i_{ff}^1 = i_{oer}$ initially. The shift in the supply curve moves the equilibrium from point 1 to point 2, but the federal funds rate remains unchanged at i_{oer} because **the interest rate paid on excess reserves, i_{oer}, sets a floor for the federal funds rate.**[2]

[2]The federal funds rate can be slightly below the floor set by the interest rate paid on excess reserves because some big lenders in the federal funds market, particularly Fannie Mae and Freddie Mac, are not banking institutions and so cannot keep deposits in the Federal Reserve and get paid the Fed's interest rate on excess reserves. Thus if they have excess funds to lend in the federal funds market, they may have to accept a federal funds rate lower than the interest rate the Fed pays on excess reserves. To make sure that the federal funds rate does not fall much below the floor set by the interest rate on excess reserves, the Federal Reserve has set up another borrowing facility, the *reverse repo facility*, in which these nonbank lenders can lend to the Fed and earn an interest rate that is close to the interest rate the Fed pays on excess reserves.

Mini-lecture

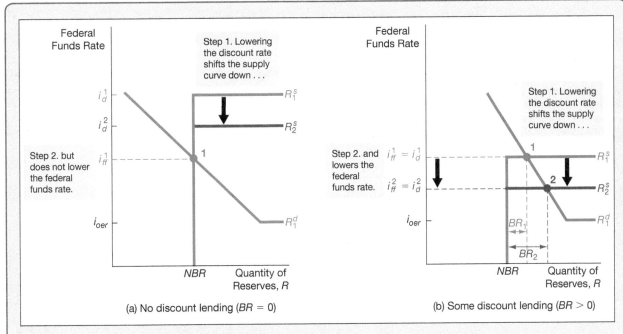

FIGURE 3   **Response to a Change in the Discount Rate**

In panel (a), when the discount rate is lowered by the Fed from i_d^1 to i_d^2, the horizontal section of the supply curve falls, as in R_2^s, and the equilibrium federal funds rate remains unchanged at i_{ff}^1. In panel (b), when the discount rate is lowered by the Fed from i_d^1 to i_d^2, the horizontal section of the supply curve R_2^s falls, and the equilibrium federal funds rate falls from i_{ff}^1 to i_{ff}^2 as borrowed reserves increase.

Discount Lending   The effect of a discount rate change depends on whether the demand curve intersects the supply curve in its vertical section or its flat section. Panel (a) of Figure 3 shows what happens if the intersection occurs on the vertical section of the supply curve so that there is no discount lending and borrowed reserves, *BR*, are zero. In this case, when the discount rate is lowered by the Fed from i_d^1 to i_d^2, the horizontal section of the supply curve falls, as in R_2^s, but the intersection of the supply and demand curves remains at point 1. Thus, in this case, no change occurs in the equilibrium federal funds rate, which remains at i_{ff}^1. Because this is the typical situation—since the Fed now usually keeps the discount rate above its target for the federal funds rate—the conclusion is that **most changes in the discount rate have no effect on the federal funds rate.**

However, if the demand curve intersects the supply curve on its flat section so that there is some discount lending (i.e., $BR > 0$), as in panel (b) of Figure 3, changes in the discount rate do affect the federal funds rate. In this case, initially discount lending is positive and the equilibrium federal funds rate equals the discount rate, $i_{ff}^1 = i_d^1$. When the discount rate is lowered by the Fed from i_d^1 to i_d^2, the horizontal section of the supply curve R_2^s falls, moving the equilibrium from point 1 to point 2, and the equilibrium federal funds rate falls from i_{ff}^1 to i_{ff}^2 ($= i_d^2$), as shown in panel (b). In this case, *BR* increases from BR_1 to BR_2.

Mini-lecture

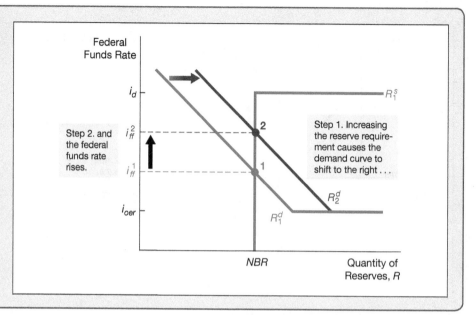

FIGURE 4
Response to a Change in Required Reserves
When the Fed raises reserve requirements, required reserves increase, which raises the demand for reserves. The demand curve shifts from R_1^d to R_2^d, the equilibrium moves from point 1 to point 2, and the federal funds rate rises from i_{ff}^1 to i_{ff}^2.

Reserve Requirements   When the required reserve ratio increases, required reserves increase and hence the quantity of reserves demanded increases for any given interest rate. Thus a rise in the required reserve ratio shifts the demand curve to the right from R_1^d to R_2^d in Figure 4, moves the equilibrium from point 1 to point 2, and in turn raises the federal funds rate from i_{ff}^1 to i_{ff}^2. The result is that **when the Fed raises reserve requirements, the federal funds rate rises.**[3]

Similarly, a decline in the required reserve ratio lowers the quantity of reserves demanded, shifts the demand curve to the left, and causes the federal funds rate to fall. **When the Fed decreases reserve requirements, the federal funds rate falls.**

Interest on Excess Reserves   The effect of a change in the interest rate paid by the Fed on excess reserves depends on whether the supply curve intersects the demand curve in its downward-sloping section or its flat section. Panel (a) of Figure 5 shows what happens if the intersection occurs on the demand curve's downward-sloping section, where the equilibrium federal funds rate is above the interest rate paid on excess reserves. In this case, when the interest rate on excess reserves is raised from i_{oer}^1 to i_{oer}^2, the horizontal section of the demand curves rises, as in R_2^d, but the intersection of the supply and demand curves remains at point 1. However, if the supply curve intersects the demand curve on its flat section, where the equilibrium federal funds rate is equal to the interest rate paid on excess reserves, as in panel (b) of Figure 5, a rise in the interest rate on excess reserves from i_{oer}^1 to i_{oer}^2 moves the equilibrium to point 2, where the equilibrium federal funds rate rises from $i_{ff}^1 = i_{oer}^1$ to $i_{ff}^2 = i_{oer}^2$. **When the federal funds rate is at the interest rate paid on excess reserves, a rise in the interest rate on excess reserves raises the federal funds rate.**

---

[3]Because an increase in the required reserve ratio means that the same amount of reserves is able to support a smaller amount of deposits, a rise in the required reserve ratio leads to a decline in the money supply. Using the liquidity preference framework from Chapter 5, the fall in the money supply results in a rise in interest rates, yielding the same conclusion given in the text—that raising reserve requirements leads to higher interest rates.

Mini-lecture

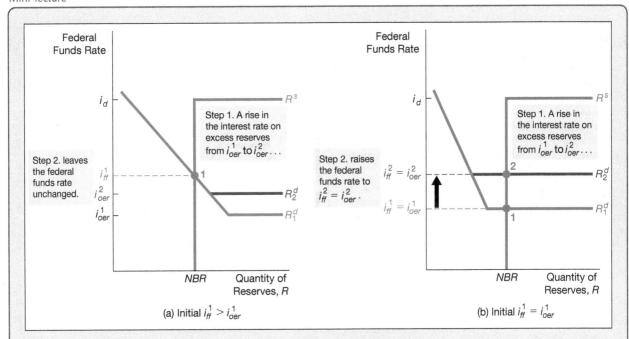

FIGURE 5   **Response to a Change in the Interest Rate on Excess Reserves**

In panel (a), when the equilibrium federal funds rate is above the interest rate paid on excess reserves, a rise in the interest rate on excess reserves from i_{oer}^1 to i_{oer}^2 raises the horizontal section of the demand curve, as in R_2^d, but the equilibrium federal funds rate remains unchanged at i_{ff}^1. In panel (b), when the equilibrium federal funds rate is equal to the interest rate paid on excess reserves, a rise in the interest rate on excess reserves from i_{oer}^1 to i_{oer}^2 raises the equilibrium federal funds rate from $i_{ff}^1 = i_{oer}^1$ to $i_{ff}^2 = i_{oer}^2$.

APPLICATION   How the Federal Reserve's Operating Procedures Limit Fluctuations in the Federal Funds Rate

An important advantage of the Fed's current procedures for operating the discount window and paying interest on excess reserves is that they limit fluctuations in the federal funds rate. We can use our supply and demand analysis of the market for reserves to see why.

Suppose that, initially, the equilibrium federal funds rate is at the federal funds rate target of i_{ff}^T in Figure 6. If the demand for reserves experiences a large unexpected increase, the demand curve shifts to the right to $R^{d''}$, where it now intersects the supply curve for reserves on the flat portion, where the equilibrium federal funds rate i_{ff}'' equals the discount rate i_d. No matter how far the demand curve shifts to the right, the equilibrium federal funds rate i_{ff}'' will stay at i_d because borrowed reserves will just continue to increase, matching the increase in demand. Similarly, if the demand for reserves experiences a large unexpected decrease, the demand curve shifts to the left to $R^{d'}$, and the supply curve intersects the demand curve on its flat portion, where the equilibrium federal funds rate i_{ff}' equals the interest rate paid on excess reserves i_{oer}. No matter how far left the demand curve shifts, the equilibrium federal funds rate stays at

Mini-lecture

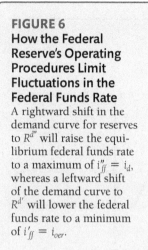

FIGURE 6
How the Federal Reserve's Operating Procedures Limit Fluctuations in the Federal Funds Rate
A rightward shift in the demand curve for reserves to $R^{d''}$ will raise the equilibrium federal funds rate to a maximum of $i''_{ff} = i_d$, whereas a leftward shift of the demand curve to $R^{d'}$ will lower the federal funds rate to a minimum of $i'_{ff} = i_{oer}$.

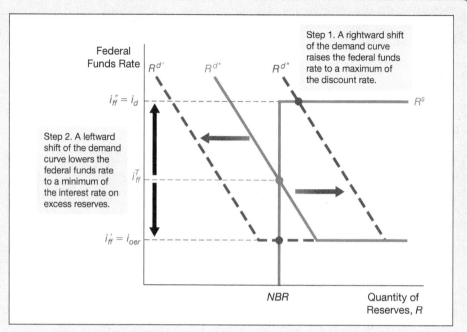

i_{oer} because excess reserves will keep on decreasing so that the quantity demanded of reserves equals the quantity of nonborrowed reserves supplied.[4]

Our analysis therefore shows that the *Federal Reserve's operating procedures limit the fluctuations of the federal funds rate so that it remains between i_{oer} and i_d*. If the range between i_{oer} and i_d is kept narrow enough, then fluctuations around the target rate will be small. ◆

15.2 CONVENTIONAL MONETARY POLICY TOOLS

LO 15.2 Summarize how conventional monetary policy tools are implemented and the relative advantages and limitations of each tool.

During normal times, the Federal Reserve uses three tools of monetary policy—open market operations, discount lending, and reserve requirements—to control the money supply and interest rates, and these three tools are referred to as **conventional monetary policy tools**. We will look at each of them in turn, and then at the additional tool of paying interest on excess reserves, to see how the Fed wields them in practice and how relatively useful each tool is.

[4]Note that, as discussed in footnote 2, the federal funds rate can be slightly below the floor of the interest rate paid on excess reserves.

Open Market Operations

Before the global financial crisis, open market operations were the most important conventional monetary policy tool because they were the primary determinants of changes in interest rates and the monetary base, the main source of fluctuations in the money supply. Open market purchases expanded reserves and the monetary base, thereby increasing the money supply and lowering short-term interest rates. Open market sales shrank reserves and the monetary base, decreasing the money supply and raising short-term interest rates.

Open market operations fall into two categories: **Dynamic open market operations** are intended to change the level of reserves and the monetary base, and **defensive open market operations** are intended to offset movements in other factors that affect reserves and the monetary base, such as changes in Treasury deposits with the Fed or changes in float. The Fed conducts conventional open market operations in U.S. Treasury and government agency securities, especially U.S. Treasury bills. The Fed conducts most of its open market operations in Treasury securities because the market for these securities is the most liquid and has the largest trading volume. It has the capacity to absorb the Fed's substantial volume of transactions without experiencing excessive price fluctuations that would disrupt the market.

As we saw in Chapter 13, the decision-making authority for open market operations is the Federal Open Market Committee (FOMC), which sets a target for the federal funds rate. The actual execution of these operations, however, is conducted by the trading desk at the Federal Reserve Bank of New York, whose operations are described in the Inside the Fed box "A Day at the Trading Desk."

Open market operations are conducted electronically through a specific set of dealers in government securities, known as **primary dealers**, by a computer system called TRAPS (Trading Room Automated Processing System). A message is electronically transmitted to all the primary dealers simultaneously over TRAPS, indicating the type and maturity of the operation being arranged. The dealers are given several minutes to respond via TRAPS with their propositions to buy or sell government securities at various prices. The propositions are then assembled and displayed on a computer screen for evaluation. The desk will select all propositions, beginning with the most attractively priced, up to the point at which the desired amount of securities is purchased or sold, and it will then notify each dealer via TRAPS on which of its propositions have been chosen. The entire selection process is typically completed in a matter of minutes.

Defensive open market operations are of two basic types. In a **repurchase agreement (often called a repo)**, the Fed purchases securities with an agreement that the seller will repurchase them in a short period of time, anywhere from 1 to 15 days from the original date of purchase. Because the effects on reserves of a repo are reversed on the day the agreement matures, a repo is actually a temporary open market purchase and is an especially desirable way of conducting a defensive open market purchase that will be reversed shortly. When the Fed wants to conduct a temporary open market sale, it engages in a **matched sale–purchase transaction (sometimes called a reverse repo)** in which the Fed sells securities and the buyer agrees to sell them back to the Fed in the near future.

At times, the desk may see the need to address a persistent reserve shortage or surplus and wish to arrange a dynamic open market operation that will have a more permanent impact on the supply of reserves. Outright transactions, which involve a purchase or sale of securities that is not self-reversing, are also conducted over TRAPS.

Inside the Fed   A Day at the Trading Desk

The manager of domestic open market operations supervises the analysts and traders who execute the purchases and sales of securities in the drive to hit the federal funds rate target. To get a grip on what might happen in the federal funds market that day, the manager's workday starts early in the morning, around 7:30 a.m., when her staff presents a review of developments in the federal funds market the previous day and an update on the actual amount of reserves in the banking system the day before. Then the staff produces updated reports that contain detailed forecasts of what will be happening to some of the short-term factors affecting the supply and demand of reserves (discussed in Chapter 14). For example, if float is predicted to decrease because good weather throughout the country is speeding up check delivery, the manager of domestic open market operations knows that she will have to conduct a defensive open market operation (in this case, a *purchase* of securities) to offset the expected decline in reserves and the monetary base from the decreased float. However, if Treasury deposits with the Fed are predicted to fall, a defensive open market *sale* would be needed to offset the expected increase in reserves. The report also predicts the change in the public's holding of currency. If currency holdings are expected to rise, then, as we saw in Chapter 14, reserves will fall, and an open market purchase is needed to raise reserves back up again.

This information helps the manager of domestic open market operations and her staff decide how large a change in nonborrowed reserves is needed to reach the federal funds rate target. If the amount of reserves in the banking system is too large, many banks will have excess reserves to lend that other banks may have little desire to hold, and the federal funds rate will fall. If the level of reserves is too low, banks seeking to borrow reserves from the few banks that have excess reserves to lend may push the funds rate higher than the desired level. Also during the morning, the staff will monitor the behavior of the federal funds rate and contact some of the major participants in the market for reserves, which may provide independent information about whether a change in reserves is needed to achieve the desired level of the federal funds rate.

Members of the manager's staff also contact several representatives of the primary dealers with whom the open market desk trades. Her staff finds out how the dealers view market conditions to get a feel for what may happen to the prices of the securities they trade in over the course of the day. They also call the Treasury to get updated information on the expected level of Treasury balances at the Fed to refine their estimates of the supply of reserves.

Members of the Monetary Affairs Division at the Board of Governors are then contacted, and the New York Fed's forecasts of reserve supply and demand are compared with the Board's. On the basis of these projections and the observed behavior of the federal funds market, the desk formulates and proposes a course of action to be taken that day, which may involve plans to add reserves to or drain reserves from the banking system through open market operations. If an operation is contemplated, the type, size, and maturity will be discussed.

At about 9 a.m., a daily conference call takes place, linking the desk with the Office of the Director of Monetary Affairs at the Board of Governors and with one of the four voting Reserve Bank presidents outside New York. During the call, a member of the open market operations unit outlines the desk's proposed reserve management strategy for the day. After the plan is approved, it is announced to the markets at 9:30 a.m., and the desk is instructed to execute immediately any temporary open market operations that are planned for that day.

At times, the desk may see the need to address a persistent reserve shortage or surplus and may wish to arrange an operation that will have a more permanent impact on the supply of reserves. These operations, referred to as *outright operations*, involve a straightforward purchase or sale of securities that is not self-reversing, and they are traditionally executed later in the day, when temporary operations are not being conducted. Even when outright operations are not being conducted, the manager of domestic open market operations and her staff do not sit idle for the rest of the day. They are continually monitoring the markets and bank reserves to plan for the next day's operations.

Discount Policy and the Lender of Last Resort

The facility at which banks can borrow reserves from the Federal Reserve is called the **discount window**. The easiest way to understand how the Fed affects the volume of borrowed reserves is by looking at how the discount window operates.

Operation of the Discount Window

The Fed's discount loans to banks are of three types: primary credit, secondary credit, and seasonal credit.[5] *Primary credit* is the discount lending that plays the most important role in monetary policy. Healthy banks are allowed to borrow all they want at very short maturities (usually overnight) from the primary credit facility, and it is therefore referred to as a **standing lending facility**.[6] The interest rate on these loans is the discount rate, and as we mentioned before, it is set higher than the federal funds rate target, usually by 100 basis points (one percentage point) because the Fed prefers that banks borrow from each other in the federal funds market so that they continually monitor each other for credit risk. As a result, in most circumstances the amount of discount lending under the primary credit facility is very small. If the amount is so small, why does the Fed have this facility?

The answer is that the facility is intended to be a backup source of liquidity for sound banks so that the federal funds rate never rises too far above the federal funds target set by the FOMC. We have already seen how this works in Figure 6. When the demand for reserves experiences a large unexpected increase, no matter how far right the demand curve shifts, the equilibrium federal funds rate i_{ff}^* will stay at i_d because borrowed reserves will just continue to increase, and the federal funds rate can rise no further. The primary credit facility has thus put a ceiling on the federal funds rate at i_d.

Secondary credit is given to banks that are in financial trouble and are experiencing severe liquidity problems. The interest rate on secondary credit is typically set at 50 basis points (0.5 percentage point) above the discount rate. The interest rate on these loans is set at a higher penalty rate to reflect the less-sound condition of these borrowers. *Seasonal credit* is given to meet the needs of a limited number of small banks in vacation and agricultural areas that have a seasonal pattern of deposits. The interest rate charged on seasonal credit is tied to the average of the federal funds rate and certificate of deposit rates. The Federal Reserve has questioned the need for the seasonal credit facility because of improvements in credit markets and is thus contemplating eliminating it at some point in the future.

Lender of Last Resort

In addition to its use as a tool to influence reserves, the monetary base, and the money supply, discounting is important in preventing and coping with financial panics. When the Federal Reserve System was created, its most important role was intended to be as the **lender of last resort**; to prevent bank failures from spinning out of control, the Fed was to provide reserves to banks when no one

---

[5]The procedures for administering the discount window were changed in January 2003. The primary credit facility replaced an adjustment credit facility whose discount rate was typically set below market interest rates, so banks were restricted in their access to this credit. In contrast, healthy banks now can borrow all they want from the primary credit facility. The secondary credit facility replaced the extended credit facility, which focused somewhat more on longer-term credit extensions. The seasonal credit facility remains basically unchanged.

[6]This type of standard lending facility is commonly called a *Lombard facility* in other countries, and the interest rate charged on these loans is often called a *Lombard rate*. (This name comes from Lombardy, a region in northern Italy that was an important center of banking in the Middle Ages.)

else would, thereby preventing bank and financial panics. Discounting is a particularly effective way to provide reserves to the banking system during a banking crisis because reserves are immediately channeled to the banks that need them most.

In performing the role of lender of last resort, the Fed must use the discount tool wisely when attempting to thwart financial panics. This is an extremely important aspect of successful monetary policymaking. Financial panics can severely damage the economy because they interfere with the ability of financial intermediaries and markets to move funds to people with productive investment opportunities (see Chapter 12).

Unfortunately, the discount tool has not always been used by the Fed to prevent financial panics, as the massive bank failures during the Great Depression attest. The Fed learned from its mistakes of that period and has performed admirably in its role of lender of last resort in the post–World War II period. The Fed has used its discount lending weapon several times to avoid bank panics by extending loans to troubled banking institutions, thereby preventing further bank failures.

At first glance, it might seem that the presence of the FDIC, which insures depositors up to a limit of $250,000 per account from losses due to a bank's failure, would make the lender-of-last-resort function of the Fed superfluous. There are two reasons why this is not the case. First, it is important to recognize that the FDIC's insurance fund amounts to about 1% of the total amount of deposits held by banks. If a large number of bank failures occurred simultaneously, the FDIC would not be able to cover all the depositors' losses. Indeed, the large number of bank failures in the 1980s and early 1990s led to large losses and a shrinkage of the FDIC's insurance fund, which reduced the FDIC's ability to cover depositors' losses. This fact has not weakened the confidence of small depositors in the banking system because the Fed has been ready to stand behind the banks to provide whatever reserves are needed to prevent bank panics. Second, the over $1.6 trillion of large-denomination deposits in the banking system are not guaranteed by the FDIC because they exceed the $250,000 limit. A loss of confidence in the banking system could still lead to runs on banks from the large-denomination depositors, and bank panics could still occur despite the existence of the FDIC. The Federal Reserve's role as lender of last resort is, if anything, more important today than ever because of the high number of bank failures experienced in the 1980s and early 1990s and during the global financial crisis from 2007 to 2009.

Not only can the Fed act as a lender of last resort to banks but it can also play the same role in the financial system as a whole. The Fed's discount window can help prevent and address financial panics that are not triggered by bank failures, such as the Black Monday stock market crash of 1987 and the terrorist destruction of the World Trade Center in September 2001 (discussed in the Inside the Fed box, "Using Discount Policy to Prevent a Financial Panic"). Although the Fed's role as the lender of last resort provides the benefit of preventing bank and financial panics, it does come with a cost. If a bank expects that the Fed will provide it with discount loans if it gets into trouble, then it will be willing to take on more risk, knowing that the Fed will come to the rescue if necessary. The Fed's lender-of-last-resort role has thus created a moral hazard problem similar to the one created by deposit insurance (discussed in Chapter 10): Banks take on more risk, thus exposing the deposit insurance agency, and hence taxpayers, to greater losses. The moral hazard problem is most severe for large banks, which may believe that the Fed and the FDIC view them as "too big to fail"; that is, they believe they will always receive Fed loans when they are in trouble because their failure would be likely to precipitate a bank panic.

Inside the Fed   Using Discount Policy to Prevent a Financial Panic

The Black Monday Stock Market Crash of 1987 and the Terrorist Destruction of the World Trade Center in September 2001. Although October 19, 1987, dubbed "Black Monday," will go down in the history books as the day of the largest one-day percentage decline in stock prices to date (the Dow Jones Industrial Average decreased by more than 20%), it was on Tuesday, October 20, 1987, that financial markets almost stopped functioning. Felix Rohatyn, one of the most prominent players on Wall Street, stated flatly: "Tuesday was the most dangerous day we had in 50 years."* Much of the credit for preventing a market meltdown after Black Monday must be given to the Federal Reserve System and then-chair of the Board of Governors, Alan Greenspan.

The stress of keeping markets functioning during the sharp decline in stock prices that occurred on Monday, October 19, meant that many brokerage houses and specialists (dealer-brokers who maintain orderly trading on the stock exchanges) were severely in need of additional funds to finance their activities. However, understandably enough, New York banks, as well as foreign and regional U.S. banks, who were growing very nervous about the financial health of securities firms, began to cut back credit to the securities industry at the very time when it was most needed. Panic was in the air. One chair of a large specialist firm commented that on Monday, "from 2 p.m. on, there was total despair. The entire investment community fled the market. We were left alone on the field." It was time for the Fed, like the cavalry, to come to the rescue.

Upon learning of the plight of the securities industry, Alan Greenspan and E. Gerald Corrigan, then president of the Federal Reserve Bank of New York and the Fed official most closely in touch with Wall Street, became fearful of a spreading collapse of securities firms. To prevent this collapse, Greenspan announced before the market opened on Tuesday, October 20, the Federal Reserve System's "readiness to serve as a source of liquidity to support the economic and financial system." In addition to this extraordinary announcement, the Fed made it clear that it would provide discount loans to any bank that would make loans to the securities industry, although this did not prove to be necessary. As one New York banker said, the Fed's message was, "We're here. Whatever you need, we'll give you."

The outcome of the Fed's timely action was that a financial panic was averted. The markets kept functioning on Tuesday, and a market rally ensued that day, with the Dow Jones Industrial Average climbing over 100 points.

A similar lender-of-last-resort operation was carried out in the aftermath of the destruction of the World Trade Center in New York City on Tuesday, September 11, 2001—the worst terrorist incident in U.S. history. Because of the disruption to the most important financial center in the world, the liquidity needs of the financial system skyrocketed. To satisfy these needs and to keep the financial system from seizing up, within a few hours of the incident, the Fed made an announcement similar to that made after the crash of 1987: "The Federal Reserve System is open and operating. The discount window is available to meet liquidity needs."[†] The Fed then proceeded to provide $45 billion to banks through the discount window, a 200-fold increase over the amount provided during the previous week. As a result of this action, along with the injection of as much as $80 billion of reserves into the banking system through open market operations, the financial system kept functioning. When the stock market reopened on Monday, September 17, trading was orderly, although the Dow Jones Average did decrease 7%.

The terrorists were able to bring down the twin towers of the World Trade Center, causing nearly 3,000 deaths. However, they were unable to bring down the U.S. financial system because of the timely actions of the Federal Reserve.

*"Terrible Tuesday: How the Stock Market Almost Disintegrated a Day After the Crash," *Wall Street Journal*, November 20, 1987, 1. This article provides a fascinating and more detailed view of the events described here and is the source of all the quotations cited.

[†]"Economic Front: How Policy Makers Regrouped to Defend the Financial System," *Wall Street Journal*, September 18, 2001, A1, provides more detail on this episode.

Similarly, Federal Reserve actions to prevent financial panics may encourage financial institutions other than banks to take on greater risk. They, too, expect that the Fed will bail them out if their failure would cause or worsen a financial panic. When the Fed considers using the discount window to prevent a panic, it needs to consider the trade-off between the moral hazard cost of its role as lender of last resort and the benefit of preventing the financial panic. This trade-off explains why the Fed must be careful not to perform its function as lender of last resort too frequently.

Reserve Requirements

As we saw in Chapter 14, changes in the required reserve ratio affect the money supply by causing the money supply multiplier to change. A rise in reserve requirements reduces the amount of deposits that can be supported by a given level of the monetary base and leads to a contraction of the money supply. A rise in reserve requirements also increases the demand for reserves and raises the federal funds rate. Conversely, a decline in reserve requirements leads to an expansion of the money supply and a fall in the federal funds rate. Because it is costly for banks to modify their reserve holdings when there is a change in reserve requirements, changes in reserve requirements are now only rarely used as a monetary policy tool.

Under the Depository Institutions Deregulation and Monetary Control Act of 1980, all depository institutions, including commercial banks, savings and loan associations, mutual savings banks, and credit unions, are subject to the same reserve requirements. Up until March 2020, required reserves on all checkable deposits—including non–interest-bearing checking accounts, NOW accounts, super-NOW accounts, and ATS (automatic transfer savings) accounts—were equal to zero for the first $16.9 million of a bank's checkable deposits, 3% on checkable deposits from $16.9 to $127.5 million, and 10% on checkable deposits over $127.5 million.[7] However, to encourage banks to lend during the coronavirus crisis, on March 15, 2020, the Fed announced a reduction in reserve requirements to zero.

Interest on Excess Reserves

Because the Fed started paying interest on excess reserves only in 2008, this tool of monetary policy does not have a long history. For the same reason the Fed sets the discount rate above the federal funds target—that is, to encourage borrowing and lending in the federal funds market so that banks monitor each other—the Fed typically sets the interest rate on excess reserves as a floor under the federal funds target. In the aftermath of the global financial crisis, banks accumulated huge quantities of reserves and, in this situation, increasing the federal funds rate would require massive amounts of open market operations to remove these reserves from the banking system. The interest-on-excess-reserves tool came to the rescue because it can be used to raise the federal funds rate, as illustrated in panel (b) of Figure 5. Indeed, this tool of monetary policy has become the primary tool to control the federal funds rate.

---

[7]These figures are for 2020. Each year, the figures are adjusted upward by 80% of the percentage increase in checkable deposits in the United States.

15.3 NONCONVENTIONAL MONETARY POLICY TOOLS AND QUANTITATIVE EASING IN THE WAKE OF THE GLOBAL FINANCIAL CRISIS AND THE CORONAVIRUS PANDEMIC

LO 15.3 Explain the key monetary policy tools that are used when conventional policy is no longer effective.

In normal times, conventional monetary policy tools, which expand the money supply and lower interest rates, are enough to stabilize the economy. However, when the economy experiences a full-scale financial crisis like the one we recently experienced, conventional monetary policy tools cannot do the job, for two reasons. First, the financial system seizes up to such an extent that it becomes unable to allocate capital to productive uses, and so investment spending and the economy collapse, as discussed in Chapter 12. Second, the negative shock to the economy can lead to the **effective-lower-bound problem**, in which the central bank is unable to lower its policy interest rate (the federal funds rate for the Fed) much below zero. A negative federal funds rate well below zero would imply that banks are willing to earn a much lower return by lending in the federal funds market than they could earn by holding cash in their vaults, with its zero rate of return, as occurred at the end of 2008. For both of these reasons, central banks needed non–interest-rate tools, known as **nonconventional monetary policy tools**, to stimulate the economy in the wake of the global financial crisis and the coronavirus pandemic. These nonconventional monetary policy tools take four forms: (1) liquidity provision, (2) asset purchases, (3) forward guidance, and (4) negative interest rates on bank deposits at a central bank.

Liquidity Provision

Because conventional monetary policy actions were not sufficient to bolster financial markets during the recent financial crisis and the coronavirus pandemic, the Federal Reserve implemented unprecedented increases in its lending facilities to provide liquidity to the financial markets.

1. **Discount Window Expansion:** At the outset of the crisis in mid-August 2007, the Fed lowered the discount rate (the interest rate on loans it makes to banks) to 50 basis points (0.50 percentage point) above the federal funds rate target from the normal 100 basis points. It then lowered it further in March 2008, to only 25 basis points above the federal funds rate target. Similarly, it lowered the discount rate by 150 basis points in March 2020 as a result of the coronavirus pandemic. However, because bank borrowing from the discount window has a "stigma" attached to it (because such borrowing suggests that the borrowing bank is desperate for funds and thus in trouble), use of the discount window has proved insufficient during crises.

2. **Term Auction Facility:** To encourage borrowing by banking institutions that avoided the stigma problem, in December 2007 the Fed set up a temporary Term Auction Facility (TAF), in which it made loans at a rate determined through competitive auctions. The TAF was more widely used than the discount window facility because it enabled banks to borrow at a rate lower than the discount rate, and the rate was determined competitively rather than being set at a penalty rate. The TAF auctions started at amounts of $20 billion, but as the crisis worsened, the Fed raised the amounts dramatically, with a total outstanding of over $400 billion. (The European Central Bank conducted similar operations, with one auction in June 2008 of over 400 billion euros.) After the global financial crisis, the TAF was discontinued.

3. **New Lending Programs:** During the global financial crisis, the Fed broadened its provision of liquidity to the financial system well beyond its traditional lending to banking institutions. These actions included lending to investment banks as well as lending to promote purchases of commercial paper, mortgage-backed securities, and other asset-backed securities. In addition, the Fed engaged in lending to J.P. Morgan to assist in its purchase of Bear Stearns and to AIG to prevent its failure. The enlargement of the Fed's lending programs during the 2007–2009 financial crisis was indeed remarkable, expanding the Fed's balance sheet by over $1 trillion by the end of 2008, with the balance sheet expansion continuing even after 2008. During the coronavirus crisis, the Fed went even further in extending credit to nonfinancial institutions. With the backing of the U.S. Treasury, it set up facilities to lend to small businesses, corporations, and state and local governments, The number of new programs introduced over the course of the crisis spawned a whole new set of abbreviations, including the TAF, TSLF, PDCF, AMLF, MMIFF, CPFF, TALF, PMCCF, SMCCF, PPPLF, MLF, MSNLF, and FIMA. These facilities are described in more detail in the Inside the Fed box "Fed Lending Facilities During the Global Financial and Coronavirus Crises."

Large-Scale Asset Purchases

The Fed's open market operations normally involve only the purchase of government securities, particularly those that are short-term. However, during the global financial crisis, the Fed started several new, large-scale-asset-purchase programs (often referred to as LSAPs) to lower interest rates for particular types of credit. Then with the coronavirus pandemic, the Fed reinstituted these large-scale-asset-purchase programs:

1. In November 2008, the Fed set up a Government Sponsored Entities Purchase Program in which the Fed eventually purchased $1.25 trillion of mortgage-backed securities (MBS) guaranteed by Fannie Mae and Freddie Mac. Through these purchases, the Fed hoped to prop up the MBS market and to lower interest rates on residential mortgages to stimulate the housing market.

2. In November 2010, the Fed announced that it would purchase $600 billion of long-term Treasury securities at a rate of about $75 billion per month. This large-scale purchase program, which became known as *QE2* (which stands for Quantitative Easing 2, not the Cunard cruise ship), was intended to lower long-term interest rates. Although *short-term* interest rates on Treasury securities hit a floor of zero during the global financial crisis, *long-term* interest rates did not. Since investment projects have a long life, long-term interest rates are more relevant to investment decisions than short-term rates. The Fed's purchase of long-term Treasuries was an effort to stimulate investment spending and the economy by lowering long-term interest rates.

3. In September 2012, the Federal Reserve announced a third large-scale-asset-purchase program, which became known as *QE3*, that combined elements of QE1 and QE2. Through QE3, the Fed conducted monthly purchases of $40 billion of mortgage-backed securities and $45 billion of long-term Treasuries. However, QE3 differed in one major way from the previous QE programs in that its goal was not to increase assets by a fixed dollar amount but instead was open-ended, with the purchase plan set to continue "if the outlook for the labor market does not improve substantially."

Inside the Fed Fed Lending Facilities During the Global Financial and Coronavirus Crises

During the global financial crisis and the coronavirus pandemic, the Federal Reserve became very creative in assembling a host of new lending facilities to help restore liquidity to different parts of the financial system. The new facilities, the dates on which they were established, and their functions are listed in the table below.

Lending Facility	Date Established	Function
Term Auction Facility (TAF)	December 12, 2007	To increase borrowing from the Fed, the TAF extends loans of fixed amounts to banks at interest rates that are determined by competitive auction rather than set by the Fed, as with normal discount lending.
Term Securities Lending Facility (TSLF)	March 11, 2008	To provide sufficient Treasury securities to act as collateral in credit markets, the TSLF lends Treasury securities to primary dealers for terms longer than overnight against a broad range of collateral.
Central Bank Liquidity Swaps	March 11, 2008, and March 15, 2020	Swap Lines lend dollars to foreign central banks in exchange for foreign currencies so that these central banks can in turn make dollar loans to their domestic banks.
Loans to J.P. Morgan to buy Bear Stearns	March 14, 2008	Buys $30 billion of Bear Stearns assets through nonrecourse loans to J.P. Morgan to facilitate its purchase of Bear Stearns
Primary Dealer Credit Facility (PDCF)	March 16, 2008, and March 17, 2020	PDCF lends to primary dealers (including investment banks) so that they can borrow on terms similar to those on which banks borrow from the traditional discount window facility.
Loans to AIG	September 16, 2008	Loans $85 billion to AIG
Asset-Backed Commercial Paper Money Market Mutual Fund Liquidity Facility (AMLF)	September 19, 2008	AMLF lends to primary dealers so that they can purchase asset-backed commercial paper from money market mutual funds so that these funds can sell this paper to meet redemptions from their investors.
Commercial Paper Funding Facility (CPFF)	October 7, 2008, and March 23, 2020	CPFF finances purchase of commercial paper from issuers.
Money Market Investor Funding Facility (MMIFF)	October 21, 2008	MMIFF lends to special-purpose vehicles that can buy a wider range of money market mutual fund assets.
Term Asset-Backed Securities Loan Facility (TALF)	November 25, 2008, and March 23, 2020	TALF lends to issuers of asset-backed securities against these securities as collateral to improve functioning of this market.
Money Market Mutual Fund Liquidity Facility (MMLF)	March 18, 2020	MMLF lends to banks that buy money market mutual fund assets.

(continued)

Lending Facility	Date Established	Function
Primary Market Credit Facility (PMCCF)	March 23, 2020	PMCCF makes loans to investment-grade companies.
Secondary Market Corporate Credit Facility (SMCCF)	March 23, 2020	SMCCF purchases secondary market, investment-grade corporate bonds.
Paycheck Protection Program Liquidity Facility (PPPLF)	April 9, 2020	PPPLF provides credit to financial institutions that originate the Small Business Administration Paycheck Protection Program loans to small businesses.
Municipal Liquidity Facility (MLF)	April 9, 2020	MLF purchases up to $500 billion of state and local government bonds.
Main Street Lending Program, which includes Main Street New Loan Facility (MSNLF) and Main Street Expanded Loan Facility (MSELF)	April 9, 2020	MSNLF and MSELF purchase 95% participations in loans made by financial institutions to small and medium-sized businesses, with the financial institution retaining 5% of the loan.
Temporary Foreign and International Monetary Authorities (FIMA) Repo Facility	March 31, 2020	FIMA Repo facility provides repurchase agreements in which international monetary authorities temporarily exchange U.S. Treasury securities for U.S. dollars.

4. At the March 15, 2020, FOMC meeting, the Fed opened a new round of large-scale asset purchases, authorizing the purchases by at least $500 billion of Treasury securities and $200 billion of mortgage-backed securities.

These liquidity-provision and large-scale-asset-purchase programs led to an unprecedented quadrupling of the Federal Reserve's balance sheet (shown in Figure 7) from 2008 to 2014, and then a further sharp increase in the Fed's balance sheet starting in March 2020.

Quantitative Easing Versus Credit Easing

As we just learned, the programs introduced by the Fed in response to the global financial crisis led to an unprecedented expansion of the Federal Reserve's balance sheet from about $900 billion to over $4 trillion by 2014. Then the Fed instituted similar programs in response to the coronavirus pandemic, leading to a further expansion to over $7 trillion in June 2020. This expansion of the balance sheet is referred to as **quantitative easing** because, as shown in Chapter 14, it leads to a huge increase in the monetary base. Because such an increase in the monetary base would usually result in an expansion of the money supply, it seems as though such an expansion could be a powerful force in stimulating the economy in the near term and possibly producing inflation down the road.

There are reasons to be very skeptical of this hypothesis. First, as we saw in the final application in Chapter 14, the huge expansion in the Fed's balance sheet and the

Real-time data

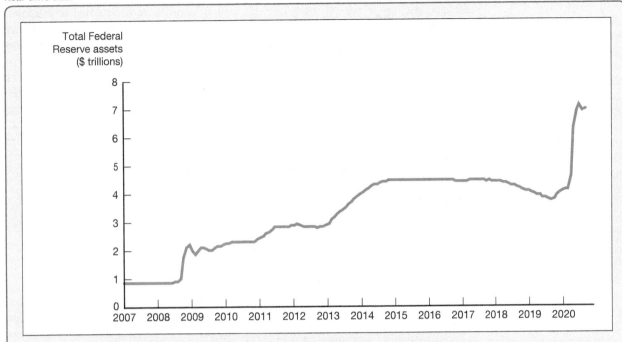

FIGURE 7 **The Expansion of the Federal Reserve's Balance Sheet, 2007–2020**
The size of the Federal Reserve's balance sheet more than quadrupled during and after the global financial crisis and then shot up again during the coronavirus pandemic.
Source: Federal Reserve Bank of St. Louis FRED database: https://fred.stlouisfed.org/series/WALCL.

monetary base did not result in a large increase in the money supply, because most of the increase in the monetary base just flowed into holdings of excess reserves. Second, because the federal funds rate had already fallen to the effective lower bound, the expansion of the balance sheet and the monetary base could not lower short-term interest rates any further and thereby stimulate the economy. Third, an increase in the monetary base does not mean that banks will increase lending, because they can just add to their holdings of excess reserves instead of making loans. Indeed, this appears to be exactly what happened during the global financial crisis, when the huge increase in the monetary base led primarily to a massive rise in excess reserves, and bank lending did not increase. A similar phenomenon seems to have occurred when the Bank of Japan engaged in quantitative easing after Japan's stock and real estate market bubbles burst in the 1990s; yet not only did the Japanese economy fail to recover, but inflation even turned negative.

Does skepticism about the merits of quantitative easing mean that the Fed's non-conventional monetary policy actions during the financial crisis were ineffective in stimulating the economy? The Fed chair at the time, Ben Bernanke, argued that the answer is no, because the Fed's policies were directed not at expanding the Fed's balance sheet but rather at **credit easing**—that is, altering the composition of the Fed's balance sheet to improve the functioning of particular segments of the credit markets. Indeed, Bernanke was adamant that the Fed's policies should not be characterized as quantitative easing.

Altering the composition of the Fed's balance sheet can stimulate the economy in several ways. First, when the Fed provides liquidity to a particular segment of the credit markets that has seized up, such liquidity can help unfreeze the market and thereby enable it to allocate capital to productive uses, consequently stimulating the economy. Second, when the Fed purchases particular securities, it increases the demand for those securities and, as we saw in Chapter 6, such an action can lower the interest rates on those securities relative to rates on other securities. Thus, even if short-term interest rates have hit a floor of the effective lower bound, asset purchases can lower interest rates for borrowers in particular credit markets and thereby stimulate spending. For example, purchases of GSE mortgage-backed securities appear to have lowered the interest rates on these securities, which led to a substantial decrease in residential mortgage rates. Purchases of long-term government securities could also lower their interest rates relative to short-term interest rates, and because long-term interest rates are likely to be more relevant to investment decisions, these asset market purchases could boost investment spending. Recent research appears to support this viewpoint, with estimates of the decline in long-term interest rates following the Fed's asset-purchase programs on the order of 100 basis points (one percentage point).[8]

Forward Guidance

Although short-term interest rates could not be driven much below zero in the aftermath of the global financial crisis, the Federal Reserve had the option of taking a different route in its efforts to achieve lower long-term interest rates, which, as we mentioned above, would stimulate the economy. This route involved a commitment by the Fed to keep the federal funds rate at zero for a long period of time. To see how this would work, recall our discussion of the expectations theory of the term structure of interest rates in Chapter 6. There we saw that long-term interest rates will equal an average of the short-term interest rates that markets expect to occur over the life of the long-term bond. By committing to the future policy action of keeping the federal funds rate at zero for an extended period, the Fed could lower the market's expectations of future short-term interest rates, thereby causing the long-term interest rate to fall. Michael Woodford of Columbia University has referred to such a strategy as **management of expectations**, but it is more commonly referred to as **forward guidance**.

The Fed pursued this forward-guidance strategy when it announced, after its FOMC meeting on December 16, 2008, that not only would it lower the federal funds rate target to between zero and ¼% but also that "the Committee anticipates that weak economic conditions are likely to warrant exceptionally low levels of the federal funds rate for some time." The Fed continued to use this type of language in its FOMC statements for several years afterward, even committing to keep the federal funds rate near zero until an actual date of mid-2013 at its FOMC meeting in August 2011 (modified to mid-2015 at later meetings). Although long-term interest rates on Treasury securities did subsequently fall, it is not clear how much of this decline was due to the Fed's forward guidance versus the general weakness of the economy.

There are two types of commitments to future policy actions: conditional and unconditional. The commitment to keep the federal funds rate at zero for an extended period starting in 2008 was *conditional* because it stated that the decision was predicated on a weak economy going forward. If economic circumstances changed, the FOMC was indicating that it might abandon the commitment. Alternatively, the Fed

---

[8]See, for example, Joseph Gagnon, Mathew Raskin, Julie Remache, and Brian Sack, "Large Scale Asset Purchases by the Federal Reserve: Did They Work?" *Federal Reserve Bank of New York Economic Policy Review* 17, no. 1 (May 2011): 41–59.

could have made an *unconditional* commitment by just stating that it would keep the federal funds rate at zero for an extended period, without indicating that this decision might change depending on the state of the economy. An unconditional commitment is stronger than a conditional commitment because it does not suggest that the commitment will be abandoned and so is likely to have a larger effect on long-term interest rates. Unfortunately, it has the disadvantage that, even if circumstances change in such a way that it would be better to abandon the commitment, the Fed may feel that it cannot go back on its word and therefore cannot abandon the commitment.

The disadvantages of an unconditional commitment are illustrated by the Fed's experience in the 2003–2006 period. In 2003, the Fed became worried that inflation was too low and that the probability of a deflation was significant. At the August 12, 2003, FOMC meeting, the FOMC stated, "In these circumstances, the Committee believes that policy accommodation can be maintained for a considerable period." Then, when the Fed started to tighten policy at its June 30, 2004, FOMC meeting, it changed its statement to "policy accommodation can be removed at a pace that is likely to be measured." For the next 17 FOMC meetings, through June 2006, the Fed raised the federal funds rate target by exactly ¼ percentage point at every single meeting. The market interpreted the FOMC's statements as indicating an unconditional commitment, and this is why the Fed may have been constrained not to deviate from a ¼ percentage point move at every FOMC meeting. In retrospect, this commitment led to monetary policy that was too easy for too long, with inflation subsequently rising to well above desirable levels and, as discussed in Chapter 12, may have helped promote the housing bubble whose bursting led to such devastating consequences for the economy.

When the Fed announced a specific date for exiting from exceptionally low rates, many market participants viewed this announcement as an unconditional commitment, despite the Federal Reserve's objections to such an interpretation. To avoid the problems associated with an unconditional commitment, in December 2012 the Fed changed its statement to be more clearly conditional by indicating that "the exceptionally low range for the federal funds rate will be appropriate at least as long as the unemployment rate remains above 6½ percent, and inflation between one and two years ahead is projected to be no more than a half percentage point above the Committee's 2 percent longer-run goal." With the unemployment rate approaching the 6½% mark, at its March 2014 meeting the FOMC dropped forward guidance based on unemployment and inflation thresholds. Subsequently, it announced that it would determine the timing and size of changes in the target for the federal funds rate, taking "into account a wide range of information, including measures of labor market conditions, indicators of inflation pressures and inflation expectations, and readings on financial and international developments."

Negative Interest Rates on Banks' Deposits

With inflation very low and their economies weak after the global financial crisis, central banks in Europe and Japan recently began experimenting with a new nonconventional monetary policy tool, setting interest rates on deposits held by banks at their central banks to be negative. In other words, banks now had to pay their central bank to keep deposits in the central bank. The central bank of Sweden was the first to set negative interest rates on bank deposits in July 2009, followed by the central bank of Denmark in July 2012, the ECB in June 2014, the central bank of Switzerland in December 2014, and the Bank of Japan in January 2016.

Setting negative interest rates on banks' deposits is supposed to work to stimulate the economy by encouraging banks to lend out the deposits they were keeping at the central bank, thereby encouraging households and businesses to spend more. However, there are doubts that negative interest rates on deposits will have the intended, expansionary effect.

First, banks might not lend out their deposits at the central bank, but instead move them into cash. There would be some cost to doing so because banks would have to build more vaults and hire security guards to protect the cash. Nonetheless, they still might prefer to do this rather than lend them out.

Second, charging banks interest on their deposits might be very costly to banks if they still have to pay positive interest rates to their depositors. In this case, bank profitability would fall. The result might then make banks less likely to lend. So instead of being expansionary, negative interest rates on banks' deposits could cause banks to cut back on lending and therefore be contractionary.

The jury is still out on whether negative interest rates on bank deposits held at central banks will stimulate the economy as intended. Indeed, doubts about the effectiveness of this nonconventional monetary policy tool has led the Fed to rule out using this tool to stimulate the economy. However, the Federal Reserve's views might change if the U.S. economy became much weaker and if the experience with negative interest rates in other countries suggested that this tool is effective in stimulating spending.

15.4 MONETARY POLICY TOOLS OF THE EUROPEAN CENTRAL BANK

LO 15.4 Identify the distinctions and similarities between the monetary policy tools of the Federal Reserve and those of the European Central Bank.

Like the Federal Reserve, the European System of Central Banks (usually referred to as the European Central Bank) signals the stance of its monetary policy by setting a **target financing rate**, which in turn sets a target for the **overnight cash rate**. Like the federal funds rate, the overnight cash rate is the interest rate for very short-term inter-bank loans. The monetary policy tools used by the European Central Bank are similar to those used by the Federal Reserve and involve open market operations, lending to banks, and reserve requirements.

Open Market Operations

Like the Federal Reserve, the European Central Bank uses open market operations as its primary tool for conducting monetary policy and setting the overnight cash rate at the target financing rate. **Main refinancing operations** are the predominant form of open market operations and are similar to the Fed's repo transactions. They involve weekly **reverse transactions** (purchase or sale of eligible assets under repurchase or credit operations against eligible assets as collateral) that are reversed within two weeks. Credit institutions submit bids, and the European Central Bank decides which bids to accept. Like the Federal Reserve, the European Central Bank accepts the most attractively priced bids and makes purchases or sales up to the point at which the desired amount of reserves is supplied. In contrast to the Federal Reserve, which conducts open market operations in one location at the Federal Reserve Bank of New York, the European Central Bank decentralizes its open market operations by conducting them through the individual national central banks.

A second category of open market operations is **longer-term refinancing operations**, which are a much smaller source of liquidity for the euro-area banking system and are similar to the Fed's outright purchases or sales of securities. These operations are carried out monthly and typically involve purchases or sales of securities with a maturity of three months. They are not used for signaling the monetary policy stance, but instead are aimed at providing euro-area banks access to longer-term funds.

Lending to Banks

As is the case for the Fed, the next most important tool of monetary policy for the European Central Bank involves lending to banking institutions, which is carried out by the national central banks, just as discount lending is performed by the individual Federal Reserve Banks. This lending takes place through a standing lending facility called the **marginal lending facility**. Through these facilities, banks can borrow (against eligible collateral) overnight loans from the national central banks at the **marginal lending rate**, which is set at 100 basis points above the target financing rate. The marginal lending rate provides a ceiling for the overnight market interest rate in the European Monetary Union, just as the discount rate does in the United States.

Interest on Excess Reserves

As in the United States, Canada, Australia, and New Zealand, the Eurosystem has another standing facility, the **deposit facility**, in which banks are paid an interest rate on excess reserves that is typically 100 basis points below the target financing rate. The prespecified interest rate on the deposit facility provides a floor for the overnight market interest rate, while the marginal lending rate sets a ceiling. The interest rate on excess reserves set by the ECB is not always positive. As discussed above, the ECB set the interest rate on excess reserves to negative values starting in June 2014.

Reserve Requirements

Like the Federal Reserve, the European Central Bank imposes reserve requirements such that all deposit-taking institutions are required to hold 2% of the total amount of checking deposits and other short-term deposits in reserve accounts with national central banks. All institutions that are subject to minimum reserve requirements have access to the European Central Bank's standing lending facilities and participate in open market operations.

SUMMARY

1. A supply and demand analysis of the market for reserves yields the following results: When the Fed makes an open market purchase or lowers reserve requirements, the federal funds rate drops. When the Fed makes an open market sale or raises reserve requirements, the federal funds rate rises. Changes in the discount rate and the interest rate paid on excess reserves may also affect the federal funds rate.

2. Conventional monetary policy tools include open market operations, discount policy, reserve requirements, and interest on excess reserves. Open market operations are the primary tool used by the Fed to implement monetary policy in normal times because they occur at the initiative of the Fed, are flexible, are easily reversed, and can be implemented quickly. Discount policy has the advantage of enabling the Fed to perform its role of lender of last resort, while raising interest rates on excess reserves to increase the federal funds rate eliminates the need to conduct massive open market operations to reduce reserves when banks have accumulated large amounts of excess reserves.

3. Conventional monetary policy tools are no longer effective when the effective-lower-bound problem occurs, in which the central bank is unable to lower short-term interest rates much below zero. In this situation, central banks use nonconventional monetary policy tools, which involve liquidity provision, asset purchases, and forward guidance. Liquidity provision and asset purchases lead to an expansion of the central bank balance sheet, which is referred to as *quantitative easing*. Expansion of the central bank balance sheet by itself is unlikely to have a large impact on the economy, but changing the composition of the balance sheet, which is accomplished by liquidity provisions and asset purchases and is referred to as *credit easing*, can have a large impact by improving the functioning of particular credit markets.

4. The monetary policy tools used by the European Central Bank are similar to those used by the Federal Reserve System and involve open market operations, lending to banks, and reserve requirements. Main financing operations—open market operations in repos that are typically reversed within two weeks—are the primary tool used to set the overnight cash rate at the target financing rate. The European Central Bank also operates standing lending facilities, which ensure that the overnight cash rate remains within 100 basis points of the target financing rate.

KEY TERMS

conventional monetary policy
tools, p. 350
credit easing, p. 361
defensive open market
operations, p. 351
deposit facility, p. 365
discount window, p. 353
dynamic open market operations, p. 351
effective-lower-bound problem, p. 357
federal funds rate, p. 343

forward guidance, p. 362
lender of last resort, p. 353
longer-term refinancing
operations, p. 365
main refinancing operations, p. 364
management of expectations, p. 362
marginal lending facility, p. 365
marginal lending rate, p. 365
matched sale–purchase transaction
(reverse repo), p. 351

nonconventional monetary policy
tools, p. 357
overnight cash rate, p. 364
primary dealers, p. 351
quantitative easing, p. 360
repurchase agreement
(repo), p. 351
reverse transactions, p. 364
standing lending facility, p. 353
target financing rate, p. 364

QUESTIONS

1. If the manager of the open market desk hears that a snowstorm is about to strike New York City, making it difficult to present checks for payment there and so raising the float, what defensive open market operations will the manager undertake?

2. During the holiday season, when the public's holdings of currency increase, what defensive open market operations typically occur? Why?

3. If the Treasury pays a large bill to defense contractors and as a result its deposits with the Fed fall, what defensive open market operations will the manager of the open market desk undertake?

4. If float decreases to below its normal level, why might the manager of domestic operations consider it more desirable to use repurchase agreements to affect the monetary base, rather than an outright purchase of bonds?

5. "The only way that the Fed can affect the level of borrowed reserves is by adjusting the discount rate." Is this statement true, false, or uncertain? Explain your answer.

6. "The federal funds rate can never be above the discount rate." Is this statement true, false, or uncertain? Explain your answer.

7. "The federal funds rate can never be below the interest rate paid on excess reserves." Is this statement true, false, or uncertain? Explain your answer.

8. Why is paying interest on excess reserves an important tool for the Federal Reserve in managing crises?

9. Why are repurchase agreements used to conduct most short-term monetary policy operations, rather than the simple, outright purchase and sale of securities?

10. Open market operations are typically repurchase agreements. What does this tell you about the likely volume of defensive open market operations relative to the volume of dynamic open market operations?

11. Following the global financial crisis in 2008, assets on the Federal Reserve's balance sheet increased dramatically, from approximately $800 billion at the end of 2007 to $4.5 trillion in 2015. Many of the assets held are longer-term securities acquired through various loan programs instituted as a result of the crisis. In this situation, how could reverse repos (matched sale–purchase transactions) help the Fed reduce its assets held in an orderly fashion, while reducing potential inflationary problems in the future?

12. "Discount loans are no longer needed because the presence of the FDIC eliminates the possibility of bank panics." Is this statement true, false, or uncertain?

13. What are the disadvantages of using loans to financial institutions to prevent bank panics?

14. "Considering that raising reserve requirements to 100% makes complete control of the money supply possible, Congress should authorize the Fed to raise reserve requirements to this level." Discuss.

15. Following the coronavirus pandemic in March of 2020, the Federal Reserve reduced the reserve requirement to zero as the size of the Fed's balance sheet approached $6 trillion. What might be the rationale for implementing such a change?

16. What are the advantages and disadvantages of *quantitative easing* as an alternative to conventional monetary policy when short-term interest rates are at the effective lower bound?

17. Why is the composition of the Fed's balance sheet a potentially important aspect of monetary policy during an economic crisis?

18. What is the main advantage and the main disadvantage of an unconditional policy commitment?

19. In which economic conditions would a central bank want to use a "forward-guidance" strategy? Based on your previous answer, can we easily measure the effects of such a strategy?

20. How do the monetary policy tools of the European System of Central Banks compare to the monetary policy tools of the Fed? Does the ECB have a discount lending facility? Does the ECB pay banks an interest rate on their deposits?

21. What is the main rationale behind paying negative interest rates to banks for keeping their deposits at central banks in Sweden, Switzerland, and Japan? What could happen to these economies if banks decide to loan their excess reserves, but no good investment opportunities exist?

22. In early 2016 as the Bank of Japan began to push policy interest rates negative, there was a sharp increase in safes for homes in Japan. Why might this be, and what does it mean for the effectiveness of negative interest-rate policy?

APPLIED PROBLEMS

23. If a switch occurs from deposits into currency, what happens to the federal funds rate? Use the supply and demand analysis of the market for reserves to explain your answer.

24. Why is it that a decrease in the discount rate does not normally lead to an increase in borrowed reserves? Use the supply and demand analysis of the market for reserves to explain.

25. Using the supply and demand analysis of the market for reserves, indicate what happens to the federal funds rate, borrowed reserves, and nonborrowed reserves, holding everything else constant, under the following situations.

   a. The economy is surprisingly strong, leading to an increase in the amount of checkable deposits.

b. Banks expect an unusually large increase in withdrawals from checking deposit accounts in the future.

c. The Fed raises the target federal funds rate.

d. The Fed raises the interest rate on excess reserves above the current equilibrium federal funds rate.

e. The Fed reduces reserve requirements.

f. The Fed reduces reserve requirements and then offsets this action by conducting an open market sale of securities.

DATA ANALYSIS PROBLEMS

The Problems update with real-time data in **MyLab Economics** and are available for practice or instructor assignment.

1. **Real-time Data Analysis** Go to the St. Louis Federal Reserve FRED database, and find data on nonborrowed reserves (NONBORRES) and the federal funds rate (FEDFUNDS).

   a. Calculate the percent change in nonborrowed reserves and the percentage point change in the federal funds rate for the most recent month of data available and for the same month a year earlier.

   b. Is your answer to part (a) consistent with what you expect from the market for reserves? Why or why not?

2. **Real-time Data Analysis** In December 2008, the Fed switched from a point federal funds target to a range target (and it's possible that it will switch back to a point target in the future). Go to the St. Louis Federal Reserve FRED database, and find data on the federal funds targets/ranges (DFEDTAR, DFEDTARU, DFEDTARL) and the effective federal funds rate (DFF). Download into a spreadsheet the data from the beginning of 2006 through the most current data available.

   a. What is the current federal funds target/range, and how does it compare to the effective federal funds rate?

   b. When was the last time the Fed missed its target or was outside the target range? By how much did it miss?

   c. For each daily observation, calculate the "miss" by taking the absolute value of the difference between the effective federal funds rate and the target (use the abs(.) function). For the periods in which the rate was a range, calculate the absolute value of the "miss" as the amount by which the effective federal funds rate was above or below the range. What was the average daily miss between the beginning of 2006 and the end of 2007? What was the average daily miss between the beginning of 2008 and December 15, 2008? What is the average daily miss for the period from December 16, 2008, to the most current date available? Since 2006, what was the largest single daily miss? Comment on the Fed's ability to control the federal funds rate during these three periods.

16 The Conduct of Monetary Policy: Strategy and Tactics

Learning Objectives

16.1 Define and recognize the importance of a nominal anchor.

16.2 Identify the six potential goals that monetary policymakers may pursue.

16.3 Summarize the distinctions between hierarchical and dual mandates.

16.4 Compare and contrast the advantages and disadvantages of inflation targeting.

16.5 Identify the key changes made over time to the Federal Reserve's monetary policy strategy.

16.6 List the four lessons learned from the global financial crisis, and discuss what they mean for inflation targeting.

16.7 Summarize the arguments for and against central bank policy responses to asset-price bubbles.

16.8 Describe and assess the four criteria for choosing a policy instrument.

16.9 Interpret and assess the performance of the Taylor rule as a hypothetical policy instrument for setting the federal funds rate.

Preview

Getting monetary policy right is crucial to the health of the economy. Overly expansionary monetary policy leads to high inflation, which decreases the efficiency of the economy and hampers economic growth. Monetary policy that is too tight can produce serious recessions in which output falls and unemployment rises. It can also lead to deflation, a fall in the price level such as occurred in the United States during the Great Depression and in Japan more recently. As we saw in Chapter 12, deflation can be especially damaging to an economy because it promotes financial instability and can worsen financial crises.

Now that we understand the tools that central banks such as the Federal Reserve use to conduct monetary policy, we can consider how central banks *should* conduct monetary policy. To explore this subject, we start by looking at the goals of monetary policy and then examine one of the most important strategies for the conduct of monetary policy, inflation targeting. We then discuss tactics—that is, the choice and setting of the monetary policy instrument.

16.1 THE PRICE STABILITY GOAL AND THE NOMINAL ANCHOR

LO 16.1 Define and recognize the importance of a nominal anchor.

Over the past few decades, policymakers throughout the world have become increasingly aware of the social and economic costs of inflation, and more concerned with maintaining a stable price level as a goal of economic policy. Indeed, **price stability**, which central bankers define as low and stable inflation, is increasingly viewed as the most important goal of monetary policy. Price stability is desirable because a rising price level (inflation) creates uncertainty in the economy, and that uncertainty might hamper economic growth. For example, when the overall level of prices is changing, the information conveyed by the prices of goods and services is harder to interpret, which complicates decision making for consumers, businesses, and governments, thereby leading to a less efficient financial system.

Not only do public opinion surveys indicate that the public is hostile to inflation, but a growing body of evidence also suggests that inflation leads to lower economic growth. The most extreme example of unstable prices is *hyperinflation*, such as occurred in Argentina, Brazil, Russia, and Zimbabwe in the recent past. Hyperinflation has proved to be very damaging to the workings of an economy.

Inflation also makes it difficult to plan for the future. For example, it is more difficult to decide how much to put aside to provide for a child's college education in an inflationary environment. Furthermore, inflation can strain a country's social fabric: Conflict might result, because each group in the society may compete with other groups to make sure that its income keeps up with the rising level of prices.

The Role of a Nominal Anchor

Because price stability is so crucial to the long-term health of an economy, a central element in successful monetary policy is the use of a **nominal anchor**—a nominal variable, such as the inflation rate or the money supply, that ties down the price level to achieve price stability. Adherence to a nominal anchor that keeps the nominal variable within a narrow range promotes price stability by directly promoting low and stable inflation expectations. A more subtle reason for a nominal anchor's importance is that it can limit the **time-inconsistency problem**, in which monetary policy conducted on a discretionary, day-by-day basis leads to poor long-term outcomes.

The Time-Inconsistency Problem

The time-inconsistency problem is something we deal with continually in everyday life. We often have a plan that we know will produce a good outcome in the long run, but when tomorrow comes, we just can't help ourselves and we renege on our plan because doing so has short-term gains. For example, we make a New Year's resolution to go on a diet, but soon thereafter we can't resist having one more bite of that rocky road ice cream—and then another bite, and then another bite—and the weight begins to pile back on. In other words, we find ourselves unable to *consistently* follow a good plan over *time*; the good plan is said to be *time-inconsistent* and will soon be abandoned.

Monetary policymakers also face the time-inconsistency problem. They are always tempted to pursue a discretionary monetary policy that is more expansionary than firms or people expect because such a policy would boost economic output (or lower unemployment) in the short run. The best policy, however, is *not* to pursue expansionary policy, because decisions about wages and prices reflect workers' and firms' expectations about policy; when they see a central bank pursuing expansionary policy, workers and firms will raise their expectations about inflation, driving wages and prices up. The rise in wages and prices will lead to higher inflation but will not result in higher output on average. (We examine this issue more formally in Chapter 24.)

A central bank will have better inflation performance in the long run if it does not try to surprise people with an unexpectedly expansionary policy, but instead keeps inflation under control. However, even if a central bank recognizes that discretionary policy will lead to a poor outcome (high inflation with no gains in output), it still may not be able to pursue the better policy of inflation control because politicians are likely to apply pressure on the central bank to try to boost output with overly expansionary monetary policy.

A clue as to how we should deal with the time-inconsistency problem comes from how-to books on parenting. Parents know that giving in to a child to keep him from acting up will produce a very spoiled child. Nevertheless, when a child throws a tantrum, many parents give him what he wants just to shut him up. Because parents don't stick to their "do not give in" plan, the child expects that he will get what he wants if he behaves badly, so he continues to throw tantrums, over and over again. Parenting books suggest a solution to the time-inconsistency problem (although they don't call it that): Parents should set behavior rules for their children and stick to them.

A nominal anchor is like a behavior rule. Just as rules can help prevent the time-inconsistency problem in parenting by helping adults resist pursuing the discretionary policy of giving in, a nominal anchor can help prevent the time-inconsistency problem in monetary policy by providing an expected constraint on discretionary policy.

16.2 OTHER GOALS OF MONETARY POLICY

LO 16.2   Identify the six potential goals that monetary policymakers may pursue.

Although price stability is the primary goal of most central banks, five other goals are continually mentioned by central bank officials when they discuss the objectives of monetary policy: (1) high employment and output stability, (2) economic growth, (3) stability of financial markets, (4) interest-rate stability, and (5) stability in foreign exchange markets.

High Employment and Output Stability

High employment is a worthy goal for two main reasons: (1) the alternative situation—high unemployment—causes much human misery; and (2) when unemployment is high, the economy has both idle workers and idle resources (closed factories and unused equipment), resulting in a loss of output (lower GDP).

Although it is clear that high employment is desirable, how high should it be? At what point can we say that the economy is at full employment? At first, it might seem that full employment is the point at which no worker is out of a job—that is, when unemployment is zero. But this definition ignores the fact that some unemployment, called *frictional unemployment*, which involves searches by workers and firms to find suitable matchups, is beneficial to the economy. For example, a worker who decides to look for a better job might be unemployed for a while during the job search. Workers often decide to leave work temporarily to pursue other activities (raising a family, travel, returning to school), and when they decide to reenter the job market, it may take some time for them to find the right job.

Another reason that unemployment is not zero when the economy is at full employment is *structural unemployment*, a mismatch between job requirements and the skills or availability of local workers. Clearly, this kind of unemployment is undesirable. Nonetheless, it is something that monetary policy can do little about.

This goal of high employment is not an unemployment level of zero but a level above zero that is consistent with full employment, the point at which the demand for labor equals the supply of labor. This level is called the **natural rate of unemployment**.

Although this definition sounds neat and authoritative, it leaves a troublesome question unanswered: What unemployment rate is consistent with full employment? In some cases, it is obvious that the unemployment rate is too high. On the one hand, the unemployment rate in excess of 20% during the Great Depression, for example, was clearly far too high. In the early 1960s, on the other hand, policymakers thought that a reasonable goal for the unemployment rate was 4%, a level that was well below more recent estimates of the natural rate of unemployment of around 6% for that period, with the result that when the unemployment rate fell to 4% in the late 1960s, inflation accelerated. The natural rate of unemployment has fallen since then, and current estimates of the natural rate of unemployment, place it around 4%, but even this estimate is subject to much uncertainty and disagreement. It is possible, for example, that appropriate government policy, such as the provision of better information about job vacancies or job training programs, might decrease the natural rate of unemployment.

The high employment goal can be thought of in another way. Because the level of unemployment is tied to the level of economic activity in the economy, a particular level of output is produced at the natural rate of unemployment, which naturally enough is referred to as the **natural rate of output** but is more often referred to as **potential output**.

Trying to achieve the goal of high employment thus means that central banks should try to move the level of output toward the natural rate of output. In other words, they should try to stabilize the level of output around its natural rate.

Economic Growth

The goal of steady economic growth is closely related to the high-employment goal because businesses are more likely to invest in capital equipment to increase productivity and economic growth when unemployment is low. Conversely, if unemployment is high and factories are idle, it does not pay for a firm to invest in additional plants and equipment. Although the two goals are closely related, policies can be aimed specifically at promoting economic growth by directly encouraging firms to invest or by encouraging people to save, which provides more funds for firms to invest. In fact, this approach is the stated purpose of *supply-side economics* policies, which are intended to spur economic growth by providing tax incentives for businesses to invest in facilities and equipment and for taxpayers to save more. Active debate continues over the role that monetary policy should play in boosting growth.

Stability of Financial Markets

As our analysis in Chapter 12 showed, financial crises can interfere with the ability of financial markets to channel funds to people with productive investment opportunities and can lead to a sharp contraction in economic activity. The promotion of a more stable financial system, in which financial crises are avoided, is thus an important goal for a central bank. Indeed, as we saw in Chapter 13, the Federal Reserve System was created to promote financial stability in the wake of the bank panic of 1907.

Interest-Rate Stability

Interest-rate stability is desirable because fluctuations in interest rates can create uncertainty in the economy and make it harder to plan for the future. Fluctuations in interest rates that affect consumers' willingness to buy houses, for example, make it more difficult for consumers to decide when to purchase a house and for construction firms to plan how many houses to build. A central bank may also want to reduce upward movements in interest rates for the reasons we discussed in Chapter 13: Upward movements in interest rates generate hostility toward central banks and lead to demands that their power be curtailed.

The stability of financial markets is also fostered by interest-rate stability, because fluctuations in interest rates create great uncertainty for financial institutions. An increase in interest rates produces large capital losses on long-term bonds and mortgages, losses that can cause the failures of the financial institutions holding them. In recent years, more pronounced interest-rate fluctuations have been a particularly severe problem for savings and loan associations and mutual savings banks, many of which got into serious financial trouble in the 1980s and early 1990s.

Stability in Foreign Exchange Markets

With the increasing importance of international trade to the U.S. economy, the value of the dollar relative to other currencies has become a major consideration for the Fed. A rise in the value of the dollar makes American industries less competitive with those abroad, and a drop in the value of the dollar stimulates inflation in the United States. In addition, preventing large changes in the value of the dollar makes it easier for firms and individuals purchasing or selling goods abroad to plan ahead. Stabilizing extreme movements in the value of the dollar in foreign exchange markets is thus an important goal of monetary policy. In other countries, which are even more dependent on foreign trade, stability in foreign exchange markets takes on even greater importance.

16.3 SHOULD PRICE STABILITY BE THE PRIMARY GOAL OF MONETARY POLICY?

LO 16.3 Summarize the distinctions between hierarchical and dual mandates.

In the long run, no inconsistency exists between the price stability goal and the other goals mentioned earlier. The natural rate of unemployment is not lowered by high inflation, so higher inflation cannot produce lower unemployment or more employment in the long run. In other words, there is no long-run trade-off between inflation and employment. In the long run, price stability promotes economic growth as well as financial and interest-rate stability. Although price stability is consistent with the other goals in the long run, in the short run price stability often conflicts with the goals of output stability and interest-rate stability. For example, when the economy is expanding and unemployment is falling, the economy may become overheated, leading to a rise in inflation. To pursue the price stability goal, a central bank would prevent this overheating by raising interest rates, an action that would initially cause output to fall and increase interest-rate instability. How should a central bank resolve this conflict among goals?

Hierarchical Versus Dual Mandates

Because price stability is crucial to the long-run health of the economy, many countries have decided that price stability should be the primary, long-run goal for central banks. For example, the Maastricht Treaty, which created the European Central Bank, states, "The primary objective of the European System of Central Banks [ESCB] shall be to maintain price stability. Without prejudice to the objective of price stability, the ESCB shall support the general economic policies in the Community," which include objectives such as "a high level of employment" and "sustainable and non-inflationary growth." Mandates of this type, which put the goal of price stability first and then state that other goals can be pursued as long as price stability is achieved, are known as **hierarchical mandates**. They are the directives governing the behavior of such central banks as the Bank of England, the Bank of Canada, and the Reserve Bank of New Zealand, as well as the European Central Bank.

In contrast, the legislation that defines the mission of the Federal Reserve states, "The Board of Governors of the Federal Reserve System and the Federal Open Market Committee shall maintain long-run growth of the monetary and credit aggregates commensurate with the economy's long-run potential to increase production, so as to promote effectively the goals of maximum employment, stable prices, and moderate long-term interest rates." Because, as we learned in Chapter 5, long-term interest rates will be very high if inflation is high, this statement in practice is a **dual mandate** to achieve two coequal objectives: price stability and maximum employment (output stability).

Is it better for an economy to operate under a hierarchical mandate or a dual mandate?

Price Stability as the Primary, Long-Run Goal of Monetary Policy

Because no inconsistency exists between achieving price stability in the long run and the natural rate of unemployment, these two types of mandates are not very different *if maximum employment is defined as the natural rate of employment*. In practice, however, a substantial difference between these two mandates might exist because the public and politicians may believe that a hierarchical mandate puts too much emphasis on inflation control and not enough on stabilizing output.

Because low and stable inflation rates promote economic growth, central bankers have come to realize that price stability should be the primary, long-run goal of monetary policy. Nevertheless, because output fluctuations should also be a concern of monetary policy, the goal of price stability should be seen as primary only in the long run. Attempts to keep inflation at the same level in the short run, no matter what else is happening in the economy, are likely to lead to excessive output fluctuations.

As long as price stability is a long-run, but not short-run, goal, central banks can focus on reducing output fluctuations by allowing inflation to deviate from the long-run goal for short periods and, therefore, can operate under a dual mandate. However, if a dual mandate leads a central bank to pursue short-run expansionary policies that increase output and employment without worrying about the long-run consequences for inflation, the time-inconsistency problem may recur. Concerns that a dual mandate might lead to overly expansionary policy is a key reason why central bankers often favor hierarchical mandates in which the pursuit of price stability takes precedence. Hierarchical mandates can also be a problem if they lead to a central bank behaving as what the former governor of the Bank of England, Mervyn King, referred to as an "inflation nutter"—that is, a central bank that focuses solely on inflation control, even in the short run, and so undertakes policies that lead to large output fluctuations. Deciding which type of mandate is better for a central bank ultimately depends on the subtleties of how the mandate will work in practice. Either type of mandate is acceptable as long as it operates to make price stability the primary goal in the long run, but not in the short run.

16.4 INFLATION TARGETING

LO 16.4 Compare and contrast the advantages and disadvantages of inflation targeting.

The recognition that price stability should be the primary long-run goal of monetary policy and that a nominal anchor is a valuable tool in helping to achieve this goal has led to a monetary policy strategy known as *inflation targeting*. **Inflation targeting** involves several elements: (1) public announcement of medium-term numerical objectives (targets) for inflation; (2) an institutional commitment to price stability as the primary, long-run goal of monetary policy and a commitment to achieving the inflation goal; (3) an information-inclusive approach in which many variables (not just monetary aggregates) are used in making decisions about monetary policy; (4) increased transparency of the monetary policy strategy through communication with the public and the markets about the plans and objectives of monetary policymakers; and (5) increased accountability of the central bank for attaining its inflation objectives. New Zealand was the first country to formally adopt inflation targeting in 1990, followed by Canada in 1991, the United Kingdom in 1992, Sweden and Finland in 1993, and Australia and Spain in 1994. Israel, Chile, and Brazil, among other countries, have also adopted a form of inflation targeting.[1]

Inflation Targeting in New Zealand, Canada, and the United Kingdom

We begin our look at inflation targeting with New Zealand, because it was the first country to adopt this strategy. We then go on to examine inflation targeting in Canada and the United Kingdom, which were the next countries to adopt it.

New Zealand   As part of a general reform of the government's role in the economy, the New Zealand parliament passed a new Reserve Bank of New Zealand Act in 1989, which became effective on February 1, 1990. In addition to increasing the independence of the central bank, which transformed it from one of the least independent central banks among developed countries to one of the most independent, the act committed the Reserve Bank to a sole objective of price stability. The act stipulated that the minister of finance and the governor of the Reserve Bank should negotiate and make public a Policy Targets Agreement, a statement that sets out the targets by which monetary policy performance will be evaluated, specifying numerical target ranges for inflation and the dates by which they are to be reached. An unusual feature of the New Zealand legislation is that the governor of the Reserve Bank is held highly accountable for the success of monetary policy. If the goals set forth in the Policy Targets Agreement are not satisfied, the governor is subject to dismissal.

The first Policy Targets Agreement, signed by the minister of finance and the governor of the Reserve Bank on March 2, 1990, directed the Reserve Bank to achieve an annual inflation rate within a 3%–5% range. Subsequent agreements lowered the range to 0%–2% until the end of 1996, when the range was changed to 0%–3%. In 2002, the range was changed again, to 1%–3%. Tight monetary policy brought the inflation rate down from above 5% to below 2% by the end of 1992 (see Figure 1, panel (a)), but at the cost of a deep recession and a sharp rise in unemployment. Since then, inflation has typically remained within the targeted range. Since 1992, New Zealand's growth rate has generally been high, and unemployment has decreased significantly.

Canada   On February 26, 1991, a joint announcement by the minister of finance and the governor of the Bank of Canada established formal inflation targets. The target ranges were to be 2%–4% by the end of 1992, 1.5%–3.5% by June 1994, and 1%–3% by December 1996. After the new government took office in late 1993, the target range was set at 1%–3% for December 1995 until December 1998 and has been kept at this level. Canadian inflation has also fallen dramatically since the adoption of inflation targets, from above 5% in 1991, to a 0% rate in 1995, and to around 2% subsequently (see Figure 1, panel (b)). As was the case in New Zealand, however, this decline was

---

[1]A precursor to the inflation-targeting strategy is monetary targeting. This strategy is discussed in an appendix to this chapter, "Monetary Targeting," which is available in **MyLab Economics**.

Real-time data

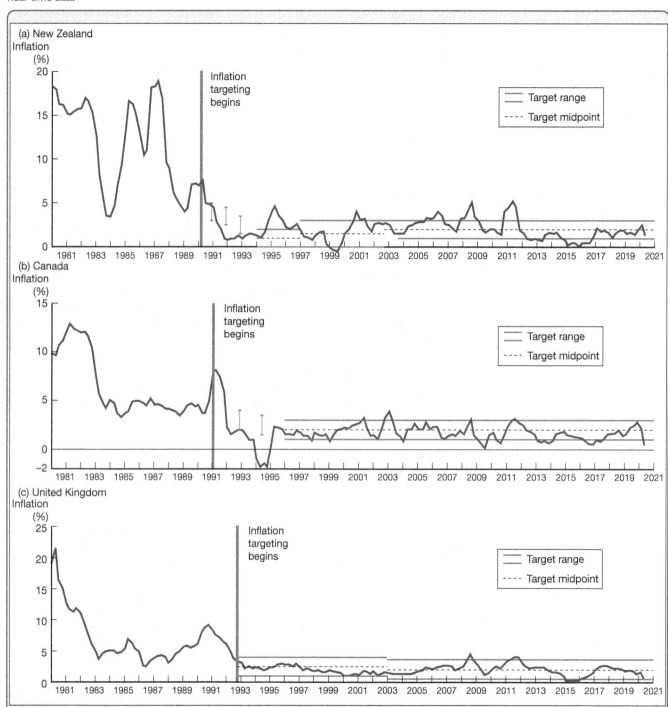

FIGURE 1   Inflation Rates and Inflation Targets for New Zealand, Canada, and the United Kingdom, 1980–2020

Inflation-targeting countries have significantly reduced the rate of inflation and over time have achieved their inflation targets.

Sources: Ben S. Bernanke, Thomas Laubach, Frederic S. Mishkin, and Adam S. Poson, *Inflation Targeting: Lessons from the International Experience* (Princeton, NJ: Princeton University Press, 1999); and Federal Reserve Bank of St. Louis FRED database: https://fred.stlouisfed.org/series/NZLCPIALLQINMEI; https://fred.stlouisfed.org/series/CPALCY01CAA661N; https://fred.stlouisfed.org/series/FPCPITOTLZGGBR.

not without cost: Unemployment soared to above 10% from 1991 until 1994, but then declined substantially.

United Kingdom In October 1992, the United Kingdom adopted an inflation target as its nominal anchor, and the Bank of England began to produce an *Inflation Report*, a quarterly report on the progress being made in achieving the target. The inflation target range was initially set at 1%–4% until the next election (spring 1997 at the latest), with the intent that the inflation rate should settle down to the lower half of the range (below 2.5%). In May 1997, the inflation target was set at 2.5% and the Bank of England was given the power to set interest rates henceforth, granting it a more independent role in monetary policy.

Before the adoption of inflation targets, inflation had already been falling in the United Kingdom, with a peak of 9% at the beginning of 1991 and a rate of 4% at the time of adoption (see Figure 1, panel (c)). By the third quarter of 1994, it was at 2.2%, within the intended range. Subsequently, inflation rose, climbing slightly above the 2.5% level by the end of 1995, but then fell and has remained close to the target since then. In December 2003, the target was changed to 2.0% for a slightly different measure of inflation. Meanwhile, growth of the U.K. economy has generally been strong, and there has been a substantial decrease in the unemployment rate since the adoption of the inflation target in 1992.[2]

Advantages of Inflation Targeting

A number of benefits are associated with inflation targeting: reduction of the time-inconsistency problem, increased transparency, increased accountability, consistency with democratic principles, and improved performance.

Reduction of the Time-Inconsistency Problem Because an explicit numerical inflation target increases the accountability of the central bank, inflation targeting can reduce the likelihood that the central bank will fall into the time-inconsistency trap of trying to expand output and employment in the short run by pursuing overly expansionary monetary policy. A key advantage of inflation targeting is that it can help focus the political debate on what a central bank can do in the long run—that is, control inflation—rather than what it cannot do, that is, permanently increase economic growth and the number of jobs through expansionary monetary policy. Thus inflation targeting can reduce political pressures on the central bank to pursue inflationary monetary policy and thereby reduce the likelihood of the time-inconsistency problem.

Increased Transparency Inflation targeting has the advantage that it is readily understood by the public and is thus highly transparent. Indeed, inflation-targeting regimes place great importance on transparency in policymaking and on regular communication with the public. Inflation-targeting central banks have frequent communications with the government, some mandated by law and some in response to informal inquiries, and their officials take every opportunity to make public speeches on their monetary policy strategy. Although these techniques are also commonly used in countries that have not adopted inflation targeting, inflation-targeting central banks have

---

[2]If you are interested in a more detailed discussion of inflation targeting in these and other countries, see Ben S. Bernanke, Thomas Laubach, Frederic S. Mishkin, and Adam S. Posen, *Inflation Targeting: Lessons from the International Experience* (Princeton, NJ: Princeton University Press, 1999).

taken public outreach a step further: Not only do they engage in extended public information campaigns, including the distribution of glossy brochures, but they also publish documents like the Bank of England's *Inflation Report*. These documents are particularly noteworthy because, unlike the usual dull-looking, formal reports of central banks, they make use of fancy graphics, boxes, and other eye-catching design elements to engage the public's interest.

The channels of communication just discussed are used by central banks in inflation-targeting countries to explain the following concepts to the general public, financial market participants, and politicians: (1) the goals and limitations of monetary policy, including the rationale for inflation targets; (2) the numerical values of the inflation targets and how they were determined; (3) how the inflation targets are to be achieved, given current economic conditions; and (4) reasons for any deviations from the targets. These communications have improved private sector planning by reducing uncertainty about monetary policy, interest rates, and inflation; they have promoted public debate of monetary policy, in part by educating the public about what a central bank can and cannot achieve; and they have helped clarify the responsibilities of the central bank and of politicians in the conduct of monetary policy.

Increased Accountability

Another key feature of inflation-targeting regimes is the tendency toward increased accountability of the central bank. Indeed, transparency and communication go hand in hand with increased accountability. The strongest case of accountability of a central bank in an inflation-targeting regime is in New Zealand, where the government has the right to dismiss the Reserve Bank's governor if the inflation targets are breached, even for one quarter. In other inflation-targeting countries, the central bank's accountability is less formalized. Nevertheless, the transparency of policy associated with inflation targeting has tended to make the central bank highly accountable to the public and the government. Sustained success in the conduct of monetary policy as measured against a preannounced and well-defined inflation target can be instrumental in building public support for a central bank's independence and for its policies. This building of public support and accountability occurs even in the absence of a rigidly defined and legalistic standard of performance evaluation and punishment.

Consistency with Democratic Principles

Not only is accountability valuable in its own right, but it also makes the institutional framework for the conduct of monetary policy more consistent with democratic principles. The inflation-targeting framework promotes the accountability of the central bank to elected officials, who are given some responsibility for setting the goals of monetary policy and then monitoring the economic outcomes. However, under inflation targeting as it generally has been practiced, the central bank has complete control over operational decisions and so can be held accountable for achieving its assigned objectives.

Improved Performance

The performance of inflation-targeting regimes has been quite good. Inflation-targeting countries seem to have significantly reduced both the rate of inflation and inflation expectations beyond what likely would have occurred in the absence of inflation targets. Furthermore, once lowered, inflation in these countries has stayed low; following disinflations, the inflation rate in inflation-targeting countries has not bounced back up during subsequent cyclical expansions of the economy.

Disadvantages of Inflation Targeting

Critics of inflation targeting cite four disadvantages of this monetary policy strategy: delayed signaling, too much rigidity, the potential for increased output fluctuations, and low economic growth. We look at each in turn and examine the validity of these criticisms.

Delayed Signaling

Inflation is not easily controlled by the monetary authorities. Furthermore, because of the long lags in the effects of monetary policy, inflation outcomes are revealed only after a substantial lag. Thus an inflation target does not send immediate signals to the public and the markets about the stance of monetary policy.

Too Much Rigidity

Some economists criticize inflation targeting because they believe it imposes a rigid rule on monetary policymakers and limits their ability to respond to unforeseen circumstances. However, useful policy strategies exist that are "rule-like" in that they involve forward-looking behavior that limits policymakers from systematically engaging in policies with undesirable long-run consequences. Such policies avoid the time-inconsistency problem and would be best described as "constrained discretion," a term coined by Ben Bernanke and the author of this book.

Indeed, inflation targeting can be described exactly in this way. Inflation targeting, as actually practiced, is far from rigid and is better described as "flexible inflation targeting." First, inflation targeting does not prescribe simple and mechanical instructions on how the central bank should conduct monetary policy. Rather, it requires the central bank to use all available information to determine which policy actions are appropriate to achieve the inflation target. Unlike simple policy rules, inflation targeting never requires the central bank to focus solely on one key variable. Second, inflation targeting, as practiced, contains a substantial degree of policy discretion. Inflation targets have been modified depending on economic circumstances, as we have seen. Moreover, central banks under inflation-targeting regimes have left themselves considerable scope to respond to output growth and fluctuations through several devices.

Potential for Increased Output Fluctuations

An important criticism of inflation targeting is that a sole focus on inflation may lead to monetary policy that is too tight when inflation is above target and thus may result in larger output fluctuations. Inflation targeting does not, however, require a sole focus on inflation—in fact, experience has shown that inflation targeters display substantial concern about output fluctuations. All the inflation targeters have set their inflation targets above zero.[3] For example, New Zealand, Canada, the United Kingdom, and Sweden currently set the midpoints of their inflation targets at 2%, while Australia sets its midpoint at 2.5%.

The decision by inflation targeters to choose inflation targets above zero reflects the concern of monetary policymakers that particularly low inflation can have substantial negative effects on real economic activity. Deflation (negative inflation, in which the price level actually falls) is especially to be feared because of the possibility that it may promote financial instability and precipitate a severe economic contraction (as discussed in Chapter 12). The deflation in Japan in recent years has been an important factor in the weakening of the Japanese financial system and economy. Inflation-targeting rates

---

[3]Consumer price indexes have been found to have an upward bias in the measurement of true inflation, so it is not surprising that inflation targets are chosen to exceed zero. However, the actual targets have been set to exceed the estimates of this measurement bias, indicating that inflation targeters have decided on targets for inflation that exceed zero even after measurement bias is accounted for.

above zero make periods of deflation less likely. This is one reason why some economists, both within and outside Japan, called on the Bank of Japan to adopt an inflation target at levels of 2%, which the Bank of Japan finally did in 2013.

Inflation targeting also does not ignore traditional stabilization goals. Central bankers in inflation-targeting countries continue to express their concern about fluctuations in output and employment, and the ability to accommodate short-run stabilization goals to some degree is built into all inflation-targeting regimes. All inflation-targeting countries have been willing to minimize output declines by gradually lowering medium-term inflation targets toward the long-run goal.

Low Economic Growth   Another common concern about inflation targeting is that it will lead to low growth in output and employment. Although inflation reduction has been associated with below-normal output during disinflationary phases in inflation-targeting regimes, once low inflation levels were achieved, output and employment returned to levels at least as high as they were before. A conservative conclusion is that once low inflation is achieved, inflation targeting is not harmful to the real economy. Given the strong economic growth after disinflation in many countries (such as New Zealand) that have adopted inflation targets, a case can be made that inflation targeting promotes real economic growth, in addition to controlling inflation.

16.5 THE EVOLUTION OF THE FEDERAL RESERVE'S MONETARY POLICY STRATEGY

LO 16.5 Identify the key changes made over time to the Federal Reserve's monetary policy strategy.

The Federal Reserve's monetary policy has evolved over time. We first discuss the Fed's monetary policy strategy prior to Ben Bernanke's term as chair of the Federal Reserve and then see how the monetary policy evolved into a flexible inflation-targeting regime starting in January 2012.

The Fed's "Just Do It" Monetary Policy Strategy

From the mid-1980s up until the time Ben Bernanke became chair of the Federal Reserve in 2006, the Federal Reserve was able to achieve excellent macroeconomic performance (including low and stable inflation), and it did so without using an explicit nominal anchor such as an inflation target. Although the Federal Reserve did not articulate an explicit strategy, a coherent strategy for the conduct of monetary policy existed nonetheless. This strategy involved an implicit, but not an explicit, nominal anchor in the form of an overriding concern on the part of the Federal Reserve to control inflation in the long run. In addition, it involved forward-looking behavior that included careful monitoring for signs of future inflation, using a wide range of information coupled with periodic "preemptive strikes" by monetary policy against the threat of inflation.

As emphasized by Milton Friedman, monetary policy effects have long lags. In industrialized countries with a history of low inflation, the inflation process seems to have tremendous inertia: Estimates from large macroeconometric models of the U.S. economy, for example, suggest that monetary policy takes over a year to affect output and over two years to have a significant impact on inflation. For countries that have experienced highly variable inflation, and therefore have more flexible prices, the lags may be shorter.

The presence of long lags means that monetary policy cannot wait for inflation to begin before it responds to it. If a central bank waits until overt signs of inflation appear, it will already be too late to maintain stable prices, at least not without a severe tightening of policy: Inflation expectations will already be embedded in the wage- and price-setting process, creating an inflation momentum that will be hard to halt. Inflation becomes much harder to control once it has been allowed to gather momentum because higher inflation expectations become ingrained in various types of long-term contracts and pricing agreements.

To prevent inflation from getting started, therefore, monetary policy needs to be forward-looking and preemptive. That is, depending on the lags from monetary policy to inflation, monetary policy needs to act long before inflationary pressures are seen in the economy. For example, suppose it takes roughly two years for monetary policy to have a significant impact on inflation. In this case, even if inflation is currently low but policymakers believe inflation will rise over the next two years with an unchanged stance of monetary policy, they must tighten monetary policy *now* to prevent the inflationary surge.

Under Alan Greenspan and Ben Bernanke, the Federal Reserve was successful in pursuing a preemptive monetary policy. For example, the Fed raised interest rates from 1994 to 1995 before a rise in inflation got a toehold. As a result, inflation did not just remain steady; it fell slightly. The Fed also conducted preemptive strikes against economic downturns. For example, the Fed started easing monetary policy in September 2007 at the onset of the global financial crisis, even though the economy was growing strongly at the time and inflation was rising.[4] (However, in this case, the Fed's preemptive policy was not sufficient to overcome the massive negative shock to the economy from the disruption to financial markets.) This preemptive, forward-looking monetary policy strategy is clearly also a feature of inflation-targeting regimes, because monetary policy instruments are adjusted to take into account the long lags in their effects on inflation.

However, the Fed's policy regime prior to the global financial crisis might best be described as a "just do it" policy, and it differed from inflation targeting in that it did not officially set a nominal anchor and was much less transparent. However, because the Fed's "just do it" approach had some of the key elements of inflation targeting, it also had many of its strengths. As with inflation targeting, the central bank used many sources of information to determine the best settings for monetary policy. The Fed's forward-looking behavior and stress on price stability helped discourage overly expansionary monetary policy, thereby ameliorating the time-inconsistency problem.

However, despite its success, the Fed's "just do it" approach had several weaknesses. First was its lack of transparency. The Fed's close-mouthed approach about its intentions gave rise to a constant guessing game about its future actions. This high level of uncertainty led to unnecessary volatility in financial markets and created doubt among producers and the general public about the future course of inflation and output. Furthermore, the opacity of the Fed's policymaking made it hard for Congress and the general public to hold the Federal Reserve accountable: The Fed could not be held accountable for its decisions if there were no predetermined criteria for judging its performance, and this lack of accountability was inconsistent with democratic principles. Low accountability might also make the Fed more susceptible to the time-inconsistency problem, whereby it might pursue short-term objectives at the expense of long-term ones.

---

[4]These episodes are discussed in the brief history of Fed policymaking given in Appendix 2 to this chapter, which is available in **MyLab Economics**.

The Long Road to Inflation Targeting

Alan Greenspan, chair of the Fed from 1987 until 2006, was not a strong advocate of increased Federal Reserve transparency. Hence, despite the weaknesses of the "just do it" approach and the successes of inflation-targeting regimes from 1991 on, Greenspan was opposed to the adoption of an inflation target and quashed movements in this direction at an FOMC meeting in 1996. When Ben Bernanke became chair of the Fed in 2006, increased Fed transparency and inflation targeting now had a strong advocate (see the Inside the Fed box "Ben Bernanke's Advocacy of Inflation Targeting").

Shortly after becoming Fed chair, Bernanke made it clear that any movement toward inflation targeting must result from a consensus within the FOMC. He then set up an internal subcommittee to discuss Federal Reserve communications, which included discussions about announcing a specific numerical inflation objective. The FOMC made a partial step in the direction of inflation targeting in November 2007, when it announced a new communication strategy that lengthened the horizon for FOMC participants' inflation projections to three years. In many cases, the three-year horizon would be sufficiently long that the projection for inflation under "appropriate policy" would reflect each participant's inflation objective, because at the three-year horizon inflation should converge to the long-run objective.[5]

In July 2008, in his last speech as a governor of the Federal Reserve, the author of this book argued that a few relatively minor modifications to the inflation objective could move the Fed even further toward inflation targeting. The Fed's first goal should be to set a date for its inflation objective that was sufficiently far off that inflation would almost surely converge to its long-run value by that date. In January 2009, the FOMC adopted this modification by adding long-term inflation forecasts under "appropriate policy" to the published FOMC participants' projections. Second, the FOMC participants should be willing to reach a consensus on a single value for the mandate-consistent inflation objective. Third, the FOMC should not modify this inflation objective unless there were valid scientific reasons for doing so. With these two additional modifications, the longer-run inflation projections would, in effect, be an announcement of a specific numerical objective for the inflation rate and so would serve as a flexible version of inflation targeting. In October 2010, then-chair Bernanke gave a speech advocating exactly this approach.[6] However, he was unable to convince his colleagues on the FOMC to adopt it.

When Janet Yellen left her position as president of the Federal Reserve Bank of San Francisco to become the vice-chair of the Board of Governors of the Federal Reserve System in 2010, Bernanke now had a strong ally for inflation targeting occupying the second-most-powerful position in the Federal Reserve System. In October 2010, Bernanke appointed Yellen as the chair of the internal subcommittee on communications, and the adoption of inflation targeting was not far off. The FOMC finally moved to inflation targeting on January 25, 2012, when it issued its "Statement on Long-Run Goals and Monetary Policy Strategy."[7] In this statement, which is renewed every January, the FOMC agreed to a single numerical value of the inflation objective,

[5]See Frederic S. Mishkin, "Whither Federal Reserve Communications," speech given at the Petersen Institute for International Economics, Washington, DC, July 28, 2008, https://www.federalreserve.gov/newsevents/speech/mishkin20080728a.htm.

[6]Ben S. Bernanke, "Monetary Policy Objectives and Tools in a Low-Inflation Environment," speech given at the Federal Reserve Bank of Boston's conference, Revisiting Monetary Policy in a Low-Inflation Environment, October 15, 2010.

[7]These statements can be found at http://www.federalreserve.gov/monetarypolicy/default.htm.

Inside the Fed   Ben Bernanke's Advocacy of Inflation Targeting

Ben Bernanke is a world-renowned expert on monetary policy who wrote extensively on inflation targeting while working in academia. While a professor at Princeton, Bernanke, in several articles and in a book co-written with the author of this book, argued that inflation targeting would be a major step forward for the Federal Reserve and would produce better economic outcomes, for many of the reasons outlined earlier.[*]

When Bernanke took his position as a governor of the Federal Reserve from 2002 to 2005, he continued to advocate the adoption of an inflation target. In an important speech given at a conference at the Federal Reserve Bank of St. Louis in 2004, he described how the Federal Reserve might approach a movement toward inflation targeting: The Fed should announce a numerical value for its long-run inflation goal.[†] Bernanke emphasized that announcing such an objective for inflation would be completely consistent with

the Fed's dual mandate of achieving price stability and maximum employment and therefore might be called a *mandate-consistent inflation objective*, since the inflation objective would be set above zero to avoid deflations, which have harmful effects on employment. In addition, the inflation objective would not be intended as a short-run target that might lead to excessively tight control of inflation at the expense of overly high employment fluctuations.

[*]Ben S. Bernanke and Frederic S. Mishkin, "Inflation Targeting: A New Framework for Monetary Policy," *Journal of Economic Perspectives* 11, no. 2 (1997); Ben S. Bernanke, Frederic S. Mishkin, and Adam S. Posen, "Inflation Targeting: Fed Policy After Greenspan," *Milken Institute Review* (Fourth Quarter, 1999): 48–56; Ben S. Bernanke, Frederic S. Mishkin, and Adam S. Posen, "What Happens When Greenspan Is Gone," *Wall Street Journal*, January 5, 2000, A22; and Ben S. Bernanke, Thomas Laubach, Frederic S. Mishkin, and Adam S. Posen, *Inflation Targeting: Lessons from the International Experience* (Princeton, NJ: Princeton University Press, 1999).

[†]Ben S. Bernanke, "Inflation Targeting," Federal Reserve Bank of St. Louis, *Review* 86, no. 4 (July/August 2004): 165–168.

2% on the personal consumption expenditure (PCE) deflator discussed in the appendix to Chapter 1. However, the statement also made it clear that the Federal Reserve would be pursuing a flexible form of inflation targeting, consistent with its dual mandate, because it not only would seek to achieve its inflation target but also would focus on promoting maximum sustainable employment.

Global   The European Central Bank's Monetary Policy Strategy

The European Central Bank (ECB) has also been slow to move toward inflation targeting, adopting a hybrid monetary policy strategy that includes some elements of inflation targeting.[*] Shortly before the ECB became fully operational in 1999, its governing council defined price stability as an inflation rate below 2%. However, in May 2003, the ECB adopted a goal for inflation over the medium term of "below, but close to, 2%." The ECB's strategy has two key "pillars." First, monetary and credit aggregates are assessed for "their implications for future inflation and economic growth." Second, many other economic variables are used to assess the future economic outlook.

The ECB's strategy is somewhat unclear and has been subject to criticism for this reason. Although the "below, but close to, 2%" goal for inflation sounds like an inflation target, the ECB has repeatedly stated that it does not have an inflation target. This central bank seems to have decided to try to "have its cake and eat it, too" by not committing too strongly to an inflation-targeting strategy. The resulting difficulty in assessing the ECB's strategy has the potential to reduce the accountability of the institution.

[*]For a description of the ECB's monetary policy strategy, go to the ECB's website at http://www.ecb.int.

The Federal Reserve is not the only central bank that has moved slowly toward inflation targeting. As the Global box "The European Central Bank's Monetary Policy Strategy" suggests, the European Central Bank also follows a weak form of inflation targeting.

16.6 LESSONS FOR MONETARY POLICY STRATEGY FROM THE GLOBAL FINANCIAL CRISIS

LO 16.6 List the four lessons learned from the global financial crisis, and discuss what they mean for inflation targeting.

Our discussion in previous chapters of the course of events that characterized the global financial crisis suggests four basic lessons for economists and policymakers on how the economy works.[8]

1. *Developments in the financial sector have a far greater impact on economic activity than was earlier realized.* Although before the crisis economists and policymakers generally recognized that financial frictions could play an important role in business cycle fluctuations, as we saw in Chapter 12, the global financial crisis made it abundantly clear that the adverse effects of financial disruptions on economic activity could be far worse than originally anticipated.

2. *The effective lower bound on interest rates can be a serious problem.* As we saw in Chapter 15, the effective lower bound on interest rates has forced the Federal Reserve to use nonconventional monetary policy tools, not only since the crisis but also during the 2003–2006 period and again during the coronavirus pandemic. Although these nonconventional tools can help stimulate the economy, they are more complicated to use than conventional tools and their impact on the economy is more uncertain, so they may be harder to use effectively.

3. *The cost of cleaning up after a financial crisis is very high.* As we saw in Chapter 12, financial crises are followed by deep recessions. In addition, recoveries from financial crises are very slow. Carmen Reinhart and Vincent Reinhart have documented that economic growth is significantly lower during the decade following financial crises, and unemployment rates stay persistently higher for a decade after crisis episodes. In addition, in the aftermath of financial crises, government indebtedness almost always sharply increases and can lead to defaults on government debt, which have become a major concern in Europe in the aftermath of the most recent crisis.[9]

4. *Price and output stability do not ensure financial stability.* Before the recent financial crisis, the common view in both academia and central banks was that achieving price and output stability would promote financial stability. However, the success of central banks in stabilizing inflation and the decreased volatility of business cycle fluctuations before 2007, which became known as the "Great Moderation," did not protect the economy from financial instability. Indeed, it may have promoted it. The low volatility of both inflation and output fluctuations may have lulled market participants into thinking less risk was present in the economic system than was really the case, leading them to take excessive risks, which in turn helped to fuel the global financial crisis.

[8]For a more detailed discussion of the lessons of the global financial crisis for monetary policy strategy, see Frederic S. Mishkin, "Monetary Policy Strategy: Lessons from the Crisis," in Marek Jarocinski, Frank Smets, and Christian Thimann, eds., *Monetary Policy Revisited: Lessons from the Crisis,* Sixth ECB Central Banking Conference (Frankfurt, Germany: European Central Bank, 2011), 67–118.

[9]See Carmen M. Reinhart and Vincent R. Reinhart, "After the Fall," *Macroeconomic Challenges: The Decade Ahead,* Federal Reserve Bank of Kansas City Economic Symposium, 2010, manuscript available at http://www.kansascityfed.org; and Carmen M. Reinhart and Kenneth S. Rogoff, *This Time Is Different: Eight Centuries of Financial Folly* (Princeton, NJ: Princeton University Press, 2009).

What implications do these lessons have for monetary policy strategy? We first consider how these lessons might affect our thinking about inflation targeting and then look at how central banks should respond to asset-price bubbles.

Implications for Inflation Targeting

Earlier in the chapter, we outlined the arguments for inflation targeting, and none of the lessons listed above contradicts these arguments. Although support for the inflation-targeting strategy is not weakened by the lessons learned from the financial crisis, these lessons do suggest that inflation targeting may need to be more flexible and also may need to be modified on several dimensions. First, we look at what these lessons might mean for the level of the inflation target.

Level of the Inflation Target

As our discussion earlier in the chapter indicated, central banks typically have an inflation target around the 2% level. The seriousness of the effective-lower-bound problem raises the question of whether this target level is too low. A controversial paper written by researchers at the IMF, including its chief economist, Olivier Blanchard, suggested that the inflation target might be raised from the 2% level to the 4% level.[10] The paper argued that with expectations of inflation anchored to this 4% target, by lowering the nominal interest rate to the effective lower bound, say, zero, the real interest rate, $i_r = i - \pi^e$, could be decreased to as low as $-4\% (= 0 - 4\%)$, rather than the rate of $-2\% (= 0 - 2\%)$ associated with the 2% inflation target. Conventional monetary policy, which involves manipulating the nominal policy rate, would then be able to become more expansionary when interest rates fell to the floor of the effective lower bound than it could with the lower inflation target. In other words, the effective lower bound on the policy rate would be less binding with a higher inflation target.

Although this argument is theoretically sound, and raising the inflation target does have its benefits, we also have to look at its costs. The benefits of a higher inflation target accrue only when the effective-lower-bound problem occurs. Although this was a major problem during the global financial crisis, such episodes have not been very frequent. If the effective-lower-bound problem is rare, then the benefits of a higher inflation target are not so large because they are available only infrequently. However, the costs of higher inflation in terms of the distortions it produces in the economy, mentioned early in the chapter, are ongoing. Thus, although these costs may not be that large in any given year, they add up over time and may outweigh the intermittent benefits of a higher inflation target when the effective lower bound occurs.

Another problem with a higher inflation target is that the history of inflation suggests that it is more difficult to stabilize the inflation rate at a 4% level than at a 2% level. Once inflation starts to rise above this level, the public is likely to believe that price stability is no longer a credible goal of the central bank. The question then arises, if a 4% level of inflation is okay, then why not 6%, or 8%, and so on? Indeed, this is what seems to have happened in the 1960s, when economists such as Paul Samuelson and Robert Solow of MIT, both eventual recipients of the Nobel Prize, argued that policymakers should be willing to tolerate higher inflation rates in the 4%–5% range. But when inflation rose to that level, the policy authorities could not contain it at that level, and it kept on rising to double-digit levels by the early 1980s. Getting inflation back down again during the Volcker era was very costly. No central banker wants to go through that cycle again, and this is why central bankers have been so hostile to the IMF researchers' suggestion.

[10]Olivier Blanchard, Giovanni Dell'Ariccia, and Paolo Mauro, "Rethinking Monetary Policy," *Journal of Money, Credit and Banking* 42, no. S1 (September 2010): 199–217.

Although central bankers have not supported raising the inflation target above the 2% level, the effective-lower-bound problem suggests that allowing inflation expectations to fall below 2% could be very costly: it would raise the real interest rate when interest rates hit the effective lower bound after there is a negative shock that hits the economy.

Even though the Federal Reserve adopted a 2% inflation objective, inflation had been running below 2% for a number of years afterwards, so the Fed became concerned that the persistent inflation undershoots of the 2% target could lead to inflation expectations declining below 2%. As a result, in August 2020, after the Fed had conducted a study of its monetary policy strategy, Jay Powell announced that the Fed was modifying its inflation target to be a 2% *average*, rather than a 2% annual target. How this modification changes the Fed's monetary policy strategy is described in the Inside the Fed box, "The Fed's New Monetary Policy Strategy: Average Inflation Targeting."

Flexibility of Inflation Targeting We have seen that inflation targeting as actually practiced would be better described as "flexible inflation targeting." However, before the global financial crisis, this flexibility involved allowing some short-run deviations of inflation from the inflation target to promote output stability as well as price stability. Two lessons from the crisis—that financial instability can have devastating effects on the economy and that achieving price and output stability does not ensure financial stability—have led to a recognition that central banks need to pay more attention to financial stability, not only in designing inflation-targeting regimes but also in any monetary policy framework. Particularly important in this regard is the issue of how central banks should respond to asset-price bubbles, the topic we discuss next.

Inside the Fed — The Fed's New Monetary Policy Strategy: Average Inflation Targeting

The Federal Reserve's original 2% point-target for inflation was one in which bygones are bygones: that is, it would continue to try to achieve a 2% annual inflation rate no matter what had happened to inflation in the past. The Fed announcement in August 2020 that it would now target an *average* inflation rate of 2% meant that bygones were no longer bygones because past inflation would affect its target in the short run. If inflation had been running below the 2% target level, as it had prior to 2020, then average inflation would fall below 2% and so to raise the average back to 2%, the Fed would seek to achieve an inflation rate above 2% for a short period of time. This would require the Fed to pursue easier monetary policy than it would have otherwise. If on the other hand, inflation had been running above 2%, then the Fed would temporarily shoot for an inflation rate below 2% and pursue a tighter monetary policy.

There are two major advantages to this new monetary policy strategy. First, it would make it less likely that inflation expectations would drift down below the 2% level because past undershoots of the target would be made up over time by pursuing easier monetary policy. The second advantage of this new monetary policy strategy is that it would generate an automatic stabilizer for the economy. When a negative shock which caused inflation to fall below the 2% target occurs, average inflation targeting would commit the Fed to temporarily raise inflation to above 2%. Inflation expectations would then likely rise above the 2% level temporarily, thus lowering the real interest rate automatically even if the Fed did not or could not lower the federal funds rate.

There is one major objection to this new monetary policy strategy. If the Fed allowed inflation to temporarily rise above the 2% level, there might be concerns that the Fed is no longer committed to keep inflation at the 2% level in the long run. To avoid this problem, the Fed would need to convince the public that an overshoot of the 2% inflation objective would not weaken the Fed's commitment to stabilize inflation at the 2% level in the long run.

16.7 SHOULD CENTRAL BANKS TRY TO STOP ASSET-PRICE BUBBLES?

LO 16.7 Summarize the arguments for and against central bank policy responses to asset-price bubbles.

Over the centuries, economies have been subject to periodic **asset-price bubbles**, pronounced increases in asset prices, or "bubbles," that depart from fundamental values and that eventually burst resoundingly. The story of the global financial crisis, discussed in Chapter 12, indicates just how costly these bubbles can be. The bursting of the asset-price bubble in the housing market brought down the financial system, leading to an economic downturn, a rise in unemployment, and direct hardship for families who were forced to leave their homes after foreclosures.

The high economic cost of asset-price bubbles raises the following questions: What should central banks do about them? Should they use monetary policy to try to pop the bubbles? Are there regulatory measures they can take to rein in asset-price bubbles? To answer these questions, we need to ask whether there are different kinds of bubbles that require different types of responses.

Two Types of Asset-Price Bubbles

To think about central banks' response to asset-price bubbles, we first need to look at the different types of bubbles and how each might best be addressed. Asset-price bubbles are of two types: One type is driven by credit, and the second type is driven purely by overly optimistic expectations (dubbed "irrational exuberance" by Alan Greenspan).

Credit-Driven Bubbles
When a credit boom begins, an asset-price bubble may begin to form. Easier-to-get credit can be used to purchase particular assets and thereby raise their prices. The rise in asset values, in turn, encourages further lending for these assets, either because it increases the value of collateral, making it easier to borrow, or because it raises the value of capital at financial institutions, which gives them more capacity to lend. The lending for these assets can then further increase demand for them and hence raise their prices even more. This feedback loop—in which a credit boom drives up asset prices, which in turn fuels the credit boom, which drives asset prices even higher, and so on—can generate a bubble in which asset prices rise well above their fundamental values.

Credit-driven bubbles are particularly dangerous, as the recent global financial crisis has demonstrated. When asset prices come back down to earth and the bubble bursts, the collapse in asset prices leads to a reversal of the feedback loop: Loans go sour, lenders cut back on the credit supply, the demand for assets declines further, and prices drop even more. These were exactly the dynamics that characterized housing markets during the global financial crisis. Driven by a credit boom in subprime lending, housing prices rose way above fundamental values; but when housing prices crashed, credit shriveled up and housing prices plummeted.

The resulting losses on subprime loans and securities eroded the balance sheets of financial institutions, causing a decline in credit (deleveraging) and a sharp fall in business and household spending, and therefore in economic activity. During the global financial crisis, the interaction between housing prices and the health of financial institutions following the collapse of the housing price bubble endangered the operation of the financial system as a whole and had dire consequences for the economy.

Bubbles Driven Solely by Irrational Exuberance Bubbles that are driven solely by overly optimistic expectations, but that are not associated with a credit boom, pose much less risk to the financial system. For example, the bubble in technology stocks in the late 1990s was not fueled by credit, and the bursting of the tech-stock bubble was not followed by a marked deterioration in financial institutions' balance sheets. The bursting of the tech-stock bubble thus did not have a very severe impact on the economy, and the recession that followed was quite mild. Bubbles driven solely by irrational exuberance are therefore far less dangerous than those driven by credit booms.

The Debate over Whether Central Banks Should Try to Pop Bubbles

Because asset prices are a central channel of monetary policy and directly affect its outcomes (the transmission mechanisms of monetary policy are discussed in Chapter 25), monetary policy certainly needs to respond to asset prices in order to obtain good outcomes in terms of inflation and output. Hence, the issue is not whether monetary policy should respond to asset price movements at all, but whether it should respond at a level over and above the level called for in terms of the objectives of stabilizing inflation and employment. Should monetary policy try to pop, or slow, the growth of potential asset-price bubbles to minimize damage to the economy when these bubbles burst? Alternatively, rather than responding directly to possible asset-price bubbles, should the monetary authorities respond only to the asset-price declines that occur after a bubble bursts, to stabilize both output and inflation? These opposing positions have been characterized as *leaning against* asset-price bubbles versus *cleaning up* after the bubbles burst, and so the debate over what to do about asset-price bubbles has been labeled the "lean versus clean" debate.

Whether central banks should try to pop, or prick, bubbles was actively debated before the global financial crisis, with Alan Greenspan arguing against such actions. Greenspan's position held great sway in central banking circles before the crisis. However, the crisis has led economists to reevaluate this viewpoint, and we look at the pro and con arguments below.

Con: Why Central Banks Should Not Try to Prick Asset-Price Bubbles but Should Just Clean Up After They Burst Alan Greenspan's argument that central banks should not take actions to prick bubbles became known as the "Greenspan doctrine." His position reflected five arguments:

1. Asset-price bubbles are nearly impossible to identify. If central banks or government officials knew that a bubble was in progress, wouldn't market participants know as well? If so, then a bubble would be unlikely to develop, because market participants would know that prices were getting out of line with fundamentals. Unless central bank or government officials are smarter than market participants, an unlikely situation given the savvy of especially talented (and high-earning) market participants, they will be unlikely to identify when bubbles of this type are occurring. A strong argument, then, exists for not responding to suspected bubbles.

2. Although some economic analysis suggests that raising interest rates can diminish asset price increases, raising interest rates may be very ineffective in restraining bubbles because market participants expect such high rates of return from buying bubble-driven assets. Furthermore, raising interest rates has often been found to cause a bubble to burst more severely, thereby increasing the damage to the economy. Another way of saying this is that bubbles are departures from normal behavior, and it is unrealistic to expect that the usual tools of monetary policy will be effective in abnormal conditions.

3. Many different asset prices exist, and at any one time a bubble may be present in only a fraction of asset markets. Monetary policy actions are a very blunt instrument in such a case, as such actions would be likely to affect asset prices in general, rather than the specific assets that are experiencing a bubble.

4. Monetary policy actions to prick bubbles can have harmful effects on the aggregate economy. If interest rates are raised significantly in an effort to curtail a bubble, the economy will slow, people will lose jobs, and inflation might fall below its desirable level. Indeed, as arguments 2 and 3 suggest, the rise in interest rates necessary to prick a bubble may be so high that it can be done only at great cost to workers and the economy. This is not to say that monetary policy should not respond to asset prices per se. The level of asset prices does affect aggregate demand (discussed in Chapter 25) and thus the evolution of the economy. Monetary policy should react to fluctuations in asset prices to the extent that they affect inflation and economic activity.

5. As long as policymakers respond in a timely fashion, by easing monetary policy aggressively after an asset bubble bursts, the harmful effects of a bursting bubble can be kept at a manageable level. Indeed, the Greenspan Fed acted in exactly this way after the stock market crash of 1987 and the bursting of the tech bubble in the stock market in 2000. Aggressive easing after the stock market bubbles burst in 1987 and 2000 was highly successful. The economy did not enter a recession after the stock market crash of 1987, and the recession that followed the tech bubble burst in 2000 was very mild.

Pro: Why Central Banks Should Try to Pop Bubbles   The recent financial crisis clearly demonstrated that the bursting of credit-driven bubbles can be not only extremely costly but also very hard to clean up. Furthermore, credit-driven bubbles can occur even if price and output stability exist in the period leading up to them. Indeed, as we have seen, price and output stability might actually encourage credit-driven bubbles because they lead market participants to underestimate the amount of risk present in the economy. The global financial crisis has therefore provided a much stronger case for leaning against potential bubbles than for just cleaning up after they burst.

However, the distinction between the two types of bubbles, one of which (credit-driven) is much more costly to the economy than the other, suggests that the lean versus clean debate may have been miscast. Rather than leaning against potential asset-price bubbles, which would include both credit-driven and irrational exuberance-type bubbles, the case is much stronger for leaning against credit *booms*, which would involve leaning against credit-driven asset-price bubbles but not against asset-price bubbles driven by irrational exuberance. It is much easier to identify credit booms than asset-price bubbles. When asset-price bubbles are rising rapidly at the same time that credit is booming, the likelihood is greater that asset prices are deviating from fundamentals because laxer credit standards are driving asset prices upward. In this case, central bank or government officials are more likely to identify that a boom is in progress; this was indeed the case during the housing market bubble in the United States, when central banks and government officials were aware that lenders had weakened lending standards and that credit extension in the mortgage markets was rising at abnormally high rates.

The case for leaning against credit-driven bubbles seems strong, but what policies would be most effective in restraining them?

Macroprudential Policies   First, it is important to recognize that the key principle to consider in designing effective policies to lean against credit booms is that such policies must curb excessive risk taking. Only when risk taking is excessive are credit booms likely to develop, and so it is natural to look to prudential regulatory measures to constrain credit booms. Regulatory policy to affect what is happening in credit markets in the aggregate is referred to as **macroprudential regulation**, and it does seem to be the right tool for reining in credit-driven bubbles.

Financial regulation and supervision, either by central banks or by other government entities, with the usual elements of a well-functioning prudential regulatory and supervisory system, as described in Chapter 10, can prevent the excessive risk taking that can trigger a credit boom, which in turn will lead to an asset-price bubble. These elements include adequate disclosure and capital requirements, prompt corrective action, close monitoring of financial institutions' risk management procedures, and close supervision to enforce compliance with regulations. More generally, regulation should focus on preventing leverage cycles. As the global financial crisis demonstrated, the rise in asset prices that accompanied the credit boom resulted in higher capital buffers at financial institutions, supporting further lending in the context of unchanging capital requirements, which led to higher asset prices, and so on; in the bust, the value of the capital dropped precipitously, leading to a cut in lending. Capital requirements that are countercyclical, that is, adjusted upward during a boom and downward during a bust, might help eliminate the pernicious feedback loops that promote credit-driven bubbles.

A rapid rise in asset prices accompanied by a credit boom provides a signal that market failures or poor financial regulation and supervision might be causing a bubble to form. Central banks and other government regulators can then consider implementing policies to rein in credit growth directly or can implement measures to make sure credit standards are sufficiently high.

Monetary Policy
The fact that the low-interest-rate policies of the Federal Reserve from 2002 to 2005 were followed by excessive risk taking suggests to many that overly easy monetary policy might promote financial instability, as was discussed in Chapter 12. Although it is far from clear that the Federal Reserve is primarily to blame for the housing bubble, research does suggest that low interest rates can encourage excessive risk taking, in what has been called the "risk-taking channel of monetary policy." Low interest rates may increase the incentives for asset managers in financial institutions to search for higher yields and hence increase risk taking. Low interest rates may also increase the demand for assets, raising their prices and leading to increased valuation of collateral, which in turn encourages lenders to lend to riskier borrowers.

The risk-taking channel of monetary policy suggests that monetary policy should be used to lean against credit booms. However, many of the Greenspan doctrine's objections to using monetary policy to prick booms are still valid, so wouldn't it be better to use macroprudential supervision to constrain credit booms, leaving monetary policy to focus on price and output stability?

This argument would be quite strong if macroprudential policies were able to do the job. However, there are doubts on this score. Prudential supervision is subject to more political pressure than monetary policy because it affects the bottom line of financial institutions more directly. Thus these institutions have greater incentives to lobby politicians to discourage macroprudential policies that would rein in credit booms, particularly during a credit boom, when they are making the most money. In addition, financial institutions are often very good at finding loopholes to avoid regulation, as we discovered in Chapter 11, and so macroprudential supervision may not be effective. The possibility that macroprudential policies may not be implemented sufficiently well to constrain credit booms suggests that monetary policy may have to be used instead.

An important lesson from the global financial crisis is that central banks and other regulators should not have a laissez-faire attitude and let credit-driven bubbles proceed without any reaction. Figuring out how to do this well, however, is indeed a daunting task.

16.8 TACTICS: CHOOSING THE POLICY INSTRUMENT

LO 16.8 Describe and assess the four criteria for choosing a policy instrument.

Now that we are familiar with the alternative strategies for implementing monetary policy, let's look at how monetary policy is conducted on a day-to-day basis. Central banks directly control the tools of monetary policy—open market operations, reserve requirements, the discount rate, the interest rate on reserves, large-scale asset purchases, and forward guidance—but knowing the tools and the strategies for implementing a monetary policy does not tell us whether that policy is easy or tight. To ascertain whether policy is easy or tight, we can observe the **policy instrument** (also called an **operating instrument**), a variable that responds to the central bank's tools and indicates the stance (easy or tight) of monetary policy. A central bank like the Fed has at its disposal two basic types of policy instruments: reserve aggregates (total reserves, nonborrowed reserves, the monetary base, and the nonborrowed base) and interest rates (the federal funds rate and other short-term interest rates). (Central banks in small countries can choose another policy instrument, the exchange rate, but we leave this topic to Chapter 18.) The policy instrument might be linked to an **intermediate target**, such as a monetary aggregate like M2 or a long-term interest rate. Intermediate targets stand between the policy instrument and the goals of monetary policy (e.g., price stability, output growth); they are not as directly affected by the tools of monetary policy but might be more closely linked to the goals of monetary policy. As a study aid, Figure 2 shows a schematic of the linkages among the tools of monetary policy, policy instruments, intermediate targets, and the goals of monetary policy.

As an example, suppose the central bank's employment and inflation goals are consistent with a nominal GDP growth rate of 5%. The central bank might believe

Mini-lecture

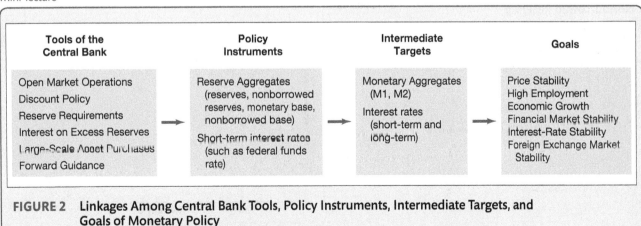

FIGURE 2 **Linkages Among Central Bank Tools, Policy Instruments, Intermediate Targets, and Goals of Monetary Policy**
The tools of the central bank are used to change the policy instrument to achieve the intermediate target and then the goals of monetary policy.

that the 5% nominal GDP growth rate will be achieved by a 4% growth rate for M2 (an intermediate target), which will in turn be achieved by a growth rate of 3% for nonborrowed reserves (the policy instrument). Alternatively, the central bank might believe that the best way to achieve its objectives would be to set the federal funds rate (a policy instrument) at, say, 4%. Can the central bank choose to target both the nonborrowed reserves and the federal-funds-rate policy instruments at the same time? The answer is no. The application of supply and demand analysis to the market for reserves, developed in Chapter 15, explains why a central bank must choose one or the other.

Let's first see why choosing an aggregate target involves losing control of the interest rate. Figure 3 contains a supply and demand diagram of the market for reserves. Although the central bank expects the demand curve for reserves to be at R^{d*}, it fluctuates between $R^{d'}$ and $R^{d''}$ because of unexpected fluctuations in deposits (and hence required reserves) and changes in banks' desire to hold excess reserves. If the central bank has a nonborrowed reserves target of NBR^* (say, because it has a target growth rate of the money supply of 4%), it expects that the federal funds rate will be i_{ff}^*. However, as the figure indicates, the fluctuations in the reserves demand curve between $R^{d'}$ and $R^{d''}$ will result in a fluctuation in the federal funds rate between i_{ff}' and i_{ff}''. Pursuing an aggregate target implies that interest rates will fluctuate.

The supply and demand diagram in Figure 4 shows the consequences of an interest-rate target set at i_{ff}^*. Again the central bank expects the reserves demand curve to be at R^{d*}, but it fluctuates between $R^{d'}$ and $R^{d''}$ due to unexpected changes in deposits or banks' desire to hold excess reserves. If the demand curve rises to $R^{d''}$, the federal funds rate will begin to rise above i_{ff}^* and the central bank will engage in open market purchases of bonds until it raises the supply of nonborrowed reserves to NBR'', at which point the equilibrium federal funds rate will return to i_{ff}^*. Conversely, if the demand curve falls to $R^{d'}$ and the federal funds rate drops, the central bank will keep making open market sales until nonborrowed reserves fall to NBR'' and the federal funds rate

Mini-lecture

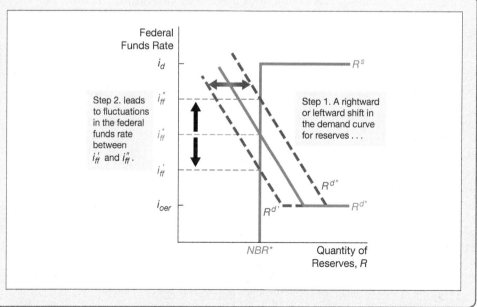

FIGURE 3

Result of Targeting on Nonborrowed Reserves

Targeting on nonborrowed reserves of NBR^* will lead to fluctuations in the federal funds rate between i_{ff}' and i_{ff}'' because of fluctuations in the demand for reserves between $R^{d'}$ and $R^{d''}$.

Mini-lecture

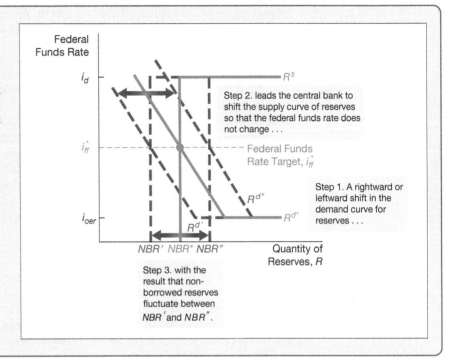

FIGURE 4

Result of Targeting on the Federal Funds Rate

Targeting on the interest rate i_{ff}^* will lead to fluctuations in nonborrowed reserves between NBR' and NBR'' because of fluctuations in the demand for reserves between $R^{d'}$ and $R^{d''}$.

returns to i_{ff}^*. The central bank's adherence to the interest-rate target thus leads to a fluctuating quantity of nonborrowed reserves and the money supply.

The conclusion from our supply and demand analysis is that interest-rate and reserve (monetary) aggregate targets are incompatible. A central bank can hit one or the other, but not both. Because a choice between them has to be made, we need to examine what criteria should be used to select a policy instrument.

Criteria for Choosing the Policy Instrument

Three criteria apply when choosing a policy instrument: The instrument must be observable and measurable, it must be controllable by the central bank, and it must have a predictable effect on the goals.

Observability and Measurability   Quick observability and accurate measurement of a policy instrument are necessary because such an instrument is useful only if it signals the policy stance rapidly. Reserve aggregates like nonborrowed reserves are easily measured, but some lag in the reporting of reserve aggregates (a delay of two weeks) exists. Short-term interest rates (like the federal funds rate), by contrast, are not only easy to measure but also immediately observable. Thus, it seems that interest rates are more observable and measurable than reserves and are therefore a better policy instrument.

However, as we learned in Chapter 4, the interest rate that is easiest to measure and observe is the nominal interest rate. It is typically a poor measure of the real cost of borrowing, which indicates with more certainty what will happen to the real GDP. The real cost of borrowing is more accurately measured by the real interest rate—that is, the nominal interest rate adjusted for expected inflation $(i_r = i - \pi^e)$. Unfortunately, real interest rates are extremely difficult to measure because we do not have a direct way of measuring expected inflation. Given that both interest rates and aggregates are associated with observability and measurability problems, it is not clear whether one should be preferred over the other as a policy instrument.

Controllability   A central bank must be able to exercise effective control over a variable if the variable is to function as a useful policy instrument. If the central bank cannot control the policy instrument, knowing that it is off track does little good because the central bank has no way of getting it back on track.

Because of shifts into and out of currency, even reserve aggregates, such as non-borrowed reserves, are not completely controllable. Conversely, the Fed can control short-term interest rates, such as the federal funds rate, very tightly. It might appear, therefore, that short-term interest rates would dominate reserve aggregates on the controllability scale. However, a central bank cannot set short-term real interest rates because it does not have control over expectations of inflation. Once again, a clear-cut case cannot be made that short-term interest rates are preferable to reserve aggregates as a policy instrument, or vice versa.

Predictable Effect on Goals   The most important characteristic of a policy instrument is that it must have a predictable effect on a goal such as high employment or price stability. If a central bank can accurately and quickly measure the price of tea in China and can completely control its price, what good does that do? The central bank cannot use the price of tea in China to affect unemployment or the price level in its own country. Because the ability of a policy instrument to affect goals is critical to its usefulness, the strength of the link between reserve or monetary aggregates and the goals (output, employment, and inflation) or, alternatively, between interest rates and these goals, has been the subject of much research and debate. In recent years, most central banks have concluded that the link between interest rates and goals such as stable inflation is stronger than the link between aggregates and inflation. For this reason, central banks throughout the world now generally use short-term interest rates as their policy instrument.

16.9 TACTICS: THE TAYLOR RULE

LO 16.9 Interpret and assess the performance of the Taylor rule as a hypothetical policy instrument for setting the federal funds rate.

As we have seen, the Federal Reserve and most other central banks currently conduct monetary policy by setting a target for short-term interest rates such as the federal funds rate. But how should this target be chosen?

John Taylor of Stanford University has come up with an answer, called the **Taylor rule**. The Taylor rule indicates that the federal (fed) funds rate should be set equal to the inflation rate plus an "equilibrium" real fed funds rate (the real fed funds rate that is consistent with full employment in the long run) plus a weighted average of two gaps: (1) an inflation gap, current inflation minus a target rate; and (2) an output gap, the percentage deviation of real GDP from an estimate of its potential (natural rate) level.[11]

---

[11]The original formulation of the Taylor rule can be found in John B. Taylor, "Discretion Versus Policy Rules in Practice," *Carnegie-Rochester Conference Series on Public Policy* 39 (1993): 195–214. However, a more intuitive discussion with a historical perspective can be found in John B. Taylor, "A Historical Analysis of Monetary Policy Rules," in *Monetary Policy Rules*, ed. John B. Taylor (Chicago: University of Chicago Press, 1999), 319–341.

This rule can be written as follows:

Federal funds rate target $=$ inflation rate $+$ equilibrium real fed funds rate

$$+ \frac{1}{2}(\text{inflation gap}) + \frac{1}{2}(\text{output gap})$$

Taylor assumed an equilibrium real fed funds rate of 2% and an appropriate target for inflation of 2%, with equal weights of $\frac{1}{2}$ on the inflation and output gaps. For a numerical example of the Taylor rule, suppose the inflation rate is at 3%, leading to a positive inflation gap of 1% ($= 3\% - 2\%$), and real GDP is 1% above its potential, resulting in a positive output gap of 1%. Then the Taylor rule suggests that the federal funds rate should be set at 6% [$= 3\%$ inflation $+ 2\%$ equilibrium real fed funds rate $+ \frac{1}{2}$ (1% inflation gap) $+ \frac{1}{2}$ (1% output gap)].

An important feature of the Taylor rule is that the coefficient on the inflation gap, $\frac{1}{2}$, is positive. If the inflation rate rises by 1 percentage point, then the federal funds target is raised by 1.5 percentage points, and so it is raised by more than a one-to-one ratio. In other words, a rise in inflation of 1 percentage point leads to an increase in the *real* federal funds rate of $\frac{1}{2}$ percentage point. The principle that the monetary authorities should raise nominal interest rates by more than the increase in the inflation rate has been named the **Taylor principle**, and it is critical to the success of monetary policy. Suppose that the Taylor principle is not followed and that the rise in nominal rates is *less* than the rise in the inflation rate, so that real interest rates *fall* when inflation rises. Serious instability then results, because a rise in inflation leads to an effective easing of monetary policy, which then leads to even higher inflation in the future. Indeed, this scenario characterizes the monetary policy of the 1970s, which led to a loss of the nominal anchor and the era of the so-called "Great Inflation," when inflation rates climbed to double-digit levels. Fortunately, since 1979, the Taylor principle has become a feature of monetary policy, with much happier outcomes on both the inflation and aggregate output fronts.

Some economists take the view that the presence of an output gap in the Taylor rule indicates that the Fed should care not only about keeping inflation under control but also about minimizing business cycle fluctuations of output around its potential level. Caring about both inflation and output fluctuations is consistent with the Fed's dual mandate and with many statements by Federal Reserve officials that controlling inflation and stabilizing real output are important concerns of the Fed.

An alternative interpretation of the presence of the output gap in the Taylor rule is that the output gap is an indicator of future inflation, as stipulated in **Phillips curve theory**. Phillips curve theory states that changes in inflation are influenced by the state of the economy relative to its productive capacity, as well as by other factors. This productive capacity can be measured by potential GDP, which is a function of the natural rate of unemployment, defined as the rate of unemployment consistent with full employment. A related concept is the **NAIRU**, the **nonaccelerating inflation rate of unemployment**, defined as the rate of unemployment at which there is no tendency for inflation to change. Simply put, the theory states that when the unemployment rate is above NAIRU, with output below potential, inflation will fall, but when it is below NAIRU, with output above potential, inflation will rise. Prior to 1995, the NAIRU was thought to reside around 6%. However, with the drop in unemployment to around the 4% level in the late 1990s, with no increase (and even a slight decrease) in inflation, some critics have questioned the value of Phillips curve theory. Either they claim that Phillips curve theory just doesn't work anymore or, alternatively, they believe that great uncertainty exists about the value of NAIRU, which may have fallen to below 5% for reasons that are not absolutely clear. Phillips curve theory is now highly controversial, and critics question whether it should be used as a guide in the conduct of monetary policy.

Real-time data

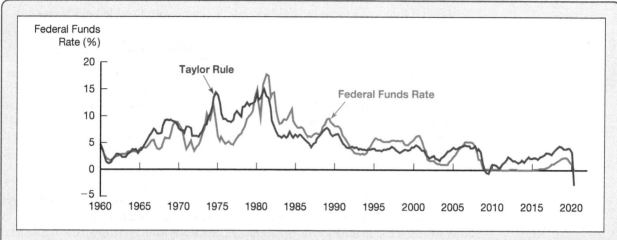

FIGURE 5   **The Taylor Rule for the Federal Funds Rate, 1960–2020**

The Taylor rule does a pretty good job of describing the Fed's setting of the federal funds rate after Alan Greenspan became the chair of the Federal Reserve in 1987, but it does not accurately describe the movement of the federal funds rate during the 1970s.

Source: Calculations with Federal Reserve Bank of St. Louis FRED database: https://fred.stlouisfed.org/series/PCEPILFE; https://fred.stlouisfed.org/series/GDPC1; https://fred.stlouisfed.org/series/GDPPOT; https://fred.stlouisfed.org/series/FEDFUNDS.

Inside the Fed   The Fed's Use of the Taylor Rule

Why hasn't the Fed put the federal funds rate on Taylor rule autopilot, guided by a computer? There are several reasons why the Fed hasn't taken this drastic action. First and foremost, no perfect model of the economy exists, so even the best and brightest economists do not know the current output gap with certainty at any given moment. Since the economy is changing all the time, the Taylor rule coefficients are unlikely to stay constant in any event.

Even if we could determine the output gap with certainty, monetary policy is by necessity a forward-looking activity, since it takes a long time for monetary policy to affect the economy. Good monetary policy requires that the Fed forecast where inflation and economic activity are headed in the future and then adjust the policy instrument accordingly. The Fed will therefore look at a much wider range of information than just the current inflation gap and output gap, the variables used in the Taylor rule, when setting its policy. In other words, the conduct of monetary policy is as much an art as it is a science, requiring both careful analytics and human judgment. The Taylor rule leaves out all of the art and so is unlikely to produce the best monetary policy outcomes. For example, financial crises, such as the crisis that occurred from 2007 to 2009, require complex monetary policy actions because changes in credit spreads (the difference between interest rates on securities with credit risk and those without) may alter how the federal funds rate affects investment decisions and therefore economic activity.

The bottom line is that putting monetary policy on autopilot by using a Taylor rule with fixed coefficients is problematic. The Taylor rule is useful, however, as a *guide* to monetary policy. If the proposed setting of the policy instrument is very different from the setting suggested by the Taylor rule, policymakers should ask whether they have a good reason for deviating from this rule. If they don't, as during the era of the 1970s when Arthur Burns was the chair of the Federal Reserve, then they might be making a mistake. Indeed, the FOMC makes use of Taylor rule estimates in exactly this way—by referring to these estimates to inform their decisions about the federal funds rate target.[*]

[*] For an in-depth discussion of the FOMC's actual use of the Taylor rule in its policy deliberations, see Pier Francesco Asso, George A. Kahn, and Robert Leeson, "The Taylor Rule and the Practice of Central Banking," Federal Reserve Bank of Kansas City Working Paper RWP 10-05 (February 2010).

As Figure 5 shows, the Taylor rule does a pretty good, but not perfect, job of describing the Fed's setting of the federal funds rate after Alan Greenspan became the chair of the Federal Reserve in 1987. (Notice in Figure 5 that the Taylor rule does not accurately describe the movement of the federal funds rate during the 1970s, which reflects the fact that the Taylor principle was not being followed at that time, which in turn explains why monetary policy outcomes were so poor.) Does this mean that the Fed should fire all of its economists and put a computer in charge to simply compute the Taylor rule setting for the federal funds rate? This would certainly save the taxpayers a lot of money. Although the Fed does not use the Taylor rule to directly compute the federal funds rate, it does make use of the Taylor rule in thinking about how to conduct monetary policy (see the Inside the Fed box "The Fed's Use of the Taylor Rule").

SUMMARY

1. The six basic goals of monetary policy are price stability (the primary goal), high employment (output stability), economic growth, stability of financial markets, interest-rate stability, and stability in foreign exchange markets.

2. A strong nominal anchor is a key element of a successful monetary policy. A strong nominal anchor helps promote price stability by tying down inflation expectations and limiting the time-inconsistency problem, in which monetary policymakers conduct monetary policy in a discretionary way that focuses on short-run objectives but produces poor long-run outcomes.

3. Inflation targeting has several advantages: (1) By focusing the political debate on long-run inflation, it can reduce the likelihood of the time-inconsistency problem; (2) it is readily understood by the public and is highly transparent; (3) it increases accountability of the central bank; and (4) it results in more stable inflation. It does have some disadvantages, however: (1) Inflation is not easily controlled by the monetary authorities, and so an inflation target does not send immediate signals to the public and the markets; (2) it might impose a rigid rule on policymakers, although this has not been the case in practice; and (3) a sole focus on inflation may lead to larger output fluctuations, or lower economic growth, although this also has not been the case in practice.

4. The Federal Reserve's monetary policy strategy has evolved over time. From the 1980s through 2006, the Federal Reserve set an implicit, not an explicit, nominal anchor. Despite its demonstrated success, this strategy lacked transparency and was inconsistent with democratic principles. Under Ben Bernanke, the Federal Reserve moved to a flexible form of inflation targeting that was consistent with the Fed's dual mandate.

5. Four lessons can be learned from the global financial crisis: (1) Developments in the financial sector have a far greater impact on economic activity than was earlier realized; (2) the effective lower bound on interest rates can be a serious problem; (3) the cost of cleaning up after a financial crisis is very high; and (4) price and output stability do not ensure financial stability.

6. The lessons of the global financial crisis provide support for more flexible inflation targeting, possibly with a higher inflation target.

7. The lessons from the crisis also suggest that monetary policy should lean against credit booms but not asset-price bubbles.

8. Because interest-rate and aggregate policy instruments are incompatible, a central bank must choose between them on the basis of three criteria: measurability, controllability, and their ability to affect goal variables predictably. Central banks now typically use short-term interest rates as their policy instrument.

9. The Taylor rule indicates that the federal funds rate should be set equal to the inflation rate plus an "equilibrium" real fed funds rate plus a weighted average of two gaps: (1) an inflation gap, current inflation minus a target rate; and (2) an output gap, the percentage deviation of real GDP from an estimate of its potential (natural rate) level. The output gap in the Taylor rule can be interpreted as an indicator of future inflation, as stipulated in Phillips curve theory. However, this theory is controversial, because high output relative to potential as measured by low unemployment has not seemed to produce higher inflation in recent years.

KEY TERMS

asset-price bubble, p. 386

dual mandate, p. 374

hierarchical mandates, p. 373

inflation targeting, p. 374

intermediate target, p. 390

macroprudential regulation, p. 389

natural rate of output, p. 372

natural rate of unemployment, p. 371

nominal anchor, p. 370

nonaccelerating inflation rate of
   unemployment (NAIRU), p. 395

operating instrument, p. 390

Phillips curve theory, p. 394

policy instrument, p. 390

potential output, p. 372

price stability, p. 369

Taylor principle, p. 394

Taylor rule, p. 394

time-inconsistency problem, p. 370

QUESTIONS

1. What are the benefits of using a nominal anchor for the conduct of monetary policy?

2. What incentives arise for a central bank to fall into the time-inconsistency trap of pursuing overly expansionary monetary policy?

3. Why would it be problematic for a central bank to have a primary goal of maximizing economic growth?

4. "Since financial crises can impart severe damage to the economy, a central bank's primary goal should be to ensure stability in financial markets." Is this statement true, false, or uncertain? Explain.

5. "A central bank with a dual mandate will achieve lower unemployment in the long run than a central bank with a hierarchical mandate in which price stability takes precedence." Is this statement true, false, or uncertain? Explain.

6. Why is a public announcement of numerical inflation rate objectives important to the success of an inflation-targeting central bank?

7. How does inflation targeting help reduce the time-inconsistency problem of discretionary policy?

8. What methods have inflation-targeting central banks used to increase communication with the public and to increase the transparency of monetary policymaking?

9. Why might inflation targeting increase support for the independence of the central bank in conducting monetary policy?

10. "Because inflation targeting focuses on achieving the inflation target, it will lead to excessive output fluctuations." Is this statement true, false, or uncertain? Explain.

11. What are the key advantages and disadvantages of the monetary strategy used by the Federal Reserve under Alan Greenspan, in which the nominal anchor was implicit rather than explicit?

12. "The effective lower bound on short-term interest rates is not a problem, since the central bank can just use quantitative easing to lower intermediate and longer-term interest rates instead." Is this statement true, false, or uncertain? Explain.

13. If higher inflation is bad, then why might it be advantageous to have a higher inflation target rather than a lower target that is closer to zero?

14. Why might macroprudential regulation be more effective in managing asset-price bubbles than monetary policy?

15. Why might it be better to *lean* against credit-driven bubbles rather than just *clean* up after asset bubbles burst?

16. According to the Greenspan doctrine, under what conditions might a central bank respond to a perceived stock market bubble?

17. Classify each of the following as either a policy instrument or an intermediate target, and explain your choice.

    a. The ten-year Treasury bond rate

    b. The monetary base

    c. M1

    d. The fed funds rate

18. "If the demand for reserves did not fluctuate, the Fed could pursue both a reserves target and an interest-rate target at the same time." Is this statement true, false, or uncertain? Explain.

19. What procedures can the Fed use to control the federal funds rate? Why does control of this interest rate imply that the Fed will lose control of nonborrowed reserves?

20. Compare the monetary base to M1 on the grounds of controllability and measurability. Which do you prefer as an intermediate target? Why?

21. "Interest rates can be measured more accurately and quickly than reserve aggregates; hence an interest rate

is preferred to the reserve aggregates as a policy instrument." Do you agree or disagree? Explain your answer.

22. How can forward guidance as a tool of the central bank affect the policy instrument, intermediate targets, and goals?

23. What does the Taylor rule imply that policymakers should do to the fed funds rate under the following scenarios?

    a. Unemployment rises due to a recession.

    b. An oil price shock causes the inflation rate to rise by 1% and output to fall by 1%.

    c. The economy experiences prolonged increases in productivity growth while actual output growth is unchanged.

    d. Potential output declines while actual output remains unchanged.

    e. The Fed revises its (implicit) inflation target downward.

    f. The equilibrium real fed funds rate decreases.

APPLIED PROBLEMS

24. If the Fed has an interest-rate target, why will an increase in the demand for reserves lead to a rise in the money supply? Use a graph of the market for reserves to explain.

25. Since monetary policy changes made through the fed funds rate occur with a lag, policymakers are usually more concerned with adjusting policy according to changes in the forecasted or expected inflation rate, rather than the current inflation rate. In light of this, suppose that monetary policymakers employ the Taylor rule to set the fed funds rate, where the inflation gap is defined as the difference between expected inflation and the target inflation rate. Assume that the weights on both the inflation and output gaps are ½, the equilibrium real fed funds rate is 2%, the inflation rate target is 2%, and the output gap is 1%.

    a. If the expected inflation rate is 4%, then at what target should the fed funds rate be set according to the Taylor rule?

    b. Suppose half of Fed economists forecast inflation to be 3%, and half of Fed economists forecast inflation to be 5%. If the Fed uses the average of these two forecasts as its measure of expected inflation, then at what target should the fed funds rate be set according to the Taylor rule?

    c. Now suppose half of Fed economists forecast inflation to be 0%, and half forecast inflation to be 8%. If the Fed uses the average of these two forecasts as its measure of expected inflation, then at what target should the fed funds rate be set according to the Taylor rule?

    d. Given your answers to parts (a)–(c) above, do you think it is a good idea for monetary policymakers to use a strict interpretation of the Taylor rule as a basis for setting policy? Why or why not?

DATA ANALYSIS PROBLEMS

The Problems update with real-time data in **MyLab Economics** and are available for practice or instructor assignment.

1. **Real-time Data Analysis** The Fed's maximum employment mandate is generally interpreted as an attempt to achieve an unemployment rate that is as close as possible to the natural rate and inflation that is close to its 2% goal for personal consumption expenditure price inflation. Go to the St. Louis Federal Reserve FRED database, and find data on the personal consumption expenditure price index (PCECTPI), the unemployment rate (UNRATE), and a measure of the natural rate of unemployment (NROU). For the price index, adjust the *units* setting to "Percent Change From Year Ago" to convert the data to the inflation rate; for the unemployment rate, change the *frequency* setting to "Quarterly." Download the data into a spreadsheet. Calculate the unemployment gap and inflation gap for each quarter. Then, using the inflation gap, create an average inflation gap measure by taking the average of the current inflation gap and the gaps for the previous three quarters. Now apply the following (admittedly arbitrary and ad hoc) test to the data from 2000:Q1 through the most recent data available: If the unemployment gap is larger than 1.0 for two or more consecutive quarters, and/or the average inflation gap is larger in absolute value than 0.5 for two or more consecutive quarters, consider the mandate "violated."

a. Based on this ad hoc test, in which quarters has the Fed "violated" the price stability portion of its mandate? In which quarters has the Fed "violated" the maximum employment mandate?

b. Is the Fed currently "in violation" of its mandate?

c. Interpret your results. What does your response to part (a) and the data imply about the challenge that monetary policy-makers face in achieving the Fed's mandate perfectly at all times?

2. **Real-time Data Analysis** Go to the St. Louis Federal Reserve FRED database, and find data on the personal consumption expenditure price index (PCECTPI), real GDP (GDPC1), an estimate of potential GDP (GDPPOT), and the federal funds rate (FEDFUNDS). For the price index, adjust the *units* setting to "Percent Change From Year Ago" to convert the data to the inflation rate; for the federal funds rate, change the *frequency* setting to "Quarterly." Download the data into a spreadsheet. Assuming the inflation target is 2% and the equilibrium real fed funds rate is 2%, calculate the inflation gap and the output gap for each quarter, from 2000 until the most recent quarter of data available. Calculate the output gap as the percentage deviation of output from the potential level of output.

a. Use the output and inflation gaps to calculate, for each quarter, the fed funds rate predicted by the Taylor rule. Assume that the weights on inflation stabilization and output stabilization are both ½ (see the formula in the chapter). Compare the current (quarterly average) federal funds rate to the federal funds rate prescribed by the Taylor rule. Does the Taylor rule accurately predict the current rate? Briefly comment.

b. Create a graph that compares the predicted Taylor rule values with the actual quarterly federal funds rate averages. How well, in general, does the Taylor rule prediction fit the average federal funds rate? Briefly explain.

c. Based on the results from the 2008–2009 period, explain the limitations of the Taylor rule as a formal policy tool. How do these limitations help explain the use of nonconventional monetary policy during this period?

d. Suppose Congress changes the Fed's mandate to a hierarchical one in which inflation stabilization takes priority over output stabilization. In this context, recalculate the predicted Taylor rule value for each quarter since 2000, assuming that the weight on inflation stabilization is ¾ and the weight on output stabilization is ¼. Create a graph showing the Taylor rule prediction calculated in part (a), the prediction using the new "hierarchical" Taylor rule, and the fed funds rate. How, if at all, does changing the mandate change the predicted policy paths? How would the fed funds rate be affected by a hierarchical mandate? Briefly explain.

e. Assume again equal weights of ½ on inflation and output stabilization, and suppose instead that beginning after the end of 2008, the equilibrium real fed funds rate declines by 0.05 each quarter (i.e., 2009:Q1 is 1. 95, then 1.90, etc.), and once it reaches zero, it remains at zero thereafter. How does it affect the prescribed fed funds rate? Why might this be important for policymakers to take into consideration?

PART 5

International Finance and Monetary Policy

Crisis and Response: Foreign Exchange Market Turmoil and the IMF

From 2002 until 2008, the U.S. dollar steadily declined in value relative to other currencies. Indeed, a major concern of policymakers was that the dollar might crash, with adverse effects on both economic activity and inflation. With the credit markets seizing up in September and October 2008, after the failure of Lehman Brothers, an amazing thing happened. Instead of continuing its decline, the dollar appreciated sharply. The same "flight to quality" that led investors to step up their purchases of U.S. Treasury securities also led them to want to hold more U.S. dollars, thereby bidding up the dollar's value.

The dollar's higher value made imported goods—ranging from flat-screen televisions to wines—cheaper to purchase and traveling abroad more affordable. But this good news for the U.S. dollar was often bad news for other currencies. Many countries in Latin America and Eastern Europe now found their currencies in free fall. The International Monetary Fund (IMF) stepped in and set up a new lending facility to make loans to distressed countries with fewer strings attached than were attached to the IMF's previous lending programs. The IMF started making loans to the tune of billions of dollars. The IMF, which had looked as though it was on the sidelines as the global financial crisis spread worldwide, now was moving to front and center.

The global financial crisis demonstrated that financial events that start in the United States can have worldwide ramifications and that international financial institutions like the IMF have an important role in responding to such events, to make sure that the international financial system continues to work well. Chapter 17 outlines how the foreign exchange market functions and how exchange rates between different countries' currencies are determined. In Chapter 18, we examine how the international financial system operates and how it affects monetary policy.

17 The Foreign Exchange Market

Learning Objectives

17.1 Explain how the foreign exchange market works and why exchange rates are important.

17.2 Identify the main factors that affect exchange rates in the long run.

17.3 Draw the demand and supply curves for the foreign exchange market and interpret the equilibrium in the market for foreign exchange.

17.4 List and illustrate the factors that affect the exchange rate in the short run.

Preview

On June 23, 2016, the United Kingdom voted to leave the European Union. This decision is referred to as *Brexit* (**Br**itian **Exit**). Within a day the British pound fell in value by 9% relative to the U.S. dollar.

The price of one currency in terms of another is called the *exchange rate*. As the Brexit example suggests, exchange rates are highly volatile. The exchange rate affects the economy and our daily lives because when the U.S. dollar becomes more valuable relative to foreign currencies, as it did relative to the British pound after Brexit, foreign goods become cheaper for Americans, and American goods become more expensive for foreigners. When the U.S. dollar falls in value, foreign goods become more expensive for Americans, and American goods become cheaper for foreigners.

Fluctuations in the exchange rate also affect both inflation and output and are an important concern to monetary policymakers. When the U.S. dollar falls in value, the higher prices of imported goods feed directly into a higher price level and inflation. At the same time, a declining U.S. dollar, which makes U.S. goods cheaper for foreigners, increases the demand for U.S. goods and leads to higher production and output.

How are currencies traded? What drives fluctuations in exchange rates? Why are exchange rates so volatile? We answer these questions by first examining the financial market in which currencies are traded. Next, we look at what affects exchange rates in the long run. We then develop a supply and demand analysis to explain what determines exchange rates in the short run. Finally, we use this supply and demand analysis to explain fluctuations in the exchange rate resulting from events such as Brexit and the global financial crisis.

17.1 FOREIGN EXCHANGE MARKET

LO 17.1 Explain how the foreign exchange market works and why exchange rates are important.

Most countries of the world have their own currencies: The United States has its dollar; the European Monetary Union, its euro; Brazil, its real; and China, its yuan. Trade between countries involves the mutual exchange of different currencies (or, more typically, bank deposits denominated in different currencies). When an American firm buys foreign goods, services, or financial assets, for example, U.S. dollars (typically, bank deposits denominated in U.S. dollars) must be exchanged for foreign currency (bank deposits denominated in the foreign currency).

The trading of currencies and bank deposits denominated in particular currencies takes place in the **foreign exchange market**. Transactions conducted in the foreign exchange market determine the rates at which currencies are exchanged, which in turn determine the cost of purchasing foreign goods and financial assets.

What Are Foreign Exchange Rates?

An **exchange rate** is the price of one currency in terms of another. There are two kinds of exchange rate transactions. The predominant ones, called **spot transactions**, involve the immediate (two-day) exchange of bank deposits. **Forward transactions** involve the exchange of bank deposits at some specified future date. The **spot exchange rate** is the exchange rate for the spot transaction, and the **forward exchange rate** is the exchange rate for the forward transaction.

When a currency increases in value, it experiences **appreciation**; when it falls in value and is worth fewer U.S. dollars, it undergoes **depreciation**. At the beginning of 1999, for example, the euro was valued at 1.18 dollars; on June 24, 2020, it was valued at 1.13 dollars, as indicated in the Following the Financial News box "Foreign Exchange Rates." The euro *depreciated* by 4%: $(1.13 - 1.18)/1.18 = -0.04 = -4\%$. Equivalently, we could say that the U.S. dollar, which went from a value of 0.85 euro per dollar at the beginning of 1999 to a value of 0.88 euro per dollar on June 24, 2020, *appreciated* by 4%: $(0.88 - 0.85)/0.85 = 0.04 = 4\%$.

Why Are Exchange Rates Important?

Exchange rates are important because they affect the relative prices of domestic and foreign goods. The dollar price of French goods to an American is determined by the interaction of two factors: the price of French goods in euros and the euro/dollar exchange rate.

Suppose that Wanda the Winetaster, an American, decides to buy a bottle of 1961 (a very good year) Château Lafite Rothschild to complete her wine cellar. If the price of the wine in France is 1,000 euros and the exchange rate is $1.13 to the euro, the wine will cost Wanda $1.130 ($= 1{,}000$ euros $\times \$1.13/\text{euro}$). Now suppose that Wanda delays her purchase by two months, at which time the euro has appreciated to $1.50

per euro. If the domestic price of the bottle of Lafite Rothschild remains 1,000 euros, its dollar cost will have risen from $1,130 to $1,500.

The same currency appreciation, however, makes the price of foreign goods in France less expensive. At an exchange rate of $1.13 per euro, a Dell computer priced at $2,000 costs Pierre the Programmer 1,770 euros; if the exchange rate increases to $1.50 per euro, the computer will cost only 1,333 euros.

A depreciation of the euro lowers the cost of French goods in America but raises the cost of American goods in France. If the euro drops in value to $1.00, Wanda's bottle of Lafite Rothschild will cost her only $1,000 instead of $1,130, and the Dell computer will cost Pierre 2,000 euros rather than 1,770 euros.

Such reasoning leads to the following conclusion: **When a country's currency appreciates (rises in value relative to other currencies), the country's goods abroad become more expensive, and foreign goods in that country become cheaper (holding domestic prices constant in the two countries). Conversely, when a country's currency depreciates, its goods abroad become cheaper, and foreign goods in that country become more expensive.**

Depreciation of a currency makes it easier for domestic manufacturers to sell their goods abroad and makes foreign goods less competitive in domestic markets. The depreciation of the U.S. dollar from 2018 to 2020 helped U.S. industries sell more goods, but it hurt American consumers because foreign goods were more expensive. The prices of French wine and cheese and the cost of vacationing abroad all rose as a result of the weak dollar.

In contrast, the appreciation of the U.S. dollar from 2016 to 2018 made goods and services produced in the United States less competitive. However, the stronger dollar was positive for American consumers because foreign goods like French cheese and vacationing abroad were less expensive.

How Is Foreign Exchange Traded?

You cannot go to a centralized location to watch exchange rates being determined; currencies are not traded on exchanges such as the New York Stock Exchange. Instead, the foreign exchange market is organized as an over-the-counter market in which several hundred dealers (mostly banks) stand ready to buy and sell deposits denominated in foreign currencies. Because these dealers are in constant telephone and computer contact, the market is very competitive; in effect, it functions no differently from a centralized market.

An important point to note is that although banks, companies, and governments talk about buying and selling currencies in foreign exchange markets, they do not take a fistful of dollar bills and sell them for British pound notes. Rather, most trades involve the buying and selling of bank deposits denominated in different currencies. So when we say that a bank is buying dollars in the foreign exchange market, what we actually mean is that the bank is buying *deposits denominated in dollars*. The volume in this market is colossal, exceeding $6 trillion per day.

Trades in the foreign exchange market consist of transactions in excess of $1 million. The market that determines the exchange rates given in the Following the Financial News box is not the market in which we would buy foreign currency for a trip abroad. Instead, we buy foreign currency in the retail market, from dealers such as American Express or from banks. Because retail prices are higher than wholesale prices, when we buy foreign exchange, we obtain fewer units of foreign currency per dollar—that is, we pay a higher price for foreign currency—than the exchange rates quoted in the newspaper.

17.2 EXCHANGE RATES IN THE LONG RUN

LO 17.2 Identify the main factors that affect exchange rates in the long run.

Like the price of any good or asset in a free market, exchange rates are determined by the interaction of supply and demand. To simplify our analysis of exchange rates in a free market, we divide it into two parts. First, we examine how exchange rates are determined in the long run; then we use our knowledge of the long-run determinants of exchange rates to help us understand how they are determined in the short run.

Theory of Purchasing Power Parity

One of the most prominent theories of how exchange rates are determined is the **theory of purchasing power parity (PPP)**. It states that the exchange rate between any two countries' currencies is such that a basket of goods and services, wherever it is produced, costs the same in both countries.

Suppose that you are buying a basket of goods and services in the United States that costs $100. The same basket costs 10,000 yen in Japan. The theory of purchasing power parity says that the exchange rate between the dollar and the yen is therefore 100 yen per dollar. At this exchange rate, the basket of goods and services in the United States would cost 10,000 yen ($= \$100 \times 100$ yen per dollar), the same cost as in Japan. Similarly, the basket of goods and services in Japan would cost $100 (10,000 yen $\times \$0.01$ per yen), the same as in the United States.

What is the intuition behind purchasing power parity? Suppose the basket of goods in Japan were shipped to the United States and there were no transportation costs or barriers to trade. It would sell for the same dollar amount in the United States as it does in Japan. Similarly, if the U.S. basket of goods were shipped to Japan, it would cost the same amount in yen. Only an exchange rate of 100 yen per dollar ensures that the prices are consistent across the two countries.

Another way of thinking about purchasing power parity is through a concept called the **real exchange rate**, the rate at which domestic goods can be exchanged for foreign goods. In effect, the real exchange rate is the price of domestic goods relative to the price of foreign goods denominated in the domestic currency. For example, if a basket of goods in New York costs $50 while the same basket of goods in Tokyo costs $75 (because the basket of goods costs 7,500 yen and the exchange rate is 100 yen per dollar), then the real exchange rate is 0.66 ($= \$50/\$75$). In our example, the real exchange rate is below 1.0, indicating that it is cheaper to buy the basket of goods in the United States than in Japan. The real exchange rate for the U.S. dollar is currently low against many other currencies, and this is why New York is overwhelmed by so many foreign tourists going on shopping sprees. The real exchange rate indicates whether a currency is relatively cheap or not. The theory of PPP can also be described in terms of the real exchange rate. PPP predicts that in the long run the real exchange rate is always equal to 1.0, so that the purchasing power of the dollar is the same as that of other currencies, such as the yen or the euro.

What happens if one country's price level changes relative to another's? For example, suppose that the price level in Japan rises by 10%, while the price level in the United States does not change. As a result, the price of the basket in Japan has risen by 10% relative to the U.S. price. Now the cost of the basket of goods and services in Japan would rise by 10% to 11,000 yen, while the price of the same basket in the United States would remain $100. For the U.S. and the Japanese baskets of goods to cost the same, the exchange rate would have to change to 110 yen per dollar. Then the U.S.

Real-time data

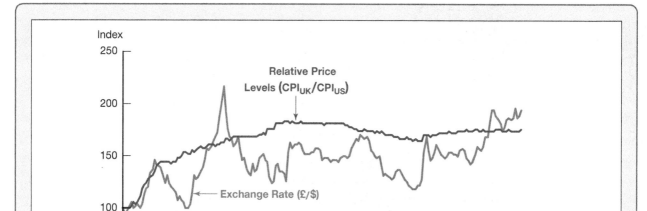

FIGURE 1   **Purchasing Power Parity, United States/United Kingdom, 1973–2020
(Index: March 1973 = 100.)**

Over the whole period shown, the rise in the British price level relative to the U.S. price level is associated with a rise in the value of the dollar, as predicted by PPP. However, the PPP relationship does not hold over shorter periods.

Source: Federal Reserve Bank of St. Louis FRED database: https://fred.stlouisfed.org/series/GBRCPIALLMINMEI; https://fred.stlouisfed.org/series/CPIAUCNS; https://fred.stlouisfed.org/series/EXUSUK.

basket would cost 11,000 yen in Japan ($100 × $100 yen per dollar), and the Japanese basket would cost $100 in the United States (11,000 yen × $0.009 per yen). Thus, according to the theory of PPP, if the price level in Japan rises 10% relative to the U.S. price level, the dollar appreciates by 10%.

Our U.S./Japanese example demonstrates the key insight of the theory of PPP: *If one country's price level rises relative to another's by a certain percentage, then the other country's currency appreciates by the same percentage.* Because one currency's appreciation is the other currency's depreciation, there is an equivalent way of stating this result: *If a country's price level rises relative to another's by a certain percentage, then its currency should depreciate by the same percentage.*

Evidence on Purchasing Power Parity   As our U.S./Japanese example demonstrates, the theory of PPP suggests that if one country's price level rises relative to another's, its currency should depreciate (and the other country's currency should appreciate). As you can see in Figure 1, this prediction is borne out in the long run. From 1973 to 2020, the British price level rose 75% relative to the U.S. price level, and as the theory of PPP predicts, the dollar appreciated against the pound—by 95%, an amount larger than the 75% increase predicted by PPP.

Yet, as the same figure indicates, PPP theory does a poor job of predicting change in the exchange rate in the short run. From early 1985 to the end of 1987, for example, the British price level rose relative to that of the United States. Instead of appreciating, as predicted by PPP theory, the U.S. dollar actually depreciated by 40% against the pound. So even though PPP theory provides some guidance as to the long-run movement of exchange rates, it does not hold particularly well in the short run.

What explains the PPP theory's failure to predict well in the short run?

Why the Theory of Purchasing Power Parity Cannot Fully Explain Exchange Rates   There are three reasons why the theory of PPP does not fully explain exchange rates in the short run.

1. PPP theory does not take into account that many goods and services (whose prices are included in a measure of a country's price level) are **nontradable**; that is, they are not traded across borders. Housing, land, and services such as restaurant meals, haircuts, and golf lessons are not traded goods. So even though the prices of these items might rise, leading to a higher price level relative to another country's, the exchange rate would experience little direct effect.

2. Similar goods typically are not identical in both countries. For example, Toyota automobiles are not the same as Chevrolets, and so their prices do not have to be equal in a country. Toyotas can be more expensive relative to Chevys, and both Americans and Japanese will still purchase Toyotas. Furthermore a rise in the price of Toyotas relative to Chevys will not necessarily mean that the yen must depreciate by the amount of the relative price increase of Toyotas over Chevys.

3. There are barriers to trade. One barrier to trade is transportation costs, but these costs have been declining dramatically over time. More important in today's world are government-imposed barriers to trade, such as **tariffs**, taxes on imported goods, and **quotas**, restrictions on the quantity of goods that can be imported. Imposition of a tariff or quota on an imported good can substantially raise its price relative to the price it would have elsewhere. For example, the U.S. government has imposed very high tariffs on imported sugar, resulting in U.S. sugar prices being several times higher than the price of sugar traded in other countries. Similarly, Japan has very high tariffs on imported rice, making it far more expensive in Japan than in other countries.

APPLICATION   # Burgernomics: Big Macs and PPP

Since 1986, *The Economist* magazine has published the Big Mac index as a "lighthearted guide to whether currencies are at their 'correct' level based on the theory of purchasing power parity." Big Macs are sold by McDonald's all around the world and are supposed to taste the same wherever they are sold. *The Economist* collects prices (in the local currency) of Big Macs sold in more than 50 different regions and countries. It then uses these prices to calculate both the exchange rate implied by PPP and the Big Mac index. Table 1 reproduces a portion of *The Economist*'s Big Mac numbers originally published in January 2020.

- Column (2) of Table 1 lists the local price of a Big Mac denominated in local currency.

- Column (3) lists the actual exchange rate.

TABLE 1	Big Mac Index, January 2020			
(1) Country	(2) Local Price of Big Mac	(3) Actual Exchange Rate (U.S. dollars per unit of local currency)	(4) Exchange Rate Implied by PPP (U.S. dollars per unit of local currency)	(5) Big Mac Index (Percent difference between actual exchange rate and implied PPP exchange rate)
Switzerland	6.50 Swiss francs	1.0328	0.8723	+18.4
Canada	6.77 Canadian dollars	0.7653	0.8375	−8.6
Euro area	4.12 euros	1.1121	1.3762	−19.2
Japan	390 yen	0.0091	0.0145	−37.5
China	21.5 yuan	0.1452	0.2637	−44.9
Russia	135 rubles	0.0162	0.0420	−61.2

Source: https://github.com/theeconomist/big-mac-data/releases/tag/2020-01

- Column (4) provides the implied exchange rate if there is purchasing power parity (that is, if the local price of the Big Mac when converted to dollars equals the dollar price of the Big Mac in the United States, which was $5.67 at the time).

- Column (5) lists the Big Mac index, the percent difference between the actual and implied exchange rates.

What conclusions can we draw from Table 1?

PPP Does Not Hold Exactly, But It Has Predictive Power Although the Big Mac prices indicate that PPP does not hold exactly, PPP does help predict exchange rates for the countries shown. According to PPP, when the Big Mac has a high price in terms of local currency, then the exchange rate quoted in U.S. dollars per unit of local currency should be low.

We see this relationship in the second and fourth columns of the table. Japan has the highest Big Mac price in terms of the local currency (390 yen), and it has the lowest exchange rate, $0.0091 per yen. The Euro area has the lowest Big Mac price in terms of the local currency (4.12 euros), and it has the highest exchange rate, $1.1121 per euro.

Departures from PPP: Overvaluations and Undervaluations The exchange rate implied by PPP often departs substantially from the actual exchange rate. This should not be surprising given that Big Macs are nontradable. Think about bringing a Big Mac from China to the United States. By the time you got it to the United States, it would be disgusting and might even give you food poisoning. The Big Mac index tells us how big the discrepancy is between the actual exchange rate and the exchange rate implied by PPP.

For example, the Big Mac index tells us that Switzerland has an actual exchange rate that is 18.4% higher than the exchange rate implied by PPP. As anyone who has visited Switzerland knows, this is a very expensive country to visit. The price of a Big Mac in Switzerland when converted into U.S. dollars using Switzerland's actual exchange rate is $6.71, which is 18.4% higher than the $5.67 you pay in the United States.

When a country's goods and services are expensive relative to other countries', we say that its currency is *overvalued* in terms of purchasing power parity.

Russia has the largest percentage difference between the actual exchange rate and the exchange rate implied by PPP. The Big Mac index indicates that the actual exchange rate is 61.2% lower than the exchange rate implied by PPP. In other words, if you are willing to fly to Russia to eat a Big Mac, you can get one for the incredibly low price of $2.17.

When a country's goods and services are cheap relative to other countries', as in the case of Russia, we say that its currency (the Russian ruble) is *undervalued* in terms of purchasing power parity. ◆

Factors That Affect Exchange Rates in the Long Run

In the long run, four major factors affect the exchange rate: relative price levels, trade barriers, preferences for domestic versus foreign goods, and productivity. We examine how each of these factors affects the exchange rate while holding the other factors constant.

The basic reasoning proceeds along the following lines: Anything that increases the demand for domestically produced goods that are traded relative to foreign traded goods tends to appreciate the domestic currency, because domestic goods will continue to sell well even when the value of the domestic currency is higher. Similarly, anything that increases the demand for foreign goods relative to domestic goods tends to depreciate the domestic currency, because domestic goods will continue to sell well only if the value of the domestic currency is lower. In other words, ***if a factor increases the demand for domestic goods relative to foreign goods, the domestic currency will appreciate; if a factor decreases the relative demand for domestic goods, the domestic currency will depreciate.***

Relative Price Levels   In line with PPP theory, when prices of American goods rise (holding prices of foreign goods constant), the demand for American goods falls, and the dollar tends to depreciate so that American goods can still sell well. By contrast, if prices of Japanese goods rise, causing the relative prices of American goods to fall, the demand for American goods increases, and the dollar tends to appreciate because American goods will continue to sell well even with a higher value of the domestic currency. ***In the long run, a rise in a country's price level (relative to the foreign price level) causes its currency to depreciate, and a fall in the country's relative price level causes its currency to appreciate.***

Trade Barriers   Barriers to free trade such as tariffs and quotas can affect the exchange rate. Suppose the United States increases its tariff or puts a lower quota on Japanese steel. These increases in trade barriers increase the demand for American steel, and the dollar tends to appreciate because American steel will still sell well even with

SUMMARY TABLE 2

Factors That Affect Exchange Rates in the Long Run

Factor	Change in Factor	Response of the Exchange Rate, E^*
Domestic price level[†]	↑	↓
Trade barriers[†]	↑	↑
Import demand	↑	↓
Export demand	↑	↑
Productivity[†]	↑	↑

*Units of foreign currency per dollar: ↑ indicates domestic currency appreciation; ↓, depreciation.

[†]Relative to other countries.

Note: Only increases (↑) in the factors are shown; the effects of decreases in the variables on the exchange rate are the opposite of those indicated in the "Response" column.

a higher value of the dollar. *Increasing trade barriers causes a country's currency to appreciate in the long run.*

Preferences for Domestic Versus Foreign Goods If the Japanese develop an appetite for American goods—say, for Florida oranges and American movies—the increased demand for American goods (exports) tends to appreciate the dollar because the American goods will continue to sell well even at a higher value of the dollar. Likewise, if Americans decide that they prefer Japanese cars to American cars, the increased demand for Japanese goods (imports) tends to depreciate the dollar. *Increased demand for a country's exports causes its currency to appreciate in the long run; conversely, increased demand for imports causes the domestic currency to depreciate.*

Productivity When productivity in a country rises, it tends to rise in domestic sectors that produce traded goods rather than nontraded goods. Higher productivity, therefore, is associated with a decline in the price of domestically produced traded goods relative to foreign traded goods. As a result, the demand for domestic traded goods rises, and the domestic currency tends to appreciate. If, however, a country's productivity lags behind that of other countries, its traded goods become relatively more expensive, and the currency tends to depreciate. *In the long run, as a country becomes more productive relative to other countries, its currency appreciates.*[1]

Our long-run theory of exchange rate behavior is summarized in Summary Table 2. We use the convention that the exchange rate E is quoted such that an appreciation of the domestic currency corresponds to a rise in the exchange rate. In the case of the

---

[1]A country might be so small that a change in productivity or the preferences for domestic or foreign goods will have no effect on the prices of these goods relative to foreign goods. In this case, changes in productivity or changes in preferences for domestic or foreign goods affect the country's income but do not necessarily affect the value of the currency. In our analysis, we are assuming that changes in productivity or preferences can affect relative prices and consequently the exchange rate.

United States, this means that we are quoting the exchange rate as units of foreign currency, say, euros, per dollar.[2]

17.3 EXCHANGE RATES IN THE SHORT RUN: A SUPPLY AND DEMAND ANALYSIS

LO 17.3 Draw the demand and supply curves for the foreign exchange market and interpret the equilibrium in the market for foreign exchange.

We have developed a theory of the long-run behavior of exchange rates. However, because factors driving long-run changes in exchange rates move slowly over time, if we are to understand why exchange rates exhibit such large changes (sometimes several percentage points) from day to day, we must develop a supply and demand analysis that explains how current exchange rates (spot exchange rates) are determined in the short run.

The key to understanding the short-run behavior of exchange rates is to recognize that an exchange rate is the price of domestic assets (bank deposits, bonds, equities, and so on, denominated in the domestic currency) in terms of foreign assets (similar assets denominated in the foreign currency). Because the exchange rate is the price of one asset in terms of another, the natural way to investigate the short-run determination of exchange rates is with a supply and demand analysis that uses an asset market approach, which relies heavily on the theory of portfolio choice developed in Chapter 5. As you will see, however, the long-run determinants of the exchange rate we have just outlined also play an important part in the short-run asset market approach.

In the past, supply and demand approaches to exchange rate determination emphasized the role of import and export demand. The more modern asset market approach used here emphasizes stocks of assets rather than the flows of exports and imports over short periods because export and import transactions are small relative to the amounts of domestic and foreign assets held at any given time. For example, the total value of foreign exchange transactions in the United States each year is well over 25 times greater than the amount of U.S. exports and imports. Thus, over short periods, decisions to hold domestic or foreign assets have a much greater role in exchange rate determination than the demand for exports and imports does.

Supply Curve for Domestic Assets

We start by discussing the supply curve. In this analysis we treat the United States as the home country, so domestic assets are denominated in dollars. For simplicity, we use euros to stand for any foreign country's currency, so foreign assets are denominated in euros.

The quantity of dollar assets supplied is primarily the quantity of bank deposits, bonds, and equities in the United States, and for all practical purposes we can take this amount as fixed with respect to the exchange rate. The quantity supplied at any exchange rate is the same, so the supply curve, *S*, is vertical, as shown in Figure 2.

[2]Exchange rates can be quoted either as units of foreign currency per domestic currency or as units of domestic currency per foreign currency. In professional writing, many economists quote exchange rates as units of domestic currency per foreign currency so that an appreciation of the domestic currency is portrayed as a fall in the exchange rate. The opposite convention is used in this text because it is more intuitive to think of an appreciation of the domestic currency as a rise in the exchange rate.

Mini-lecture

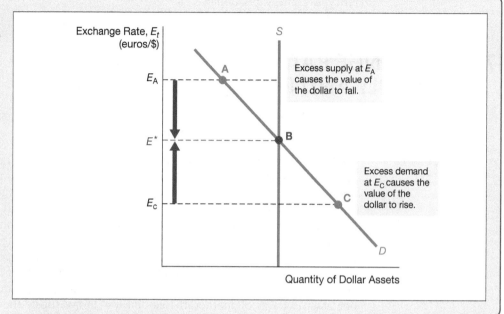

FIGURE 2

Equilibrium in the Foreign Exchange Market

Equilibrium in the foreign exchange market occurs at point B, the intersection of the demand curve D and the supply curve S at an exchange rate of E^*.

(Figure labels: Exchange Rate, E_t (euros/$); S; A; E_A; Excess supply at E_A causes the value of the dollar to fall.; E^*; B; Excess demand at E_C causes the value of the dollar to rise.; E_C; C; D; Quantity of Dollar Assets)

Demand Curve for Domestic Assets

The demand curve traces out the quantity of domestic (dollar) assets demanded at each current exchange rate by holding everything else constant, particularly the expected future value of the exchange rate. We write the current exchange rate (the spot exchange rate) as E_t and the expected exchange rate for the next period as E_{t+1}^e. As suggested by the theory of portfolio choice, the most important determinant of the quantity of domestic (dollar) assets demanded is the relative expected return on domestic assets. Let's see what happens as the current exchange rate E_t falls.

Suppose we start at point A in Figure 2, where the current exchange rate is at E_A. With the future expected value of the exchange rate held constant at E_{t+1}^e, a lower value of the current exchange rate—say, at E^*—implies that the dollar is more likely to rise in value, that is, appreciate. The greater the expected rise (appreciation) of the dollar, the higher is the relative expected return on dollar (domestic) assets. According to the theory of portfolio choice, because dollar assets are now more desirable to hold, the quantity of dollar assets demanded will rise, as shown by point B in Figure 2. If the current exchange rate falls even further to E_C, there will be an even higher expected appreciation of the dollar, a higher expected return, and therefore an even greater quantity of dollar assets demanded. This effect is shown at point C at Figure 2. The resulting demand curve D, which connects these points, is downward-sloping, indicating that at lower current values of the dollar (everything else being equal), the quantity demanded of dollar assets is higher.

A numerical example may make this clearer. Suppose that the future expected value of the dollar, E_{t+1}^e, is 1.20 euros per dollar, and E_A is 1.10 euros per dollar, E^* is 1.00 euros per dollar and E_C is 0.90 euro per dollar. At E_A where the exchange rate is 1.10 euros per dollar, the expected appreciation of the dollar is 10% $(= (1.20 - 1.10)/1.10 = +0.10 = +10\%)$. When the exchange rate drops to E^* of 1.00 euros per dollar, the expected appreciation is now a larger 20% $(= (1.20 - 1.00)/1.00 = +0.20 = +20\%)$, and so the quantity of dollar assets demanded is higher. When the exchange rate declines even further to E_C of 0.90 euro per dollar, the expected appreciation of the dollar rises further to 30% $(= (1.20 - 0.90)/0.90 = +0.30 = +30\%)$ and so the quantity demanded of dollar assets is even higher.

Equilibrium in the Foreign Exchange Market

As in the usual supply and demand analysis, the market is in equilibrium when the quantity of dollar assets demanded equals the quantity supplied. In Figure 2, equilibrium occurs at point B, the intersection of the demand and supply curves. At point B, the exchange rate is E^*.

Suppose the exchange rate is at E_A, which is higher than the equilibrium exchange rate of E^*. As we can see in Figure 2, the quantity of dollar assets supplied is now greater than the quantity demanded, a condition of excess supply. Given that more people want to sell dollar assets than want to buy them, the value of the dollar will fall. As long as the exchange rate remains above the equilibrium exchange rate, an excess supply of dollar assets will continue to be available, and the dollar will fall in value until it reaches the equilibrium exchange rate of E^*.

Similarly, if the exchange rate is less than the equilibrium exchange rate at E_C, the quantity of dollar assets demanded will exceed the quantity supplied, a condition of excess demand. Given that more people want to buy dollar assets than want to sell them, the value of the dollar will rise until the excess demand disappears and the value of the dollar is again at the equilibrium exchange rate of E^*.

17.4 EXPLAINING CHANGES IN EXCHANGE RATES

LO 17.4 List and illustrate the factors that affect the exchange rate in the short run.

The supply and demand analysis of the foreign exchange market illustrates how and why exchange rates change.[3] We have simplified this analysis by assuming that the amount of dollar assets is fixed: The supply curve is vertical at a given quantity and does not shift. Under this assumption, we need to look at only those factors that shift the demand curve for dollar assets to explain how exchange rates change over time.

Shifts in the Demand for Domestic Assets

As we have seen, the quantity of domestic (dollar) assets demanded depends on the relative expected return on dollar assets. To see how the demand curve shifts, we need to determine how the quantity demanded changes, holding the current exchange rate, E_t, constant, when other factors change.

For insight into the direction in which the demand curve will shift, suppose you are an investor who is considering putting funds into domestic (dollar) assets. When a factor changes, you must decide whether, at a given level of the current exchange rate and holding all other variables constant, you would earn a higher or lower expected return on dollar assets versus foreign assets. This decision will tell you whether you want to hold more or fewer dollar assets and thus whether the quantity demanded will increase or decrease at each level of the exchange rate. The direction of the change in

---

[3]How and why exchange rates change can also be modeled using the *interest parity condition*, an important concept in international finance that shows the relationships among domestic interest rates, foreign interest rates, and the expected appreciation of domestic currency. The interest parity condition and how it explains the determination of exchange rates is discussed in an appendix to this chapter found in **MyLab Economics**.

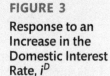

FIGURE 3

Response to an Increase in the Domestic Interest Rate, i^D

When the domestic interest rate i^D increases, the relative expected return on domestic (dollar) assets increases and the demand curve shifts to the right. The equilibrium exchange rate rises from E_1 to E_2.

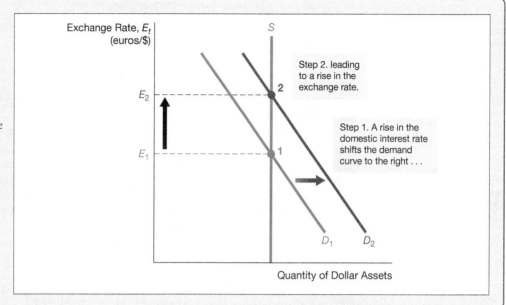

the quantity demanded at each exchange rate indicates which way the demand curve will shift. In other words, if the relative expected return on dollar assets rises, holding the current exchange rate constant, the demand curve will shift to the right. If the relative expected return falls, the demand curve will shift to the left.

Domestic Interest Rate, i^D   Suppose that dollar assets pay an interest rate of i^D. When the domestic interest rate on dollar assets i^D rises, holding the current exchange rate E_t and everything else constant, the return on dollar assets increases relative to the return on foreign assets, and so people will want to hold more dollar assets. The quantity of dollar assets demanded increases at every value of the exchange rate, as shown by the rightward shift of the demand curve from D_1 to D_2 in Figure 3. The new equilibrium is reached at point 2, the intersection of D_2 and S, and the equilibrium exchange rate rises from E_1 to E_2. *An increase in the domestic interest rate i^D shifts the demand curve for domestic assets D to the right and causes the domestic currency to appreciate ($E\uparrow$).*

Conversely, if i^D falls, the relative expected return on dollar assets falls, the demand curve shifts to the left, and the exchange rate falls. *A decrease in the domestic interest rate i^D shifts the demand curve for domestic assets D to the left and causes the domestic currency to depreciate ($E\downarrow$).*

Foreign Interest Rate, i^F   Suppose foreign assets pay an interest rate of i^F. When the foreign interest rate i^F rises, holding the current exchange rate and everything else constant, the return on foreign assets rises relative to the return on dollar assets. Thus the relative expected return on dollar assets falls. Now people want to hold fewer dollar assets, and the quantity demanded decreases at every value of the exchange rate. This scenario is shown by the leftward shift of the demand curve from D_1 to D_2 in Figure 4. The new equilibrium is reached at point 2, when the value of the dollar has fallen. Conversely, a decrease in i^F raises the relative expected return on dollar assets, shifts the demand curve to the right, and raises the exchange rate. To summarize, *an increase in*

Mini-lecture

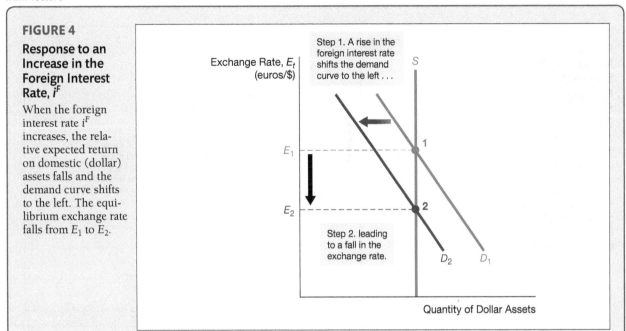

FIGURE 4

Response to an Increase in the Foreign Interest Rate, i^F

When the foreign interest rate i^F increases, the relative expected return on domestic (dollar) assets falls and the demand curve shifts to the left. The equilibrium exchange rate falls from E_1 to E_2.

Step 1. A rise in the foreign interest rate shifts the demand curve to the left . . .

Step 2. leading to a fall in the exchange rate.

Exchange Rate, E_t (euros/$)

Quantity of Dollar Assets

the foreign interest rate i^F shifts the demand curve D to the left and causes the domestic currency to depreciate; a fall in the foreign interest rate i^F shifts the demand curve D to the right and causes the domestic currency to appreciate.

Changes in the Expected Future Exchange Rate, E^e_{t+1} Expectations about the future value of the exchange rate play an important role in shifting the current demand curve because the demand for domestic assets, like that for any physical or financial asset, depends on the future resale price. Given the current exchange rate E_t, any factor that causes the expected future exchange rate E^e_{t+1} to rise increases the expected appreciation of the dollar. The result is a higher relative expected return on dollar assets, which increases the demand for dollar assets at every exchange rate, thereby shifting the demand curve to the right from D_1 to D_2 in Figure 5. The equilibrium exchange rate rises to point 2 at the intersection of the D_2 and S curves. *A rise in the expected future exchange rate E^e_{t+1} shifts the demand curve to the right and causes an appreciation of the domestic currency.* According to the same reasoning, *a fall in the expected future exchange rate E^e_{t+1} shifts the demand curve to the left and causes a depreciation of the currency.*

Earlier in the chapter we discussed the determinants of the exchange rate in the long run: the relative price level, relative trade barrier, import and export demand, and relative productivity (refer to Summary Table 2). These four factors influence the expected future exchange rate. The theory of purchasing power parity suggests that if a higher American price level relative to the foreign price level is expected to persist, then the dollar will depreciate in the long run. A higher expected relative American price level should thus have a tendency to lower E^e_{t+1}, lower the relative expected return on dollar assets, shift the demand curve to the left, and lower the current exchange rate.

Mini-lecture

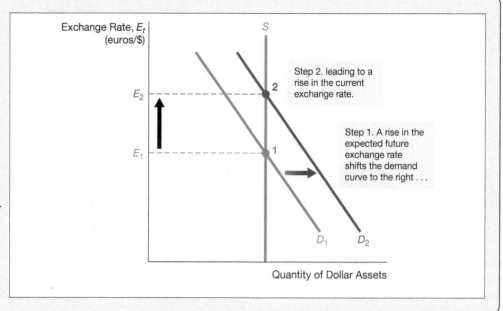

Response to an Increase in the Expected Future Exchange Rate, E_{t+1}^e

When the expected future exchange rate increases, the relative expected return on domestic (dollar) assets rises and the demand curve shifts to the right. The equilibrium exchange rate rises from E_1 to E_2.

Similarly, the other long-run determinants of the exchange rate can influence the relative expected return on dollar assets and the current exchange rate. Briefly, the following changes, all of which increase the demand for domestic goods relative to foreign goods, will raise E_{t+1}^e: (1) expectations of a fall in the American price level relative to the foreign price level; (2) expectations of higher American trade barriers relative to foreign trade barriers; (3) expectations of lower American import demand; (4) expectations of higher foreign demand for American exports; and (5) expectations of higher American productivity relative to foreign productivity. By increasing E_{t+1}^e, all of these changes increase the relative expected return on dollar assets, shift the demand curve to the right, and cause an appreciation of the domestic currency, the dollar.

The fact that exchange rates are so volatile is explained by the analysis here. Because expected appreciation of the domestic currency affects the expected return on domestic assets, expectations about the price level, inflation, trade barriers, productivity, import demand, export demand, and monetary policy play important roles in determining the exchange rate. When expectations about any of these variables change, as they do—and often, at that—our analysis indicates that the expected return on domestic assets, and therefore the exchange rate, will be immediately affected. Because expectations on all these variables change with just about every bit of news that appears, it is not surprising that the exchange rate is volatile.

Recap: Factors That Change the Exchange Rate

Summary Table 3 outlines all of the factors that shift the demand curve for domestic assets and thereby cause the exchange rate to change. Shifts in the demand curve occur when one factor changes, holding everything else constant, including the current

SUMMARY TABLE 3

Factors That Shift the Demand Curve for Domestic Assets and Affect the Exchange Rate

Factor	Change in Factor	Change in Quantity Demanded of Domestic Assets at Each Exchange Rate	Response of Exchange Rate, E_t	
Domestic interest rate, i^D	↑	↑	↑	
Foreign interest rate, i^F	↑	↓	↓	
Expected domestic price level*	↑	↓	↓	
Expected trade barriers*	↑	↑	↑	
Expected import demand	↑	↓	↓	
Expected export demand	↑	↑	↑	
Expected productivity*	↑	↑	↑	

*Relative to other countries.

Note: Only increases (↑) in the factors are shown; the effects of decreases in the variables on the exchange rate are the opposite of those indicated in the "Response" column.

exchange rate. Again, the theory of portfolio choice asserts that changes in the relative expected return on dollar assets are the source of shifts in the demand curve.

Let's review what happens when each of the seven factors in Table 3 changes. Remember that to understand the direction in which the demand curve will shift, we must consider what happens to the relative expected return on dollar assets when the factor changes. If the relative expected return rises, holding the current exchange rate constant, the demand curve shifts to the right. If the relative expected return falls, the demand curve shifts to the left.

1. When the interest rates on domestic assets i^D rise, the expected return on dollar assets rises at each exchange rate and so the quantity demanded increases. The demand curve therefore shifts to the right, and the equilibrium exchange rate rises, as shown in the first row of Table 3.
2. When the foreign interest rate i^F rises, the return on foreign assets rises, and so the relative expected return on dollar assets falls. The quantity demanded of dollar assets then falls, the demand curve shifts to the left, and the exchange rate falls, as shown in the second row of Table 3.
3. When the expected domestic price level rises relative to the foreign price level, our analysis of the long-run determinants of the exchange rate indicates that the value of the dollar will fall in the future. The expected return on dollar assets thus falls, the quantity demanded declines, the demand curve shifts to the left, and the exchange rate falls, as indicated in the third row of Table 3.
4. With higher expected trade barriers, the value of the dollar is higher in the long run and the expected return on dollar assets is higher. The quantity demanded of dollar assets thus rises, the demand curve shifts to the right, and the exchange rate rises, as shown in the fourth row of Table 3.
5. When the expected import demand rises, we expect the exchange rate to depreciate in the long run, so the expected return on dollar assets falls. The quantity demanded of dollar assets at each value of the current exchange rate therefore falls, the demand curve shifts to the left, and the exchange rate falls, as shown in the fifth row of Table 3.
6. When the expected export demand rises, the exchange rate is expected to appreciate in the long run. Thus the expected return on dollar assets rises, the demand curve shifts to the right, and the exchange rate rises, as indicated in the sixth row of Table 3.
7. When expected domestic productivity rises, the exchange rate is expected to appreciate in the long run, so the expected return on domestic assets rises. The quantity demanded at each exchange rate therefore rises, the demand curve shifts to the right, and the exchange rate rises, as shown in the seventh row of Table 3.

APPLICATION   # Effects of Changes in Interest Rates on the Equilibrium Exchange Rate

Our analysis has revealed the factors that affect the value of the equilibrium exchange rate. Now we use this analysis to take a closer look at the response of the exchange rate to changes in interest rates and money growth.

Changes in domestic interest rates i^D are often cited as a major factor affecting exchange rates. For example, we see headlines in the financial press like this one: "Dollar Recovers as Interest Rates Edge Upward." But is the positive correlation suggested in this headline true in every case?

Mini-lecture

FIGURE 6

Effect of a Rise in the Domestic Interest Rate as a Result of an Increase in Expected Inflation

Because a rise in domestic expected inflation leads to a decline in expected dollar appreciation that is larger than the increase in the domestic interest rate, the relative expected return on domestic (dollar) assets falls. The demand curve shifts to the left, and the equilibrium exchange rate falls from E_1 to E_2.

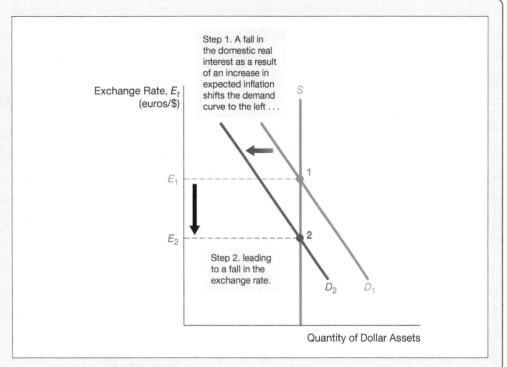

Not necessarily, because to analyze the effects of interest rate changes, we must carefully distinguish the sources of the changes. The Fisher equation (Chapter 4) states that a nominal interest rate such as i^D equals the *real* interest rate plus expected inflation: $i = i_r + \pi^e$. The Fisher equation thus indicates that the interest rate i^D can change for two reasons: Either the real interest rate i_r changes or the expected inflation rate π^e changes. The effect on the exchange rate is quite different, depending on which of these two factors is the source of the change in the nominal interest rate.

Suppose the domestic real interest rate increases, so that the nominal interest rate i^D rises while expected inflation remains unchanged. In this case, it is reasonable to assume that the expected appreciation of the dollar will be unchanged because expected inflation is unchanged. In this case, the increase in i^D increases the relative expected return on dollar assets, raises the quantity of dollar assets demanded at each level of the exchange rate, and shifts the demand curve to the right. We end up with the situation depicted in Figure 3, which analyzes an increase in i^D, holding everything else constant. Our model of the foreign exchange market produces the following result: *When domestic real interest rates rise, the domestic currency appreciates.*

When the nominal interest rate rises because of an increase in expected inflation, we get a different result from the one shown in Figure 3. The rise in expected domestic inflation leads to a decline in the expected appreciation of the dollar, which is typically found to be larger than the increase in the domestic interest rate i^D. As a result, at any given exchange rate, the relative expected return on domestic (dollar) assets falls, the demand curve shifts to the left, and the exchange rate falls from E_1 to E_2, as shown in Figure 6. Our analysis leads to this conclusion: **When domestic interest rates rise due to an expected increase in inflation, the domestic currency depreciates.**

Because this result is completely different from the result that is obtained when the rise in the domestic interest rate is associated with a higher real interest rate, we must always distinguish between *real* and *nominal* measures when analyzing the effects of interest rates on exchange rates.

APPLICATION The Global Financial Crisis and the Dollar

With the start of the global financial crisis in August 2007, the dollar began an accelerated decline in value, falling by 9% against the euro until mid-July of 2008. After hitting an all-time low against the euro on July 11, the value of the dollar suddenly shot upward, by over 20% against the euro by the end of October. What is the relationship between the global financial crisis and these large swings in the value of the dollar?

Supply and demand analysis of what happened to the dollar is illustrated in Figure 7. Because we are analyzing what happened to the value of the dollar, we are again treating

Mini-lecture

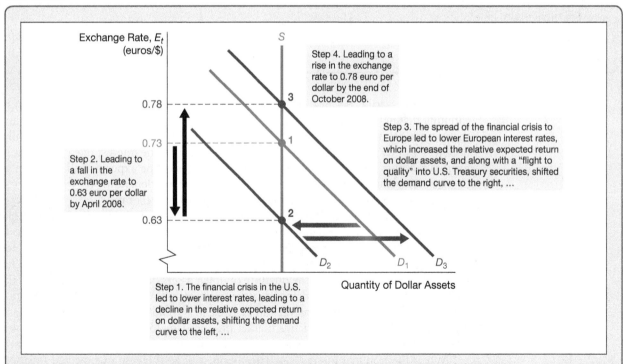

FIGURE 7 Global Financial Crisis and the Dollar

The financial crisis in the United States led to lower interest rates, leading to a decline in the relative expected return on dollar assets, which shifted the demand curve to the left and lowered the exchange rate to 0.63 euro per dollar by April 2008. The spread of the global financial crisis to Europe led to lower European interest rates, which increased the relative expected return of dollar assets, and along with a "flight to quality" to U.S. Treasury securities, shifted the demand curve to the right and raised the exchange rate to 0.78 euro per dollar by the end of October 2008.

the U.S. dollar as the domestic currency. The exchange rate on the vertical axis in the diagram is therefore quoted as euros per U.S. dollar, so a rise in the exchange rate is an appreciation of the dollar. The horizontal axis is the quantity of U.S. (dollar) assets. In August 2007 before the crisis started, the exchange rate for the dollar was 0.73 euro per dollar at equilibrium point 1.

During 2007, the negative effects of the financial crisis on economic activity were mostly confined to the United States. The Federal Reserve acted aggressively to lower interest rates to counter the contractionary effects, decreasing the federal funds rate target by 325 basis points from September 2007 to April 2008. In contrast, other central banks like the ECB did not see the need to lower interest rates, particularly because high energy prices had led to a surge in inflation. The relative expected return on dollar assets thus declined, shifting the demand curve for dollar assets to the left in Figure 7, from D_1 to D_2. The equilibrium moved from point 1 in August 2007 to point 2 in April 2008, leading to a decline in the equilibrium exchange rate to 0.63 euro per dollar. Our analysis of the foreign exchange market thus explains why the early phase of the global financial crisis led to a decline in the value of the dollar.

We now turn to the rise in the value of the dollar. Starting in the summer of 2008, the effects of the global financial crisis on economic activity began to spread more widely throughout the world. The European Central Bank started to cut interest rates, with the expectation that further rate cuts would follow, as indeed did occur. The expected decline in foreign interest rates then increased the relative expected return on dollar assets, leading to a rightward shift in the demand curve from D_2 to D_3, with the equilibrium moving to point 3 where the dollar rose to 0.78 euro per dollar by the end of October 2008. Another factor driving the dollar upward was the "flight to quality" that occurred when the global financial crisis reached a particularly virulent stage in September and October. Both Americans and foreigners now wanted to put their money into the safest assets possible: U.S. Treasury securities. The resulting increase in the demand for dollar assets provided an additional reason for the demand curve for dollar assets to shift out to the right, thereby helping to produce a sharp appreciation of the dollar. ◆

APPLICATION   Brexit and the British Pound

As noted in the introduction, the Brexit vote in the United Kingdom on June 23, 2016, led to nearly a 10% depreciation in the British pound, from $1.48 to the pound on June 23, just before the vote, to $1.36 per pound on June 24. What explains the large one-day decline in the exchange rate for the pound?

Here we use our supply and demand analysis of the foreign exchange market in Figure 8 to answer this question. Because we are analyzing what happened to the value of the British pound, we are treating the pound as the domestic currency and thus are looking at the supply of and demand for pounds. The exchange rate on the vertical axis in the figure is therefore quoted as U.S. dollars per pound, so a rise in the exchange rate is an appreciation of the pound. The horizontal axis is the quantity of British pound assets. On June 23, right before the Brexit vote, the initial equilibrium was at point 1, with the equilibrium exchange rate for the pound at $1.48 per pound.

Mini-lecture

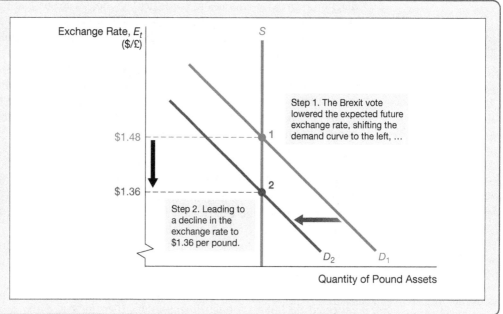

FIGURE 8

Brexit and the British Pound

The Brexit vote lowered the expected return on British pound assets, which shifted the demand curve to the left and lowered the exchange rate to $1.36 per pound.

Step 1. The Brexit vote lowered the expected future exchange rate, shifting the demand curve to the left, ...

Step 2. Leading to a decline in the exchange rate to $1.36 per pound.

The Brexit vote would result in the United Kingdom no longer having access to the "one market" of the European Union, thereby likely erecting significant trade barriers to the export of British goods and services, especially financial services, which is one of Britain's most important industries. With higher expected European Union trade barriers, the demand for British goods and services would fall in the future, so the expected value of the pound would be lower in the future. The relative expected return on British (pound) assets therefore fell, and so the quantity demanded of pound assets declined at any given exchange rate, shifting the demand curve for pound assets to the left. The result was the sharp fall in the equilibrium exchange rate for the British pound to $1.36 per pound. ◆

SUMMARY

1. Foreign exchange rates (the price of one country's currency in terms of another's) are important because they affect the price of domestically produced goods sold abroad and the cost of foreign goods bought domestically.

2. The theory of purchasing power parity suggests that long-run changes in the exchange rate between the currencies of two countries are determined by changes in the relative price levels in the two countries. Other factors that affect exchange rates in the long run are tariffs and quotas, import demand, export demand, and productivity.

3. In the short run, exchange rates are determined by changes in the relative expected return on domestic assets, which cause the demand curve to shift. Any factor that changes the relative expected return on domestic assets will lead to changes in the exchange rate. Such factors include changes in the interest rates on domestic and foreign assets, as well as changes in any of the factors that affect the long-run exchange rate and hence the expected future exchange rate.

4. The asset market approach to exchange rate determination can explain the changes in the value of the dollar during the global financial crisis, and the sharp decline in the value of the British pound after the Brexit vote.

KEY TERMS

appreciation, p. 403
depreciation, p. 403
exchange rate, p. 403
foreign exchange market, p. 403
forward exchange rate, p. 403

forward transaction, p. 403
nontradable, p. 407
quotas, p. 407
real exchange rate, p. 405
spot exchange rate, p. 403

spot transaction, p. 403
tariffs, p. 407
theory of purchasing power parity
  (PPP), p. 405

QUESTIONS

1. Suppose that you are considering going on vacation abroad and that the euro has appreciated by 15% with respect to the U.S. dollar. Would you be more or less willing to visit Rome and Paris?

2. "A country is always worse off when its currency is weak (falls in value)." Is this statement true, false, or uncertain? Explain your answer.

3. When the U.S. dollar depreciates, what happens to exports and imports in the United States?

4. If the Japanese price level rises by 5% relative to the price level in the United States, what does the theory of purchasing power parity predict will happen to the value of the Japanese yen in terms of dollars?

5. If the demand for a country's exports falls at the same time that tariffs on imports are raised, will the country's currency tend to appreciate or depreciate in the long run?

6. When the Federal Reserve conducts an expansionary monetary policy, what happens to the money supply? How does this affect the supply of dollar assets?

7. From 2009 to 2011, the economies of Australia and Switzerland suffered relatively mild effects from the global financial crisis. At the same time, many countries in the euro area were hit hard by high unemployment and burdened with unsustainably high government debts. How should this have affected the euro/Swiss franc and euro/Australian dollar exchange rates?

8. In the mid to late 1970s, the yen appreciated in value relative to the dollar, even though Japan's inflation rate was higher than America's. How can this be explained by improvements in the productivity of Japanese industry relative to U.S. industry?

9. Suppose the president of the United States announces a new set of reforms that includes a new anti-inflation program. Assuming the announcement is believed by the public, what will happen to the exchange rate on the U.S. dollar?

10. If the Indian government unexpectedly announces that it will be imposing higher tariffs on foreign goods one year from now, what will happen to the value of the Indian rupee today?

11. If nominal interest rates in America rise but real interest rates fall, predict what will happen to the U.S. dollar exchange rate.

12. If American auto companies make a breakthrough in automobile technology and are able to produce a car that gets 200 miles to the gallon, what will happen to the U.S. dollar exchange rate?

13. If Mexicans go on a spending spree and buy twice as much French perfume and twice as many Japanese TVs, English sweaters, Swiss watches, and bottles of Italian wine, what will happen to the value of the Mexican peso?

14. Through the summer and fall of 2008, as the global financial crisis began to take hold, international financial institutions and sovereign wealth funds significantly increased their purchases of U.S. Treasury securities as a safe haven investment. How should this have affected U.S. dollar exchange rates?

15. In September 2012, the Federal Reserve announced a large-scale asset-purchase program (known as QE3) designed to lower intermediate and longer-term interest rates. What effect should this have had on the dollar/euro exchange rate?

16. On June 23, 2016, voters in the United Kingdom voted to leave the European Union. From June 16 to June 23, 2016, the exchange rate between the British pound and the U.S. dollar increased from 1.41 dollars per pound to 1.48 dollars per pound. What can you say about market expectations regarding the result of the referendum?

APPLIED PROBLEMS

17. A German sports car is selling for 70,000 euros. What is the dollar price in the United States of the German car if the exchange rate is 0.90 euro per dollar?

18. If the Canadian dollar to U.S. dollar exchange rate is 1.28 and the British pound to U.S. dollar exchange rate is 0.62, what must be the Canadian dollar to British pound exchange rate?

19. The New Zealand dollar to U.S. dollar exchange rate is 1.36, and the British pound to U.S. dollar exchange rate is 0.62. If you find that the British pound to New Zealand dollar is trading at 0.49, what can you do to earn a riskless profit?

20. In 1999, the euro was trading at $0.90 per euro. If the euro is now trading at $1.16 per euro, what is the percentage change in the euro's value? Is this an appreciation or a depreciation?

21. The Mexican peso is trading at 10 pesos per dollar. If the expected U.S. inflation rate is 2% while the expected Mexican inflation rate is 23% over the next year, given PPP, what is the expected exchange rate in one year?

22. If the price level recently increased by 20% in England while falling by 5% in the United States, by how much must the exchange rate change if PPP holds? Assume that the current exchange rate is 0.55 pound per dollar.

For Problems 23–25, use a graph of the foreign exchange market for dollars to illustrate the effects described in each problem.

23. If expected inflation drops in Europe, so that interest rates fall there, what will happen to the exchange rate on the U.S. dollar?

24. If the European Central Bank decides to pursue a contractionary monetary policy to fight inflation, what will happen to the value of the U.S. dollar?

25. If a strike takes place in France, making it harder to buy French goods, what will happen to the value of the U.S. dollar?

DATA ANALYSIS PROBLEMS

The Problems update with real-time data in **MyLab Economics** and are available for practice or instructor assignment.

1. Real-time Data Analysis Go to the St. Louis Federal Reserve FRED database, and find data on the exchange rate of U.S. dollars per British pound (DEXUSUK). A Mini Cooper can be purchased in London, England, for £17,865 or in Boston, United States, for $23,495.

   a. Use the most recent exchange rate available to calculate the real exchange rate of the London Mini per Boston Mini.
   b. Based on your answer to part (a), are Mini Coopers relatively more expensive in Boston or in London?
   c. What price in British pounds would make the Mini Cooper equally expensive in both locations, all else being equal?

2. Real-time Data Analysis Go to the St. Louis Federal Reserve FRED database, and find data on the daily dollar exchange rates for the euro (DEXUSEU), British pound (DEXUSUK), and Japanese yen (DEXJPUS). Also find data on the daily three-month London Interbank Offer Rate, or LIBOR, for the United States dollar (USD3MTD156N), euro (EUR3MTD156N), British pound (GBP3MTD156N), and Japanese yen (JPY3MTD156N). LIBOR is a measure of interest rates denominated in each country's respective currency.

   a. Calculate the difference between the LIBOR rate in the United States and the LIBOR rates in the three other countries using the data from one year ago and the most recent data available.
   b. Based on the changes in interest rate differentials, do you expect the dollar to depreciate or appreciate against the other currencies?
   c. Report the percentage change in the exchange rates over the past year. Are the results you predicted in part (b) consistent with the actual exchange rate behavior?

18 The International Financial System

Learning Objectives

18.1 Use graphs and T-accounts to illustrate the distinctions between the effects of sterilized and unsterilized interventions on foreign exchange markets.

18.2 Interpret the relationships among the current account and the financial account in the balance of payments.

18.3 Identify the mechanisms for maintaining a fixed exchange rate, and assess the challenges faced by fixed exchange rate regimes.

18.4 Summarize the advantages and disadvantages of capital controls.

18.5 Assess the role of the IMF as an international lender of last resort.

18.6 Identify the ways in which international monetary policy and exchange rate arrangements can affect domestic monetary policy operations.

18.7 Summarize the advantages and disadvantages of exchange-rate targeting.

Preview

As the U.S. economy and the economies of the rest of the world grow more interdependent, a country's monetary policy can no longer be conducted without taking international considerations into account. In this chapter, we examine how international financial transactions and the structure of the international financial system affect monetary policy. We also examine the evolution of the international financial system during the past half century and consider where it may be headed in the future.

18.1 INTERVENTION IN THE FOREIGN EXCHANGE MARKET

LO 18.1 Use graphs and T-accounts to illustrate the distinctions between the effects of sterilized and unsterilized interventions on foreign exchange markets.

In Chapter 17, we analyzed the foreign exchange market as if it were a completely free market that responds to all conventional market pressures. Like many other markets, however, the foreign exchange market is not free of government intervention; central banks regularly engage in international financial transactions, the purchase and sale of their currencies, called **foreign exchange interventions**, to influence exchange rates. In our current international environment, exchange rates fluctuate from day to day, but central banks attempt to influence their countries' exchange rates by buying and selling currencies. We can use the exchange rate analysis we developed in Chapter 17 to explain the impact of central bank intervention on the foreign exchange market.

Foreign Exchange Intervention and the Money Supply

The first step in understanding how central bank intervention in the foreign exchange market affects exchange rates is to explore the impact on the monetary base of a central bank sale in the foreign exchange market of some of its holdings of assets denominated in a foreign currency (called **international reserves**). Suppose the Fed decides to sell $1 billion of its foreign assets in exchange for $1 billion of U.S. currency. (This type of transaction is conducted at the foreign exchange desk at the Federal Reserve Bank of New York—see the Inside the Fed box, "A Day at the Federal Reserve Bank of New York's Foreign Exchange Desk.") The Fed's purchase of dollars has two effects. First, it reduces the Fed's holdings of international reserves by $1 billion. Second, because the Fed's purchase

425

Inside the Fed   A Day at the Federal Reserve Bank of New York's Foreign Exchange Desk

Although the U.S. Treasury holds primary responsibility for foreign exchange policy, decisions to intervene in the foreign exchange market are made jointly by the U.S. Treasury and the Federal Reserve's FOMC (Federal Open Market Committee). The actual conduct of foreign exchange intervention is the responsibility of the foreign exchange desk at the Federal Reserve Bank of New York, which is right next to the open market desk.

The manager of foreign exchange operations at the New York Fed supervises the traders and analysts, who follow developments in the foreign exchange market. Every morning at 7:30, a trader on staff who has arrived at the New York Fed in the predawn hours speaks on the telephone with counterparts at the U.S. Treasury and provides an update on overnight activity in overseas financial and foreign exchange markets. Later in the morning, at 9:30, the manager and his or her staff hold a conference call with the senior staff members at the Board of Governors of the Federal Reserve in Washington. In the afternoon, at 2:30, the manager and staff hold a second conference call, which is a joint briefing of officials at the Board and at

the Treasury. Although by statute the Treasury has the lead role in setting foreign exchange policy, it strives to reach a consensus among all three parties—the Treasury, the Board of Governors, and the Federal Reserve Bank of New York. If the three parties decide that a foreign exchange intervention is necessary that day—an unusual occurrence, as a year may go by without a U.S. foreign exchange intervention—the manager instructs his traders to carry out the agreed-on purchase or sale of foreign currencies. Because funds for exchange rate intervention are held separately by the Treasury (in its Exchange Stabilization Fund) and the Federal Reserve, the manager and his or her staff are not trading the funds of the Federal Reserve Bank of New York; rather, they act as an agent for the Treasury and the FOMC in conducting these transactions.

As part of their duties, before every FOMC meeting, the staff help prepare a lengthy document full of data for the FOMC members, other Reserve Bank presidents, and Treasury officials, a task that keeps them especially busy. The document describes developments in the domestic and foreign markets over the previous five or six weeks.

of currency removes it from the hands of the public, currency in circulation falls by $1 billion. We can see this in the following T-account for the Federal Reserve:

Federal Reserve System			
Assets		**Liabilities**	
Foreign assets (international reserves)	−$1 billion	Currency in circulation	−$1 billion

Because the monetary base is made up of currency in circulation plus reserves, this decline in currency implies that the monetary base has fallen by $1 billion.

If, as is more likely, the persons buying the foreign assets pay for them with checks written on accounts at domestic banks rather than with currency, then the Fed deducts the $1 billion from the reserve deposits it holds for these banks. The result is that deposits with the Fed (reserves) decline by $1 billion, as shown in the following T-account:

Federal Reserve System			
Assets		**Liabilities**	
Foreign assets (international reserves)	−$1 billion	Deposits with the Fed (reserves)	−$1 billion

In this case, the outcome of the Fed sale of foreign assets and the purchase of dollar deposits is a $1 billion decline in reserves and, as before, a $1 billion decline in the monetary base, because reserves are also a component of the monetary base.

We now see that the outcome for the monetary base is exactly the same when a central bank sells foreign assets to purchase domestic bank deposits or domestic currency. This is why, when we say that a central bank has purchased its domestic currency, we do not have to distinguish between currency and bank deposits denominated in the domestic currency. We have thus reached an important conclusion: *A central bank's purchase of domestic currency and corresponding sale of foreign assets in the foreign exchange market leads to an equal decline in its international reserves and the monetary base.*

We could have reached the same conclusion by a more direct route. A central bank sale of a foreign asset is no different from an open market sale of a government bond. We learned in our exploration of the money supply process that an open market sale leads to an equal decline in the monetary base; therefore, a sale of foreign assets also leads to an equal decline in the monetary base. By similar reasoning, a central bank purchase of foreign assets paid for by selling domestic currency, like an open market purchase, leads to an equal rise in the monetary base. Thus we reach the following conclusion: *A central bank's sale of domestic currency to purchase foreign assets in the foreign exchange market results in an equal rise in its international reserves and the monetary base.*

The intervention we have just described, in which a central bank allows the purchase or sale of domestic currency to have an effect on the monetary base, is called an **unsterilized foreign exchange intervention**. But what if the central bank does not want the purchase or sale of domestic currency to affect the monetary base? All it has to do is counteract the effect of the foreign exchange intervention by conducting an offsetting open market operation in the government bond market. For example, in the case of a $1 billion purchase of dollars by the Fed and a corresponding $1 billion sale of foreign assets, which, as we have seen, would decrease the monetary base by $1 billion, the Fed can conduct an open market purchase of $1 billion of government bonds, which will increase the monetary base by $1 billion. The resulting T-account for the foreign exchange intervention and the offsetting open market operation leaves the monetary base unchanged:

Federal Reserve System			
Assets		**Liabilities**	
Foreign assets (international reserves)	−$1 billion	Monetary base	0
Government bonds	+$1 billion		

Mini-lecture

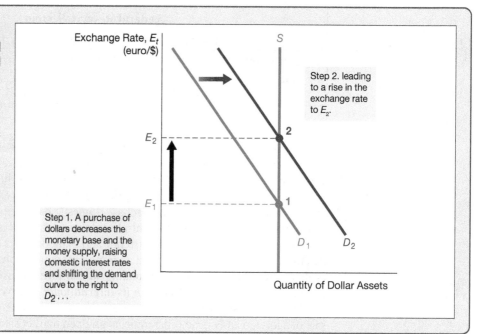

FIGURE 1

Effect of an Unsterilized Purchase of Dollars and Sale of Foreign Assets

A purchase of dollars and the consequent open market sale of foreign assets decrease the monetary base and the money supply. The resulting fall in the money supply leads to a rise in domestic interest rates, which raises the relative expected return on dollar assets. The demand curve shifts to the right from D_1 to D_2, and the equilibrium exchange rate rises from E_1 to E_2.

A foreign exchange intervention with an offsetting open market operation that leaves the monetary base unchanged is called a **sterilized foreign exchange intervention**.

Now that we understand that there are two types of foreign exchange interventions—unsterilized and sterilized—let's look at how each affects the exchange rate.

Unsterilized Intervention

Intuition might lead you to suspect that if a central bank wants to raise the value of the domestic currency, it should buy its currency in the foreign exchange market and sell foreign assets. Indeed, this intuition is correct in the case of an unsterilized intervention.

Recall that in an unsterilized intervention, if the Federal Reserve decides to buy dollars and therefore sells foreign assets in exchange for dollar assets, this exchange works just like an open market sale of bonds to decrease the monetary base. Hence the purchase of dollars leads to a decrease in the money supply, which raises the domestic interest rate and increases the relative expected return on dollar assets. As a result, the demand curve shifts to the right from D_1 to D_2, as shown in Figure 1, and the exchange rate rises to E_2.[1]

Our analysis leads us to the following conclusion about unsterilized interventions in the foreign exchange market: *An unsterilized intervention in which domestic currency is bought and foreign assets are sold leads to a fall in international reserves, a fall in the money supply, and an appreciation of the domestic currency*.

[1]An unsterilized intervention in which the Fed buys dollars decreases the amount of dollar assets slightly because it leads to a decrease in the monetary base while leaving the amount of government bonds in the hands of the public unchanged. The curve depicting the supply of dollar assets thus shifts to the left slightly, which also works toward raising the exchange rate, yielding the same conclusion derived in Figure 1. Because the resulting increase in the monetary base is only a minuscule fraction of the total amount of dollar assets outstanding, the supply curve shifts by an imperceptible amount. This is why Figure 1 is drawn with the supply curve unchanged.

The reverse result is found for an unsterilized intervention in which domestic currency is sold and foreign assets are purchased. The sale of domestic currency and purchase of foreign assets (which increases international reserves) work like an open market purchase to increase the monetary base and the money supply. The increase in the money supply lowers the interest rate on dollar assets. The resulting decrease in the relative expected return on dollar assets means that people will buy less dollar assets, so the demand curve shifts to the left and the exchange rate falls. *An unsterilized intervention in which domestic currency is sold and foreign assets are purchased leads to a rise in international reserves, a rise in the money supply, and a depreciation of the domestic currency.*

Sterilized Intervention

The key point to remember about a sterilized intervention is that the central bank engages in offsetting open market operations, and so there is no impact on the monetary base and the money supply. In the context of the model of exchange rate determination we have developed here, it is a straightforward task to show that a sterilized intervention has almost *no effect* on the exchange rate. A sterilized intervention leaves the money supply unchanged and thus has no direct way of affecting interest rates.[2] Because the relative expected return on dollar assets is unaffected, the demand curve remains at D_1 in Figure 1, and the exchange rate remains unchanged at E_1.

At first it might seem puzzling that a central bank purchase or sale of domestic currency that is sterilized does not lead to a change in the exchange rate. A central bank–sterilized purchase of domestic currency cannot raise the exchange rate because, with no effect on the domestic money supply or interest rates, any resulting rise in the exchange rate would lead to an excess supply of dollar assets. With more people willing to sell dollar assets than willing to buy them, the exchange rate would fall back to its initial equilibrium level, where the demand and supply curves intersect.

18.2 BALANCE OF PAYMENTS

LO 18.2 Interpret the relationships among the current account and the financial account in the balance of payments.

Because international financial transactions strongly affect a country's monetary policy, it is worth knowing how these transactions are measured. The **balance of payments** is a bookkeeping system that records the transactions between a nation (private sector and government) and foreign countries. Here we examine the key items in the balance of payments, which you often hear about in the media.

---

[2]A sterilized intervention changes the amount of foreign securities relative to domestic securities in the hands of the public, called a *portfolio balance effect*. Through this effect, the central bank might be able to influence the interest differential between domestic and foreign assets, which in turn affects the relative expected return on domestic assets. Empirical evidence has not revealed this portfolio balance effect to be significant. However, a sterilized intervention *could* indicate what central banks want to happen to the future exchange rate and so might provide a signal about the course of future monetary policy and change the expected future exchange rate, E_{t+1}^e. In this way, a sterilized intervention could lead to a shift in the demand curve for domestic assets and ultimately affect the exchange rate. However, the future change in monetary policy—not the sterilized intervention—is the source of the exchange rate effect. For a further discussion of the signaling and portfolio balance effects and the possible differential effects of sterilized versus unsterilized intervention, see Paul Krugman, Maurice Obstfeld, and Mark Melitz, *International Economics: Theory and Policy*, 11th ed. (New York: Pearson, 2018).

Current Account

The **current account** shows a country's current international transactions (that is, transactions that do not involve the purchase or sale of financial assets) for a given year. The current account is composed of three items: the trade balance, net investment income, and transfers.

The **trade balance on goods and services** (often called simply the **trade balance**) equals the total value of exports of goods and services minus the total value of imports of goods and services. (The trade balance is also referred to as to **net exports**.) When merchandise imports are greater than exports (as they were by $577 billion in 2019 in the United States), the country runs a trade deficit. If exports of goods and services exceed imports, the country runs a trade surplus.

In 2019 *net investment income* was $236 billion for the United States because Americans received more investment income from abroad than they paid out. *Transfers* are funds sent by domestic residents and the government to foreigners; they include *remittances* (money sent by domestic workers to foreigners, usually relatives), pensions, and foreign aid. Because Americans made more transfers to foreigners than foreigners made to the United States, transfers were −$139 billion in 2019. The sum of these two items plus the trade balance (net exports) is the **current account balance**, which in 2019 had a deficit of $480 billion:

$$-\$480 \text{ billion} = (-\$577 \text{ billion}) + (\$236 \text{ billion}) + (-\$139 \text{ billion})$$

Current account balance = trade balance + net investment income + transfers

When a country is running a current account deficit, as the United States does, then it is making more payments to foreigners on a current basis than it is receiving from foreigners. Like any deficit, a current account deficit has to be financed. To see how, we now turn to the financial account.

Financial Account

The **financial account** shows the international transactions that involve the purchase or sale of assets. When Americans increase their net holdings of foreign assets, this change is recorded as a *net U.S. acquisition of financial assets* in the financial account. When foreigners increase their net holdings of U.S. assets, this change is recorded as a *net U.S. incurrence of liabilities* because foreigners' claims on U.S. assets are liabilities for Americans. The difference between the *net U.S. acquisition of financial assets* and *net U.S. incurrence of liabilities* is the **financial account balance**. In 2019, the financial account balance plus other items, which for practical purposes we will include with the financial account balance, was −$480 billion.[3] This financial account balance tells us that in 2019, the United States experienced an increase of liabilities to foreigners that exceeded the increase in U.S. foreign asset holdings by $480 billion. In other words, our U.S. indebtedness to foreigners increased by $480 billion.

[3]In the balance of payments, the financial account balance is officially the *net U.S. acquisition of assets* minus the *net U.S. incurrence of liabilities*. In 2019, this number was −$395 billion. However, there is another important component that makes sense to include in the financial account balance, the *statistical discrepancy*, which represents errors due to unrecorded transactions and keeps the balance of payments in overall balance. The statistical discrepancy was $91 billion in 2019. Because many experts believe that the statistical discrepancy is primarily the result of large hidden capital flows, we include it in the financial account balance. Another component of the financial account balance is the *balance on the capital account*, which includes (1) goods and assets that people take with them when they move to another country and (2) net purchases of nonproduced, nonfinancial assets, such as intellectual property rights or mineral rights. The balance on the capital account was −$6 billion in 2019. The sum of the 2019 financial account balance, the statistical discrepancy and the capital account balance, $395 billion + $91 billion −$6 billion, is the $480 billion number in the text.

Global   Should We Worry About the Large U.S. Current Account Deficit?

The large U.S. current account deficit in recent years—in 2019 it was $480 billion, 2.2% of GDP—raises concerns for several reasons. First, because a large part of the deficit comes from a trade deficit, we can conclude that at current exchange rates, foreigners' demand for U.S. exports is far less than Americans' demand for imports. Our supply-and-demand analysis of the foreign exchange market suggests that low demand for U.S. exports and high U.S. demand for imports may lead to a decline in the value of the U.S. dollar.

Second, a large current account deficit means that the United States is becoming more indebted to foreigners. This borrowing will have to be paid back at some point in the future. When the bill comes due, Americans will not be as rich as they otherwise would be.

However, a large current account deficit indicates large capital inflows into the United States. These capital inflows might be funding highly attractive investment opportunities in the United States. These investments might increase U.S. wealth so much in the future that even when foreigners are paid back, Americans, on net, are richer.

The financial account balance tells us the amount of *net capital inflows* into the United States. When foreigners increase their holdings of U.S. assets, capital has flowed into the United States. In contrast, when Americans increase their holdings of foreign assets, capital has flowed out of the United States. So, in 2019, foreigners increased their holdings of U.S. assets by $480 billion more than Americans increased their holdings of foreign assets. The result was a net capital inflow of $480 billion into the United States.

You probably have noticed that this financial account balance is equal in absolute value to the current account deficit. This equality makes sense because if Americans are spending more than they are taking in on the current account, they must be financing this spending by borrowing an equal amount from foreigners. Another way to see this equality is to use the accounting principle that the uses of funds must equal the sources of funds. Hence the current account deficit, which provides the net uses of funds for current items, must equal the sources of funds, which is what the financial account balance tells us. The large current account deficit in recent years, which in 2019 was over $480 billion, has raised serious concerns that these large deficits may have negative consequences for the U.S. economy (see the Global box "Should We Worry About the Large U.S. Current Account Deficit?").

18.3 EXCHANGE RATE REGIMES IN THE INTERNATIONAL FINANCIAL SYSTEM

LO 18.3 Identify the mechanisms for maintaining a fixed exchange rate, and assess the challenges faced by fixed exchange rate regimes.

Exchange rate regimes in the international financial system are classified into two basic types: fixed and floating. In a **fixed exchange rate regime**, the value of a currency is pegged relative to the value of another currency (called the **anchor currency**) so that the exchange rate is fixed in terms of the anchor currency. In a **floating exchange rate regime**, the value of a currency is allowed to fluctuate against all other currencies. When countries intervene in foreign exchange markets in an attempt to influence their exchange rates by buying and selling foreign assets, the regime is referred to as a **managed float regime (or a dirty float)**.

In examining past exchange rate regimes, we start with the gold standard of the late nineteenth and early twentieth centuries.

Gold Standard

Before World War I, the world economy operated under the **gold standard**, a fixed exchange rate regime in which the currencies of most countries were convertible directly into gold at fixed rates, so that exchange rates between currencies were also fixed. One American dollar bill, for example, could be turned in to the U.S. Treasury and exchanged for approximately $\frac{1}{20}$ ounce of gold. Likewise, the British Treasury would exchange $\frac{1}{4}$ ounce of gold for £1 sterling. Because an American could convert $20 into 1 ounce of gold, which could be used to buy £4, the exchange rate between the pound and the dollar was effectively fixed at $5 to the pound. The fixed exchange rates under the gold standard had the important advantage of encouraging world trade by eliminating the uncertainty that occurs when exchange rates fluctuate.

One problem with the gold standard was that monetary policy throughout the world was greatly influenced by the production of gold and gold discoveries. When gold production was low in the 1870s and 1880s, the money supply throughout the world grew slowly and did not keep pace with the growth of the world economy. The result was deflation (falling price levels). Gold discoveries in Alaska and South Africa in the 1890s greatly expanded gold production, causing money supplies to increase rapidly and price levels to rise (inflation) until World War I.

The Bretton Woods System

After World War II, the victors set up a fixed exchange rate system that became known as the **Bretton Woods system**, after the New Hampshire town in which the agreement was negotiated in 1944. The Bretton Woods system remained in effect until 1971.

The Bretton Woods agreement created the **International Monetary Fund (IMF)**, headquartered in Washington, DC, which had 30 original member countries in 1945 and currently has over 180. The IMF was given the task of promoting the growth of world trade by setting rules for the maintenance of fixed exchange rates and by making loans to countries that were experiencing balance-of-payments difficulties. In addition to monitoring the compliance of member countries with its rules, the IMF also took on the job of collecting and standardizing international economic data.

The Bretton Woods agreement also set up the International Bank for Reconstruction and Development, commonly referred to as the **World Bank**. Headquartered in Washington, DC, it provides long-term loans to help developing countries build dams, roads, and other physical capital that will contribute to their economic development. The funds for these loans are obtained primarily by the issuance of World Bank bonds, which are sold in the capital markets of the developed countries. In addition, the General Agreement on Tariffs and Trade (GATT), headquartered in Geneva, Switzerland, was set up to monitor rules for the conduct of trade between countries (tariffs and quotas). The GATT has since evolved into the **World Trade Organization (WTO)**.

Because the United States emerged from World War II as the world's largest economic power, with over half of the world's manufacturing capacity and the greater part of the world's gold, Bretton Woods put in place a system of fixed exchange rates that was based on the convertibility of U.S. dollars into gold (for foreign governments and central banks only) at $35 per ounce. The fixed exchange rates were to be maintained by intervention in the foreign exchange market by central banks in countries besides the United States that bought and sold dollar assets, which these countries held as international reserves. The U.S. dollar, which was used by other countries to denominate the assets that they held as international reserves, was called the **reserve currency**. Thus an important feature of the Bretton Woods system was the establishment of the United States as the reserve currency country. Even after the breakup of the Bretton Woods system, the U.S. dollar kept its position as the reserve currency in which most international financial transactions are conducted.

The fixed exchange rate, which was a feature of the Bretton Woods system, was finally abandoned in 1973. From 1979 to 1990, the European Union instituted among its members its own fixed exchange rate system, called the European Monetary System (EMS). In theory, in the *exchange rate mechanism (ERM)* of this system, the exchange rate between any pair of currencies of the participating countries was not supposed to fluctuate outside narrow limits, called the "snake." In practice, all of the countries in the EMS pegged their currencies to the German mark.

How a Fixed Exchange Rate Regime Works

Figure 2 uses the supply and demand analysis of the foreign exchange market that we learned in the previous chapter to show how a fixed exchange rate regime works in practice. Panel (a) describes a situation in which the domestic currency is fixed relative to an anchor currency at E_{par}, while the demand curve has shifted left to D_1, perhaps

Mini-lecture

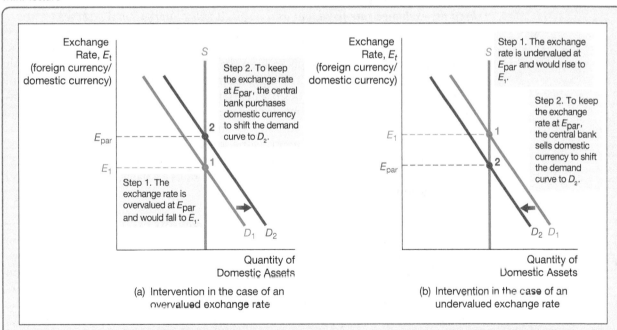

(a) Intervention in the case of an overvalued exchange rate

(b) Intervention in the case of an undervalued exchange rate

FIGURE 2 **Intervention in the Foreign Exchange Market Under a Fixed Exchange Rate Regime**

In panel (a), the exchange rate at E_{par} is overvalued. To keep the exchange rate at E_{par} (point 2), the central bank must purchase domestic currency to shift the demand curve to D_2. In panel (b), the exchange rate at E_{par} is undervalued, so the central bank must sell domestic currency to shift the demand curve to D_2 and keep the exchange rate at E_{par} (point 2).

because foreign interest rates have risen, thereby lowering the relative expected return on domestic assets. At E_{par}, the exchange rate is now *overvalued:* The demand curve D_1 intersects the supply curve at an exchange rate E_1 that is lower than the fixed (par) value of the exchange rate E_{par}. To keep the exchange rate at E_{par}, the central bank must intervene in the foreign exchange market and purchase domestic currency by selling foreign assets. This action, like an open market sale, causes both the monetary base and the money supply to decrease, driving up the interest rate on domestic assets, i^D.[4] This increase in the domestic interest rate raises the relative expected return on domestic assets, shifting the demand curve to the right. The central bank will continue to purchase domestic currency until the demand curve reaches D_2 and the equilibrium exchange rate is at E_{par}, at point 2 in panel (a).

We thus conclude that **when the domestic currency is overvalued, the central bank must purchase domestic currency to keep the exchange rate fixed, but as a result it loses international reserves**.

Panel (b) in Figure 2 describes the situation in which the demand curve has shifted to the right to D_1 because the relative expected return on domestic assets has risen and hence the exchange rate at E_{par} is *undervalued:* The initial demand curve D_1 intersects the supply curve at exchange rate E_1, which is above E_{par}. In this situation, the central bank must sell domestic currency and purchase foreign assets. This action works like an open market purchase; it increases the money supply and lowers the interest rate on domestic assets i^D. The central bank keeps selling domestic currency and lowering i^D until the demand curve shifts all the way to D_2, where the equilibrium exchange rate is at E_{par}—point 2 in panel (b). Our analysis thus leads us to the following result: **When the domestic currency is undervalued, the central bank must sell domestic currency to keep the exchange rate fixed, but as a result, it gains international reserves**.

Devaluation and Revaluation   As we have seen, if a country's currency is overvalued, its central bank's attempts to keep the currency from depreciating will result in a loss of international reserves. If the country's central bank eventually runs out of international reserves, it cannot keep its currency from depreciating, and a **devaluation**, in which the par exchange rate is reset at a lower level, must occur.

If, by contrast, a country's currency is undervalued, its central bank's intervention to keep the currency from appreciating leads to a gain of international reserves. As we will see shortly, the central bank might not want to acquire these international reserves, and so it might want to reset the par value of its exchange rate at a higher level (a **revaluation**).

Perfect Capital Mobility   If perfect **capital mobility** exists—that is, if there are no barriers to domestic residents purchasing foreign assets or to foreigners purchasing domestic assets—then a sterilized exchange rate intervention cannot keep the exchange rate at E_{par} because, as we saw earlier in the chapter, the relative expected return on domestic assets is unaffected. For example, if the exchange rate is overvalued, a sterilized purchase of domestic currency will leave the relative expected return and the demand curve unchanged, so pressure for a depreciation of the domestic currency is not removed. If the central bank keeps purchasing its domestic currency but continues to sterilize, it will just keep losing international reserves until it finally runs out of them and is forced to let the value of the currency seek a lower level.

---

[4]Because the exchange rate will continue to be fixed at E_{par}, the expected future exchange rate remains unchanged and so is not addressed in the analysis.

Speculative Attacks

A serious shortcoming of fixed exchange rate systems such as the Bretton Woods system and the European Monetary System is that such systems can lead to foreign exchange crises involving a **speculative attack** on a currency. A speculative attack involves massive sales of a weak currency or purchases of a strong currency that cause a sharp change in the exchange rate. In the following application, we use our model of exchange rate determination to understand how the September 1992 exchange rate crisis that rocked the European Monetary System came about.

APPLICATION   The Foreign Exchange Crisis of September 1992

In the aftermath of German reunification in October 1990, the German central bank, the Bundesbank, faced rising inflationary pressures, with inflation having accelerated from below 3% in 1990 to near 5% by 1992. To get monetary growth under control and to dampen inflation, the Bundesbank raised German interest rates to near double-digit levels. Figure 3 shows the consequences of these actions by the Bundesbank in the foreign

Mini-lecture

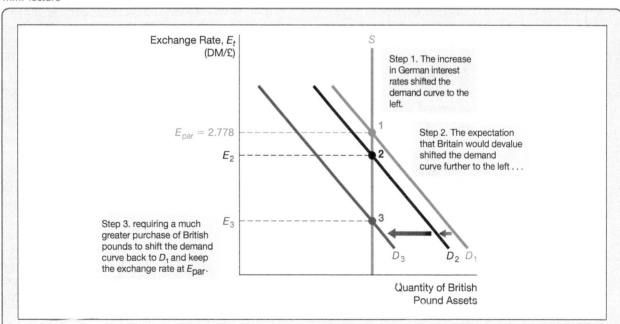

FIGURE 3   **Foreign Exchange Market for British Pounds in 1992**

The realization by speculators that the United Kingdom would soon devalue the pound decreased the relative expected return on British pound assets, resulting in a leftward shift of the demand curve from D_2 to D_3. As a result, the British central bank was forced to purchase a large amount of pounds in an effort to raise the interest rate so that the demand curve would shift back to D_1 and the exchange rate E_{par} would remain at 2.778 German marks per pound.

exchange market for British pounds. Note that in the diagram, the pound is the domestic currency and the German mark (deutsche mark, DM, Germany's currency before the advent of the euro in 1999) is the foreign currency.

The increase in German interest rates i^F lowered the relative expected return on British pound assets and shifted the demand curve to D_2, as shown in Figure 3. The intersection of the supply and demand curves at point 2 was now below the lower exchange rate limit at that time (2.778 marks per pound, denoted E_{par}). To increase the value of the pound relative to the mark and to restore the mark/pound exchange rate to within the exchange rate mechanism limits, one of two things had to happen. In the first option, the Bank of England would have to pursue a contractionary monetary policy, thereby raising British interest rates sufficiently to shift the demand curve back to D_1, so that the equilibrium would remain at point 1 and the exchange rate would remain at E_{par}. Alternatively, the Bundesbank would have to pursue an expansionary monetary policy, thereby lowering German interest rates. Lower German interest rates would raise the relative expected return on British assets and shift the demand curve back to D_1, so that the exchange rate would remain at E_{par}.

The catch was that the Bundesbank, whose primary goal was to fight inflation, was unwilling to pursue an expansionary monetary policy, and the British, who were facing their worst recession in the postwar period, were unwilling to pursue a contractionary monetary policy to prop up the pound. This impasse became clear when, in response to great pressure from other members of the EMS, the Bundesbank was willing to lower its lending rates by only a token amount on September 14 after a speculative attack was mounted on the currencies of the Scandinavian countries. So, at some point in the near future, the value of the pound would have to decline to point 2. Speculators now knew that depreciation of the pound was imminent and so the expected future exchange rate, E_{t+1}^e, fell. As a result, the relative expected return on the pound fell sharply, shifting the demand curve left to D_3 in Figure 3.

As a result of the large leftward shift of the demand curve, a huge excess supply of pound assets now existed at the par exchange rate E_{par}, which caused a massive sell-off of pounds (and purchases of marks) by speculators. The need for the British central bank to intervene to raise the value of the pound now became much greater and required a huge rise in British interest rates. A major intervention effort on the part of the Bank of England, which led to a rise in its lending rate from 10% to 15%, still wasn't enough to save the pound. The British were finally forced to give up on September 16: They pulled out of the ERM indefinitely and allowed the pound to depreciate by 10% against the mark.

Speculative attacks on other currencies forced devaluation of the Spanish peseta by 5% and of the Italian lira by 15%. To defend its currency, the Swedish central bank was forced to raise its daily lending rate to the astronomical level of 500%! By the time the crisis was over, the British, French, Italian, Spanish, and Swedish central banks had intervened to the tune of $100 billion; the Bundesbank alone had laid out $50 billion for foreign exchange intervention.

The attempt to prop up the European Monetary System was not cheap for these central banks. It is estimated that they lost $4 to $6 billion as a result of exchange rate intervention during the crisis. What the central banks lost, the speculators gained. A speculative fund run by George Soros ran up $1 billion of profits during the crisis, and Citibank traders reportedly made $200 million. When an exchange rate crisis arises, life certainly can be sweet for exchange rate speculators. ◆

The Policy Trilemma

An important implication of the foregoing analysis is that a country that ties its exchange rate to an anchor currency of a larger country loses control of its monetary policy. If the larger country pursues a more contractionary monetary policy and raises interest rates, this action will lead to lower expected inflation in the larger country, thus causing an appreciation of the larger country's currency and a depreciation of the smaller country's currency. The smaller country, having locked its exchange rate to the anchor currency, will now find its currency overvalued and will therefore have to sell the anchor currency and buy its own to keep its currency from depreciating. The result of this foreign exchange intervention will be a decline in the smaller country's international reserves, a contraction of its monetary base, and a rise in interest rates. Sterilization of this foreign exchange intervention is not an option because this course of action would just lead to a continuing loss of international reserves, until the smaller country was forced to devalue its currency. The smaller country no longer controls its monetary policy because movements in its interest rates are completely determined by movements in the larger country's interest rates.

Our analysis therefore indicates that a country (or a monetary union like the Eurozone) can't pursue the following three policies at the same time: (1) free capital mobility, (2) a fixed exchange rate, and (3) an independent monetary policy. Economists call this result the **policy trilemma** (or, more colorfully, the **impossible trinity**). Figure 4 illustrates the policy trilemma. A country can choose only two of the three options, which are denoted by the sides of the triangle. In option 1, a country (or monetary union) chooses to have capital mobility and an independent monetary policy, but not a fixed exchange rate. The Eurozone and the United States have made this choice. Hong Kong and Belize have chosen option 2, in which there is free capital mobility and the exchange rate is fixed, but the country does not have an independent monetary policy. Other countries, like China, have chosen option 3, in which the country has a fixed exchange rate and

Mini-lecture

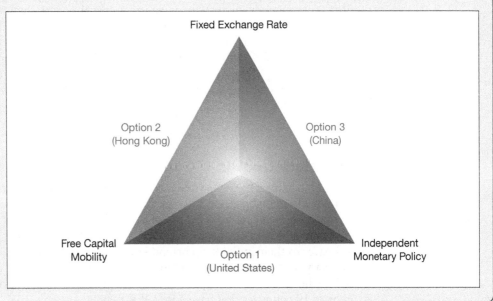

FIGURE 4

The Policy Trilemma

A country (or monetary union) cannot pursue the following three policies at the same time: (1) free capital mobility, (2) a fixed exchange rate, and (3) an independent monetary policy. Instead, it must choose two of the three policies denoted by the sides of the triangle.

pursues an independent monetary policy but does not have free capital mobility because of **capital controls**, or restrictions on the free movement of capital across the borders.

The policy trilemma thus leaves countries with a difficult choice. Do they accept exchange rate volatility (option 1), give up an independent monetary policy (option 2), or restrict capital flows (option 3)?

APPLICATION

How Did China Accumulate $4 Trillion of International Reserves?

By 2014, China had accumulated $4 trillion of international reserves (which, however, declined to $3 trillion by 2020). How did the Chinese get their hands on this vast amount of foreign assets? After all, China is not yet a rich country.

The answer is that in 1994, China pegged its exchange rate to the U.S. dollar at a fixed rate of 12 cents to the yuan (also called the renminbi). China's rapidly growing productivity, accompanied by an inflation rate lower than that of the United States, caused the long-run value of the yuan to increase, leading to a higher relative expected return on yuan assets and a rightward shift of the demand curve for yuan assets. As a result, the Chinese found themselves in the situation depicted in panel (b) of Figure 2, a situation in which the yuan was undervalued. To keep the yuan from appreciating above E_{par} to E_1 in the figure, the Chinese central bank has engaged in massive purchases of U.S. dollar assets. Today the Chinese government is one of the largest holders of U.S. government bonds in the world.

The Chinese pegged the yuan at 12 cents from 1994 until 2005. Because the Chinese authorities created substantial roadblocks to capital mobility, they were able to sterilize most of their exchange rate interventions while maintaining the exchange rate peg. Nevertheless, their foreign exchange rate interventions led to a rapidly growing money supply that produced inflationary pressures. As a result, in July 2005, China finally made its peg somewhat more flexible by letting the value of the yuan rise 2.1%, and China subsequently allowed the yuan to appreciate at a gradual pace. The Chinese central bank also indicated that it would no longer fix the value of the yuan to the U.S. dollar, but would instead maintain its value relative to a basket of currencies.

After 2014, the Chinese yuan was no longer undervalued, and the Chinese central bank began to purchase yuan, leading to a decline in foreign exchange reserves. By 2020, Chinese international reserves had fallen to $3 trillion. ◆

Monetary Unions

A variant of a fixed exchange rate regime is a **monetary (or currency) union**, in which a group of countries decides to adopt a common currency, thereby fixing the countries' exchange rates in relation to each other. One of the earliest monetary unions was formed in 1787, when the 13 American colonies formed the United States of America and gave up their individual currencies for the U.S. dollar. The most recently formed monetary union is the European Monetary Union (EMU), which was formed in January 1999, when 11 initial member countries adopted a new joint currency, the euro. There are now 19 countries that have adopted the euro.

The key economic advantage of a monetary union is that it makes trade across borders easier because goods and services in all of the member countries are now priced in the same currency. However, as with any fixed exchange rate regime and free capital mobility, a currency union means that individual countries no longer have their own independent monetary policies with which to address shortfalls of aggregate demand. This disadvantage of a currency union has raised questions about whether the Eurozone will break up, as discussed in the Global box "Will the Euro Survive?"

Managed Float

With the demise of the Bretton Woods system, most exchange rates now change daily in response to market forces, but central banks have not been willing to give up the option of intervening in the foreign exchange market. The ability to prevent large changes in exchange rates makes it easier for firms and individuals purchasing or selling goods abroad to plan for the future. Furthermore, countries with surpluses in their balances of payments frequently do not want to see their currencies appreciate, because it makes their goods more expensive abroad and foreign goods cheaper in the home country. Because an appreciation might hurt sales for domestic businesses and increase unemployment, countries with balance-of-payments surpluses often have sold their currencies in the foreign exchange market and acquired international reserves.

Countries with balance-of-payments deficits do not want to see their currencies lose value because it makes foreign goods more expensive for domestic consumers and can stimulate inflation. To keep the value of the domestic currency high, countries with

---

Global Will the Euro Survive?

The global financial crisis of 2007–2009 led to economic contraction throughout Europe, with the countries in the southern part of the Eurozone hit especially hard. Unemployment in the hard-hit southern countries climbed much faster than in the northern countries such as Germany. Furthermore, with the contraction of their economies, many of the southern countries began to experience large government budget deficits and sovereign debt crises, as described in Chapter 12, in which investors pulled back from purchasing these countries' bonds, sending interest rates to extremely high levels. The resulting collapse of the southern countries' economies could have been alleviated by easier monetary policy that would have stimulated economic activity, but this option was unavailable to these countries because the European Central Bank had to conduct monetary policy for the Eurozone as a whole, which was not suffering as badly as the individual southern countries.

This "straightjacket" effect of the euro has weakened support for the euro in the southern countries, leading to increased talk of abandoning the euro. Support for the euro has also weakened in the stronger, northern countries, since they have been called upon to provide bailouts to the weaker member countries. Because the stronger countries might wish to abandon their commitment to the euro in order to limit their transfers of funds to the weaker countries, and the weaker countries might wish to abandon their commitment to the euro so that they can boost their economies through more expansionary monetary policy and depreciation of their currencies, there are doubts that the European Monetary Union will survive. However, the euro is still seen by many as an important step in the creation of a more united and powerful Europe, and this political consideration has created strong support for retaining the monetary union.

deficits have often bought their own currencies in the foreign exchange market and given up international reserves.

The current international financial system is a hybrid of a fixed and a flexible exchange rate system. Rates fluctuate in response to market forces but are not determined solely by them. Furthermore, many countries continue to keep the value of their currency fixed against other currencies, as was the case in the European Monetary System before the introduction of the euro, and China from 1994 until 2005.

18.4 CAPITAL CONTROLS

LO 18.4 Summarize the advantages and disadvantages of capital controls.

Emerging market countries are countries that have recently opened up to flows of goods, services, and capital from the rest of the world. Politicians and some economists have advocated that these countries avoid financial instability by restricting capital mobility. Are capital controls a good idea?

Controls on Capital Outflows

Capital outflows can promote financial instability because, when domestic residents and foreigners pull their capital out of a country, the resulting capital outflow forces the country to devalue its currency. Because they want to avoid such instability, politicians in emerging market countries may find capital controls particularly attractive.

Although these controls sound like a good idea, they suffer from several disadvantages. First, empirical evidence indicates that controls on capital outflows are seldom effective during a crisis, because the private sector will find ingenious ways to evade them and will have little difficulty in moving funds out of the country. Second, the evidence suggests that capital flight may actually increase after controls are put into place because confidence in the government is weakened. Third, controls on capital outflows can lead to corruption, since government officials are often paid to look the other way while domestic residents try to move funds abroad. Fourth, controls on capital outflows may lull governments into thinking they do not have to act to reform their financial systems to deal with the crisis, and so opportunities to improve the functioning of the economy are lost.

Controls on Capital Inflows

Although most economists find the arguments against controls on capital outflows persuasive, the idea of controls on capital inflows receives more support. Supporters reason that if speculative capital cannot come in, then it cannot go out suddenly. Thus a potential crisis is averted. Our analysis of financial crises in Chapter 12 provides support for this view by suggesting that capital inflows can lead to credit booms and excessive risk taking on the part of banks, factors that can help trigger a financial crisis.

However, controls on capital inflows have the undesirable feature of possibly blocking funds that could be used for productive investment opportunities from entering a country. Although controls on capital inflows may limit the amount of fuel supplied to lending booms through capital flows, over time they produce substantial distortions and misallocations of resources as households and businesses try to get around them. Indeed, as with controls on capital outflows, controls on capital inflows can lead to corruption. Serious doubts exist over whether capital controls can be effective in today's environment, in which trade is open and in which the variety of financial instruments makes it easier to get around these controls.

A strong case can be made, however, for improving bank regulation and supervision so that capital inflows are less likely to produce a lending boom that would encourage excessive risk taking by banking institutions. For example, restrictions on the growth of bank borrowing might substantially limit capital inflows. Supervisory controls that focus on the sources of financial fragility, rather than the symptoms, can enhance the efficiency of the financial system rather than hamper it.

18.5 THE ROLE OF THE IMF

LO 18.5 Assess the role of the IMF as an international lender of last resort.

The International Monetary Fund (IMF) was originally set up under the Bretton Woods system to help countries deal with balance-of-payments problems and stand by the fixed exchange rates by lending to deficit countries. When the Bretton Woods system of fixed exchange rates collapsed in 1973, the IMF took on new roles.

The IMF continues to function as a data collector and continues to provide technical assistance to its member countries. Although the IMF no longer attempts to encourage fixed exchange rates, its role as an international lender has become more important in recent years. This role first came to the fore in the 1980s during the Third World debt crisis, during which the IMF assisted developing countries in repaying their loans. During the financial crises in Mexico from 1994–1995 and in East Asia from 1997–1998, the IMF made huge loans to these and other affected countries to help them recover financially and to prevent the spread of the crises to other countries. Then, starting in 2010, the IMF made large loans to Greece, Ireland, and Portugal to help these countries avoid defaults on their government debt. This role of the IMF, in which it acts as an international lender of last resort and helps countries cope with financial instability, is indeed highly controversial.

Should the IMF Act as an International Lender of Last Resort?

We have seen that when a central bank engages in a lender-of-last-resort operation, as the Federal Reserve did during the recent global financial crisis, such an action can minimize the severity of the financial crisis and sometimes even prevent it from happening. When the IMF acts as an international lender of last resort, this role can have similar benefits, particularly when the central bank of the country it is lending to does not have the capacity to cope with the crisis.

However, when the IMF acts as an international lender of last resort, it can lead to serious moral hazard problems. First, knowing that the IMF is willing to take on this role may encourage governments to be profligate, because they know they are likely to be bailed out by the IMF if things get out of hand. Second, governments use IMF funds to protect depositors and other creditors of banking institutions from losses. This safety net creates the moral hazard problem discussed in Chapter 10, because depositors and other creditors have less incentive to monitor these banking institutions and to withdraw their deposits if the institutions are taking on too much risk.

An international lender of last resort must find ways to limit these two moral hazard problems or it can actually make the situation worse. The international lender of last resort can make it clear that it will extend liquidity only to governments that both put their fiscal houses in order and implement measures to prevent excessive risk taking by financial institutions. Critics of the IMF, however, believe that the IMF has not put enough pressure on the governments to which it lends to contain these two moral hazard problems, and for this reason they believe the IMF should abandon its role as an international lender of last resort. The IMF has also been criticized for imposing so-called austerity programs that force borrowing governments to cut government spending, raise taxes, and raise interest rates. These austerity programs can be highly contractionary (see Chapter 22) and can lead to high unemployment and even political instability.

The debate over whether the world would be better off with the IMF operating as an international lender of last resort is currently a hot one. Much attention is being focused on efforts to make the IMF more effective in performing this role, and redesign of the IMF is at the center of proposals for a new international financial architecture that will help reduce international financial instability.

18.6 INTERNATIONAL CONSIDERATIONS AND MONETARY POLICY

LO 18.6 Identify the ways in which international monetary policy and exchange rate arrangements can affect domestic monetary policy operations.

Our analysis in this chapter so far has suggested several ways in which monetary policy can be affected by international matters. Awareness of these effects can have significant implications for the way in which monetary policy is conducted.

Direct Effects of the Foreign Exchange Market on Monetary Policy

When central banks intervene in the foreign exchange market, they acquire or sell off international reserves and their monetary base is affected. When a central bank intervenes in the foreign exchange market, it gives up some control of its monetary policy. For example, in the early 1970s, the German central bank faced a dilemma. In attempting to keep the German mark from appreciating too much against the U.S. dollar, the Germans acquired huge quantities of international reserves, leading to a high rate of money growth and lower interest rates that the German central bank considered inflationary.

The Bundesbank could have stopped its intervention in the foreign exchange market, thereby reasserting control over its own monetary policy. Such a strategy has a major drawback when a central bank is under pressure not to allow its currency to appreciate: The lower price of imports and higher price of exports that result from an appreciation of its currency will hurt domestic producers and increase unemployment.

Because the U.S. dollar has been a reserve currency, the U.S. monetary base and money supply have not been greatly affected by developments in the foreign exchange market. As long as foreign central banks, rather than the Fed, intervene to keep the value of the dollar from changing, American holdings of international reserves will remain unaffected. Conducting monetary policy is typically easier when a country's currency is a reserve currency.[5]

---

[5]However, the central bank of a reserve currency country must worry about a shift away from the use of its currency for international reserves.

Exchange Rate Considerations

If a central bank does not want to see its currency fall in value, it may pursue a more contractionary monetary policy to raise the domestic interest rate, thereby strengthening its currency. Similarly, if a country experiences an appreciation in its currency, its domestic industry may suffer from increased foreign competition and may pressure the central bank to ease monetary policy in order to lower the exchange rate.

18.7 TO PEG OR NOT TO PEG: EXCHANGE-RATE TARGETING AS AN ALTERNATIVE MONETARY POLICY STRATEGY

LO 18.7 Summarize the advantages and disadvantages of exchange-rate targeting.

In Chapter 16, we discussed two monetary policy strategies that could be used to promote price stability: inflation targeting and the Federal Reserve's "just do it" strategy. Another strategy that uses a strong nominal anchor to promote price stability is called **exchange-rate targeting** (sometimes referred to as an **exchange-rate peg**).

Targeting the exchange rate is a monetary policy strategy with a long history. It can take the form of fixing the value of the domestic currency to a commodity such as gold, the key feature of the gold standard described earlier in the chapter. More recently, fixed exchange rate regimes have involved fixing the value of the domestic currency to that of a large, low-inflation country like the United States (the *anchor country*). Another alternative is to adopt a *crawling target* or *peg*, in which a currency is allowed to depreciate at a steady rate so that the inflation rate of the pegging country can be higher than that of the anchor country.

Advantages of Exchange-Rate Targeting

Exchange-rate targeting has several advantages. First, the nominal anchor of an exchange-rate target directly contributes to the goal of keeping inflation under control by tying the inflation rate for internationally traded goods to the rate in the anchor country. The exchange-rate target is able to do this because the foreign price of internationally traded goods is set by the world market, whereas the domestic price of these goods is fixed by the exchange-rate target. For example, until 2002, the exchange rate for the Argentine peso was exactly one to the dollar, so a bushel of wheat traded internationally at five dollars had its price set at five pesos. If the exchange-rate target is credible (i.e., expected to be adhered to), the exchange-rate target has the added benefit of anchoring inflation expectations to the inflation rate in the anchor country.

Second, an exchange-rate target provides an automatic rule for the conduct of monetary policy that helps mitigate the time-inconsistency problem described in Chapter 16. As we saw earlier in the chapter, an exchange-rate target forces a tightening of monetary policy when there is a tendency for the domestic currency to depreciate and a loosening of policy when there is a tendency for the domestic currency to appreciate, so discretionary monetary policy is less of an option. The central bank will therefore be constrained from falling into the time-inconsistency trap of trying to expand output and employment in the short run by pursuing overly expansionary monetary policy.

Third, an exchange-rate target has the advantage of simplicity and clarity, which makes it easily understood by the public. A "sound currency" is an easy-to-understand rallying cry for monetary policy. In the past, for example, this aspect of simplicity was important in France, where an appeal to the "franc fort" (strong franc) was often used to justify tight monetary policy.

Given its advantages, it is not surprising that exchange-rate targeting has been used successfully to control inflation in industrialized countries. Both France and the United Kingdom, for example, successfully used exchange-rate targeting to lower inflation by tying the values of their currencies to the German mark. In 1987, when France first pegged its exchange rate to the mark, its inflation rate was 3%, two percentage points above the German inflation rate. By 1992, its inflation rate had fallen to 2%, a level that can be argued is consistent with price stability and that was actually below the German inflation rate. By 1996, the French and German inflation rates had converged to a number slightly below 2%. Similarly, after pegging its currency to the German mark in 1990, the United Kingdom was able to lower its inflation rate from 10% to 3% by 1992, when it was forced to abandon the exchange rate mechanism (ERM).

Exchange-rate targeting has also been an effective means of reducing inflation quickly in emerging market countries. For example, before the devaluation in Mexico in 1994, its exchange-rate target enabled it to bring inflation down from levels above 100% in 1988 to levels below 10% in 1994.

Disadvantages of Exchange-Rate Targeting

Despite the inherent advantages of exchange-rate targeting, several serious criticisms of this strategy can be made. The problem (as we saw earlier in the chapter) is that with capital mobility, the targeting country can no longer pursue its own independent monetary policy and use it to respond to domestic shocks that are independent of those hitting the anchor country. Furthermore, an exchange-rate target means that shocks to the anchor country are directly transmitted to the targeting country, because changes in interest rates in the anchor country lead to corresponding changes in interest rates in the targeting country.

A striking example of these weaknesses occurred when Germany was reunified in 1990. In response to concerns about inflationary pressures arising from reunification and the massive fiscal expansion required to rebuild East Germany, long-term German interest rates rose until February 1991, and short-term rates rose until December 1991. This shock to the anchor country in the exchange rate mechanism (ERM) was transmitted directly to the other countries in the ERM whose currencies were pegged to the mark, and their interest rates rose in tandem with the German rates. Continued adherence to the exchange-rate target slowed economic growth and increased unemployment in countries such as France that remained in the ERM exchange-rate peg.

A second problem with exchange-rate targets is that they leave countries open to speculative attacks on their currencies. Indeed, one aftermath of German reunification was the foreign exchange crisis of September 1992. As we saw earlier, the tight monetary policy practiced in Germany following reunification subjected the countries of the ERM to a negative demand shock that led to declines in economic growth and increases in unemployment. It was certainly feasible for the governments of these countries to keep their exchange rates fixed relative to the mark under these circumstances, but speculators began to question whether these countries' commitment to the exchange-rate peg would eventually weaken. Speculators reasoned that these countries would not tolerate the rise in unemployment that resulted from keeping interest rates high enough to fend off attacks on their currencies.

At this stage, speculators were, in effect, presented with a one-way bet, because the currencies of countries like France, Spain, Sweden, Italy, and the United Kingdom could go in only one direction and depreciate against the mark. Selling these currencies before the likely depreciation occurred gave speculators an attractive profit opportunity with potentially high expected returns. The result was the speculative attack of September 1992. Only in France was the commitment to the fixed exchange rate strong enough that France did not devalue. The governments of the other ERM countries were unwilling to defend their currencies at all costs and eventually allowed their currencies to fall in value.

The different responses of France and the United Kingdom after the September 1992 exchange rate crisis illustrate the potential cost of an exchange-rate target. On the one hand, France, which continued to peg its currency to the mark and thus was unable to use monetary policy to respond to domestic conditions, found that economic growth remained slow after 1992, and unemployment increased. The United Kingdom, on the other hand, which dropped out of the ERM exchange-rate peg and adopted inflation targeting, enjoyed much better economic results: Economic growth was higher, the unemployment rate fell, and yet the inflation rate was not much worse than France's.

In contrast to industrialized countries, emerging market countries (including the transition countries of Eastern Europe) may not lose all that much by giving up an independent monetary policy when they target exchange rates. Because many emerging market countries have not developed the political or monetary institutions that are necessary for the successful use of discretionary monetary policy, they may have little to gain but a lot to lose from an independent monetary policy. Thus they are better off if they adopt, in effect, the monetary policy of a country like the United States through targeting exchange rates than if they pursue their own independent policy. This is one of the reasons so many emerging market countries have adopted exchange-rate targeting.

Nonetheless, exchange-rate targeting is highly dangerous for these countries because it leaves them open to speculative attacks that can have far more serious consequences for their economies than for those of industrialized countries. Indeed, the successful speculative attacks on Mexico in 1994, East Asia in 1997, and Argentina in 2002 plunged their economies into full-scale financial crises that devastated their countries.

An additional disadvantage of an exchange-rate target is that it can weaken the accountability of policymakers, particularly in emerging market countries. Because exchange-rate targeting fixes the exchange rate, it eliminates an important signal that can help constrain monetary policy from becoming too expansionary and thereby limit the time-inconsistency problem. In industrialized countries, particularly in the United States, the bond market provides an important signal about the stance of monetary policy. Overly expansionary monetary policy or strong political pressure to engage in overly expansionary monetary policy produces an inflation scare, in which inflation expectations surge, interest rates rise (because of the Fisher effect, described in Chapter 5), and long-term bond prices decline sharply. Because both central banks and politicians want to avoid this kind of scenario, overly expansionary monetary policy is less likely.

In many countries, particularly emerging market countries, the long-term bond market is essentially nonexistent. Under a floating exchange rate regime, however, if monetary policy is too expansionary, the exchange rate will depreciate. In these countries, the daily fluctuations of the exchange rate can, like the bond market in the United States, provide an early warning signal that monetary policy is too expansionary. Just as the fear of a visible inflation scare in the bond market constrains central bankers from pursuing overly expansionary monetary policy and constrains politicians from putting pressure on the central bank to do so, fear of exchange rate depreciations can make overly expansionary monetary policy, and therefore the time-inconsistency problem, less likely.

The need for signals from the foreign exchange market may be even more acute for emerging market countries because the balance sheets and actions of their central banks are not as transparent as those of industrialized countries. Targeting the exchange rate can make it even harder to ascertain the central bank's policy actions. The public is less able to keep a watch on the central bank and the politicians pressuring it, which makes it easier for monetary policy to become too expansionary.

When Is Exchange-Rate Targeting Desirable for Industrialized Countries?

Given the above disadvantages of exchange-rate targeting, when might it make sense? In industrialized countries, the biggest cost to exchange-rate targeting is the loss of an independent monetary policy to deal with domestic considerations. If an independent, domestic monetary policy can be conducted responsibly, the loss of such a policy can be a serious cost indeed, as the comparison between the post-1992 experiences of France and the United Kingdom indicates. However, not all industrialized countries are capable of conducting their own monetary policies successfully, either because the central bank is not independent or because political pressures on the central bank lead to an inflationary bias in monetary policy. In these cases, giving up independent control of domestic monetary policy may not be such a great loss, while the advantages of having monetary policy determined by a better-performing central bank in the anchor country can be substantial.

Italy provides a good example. It is not a coincidence that the Italian public had the most favorable attitude of all the European countries toward the European Monetary Union. The past record of Italian monetary policy was not good, and the Italian public recognized that a monetary policy controlled by more responsible outsiders had benefits that far outweighed the costs to the country of losing the ability to focus monetary policy on domestic considerations.

A second reason why industrialized countries might find exchange-rate targeting useful is that it encourages integration of the domestic economy with the economies of neighboring countries. Clearly, this was the rationale for the long-standing pegging of the exchange rate to the deutsche mark by countries such as Austria and the Netherlands and the more recent exchange-rate pegs that preceded the formation of the European Monetary Union.

To sum, exchange-rate targeting for industrialized countries is probably not the best monetary policy strategy for controlling the overall economy unless (1) domestic monetary and political institutions are not conducive to good monetary policymaking or (2) an exchange-rate target has other important benefits that have nothing to do with monetary policy.

When Is Exchange-Rate Targeting Desirable for Emerging Market Countries?

In countries with particularly weak political and monetary institutions that have experienced continued bouts of hyperinflation, a characterization that applies to many emerging market (including transition) countries, exchange-rate targeting may be the only way to break inflationary psychology and stabilize the economy. In this situation, exchange-rate targeting is the stabilization policy of last resort. However, if the exchange-rate targeting regimes in emerging market countries are not transparent, they are more likely to break down, often resulting in disastrous financial crises.

Are there exchange rate strategies that will make it less likely that the exchange rate regime will break down in an emerging market country? Two such strategies, currency boards and dollarization, have received increased attention in recent years.

Currency Boards

A **currency board** is an arrangement in which the domestic currency is backed 100% by a foreign currency (say, dollars), and the note-issuing authority, whether it be the central bank or the government, establishes a fixed exchange rate to this foreign currency and stands ready to exchange domestic currency for the foreign currency at this rate whenever the public so requests. A currency board is just a variant of a fixed exchange-rate target in which the commitment to the fixed exchange rate is especially strong because the conduct of monetary policy is, in effect, put on autopilot and taken completely out of the hands of the central bank and the government. In contrast, the typical fixed or pegged exchange rate regime does allow the monetary authorities some discretion in their conduct of monetary policy because they can still adjust interest rates or print money.

A currency board arrangement thus has important advantages over a monetary policy strategy that just uses an exchange-rate target. First, the money supply can expand only when foreign currency is exchanged for domestic currency at the central bank. Therefore, the increased amount of domestic currency is matched by an equal increase in foreign exchange reserves. The central bank no longer has the ability to print money and thereby cause inflation. Second, the currency board setup involves a stronger commitment by the central bank to the fixed exchange rate and may therefore be effective in bringing inflation down quickly and in decreasing the likelihood of a successful speculative attack against the currency.

Although currency boards solve the transparency and commitment problems inherent in an exchange-rate target regime, they suffer from some of the same shortcomings: the loss of an independent monetary policy, increased exposure of the economy to shocks from the anchor country, and the loss of the central bank's ability to create money and act as a lender of last resort. Other means must therefore be used to cope with potential banking crises. In addition, if a speculative attack on a currency board occurs, the exchange of domestic currency for foreign currency leads to a sharp contraction of the money supply, which can be highly damaging to the economy.

Currency boards have been established in the territory of Hong Kong (1983) and in countries such as Argentina (1991), Estonia (1992), Lithuania (1994), Bulgaria (1997), and Bosnia (1998). Argentina's currency board, which operated from 1991 until 2002 and required the central bank to exchange U.S. dollars for new pesos at a fixed exchange rate of 1 to 1, is one of the most interesting. For more on this subject, see the Global box "Argentina's Currency Board."

Global Argentina's Currency Board

Argentina has a long history of monetary instability, with inflation rates fluctuating dramatically over the years, sometimes surging to beyond 1,000% per year. To end this cycle of inflationary surges, Argentina decided to adopt a currency board in April 1991. The Argentine currency board worked as follows. Under Argentina's convertibility law, the peso/dollar exchange rate was fixed at 1 to 1, and a member of the public could go to the Argentine central bank and exchange a peso for a dollar, or vice versa, at any time.

The early years of Argentina's currency board looked stunningly successful. Inflation, which was running at an 800% annual rate in 1990, fell to less than 5% by the end of 1994, and economic growth was rapid, averaging almost 8% per year from 1991 to 1994. In the aftermath of the Mexican peso crisis, however, concern about the health of the Argentine economy led the public to pull money out of the banks (deposits fell by 18%) and exchange pesos for dollars, thus causing a contraction of the Argentine money supply. The result was a sharp drop in Argentine economic activity, with real GDP shrinking by more than 5% in 1995 and the unemployment rate jumping above 15%. Only in 1996 did the economy begin to recover.

Because the central bank of Argentina had no control over monetary policy under the currency board system, it was virtually helpless to counteract the contractionary monetary effects stemming from the public's behavior. Furthermore, because the currency board did not allow the central bank to create pesos and lend them to the banks, it had very

little capability to act as a lender of last resort. With help from international agencies such as the IMF, the World Bank, and the Inter-American Development Bank, which lent Argentina more than $5 billion in 1995 to help shore up its banking system, the currency board survived.

In 1998, however, Argentina entered another recession, one that was both severe and very long-lasting. By the end of 2001, unemployment had reached nearly 20%, a level comparable to that experienced in the United States during the Great Depression of the 1930s. The result was civil unrest and the fall of the elected government, as well as a major banking crisis and a default on nearly $150 billion of government debt. Because the Central Bank of Argentina had no control over monetary policy under the currency board system, it was unable to use monetary policy to expand the economy and get Argentina out of its recession. In addition, because the currency board limited the central bank's ability to create pesos and act as a lender of last resort, the central bank was unable to help banks weather the banking crisis. In January 2002, the currency board finally collapsed, the peso depreciated by more than 70%, and inflation shot through the roof. The result was a full-scale financial crisis that led to an extremely severe depression. Clearly, the Argentine public is not as enamored of its currency board as it once was.*

*The Argentine financial crisis is described in detail in an additional chapter, "Financial Crises in Emerging Market Economies," which can be found in **MyLab Economics**.

Dollarization

Another solution to the transparency problem and doubts about commitment to the exchange-rate target is **dollarization**, the adoption of a sound currency, like the U.S. dollar, as a country's money. Indeed, dollarization is just another variant of a fixed exchange-rate target, but with an even stronger commitment mechanism than that provided by a currency board. A currency board can be abandoned, allowing a change in the value of the currency, but a change of value is impossible with dollarization: A dollar bill is always worth one dollar, whether it is held in the United States or outside it.

Dollarization has been advocated as a monetary policy strategy for emerging market countries: It was discussed actively by Argentine officials in the aftermath of the devaluation of the Brazilian real in January 1999 and was adopted by Ecuador in March 2000. Dollarization's key advantage is that it completely eliminates the possibility of a speculative attack on the domestic currency (because there is no such currency). (Such an attack is still a danger under a currency board arrangement.)

Dollarization is subject to the usual weaknesses of an exchange-rate target (the loss of an independent monetary policy, increased exposure of the economy to shocks from the anchor country, and the inability of the central bank to create money and act as a lender of last resort). Dollarization has one additional weakness not characteristic of currency boards or other exchange-rate target regimes. Because a country adopting dollarization no longer has its own currency, it loses the revenue that a government receives by issuing money, which is called **seignorage**. Because governments (or their central banks) do not have to pay interest on their domestic currency, they earn revenue (seignorage) by using this currency to purchase income-earning assets such as bonds. In the case of the Federal Reserve in the United States, this revenue is usually in excess of $30 billion per year. If an emerging market country dollarizes and gives up its currency, it needs to make up this loss of revenue somehow, and this is not always easy for a poor country.

SUMMARY

1. An unsterilized central bank intervention in which the domestic currency is sold to purchase foreign assets leads to a gain in international reserves, an increase in the money supply, and a depreciation of the domestic currency. Available evidence suggests, however, that sterilized central bank interventions have little long-term effect on the exchange rate.

2. The balance of payments is a bookkeeping system used to record all transactions between a country and foreign countries. The current account balance is the sum of the trade balance, net investment income, and transfers. A current account deficit is financed by the financial account balance, and so a current account deficit indicates that a country is becoming more indebted to foreigners.

3. Before World War I, the gold standard was predominant. Currencies were convertible into gold, thus fixing exchange rates between them. After World War II, the Bretton Woods system and the IMF were established to promote a fixed exchange rate system in which the U.S. dollar, the reserve currency, was convertible into gold. The Bretton Woods system collapsed in 1971. We now have an international financial system that has elements of a managed float and a fixed exchange rate system. Some exchange rates fluctuate from day to day, even though central banks intervene in the foreign exchange market, while other exchange rates are fixed.

4. Controls on capital outflows receive support because they may prevent domestic residents and foreigners from pulling capital out of a country during a crisis and thereby make devaluation less likely. Controls on capital inflows make sense under the theory that, if speculative capital cannot flow in, then it also cannot go out suddenly. Thus a crisis is averted. However, capital controls suffer from several disadvantages: They are seldom effective, they often lead to corruption, and they may encourage governments to avoid taking the steps that are necessary to reform their financial systems to deal with the crisis.

5. The IMF's role as an international lender of last resort can help lessen the severity of financial crises. However, the IMF's role as an international lender of last resort also creates serious moral hazard problems because it encourages governments to be profligate and also encourages excessive risk taking by financial institutions, making a financial crisis more likely.

6. Two international considerations affect the conduct of monetary policy: direct effects of the foreign exchange market on monetary policy and exchange rate

considerations. Inasmuch as the United States has been a reserve currency country in the post–World War II period, U.S. monetary policy has been less affected than that of other countries by developments in the foreign exchange market. However, in recent years, exchange rate considerations have played a more prominent role in influencing U.S. monetary policy.

7. Exchange-rate targeting has the following advantages as a monetary policy strategy: (1) It directly keeps inflation under control by tying the inflation rate for internationally traded goods to that found in the anchor country to which the targeting country's currency is pegged; (2) it provides an automatic rule for the conduct of monetary policy that helps mitigate the time-inconsistency problem; and (3) it is simple and clear. Exchange-rate targeting also has some serious disadvantages: (1) It results in a loss of independent monetary policy in the pegging country; (2) it leaves the pegging country open to speculative attacks; and (3) it can weaken the accountability of policymakers because the exchange rate signal is lost. Two strategies that make it less likely that exchange-rate targeting will break down are currency boards, in which the central bank stands ready to automatically exchange domestic currency for foreign currency at a fixed rate, and dollarization, in which a sound currency like the U.S. dollar is adopted as a country's money.

KEY TERMS

anchor currency, p. 431
balance of payments, p. 429
Bretton Woods system, p. 432
capital controls, p. 438
capital mobility, p. 434
currency board, p. 447
current account, p. 430
current account balance, p. 430
devaluation, p. 434
dollarization, p. 448
emerging market countries, p. 440
exchange-rate peg, p. 443
exchange-rate targeting, p. 443
financial account, p. 430

financial account balance, p. 430
fixed exchange rate regime, p. 431
floating exchange rate regime, p. 431
foreign exchange interventions, p. 425
gold standard, p. 432
impossible trinity, p. 437
International Monetary Fund (IMF), p. 432
international reserves, p. 425
managed float regime (dirty float), p. 431
monetary (or currency) union, p. 438
net exports, p. 430
policy trilemma, p. 437

reserve currency, p. 433
revaluation, p. 434
seignorage, p. 449
speculative attack, p. 435
sterilized foreign exchange intervention, p. 428
trade balance on goods and services (trade balance), p. 430
unsterilized foreign exchange intervention, p. 427
World Bank, p. 432
World Trade Organization (WTO), p. 432

QUESTIONS

1. If the Federal Reserve sells dollars in the foreign exchange market but conducts an offsetting open market operation to sterilize the intervention, what will be the effect on international reserves, the money supply, and the exchange rate?

2. If the Federal Reserve buys dollars in the foreign exchange market but does not sterilize the intervention, what will be the impact on international reserves, the money supply, and the exchange rate?

3. For each of the following, identify whether they increase or decrease the current account balance:

a. An American citizen's purchase of an airline ticket from Air France

b. A Japanese citizen's purchase of California oranges

c. $50 million of foreign aid to Honduras

d. A worker in California who sends money to his parents in Mexico

e. The services an American accounting firm provides to a German firm

4. Suppose that you travel to Cali (Colombia), where the exchange rate is 1 USD to 2,900 Colombian pesos. As

you enter a McDonald's restaurant, you realize you need 17,400 Colombian pesos to buy a Big Mac. Assuming a Big Mac sells for $5 in the United States, would you say that the Colombian peso is over- or undervalued in terms of PPP?

5. Refer to the previous exercise. Which type of foreign market intervention must the central bank of Colombia conduct to keep the exchange rate at a level where the currency is not under- or overvalued in terms of PPP?

6. What would be the effect of a devaluation on a country's imports and exports? If a country imports most of the goods included in the basket of goods and services used to calculate the CPI, what do you think the effect will be on this country's inflation rate?

7. Under the gold standard, if Britain became more productive relative to the United States, what would happen to the money supply in the two countries? Why would the changes in the money supply help preserve a fixed exchange rate between the United States and Britain?

8. What is the exchange rate between dollars and Swiss francs if one dollar is convertible into 1/20 ounce of gold, and one Swiss franc is convertible into 1/40 ounce of gold?

9. "Inflation is not possible under the gold standard." Is this statement true, false, or uncertain? Explain your answer.

10. What are some of the disadvantages of China's pegging the yuan to the dollar?

11. If a country's par exchange rate was undervalued during the Bretton Woods fixed exchange rate regime, what kind of intervention would that country's central bank be forced to undertake, and what effect would the intervention have on the country's international reserves and money supply?

12. Why might a country that is suffering a recession not want to intervene in the foreign exchange market if its currency is overvalued? Assume this country participates in a fixed exchange rate regime.

13. "If a country wants to keep its exchange rate from changing, it must give up some control over its monetary policy." Is this statement true, false, or uncertain? Explain your answer.

14. Why is it that in a pure, flexible exchange rate system, the foreign exchange market has no direct effect on the money supply? Does this mean that the foreign exchange market has no effect on monetary policy?

15. Why did the exchange-rate peg lead to difficulties for the countries in the ERM after the German reunification?

16. How can exchange-rate targets lead to a speculative attack on a currency?

17. The IMF does not enjoy a great reputation in many countries that were recipients of IMF loans or bailouts. Explain why many citizens were not happy with the role played by the IMF.

18. How can the long-term bond market help reduce the time-inconsistency problem for monetary policy? Can the foreign exchange market also perform this role?

19. What are the key advantages of exchange-rate targeting as a monetary policy strategy?

20. When is exchange-rate targeting likely to be a sensible strategy for industrialized countries? When is exchange-rate targeting likely to be a sensible strategy for emerging market countries?

21. What are the advantages and disadvantages of currency boards and dollarization over a monetary policy that uses only an exchange-rate target?

APPLIED PROBLEMS

22. Calculate the overvaluation of the Thai baht (THB) if you can get 34.6 THB per USD at the exchange counter, but a lunch menu that costs 25 USD in Boston sells for 948.25 THB in Bangkok.

23. Suppose the Federal Reserve purchases $1,000,000 worth of foreign assets.

a. If the Federal Reserve purchases the foreign assets with $1,000,000 in currency, show the effect of this open market operation, using T-accounts. What happens to the monetary base?

b. If the Federal Reserve purchases the foreign assets by selling $1,000,000 in T-bills, show the effect of this open market operation, using T-accounts. What happens to the monetary base?

24. Suppose the Mexican central bank chooses to peg the peso to the U.S. dollar and commits to a fixed peso/dollar exchange rate. Use a graph of the market for peso assets (foreign exchange) to show and explain how the peg must be maintained if a shock in the U.S. economy forces the Fed to pursue contractionary monetary policy. What does this say about the ability of central banks to address domestic economic problems while maintaining a pegged exchange rate?

DATA ANALYSIS PROBLEMS

The Problems update with real-time data in **MyLab Economics** and are available for practice or instructor assignment.

1. **Real-time Data Analysis** Go to the St. Louis Federal Reserve FRED database, and find data on net exports (NETEXP), transfers (A123RC1Q027SBEA), and the current account balance (NETFI).

    a. Calculate net investment income for the most recent quarter available, and for the same quarter a year earlier.

    b. Calculate the percentage change in the current account balance from the same quarter one year earlier. Which one of the three items making up the current account balance had the largest effect in percentage terms on the change of the current account? Which one had the smallest effect?

2. **Real-time Data Analysis** Go to the St. Louis Federal Reserve FRED database, and find data on the monthly U.S. dollar exchange rate to the Chinese yuan (EXCHUS), the Canadian dollar (EXCAUS), and the South Korean won (EXKOUS). Download the data into a spreadsheet.

    a. For the most recent five-year period of data available, use the average, max, min, and stdev functions in Excel to calculate the average, highest, and lowest exchange rate values, as well as the standard deviation of the exchange rate to the dollar (this is an absolute measure of the volatility of the exchange rate).

    b. Using the maximum and minimum values of each exchange rate over the past five years, calculate the ratio of the difference between the maximum and minimum values to the average level of the exchange rate (expressed as a percentage by multiplying by 100). This value gives an indication of how tightly the exchange rate moves. Based on your results, which of the three countries is most likely to peg its currency to the U.S. dollar? How does this country's currency compare with the other two?

    c. Calculate the ratio of the standard deviation to the average exchange rate over the past five years (expressed as a percentage by multiplying by 100). This value gives an indication of how volatile the exchange rate is. Based on your results, which of the three currencies is most likely to be pegged to the U.S. dollar? How does this currency compare with the other two?

Monetary Theory

Crisis and Response: The Great Recession and the Coronavirus Recession

In 2007 and 2008, the U.S. economy was hit by a perfect storm of formidable shocks. By the end of 2007, oil prices had risen from $60 per barrel at the beginning of the year to $100, reaching a peak of over $140 per barrel in July 2008. The oil price shock was both contractionary and inflationary, and as a result led to both higher inflation and higher unemployment—not to mention many unhappy drivers at the gas pumps. If this supply shock were not bad enough, the global financial crisis hit the economy starting in August 2007 and caused a contraction in both household and business spending. This shock led to a further rise in unemployment, with some weakening of inflationary pressure further down the road.

The result of this perfect storm of adverse shocks was the most severe economic contraction since the Great Depression, now named the Great Recession, with unemployment rising from the 4.6% level in 2006 and 2007 to the 10% level by the end of 2009. Inflation also accelerated from 2.5% in 2006 to over 5% by the middle of 2008, but with the increase in the unemployment rate and the decline of oil and other commodity prices by the fall of 2008, inflation rapidly came back down again.

The U.S. economy was hit by an even larger adverse shock in March 2020, when the coronavirus pandemic led to massive lockdowns. Not only was there a dramatic cut in production, but also household and business spending collapsed. The result was that from February 2020 to April 2020, the unemployment rate rose from 3½ percent to almost 15%, a far higher level than it reached in 2009. With the collapse of oil prices and the rise in unemployment, inflation fell from around the 2% level before the pandemic to less than 0.5% in April.

Both recessions led to aggressive monetary policy actions to address the contractionary forces in the economy, with the Federal Reserve cutting its policy rate, the federal funds rate, to zero, while also creating new lending programs to shore up both financial institutions and businesses. The federal government also took actions to stabilize the economy by implementing massive fiscal stimulus packages of close to a trillion dollars in 2008–2009 and then over $3 trillion in 2020. Although these stimulus packages helped boost GDP, however, they were overwhelmed by the negative shocks from the global financial crisis and the coronavirus pandemic, so in both instances the economy went into a tailspin.

The impact of adverse shocks highlights the need to understand how monetary and other government policies affect inflation and economic activity. Chapter 19 discusses how the quantity theory of money explains inflation in the long run and how theories of the demand for money have evolved. Aggregate supply and demand analysis, the basic framework that will enable us to study the effects of monetary policy on output and inflation, is then developed in Chapters 20–23. In Chapter 24, we expand on aggregate supply and demand analysis to understand how monetary policy can be used to stabilize the economy and inflation. Chapter 25 outlines the transmission mechanisms through which monetary policy affects the aggregate economy.

19 Quantity Theory, Inflation, and the Demand for Money

Learning Objectives

19.1 Assess the relationship between money growth and inflation in the short run and the long run, as implied by the quantity theory of money.

19.2 Identify the circumstances under which budget deficits can lead to inflationary monetary policy.

19.3 Summarize the three motives underlying the liquidity preference theory of money demand.

19.4 Identify the factors underlying the portfolio choice theory of money demand.

19.5 Assess and interpret the empirical evidence on the validity of the liquidity preference and portfolio theories of money demand.

Preview

In earlier chapters, we spent a lot of time and effort learning what the money supply is, how it is determined, and what part the Federal Reserve System plays in it. Now we are ready to explore the role of the money supply and monetary policy in determining inflation and total production of goods and services (aggregate output) in the economy. The study of the effects of money and monetary policy on the economy is called **monetary theory**, and we examine this branch of economics in the chapters of Part 6.

When economists mention *supply*, the word *demand* is sure to follow, and the discussion of money is no exception. Understanding the supply of money is an essential building block in understanding how monetary policy affects the economy, because understanding the supply of money suggests the factors that influence the quantity of money in the economy. Not surprisingly, another essential part of monetary theory is the demand for money.

After discussing the quantity theory of money and its link to the demand for money, we delve more deeply into the factors that determine the demand for money. A central question in monetary theory is whether or to what extent the quantity of money demanded is affected by changes in interest rates. Because this issue is crucial to how we view money's effects on aggregate economic activity, we will focus on the role of interest rates in the demand for money.

19.1 QUANTITY THEORY OF MONEY

LO 19.1 Assess the relationship between money growth and inflation in the short run and the long run, as implied by the quantity theory of money.

Developed by the classical economists in the nineteenth and early twentieth centuries, the quantity theory of money explains how the nominal value of aggregate income is determined. Because the theory also tells us how much money is held for a given amount of aggregate income, it is a theory of the demand for money. The most important feature of this theory is that it suggests that interest rates have no effect on the demand for money.

Velocity of Money and Equation of Exchange

The clearest exposition of the classical quantity theory approach is found in the work of the American economist Irving Fisher, in his influential book *The Purchasing Power of Money*, published in 1911. Fisher wanted to examine the link between the total quantity of money M (the money supply) and the total amount of spending on final goods and services produced in the economy $P \times Y$, where P is the price level and Y is aggregate output (income). (Total spending $P \times Y$ is also thought of as aggregate nominal income for the economy or as nominal GDP.) The concept that provides the link between M and $P \times Y$ is called the **velocity of money** (often abbreviated to *velocity*), the average number of times per year (turnover) that a dollar is spent in buying the total amount of goods and services produced in the economy. Velocity V is defined more precisely as total spending $P \times Y$ divided by the quantity of money M:

$$V = \frac{P \times Y}{M} \tag{1}$$

If, for example, nominal GDP $(P \times Y)$ in a year is \$10 trillion and the quantity of money (M) is \$2 trillion, we can calculate velocity as follows:

$$V = \frac{\$10 \text{ trillion}}{\$2 \text{ trillion}} = 5$$

The value of 5 for velocity means that the average dollar is spent five times in purchasing final goods and services in the economy.

By multiplying both sides of Equation 1 by M, we obtain the **equation of exchange**, which relates nominal income to the quantity of money and velocity:

$$M \times V = P \times Y \tag{2}$$

The equation of exchange thus states that the quantity of money multiplied by the number of times this money is spent in a given year must equal nominal income (the total nominal amount spent on goods and services in that year).[1]

As it stands, Equation 2 is nothing more than an identity—a relationship that is true by definition. It does not tell us, for instance, that when the money supply M changes, nominal income $(P \times Y)$ changes in the same direction; a rise in M, for example, might be offset by a fall in V, leaving $M \times V$ (and therefore $P \times Y$) unchanged. To convert the equation of exchange (an *identity*) into a *theory* of how nominal income is determined, we must first understand the factors that determine velocity.

Determinants of Velocity Irving Fisher reasoned that velocity is determined by the institutions within an economy that affect the ways in which individuals conduct transactions. If people use charge accounts and credit cards to conduct their transactions, as they often do today, and consequently use money less often when making purchases, less money is required to conduct the transactions generated by nominal income (M falls relative to $P \times Y$), and so velocity $(P \times Y)/M$ increases. Conversely, if it is more convenient for purchases to be paid for with cash, checks, or debit cards

---

[1]Fisher actually first formulated the equation of exchange in terms of the nominal value of transactions in the economy PT:

$$MV_T = PT$$

where
$$P = \text{average price per transaction}$$
$$T = \text{number of transactions conducted in a year}$$
$$V_T = PT/M = \text{transactions velocity of money}$$

Because the nominal value of transactions T is difficult to measure, the quantity theory has been formulated in terms of aggregate output Y as follows: T is assumed to be proportional to Y so that $T = vY$, where v is a constant of proportionality. Substituting vY for T in Fisher's equation of exchange yields $MV_T = vPY$, which can be written as Equation 2 in the text, in which $V = V_T/v$.

(all of which are money), more money is used to conduct the transactions generated by the same level of nominal income, and so velocity falls. Fisher took the view that the institutional and technological features of the economy would affect velocity only slowly over time, so velocity would normally be reasonably constant in the short run.

Demand for Money   Fisher's quantity theory can also be interpreted in terms of the **demand for money**, the quantity of money that people want to hold.

Because the quantity theory of money tells us how much money is held for a given amount of nominal spending, it is, in fact, a theory of the demand for money. To illustrate, let's first divide both sides of the equation of exchange (Equation 2) by V to yield the following:

$$M = \frac{1}{V} \times PY$$

When the money market is in equilibrium, money supply equals money demand, so we can replace M in the equation by M^d. In addition, since velocity is assumed to be constant in the quantity theory of money, we can replace $1/V$ with a constant k. Substituting k for $1/V$ and M^d for M, we can rewrite the equation as

$$M^d = k \times PY \tag{3}$$

Equation 3 tells us that because k is constant, the level of transactions generated by a fixed level of nominal income PY determines the quantity of money M^d that people will demand. Therefore, Fisher's theory suggests that the demand for money is purely a function of income, and interest rates have no effect on the demand for money.[2]

From the Equation of Exchange to the Quantity Theory of Money

Fisher's view that velocity is fairly constant in the short run, so that $V = \overline{V}$, transforms the equation of exchange into the **quantity theory of money**, which states that nominal income (spending) is determined solely by movements in the quantity of money M.

$$P \times Y = M \times \overline{V} \tag{4}$$

The quantity theory equation above indicates that when the quantity of money M doubles, $M \times \overline{V}$ doubles, and so must $P \times Y$, the value of nominal income. To illustrate, let's assume that velocity is 5, nominal income (GDP) is initially $10 trillion, and the money supply is $2 trillion. If the money supply doubles to $4 trillion, the quantity theory of money suggests that nominal income will double to $20 trillion ($= 5 \times \$4$ trillion).

Quantity Theory and the Price Level

Because the classical economists (including Fisher) thought that wages and prices were completely flexible, they believed that the level of aggregate output Y produced in the economy during normal times would remain at the full-employment level. Hence Y in the equation of exchange could be treated as reasonably constant in the short run and

[2]While Fisher was developing his quantity theory approach to the demand for money, a group of classical economists in Cambridge, England, led by Alfred Marshall and A. C. Pigou, came to similar conclusions, although via slightly different reasoning. They derived Equation 3 by recognizing that two properties of money motivate people to hold it: its utility as a medium of exchange, and its value as a store of wealth.

thus could be assigned a fixed value of $\overline{Y}$ in Equation 4. Dividing both sides of Equation 4 by $\overline{Y}$, we can write the price level as follows:

$$P = \frac{M \times \overline{V}}{\overline{Y}} \tag{5}$$

The quantity theory of money as represented by Equation 5 implies that if M doubles, P must also double in the short run, because $\overline{V}$ and $\overline{Y}$ are constant. In our example, if aggregate output is \$10 trillion, velocity is 5, and the money supply is \$2 trillion, then the price level equals 1.0.

$$P = \frac{\$2 \text{ trillion} \times 5}{\$10 \text{ trillion}} = \frac{\$10 \text{ trillion}}{\$10 \text{ trillion}} = 1.0$$

When the money supply doubles to \$4 trillion, the price level must also double, to 2.0, because

$$P = \frac{\$4 \text{ trillion} \times 5}{\$10 \text{ trillion}} = \frac{\$20 \text{ trillion}}{\$10 \text{ trillion}} = 2.0$$

Classical economists relied on the quantity theory of money to explain movements in the price level. In their view, **changes in the quantity of money lead to proportional changes in the price level.**

Quantity Theory and Inflation

We now transform the quantity theory of money into a theory of inflation. You might recall from high school the mathematical fact that the percentage change ($\%\Delta$) of a product of two variables is approximately equal to the sum of the percentage changes of the individual variables. In other words,

$$\text{percentage change in } (x \times y) = (\text{percentage change in } x)$$
$$+ (\text{percentage change in } y)$$

Using this mathematical fact, we can rewrite the equation of exchange as follows:

$$\%\Delta M + \%\Delta V = \%\Delta P + \%\Delta Y$$

Subtracting $\%\Delta Y$ from both sides of the preceding equation, and recognizing that the inflation rate π is equal to the growth rate of the price level $\%\Delta P$, we can write:

$$\pi - \%\Delta P = \%\Delta M + \%\Delta V - \%\Delta Y$$

Since we assume velocity is constant, its growth rate is zero, and so the quantity theory of money is also a theory of inflation:

$$\pi = \%\Delta M - \%\Delta Y \tag{6}$$

Because the percentage change in a variable at an annual rate is the same as the growth rate of that variable, Equation 6 can be stated in words as follows: **The quantity theory**

Real-time data

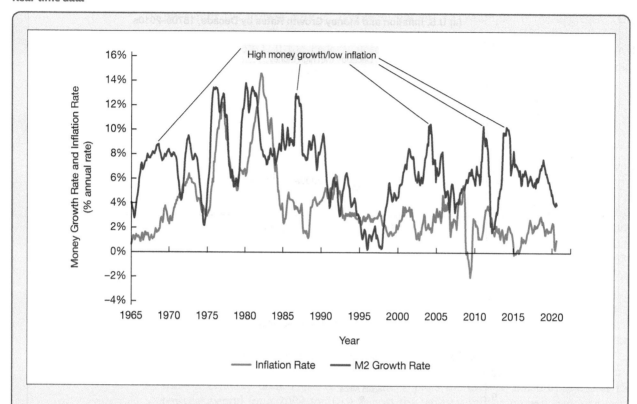

FIGURE 2 **Annual U.S. Inflation and Money Growth Rates, 1965–2019**

Plots of the annual U.S. inflation rate against the annual money (M2) growth rate from two years earlier (to allow for lag effects from money growth to inflation) do not support a short-run link between inflation and money growth. There were many years (1963–1967, 1983–1985, 2003–2005, 2010–2011, and 2013–2015) in which money growth was high yet inflation was low.

Source: Federal Reserve Bank of St. Louis, FRED database: https://fred.stlouisfed.org/series/CPIAUCSL; https://fred.stlouisfed.org/series/M2SL.

19.2 BUDGET DEFICITS AND INFLATION

LO 19.2 Identify the circumstances under which budget deficits can lead to inflationary monetary policy.

Budget deficits can be an important source of inflationary monetary policy. To see why this is the case, we need to look at the ways in which a government finances its budget deficits.

Government Budget Constraint

Because the government has to pay its bills just as we do, it has a budget constraint. We can pay for our spending in two ways: We can raise revenue (by working), or we can borrow. The government also enjoys these two options: It can raise revenue by levying taxes, or it can go into debt by issuing government bonds. Unlike us, however, it has a third option: The government can create money and use it to pay for the goods and services it buys.

The methods used to finance government spending are described by an expression called the **government budget constraint**, which states the following: The government budget deficit *DEF*, which equals the excess of government spending *G* over tax revenue *T*, must equal the sum of the change in the monetary base ΔMB and the change in government bonds held by the public ΔB. Algebraically, this expression can be written as follows:

$$DEF = G - T = \Delta MB + \Delta B \tag{7}$$

To see what the government budget constraint means in practice, let's look at the case in which the only government purchase is a $100 million supercomputer. If the government convinces the electorate that such a computer is worth paying for, it will probably be able to raise the $100 million in taxes to pay for it, and the budget deficit will equal zero. According to the government budget constraint, no issue of money or bonds is needed to pay for the computer because the budget is balanced. If taxpayers think the supercomputer is too expensive and refuse to pay taxes to sponsor its purchase, the budget constraint indicates that the government must pay for the computer by selling $100 million of new bonds to the public or by, in effect, printing $100 million of currency. In either case, the budget constraint is satisfied. The $100 million deficit is balanced by the change in the stock of government bonds held by the public ($\Delta B = \$100$ million) or by the change in the monetary base ($\Delta MB = \$100$ million).

The government budget constraint thus reveals two important facts: *If the government deficit is financed by an increase in bond holdings by the public, there is no effect on the monetary base and hence no effect on the money supply. But if the deficit is not financed by increased bond holdings by the public, both the monetary base and the money supply increase*.

There are several ways to understand why a deficit leads to an increase in the monetary base when the public's bond holdings do not increase. The simplest case is the case in which a government's treasury has the legal right to issue currency to finance its deficit. Financing the deficit is then very straightforward: The government just pays for the spending that is in excess of its tax revenues by issuing new currency. Because this increase in currency adds directly to the monetary base, the monetary base rises, and the money supply rises with it through the process of multiple deposit creation described in Chapter 14.

In the United States, however, and in many other countries, the government does not have the right to issue currency to pay for its bills. In this case, the government must finance its deficit by first issuing bonds to the public. If these bonds do not actually end up in the hands of the public, however, the only alternative is for the central bank to purchase them. To keep the newly issued government bonds from ending up in the hands of the public, the central bank must conduct an open market purchase, which, as we saw in Chapter 14, leads to an increase in the monetary base and in the money supply through the process of multiple deposit creation. This method of financing government spending is called **monetizing the debt** because, as indicated by the two-step process just described, government debt issued to finance government spending has been removed from the hands of the public and has been

FYI   Modern Monetary Theory

Modern Monetary Theory argues that the Green New Deal can be easily paid for by having the Federal Reserve buy government bonds to fund the resulting large budget deficits. As our analysis here suggests, Modern Monetary Theory is correct that the large budget deficit resulting from a large increase in government spending can be paid for by a central bank's purchases of government bonds. However, it ignores that this financing of a persistent budget deficit by a central bank's purchase of government bonds leads to an expansion in the money supply. The result of massive government spending financed by central bank purchases of government bonds can thus be very rapid growth of the money supply. As the quantity theory of money indicates, this very rapid

growth of the money supply would then cause very high inflation.

Financing of the Green New Deal by the Fed's purchase of government bonds would thus not be "free" because it would likely result in very high inflation. Most mainstream economists, even those on the left, such as Paul Krugman, have rejected Modern Monetary Theory along the lines discussed above. Their criticisms are much in keeping with the economics adage "There is no such thing as a free lunch." A Green New Deal would need to be paid for by higher taxes at some point in the future if inflation is to be avoided, and so should be evaluated on whether it is productive spending that will pay for itself or have sufficient benefits for the society that make it worth the cost.

replaced by high-powered money. This method of financing is somewhat inaccurately referred to as **printing money** because high-powered money (the monetary base) is created in the process. The use of the word *printing* is misleading because no new currency is actually printed; instead, the monetary base increases when the central bank conducts open market purchases, just as it would increase if more currency were put into circulation.

We thus see that a budget deficit can lead to an increase in the money supply if it is financed by the creation of high-powered money. However, because the quantity theory of money explains inflation only in the long run, in order to produce inflation, the budget deficit must be *persistent*—that is, it must last for a substantial period of time. This leads us to the following conclusion: ***The financing of a persistent deficit by means of money creation will lead to sustained inflation.***

Progressives from the Democratic Party have recently proposed a "Green New Deal," a massive government spending program to cope with climate change and economic inequality. They have argued that a new theory referred to as *Modern Monetary Theory* (discussed in the FYI box, "Modern Monetary Theory") makes it easy to pay for the Green New Deal.

Hyperinflation

The analysis here can be used to explain **hyperinflations**, periods of extremely high inflation of more than 50% per month. Many economies—both poor and developed—have experienced hyperinflation over the past century, but the United States has been spared such turmoil. One of the most extreme examples of hyperinflation throughout world history occurred in Zimbabwe in the 2000s, and it is discussed in the application that follows.

APPLICATION   The Zimbabwean Hyperinflation

We now use our analysis of the quantity theory of money to explain the Zimbabwean hyperinflation that started in the early 2000s.

After the government expropriation of farms in 2000, which were redistributed to supporters of Robert Mugabe, the president of the country, Zimbabwean agricultural output plummeted and, along with it, tax revenue. As a result, the government's expenditures now massively exceeded revenues. The government could have obtained revenues to cover its expenditures by raising taxes, but given the depressed state of the economy, generating revenue in this way was both hard to do and would have been politically unpopular. Alternatively, the government could have tried to finance its expenditure by borrowing from the public, but given the public's distrust of the government, this was not an option. There was only one route left: the printing press. The government could pay for its expenditures by simply printing more currency (increasing the money supply) and using it to make payments to individuals and businesses. This is exactly what the Zimbabwean government did, and the money supply began to increase rapidly.

As predicted by the quantity theory, the surge in the money supply led to a rapidly rising price level. In February 2007, the Reserve Bank of Zimbabwe, the central bank, outlawed price increases on many commodities. Although this tactic has been tried before by governments in countries experiencing hyperinflations, it has never worked: Criminalizing inflation cannot stop inflation when the central bank keeps on printing money. In March 2007, the inflation rate hit a record of over 1,500%. By 2008, Zimbabwe's official inflation rate was officially over 2 million percent (but unofficially over 10 million percent). In July 2008, the Zimbabwean central bank issued a new $100 billion bank note and shortly later issued a $100 trillion dollar bill, the highest denomination dollar note on record. That's a lot of zeros, but don't be too impressed. Although holding one of these bills made you a trillionaire, such a bill could not even buy you a bottle of beer. Zimbabwean currency became worth less than toilet paper.

In 2009, the Zimbabwean government allowed the use of foreign currencies like the U.S. dollar for all transactions, but the damage had already been done. The hyperinflation wreaked havoc on the economy, and an extremely poor country became even poorer. ◆

19.3 KEYNESIAN THEORIES OF MONEY DEMAND

LO 19.3 Summarize the three motives underlying the liquidity preference theory of money demand.

In his famous 1936 book *The General Theory of Employment, Interest and Money*, John Maynard Keynes abandoned the quantity theory view that velocity is a constant and developed a theory of money demand that emphasized the importance of interest rates. In his theory of the demand for money, which he called the **liquidity preference theory**, Keynes presented three motives behind the demand for money: the transactions motive, the precautionary motive, and the speculative motive.

Transactions Motive

In the quantity theory approach, individuals are assumed to hold money because it is a medium of exchange that can be used to carry out everyday transactions. Keynes initially accepted the quantity theory view that the transactions component is proportional to income. Later, he and other economists recognized that new methods of payment, referred to as **payment technology**, could also affect the demand for money. For example, credit cards enable consumers to make even very small purchases without needing to hold money. Electronic payments that can be made from investors' brokerage accounts also reduce money demand. In Keynes's view, as payment technology advanced, the demand for money would be likely to decline relative to income.

Precautionary Motive

Keynes also recognized that people hold money as a cushion against unexpected opportunities. Suppose you have been thinking about buying a new Xbox gaming console and now see that it is on sale at 25% off. If you are holding money as a precaution for just such an occurrence, you can immediately buy it. Keynes argued that the precautionary money balances people would want to hold would also be proportional to income.

Speculative Motive

Keynes also believed that people choose to hold money as a store of wealth, which he called the *speculative motive*. Because the definition of money in Keynes's analysis includes currency (which earns no interest) and checking account deposits (which typically earn little interest), he assumed that money earns no interest and hence its opportunity cost relative to holding other assets, such as bonds, is the nominal interest rate on bonds, i. As the interest rate i rises, the opportunity cost of money rises (it becomes more costly to hold money relative to bonds), and the quantity of money demanded falls.

Putting the Three Motives Together

In combining the three motives for holding money balances into a demand-for-money equation, Keynes was careful to distinguish between nominal quantities and real quantities. Money is valued in terms of what it can buy. If, for example, all prices in the economy doubled (the price level doubled), the same nominal quantity of money would be able to buy only half as many goods. Keynes thus reasoned that people want to hold a certain amount of **real money balances** (the quantity of money in real terms). By combining the three motives for holding money balances into a demand for real money balances, Keynes formulated what is called the liquidity preference function, which is written as follows:

$$\frac{M^d}{P} = L(\underset{-}{i}, \underset{+}{Y}) \tag{8}$$

Equation 8 states that the demand for real money balances is negatively related to the nominal interest rate and is positively related to real income.

Later Keynesian economists, such as Nobel Prize winner James Tobin, expanded the analysis and showed that interest rates play a more important role in money demand than even Keynes supposed. These economists demonstrated that even the transactions and precautionary demands for money would be negatively related to the interest rate.[3]

An important implication of Keynesian theories of money demand is that velocity is not a constant but will fluctuate with changes in interest rates. To illustrate, we write the liquidity preference function as follows:

$$\frac{P}{M^d} = \frac{1}{L(i, Y)}$$

Multiplying both sides of this equation by Y and recognizing that we can replace M^d by M (because they must be equal in money market equilibrium), we can solve for velocity:

$$V = \frac{PY}{M} = \frac{Y}{L(i, Y)} \tag{9}$$

We know that the demand for money is negatively related to interest rates; when i goes up, $L(i, Y)$ declines, and therefore velocity rises. Because interest rates undergo substantial fluctuations, Keynesian theories of the demand for money indicate that velocity undergoes substantial fluctuations as well. Thus Keynesian theories cast doubt on the classical quantity theory view that nominal income is determined primarily by movements in the quantity of money.

19.4 PORTFOLIO THEORIES OF MONEY DEMAND

LO 19.4 Identify the factors underlying the portfolio choice theory of money demand.

Related to Keynes's analysis of the demand for money are so-called portfolio theories of money demand, in which people decide how much of an asset such as money they want to hold as part of their overall portfolio of assets.[4]

Theory of Portfolio Choice and Keynesian Liquidity Preference

In Chapter 5, we developed the theory of portfolio choice, which stated that the demand for an asset is positively related to wealth, the expected return on the asset relative to other assets, and relative liquidity, whereas it is negatively related to its risk relative to other assets. This theory of portfolio choice can justify the conclusion from the Keynesian liquidity preference function that the demand for real money balances is positively related to income and negatively related to the nominal interest rate.

Because income and wealth tend to move together, when income is higher, wealth is likely to be as well. Hence, higher income means greater wealth, and the theory of

---

[3] Three famous papers that elaborated on Keynes's approach to the demand for money are as follows: William J. Baumol, "The Transactions Demand for Cash: An Inventory Theoretic Approach," *Quarterly Journal of Economics* 66 (1952): 545–556; James Tobin, "The Interest Elasticity of the Transactions Demand for Cash," *Review of Economics and Statistics* 38 (1956): 241–247; and James Tobin, "Liquidity Preference as Behavior Towards Risk," *Review of Economic Studies* 25 (1958): 65–86.

[4] This is the approach taken by Milton Friedman in his famous paper "The Quantity Theory of Money: A Restatement," in *Studies in the Quantity Theory of Money*, ed. Milton Friedman (Chicago: University of Chicago Press, 1956), 3–21.

portfolio choice then indicates that the demand for the money assets will rise and the demand for real money balances will be higher.

As interest rates rise, the expected return on money does not change. However, the return on bonds, an alternative asset, goes up. Thus, although the expected *absolute* return on money did not change, money's expected return *relative* to bonds went down. In other words, as the theory of portfolio choice indicates, higher interest rates make money less desirable, and the demand for real money balances falls.

Other Factors That Affect the Demand for Money

The theory of portfolio choice indicates that other factors besides income and the nominal interest rate can affect the demand for money. We look at each of these in turn.

Wealth The theory of portfolio choice posits that as wealth increases, investors have more resources with which to purchase assets, increasing the demand for money. However, when income is held constant, greater wealth has only a small effect on the demand for money. In general, investors will hold only a small amount of money in their investment portfolio, preferring interest-bearing assets with similar risk and liquidity profiles, such as money market mutual funds, that are not included in measures of money such as M1. Currency and checkable deposits are sometimes said to be **dominated assets** because investors can hold other assets that pay higher returns and yet are perceived to be just as safe.

Risk It's hard to imagine an asset less risky than money. Currency will always be accepted, unless there's a revolution and the new government does not accept the old government's currency. And bank deposits are safe as long as deposit insurance exists. In the theory of portfolio choice, however, risk is always measured relative to another asset. Thus, if the stock market becomes more volatile, money can become less risky relative to stocks and demand for it will increase. In addition, although money is extremely safe on a nominal basis, its real return (the nominal return minus expected inflation) can become highly variable when inflation becomes very variable. Higher variability in the real return of money lowers the demand for money, as people shift into alternative assets known as **inflation hedges**, whose real returns are less affected than that of money when inflation varies. Popular inflation hedges include TIPS (Treasury Inflation Protected Securities), gold, and real estate.

Liquidity of Other Assets In recent years, financial innovation has led to the development of new liquid assets, such as money market mutual funds or home equity lines of credit that allow households to write checks that are backed by their homes. As these alternative assets become more liquid, the relative liquidity of money falls, and so the demand for money falls as well.

Summary

Our analysis of the demand for money using Keynesian and portfolio theories indicates that seven factors affect the demand for money: interest rates, income, payment technology, wealth, riskiness of other assets, inflation risk, and liquidity of other assets. As a study aid, Summary Table 1 indicates the response of money demand to changes in each of these factors and gives a brief synopsis of the reasoning behind each response.

SUMMARY TABLE 1			
Factors That Determine the Demand for Money			
Variable	**Change in Variable**	**Money Demand Response**	**Reason**
Interest rates	↑	↓	Opportunity cost of money rises
Income	↑	↑	Higher value of transactions
Payment technology	↑	↓	Less need for money in transactions
Wealth	↑	↑	More resources to put into money
Riskiness of other assets	↑	↑	Money relatively less risky and so more desirable
Inflation risk	↑	↓	Money relatively more risky and so less desirable
Liquidity of other assets	↑	↓	Money relatively less liquid and so less desirable

Note: Only increases (↑) in the factors are shown; the effects of decreases in the variables on the exchange rate are the opposite of those indicated in the "Response" column.

19.5 EMPIRICAL EVIDENCE ON THE DEMAND FOR MONEY

LO 19.5 Assess and interpret the empirical evidence on the validity of the liquidity preference and portfolio theories of money demand.

Here we examine the empirical evidence on the two key issues that distinguish different theories of money demand and affect their conclusions about whether the quantity of money is the primary determinant of aggregate spending: Is the demand for money sensitive to changes in interest rates, and is the demand-for-money function stable over time?

Interest Rates and Money Demand

We have established that if interest rates do not affect the demand for money, velocity is more likely to be constant—or at least predictable—and so the quantity theory view that aggregate spending is determined by the quantity of money is more likely to be true. However, the more sensitive to interest rates the demand for money is, the more unpredictable velocity will be, and the less clear the link between the money supply and aggregate spending becomes. Indeed, there exists an extreme case of ultrasensitivity of the demand for money to interest rates, called the **liquidity trap**, in which conventional monetary policy has no direct effect on aggregate spending because a change in the money supply has no effect on interest rates.[5]

[5]If the demand for money is ultrasensitive to interest rates, a tiny change in interest rates produces a very large change in the quantity of money demanded. Hence, in this case, the demand for money would be completely flat in the supply and demand diagrams of Chapter 5. Therefore, a change in the money supply that shifts the money supply curve to the right or left causes it to intersect the flat money demand curve at the same unchanged interest rate.

The evidence for the interest sensitivity of the demand for money is remarkably consistent. In situations in which nominal interest rates have not hit a floor of zero, the demand for money is sensitive to interest rates. However, when nominal interest rates fall to zero, they can go no lower. In this situation, a liquidity trap occurs because the demand for money is now completely flat. Indeed, this is exactly the situation that has occurred in the United States in recent years, which is why the Federal Reserve has had to resort to nonconventional monetary policy.

Stability of Money Demand

If the money demand function, like the one in Equation 8, is unstable and undergoes substantial, unpredictable shifts, as Keynes believed, then velocity is unpredictable, and the quantity of money may not be tightly linked to aggregate spending, as it is in the quantity theory. The stability of the money demand function is crucial to whether the Federal Reserve should target interest rates or the money supply. If the money demand function is unstable and so the money supply is not closely linked to aggregate spending, then the level of interest rates set by the Fed will provide more information about the stance of monetary policy than will the money supply.

Until the early 1970s, the evidence strongly supported the stability of the money demand function. However, after 1973, the rapid pace of financial innovation, which changed the items that could be used as money, led to substantial instability in estimated money demand functions. The instability of the money demand function calls into question whether our theories and empirical analyses are adequate. It also has important implications for the conduct of monetary policy, because it casts doubt on the usefulness of the money demand function as a tool for providing guidance to policymakers. In particular, because the money demand function has become unstable, velocity is now harder to predict. Monetary policymakers have found that the money supply does not provide reliable information on the future course of the economy, leading them to think of monetary policy in terms of the setting of interest rates. The instability of money demand has thus led to a downgrading of the focus on money supply in the conduct of monetary policy.

SUMMARY

1. The quantity theory of money as expressed by the equation of exchange, $M \times V = P \times Y$, indicates that nominal spending is determined solely by movements in the quantity of money. The quantity theory indicates that (1) changes in the quantity of money lead to proportional changes in the price level, because $P = (M \times \overline{V})/\overline{Y}$, and (2) the inflation rate is the growth rate of the money supply minus the growth rate of aggregate output—that is, $\pi = \%\Delta M - \%\Delta Y$. These implications of the quantity theory are borne out by the data in the long run, but not in the short run.

2. The government budget constraint indicates that a deficit must be financed by either money creation or by the issuance of government bonds. That is, $DEF = G - T = \Delta MB + \Delta B$. Combining this fact with the quantity theory indicates that financing a persistent deficit by money creation will lead to sustained inflation. This analysis helps explain hyperinflations, in which inflation and money growth rise to extremely high levels because of massive budget deficits.

3. John Maynard Keynes suggested three motives for holding money: the transactions motive, the precautionary motive, and the speculative motive. His resulting liquidity preference theory views the transactions and precautionary components of money demand as proportional to income. However, the speculative component of

money demand is viewed as sensitive to interest rates as well as to expectations about the future movements of interest rates. This theory, then, implies that velocity is unstable and cannot be treated as a constant.

4. Portfolio theories of money demand indicate that the demand for money is determined not only by interest rates, income, and payment technology, as in the Keynesian analysis, but also by wealth, riskiness of other assets, inflation risk, and liquidity of other assets.

5. Two main conclusions can be reached from the research on the demand for money: The demand

for money is sensitive to interest rates, as long as the interest rate is above zero. Since 1973, money demand has been found to be unstable, with the most likely source of the instability being the rapid pace of financial innovation. Because the money demand function is found to be both unstable and sensitive to interest rates, velocity cannot be viewed as constant and is not easily predicted. These conclusions have led to a downgrading of the focus on money supply and a greater emphasis on interest rates in the conduct of monetary policy.

KEY TERMS

demand for money, p. 456
dominated assets, p. 466
equation of exchange, p. 455
government budget constraint, p. 461
hyperinflations, p. 462

inflation hedges, p. 466
liquidity preference theory, p. 463
liquidity trap, p. 467
monetary theory, p. 454
monetizing the debt, p. 461

payment technology, p. 464
printing money, p. 462
quantity theory of money, p. 456
real money balances, p. 464
velocity of money, p. 455

QUESTIONS

1. How would you expect velocity to typically behave over the course of the business cycle?

2. If velocity and aggregate output are reasonably constant (as the classical economists believed), what will happen to the price level when the money supply increases from $1 trillion to $4 trillion?

3. If credit cards were made illegal by congressional legislation, what would happen to velocity? Explain your answer.

4. "If nominal GDP rises, velocity must rise." Is this statement true, false, or uncertain? Explain your answer.

5. Why would a central bank be concerned about persistent, long-term budget deficits?

6. "Persistent budget deficits always lead to higher inflation." Is this statement true, false, or uncertain? Explain your answer.

7. Why might a central bank choose to monetize the debt, knowing that it could lead to higher inflation?

8. Consider two central banks: one with a history of maintaining price stability and low inflation, and

the other with a history of high inflation and poor inflation management. All else equal, if the same level of government budget deficit is monetized in both countries, how is inflation likely to behave in each country?

9. Some payment technologies require infrastructure (e.g., merchants need to have access to credit card swiping machines). In most developing countries historically this infrastructure has either been nonexistent or very costly. However, recently mobile payment systems have expanded rapidly in developing countries as they have become cheaper. Everything else being equal, would you expect the transaction component of the demand for money to be increasing or decreasing in a developing country relative to a rich country?

10. What three motives for holding money did Keynes consider in his liquidity preference theory of the demand for real money balances? On the basis of these motives, what variables did he think determined the demand for money?

11. In many countries, people hold money as a cushion against unexpected needs arising from a variety of potential scenarios (e.g., banking crises, natural

disasters, health problems, unemployment, etc.) that are not usually covered by insurance markets. Explain the effect of such behavior on the precautionary component of the demand for money.

12. Why is Keynes's analysis of the speculative demand for money important to his view that velocity will undergo substantial fluctuations and thus cannot be treated as constant?

13. According to the portfolio theories of money demand, what are the four factors that determine money demand? What changes in these factors can increase the demand for money?

14. Explain how the following events will affect the demand for money according to the portfolio theories of money demand:

a. The economy experiences a business cycle contraction.

b. Brokerage fees decline, making bond transactions cheaper.

c. The stock market crashes. (*Hint:* Consider both the increase in stock price volatility following a market crash and the decrease in wealth of stockholders.)

15. Suppose a given country experienced low and stable inflation rates for quite some time, but then inflation picked up and over the past decade had been relatively high and quite unpredictable. Explain how this new inflationary environment would affect the demand for money according to portfolio theories of money

demand. What would happen if the government decided to issue inflation-protected securities?

16. Consider the portfolio choice theory of money demand. How do you think the demand for money would be affected during a hyperinflation (i.e., monthly inflation rates in excess of 50%)?

17. Both the portfolio choice and Keynes's theories of the demand for money suggest that as the relative expected return on money falls, demand for it will fall. Why does the portfolio choice approach predict that money demand is affected by changes in interest rates? Why did Keynes think that money demand is affected by changes in interest rates?

18. Why does the Keynesian view of the demand for money suggest that velocity is unpredictable?

19. What evidence is used to assess the stability of the money demand function? What does the evidence suggest about the stability of money demand, and how has this conclusion affected monetary policymaking?

20. Suppose that a plot of the values of M2 and nominal GDP for a given country over 40 years shows that these two variables are very closely related. In particular, a plot of their ratio (nominal GDP/M2) yields very stable and easy-to-predict values. On the basis of this evidence, would you recommend that the monetary authorities of this country conduct monetary policy by focusing mostly on the money supply rather than on setting interest rates? Explain.

APPLIED PROBLEMS

21. Suppose the money supply M has been growing at 10% per year, and nominal GDP, PY, has been growing at 20% per year. The data are as follows (in billions of dollars):

	2021	2022	2023
M	100	110	121
PY	1,000	1,200	1,440

Calculate the velocity for each year. At what rate is the velocity growing?

22. Calculate what happens to nominal GDP if velocity remains constant at 5 and the money supply increases from $200 billion to $300 billion.

23. What happens to nominal GDP if the money supply grows by 20% but velocity declines by 30%?

24. If velocity and aggregate output remain constant at 5 and $1,000 billion, respectively, what happens to the price level if the money supply declines from $400 billion to $300 billion?

25. Suppose the liquidity preference function is given by

$$L(i, Y) = \frac{Y}{8} - 1{,}000i$$

Use the money demand equation, along with the following table of values, to calculate the velocity for each period.

	Period 1	Period 2	Period 3	Period 4	Period 5	Period 6	Period 7
Y (in billions)	12,000	12,500	12,250	12,500	12,800	13,000	13,200
Interest rate	0.05	0.07	0.03	0.05	0.07	0.04	0.06

DATA ANALYSIS PROBLEMS

The Problems update with real-time data in **MyLab Economics** and are available for practice or instructor assignment.

1. **Real-time Data Analysis** Go to the St. Louis Federal Reserve FRED database, and find data on the M1 Money Stock (M1SL), M1 Money Velocity (M1V), and Real GDP (GDPC1). Convert the M1SL data series to "quarterly" using the *frequency* setting, and for all three series, use the "Percent Change from Year Ago" setting for *units*.
   a. Calculate the average percentage change in real GDP, the M1 money stock, and velocity since 2000:Q1.
   b. Based on your answer to part (a), calculate the average inflation rate since 2000 as predicted by the quantity theory of money.
   c. Next, find the data on the GDP deflator price index (GDPDEF), download the data using the "Percent Change from Year Ago" setting, and calculate the average inflation rate since 2000:Q1. Comment on the value relative to your answer in part (b).

2. **Real-time Data Analysis** Go to the St. Louis Federal Reserve FRED database, and find data on the budget deficit (FYFSD), the amount of federal debt held by the public (FYGFDPUN), and the amount of federal debt held by the Federal Reserve (FDHBFRBN). Convert the two "debt held" series to "Annual" using the *frequency* setting. Download all three series into a spreadsheet. Make sure that the rows of data align properly to the correct dates. Note that for the deficit series, a negative number indicates a deficit; multiply the series by −1 so that a deficit is indicated by a positive number. Manipulate the three series so that all data are given in terms of the same units (either millions or billions of dollars). To do this, if a series is in millions and you are converting it to billions, divide the series by 1,000. Finally, for each year, convert the two "debt held" series into one "changes in debt holdings by the public and the Federal Reserve" series by calculating, for each year, the difference in bond holdings from the preceding year.
   a. Create a scatter plot showing the deficit on the horizontal axis and the change in bond holdings by the public on the vertical axis, using the data from 1980 through the most recent period of data available. Insert a fitted line into the scatter plot, and comment on the relationship between the deficit and the change in public bond holdings.
   b. Create a scatter plot showing the deficit on the horizontal axis and the change in bond holdings by the Federal Reserve on the vertical axis, using the data from 1980 through the most recent period of data available. Insert a fitted line into the scatter plot, and comment on the relationship between the deficit and the change in Federal Reserve bond holdings.
   c. Now repeat part (b), but create separate scatter plots for the period from 1980 to 2007 and from 2008 to the most recent year. Comment on how, if at all, the monetizing of the debt is exhibited in the data. Do you think the relationship between the deficit and the change in bond holdings of the Federal Reserve has changed since 2008? Why or why not?

20 The *IS* Curve

Learning Objectives

20.1 Explain the relationship of planned expenditure and aggregate demand.

20.2 List and describe the factors that determine the four components of aggregate demand (or planned expenditure).

20.3 Solve for the goods market equilibrium.

20.4 Describe why the *IS* curve slopes downward and why the economy heads to a goods market equilibrium.

20.5 List the factors that shift the *IS* curve, and describe how they shift the *IS* curve.

Preview

During the Great Depression of the 1930s, aggregate output fell precipitously, by 30%, with unemployment rising to 25%. Although the recession of 2007–2009 was not as severe, the contraction in economic activity led unemployment to rise to over 10%. With the coronavirus pandemic, the unemployment rate rose to a peak of 14.7% in April 2020. To understand why these contractions in economic activity occur, economists make use of the concept of *aggregate demand*, the total amount of output demanded in the economy. This concept was developed by John Maynard Keynes in his revolutionary book *The General Theory of Employment, Interest, and Money*, published in 1936, in which he argued that short-run changes in aggregate output, such as the decline in output that occurred during the Great Depression, are determined by changes in aggregate demand. The concept of aggregate demand is a central element in the *aggregate demand–aggregate supply (AD/AS) model*, the basic macroeconomic model used to explain short-run fluctuations in aggregate output.

In this chapter, we develop the first building block in understanding aggregate demand, the *IS curve*, which describes the relationship between real interest rates and aggregate output when the market for goods and services (more simply referred to as the *goods market*) is in equilibrium. We begin by deriving the *IS* curve and then go on to explain what factors cause the *IS* curve to shift. With our understanding of the *IS* curve, we can examine why fluctuations in economic activity occur and how the fiscal stimulus package of 2009 affected the economy. Then, in the next chapter, we make use of the *IS* curve to understand the role played by monetary policy in economic fluctuations.

20.1 PLANNED EXPENDITURE AND AGGREGATE DEMAND

LO 20.1 Explain the relationship of planned expenditure and aggregate demand.

We start our analysis by discussing the concept of **planned expenditure**, the total amount that households, businesses, the government, and foreigners want to spend on domestically produced goods and services. In contrast, *actual expenditure* is the amount that these entities actually do spend, which equals the total amount of output produced in the economy. Note that all of the analysis in this chapter refers to expenditure in real terms, that is, in terms of actual physical amounts of goods and services. Keynes viewed **aggregate demand**, the total amount of output demanded in the economy, as being the same as planned expenditure. As we shall see shortly, planned expenditure—and hence aggregate demand—explains the level of aggregate output when the goods market is in equilibrium, that is, when aggregate demand for goods and services is equal to the actual amount of goods and services produced.

The total amount of aggregate demand (planned expenditure) is the sum of four types of spending:

1. **Consumption expenditure** (*C*), the total demand for consumer goods and services (e.g., hamburgers, iPhones, rock concerts, visits to the doctor)
2. **Planned investment spending** (*I*), the total planned spending by businesses on new physical capital (e.g., machines, computers, factories), plus planned spending on new homes
3. **Government purchases** (*G*), the spending by all levels of government on goods and services (e.g., aircraft carriers, salaries of government employees, red tape), not including transfer payments (which redistribute income from one person to another)
4. **Net exports** (*NX*), the net foreign spending on domestic goods and services, equal to exports minus imports

We represent the total aggregate demand (Y^{ad}) with the following equation:

$$Y^{ad} = C + I + G + NX \tag{1}$$

20.2 THE COMPONENTS OF AGGREGATE DEMAND

LO 20.2 List and describe the factors that determine the four components of aggregate demand (or planned expenditure).

To understand what determines aggregate demand (total planned expenditure) in the economy, let's look at each of its components in detail.

Consumption Expenditure

What determines how much you spend on consumer goods and services? Your income is likely the most important factor; if your income rises, you most likely will be willing to spend more. Keynes reasoned similarly that consumption expenditure is related to **disposable income** (denoted by Y_D), the total amount of income available for spending, equal to aggregate output Y minus taxes $T(Y - T)$.[1]

Consumption Function Keynes called the relationship between disposable income Y_D and consumption expenditure C the **consumption function**, and expressed it as follows:

$$C = \overline{C} + mpc \times Y_D \tag{2}$$

or, alternatively,

$$C = \overline{C} + mpc \times (Y - T) \tag{3}$$

---

[1]More precisely, taxes T refers to taxes minus net transfers (government payments to households and businesses that are, in effect, negative taxes). Examples of government transfers include Social Security payments and unemployment insurance payments.

The term $\overline{C}$ stands for **autonomous consumption expenditure**, the amount of consumption expenditure that is **exogenous** (independent of variables in the model, such as disposable income). Autonomous consumption is related to consumers' optimism about their future income and household wealth, both of which are positively related to consumer spending.

The term *mpc*, the **marginal propensity to consume**, reflects the change in consumption expenditure that results from an additional dollar of disposable income. Keynes assumed that *mpc* was a constant between the values of 0 and 1. If, for example, a $1.00 increase in disposable income leads to an increase in consumption expenditure of $0.60, then $mpc = 0.6$.

Planned Investment Spending

Investment spending is another key component of total expenditure. There are two types of investment spending: *fixed* and *inventory*. (Note that economists' use of the word *investment* differs from the everyday use of the term, as explained in the FYI box.)

Fixed Investment **Fixed investment** is planned spending by firms on equipment (machines, computers, airplanes) and structures (factories, office buildings, shopping centers), plus planned spending on new residential housing.

Inventory Investment **Inventory investment** is spending by firms on additional holdings of raw materials, parts, and finished goods, calculated as the change in holdings of these items in a given time period—say, a year.

Inventory investment is a much smaller component of investment than fixed investment. We discuss inventory investment in detail at this juncture because it plays an important role in the determination of aggregate output. To illustrate, consider the following scenarios:

1. Suppose that Ford Motor Company has 100,000 cars sitting in its factory lots on December 31, 2022, ready to be shipped to dealers. If each car has a wholesale price of $20,000, Ford has an inventory worth $2 billion. If by December 31, 2023, its inventory of cars has risen to 150,000, with a value of $3 billion, its inventory investment in 2023 is $1 billion, the *change* in the level of its inventory over the course of the year ($3 billion in 2023 minus $2 billion in 2022).

2. Instead suppose that by December 31, 2023, Ford's inventory of cars has dropped to 50,000, with a value of $1 billion. Its inventory investment in 2023 is now −$1 billion, the *change* in the level of its inventory over the course of the year ($1 billion in 2023 minus $2 billion in 2022).

3. Ford will have additional inventory investment if the level of raw materials and parts that it is holding to produce these cars increases over the course of the year. If on December 31, 2022, it holds $50 million of steel to be used to produce its cars, and on December 31, 2023, it holds $100 million of steel, it has an additional $50 million of inventory investment in 2023.

An important feature of inventory investment is that some inventory investment can be unplanned (in contrast, fixed investment is always planned). Suppose that the reason Ford finds itself with an additional $1 billion of cars on December 31, 2023, is because it sold $1 billion less of its cars than expected in 2023. This $1 billion of inventory investment in 2023 was unplanned. In this situation, Ford is producing more cars than it can sell, and it will cut production to avoid accumulating unsold goods. The act of adjusting production to eliminate unplanned inventory investment plays a key role in the determination of aggregate output, as we shall see.

Planned Investment Spending and Real Interest Rates   Planned investment spending, a component of aggregate demand Y^{ad}, is equal to planned fixed investment plus the amount of inventory investment *planned* by firms. Keynes considered the level of the real interest rate for investments as a key determinant of planned investment spending.

To understand Keynes's reasoning, we need to recognize that businesses make investments in physical capital (machines and factories) as long as they expect to earn more from the physical capital than the interest cost of a loan to finance the investment. When the real interest rate for investments is high—say, at 10%—few investments in physical capital will earn more than the 10% interest cost of borrowing funds, and so planned investment spending will be low. When the real interest rate for investments is low—say, 1%—many investments in physical capital will earn more than the 1% interest cost of borrowing funds. Therefore, when the real interest rate for investments and hence the cost of borrowing are low, business firms are more likely to undertake investments in physical capital, and planned investment spending increases.

Even if a company has surplus funds and does not need to borrow to undertake an investment in physical capital, its planned investment spending still will be affected by the real interest rate for investments. Instead of investing in physical capital, the company could purchase a corporate bond. If the real interest rate on this security were high—say, 10%—the opportunity cost (forgone interest earnings) of an investment in physical capital would be high. Planned investment spending would then be low, because the firm probably would prefer to purchase the security and earn the high 10% return than to invest in physical capital. As the real interest rate for investments and the opportunity cost of investing fall—say, to 1%—planned investment spending will increase because investments in physical capital are likely to earn greater income for the firm than the measly 1% that would be earned by investing in the security.

Planned Investment and Business Expectations   Keynes also believed that planned investment spending is heavily influenced by business expectations about the future. Businesses that are optimistic about future profit opportunities are willing to spend more, whereas pessimistic businesses cut back their spending. Thus Keynes posited a component of planned investment spending, which he called **autonomous investment**, $\bar{I}$, that is completely exogenous and so is unexplained by variables in his model, such as output or interest rates.

Keynes believed that changes in autonomous spending are dominated by these unstable exogenous fluctuations in planned investment spending, which are influenced by emotional waves of optimism and pessimism—factors he labeled **"animal spirits."** His view was colored by the collapse in investment spending during the Great Depression, which he saw as the primary reason for the economic contraction.

Investment Function   By combining the two factors that Keynes theorized drive investment, we can derive an investment function that describes how planned investment spending is related to autonomous investment and the real interest rate for investments. We write this function as follows:

$$I = \bar{I} - dr_i \qquad (4)$$

where d is a parameter reflecting the responsiveness of investment to the real interest rate for investments, which is denoted by r_i.

However, the real interest rate for investments reflects not only the real interest rate r on short-term, safe, debt instruments, which is controlled by the central bank, but also **financial frictions**, denoted by $\bar{f}$, which are additions to the real cost of borrowing caused by barriers to the efficient functioning of financial markets. (We discussed the origins of these frictions—the asymmetric information problems of adverse selection and moral hazard—in detail in Chapter 8.) Financial frictions make it harder for lenders to ascertain the creditworthiness of a borrower. Lenders need to charge a higher interest rate to protect themselves against the possibility that the borrower may not pay back the loan, which leads to an increase in the *credit spread*, the difference between the interest rate on loans to businesses and the interest rate on completely safe assets that are sure to be paid back. Hence financial frictions add to the real interest rate for investments, and we can write:

$$r_i = r + \bar{f} \qquad (5)$$

Substituting in Equation 4 the real cost of borrowing from Equation 5 yields:

$$I = \bar{I} - d(r + \bar{f}) \qquad (6)$$

Equation 6 states that investment is positively related to business optimism as represented by autonomous investment and negatively related to the real interest rate and financial frictions.

Government Purchases and Taxes

Now we bring the government into the picture. The government affects aggregate demand in two ways: through its purchases and through taxes.

Government Purchases   As we saw in the aggregate demand equation, Equation 1, government purchases add directly to aggregate demand. Here we assume that government purchases are exogenous, and we write government purchases as follows:

$$G = \overline{G} \qquad (7)$$

Equation 7 states that government purchases are set at a fixed amount $\overline{G}$.

Taxes   The government affects spending through taxes because, as discussed earlier, disposable income is equal to income minus taxes, $Y - T$, and disposable income affects consumption expenditure. Higher taxes T reduce disposable income for a given level of income and hence cause consumption expenditure to fall. The tax laws in a country like the United States are very complicated, so to keep the model simple, we assume that government taxes are exogenous and are set at a fixed amount $\overline{T}$:[2]

$$T = \overline{T} \tag{8}$$

Net Exports

As with planned investment spending, we can think of net exports as being made up of two components: *autonomous net exports* and the part of net exports that is affected by changes in real interest rates.

Real Interest Rates and Net Exports   Real interest rates influence the amount of net exports through the **exchange rate**. Recall that the exchange rate is the price of one currency, say, the dollar, in terms of another currency, say, the euro.[3] We examined a model that explains the link between the exchange rate and real interest rates in Chapter 17, but here we will only outline the intuition. When U.S. real interest rates rise, U.S. dollar assets earn higher returns relative to foreign assets. People then want to hold more dollars, so they bid up the value of a dollar and thereby increase its value relative to the values of other currencies. Thus a rise in U.S. real interest rates leads to a higher value of the dollar.

A rise in the value of the dollar makes U.S. exports more expensive in foreign currencies, so foreigners will buy less of these exports, thereby driving down net exports. A rise in the value of the dollar also makes foreign goods less expensive in terms of dollars, so U.S. imports will rise, also causing a decline in net exports. We therefore see that a rise in the real interest rate, which leads to an increase in the value of the dollar, in turn leads to a decline in net exports.

Autonomous Net Exports   The amount of exports is also affected by the demand by foreigners for domestic goods, while the amount of imports is affected by the demand by domestic residents for foreign goods. For example, if the Chinese have a poor harvest and want to buy more U.S. wheat, U.S. exports will rise. If the Brazilian economy is booming, then Brazilians will have more money to spend on U.S. goods, and U.S. exports will rise. In contrast, if U.S. consumers discover how good Chilean wine is and want to buy more, then U.S. imports will rise. Thus we can think of net exports as being determined by real interest rates as well as by a component called **autonomous net exports**, $\overline{NX}$, which is the level of net exports that is treated as exogenous (outside the model).[4]

---

[2]For simplicity, we assume here that taxes are unrelated to income. However, because taxes increase with income, we can describe taxes more realistically with the following tax function:

$$T = \overline{T} + tY$$

Using this equation instead of Equation 9 in the derivation of Equation 12 later in the chapter would lead to *mpc* being replaced by $mpc(1 - t)$ in Equation 12.

[3]If a government pegs the exchange rate to another country's currency, so that the rate is fixed in what is called a *fixed exchange rate regime* (see Chapter 18), then real interest rates do not directly affect net exports as in Equation 9, and $NX = \overline{NX}$. Taking out the response of net exports to the real interest rates does not change the basic analysis of the chapter but does lead to a slightly different Equation 12 later in the chapter.

[4]Foreign aggregate output is outside the model, and so its effect on net exports is exogenous and hence is a factor that affects autonomous net exports. U.S. domestic output, Y, could also affect net exports because greater domestic disposable income would increase spending on imports and thus would lower net exports. To build this factor into the *IS* curve, we could modify the net export function given in Equation 9 as follows:

$$NX = \overline{NX} - xr - iY$$

where i is the marginal propensity to spend on imports. This change would lead to a modification of Equation 12 later in the chapter, in which the *mpc* term would be replaced by $mpc - i$.

Net Export Function   Putting these two components of net exports together, we can write a net export function:

$$NX = \overline{NX} - xr \tag{9}$$

where x is a parameter that indicates how net exports respond to the real interest rate. This equation tells us that net exports are positively related to autonomous net exports and are negatively related to the level of real interest rates.

20.3 GOODS MARKET EQUILIBRIUM

LO 20.3 Solve for the goods market equilibrium.

Keynes recognized that equilibrium will occur in the economy when the total quantity of output is equal to the total amount of aggregate demand (planned expenditure). That is,

$$Y = Y^{ad} \tag{10}$$

When this equilibrium condition is satisfied, planned spending for goods and services is equal to the amount that is produced. Producers are able to sell all of their output and have no reason to change their production levels, because there is no unplanned inventory investment. By examining the factors that affect each component of planned spending, we can understand why aggregate output goes to a certain level.

Solving for Goods Market Equilibrium

With our understanding of the factors that drive the components of aggregate demand, we can see how aggregate output is determined by using Equation 1, the aggregate demand equation, to rewrite the equilibrium condition given in Equation 10 as follows:

$$Y = C + I + G + NX \tag{11}$$

aggregate output = consumption expenditure + planned investment spending
+ government purchases + net exports

Now we can use our consumption, investment, and net export functions in Equations 3, 6, and 7, along with Equations 8 and 9, to determine aggregate output. Substituting all of these equations into the equilibrium condition given by Equation 11 yields the following:

$$Y = \overline{C} + mpc \times (Y - \overline{T}) + \overline{I} - d(r + \overline{f}) + \overline{G} + \overline{NX} - xr$$

Collecting terms, we can rewrite this equation as follows:

$$Y = \overline{C} + \overline{I} - d\overline{f} + \overline{G} + \overline{NX} + mpc \times Y - mpc \times \overline{T} - (d + x)r$$

Subtracting $mpc \times Y$ from both sides of the equation, we have

$$Y - mpc \times Y = Y(1 - mpc) = \overline{C} + \overline{I} - d\overline{f} + \overline{G} + \overline{NX} - mpc \times \overline{T} - (d + x)r$$

Then, dividing both sides of the equation by $1 - mpc$, we obtain an equation that gives us a means of determining aggregate output when the goods market is in equilibrium:[5]

$$Y = [\overline{C} + \overline{I} - d\overline{f} + \overline{G} + \overline{NX} - mpc \times \overline{T}] \times \frac{1}{1 - mpc} - \frac{d + x}{1 - mpc} \times r \quad (12)$$

Deriving the *IS* Curve

We refer to Equation 12 as the **IS curve**, and it shows the relationship between aggregate output and the real interest rate when the goods market is in equilibrium. Equation 12 is made up of two terms. Since mpc is between 0 and 1, $1/(1 - mpc)$ is positive, so the first term tells us that an increase in autonomous consumption, investment, government purchases, or net exports, or a decrease in taxes or financial frictions, leads to an increase in output at any given real interest rate. In other words, the first term tells us about shifts in the *IS* curve. The second term tells us that an increase in real interest rates results in a decrease in output, which can be shown as a movement along the *IS* curve.

20.4 UNDERSTANDING THE *IS* CURVE

LO 20.4 Describe why the *IS* curve slopes downward and why the economy heads to a goods market equilibrium.

To gain a deeper understanding of the *IS* curve, we will proceed in several steps. In this section, we begin by looking at the intuition behind the *IS* curve, and then we discuss a numerical example. Then, in the following section, we outline the factors that shift the *IS* curve.

What the *IS* Curve Tells Us: Intuition

The *IS* curve traces out the points at which the goods market is in equilibrium. For each given level of the real interest rate, the *IS* curve tells us the level of aggregate output that is necessary for the goods market to be in equilibrium. As the real interest rate rises, planned investment spending and net exports fall, which in turn lowers aggregate demand; aggregate output must be lower if it is to equal aggregate demand and satisfy goods market equilibrium. Hence the *IS* curve is downward-sloping.

What the *IS* Curve Tells Us: Numerical Example

We can analyze the *IS* curve with the following numerical example, which gives specific values for the exogenous variables and the parameters in Equation 12.

$$\overline{C} = \$1.4 \text{ trillion}$$
$$\overline{I} = \$1.2 \text{ trillion}$$
$$\overline{G} = \$3.0 \text{ trillion}$$
$$\overline{T} = \$3.0 \text{ trillion}$$
$$\overline{NX} = \$1.3 \text{ trillion}$$
$$\overline{f} = 1$$
$$mpc = 0.6$$
$$d = 0.3$$
$$x = 0.1$$

---

[5]Note that the term $1/(1 - mpc)$ that multiplies $\overline{G}$ is known as the *expenditure multiplier*, and the term $-mpc/(1 - mpc)$ that multiplies $\overline{T}$ is called the *tax multiplier*. The tax multiplier is smaller in absolute value than the expenditure multiplier because mpc < 1.

Mini-lecture

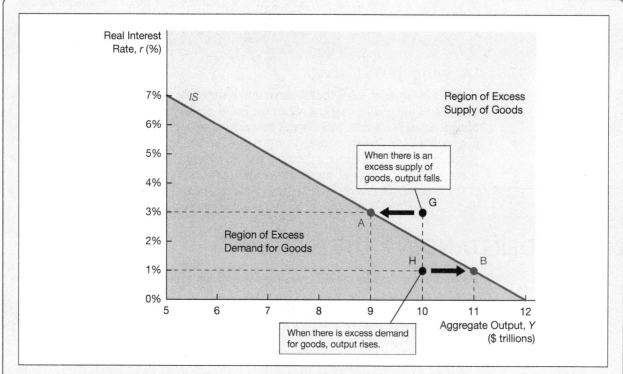

FIGURE 1 **The *IS* Curve**

The downward-sloping *IS* curve represents points at which the goods market is in equilibrium—for example, points A and B. Notice that output changes as necessary to return the market to equilibrium. For example, at point G in the orange-shaded area, an excess supply of goods exists and firms will cut production, decreasing aggregate output to the equilibrium level at point A. At point H in the blue-shaded area, an excess demand for goods exists, so firms will increase production, and aggregate output will increase toward the equilibrium level at point B.

Using these values, we can rewrite Equation 12 as follows:

$$Y = [1.4 + 1.2 - 0.3 + 3.0 + 1.3 - 0.6 \times 3.0] \times \frac{1}{1 - 0.6} - \frac{0.3 + 0.1}{1 - 0.6} \times r$$

Plugging these values into Equation 12 yields the equation of the *IS* curve shown in Figure 1:

$$Y = \frac{4.8}{0.4} - \frac{0.4}{0.4} \times r = 12 - r \tag{13}$$

At a real interest rate of $r = 3\%$, the equilibrium output Y is equal to 12 trillion $-$ 3 trillion $=$ 9 trillion. We plot this combination of the real interest rate and equilibrium output as point A in Figure 1. At a real interest rate of $r = 1\%$, the equilibrium output Y is equal to 12 trillion $-$ 1 trillion $=$ 11 trillion, which we plot as point B. The line connecting these points is the *IS* curve and, as you can see, it is downward-sloping.

Why the Economy Heads Toward Equilibrium

The concept of equilibrium is useful only if there is a tendency for the economy to settle there. Let's first consider what happens if the economy is located to the right of the *IS* curve (the orange shaded area), where an excess supply of goods exists. In Figure 1 at point G, actual output is above aggregate demand, and firms are saddled with unsold inventory. To keep from accumulating unsold goods, firms will continue cutting production. As long as production is above the equilibrium level, output will exceed aggregate demand and firms will continue cutting production, sending aggregate output toward the equilibrium level, as indicated by the leftward arrow from point G to point A. Only when the economy moves to point A on the *IS* curve will there be no further tendency for output to change.

What happens if aggregate output is below the equilibrium level of output (the blue shaded area to the left of the *IS* curve), where an excess demand for goods exists? At point H in Figure 1, actual output is below aggregate demand, so firms will want to increase production because inventories are declining more than they desire, and aggregate output will increase, as shown by the rightward arrow. When the economy has moved to point B on the *IS* curve, there will again be no further tendency for output to change.

20.5 FACTORS THAT SHIFT THE *IS* CURVE

LO 20.5 List the factors that shift the *IS* curve, and describe how they shift the *IS* curve.

You have now learned that the *IS* curve describes equilibrium points in the goods market—the combinations of the real interest rate and equilibrium output. The *IS* curve shifts whenever change occurs in autonomous factors (factors independent of aggregate output and the real interest rate). Note that a change in the real interest rate that affects equilibrium aggregate output causes only a *movement along* the *IS* curve. A *shift* in the *IS* curve, by contrast, occurs when equilibrium output changes *at each given real interest rate*.

In Equation 12, we identified six autonomous factors that can shift aggregate demand and hence affect the level of equilibrium output. Although Equation 12 directly tells us how these factors shift the *IS* curve, we will develop some intuition as to how each autonomous factor does so.

Changes in Government Purchases

Let's look at what happens if government purchases rise from $3 trillion to $4 trillion in Figure 2. IS_1 represents the same *IS* curve that we developed in Figure 1. We determine the equation for IS_2 by substituting the $4 trillion value into Equation 12:

$$Y = [1.4 + 1.2 - 0.3 + 4.0 + 1.3 - 0.6 \times 3.0] \times \frac{1}{1 - 0.6} - \frac{0.3 + 0.1}{1 - 0.6} \times r$$

$$= \frac{5.8}{0.4} - r = 14.5 - r$$

On the basis of these results, at a real interest rate of $r = 3\%$, equilibrium output Y is equal to $14.5 trillion $-$ $3 trillion $=$ $11.5 trillion, which we mark as point C on Figure 2. At a real interest rate of $r = 1\%$, equilibrium output has increased to $Y = $14.5 trillion $-$ $1 trillion $=$ $13.5 trillion, which we mark as point D. The increase in government purchases therefore shifts the *IS* curve to the right from IS_1 to IS_2.

Mini-lecture

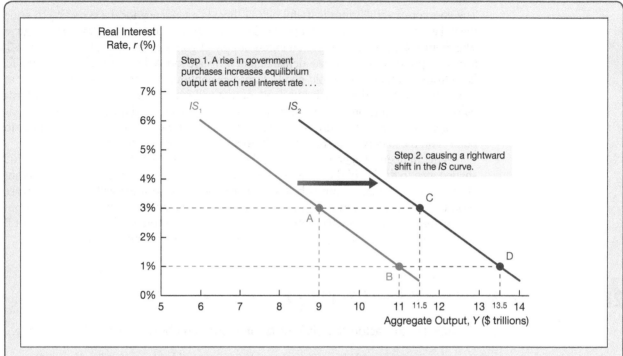

FIGURE 2 **Shift in the *IS* Curve from an Increase in Government Purchases**

IS_1 represents the *IS* curve we derived in Figure 1. IS_2 reflects a \$1.0 trillion increase in government purchases. The increase in government purchases causes aggregate output to rise, shifting the *IS* curve to the right by \$2.5 trillion at each real interest rate, from IS_1 to IS_2.

Intuitively, we can see why an increase in government purchases leads to a rightward shift of the *IS* curve by recognizing that an increase in government purchases causes aggregate demand to increase at any given real interest rate. Since aggregate output equals aggregate demand when the goods market is in equilibrium, *an increase in government purchases that causes aggregate demand to rise also causes equilibrium output to rise, thereby shifting the IS curve to the right. Conversely, a decrease in government purchases causes aggregate demand to fall at any given real interest rate and leads to a leftward shift of the IS curve.*

APPLICATION The Vietnam War Buildup, 1964–1969

The United States' involvement in Vietnam began to escalate in the early 1960s. After 1964, the United States was fighting a full-scale war. Beginning in 1965, the resulting increases in military expenditure raised government purchases. When government purchases are rising rapidly, central banks will usually raise real interest rates to keep the economy from overheating. The Vietnam War period, however, was unusual in that the Federal Reserve decided to keep real interest rates constant. Hence, this period provides an excellent example of how policymakers might make use of *IS* curve analysis to inform policy.

Mini-lecture

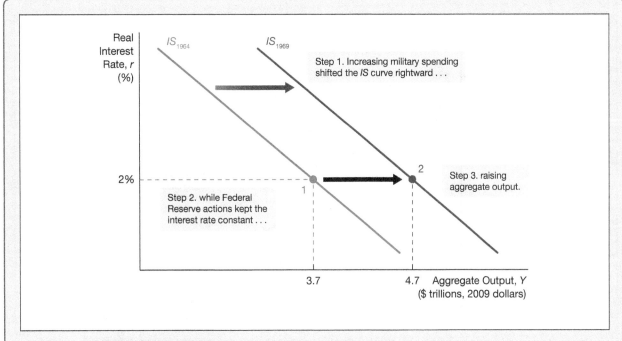

FIGURE 3   **Vietnam War Buildup**

Increases in military spending beginning in 1965 caused the *IS* curve to shift from IS_{1964} to IS_{1969}. Because the Federal Reserve decided to keep real interest rates constant at 2% during this period, equilibrium output rose from $3.7 trillion (in 2009 dollars) in 1964 to $4.7 trillion in 1969, setting the stage for an increase in inflation.

The rise in government purchases shifted the *IS* curve to the right, from IS_{1964} to IS_{1969} in Figure 3. Because the Federal Reserve decided to keep real interest rates constant at 2% during this period, equilibrium output rose from $3.7 trillion (in 2009 dollars) in 1964 to $4.7 trillion by 1969, with the unemployment rate falling steadily from 5% in 1964 to 3.4% in 1969. However, all was not well for the economy: The combination of an increase in government purchases and a constant real interest rate led to an overheating of the economy that eventually resulted in high inflation. (We will discuss the link between an overheating economy and inflation in the coming chapters.) ◆

Changes in Taxes

Now let's look at Figure 4 to see what happens if the government raises taxes from $3 trillion to $4 trillion. IS_1 represents the same *IS* curve that we developed in Figure 1. We determine the equation for IS_2 by substituting the $4 trillion value into Equation 12:

$$Y = [1.4 + 1.2 - 0.3 + 3.0 + 1.3 - 0.6 \times 4.0] \times \frac{1}{1 - 0.6} - \frac{0.3 + 0.1}{1 - 0.6} \times r$$

$$= \frac{4.2}{0.4} - r = 10.5 - r$$

Mini-lecture

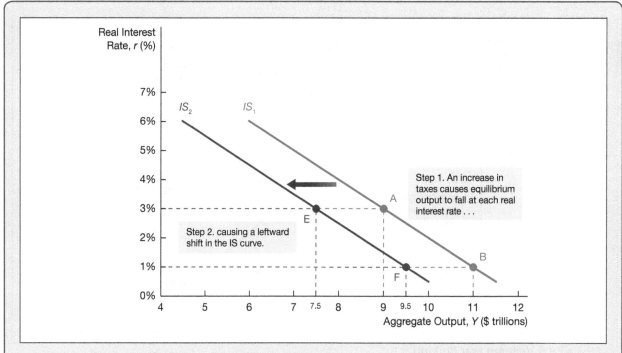

FIGURE 4   Shift in the *IS* Curve from an Increase in Taxes

IS_1 represents the *IS* curve we derived in Figure 1. IS_2 reflects a $1.0 trillion increase in government tax revenues. The increase in taxes decreases aggregate output levels by $1.5 trillion, shifting the *IS* curve to the left, from IS_1 to IS_2.

At a real interest rate of $r = 3\%$, equilibrium output $Y = \$10.5$ trillion − $3 trillion = $7.5 trillion, which we mark as point E in Figure 4. At this real interest rate, equilibrium output has decreased from point A to point E, as shown by the leftward arrow. Similarly, at a real interest rate of $r = 1\%$, equilibrium output has decreased to $Y = \$10.5$ trillion − $1 trillion = $9.5 trillion, causing a leftward shift from point B to point F. The *IS* curve shifts to the left, from IS_1 to IS_2, as a result of the increase in taxes.

We have the following result: ***At any given real interest rate, a rise in taxes causes aggregate demand and hence equilibrium output to fall, thereby shifting the IS curve to the left. Conversely, a cut in taxes at any given real interest rate increases disposable income and causes aggregate demand and equilibrium output to rise, shifting the IS curve to the right.***

Policymakers use both tax and government purchase policies to stimulate the economy when it enters a recession, as illustrated in the following Application.

APPLICATION   The Fiscal Stimulus Package of 2009

In the fall of 2008, the U.S. economy was in crisis. By the time the new Obama administration took office, the unemployment rate had risen from 4.7% just before the recession began in December 2007 to 7.6% in January 2009. To stimulate the economy, the

Obama administration proposed a fiscal stimulus package that, when passed by Congress, included $288 billion in tax cuts for households and businesses and $499 billion in increased federal spending, including transfer payments. What does our *IS* curve analysis suggest should have happened to the economy?

As the analyses in Figure 2 and Figure 4 indicate, these tax cuts and spending increases should have increased aggregate demand, thereby raising the equilibrium level of aggregate output at any given real interest rate and so shifting the *IS* curve to the right. Unfortunately, things didn't work out quite as the Obama administration had planned. Most of the government purchases did not kick in until after 2010, while the declines in autonomous consumption and investment were much larger than anticipated. The fiscal stimulus was more than offset by the weak consumption and investment caused by an increase in financial frictions and worries about the economy. As a result, aggregate demand ended up contracting rather than rising, and the *IS* curve did not shift to the right as hoped. Despite the good intentions of the fiscal stimulus package, the unemployment rate ended up rising to 10% in 2009. Without the fiscal stimulus package, however, the *IS* curve likely would have shifted even further to the left, resulting in even more unemployment. ◆

Changes in Autonomous Spending

As you can see from Equation 12, autonomous consumption, investment, and net exports—$\overline{C}$, $\overline{I}$, and $\overline{NX}$, respectively—all are multiplied by the term $1/(1 - mpc)$ in the same way the $\overline{G}$ term is. Thus an increase in any of these variables has the same impact on the *IS* curve as an increase in government purchases. For this reason, we can lump these variables together as **autonomous spending**, exogenous spending that is unrelated to variables in the model such as output or real interest rates. We look intuitively at how changes in each of these variables affect the *IS* curve in turn.

Autonomous Consumption   Suppose consumers find that their wealth has increased courtesy of a stock market boom or that they have become increasingly optimistic about their future income prospects because a positive productivity shock to the economy has occurred. Both of these events are autonomous; that is, they are not affected by the level of the real interest rate. *The resulting rise in autonomous consumption would raise aggregate demand and equilibrium output at any given real interest rate, shifting the IS curve to the right. Conversely, a decline in autonomous consumption expenditure would cause aggregate demand and equilibrium output to fall, shifting the IS curve to the left.*

Autonomous Investment Spending   Earlier in the chapter, we learned that changes in the real interest rate affect planned investment spending and hence the equilibrium level of output. This change in investment spending merely causes a movement along the *IS* curve, not a shift. An autonomous rise in planned investment spending unrelated to the real interest rate—say, because companies become more confident about investment profitability after the stock market rises—increases aggregate demand. *An increase in autonomous investment spending therefore increases equilibrium output at any given real interest rate, shifting the IS curve to the right. In contrast, a decrease in autonomous investment spending causes aggregate demand and equilibrium output to fall, shifting the IS curve to the left.*

SUMMARY TABLE 1

Shifts in the *IS* Curve from Autonomous Changes in $\overline{C}, \overline{I}, \overline{G}, \overline{T}, \overline{NX},$ and $\overline{f}$

Variable	Change in Variable	Shift in *IS* Curve	Reason
Autonomous consumption expenditure, $\overline{C}$	↑	r ... IS_1 IS_2 ... Y	$C\uparrow Y\uparrow$
Autonomous investment, $\overline{I}$	↑	r ... IS_1 IS_2 ... Y	$I\uparrow Y\uparrow$
Government spending, $\overline{G}$	↑	r ... IS_1 IS_2 ... Y	$G\uparrow Y\uparrow$
Taxes, $\overline{T}$	↑	r ... IS_2 IS_1 ... Y	$T\uparrow \Rightarrow C\downarrow Y\downarrow$
Autonomous net exports, $\overline{NX}$	↑	r ... IS_1 IS_2 ... Y	$\overline{NX}\uparrow Y\uparrow$
Financial frictions, $\overline{f}$	↑	r ... IS_2 IS_1 ... Y	$I\downarrow Y\downarrow$

Note: Only increases (↑) in the variables are shown; the effects of decreases in the variables on aggregate output would be the opposite of those indicated in the last two columns.

Autonomous Net Exports   An autonomous rise in net exports unrelated to the real interest rate—say, because American-made handbags become more chic than French-made handbags, or because foreign countries have a boom and thus buy more U.S. goods—causes aggregate demand to rise. *An autonomous increase in net exports thus leads to an increase in equilibrium output at any given real interest rate and shifts the IS curve to the right. Conversely, an autonomous fall in net exports causes aggregate demand and equilibrium output to decline, shifting the IS curve to the left.*

Changes in Financial Frictions

An increase in financial frictions, as occurred during the financial crisis of 2007–2009, raises the real interest rate for investments and hence causes investment spending and aggregate demand to fall. *An increase in financial frictions leads to a decline in equilibrium output at any given real interest rate and shifts the IS curve to the left. Conversely, a decrease in financial frictions causes aggregate demand and equilibrium output to rise, shifting the IS curve to the right.*

Summary of Factors That Shift the *IS* Curve

As a study aid, Summary Table 1 on the previous page shows how each factor shifts the *IS* curve and the reason the shift occurs. Now that we have a full understanding of the *IS* curve, we can use this building block to examine the relationship between monetary policy and the aggregate demand curve in the following chapter.

SUMMARY

1. Planned expenditure, the total amount of goods demanded in the economy, is the same as aggregate demand, which is the sum of four types of spending: consumption expenditure, planned investment spending, government purchases, and net exports. We represent the total aggregate demand (Y^{ad}) with Equation 1: $Y^{ad} = C + I + G + NX$.

2. Consumption expenditure is described by the consumption function, which indicates that consumption expenditure will rise as disposable income increases. Planned expenditure and hence aggregate demand are negatively related to the real interest rate because a rise in the real interest rate reduces both planned investment spending and net exports. An increase in financial frictions raises the real interest rate for investments and hence lowers planned investment spending and aggregate demand. The government also affects planned expenditure via spending, which directly changes

aggregate demand, or via taxes, which indirectly affect aggregate demand by influencing disposable income and hence consumption expenditure.

3. The level of aggregate output when the goods market is in equilibrium is determined by the condition that aggregate output equals aggregate demand.

4. The *IS* curve traces out the combinations of the real interest rate and aggregate output at which the goods market is in equilibrium. The *IS* curve slopes downward because higher real interest rates lower planned investment spending and net exports and so lower equilibrium output.

5. The *IS* curve shifts to the right when there is a rise in autonomous consumption, a rise in autonomous investment, a rise in government purchases, a rise in autonomous net exports, a fall in taxes, or a decline in financial frictions. Movements of these six factors in the opposite direction will shift the *IS* curve to the left.

KEY TERMS

aggregate demand, p. 472
"animal spirits", p. 476
autonomous consumption
   expenditure, p. 474
autonomous investment, p. 475
autonomous net exports,
   p. 477
autonomous spending, p. 485

consumption expenditure, p. 473
consumption function, p. 473
disposable income, p. 473
exchange rate, p. 477
exogenous, p. 474
financial frictions, p. 476
fixed investment, p. 474
government purchases, p. 473

inventory investment, p. 474
IS curve, p. 479
marginal propensity to
   consume, p. 474
net exports, p. 473
planned investment
   spending, p. 473

QUESTIONS

1. "When the stock market rises, investment spending is increasing." Is this statement true, false, or uncertain? Explain your answer.

2. Why is inventory investment counted as part of aggregate spending if it isn't actually sold to the final end user?

3. "Since inventories can be costly to hold, firms' planned inventory investment should be zero, and firms should acquire inventory only through unplanned inventory accumulation." Is this statement true, false, or uncertain? Explain your answer.

4. During and in the aftermath of the financial crisis of 2007–2009, planned investment fell substantially despite significant decreases in the real interest rate. What factors related to the planned investment function could explain this?

5. If households and firms believe the economy will be in a recession in the future, will this necessarily cause a recession, or have any impact on output at all?

6. Why do increases in the real interest rate lead to decreases in net exports, and vice versa?

7. How would a decline in house prices or decrease in stock market prices affect the *IS* curve?

8. If firms suddenly become more optimistic about the profitability of investment and planned investment spending rises by $100 billion, while consumers become more pessimistic and autonomous consumer spending falls by $100 billion, what happens to aggregate output?

9. If an increase in autonomous consumer expenditure is matched by an equal increase in taxes, will aggregate output rise or fall?

10. If a change in the real interest rate has no effect on planned investment spending or net exports, what does this imply about the slope of the *IS* curve?

11. Inventories typically increase starting at the beginning of recessions, and begin to decline near the end of recessions. What does this say about the relationship between planned spending and aggregate output over the business cycle?

12. Why do companies cut production when they find that their unplanned inventory investment is greater than zero? If they didn't cut production, what effect would this have on their profits? Why?

13. "Firms will increase production when planned investment is less than (actual) total investment." Is this statement true, false, or uncertain? Explain your answer.

14. In each of the following cases, determine whether the *IS* curve shifts to the right or left, does not shift, or is indeterminate in the direction of shift.

    a. The real interest rate rises.

    b. The marginal propensity to consume declines.

    c. Financial frictions increase.

    d. Autonomous consumption decreases.

    e. Both taxes and government spending decrease by the same amount.

    f. The sensitivity of net exports to changes in the real interest rate decreases.

    g. The government provides tax incentives for research and development programs for firms.

15. "Financial frictions are not a problem for the economy, since they do not affect the safe policy rate which is controlled by the central bank." Is this statement true, false, or uncertain? Explain your answer.

16. When the Federal Reserve reduces its policy interest rate, how, if at all, is the *IS* curve affected? Briefly explain.

17. Suppose you read that prospects for stronger future economic growth have led the dollar to strengthen and stock prices to increase.

    a. What effect does the strengthened dollar have on the *IS* curve?

    b. What effect does the increase in stock prices have on the *IS* curve?

    c. What is the combined effect of these two events on the *IS* curve?

APPLIED PROBLEMS

18. Calculate the value of the consumption function at each level of income in the following table if autonomous consumption = 300, taxes = 200, and *mpc* = 0.9.

Income Y	Disposable Income Y^D	Consumption C
0		
100		
200		
300		
400		
500		
600		

19. Assume that autonomous consumption is $1,625 billion and disposable income is $11,500 billion. Calculate consumption expenditure if an increase of $1,000 in disposable income leads to an increase of $750 in consumption expenditure.

20. Suppose that Dell Corporation has 20,000 computers in its warehouses on December 31, 2022, ready to be shipped to merchants (each computer is valued at $500). By December 31, 2023, Dell Corporation has 25,000 computers ready to be shipped, each valued at $450.

  a. Calculate Dell's inventory on December 31, 2022.

  b. Calculate Dell's inventory investment in 2023.

  c. What happens to inventory spending during the early stages of an economic recession?

21. If the consumption function is $C = 100 + 0.75Y_D$, $I = 200$, government spending is 200, and net exports are zero, what will be the equilibrium level of output? What will happen to aggregate output if government spending rises by 100?

22. If the marginal propensity to consume is 0.75, by how much would government spending have to rise to increase output by $1,000 billion? By how much would taxes need to decrease to increase output by $1,000 billion?

23. Assuming both taxes and government spending increase by the same amount, derive an expression for the effect on equilibrium output.

24. Consider an economy described by the following data:

$$\overline{C} = \$3.25 \text{ trillion}$$
$$\overline{I} = \$1.3 \text{ trillion}$$
$$\overline{G} = \$3.5 \text{ trillion}$$
$$\overline{T} = \$3.0 \text{ trillion}$$
$$\overline{NX} = -\$1.0 \text{ trillion}$$
$$\overline{f} = 1$$
$$mpc = 0.75$$
$$d = 0.3$$
$$x = 0.1$$

  a. Derive simplified expressions for the consumption function, the investment function, and the net export function.

  b. Derive an expression for the *IS* curve.

  c. If the real interest rate is $r = 2$, what is equilibrium output? If $r = 5$, what is equilibrium output?

  d. Draw a graph of the *IS* curve showing the answers from part (c) above.

  e. If government purchases increase to $4.2 trillion, what will happen to equilibrium output at $r = 2$? What will happen to equilibrium output at $r = 5$? Show the effect of the increase in government purchases in your graph from part (d).

25. Consider an economy described by the following data:

$$\overline{C} = \$4 \text{ trillion}$$
$$\overline{I} = \$1.5 \text{ trillion}$$
$$\overline{G} = \$3.0 \text{ trillion}$$
$$\overline{T} = \$3.0 \text{ trillion}$$
$$\overline{NX} = \$1.0 \text{ trillion}$$
$$\overline{f} = 0$$
$$mpc = 0.8$$
$$d = 0.35$$
$$x = 0.15$$

  a. Derive an expression for the *IS* curve.

  b. Assume that the Federal Reserve controls the interest rate and sets the interest rate at $r = 4$. What is the equilibrium level of output?

  c. Suppose that a financial crisis begins and $\overline{f}$ increases to $\overline{f} = 3$. What will happen to equilibrium output?

If the Federal Reserve can set the interest rate, then at what level should the interest rate be set to keep output from changing?

d. Suppose the financial crisis causes $\bar{f}$ to increase as indicated in part (c) and also causes planned autonomous investment to decrease to $\bar{I} = \$1.1$ trillion.

Will the change in the interest rate implemented by the Federal Reserve in part (c) be effective in stabilizing output? If not, what additional monetary or fiscal policy changes could be implemented to stabilize output at the original equilibrium output level given in part (b)?

DATA ANALYSIS PROBLEMS

The Problems update with real-time data in **MyLab Economics** and are available for practice or instructor assignment.

1. **Real-time Data Analysis** Go to the St. Louis Federal Reserve FRED database, and find data on Personal Consumption Expenditures (PCEC), Personal Consumption Expenditures: Durable Goods (PCDG), Personal Consumption Expenditures: Nondurable Goods (PCND), and Personal Consumption Expenditures: Services (PCESV).
    a. According to the most recent data, what percentage of total household expenditures is devoted to the consumption of goods (both durable and nondurable goods)? What percentage is devoted to services?
    b. Given these data, which specific component of household expenditures would be most impacted by a reduction in overall household spending? Explain.

2. **Real-time Data Analysis** Go to the St. Louis Federal Reserve FRED database, and find data on Real Private Domestic Investment (GPDIC1), a measure of the real interest rate; the 10-year Treasury Inflation-Indexed Security, *TIIS* (FII10); and the spread between Baa corporate bonds and the 10-year U.S. treasury (BAA10YM), a measure of financial frictions. For (FII10) and (BAA10YM), convert the *frequency* setting to

"quarterly," and download the data into a spreadsheet. For each quarter, add the (FII10) and (BAA10YM) series to create r_i, the real interest rate for investments for that quarter. Then calculate the change in both investment and r_i as the change in each variable from the previous quarter.
    a. For the eight most recent quarters of data available, calculate the change in investment from the previous quarter, and then calculate the average change over the eight most recent quarters.
    b. Assume there is a one-quarter lag between movements in r_i and changes in investment; in other words, if r_i changes in the current quarter, it will affect investment in the next quarter. For the eight most recent lagged quarters of data available, calculate the one-quarter-lagged average change in r_i.
    c. Take the ratio of your answer from part (a) divided by your answer from part (b). What does this value represent? Briefly explain.
    d. Repeat parts (a) through (c) for the period 2008:Q3 to 2009:Q2. How do financial frictions help explain the behavior of investment during the financial crisis? How do the coefficients on investment compare between the current period and the financial crisis period? Briefly explain.

21 The Monetary Policy and Aggregate Demand Curves

Learning Objectives

21.1 Recognize the impact of changes in the nominal federal funds rate on short-term real interest rates.

21.2 Define and illustrate the monetary policy (*MP*) curve, and explain shifts in the *MP* curve.

21.3 Explain why the aggregate demand (*AD*) curve slopes downward, and explain shifts in the *AD* curve.

Preview

At the height of the financial crisis in December 2008, the Federal Open Market Committee of the Federal Reserve announced a surprisingly bold policy decision that sent the markets into a frenzy. The committee lowered the federal funds rate, the interest rate charged on overnight loans between banks, by 75 basis points (0.75 percentage point), moving the federal funds rate almost all the way to zero.

To see how a monetary policy action like the one described above affects the economy, we need to analyze how monetary policy affects aggregate demand. We start this chapter by explaining why monetary policy leads to higher interest rates when inflation increases, leading to a positive relationship between real interest rates and inflation that can be illustrated using the *monetary policy (MP) curve*. Then, by combining the *MP* curve with the *IS* curve we developed in the previous chapter, we derive the *aggregate demand curve*, a key element in the aggregate demand/aggregate supply model framework used in the rest of this book to discuss short-run economic fluctuations.

21.1 THE FEDERAL RESERVE AND MONETARY POLICY

LO 21.1 Recognize the impact of changes in the nominal federal funds rate on short-term real interest rates.

Central banks throughout the world use a very short-term interest rate as their primary policy tool. In the United States, the Federal Reserve conducts monetary policy via its setting of the federal funds rate. For example, after the FOMC meeting of March 15, 2020, the Federal Reserve issued a statement that "the Committee decided to lower the target range for the federal funds rate to 0 to ¼ percent."

As we saw in Chapter 15, the Federal Reserve controls the federal funds rate by varying the reserves it provides to the banking system. When it provides more reserves, banks have more money to lend to each other, and this excess liquidity causes the federal funds rate to fall. When the Fed drains reserves from the banking system, banks have less to lend, and the lack of liquidity leads to a rise in the federal funds rate.

The federal funds rate is a *nominal* interest rate, but as we learned in the previous chapter, it is the *real* interest rate that affects net exports and business spending, thereby determining the level of equilibrium output. How does the Federal Reserve's control of the federal funds rate enable it to control the real interest rate, through which monetary policy affects the economy?

Recall from Chapter 4 that the real interest rate, r, is the nominal interest rate, i, minus expected inflation, π^e.

$$r = i - \pi^e$$

Changes in nominal interest rates can change the real interest rate only if actual and expected inflation do not change much in the short run. Because prices typically are slow to move, changes in monetary policy will not have an immediate effect on inflation and expected inflation in the short run. As a result, **when the Federal Reserve lowers the federal funds rate, real interest rates fall; when the Federal Reserve raises the federal funds rate, real interest rates rise.**

21.2 THE MONETARY POLICY CURVE

LO 21.2 Define and illustrate the monetary policy (*MP*) curve, and explain shifts in the *MP* curve.

We have seen how the Federal Reserve can control real interest rates in the short run. The next step in our analysis is to examine how monetary policy reacts to inflation. The **monetary policy (MP) curve** indicates the relationship between the real interest rate set by the central bank and the inflation rate. We can write the equation of this curve as follows:

$$r = \bar{r} + \lambda\pi \tag{1}$$

where $\bar{r}$ is the autonomous (exogenous) component of the real interest rate set by the monetary policy authorities, which is unrelated to the current level of the inflation rate or any other variable in the model, and λ is the responsiveness of the real interest rate to the inflation rate.

To make our discussion of the monetary policy curve more concrete, Figure 1 shows an example of a monetary policy curve *MP* in which $\bar{r} = 1.0$ and $\lambda = 0.5$:

$$r = 1.0 + 0.5\pi \tag{2}$$

At point A, where inflation is 1%, the Federal Reserve sets the real interest rate at 1.5%; at point B, where inflation is 2%, the Fed sets the real interest rate at 2%; and at point C, where inflation is 3%, the Fed sets the real interest rate at 2.5%. The line going through points A, B, and C is the monetary policy curve *MP*, and it is upward-sloping, indicating that monetary policymakers raise real interest rates when the inflation rate rises.

Why the Monetary Policy Curve Has an Upward Slope

The simplest way to see why the *MP* curve has an upward slope is to recognize that central banks seek to keep inflation stable. To stabilize inflation, monetary policymakers tend to follow the **Taylor principle**, named after John Taylor of Stanford University: They raise real interest rates when there is a rise in inflation, as illustrated by the *MP* curve.[1] Central banks raise real interest rates when inflation increases because the rise in the real interest rate would be needed to contract the economy in order to bring inflation back down.

---

[1]Note that the Taylor principle differs from the Taylor rule, described in Chapter 16, in that it does not provide a rule for how monetary policy should react to conditions in the economy, whereas the Taylor rule does.

Mini-lecture

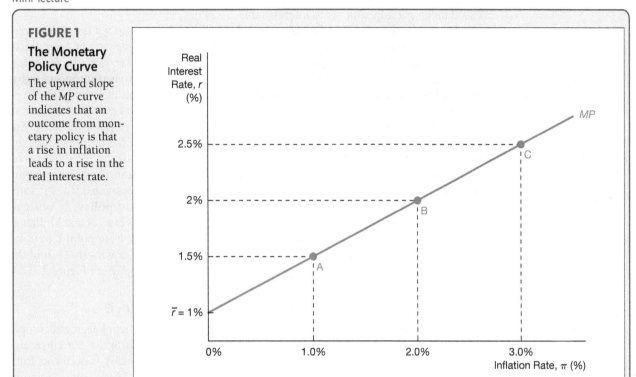

FIGURE 1

The Monetary Policy Curve

The upward slope of the *MP* curve indicates that an outcome from monetary policy is that a rise in inflation leads to a rise in the real interest rate.

An alternative rationale for why monetary policy leads to an upward-sloping *MP* curve results from the central bank not increasing liquidity in the banking system when there is a rise in inflation. Firms and households hold money to carry out transactions. When the inflation rate rises, the price level is higher than it otherwise would be, so more money is needed to pay for the goods and services they want to buy. If the central bank does not increase liquidity in the banking system and create more money for households and firms when inflation rises, households and firms would try to increase their money holdings by moving funds from interest-bearing assets into money. For example, they might increase their money holdings by selling bonds, which would drive down bond prices and therefore raise interest rates. Alternatively, they would try to increase their money holdings by reducing their interest-bearing savings accounts at banks, which would then have less funds to lend out, which would also drive interest rates up. The resulting rise in the nominal interest rate when the monetary policy does not increase liquidity in the banking system would raise the real interest rate, because in the short run, inflation expectations are unchanged, so nominal and real interest rates move together.

Shifts in the *MP* Curve

In common parlance, the Federal Reserve is said to "tighten" monetary policy when it raises real interest rates and to "ease" it when it lowers real interest rates. It is important, however, to distinguish between changes in monetary policy that shift the monetary policy curve, which we call *autonomous* changes, and the Taylor principle–driven changes that are reflected in movements along the monetary policy curve, which are called *automatic* adjustments to interest rates.

Central banks may make autonomous changes to monetary policy for various reasons. They may wish to change the inflation rate from its current value. For example, to lower inflation, they could increase $\bar{r}$ by one percentage point and so raise the real interest rate at any given inflation rate, a move that we will refer to as an **autonomous tightening of monetary policy**. At a 2% inflation rate, the real interest rate would rise from 2% to, say, 3%—that is, from point B to point B_2. This autonomous monetary tightening would shift the monetary policy curve upward by one percentage point, from MP_1 to MP_2 in Figure 2, thereby causing the economy to contract and inflation to fall. Or, the central banks may have other information, unrelated to inflation, suggesting that interest rates must be adjusted to achieve good economic outcomes. For example, if the economy is going into a recession, monetary policymakers will want to lower real interest rates at any given inflation rate, an **autonomous easing of monetary policy**, in order to stimulate the economy and to prevent inflation from falling. In this case, at a 2% inflation rate, the real interest rate would fall from 2% to, say, 1%—that is, from point B to point B_3. This autonomous easing of monetary policy would result in a downward shift of the monetary policy curve by, say, one percentage point, from MP_1 to MP_3 in Figure 2.

Movements Along Versus Shifts in the *MP* Curve

A stumbling block for many students studying the aggregate demand/aggregate supply (*AD/AS*) framework is understanding the distinction between *shifts in* the *MP* curve and *movements along* the *MP* curve. Movements along the *MP* curve—that is, movements from

Mini-lecture

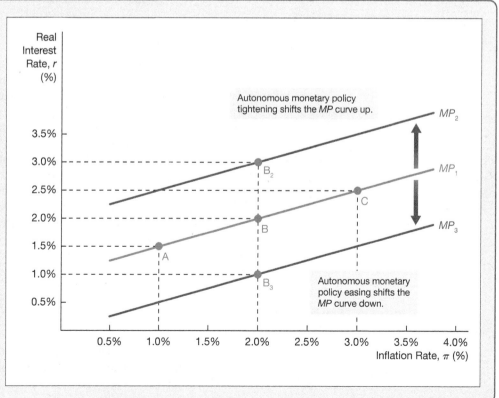

FIGURE 2

Shifts in the Monetary Policy Curve

Autonomous changes in monetary policy—for example, when a central bank changes the real interest rate at any given inflation rate—shift the *MP* curve. An autonomous tightening of monetary policy that increases the real interest rate shifts the *MP* curve up to MP_2, whereas an autonomous easing of monetary policy that lowers the real interest rate shifts the *MP* curve down to MP_3.

point A to B to C in Figure 1—should be viewed as a central bank's normal response (also known as an endogenous response) of raising interest rates when inflation is rising. Thus we can think of a movement along the *MP* curve as an *automatic* response of the central bank to a change in inflation. Such an automatic response does not involve a shift in the *MP* curve.

However, when the central bank raises interest rates *at a given level of the inflation rate*, this action is not an automatic response to higher inflation but is instead an autonomous tightening of monetary policy that shifts the *MP* curve up, from MP_1 to MP_2 in Figure 2.

The distinction between autonomous monetary policy changes and movements along the monetary policy curve is illustrated by the two following applications, which describe the monetary policy actions taken by the Federal Reserve in the period from 2004 to 2006 and at the onset of the global financial crisis in the fall of 2007.

APPLICATION

Movements Along the *MP* Curve: The Rise in the Federal Funds Rate Target, 2004–2006 and 2015–2019

Fears of deflation—i.e., fears that inflation could turn negative—led the Federal Reserve to commit to the very low federal funds rate of 1% from June 2003 to June 2004. However, with the economy growing rapidly, inflationary pressures began to rise, and at its June 2004 meeting the FOMC decided to increase the federal funds rate by ¼ of a percentage point. Furthermore, the FOMC made this increase a very automatic process, raising the federal funds rate by exactly the same amount at every subsequent FOMC meeting through June 2006 (see Figure 3). Then, from 2015 to 2019, inflation began to rise, and the FOMC raised the federal funds rate starting in December of 2015 until it reached a level of 2% in 2019. What do these episodes tell us about the monetary policy curve during these time periods?

Because the Federal Reserve was reacting to inflationary pressures in both periods, its monetary policy actions were clearly movements along the *MP* curve, say, from point A to B to C in Figure 1. The Fed was following the Taylor principle, reacting to higher inflation by raising the real interest rate. ◆

APPLICATION

Shift in the *MP* Curve: Autonomous Monetary Easing During the Global Financial and Coronavirus Crises

When the global financial crisis started in August 2007, inflation was rising and the unemployment rate was quite low, yet the Fed began an aggressive easing of monetary policy, lowering the federal funds rate as shown in Figure 3. In February 2020, the inflation rate was near its target level of 2%, and the unemployment rate was again very low. When it became clear that the coronavirus was beginning to spread out of control, the FOMC decided to lower the federal funds rate by 50 basis points (0.50 percentage point) on March 3, 2020, and then by another 100 basis points on March 15, 2020, down to zero. What were the implications for the monetary policy curve?

Real-time data

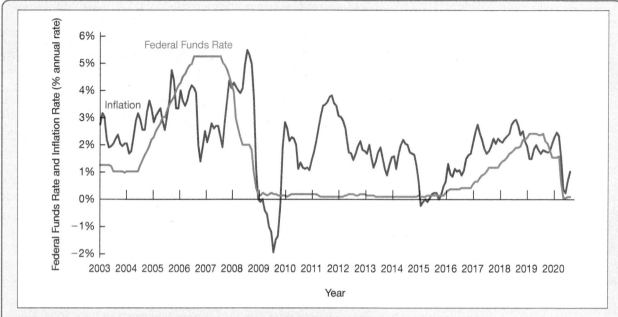

FIGURE 3 **The Federal Funds Rate and Inflation Rate, 2003–2020**

From June 2004 through June 2006, because of pressures from rising inflation, the Fed increased its policy rate, the federal funds rate, by 1/4 of a percentage point at every FOMC meeting. Then, from 2015 to 2019, rises in inflation led to the Fed raising the federal funds rate from zero to 2%. These Fed actions were a movement along the *MP* curve. In contrast, the Fed began an autonomous easing of monetary policy in September 2007 and in March 2020, bringing down the federal funds rate sharply, even though inflation at the time was not falling.

Source: Federal Reserve Bank of St. Louis FRED database: http://research.stlouisfed.org/fred2/series/CPIAUCSL; http://research.stlouisfed.org/fred2/series/FEDFUNDS.

A movement along the *MP* curve when the global financial crisis first started would have suggested that the Fed planned to continue hiking interest rates because inflation was rising, but instead the Fed did the opposite. Similarly, with unemployment low and the inflation rate near the target level, when the coronavirus crisis was first beginning, the Taylor principle would not have suggested that the Fed would lower interest rates, although it did do so dramatically in March. The Fed's actions in both cases thus shifted the monetary policy curve down, from MP_1 to MP_3, as shown in Figure 2. The Fed pursued this autonomous monetary policy easing because the negative shock to the economy caused by the disruption to financial markets and the coronavirus pandemic (discussed in Chapter 12) indicated that the economy was likely to weaken in the near future, and the inflation rate would then fall. Indeed, this is exactly what came to pass, with the economy going into a recession after the onset of the global financial and coronavirus crises. ◆

21.3 THE AGGREGATE DEMAND CURVE

LO 21.3 Explain why the aggregate demand (*AD*) curve slopes downward, and explain shifts in the *AD* curve.

We are now ready to derive the relationship between the inflation rate and aggregate output when the goods market is in equilibrium: the **aggregate demand curve**. The *MP* curve that we just developed demonstrates how central banks respond to changes in inflation by changing the interest rate in line with the Taylor principle. The *IS* curve we developed in Chapter 20 showed that changes in real interest rates, in turn, affect equilibrium output. With these two curves, we can now link the quantity of aggregate output demanded with the inflation rate, given the public's expectations of inflation and the stance of monetary policy. The aggregate demand curve is central to the aggregate demand and supply analysis we will develop further in the next chapter, which will enable us to explain short-run fluctuations in both aggregate output and inflation.

Deriving the Aggregate Demand Curve Graphically

Using the hypothetical *MP* curve from Equation 2, we know that when the inflation rate rises from 1% to 2% to 3%, the Federal Reserve reacts by raising the real interest rate from 1.5% to 2% to 2.5%. We plot these points in panel (a) of Figure 4 as the *MP* curve. In panel (b), we graph the *IS* curve described in Equation 13 of Chapter 20 ($Y = 12 - r$). As the real interest rate rises from 1.5% to 2% to 2.5%, the equilibrium moves from point 1 to point 2 to point 3, and aggregate output falls from $10.5 trillion to $10 trillion to $9.5 trillion. In other words, as real interest rates rise, investment and net exports decline, leading to a reduction in aggregate demand. Using the information from panels (a) and (b), we can create the curve shown in panel (c). As inflation rises from 1% to 2% to 3%, the equilibrium moves from point 1 to point 2 to point 3 in panel (c), and aggregate output falls from $10.5 trillion to $10 trillion to $9.5 trillion.

The line that connects the three points shown in panel (c) is the aggregate demand curve, *AD,* and it indicates the level of aggregate output corresponding to each of the three real interest rates consistent with equilibrium in the goods market for any given inflation rate. The aggregate demand curve has a downward slope because a higher inflation rate leads the central bank to raise the real interest rate, thereby lowering planned spending and hence lowering the level of equilibrium aggregate output.

By using some algebra (see the FYI box "Deriving the Aggregate Demand Curve Algebraically"), the *AD* curve in Figure 4 can be written numerically as follows:

$$Y = 11 - 0.5\pi \qquad (3)$$

FYI   **Deriving the Aggregate Demand Curve Algebraically**

To derive a numerical *AD* curve, we start by taking the numerical *IS* curve given by Equation 13 in Chapter 20:

$$Y = 12 - r$$

We then use the numerical *MP* curve given in Equation 2, $r = 1.0 + 0.5\pi$, to substitute for *r*, yielding

$$Y = 12 - (1.0 + 0.5\pi)$$
$$= (12 - 1) - 0.5\pi$$
$$= 11 - 0.5\pi$$

which is the same as Equation 3 in the text.

Similarly, we can derive a more general version of the *AD* curve by using the algebraic version of the *IS* curve given by Equation 12 in Chapter 20:

$$Y = [\overline{C} + \overline{I} - d\overline{f} + \overline{G} + \overline{NX} - mpc \times \overline{T}]$$
$$\times \frac{1}{1 - mpc} - \frac{d + x}{1 - mpc} \times r$$

We then substitute for *r* using the algebraic *MP* curve given in Equation 1, $r = \overline{r} + \lambda\pi$, to get the more general equation of the *AD* curve:

$$Y = [\overline{C} + \overline{I} - d\overline{f} + \overline{G} + \overline{NX} - mpc \times \overline{T}]$$
$$\times \frac{1}{1 - mpc} - \frac{d + x}{1 - mpc} \times (\overline{r} + \lambda\pi)$$

Mini-lecture

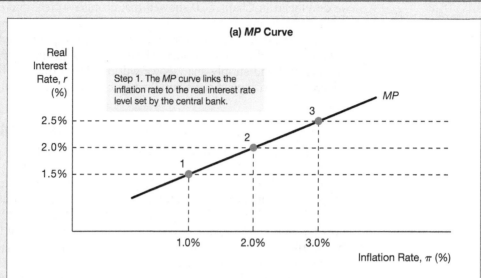

(a) *MP* Curve

Step 1. The *MP* curve links the inflation rate to the real interest rate level set by the central bank.

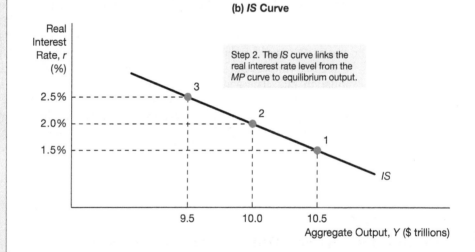

(b) *IS* Curve

Step 2. The *IS* curve links the real interest rate level from the *MP* curve to equilibrium output.

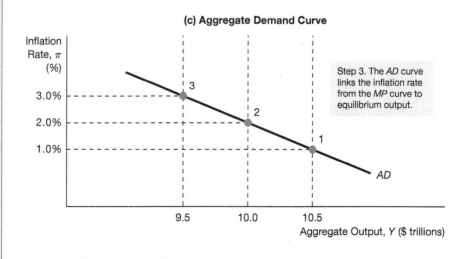

(c) Aggregate Demand Curve

Step 3. The *AD* curve links the inflation rate from the *MP* curve to equilibrium output.

Factors That Shift the Aggregate Demand Curve

Movements along the aggregate demand curve describe how the equilibrium level of aggregate output changes when the inflation rate changes. When factors other than the inflation rate change, however, the aggregate demand curve shifts. We first review the factors that shift the *IS* curve, and then consider the factors that shift the *AD* curve.

Shifts in the *IS* Curve   We saw in the preceding chapter that there are six factors that cause the *IS* curve to shift. It turns out that these same factors will cause the aggregate demand curve to shift as well:

1. Autonomous consumption expenditure
2. Autonomous investment spending
3. Government purchases
4. Taxes
5. Autonomous net exports
6. Financial frictions

We examine how changes in these factors lead to a shift in the aggregate demand curve, as shown in Figure 5.

Suppose that inflation is at 2.0%, and so the *MP* curve in panel (a) of Figure 5 shows that the real interest rate is at 2.0%. The IS_1 curve in panel (b) then shows that the equilibrium level of output is at $10 trillion at point A_1, which corresponds to an equilibrium level of output of $10 trillion at point A_1 on the AD_1 curve in panel (c). Now suppose there is a rise in, for example, government purchases of $1 trillion. Panel (b) shows that with both the inflation rate and the real interest rate held constant at 2.0%, the equilibrium moves from point A_1 to point A_2, with output rising to $12.5 trillion[2] and so the *IS* curve shifts to the right from IS_1 to IS_2. The rise in output to $12.5 trillion means that, holding inflation and the real interest rate constant, the equilibrium in panel (c) also moves from point A_1 to point A_2, and so the *AD* curve also shifts to the right, from AD_1 to AD_2.

Figure 5 shows that ***any factor that shifts the IS curve shifts the aggregate demand curve in the same direction***. Therefore, any factor that shifts the *IS* curve to the right—a rise in autonomous consumption expenditure or planned investment spending encouraged by "animal spirits," a rise in government purchases, an autonomous rise in net exports, a fall in taxes, or a decline in financial frictions—will also shift the aggregate demand curve to the right. Conversely, any factor that shifts the *IS* curve to the left—a fall in autonomous consumption expenditure, a fall in planned investment spending, a fall in government purchases, a fall in net exports, a rise in taxes, or a rise in financial frictions—will shift the aggregate demand curve to the left.

Shifts in the *MP* Curve   We now examine what happens to the aggregate demand curve when the *MP* curve shifts. Suppose the Federal Reserve is worried about the economy overheating and so decides to autonomously tighten monetary policy by raising the real interest rate by one percentage point at any given level of the inflation rate. At an inflation rate of 2.0%, the real interest rate rises from 2.0% to 3.0% in Figure 6. The *MP* curve shifts up from MP_1 to MP_2 in panel (a). Panel (b) shows that when the inflation rate is at 2.0%, the higher real interest rate of 3.0% causes the equilibrium to

---

[2]As we saw in the numerical example in Chapter 20, a rise in government purchases of $1 trillion leads to a $2.5 trillion increase in equilibrium output at any given real interest rate, and this is why output rises from $10 trillion to $12.5 trillion when the real interest rate is at 2.0%.

Mini-lecture

FIGURE 5

Shift in the AD Curve from Shifts in the IS Curve

At a 2% inflation rate in panel (a), the monetary policy curve indicates that the real interest rate is 2%. An increase in government purchases shifts the IS curve to the right in panel (b). At a given inflation rate and real interest rate of 2%, equilibrium output rises from $10 trillion to $12.5 trillion, which is shown as a movement from point A_1 to point A_2 in panel (c), shifting the aggregate demand curve to the right from AD_1 to AD_2. Any factor that shifts the IS curve shifts the AD curve in the same direction.

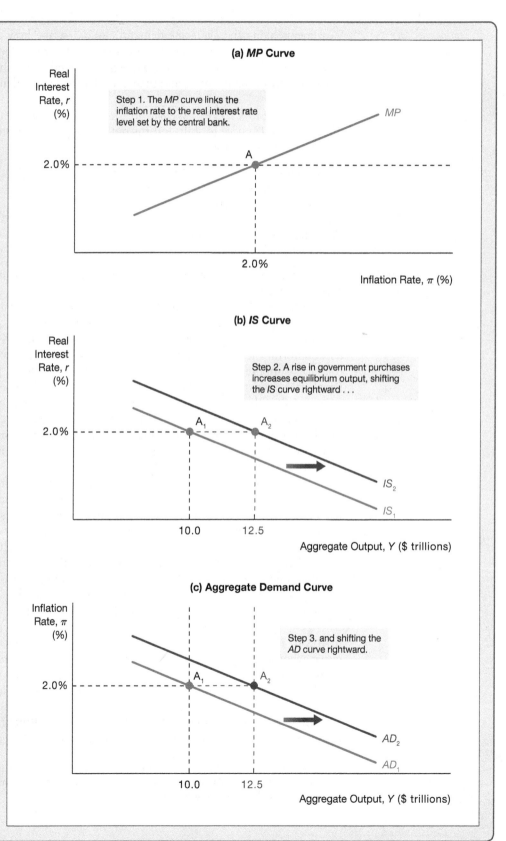

(a) MP Curve

Real Interest Rate, r (%)

Step 1. The MP curve links the inflation rate to the real interest rate level set by the central bank.

MP

A

2.0%

2.0%

Inflation Rate, π (%)

(b) IS Curve

Real Interest Rate, r (%)

Step 2. A rise in government purchases increases equilibrium output, shifting the IS curve rightward . . .

A_1 A_2

2.0%

IS_2

IS_1

10.0   12.5

Aggregate Output, Y ($ trillions)

(c) Aggregate Demand Curve

Inflation Rate, π (%)

Step 3. and shifting the AD curve rightward.

A_1 A_2

2.0%

AD_2

AD_1

10.0   12.5

Aggregate Output, Y ($ trillions)

Mini-lecture

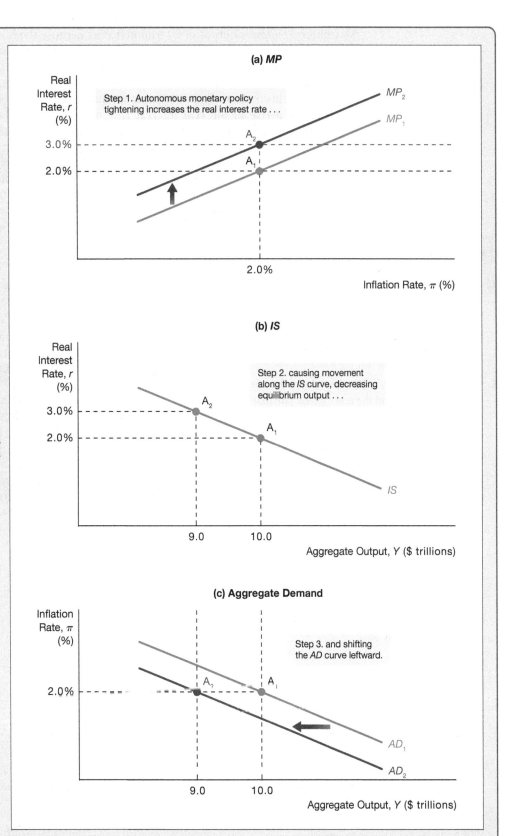
(a) MP

Real Interest Rate, r (%)

Step 1. Autonomous monetary policy tightening increases the real interest rate . . .

MP_2

MP_1

A_2 — 3.0%

A_1 — 2.0%

2.0%

Inflation Rate, π (%)

(b) IS

Real Interest Rate, r (%)

Step 2. causing movement along the *IS* curve, decreasing equilibrium output . . .

A_2 — 3.0%

A_1 — 2.0%

IS

9.0   10.0

Aggregate Output, Y ($ trillions)

(c) Aggregate Demand

Inflation Rate, π (%)

Step 3. and shifting the *AD* curve leftward.

2.0%

A_2 A_1

AD_1

AD_2

9.0   10.0

Aggregate Output, Y ($ trillions)

move from point A_1 to point A_2 on the *IS* curve, with output falling from $10 trillion to $9 trillion. The lower output of $9 trillion occurs because the higher real interest leads to a decline in investment and net exports, which lowers aggregate demand. The lower output of $9 trillion then decreases the equilibrium output level from point A_1 to point A_2 in panel (c), and so the *AD* curve shifts to the left, from AD_1 to AD_2.

Our conclusion from Figure 6 is that ***an autonomous tightening of monetary policy—that is, a rise in the real interest rate at any given inflation rate—shifts the aggregate demand curve to the left. Conversely, an autonomous easing of monetary policy shifts the aggregate demand curve to the right.***

We have now derived and analyzed the aggregate demand curve, an essential element in the aggregate demand and supply framework, that we will examine in the next chapter. We will use the aggregate demand curve in this framework to determine both aggregate output and inflation, as well as to examine events that cause these variables to change.

SUMMARY

1. When the Federal Reserve lowers the federal funds rate by providing more liquidity to the banking system, real interest rates fall in the short run; when the Federal Reserve raises the federal funds rate by reducing the amount of liquidity in the banking system, real interest rates rise in the short run.

2. The monetary policy (*MP*) curve shows the relationship between inflation and the real interest rate that arises from monetary authorities' actions. Monetary policymakers follow the Taylor principle by raising real interest rates in response to higher inflation, represented by the upward slope of the monetary policy curve. An autonomous tightening of monetary policy occurs when monetary policymakers raise the real interest rate at any given inflation rate, resulting in an upward shift of the monetary policy curve. An autonomous easing of monetary policy and a downward shift of the monetary

policy curve occur when monetary policymakers lower the real interest rate at any given inflation rate.

3. The aggregate demand curve gives the level of equilibrium aggregate output (which equals the total quantity of output demanded) for any given inflation rate. It slopes downward because a higher inflation rate leads the central bank to raise real interest rates, which leads to a lower level of equilibrium output. The aggregate demand curve will shift in the same direction as the *IS* curve; hence the *AD* curve shifts to the right when government purchases increase, taxes decrease, "animal spirits" encourage consumer and business spending, autonomous net exports increase, or financial frictions decrease. An autonomous tightening of monetary policy—that is, an increase in the real interest rate at any given inflation rate—leads to a decline in aggregate demand, and the aggregate demand curve shifts to the left.

KEY TERMS

aggregate demand curve, p. 496
autonomous easing of monetary policy,
   p. 494

autonomous tightening of monetary
   policy, p. 494

monetary policy (*MP*) curve, p. 492
Taylor principle, p. 492

QUESTIONS

1. When the inflation rate increases, what happens to the federal funds rate? Operationally, how does the Fed adjust the federal funds rate?

2. What is the key assumption underlying the Fed's ability to control the real interest rate?

3. Why does the *MP* curve necessarily have an upward slope?

4. If $\lambda = 0$, what does this imply about the relationship between the nominal interest rate and the inflation rate?

5. How does an autonomous tightening or easing of monetary policy by the Fed affect the *MP* curve?

6. How is an autonomous tightening or easing of monetary policy different from a change in the real interest rate caused by a change in the current inflation rate?

7. Suppose that a new Fed chair is appointed and that his or her approach to monetary policy can be summarized by the following statement: "I care only about increasing employment. Inflation has been at very low levels for quite some time; my priority is to ease monetary policy to promote employment." How would you expect the monetary policy curve to be affected, if at all?

8. "The Fed decreased the fed funds rate in late 2007, even though inflation was increasing. This action demonstrated a violation of the Taylor principle." Is this statement true, false, or uncertain? Explain your answer.

9. What factors affect the slope of the aggregate demand curve?

10. "Autonomous monetary policy is more effective at changing output when λ is higher." Is this statement true, false, or uncertain? Explain your answer.

11. If net exports were not sensitive to changes in the real interest rate, would monetary policy be more or less effective in changing output?

12. If an asset-price bubble begins to form, assuming the central bank responds, how is it likely to respond, and what will be the effect on the *MP* curve?

13. For each of the following situations, describe how (if at all) the *IS*, *MP*, and *AD* curves are affected.

  a. A decrease in financial frictions

  b. An increase in taxes and an autonomous easing of monetary policy

  c. An increase in the current inflation rate

  d. A decrease in autonomous consumption

  e. Firms become more optimistic about the future of the economy.

  f. The new Federal Reserve chair begins to care more about fighting inflation.

14. What would be the effect of an increase in U.S. net exports on the aggregate demand curve? Would an increase in net exports affect the monetary policy curve? Explain.

15. Why does the aggregate demand curve shift when "animal spirits" change?

16. Suppose that government spending is increased at the same time that an autonomous monetary policy tightening occurs. What will happen to the position of the aggregate demand curve?

17. If financial frictions increase, how will this affect credit spreads, and how might the central bank respond? Why?

18. "If $\bar{f}$ increases, then the Fed can keep output constant by reducing the real interest rate by the same amount as the increase in financial frictions." Is this statement true, false, or uncertain? Explain your answer.

APPLIED PROBLEMS

19. Assume that the monetary policy curve is given by $r = 1.5 + 0.75\pi$.

  a. Calculate the real interest rate when the inflation rate is 2%, 3%, and 4%.

  b. Draw a graph of the *MP* curve, labeling the points from part (a).

  c. Assume now that the monetary policy curve is given by $r = 2.5 + 0.75\pi$. Does the new monetary policy curve represent an autonomous tightening or loosening of monetary policy?

  d. Calculate the real interest rate when the inflation rate is 2%, 3%, and 4%, and draw the new *MP* curve, showing the shift from part (b).

20. Use an *IS* curve and an *MP* curve to derive graphically the *AD* curve.

21. Suppose the monetary policy curve is given by $r = 1.5 + 0.75\pi$, and the *IS* curve is given by $Y = 13 - r$.

  a. Calculate an expression for the aggregate demand curve.

  b. Calculate the real interest rate and aggregate output when the inflation rate is 2%, 3%, and 4%.

  c. Draw graphs of the *IS*, *MP*, and *AD* curves, labeling the points from part (b) on the appropriate graphs.

22. Consider an economy described by the following:

$$\overline{C} = \$4 \text{ trillion}$$
$$\overline{I} = \$1.5 \text{ trillion}$$
$$\overline{G} = \$3.0 \text{ trillion}$$
$$\overline{T} = \$3.0 \text{ trillion}$$

$\overline{NX} = \$1.0$ trillion

$\bar{f} = 0$

$mpc = 0.8$

$d = 0.35$

$x = 0.15$

$\lambda = 0.5$

$\bar{r} = 2$

a. Derive expressions for the *MP* curve and the *AD* curve.

b. Calculate the real interest rate and aggregate output when $\pi = 2$ and $\pi = 4$.

c. Draw a graph of the *MP* curve and the *AD* curve, labeling the points given in part (b).

23. Consider an economy described by the following:

$\overline{C} = \$3.25$ trillion

$\overline{I} = \$1.3$ trillion

$\overline{G} = \$3.5$ trillion

$\overline{T} = \$3.0$ trillion

$\overline{NX} = -\$1.0$ trillion

$\bar{f} = 1$

$mpc = 0.75$

$d = 0.3$

$x = 0.1$

$\lambda = 1$

$\bar{r} = 1$

a. Derive expressions for the *MP* curve and the *AD* curve.

b. Assume that $\pi = 1$. Calculate the real interest rate, the equilibrium level of output, consumption, planned investment, and net exports.

c. Suppose the Fed increases $\bar{r}$ to $\bar{r} = 2$. Calculate the real interest rate, the equilibrium level of output, consumption, planned investment, and net exports at this new level of $\bar{r}$.

d. Considering that output, consumption, planned investment, and net exports all decreased in part (c), why might the Fed choose to increase $\bar{r}$?

24. Consider the economy described in Applied Problem 23.

a. Derive expressions for the *MP* curve and the *AD* curve.

b. Assume that $\pi = 2$. What are the real interest rate and the equilibrium level of output?

c. Suppose government spending increases to $4 trillion. What happens to equilibrium output?

d. If the Fed wants to keep output constant, then what monetary policy change should it make?

25. Suppose the *MP* curve is given by $r = 2 + \pi$, and the *IS* curve is given by $Y = 20 - 2r$.

a. Derive an expression for the *AD* curve, and draw a graph labeling points at $\pi = 0$, $\pi = 4$, and $\pi = 8$.

b. Suppose that λ increases to $\lambda = 2$. Derive an expression for the new *AD* curve, and draw the new *AD* curve using the graph from part (a).

c. What does your answer to part (b) imply about the relationship between a central bank's distaste for inflation and the slope of the *AD* curve?

DATA ANALYSIS PROBLEMS

The Problems update with real-time data in **MyLab Economics** and are available for practice or instructor assignment.

1. Real-time Data Analysis A measure of real interest rates can be approximated by the Treasury Inflation-Indexed Security, or *TIIS*. Go to the St. Louis Federal Reserve FRED database, and find data on the five-year *TIIS* (FII5) and the personal consumption expenditure price index (PCECTPI), a measure of the price index. Choose "Quarterly" for the *frequency* setting of the *TIIS*, and download both data series. Convert the price index data to annualized inflation rates by taking the quarter-to-quarter percent change in the price index and multiplying it by 4. Be sure to multiply by 100 so that your results are percentages.

a. Calculate the average inflation rate and the average real interest rate over the most recent four quarters of data available and the four quarters prior to that.

b. Calculate the change in the average inflation rate between the most recent annual period and the year prior. Then calculate the change in the average real interest rate over the same period.

c. Using your answers to part (b), compute the ratio of the change in the average real interest rate to the change in the average inflation rate. What does this ratio represent? Comment on how it relates to the Taylor principle.

2. **Real-time Data Analysis** A measure of real interest rates can be approximated by the Treasury Inflation-Indexed Security, or *TIIS*. Go to the St. Louis Federal Reserve FRED database, and find data on the five-year *TIIS* (FII5) and the personal consumption expenditure price index (PCECTPI), a measure of the price index. Choose "Quarterly" for the *frequency* setting for the *TIIS*, and choose "Percent Change From Year Ago" for the *units* setting on (PCECTPI). Plot both series on the same graph, using data from 2007 through the most current data available. Use the graph to identify periods of autonomous monetary policy changes. Briefly explain your reasoning.

22

Aggregate Demand and Supply Analysis

Learning Objectives

22.1 Describe the variables that aggregate demand and supply analysis is trying to explain.

22.2 Summarize and illustrate the aggregate demand curve and the factors that shift it.

22.3 Illustrate and interpret the short-run and long-run aggregate supply curves.

22.4 Illustrate and interpret shifts in the short-run and long-run aggregate supply curves.

22.5 Illustrate and interpret the short-run and long-run equilibria and the role of the self-correcting mechanism.

22.6 Illustrate and interpret the short-run and long-run effects of a shock to aggregate demand.

22.7 Illustrate and interpret the short-run and long-run effects of supply shocks.

22.8 Summarize the conclusions from aggregate demand and supply analysis.

Preview

In earlier chapters, we focused considerable attention on monetary policy because it touches our everyday lives by affecting both inflation and the quantity of jobs available. In this chapter, we develop aggregate demand and supply analysis, a basic tool that will enable us to explain the effects of monetary policy on fluctuations in inflation, aggregate output, and unemployment. (The Following the Financial News box, "Aggregate Output, Unemployment, and Inflation" indicates where and how often data on aggregate output, unemployment, and the inflation rate are published.) Not only will the analysis help us interpret the past but it also will help us understand recent episodes in the business cycle, such as the severe recessions resulting from the global financial crisis of 2007–2009 and the coronavirus pandemic in 2020. It also will help predict how future events may affect aggregate output, unemployment, and inflation.

22.1 BUSINESS CYCLES AND INFLATION

LO 22.1 Describe the variables that aggregate demand and supply analysis is trying to explain.

Before we develop aggregate demand and supply analysis, let's look at what this analysis is trying to explain: business cycles and inflation. First, let's discuss business cycles.

Business Cycles

Business cycles are the upward and downward movements of aggregate economic activity produced in the economy. Real GDP, the total of goods and services produced in a year, using constant prices, is the most widely used measure of aggregate economic activity, also referred to as **aggregate output**. Many economic variables move up and down together during business cycles. Most importantly, as Figure 1 shows, employment rises when real GDP is rising, and employment falls when real GDP falls. **Recessions**, the shaded areas in the figure, are periods when aggregate economic activity is decreasing or contracting. **Expansions** (also called **booms**) are periods when aggregate economic activity is increasing or expanding.

One way to look at business cycles is to divide aggregate output (real GDP) into two components, the long-run trend, which grows smoothly over time, and fluctuations around this trend. The long-run trend of aggregate output, which grows smoothly over time, is referred to as **potential output** (or **potential GDP**). It is the level of

Real-time data

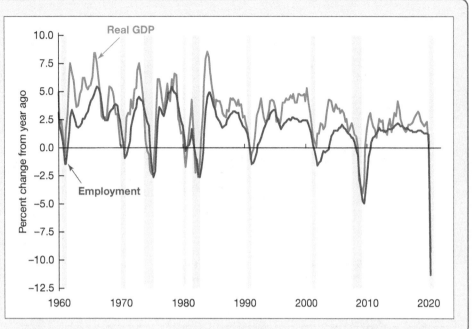

FIGURE 1

GDP and Employment Growth, 1960–2020

The figure shows the growth rate of real GDP and employment from four quarters earlier, with the recession periods (peak to trough) shaded. Note how closely real GDP and employment growth move together. (*Note:* Shaded areas indicate recessions.)

Source: Federal Reserve Bank of St. Louis, FRED database: https://fred.stlouisfed.org/series/ GDPC1; https://fred.stlouisfed. org/series/PAYEMS.

aggregate output that is generated when the economy is at full employment and firms on average are producing at their long-run, profit-maximizing level.

We can think about the business cycle as a series of short-run deviations of aggregate output from its long-run trend (that is, from potential output). The **output gap** is the percentage difference between actual aggregate output and potential output.[1] The output gap is measured as the *percentage* difference between actual real GDP and potential GDP. For example, in the second quarter of 2020, the output gap was –10.0%, indicating that aggregate output was 10% *below* potential output. Figure 2 shows how the output gap has fluctuated since 1960, with the shaded areas indicating recessions. The output gap allows us to compare the magnitude of different business cycle fluctuations. For example, it shows that the 1981–1982 recession, the 2007–2009 Great Recession, and the 2020 Covid-19 Recession had output gaps that were large and negative, with real GDP falling more than 6% below potential GDP. Other recessions, like those of 1960–1961, 1969–1970, 1990–1991, and 2000–2001, were far milder, with output gaps never becoming more negative than –3%.

Although the output gap fell to a similar level in the 1981–1982 and 2007–2009 recessions, the figure shows that the recovery from the 2007–2009 recession has been much slower, with the output gap not returning to zero where there is full employment until nine years after the recession ended in June 2009. For this reason, the 2007–2009 recession is viewed as much more severe than the 1981–1982 recession. Indeed, the 2007–2009 recession was, at that time, the most severe since the Great Depression of 1929–1933 and has become known as the "Great Recession."

[1]The output gap is calculated as the difference between real GDP and potential GDP, divided by potential GDP, which is then expressed as a percent by multiplying 100.

In the second quarter of 2020, real GDP was $17.282 trillion, while potential GDP was $19.204 trillion. The calculation for the output gap for that quarter is:

$$\text{Output Gap} = \frac{\text{Real GDP} - \text{Potential GDP}}{\text{Potential GDP}} = \frac{17.282 - 19.204}{19.204} = -0.100 = -10.0\%$$

Real-time data

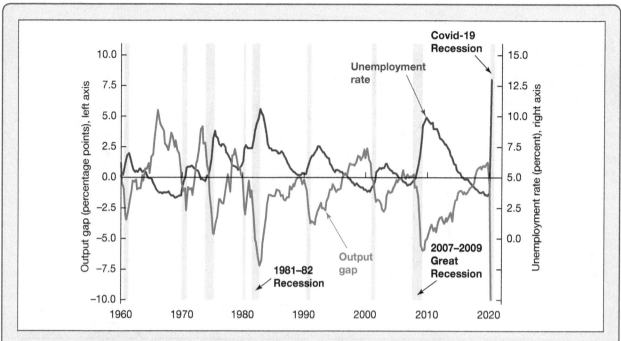

FIGURE 2   Output Gap and Unemployment Rate, 1960–2020

The output gap is a measure of the magnitude of business cycle fluctuations, and it shows that the three most severe recessions since 1960 were the 1981–1982 recession, the 2007–2009 Great Recession, and the 2020 Covid-19 recession. The figure shows that the output gap is strongly negatively related to the unemployment rate, so that when the output gap falls, the unemployment rate rises, and vice versa. (*Note:* Shaded areas indicate recessions.)

Source: Federal Reserve Bank of St. Louis, FRED database: https://fred.stlouisfed.org/series/GDPC1; https://fred.stlouisfed.org/series/GDPPOT; https://fred.stlouisfed.org/series/UNRATE.

One of the key reasons we care about business cycles is also shown in Figure 2, which plots not only business cycle fluctuations as represented by the output gap, but also the **unemployment rate**, the percentage of workers looking for work but who do not have jobs. As Figure 2 shows, there is a strong negative relationship between the unemployment rate and the output gap. During booms, aggregate output is rising relative to potential output and the output gap rises. (Note that as you can see in the figure, if output is below potential output so the output gap is negative, when the output gap rises, then the output gap becomes less negative. When output is above potential output, then the output gap becomes more positive as it rises.) During business cycle booms when the output gap is rising, firms hire more workers, so the unemployment rate declines.

For example, during the business cycle expansion from November 2001 to December 2007, actual real GDP rose relative to potential GDP, with the output gap rising (becoming less negative) from –2.0% to +0.2%. This rising output gap was accompanied by a fall in the unemployment rate from 5.5% to 5.0%. Then during the Great Recession from December 2007 to June 2009, aggregate real GDP fell sharply, the output gap declined to –6.0%, and the unemployment rate rose to 9.5%. An important fact to note from the figure is that the unemployment rate can remain very high during a business cycle expansion, particularly in its early phase. For example, even a year and a half after the business cycle expansion began in June 2009, the unemployment rate remained above 9%.

Clearly, business cycle fluctuations produce large swings in the unemployment rate, with recessions hitting workers very hard when the unemployment rate rises sharply. When unemployment is high, it is more likely that you might lose your job.

Furthermore, if you are unlucky enough to graduate when unemployment is high, you will have a hard time finding the dream job you were anticipating.

When people lose their jobs during a recession, many of them can no longer afford to make their mortgage payments and end up losing their homes. Poverty rates also rise. Many people also become depressed during recessions because their self-worth is damaged when they are unemployed and cannot find a job. Their health can further deteriorate if they are unable to pay for adequate health care.

Just as workers do not fare well during recessions, neither do businesses, which often find that (1) they cannot sell all the goods they have produced and (2) they receive lower prices for their products. During recessions, business profits decline. Many firms now have to close their factories or can no longer pay back their loans and end up declaring bankruptcy. Many businesses close their doors, never to open them again.

We care about business cycles because they lead to large fluctuations in unemployment and output. Booms are good for workers and businesses, while recessions lead to great economic hardship. We need to understand what drives business cycles, and as we will see, aggregate demand and supply analysis enables us to do exactly that. Indeed, we will use this analysis to explain major business cycle episodes such as the 1981–1982 recession, the Great Recession of 2007–2009, and the Covid-19 recession that started in 2020.

Inflation

We also care about inflation because low and stable inflation reduces the need for businesses to change prices frequently, which otherwise would be costly. Low and stable inflation also lowers uncertainty in the economy, which makes it easier for households and businesses to make economic decisions, thus increasing the efficiency of the economy.

Figure 3 shows that inflation has not always been low and stable. For example, the inflation rate reached a peak of over 14% in 1980. In contrast, the inflation rate fell precipitously during the 2007–2009 recession, even going negative for a brief period of time. We will also use aggregate demand and supply analysis to explain fluctuations in inflation, such as those that occurred in these two episodes.

Real-time data

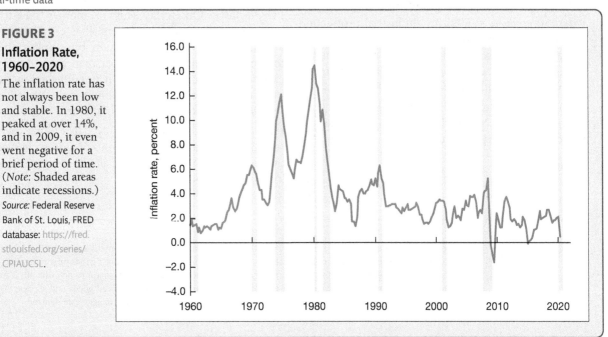

FIGURE 3

Inflation Rate, 1960–2020

The inflation rate has not always been low and stable. In 1980, it peaked at over 14%, and in 2009, it even went negative for a brief period of time. (*Note:* Shaded areas indicate recessions.)

Source: Federal Reserve Bank of St. Louis, FRED database: https://fred.stlouisfed.org/series/CPIAUCSL.

22.2 AGGREGATE DEMAND

LO 22.2 Summarize and illustrate the aggregate demand curve and the factors that shift it.

We start our analysis of aggregate demand by examining the components of aggregate demand.

Components of Aggregate Demand

Aggregate quantity demanded is the total quantity of goods and services that households, businesses, governments, and foreigners want to buy (demand) at any given inflation rate during a specific period, such as a year. To understand what determines the aggregate quantity demanded, we examine its components.

Aggregate quantity demanded is made up of four component parts: **consumption expenditure**, the total demand for consumer goods and services; **planned investment spending**,[2] the total planned spending by business firms on new machines,

---

Following the Financial News | Aggregate Output, Unemployment, and Inflation

Newspapers and Internet sites periodically report data that provide information on the level of aggregate output, unemployment, and the inflation rate. Here is a list of the relevant data series, their frequencies of publication, and the times at which they are published.

Aggregate Output and Unemployment

Real GDP: Quarterly (January–March, April–June, July–September, October–December); published three to four weeks after the end of a quarter.

Industrial production: Monthly. Industrial production is not as comprehensive a measure of aggregate output as real GDP because it measures only manufacturing output; the estimate for the previous month is reported in the middle of the following month.

Unemployment rate: Monthly. The previous month's figure is usually published on the Friday of the first week of the following month.

Inflation Rate

Several different measures of the inflation rate are calculated from different measures of the price level.

GDP deflator: Quarterly. This comprehensive measure of the price level (described in the appendix to Chapter 1) is published at the same time as the real GDP data.

Consumer price index (CPI): Monthly. The CPI is a measure of the price level for consumers (also described in the appendix to Chapter 1); the value for the previous month is published in the third or fourth week of the following month.

PCE deflator: Quarterly. This is another measure of the price level for consumers. It is calculated in a similar way to the GDP deflator but applies only to the items that are in the personal consumption expenditure category of GDP. It is published at the same time as the real GDP data and is the preferred inflation measure of the Federal Reserve.

Producer price index (PPI): Monthly. The PPI is a measure of the average level of wholesale prices charged by producers and is published at the same time as industrial production data.

---

[2]Recall that economists restrict the definition of the word *investment* to mean the purchase of new physical capital, such as a new machine or a new house, which adds to spending on newly produced goods or services. This differs from the everyday use of the term by noneconomists, who use the word *investment* to describe purchases of common stocks or bonds, purchases that do not necessarily involve newly produced goods and services. When economists speak of investment spending, they are referring to purchases that add to aggregate demand.

factories, and other capital goods, plus planned spending on new homes; **government purchases**, spending by all levels of government (federal, state, and local) on goods and services (paper clips, computers, computer programming, missiles, government employees, and so on); and **net exports**, the net foreign spending on domestic goods and services, equal to exports minus imports. Using the symbols C for consumption expenditure, I for planned investment spending, G for government spending, and NX for net exports, we can write the following expression for aggregate demand Y^{ad}:

$$Y^{ad} = C + I + G + NX \qquad (1)$$

Deriving the Aggregate Demand Curve

The first building block of aggregate demand and supply analysis is the **aggregate demand curve**, which describes the relationship between the aggregate quantity demanded and the inflation rate when all other variables are held constant.

The first step in deriving the aggregate demand curve is to recognize that when the inflation rate rises ($\pi \uparrow$), the real interest rate rises ($r \uparrow$). This occurs for either of two reasons: When the inflation rate rises, (1) the monetary authorities take actions to raise the real interest rate to keep inflation from spiraling out of control or (2) the monetary authorities just do not increase liquidity in the banking system when inflation rises, so the real interest rate rises.

Next we can examine the effects of the higher real interest rate on the individual components of aggregate demand. When the real interest rate is higher, the cost of financing purchases of new physical capital becomes higher, making investment less profitable and causing planned investment spending to decline ($I \downarrow$). Because, as shown in Equation 1, planned investment spending is included in aggregate demand, the decline in planned investment spending causes aggregate demand to fall ($Y^{ad} \downarrow$). A higher inflation rate therefore leads to a lower level of the quantity of aggregate output demanded ($\pi \uparrow \implies Y^{ad} \downarrow$), and so the aggregate demand curve slopes downward, as in Figure 4.

Schematically, we can describe why the aggregate demand curve slopes downward, as follows:[3]

$$\pi \uparrow \implies r \uparrow \implies I \downarrow \implies Y^{ad} \downarrow$$

Factors That Shift the Aggregate Demand Curve

Seven basic factors (often referred to as **demand shocks**) can shift the aggregate demand curve to a new position: (1) autonomous monetary policy, (2) government purchases, (3) taxes, (4) autonomous net exports, (5) autonomous consumption expenditure, (6) autonomous investment, and (7) financial frictions. (The use of the term *autonomous* in the factors listed above sometimes confuses students, and so it is discussed in the FYI box "What Does *Autonomous* Mean?") As we examine each case, we ask what happens to the aggregate demand curve when each of these factors changes while the inflation rate is held constant.

---

[3]If you have already read Chapters 20 and Chapter 21, this discussion of aggregate demand is just a recap of the analysis given in those chapters. Note that an additional mechanism for a downward-sloping aggregate demand curve operates through net exports, as discussed in Chapters 20 and 21.

FIGURE 4

Leftward Shift in the Aggregate Demand Curve

The aggregate demand curve shifts to the left from AD_1 to AD_2 when there is an autonomous tightening of monetary policy ($\bar{r}\uparrow$), a decrease in government purchases ($\bar{G}\downarrow$), an increase in taxes ($\bar{T}\uparrow$), a decrease in autonomous net exports ($\overline{NX}\downarrow$), a decrease in autonomous consumption expenditure ($\bar{C}\downarrow$), a decrease in autonomous investment ($\bar{I}\downarrow$), or an increase in financial frictions ($\bar{f}\uparrow$).

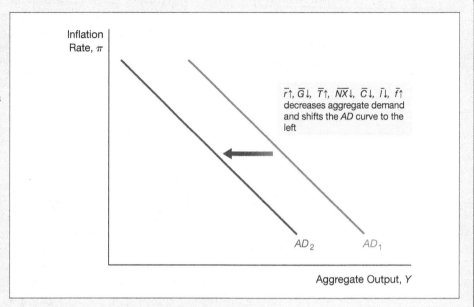

$\bar{r}\uparrow, \bar{G}\downarrow, \bar{T}\uparrow, \overline{NX}\downarrow, \bar{C}\downarrow, \bar{I}\downarrow, \bar{f}\uparrow$ decreases aggregate demand and shifts the *AD* curve to the left

1. *Autonomous monetary policy.* We have already noted that when inflation rises, the real interest rate rises. However, the central bank often wants to make changes in the real interest rate that are autonomous, denoted by $\bar{r}$, which are movements unrelated to the variables in the model, such as the current level of the inflation rate. When the Federal Reserve decides to increase this autonomous component of the real interest rate, $\bar{r}$, the higher real interest rate at any given inflation rate leads to a higher cost of financing investment projects, which leads to a decline in investment spending and the quantity of aggregate demand, as demonstrated by the following schematic:

$$\bar{r}\uparrow \;\Rightarrow\; I\downarrow \;\Rightarrow\; Y^{ad}\downarrow$$

Therefore, aggregate demand falls at any given inflation rate, and the aggregate demand curve shifts to the left, as in Figure 4.

FYI   What Does *Autonomous* Mean?

When economists use the word *autonomous*, they mean that this component of the variable is exogenous (independent of other variables in the model). For example, autonomous monetary policy is the component of the real interest rate set by the central bank that is unrelated to inflation or to any other variable in the model. Changes in autonomous components therefore are never associated with *movements along* a curve, but rather are associated with *shifts in* the curve. Hence a change in autonomous monetary policy shifts the *AD* curve but is never a movement along the curve.

2. *Government purchases.* An increase in government purchases at any given inflation rate adds directly to aggregate demand expenditure, and hence aggregate demand rises:

$$\overline{G}\uparrow \Rightarrow Y^{ad}\uparrow$$

Aggregate demand, therefore, rises at any given inflation rate, and the aggregate demand curve shifts to the right, as in Figure 5.

3. *Taxes.* At any given inflation rate, an increase in taxes lowers disposable income, which leads to lower consumption expenditure and aggregate demand, so that aggregate demand falls:

$$\overline{T}\uparrow \Rightarrow C\downarrow \Rightarrow Y^{ad}\downarrow$$

Aggregate demand falls at any given inflation rate, and the aggregate demand curve shifts to the left, as in Figure 4.

4. *Autonomous net exports.* An autonomous increase in net exports at any given inflation rate adds directly to aggregate demand and so raises aggregate demand:

$$\overline{NX}\uparrow \Rightarrow Y^{ad}\uparrow$$

Aggregate demand rises at any given inflation rate, and the aggregate demand curve shifts to the right, as in Figure 5.

5. *Autonomous consumption expenditure.* When consumers become more optimistic, autonomous consumption expenditure rises, and so consumers spend more at any given inflation rate. Aggregate demand therefore rises:

$$\overline{C}\uparrow \Rightarrow Y^{ad}\uparrow$$

Aggregate demand rises at any given inflation rate, and the aggregate demand curve shifts to the right, as in Figure 5.

Mini-lecture

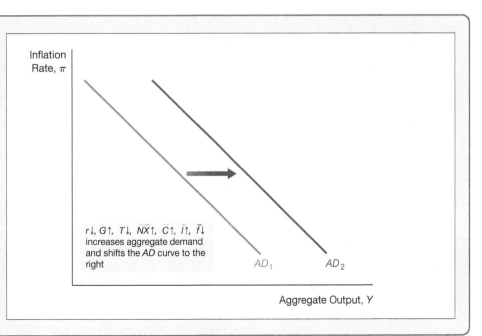

FIGURE 5

Rightward Shift in the Aggregate Demand Curve

The aggregate demand curve shifts to the right, from AD_1 to AD_2, when there is an autonomous easing of monetary policy ($\overline{r}\downarrow$), an increase in government purchases ($\overline{G}\uparrow$), a decrease in taxes ($\overline{T}\downarrow$), an increase in autonomous net exports ($\overline{NX}\uparrow$), an increase in autonomous consumption expenditure ($\overline{C}\uparrow$), an increase in autonomous investment ($\overline{I}\uparrow$), or a decrease in financial frictions ($\overline{f}\downarrow$).

Inflation Rate, π

$r\downarrow, G\uparrow, T\downarrow, \overline{NX}\uparrow, \overline{C}\uparrow, \overline{I}\uparrow, \overline{f}\downarrow$ increases aggregate demand and shifts the *AD* curve to the right

AD_1 AD_2

Aggregate Output, *Y*

SUMMARY TABLE 1

Factors That Shift the Aggregate Demand Curve

Factor	Change	Shift in Aggregate Demand Curve
Autonomous monetary policy, $\bar{r}$	↑	π ... AD_2 AD_1 / Y
Government purchases, $\overline{G}$	↑	π ... AD_1 AD_2 / Y
Taxes, $\overline{T}$	↑	π ... AD_2 AD_1 / Y
Autonomous net exports, $\overline{NX}$	↑	π ... AD_1 AD_2 / Y
Autonomous consumption expenditure, $\overline{C}$	↑	π ... AD_1 AD_2 / Y
Autonomous investment, $\bar{I}$	↑	π ... AD_1 AD_2 / Y
Financial frictions, $\bar{f}$	↑	π ... AD_2 AD_1 / Y

Note: Only increases (↑) in the factors are shown. The effect of decreases in the factors would be the opposite of those indicated in the "Shift" column.

6. *Autonomous investment.* When businesses become more optimistic, autonomous investment rises and businesses spend more at any given inflation rate. Planned investment increases and aggregate demand rises:

$$\bar{I}\uparrow \Rightarrow Y^{ad}\uparrow$$

Aggregate demand rises at any given inflation rate, and the aggregate demand curve shifts to the right, as in Figure 5.

7. *Financial frictions.* The real cost of borrowing reflects not only the real interest rate on default-free debt instruments, r, but also financial frictions, denoted by $\bar{f}$, which are additions to the real cost of borrowing caused by asymmetric information problems in financial markets (described in Chapter 8). When financial frictions increase, the real cost of borrowing increases, so planned investment spending falls at any given inflation rate, and aggregate demand falls:

$$\bar{f}\uparrow \Rightarrow I\downarrow \Rightarrow Y^{ad}\downarrow$$

Aggregate demand falls at any given inflation rate, and the aggregate demand curve shifts to the left as in Figure 4.

The conclusion from our analysis is as follows: *Aggregate demand increases at any given inflation rate, and the aggregate demand curve shifts to the right when there is (1) an autonomous easing of monetary policy ($\bar{r}\downarrow$), (2) an increase in government purchases ($\overline{G}\uparrow$), (3) a decrease in taxes ($\overline{T}\downarrow$), (4) an increase in autonomous net exports ($\overline{NX}\uparrow$), (5) an increase in autonomous consumption expenditure ($\overline{C}\uparrow$), (6) an increase in autonomous investment ($\bar{I}\uparrow$), or (7) a decrease in financial frictions ($\bar{f}\downarrow$). Conversely, the aggregate demand curve shifts to the left when any of these factors change in the opposite direction.* As a study aid, Summary Table 1 summarizes the shifts in the aggregate demand curve that occur with changes in each of these seven factors.

22.3 AGGREGATE SUPPLY

LO 22.3 Illustrate and interpret the short-run and long-run aggregate supply curves.

To complete our analysis, we need to derive an **aggregate supply curve**, a curve that shows the relationship between the quantity of output supplied and the inflation rate. In the typical supply and demand analysis, we have only one supply curve, but because prices and wages take time to adjust to their long-run levels, the aggregate supply curve differs in the short and long runs. First we examine the long-run aggregate supply curve; then we derive the short-run aggregate supply curve. Finally, we look at how both of these curves shift over time and at how the economy moves from the short run to the long run.

Long-Run Aggregate Supply Curve

The amount of output that can be produced in the economy in the long run is determined by the amount of capital in the economy, the amount of labor supplied at full employment, and the available technology. As discussed in Chapter 16, some unemployment cannot be helped because it is either frictional or structural. Thus, at full employment, unemployment is not at zero but is rather at a level above zero at which the labor market is in equilibrium. This **natural rate of unemployment** is the rate to

Mini-lecture

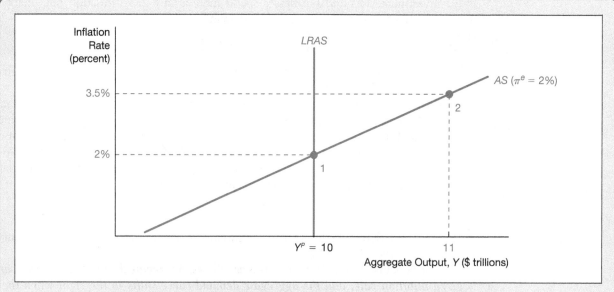

FIGURE 6   Long- and Short-Run Aggregate Supply Curves

The amount of aggregate output supplied at any given inflation rate is at potential output in the long run, $10 trillion, so that the long-run aggregate supply curve *LRAS* is a vertical line at $Y^P = \$10$ trillion. The short-run aggregate supply curve, *AS*, where $\pi^e = 2\%$, is upward-sloping because as *Y* rises relative to Y^P, labor markets get tighter and inflation rises. *AS* intersects *LRAS* at point 1, where current inflation equals expected inflation of 2%.

which the economy gravitates in the long run.[4] Many economists believe that the natural rate of unemployment is currently around 4%.

The level of aggregate output produced at the natural rate of unemployment is called the **natural rate of output** but is more often referred to as **potential output**: It is the level of output generated when all firms on average are operating at their long-run, profit-maximizing level, and is where the economy settles in the long run for any inflation rate. Suppose potential output is at $10 trillion. The long-run aggregate supply curve (*LRAS*) is then vertical at the $10 trillion of potential output, denoted by Y^P, as drawn in Figure 6.

Short-Run Aggregate Supply Curve

The short-run aggregate supply curve is based on the idea that three factors drive inflation: (1) expectations of inflation, (2) the output gap, and (3) inflation (supply) shocks.

Expected Inflation, π^e   Workers and firms care about wages in real terms—that is, in terms of the goods and services that wages can buy. When workers expect a positive inflation rate, they will adjust nominal wages upward one-to-one with the expected inflation rate so that the real wage rate does not decrease. Thus, holding everything else constant, wage inflation will rise one-to-one with rises in expected inflation. Because

---

[4]A more detailed derivation of the short-run aggregate supply curve, based on the Phillips curve (which gives the relationship between unemployment and inflation), can be found in the appendix to this chapter.

wages are the most important cost of producing goods and services, overall inflation will also rise on a one-to-one basis with increases in expected inflation.

Output Gap

The **output gap** is defined as the percentage difference between aggregate output and potential output, $Y - Y^P$. When output exceeds its potential level and the output gap is positive, there is very little slack in the economy. Workers will demand higher wages, and firms will take the opportunity to raise prices. The end result will be higher inflation. Conversely, when the output gap is negative, there will be a lot of slack in the economy. Thus workers will accept smaller increases in wages, and firms will need to lower prices to sell their goods, resulting in lower inflation.

Inflation (Supply) Shocks

Supply shocks occur when there are shocks to the supply of goods and services produced in the economy that translate into **inflation shocks**, that is, shifts in inflation that are independent of the amount of slack in the economy or expected inflation. For example, when the supply of oil is restricted, as has occurred several times when Middle East countries were at war, the resulting rise in the price of oil leads firms to raise prices more to reflect the increased costs of production, thus driving up inflation. Energy inflation shocks can also occur when demand increases—for example, increased demand from developing countries like China such as occurred in 2007–2008—again driving up inflation. Inflation shocks can also come from rises in import prices or from **cost-push shocks** in which workers push for wages that are higher than productivity gains, thereby driving up costs and inflation.

Short-Run Aggregate Supply Curve

Putting all of our analysis together, we can write the following equation for the short-run aggregate supply curve:

$$\pi = \pi^e + \gamma(Y - Y^P) + \rho$$

$$\text{inflation} = \text{expected inflation} + \gamma \times \text{output gap} + \text{inflation shock} \tag{2}$$

where

$$\pi = \text{inflation}$$
$$\pi^e = \text{expected inflation}$$
$$Y - Y^P = \text{the output gap}$$
$$\gamma = \text{the sensitivity of inflation to the output gap}$$
$$\rho = \text{the inflation shock}$$

The short-run aggregate supply curve given in Equation 2 tells us that inflation is driven by three factors: (1) expectations of inflation, (2) output gaps, and (3) inflation shocks.

Why the Short-Run Aggregate Supply Curve Is Upward-Sloping

To see why the short-run aggregate supply curve, *AS*, in Figure 6 is upward-sloping, let's assume that expected inflation is at 2% and that there are no inflation shocks. When actual output equals potential output at $10 trillion, the output gap, $Y - Y^P$, is zero, and so Equation 2 indicates that the inflation rate will equal the expected inflation rate of 2%. The combination of $10 trillion of aggregate output and a 2% inflation rate is shown by point 1 on the *AS* curve. (Note that the short-run aggregate supply curve in Figure 6 is marked as $AS\ (\pi^e = 2\%)$ to indicate it is drawn assuming $\pi^e = 2\%$.)

Now suppose that aggregate output rises to $11 trillion. Because there is a positive output gap ($Y = \$11$ trillion $> Y^P = \$10$ trillion), Equation 2 indicates that inflation will rise above 2%, say, to 3.5%, marked as point 2. The curve connecting points 1 and 2 is the short-run aggregate supply curve, AS, and it is upward-sloping. When Y rises relative to Y^P and $Y > Y^P$, the labor market is tighter and firms raise their prices at a more rapid rate, causing the inflation rate to rise. Thus the AS curve is upward-sloping.

Price Stickiness and the Short-Run Aggregate Supply Curve

In the short run, wages and prices are **sticky**, which means that wages and prices are slow to adjust. The more flexible wages and prices are—that is, the less sticky they are—the more rapidly they, and inflation, respond to deviations of output from potential output; that is, more flexible wages and prices imply that the value of γ is higher, which in turn implies that the short-run aggregate supply curve is steeper. If wages and prices are completely flexible, then γ becomes so large that the short-run aggregate supply curve becomes vertical and is identical to the long-run aggregate supply curve.

22.4 SHIFTS IN THE AGGREGATE SUPPLY CURVES

LO 22.4 Illustrate and interpret shifts in the short-run and long-run aggregate supply curves.

Now that we have examined the long-run and short-run aggregate supply curves, we can look at why each of these curves shifts.

Shifts in the Long-Run Aggregate Supply Curve

The quantity of output supplied in the long run is determined by the three factors that cause potential output to change and thus shift the long-run aggregate supply curve: (1) the total amount of capital in the economy, (2) the total amount of labor supplied in the economy, and (3) the available technology that puts labor and capital together to produce goods and services. When any of these three factors increases, potential output rises, say, from $Y_1^P = \$10$ trillion to $Y_2^P = \$11$ trillion, and the long-run aggregate supply curve shifts to the right, from $LRAS_1$ to $LRAS_2$ in Figure 7.

Because all three of these factors typically grow fairly steadily over time, Y^P and the long-run aggregate supply curve will keep shifting to the right at a steady pace. To keep things simple in later diagrams in this and following chapters, when Y^P is growing at a steady rate, we will represent Y^P and the long-run aggregate supply curve as fixed.

Another source of shifts in the long-run aggregate supply curve is changes in the natural rate of unemployment. If the natural rate of unemployment declines, it means that labor is being more heavily utilized, and so potential output will increase. A decline in the natural rate of unemployment thus shifts the long-run aggregate supply curve to the right, from $LRAS_1$ to $LRAS_2$ in Figure 7. A rise in the natural rate of unemployment would have the opposite effect, shifting the long-run aggregate supply curve to the left.

The conclusion from our analysis is as follows: *The long-run aggregate supply curve shifts to the right when there is (1) an increase in the total amount of capital in the economy, (2) an increase in the total amount of labor supplied in the economy, (3) an increase in available technology, or (4) a decline in the natural rate of unemployment. An opposite movement in these variables shifts the LRAS curve to the left.*

Mini-lecture

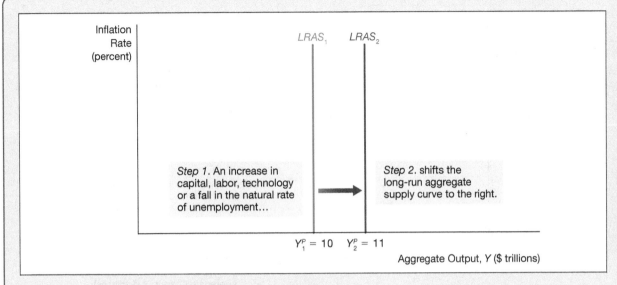

FIGURE 7   **Shift in the Long-Run Aggregate Supply Curve**

The long-run aggregate supply curve shifts to the right from $LRAS_1$ to $LRAS_2$ when there is (1) an increase in the total amount of capital in the economy, (2) an increase in the total amount of labor supplied in the economy, (3) an increase in the available technology, or (4) a decline in the natural rate of unemployment. An opposite movement in these variables shifts the $LRAS$ curve to the left.

Shifts in the Short-Run Aggregate Supply Curve

The three terms on the right-hand side of Equation 2 suggest that three factors can shift the short-run aggregate supply curve: (1) expected inflation, (2) a persistent output gap, and (3) inflation shocks.

Expected Inflation   What if a newly appointed chair of the Federal Reserve does not think that inflation is costly and so is willing to tolerate an inflation rate that is two percentage points higher than the current rate? Households and firms will then expect that the Fed will pursue policies that will let inflation rise by, say, two percentage points in the future, and will want to raise wages and prices by this additional amount. In such a situation, expected inflation π^e will jump by two percentage points, and the short-run aggregate supply curve will shift upward and to the left, from AS_1 to AS_2 in Figure 8. *A rise in expected inflation causes the short-run aggregate supply curve to shift upward and to the left. Conversely, a fall in expected inflation causes the short-run aggregate supply curve to shift down and to the right. The larger the change in expected inflation, the larger is the shift.*

Inflation Shock   Suppose that energy prices suddenly shoot up because terrorists destroy a number of oil fields. This supply restriction (referred to as a *negative supply shock*) causes the inflation-shock term ρ in Equation 2 to increase, and so the short-run aggregate supply curve shifts up and to the left, from AS_1 to AS_2 in Figure 8. In contrast, a favorable (positive) supply shock drives down inflation, and so has the opposite

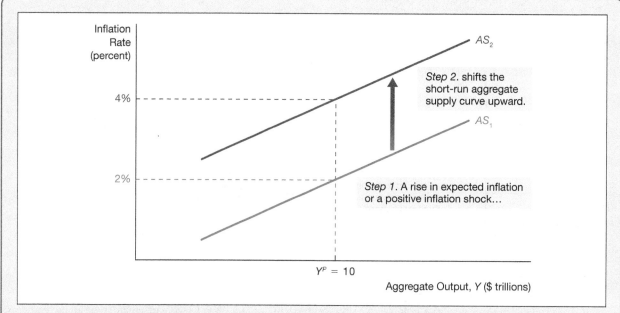

FIGURE 8 **Shift in the Short-Run Aggregate Supply Curve from Changes in Expected Inflation and Supply (Inflation) Shocks**

A rise in expected inflation or a negative supply shock (a positive inflation shock) shifts the short-run aggregate supply curve upward from AS_1 to AS_2. (A decrease in expected inflation or a negative inflation shock would lead to a downward shift of the AS curve.)

effect: It causes the short-run aggregate supply curve to shift down and to the right. *Negative supply shocks drive up inflation and cause the short-run aggregate supply curve to shift up and to the left, while positive supply shocks lower inflation and cause the short-run aggregate supply curve to shift down and to the right.*

Persistent Output Gap We have already seen that a higher output gap leads to higher inflation, causing a movement along the short-run aggregate supply curve. We can represent this scenario by the movement from point 1 to point 2 on the initial short-run aggregate supply curve AS_1 in Figure 9. A persistent output gap, however, will cause the short-run aggregate supply curve to shift by affecting expected inflation. To see this, consider what happens if the aggregate output stays at $11 trillion, which is greater than the potential output of $Y^P = \$10$ trillion, so that the output gap remains persistently positive. At point 2 on the initial short-run aggregate supply curve, AS_1, output has risen to $11 trillion and inflation has risen from 2% to 3.5%. This higher level of inflation will cause expected inflation to rise during the next period, and so the short-run aggregate supply curve for the next period, AS_2, will shift upward. If output remains above potential output at point 3, inflation will rise further, to 5.0%. This higher inflation will then lead to higher expected inflation and, as the vertical arrow indicates, the short-run aggregate supply curve will shift upward to AS_3 during the next period.

When will the short-run aggregate supply curve stop rising? It will stop only when output returns to its potential level and the output gap disappears. At this point, there

Mini-lecture

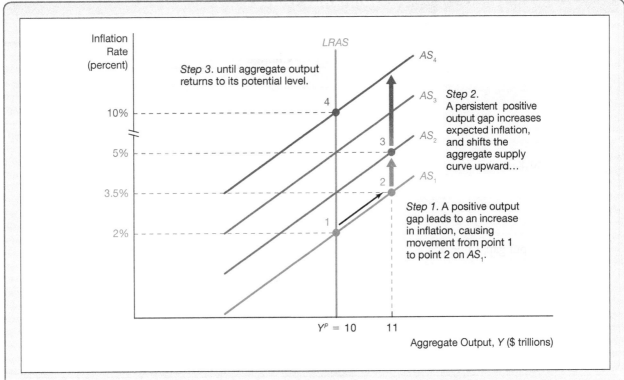

FIGURE 9   Shift in the Short-Run Aggregate Supply Curve from a Persistent Positive Output Gap

When output is above potential, the economy moves along the AS_1 curve from point 1 to point 2 and inflation rises to 3.5%. If output continues to remain above potential output, where the output gap is positive, the short-run aggregate supply curve will shift upward, to AS_2 and then to AS_3. The short-run aggregate supply curve stops shifting upward when the economy reaches point 4 on the short-run aggregate supply curve AS_4, where the output gap is once again zero.

is no longer a reason for actual and hence expected inflation to rise. Suppose this happens when inflation is at 10% and aggregate output $Y = \$10$ trillion $= Y^P$. Because the output gap is now zero, the aggregate supply curve drawn through point 4, AS_4, has no reason to shift because inflation and expected inflation have stopped rising.

The same reasoning indicates that if aggregate output is kept below potential for a period of time, $Y < Y^P$, then the short-run aggregate supply curve will shift downward and to the right. This downward shift of the aggregate supply curve will stop only when output returns to its potential level and the economy is back on the long run aggregate supply curve.

Our analysis yields the following conclusion: **When aggregate output is above potential output, so that a persistent positive output gap exists, the short-run aggregate supply curve shifts up and to the left. Conversely, when aggregate output falls below potential output, the short-run aggregate supply curve shifts down and to the right. Only when aggregate output returns to potential output does the short-run aggregate supply curve stop shifting.** As a study aid, Summary Table 2 summarizes the shifts in the short-run aggregate supply curve caused by each of these three factors.

In the third quarter of 2007, just before the Great Recession began, the output gap was +0.2%, but it rose to only +1.2% by the fourth quarter of 2019, even though real GDP had risen over the same period by 23%, from $15.7 trillion to $19.3 trillion in 2012 dollars. To examine business cycle fluctuations, it is useful to modify the *AD/AS* diagram to show the level of equilibrium aggregate output relative to potential GDP (and therefore the output gap). To modify the *AD/AS* diagram, we express real GDP in terms of an **aggregate output index**, in which potential GDP is designated as 100 and all other values of real GDP are set relative to 100.

Calculating an Aggregate Output Index.

An aggregate output index is calculated as

$$\text{Aggregate Output Index} = \frac{\text{Aggregate Output}}{\text{Potential Output}} \times 100$$

To see how the aggregate output index is calculated, suppose that potential GDP is $10 trillion, then:

- At $9 trillion, the aggregate output index is 90 ($=[\$9 \text{ trillion}/\$10 \text{ trillion}] \times 100 = 0.90 \times 100$). In other words, aggregate output is 10% below potential output and the output gap is –10%.
- At $10 trillion, which equals potential GDP, the aggregate output index is 100 ($=[\$10 \text{ trillion}/\$10 \text{ trillion}] \times 100 = 1.00 \times 100$). In other words, aggregate output equals potential output and the output gap is zero.
- At $11 trillion, the aggregate output index is 110 ($=[\$11 \text{ trillion}/\$10 \text{ trillion}] \times 100 = 1.10 \times 100$). In other words, aggregate output is 10% above potential output and the output gap is +10%.

An *AD/AS* Diagram with an Aggregate Output Index

In Figure 11, we draw an *AD/AS* diagram with an aggregate output index. We replace aggregate output on the horizontal axis with the aggregate output index.

We replace the aggregate output value of $9 trillion with its aggregate output index value of 90. The aggregate output value of $10 trillion, which equals potential GDP, is replaced by its aggregate output index value of 100. Aggregate output of $11 trillion is replaced by its aggregate output index value of 110. The equilibrium at point *E* now indicates that the equilibrium aggregate output $Y^* = 100$, where, as in the previous figure, aggregate output is at the $10 trillion, potential output level.

The value of the output gap is readily obtained from the aggregate output index, as is shown by the boxes in the figure. At the equilibrium, the aggregate output index $Y^* = 100$, so the output gap is zero. When the value of the aggregate output index is 90, aggregate output is 10% below potential GDP, so the output gap is –10%. When the value of the aggregate output index is 110, aggregate output is 10% above potential output, so the output gap is 110.

How the Short-Run Equilibrium Moves to the Long-Run Equilibrium over Time

In supply and demand analysis, once we find the equilibrium point at which the quantity demanded equals the quantity supplied, additional analysis typically is not needed. In *aggregate* supply and demand analysis, however, that is not the case. Even when the

Mini-lecture

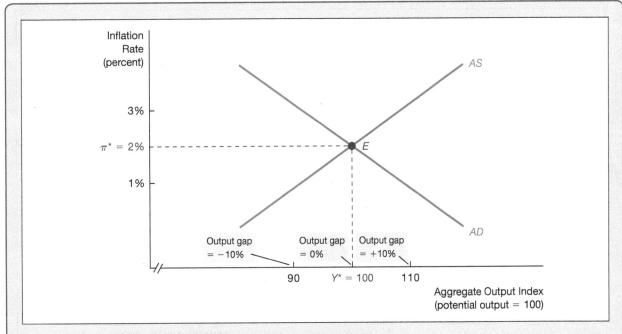

FIGURE 11   *AD/AS* Diagram Using an Aggregate Output Index

With the horizontal axis changed to an aggregate output index and potential output of $10 trillion, the aggregate output value of $9 trillion is replaced by an aggregate output index of 90, the aggregate output value of $10 trillion is replaced by the aggregate output index of 100, and the aggregate output value of $11 trillion is replaced by the aggregate output index of 110. The corresponding output gap that corresponds to each value of the aggregate output index is also shown.

quantity of aggregate output demanded equals the quantity supplied at the intersection of the aggregate demand curve and the short-run aggregate supply curve, if output differs from its potential level ($Y^* \neq Y^P$), the short-run equilibrium will move over time. To understand why, recall that if the current level of inflation changes from its initial level, the short-run aggregate supply curve will shift as wages and prices adjust to a new expected rate of inflation.

We look at how the short-run equilibrium changes over time in response to two situations: when short-run equilibrium output is initially above potential output (the natural rate of output) and when it is initially below potential output.

In panel (a) of Figure 12, the initial equilibrium occurs at point 1, the intersection of the aggregate demand curve *AD* and the initial short-run aggregate supply curve AS_1. The long-run aggregate supply curve, *LRAS*, is a vertical line at an aggregate output index of 100, because on the long-run aggregate supply curve, aggregate output is always equal to potential output at any given inflation rate. The level of the aggregate output index at point 1 is 110, so aggregate output is greater than potential output, and there is excessive tightness in the labor market. Hence, the positive output gap at 110 drives wages up and causes firms to raise their prices at a more rapid rate. Inflation then rises above the initial inflation rate, say, to 2.5%. At this higher inflation rate, firms and households adjust their expectations next period, and expected inflation becomes higher. Wages and prices then rise more rapidly, and the aggregate supply curve shifts up and to the left, from AS_1 to AS_2.

Mini-lecture

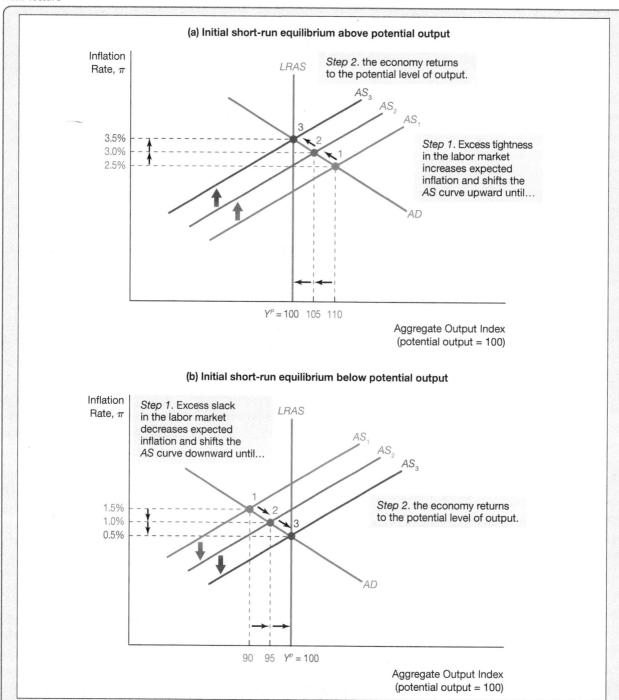

FIGURE 12 **Adjustment to Long-Run Equilibrium in Aggregate Supply and Demand Analysis**

In both panels, the initial short-run equilibrium is at point 1, at the intersection of *AD* and AS_1. In panel (a), initial short-run equilibrium is above potential output, the long-run equilibrium, and so the short-run aggregate supply curve shifts upward until it reaches AS_3, where the aggregate output index returns to 100 and inflation rises to 3.5%. In panel (b), the initial short-run equilibrium is below potential output, and so the short-run aggregate supply curve shifts downward until the aggregate output index returns to 100 and inflation falls to 0.5%. In both panels, the economy's self-correcting mechanism returns the economy to the level of potential output.

The new short-run equilibrium at point 2 is an upward movement along the aggregate demand curve, and the aggregate output index falls to 105 and inflation rises to 3.0%. However, because aggregate output is still above potential output, inflation continues to be above its value last period. Expected inflation rises further, eventually shifting the aggregate supply curve up and to the left to AS_3. The economy reaches long-run equilibrium at point 3 on the vertical long-run aggregate supply curve ($LRAS$), at an aggregate output index of 100 and an inflation rate of 3.5%. Because output now is at potential, there is no further pressure on inflation to rise and thus no further tendency for the aggregate supply curve to shift.

The movements in panel (a) indicate that the economy will not remain at a level of output higher than potential output over time. Specifically, the short-run aggregate supply curve will shift up and to the left, raising the inflation rate and causing the economy (equilibrium) to move upward along the aggregate demand curve until it comes to rest at a point on the long-run aggregate supply curve ($LRAS$) that is at potential output, where the aggregate output index is 100.

In panel (b), at the initial equilibrium at point 1, the aggregate output index is at 90, which is 10% below the level of potential output. Because unemployment is now above its natural rate, there is excess slack in the labor markets. This slack at an aggregate output index of 90 decreases inflation to 1.5%, which decreases expected inflation and shifts the short-run aggregate supply curve in the next period down and to the right, to AS_2.

The equilibrium now moves to point 2, and the aggregate output index rises to 95, while the inflation rate falls to 1.0%. However, because aggregate output at an aggregate output index of 95 is still below potential output, inflation again is below its value last period, causing expected inflation to fall further. This decline in expected inflation shifts the aggregate supply curve down until it comes to rest at AS_3. The economy (equilibrium) moves downward along the aggregate demand curve until it reaches the long-run equilibrium at point 3, at the intersection of the aggregate demand curve (AD) and the long-run aggregate supply curve ($LRAS$) at an aggregate output index of 100 and an inflation rate of 0.5%. Here, as in panel (a), the economy comes to rest when output has again returned to its potential level.

Self-Correcting Mechanism

Notice that in both panels of Figure 12, regardless of where output is initially, it returns eventually to potential output, a feature we call the **self-correcting mechanism**. The self-correcting mechanism occurs because the short-run aggregate supply curve shifts up or down to restore the economy to the long-run equilibrium at full employment (aggregate output at potential) over time.

22.6 CHANGES IN EQUILIBRIUM: AGGREGATE DEMAND SHOCKS

LO 22.6 Illustrate and interpret the short-run and long-run effects of a shock to aggregate demand.

With an understanding of the distinction between the short-run and long-run equilibria, we are now ready to analyze what happens when the economy experiences demand shocks, shocks that cause the aggregate demand curve to shift. Figure 13 depicts the effects of a rightward shift in the aggregate demand curve due to positive demand shocks, which may be caused by the following:

- An autonomous easing of monetary policy ($\bar{r}\downarrow$, a lowering of the real interest rate at any given inflation rate)
- An increase in government purchases ($\overline{G}\uparrow$)
- A decrease in taxes ($\overline{T}\downarrow$)
- An increase in autonomous net exports ($\overline{NX}\uparrow$)
- An increase in autonomous consumption expenditure ($\overline{C}\uparrow$)
- An increase in autonomous investment ($\bar{I}\uparrow$)
- A decrease in financial frictions ($\bar{f}\downarrow$)

Figure 13 shows the economy initially in long-run equilibrium at point 1, where the initial aggregate demand curve AD_1 intersects the short-run aggregate supply AS_1 curve at an aggregate output index of 100 and the inflation rate is 2%. Suppose that consumers and businesses become more optimistic and that the resulting increases in autonomous consumption and investment create a positive demand shock that shifts the aggregate demand curve to the right to AD_2. The economy moves up the short-run aggregate supply curve AS_1 to point 2, and the aggregate output index and inflation rise to 110 and 3.5%, respectively. However, the economy will not remain at point 2 in the long run because the aggregate output index at 110 is above potential output.

Mini-lecture

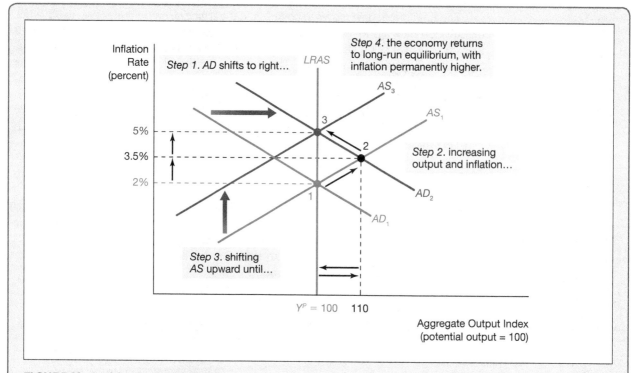

FIGURE 13 Positive Demand Shock

A positive demand shock shifts the aggregate demand curve upward from AD_1 to AD_2 and moves the economy from point 1 to point 2, resulting in higher inflation at 3.5% and a higher aggregate output index of 110. Because output is greater than potential output and therefore expected inflation increases, the short-run aggregate supply curve begins to shift up, eventually reaching AS_3. At point 3, the economy returns to long-run equilibrium, with the aggregate output index at 100 and the inflation level rising to 5%.

Source: Economic Report of the President.

Expected inflation will rise, and the short-run aggregate supply curve will eventually shift upward to AS_3. The economy (equilibrium) thus will move up the AD_2 curve from point 2 to point 3, which is the point of long-run equilibrium at which inflation equals 5% and output returns to potential with the aggregate output index at 100. *Although the initial short-run effect of the rightward shift in the aggregate demand curve is a rise in both inflation and output, the ultimate long-run effect is a rise in inflation only, because the aggregate output index returns to its initial level of 100.*[6]

We now apply the aggregate demand and supply model to demand shocks, as a payoff for our hard work in constructing the model. Throughout the remainder of this chapter, we will apply aggregate supply and demand analysis to a number of business cycle episodes. To simplify our analysis, we will assume in all examples that aggregate output is initially at the level of potential output.

APPLICATION   The Volcker Disinflation, 1980–1986

When Paul Volcker became the chair of the Federal Reserve in August 1979, inflation had spun out of control and the inflation rate exceeded 10%. Volcker was determined to get inflation down. The inflation rate fell from 11.3% in 1979 to 6.2% in 1982, and then to 4.1% in 1988. But the decline in inflation came at a high cost: The economy experienced its worst recession since World War II, with the aggregate output index falling to 93.9 in 1982 (which corresponded to an output gap of –6.1% and an unemployment rate of 9.7%). By 1988, the economy had recovered and the aggregate output index rose to 99.3, where aggregate output was close to its potential output level, and the unemployment rate fell back to 5.5%.

Figure 14 shows how aggregate demand and supply analysis can explain these outcomes. Note that to keep this and later figures in applications less cluttered, we no longer draw the long-run aggregate supply curve in the *AD/AS* diagram, because it is always just a vertical line at an aggregate output index of 100. Instead, there is a tick mark at an aggregate output index of 100 to remind you where the long-run aggregate would otherwise be.

The initial equilibrium is at point *1979*. The initial equilibrium in 1979 occurred at the intersection of the aggregate demand curve, AD_{1979}, and the short-run aggregate supply curve, AS_{1979}. The resulting inflation rate in 1979 was 11.3%, and the aggregate output index was 100.8, so the economy was close to the long-run equilibrium.

The monetary tightening led to a higher real interest rate at any given inflation rate. As a result, consumption expenditure and investment spending fell precipitously, leading to a decrease in in the quantity of aggregate output demanded at any given inflation rate. By 1982, the monetary tightening that started in 1979 and continued through 1981 had shifted the aggregate demand curve to the left to AD_{1982}. The equilibrium moved down the short-run aggregate supply curve to point *1982*, at the intersection of the initial short-run aggregate supply curve, AS_{1979}, and the aggregate demand curve, AD_{1982}. The equilibrium inflation rate then fell to 6.2% in 1982, while the equilibrium output index fell to 93.9, that is, 6.1% below potential output. The resulting recession was very severe, with the unemployment rate rising from an average of 5.9% in 1979 to 9.7% in 1982.

[6]The analysis here assumes that each of these positive demand shocks occurs while everything else is held constant, the usual *ceteris paribus* ("other things being equal") assumption that is standard in supply and demand analysis. Specifically, this means that the central bank is assumed not to be responding to demand shocks. In the next chapter, we relax this assumption and allow monetary policymakers to respond to these shocks. As we will see, if monetary policymakers want to keep inflation caused by a positive demand shock from rising, they will respond by autonomously tightening monetary policy.

Mini-lecture

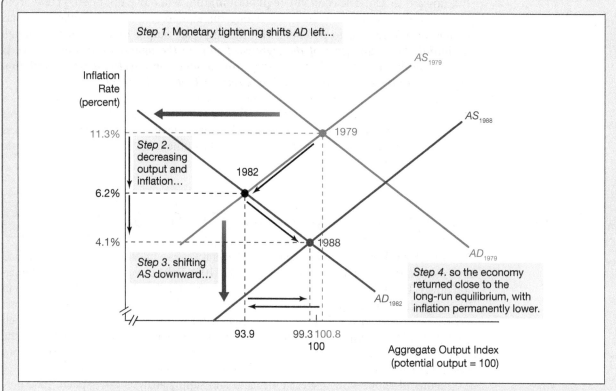

FIGURE 14   The Volcker Disinflation

The figure shows that former Fed chair Volcker's actions to decrease inflation were successful but costly: The autonomous monetary policy tightening caused a negative demand shock that shifted the aggregate demand curve to the left from AD_{1979} to AD_{1982} and led to a decline in inflation from 11.1% to 6.2% and a decline in the aggregate output index from 100.4 to 99.3. Then with a further downward shift of the short-run aggregate supply curve to AS_{1988}, the inflation rate fell to 4.1% in 1988, while the aggregate output index recovered to 99.4.

With aggregate output well below its potential output level, the short-run aggregate supply curve shifted downward and to the left to AS_{1988}. By 1988, the economy moved toward the equilibrium at point *1988*. The inflation rate fell further to 4.1% and output rose back near potential output, with the aggregate output index rising to 99.4. The rise in the aggregate output index then led to the unemployment rate falling back to 5.5%. ◆

22.7 CHANGES IN EQUILIBRIUM: AGGREGATE SUPPLY (INFLATION) SHOCKS

LO 22.7 Illustrate and interpret the short-run and long-run effects of supply shocks.

In our discussion earlier in the chapter of the short-run aggregate supply curve, we showed that inflation will rise independently of tightness in the labor markets or increases in expected inflation if there are supply shocks, such as a decrease in the supply of oil that causes prices to rise. When the shock involves a restriction in supply, we refer to this type of supply shock as a *negative* (or *unfavorable*) *supply shock*, and it results in a rise in commodity prices. Examples of negative supply shocks include a disruption in oil supplies, a rise in import prices when a currency declines in value, or a cost-push shock from workers pushing for higher wages that outpace productivity growth, driving up costs and inflation. When the supply shock involves an increase in supply, it is called a *positive* (or *favorable*) *supply shock*. Positive supply shocks include a particularly good harvest or a fall in import prices.

To see how a supply shock affects the economy, we can use our aggregate supply and demand analysis. We start by assuming that output is at its potential level, with the aggregate output index at 100, and inflation is at 2%, at point 1 in Figure 15. Suppose that a war in the Middle East causes a negative supply shock. When the negative supply shock hits the economy and oil prices rise, the change in the price shock term ρ indicates that inflation will rise to above 2% and the short-run aggregate supply curve will shift up and to the left, from AS_1 to AS_2.

The economy then will move up the aggregate demand curve, from point 1 to point 2, where inflation rises to 3.5% but the aggregate output index *falls* below 100. We use the term **stagflation** (a combination of the words *stagnation* and *inflation*) to describe a

Mini-lecture

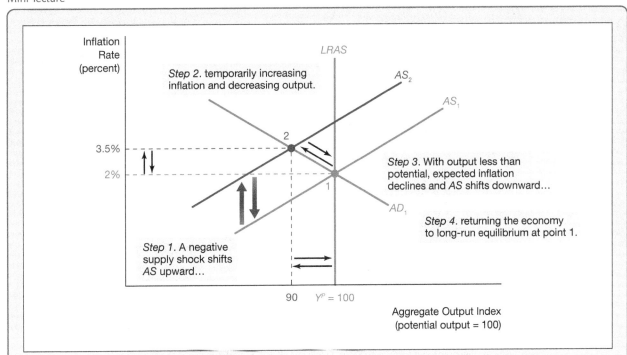

FIGURE 15 **Negative Supply Shock**

A negative supply shock shifts the short-run aggregate supply curve from AS_1 to AS_2, and the economy moves from point 1 to point 2, where inflation increases to 3.5% and the aggregate output index declines to 90. Because output is less than potential, the negative output gap lowers inflation and hence expected inflation. The decline in expected inflation shifts the short-run aggregate supply curve back down, and eventually it returns to AS_1, where the economy is again at the initial long-run equilibrium at point 1.

situation defined by rising inflation but a falling level of aggregate output, as pictured in Figure 15. At point 2, output is therefore below its potential level (the aggregate output index is, say, at 90), and so inflation falls. The decline in inflation causes expected inflation to fall and shifts the short-run aggregate supply curve back down to where it was initially, at AS_1. The economy (equilibrium) slides down the aggregate demand curve AD_1 (assuming the aggregate demand curve remains in the same position) and returns to the long-run equilibrium at point 1, where the aggregate output index is again at 100 and inflation is again at 2%.

Although a negative supply shock leads to an upward and leftward shift of the short-run aggregate supply curve, which initially raises inflation and lowers output, the ultimate long-run effect is that output and inflation are unchanged.

A favorable (positive) supply shock—say, an excellent harvest of wheat in the Midwest—moves all the curves in Figure 15 in the opposite direction and so has the opposite effects. *A positive supply shock shifts the short-run aggregate supply curve downward and to the right, initially leading to a fall in inflation and a rise in output. In the long run, however, output and inflation are unchanged (holding the aggregate demand curve constant).*

We now will apply the aggregate demand and supply model to studying the negative supply shocks of 1973–1975 and 1978–1980. (Recall we assume that aggregate output is initially at its potential level, with the aggregate output index at 100.)

APPLICATION   # Negative Supply Shocks, 1973–1975 and 1978–1980

In 1973, the U.S. economy was hit by a series of negative supply shocks:

1. As a result of the oil embargo stemming from the Arab–Israeli war of 1973, the Organization of Petroleum Exporting Countries (OPEC) engineered a quadrupling of oil prices by restricting oil production.
2. A series of crop failures throughout the world led to a sharp increase in food prices.
3. The termination of U.S. wage and price controls in 1973 and 1974 led to a push by workers to obtain wage increases that had been prevented by the controls.

In 1973, the inflation rate was 6.3%, while the aggregate output index was at 103.4, as is indicated by the equilibrium point, *1973*, in Figure 16. The triple thrust of these negative supply shocks shifted the short-run aggregate supply curve sharply upward and to the left, from AS_{1973} to AS_{1975}, and the economy moved to point *1975*. As shown in Figure 16, inflation rose to 9.1% in 1975 and the aggregate output index fell to 95.9. The decline in aggregate output led to a steep rise in the unemployment rate from 4.8% to 8.3%.

The 1978–1980 period was almost an exact replay of the 1973–1975 period. By 1978, the economy had just about fully recovered from the 1973–1975 supply shocks when poor harvests and a doubling of oil prices (resulting from the overthrow of the Shah of Iran) led to another sharp upward and leftward shift of the short-run aggregate supply curve in 1979. The pattern predicted by Figure 16 played itself out again— inflation and unemployment both shot upward. ◆

Mini-lecture

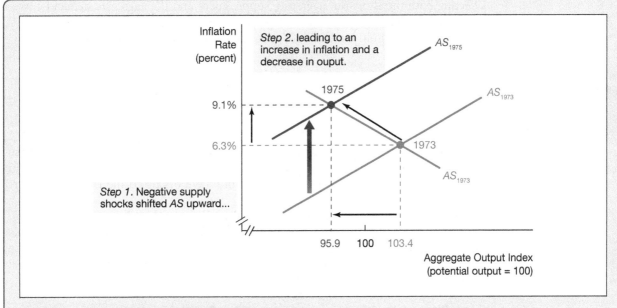

FIGURE 16   Negative Supply Shocks, 1973–1975

The negative supply shocks in 1973 led to an upward shift in the short-run aggregate supply curve, from AS_{1973} to AS_{1975}. The economy moved from point *1973* to point *1975*, where the aggregate output index fell from 103.4 to 95.9, while the inflation rate rose from 6.3% to 9.1%.

22.8 CONCLUSIONS FROM AGGREGATE DEMAND AND SUPPLY ANALYSIS

LO 22.8 Summarize the conclusions from aggregate demand and supply analysis.

Aggregate demand and supply analysis leads us to the following conclusions.[7]

1. The economy has a self-correcting mechanism that returns it to potential output and the natural rate of unemployment over time.

2. A shift in the aggregate demand curve—caused by changes in autonomous monetary policy (changes in the real interest rate at any given inflation rate), government purchases, taxes, autonomous net exports, autonomous consumption expenditure, autonomous investment, or financial frictions—affects the output gap only in the short run and not in the long run. Furthermore, the initial change in inflation is lower than the long-run change in inflation when the short-run aggregate supply curve has fully adjusted.

3. A supply shock affects the output gap and inflation only in the short run and has no effect in the long run (holding the aggregate demand curve constant).

---

[7]Aggregate demand and supply analysis also can be used to understand the effects of macroeconomic shocks on asset prices. This analysis can be found in the second appendix to this chapter that is in **MyLab Economics**.

Often, aggregate demand and aggregate supply shocks occur simultaneously, affecting both the short-run aggregate supply curve and the aggregate demand curve. This is what happened both in the Great Recession of 2007–2009 and in the Covid-19 recession that began in March 2020, as is illustrated in the following applications.

APPLICATION # AD/AS Analysis of the Great Recession of 2007–2009

We break the *AD/AS* analysis of the Great Recession into two phases. The first phase occurs prior to the bankruptcy of Lehman Brothers, a global financial services firm, in fall 2008, the largest bankruptcy in U.S. history. (We discussed the Lehman Brothers bankruptcy in Chapter 12.)

The second phase occurs from fall 2008 until the end of the recession in 2009. With the bankruptcy of Lehman Brothers in fall 2008, major lenders such as banks stopped lending money, which caused a collapse in investment spending. At the same time, the stock market crashed and consumer optimism plummeted. The result was a sharp cutback in consumer spending.

First Phase.   In 2006, the inflation rate was 2.4% and aggregate output was near potential output, with the aggregate output index at 100.4. This equilibrium at point *2006* is shown in the *AD/AS* diagram in Figure 17, which illustrates what happened in the first phase of the Great Recession.

At the beginning of 2007, high demand for oil in rapidly growing developing countries like China and India, and the slowing of oil production in places like Mexico, Russia, and Nigeria, drove oil prices up sharply. Oil prices rose from around $60 per barrel at the beginning of 2007 to $100 per barrel at the end of 2007, and they reached a peak of over $140 per barrel in July 2008. The rise in oil prices, along with increases in other commodity prices, led to a negative supply shock that shifted the short-run aggregate supply curve sharply upward, from AS_{2006} to AS_{2008} in Figure 17. To make matters worse, a financial crisis hit the economy starting in August 2007, causing a sharp increase in financial frictions, which led to contraction in both household and business spending (discussed in Chapter 12). This negative demand shock shifted the aggregate demand curve to the left, from AD_{2006} to AD_{2008}, and moved the economy to point *2008*, with inflation rising to 3.8%, and the aggregate output index falling to 98.1. As predicted by our aggregate demand and supply analysis, this perfect storm of negative shocks led to a recession starting in December 2007, with the unemployment rate rising from 4.6% in 2006 to 5.8% in 2008.

Second Phase.   Figure 18 provides an *AD/AS* diagram of the second phase of the Great Recession. The initial equilibrium is at point *2008*, the same as in the previous figure, where the aggregate output index was at 98.1 and the inflation rate was 3.8%. The second phase of the Great Recession began in fall 2008, with the bankruptcy of Lehman Brothers. The shockwave that hit the financial system led to a massive contraction of lending, which caused a collapse in investment spending. At the same time, the stock market crashed, with stock prices falling by more than 50%. Consumer optimism plummeted. The result was a sharp cutback in consumer spending, which shifted the aggregate demand curve sharply to the left from AD_{2008} to AD_{2009}.

As the financial crisis spread to the rest of the world, commodity prices plummeted. In particular, the price of oil fell to $40 per barrel by early 2009, well below the $60

Mini lecture

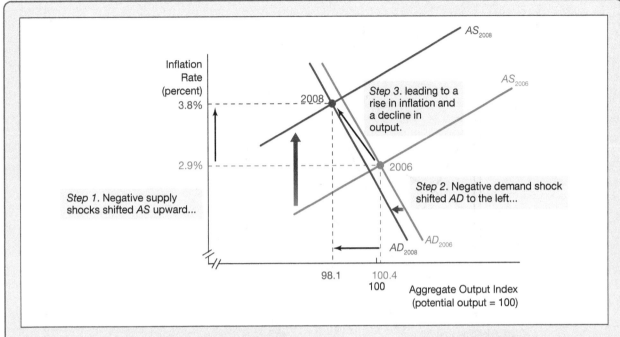

FIGURE 17 **First Phase of the Great Recession**
The negative supply shock caused by a rise in the price of oil shifted the short-run aggregate supply curve up from AS_{2006} to AS_{2008}, while the negative demand shock caused by the financial crisis led the aggregate demand curve to shift leftward from AD_{2006} to AD_{2008}. The economy moved to point *2008*, with the aggregate output index falling from 100.4 to 98.1, and the inflation rate rising from 2.9% to 3.8%.

price at the beginning of 2007. This decline in oil prices, and the fact that aggregate output was below its potential level, led to a sharp decline in the short-run aggregate supply curve to AS_{2009}. As shown in Figure 18, the equilibrium moved to point *2009*, where the aggregate output index fell to 94.3 and inflation fell to –0.3%. The large decline in aggregate output led to a rise in the unemployment rate to 9.3% in 2009, but in the aftermath of the financial crisis, the economic recovery was very slow, with aggregate output not returning to its potential level until ten years after the financial crisis started (see Figure 3). This is why the recession of 2007–2009 has been given the name the Great Recession. ◆

APPLICATION An *AD/AS* Analysis of the Covid-19 Recession

When the coronavirus began to spread exponentially in March 2020 and lockdowns were implemented throughout the United States, the economy went into a tailspin. The economy declined at the steepest rate in U.S. history, with the aggregate output index falling from 101.2 in the fourth quarter of 2019 to 90.0 in the second quarter of 2020.

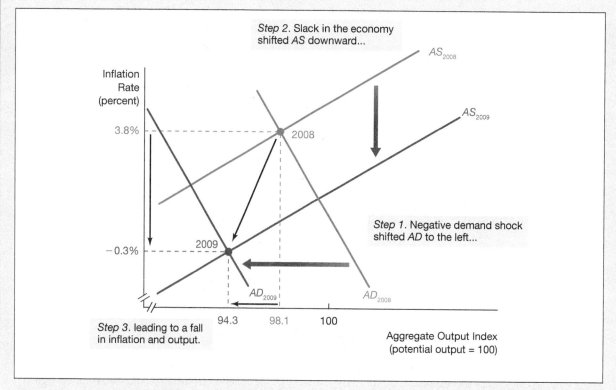

FIGURE 18 **Second Phase of the Great Recession**

After the Lehman bankruptcy, the worsening financial crisis led to a large leftward shift in the aggregate demand curve from AD_{2008} to AD_{2009}. With commodity prices falling worldwide and aggregate output below potential output, the short-run aggregate supply curve shifted down from AD_{2008} to AS_{2009}. The economy moved to point *2009*, where the inflation rate fell to −0.3% and the aggregate output index fell to 94.3.

With this precipitous drop in output, the unemployment rate rose from 3.5% in the fourth quarter of 2019 to 13% in the second quarter of 2020. At the same time, the inflation rate fell from 2.0% to 0.4%.

What is unusual about the resulting Covid-19 recession is that it was triggered by a massive aggregate supply shock that induced a massive aggregate demand shock. The lockdowns that began in March 2020 led to production shutting down in many parts of the U.S. economy. The result was that the short-run aggregate supply curve shifted up and to the left from $AS_{2019:Q4}$ to $AS_{2020:Q2}$ in Figure 19. Because the lockdowns meant that households were unable to venture out to stores, they sharply cut back their spending. In addition, because it was hard to know how long the coronavirus pandemic would last and when the economy might reopen, uncertainty increased greatly, so businesses shelved a lot of their investment plans. Uncertainty and the collapse in stock prices also further reduced the willingness of consumers to spend. The result was a large decline in the quantity of aggregate output demanded at any given inflation rate, so the aggregate demand curve shifted sharply to the left from $AD_{2019:Q4}$ to $AD_{2020:Q2}$.

Mini-lecture

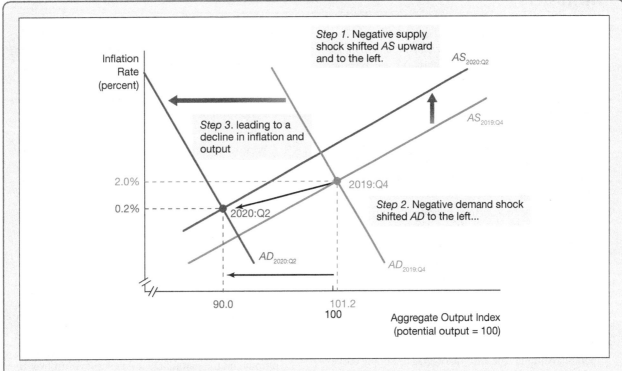

FIGURE 19 The Covid-19 Recession

The lockdown of the U.S. economy led to the short-run aggregate supply curve shifting from $AD_{2019:Q4}$ to $AD_{2020:Q2}$, which also led to a leftward shift of the aggregate demand curve from $AD_{2019:Q4}$ to $AD_{2020:Q2}$. The macroeconomic equilibrium moved from point *2019:Q4* to point *2020:Q2*, and the aggregate output index fell to 90.0 and inflation fell to 0.4%.

The new equilibrium moved from point *2019:Q4* to point *2020:Q2*. The aggregate output index fell from 101.2 in the 2019:Q4 to 90.0 in 2020:Q2, with the unemployment rate rising to 13%. Although our analysis predicts that aggregate output would necessarily fall because both the aggregate demand and short-run aggregate supply curves shifted to the left, it was not clear whether inflation would rise or fall because the restriction in supply would raise inflation, while the decline in aggregate demand would lower inflation. However, another event that occurred was a price war between Saudi Arabia and Russia, which led to a drop in the price of oil from around $60 a barrel to less than $30 per barrel in the second quarter of 2020. This precipitous drop in the price of oil acted as a positive supply shock that offset some of the negative supply shock from the pandemic. As a result, the short-run aggregate supply curve shifted by less than the aggregate demand curve, and the inflation rate fell from 2.0% in the fourth quarter of 2019 to 0.4% in the second quarter of 2020. ◆

SUMMARY

1. Business cycles are the upward and downward movement of aggregate economic activity and are important for aggregate demand and supply analysis to explain because declines in aggregate output are associated with increases in unemployment, which lead to economic hardship. Aggregate demand and supply analysis is also used to explain fluctuations in inflation, which are important because low and stable inflation reduces the need for businesses to engage in costly changes in price for their products and reduces uncertainty in the economy, making it easier for households and businesses to make economic decisions.

2. The aggregate demand curve indicates the quantity of aggregate output demanded at each inflation rate, and it is downward-sloping. The primary sources of shifts in the aggregate demand curve are (1) autonomous monetary policy, (2) government purchases, (3) taxes, (4) autonomous net exports, (5) autonomous consumption expenditure, (6) autonomous investment, and (7) financial frictions.

3. The long-run aggregate supply curve is vertical at potential output. The long-run aggregate supply curve shifts when technology changes, when there are long-run changes to the amount of labor or capital, or when the natural rate of unemployment changes. The short-run aggregate supply curve slopes upward because inflation rises as output rises relative to potential output. The short-run supply curve shifts when there are changes in expected inflation, inflation shocks, or persistent output gaps.

4. Equilibrium in the short run occurs at the point at which the aggregate demand curve intersects the short-run aggregate supply curve. Although this is the level to which the economy heads temporarily, the self-correcting mechanism leads the economy to settle permanently at the long-run equilibrium, the point at which the aggregate demand curve intersects the long-run aggregate supply curve and aggregate output is at its potential. Shifts in either the aggregate demand curve or the short-run or long-run aggregate supply curves can produce changes in aggregate output and inflation.

5. A positive demand shock shifts the aggregate demand curve to the right and initially leads to a rise in both inflation and output. However, in the long run, such a shock leads only to a rise in inflation, because output returns to its potential initial level.

6. A positive supply shock leads to a downward and rightward shift in the short-run aggregate supply curve, which initially lowers inflation and raises output. However, in the long run, the output gap and inflation are unchanged.

7. Three conclusions can be drawn from aggregate demand and supply analysis: (1) The economy has a self-correcting mechanism that returns it to potential output and the natural rate of unemployment over time; (2) a shift in the aggregate demand curve—caused by changes in autonomous monetary policy (changes in the real interest rate at any given inflation rate), government purchases, taxes, autonomous net exports, autonomous consumption expenditure, autonomous investment, or financial frictions—affects the output gap only in the short run and not in the long run; furthermore, the initial change in inflation is lower than the change in the long run; and (3) a supply shock affects the output gap and inflation only in the short run and has no effect in the long run (holding the aggregate demand curve constant).

KEY TERMS

AD/AS diagram, p. 523
aggregate demand curve, p. 511
aggregate output, p. 506
aggregate output index, p. 524
aggregate quantity demanded, p. 510
aggregate supply curve, p. 515
booms, p. 506
business cycle, p. 506
consumption expenditure, p. 510
cost-push shocks, p. 517

demand shocks, p. 511
expansion, p. 506
government purchases, p. 511
inflation shocks, p. 517
macroeconomic equilibrium, p. 522
natural rate of output, p. 516
natural rate of unemployment, p. 515
net exports, p. 511
output gap, p. 517
planned investment spending, p. 510

potential GDP, p. 506
potential output, p. 506
recession, p. 506
self-correcting mechanism, p. 527
stagflation, p. 531
sticky, p. 518
supply shocks, p. 517
unemployment rate, p. 508

QUESTIONS

1. Explain why the aggregate demand curve slopes downward and the short-run aggregate supply curve slopes upward.

2. Identify three factors that can shift the aggregate demand curve to the right and three different factors that can shift the aggregate demand curve to the left.

3. "The appreciation of the dollar from 2012 to 2018 had a negative effect on aggregate demand in the United States." Is this statement true, false, or uncertain? Explain your answer.

4. In many countries around the world, the population is aging and large segments of the population are retiring or close to retirement. What effect would this have on a country's long-run aggregate supply curve? What will happen to aggregate output as a result?

5. If the labor force becomes more productive over time, how would the long-run aggregate supply curve be affected?

6. Why are central banks so concerned with inflation expectations?

7. "If prices and wages are perfectly flexible, then $\gamma = 0$ and changes in aggregate demand have a smaller effect on output." Is this statement true, false, or uncertain? Explain your answer.

8. What factors shift the short-run aggregate supply curve? Do any of these factors shift the long-run aggregate supply curve? Why?

9. If large budget deficits cause the public to think there will be higher inflation in the future, what is likely to happen to the short-run aggregate supply curve when budget deficits rise?

10. In the aftermath of the financial crisis in the United States, labor mobility has decreased significantly. How, if at all, might this affect the natural rate of unemployment?

11. When aggregate output is below the natural rate of output, what happens to the inflation rate over time if the aggregate demand curve remains unchanged? Why?

12. Suppose the public believes that a newly announced anti-inflation program will work and so lowers its expectations of future inflation. What will happen to aggregate output and the inflation rate in the short run?

13. If the unemployment rate is above the natural rate of unemployment, holding other factors constant, what will happen to inflation and output?

14. What happens to inflation and output in the short run and the long run when taxes decrease?

15. If stagflation is bad (high inflation and high unemployment), does this necessarily mean low inflation and low unemployment is good?

16. Why did the Federal Reserve pursue inherently recessionary policies in the early 1980s?

17. In what ways is the Volcker disinflation considered a success? In what ways is it considered a failure?

APPLIED PROBLEMS

18. Suppose the president gets Congress to pass legislation that encourages investment in research and the development of new technologies. Assuming this policy leads to a positive productivity change for the U.S. economy, use aggregate demand and supply analysis to predict the effects on inflation and output. Demonstrate these effects on a graph.

19. Proposals advocating the implementation of a national sales tax have been presented before Congress. Predict the effects of such a tax on the aggregate supply and demand curves, showing the effects on output and inflation. Use a graph of aggregate supply and demand to demonstrate these effects.

20. Suppose the inflation rate remains relatively constant while output decreases and the unemployment rate increases. Using an aggregate demand and supply graph, show how this scenario is possible.

21. Classify each of the following as a supply shock or a demand shock. Use a graph to show the effects on inflation and output in the short run and in the long run.

   a. Financial frictions increase.

   b. Households and firms become more optimistic about the economy.

   c. Favorable weather produces a record crop of wheat and corn in the Midwest.

   d. Auto workers go on strike for four months.

22. During 2017, some Fed officials discussed the possibility of increasing interest rates as a way of fighting potential increases in expected inflation. If the public came to expect higher inflation rates in the future, what would be the effect on the short-run aggregate supply curve? Use an aggregate demand and supply graph to illustrate your answer.

DATA ANALYSIS PROBLEMS

The Problems update with real-time data in **MyLab Economics** and are available for practice or instructor assignment.

1. **Real-time Data Analysis** Go to the St. Louis Federal Reserve FRED database, and find data on real GDP (GDPC1), potential GDP (GDPPOT), and the unemployment rate (UNRATE) from 1960 to the most recent period. For the unemployment rate data, convert the frequency to Quarterly. Download all of the data into a spreadsheet, and calculate the output gap and aggregate output index for each quarter.

   a. In which quarter is the output gap the most negative? What is the Aggregate Output Index for that quarter?

   b. In which quarter is the unemployment rate highest?

   c. Are these periods of time close to each other? What does this tell you about the relationship between output gaps and the unemployment rate?

2. **Real-time Data Analysis** Go to the St. Louis Federal Reserve FRED database, and find data on real government spending (GCEC1), real GDP (GDPC1), taxes (W006RC1Q027SBEA), and the personal consumption expenditure price index (PCECTPI), a measure of the price level. Download all of the data into a spreadsheet, and convert the tax data series into real taxes. To do this, for each quarter, divide taxes by the price index and then multiply by 100.

   a. Calculate the level change in real GDP over the four most recent quarters of data available and the four quarters prior to that.

   b. Calculate the level change in real government spending and real taxes over the four most recent quarters of data available and the four quarters prior to that.

   c. Are your results consistent with what you would expect? How do your answers to part (b) help explain, if at all, your answer to part (a)? Explain using the *IS* and *AD* curves.

3. **Real-time Data Analysis** Go to the St. Louis Federal Reserve FRED database, and find data on the personal consumption expenditure price index (PCECTPI), a measure of the price level; real compensation per hour (COMPRNFB); the nonfarm business sector real output per hour (OPHNFB), a measure of worker productivity; the price of a barrel of oil (MCOILWTICO); and the University of Michigan survey of inflation expectations (MICH). Use the *frequency* setting to convert the oil price and inflation expectations data series to "Quarterly," and use the *units* setting to convert the price index to "Percent Change from Year Ago." Download all of the data into a spreadsheet, and convert the compensation and productivity measures to a single indicator. To do this, for each quarter, take the compensation number and subtract the productivity number. Call this difference "Net Wages Above Productivity."

   a. Calculate the change in the inflation rate over the four most recent quarters of data available and the four quarters prior to that.

   b. Calculate the changes in net wages above productivity, the price of oil, and inflation expectations over the four most recent quarters of data available and the four quarters prior to that.

   c. Are your results consistent with what you would expect? How do your answers to part (b) help explain, if at all, your answer to part (a)? Explain using the short-run aggregate supply curve.

22 The Phillips Curve and the Short-Run Aggregate Supply Curve

This appendix discusses the *Phillips curve*, which describes the relationship of unemployment and inflation, and this appendix shows how this relationship can be used to derive the short-run aggregate supply curve presented in the chapter.

22.A1 THE PHILLIPS CURVE

In 1958, New Zealand economist A. W. Phillips published a famous empirical paper that examined the relationship between unemployment and wage growth in the United Kingdom.[1] For the years 1861 to 1957, he found that periods of low unemployment were associated with rapid rises in wages, whereas periods of high unemployment were associated with low growth in wages. Other economists soon discovered that this relationship extended to many other countries. Because inflation is more central to macroeconomic issues than wage growth, these economists studied the relationship between unemployment and inflation. The negative correlation between unemployment and inflation that they found in many countries became known, naturally enough, as the *Phillips curve*.

The idea behind the Phillips curve is quite intuitive. When labor markets are *tight*—that is, the unemployment rate is low—firms may have difficulty hiring qualified workers and may even have a hard time keeping their present employees. Because of the shortage of workers in the labor market, firms will raise wages to attract workers and also raise their prices at a more rapid rate.

Phillips Curve Analysis in the 1960s

Because wage inflation feeds directly into overall inflation, in the 1960s the Phillips curve became extremely popular as a model for inflation fluctuations because it seemed to fit the data so well. Panel (a) of Figure 1 shows a plot of the U.S. inflation rate against the unemployment rate from 1950 to 1969. From this plot, we can see that a very clear negative correlation exists between unemployment and inflation. The Phillips curve for this period seems to imply that there is a long-run trade-off between unemployment and inflation—that is, policymakers can choose policies that will lead to a higher rate of inflation and end up with a lower unemployment rate on a sustained basis. This apparent trade-off was very influential in policy circles in the 1960s, as we can see in the FYI box "The Phillips Curve Trade-off and Macroeconomic Policy in the 1960s."

[1] A.W. Phillips, "The Relationship Between Unemployment and the Rate of Change of Money Wages in the United Kingdom, 1861–1957," *Economica* 25 (November 1958): 283–299.

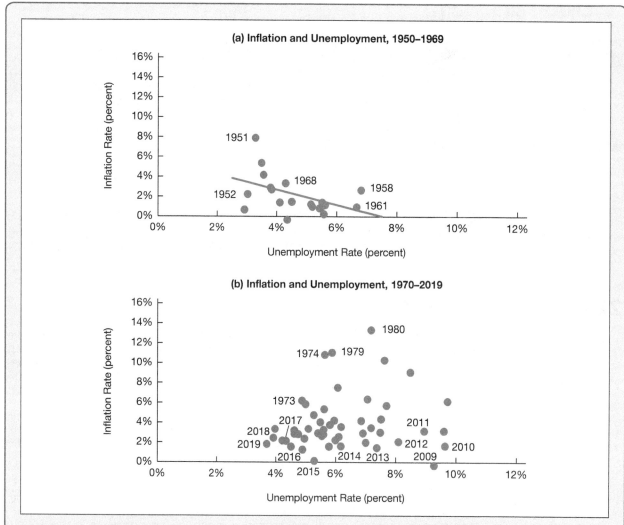

FIGURE 1   Inflation and Unemployment in the United States, 1950–1969 and 1970–2019
The plot of inflation against unemployment over the 1950–1969 period in panel (a) shows that a higher inflation rate was generally associated with a lower rate of unemployment. Panel (b) shows that after 1970, the negative correlation between inflation and unemployment disappeared.
Source: Federal Reserve Bank of St. Louis, FRED database: https://fred.stlouisfed.org/series/UNRATE; https://fred.stlouisfed.org/series/CPIAUCSL.

The Friedman-Phelps Phillips Curve Analysis

In 1967 and 1968, Nobel Prize winners Milton Friedman and Edmund Phelps pointed out a severe theoretical flaw in the Phillips curve analysis.[2] Phillips curve analysis was inconsistent with the view that workers and firms care about *real* wages, the amount

---

[2]As we discussed in Chapter 16, there will always be some unemployment—either *frictional unemployment*, unemployment that occurs because workers are searching for jobs, or *structural unemployment*, unemployment that arises from a mismatch of skills with available jobs and is a structural feature of the labor markets. Thus even when wages and prices are fully flexible, the natural rate of unemployment is at a level above zero.

FYI   The Phillips Curve Trade-Off and Macroeconomic Policy in the 1960s

In 1960, Paul Samuelson and Robert Solow published a paper outlining how policymakers could exploit the Phillips curve trade-off. The policymaker could choose between two competing goals—inflation and unemployment—and decide how high an inflation rate he or she would be willing to accept to attain a lower unemployment rate.[*] Indeed, Samuelson and Solow even stated that policymakers could achieve a "nonperfectionist" goal of a 3% unemployment rate at what they considered to be a tolerable inflation rate of 4%–5% per year. This thinking was influential in the Kennedy and then Johnson administrations and contributed to the adoption of policies in the mid-1960s to stimulate the economy and bring the unemployment rate down to low levels. At first, these policies seemed to be successful because the subsequent higher inflation rates were accompanied by lower unemployment rates. However, the good times were not to last: From the late 1960s through the 1970s, inflation accelerated yet the unemployment rate remained stubbornly high.

[*]Paul A. Samuelson and Robert M. Solow, "Analytical Aspects of Anti-Inflation Policy," *American Economic Review* 50 (May 1960, Papers and Proceedings): 177–194.

of real goods and services that wages can purchase, not *nominal* wages. Thus when workers and firms expect the price level to be rising, they will adjust nominal wages upward so that the real wage rate does not decrease. In other words, wages and overall inflation will rise on a one-to-one basis with increases in expected inflation, as well as respond to tightness in the labor market. In addition, the Friedman-Phelps analysis suggested that in the long run the economy would reach the level of unemployment that would occur if all wages and prices were flexible, which they called the *natural rate of unemployment*.[3] The natural rate of unemployment is the full-employment level of unemployment, because some unemployment will still exist even when wages and prices are flexible.

The Friedman-Phelps reasoning suggested a Phillips curve that we can write as follows:

$$\pi = \pi^e - \omega(U - U_n) \tag{1}$$

where π represents inflation, π^e expected inflation, U the unemployment rate, U_n the natural rate of unemployment, and ω the sensitivity of inflation to $U - U_n$. The presence of the π^e term explains why Equation 1 is also referred to as the *expectations-augmented Phillips curve*: It indicates that inflation is negatively related to the difference between the unemployment rate and the natural rate of unemployment $(U - U_n)$, a measure of tightness in the labor markets called the *unemployment gap*.

The expectations-augmented Phillips curve implies that long-run unemployment will be equal to the natural rate level, as Friedman and Phelps theorized. Recognize that in the long run, expected inflation must gravitate to actual inflation, and Equation 1 therefore indicates that U must be equal to U_n.

The Friedman-Phelps expectations-augmented version of the Phillips curve displays no long-run trade-off between unemployment and inflation. To show this, Figure 2

[3]Milton Friedman outlined his criticism of the Phillips curve in his 1967 presidential address to the American Economic Association: Milton Friedman, "The Role of Monetary Policy," *American Economic Review* 58 (1968): 1–17. Phelps's reformulation of the Phillips curve analysis was outlined in Edmund Phelps, "Money-Wage Dynamics and Labor-Market Equilibrium," *Journal of Political Economy* 76 (July/August 1968, Part 2): 687–711.

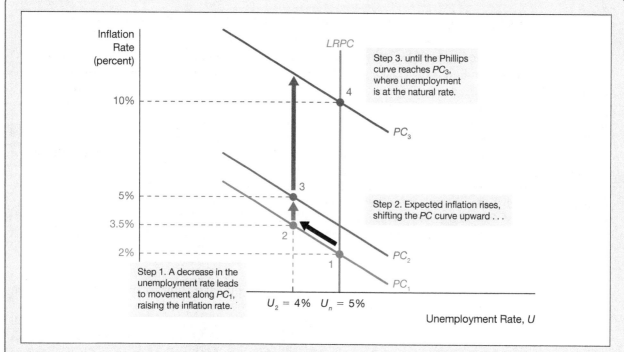

Step 3. until the Phillips curve reaches PC_3, where unemployment is at the natural rate.

Step 2. Expected inflation rises, shifting the PC curve upward . . .

Step 1. A decrease in the unemployment rate leads to movement along PC_1, raising the inflation rate.

$U_2 = 4\%$ $U_n = 5\%$

FIGURE 2   **The Short- and Long-Run Phillips Curve**
The expectations-augmented Phillips curve is downward-sloping because a lower unemployment rate results in a higher inflation rate for any given level of expected inflation. If the economy moves, due to a decline in the unemployment rate, from point 1 to point 2 on PC_1, the inflation rate rises. If unemployment remains at 4%, inflation rises further, shifting the short-run expectations-augmented Phillips curve upward to PC_2 and to point 3. Eventually, when the economy reaches point 4, where $\pi^e = \pi = 10\%$, the expectations-augmented Phillips curve PC_3 stops shifting because unemployment is at the natural rate of unemployment. The line connecting points 1 and 4 is the long-run Phillips curve, $LRPC$, and shows that long-run unemployment is at the natural rate of unemployment for any inflation rate.

presents the expectations-augmented Phillips curve, marked as PC_1, for a given expected inflation rate of 2% and a natural rate of unemployment of 5%. (PC_1 goes through point 1 because Equation 1 indicates that when $\pi = \pi^e = 2\%$, $U = U_n = 5\%$, and the curve's slope is $-\omega$.) Suppose the economy is initially at point 1, where the unemployment rate is at the natural rate level of 5%, but then government policies to stimulate the economy cause the unemployment rate to fall to 4%, a level that is below the natural rate level. The economy then moves along PC_1 to point 2, with inflation rising above 2% to, say, 3.5%. Expected inflation then rises as well, and so the expectations-augmented Phillips curve shifts upward from PC_1 to PC_2. Continued efforts to stimulate the economy and keep the unemployment rate at 4%, below the natural rate level, will cause further increases in the actual and expected inflation rates, causing the expectations-augmented Phillips curve to continue to shift upward.

When will the expectations-augmented Phillips curve stop rising? It will stop only when unemployment is back at the natural rate level, that is, when $U = U_n = 5\%$. Suppose this happens when inflation is at 10%; then expected inflation will also be at 10% because inflation has settled down to that level, with the expectations-augmented

Phillips curve at PC_3 in Figure 2. The economy will now move to point 4, where $\pi = \pi^e = 10\%$ and unemployment is at the natural rate $U = U_n = 5\%$. We thus see that in the long run, when the expectations-augmented Phillips curve has stopped shifting, the economy will be at points such as 1 and 4. The line connecting these points is thus the *long-run Phillips curve*, which we mark as *LRPC* in Figure 2.

Figure 2 leads us to three important conclusions:

1. *There is no long-run trade-off between unemployment and inflation* because, as shown by the vertical long-run Phillips curve, a higher long-run inflation rate is not associated with a lower level of unemployment.
2. *There is a short-run trade-off between unemployment and inflation* because, at a given expected inflation rate, policymakers can attain a lower unemployment rate at the expense of a somewhat higher inflation rate, as indicated by point 2 in Figure 2.
3. *There are two types of Phillips curves, long-run and short-run.* The expectations-augmented Phillips curves—PC_1, PC_2, and PC_3—are actually short-run Phillips curves: They are drawn for given values of expected inflation and will shift if deviations of unemployment from the natural rate cause inflation and expected inflation to change.

The Phillips Curve After the 1960s

As indicated in Figure 2, the expectations-augmented Phillips curve shows that the negative correlation between unemployment and inflation breaks down when the unemployment rate remains below the natural rate of unemployment for any extended period of time. This prediction of the Friedman and Phelps analysis turned out to be exactly right. Starting in the 1970s, after a period of very low unemployment rates, the negative correlation between unemployment and inflation that was so visible in the 1950s and 1960s disappeared, as shown in panel (b) of Figure 1. Not surprisingly, given the brilliance of Friedman's and Phelps's work, they were both awarded Nobel Prizes.

The Modern Phillips Curve

Inflation jumped up sharply with the sharp rise in oil prices in 1973 and 1979 (see panel (b) of Figure 1), and Phillips-curve theorists realized that they had to add one more feature to the expectations-augmented Phillips curve. *Supply shocks* are shocks to supply that change the amount of output an economy can produce from the same amount of capital and labor. These supply shocks translate into *inflation shocks*, that is, shifts in inflation that are independent of the tightness of the labor markets or of expected inflation. For example, when the supply of oil was restricted following the war between the Arab states and Israel in 1973, the price of oil more than quadrupled, and firms had to raise prices to reflect their increased costs of production, thus driving up inflation. Adding inflation shocks (ρ) to the expectations-augmented Phillips curve leads to the modern form of the short-run Phillips curve.

$$\pi = \pi^e - \omega(U - U_n) + \rho \tag{2}$$

The modern, short-run Phillips curve implies that wages and prices are sticky. The more flexible wages and prices are, the more they, and inflation, respond to deviations of unemployment from the natural rate. That is, more flexible wages and prices imply that the absolute value of ω is higher, which in turn implies that the short-run Phillips curve is steeper. If wages and prices are completely flexible, then ω becomes so large that the short-run Phillips curve is vertical and identical to the long-run Phillips curve. In this case, there is no long-run or short-run trade-off between unemployment and inflation.

The Modern Phillips Curve with Adaptive (Backward-Looking) Expectations

To complete our analysis of the Phillips curve, we need to understand how firms and households form expectations about inflation. One simple model assumes that they do so by looking at past inflation:

$$\pi^e = \pi_{-1}$$

where π_{-1} is the inflation rate for the previous period. This form of expectations is known as *adaptive expectations* or *backward-looking expectations* because expectations are formed by looking at the past and therefore change only slowly over time.[4] Substituting π_{-1} for π^e in Equation 2 yields the following short-run Phillips curve:

$$\pi = \pi_{-1} - \omega(U - U_n) + \rho$$

inflation = expected inflation − ω × unemployment gap + inflation shock (3)

This form of the Phillips curve has two advantages over the more general formulation given in Equation 2. First, it takes on a very simple mathematical form that is convenient to use. Second, it provides two additional, realistic reasons why inflation might be sticky. One reason is that inflation expectations adjust only slowly as inflation changes over time. Inflation expectations are therefore sticky, which results in some inflation stickiness. Another reason is that the presence of past inflation in the Phillips curve formulation can reflect the fact that some wage and price contracts might be backward-looking, that is, tied to past inflation, and so inflation might not fully adjust to changes in inflation expectations in the short run.

There is, however, one important weakness of the adaptive-expectations form of the Phillips curve given in Equation 3: It takes a very mechanical view of how inflation expectations are formed. More sophisticated analysis of expectations formation has important implications for the conduct of macroeconomic policy and is discussed in Chapter 24. For the time being, we will make use of the simple form of the Phillips curve with adaptive expectations, keeping in mind that the π_{-1} term represents expected inflation.

There is another convenient way of looking at the adaptive-expectations form of the Phillips curve. By subtracting π_1 from both sides of Equation 3, we can rewrite it as follows:

$$\Delta\pi = \pi - \pi_{-1} = -\omega(U - U_n) + \rho \tag{4}$$

Written in this form, the Phillips curve indicates that a negative unemployment gap (tight labor market) causes the inflation rate to rise, or *accelerate*. Thus the Equation 4 version of the Phillips curve is often referred to as an *accelerationist Phillips curve*. In this formulation, the term U_n has another interpretation. Since inflation stops accelerating (changing) when the unemployment rate is at U_n, we can refer to this term as the *nonaccelerating inflation rate of unemployment* or, more commonly, *NAIRU*.

---

[4]An alternative, modern form of expectations makes use of the concept of *rational expectations*, whereby expectations are formed using all available information and so may react more quickly to new information. We discuss rational expectations and their role in macroeconomic analysis in Chapter 24.

22.A2 THE SHORT-RUN AGGREGATE SUPPLY CURVE

To complete our aggregate demand and supply model, we need to use our analysis of the Phillips curve to derive a *short-run aggregate supply curve,* which represents the relationship between the total quantity of output that firms are willing to produce and the inflation rate.

We can translate the modern Phillips curve into a short-run aggregate supply curve by replacing the unemployment gap $(U - U_n)$ with the *output gap*, the difference between output and potential output $(Y - Y^P)$. To do this, we need to make use of a relationship between unemployment and aggregate output that was discovered by the economist Arthur Okun, once the chair of the Council of Economic Advisors and later an economist with the Brookings Institution.[5] **Okun's law** describes the negative relationship between the unemployment gap and the output gap.

Okun's Law   We show Okun's law in Figure 3, which plots the unemployment gap against the output gap. A tight negative relationship exists between the two variables. When output is above potential, so that the output gap is positive, the unemployment rate is below the natural rate of unemployment; that is, the unemployment gap is negative. The line through the data points in Figure 3 describes this negative relationship, which is given algebraically as follows:[6]

$$U - U_n = -0.5 \times (Y - Y^P) \tag{5}$$

Okun's law thus states that for each percentage point that output is above potential, the unemployment rate is one-half of a percentage point below the natural rate of unemployment. Alternatively, for every percentage point that unemployment is above its natural rate, output is two percentage points below potential output.

Another way of thinking about Okun's law is to realize that a one percentage point increase in output leads to a one-half percentage point decrease in unemployment.[7] Why is the decrease in the unemployment rate only half the increase in the output rate?

---

[5]The output gap, $Y - Y^P$, in Okun's law is most accurately expressed in percentage terms, so the units of Y and Y^P would be in logarithims. However, to keep the algebra simple in this and later chapters, we will treat Y and Y^P as levels and not logarithms in both the Okun's law equation and the short-run aggregate supply curve developed here.
[6]Arthur M. Okun, "Potential GNP: Its Measurement and Significance," in *Proceeding of the Business and Economics Section: American Statistical Association* (Washington, DC: American Statistical Association, 1962), 98–103; reprinted in Arthur M. Okun, *The Political Economy of Prosperity* (Washington, DC: Brookings Institution, 1970), pp. 132–145.
[7]To see this algebraically, take the differences of Equation 5 and assume that U_n remains constant (a reasonable assumption because the natural rate of unemployment changes only very slowly over time). Then,

$$\%\Delta U = -0.5 \times (\%\Delta Y - \%\Delta Y^P)$$

where $\%\Delta$ indicates a percentage point change. Since potential output grows at a fairly steady rate of around three percent per year, $\%\Delta Y^P = 3\%$, we can also write Okun's law as follows:

$$\%\Delta U = -0.5 \times (\%\Delta Y - 3)$$

or

$$\%\Delta Y = 3 - 2 \times \%\Delta U$$

Hence we can state Okun's law in the following way: For every percentage point rise in output (real GDP), unemployment falls by one-half of a percentage point. Alternatively, for every percentage point rise in unemployment, real GDP falls by two percentage points.

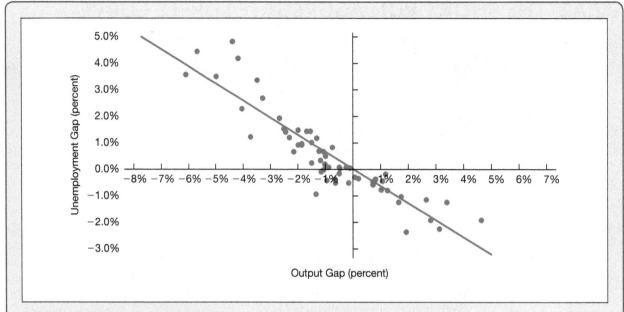

FIGURE 3   **Okun's Law, 1960–2019**

The plot of the unemployment gap and the output gap reveals a linear relationship, represented by the solid line with a slope of $-\frac{1}{2}$.

Source: Federal Reserve Bank of St. Louis, FRED database: https://fred.stlouisfed.org/series/UNRATE; https://fred.stlouisfed.org/series/GDPC1; https://fred.stlouisfed.org/series/GDPPOT; https://fred.stlouis.org/series/NROU.

When output rises, firms do not increase employment commensurately with the increase in output, a phenomenon that is known as *labor hoarding*. Rather, firms work their employees harder, increasing their hours. Furthermore, when the economy is expanding, more people enter the labor force because job prospects are better, and so the unemployment rate does not fall by as much as employment increases.

Deriving the Short-Run Aggregate Supply Curve   We can use Okun's law as given in Equation 5 to substitute for $U - U_n$ in the short-run Phillips curve (Equation 2 of this appendix) to yield the following:

$$\pi = \pi^e + 0.5\omega(Y - Y^P) + \rho$$

Replacing 0.5ω by γ, which describes the sensitivity of inflation to the output gap, we get the short-run aggregate supply curve given as Equation 2 in the chapter:

$$\pi = \pi^e + \gamma(Y - Y^P) + \rho$$

inflation = expected inflation $+ \gamma \times$ output gap $+$ inflation shock

23 Monetary Policy Theory

Learning Objectives

23.1 Illustrate and explain the policy choices that monetary policymakers face under the conditions of aggregate demand and aggregate supply shocks.

23.2 Identify the lags in the policy process, and summarize why they weaken the case for an activist policy approach.

23.3 Explain why monetary policymakers can target any inflation rate in the long run but cannot target a level of aggregate output in the long run.

23.4 Identify the sources of inflation and the role of monetary policy in propagating inflation.

23.5 Explain the unique challenges that monetary policymakers face at the effective lower bound, and illustrate how non-conventional monetary policy can be effective under such conditions.

Preview

Between September 2007 and December 2008, the Federal Reserve lowered the target for its policy interest rate, the federal funds rate, from $5\frac{1}{4}$% all the way down to zero and continued to keep it there for more than seven years afterward. Why did the Fed lower interest rates so aggressively and continue to keep them so low?

Could this monetary policy easing have sparked undesirable inflation? Many commentators in the media thought so. Starting in the early 1960s, when the inflation rate hovered between 1% and 2%, the economy began to suffer from higher and more variable rates of inflation. By the late 1960s, the inflation rate had climbed to beyond 5%, and by 1974, it reached the double-digit level. After moderating somewhat during the 1975–1978 period, it shot above 10% in 1979 and 1980, decreased to around 5% from 1982 to 1990, declined further to around 2% in the late 1990s, and then climbed above the 5% level in 2008. Subsequently, the inflation rate fell to below the 2% level. Inflation has become a major concern of politicians and the public, and how best to control it is an issue that frequently dominates the discussion of economic policy.

In this chapter, we will use the aggregate demand/aggregate supply (*AD/AS*) framework developed in Chapter 22 to develop a theory of monetary policy. Specifically, we will examine the role of monetary policy in stabilizing the economy and creating inflation. We apply the theory to four big questions: Does stabilizing inflation stabilize output? Should policy be *activist*, responding aggressively to fluctuations in economic activity, or passive and *nonactivist*? What are the roots of inflation? How can monetary policy work when interest rates cannot go much below zero?

23.1 RESPONSE OF MONETARY POLICY TO SHOCKS

LO 23.1 Illustrate and explain the policy choices that monetary policymakers face under the conditions of aggregate demand and aggregate supply shocks.

As we saw in Chapter 16, the primary goal of central banks is price stability: That is, they try to maintain inflation, π, close to a target level (π^T), referred to as an **inflation target**, that is slightly above zero. Most central banks set π^T between 1% and 3%. In other words, central banks pursue price stability through monetary policy that aims to minimize the difference between inflation and the inflation target ($\pi - \pi^T$), a difference economists refer to as the **inflation gap**.

In Chapter 16, we learned that central banks also care about stabilizing economic activity. Because economic activity can be sustained only at potential output, we can describe this objective of monetary policy by saying that monetary policymakers want aggregate output to be close to its potential level, Y^P. Central banks want to minimize the difference between aggregate output and potential output ($Y - Y^P$), i.e., the *output gap*. In our analysis of aggregate demand and supply in Chapter 22, we examined two categories of economic shocks—demand shocks and supply shocks—and the effects of each on inflation and output. In this section, we describe a central bank's policy responses, given its objectives, to each of these types of shocks. In the case of demand shocks, policymakers can simultaneously pursue price stability and stability of economic activity. In the aftermath of a supply shocks, however, policymakers can achieve either price stability or economic activity stability, but not both. This trade-off poses a thorny dilemma for central banks with dual mandates.

Response to an Aggregate Demand Shock

Because we are discussing stabilizing economic activity, we need to focus on output gaps rather than the level of aggregate output. Thus, in this and the next chapter, we will conduct all *AD/AS* analysis in terms of the aggregate output index, in which potential output has a value of 100, rather than in terms of aggregate output. In all the following *AD/AS* diagrams, the label on the horizontal axis is now always going to be the aggregate output index, and Y represents the aggregate output index rather than aggregate output.

We begin by considering the effects of an aggregate demand shock, illustrated in Figure 1. For example, the coronavirus pandemic began, in March 2020, to cause both consumer and business spending to fall. In the figure, the economy is initially at point 1, where output is at its potential level so the aggregate output index is at $Y^P = 100$, and inflation is at π^T. The negative demand shock decreases aggregate demand, shifting AD_1 to the left to AD_2. Policymakers can respond to this shock in two possible ways.

No Policy Response If the central bank does not respond by changing the autonomous component of monetary policy, the aggregate demand curve remains at AD_2, and so the economy moves to the intersection of AS_1 and AD_2. Here, the aggregate output index falls to Y_2, so aggregate output is below potential output, and inflation falls to π_2, below the inflation target of π^T. With inflation falling and output below potential, expected inflation will decline and the short-run aggregate supply curve will shift down and to the right until it reaches AS_3, and the economy will move to point 3. Output will be back to its potential level at an aggregate output index of $Y^P = 100$ and inflation will fall to a lower level of π_3. At first glance, this outcome looks favorable—inflation is lower and output is back at its potential. But aggregate output will remain below potential for some time, and if inflation was initially at its target level, the fall in inflation is undesirable for the reasons outlined in Chapters 12 and 16.

Policy Stabilizes Economic Activity and Inflation in the Short Run Policymakers can eliminate both the output gap and the inflation gap in the short run by pursuing policies aimed at increasing aggregate demand to its initial level and returning the economy to its preshock state. The central bank does this by autonomously easing monetary policy by cutting the real interest rate at any given inflation rate. This action stimulates investment spending and increases the quantity of aggregate output demanded at any given inflation rate, thereby shifting the *AD* curve to the right. As a result, the aggregate demand curve shifts from AD_2 back to AD_1 in Figure 2,

Mini-lecture

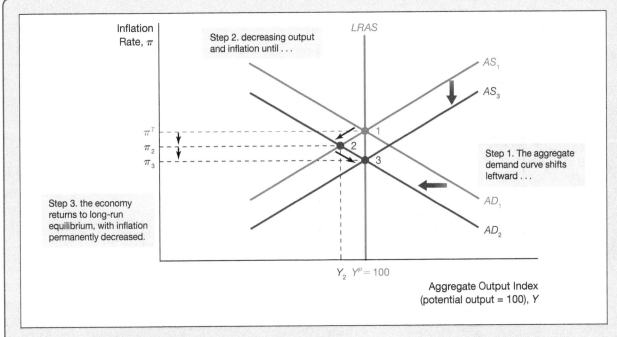

FIGURE 1   Aggregate Demand Shock: No Policy Response

An aggregate demand shock shifts the aggregate demand curve leftward from AD_1 to AD_2 and moves the economy from point 1 to point 2, where the aggregate output index falls to Y_2 and inflation falls to π_2. With output below potential, the short-run aggregate supply curve shifts down to AS_3 and the economy moves to point 3, where output is back at $Y^P = 100$ but inflation has fallen to π_3.

and the economy returns to point 1. (The Federal Reserve took exactly these steps by lowering the federal funds rate from 5% to $\frac{1}{4}$% to zero over 15 months starting in September 2007.)

Our analysis of this monetary policy response shows that *in the case of aggregate demand shocks, there is no trade-off between the pursuits of price stability and economic activity stability.* A monetary policy response that focuses on stabilizing inflation is exactly the monetary policy response that will stabilize economic activity. No conflict exists between the dual objectives of stabilizing inflation and stabilizing economic activity, a result that Olivier Blanchard (the chief economist at the International Monetary Fund at the time, formerly a professor at MIT) referred to as the **divine coincidence**.

Response to a Supply Shock

When a supply shock occurs—for example, when the price of oil surges because of political unrest in the Middle East or because of an act of God such as a devastating hurricane in Florida—the divine coincidence does not hold. Policymakers face a short-run trade-off between stabilizing inflation and stabilizing economic activity. To illustrate, we start with the economy at point 1 in Figure 3, where aggregate output is at the natural rate, so the aggregate output index is at $Y^P = 100$ and inflation is at π^T.

Mini-lecture

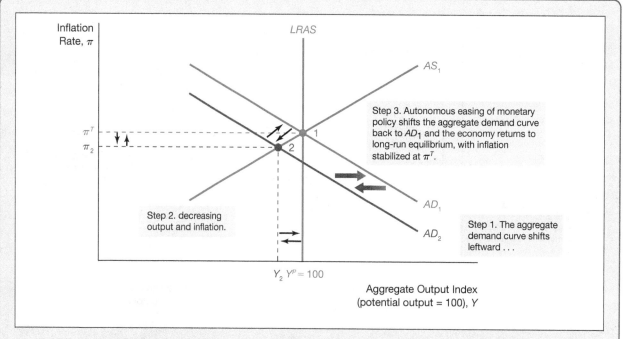

FIGURE 2 **Aggregate Demand Shock: Policy Stabilizes Output and Inflation in the Short Run**

An aggregate demand shock shifts the aggregate demand curve leftward from AD_1 to AD_2 and moves the economy from point 1 to point 2, where the aggregate output index falls to Y_2 and inflation falls to π_2. An autonomous easing of monetary policy lowers the real interest rate at any given inflation rate and shifts the AD curve back to AD_1. Aggregate output returns to potential at point 1, and inflation returns to its target level.

The negative supply shock—from, say, a rise in the price of oil—shifts the short-run aggregate supply curve up and to the left, from AS_1 to AS_2. The economy moves to point 2, with inflation rising to π_2 and the aggregate output indexing falling to Y_2. Policymakers can respond to the supply shock in three possible ways.

No Policy Response   One potential policy choice is to refrain from making an autonomous change in monetary policy so that the aggregate demand curve does not shift. Since aggregate output is less than potential output, eventually the short-run aggregate supply curve will shift back down to the right, returning to AS_1. The economy will return to point 1 in Figure 3, and both the output and inflation gaps will close as output and inflation return to their initial levels of $Y^P = 100$ and π^T, respectively. Both inflation and economic activity will stabilize over time. While we wait for the long run, however, the economy will undergo a painful period of reduced output and higher inflation rates. To avoid this period of reduced output and high inflation, monetary policymakers might decide to try to stabilize economic activity or inflation in the short run.

Policy Stabilizes Inflation in the Short Run   A second policy choice for monetary authorities is to keep inflation at the target level of π^T in the short run by autonomously tightening monetary policy and raising the real interest rate at any given inflation rate. Doing so will cause investment spending and aggregate demand to fall at

Mini-lecture

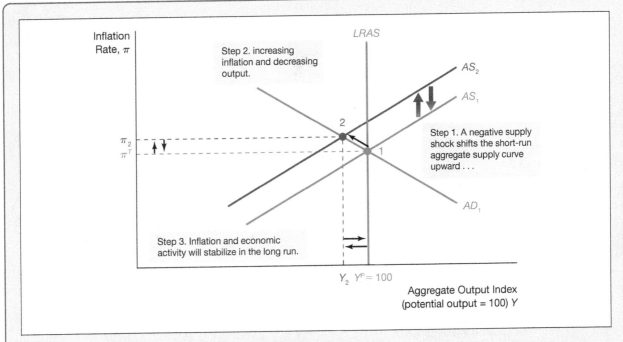

FIGURE 3   Response to a Supply Shock: No Policy Response

A negative supply shock shifts the short-run aggregate supply curve upward from AS_1 to AS_2, moving the economy to point 2, with inflation rising to π_2 and the aggregate output index falling to Y_2. If the autonomous monetary policy remains unchanged, the short-run aggregate supply curve will shift back down and to the right in the long run, eventually returning to AS_1, and the economy will move back to point 1.

each inflation rate, shifting the aggregate demand curve to the left to AD_3 in Figure 4. The economy now will move to point 3, where the aggregate demand curve AD_3 intersects the short-run aggregate supply curve AS_2 at an inflation rate of π^T. Because output is below potential at point 3, the short-run aggregate supply curve will shift back down to AS_1. To keep the inflation rate at π^T, the monetary authorities will need to move the short-run aggregate demand curve back to AD_1 by reversing the autonomous tightening, and eventually the economy will return to point 1.

As Figure 4 illustrates, stabilizing inflation reduces the aggregate output index to Y_3 in the short run, and only over time will output return to potential output at an aggregate output index of $Y^P = 100$. *Stabilizing inflation in response to a supply shock leads to a larger deviation of aggregate output from potential, so this action does not stabilize economic activity.*

Policy Stabilizes Economic Activity in the Short Run   A third policy choice is for monetary policymakers to stabilize economic activity rather than inflation in the short run by increasing aggregate demand. According to Figure 5, this policy decision will shift the aggregate demand curve to the right to AD_3, where it intersects the short-run aggregate supply curve AS_2 and the long-run aggregate supply curve *LRAS* at point 3. To achieve this result, policymakers will have to autonomously ease monetary policy by lowering the real interest rate at any given inflation rate. At point 3, the output gap

Mini-lecture

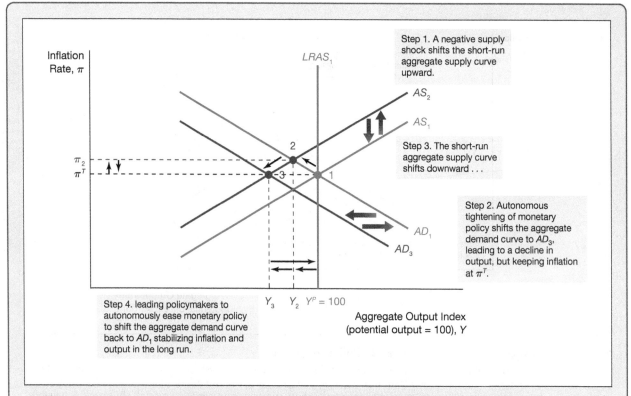

FIGURE 4 **Response to a Supply Shock: Short-Run Inflation Stabilization**

A negative supply shock shifts the short-run aggregate supply curve from AS_1 to AS_2, moving the economy to point 2, with inflation rising to π_2 and the aggregate output index falling to Y_2. Autonomous tightening of monetary policy shifts the aggregate demand curve to the left to AD_3, and the economy moves to point 3, where inflation is at π^T. With output below potential at point 3, the short-run aggregate supply curve shifts back to AS_1. To keep the inflation rate at π^T, the autonomous tightening of monetary policy is reversed, shifting the aggregate demand curve back to AD_1 and the economy back to point 1.

returns to zero, so monetary policy has stabilized economic activity. However, inflation has risen to π_3, which is greater than π^T, and so inflation has *not* been stabilized. **Stabilizing economic activity in response to a supply shock results in a larger deviation of inflation from the inflation target rather than a stabilization of inflation.**

The Bottom Line: The Relationship Between Stabilizing Inflation and Stabilizing Economic Activity

We can draw the following conclusions from our analysis:

1. *If most shocks to the economy are aggregate demand shocks, then policy that stabilizes inflation will also stabilize economic activity, even in the short run.*
2. *If supply shocks are the most common type of shock, then a central bank must choose between the two stabilization objectives in the short run.*

Mini-lecture

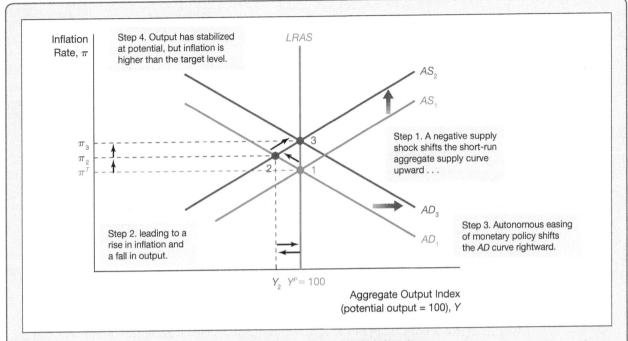

FIGURE 5   **Response to a Supply Shock: Short-Run Output Stabilization**

A negative supply shock shifts the short-run aggregate supply curve from AS_1 to AS_2, moving the economy to point 2, with inflation rising to π_2 and the aggregate output index falling to Y_2. To stabilize output, autonomous monetary policy easing shifts the aggregate demand curve rightward to AD_3. At point 3, the monetary policy action has stabilized economic activity, but inflation at π_3 is greater than the target level π^T.

23.2 HOW ACTIVELY SHOULD POLICYMAKERS TRY TO STABILIZE ECONOMIC ACTIVITY?

LO 23.2 Identify the lags in the policy process, and summarize why they weaken the case for an activist policy approach.

All economists have similar policy goals (to promote high employment and price stability), yet they often disagree on the best approach for achieving these goals. Suppose policymakers confront an economy that has high unemployment resulting from a negative demand or supply shock that has reduced aggregate output. **Nonactivists** believe that wages and prices are very flexible and that the self-correcting mechanism works very rapidly. They argue that the short-run aggregate supply curve will shift downward quickly, returning the economy to full employment rapidly. They thus believe that government action to eliminate unemployment is unnecessary. **Activists**, many of whom are followers of Keynes and are thus referred to as **Keynesians**, regard the self-correcting mechanism, which works through wage and price adjustment, as a very slow-working mechanism because of the stickiness of wages and prices. Thus they believe it will take the economy a very long time to reach the long run, agreeing with Keynes's famous adage that "In the long-run, we are all dead." Activists therefore believe that the government should pursue active policies to increase aggregate demand and eliminate high unemployment when it develops.

Lags and Policy Implementation

If policymakers could shift the aggregate demand curve instantaneously, activist policies could be used to move the economy immediately to the full-employment level, as we saw in the previous section. However, several types of lags prevent this immediate shift from occurring, and there are differences in the lengths of these lags for monetary versus fiscal policy.

1. The **data lag** is the time it takes for policymakers to obtain the data that describe what is happening in the economy. Accurate data on GDP, for example, are not available until several months after a given quarter is over.

2. The **recognition lag** is the time it takes for policymakers to feel confident about the signals the data are sending about the future course of the economy. For example, to minimize errors, the National Bureau of Economic Research (the private organization that officially dates business cycles) will not declare the economy to be in recession until at least six months after it has determined that a recession has begun.

3. The **legislative lag** represents the time it takes to get legislation passed to implement a particular policy. The legislative lag does not apply to most monetary policy actions, such as the lowering of interest rates. It is, however, important in the implementation of fiscal policy, because it can sometimes take six months to a year to get legislation passed to change taxes or government purchases.

4. The **implementation lag** is the time it takes for policymakers to change policy instruments once they have decided on a new policy. Again, this lag is less important for the conduct of monetary policy, because the Federal Reserve can immediately change its policy interest rate, whereas it is more important for the implementation of fiscal policy. The implementation of new fiscal policy can take substantial time; for example, getting government agencies to change their spending habits takes time, as does changing tax tables.

5. The **effectiveness lag** is the time it takes for the policy to have a real impact on the economy. The effectiveness lag is both long (often a year long or longer) and variable (that is, substantial uncertainty exists about the length of this lag).

The existence of these lags makes the policymakers' job far more difficult and therefore weakens the case for activism. When unemployment is high, activist policy aimed at shifting the aggregate demand curve rightward to restore the economy to full employment may not produce desirable outcomes. Indeed, if the policy lags described above are very long, then by the time the aggregate demand curve shifts to the right, the self-correcting mechanism may have already returned the economy to full employment. Then, when the activist policy kicks in, it may cause output to rise above potential, leading to a rise in inflation. In situations in which policy lags are longer than the time it takes the self-correcting mechanism to work, a policy of nonactivism may produce better outcomes.

The activist/nonactivist debate came to the fore when the Obama administration advocated a fiscal stimulus package early in its administration in 2009 (see the FYI box "The Activist/Nonactivist Debate over the Obama Fiscal Stimulus Package"). In Chapter 24, we will return to the issue of just how active policy should be when we look at the role that expectations play in monetary policy.

FYI   **The Activist/Nonactivist Debate over the Obama Fiscal Stimulus Package**

When President Obama took office in January 2009, he faced a very serious recession, with unemployment at over 7% and rising rapidly. Although policymakers had been using monetary policy aggressively to stabilize the economy (see Chapters 12 and 15), many activists argued that the government needed to do more by implementing a massive fiscal stimulus package. They argued that without the stimulus package, monetary policy, which had already lowered the federal funds rate to close to zero and so could not lower nominal interest rates further, would be unable to increase aggregate demand to the full-employment level. In contrast, nonactivists opposed the fiscal stimulus package, arguing that fiscal stimulus would take too long to work because of long implementation lags. They cautioned that if the fiscal stimulus kicked in after the economy had already recovered, the result would be increased volatility in inflation and economic activity.

The economics profession was split over the desirability of fiscal stimulus. Approximately 200 economists who opposed fiscal stimulus signed a petition published in the *Wall Street Journal* and the *New York Times* on January 28, 2009. An opposing petition, also signed by about 200 economists, was sent to the U.S. Congress on February 8. The Obama administration came down squarely on the side of the activists and proposed the American Recovery and Reinvestment Act of 2009, a $787 billion fiscal stimulus package that was passed by Congress on February 13, 2009. In the House, the vote in favor of the stimulus package was 244 to 188, with 177 Republicans and 11 Democrats opposing the bill. In the Senate, the vote was 61 to 37, with all 58 Democrats and 3 Republicans supporting the bill. Even after the fact, the value of the 2009 stimulus package is still hotly debated, with some believing it helped stabilize the economy and others believing it was not effective.

23.3 INFLATION: ALWAYS AND EVERYWHERE A MONETARY PHENOMENON

LO 23.3 Explain why monetary policymakers can target any inflation rate in the long run but cannot target a level of aggregate output in the long run.

Milton Friedman is famous for his adage that in the long run, "Inflation is always and everywhere a monetary phenomenon." This adage is supported by our aggregate demand and supply analysis, which asserts that monetary policymakers can target any inflation rate in the long run by shifting the aggregate demand curve through autonomous monetary policy. As an illustration, look at Figure 6, where the economy is at point 1, with aggregate output at potential output, so the aggregate output index is at $Y^P = 100$, and inflation is at an initial inflation target of π_1^T.

Suppose the central bank believes that this inflation target is too low and chooses to raise it to π_3^T. The central bank eases monetary policy autonomously by lowering the real interest rate at any given inflation rate, thereby increasing investment spending and aggregate demand. In Figure 6, the aggregate demand curve shifts to AD_3. The economy then moves to point 2, at the intersection of AD_3 and AS_1, with inflation rising to π_2. Because aggregate output is above potential output, $Y_2 > Y^P$, the short-run aggregate supply curve shifts up and to the left, eventually stopping at AS_3. The economy moves to point 3, where inflation is at the higher target level of π_3^T and the output gap is back at zero.

Mini-lecture

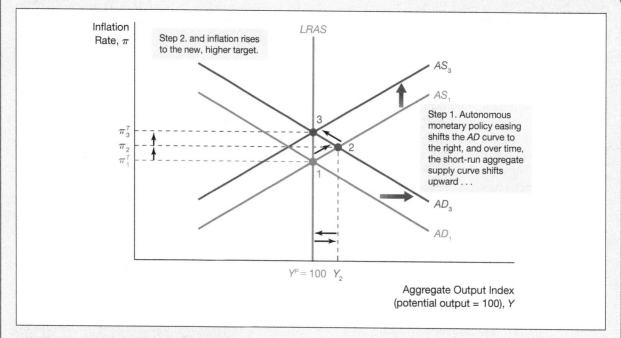

FIGURE 6   A Rise in the Inflation Target

To raise the inflation target to π_3^T, the central bank undertakes an autonomous monetary policy easing by lowering the real interest rate at any given inflation rate, thereby shifting the aggregate demand curve rightward to AD_3. The economy then moves to point 2, and the short-run aggregate supply curve shifts up and to the left, eventually stopping at AS_3. The economy then moves to point 3, with the output gap at zero and inflation at π_3^T.

The analysis in Figure 6 demonstrates the following key points:

1. *The monetary authorities can target any inflation rate in the long run with autonomous monetary policy adjustments.*
2. *Potential output—and therefore the quantity of aggregate output produced in the long run—is independent of monetary policy.*

23.4 CAUSES OF INFLATIONARY MONETARY POLICY

LO 23.4 Identify the sources of inflation and the role of monetary policy in propagating inflation.

If everyone agrees that high inflation is bad for an economy, why do we see so much of it? Do governments pursue inflationary monetary policies intentionally? We know that monetary authorities can set the inflation rate in the long run, so it must be that in trying to achieve other goals, governments end up with overly expansionary monetary policies and high inflation. In this section, we will examine the government policies that are the most common sources of inflation.

High Employment Targets and Inflation

One important goal of most governments is high employment, and the pursuit of this goal can bring on high inflation. The U.S. government is committed by law (the Employment Act of 1946 and the Humphrey-Hawkins Act of 1978) to engage in activist policy to promote high employment. Both laws require a commitment to a high level of employment consistent with stable inflation—yet in practice, the U.S. government and the Federal Reserve have often pursued a high employment target with little concern for the inflationary consequences of such a policy. This tendency was especially apparent in the mid-1960s and 1970s, when the government and the Fed began taking an active role in attempting to stabilize unemployment.

Two types of inflation can result from an activist stabilization policy aimed at promoting high employment:

1. **Cost-push inflation** results from either a negative supply shock or a push by workers for wage hikes that are beyond those justified by productivity gains.
2. **Demand-pull inflation** results when policymakers pursue policies that increase aggregate demand.

We will now use aggregate demand and supply analysis to examine the effects of a high employment target on both types of inflation.

Cost-Push Inflation

Consider the economy shown in Figure 7, which is initially at point 1, the intersection of the aggregate demand curve AD_1 and the short-run aggregate supply curve AS_1. Suppose workers succeed in pushing for higher wages, either because they want to increase their real wages (their wages in terms of the goods and services they can buy) above the level justified by productivity gains or because they expect inflation to increase and therefore want their wages to increase accordingly. This cost-push shock, which acts like a negative supply shock, raises the inflation rate and shifts the short-run aggregate supply curve up and to the left, to AS_2. If the central bank takes no action to change the equilibrium interest rate and the monetary policy curve remains unchanged, the economy will move to point 2′, at the intersection of the new short-run aggregate supply curve AS_2 and the aggregate demand curve AD_1. The aggregate output index will decline to Y', where output is below potential output, and the inflation rate will rise to $\pi_{2'}$, leading to an increase in unemployment.

In contrast, activist policymakers with a high employment target would implement policies to increase aggregate demand, such as tax cuts, increases in government purchases, or an autonomous easing of monetary policy. These policies would shift the aggregate demand curve in Figure 7 to AD_2, quickly returning the economy to potential output at point 2 and increasing the inflation rate to π_2. The workers would fare quite well, earning both higher wages and government protection against excessive unemployment.

The workers' success might encourage them to seek even higher wages. In addition, other workers might now realize that their wages have fallen relative to their fellow workers' wages, leading them to seek wage increases. These actions will lead to another negative supply shock, which will cause the short-run aggregate supply curve in Figure 7 to shift up and to the left again, to AS_3. Unemployment will develop again when we move to point 3′, prompting additional activist policies that will shift the aggregate demand curve rightward to AD_3 and return the economy to full employment at a higher inflation rate of π_3. If this process continues, the result will be a continuing increase in inflation—a cost-push inflation.

Mini-lecture

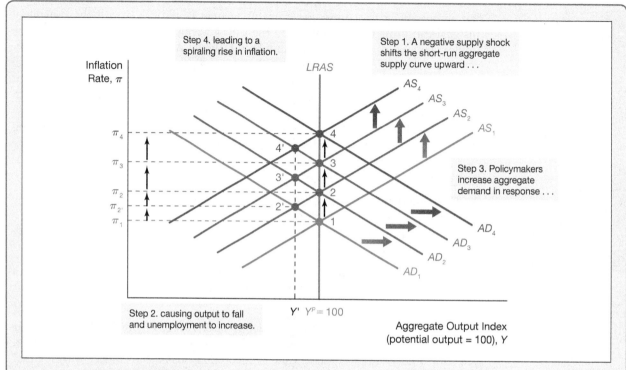

FIGURE 7 **Cost-Push Inflation**

A cost-push shock (which acts like a negative supply shock) shifts the short-run aggregate supply curve up and to the left to AS_2, and the economy moves to point 2′. To keep aggregate output at potential output and to lower the unemployment rate, policymakers shift the aggregate demand curve to AD_2 so that the economy will return quickly to potential output at point 2 and an inflation rate of π_2. Further upward and leftward shifts of the short-run aggregate supply curve, to AS_3 and beyond, lead the policymakers to continue increasing aggregate demand, leading to a continuing increase in inflation—a cost-push inflation.

Demand-Pull Inflation A goal of high employment can lead to inflationary fiscal and monetary policy in another way. Even at full employment (the natural rate of unemployment), some unemployment is always present because of frictions in the labor market that complicate the matching of unemployed workers with employers. Consequently, the unemployment rate when employment is full is still greater than zero. When policymakers mistakenly underestimate the natural rate of unemployment and so set a target for unemployment that is too low (i.e., less than the natural rate of unemployment), they set the stage for expansionary monetary policy that produces inflation.

Figure 8 uses aggregate supply and demand analysis to show how this scenario can unfold. If policymakers set a 4% unemployment target when the natural rate of unemployment is 5%, they are trying to achieve an output target greater than potential output. We mark this target level of the aggregate output index in Figure 8 as Y^T. Suppose the economy is initially at point 1: At this point, the economy is at potential output but below the target level of the aggregate output index Y^T. To hit the unemployment target of 4%, policymakers must enact policies, such as expansionary fiscal policy or an autonomous easing of monetary policy, to increase aggregate demand. The aggregate

Mini-lecture

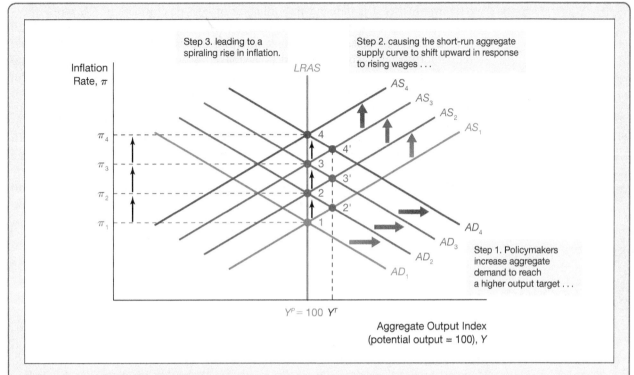

FIGURE 8 **Demand-Pull Inflation**

Too low an unemployment target (too high a target for the aggregate output index of Y^T) causes the government to increase aggregate demand, shifting the AD curve rightward from AD_1 to AD_2 to AD_3 and so on. Because at Y^T the unemployment rate is below the natural rate level, wages will rise and the short-run aggregate supply curve will shift up and leftward, from AS_1 to AS_2 to AS_3 and so on. The result is a continuing rise in inflation known as a demand-pull inflation.

demand curve in Figure 8 shifts to the right until it reaches AD_2 and the economy moves to point 2′, where the aggregate output index is at Y^T and policymakers have achieved the 4% unemployment rate goal. But there is more to the story. At Y^T, the 4% unemployment rate is below the natural rate level and output is above potential, causing wages to rise. The short-run aggregate supply curve will now shift up and to the left, eventually reaching AS_2 and moving the economy from point 2′ to point 2, where it is back at potential output but at a higher inflation rate of π_2. Because unemployment is again higher than the target level, policymakers will once more shift the aggregate demand curve rightward to AD_3 in order to hit the output target at point 3′—and the whole process will continue to drive the economy to point 3 and beyond. The overall result is a steadily rising inflation rate.

Pursuing too low an unemployment rate target or, equivalently, too high an output target thus leads to inflationary monetary or fiscal policy. Policymakers fail on two counts: They have not achieved their unemployment target, and they have caused higher inflation. If the target rate of unemployment is below the natural rate, the process we see in Figure 8 will be well under way before the policymakers realize their mistake.

Cost-Push Versus Demand-Pull Inflation   When inflation occurs, how do we know whether it is demand-pull inflation or cost-push inflation? We would normally expect to see demand-pull inflation when unemployment is below the natural rate level, and to see cost-push inflation when unemployment is above the natural rate level. Unfortunately, economists and policymakers still struggle with accurately measuring the natural rate of unemployment. Complicating matters further, a cost-push inflation can be initiated by a demand-pull inflation, blurring the distinction. When a demand-pull inflation produces higher inflation rates, expected inflation will eventually rise and workers will demand higher wages (cost-push inflation) so that their real wages do not fall. Finally, expansionary monetary and fiscal policies produce both kinds of inflation, so we cannot distinguish between the two types of inflation on the basis of their source.

In the United States, as we will see in the following application, the primary reason for inflationary policy has been policymakers' adherence to a high employment target. As we saw in Chapter 19, high inflation can also be caused by persistent government budget deficits that are financed by increases in the monetary base.

APPLICATION   The Great Inflation

Now that we have examined the roots of inflationary monetary policy, we can investigate the causes of the rise in U.S. inflation that occurred from 1965 to 1982, a period dubbed the "Great Inflation."

Panel (a) of Figure 9 documents the rise in inflation during these years. Just before the Great Inflation started, the inflation rate was below 2% at an annual rate; by the late 1970s, it averaged around 8%. It peaked at over 14% in 1980 after an oil price shock in 1979. Panel (b) of Figure 9 compares the actual unemployment rate to estimates of the natural rate of unemployment. Notice that the economy experienced unemployment below the natural rate in every year but one between 1960 and 1973, as represented by the shaded areas. This insight suggests that from 1960–1973, the U.S. economy experienced the demand-pull inflation we described in Figure 9. That is, in trying to achieve an output target that was too high, policymakers pursued a policy of autonomous monetary policy easing that shifted the aggregate demand curve to the right and created a positive output gap, thereby increasing inflation. Policymakers, economists, and politicians were committed in the mid-1960s to a target unemployment rate of 4%, a level of unemployment they believed to be consistent with price stability. In hindsight, most economists today agree that the natural rate of unemployment was substantially higher in the 1960s and 1970s, between 5% and 6%, as shown in panel (b) of Figure 9. The inappropriate 4% unemployment target initiated the most sustained inflationary episode in U.S. history.

Panel (b) of Figure 9 shows that after 1974, the unemployment rate remained above the natural rate of unemployment (see shaded area), with the exception of a brief period in 1978 and 1979, and yet inflation continued, per panel (a), indicating a cost-push inflation such as we described in Figure 7 (the impetus for which was the earlier demand-pull inflation). The public's knowledge that government policy was aimed squarely at high employment explains the persistence of inflation. The higher rate of expected inflation from the demand-pull inflation shifted the short-run aggregate supply curve in Figure 7 upward and to the left, causing a rise in unemployment that policymakers tried to eliminate by autonomously easing monetary

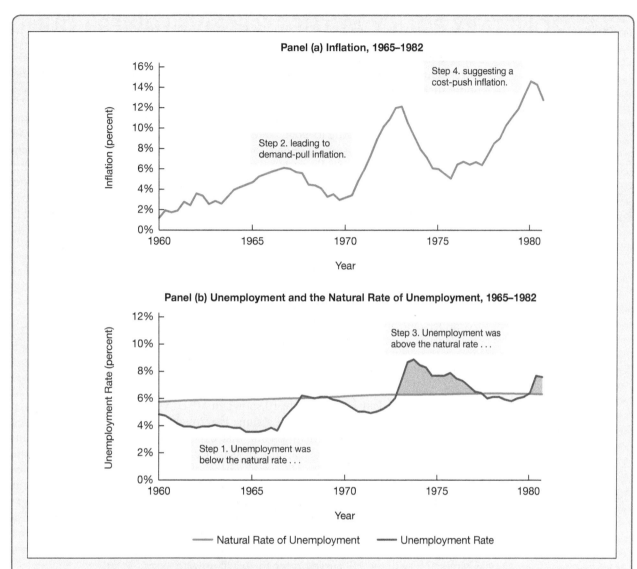

Panel (a) Inflation, 1965–1982

Step 4. suggesting a cost-push inflation.

Step 2. leading to demand-pull inflation.

Panel (b) Unemployment and the Natural Rate of Unemployment, 1965–1982

Step 3. Unemployment was above the natural rate . . .

Step 1. Unemployment was below the natural rate . . .

— Natural Rate of Unemployment   — Unemployment Rate

FIGURE 9 **Inflation and Unemployment, 1965–1982**

As shown in panel (a), the CPI inflation rate was below 2% at an annual rate in the early 1960s, but by the late 1970s, it was averaging around 8%. It peaked at over 14% in 1980 following an oil price shock in 1979. As shown in panel (b), the economy experienced unemployment below the natural rate in every year but one between 1960 and 1973, suggesting a demand-pull inflation as described in Figure 8. After 1975, the unemployment rate was regularly above the natural rate of unemployment, suggesting a cost-push inflation as delineated in Figure 7.

Source: Economic Report of the President.

policy, shifting the aggregate demand curve to the right. The result was a continuing rise in inflation.

Only when the Federal Reserve, under Fed chair Paul Volcker, committed to an anti-inflationary monetary policy, which involved hiking the federal funds rate to the 20% level, did inflation come down, ending the Great Inflation. ◆

23.5 MONETARY POLICY AT THE EFFECTIVE LOWER BOUND

LO 23.5 Explain the unique challenges that monetary policymakers face at the effective lower bound, and illustrate how nonconventional monetary policy can be effective under such conditions.

So far we have assumed that a central bank can continue to lower the real interest rate as inflation falls by lowering its policy rate—say, the federal funds rate—so that the *MP* curve is always upward-sloping. However, because the federal funds rate is a nominal interest rate, it can never fall much below a value of zero. A negative federal funds rate well below zero would imply that banks are willing to earn a much lower return by lending in the federal funds market than they could earn by holding cash in their vaults, with its zero rate of return. As discussed in Chapter 15, the floor on the policy rate is referred to as the *effective lower bound*, and it creates a particular problem for the conduct of monetary policy.

Deriving the Aggregate Demand Curve with the Effective Lower Bound

To understand more deeply the problems created by the effective lower bound with regard to the conduct of monetary policy, let's look at what happens to the aggregate demand curve when a central bank cannot lower its policy rate much below zero. A key fact in this analysis is that the real interest rate is the interest rate that is adjusted for expected inflation, i.e., the real rate equals the nominal rate minus expected inflation, $r = i - \pi^e$. Panel (a) of Figure 10 shows an *MP* curve that hits the effective lower bound, which, for simplicity, we will assume is zero, although it could be slightly less than zero. For our purposes, let's assume that expected inflation moves closely with the actual inflation rate (as it usually does), as indicated on the horizontal axis in panel (a). Let's start at point 3 on the *MP* curve, where inflation is at 3% and the real interest rate is at 2%. Now let's see what happens as inflation falls from 3% to 2%. At this inflation level, the monetary authorities will want to lower the real interest rate to, say, −2% (point 2 in panel (a)), which will require them to lower the policy rate to zero ($r = 0 - 2\% = -2\%$). At point 2 in panel (a), the effective lower bound has been reached on the *MP* curve. So far, our analysis is identical to the analysis given in Chapter 21, with the MP curve having the usual upward slope.

Now, what happens if the inflation rate falls even further—say, to 1%? The monetary authorities would like to lower the real interest rate by lowering the policy rate again, but they can't because the policy rate has already hit the floor of the effective lower bound (which we are assuming is equal to zero). Indeed, as indicated by point 1 on the *MP* curve, with the nominal policy rate at the effective lower bound at zero, the real interest rate at an inflation rate of 1% has now risen to −1% ($r = 0 - 1\% = -1\%$). Hence, we see that the segment of the *MP* curve that connects point 2 to point 1 is downward-sloping, the opposite of what we found in Chapter 21.

Now let's see what happens to the aggregate demand curve, shown in panel (b) of Figure 10. At a 3% inflation rate and a real interest rate of 2% (point 3 on the *MP* curve in panel (a)), the equilibrium level of the aggregate output index is, say, 90, marked as point 3 on the aggregate demand curve in panel (b). Now, when inflation falls to 2% and the real interest rate is at −2%, as indicated by point 2 on the *MP* curve in panel (a), the aggregate output index rises to 100 because planned investment spending rises with the lower real interest rate. The inflation rate of 2% and level of the aggregate output

Mini-lecture

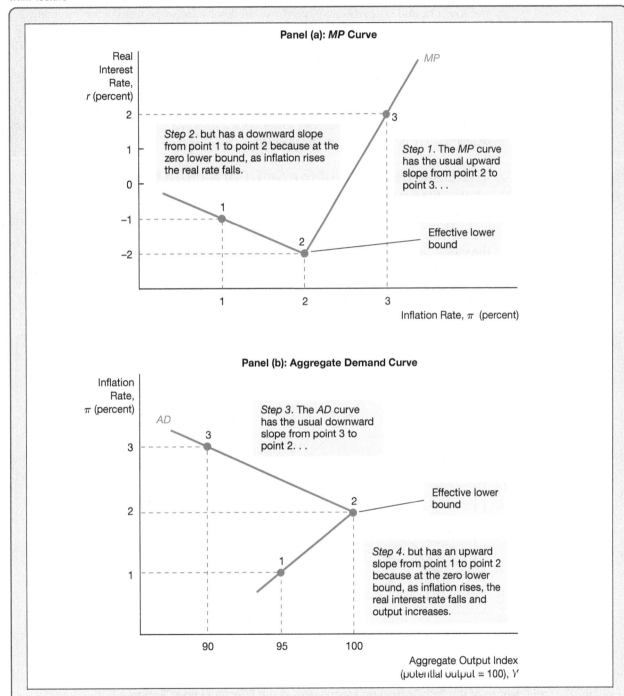

FIGURE 10   Derivation of the Aggregate Demand Curve with an Effective Lower Bound

In panel (a), the *MP* curve has the usual upward slope in going from point 2 to point 3, but it slopes downward in the segment from point 1 to point 2 because, with the policy rate at the floor of the effective lower bound, as inflation and expected inflation fall, the real interest rate rises. This produces a kink in the aggregate demand curve, as shown in panel (b).

index is marked as point 2 on the *AD* curve in panel (b). This point is also at the effective lower bound. The *AD* curve has the usual downward slope from point 3 to point 2.

However, if inflation falls to 1%, point 1 on the *MP* curve indicates that the real interest rate will rise to −1% because, at the effective lower bound, where the nominal policy rate is stuck near zero the decrease in both inflation and expected inflation will raise the real interest rate. The rise in the real interest rate will cause the aggregate output index to fall, to 95 at point 1 on the *AD* curve in panel (b). Therefore, in going from point 1 to point 2, the aggregate demand curve slopes upward rather than downward. The presence of the effective lower bound thus can produce a kinked aggregate demand curve of the type seen in panel (b).

The Disappearance of the Self-Correcting Mechanism at the Effective Lower Bound

Now let's analyze what happens in our aggregate demand and supply diagram when the economy is hit by a large negative shock, such as the shock that occurred during the global financial crisis from 2007 to 2009 (see Chapter 12), so that the effective lower bound becomes binding. In this situation, the initial short-run aggregate supply curve intersects the upward-sloping part of the aggregate demand curve at point 1 in Figure 11, where the aggregate output index is at Y_1, which is less than $Y^P = 100$.

Mini-lecture

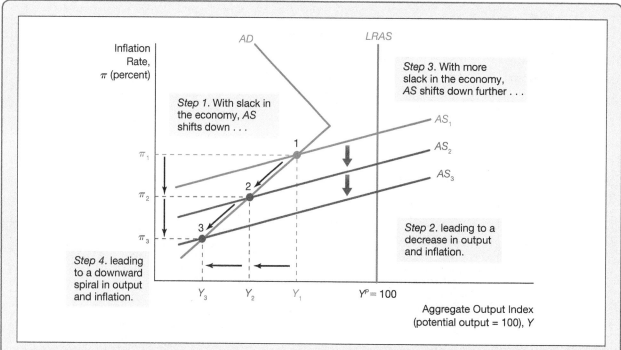

FIGURE 11   **The Absence of the Self-Correcting Mechanism at the Effective Lower Bound**

At the initial equilibrium at point 1, $Y_1 < Y^P$, so the short-run aggregate supply curve shifts down to AS_2 and the economy moves to point 2, where the aggregate output index and inflation have fallen to Y_2 and π_2, respectively. Because Y_2 is even lower relative to Y^P, the short-run aggregate supply curve shifts down even further to AS_2, and the economy moves to point 3, where the aggregate output index and inflation have fallen even further, to Y_3 and π_3, respectively. Both output and inflation therefore experience downward spirals.

Because $Y_1 < Y^P$, there is slack in the economy, and so the short-run aggregate supply curve will fall to AS_2 and the economy will move to point 2, at the intersection of the AS_2 and AD curves, where inflation and the aggregate output index will have declined to π_2 and Y_2, respectively. Now, Y_2 is even lower relative to Y^P, so the short-run aggregate supply curve will shift down even further, to AS_3, and the economy will move to point 3, where inflation and the aggregate output index have fallen even further, to π_3 and Y_3, respectively.

Our analysis of Figure 11 reveals two key results:

- First, the self-correcting mechanism is no longer operational. When the economy is in a situation in which equilibrium output is below potential output and the effective lower bound on the policy rate has been reached, output is not restored to its potential level if policymakers do nothing. Indeed, the opposite occurs—the economy goes into a downward spiral.
- Second, in this situation, the economy goes into a deflationary spiral, characterized by continually falling inflation and output.

The intuition behind these two results is fairly straightforward. When output is below potential and the policy rate has hit the floor of the effective lower bound, the resulting fall in inflation leads to higher real interest rates, which depress output further, which causes inflation to fall further, and so on. Schematically, this chain of events can be expressed as follows:

$$Y < Y^P \Rightarrow \pi\downarrow \Rightarrow r\uparrow \Rightarrow Y\downarrow \Rightarrow Y \ll Y^P \Rightarrow \pi\downarrow \Rightarrow r\uparrow \Rightarrow Y\downarrow$$

The final outcome is that both output and inflation go into downward spirals.

APPLICATION   # Nonconventional Monetary Policy and Quantitative Easing

At the effective lower bound, conventional expansionary monetary policy is no longer an option because the monetary policy authorities are unable to lower the policy rate. As a result, the central bank has to turn to the nonconventional policies discussed in Chapter 15 to stimulate the economy. Here we will analyze how these different nonconventional policies lead to economic expansion while avoiding the downward spirals in output and inflation that characterized the situation described in Figure 11.

Recall that nonconventional monetary policy takes three forms: liquidity provision, asset purchases (quantitative easing), and management of expectations. To see how each of these forms works, recall from Chapter 20 that the real interest rate for investments r_i reflects not only the short-term real interest rate set by the central bank, r, but also an additional term $\bar{f}$, which we referred to previously as financial frictions. This relationship can be written mathematically as follows

$$r_i = r + \bar{f} \tag{1}$$

Each of these nonconventional monetary policy measures helps raise aggregate output and inflation by lowering $\bar{f}$ in the *AD/AS* model. Let's look at each of these measures in turn.

Mini-lecture

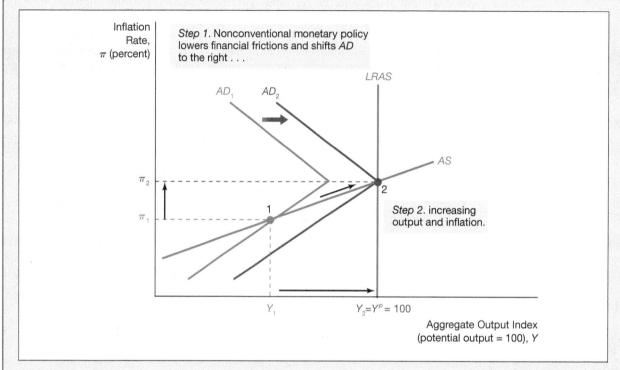

FIGURE 12 Response to Nonconventional Monetary Policy

Nonconventional monetary policy, whether it involves liquidity provision, asset purchases, or management of expectations, lowers $\bar{f}$, which in turn lowers the real interest rate for investments at any given inflation rate and shifts the aggregate demand curve to AD_2. The economy moves to point 2, where the aggregate output index and inflation have risen to Y_2 and π_2, respectively.

Liquidity Provision

The effective lower bound situation depicted in Figure 12 often arises when credit markets seize up and there is a sudden shortage of liquidity, as occurred during the 2007-2009, global financial crisis. The shortage of liquidity results in a sharp rise in financial frictions, which shifts the aggregate demand curve to AD_1 in Figure 12 to point 1, where it intersects the aggregate supply curve and where the policy rate has hit a floor of the effective lower bound and output is below potential. A central bank can bring down financial frictions directly by increasing its lending facilities in order to provide more liquidity to impaired markets so that they can return to their normal functions, thereby bringing down the $\bar{f}$ term. As we saw in Chapter 22, this decline in financial frictions lowers the real interest rate for investments, $r_i = r + \bar{f}$, and so increases investment spending and the quantity of aggregate output demanded at any given inflation rate. The aggregate demand curve then shifts to the right to AD_2 and the economy moves to point 2, where both output and inflation have risen. Indeed, if liquidity provisions are sufficiently successful, the economy can move back to its full employment level, where output will return to potential, as indicated by point 2 in the figure.

Asset Purchases and Quantitative Easing

The monetary authorities can also lower the $\bar{f}$ term by lowering credit spreads through the purchase of privately issued securities. When the monetary authorities purchase a private security, such a purchase raises the security's price and therefore lowers its interest rate, thereby lowering the credit spread and hence $\bar{f}$ and the real interest rate for investments. The decline in the real interest rate for investments at any given inflation rate then causes the aggregate demand curve to shift to the right, as shown in Figure 12, and raises both output and inflation.

Because investments typically are associated with long-term projects, the real interest rate for investments is likely to be a long-term interest rate and therefore differs from the short-term real interest rate r. Hence the $\bar{f}$ term in Equation 1 can be viewed as reflecting not only financial frictions and credit spreads but also the spread between long-term and short-term rates. This means that asset purchases of long-term government securities also can lower the real interest rate for investments. When the Federal Reserve purchases long-term U.S. Treasury bonds, for example, this action raises their price and lowers long-term interest rates. The result is a decline in $\bar{f}$ and the real interest rate for investments at any given inflation rate, and so the aggregate demand curve will shift to the right, to AD_2 in Figure 12, thereby raising output and inflation.

When a central bank engages in liquidity provision or asset purchases, its balance sheet necessarily expands. Indeed, as we saw in Chapter 15, from before the financial crisis began in September 2007 through 2014, the value of Federal Reserve assets rose from about $800 billion to over $4 trillion, and then rose again dramatically starting in March 2020 in response to the coronavirus pandemic. Such an expansion of the balance sheet is referred to as *quantitative easing* because it leads to a huge increase in liquidity in the economy, which can be a powerful force in stimulating the economy in the near term and possibly producing inflation down the road.

However, an expansion in the central bank's balance sheet in and of itself may not be enough to stimulate the economy. As we saw in our *AD/AS* analysis of the effective lower bound, unless quantitative easing is able to lower the real interest rate for investments, in what former Fed chair Ben Bernanke referred to as a *credit easing*, there will be no impact on the aggregate demand curve and hence no impact on output and inflation. If the asset-purchase program involves only the purchase of short-term government securities, the program is unlikely to affect credit spreads or the spread between long- and short-term interest rates, and so $\bar{f}$ and the real interest rate for investments will remain unchanged. The result will be a minimal impact on the aggregate economy.[1] Indeed, this was the experience in Japan when the Bank of Japan pursued a large-scale asset-purchase program that primarily involved purchases of short-term government bonds. Not only did the economy fail to recover but inflation even turned negative.

[1]There are two other reasons that quantitative easing in and of itself will not necessarily be stimulative. First, large expansions in a central bank's balance sheet do not necessarily result in large increases in the money supply. As indicated in the application in Chapter 14, "Quantitative Easing and the Money Supply, 2007-2020," this was exactly the case in the United States from 2007 to 2014 and again in 2020, when huge expansions in the Fed's balance sheet and the monetary base did not result in a large increase in the money supply because most of the increase in the monetary base just flowed into holdings of excess reserves. Second, an increase in the monetary base does not mean that banks will increase lending, because they have the option of just adding to their holdings of excess reserves instead of making loans. This is exactly what happened during the global financial crisis and the coronavirus pandemic, when a huge increase in the monetary base led primarily to a massive rise in excess reserves, and bank lending did not increase.

Management of Expectations

One form of management of expectations is forward guidance in which the central bank commits to keeping the policy rate low for a long period of time, another way of lowering long-term interest rates relative to short-term rates and thereby lowering $\bar{f}$ and the real interest rate for investments. Because investors can choose to invest in a long-term bond rather than investing in a sequence of short-term bonds, as we saw in Chapter 6, the interest rate on long-term bonds will be closely related to an average of the short-term interest rates that markets expect to occur over the life of the long-term bond. By committing to the future policy action of keeping the federal funds rate at zero for an extended period, a central bank can lower the market's expectations of future short-term interest rates, thereby causing the long-term interest rate to fall. The result will be a decline in $\bar{f}$ and the real interest rate for investments, which will shift the aggregate demand curve to the right as in Figure 12, raising both output and inflation.

So far, the mechanisms for the efficacy of nonconventional monetary policies have operated through the $\bar{f}$ term and rightward shifts in the aggregate demand curve as in Figure 12. However, management of expectations can also operate through shifts in the short-run aggregate supply curve that can be achieved by raising expectations of inflation, as shown in Figure 13. Recall from Chapter 22 that a rise in inflation expectations—say, because the central bank commits to doing whatever it takes to raise inflation in the future—will shift the short-run aggregate supply curve up, to AS_2 in Figure 13, moving the economy to point 2, where the aggregate output index and inflation rise to Y_2 and π_2, respectively. The intuition behind this result is straightforward: With the policy rate fixed at the effective lower bound, the rise in expected inflation will lead to a decline in the real interest rate, which will cause investment spending and aggregate output to rise as the economy slides up the aggregate demand curve from point 1 to point 2, as shown in the figure. One problem with this strategy, however, is that the public must believe that inflation will actually rise in the future. If the central bank's commitment to raising inflation is not credible, then inflation expectations may not rise and this particular type of management of expectations will not work.

APPLICATION Abenomics and the Shift in Japanese Monetary Policy in 2013

By 2012, the Japanese economy had been in a funk for well over ten years, with very low growth, the policy rate stuck at the effective lower bound near zero, and the economy experiencing deflation. With this scenario as his backdrop, Shinzo Abe won the general election for prime minister of Japan in December 2012, and after taking office he promoted a major shift in economic policy aimed at stimulating economic growth, a policy that the media has since dubbed "Abenomics." A key element of Abenomics was a sea change in monetary policy. First, Abe pressured the Bank of Japan to double its inflation target from 1% to 2% in January 2013, over the objections of the former governor of the Bank of Japan, Masaaki Shirakawa, who then resigned in March. After taking over the former governor's position in March 2013, the new Bank of Japan Governor, Haruhiko Kuroda, announced a major change in the way the Bank of Japan would conduct

Mini-lecture

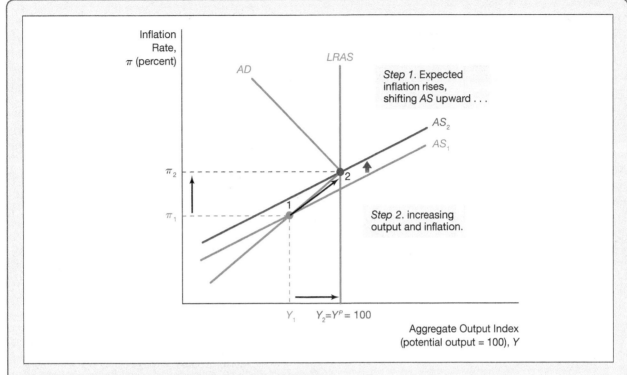

FIGURE 13 **Response to a Rise in Inflation Expectations**
A rise in inflation expectations causes the short-run aggregate supply curve to shift up to AS_2 and the economy to move to point 2, where the aggregate output index and inflation rise to Y_2 and π_2, respectively.

monetary policy in the future. First, in contrast to the previous governor, who never formally committed to achieving the 1% inflation target, Kuroda committed to achieving the higher 2% inflation objective within two years. Second, he indicated that the Bank of Japan would now engage in a massive asset-purchase (quantitative easing) program that would not only double the size of the Bank of Japan's balance sheet but would also involve the purchase of a very different set of assets. Specifically, rather than purchasing short-term government bonds, the Bank of Japan would now purchase long-term bonds, including private securities such as real estate investment trusts.

We can use our analysis from the previous section to predict why this approach was taken to fix the Japanese economy. First, in contrast to the previous quantitative easing, the Abenomics program sought to lower $\bar{f}$ through the purchase of long-term assets. Specifically, the program would lower $\bar{f}$ by lowering credit spreads through the purchase of private securities and also by lowering long-term interest rates through the purchase of long-term government bonds. As we have seen, with the policy rate at the effective lower bound, a lower $\bar{f}$ would lead to a lower real interest rate for investments, thereby shifting the aggregate demand curve to the right, to AD_2 in Figure 14.

Second, the higher inflation target, and even more importantly the stronger commitment by Kuroda to achieving this higher target, should, according to our analysis,

Mini-lecture

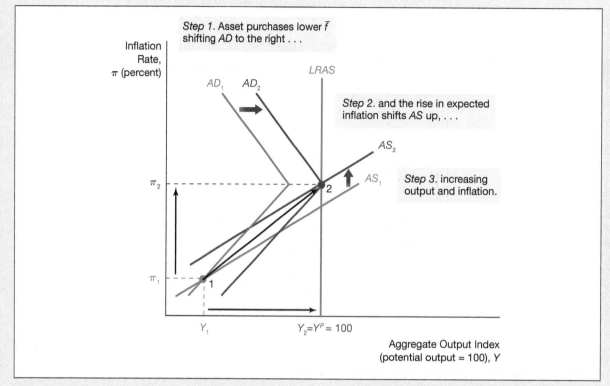

Step 1. Asset purchases lower $\bar{f}$ shifting *AD* to the right . . .

Inflation Rate, π (percent)

LRAS

AD_1 AD_2

Step 2. and the rise in expected inflation shifts *AS* up, . . .

AS_2

AS_1

π_2

2

Step 3. increasing output and inflation.

π_1

1

Y_1 $Y_2 = Y^P = 100$

Aggregate Output Index (potential output = 100), Y

FIGURE 14 Response to the Shift in Japanese Monetary Policy in 2013

The Bank of Japan's revised asset-purchase program lowers $\bar{f}$, which lowers the real interest rate on investments at any given inflation rate and shifts the aggregate demand curve to the right, from AD_1 to AD_2. The rise in inflation expectations causes the short-run aggregate supply curve to shift upward from AS_1 to AS_2. The economy moves to point 2, where the aggregate output index and inflation rise to Y_2 and π_2, respectively.

raise expected inflation and hence shift the short-run aggregate supply curve to AS_2. As we can see in Figure 14, the economy would then move to point 2, where both output and inflation would rise.

In other words, the new monetary policy's two-pronged attack would both lower the real interest rate for investments directly through the asset-purchase program and also directly raise inflation expectations, providing another factor that would drive down the real interest rate. Both of these mechanisms would then operate to promote an economic expansion and an exit from the deflationary environment that the Japanese had been experiencing for the past 15 years. Although this new policy strategy has helped raise Japanese inflation above zero and has led to lower unemployment, it has not been successful in raising Japanese inflation to the 2% target. This failure illustrates how difficult it is to raise inflation expectations once a prolonged period of deflation has occurred. ◆

SUMMARY

1. For aggregate demand shocks, the price stability and economic activity stability objectives are consistent: Stabilizing inflation stabilizes economic activity, even in the short run. For supply shocks, however, there is a trade-off between stabilizing inflation and stabilizing economic activity in the short run. In the long run, however, there is no conflict between stabilizing inflation and stabilizing economic activity.

2. Activists regard the self-correcting mechanism, which works through wage and price adjustment, as very slow and hence feel that the government should pursue active, accommodating policy to address high unemployment when it develops. Nonactivists, by contrast, believe that the self-correcting mechanism works quickly and therefore advocate that the government should avoid the implementation of active policies aimed at eliminating unemployment.

3. Milton Friedman's view that in the long run inflation is always and everywhere a monetary phenomenon is borne out by aggregate demand and supply analysis: Such analysis shows that monetary policymakers can target any inflation rate in the long run through autonomous monetary policy, which makes use of the federal funds rate policy tool to change the level of aggregate demand and thereby adjust the equilibrium inflation rate.

4. Two types of inflation can result from an activist stabilization policy aimed at promoting high employment: cost-push inflation, which is caused by negative supply shocks or a push by workers for wages that are higher than the level justified by productivity gains; and demand-pull inflation, which results when policymakers pursue high output and employment targets through policies that increase aggregate demand. Both demand-pull and cost-push inflation led to the Great Inflation that occurred in the United States from 1965 to 1982.

5. When the nominal policy rate hits the floor of the effective lower bound, the aggregate demand curve becomes upward-sloping, which means that the self-correcting mechanism that returns the economy to full employment is no longer operational. At the effective lower bound, in order to boost output and inflation, the monetary authorities must turn to nonconventional policies of three types: liquidity provision, asset purchases (typically referred to as quantitative easing), and management of expectations.

KEY TERMS

activists, p. 555
cost-push inflation, p. 559
data lag, p. 556
demand-pull inflation, p. 559
divine coincidence, p. 551

effectiveness lag, p. 556
implementation lag, p. 556
inflation gap, p. 549
inflation target, p. 549
Keynesians, p. 555

legislative lag, p. 556
nonactivists, p. 555
recognition lag, p. 556

QUESTIONS

1. What does it mean when we say that the inflation gap is negative?

2. "If autonomous spending falls, the central bank should lower its inflation target in order to stabilize inflation." Is this statement true, false, or uncertain? Explain your answer.

3. For each of the following shocks, describe how monetary policymakers would respond (if at all) to stabilize economic activity. Assume the economy starts at a long-run equilibrium.

a. Consumers reduce autonomous consumption.

b. Financial frictions decrease.

c. Government spending increases.

d. Taxes increase.

e. The domestic currency appreciates.

4. During the global financial crisis, how was the Fed able to help offset the sharp increase in financial frictions without the option of lowering interest rates further? Did the Fed's plan work?

5. Why does the divine coincidence simplify the job of policymakers?

6. Why do negative supply shocks pose a dilemma for policymakers?

7. Suppose three economies are hit with the same negative supply shock. In country A, inflation initially rises and output falls; then inflation rises more and output increases. In country B, inflation initially rises and output falls; then both inflation and output fall. In country C, inflation initially rises and output falls; then inflation falls and output eventually increases. What type of stabilization approach did each country take?

8. "Policymakers would never respond by stabilizing output in response to a positive supply shock." Is this statement true, false, or uncertain? Explain your answer.

9. The fact that it takes a long time for firms to get new plants and equipment up and running is an illustration of what policy problem?

10. In the United States, many observers have commented in recent years on the "political gridlock in Washington, D.C.," and referred to Congress as a "Do Nothing Congress." What type of policy lag is this describing?

11. Is stabilization policy more likely to be conducted through monetary policy or through fiscal policy? Why?

12. "If the data and recognition lags could be reduced, activist policy probably would be more beneficial to the economy." Is this statement true, false, or uncertain? Explain your answer.

13. If the economy's self-correcting mechanism works slowly, should the government necessarily pursue discretionary policy to eliminate unemployment? Why or why not?

14. In the early 1970s, an unexpected productivity slowdown led most economists to believe that potential output was larger than it actually was. How are policymakers likely to respond under this situation, and what do you expect to be the outcome?

15. In both the 1960s and the 1970s in the United States, inflation increased significantly. However, unemployment behaved very differently in the two decades. Why is this?

16. Given a relatively steep and a relatively flat short-run aggregate supply curve, which curve would support the case for nonactivist policy? Why?

17. "Because government policymakers do not consider inflation desirable, their policies cannot be the source of inflation." Is this statement true, false, or uncertain? Explain your answer.

18. How can monetary authorities target any inflation rate they wish?

19. What will happen if policymakers erroneously believe that the natural rate of unemployment is 7% when it is actually 5% and therefore pursue stabilization policy?

20. How can demand-pull inflation lead to cost-push inflation?

21. How does the policy rate hitting a floor a little below zero lead to an upward-sloping aggregate demand curve?

22. Why does the self-correcting mechanism stop working when the policy rate hits the effective lower bound?

23. In what ways can nonconventional monetary policy affect the real interest rate for investments when the economy reaches the effective lower bound? How are credit spreads affected?

APPLIED PROBLEMS

24. Suppose the current administration decides to decrease government expenditures as a means of cutting the existing government budget deficit.
    a. Using a graph of aggregate demand and supply, show the effects of such a decision on the economy in the short run. Describe the effects on inflation and output.
    b. What will be the effect on the real interest rate, the inflation rate, and the aggregate output index if the Federal Reserve decides to stabilize the inflation rate?

25. Use a graph of aggregate demand and supply to demonstrate how lags in the policy process can result in undesirable fluctuations in output and inflation.

26. As monetary policymakers become more concerned with inflation stabilization, the slope of the aggregate demand curve becomes flatter. How does the resulting change in the slope of the aggregate demand curve help stabilize inflation when the economy is hit with a negative supply shock? How does this affect output? Use a graph of aggregate demand and supply to demonstrate.

27. In 2003, as the U.S. economy finally seemed poised to exit its ongoing recession, the Fed began to worry about a "soft patch" in the economy, in particular the possibility of a deflation. As a result, the Fed proactively lowered the federal funds rate from 1.75% in late 2002 to 1% by mid-2003, the lowest federal funds rate on record up to that point in time. In addition, the Fed committed to keeping the federal funds rate at this level for a considerable period of time. This policy was considered highly expansionary and was seen by some as potentially inflationary and unnecessary.

a. How might fears of the effective lower bound justify such a policy, even if the economy was not actually in a recession?

b. Show the impact of these policies on the *MP* curve and the *AD/AS* graph. Be sure to show the initial conditions in 2003 and the impact of the policy on the deflation threat.

28. Suppose that $\bar{f}$ is determined by two factors: financial panic and asset purchases.

a. Using an *MP* curve and an *AS/AD* graph, show how a sufficiently large financial panic can pull the economy below the effective lower bound and into a destabilizing deflationary spiral.

b. Using an *MP* curve and an *AS/AD* graph, show how a sufficient amount of asset purchases can reverse the effects of the financial panic depicted in part (a).

DATA ANALYSIS PROBLEMS

The Problems update with real-time data in **MyLab Economics** and are available for practice or instructor assignment.

1. Real-time Data Analysis On January 28, 2019, the Federal Reserve released its amended statement on longer-run goals and monetary policy strategy. It stated: "The Committee reaffirms its judgment that inflation at the rate of 2 percent, as measured by the annual change in the price index for personal consumption expenditures, is most consistent over the longer run with the Federal Reserve's statutory mandate" and that "the median of FOMC participants' estimates of the longer-run normal rate of unemployment was 4.4 percent." Assume this statement implies that the natural rate of unemployment is believed to be 4.4%. Go to the St. Louis Federal Reserve FRED database, and find data on the personal consumption expenditure price index (PCECTPI), the unemployment rate (UNRATE), real GDP (GDPC1), and real potential gross domestic product (GDPPOT), an estimate of potential GDP. For the price index, adjust the *units* setting to "Percent Change From Year Ago." Download the data into a spreadsheet.

a. For the most recent four quarters of data available, calculate the average inflation gap using the 2% target referenced by the Fed. Calculate this value as the average of the inflation gaps over the four quarters.

b. For the most recent four quarters of data available, calculate the average output gap using the GDP measure and the potential GDP estimate. Calculate the gap as the percentage deviation of output from the potential level of output. Calculate the average value over the most recent four quarters of data available.

c. For the most recent 12 months of data available, calculate the average unemployment gap, using 4.4% as the presumed natural rate of unemployment. Based on your answers to parts (a) through (c), does the divine coincidence apply to the current economic situation? Why or why not? What does your answer imply about the sources of shocks that have impacted the current economy? Briefly explain.

2. Real-time Data Analysis Go to the St. Louis Federal Reserve FRED database, and find data on the personal consumption expenditure price index (PCECTPI), the unemployment rate (UNRATE), and an estimate of the natural rate of unemployment (NROU). For the price index, adjust the *units* setting to "Percent Change From Year Ago." For the unemployment rate, adjust the *frequency* setting to "Quarterly." Select the data from 2000 through the most current data available, download the data, and plot all three variables on the same graph. Using your graph, identify periods of demand pull or cost-push movements in the inflation rate. Briefly explain your reasoning.

24 The Role of Expectations in Monetary Policy

Learning Objectives

24.1 Summarize the Lucas critique.

24.2 Compare and contrast the use of policy rules versus discretionary policy.

24.3 Summarize and illustrate the benefits of a credible central bank.

24.4 Identify the ways in which central banks can establish and maintain credibility.

Preview

After World War II, economists, armed with models like the ones we developed in Chapters 20–23, felt that discretionary policies could reduce the severity of business cycle fluctuations without creating inflation. In the 1960s and 1970s, these economists got their chance to put their policies into practice, but the results were not what they had anticipated. The economic record for that period is not a happy one: Inflation accelerated, with the inflation rate often climbing to above 10%, and unemployment figures deteriorated from those of the 1950s.[1]

In the 1970s and 1980s, economists, including Nobel Prize winners Robert Lucas of the University of Chicago and Thomas Sargent, now at New York University, used the rational expectations theory discussed in Chapter 7 to examine why discretionary policies appear to have performed so poorly. Their analysis cast doubt on whether macroeconomic models can be used to evaluate the potential effects of policy and on whether policy can be effective when the public *expects* that it will be implemented. Because the analysis of Lucas and Sargent has such strong implications for the way in which policy should be conducted, it has been labeled the *rational expectations revolution*.[2]

This chapter examines the analysis behind the rational expectations revolution. We start first with the Lucas critique, which indicates that because expectations are an important part of economic behavior, it may be quite difficult to predict what the outcome of a discretionary policy will be. We then discuss the effect of rational expectations on the aggregate demand and supply analysis we developed in Chapter 22, and explore how this theoretical breakthrough has shaped current policymaking models and debates.

24.1 LUCAS CRITIQUE OF POLICY EVALUATION

LO 24.1 Summarize the Lucas critique.

Economists have long used **macroeconometric models** to forecast economic activity and to evaluate the potential effects of policy options. In essence, the models are collections of equations that describe statistical relationships among many economic variables. Economists can feed data into such models, which then churn out a forecast or prediction.

[1]Some of the deterioration can be attributed to supply shocks in 1973–1975 and 1978–1980.

[2]Other economists who have been active in promoting the rational expectations revolution are Robert Barro of Harvard University, Bennett McCallum of Carnegie-Mellon University, Nobel Prize winner Edward Prescott of Arizona State University, and Neil Wallace of Pennsylvania State University.

In his famous paper "Econometric Policy Evaluation: A Critique," Robert Lucas spurred the rational expectations revolution by presenting a devastating argument against the use of the macroeconometric models used at the time for evaluating policy.[3]

Econometric Policy Evaluation

To understand Lucas's argument, we must first understand how econometric policy evaluation is done. Say, for example, that the Federal Reserve wants to evaluate the potential effects of changes in the federal funds rate from the existing level of, say, 5%. Using conventional methods, the Fed economists would feed different fed funds rate options—say, 4% and 6%—into a computer version of a model. The model would then predict how unemployment and inflation would change under the different scenarios. Then, the policymakers would select the policy that the model predicted would have the most desirable outcomes.

Relying on rational expectations theory, Lucas identified faulty reasoning in this approach if the model did not incorporate rational expectations, as was true for the macroeconometric models used by policymakers at the time: When policies change, public expectations shift as well. For example, if the Fed raises the federal funds rate to 6%, this action might change the way the public forms expectations about where interest rates will head in the future. Those changing expectations, as we've seen, can have a real effect on economic behavior and outcomes. Yet econometric models that do not incorporate rational expectations ignore the effects of changing expectations and thus are unreliable for evaluating policy options.

APPLICATION   The Term Structure of Interest Rates

Let's now apply Lucas's argument to a concrete example involving only one equation typically found in econometric models: the term structure equation. The equation relates the long-term interest rate to current and past values of the short-term interest rate. It is one of the most important equations in macroeconometric models because the long-term interest rate, not the short-term rate, is the one believed to have the larger impact on aggregate demand.

In Chapter 6, we learned that the long-term interest rate is related to an average of expected future short-term interest rates. Suppose that in the past, when the short-term rate rose, it quickly fell back down again; that is, any increase was temporary. Because rational expectations theory suggests that any rise in the short-term interest rate is expected to be only temporary, such a rise should have only a minimal effect on the average of expected future short-term rates. Therefore, the rise in the short-term rate should cause the long-term interest rate to rise by only a negligible amount. The term structure relationship as estimated using past data thus indicates that changes in the short-term interest rate will have only a weak effect on the long-term interest rate.

Suppose the Fed wants to evaluate the effects on the economy of a policy that is likely to raise the short-term interest rate from its existing level of, say, 5% to a higher level of 6% for the foreseeable future. The term structure equation, which has been estimated using past data, will indicate that just a small change in the long-term interest

---

[3]*Carnegie-Rochester Conference Series on Public Policy* 1 (1976): 19–46.

rate will occur. However, if the public expects that the short-term rate is rising to a permanently higher level, rational expectations theory indicates that people will no longer expect a rise in the short-term rate to be temporary. Instead, when they see the interest rate rise to 6%, they will expect the average of future short-term interest rates to rise substantially, and so the long-term interest rate will rise greatly, not minimally, as suggested by the term structure equation. You can see that using an econometric model to evaluate the likely outcome of the change in Fed policy can lead to highly misleading information.

The term structure application demonstrates another aspect of the Lucas critique. The effects of a particular policy depend critically on the public's expectations about the policy. If the public expects the rise in the short-term interest rate to be merely temporary, then the response of the long-term interest rate, as we have seen, will be negligible. If, however, the public expects the rise to be more permanent, the response of the long-term rate will be far greater. *The Lucas critique points out not only that conventional econometric models cannot be used for policy evaluation but also that the public's expectations about a policy will influence the response to that policy.*

The term structure equation discussed here is only one of many equations in the econometric models to which the Lucas critique applies. In fact, Lucas uses examples of consumption and investment equations in his paper. One attractive feature of the term structure example is that it deals with expectations in the financial market, a sector of the economy for which the empirical evidence supporting rational expectations is much stronger. The Lucas critique should also apply, however, to sectors of the economy with regard to which rational expectations theory is more controversial, because the basic principle of the Lucas critique is not that expectations are always rational but rather that the formation of expectations changes when the behavior of a forecasted variable changes. This less stringent principle is supported by the evidence in sectors of the economy other than financial markets. ◆

24.2 POLICY CONDUCT: RULES OR DISCRETION?

LO 24.2 Compare and contrast the use of policy rules versus discretionary policy.

The Lucas critique exposed the need for new policy models that reflected the insights of rational expectations theory. Here, we explore the implications of the critique on a long-running debate among economists: whether monetary policymakers should have the flexibility to adapt their policies to a changing situation, or whether they should adopt **rules**, binding plans that specify how policy will respond (or not respond) to particular data such as unemployment and inflation data.

Discretion and the Time-Inconsistency Problem

We say that policymakers operate with **discretion** when they make no commitment to future actions but instead make what they believe in that moment to be the right policy decision for the situation. Complexities are introduced when policymakers are empowered to shape policy "on the fly." The *time-inconsistency problem* discussed in Chapter 16 reveals the potential limitations of discretionary policy. Recall that the time-inconsistency problem is the tendency of policymakers to deviate from good long-run plans when making short-run decisions. Policymakers are always tempted to pursue policies that are more expansionary than firms or people expect because such a policy will boost economic output (and lower unemployment) in the short run. The best policy, however, is *not* to pursue expansionary policy, because decisions about wages and prices reflect workers' and firms' expectations about policy (an implication of the rational expectations revolution). For example, when workers and firms see a central bank pursuing discretionary expansionary policy, they will recognize that this policy is likely to lead to higher inflation in the future. They will therefore raise their expectations of inflation, driving wages and prices up. The rise in wages and prices will lead to higher inflation but may not result in higher output on average.

Policymakers will promote better inflation performance in the long run if they do not try to surprise people with an unexpectedly expansionary policy but instead keep inflation under control. One way of doing this is to abandon discretion and adopt rules to govern policymaking.

Types of Rules

In contrast to discretion, rules are essentially automatic. One famous type of rule, advocated by Milton Friedman and his followers, who are known as **monetarists**, is the **constant-money-growth-rate rule**, whereby policymakers keep the money supply growing at a constant rate regardless of the state of the economy. Other monetarists, such as Bennett McCallum and Alan Meltzer, have proposed variants of this rule that allow the rate of money supply growth to be adjusted for shifts in velocity, nominal income divided by the quantity of money, which has often been found to be unstable in the short run. Rules of this type are deemed nonactivist because they do not "react" to economic conditions. Monetarists advocate rules of this type because they believe that money is the sole source of fluctuations in aggregate demand and that long and variable lags in the effects of monetary policy will lead to greater volatility in economic activity and inflation if policy actively responds to unemployment (as discussed in Chapter 23).

Activist rules, in contrast, specify that monetary policy should react to the level of output as well as to inflation. The most famous rule of this type is the *Taylor rule*, discussed in Chapter 16. It specifies that the Fed should set its federal funds rate target by using a formula that considers both the output gap ($Y - Y^P$) and the inflation gap ($\pi - \pi^T$).

The Case for Rules

As suggested by our discussion of the time-inconsistency problem, discretionary monetary policy can lead to poor economic outcomes. If monetary policymakers operate with discretion, they will be tempted to pursue overly expansionary monetary policies that will boost employment in the short run but generate higher inflation (but not higher employment) in the long run. A commitment to a policy rule like the Taylor rule or the constant-money-growth-rate rule solves the time-inconsistency problem because policymakers are forced to follow a set plan that does not allow them to exercise discretion and therefore prevents them from exploiting the short-run trade-off between inflation and employment. With their hands bound by a policy rule, policymakers can achieve desirable long-run outcomes.

Another argument in support of rules posits that policymakers and politicians simply cannot be trusted to make good decisions. Milton Friedman and Anna Schwartz's monumental work, *A Monetary History of the United States*,[4] documents numerous instances in which the Federal Reserve made serious policy errors, with the worst

[4]Milton Friedman and Anna Jacobson Schwartz, *A Monetary History of the United States, 1867–1960* (Princeton, NJ: Princeton University Press, 1963).

FYI   **The Political Business Cycle and Richard Nixon**

You might know that Richard Nixon and his aides took some extraordinary actions to ensure a landslide victory in the 1972 presidential election, such as breaking into the offices of political rivals at the Watergate Hotel. Less well known are similar actions on the economic front prior to the election. Before the 1972 election, the Nixon administration imposed wage and price controls on the economy, which temporarily lowered the inflation rate. After the election, those same actions contributed to a surge in inflation. Nixon also pursued expansionary fiscal policy by cutting taxes. And it has been rumored that the chair of the Federal Reserve at the time, Arthur Burns, succumbed to direct pressure from Nixon to maintain low interest rates through election day. The aftermath was ugly. The economy overheated and inflation rose to over 10% by the late 1970s, a rate that was abetted by the negative supply shocks during that period (see Chapter 22).

The Nixon episode led economists and political scientists to theorize that politicians will take steps to make themselves look good during election years. Specifically, the theory went, they will take steps to stimulate the economy prior to the election, in the hope of stimulating a boom and low unemployment, outcomes that will increase their electoral chances. Unfortunately, the result of these actions will be higher inflation down the road, which then will require contractionary policies to get inflation under control, leading to a recession in the future. The resulting ups and downs of the economy would be the direct result of political machinations and so could be characterized as a political business cycle. Although the Nixon episode provided support for the existence of a political business cycle, the research has not led to a definitive answer regarding whether this phenomenon is a general one.*

*The paper that launched research on the political business cycle was William Nordhaus, "The Political Business Cycle," *Review of Economic Studies* 42 (1975): 169–190.

---

occurring during the Great Depression, when the Fed just stood by and let the banking system and the economy collapse (Chapter 12 discusses the Fed's actions during the Great Depression). Proponents of this argument believe that the politicians who make fiscal policy are not to be trusted because they have strong incentives to pursue policies that will help them win the next election. They are therefore more likely to focus on increasing employment in the short run without worrying that their actions might lead to higher inflation further down the road. Their advocacy for expansionary policies can lead to a so-called **political business cycle**, in which fiscal and monetary policy are expansionary right before elections, with higher inflation following later. (For an example, see the FYI box "The Political Business Cycle and Richard Nixon.")

The Case for Discretion

Although policy rules have important advantages, they also have serious drawbacks. First, rules can be too rigid because they cannot account for every contingency. For example, almost no one could have predicted that problems in one small part of the financial system, subprime mortgage lending, would lead to the worst financial crisis in over 70 years, with such devastating effects on the world economy. The unprecedented steps taken by the Federal Reserve during this crisis to prevent it from causing a depression (described in Chapters 12 and 15) could not have been written into a policy rule ahead of time. The ability to act flexibly through discretion can thus be a key factor in a successful monetary policy.

The second problem with policy rules is that they do not easily incorporate the tool of judgment. Monetary policy is as much an art as it is a science. Monetary policymakers must look at a wide range of information to decide on the best course for monetary policy, and some of this information is not easily quantifiable. Judgment is thus an essential element of good monetary policy, and it is very hard to write it into a rule. Only through discretion can monetary policy bring judgment to bear.

Third, no one really knows what the true model of the economy is, and so any policy rule that is based on a particular model will prove to be wrong if the model is flawed. Discretion avoids the straightjacket that would lock in the wrong policy if the model that was used to derive the policy rule proved to be a poor one.

Fourth, even if the model is a good one, any structural changes in the economy will necessitate changes in the coefficients of the model. For example, the Lucas critique points out that the structural shifts caused by changes in policies can lead to changes in the coefficients of macroeconometric models. Another example of structural economic change occurred in the 1980s, when the relationship between monetary aggregates, such as M1 and M2, and aggregate spending broke down as a result of financial innovation. Following a rule that assumed a constant growth rate in one of these aggregates would have produced bad outcomes. Indeed, this is what happened in Switzerland in the late 1980s and early 1990s when adherence to a rule that assumed a particular growth rate of monetary aggregates led to a surge in inflation (as discussed in the Global box "The Demise of Monetary Targeting in Switzerland"). Discretion enables policymakers to change policy settings when an economy undergoes structural changes.

Constrained Discretion

The tug-of-war between rules and discretion has strongly influenced academic debates about monetary policy for many decades. But either choice may be too rigid. As we have seen, both rules and discretion are subject to problems, and so the dichotomy between rules and discretion may be too simple to capture the realities that macroeconomic

---

Global   The Demise of Monetary Targeting in Switzerland

In 1975, the Swiss National Bank (Switzerland's central bank) adopted monetary targeting in which it announced a growth rate target for the monetary aggregate M1. In 1980, the Swiss switched their growth rate target to an even narrower monetary aggregate, the monetary base. Although monetary targeting had been quite successful in Switzerland for many years, the Swiss economy ran into serious problems with the introduction of a new interbank payment system, the Swiss Interbank Clearing (SIC), and a wide-ranging revision of commercial banks' liquidity requirements in 1988. These structural changes caused a severe drop in banks' desired holdings of deposits at the Swiss National Bank, and these holdings were the major component of the monetary base. A smaller amount of the monetary base was now needed to conduct transactions, altering the relationship between the monetary base and aggregate spending, and so the 2% target growth rate for the monetary base was suddenly far too expansionary. Inflation subsequently rose to over 5%, well above that in other European countries.

High inflation rates horrified the Swiss, who had always prided themselves on maintaining a low-inflation environment even when the rest of Europe did not. These problems with monetary targeting led the Swiss to abandon it in the 1990s and adopt a much more flexible framework for the conduct of monetary policy.*

*For a further discussion of monetary targeting in Switzerland, see Chapter 4 of Ben S. Bernanke, Thomas Laubach, Frederic S. Mishkin, and Adam S. Posen, *Inflation Targeting: Lessons from the International Experience* (Princeton, NJ: Princeton University Press, 1999).

policymakers face. Discretion can be a matter of degree. Discretion can be a relatively undisciplined approach that leads to policies that change with the personal views of policymakers or with the direction of political winds, or it might operate within a more clearly articulated framework in which the general objectives and tactics of the policymakers—although not their specific actions—are committed to in advance. Ben Bernanke, former chair of the Federal Reserve, along with the author of this textbook, came up with a name for this type of framework: **constrained discretion**.[5] Constrained discretion imposes a conceptual structure and inherent discipline on policymakers, but without eliminating all flexibility. It combines some of the advantages ascribed to rules with those ascribed to discretion.

24.3 THE ROLE OF CREDIBILITY AND A NOMINAL ANCHOR

LO 24.3 Summarize and illustrate the benefits of a credible central bank.

An important way to constrain discretion, as discussed in Chapter 16, is to commit to a *nominal anchor*, a nominal variable—such as the inflation rate, the money supply, or an exchange rate—that ties down the price level or inflation to achieve price stability. For example, if a central bank has an explicit target for the inflation rate—say, 2%—and takes steps to achieve this target, then the inflation target becomes a nominal anchor. Alternatively, a government could commit to a fixed exchange rate between its currency and a sound currency like the dollar and use this as its nominal anchor. If the commitment to a nominal anchor has **credibility**—that is, it is believed by the public—then it has important benefits.

Benefits of a Credible Nominal Anchor

First, a credible nominal anchor has elements of a behavior rule. Just as rules help to prevent the time-inconsistency problem in parenting by helping adults resist pursuit of the discretionary policy of giving in, a nominal anchor can help overcome the time-inconsistency problem by providing an expected constraint on discretionary policy. For example, if monetary policymakers commit to a nominal anchor of achieving a specific inflation objective—say, a 2% inflation rate—then they know that they will be subject to public scrutiny and criticism if they miss this objective or pursue policies that are clearly inconsistent with this objective, such as an interest rate target that is too low. Because policymakers wish to avoid embarrassment and possibly legal punishment, they will be less tempted to pursue overly expansionary, discretionary policies in the short run, policies that would be inconsistent with their commitment to the nominal anchor.

Second, a credible commitment to a nominal anchor helps to anchor inflation expectations, which leads to smaller fluctuations in inflation. Such a commitment thus contributes to price stability and also helps stabilize aggregate output. The credibility of a commitment to a nominal anchor is therefore a critical element in enabling monetary policy to achieve both of its objectives, price stability and stabilization of economic activity. In other words, a credible nominal anchor helps make monetary policy more efficient.

[5]See Ben S. Bernanke and Frederic S. Mishkin, "Inflation Targeting: A New Framework for Monetary Policy?" *Journal of Economic Perspectives* 11 (Spring 1997): 97–116.

We will use the aggregate demand and supply framework to show analytically why a credible nominal anchor helps produce this desirable outcome. First we will look at the effectiveness of stabilization policy when it is responding to an aggregate demand shock, and then we will look at its effectiveness when it is responding to an aggregate supply shock. We will also look at the benefits of credibility for anti-inflation policy.

Credibility and Aggregate Demand Shocks

We now examine the importance of credibility in the short run when positive and negative demand shocks are present.

Positive Demand Shock   Let's first look at what happens in the short run when a positive aggregate demand shock occurs. For example, suppose businesses suddenly get new information that makes them more optimistic about the future, and so they increase their investment spending. As a result of this positive demand shock, the aggregate demand curve shifts to the right from AD_1 to AD_2, moving the economy from point 1 to point 2 in panel (a) of Figure 1. The aggregate output index rises to Y_2 and inflation rises above the inflation target of π^T to π_2. As we saw in Chapter 23, the appropriate response, if the monetary authorities wish to stabilize inflation and economic activity, is to tighten monetary policy and shift the short-run aggregate demand curve back down to AD_1 in order to move the economy back to point 1. However, because of the long lags between monetary policy actions and their effects on aggregate demand, it will take some time before the short-run aggregate demand curve shifts back to AD_1.

Now let's look at what happens to the short-run aggregate supply curve. Recall from Chapter 22 that the short-run aggregate supply curve can be expressed as follows:

$$\pi \quad = \quad \pi^e \quad + \quad \gamma(Y - Y^P) + \quad \rho$$

inflation = expected inflation + γ × output gap + inflation shock

If the commitment to the nominal anchor is credible, then the public's expected inflation rate π^e will remain unchanged and the short-run aggregate supply curve will remain at AS_1. Inflation therefore will not go higher than π_2, and over time, as the short-run aggregate demand curve shifts back down to AD_1, inflation will fall back down to the inflation target of π^T.

But what if monetary policy is not credible? The public will worry that the monetary authorities are willing to accept a higher inflation rate than π^T and are not willing to drive the short-run aggregate demand curve back to AD_1 quickly. In this case, the weak credibility of the monetary authorities will cause expected inflation π^e to rise and so the short-run aggregate supply curve will rise, shifting from AS_1 to AS_3 and sending the economy to point 3 in the short run, where inflation has risen further to π_3. Even if the monetary authorities tighten monetary policy and return the aggregate demand curve to AD_1, the damage is done: Inflation has risen more than it would have if the central bank had credibility. Our aggregate demand and supply analysis thus yields the following conclusion: *Monetary policy credibility has the benefit of stabilizing inflation in the short run when faced with positive demand shocks.*

Negative Demand Shock   Panel (b) of Figure 1 illustrates a negative demand shock. For example, suppose consumer confidence dips and consumer spending declines. The aggregate demand curve shifts left from AD_1 to AD_2, and the economy moves to point 2 in the short run, where the aggregate output index has fallen to Y_2,

Mini-lecture

FIGURE 1

Credibility and Aggregate Demand Shocks

In panel (a), the positive aggregate demand shock shifts the aggregate demand curve to the right from AD_1 to AD_2, moving the economy from point 1 to point 2. If monetary policy is not credible, expected inflation will rise and so the short-run aggregate supply curve will rise and shift to the left to AS_3, sending the economy to point 3, where inflation has risen further to π_3. In panel (b), the negative aggregate demand shock shifts the aggregate demand curve left from AD_1 to AD_2, and the economy moves to point 2. If the central bank is not credible, inflation expectations might increase, and the short-run aggregate supply curve will rise and shift to the left to AS_3. Monetary policy easing then will move the economy to point 3, where the aggregate output index at Y_3 is still below its potential level at $Y^P = 100$.

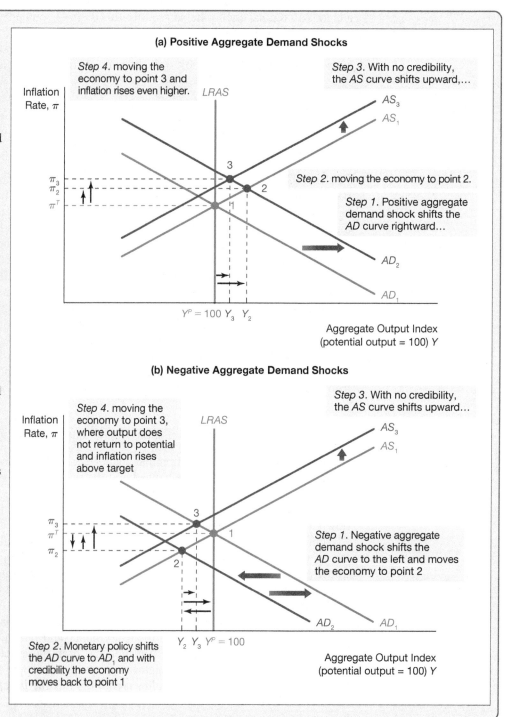

(a) Positive Aggregate Demand Shocks

Step 4. moving the economy to point 3 and inflation rises even higher.

Step 3. With no credibility, the AS curve shifts upward,...

Step 2. moving the economy to point 2.

Step 1. Positive aggregate demand shock shifts the AD curve rightward...

(b) Negative Aggregate Demand Shocks

Step 3. With no credibility, the AS curve shifts upward...

Step 4. moving the economy to point 3, where output does not return to potential and inflation rises above target

Step 1. Negative aggregate demand shock shifts the AD curve to the left and moves the economy to point 2

Step 2. Monetary policy shifts the AD curve to AD_1 and with credibility the economy moves back to point 1

so output is below potential output, and inflation has fallen to π_2, which is below the target level of π^T. To stabilize output and inflation, the central bank will ease monetary policy to move the aggregate demand curve back to AD_1. If the central bank has high credibility, expected inflation will remain unchanged, the short-run aggregate supply curve will remain at AS_1, and the economy will return to point 1, where the aggregate output index is back at its potential level Y^P.

However, what if the central bank's credibility is weak? When the public sees an easing of monetary policy, it might become concerned that the central bank is weakening its commitment to the nominal anchor and intends to pursue inflationary policy in the future. In this situation, inflation expectations might increase, and so the short-run aggregate supply curve will rise to AS_3, sending the economy to point 3, where the aggregate output index rise only from Y_2 to Y_3, still leaving it below the potential level of Y^P. Weak credibility in the face of a negative demand shock will keep output below potential output for a longer period than would occur if credibility was strong. We have the following additional result: ***Monetary policy credibility has the benefit of stabilizing economic activity in the short run when faced with negative demand shocks.***

Credibility and Aggregate Supply Shocks

Now let's look at what happens in Figure 2 if a negative aggregate supply shock occurs. If energy prices increase, the short-run aggregate supply curve will shift up and to the left. How much the aggregate supply curve will shift, however, depends on the amount

Mini-lecture

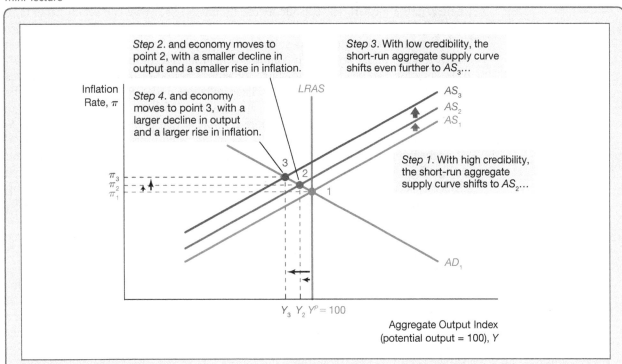

FIGURE 2   Credibility and Aggregate Supply Shocks

If the credibility of monetary policy is high, the negative aggregate supply shock will shift the short-run aggregate supply curve only to AS_2 and the economy will move to point 2, where the rise in inflation to π_2 will be minor and the fall in output to Y_2 will also be minor. If credibility is weak, then inflation expectations will rise substantially and the upward shift of the short-run aggregate supply curve will be much larger, moving the curve up and to the left to AS_3. The economy will move to point 3, with worse outcomes for both inflation and output—inflation will be higher at π_3 and the aggregate output index will be lower at Y_3.

of credibility the monetary authorities have. If the credibility of the nominal anchor is strong, inflation expectations will not rise, and so the upward and leftward shift of the short-run aggregate supply curve to AS_2 will be small. When the economy moves to point 2 in the short run, the rise in inflation to π_2 will then be minor, and the fall in the aggregate output index to Y_2 will also be minor. If, however, the central bank's commitment to the nominal anchor is perceived as weak, then inflation expectations will rise substantially and the upward and leftward shift of the short-run aggregate supply curve will be much larger, moving the curve up to AS_3. Now the economy will move to point 3 in the short run, with worse outcomes for both inflation and output—inflation will be higher at π_3 and the aggregate output index will be lower at Y_3. We reach the following conclusion: *Monetary policy credibility has the benefit of producing better outcomes for both inflation and output in the short run when faced with negative supply shocks.*

The theoretical benefits of credibility when the economy is hit by negative supply shocks are confirmed by the data, as illustrated in the following application.

APPLICATION   A Tale of Three Oil Price Shocks

In 1973, 1979, and 2007, the U.S. economy was hit by major negative supply shocks when the price of oil rose sharply; yet in the first two episodes inflation rose sharply, whereas in the most recent episode it rose by much less, as we can see in panel (a) of Figure 3. In the case of the first two episodes, monetary policy credibility was extremely weak because the economy was suffering from high inflation that the Fed had been unable to keep under control. In contrast, when the third oil price shock hit in 2007–2008, inflation had been low and stable for quite a period of time, and so the Fed had more credibility regarding its intent to keep inflation under control. One reason that might explain why the third oil price shock appears to have had a smaller effect on inflation is that monetary policy was more credible at that point in time. Our aggregate demand and supply analysis provides the reasoning behind this view.

In the first two episodes, during which both the Fed's commitment to a nominal anchor and the Fed's credibility were weak, the oil price shocks would have produced a surge in inflation expectations and a large upward and leftward shift of the short-run aggregate supply curve, to AS_3 in Figure 2. Thus, our aggregate demand and supply analysis predicts that there would have been a sharp contraction in economic activity and a sharp rise in inflation. This is exactly what we see in panels (a) and (b) of Figure 3. The economic contractions were very severe, with unemployment rising to above 8% in the aftermath of the 1973 and 1979 oil price shocks. In addition, inflation shot up to double-digit levels during these periods.

In the 2007–2008 episode, the outcome was quite different. Through greater policy credibility was established over many years, inflation expectations remained grounded when the oil price shock occurred. As a result, the short-run aggregate supply curve shifted up and to the left by much less, to only AS_2 in Figure 2. Our aggregate demand and supply analysis predicts that a much smaller increase in inflation would result from the negative supply shock and that the contraction in economic activity also would be less. Indeed, this is exactly what transpired until the global financial crisis entered its virulent phase in the fall of 2008. Inflation rose by much less than in the previous episodes, and the economy held up fairly well until the financial crisis took a disastrous turn in October 2008 (see Chapter 12). Only then did the economy go into a tailspin, but it is clear that this economic contraction was not the result of the negative supply shock. Inflation actually fell quite dramatically, indicating that a massive negative demand shock was the source of the sharp contraction in economic activity. ◆

Real-time data

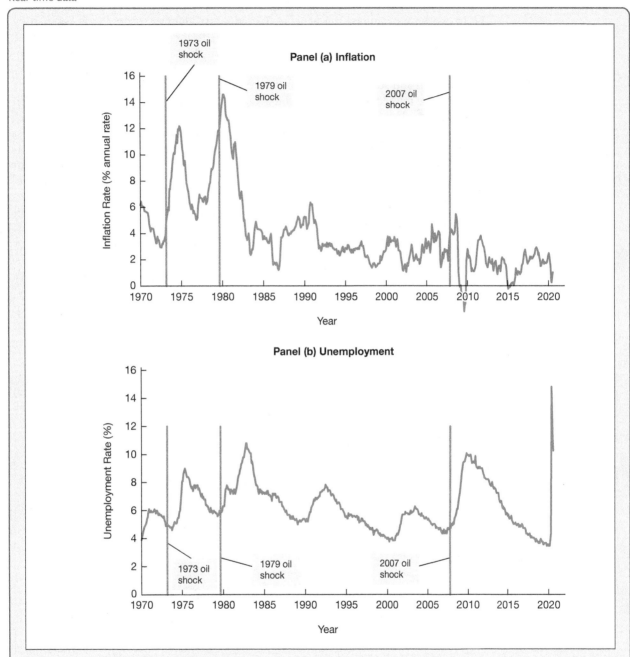

FIGURE 3 **Inflation and Unemployment, 1970–2020**

During the 1973 and 1979 oil shock episodes, inflation was initially high and the Fed's commitment to a nominal anchor was weak, whereas during the 2007 episode, inflation was initially low and the Fed's credibility was high. As a result, inflation and unemployment rose more in the first two episodes than in the last episode, with unemployment rising sharply in the third episode only after the 2007–2009 global financial crisis took a disastrous turn in October 2008.

Source: Federal Reserve Bank of St. Louis, FRED database: https://fred.stlouisfed.org/series/UNRATE; https://fred.stlouisfed.org/series/CPIAUCSL.

Credibility and Anti-Inflation Policy

So far we have examined the benefits of credibility when the economy is buffeted by demand and supply shocks. By the end of the 1970s, the high inflation rate (then over 10%) helped shift the primary concern of policymakers to the reduction of inflation. What role does credibility play in the effectiveness of anti-inflation policies? The aggregate demand and supply diagram given in Figure 4 will help us answer this question.

Suppose the economy has settled into a sustained 10% inflation rate at point 1, with the aggregate demand curve at AD_1 and the short-run aggregate supply curve at AS_1. Now suppose a new Federal Reserve chair is appointed who decides that inflation must be stopped. The new chair convinces the FOMC to autonomously tighten monetary policy so that the aggregate demand curve is shifted to the left to AD_4, which in the long run will move the economy to point 4 and slow inflation down to the 2% inflation objective.

If the central bank has very little credibility, then the public will not be convinced that the central bank will stay the course to reduce inflation and therefore they will not revise their inflation expectations down from the 10% level. As a result, the short-run aggregate supply curve will remain at AS_1 and the economy will move to point 2. Although inflation will fall to π_2, the aggregate output index will decline to Y_2.

Now consider what will happen if, instead, the central bank has high credibility and so the public believes that the central bank will do whatever it takes to lower inflation. In this case, expectations of inflation will fall, the short-run aggregate supply curve will fall to AS_3, and the economy will move to point 3. Inflation then will fall even

Mini-lecture

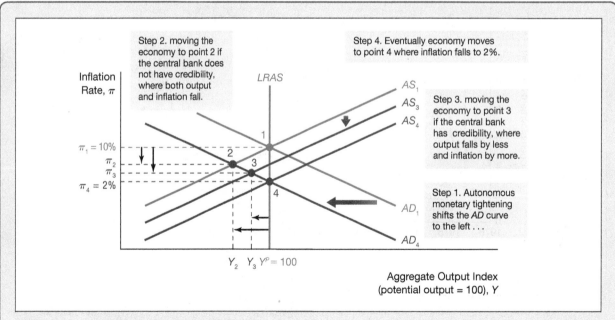

FIGURE 4   Credibility and Anti-Inflation Policy

Anti-inflation policy shifts the aggregate demand curve to the left from AD_1 to AD_4. If the central bank lacks credibility, the short-run aggregate supply curve remains at AS_1 and the economy moves to point 2, where the aggregate output index falls to Y_2 and inflation falls to π_2. If the central bank has credibility, then expected inflation declines and the short-run aggregate supply curve shifts down to AS_3. The economy moves to point 3, where the aggregate output index has fallen by less, to Y_3, and inflation has fallen by more, to π_3. Eventually the economy moves to point 4, but with credibility, the anti-inflation policy is more effective, lowering inflation faster and at less cost in terms of output.

further to π_3, and the aggregate output index will decline by less, to Y_3. Indeed, in the extreme case in which the central bank is perfectly credible, there is even a possibility that inflation expectations will immediately decline to the 2% level and that the short-run aggregate supply curve will shift all the way down to AS_4. In this case, the economy will immediately move to point 4, where inflation has declined to the 2% inflation objective, and yet the aggregate output index will remain at Y^P, so the economy stays at full employment. In this case, the anti-inflation policy will be costless because it will not require any loss of output. Although this last scenario is unlikely, we have shown the following result to be true: ***The greater the credibility of the central bank as an inflation fighter, the more rapid the decline in inflation and the lower the loss of output will be in the attempt to achieve the inflation objective.***

Evidence that credibility plays an important role in successful anti-inflation policies is provided by the dramatic end of the Bolivian hyperinflation in 1985 (see the Global box, "Ending the Bolivian Hyperinflation: A Successful Anti-Inflation Program"). But establishing credibility is easier said than done. You might think that an announcement by policymakers at the Federal Reserve that they plan to pursue an anti-inflation policy might do the trick. The public will expect that this policy will be adhered to and will act accordingly. However, this conclusion assumes that the public will believe the policymakers' announcement. Unfortunately, that is not how the real world works.

The history of Federal Reserve policymaking suggests that the Fed has not always done what it set out to do. In fact, during the 1970s, the chair of the Federal Reserve Board at the time, Arthur Burns, repeatedly announced that the Fed would pursue a vigorous anti-inflation policy, yet instead of raising real interest rates when inflation rose, he actually lowered them. Such episodes reduced the credibility of the Federal Reserve in the eyes of the public and, as predicted in Figure 4, the resulting lack of credibility had serious consequences. The reduction of inflation that occurred from 1981 to 1984 was bought at a very high cost; the 1981–1982 recession that helped bring down the inflation rate was one of the most severe recessions of the post–World War II period.

Global   Ending the Bolivian Hyperinflation: A Successful Anti-Inflation Program

The most remarkable anti-inflation program of recent times was implemented in Bolivia. In the first half of 1985, Bolivia's inflation rate was running at 20,000% and rising. Indeed, the inflation rate was so high that the price of a movie ticket often rose while people waited in line to buy it. In August 1985, Bolivia's new president announced his anti-inflation program, the New Economic Policy. To rein in money growth and establish credibility, the new government took drastic actions to slash the budget deficit by shutting down many state-owned enterprises, eliminating subsidies, freezing public sector salaries, and collecting a new wealth tax. The finance ministry was put on new footing; the budget was balanced on a day-by-day basis. Without exception, the finance minister would not authorize spending in excess of the amount of tax revenue that had been collected the day before. The Bolivian inflation was stopped in its tracks within one month, and the output loss was minor (less than 5% of GDP).

Certain hyperinflations before World War II were also ended with small losses of output through the implementation of policies similar to Bolivia's,* and a 1985 anti-inflation program in Israel, which also involved substantial reductions in budget deficits, sharply reduced inflation without any clear loss of output. Without a doubt, credible anti-inflation policies can be highly successful in eliminating inflation.

*For an excellent discussion of the end of four hyperinflations in the 1920s, see Thomas Sargent, "The Ends of Four Big Inflations," in *Inflation: Causes and Consequences,* ed. Robert E. Hall (Chicago: University of Chicago Press, 1982), 41–98.

The U.S. government can play an important role in establishing the credibility of anti-inflation policy. We have seen that large budget deficits may help stimulate inflationary monetary policy, and when the government and the Fed announce that they will pursue a restrictive anti-inflation policy, they are unlikely to be believed *unless* the federal government demonstrates fiscal responsibility. This is a good economic example of the old adage "Actions speak louder than words." When the government takes actions that will help the Fed adhere to an anti-inflation policy, the policy becomes more credible. Unfortunately, this lesson has sometimes been ignored by politicians in the United States and in other countries.

24.4 APPROACHES TO ESTABLISHING CENTRAL BANK CREDIBILITY

LO 24.4 Identify the ways in which central banks can establish and maintain credibility.

Our analysis has demonstrated that a credible nominal anchor that anchors inflation expectations is a key element in the success of monetary policy. But how do the monetary authorities achieve this credibility? We discussed several approaches in earlier chapters. One approach to credibility, discussed in Chapter 16, is through continued success at keeping inflation under control through concerted policy actions. This approach proved successful for the Federal Reserve during the Greenspan and Bernanke years. An approach that has been growing in popularity in recent years, also discussed in Chapter 16, is *inflation targeting*, which involves the public announcement of a medium-term numerical target for inflation and a commitment to achieving it. Some countries have successfully kept inflation under control by pegging their currency's exchange rate to the currency of an anchor country that already has a strong nominal anchor. We discussed this strategy, sometimes called *exchange-rate targeting*, in Chapter 18. Another way to increase central bank credibility is to give the central bank more independence from the political process, as discussed in Chapter 13. Two additional approaches, not discussed in earlier chapters but discussed below, are nominal GDP targeting and the appointment of "conservative" central bankers.

Nominal GDP Targeting

A variant of inflation targeting that recently has received increased attention is **nominal GDP targeting**, in which the central bank announces an objective of hitting a particular level of nominal GDP growth (recall that nominal GDP is real GDP times the price level). For example, if the inflation objective for the central bank were 2% and potential GDP were expected to grow at an annual rate of 3%, then nominal GDP targeting would mean a commitment by the central bank to keeping nominal GDP growing at 5% per year. Nominal GDP targeting has elements of an inflation targeting regime because the targeted growth rate of nominal GDP is tied to the chosen numerical inflation objective. In addition, nominal GDP targeting implies that the central bank will respond to slowdowns in the real economy even if inflation is not falling. To see this, note that with inflation unchanged, a slowdown in real GDP will result in a slowdown in nominal GDP, and so the monetary authorities will be prompted to pursue more expansionary monetary policy.

A potential advantage of nominal GDP targeting is that it focuses not only on controlling inflation but also explicitly on stabilizing real GDP. Another potential advantage is that with nominal GDP targeting, real GDP growth that is below potential or inflation that is below the inflation objective will encourage more expansionary monetary policy, because actual nominal GDP will fall further below its target. Expectations of this more expansionary policy will help stimulate aggregate demand, which will be particularly useful if the zero-lower-bound problem occurs and the monetary authorities are unable to lower the policy interest rate.

Critics cite two major weaknesses of nominal GDP targeting. First, nominal GDP targeting requires accurate estimates of potential GDP growth, which are not easy to achieve. Second, nominal GDP targeting is more complicated to explain to the public than inflation targeting and thus the public might be confused about the objectives of the central bank. At this time, no central bank has adopted nominal GDP targeting, but this may change in the future.

Appoint "Conservative" Central Bankers

Kenneth Rogoff of Harvard University suggested that another way of establishing central bank credibility is for the government to appoint central bankers who have a strong aversion to inflation.[6] He characterized these central bankers as "conservative,"

Inside the Fed   The Appointment of Paul Volcker, Anti-Inflation Hawk

President Jimmy Carter appointed Paul Volcker as chair of the Federal Reserve in August 1979. Prior to that, inflation had been climbing steadily, and at the time of Volcker's appointment, the annual CPI inflation rate had reached 11.8%. Volcker was the quintessential "conservative" central banker, a well-known inflation hawk who had made it clear to the president that he would take on inflation and wring it out of the system. In October 1979, shortly after Volcker took the helm of the Fed, the FOMC began to raise interest rates dramatically, increasing the federal funds rate by over 8 percentage points to nearly 20% by April 1980. However, with the sharp economic contraction that began in January 1980, Volcker blinked and took his foot off the brake, allowing the federal funds rate to decline to around the 10% level by July, at which time the economy started to recover. Unfortunately, this monetary medicine had not done the trick, and inflation remained very high, with CPI inflation above 13%. Volcker then showed his anti-inflation, hawkish mettle: The Fed raised the federal funds rate to the 20% level by January 1981 and kept it there until July of the same year. Then, in the face of the most

severe recession of the post–World War II period up to that point, the Fed kept the federal funds rate at a level of around 15% from July 1981 until July 1982, despite a rise in the unemployment rate to nearly 10%. Finally, only with the inflation rate starting to fall in July of 1982 did the Fed begin to lower the federal funds rate.

Volcker's anti-inflation credentials had now been fully established, and by 1983 inflation had fallen to below 4% and remained around that level for the rest of Volcker's tenure at the Fed through 1987. Volcker had reestablished the credibility of the Fed as an inflation fighter, with the result that inflation expectations had now stabilized, ending the period of high inflation in the United States that became known as the "Great Inflation." Volcker became a monetary policy hero and has been lauded ever since as one of the greatest central bankers of all time. Indeed, even after he left the Fed, he continued to play a prominent role in policy discussions. For example, he served on the Economic Advisory Board under President Obama and authored the so-called "Volcker rule" (discussed in Chapter 10) that restricted banks from trading with their own money (proprietary trading).

---

[6]Kenneth Rogoff, "The Optimal Degree of Commitment to an Intermediary Monetary Target," *Quarterly Journal of Economics* (November 1985): 169–189.

although a better description would be "tough" or "hawkish on inflation." (See the Inside the Fed box, "The Appointment of Paul Volcker, Anti-Inflation Hawk," to read about the appointment of a "conservative" central banker.)

When the public sees the appointment of a "conservative" central banker, it will expect that he or she will be less tempted to pursue expansionary monetary policy to exploit the short-run trade-off between inflation and unemployment and will do whatever it takes to keep inflation under control. As a result, inflation expectations and realized inflation are likely to be more stable, with the benefits outlined previously.

The problem with this approach to solving the credibility problem is that it is not clear that it will continue to work over time. If a central banker has more "conservative" preferences than the public, won't the public demand the appointment of central bankers who are more in tune with their preferences? After all, in a democratic society, government officials are supposed to represent the will of the people.

SUMMARY

1. The simple principle (derived from rational expectations theory) that the manner in which expectations are formed changes when the behavior of forecasted variables changes led to the famous Lucas critique of econometric policy evaluation. Lucas argued that when policy changes, the method of expectations formation changes; hence the relationships in an econometric model will change. An econometric model that has been created on the basis of past data will no longer be a valid model for evaluating the effects of a policy change and may prove to be highly misleading. The Lucas critique also points out that the effects of a particular policy depend critically on the public's expectations of the policy.

2. Advocates of rules for the conduct of monetary policy believe that rules solve the time-inconsistency problem because policymakers are forced to follow a set plan, which eliminates the temptation to deviate from the plan and ensures the achievement of desirable long-run outcomes. Advocates of discretion believe that rules are much too rigid because they cannot predict every contingency and do not allow for the use of judgment. Constrained discretion imposes a conceptual structure and inherent discipline on policymakers, but it does so without eliminating all flexibility, so that it combines some of the advantages ascribed to rules with those ascribed to discretion.

3. An important way for the monetary authorities to constrain discretion is by committing to a credible nominal anchor—a nominal variable, such as the inflation rate, the money supply, or an exchange rate—that ties down the price level or inflation to achieve price stability. A credible nominal anchor helps solve the time-inconsistency problem and helps anchor inflation expectations. Credibility has the benefit of stabilizing both output and inflation fluctuations and also enables anti-inflation policies to lower inflation at a lower cost in terms of lost output.

4. Approaches to establishing credibility include implementing actual policies to keep inflation low, inflation targeting, exchange-rate targeting, and the promotion of central bank independence. Two other approaches to establishing central bank credibility are nominal GDP targeting, in which the central bank announces an objective of hitting a particular level of nominal GDP growth, and the appointment of a "conservative" central banker (like Paul Volcker) who is hawkish on controlling inflation.

KEY TERMS

constant-money-growth-rate rule, p. 579
constrained discretion, p. 582
credibility, p. 582

discretion, p. 578
macroeconometric models, p. 576
monetarists, p. 579

nominal GDP targeting, p. 590
political business cycle, p. 580
rules, p. 578

QUESTIONS

1. What does the Lucas critique state about the limitations of our current understanding of the way in which the economy works?

2. "The Lucas critique casts doubt on the ability of discretionary stabilization policy to be beneficial." Is this statement true, false, or uncertain? Explain your answer.

3. Suppose an econometric model based on past data predicts a small decrease in domestic investment when the Federal Reserve increases the federal funds rate. Assume the Federal Reserve is considering an increase in the federal funds rate target to fight inflation and promote a low inflation environment that will encourage investment and economic growth.

   a. Discuss the implications of the econometric model's predictions if individuals interpret the increase in the federal funds rate target as a sign that the Fed will keep inflation at low levels in the long run.

   b. What would be Lucas's critique of this model?

4. If the public expects the Fed to pursue a policy that is likely to raise short-term interest rates permanently to 5%, but the Fed does not go through with this policy change, what will happen to long-term interest rates? Explain your answer.

5. In what sense can greater central bank independence make the time-inconsistency problem worse?

6. What are the arguments for and against policy rules?

7. If, in a surprise victory, a new administration that the public believes will pursue inflationary policy is elected to office, predict what might happen to the level of output and inflation even before the new administration comes into power.

8. Many economists are worried that a high level of budget deficits may lead to inflationary monetary policies in the future. Could these budget deficits have an effect on the current rate of inflation?

9. In some countries, the president chooses the head of the central bank. The same president can fire the head of the central bank and replace him or her with another director at any time. Explain the implications of such a situation for the conduct of monetary policy. Do you think the central bank will follow a monetary policy rule, or will it engage in discretionary policy?

10. How would an unexpected change in the equilibrium real fed funds rate be an argument against using a Taylor rule for monetary policy implementation?

11. How is *constrained discretion* different from *discretion* in monetary policy? How are the outcomes of these policies likely to differ?

12. In general, how does credibility (or lack thereof) affect the aggregate supply curve?

13. In Japan, the government and central bank have enacted policies recently to raise inflation permanently from persistently low levels, however inflation continues to remain near zero. How, if at all, might credibility of the central bank explain the low inflation persistence?

14. As part of its response to the global financial crisis, the Fed lowered the federal funds rate target to nearly zero by December 2008 and quadrupled the monetary base between 2008 and 2014, a considerable easing of monetary policy. However, survey-based measures of five- to ten-year inflation expectations remained low throughout most of this period. Comment on the Fed's credibility in fighting inflation.

15. "The more credible the policymakers who pursue an anti-inflation policy, the more successful that policy will be." Is this statement true, false, or uncertain? Explain your answer.

16. Why did the oil price shocks of the 1970s affect the economy differently than the oil price shocks of 2007?

17. Central banks that engage in inflation targeting usually announce the inflation target and time period for which that target will be relevant. In addition, central bank officials are held accountable for their actions (e.g., they could be fired if the target is not reached), and their success or lack thereof is also public information. Explain why transparency is such a fundamental ingredient of inflation targeting.

18. In recent years, central banks have dramatically increased the amount of communication with market participants and the public, and at the same time in many of these countries, average inflation has declined and become less volatile. Is this coincidence, or is there a connection? Explain.

19. What are the purposes of inflation targeting, and how does this monetary policy strategy achieve them?

20. How can the establishment of an exchange-rate target bring credibility to a country with a poor record of inflation stabilization?

21. What traits characterize a "conservative" central banker?

APPLIED PROBLEMS

22. Suppose the central bank is following a constant-money-growth-rate rule and the economy is hit with a severe economic downturn. Use an aggregate supply and demand graph to show the possible effects on the economy. How does this situation reflect on the credibility of the central bank if it maintains the money growth rule? How does it reflect on the central bank's credibility if it abandons the money growth rule to respond to the downturn?

23. Suppose country A has a central bank with full credibility, and country B has a central bank with no credibility. How does the credibility of each country's central bank affect the speed of adjustment of the aggregate supply curve to policy announcements? How does this result affect output stability? Use an aggregate supply and demand diagram to demonstrate.

24. Suppose two countries have identical aggregate demand curves and potential levels of output, and γ is the same in both countries. Assume that in 2022, both countries are hit with the same negative supply shock. Given the table of values below for inflation in each country, what can you say, if anything, about the credibility of each country's central bank? Explain your answer.

	Country A	Country B
2021	3.0%	3.0%
2022	3.8%	5.5%
2023	3.5%	5.0%
2024	3.2%	4.3%
2025	3.0%	3.8%

25. How does a credible nominal anchor help improve the economic outcomes that result from a positive aggregate demand shock? How does a credible nominal anchor help if a negative aggregate supply shock occurs? Use graphs of aggregate supply and demand to demonstrate.

DATA ANALYSIS PROBLEMS

The Problems update with real-time data in **MyLab Economics** and are available for practice or instructor assignment.

1. Real-time Data Analysis Go to the St. Louis Federal Reserve FRED database, and find data on the personal consumption expenditure price index (PCECTPI). Convert the *units* setting to "Percent Change from Year Ago," and download the data. Beginning in January 2012, the Fed formally announced a 2% inflation goal over the "longer-term."

   a. Calculate the average inflation rate over the last four and the last eight quarters of data available. How does it compare to the 2% inflation goal?

   b. What, if anything, does your answer to part (a) imply about Federal Reserve credibility?

2. Real-time Data Analysis Go to the St. Louis Federal Reserve FRED database, and find data on the core PCE price index (PCEPILFE) and the spot price of a barrel of oil (WTISPLC). For both variables, convert the *units* setting to "Percent Change from Year Ago," and download the data from 1960 to the most recent available data.

   a. Identify periods in which oil price inflation is 80% or higher.

   b. In the periods identified in part (a), how many months was oil price inflation 80% or higher? What was the average core inflation rate during each of those episodes?

   c. On the basis of your answers to parts (a) and (b) above, what can you conclude about the credibility of more recent monetary policy compared to its credibility in the earlier periods?

25 Transmission Mechanisms of Monetary Policy

Learning Objectives

25.1 List and summarize the transmission mechanisms through which monetary policy can affect the real economy.

25.2 Summarize and apply the four lessons outlined in this chapter for the conduct of monetary policy.

Preview

Since 1980, the U.S. economy has been on a roller coaster, with output, unemployment, and inflation undergoing drastic fluctuations. At the start of the 1980s, inflation was running at double-digit levels, and the recession of 1980 was followed by one of the shortest economic expansions on record. After a year, the economy plunged into the 1981–1982 recession, with the unemployment rate climbing to over 10%, and only then did the inflation rate begin to come down to below the 5% level. The 1981–1982 recession was followed by a long economic expansion that reduced the unemployment rate to below 6% during the 1987–1990 period. With Iraq's invasion of Kuwait and a rise in oil prices in the second half of 1990, the economy again plunged into recession. Subsequent growth in the economy was sluggish at first but eventually sped up, and the unemployment rate fell to below 5% in the late 1990s. In March 2001, after a 10-year expansion, the longest in U.S. history, the economy slipped into a recession, with the unemployment rate climbing to around 6%. By 2007, an economic recovery had brought the unemployment rate below 5%, but with the onset of the global financial crisis, the economy entered a recession in December 2007, with the unemployment rate rising to 10%. Only in July 2009 did the economy start to recover, making the recession of 2007–2009 the longest recession since World War II. After a more than ten-year expansion, the coronavirus pandemic led to another recession that started in February 2020, with the unemployment rate rising to 14.7% in April. In light of large fluctuations in aggregate output (reflected in the unemployment rate) and inflation, and the economic instability that accompanies them, policymakers face the following dilemma: What policy or policies, if any, should be implemented to reduce fluctuations in output and inflation in the future?

To answer this question, monetary policymakers must be able to accurately assess the timing and effect of their policies on the economy. To make this assessment, they need to understand the mechanisms through which monetary policy affects the economy. In this chapter, we examine the transmission mechanisms of monetary policy and evaluate the empirical evidence on these mechanisms to better understand the role that monetary policy plays in the economy. We will see that these monetary transmission mechanisms emphasize the link between the financial system (which we studied in the first three parts of this book) and monetary theory, the subject of this part of the book.

25.1 TRANSMISSION MECHANISMS OF MONETARY POLICY

LO 25.1 List and summarize the transmission mechanisms through which monetary policy can affect the real economy.

In this section, we examine the ways in which monetary policy affects aggregate demand and the economy, which are referred to as **transmission mechanisms of monetary policy**. We start with interest-rate channels because they are the key monetary transmission mechanism of the *AD/AS* model developed in Chapters 20, 21, and 22 and applied to monetary policy in Chapters 23 and 24.[1]

Traditional Interest-Rate Channels

The traditional view of the monetary transmission mechanism can be characterized by the following schematic, which shows the effect of an easing of monetary policy accomplished by lowering the real interest rate:

$$r\downarrow \;\Rightarrow\; I\uparrow \;\Rightarrow\; Y^{ad}\uparrow \tag{1}$$

This schematic shows that an easing of monetary policy leads to a fall in real interest rates $(r\downarrow)$, which in turn lowers the real cost of borrowing, causing a rise in investment spending $(I\uparrow)$, thereby leading to an increase in aggregate demand $(Y^{ad}\uparrow)$.

Although Keynes originally emphasized this channel as operating through businesses' decisions about investment spending, the search for new monetary transmission mechanisms led economists to recognize that consumers' decisions about housing and **consumer durable expenditure** (spending by consumers on durable items such as automobiles and refrigerators) also are investment decisions. Thus the interest-rate channel of monetary transmission outlined in Equation 1 applies equally to consumer spending, and in this case I represents investments in residential housing and consumer durable expenditure.

An important feature of the interest-rate transmission mechanism is its emphasis on the *real* (rather than the nominal) interest rate as the rate that affects consumer and business decisions. In addition, it is often the real *long-term* interest rate (not the real short-term interest rate) that is viewed as having the major impact on spending. How is it that a change in the short-term nominal interest rate induced by a central bank results in a corresponding change in the real interest rate on both short- and long-term bonds? We have already seen that the answer lies in the phenomenon of *sticky prices*—the fact that the aggregate price level adjusts slowly over time, so expansionary monetary policy, which lowers the short-term nominal interest rate, also lowers the short-term real interest rate. The expectations hypothesis of the term structure described in Chapter 6, which states that the long-term interest rate is an average of expected future short-term interest rates, suggests that a lower real short-term interest rate, as long as it is expected to persist, leads to a fall in the real long-term interest rate. These lower real interest rates then lead to increases in business fixed investment, residential housing investment, inventory investment, and consumer durable expenditure, all of which produce the rise in aggregate demand.

The fact that the real interest rate rather than the nominal rate affects spending suggests an important mechanism through which monetary policy can stimulate the

---

[1]An appendix to this chapter found in **MyLab Economics** examines the empirical evidence on the importance of money to economic fluctuations.

economy, even if nominal interest rates hit a floor of zero (the effective lower bound) during a deflationary episode. With nominal interest rates at a floor of zero, a commitment to future expansionary monetary policy can raise expected inflation (π^e), thereby lowering the real interest rate $(r = i - \pi^e)$ even when the nominal interest rate is fixed at zero and stimulating spending through the interest-rate channel:

$$\pi^e \uparrow \Rightarrow r\downarrow \Rightarrow I\uparrow \Rightarrow Y^{ad}\uparrow \tag{2}$$

This mechanism thus indicates that monetary policy can still be effective even when nominal interest rates have already been driven down to zero by the monetary authorities. Indeed, this mechanism explains why the Federal Reserve resorted in December 2008 to the nonconventional monetary policy of committing to keep the federal funds rate at zero for an extended period of time. By so doing, the Fed was trying to keep inflation expectations from falling in order to make sure that real interest rates remained low, so as to stimulate the economy. In addition, the commitment to keep interest rates low for an extended period of time would help lower long-term interest rates, which would also induce greater spending.

Some economists, such as John Taylor of Stanford University, take the position that strong empirical evidence exists for substantial interest-rate effects on consumer and investment spending through the real cost of borrowing, making the interest-rate monetary transmission mechanism a strong one. His position is highly controversial, and many researchers, including Ben Bernanke, former chair of the Fed, and Mark Gertler of New York University, believe that the empirical evidence does not support strong interest-rate effects that operate through the real cost of borrowing.[2] Indeed, these researchers see the empirical failure of traditional interest-rate monetary transmission mechanisms as having provided the stimulus for the search for other transmission mechanisms of monetary policy.

These other transmission mechanisms fall into two basic categories: those operating through asset prices other than interest rates and those operating through asymmetric information effects on credit markets (the **credit view**). These mechanisms are summarized in the schematic diagram in Figure 1.

Other Asset Price Channels

One drawback of the aggregate demand analysis in previous chapters is that it focuses on only one asset price, the interest rate, rather than on many asset prices. In addition to bond prices, two other asset prices receive substantial attention as channels for monetary policy effects: foreign exchange rates and the prices of equities (stocks).

Exchange Rate Effects on Net Exports
With the growing internationalization of economies throughout the world and the advent of flexible exchange rates, more attention has been paid to how monetary policy affects exchange rates, which in turn affect net exports and aggregate demand.

The foreign exchange rate channel also involves interest-rate effects because, as we saw in Chapter 17, when domestic real interest rates fall, domestic dollar assets become less attractive relative to assets denominated in foreign currencies. As a result, the value of dollar assets relative to other currency assets falls, and the dollar depreciates

[2]See John Taylor, "The Monetary Transmission Mechanism: An Empirical Framework," *Journal of Economic Perspectives* 9 (Fall 1995): 11–26, and Ben Bernanke and Mark Gertler, "Inside the Black Box: The Credit Channel of Monetary Policy Transmission," *Journal of Economic Perspectives* 9 (Fall 1995): 27–48.

Mini-lecture

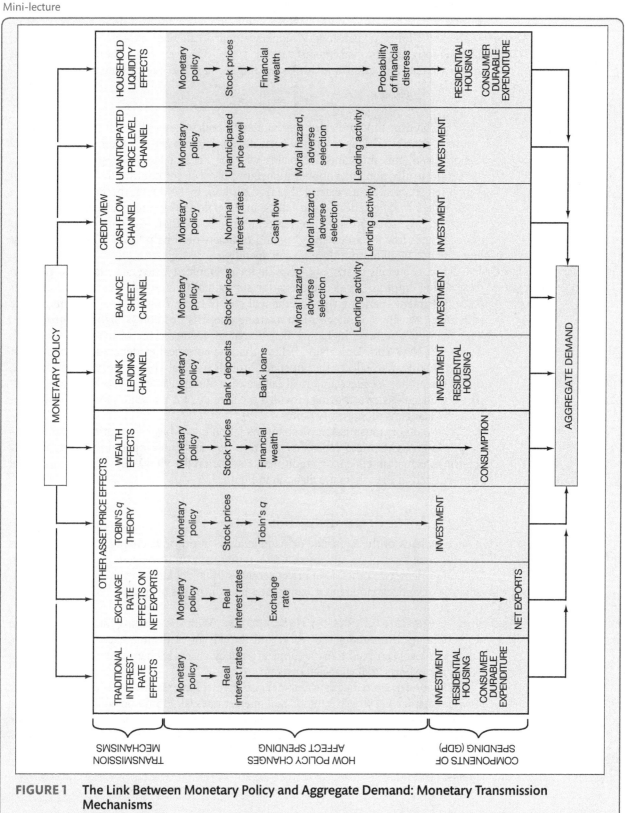

FIGURE 1   The Link Between Monetary Policy and Aggregate Demand: Monetary Transmission Mechanisms

This figure shows the different channels through which monetary policy affects aggregate demand.

(denoted by $E\downarrow$). The lower value of the domestic currency makes domestic goods cheaper than foreign goods, thereby causing a rise in net exports ($NX\uparrow$) and hence in aggregate demand ($Y^{ad}\uparrow$). The schematic for the monetary transmission mechanism that operates through the exchange rate is

$$r\downarrow \Rightarrow E\downarrow \Rightarrow NX\uparrow \Rightarrow Y^{ad}\uparrow \tag{3}$$

Tobin's q Theory   Nobel Prize winner James Tobin developed a theory, referred to as *Tobin's q theory*, that explains how monetary policy can affect the economy through its effects on the valuation of equities (stock). Tobin defines q as the market value of firms divided by the replacement cost of capital. If q is high, the market price of firms is high relative to the replacement cost of capital, and new plant and equipment capital is cheap relative to the market value of firms. Companies then can issue stock and get a high price for it relative to the cost of the facilities and equipment they are buying. Investment spending will rise because firms can buy a lot of new investment goods with only a small issue of stock.

Conversely, when q is low, firms will not purchase *new* investment goods because the market value of firms is low relative to the cost of capital. If companies want to acquire capital when q is low, they can buy another firm cheaply and acquire old capital instead. Investment spending, the purchase of new investment goods, will then be very low. Tobin's q theory gives a good explanation for the extremely low rate of investment spending during the Great Depression. In that period, stock prices collapsed, and by 1933, stocks were worth only one-tenth of their value in late 1929; q fell to unprecedentedly low levels.

The crux of this discussion is that a link exists between Tobin's q and investment spending. But how might monetary policy affect stock prices? Quite simply, lower real interest rates on bonds mean that the expected return on this alternative to stocks falls. This makes stocks more attractive relative to bonds, and so demand for them increases, which raises their price.[3] By combining this result with the fact that higher stock prices (P_s) will lead to a higher q and thus higher investment spending I, we can write the following transmission mechanism of monetary policy:

$$r\downarrow \Rightarrow P_s\uparrow \Rightarrow q\uparrow \Rightarrow I\uparrow \Rightarrow Y^{ad}\uparrow \tag{4}$$

Wealth Effects   In their search for new monetary transmission mechanisms, researchers also looked at how consumers' balance sheets might affect their spending decisions. Franco Modigliani was the first to take this tack, using his famous life cycle hypothesis of consumption. **Consumption** is spending by consumers on nondurable goods and services.[4] It differs from *consumer expenditure* in that it does not include spending on consumer durables. The basic premise of Modigliani's theory is that consumers smooth out their consumption over time. Therefore, consumption spending is determined by the lifetime resources of consumers, not just today's income.

---

[3]An alternative way of looking at this transmission mechanism is to use the model discussed in Chapter 7 in which a decrease in the real interest rate lowers the required return on investments in stocks and so increases stock prices. Then the lower yield on stocks reduces the cost of financing investment spending through the issuance of equity. This way of looking at the link between stock prices and investment spending is formally equivalent to Tobin's q theory.

[4]Consumption also includes another small component, the services that a consumer receives from the ownership of housing and consumer durables.

An important component of consumers' lifetime resources is their financial wealth, a major part of which is common stocks. When stock prices rise, the value of financial wealth increases, thereby increasing the lifetime resources of consumers, which means that consumption should rise. Considering that, as we have seen, monetary easing can lead to a rise in stock prices, we now have another monetary transmission mechanism:

$$r\downarrow \Rightarrow P_s\uparrow \Rightarrow \text{wealth}\uparrow \Rightarrow \text{consumption}\uparrow \Rightarrow Y^{ad}\uparrow \qquad (5)$$

Modigliani's research found this relationship to be an extremely powerful mechanism that adds substantially to the potency of monetary policy.

The wealth and Tobin's q channels allow for a general definition of equity, so they can also be applied to the housing market, where housing is equity. An increase in home prices, which raises their prices relative to replacement cost, leads to a rise in Tobin's q for housing, thereby stimulating its production. Similarly, housing prices are extremely important components of wealth, so rises in these prices increase wealth, thereby increasing consumption. Monetary expansion, which raises housing prices through the Tobin's q and wealth mechanisms described here, thus leads to a rise in aggregate demand.

Credit View

Dissatisfaction with the conventional story that interest-rate effects explain the impact of monetary policy on spending on durable assets has led to a new explanation that is based on the concept of asymmetric information, a problem that leads to financial frictions in financial markets (see Chapter 8). This explanation, referred to as the *credit view*, proposes that two types of monetary transmission channels arise as a result of financial frictions in credit markets: those that operate through effects on bank lending and those that operate through effects on firms' and households' balance sheets.

Bank Lending Channel   The concept of the bank lending channel is based on the analysis in Chapter 8, which demonstrated that banks play a special role in the financial system because they are especially well suited to solving asymmetric information problems in credit markets. Because of banks' special role, certain borrowers will not have access to the credit markets unless they borrow from banks. As long as there is no perfect substitutability of retail bank deposits with other sources of funds, the bank lending channel of monetary transmission operates as follows: Expansionary monetary policy, which increases bank reserves and bank deposits, raises the quantity of bank loans available. Because many borrowers are dependent on bank loans to finance their activities, this increase in loans causes investment (and possibly consumer) spending to rise. Schematically, the monetary policy effect is written as follows:

$$\text{bank reserves}\uparrow \Rightarrow \text{bank deposits}\uparrow \Rightarrow \text{bank loans}\uparrow \Rightarrow I\uparrow \Rightarrow Y^{ad}\uparrow \qquad (6)$$

An important implication of the credit view is that monetary policy will have a greater effect on expenditure by smaller firms, which are more dependent on bank loans, than it will on large firms, which can get funds directly through the stock and bond markets (and not only through banks).

Although this mechanism has been confirmed by researchers, doubts about the influence of the bank lending channel have been raised in the literature, and there are reasons to suspect that the bank lending channel in the United States may not be as powerful as it once was. The first reason this channel is less powerful than it once was is that current U.S. regulations no longer impose restrictions on banks that hinder their ability to raise funds (see Chapter 11). Prior to the mid-1980s, certificates of deposit (CDs) were subjected to reserve requirements and Regulation Q deposit rate ceilings, which made it hard for banks to replace deposits that flowed out of the banking system during a monetary contraction. With these regulatory restrictions abolished, banks can more easily respond to a decline in bank reserves and a loss of retail deposits by issuing CDs at market interest rates that do not have to be backed up by required reserves. Second, the worldwide decline of the traditional bank lending business (also discussed in Chapter 11) has rendered the bank lending channel less potent. Nonetheless, many economists believe that the bank lending channel played an important role in the slow recovery of the United States from the 2007–2009 recession. However, this channel is likely to be even less potent in recent years because banks are now paid interest on their excess reserves and so have less incentive to lend them out.

Balance Sheet Channel Even though the bank lending channel may be declining in importance, it is by no means clear that this is the case for the other credit channel, the balance sheet channel. Like the bank lending channel, the balance sheet channel arises from the presence of financial frictions in credit markets. In Chapter 8, we saw that the lower the net worth of business firms, the more severe the adverse selection and moral hazard problems in lending to these firms become. Lower net worth means that lenders in effect have less collateral for their loans, so their potential losses from adverse selection are higher. A decline in firms' net worth, which raises the adverse selection problem, thus leads to decreased lending to finance investment spending. The lower net worth of businesses also increases the moral hazard problem because it means that owners have a lower equity stake in their firms, giving them more incentive to engage in risky investment projects. When borrowers take on more risky investment projects, it is more likely that lenders will not be paid back, and so a decrease in businesses' net worth leads to a reduction in lending and hence in investment spending.

Monetary policy can affect firms' balance sheets in several ways. Easing of monetary policy, which causes a rise in stock prices ($P_s\uparrow$) along the lines described earlier, raises the net worth of firms and so leads to higher investment spending ($I\uparrow$) and higher aggregate demand ($Y^{ad}\uparrow$) because of the decrease in adverse selection and moral hazard problems. This leads to the following schematic for this particular balance sheet channel of monetary transmission:

$$r\downarrow \Rightarrow P_s\uparrow \Rightarrow \text{firms' net worth}\uparrow \Rightarrow \text{adverse selection}\downarrow, \atop \text{moral hazard}\downarrow \Rightarrow \text{lending}\uparrow \Rightarrow I\uparrow \Rightarrow Y^{ad}\uparrow \tag{7}$$

Cash Flow Channel Another balance sheet channel operates by affecting *cash flow*, the difference between firms' cash receipts and cash expenditures. An easing of monetary policy, which lowers nominal interest rates, also causes an improvement in firms' balance sheets because it raises cash flow. The increase in cash flow increases the liquidity of the firm (or household) and thus makes it easier for lenders to know whether the firm (or household) will be able to pay its bills. The result is that adverse selection and moral hazard problems become less severe, leading to an increase in lending and economic activity. The following schematic describes this alternative balance sheet channel:

$$i\downarrow \Rightarrow \text{firms' cash flow}\uparrow \Rightarrow \text{adverse selection}\downarrow,$$
$$\text{moral hazard}\downarrow \Rightarrow \text{lending}\uparrow \Rightarrow I\uparrow \Rightarrow Y^{ad}\uparrow \tag{8}$$

An important feature of this transmission mechanism is that *nominal* interest rates affect firms' cash flow. Thus this interest-rate mechanism differs from the traditional interest-rate mechanism discussed earlier in which the real interest rate affects investment. Furthermore, the short-term interest rate plays a special role in this transmission mechanism because interest payments on short-term (rather than long-term) debt typically have the greatest impact on the cash flow of households and firms.

A related transmission mechanism involving adverse selection is the credit-rationing phenomenon. Through this mechanism, expansionary monetary policy that lowers interest rates can stimulate aggregate demand. As discussed in Chapter 9, credit rationing occurs when borrowers are denied loans even though they are willing to pay a higher interest rate. The loans are denied because individuals and firms with the riskiest investment projects are exactly the ones who are willing to pay the highest interest rates because, if the high-risk investment succeeds, they will be the primary beneficiaries. Thus higher interest rates increase the adverse selection problem, and lower interest rates reduce it. When expansionary monetary policy lowers interest rates, risk-prone borrowers make up a smaller fraction of those demanding loans, and so lenders are more willing to lend, raising both investment and aggregate demand, along the lines of parts of the schematic given in Equation 8.

Unanticipated Price Level Channel

A third balance sheet channel operates through monetary policy effects on the general price level. Because in industrialized countries debt payments are contractually fixed in nominal terms, an unanticipated rise in the price level lowers the value of firms' liabilities in real terms (decreases the burden of the debt) but should not lower the real value of the firms' assets. An easing of monetary policy, which raises inflation and hence leads to an unanticipated rise in the price level ($P\uparrow$), therefore raises real net worth, which lowers adverse selection and moral hazard problems, thereby leading to a rise in investment spending and aggregate demand, as in the following schematic:

$$r\downarrow \Rightarrow \pi\uparrow \Rightarrow \text{unanticipated } P\uparrow \Rightarrow \text{firms' real net worth}\uparrow$$
$$\Rightarrow \text{adverse selection}\downarrow, \text{moral hazard}\downarrow \Rightarrow \text{lending}\uparrow \Rightarrow I\uparrow \Rightarrow Y^{ad}\uparrow \tag{9}$$

The view that unanticipated movements in the price level affect aggregate demand has a long tradition in economics: It is the key feature in the debt-deflation view of the Great Depression, outlined in Chapter 12.

Household Liquidity Effects

Although most literature on the credit channel focuses on spending by businesses, the credit view should apply equally well to consumer spending, particularly spending on consumer durables and housing. Declines in bank lending induced by a monetary contraction should cause corresponding declines in durable and housing purchases by consumers who do not have access to other sources of credit. Similarly, increases in interest rates should cause deteriorations in household balance sheets, because consumers' cash flow is adversely affected.

The balance sheet channel also operates through liquidity effects on consumer durable and housing expenditures. These effects were found to be important factors during the Great Depression (see the FYI box "Consumers' Balance Sheets and the Great Depression"). In the liquidity effects view, balance sheet effects work through their impact on consumers' desire to spend rather than on lenders' desire to lend. Because of asymmetric information regarding their quality, consumer durables and housing are very illiquid assets. If, as a result of a severe income shock, consumers needed to sell their consumer durables or housing immediately to raise money, they would expect to suffer a big financial loss because they would not be able to get the full value of these assets in a distress sale. (This is just a manifestation of the lemons problem described in Chapter 8.) In contrast, if consumers held financial assets (such as money in the bank, stocks, or bonds), they could sell them quickly and easily for their full market value and raise the cash. Hence, if consumers expect that they are likely to find themselves in financial distress, they will prefer to hold fewer illiquid consumer durable and housing assets and a greater amount of liquid financial assets.

A consumer's balance sheet should be an important influence on his or her estimate of the likelihood of future suffering from financial distress. Specifically, when consumers have a large amount of financial assets relative to their debts, their estimate of the probability of financial distress is low, and they are more willing to purchase consumer durables or housing. When stock prices rise, the value of financial assets increases as well; consumer durable expenditure will also rise because consumers have a more secure financial position and therefore a lower estimate of the likelihood of future financial distress. This leads to another transmission mechanism for monetary policy, one that operates through the link between money and stock prices:

$$r\downarrow \Rightarrow P_s\uparrow \Rightarrow \text{value of households' financial assets}\uparrow$$
$$\Rightarrow \text{likelihood of financial distress}\downarrow \qquad (10)$$
$$\Rightarrow \text{consumer durable and housing expenditure}\uparrow \Rightarrow Y^{ad}\uparrow$$

The illiquidity of consumer durable and housing assets provides another reason why a monetary easing, which lowers interest rates and thereby increases cash flow to consumers, leads to a rise in spending on consumer durables and housing. An increase in consumer cash flow decreases the likelihood of financial distress, which increases the desire of consumers to hold durable goods and housing, thus increasing spending on these items and hence increasing aggregate demand. The only difference between this view of cash flow effects and that outlined in Equation 8 is that in this view, it is not

---

FYI   Consumers' Balance Sheets and the Great Depression

The years between 1929 and 1933 witnessed the worst deterioration in consumers' balance sheets ever seen in the United States. The stock market crash in 1929, which caused an economic slump that lasted until 1933, reduced the value of consumers' wealth by $1,020 billion (in 2009 dollars), and as expected, consumption dropped sharply (by $199 billion). Because of the decline in the price level during that period, the level of real debt that consumers owed also increased sharply (by over 20%). Consequently, the value of financial assets relative to the amount of debt declined sharply, increasing the likelihood of financial distress. Not surprisingly, spending on consumer durables and housing fell precipitously: From 1929 to 1933, consumer durable expenditure declined by over 50%, while expenditure on housing declined by 80%.*

*For further discussion of the effect of consumers' balance sheets on spending during the Great Depression, see Frederic S. Mishkin, "The Household Balance Sheet and the Great Depression," *Journal of Economic History* 38 (1978): 918–937.

the willingness of lenders to lend to consumers that causes expenditure to rise, but the willingness of consumers to spend.

Why Are Credit Channels Likely to Be Important?

There are three reasons to believe that credit channels are important monetary transmission mechanisms. First, a large body of evidence on the behavior of individual firms supports the view that financial frictions of the type crucial to the operation of credit channels do affect firms' employment and spending decisions. Second, evidence shows that small firms (which are more likely to be credit-constrained) are hurt more by tight monetary policy than large firms, which are unlikely to be credit-constrained. Third, and maybe most compelling, the asymmetric information view of financial frictions, which is at the core of credit channel analysis, is a theoretical construct that has proved useful in explaining many other important economic phenomena, such as why many of our financial institutions exist, why our financial system has the structure that it has, and why financial crises are so damaging to the economy (topics discussed in Chapters 8 and 12). The best support for a theory is its demonstrated usefulness in a wide range of applications. By this standard, the asymmetric information theory, which supports the existence of credit channels as an important monetary transmission mechanism, has much to recommend it.

APPLICATION The Great Recession

With the advent of the financial crisis in the summer of 2007, the Fed began a very aggressive easing of monetary policy. The Fed dropped the target federal funds rate from $5\frac{1}{4}\%$ to 0% over a 15-month period from September 2007 to December 2008. At first, it appeared that the Fed's actions would keep the growth slowdown mild and prevent a recession. However, the economy proved to be weaker than the Fed or private forecasters expected, with the most severe recession of the post–World War II period up until that time beginning in December 2007. Why did the economy become so weak despite this unusually rapid reduction in the Fed's policy instrument?

The financial meltdown led to negative effects on the economy from many of the channels we have outlined above. The rising level of subprime mortgage defaults, which led to a decline in the value of mortgage-backed securities and CDOs, led to large losses on the balance sheets of financial institutions. With weaker balance sheets, these financial institutions began to deleverage and cut back on their lending. With no one else available to collect information and make loans, adverse selection and moral hazard problems, and hence financial frictions, increased in credit markets, leading to a slowdown of the economy. Credit spreads also went through the roof with the increase in uncertainty caused by the failure of so many financial markets. The declines in the stock market and housing prices also weakened the economy because they lowered household wealth. The decrease in household wealth led to a drop in Tobin's q, which led to restrained consumer spending and weaker investment spending.

With all these channels operating, it is no surprise that despite the Fed's aggressive lowering of the federal funds rate, the economy still took a big hit. ◆

25.2 LESSONS FOR MONETARY POLICY

LO 25.2 Summarize and apply the four lessons outlined in this chapter for the conduct of monetary policy.

What useful lessons regarding the appropriate conduct of monetary policy can we draw from the analysis in this chapter? Four basic lessons can be learned.

1. *It is dangerous to consistently associate an easing or tightening of monetary policy with a fall or rise in short-term nominal interest rates.* Because most central banks use short-term nominal interest rates—typically, the interbank rate—as the key operating instrument in their monetary policies, the danger exists that central banks and the public will focus too much on short-term nominal interest rates as an indicator of the stance of monetary policy. Indeed, it is quite common to see statements that always associate monetary tightenings with a rise in the interbank rate and monetary easings with a decline in the interbank rate. We do not make this mistake in this book because we have been careful to associate monetary easing or tightening with changes in *real* and not *nominal* interest rates.

2. *Other asset prices besides those on short-term debt instruments contain important information about the stance of monetary policy because they are important elements in various monetary policy transmission mechanisms.* As we have seen in this chapter, economists have come a long way in understanding that other asset prices besides interest rates have major effects on aggregate demand. As we saw in Figure 1, asset prices such as stock prices, foreign exchange rates, and housing prices play an important role in monetary transmission mechanisms. Furthermore, additional channels, such as those that operate through the exchange rate, Tobin's q, and wealth effects, provide additional evidence that other asset prices play an important role in monetary transmission mechanisms. Although economists strongly disagree among themselves about which channels of monetary transmission are the most important—not surprising, given that economists, particularly those in academia, always enjoy a good debate—they do concur that asset prices other than those on short-term debt instruments play an important role in the effects of monetary policy on the economy.

   The view that asset prices other than short-term interest rates matter has important implications for monetary policy. When we try to assess the stance of policy, it is critical that we look at other asset prices in addition to short-term interest rates. For example, if short-term interest rates are low or even zero and yet stock prices are low, housing prices are low, and the value of the domestic currency is high, monetary policy is clearly tight, not easy.

3. *Monetary policy can be effective in reviving a weak economy even if short-term interest rates are already near zero.* We have recently entered a world in which inflation is not always the norm. Japan, for example, recently experienced a period of deflation during which the price level was actually falling. In the United States, the federal funds rate hit a floor of zero from the end of 2008 until the end of 2015 and then again in March 2020. One common view is that when a central bank has driven down short-term nominal interest rates to nearly zero, monetary policy can do nothing more to stimulate the economy. The transmission mechanisms of monetary policy described here indicate that this view is false. As indicated in our discussion of the factors that affect the monetary base in Chapter 14, expansionary monetary policy aimed at increasing liquidity in the economy can be conducted through open market purchases, which do not have to be solely in short-term

government securities. For example, purchases of private securities, as the Federal Reserve made in 2009 and in 2020, can reduce financial frictions by lowering credit spreads and stimulating investment spending. In addition, a commitment to future expansionary monetary policy helps revive the economy by raising inflation expectations and by reflating other asset prices, which then stimulate aggregate demand through the channels outlined here. The nonconventional monetary policies we discussed in Chapter 15 are policies of this type. Nonconventional monetary policies can be a potent force in reviving economies that are undergoing deflation and that have short-term interest rates near zero. Indeed, as we saw in Chapter 12, aggressive nonconventional monetary policy during the recent financial crisis helped prevent the Great Recession from turning into a Great Depression and also helped the economy avoid a deflationary episode like the one that occurred during the Great Depression era. Aggressive nonconventional monetary policy has again been implemented to boost the economy in the aftermath of the coronavirus pandemic.

4. *Avoiding unanticipated fluctuations in the price level is an important objective of monetary policy, thus providing a rationale for price stability as the primary long-run goal of monetary policy.* As we saw in Chapter 16, central banks in recent years have been placing greater emphasis on price stability as the primary long-run goal of monetary policy. Several rationales for this goal have been proposed, including the undesirable effects of uncertainty about the future price level on business decisions and hence on productivity, distortions associated with the interaction of nominal contracts and the tax system with inflation, and increased social conflict stemming from inflation. Our discussion of monetary transmission mechanisms provides an additional reason why price stability is so important. As we have seen, unanticipated movements in the inflation rate can cause unanticipated fluctuations in output, an undesirable outcome. Particularly important in this regard is the knowledge that, as we saw in Chapter 12, price deflation can be an important factor leading to a prolonged financial crisis, as occurred during the Great Depression. An understanding of the monetary transmission mechanisms thus makes it clear that the goal of price stability is desirable because it reduces uncertainty about the future price level. The price stability goal implies that a negative inflation rate is at least as undesirable as too high an inflation rate. Indeed, because of the threat of financial crises, central banks must work very hard to prevent price deflation.

APPLICATION Applying the Monetary Policy Lessons to Japan's Two Lost Decades

Until 1990, it looked as if Japan might overtake the United States in per capita income. From the early 1990s until 2012, during the years that have become known as the "two lost decades," the Japanese economy stagnated, with deflation and low growth. As a result, Japanese living standards fell further and further behind those of the United States. Many economists take the view that Japanese monetary policy is in part to blame for the poor performance of the Japanese economy during this period. Could Japanese monetary policy have performed better if Japan had applied the four lessons outlined in the previous section?

The first lesson suggests that it is dangerous to think that declines in interest rates always mean that monetary policy has been easing. In the mid-1990s, when short-term interest rates began to decline, falling to nearly zero in the late 1990s and early 2000s, the monetary authorities in Japan took the view that monetary policy was sufficiently expansionary. Now it is widely recognized that this view was incorrect, because the falling and eventually negative inflation rates in Japan meant that real interest rates were actually quite high and that monetary policy was tight, not easy. If the monetary authorities in Japan had followed the advice of the first lesson, they might have pursued a more expansionary monetary policy, which would have helped boost the economy.

The second lesson suggests that monetary policymakers should pay attention to other asset prices, in addition to those on short-term debt instruments, in assessing the stance of monetary policy. At the same time that interest rates were falling in Japan, stock and real estate prices were collapsing, thus providing another indication that Japanese monetary policy was not easy. Knowledge of the second lesson might have led Japanese monetary policymakers to recognize sooner that they needed a more expansionary monetary policy.

The third lesson indicates that monetary policy can still be effective even if short-term interest rates are near zero. Officials at the Bank of Japan frequently claimed that they were helpless to stimulate the economy because short-term interest rates had fallen to nearly zero. By recognizing that monetary policy can be effective even when interest rates are near zero, as suggested by the third lesson, the Japanese monetary authorities could have taken monetary policy actions that would have stimulated aggregate demand by raising other asset prices and inflationary expectations.

The fourth lesson indicates that unanticipated fluctuations in the price level should be avoided. If the Japanese monetary authorities had adhered to this lesson, they might have recognized that allowing deflation to occur could be very damaging to the economy and that such deflation was inconsistent with the goal of price stability.

These four lessons of monetary policy were finally taken to heart by the Bank of Japan. As we discussed in Chapter 23, monetary policy in Japan has undergone a dramatic shift since 2013, to a highly expansionary, nonconventional monetary policy with a higher inflation target. Since then the Japanese economy has improved, with the unemployment rate falling. However, although the inflation rate has risen, it still remains stubbornly low, well below the Bank of Japan's 2% inflation target. ◆

SUMMARY

1. The transmission mechanisms of monetary policy include traditional interest-rate channels that operate through the real cost of borrowing and affect investment; other asset price channels such as exchange rate effects, Tobin's *q* theory, and wealth effects; and the credit view channels—the bank lending channel, the balance sheet channel, the cash flow channel, the unanticipated price level channel, and household liquidity effects.

2. Four lessons for monetary policy can be drawn from this chapter: (1) It is dangerous to consistently associate monetary policy easing or tightening with a fall or rise in short-term nominal interest rates; (2) other asset prices besides those on short-term debt instruments contain important information about the stance of monetary policy because they are important elements in the monetary policy transmission mechanisms; (3) monetary policy can be effective in reviving a weak economy even if short-term interest rates are already near zero; and (4) avoiding unanticipated fluctuations in the price level is an important objective of monetary policy, thus providing a rationale for price stability as the primary long-run goal of monetary policy.

KEY TERMS

consumer durable expenditure, p. 596

consumption, p. 599
credit view, p. 597

transmission mechanisms of monetary policy, p. 596

QUESTIONS

1. From 2008 to 2015, auto loan rates in the United States declined from around 8% to near historic lows of around 4%. At the same time, auto sales increased dramatically. How, if at all, does this relate to the monetary transmission mechanisms?

2. "Considering that consumption accounts for nearly two-thirds of total GDP, this means that the interest rate, wealth, and household liquidity channels are the most important monetary policy channels in the U.S." Is this statement true, false, or uncertain? Explain your answer.

3. How can the interest rate channel still function when short-term nominal interest rates are at the effective lower bound?

4. Lars Svensson, a former Princeton professor and deputy governor of the Swedish central bank, proclaimed that when an economy is at risk of falling into deflation, central bankers should be "responsibly irresponsible" with monetary expansion policies. What does this mean, and how does it relate to the monetary transmission mechanisms?

5. Describe an advantage and a disadvantage of the fact that monetary policy has so many different channels through which it can operate.

6. "If countries fix their exchange rate, the exchange rate channel of monetary policy does not exist." Is this statement true, false, or uncertain? Explain your answer.

7. During the 2007–2009 recession, the value of common stocks in real terms fell by more than 50%. How might this decline in the stock market have affected aggregate demand and thus contributed to the severity of the recession? Be specific about the mechanisms through which the stock market decline affected the economy.

8. "The costs of financing investment are related only to interest rates; therefore, the only way that monetary policy can affect investment spending is through its effects on interest rates." Is this statement true, false, or uncertain? Explain your answer.

9. From March 2009 to February 2020, the S&P 500 stock index increased by over 350%. Over the same period, University of Michigan's index of consumer confidence increased from 57.3 to 101.0 (an increase of 75%). Explain how this relates to the monetary transmission mechanisms.

10. From mid-2008 to early 2009, the Dow Jones Industrial Average declined by more than 50%, while real interest rates were low or falling. What does this scenario suggest should have happened to investment?

11. Nobel Prize winner Franco Modigliani found that the most important transmission mechanisms of monetary policy involve consumer expenditure. Describe how at least two of these mechanisms work.

12. In the late 1990s, the stock market was rising rapidly, the economy was growing, and the Federal Reserve kept interest rates relatively low. Comment on how this policy stance would affect the economy as it relates to the Tobin q transmission mechanisms.

13. During and after the global financial crisis, the Fed reduced the fed funds rate to nearly zero. At the same time, the stock market fell dramatically and housing market values declined sharply. Comment on the effectiveness of monetary policy during this period with regard to the wealth channel.

14. From August 2014 to August 2017, the Fed continued to reiterate that monetary policy was "accommodative." And during this time, excess reserves by banks decreased from around $2.67 trillion to around $2 trillion, a decline of about 25%. What does this say about the bank lending channel?

15. Why does the credit view imply that monetary policy has a greater effect on small businesses than on large firms?

16. Why might the bank lending channel be less effective today than it once was?

17. If adverse selection and moral hazard increase, how does this affect the ability of monetary policy to address economic downturns?

18. How does the Great Depression demonstrate the unanticipated price level channel?

19. How are the wealth effect and the household liquidity effect similar? How are they different?

20. After the coronavirus pandemic hit the economy, mortgage rates reached record-low levels in 2020.
    a. What effect should this have had on the economy, according to the household liquidity effect channel?
    b. During much of this time, most banks raised their credit standards significantly, making it much more difficult to qualify for home loans and to refinance

existing loans. How does this information alter your answer to part (a)?

21. "If the fed funds rate is at zero, the Fed can no longer implement effective accommodative policy." Is this statement true, false, or uncertain? Explain.

22. In December 2015, the Fed raised the fed funds rate for the first time in nearly a decade, and gradually increased interest rates over a prolonged period of time after that. However, the Fed continued to reiterate in its policy statements during this time that "the stance of monetary policy remains accommodative." Explain this seeming contradiction.

23. In general, if stock prices are rising, consumption growth is strong, house price appreciation is high, and unemployment is low, would you classify monetary policy as likely to be tight or easy?

24. How does the experience of Japan during the "two lost decades" lend support to the four lessons for monetary policy outlined in this chapter?

APPLIED PROBLEMS

25. Suppose the economy is in recession and the monetary policymakers lower interest rates in an effort to stabilize the economy. Use an aggregate supply and demand diagram to demonstrate the effects of a monetary easing when the transmission mechanisms are functioning normally and when the transmission mechanisms are weak, such as during a deep downturn or when significant financial frictions are present.

DATA ANALYSIS PROBLEMS

The Problems update with real-time data in **MyLab Economics** and are available for practice or instructor assignment.

1. **Real-time Data Analysis** A "rate cycle" is a period of monetary policy during which the federal funds rate moves from its low point toward its high point, or vice versa, in response to business cycle conditions. Go to the St. Louis Federal Reserve FRED database, and find data on the federal funds rate (FEDFUNDS), real business fixed investment (PNFIC1), real residential investment (PRFIC1), and consumer durable expenditures (PCDGCC96). Use the *frequency* setting to convert the federal funds rate data to "quarterly," and download the data.

    a. When did the last rate cycle begin and end? (*Note*: If a rate cycle is currently in progress, use the current period as the end.) Is this rate cycle a contractionary or an expansionary rate cycle?

    b. Calculate the percentage change in business fixed investment, residential (housing) investment, and consumer durable expenditures over this rate cycle.

    c. Based on your answers to parts (a) and (b), how effective was the traditional interest rate channel of monetary policy over this rate cycle?

2. **Real-time Data Analysis** As defined in Exercise 1, a "rate cycle" is a period of monetary policy during which the federal funds rate moves from its low point toward its high point, or vice versa, in response to business cycle conditions. Go to the St. Louis Federal Reserve FRED database, and find data on the federal funds rate (FEDFUNDS), bank reserves (TOTRESNS), bank deposits (TCDSL), commercial and industrial loans (BUSLOANS), real estate loans (REALLN), real business fixed investment (PNFIC96), and real residential investment (PRFIC1). Use the *frequency* setting to convert the federal funds rate, bank reserves, bank deposits, commercial and industrial loans, and real estate loans data to "quarterly," and download the data.

    a. When did the last rate cycle begin and end? (*Note*: If a rate cycle is currently in progress, use the current period as the end.) Is this rate cycle a contractionary or an expansionary rate cycle?

    b. Calculate the percentage change in bank deposits, bank lending, real business fixed investment, and real residential (housing) investment over this rate cycle.

    c. Based on your answers to parts (a) and (b), how effective was the bank lending channel of monetary policy over this rate cycle?

Glossary

activists   Economists who regard the self-correcting mechanism, which works through wage and price adjustment, as very slow because wages and prices are sticky. Activists see the need to pursue active policy to eliminate high unemployment when it develops.

adaptive expectations   Expectations for the value of a variable that are based on an average of past values of the variable.

AD/AS diagram   A graph that shows the aggregate demand curve, the short-run aggregate supply curve, and the macroeconomic equilibrium.

adverse selection   The problem created by asymmetric information prior to a financial transaction: it occurs when one party to a transaction has information about a hidden characteristic and takes economic advantage of this information by making an agreement (transaction) with less informed parties.

agency theory   The analysis of how asymmetric information problems affect economic behavior.

aggregate demand   The total quantity of output demanded in an economy at different price levels.

aggregate demand curve   The curve showing the relationship between the price level and the quantity of aggregate output demanded when the goods and money markets are in equilibrium.

aggregate income   The total income of factors of production (land, labor, capital) in an economy.

aggregate output   The total production of final goods and services in an economy.

aggregate output index   An index in which potential GDP is designated as 100 and all other values of real GDP are set relative to 100.

aggregate price level   The average price of goods and services in an economy.

aggregate quantity demanded   The total quantity of goods and services that households, businesses, governments, and foreigners want to buy (demand) at any given inflation rate during a specific period, such as a year.

aggregate supply curve   The curve showing the relationship between the quantity of output supplied and the price level.

anchor currency   A currency to which other countries' currencies are pegged.

"animal spirits"   Waves of optimism and pessimism that affect consumers' and businesses' willingness to spend.

appreciation   Increase in a currency's value.

arbitrage   Elimination of a riskless profit opportunity in a market.

asset   A financial claim or piece of property that is a store of value.

asset management   The acquisition of assets that have a low rate of default and the diversification of asset holdings to increase profits.

asset market approach   An approach to determining asset prices that makes use of stocks of assets rather than flows.

asset-price bubbles   Occur when asset prices in the stock and real estate markets are driven well above the assets' fundamental economic values by investor psychology.

asset transformation   The process of turning risky assets into safer assets, accomplished by creating and selling assets with risk characteristics that people are comfortable with and then using the funds acquired by selling these assets to purchase other assets that have far more risk.

asymmetric information   The unequal knowledge that each party to a transaction has about the other party.

automated teller machine (ATM)   An electronic machine that provides banking services 24 hours a day.

autonomous consumption expenditure   The amount of consumer expenditure that is independent of disposable income.

autonomous easing of monetary policy   The lowering of real interest rates at any given inflation rate.

autonomous investment   A component of planned investment spending that is completely exogenous and so is unexplained by the variables in a model.

autonomous net exports   The level of net exports that is treated as exogenous (outside the model).

autonomous spending   Exogenous spending that is unrelated to variables in the model such as output or the real interest rate.

autonomous tightening of monetary policy   The raising of real interest rates at any given inflation rate.

balance of payments   A bookkeeping system for recording all payments that have a direct bearing on the movement of funds between a country and other countries.

balance sheet   A balanced list of the assets and liabilities of a bank (or firm): Total assets equal total liabilities plus capital.

bank failure   A situation in which a bank cannot satisfy its obligations to pay its depositors and other creditors and so goes out of business.

bank holding companies   Companies that own one or more banks.

bank panic   The simultaneous failure of many banks, as during a financial crisis.

banks   Financial institutions (such as commercial banks, savings and loan associations, and credit unions) that accept money deposits and make loans.

Basel Accord   An agreement that required that banks hold as capital at least 8% of their risk-weighted assets.

Basel Committee on Banking Supervision   An international committee of bank supervisors that meets under the auspices of the Bank for International Settlements in Basel, Switzerland.

behavioral finance   A subfield of finance that applies concepts from other social sciences, such as anthropology, sociology, and particularly psychology, to explain the behavior of securities prices.

Board of Governors of the Federal Reserve System A board with seven governors (including the chair) that plays an essential role in decision making within the Federal Reserve System.

bond A debt security that promises to make periodic payments to the holder for a specified period of time.

boom See *expansion.*

borrowed reserves A bank's borrowings from the Fed.

branches A main bank's additional offices in which banking operations are conducted.

Bretton Woods system The international monetary system, in use from 1945 to 1971, in which exchange rates were fixed and the U.S. dollar was freely convertible into gold (by foreign governments and central banks only).

brokers Agents for investors; brokers match buyers with sellers.

bubble A situation in which the price of an asset differs from its fundamental market value.

budget deficit Government expenditures in excess of tax revenues.

budget surplus Tax revenues in excess of government expenditures.

business cycles The upward and downward movement of aggregate economic activity.

capital Wealth, either financial or physical in form, that is employed to produce more wealth.

capital adequacy management A bank's decisions about the amount of capital it should maintain and the best ways to acquire the needed capital.

capital controls Restrictions on the free movement of capital across borders.

capital market A financial market in which longer-term debt (generally with an original maturity of greater than one year) and equity instruments are traded.

capital mobility A situation in which foreigners can easily purchase a country's assets, and the country's residents can easily purchase foreign assets.

cash flows Cash payments to the holder of a security.

central bank The government agency that oversees a country's banking system and is responsible for the amount of money and credit supplied in the economy; in the United States, the Federal Reserve System.

collateral Property that is pledged to the lender to guarantee payment in the event that the borrower is unable to make debt payments.

commodity money Money made up of precious metals or another valuable commodity.

common stock A security that is a claim on the earnings and assets of a company.

community banks Small banks with local roots.

compensating balance The required minimum amount of funds that a firm receiving a loan must keep in a checking account at the lending bank.

conflicts of interest A manifestation of the moral hazard problem. Conflicts of interest occur when a financial institution provides multiple services with conflicting goals, a situation that may lead the firm to conceal important information or disseminate misleading information.

consol A perpetual bond with no maturity date and no repayment of principal, and that makes periodic, fixed coupon payments.

constant-money-growth-rate rule Monetary policy rule, advocated by monetarists, in which policymakers keep the money supply growing at a constant rate, regardless of the state of the economy.

constrained discretion A framework in which the general objectives and tactics of policymakers—but not specific actions—are committed to in advance; this framework imposes a conceptual structure and inherent discipline on policymakers without eliminating all flexibility.

consumer durable expenditure Spending by consumers on durable items such as automobiles and household appliances.

consumption Spending by consumers on nondurable goods and services (including services related to the ownership of homes and consumer durables).

consumption expenditure The total demand for consumer goods and services.

consumption function The relationship between disposable income and consumer expenditure.

conventional monetary policy tools The classic tools of monetary policy that the Federal Reserve uses to control the money supply and interest rates: open market operations, discount lending, and reserve requirements.

cost-push inflation Inflation that occurs when workers push to obtain higher wages.

cost-push shocks Price shocks that occur when workers push for wages that are higher than productivity gains, thereby driving up costs and inflation.

costly state verification Monitoring of a firm's activities, an expensive process in terms of both time and money.

coupon bond A credit market instrument that pays the owner a fixed interest payment every year until the maturity date, at which time a specified final amount is repaid.

coupon rate The dollar amount of the yearly coupon payment expressed as a percentage of the face value of a coupon bond.

credibility A commitment to policy actions that is believed by the public.

credit boom A lending spree in which financial institutions expand their lending at a rapid pace.

credit default swaps Financial insurance contracts that provide payments to holders of bonds if they default.

credit easing Altering the composition of the Fed's balance sheet in order to improve the functioning of particular segments of the credit markets.

credit rationing Occurs when a lender refuses to make loans even though borrowers are willing to pay the stated interest rate or even a higher rate, or when a lender restricts the sizes of loans so that the loans are made for less than the full amount sought.

credit risk The risk arising from the possibility that the borrower will default.

credit spread The difference between the interest rate on loans to households and businesses and the interest rate on completely safe assets that are sure to be paid off, such as U.S. Treasury securities.

credit view Monetary transmission mechanisms that operate through asymmetric information effects on credit markets.

credit-rating agencies Investment advisory firms that rate the quality of corporate and municipal bonds in terms of the probability of default.

currency Paper money (such as dollar bills) and coins.

currency board A monetary regime in which the domestic currency is backed 100% by a foreign currency (say, dollars) and in which the note-issuing authority, whether it be the central bank or the government, establishes a fixed exchange rate to this foreign currency and stands ready to exchange domestic currency at this rate whenever the public so requests.

current account An account that shows international transactions involving currently produced goods and services.

current account balance The sum of trade balance, net interest income, and transfers.

current yield An approximation of the yield to maturity; equal to the yearly coupon payment divided by the price of a coupon bond.

data lag The time it takes for policymakers to obtain data on the state of the economy.

dealers People who link buyers with sellers by buying and selling securities at stated prices.

debt deflation A situation in which a substantial decline in the price level sets in, leading to a further deterioration in firms' net worth because of the increased burden of indebtedness.

default A situation in which the party issuing a debt instrument is unable to make interest payments or pay off the amount owed when the instrument matures.

default-free bonds Bonds with no default risk, such as U.S. government bonds.

defensive open market operations Open market operations intended to offset movements in other factors that affect the monetary base (such as changes in Treasury deposits with the Fed or changes in float).

deleveraging Occurs when financial institutions cut back on their lending because they have less capital.

demand curve The curve depicting the relationship between quantity demanded and price when all other economic variables are held constant.

demand for money The quantity of money that people want to hold.

demand shocks Shocks that can shift the aggregate demand curve, including changes in the money supply, changes in

government expenditure and taxes, changes in net exports, changes in consumer and business spending, and financial frictions.

demand-pull inflation Inflation that results when policymakers pursue policies that shift the aggregate demand curve.

deposit facility The European Central Bank's standing facility, in which banks are paid a fixed interest rate 100 basis points below the target financing rate.

deposit outflows Losses of deposits when depositors make withdrawals or demand payment.

deposit rate ceiling A restriction on the maximum interest rate payable on deposits.

depreciation A decrease in a currency's value.

devaluation The resetting of the fixed value of a currency to a lower level.

discount bond A credit market instrument that is bought at a price below its face value and whose face value is repaid at the maturity date; it does not make any interest payments. Also called a *zero-coupon bond*.

discount loans A bank's borrowings from the Federal Reserve System; also known as *advances*.

discount rate The interest rate that the Federal Reserve charges banks on discount loans.

discount window The Federal Reserve facility at which discount loans are made to banks.

discretion When policymakers make decisions that they believe are the best policies to address a given situation at a given point in time.

disintermediation A reduction in the flow of funds into the banking system that causes the amount of financial intermediation to decline.

disposable income Total income available for spending, equal to aggregate income minus taxes.

diversification Investing in a collection (portfolio) of assets whose returns do not always move together, with the result that the overall risk is lower than that on the individual assets.

dividends Periodic payments made by equities to shareholders.

divine coincidence A phrase coined by Olivier Blanchard, referring to the situation in which a policy meant to stabilize inflation is also the best policy for stabilizing economic activity.

dollarization The adoption of a sound currency, like the U.S. dollar, as a country's money.

dominated assets Assets such as currency and checkable assets, which earn lower returns than other assets that are just as safe.

dual banking system The banking system in place in the United States, in which banks supervised by the federal government and banks supervised by the states operate side by side.

dual mandate A central bank mandate that features two co-equal objectives: price stability and maximum employment.

duration analysis A measurement of the sensitivity of the market value of a bank's assets and liabilities to changes in interest rates.

dynamic open market operations   Open market operations that are intended to change the level of reserves and the monetary base.

e-cash   Electronic money that is used on the Internet to purchase goods or services.

e-finance   A new means of delivering financial services electronically.

easing of monetary policy   The lowering of the federal funds rate.

economies of scale   The reduction in transaction costs per dollar of transaction as the size (scale) of transactions increases.

economies of scope   The ability to use one resource to provide many different products and services.

Edge Act corporation   A special subsidiary of a U.S. bank that is engaged primarily in international banking.

effectiveness lag   The time it takes for a policy to actually have an impact on the economy.

effective-lower-bound problem   A situation in which the central bank is unable to lower short-term interest rates much below zero.

efficient market hypothesis   The application of the theory of rational expectations to financial markets. Also called the *theory of efficient capital markets*.

electronic money (e-money)   Money that exists only in electronic form and substitutes for cash as well.

emerging market countries   Countries that have recently opened up to flows of goods, services, and capital from the rest of the world.

equation of exchange   The equation $MV = PY$, which relates nominal income to the quantity of money.

equities   Claims to share in the net income and assets of a corporation (such as common stock).

equity capital   See *net worth*.

equity multiplier (EM)   The amount of assets per dollar of equity capital.

Eurobonds   Bonds denominated in a currency other than that of the country in which they are sold.

Eurocurrencies   A variant of the Eurobond; foreign currencies deposited in banks outside the home country.

Eurodollars   U.S. dollars that are deposited in foreign banks outside the United States or in foreign branches of U.S. banks.

excess demand   A situation in which the quantity demanded is greater than the quantity supplied.

excess reserves   Reserves in excess of required reserves.

excess supply   A situation in which the quantity supplied is greater than the quantity demanded.

exchange rate   The price of one currency stated in terms of another currency.

exchange-rate peg   The fixing of the value of the domestic currency to the value of another currency, so that the exchange rate is fixed. Also called *exchange-rate targeting*.

exchange-rate targeting   See *exchange-rate peg*.

exchanges   Secondary markets in which buyers and sellers of securities (or their agents or brokers) meet in one central location to conduct trades.

exogenous   Independent of variables in the model.

expansion   A period when aggregate economic activity is increasing or expanding (also called a *boom*).

expectations theory   The proposition that the interest rate on a long-term bond will equal the average of the short-term interest rates that people expect to occur over the life of the long-term bond.

expected return   The return on an asset expected over the next period.

face value   A specified final amount paid to the owner of a coupon bond at the maturity date. Also called *par value*.

federal funds rate   The interest rate on overnight loans of deposits at the Federal Reserve.

Federal Open Market Committee (FOMC)   The committee that makes decisions regarding the conduct of open market operations; composed of the seven members of the Board of Governors of the Federal Reserve System, the president of the Federal Reserve Bank of New York, and the presidents of four other Federal Reserve banks (on a rotating basis).

Federal Reserve Banks   The 12 district banks in the Federal Reserve System.

Federal Reserve System (the Fed)   The central banking authority responsible for monetary policy in the United States.

fiat money   Paper currency decreed by a government as legal tender but not convertible into coins or precious metal.

financial account   Account that shows the international transactions that involve the purchase or sale of assets.

financial account balance   The difference between the net acquisition of financial assets and the net incurrence of financial liabilities.

financial crisis   A major disruption in financial markets that is characterized by sharp declines in asset prices and the failures of many financial and nonfinancial firms.

financial derivatives   Instruments that have payoffs that are linked to previously issued securities; used as risk reduction tools.

financial engineering   The process of researching and developing new financial products and services that will meet customer needs and also prove profitable.

financial frictions   Asymmetric information problems that act as barriers to the efficient allocation of capital.

financial innovation   The introduction of new types of financial products in an economy.

financial intermediaries   Institutions (such as banks, insurance companies, mutual funds, pension funds, and finance companies) that borrow funds from people who have saved and then make loans to others.

financial intermediation   The process of indirect finance whereby financial intermediaries link lender-savers with borrower-spenders.

financial liberalization   The elimination of restrictions on financial markets.

financial markets   Markets in which funds are transferred from people who have a surplus of available funds to people who have a shortage of available funds.

financial panic   The widespread collapse of financial markets and intermediaries in an economy.

financial supervision (prudential supervision)   The oversight of financial institutions and their operations.

fire sales   Forced, rapid sales of assets to raise needed funds.

fiscal policy   Policy that involves decisions about government spending and taxation.

Fisher effect   Describes the rise in interest rates that occurs when inflation is at the level of expected inflation; named after economist Irving Fisher.

fixed exchange rate regime   A regime in which central banks buy and sell their own currencies to keep their exchange rates fixed at a certain level.

fixed investment   Spending by firms on equipment (computers, airplanes) and structures (factories, office buildings), and planned spending on residential housing.

fixed-payment loan   A credit market instrument that provides the borrower with an amount of money that is repaid through fixed periodic (usually monthly) payments made over a set number of years.

float   Cash items in process of collection at the Fed minus deferred-availability cash items.

floating exchange rate regime   An exchange rate regime in which the values of currencies are allowed to fluctuate against one another.

foreign bonds   Bonds sold in a foreign country and denominated in that country's currency.

foreign exchange intervention   An international financial transaction in which a central bank buys or sells currency to influence foreign exchange rates.

foreign exchange market   The market in which exchange rates are determined.

foreign exchange rate   See *exchange rate*.

forward exchange rate   The exchange rate for a forward transaction.

forward guidance   A central bank commitment to a future path of the policy interest rate.

forward transaction   A transaction that involves the exchange of bank deposits denominated in different currencies at some specified future date.

free-rider problem   The problem that occurs when people who do not pay for information take advantage of the information that other people have paid for.

fully amortized loan   See *fixed-payment loan*.

fundamental economic values   Values of assets based on realistic expectations of their future income streams.

futures contract   A contract in which the seller agrees to provide a certain standardized commodity to the buyer on a specific future date at an agreed-on price.

gap analysis   A measurement of the sensitivity of bank profits to changes in interest rates, calculated by subtracting the amount of rate-sensitive liabilities from the amount of rate-sensitive assets.

generalized dividend model   A model in which the price of a stock is determined only by the present value of the dividends.

goal independence   The ability of the central bank to set the goals of monetary policy.

gold standard   A fixed exchange rate regime under which a currency is directly convertible into gold.

Gordon growth model   A simplified model used to compute the value of a stock by assuming constant dividend growth.

government budget constraint   The requirement that the government budget deficit must equal the sum of the change in the monetary base and the change in government bonds held by the public.

government purchases   Spending by all levels of government (federal, state, and local) on goods and services.

gross domestic product (GDP)   The value of all final goods and services produced in the economy during the course of a year.

haircuts   The excess amount of collateral above the amount of a loan.

hedge   To protect oneself against risk.

hierarchical mandate   A central bank mandate in which the goal of price stability comes first; once price stability has been achieved, other goals can be pursued.

high-powered money   The monetary base.

hyperinflation   An extreme inflation in which the inflation rate exceeds 50% per month.

implementation lag   The time it takes for policymakers to change policy instruments once they have decided on a new policy.

impossible trinity   Another term for the policy trilemma, in which a country cannot pursue the following three policies at the same time: free capital mobility, a fixed exchange rate, and an independent monetary policy.

incentive-compatible   Used to describe a contract in which the incentives of both parties to the contract are in alignment.

income   The flow of earnings.

inflation   The economic condition of a continually rising price level.

inflation gap   The difference between inflation and the inflation target.

inflation hedges   Alternative assets whose real returns are less affected than that of money when inflation varies.

inflation rate   The rate of change of the price level, usually measured as a percentage change per year.

inflation shocks   Shifts in inflation that are independent of the amount of slack in the economy or expected inflation.

inflation target   A central bank target for the inflation rate.

inflation targeting   A monetary policy strategy that involves the public announcement of a medium-term numerical target for inflation.

instrument independence The ability of the central bank to set monetary policy instruments.

interest parity condition The observation that the domestic interest rate equals the foreign interest rate plus the expected appreciation in the foreign currency.

interest rate The cost of borrowing or the price paid for the rental of funds (usually expressed as a percentage per year).

interest-rate risk The possible reduction in returns associated with changes in interest rates.

intermediate target Any of a number of variables, such as monetary aggregates or interest rates, that have a direct effect on employment and the price level and that the Fed seeks to influence.

intermediate-term With reference to a debt instrument, having a maturity of between one and ten years.

international banking facilities (IBFs) Banking establishments in the United States that can accept time deposits from foreigners but are not subject to reserve requirements or restrictions on interest payments.

International Monetary Fund (IMF) The international organization created by the Bretton Woods agreement whose objective it is to promote the growth of world trade by making loans to countries experiencing balance-of-payments difficulties.

international reserves Central bank holdings of assets denominated in foreign currencies.

inventory investment Spending by firms on additional holdings of raw materials, parts, and finished goods.

inverted yield curve A yield curve that is downward-sloping.

investment banks Firms that assist in the initial sale of securities in the primary market.

IS curve The relationship that describes the combinations of aggregate output and interest rates for which the total quantity of goods produced equals the total quantity demanded (goods market equilibrium).

junk bonds Bonds with ratings below Baa (or BBB) that have a high default risk.

Keynesian A follower of John Maynard Keynes who believes that movements in the price level and aggregate output are driven by changes not only in the money supply but also in government spending and fiscal policy, and who does not regard the economy as inherently stable.

legislative lag The time it takes to pass legislation to implement a particular policy.

lender of last resort A lender that provides reserves to financial institutions when no one else is willing to do so; such lending is usually done to prevent a financial crisis.

leverage cycle A feedback loop in which a boom in the issuance of credit leads to higher asset prices, which results in higher capital buffers at financial institutions, which supports further lending, which raises prices further, etc.; during the subsequent bust, asset prices fall, leading to cuts in lending, declines in asset prices, and so on.

leverage ratio A bank's capital divided by its assets.

liabilities IOUs or debts.

liability management The acquisition of funds at low cost to increase profits.

liquid Easily converted into cash.

liquidity The relative ease and speed with which an asset can be converted into cash.

liquidity management The decisions made by a bank in order to maintain enough liquid assets to meet the bank's obligations to depositors.

liquidity preference framework A model developed by John Maynard Keynes that predicts the equilibrium interest rate on the basis of the supply of and demand for money.

liquidity preference theory John Maynard Keynes's theory of the demand for money.

liquidity premium theory The theory that the interest rate on a long-term bond will equal an average of the short-term interest rates expected to occur over the life of the long-term bond, plus a positive term (liquidity) premium.

liquidity services Services that financial intermediaries provide to their customers to make it easier for the customers to conduct their transactions.

liquidity trap A case of ultrasensitivity of the demand for money to interest rates, in which conventional monetary policy has no direct effect on aggregate spending because a change in the money supply has no effect on the interest rate.

loan commitment A bank's commitment to provide a firm with loans (for a specified period of time) up to a given amount at an interest rate that is tied to some market interest rate.

loan sale The sale through a contract (also called a *secondary loan participation*) of all or part of the cash stream from a specific loan, thereby removing the loan from the bank's balance sheet.

long-term With reference to a debt instrument, having a maturity of ten years or more.

longer-term refinancing operations A category of open market operations conducted by the European Central Bank; similar to the Fed's outright purchases or sales of securities.

M1 A measure of money that includes currency, traveler's checks, and checkable deposits.

M2 A measure of money that includes M1 plus the following: money market deposit accounts, money market mutual fund shares, small-denomination time deposits, savings deposits, overnight repurchase agreements, and overnight Eurodollars.

macroeconometric models Models used to forecast the effects of policy on economic activity; macroeconometric models use collections of equations that describe statistical relationships among many economic variables.

macroeconomic equilibrium Occurs when all markets are simultaneously in equilibrium, at the point where the quantity of aggregate output demanded equals the quantity of aggregate output supplied.

macroprudential regulation Regulatory policy that affects the credit markets in the aggregate.

macroprudential supervision Supervision that focuses on the safety and soundness of the financial system in the aggregate.

main refinancing operations Weekly reverse transactions (purchases or sales of eligible assets through repurchase agreements or credit operations, with eligible assets as collateral) that are reversed within two weeks and are the primary monetary policy tool of the European Central Bank.

managed float regime An exchange rate regime in which countries attempt to influence their exchange rates by buying and selling currencies (also called a *dirty float*).

management of expectations A term coined by Michael Woodford that refers to a commitment by the Fed to keep the federal funds rate at zero for an extended period in order to generate a fall in the long-term interest rate.

marginal lending facility The European Central Bank's standing lending facility, in which banks can borrow (against eligible collateral) overnight loans from the national central bank at a rate that is 100 basis points above the target financing rate.

marginal lending rate The interest rate charged by the European Central Bank for borrowing at its marginal lending facility.

marginal propensity to consume The slope of the consumption function line that measures the change in consumer expenditure that results from an additional dollar of disposable income.

market equilibrium Occurs in an economy when the quantity that people are willing to buy (demand) is equal to the quantity that people are willing to sell (supply).

market fundamentals Items that have a direct impact on the future income streams of a security.

matched sale–purchase transaction An arrangement whereby the Fed sells securities and the buyer agrees to sell them back to the Fed in the near future; sometimes called a *reverse repo*.

maturity The time to the expiration date (maturity date) of a debt instrument.

medium of exchange Anything that is used to pay for goods and services.

microprudential supervision Supervision that focuses on the safety and soundness of individual financial institutions.

monetarist A follower of Milton Friedman who sees changes in the money supply as the primary source of movements in the price level and aggregate output, and who views the economy as inherently stable.

monetary aggregates The measures of the money supply (M1 and M2) used by the Federal Reserve System.

monetary base The sum of the Fed's monetary liabilities (currency in circulation and reserves) and the U.S. Treasury's monetary liabilities (Treasury currency in circulation, primarily coins).

monetary policy The management of the money supply and interest rates.

monetary policy (*MP*) curve The curve showing the relationship between the real interest rate set by the central bank and the inflation rate.

monetary theory The theory that relates changes in the quantity of money to changes in economic activity.

monetary (currency) union A group of countries that decides to adopt a common currency, thereby fixing the countries' exchange rates in relation to each other.

monetizing the debt A method of financing government spending whereby the government debt issued to finance government spending is removed from the hands of the public and is replaced by high-powered money instead. Also called *printing money*.

money (money supply) Anything that is generally accepted as payment for goods or services or in the repayment of debts.

money center banks Large banks in key financial centers (New York, Chicago, San Francisco).

money market A financial market in which only short-term debt instruments (generally those with original maturities of less than one year) are traded.

money multiplier A ratio that relates the change in the money supply to a given change in the monetary base.

money supply The quantity of money.

moral hazard The risk that occurs when an informed party takes a hidden (unobserved) action that harms the less-informed party.

mortgage-backed securities Securities that cheaply bundle and quantify the default risk of the underlying high-risk mortgages.

mortgages Loans to households or firms that wish to purchase housing, land, or other real structures; the structure or land itself serves as collateral for the loan.

multiple deposit creation The process whereby, when the Fed supplies the banking system with $1 of additional reserves, deposits increase by a multiple of this amount.

national banks Federally chartered banks.

natural rate of output See *potential output*.

natural rate of unemployment The rate of unemployment consistent with full employment; the rate at which the demand for labor equals the supply of labor.

net exports Net foreign spending on domestic goods and services, equal to exports minus imports.

net worth The difference between a firm's assets (what it owns or is owed) and its liabilities (what it owes). Also called *equity capital*.

nominal anchor A nominal variable, such as the inflation rate, an exchange rate, or the money supply, that monetary policymakers use to tie down the price level.

nominal GDP targeting A monetary policy strategy in which the central bank announces an objective of hitting a particular level of nominal GDP (real GDP times the price level) that grows over time.

nominal interest rate An interest rate that does not take inflation into account.

nonaccelerating inflation rate of unemployment (NAIRU) The rate of unemployment at which there is no tendency for inflation to change.

nonactivists Economists who believe that wages and prices are very flexible and so the self-correcting mechanism works very rapidly; nonactivists do not see the need to pursue policies to return the economy to full employment.

nonborrowed monetary base The monetary base minus discount loans (borrowed reserves).

nonconventional monetary policy tools The non-interest-rate tools used by central banks to stimulate the economy: liquidity provision, asset purchases, and commitments to future monetary policy actions.

nontradable Goods and services that are not traded across borders.

off-balance-sheet activities Bank activities that involve the trading of financial instruments and the generation of income from fees and loan sales, all of which affect bank profits but are not visible on bank balance sheets.

open market operations The Fed's buying or selling of bonds in the open market.

open market purchase A purchase of bonds by the Fed.

open market sale A sale of bonds by the Fed.

operating instrument A variable that is very responsive to the central bank's tools and indicates the stance of monetary policy (also called a *policy instrument*).

opportunity cost The amount of interest (expected return) sacrificed by not holding an alternative asset.

optimal forecast The best guess of future conditions, made using all available information.

originate-to-distribute model A business model in which a mortgage is originated by a separate party, typically a mortgage broker, and then distributed to an investor as an underlying asset in a security.

output gap The percentage difference between aggregate output and potential output.

over-the-counter (OTC) market A secondary market in which dealers at different locations who have an inventory of securities stand ready to buy and sell securities "over the counter" to anyone who comes to them and is willing to accept their prices.

overnight cash rate The interest rate for very-short-term interbank loans in the euro area.

par value See *face value*.

payment technology Methods of payment that include credit cards and electronic payments.

payments system The method of conducting transactions in an economy.

perpetuity See *consol*.

Phillips curve theory A theory suggesting that changes in inflation are influenced by the state of the economy relative to its production capacity, as well as other factors.

planned expenditure The total amount that households, businesses, the government, and foreigners want to spend on domestically produced goods and services.

planned investment spending Total planned spending by businesses on new physical capital (e.g., machines, computers, apartment buildings) plus planned spending on new homes.

policy instrument A variable that is very responsive to the central bank's tools and that indicates the stance of monetary policy (also called an *operating instrument*).

policy trilemma The idea that a country cannot pursue the following three policies at the same time: free capital mobility, a fixed exchange rate, and an independent monetary policy.

political business cycle A business cycle caused by expansionary policies that are pursued prior to an election.

portfolio A collection or group of assets.

potential GDP See *potential output*.

potential output The level of aggregate output produced when the economy is at full employment (the unemployment rate is at the at the natural rate of unemployment) and firms are on average producing at their long-run, profit maximizing level (also called the *natural rate of output*).

preferred habitat theory A theory that holds that the interest rate on a long-term bond is equal to an average of the short-term interest rates expected to occur over the life of the long-term bond, plus a positive term premium. Closely related to the liquidity premium theory.

present discounted value See *present value*.

present value Today's value of a payment to be received in the future, when the interest rate is i. Also called *present discounted value*.

price stability Low and stable inflation.

primary dealers Government securities dealers, operating out of private firms or commercial banks, with whom the Fed's open market desk trades.

primary market A financial market in which new issues of a security are sold to initial buyers.

principal–agent problem A moral hazard problem that occurs when the managers in control (the agents) act in their own interest rather than in the interest of the owners (the principals), due to differing sets of incentives.

printing money See *monetizing the debt*.

private-equity firm A financial intermediary that has a similar structure to a venture capital firm but instead of investing in new businesses, it buys the shares of *existing* corporations.

prudential supervision See *financial supervision*.

quantitative easing An expansion of the Federal Reserve's balance sheet.

quantity theory of money The theory that nominal income is determined solely by movements in the quantity of money.

quotas Restrictions on the quantity of foreign goods that can be imported.

random walk Movements of a variable whose future values cannot be predicted (are random) because, given today's value, the value of the variable is just as likely to fall as it is to rise.

rate of capital gain The change in a security's price relative to its initial purchase price.

rate of return See *return*.

rational expectations Expectations that reflect optimal forecasts (the best guess of future conditions) made using all available information.

real exchange rate The rate at which domestic goods can be exchanged for foreign goods; i.e., the price of domestic goods relative to foreign goods denominated in domestic currency.

real interest rate The interest rate adjusted for expected changes in the price level (inflation) so that it more accurately reflects the true cost of borrowing.

real money balances The quantity of money in real terms.

real terms Terms that reflect the actual amount of goods and services that one can buy.

recession A period during which aggregate output is declining.

recognition lag The time it takes for policymakers to feel confident about the signals the data are sending regarding the future course of the economy.

regulatory arbitrage A process in which banks keep on their books assets that are relatively risky, such as a loan to a company with a very low credit rating, while taking off their books low-risk assets, such as a loan to a company with a very high credit rating. In regulatory arbitrage, the risky and low-risk assets have the same risk-based capital requirements.

repurchase agreement (repo) An arrangement whereby the Fed or another party purchases securities with the understanding that the seller will repurchase them in a short period of time, usually less than a week.

required reserve ratio The fraction of deposits that the Fed requires be kept as reserves.

required reserves Reserves that are held to meet the Fed's requirement that for every dollar of deposits at a bank, a certain fraction must be kept as reserves.

reserve currency A currency, such as the U.S. dollar, that is used by other countries to denominate the assets they hold as international reserves.

reserve requirements Regulations that oblige depository institutions to keep a certain fraction of their deposits in accounts with the Fed.

reserves Banks' holding of deposits in accounts with the Fed plus currency that is physically held by banks (vault cash).

residual claimant A stockholder's right to receive whatever remains after all other claims against a firm's assets have been satisfied.

restrictive covenants Provisions that restrict and specify certain activities that a borrower can engage in.

return The payments to the owner of a security plus the change in the security's value, expressed as a fraction of its purchase price. More precisely called the *rate of return*.

return on assets (ROA) Net profit after taxes per dollar of assets.

return on equity (ROE) Net profit after taxes per dollar of equity capital.

revaluation The resetting of the fixed value of a currency at a higher level.

reverse transactions Purchases or sales of eligible assets by the European Central Bank under repurchase agreements or credit operations, with eligible assets as collateral, that are reversed within two weeks.

risk The degree of uncertainty associated with the return on an asset.

risk premium The spread between the interest rate on bonds with default risk and the interest rate on default-free bonds.

risk sharing The process of creating and selling assets with risk characteristics that people are comfortable with and then using the funds acquired by selling these assets to purchase other assets that have far more risk.

risk structure of interest rates The relationships among the interest rates on various bonds with the same term to maturity.

rules Binding plans that specify how policy will respond (or not respond) to particular data, such as data on unemployment and inflation.

secondary market A financial market in which securities that have previously been issued (and are thus secondhand) can be resold.

secondary reserves Short-term U.S. government and agency securities held by banks.

secured debt Debt guaranteed by collateral.

securitization The process of transforming illiquid financial assets into marketable capital market instruments.

security A claim on a borrower's future income that is sold by the borrower to the lender. Also called a *financial instrument*.

segmented markets theory A theory of term structure that sees the markets for different-maturity bonds as completely separated and segmented, so that the interest rate on bonds of a given maturity is determined solely by supply of and demand for bonds of that maturity.

seignorage The revenue that a government receives by issuing money.

self-correcting mechanism A characteristic of the economy that causes output to return eventually to the natural rate level, regardless of where it lies initially.

shadow banking system A system in which bank lending is replaced by lending via the securities market.

short sales Borrowing stock from brokers and then selling the stock in the market, with the hope that a profit will be earned by buying the stock back again ("covering the short") after it has fallen in price.

short-term With reference to a debt instrument, having a maturity of one year or less.

simple deposit multiplier The multiple increase in deposits generated by an increase in the banking system's reserves. The behavior of depositors and banks plays no role in this simple model.

simple loan A credit market instrument that provides the borrower with an amount of funds that must be repaid to the lender at the maturity date, along with an additional payment (interest).

smart card A stored-value card that contains a computer chip that allows the card to be loaded with digital cash from the owner's bank account whenever needed.

speculative attack Involves massive sales of a weak currency or purchases of a strong currency that can cause a sharp change in the exchange rate.

spot exchange rate The exchange rate for a spot transaction.

spot transaction The predominant type of exchange rate transaction, involving the immediate exchange of bank deposits denominated in different currencies.

stagflation A situation of rising inflation but a falling level of aggregate output.

standing lending facility A lending facility in which healthy banks are allowed to borrow all they want from a central bank.

state banks State-chartered banks.

state-owned banks Banks that are owned by governments.

sterilized foreign exchange intervention A foreign exchange intervention that is accompanied by an offsetting open market operation that leaves the monetary base unchanged.

sticky When wages and prices are slow to adjust.

stock A security that is a claim on the earnings and assets of a company.

stockholders Those who hold stock in a corporation.

store of value A repository of purchasing power over time.

stress tests Tests used by financial institutions to calculate potential losses and capital needs under fictional dire scenarios.

structured credit products Securities that are derived from the cash flows of underlying assets and are tailored to have particular risk characteristics that appeal to investors with different preferences.

subprime mortgages Mortgages made to borrowers with less-than-stellar credit records.

superregional banks Bank holding companies that are similar in size to money center banks but whose headquarters are not based in one of the money center cities (New York, Chicago, San Francisco).

supply curve A curve depicting the relationship between quantity supplied and price when all other economic variables are held constant.

supply shock Any change in technology or the supply of raw materials that can shift the aggregate supply curve.

sweep account An arrangement whereby any balances above a certain amount that remain in a corporation's checking account at the end of the business day are "swept out" of the account and invested in overnight repos that pay the corporation interest.

systemically important financial institutions (SIFIs) Firms that are designated by the Financial Stability Oversight Council as systemically important and so are subject to additional oversight and regulation by the Federal Reserve.

T-account A simplified balance sheet with lines in the form of a T that lists only the changes that occur in balance sheet items starting from some initial balance sheet position.

target financing rate The European Central Bank's target for the overnight cash rate, the interest rate for very-short-term interbank loans in the euro area.

tariffs Taxes on imported goods.

Taylor principle The principle that the monetary authorities should raise nominal interest rates by more than the increase in the inflation rate.

Taylor rule Economist John Taylor's monetary policy rule that explains how the federal funds rate target is set.

term structure of interest rates The relationships among interest rates on bonds with different terms to maturity.

theory of efficient capital markets See *efficient market hypothesis.*

theory of portfolio choice A theory that outlines how much of an asset people will want to hold in their portfolios, as determined by wealth, expected returns, risk, and liquidity.

theory of purchasing power parity (PPP) The theory that exchange rates between any two currencies will adjust to reflect changes in the price levels of the two countries.

thrift institutions (thrifts) Savings and loan associations, mutual savings banks, and credit unions.

tightening of monetary policy An increase in the federal funds rate.

time-inconsistency problem The problem that occurs when monetary policymakers conduct monetary policy in a discretionary way and pursue expansionary policies that are attractive in the short run but lead to poor long-run outcomes.

too-big-to-fail problem Problem in which regulators are reluctant to close down large financial institutions because doing so might precipitate a financial crisis.

trade balance on goods and services (trade balance) The difference between merchandise exports and imports.

transaction costs The time and money spent trying to exchange financial assets, goods, or services.

transmission mechanisms of monetary policy The channels through which the money supply affects economic activity.

Troubled Asset Relief Plan (TARP) A provision of the Bush administration's Economic Recovery Act of 2008 that authorized the Treasury to spend $700 billion on purchases of subprime mortgage assets from troubled financial institutions or on injections of capital into these institutions.

underwrite To purchase securities from a corporation at a predetermined price and then resell them in the market.

underwriting Guaranteeing the price for a corporation's securities and then selling them to the public.

unemployment rate The percentage of the labor force not working.

unexploited profit opportunity A situation in which an investor can earn a higher-than-normal return.

unit of account Anything used to measure value in an economy.

unsecured debt   Debt not guaranteed by collateral.

unsterilized foreign exchange intervention   A foreign exchange intervention in which a central bank allows the purchase or sale of domestic currency to affect the monetary base.

value at risk (VaR)   Calculations that measure the size of the loss on a trading portfolio that might happen 1% of the time over a short period—say, 2 weeks.

vault cash   Currency that is physically held by banks and stored in vaults overnight.

velocity of money   The rate of turnover of money; the average number of times per year that a dollar is spent in buying the total amount of final goods and services produced in the economy.

venture capital firm   A financial intermediary that pools the resources of its partners and uses the funds to help entrepreneurs start up new businesses.

virtual bank   A bank that has no building but rather exists only in cyberspace.

wealth   All resources owned by an individual, including all assets.

World Bank   The International Bank for Reconstruction and Development, an international organization that provides long-term loans to assist developing countries in building dams, roads, and other physical capital that will contribute to their economic development.

World Trade Organization (WTO)   An organization headquartered in Geneva, Switzerland, that monitors rules for the conduct of trade between countries (tariffs and quotas).

yield curve   A plot of the interest rates on particular types of bonds with different terms to maturity.

yield to maturity   The interest rate that equates the present value of payments received from a credit market instrument with its value today.

zero-coupon bond   See *discount bond*.

Index

Note: Page numbers followed by *b* refer to boxed material; those followed by *f* refer to figures; those followed by n refer to footnotes; and those followed by *t* refer to tables.

A

Abe, Shinzo, 570
Accelerationist Phillips curve, 546
Account, money as unit of, 51
Accountability, increased by inflation targeting, 378
Activists, 555–556
Activities, financial intermediary restrictions on, 44
Actual expenditure, 472
AD/AS (aggregate demand–aggregate supply) model, 472
Adaptive expectations, 147
  modern Phillips curve with, 546
Adaptive expectations hypothesis, 147
Adjustable-rate mortgages, 239
Advances, 190, 320
Adverse selection, 36–37, 169–175
  with government safety nets, 219
  influence on financial structure, 169–175
  in loan markets. *See* Credit risk
  tools to solve problems of, 171–175
After-tax real interest rate, 81
Agency theory, 169
Aggregate demand, 472, 510–513
  components of, 473–478, 510–511
  planned expenditure and, 472–473

Aggregate demand–aggregate supply (*AD/AS*) model, 472
  AD/AS analysis of the Covid-19 recession, 535–537, 537*f*
Aggregate demand and supply analysis, 506–540. *See also* Aggregate demand curve; Aggregate supply curve; Short-run aggregate supply curve
  business cycles and, 506–509, 507*f*, 508*f*
  conclusions from, 533–537
  of coronavirus recession, 535–537, 537*f*
  equilibrium in. *See* Macroeconomic equilibrium
  of Great Recession, 534–535, 535*f*, 536*f*
  inflation and, 509, 509*f*
  using an aggregate output index, 523–524
Aggregate demand curve, 496–502
  derivation of, 511, 512*f*
  deriving with effective lower bound, 564, 565*f*, 566
  factors shifting, 499–502, 511–515, 513*f*, 514*t*
  graphical derivation of, 497, 497*b*, 498*f*
  shifts of, factors causing, 499–502, 511–515, 513*f*, 514*t*
Aggregate demand shocks, 527–530, 528*f*
  credibility and, 583–585, 584*f*
  monetary policy response to, 550–551, 551*f*, 552*f*
Aggregate income, 19
Aggregate output, 7–8, 506
  in financial news, 510*b*
  GDP as measure of. *See* Gross domestic product (GDP)

Aggregate output indexes, 523–524
  AD/AS diagram with, 524, 525*f*
  calculating, 524
Aggregate price level, 8, 20
Aggregate quantity demanded, 510–511
Aggregate supply curve, 515–518
  long-run, 515–516, 516*f*, 518, 519*f*
  shifts of, 518–521
  short-run. *See* Short-run aggregate supply curve
Aggregate supply shocks, 530–532, 531*f*
  credibility and, 585–586, 585*f*, 587*f*
Agricultural Bank of China, 263*t*
AIG
  credit default swaps and, 275
  failure of, 218, 220, 270
  Fed loans to, 281, 358, 359*b*
Airline industry, losses suffered by, 118
Akerlof, George, 169, 170n
ALM (asset-liability management) committee, 199
American Airlines, 118
American Express, 240
American Recovery and Reinvestment Act of 2009, 282, 558*b*
AMLF (Asset-Backed Commercial Paper Money Market Mutual Fund Liquidity Facility), 359*b*
Anchor country, 443
Anchor currencies, 431
Animal spirits, 476
Anti-inflation policy, credibility and, 588–590, 588*f*
Applications
  Abenomics and the shift in Japanese monetary policy in 2013, 570–572, 572*f*

Applications (*Cont.*)

AD/AS analysis of the Great Recession of 2007–2009, 534

applying the monetary policy lessons to Japan's two lost decades, 606–607

autonomous monetary easing during the global financial and coronavirus crises, 495–496

bank capital management strategies, 202

Big Mac index, 407*b*–409*b*, 408*t*

bond interest rates and Trump tax cuts, 124–125

bond price for a coupon bond, 71–72

Brexit and the British pound, 421–422, 422*f*

China as counterexample to the importance of financial development, 183–184

Chinese accumulation of $4 trillion of international reserves, 438

coronavirus pandemic and Baa-Treasury spread, 122

coronavirus pandemic and possibility of a financial crisis, 283

coronavirus stock market crash of 2020, 146

credit crunch caused by a capital crunch during the global financial crisis, 203

equilibrium exchange rate and changes in the interest rate, 418–420, 419*f*

equilibrium interest rate changes due to changes in income, price level, or money supply, 106, 106*t*

Fiscal stimulus package of 2009, 484–485

Fisher effect, 98–99, 98*f*, 99*f*

foreign exchange crisis of September 1992, 435–436, 435*f*

global financial crisis and the dollar, 420–421, 420*f*

Great Depression, 272–274, 272*f*, 273*f*

Great Inflation, 562–563, 563*f*

Great Recession, 604*b*

how the Fed's operating procedures limit fluctuations in the federal funds rate, 349*b*–350*b*, 350*f*

interest rate calculation, 81

interest rate changes due to a business cycle expansion, 100–101, 100*f*, 101*t*

interest-rate risk management strategies, 209

jackpot valuation, 67

low interest rates following the global financial crisis, 101–102

monetary policy and stock prices, 146

money supply growth rate and interest rates, 110–112, 111*f*, 112*f*

negative supply shocks, 1973-1975 and 1978-1980, 532, 533*f*

nonconventional monetary policy and quantitative easing, 567–570

oil price shocks, 586, 587*f*

practical guide to investing in the stock market, 153–156

quantitative easing and the money supply during the global financial and coronavirus crises, 337*b*–339*b*, 338*f*

quantity theory of money, 458, 459*f*, 460*f*

rise in the federal funds rate target, 2004-2006 and 2015-2019, 495, 495*f*

simple present value, 66

stock market crashes and efficient market hypothesis and efficiency of financial markets, 157

term structure of interest rates, 577–578

Trump tax cuts and bone interest rates, 124–125

Vietnam War buildup, 482–483, 483*f*

Volcker disinflation, 1980-1986, 529–530, 530*f*

yearly payment on a fixed-payment loan, 70

yield curve interpretation, 135–137, 136*f*

yield to maturity for a coupon bond, 71–72

yield to maturity on a discount bond, 74

yield to maturity on a fixed-payment loan, 70

yield to maturity on a perpetuity, 73–74

yield to maturity on a simple loan, 68–69

Zimbabwean hyperinflation, 463*b*

Appreciation, 403

APR (annual percentage rate), 227

Arbitrage, 151
regulatory, 222

Argentina
currency board in, 447, 448*b*
hyperinflation in, 369

ARM (adjustable rate mortgage) rate, 30*b*

Asset-Backed Commercial Paper Money Market Mutual Fund Liquidity Facility (AMLF), 359*b*

Asset demand, determinants of, 86–88

Asset-liability management (ALM) committee, 199

Asset management, 195

Asset market approach, 92

Asset-price bubbles, 270, 387–391
credit-driven, 387
debate over whether central bubbles should try to pop, 388–391
driven solely by irrational exuberance, 387, 388
in housing market, 276–278, 276*f*, 277*b*
macroprudential policies and, 389–390

monetary policy and, 390–391
Asset prices, decline in, Great Recession and, 278–279, 279*f*
Asset transformation, 36, 192
Assets, 3
  on bank balance sheet, 191–192
  decline in income advantages on, 248
  demand for, determinants of, 86–88
  demand for, domestic, 412–416
  dominated, 466
  on Fed balance sheet, 320
  financial intermediary restrictions on, 44
  large-scale purchases of, as monetary policy tool, 358, 360, 361*f*
  purchases of, quantitative easing and, 569
  restrictions on holdings of, 221
  return on, bank capital adequacy management and, 201
Asso, Pier Francesco, 396*b*
Asymmetric information, 36–38, 169. *See also* Adverse selection; Moral hazard
  credit-rating agencies and, 276
  as rationale for financial regulation, 216–221
  regulation to reduce, 42
ATMs (automated teller machines), 241, 251–252
ATS (automatic transfer from savings) accounts, 58
AT&T, 240
Australia
  British-style universal banking system in, 258
  decline of traditional banking in, 249
  inflation targeting in, 375, 379
Auto loans, 30*b*
Automated teller machines (ATMs), 241, 251–252
Automatic transfer from savings (ATS) accounts, 58

Autonomous consumption expenditure, 474
  changes in, shifts of *IS* curve and, 485
  shifts of aggregate demand curve and, 513
Autonomous easing of monetary policy, 494, 494*f*, 495–496
Autonomous investment, 475
  changes in, shifts of *IS* curve and, 485
  shifts of aggregate demand curve and, 515
Autonomous monetary policy, shifts of aggregate demand curve and, 512
Autonomous net exports, 477
  changes in, shifts of *IS* curve and, 486
  shifts of aggregate demand curve and, 513
Autonomous spending, changes in, shifts of *IS* curve and, 485–486
Autonomous tightening of monetary policy, 494, 494*f*

B
Backward-looking expectations, modern Phillips curve with, 546
Bahamas, as tax haven, 261
Balance of payments
  current account and, 430, 431*b*
  financial account and, 430–431
  sterilized, 429–431
Balance sheet channel, monetary transmission and, 601
Balance sheets
  of a bank. *See* Bank balance sheet
  consumer, Great Depression and, 603*b*
  of Fed, 319–320
Banc One, 253
Bank Act of 1946 (England), 314
Bank Americard, 240
Bank balance sheet, 188–192, 189*t*

assets on, 191–192
  deterioration of, Great Recession and, 278
  liabilities on, 188–190
Bank capital, 190
  requirements for, 202, 222, 287
Bank commercial loans, 29*t*, 31
Bank deposits, negative interest rates on, as monetary policy tool, 363–364
Bank failures
  financial regulation to prevent, 216–217
  during Great Depression, 237, 354
  during 1980s and 1990s, 253, 256
  prevention by bank capital, 200
Bank for International Settlements, 212, 222
Bank holding companies, 238
  growth of, 251
  resolution authority over, 285–286
Bank Holding Company Act and Douglas Amendment of 1956, 230*t*
Bank holiday, 272–273
Bank lending channel, monetary transmission and, 600–601
Bank of America, 250*t*, 253, 263*t*
  entry into virtual banking market, 241
  merger with NationsBank, 254
  sale of Merrill Lynch to, 258*b*, 280
Bank of Canada, 314
  hierarchical mandates and, 373
Bank of China, 263*t*
Bank of England, 314–315
  foreign exchange crisis of 1992 and, 436
  hierarchical mandates and, 373
Bank of Japan, 315
Bank of North America, 235
Bank of the United States, First, 236
  failure of, 270

Bank of the United States, Second, 236, 294–295
Bank panics, 217
  during Great Depression, 272–273
Banking
  correspondent, 191
  electronic, 241
  home, 241
  international. *See* International banking
  interstate, breakdown of barriers to, 253
  reasons to study, 5–7, 14
  universal, 257–258
Banking Act of 1933, 228, 229*t*
Banking Act of 1935, 229*t*
Banking crises, 270–271
Banking industry, 235–266
  consolidation in, 252–256, 252*f*
  financial innovation and. *See* Financial innovation
  historical development of, 235–238, 236*f*
  international. *See* International banking
  separation of other financial service industries from, 256–258
  structure of, 249–252, 250*t*, 255*b*
  thrift industry and, 258–260
  U.S., future of, 254–255
Banking system
  dual, 237
  multiple deposit creation and, 326–329, 328*t*
  shadow. *See* Shadow banking system
Banknotes, 49, 237
Banks, 6, 38–40, 39*t*, 40*t*, 188–215
  asset management by, 195, 198–199
  balance sheet of. *See* Bank balance sheet
  branches of, 241
  capital adequacy management by, 195, 200–202

central. *See* Central banks
commercial, 235, 236–237
community, 255
credit crunch and, 203
credit risk and. *See* Credit risk
failures of. *See* Bank failures
Fed as lender of last resort and, 353–354, 355*b*, 356
interest-rate risk and, 195, 207–209
investment. *See* Investment banks
lending to, by European Central Bank, 365
liability management by, 195, 199
liquidity management and role of reserves and, 195–198
money center, 199
money supply process and, 318
national, 237
off-balance sheet activities of. *See* Off-balance-sheet activities
regulation of. *See* Financial regulation
state, 237
state-owned, 183
superregional, 253
too-big-to-fail, 219–220, 287
virtual, 241
Barings Bank, 210, 211*b*, 212
Barro, Robert, 576n
Barter economy, 50
Basel Accords, 222, 223*b*, 226, 262
Basel Committee on Banking Supervision, 222
Basic gap analysis, 208
Baumol, William J., 465n
Bear Stearns, 218, 220, 258*b*, 270
  Fed loan to, 358
  sale to J.P. Morgan, 279–280
Behavioral finance, 157–158
Beige book, 303*b*
Belgium, government intervention during 2007–2009 financial crisis in, 282*b*
Belize, policy trilemma and, 437
Bent, Bruce, 245, 246*b*, 246

Bernanke, Ben, 377n, 581*b*
  appointment as Fed chair, 306, 306n
  on collateralized debt obligations, 275*b*
  on constrained discretion, 379, 582
  on credit easing, 569
  on Fed communication, 311*b*
  on housing price bubble, 277*b*
  inflation targeting under, 382, 383*b*
  on interest rates as monetary transmission mechanism, 597
  monetary policy strategy under, 380, 381
  style as Fed chair, 304, 304*b*–305*b*
Big Mac index, 407–409, 408*t*
Bitcoin, 55–56
Bitcoin Cash, 55
Black Monday, 4, 157, 355*b*
Blanchard, Olivier
  on divine coincidence, 551
  on inflation targeting, 385
Blue book, 303*b*
BNP Paribas, 263*t*, 279
Board of Governors of the Federal Reserve System, 295, 300
  chairs of, 303–304, 304*b*–305*b*
Bolivia, hyperinflation in, 589*b*
Bond markets, 3
  demand in, 89–90, 92
  equilibrium in, 91–92
  international, 32–33
  lemons in, 170
  supply in, 82, 90–91, 90*f*
Bond ratings, 120–121, 120*t*
Bonds, 3, 31
  convertible, 31
  corporate. *See* Corporate bonds
  coupon. *See* Coupon bonds
  default-free, 118
  default risk of, 118–121, 119*f*, 120*t*
  definition of, 3n
  discount (zero-coupon). *See* Discount bonds

eurobonds. *See* Eurobonds
foreign, 32–33
government. *See* U.S. Treasury bonds
income taxes and, 123, 124–125, 124*f*
junk, 121, 241–242
municipal. *See* Municipal bonds
prices of, for a coupon bond, 71–74, 72*t*
risk structure of interest rates and. *See* Risk structure of interest rates
term structure of interest rates and. *See* Term structure of interest rates
Booms, 506
Borrowed reserves (BR), 320, 324, 345
changes in, money supply and, 331
Borrowings
on bank balance sheet, 190
from the Fed, 190, 320
Bosnia, currency board in, 447
BR (borrowed reserves), 320, 324, 345
Branching restrictions, 251–252
Brazil
hyperinflation in, 369
inflation targeting in, 375
Breaking the buck, 245*b*
Bretton Woods system, 432–433
Brexit, 402, 421–422, 422*f*
British-style universal banking system, 258
Brokers, 26
Brown, Gordon, 314
Brown, Henry, 245
Bubbles, 156. *See also* Asset-price bubbles
Budget constraint, government, 460–462
Budget deficits, 11
government budget constraint and, 461
supply of bonds and, 96*t*, 97–98
Budget surpluses, 11
Bulgaria, currency board in, 447

Bull markets, 4
Bundesbank
foreign exchange crisis of 1992 and, 435–436, 435*f*
intervention in foreign exchange market, 442
Bundlers, 243
Bureaucratic behavior, theory of, 310–311
Burns, Arthur, 304, 307*b*, 580*b*, 589
Bush, George H. W., 306n, 307*b*
Bush, George W., 306n, 307*b*
Business cycle expansions, 506
interest rate changes due to, 100–101, 100*f*, 101*f*
Business cycles, 7–8, 8*f*, 506–509, 508*f*
political, 308, 580, 580*b*
unemployment rate and, 508–509
yield curve as forecasting tool for, 135*b*
Business expectations, planned investment spending and, 475–476

C
CAC 40 index, 34*b*
Call reports, 224
Calling in loans, 198
CAMELS ratings, 225, 226
Canada
British-style universal banking system in, 258
inflation targeting in, 375, 376*f*, 377, 379
Capital, 24
bank. *See* Bank capital
equity. *See* Net worth
mobility of, perfect, 434
Capital account, balance on, 430n
Capital adequacy management, 195, 200–202
capital requirements and, 202
prevention of bank failure and, 200
returns to equity holders and, 200–201
strategies for, 202

trade-off between safety and returns to equity holders and, 201–202
Capital controls, 261, 438, 440–441
on capital inflows, 440–441
on capital outflows, 440
Capital markets, 27
instruments in, 29–31, 29*t*
interest rates in, 30*b*
U. S. loss of international dominance and, 32*b*
Capital One Financial Corp., 250*t*
Car loans, 30*b*
CARES (Coronavirus Aid, Relief, and Economic Security) Act, 283
Carney, Mark, 315
Carte Blanche, 240
Carter, Jimmy, 306n, 591*b*
Cash flow channel, monetary transmission and, 601–602
Cash flows, 64, 142
Cash items in process of collection, 191
Cashless society, 55*b*
Cayman Islands, 261
CDOs. *See* Collateralized debt obligations
CDs. *See* Certificates of deposit
Cease and desist orders, 225
CEBA (Competitive Equality in Banking Act) of 1987, 230*b*
Central Bank Liquidity Swaps, 359*b*
Central banks, 10, 236, 237. *See also* specific banks
asset-price bubbles and. *See* Asset-price bubbles
behavior of, 310–311
of Canada, 314, 373
of China, 263*t*
credibility of. *See* Credibility
of England. *See* Bank of England
European. *See* European Central Bank (ECB)
of Germany. *See* Bundesbank
global independence and macroeconomic performance of, 310

Central banks (*Cont.*)
of Japan, 315
monetary policy and. *See*
Monetary policy
money supply process and,
318
of New Zealand, 373
trend toward independence
of, 315
of United States. *See* Federal
Reserve System (Fed)
of Zimbabwe, 463
Certificates of deposit (CDs),
27*t*, 28, 190
negotiable, 199
Ceteris paribus assumption, 89,
106, 529n
CFTC (Commodities Futures
Trading Commission), 43*t*
Chancellor of the Exchequer, 314
Checkable deposits, 189–190
other, in M1 monetary aggregate, 57–58
Checks, 53–54
Chicago Board of Trade, 239
Chile, inflation targeting in, 375
China
financial development of,
183–184
pegging of exchange rate to
U.S. dollar, 438
policy trilemma and, 437–438
China Construction Bank, 263*t*
Cirrus, 252
Citibank, 436
Citicorp, 204
merger with Travelers Group,
257
Citigroup, 12, 172*b*, 250*t*
Clinton, Bill, 306n, 307*b*
Collateral, 28, 167
credit risk management and,
206
haircuts and, 278
to reduce adverse selection, 174
to reduce moral hazard,
178–179
tyranny of, 182*b*
Collateralized debt obligations
(CDOs), 274, 275*b*

bank balance sheets and, 278
Commercial banks, 39
assets and liabilities of, 39*t*, 40*t*
branching restrictions and,
251–252
consolidation of, 252–256,
252*f*
declining importance of, 246,
247*f*
historical development of,
235, 236–237
industry structure and, 249–
252, 250*t*
pursuit of off-balance-sheet
activities by, 248–249
Commercial paper, 27*t*, 28, 242
Commercial Paper Funding
Facility (CPFF), 359*b*
Commodities Futures Trading
Commission (CFTC), 43*t*
Commodity money, 53
Common stock, 3. *See also*
Stock *entries*
Community banks, 255
Community Reinvestment Act
(CRA) of 1974, 227, 301*b*
Compensating balances, credit
risk management and, 206
Competition
financial intermediary
restrictions on, 44
restrictions on, 227–228
Competitive Equality in Bank-
ing Act (CEBA) of 1987,
230*b*
Conflicts of interest, 37
Consolidation, 252–256, 252*f*
Constant-money-growth-rate
rule, 579
Constrained discretion, 379,
581–582
Consumer balance sheets, Great
Depression and, 603*b*
Consumer durable expendi-
tures, 596
Consumer expenditure, 599
Consumer Financial Protection
Bureau, 285
opposition of, 288
Consumer loans, 29*t*, 31

Consumer price index (CPI), 20
in financial news, 510*b*
Consumer protection, 227
Consumer Protection Act of
1969, 227
Consumer Reports, 173
Consumption expenditure, 599
as aggregate demand component, 473–474, 510
autonomous. *See* Autonomous
consumption expenditure
exogenous, 474
Consumption function, 473–474
Contagion effect, 217
Continental Illinois, 219–220
Contractual savings institutions,
39*t*, 40–41, 40*t*
Controllability, as criterion for
choosing a policy instru-
ment, 393
Conventional monetary policy
tools, 350–356
discount policy as, 353, 355*b*
interest on excess reserves as,
356
lender of last resort as,
353–354, 356
open market operations as, 351
reserve requirements as, 356
Convertible bonds, 31
Coronavirus Aid, Relief,
and Economic Security
(CARES) Act, 283
Coronavirus pandemic
aggregate demand and supply
analysis of, 535–537, 537*f*
autonomous monetary easing
during, 495–496
credit spreads during, 122, 283
economic impact of, 283
Fed lending facilities during,
359*b*–360*b*
interest rates and, 101
quantitative easing and
money supply during, 337,
338*f*, 339
stock market and, 4, 146
unemployment due to, 472
Corporate bonds, 29*t*, 31
convertible, 31

default risk of, 118–120, 119*f*
during Great Depression, 121
interest rates on, 117
liquidity of, 122–123
Corrective action, for bank capital problems, 224
Correspondent banking, 191
Corrigan, E. Gerald, 355*b*
Cost-push inflation, 559, 560*f*
demand-pull inflation vs., 562
Cost-push shocks, 517
Costly state verification, 176
Coupon bonds, 67
price and yield to maturity for, 71–74, 72*t*
Coupon rate, 67
Covid-19 pandemic. *See* Coronavirus pandemic
CPFF (Commercial Paper Funding Facility), 359*b*
CPI. *See* Consumer price index
CRA (Community Reinvestment Act) of 1974, 227, 301*b*
Crawling target (crawling peg), 443
Credibility, 582–590
aggregate demand shocks and, 583–585, 584*f*
aggregate supply shocks and, 585–586, 585*f*, 587*f*
anti-inflation policy and, 588–590, 588*f*, 589*b*
of central bank, establishing, 590–592
of nominal anchor, benefits of, 582–583
Credit
asset bubbles driven by, 387
seasonal, 353
secondary, 353
Credit Agricole Group, 263*t*
Credit booms, 268–270
Credit cards, 240
Credit crunches, capital crunch causing, 203
Credit default swaps, 275
Credit easing, 569
quantitative easing vs., 360–362
Credit market instruments, 67–68

Credit-rating agencies, 120–121, 120*t*, 121*b*
asymmetric information and, 276
conflicts of interest at, global financial crisis and, 120
Great Recession and, 279
Credit rationing, credit risk management and, 206–207
Credit risk, 195, 203–207
collateral and, 206
compensating balances and, 206
credit rationing and, 206–207
loan commitments and, 206
long-term customer relationships and, 205
monitoring to manage, 205
restrictive covenants to manage, 205
screening to manage, 204
specialization in lending and, 204–205
Credit spreads, 476
during coronavirus pandemic, 283
during Great Depression, 273, 273*f*
during Great Recession, 281, 281*f*
Credit unions, 38, 39*t*, 40, 40*t*, 259–260
Credit view transmission mechanisms, 597, 600–604
balance sheet channel and, 601
bank lending channel and, 600–601
cash flow channel and, 601–602
household liquidity effects and, 602–604
unanticipated price level channel and, 602
Cryptocurrencies, 55–56
Currencies, 49
anchor, 431
appreciation of, 403
changes in holdings of, money supply and, 332
cryptocurrencies, 55–56

depreciation of, 403
devaluation of, 434
Eurocurrencies, 33
exchange rates and. *See* Exchange rate *entries*; Foreign exchange *entries*
issuance of, 28
in M1 monetary aggregate, 57
paper, 53
reserve, 433
revaluation of, 434
shifts from deposits to, 322
Currency boards, 447, 448*b*
Currency in circulation, on Fed balance sheet, 319–320
Currency unions, 438–439
Current account, 430
Current account balance, 430
Current yield, 74

D
Dai-Ichi Kangyo Bank, 262–263
Daiwa Bank, 211*b*
Data lag, 556
DAX index, 34*b*
De Soto, Hernando, 182*b*
Dealers, 26
Debit cards, 54, 240–241
Debt
monetizing, 461–462
secured (collateralized), 167
unsecured, 167
Debt contracts
incentive-compatible, 179
to reduce moral hazard, 177
tools to solve moral hazard in, 178–180
Debt deflation, 271
during Great Depression, 273–274
Debt instruments, 25
Debt markets, 25. *See also* Bond markets
Debt securities. *See also* Bonds; Mortgages
external financing provided by, 166
short-term, 242
Default, 28
Default-free bonds, 118

Default risk, 118–121, 119*f*, 120*t*
Defensive open market operations, 351
Deficits
  budget. *See* Budget deficits
  in current account, 431*b*
Deleveraging, 268
Dell'Ariccia, Giovanni, 385n
Delta, 118
Demand
  aggregate. *See* Aggregate demand *entries*
  for assets, determinants of, 86–88
  for assets, domestic, 412–416
  for money. *See* Money demand
  for reserves, 344, 344*f*
Demand curve
  aggregate. *See* Aggregate demand curve
  bond, 89–90
  for domestic assets, exchange rates and, 412–413
  for domestic assets, shifts in, exchange rates and, 413–416
  excess, 91
  movement along, 92
  shifts in. *See* Shifts in demand
Demand deposits
  for assets, determinants of, 86–88
  in M1 monetary aggregate, 57
Demand-pull inflation, 559–561, 561*f*
  cost-push inflation vs., 562
Demand shocks, 511–515, 513*f*, 514*t*, 527–530, 528*f*
Democratic principles, consistency of inflation targeting with, 378
Denmark, negative interest rate in, 76*b*
Deposit facilities, 365
Deposit insurance, 44, 217–218. *See also* Federal Deposit Insurance Corporation (FDIC)
  for credit unions, 259
  global, 218*b*

S&Ls and, 259
Deposit outflows, 195
Deposit rate ceilings, avoidance of, 244, 247
Depositors, money supply process and, 318
Depository institutions, 38–40, 39*t*, 40*t*. *See also* Banks; Credit unions; Savings and loan associations; Thrift institutions (thrifts)
Depository Institutions Act of 1982, 230*t*
Depository Institutions Deregulation and Monetary Control Act (DIDMCA) of 1980, 230*t*, 299, 356
Deposits, 57–58. *See also* Multiple deposit creation
  bank, negative interest rates on, as monetary policy tool, 363–364
  checkable, 189–190
  demand. *See* Demand deposits
  nontransaction, 190
  at other banks, 191
  savings, 39, 58
  shifts into currency from, 322
  time, 190
  treasury, monetary base and, 324
Deposits (shares), 39, 40
Depreciation, 403
Depressions. *See* Great Depression
Derivatives, regulation of trading of, 286, 288
Deutsche Bank, 12
Devaluation, 434
Developing countries, tyranny of collateral in, 182*b*
DIDMCA (Depository Institutions Deregulation and Monetary Control Act) of 1980, 230*t*, 299, 356
Diners Club, 240
Direct finance, 23
Dirty float, 431, 439–440
Disclosure
  financial intermediary requirements for, 44

requirements for, 226–227
Discount bonds, 68
  yield to maturity on, 74–75
Discount loans, 190, 320
  borrowings from, 190
  federal funds rate and, 347, 347*f*
Discount policy
  as monetary policy tool, 353, 355*b*
  to prevent financial panics, 355*b*
Discount rate, 197, 320
Discount window
  expansion of, as monetary policy tool, 357
  operation of, 353
Discounting the future, 66
Discover card, 240
Discretion
  case for, 580–581
  constrained, 581–582
  time-inconsistency problem and, 578–579
Disinflation, Volcker, 529–530, 530*f*
Disintermediation, 244, 247
Disposable income, 473
Distributors, 243
Diversification, 36
Dividends, 25, 142
Divine coincidence, 551
DJIA. *See* Dow Jones Industrial Average (DJIA)
Dodd-Frank Wall Street Reform and Consumer Protection Act of 2010, 231*b*, 285–286
  annual stress tests and, 285
  consumer protection and, 285
  critics of, 287–288
  derivatives and, 286
  Federal Reserve Bank directors and, 298
  limits on Fed lending under, 286
  resolution authority and, 285–286
  systemic risk regulation and, 286
  Volcker rule and, 286

Dollarization, 448–449
Dominated assets, 466
Douglas Amendment, overturning of, 254
Dow Jones Industrial Average (DJIA), 4, 33, 34*b*, 141
  Black Monday and, 157
Draghi, Mario, 280*b*
Drexel Burnham Lambert, 242
Dual banking system, 237
Dual mandates, 373–374
Duration, 78n
Duration analysis, 208–209
Dynamic open market operations, 351

E
E-cash, 54–55
E-finance, 6
E-money, 54–55, 55*b*
Easing of monetary policy, 303
East Asia, speculative attack on, 445
ECB. *See* European Central Bank
Eccles, Marriner S., 304
Economic activity, stabilization of, as monetary policy response to supply shocks, 553–554, 555*f*
Economic growth
  financial development and, 181–183
  low, inflation targeting and, 380
  as monetary policy goal, 372
  rate of, 21
Economic Stimulus Act of 2008, 282
Economies of scale, 35
  transaction cost reduction by, 168
Economies of scope, 37
  information technology and, 253–254
Ecuador, dollarization by, 449
Edge Act corporations, 262
Effective lower bound, 564–572
  Abenomics and, 570–572, 572*f*
  asset purchases and quantitative easing and, 569

deriving aggregate demand curve with, 564–566, 565*f*
  disappearance of self-correcting mechanism at, 566–567, 566*f*
  liquidity provision and, 568, 568*f*
  management of expectations and, 570, 571*f*
  nonconventional monetary policy and, 567–570
Effective-lower-bound problem, 357
Effectiveness lag, 556
Efficient market hypothesis, 141, 149, 150–157
  implications for financial markets, 156–157
  practical guide to investing in the stock market and, 153–156, 155*b*
  random-walk behavior of stock prices and, 152–153, 153*b*
  rationale behind, 151–152
Eisenhower, Dwight D., 306n
Electronic banking, 241
Electronic money, 54–55, 55*b*
Electronic payment, 54
EM (equity multiplier), 201, 202
Emergency Economic Stabilization Act of 2008, 281
Emerging market countries, 267n
  capital controls and, 440–441
  desirability of exchange-rate targeting for, 447
Employment. *See also* Unemployment *entries*
  high, as goal of monetary policy, 371–372
Employment Act of 1946, 558
EMS. *See* European Monetary System
EMU (European Monetary Union), 312, 438
Enron Corporation, 172*b*
EOS, 55
Equal Credit Opportunity Act of 1974, 227

Equation of exchange, 455–456
Equilibrium
  macroeconomic. *See* Macroeconomic equilibrium
  market. *See* Market equilibrium
  reasons the economy heads toward, 481
Equilibrium interest rates, 86, 92–102
  business cycle expansions and, 100–101, 100*f*, 101*f*
  changes in due to changes in income, price level, or money supply, 106, 106*t*
  Fisher effect and, 98–99, 98*f*, 99*f*
  low, secular stagnation and, 101–102
  shifts in demand for bonds and, 92–96, 94*t*
  shifts in supply of bonds and, 96–98, 96*t*
Equilibrium price, 91
Equities, 25. *See also* Stock *entries*
Equity, return on, bank capital adequacy management and, 201
Equity capital. *See* Net worth
Equity contracts. *See also* Stock *entries*
  costly state verification and, 176
  moral hazard in, 175–177
Equity markets. *See* Stock markets
Equity multiplier (EM), 201, 202
Equity securities. *See* Stock *entries*
Equity tranches, 275*b*
ERM (exchange rate mechanism), 433
ESCB (European System of Central Banks), 312, 373
Estonia, currency board in, 447
Ethereum, 55
Eurobonds, 33
  adoption of, 438
  survival of, 439*b*
Eurocurrencies, 33

Eurodollar market, 260–261
   birth of, 261*b*
Eurodollars, 33
Europe. *See also* specific countries
   low interest rates in, 101–102
European Central Bank (ECB),
      312–313
   Fed compared with, 312
   global financial crisis and, 421
   Governing Council of, 312–313
   hierarchical mandates and, 373
   independence of, 313
   interest on excess reserves
      and, 365
   lending to banks by, 365
   monetary policy strategy of,
      383*b*
   monetary policy tools of,
      364–365
   open market operations of,
      364–365
   reserve requirements and, 365
   response to financial crisis of
      2007–2009, 280*b*
   response to Great Recession, 279
European Monetary System
      (EMS), 433
   speculative attacks and, 435–
      436, 435*f*
European Monetary Union
      (EMU), 312, 438
European System of Central
      Banks (ESCB), 312, 373
Euroyen deposits, 261n
Eurozone
   negative interest rate in, 76*b*
   policy trilemma and, 437
Ex ante real interest rate, 80
Ex post real interest rate, 80
Excess demand curve, 91
Excess reserves, 191, 320
   changes in, money supply
      and, 332
   interest on, as monetary pol-
      icy tool, 356, 365
   opportunity cost of holding,
      344
Excess supply, 91
Exchange, money as medium
   of, 50–51

Exchange rate mechanism
      (ERM), 433
Exchange-rate peg. *See*
      Exchange-rate targeting
Exchange rate regimes, 431–440
   Bretton Woods system and,
      432–433
   fixed, 431, 433–434, 433*f*
   floating, 431
   gold standard and, 432
   managed (dirty) float and,
      431, 439–440
   monetary unions and, 438–439
   pegging of Chinese exchange
      rate to U.S. dollar and, 438
   policy trilemma and, 437–
      438, 437*f*
   speculative attacks and, 435–
      436, 435*f*
Exchange-rate targeting, 443–
      449, 590
   advantages of, 443–444
   currency boards and, 447, 448*b*
   desirability for emerging mar-
      ket countries, 447
   desirability for industrialized
      countries, 446
   disadvantages of, 444–446
   dollarization and, 448–449
Exchange rates, 13, 13*f*, 402–
      424, 403*b*
   definition of, 403
   demand curve for domestic
      assets and, 412–413
   equilibrium, changes in inter-
      est rates and, 418–420, 419*f*
   equilibrium in the foreign
      exchange market and, 413
   factors affecting in long run,
      409–411
   factors affecting in short run,
      416–422, 417*t*
   forward, 403
   future, expected, changes in,
      415–416, 416*f*
   importance of, 403–404
   in long run, 405–411
   net exports and, 597, 599
   purchasing power parity and,
      405–409

   real, 405
   real interest rates and, 477
   shifts in the demand for domes-
      tic assets and, 413–416
   in short run, 411–413
   spot, 403
   supply curve for domestic
      assets and, 411, 412*f*
Exchanges, 26
Exogenous consumption
   expenditure, 474
Expansions. *See* Business cycle
   expansions
Expectations
   adaptive, 147, 546
   business, planned investment
      spending and, 475–476
   management of, as monetary
      policy tool, 362–363, 570,
      571*f*
   rational, theory of. *See* Theory
      of rational expectations
Expectations-augmented Phil-
      lips curve, 543
Expectations theory, 127–130
Expected future exchange rate,
      changes in, 415–416, 416*f*
Expected inflation
   change in, Fisher effect and,
      98–99, 98*f*, 99*f*
   short-run aggregate supply
      curve and, 516–517, 519
   supply of bonds and, 96*t*, 97
Expected-inflation effect,
      money growth and interest
      rates and, 109
Expected profitability, supply of
      bonds and, 96*t*, 97, 97*f*
Expected returns
   asset demand and, 87
   demand for bonds and, 94*t*, 95
Expenditure multiplier, 479n
Expenditures
   actual, 472
   consumer, 599
   consumption. *See* Autonomous
      consumption expenditure;
      Consumption expenditure
   planned, aggregate demand
      and, 472–473

Expertise, transaction cost reduction by, 168
Exports, net. *See* Net exports

F

Face value, 67
Factors of production, total income of, 19
Fair Credit Billing Act of 1974, 227
Fair Isaac Corporation, 243
Fallen angels, 242
Fama, Eugene, 150
Fannie Mae
    housing price bubble and, 277
    proposals to reform, 288–289
    put into conservatorship, 280
FDIC. *See* Federal Deposit Insurance Corporation
FDICIA (Federal Deposit Insurance Corporation Improvement Act) of 1991, 224, 230*b*–231*b*
Federal Deposit Insurance Corporation (FDIC), 43*t*, 44, 237, 238
    Fed as lender of last resort and, 354
    methods for handling failed banks, 217–218
    mutual savings banks and, 259
    resolution authority and, 285–286
    response to Great Recession, 282
    S&Ls and, 259
Federal Deposit Insurance Corporation Improvement Act (FDICIA) of 1991, 224, 230*b*–231*b*
Federal Deposit Insurance Reform Act of 2005, 231*b*
Federal Farm Credit Bank, 31
Federal funds, 27*t*, 29
Federal funds loans, 27*t*, 29
Federal funds rate, 2, 28*b*, 29, 300–301, 491
    announcement of, 343
    discount lending and, 347, 347*f*

Fed limitation of fluctuations in, 349–350, 350*f*
    open market operations and, 345–346, 346*f*
    reserve requirements and, 348, 348*f*
    rise in target for during 2004-2006 and 2015-2019, 495, 496*f*
    Taylor rule and, 394–395, 396*b*, 396*f*, 397
Federal Home Loan Bank System (FHLBS), 259
Federal Home Loan Mortgage Corporation (FHLMC). *See* Freddie Mac
Federal Housing Finance Agency, 259
Federal National Mortgage Association (FNMA). *See* Fannie Mae
Federal Open Market Committee (FOMC), 295, 300–303, 351
    beige book and, 303*b*
    blue book and, 303*b*
    directives of, release of, 311*b*
    federal funds rate and. *See* Federal funds rate
    foreign exchange policy and, 426*b*
    green books and, 303*b*
    inflation targeting and, 382
    meetings of, 302*b*
    teal book and, 303*b*
Federal Reserve Act of 1913, 229*t*, 295
Federal Reserve Banks, 295, 296–299, 297*f*, 298*b*
    monetary policy and, 298–299
    of New York, foreign exchange desk at, 426*b*
    of New York, special role of, 298*b*
Federal Reserve System (Fed), 10–11, 43*t*, 294–309, 491–492
    balance sheet of, 319–320
    Board of Governors of, 295, 300

borrowings from, 190
case against independence of, 309
case for independence of, 308–309
chairs of Board of Governors of, 303–304, 304*b*–305*b*, 591–592
communication strategy of, 311*b*
Congressional influence on, 306
degree of independence of, 305–307, 307*b*
dual mandate and, 373–374
European Central Bank compared with, 312
federal funds rate and. *See* Federal funds rate
Federal Open Market Committee of. *See* Federal Open Market Committee (FOMC)
Federal Reserve Bank
    branches of, 296–299, 297*f*, 298*b*
    inflation targeting and. *See* Inflation targeting
    as lender of last resort, 219, 353–354, 355*b*, 356
    lending by, limits under Dodd-Frank, 286
    member banks of, 237, 299
    monetary policy and. *See* Monetary policy
    monetary policy strategy of, 380–384
    money supply process and. *See* Monetary base; Money multiplier; Money supply process
    open market operations of. *See* Open market operations
    operating procedures of, 349–350, 350*f*
    origins of, 294–295, 295*b*
    presidential influence on, 306, 307*b*
    Regulation Q and, 44
    regulatory responsibility of, 237–238

Federal Reserve System (*Cont.*)
  research staff of, 301*b*
  response to coronavirus pan-
    demic, 283
  response to Great Recession,
    279, 281
  structure of, 295–310, 296*f*
  Taylor rule and, 394–395,
    396*b*, 396*f*, 397
  trading desk and, 352*b*
Fee income, generation of, 210
FHLBS (Federal Home Loan
    Bank System), 259
FHLMC (Federal Home Loan
    Mortgage Corporation). *See*
    Freddie Mac
Fiat money, 53
FICO scores, 243
FIMA (Temporary Foreign and
    International Monetary
    Authorities) Repo Facility,
    360*b*
Finance companies, 39*t*, 40*t*, 41
Financial account, 430–431
Financial account balance,
    430–431
Financial consolidation, gov-
    ernment safety net and,
    220–221
Financial crises, 7, 267–291
  banking crisis phase of,
    270–271
  debt deflation stage of, 271
  definition of, 267–268
  future regulation and, 287–289
  Great Depression as. *See*
    Great Depression
  Great Recession as. *See* Finan-
    cial crisis of 2007–2009
  initial phase of, 268–270
  sequence of events in, 268, 269*f*
  too-big-to-fail problem and,
    286–287
  of 2007–2009. *See* Financial
    crisis of 2007–2009
Financial crisis of 2007–2009,
    7, 267, 274–283
  aggregate demand and supply
    analysis of, 534–535, 535*f*,
    536*f*

autonomous monetary easing
    during, 495–496
bank balance sheets and, 278
Basel Accord after, 223*b*
causes of, 274–276
changes to financial regula-
    tion following, 284–286
dollar and, 420–421, 420*f*
effects of, 276–281
Fed lending facilities during,
    359*b*–360*b*
global financial markets and,
    279, 280*b*, 282*b*
government intervention and
    recovery from, 282–283
height of, 281, 281*f*
high-profile firm failures and,
    279–281
housing prices and, 276–278,
    276*f*
lessons for monetary policy
    strategy from, 384–386
monetary transmission mech-
    anisms and, 604
output gap and, 507, 508*f*
quantitative easing and
    money supply during, 337,
    338*f*, 339
run on shadow banking sys-
    tem and, 278–279, 279*f*
Financial derivatives, 239–240,
    275
Financial development
  of China, 183–184
  economic growth and, 181–183
Financial engineering, 238
Financial frictions, 268, 476
  changes in, shifts of *IS* curve
    and, 487
  shifts of aggregate demand
    curve and, 515
Financial innovation, 6, 238–249
  avoidance of existing regula-
    tions and, 244–246
  credit booms and busts and,
    268–270
  decline of traditional banking
    and, 246–249, 247*f*
  information technology and,
    240–242

interest-rate volatility and,
    239–240
  in mortgage markets, Great
    Recession and, 274
  securitization and, 242–243
Financial institutions. *See also*
    Banks; Central banks;
    Commercial banks; Credit
    unions; Investment banks;
    Savings and loan associations
  Fed loans to, on Fed balance
    sheet, 320, 323
  reasons to study, 5–7
Financial instruments. *See* Bond
    entries; Securities; Stock
    entries
Financial intermediaries, 6. *See
    also* Commercial banks;
    Insurance companies; Invest-
    ment banks; Mutual funds
  ensuring soundness of, 43–45
  external financing provided
    by, 166
  importance relative to securi-
    ties markets, 35*b*
  indirect finance and. *See*
    Indirect finance
  transaction costs and, 167–
    168
  types of, 38–42, 39*t*, 40*t*
Financial intermediation, 34
  to reduce adverse selection,
    172–174
  to reduce moral hazard, 177,
    180
Financial liberalization, credit
    booms and busts and,
    268–270
Financial markets. *See also*
    Bond markets; Capital mar-
    kets; Money market; Stock
    market
  efficiency of, 156–157
  flow of funds through, 22–
    24, 23*f*
  function of, 22–24, 23*f*
  global, Great Recession and,
    279
  instruments in, 27–31
  internationalization of, 31–33

reasons to study, 2–5, 14
stability of, as monetary policy goal, 372
structure of, 25–27
Financial news
aggregate output, unemployment, and inflation, 510*b*
capital market interest rates in, 30*b*
foreign exchange rates, 403*b*
foreign stock market indexes, 34*b*
monetary aggregates, 57*b*
money market rates in, 28*b*
Financial panics, 43
discount policy to prevent, 355*b*
Financial Reform, Recovery and Enforcement Act (FIRREA) of 1989, 230*b*
Financial regulation, 42–45, 43*t*, 216–234. *See also specific legislation and agencies*
abroad, 45
asymmetric information as rationale for, 216–221
bank panics as reason for, 216–218
Basel Accord as, 222, 223*b*
capital requirements as, 222
changes in, following Great Recession, 284–286
of competition, 227–228
consolidation of, 238
for consumer protection, 227
corrective action and, 224
of credit unions, 259–260
of derivatives trading, 286, 288
disclosure requirements and, 226–227
drawbacks of, 219–221
to ensure soundness of financial intermediaries, 43–45
financial supervision and, 224–225
of financial system, 166
future of, 287–289
to increase information, 171–172, 176–177
international, 229*b*

legislation for, 229*t*–231*t*
macroprudential, asset-price bubbles and, 389–390
of mutual savings banks, 259
to reduce asymmetric information, 42
regulatory agencies and, 237–238
restrictions on asset holdings as, 221
of risk management processes, 225–226
of savings and loan associations, 259
types of, 221–231
Financial repression, 181–183
Financial structure, adverse selection and, 169–175
Financial structure analysis, 164–187
asymmetric information and. *See* Adverse selection; Moral hazard
global, 164–167, 165*f*
transaction costs and, 167–168
Financial supervision, 224–225
Financial system
international. *See* International financial system
regulation of, 42–45, 43*t*, 166. *See also* Financial regulation; *specific legislation and agencies*
structure of, 6
Financial Times Stock Exchange (FTSE) 100-Share Index, 33, 34*b*
Finland, inflation targeting in, 375
Fire and casualty insurance companies, 39*t*, 40*t*, 41
Fire sales, 271
FIRREA (Financial Reform, Recovery and Enforcement Act) of 1989, 230*b*
First Bank of the United States, 294
First Boston Corporation, 237
First National Bank of Boston, 237

Fiscal policy, 11–12, 12*f*
Fiscal stimulus package of 2009, 484–485, 558*b*
Fischer, Stanley, 305
Fisher, Irving, 454–456
Fisher effect, 98–99, 98*f*, 99*f*
Fisher equation, 80
Fitch Ratings, 120*t*, 121
Great Recession and, 279
Five-year adjustable rate mortgage (ARM) rate, 30*b*
Fixed exchange rate regimes, 431, 477n
abandonment by United States, 433
instituted by European Union, 433
operation of, 433–434, 433*f*
speculative attacks and, 435–436, 435*f*
Fixed investment, 474
Fixed-payment loans, 67
Float, monetary base and, 324
Floating exchange rate regimes, 431
Flows, 92
FNMA (Federal National Mortgage Association). *See* Fannie Mae
FOMC. *See* Federal Open Market Committee
Ford, 32*b*
Ford Motor Credit Company, 41
Forecasting, of business cycles, yield curve as tool for, 135*b*
Foreign bonds, 32–33
Foreign exchange market interventions
monetary policy and, 442
money supply and, 425–428
sterilized, 428, 429
unsterilized, 428–429, 428*f*
Foreign exchange markets, 13–14, 13*f*, 402–404. *See also* Exchange rate *entries*
equilibrium in, 413
stability of, as monetary policy goal, 373
trades in, 404

Foreign exchange rates. *See*
    Exchange rate *entries*
Fortis, 282*b*
Forward exchange rate, 403
Forward guidance, as monetary
    policy tool, 362–363
Forward transactions, 403
France
    exchange-rate targeting by, 444
    government intervention dur-
        ing 2007–2009 financial
        crisis in, 282*b*
    speculative attack on, 445
Freddie Mac
    housing price bubble and,
        277
    proposals to reform, 288–289
    put into conservatorship, 280
Free-rider problem, 171
Frictional unemployment, 371,
    542n
Friedman, Milton, 465n
    on inflation, 9, 557
    on liquidity effect, 108–109
    on monetary policy, 380
    on Phillips curve, 542–545,
        543n, 544*f*
    on rules vs. discretion, 579–580
FTSE (Financial Times Stock
    Exchange) 100-Share
    Index, 33, 34*b*
Fuji Bank, 262–263
Fully amortized loans, 67
Fundamental economic values,
    270
Futures contracts, 240
FYI topics
    activist/nonactivist debate
        over the Obama stimulus
        package, 558*b*
    algebraic derivation of the aggre-
        gate demand curve, 497*b*
    apes as investment advisers,
        155*b*
    Bruce Bent and the money
        market mutual fund panic
        of 2008, 245*b*
    cashless society, 55*b*
    collateralized debt obliga-
        tions, 275*b*

conflicts of interest at credit-
        rating agencies and the
        global financial crisis, 121*b*
    consumers' balance sheets
        and the Great Depression,
        603*b*
    Enron implosion, 172*b*
    financial development
        and economic growth,
        181*b*–183*b*
    global financial crisis and the
        demise of large, free-stand-
        ing investment banks, 258*b*
    meaning of autonomous,
        512*b*
    meaning of the word *invest-
        ment,* 474*b*
    modern monetary theory,
        462*b*
    Phillips curve trade-off and
        macroeconomic policy in
        the 1960s, 543*b*
    political business cycle and
        Richard Nixon, 580*b*
    tyranny of collateral, 182*b*
    U.S. dollars held abroad, 58*b*
    yield curve as a forecasting
        tool for inflation and the
        business cycle, 135*b*

G

Gagnon, Joseph, 362n
GAO (Government Account-
    ability Office), 306
Gap analysis, 208, 209
Garn-St. Germain Act of 1982,
    230*t*
GATT (General Agreement on
    Tariffs and Trade), 432
GDP. *See* Gross domestic product
GDP deflator, 20
    in financial news, 510*b*
General Agreement on Tariffs
    and Trade (GATT), 432
General Motors, 32*b*, 240
*The General Theory of Employ-
    ment, Interest and Money*
    (Keynes), 463, 472
Generalized dividend valuation
    model, 143

Germany
    central bank of. *See* Bundesbank
    exchange-rate targeting by,
        444
    foreign exchange crisis of
        1992 and, 435–436, 435*f*
    government intervention dur-
        ing 2007–2009 financial
        crisis in, 282*b*
    hyperinflation in, 52
    universal banking in, 257
Gertler, Mark, on interest rates
    as monetary transmission
    mechanism, 597
Ginnie Mae, 30, 31
Glass-Steagall Act of 1933, 228,
    229*t*, 237
    erosion of, 256
    repeal of, 254, 257
Global financial crisis of 2007–
    2009. *See* Financial crisis of
    2007–2009
Global topics
    Argentina's currency board,
        448*b*
    banking structure in the
        United States and abroad
        compared, 255*b*
    Basel Accord after global
        financial crisis, 223*b*
    birth of the Eurodollar
        market, 261*b*
    demise of monetary targeting
        in Switzerland, 581*b*
    ending the Bolivian hyperin-
        flation, 589*b*
    European Central Bank's
        monetary policy strategy,
        383*b*
    European sovereign debt
        crisis, 280*b*
    financial intermediary impor-
        tance relative to securities
        markets, 35*b*
    foreign exchange rates,
        following of a random walk
        by, 153*b*
    international financial regula-
        tion, 229*b*
    negative interest rates, 76*b*

relative decline of U.S. capital markets, 30*b*

rogue traders and the principal-agent problem, 211*b*

spread of government deposit insurance, 218*b*

survival of the euro, 439*b*

U.S. current account deficit, 431*b*

worldwide government bailouts during the global financial crisis, 282*b*

GNMA (Ginnie Mae, Government National Mortgage Association), 30, 31

Goal independence, 305

Gold standard, 432

Goldman Sachs, 250*t*, 258*b*

Goods and services

nontradable, 407

total production of. *See* Aggregate output

trade balance on, 430

Goods market equilibrium, 478–479

Gordon growth model, 143–144, 146

Gorton, Gary, 278*n*

Governing Council of European Central Bank, 312–313

Government Accountability Office (GAO), 306

Government bonds. *See* U.S. Treasury bonds

Government budget constraint, 460–462

Government deficits. *See* Budget deficits

Government intervention

during coronavirus pandemic, 283

following financial crisis of 2007–2009, 279, 281, 282–283, 282*b*

Government National Mortgage Association (GNMA, Ginnie Mae), 30, 31

Government purchases

as aggregate demand component, 473, 476–477, 511

changes in, shifts of *IS* curve and, 481–483, 482*f*, 483*f*

shifts of aggregate demand curve and, 513, 513*f*

Government retirement funds, 39*t*, 40*t*, 41

Government-sponsored enterprises (GSEs). *See also* Fannie Mae; Freddie Mac

proposals to reform, 288–289

Government Sponsored Entities Purchase Program, 358

Gramm-Leach-Bliley Financial Services Modernization Act of 1999, 220, 231*b*, 257

Grant and Ward failure, 270

Great Depression, 272–274

bank failures during, 237, 354

bank panics and, 272–273

consumers' balance sheets and, 603*b*

corporate bond interest rates during, 121

debt deflation and, 271, 273–274

falling stock prices during, 273, 273*f*

global impact of, 274

government bond interest rates during, 117

stock market crash and, 272

unemployment during, 371

Great Inflation, 307*b*, 395, 562–563, 563*f*

Great Recession. *See* Financial crisis of 2007–2009

Greece, financial crisis of 2007–2009 and, 279, 280*b*, 282*b*

Green book, 303*b*

Green New Deal, 462*b*

Greenlaw, David, 280*b*

Greenspan, Alan

appointment as Fed chair, 306

on asset-price bubbles, 388–389

on Fed communication, 311*b*

on financial crisis of 2007–2009, 267

financial panic prevented by, 355*b*

inflation targeting under, 382

on irrational exuberance, 270

monetary policy strategy under, 381

retirement as Fed chair, 300*n*

style as Fed chair, 304, 304*b*, 305*b*

Taylor rule under, 397

Greenspan doctrine, 388–389, 390

Greenwald, Bruce, 170*n*

Gross domestic product (GDP), 11, 19. *See also* Aggregate output; Aggregate output indexes

potential, 506–507

real, 510*b*

GSEs. *See* Fannie Mae; Freddie Mac; Government-sponsored enterprises

H

Haircuts, 278

Hamanaka, Yasuo, 211*b*

Hamilton, Alexander, 236

Hamilton, James D., 280*b*

Hang Seng index, 34*b*

Hedge funds, 39*t*, 40*t*, 42

Hedges, inflation, 466

Hedging of interest-rate risk, 239–240

Hierarchical mandates, 373–374

High employment targets, inflation and, 558–562

High-powered money. *See* Monetary base

Holding period, 79

Home banking, 241

Honda, 32*b*

Hong Kong

currency board in, 447

policy trilemma and, 437

Hooper, Peter, 280*b*

Hot tips, for investing in the stock market, 154–155

Household liquidity, monetary transmission and, 602–604

Housing market
  bubble in. *See* Asset-price
    bubbles
  Great Recession and,
    276–278, 276f, 277b
HSBC Holdings plc, 263t
Humphrey-Hawkins Act of
  1978, 306, 311b, 558
Hyperinflation, 52, 369,
  462–463
  Bolivian, 589b
  German, 52
  Zimbabwean, 369, 462–463
Hypo Real Estate Holdings, 282b

I

IBFs (international banking
  facilities), 262
Iceland, government intervention during 2007–2009
  financial crisis in, 282b
Iguchi, Toshihide, 211b
Iksill, Bruno, 211b
IMF. *See* International Monetary
  Fund
Implementation lag, 556
Impossible trinity, 437–438, 437f
Incentive-compatible debt contracts, 179
Income, 50
  aggregate, 19
  changes in equilibrium inter-
    est rate due to changes in,
    106t, 107, 107f
  disposable, 473
  as flow, 50
  net, 25
Income effect
  money growth and interest
    rates and, 109
  shifts in the demand for
    money and, 105, 106t
Income taxes. *See* Taxes
Independence of central banks,
  305–310
  case against, 309–310
  case for, 308–309
  of European Central Bank, 313
  goal independence, 305
  instrument independence, 305

trend toward increase in, 315
  in United States, 305–310
Indirect finance, 23f, 33–38
  asymmetric information and,
    36–38
  conflicts of interest and, 38
  economies of scope and, 38
  external financing provided
    by, 166
  risk sharing and, 36
  transaction costs and, 34–35
Industrial and Commercial
  Bank of China, 263t
Industrial Bank of Japan,
  262–263
Industrial production, in financial news, 510b
Industrialized countries. *See
  also specific countries*
  decline of traditional banking
    in, 249
  desirability of exchange-rate
    targeting for, 446
Inflation, 8–9, 9f, 10f, 509, 509f
  cost-push, 559, 560f, 562
  demand-pull, 559–562, 561f
  expected. *See* Expected inflation
  Great Inflation and, 307b,
    395, 562–563, 563f
  high employment targets and,
    558–562
  monetary policy and, 369–370
  monetary policy response to
    supply shocks and, 552–
    553, 554f
  propagation by monetary
    policy, 558–563
  quantity theory of money
    and, 457–458
  unemployment and. *See*
    Phillips curve
  yield curve as forecasting tool
    for, 135b
Inflation gap, 549
Inflation hedges, 466
Inflation nutter, 374
Inflation rate, 9, 10f, 21
  in financial news, 510b
  as monetary policy target. *See*
    Inflation targeting

Inflation Report (United Kingdom), 377, 378
Inflation shocks, short-run
  aggregate supply curve and,
    517, 519–520, 520f
Inflation targeting, 374–380,
  549, 557–558, 557f, 590
  advantages of, 377–378
  average, 386b
  in Canada, 375, 376f, 377
  disadvantages of, 379–380
  flexibility of, 386
  level of, 385–386
  in New Zealand, 375, 376f
  in United Kingdom, 375,
    376f, 377
Information
  asymmetric. *See* Adverse
    selection; Moral hazard
  government regulation to
    increase, 171–172
  private production and sale
    of, 171
Information technology, 240–
  242
  decline in income advantages
    on assets and, 248
ING, 282b
Initial public offerings (IPOs),
  32b
Inside the Fed topics
  appointment of Paul Volcker
    as chair, 591b
  average inflation targeting,
    386b
  Bernanke's advocacy of infla-
    tion targeting, 383b
  discount policy to prevent a
    financial panic, 355b
  evolution of the Fed's com-
    munication strategy, 311b
  Fed lending facilities dur-
    ing the global financial
    and coronavirus crises,
    359b–360b
  Federal Reserve Bank of New
    York's foreign exchange
    desk, 426b
  Fed's use of the Taylor rule,
    396b

FOMC meeting, 302*b*
green, blue, teal, and beige books, 303*b*
housing price bubble responsibility, 277*b*
political genius of the founders of the Fed, 295*b*
presidential attacks in the independence of the Fed, 307*b*
research staff's role, 301*b*
special role of the Federal Reserve Bank of New York, 298*b*
styles of Fed chairs, 304*b*–305*b*
trading desk of the Fed, 352*b*
Insiders, 42
Instrument independence, 305
Insurance
deposit. *See* Deposit insurance; Federal Deposit Insurance Corporation
state insurance commissions and, 43*t*
Insurance companies, 39*t*, 40, 40*t*. *See also* AIG; Ohio Life Insurance and Trust Company failure
Inter-American Development Bank, 448*b*
Interest, on excess reserves, as monetary policy tool, 356
Interest-rate risk, 78–79, 195, 207–209
gap analysis and duration analysis and, 208–209
strategies for managing, 209
volatility of rates and, 239–240
Interest-rate volatility
adjustable-rate mortgages and, 239
financial derivatives and, 239–240
Interest rates, 3, 4*f*, 10, 11*f*, 64–85, 86–116
asset demand determinants and, 86–88
bond market and. *See* Bond markets; Bonds
calculating, 81

in capital market, 30*b*
changes in, equilibrium exchange rate and, 418–420, 419*f*
credit market instruments and, 67–68
discount, 197, 320
domestic, exchange rates and, 414, 414*f*
effective lower bound and. *See* Effective lower bound
equilibrium. *See* Equilibrium interest rates
federal funds. *See* Federal funds rate
financial intermediary restrictions on, 44–45
foreign, exchange rates and, 414–415, 415*f*
Libor, 28*b*
liquidity preference framework and. *See* Liquidity preference framework
marginal lending rate, 365
mean-reverting, 130n
measuring, 64–75
as monetary transmission mechanism, 596–597, 598*f*
money demand and, 467–468
in money market, 28*b*
money supply and, 108–113
negative, 76*b*, 363–364
overnight cash rate, 364
present value and, 65–66
prime, 28*b*
real. *See* Real interest rate
returns vs., 75–80, 78*t*
risk structure of. *See* Risk structure of interest rates
simple, 65
stability of, as monetary policy goal, 372
target financing rate, 364
term structure of. *See* Term structure of interest rates; Yield curves
treasury bill, 28*b*
Trump tax cuts and, 124–125
yield to maturity and, 64, 68–75
Intermediate targets, 391

Intermediate-term debt instruments, 25
International banking, 260–263
Eurodollar market and, 260–261
foreign banks in the United States and, 262–263, 263*t*
overseas U.S. banking and, 261–262
International Banking Act of 1978, 262
International banking facilities (IBFs), 262
International finance, reasons to study, 12–14
International financial system, 14, 425–452
balance of payments and, 429–431
basic facts about, 164–167, 165*f*
capital controls in, 440–441
current account and, 430
exchange rates and. *See* Exchange rate *entries*
financial account and, 430–431
foreign exchange intervention in, money supply and, 425–428
IMF's role in, 441–442
monetary policy and, 442–443
sterilized intervention in, 429
unsterilized intervention in, 428–429, 428*f*
International Monetary Fund (IMF), 432, 441–442
as international lender of last resort, 441–442
International reserves, 425
Interstate banking, breakdown of barriers to, 253
Inventory investment, 474–475
Inverted yield curves, 126
Investment
autonomous, 475, 485
autonomous, shifts of aggregate demand curve and, 515
definition of, 474*b*
fixed, 474
inventory, 474–475
planned, 473, 474–476, 510

Investment Advisers Act of 1940, 230t
Investment advisors
  reports published by, 153–154
  success of, 155b
Investment banks, 26, 42. *See also* Bear Stearns; Lehman Brothers
  failure of, 218, 220, 258b
Investment Company Act of 1940, 230t
Investment function, 476
Investment intermediaries, 39t, 40t, 41–42
IPOs (initial public offerings), 32b
Ireland
  financial crisis of 2007–2009 and, 279
  government intervention during 2007–2009 financial crisis in, 282b
  sovereign debt crisis in, financial crisis of 2007–2009 and, 280b
Irrational exuberance, 270, 387, 388
IS curve, 472–490
  aggregate demand components and, 473–478
  derivation of, 479
  factors shifting, 481–487, 486t
  goods market equilibrium and, 478–479
  planned expenditure and aggregate demand and, 472–473
  shifts in, shifts of aggregate demand curve and, 499, 500f
Israel, inflation targeting in, 375
Italy
  sovereign debt crisis in, 280b
  speculative attack on, 436

J
J.P. Morgan, 12, 172b
  assets of, 250t, 263t
  Bear Stearns purchased by, 258b, 279–280
  Fed loans to, 358, 359b
  reorganization as commercial bank, 237
  stock underwriting privilege extended to, 256
Jackson, Andrew, 236, 294
Japan
  Abenomics and, 570–572, 572f
  British-style universal banking system in, 258
  decline of traditional banking in, 249
  inflation targeting in, 380
  low interest rates in, 101–102
  monetary policy in, 606–607
  negative interest rate in, 76b
Jay Cooke and Company failure, 270
Johnson, Lyndon B., 306n, 307b
Jumbo mortgage rate, 30b
Junk bonds, 121, 241–242

K
Kahn, George A., 396b
Kane, Edward, 244
Kennedy, John F., 306n
Kerviel, Jerome, 211b
Keynes, John Maynard
  aggregate demand concept and, 472
  liquidity preference theory of, 102–105, 104f, 463–464
  on planned investment spending, 475–476
Keynesians, 555
King, Mervyn, 374
Knickerbocker Trust Company failure, 270
Krugman, Paul, 429n
Kuroda, Haruhiko, 570–572

L
Labor hoarding, 548
Lags, monetary policy implementation and, 556
Large-denomination time deposits, 190
Large-scale asset purchases (LSAPs), as monetary policy tool, 358, 360, 361f
Laubach, Thomas, 377n, 383b, 581b
Leeson, Nick, 211b
Leeson, Robert, 396b
Legislation. *See also specific legislation*
  major, in United States, 229t–231t
Legislative lag, 556
Lehman Brothers
  failure of, 218, 220, 245b, 258b, 270
  lack of resolution authority over, 285
Lemons problem, 169–175
Lender of last resort
  Fed as, 353–354, 356
  IMF as, 441–442
Leverage cycle, 284
Leverage ratio, 222
Liabilities, 23
  on bank balance sheet, 188–190
  on Fed balance sheet, 319–320
Liability management, 195
Libor rate, 28b
Life insurance companies, 39t, 40, 40t
Lines of credit, backup, 210
Liquidity, 26, 52
  asset demand and, 88
  bond interest rates and, 122–123
  demand for bonds and, 94t, 95–96
  effective lower bound and, 568, 568f
  of other assets, money demand and, 466
  provision of, as monetary policy tool, 357–358
Liquidity management, 195–198
Liquidity preference framework, 102–108, 104f
  changes in equilibrium interest rates in, 105–108
Liquidity preference theory, 463–466
Liquidity premium theory, 131–133, 132f, 134f

Liquidity services, 35, 168
Liquidity trap, 467
Lithuania, currency board in, 447
Loan commitments, credit risk management and, 206
Loan originators, 243
Loan sales, 210
Loans
  on bank balance sheet, 191–192
  calling in, 198
  commercial, bank, 29t, 31
  consumer, 29t, 31
  discount. *See* Discount loans
  federal funds, 27t, 29
  to financial institutions, on Fed balance sheet, 320, 323
  fixed-payment, 67
  fully amortized, 67
  monetary transmission and, 600–601
  new, as monetary policy tool, 358
  new-car, 30b
  NINJA, 227
  private, avoidance of free-rider problem and, 180
  simple, 65
Lombard facility, 353n
Lombard rate, 353n
Long-run aggregate supply curve, 515–516, 516f
  shifts of, 518, 519f
Long-term customer relationships, credit risk management and, 205
Long-term debt instruments, 25
Longer-term refinancing operations, 365
LSAPs (large-scale asset purchases), as monetary policy tool, 358, 360, 361f
Lucas, Robert, 576, 577
Lucas critique, 576–578, 581
Luxembourg, government intervention during 2007–2009 financial crisis in, 282b

M
Maastricht Treaty, 312, 313, 373
Macaulay's concept of duration, 208
Macroeconomic equilibrium, 522–527
  aggregate demand shocks and, 527–530, 528f
  movement from short- to long-term, 524–527, 526f
  self-correcting mechanism and, 527
  short-run, 523, 523f
Macroeconomic models, 576
Macroprudential regulation, asset-price bubbles and, 389–390
Macroprudential supervision, 284–285
Macys, 240
Main refinancing operations, of European Central Bank, 364
Main Street Expanded Loan Facility (MSELF), 360b
Main Street New Loan Facility (MSNLF), 360b
Majluf, N. S., 170n
Managed float, 431, 439–440
Management of expectations, as monetary policy tool, 362–363
Mandate-consistent inflation objectives, 383b
Marginal lending facility, 365
Marginal lending rate, 365
Marginal propensity to consume, 474
Market-clearing price, 91
Market equilibrium, 86
  in bond market, 91–92
  in foreign exchange market, 413
  in goods market, 478–479
  in market for reserves, 344f, 345
Market for reserves, 343–345
  demand in, 344, 344f
  equilibrium in, 344f, 345
  supply in, 345
Market fundamentals, 156

Markets. *See specific markets*
Marshall, Alfred, 456n
Martin, William McChesney, Jr., 300n, 304, 306n, 307b
MasterCard, 240
MasterCharge, 240
Matched sale-purchase transactions, 351
Maturity, of a debt instrument, 25
Maturity bucket approach, 208
Maturity buckets, 208
Maturity date, 65
Mauro, Paulo, 385n
MBSs. *See* Mortgage-backed securities
McCallum, Bennett, 576n, 579
McFadden Act of 1927, 229t, 251
  overturning of, 254
McKinney, Stewart, 220
Mean-reverting interest rates, 130n
Measurability, as criterion for choosing a policy instrument, 393–394
Medium of exchange, money as, 50–51
Melitz, Mark, 429n
Meltzer, Alan, 579
Mergers, 252–256, 252f
Merrill Lynch, sale to Bank of America, 258b, 280
Metrick, Andrew, 278n
Mexico, speculative attack on, 445
Mezzanine tranches, 275b
Microprudential supervision, 284
Microsoft, 28–29
Milken, Michael, 242
Mishkin, Frederic S., 181n, 280b, 377n, 384n, 581b, 603b
  on constrained discretion, 582
  on inflation targeting, 382
Mitsubishi UFJ Financial Group, 263t
MLF (Municipal Liquidity Facility), 360b

MMIFF (Money Market Investor Funding Facility), 359*b*

MMLF (Money Market Mutual Fund Liquidity Facility), 359*b*

Modigliani, Franco, 599

M1 and M2 monetary aggregates, 57–59, 57*b*, 57*t*, 59*f*

Monetarists, 579

Monetary aggregates, 57–59, 57*b*, 57*t*, 59*f*

Monetary base, 321–325
  definition of, 320
  Fed's ability to control, 324–325
  float and, 324
  loans to financial institutions and, 323
  nonborrowed, 324
  open market operations and, 321–322
  shifts from deposits into currency and, 322–323
  Treasury deposits at the Fed and, 324

A Monetary History of the United States, 1867–1960 (Friedman and Schwartz), 579–580

Monetary liabilities, of Fed, 320–321

Monetary policy, 343–400, 491–492, 549–575, 576–594
  activist vs. nonactivist, 555–556, 558*b*
  asset-price bubbles and, 390–391
  autonomous, shifts of aggregate demand curve and, 512
  autonomous easing of, 494, 494*f*, 495–496
  autonomous tightening of, 494, 494*f*
  conduct of, 10–11
  conventional tools of, 350–356
  credibility and. *See* Credibility
  discount lending and, 347, 347*f*
  discount policy and, 353, 355*b*
  easing of, 303

econometric policy evaluation and, 577
economic growth as goal of, 372
at effective lower bound. *See* Effective lower bound
European Central Bank and, 364–365
Fed as lender of last resort and, 353–354, 356
federal funds rate and market for reserves and, 343–350
Fed's strategy for, 380–384
financial market stability as goal of, 372
foreign exchange market effects on, 442
foreign exchange market stability as goal of, 373
forward guidance and, 362–363
goals of, 369–374
high employment as goal of, 371–372
inflation and, 557–558, 557*f*
inflation targeting and. *See* Inflation targeting
inflationary, causes of, 558–563
interest on excess reserves and, 348, 349*f*, 356
interest-rate stability as goal of, 372
lags and implementation of, 556
large-scale asset purchases and, 358, 360, 361*f*
lessons learned from global financial crisis and, 384–386
liquidity provision and, 357–358
Lucas critique of policy evaluation and, 576–578
market for reserves and, 343–345
negative interest rates and, 363–364
nominal anchor and, 370
nonconventional tools of, 357–360, 567–570

open market operations and, 345–346, 346*f*, 351
output stability as goal of, 372
policy instrument choice and, 391–394, 391*f*–393*f*
price stability as goal of, 369–370, 373–374
quantitative easing vs. credit easing and, 360–362
reasons to study, 7–12
reserve requirements and, 348, 348*f*, 356
response to shocks, 549–554
rules vs. discretion and, 578–582
stock prices and, 146
Taylor rule and, 394–395, 396*f*, 397
tightening of, 303
time-inconsistency problem and, 370–371
transmission mechanisms of. *See* Transmission mechanisms of monetary policy

Monetary policy (*MP*) curve, 492–496, 493*f*
  movements along, 495, 496*f*
  movements along vs. shifts in, 494–495
  shifts in, 493–494, 494*f*, 495–496, 499, 501*f*, 502
  shifts of aggregate demand curve and, 499, 501*f*, 502
  upward slope of, 492–493

Monetary Policy Report to the Congress, 306

Monetary theory, 8, 454–609
  aggregate demand and supply analysis and. *See* Aggregate demand and supply analysis; Aggregate demand curve; Aggregate supply curve
  government budget constraint and, 460–462
  hyperinflation and, 462–463
  interest rates and money demand and, 467–468
  IS *curve and. See* IS curve
  liquidity preference theory and, 463–465

modern, 462*b*
monetary policy and. *See*
    Monetary policy; Monetary
    policy curve
portfolio theories of money
    demand and, 465–466
quantity theory of money
    and. *See* Quantity theory of
    money
stability of money demand
    and, 468
Monetary unions, 438–439
Monetizing the debt, 461–462
Money, 49–62. *See also* Money
    supply; Money supply
    process
checks and, 53–54
commodity, 53
cryptocurrencies as, 55–56
demand for. *See* Money
    demand
electronic (e-money), 54–55
electronic payment and, 54
fiat, 53
functions of, 50–52
high-powered. *See*
    Monetary base
inflation and. *See* Inflation
interest rates and, 10, 11*f*
meaning of, 49–50
measuring, 56–59
as medium of exchange,
    50–51
motives for holding, 464
printing, 462
quantity theory of. *See*
    Quantity theory of money
reasons to study, 7–12, 14
as stock, 50
as store of value, 52
as unit of account, 51–52
velocity of, 454–456
Money center banks, 199
Money demand, 456
empirical evidence on,
    467–468
interest rates and, 467–468
liquidity preference frame-
    work and, 102–105, 104*f*
portfolio theories of, 465–466

shifts in, 105
stability of, 468
Money market, 27
definition of, 102n
interest rates in, 28*b*
Money market deposit
    accounts, in M2 monetary
    aggregate, 58
Money market instruments,
    27–29, 27*t*
Money Market Investor Fund-
    ing Facility (MMIFF), 359*b*
Money Market Mutual Fund
    Liquidity Facility (MMLF),
    359*b*
Money market mutual fund
    shares, in M2 monetary
    aggregate, 58
Money market mutual funds,
    39*t*, 40*t*, 41, 242, 245–246
panic of 2008 and, 245*b*
Money multiplier, 333–339
derivation of, 333–335
intuition behind, 335–336
money supply response to
    changes in factors and,
    336–337
quantitative easing during
    financial crises and, 337,
    338*f*, 339
Money supply, 7–12, 49
changes in equilibrium inter-
    est rate due to changes in,
    106*t*, 107–108, 108*f*
factors determining, 331–332
during financial crises, 337,
    338*f*, 339
foreign exchange intervention
    and, 425–428
interest rates and, 108–113
liquidity preference frame-
    work and, 102–105, 104*f*
shifts in, 105
Money supply process, 318–342
borrowed reserves changes
    and, 331
control of monetary base and,
    321–325
currency holdings changes
    and, 332

excess reserves changes and,
    332
factors determining money
    supply and, 331–332
Fed balance sheet and,
    319–320
monetary base and. *See*
    Monetary base
money multiplier and. *See*
    Money multiplier
multiple deposit creation
    and, 325–331
nonborrowed monetary base
    changes and, 331
overview of, 332, 333*t*
players in, 318
required reserve ratio changes
    and, 331–332
Monitoring
credit risk management and,
    205
to reduce moral hazard, 179
to solve the principal-agent
    problem, 176
Moody's Investor Service, 120*t*,
    121
Moral hazard, 37, 169
asset holding restrictions and,
    221
capital requirements and,
    222
choice between debt and
    equity contracts and,
    175–177
financial consolidation and,
    220–221
financial structure in debt
    markets and, 178–184
with government safety nets,
    219
in loan markets. *See*
    Credit risk
Morgan Stanley, 237, 250*t*,
    258*b*
Mortgage-backed securities
    (MBSs), 30
bank balance sheets and,
    278
Fed purchase of, 358
Mortgage brokers, 243

Mortgage markets
  agency problems in, Great
    Recession and, 274–275
  financial innovation in, Great
    Recession and, 274
Mortgages, 29t, 30
  adjustable-rate, 239
  subprime, 243
Movement along the demand
  curve, 92
Movement along the monetary
  policy curve, 494–495, 496f
Movement along the supply
  curve, 92
MP curve. *See* Monetary policy curve
MSELF (Main Street Expanded
  Loan Facility), 360b
MSNLF (Main Street New Loan
  Facility), 360b
Mugabe, Robert, 463
Multiple deposit creation, 325–331
  banking system and, 326–
    329, 328t
  critique of simple model of,
    330–331
  formula for, derivation of,
    329–330
  at a single bank, 325–326
Multiplier. *See* Money multiplier
Municipal bonds, 31
  income taxes and, 123, 124f
  interest rates on, 117
Municipal Liquidity Facility
  (MLF), 360b
Muth, John, 147
Mutual funds, 39t, 40t, 41, 168
Mutual savings banks, 38, 39,
  39t, 40t, 259
Myers, Stewart, 170n
The Mystery of Capital
  (De Soto), 182b

N

NAIRU (nonaccelerating
  inflation rate of unemployment), 395, 546
Nakamoto, Satoshi, 55
NASDAQ Composite index, 26,
  34b, 141
  Black Monday and, 157

National Bank Act of 1863, 237
National banks, 237, 299
National Bureau of Economic
  Research, 556
National Central Banks (NCBs),
  312
National Credit Union Admin-
  istration (NCUA), 43t, 259
National Credit Union Share
  Insurance Fund (NCUSIF),
  44, 259
NationsBank, merger with Bank
  of America, 254
Natural rate of output, 372,
  506–507, 516
Natural rate of unemployment,
  371, 515–516, 543
NBR (nonborrowed reserves),
  345
NCBs (National Central Banks),
  312
NCUA (National Credit Union
  Administration), 43t, 259
NCUSIF (National Credit
  Union Share Insurance
  Fund), 44, 259
Negative interest rates, as mon-
  etary policy tool, 363–364
Negative supply shocks,
  531–532, 531f, 533f
Negotiable bank certificates of
  deposit, 27t, 28
Negotiated order of withdrawal
  (NOW) accounts, 58
Net capital inflows, 431
Net export function, 478
Net exports, 430
  as aggregate demand compo-
    nent, 473, 477–478, 511
  autonomous, 477, 486
  autonomous, shifts of aggre-
    gate demand curve and, 513
  exchange rates and, 597, 599
Net income, 25
Net stable funding ration
  (NSFR), 285
Net U.S. acquisition of financial
  assets, 430
Net U.S. incurrence of financial
  assets, 430

Net worth
  to reduce adverse selection,
    174
  to reduce moral hazard,
    178–179
Netherlands
  government intervention dur-
    ing 2007–2009 financial
    crisis in, 282b
  universal banking in, 257
New-car loan rate, 30b
New York Stock Exchange, 26
New Zealand
  central bank accountability
    in, 378
  inflation targeting in, 375,
    376f, 379
NIFs (note issuance facilities),
  210
Nikkei 300 Average, 33
NINJA loans, 227
Nippon Ginko, 315
Nixon, Richard, 306n, 307b,
  580b
Nominal anchors, 370, 582
  credible, benefits of, 582–583
Nominal GDP targeting,
  590–591
Nominal interest rate, real inter-
  est rate vs., 80–83, 82f
Nominal variables, real vari-
  ables vs., 19–20
Nonaccelerating inflation
  rate of unemployment
  (NAIRU), 395, 546
Nonactivists, 555
Nonborrowed monetary base,
  324
  changes in, money supply
    and, 331
Nonborrowed reserves (NBR),
  345
Nonconventional monetary
  policy tools, 357–364
  forward guidance as, 362–
    363
  large-scale asset purchases as,
    358, 360, 361f
  liquidity provision as,
    357–358

negative interest rates as, 363–364

quantitative easing vs. credit easing as, 360–362

Nontradable goods and services, 407

Nontransaction deposits, 190

Northern Rock, 279

Northwest, 118

Note issuance facilities (NIFs), 210

NOW (negotiated order of withdrawal) accounts, 58

NSFR (net stable funding ration), 285

NYCE, 252

O

Obama, Barack

Bernanke's reappointment as Fed chair by, 306n

Rubin doctrine and, 307b

stimulus package under, 484–485, 558b

Observability, as criterion for choosing a policy instrument, 393–394

Obstfeld, Maurice, 429n

OECD (Organization for Economic Cooperation and Development), 222

Off-balance-sheet activities, 209–212, 222

commercial banks' pursuit of, 248–249

fee income generation as, 210

loan sales as, 210

risk management techniques and, 210, 212

trading activities as, 210, 212

Office of the Comptroller of the Currency, 225

commercial bank regulation by, 237

financial intermediaries and, 43–44, 43t

regulatory responsibility of, 257

S&Ls and, 259

Ohio Life Insurance and Trust Company failure, 270

Oil price shocks, 586, 587f

Okun, Arthur, 547

Okun's law, 547, 548f

One-period valuation model, 142–143

OPEC (Organization of Petroleum Exporting Countries), 532

Open market operations, 299, 321–322

defensive, 351

dynamic, 351

of European Central Bank, 364–365

federal funds rate and, 345–346, 346f

as monetary policy tool, 351

Open market purchases, 321–322

Open market sales, 321, 322

Operating instruments. *See* Policy instruments

Opportunity cost

of holding excess reserves, 344

quantity of money and the interest rate and, 103

Optimal forecast, 147

Orderly Liquidation Authority, 285–286

opposition of, 288

Organization for Economic Cooperation and Development (OECD), 222

Organization of Petroleum Exporting Countries (OPEC), 532

Originate-to-distribute business model, 243

OTC (over-the-counter) markets, 26

Other checkable deposits, in M1 monetary aggregate, 57–58

Output

aggregate. *See* Aggregate output; Aggregate output indexes; Gross domestic product (GDP)

fluctuations in, inflation targeting and, 379–380

natural rate of (potential), 372, 506–507, 516

Output gap, 507, 508f

short-run aggregate supply curve and, 517, 520–521, 521f, 522t

unemployment and, 547, 548f

Outright operations, 352b

Over-the-counter (OTC) markets, 26

Overconfidence, investing in stock market and, 158

Overnight cash rate, 364

Overvaluations, purchasing power parity and, 408–409

P

Panic of 1907, 295

Paper currency, 53

Par value, 67

Parmalat, 172

Paul, Ron, 306

Paycheck Protection Program Liquidity Facility (PPPLF), 360b

Payment technology, 464

Payments system, 53–56

Payoff method, of FDIC, 217

PayPal, 55

PCAOB (Public Company Accounting Oversight Board), 227

PCE (personal consumption expenditures), 20

PCE deflator, 20

in financial news, 510b

PDCF (Primary Dealer Credit Facility), 359b

Pension funds, 39t, 40t, 41

Perfect substitutes, 127

Performance, improved by inflation targeting, 378

Perpetuities, yield to maturity on, 73–74

Personal consumption expenditures (PCE), 20

Phelps, Edmund, 543n

Phillips curve analysis of, 542–545, 544f

Phillips, A. W., 541

Phillips curve, 541–546
  accelerationist, 546
  expectations-augmented, 543
  Friedman-Phelps analysis of, 542–545, 544*f*
  macroeconomic policy in 1960s and, 543*b*
  modern, 545–546
  after 1960s, 545
  in 1960s, 541, 542*f*, 543*b*
Phillips curve theory, 395
Pieces of eight, 49
Pigou, A. C., 456n
Planned expenditure, aggregate demand and, 472–473
Planned investment spending
  as aggregate demand component, 473, 474–476, 510
  business expectations and, 475–476
  real interest rates and, 475
PMCCF (Primary Market Credit Facility), 360*b*
PNC Financial Services Group, 250*t*
Policy instruments, 391–394, 391*f*–393*f*
  criteria for choosing, 393–394
Policy Targets Agreement (New Zealand), 375
Policy trilemma, 437–438, 437*f*
Political business cycle, 308, 580, 580*b*
Politics
  influence on the Fed, 306, 307*b*, 308–309
  structure of Fed and, 295
Portfolio, 36
Portfolio balance effect, 429n
Portfolio choice theory, 86, 88, 88*t*
Portugal, financial crisis of 2007–2009 and, 279, 280*b*
Posen, Adam S., 377n, 383*b*, 581*b*
Positive supply shocks, 531
Potential GDP, 506–507
Potential output, 372, 506–507, 516
Powell, Jay, 304, 304*b*–305*b*, 307*b*

PPI (producer price index), in financial news, 510*b*
PPP. *See* Theory of purchasing power parity
PPPLF (Paycheck Protection Program Liquidity Facility), 360*b*
Precautionary motive for holding money, 464
Preferences, for domestic vs. foreign goods, exchange rates and, 410
Preferred habitat theory, 131–133, 132*f*, 134*f*
Present value (present discounted value), 65–67
  simple, 66
President of the United States. *See also* individual presidents
  influence on the Fed, 306, 307*b*
Price, equilibrium (market-clearing), 91
Price-level effect
  money growth and interest rates and, 109
  shifts in the demand for money and, 105, 106*t*
Price levels, 8
  aggregate, 20
  changes in equilibrium interest rate due to changes in, 106*t*, 107, 107*f*
  debt deflation and, 271
  quantity theory of money and, 456–457
  relative, exchange rates and, 409
Price stability
  hierarchical vs. dual mandates to achieve, 373–374
  as monetary policy goal, 369–370, 373–374
Price stickiness, 596
  short-run aggregate supply curve and, 518
Primary Dealer Credit Facility (PDCF), 359*b*
Primary dealers, 321
Primary Market Credit Facility (PMCCF), 360*b*
Primary markets, 25–26

Prime rate, 28*b*
Principal-agent problem, 175–177
  in mortgage markets, Great Recession and, 274–275
  rogue traders and, 211*b*, 212
  tools to help resolve, 176–177
Private-equity firms, 177
Private loans, avoidance of free-rider problem and, 180
Producer price index (PPI), in financial news, 510*b*
Productivity, exchange rates and, 410–411, 410*t*
Prudential supervision, 224–225
Public Company Accounting Oversight Board (PCAOB), 227
Public interest view, of government behavior, 310
Purchase and assumption method, of FDIC, 217–218
Purchases
  government. *See* Government purchases
  open market, 321–322
The Purchasing Power of Money (Fisher), 454
Purchasing power parity. *See* Theory of purchasing power parity (PPP)
Pure arbitrage, 151

Q
Quantitative easing, 358, 360, 361*f*, 569
  credit easing vs., 360–362
  during financial crises, 337, 338*f*, 339
Quantity theory of money, 454–458
  equation of exchange and, 454–456
  inflation and, 457–458
  in long run, 458, 459*f*
  price level and, 456–457
  in short run, 458, 460*f*
  testing, 458, 459*f*, 460*f*
  velocity of money and, 454–456
Quotas, 407

R

Rajan, Raghuram, 182*b*
Random walk, 152–153, 153*b*
Raskin, Matthew, 362n
Rate of return, interest rates vs.,
  68*t*, 75–80
Rational expectations. *See* Efficient
  market hypothesis; Theory of
  rational expectations
Rational expectations revolu-
  tion, 576
Reagan, Ronald, 306n, 307*b*
Real exchange rate, 405
Real GDP, in financial news,
  510*b*
Real interest rates
  after-tax, 81
  ex ante, 80
  ex post, 80
  exchange rates and, 477
  nominal interest rate vs.,
    80–83, 82*f*
  planned investment spending
    and, 475
Real money balances, 464
Real terms, 80–81
Real variables, nominal vari-
  ables vs., 19–20
Recessions, 7–8, 506. *See also*
  Financial crisis of 2007–
  2009
  output gap and, 507, 508*f*
Recognition lag, 556
Regulation. *See* Financial regu-
  lation; *specific legislation*
Regulation Q, 44, 244
  elimination of ceilings on inter-
    est rates under, 247–248
  money market mutual funds
    and, 245–246
Regulatory agencies, 43*t*
Regulatory arbitrage, 222
Reinhart, Carmen M., 384
Reinhart, Vincent R., 384
Reinvestment risk, 79n
Remache, Julie, 362n
Repurchase agreements (repos),
  27*t*, 28–29, 278, 351
  reverse (matched sale-pur-
    chase transactions), 351

Required reserve ratio, 191
  changes in, money supply
    and, 331–332
Required reserves, 191, 320
Reserve Bank of New Zealand,
  hierarchical mandates and,
  373
Reserve Bank of New Zealand
  Act of 1989, 375
Reserve Bank of Zimbabwe, 463
Reserve currencies, 433
Reserve Primary Fund, 245*b*
Reserve requirements, 191
  avoidance of, 244
  federal funds rate and, 348,
    348*f*
  as monetary policy tool, 356,
    365
Reserves, 191
  borrowed, 320, 324, 345
  excess. *See* Excess reserves
  on Fed balance sheet, 320
  international, 425
  liquidity management and,
    195–198
  market for. *See* Market for
    reserves
  nonborrowed, 345
  required, 191, 320
  secondary, 191
Residual claimants, 25, 142
Resolution authority, opposition
  to, 288
Restrictive covenants, 167
  credit risk management and,
    205
  to reduce moral hazard,
    179–180
Return on assets (ROA), bank
  capital adequacy management and, 201
Return on equity (ROE), bank
  capital adequacy management and, 201
Returns
  expected, asset demand and, 87
  interest rates vs., 68*t*, 75–80
Revaluation, 434
Reverse repo facilities, 346n
Reverse repos, 351

Reverse transactions, of European Central Bank, 364
Revolving underwriting facilities (RUFs), 210
Riegle-Neal Interstate Banking
  and Branching Efficiency
  Act of 1994, 220, 231*b*, 254
  consolidation and, 257
Rigidity, inflation targeting and,
  379
Ripple, 55
Risk, 36
  asset demand and, 87–88
  credit. *See* Credit risk
  default, 118–121, 119*f*, 120*t*
  demand for bonds and, 94*t*, 95
  interest-rate. *See* Interest-rate risk
  money demand and, 466
  reinvestment, 79n
Risk averse persons, 87–88
Risk management, by banks,
  assessment of, 225–226
Risk preferers (risk lovers), 87
Risk premium, 118, 123
Risk sharing, 36
Risk structure of interest rates,
  117–125, 118*f*
  default risk and, 118–121,
    119*f*, 120*t*
  income taxes and, 123, 124–
    125, 124*f*
  liquidity and, 122–123
ROA (return on assets), bank
  capital adequacy management and, 201
ROE (return on equity), bank
  capital adequacy manage-
  ment and, 201
Rogoff, Kenneth S., 384n, 591
Rogue traders, principal-agent
  problem and, 211*b*, 212
Rohatyn, Felix, 355*b*
Roosevelt, Franklin D., bank
  holiday declared by, 272–
  273
Royal Bank of Canada, 241
Rubin, Robert, 307*b*
Rubin doctrine, 307*b*
RUFs (revolving underwriting
  facilities), 210

Rules, 578
    case for, 579–580
    types of, 579
Russia, hyperinflation in, 369

S

Sack, Brian, 362n
Sales, open market, 321, 322
Salomon Smith Barney, 257
Samuelson, Paul, 543*b*
    on inflation targeting, 385
Sarbanes-Oxley Act of 2002,
    32*b*, 227, 231*b*
Sargent, Thomas, 576, 589*b*
Savings accounts, 190
Savings and loan associations
    (S&Ls), 38, 39, 39*t*, 40*t*,
    259
    adjustable-rate mortgages
        issued by, 239
Savings deposits, 39
    in M2 monetary aggregate, 58
Schwartz, Anna, 579
Screening, credit risk manage-
    ment and, 204
Sears, 240
Seasonal credit, 353
Secondary credit, 353
Secondary loan participations,
    210
Secondary Market Corporate
    Credit Facility (SMCCF),
    360*b*
Secondary markets, 25, 26
Secondary reserves, 191
Secular stagnation, 101–102
Secured debt, 167
Securities, 3
    on bank balance sheet, 191
    debt. *See* Bonds; Debt securi-
        ties; Mortgages
    equity. *See* Stock entries
    on Fed balance sheet, 320
    in financial markets, 23
    mortgage-backed, 30, 278,
        358
    primary markets for, 25–26
    secondary markets for, 25, 26
Securities Act of 1933, 42, 226,
    230*t*

Securities and Exchange Com-
    mission (SEC), 42, 43*t*,
    172, 226
    regulatory responsibility of, 257
Securities Exchange Act of
    1934, 230*t*
Securities markets. *See also* Bond
    markets; Stock markets
    external financing provided
        by, 166
Securitization, 242–243
    shadow banking system and,
        242–243
    subprime mortgages and, 243
Security First Network Bank, 241
Segmented markets theory,
    130–131
Seigniorage, 449
Self-correcting mechanism, 527
    disappearance at effective
        lower bound, 566–567, 566*f*
Senior tranches, 275*b*
Servicers, 243
Shadow banking system, 238
    run on, 278–279, 279*f*
    securitization and, 242–243
Shares (deposits), 39, 40
Shefrin, Hersh, 157n
Shifts in demand
    for bonds, 92–96, 94*t*
    for money, 105
Shifts in supply
    of bonds, 96–98, 96*t*
    of money, 105
Shifts of the aggregate demand
    curve, factors causing, 499–
    502, 511–515, 513*f*, 514*t*
Shifts of the aggregate supply
    curve, 518–521
Shifts of the *IS* curve
    factors causing, 481–487, 486*t*
    shifts of aggregate demand
        curve and, 499, 500*f*
Shifts of the long-run aggregate
    supply curve, 518, 519*f*
Shifts of the monetary policy
    curve, 493–494, 494*f*,
    495–496
    shifts of aggregate demand
        curve and, 499, 501*f*, 502

Shifts of the short-run aggregate
    supply curve, 519–521
Shiller, Robert, 157
Shirakawa, Masaaki, 570
Shleifer, Andrei, 157n
Shocks
    aggregate demand. *See*
        Aggregate demand shocks
    aggregate supply. *See*
        Aggregate supply shocks
    cost-push, 517
    demand, 511–515, 513*f*,
        514*t*, 527–530, 528*f*
    inflation, short-run aggregate
        supply curve and, 517,
        519–520, 520*f*
    oil price, 586, 587*f*
    supply. *See* Supply shocks
Short-run aggregate supply
    curve, 516–518, 547–548
    derivation of, 548
    expected inflation and,
        516–517, 519
    inflation shocks and, 517,
        519–520, 520*f*
    output gap and, 517,
        520–521, 521*f*, 522*t*
    price stickiness and, 518
    shifts of, 519–521
    upward slope of, 517–518
Short sales, 158
Short-term debt instruments, 25
SIFIs. *See* Systematically impor-
    tant financial institutions
Signaling, delayed by inflation
    targeting, 379
Simple interest rate, 65
Simple loans, 65
Simple present value, 66
S&Ls. *See* Savings and loan
    associations
Small-denomination time
    deposits, in M2 monetary
    aggregate, 58
Smart cards, 54
Smart money, efficient market
    hypothesis and, 152, 158
SMCCF (Secondary Market
    Corporate Credit Facility),
    360*b*

Social contagion, investing in stock market and, 158
Société Générale, 211*b*
Solow, Robert, 543*b*
on inflation targeting, 385
Soros, George, 436
Sources of funds, 188
South Korea, government intervention during 2007–2009 financial crisis in, 282*b*
Sovereign debt crisis, European, financial crisis of 2007–2009 and, 280*b*
Sowell, Thomas, 277n
S&P 500 index, 34*b*, 141
Spain
financial crisis of 2007–2009 and, 279, 280*b*, 282*b*
inflation targeting in, 375
sovereign debt crisis in, 280*b*
speculative attack on, 436
Special purpose vehicles (SPVs), 275*b*
Specialization in lending, credit risk management and, 204–205
Speculative attacks, 435–436, 435*f*
Speculative motive for holding money, 464
Spot exchange rate, 403
Spot transactions, 403
SPVs (special purpose vehicles), 275*b*
Standard & Poor's, 120*t*, 121
Great Recession and, 279
Standardized gap analysis, 208
Standing lending facility, 353
State banking commissions, 43*t*
State banks, 237
State insurance commissions, 43*t*
State-owned banks, 183
Statistical discrepancy, 430n
Sterilized foreign exchange interventions, 428, 429
Sticky prices, 596
Stiglitz, Joseph E., 170n
Stimulus package, 484–485, 558*b*
Stock market indexes
Dow Jones Industrial Average, 4, 33, 34*b*, 141, 157

foreign, 34*b*
NASDAQ, 26, 34*b*, 141, 157
S&P 500, 34*b*, 141
Stock markets, 3–5, 5*f*, 25, 141
crashes of, 146, 157, 272, 272*f*, 281, 281*f*
external financing provided by, 165, 165*f*
foreign, 34*b*
IPOs of, 32*b*
lemons in, 170
practical guide to investing in, 153–156
stock price setting in, 144–146
world, 33
Stock prices, 4–5, 5*f*, 141–144
coronavirus stock market crash of 2020 and, 146
decline during Great Depression, 273, 273*f*
generalized dividend valuation model and, 143
Gordon growth model and, 143–144, 146
monetary policy and, 146
one-period valuation model and, 142–143
random walk behavior of, 152–153, 153*b*
response to news, 155
stock valuation and, 144–146
Stockholders, 141–142
insiders, 42
Stocks (amounts), 92
Stocks (securities), 3, 29*t*, 30
external financing provided by, 166
Store of value, money as, 52
Stored-value cards, 54
Strait Times index, 33, 34*b*
Stress tests, 226
under Dodd-Frank, 285
Structural unemployment, 371, 542n
Structured credit products, 274. *See also* Collateralized debt obligations (CDOs)
Subprime mortgages, 243, 267
Substitutes, perfect, 127
Sumitomo Corporation, 211*b*

Summers, Lawrence, 102
Super senior tranches, 275*b*
Superregional banks, 253
Supply
excess, 91
of money. *See* Money supply
of reserves, 345
Supply curve
aggregate. *See* Aggregate supply curve; Long-run aggregate supply curve; Short-run aggregate supply curve
bond, 90–91, 90*f*
for domestic assets, exchange rates and, 411, 412*f*
movement along, 92
shifts of. *See* Shifts in supply; Shifts of the aggregate supply curve; Shifts of the long-run aggregate supply curve; Shifts of the short-run aggregate supply curve
Supply shocks, 530–532, 531*f*
monetary policy response to, 551–554, 553*f*
negative, 531–532, 531*f*, 533*f*
positive, 531
short-run aggregate supply curve and, 517
Supply-side economics, 372
Sweden
government intervention during 2007–2009 financial crisis in, 282*b*
inflation targeting in, 375, 379
negative interest rate in, 76*b*
speculative attack on, 436
Sweep accounts, 246
Swiss National Bank, 581*b*
Switzerland
capital requirements for large financial institutions in, 287
demise of monetary targeting in, 581*b*
negative interest rate in, 76*b*
universal banking in, 257
Systematically important financial institutions (SIFIs), 286
solutions to too-big-to-fail problem and, 287

T

T-accounts, 192–194
   open market operations and,
      321–322
TAF (Term Auction Facility),
   357, 359*b*
TALF (Term Asset-Backed Securities Loan Facility), 359*b*
Target financing rate, 364
Tariffs, 407
TARP (Troubled Asset Relief
   Program), 282
Tax cuts, under Trump, bond
   interest rates and, 124–125
Tax havens, 261
Tax multiplier, 479n
Taxes
   aggregate demand and,
      476–477
   bonds and, 123, 124–125, 124*f*
   changes in, shifts of *IS* curve
      and, 483–485, 484*f*
   shifts of aggregate demand
      curve and, 513
Taylor, John
   on federal funds rate, 394, 395
   on housing price bubble, 277*b*
   on interest rates as monetary
      transmission mechanism, 597
   on stabilization of inflation,
      395, 492
Taylor principle, 395, 492
Taylor rule, 394–395, 396*b*,
   396*f*, 397, 579
TD Group US, 250*t*
Teal book, 303*b*
Temporary Foreign and Interna-
   tional Monetary Authorities
   (FIMA) Repo Facility, 360*b*
10-year Treasury rate, 30*b*
Tennessee Valley Authority, 31
Term Asset-Backed Securities
   Loan Facility (TALF), 359*b*
Term Auction Facility (TAF),
   357, 359*b*
Term Securities Lending Facility
   (TSLF), 359*b*
Term structure of interest rates,
   117, 125–137, 126*f*, 577–
   578. *See also* Yield curves

evidence on, 134–135
expectations theory and,
   127–130
liquidity premium theory
   and, 131–133, 132*f*, 134*f*
preferred habitat theory and,
   131–133, 132*f*, 134*f*
segmented markets theory
   and, 130–131
Theory of bureaucratic
   behavior, 310–311
Theory of efficient capital
   markets, 149
Theory of portfolio choice, 88,
   88*t*, 465–466
Theory of purchasing power
   parity (PPP), 405–409
   Big Mac index and, 407–409,
      408*t*
   departures from, 408–409
   evidence on, 406–407, 406*f*
   inability to fully explain
      exchange rates, 407
   predictive power of, 408
Theory of rational expectations,
   141, 146–149
   formal statement of, 148
   implications of, 149
   rationale behind, 148–149
30-year mortgage rate, 30*b*
Thrift industry, 258–260
Thrift institutions (thrifts), 38,
   39*t*, 40*t*
Tightening of monetary policy, 303
Time deposits, 190
Time-inconsistency problem,
   370–371
   discretion and, 578–579
   reduction by inflation
      targeting, 377
Tobin, James, 464, 465n, 599
Tobin's q theory, 599
Too-big-to-fail problem, 219–
   220, 287
Toyota, 32*b*
Trade balance on goods and
   services, 430
Trade barriers, exchange rates
   and, 407, 409–410
Trading Activities Manual, 226

Trading desk, of Fed, 352*b*
Trading Room Automated Processing System (TRAPS), 351
Tranches, 275*b*
Transaction costs, 34–35,
   167–168
   influence on financial struc-
      ture, 167–168
   reduction by financial inter-
      mediaries, 168
Transactions motive for holding
   money, 464
Transition countries, economic
   growth of, 181–183
Transmission mechanisms of
   monetary policy, 595–609
   balance sheet channel as, 601
   bank lending channel as,
      600–601
   cash flow channel as, 601–602
   exchange rate effects on net
      exports and, 597, 599
   Great Recession and, 604
   household liquidity effects
      and, 602–604
   importance of credit channels
      for, 604
   lessons for monetary policy
      and, 605–607
   Tobin's q theory and, 599
   traditional interest-rate chan-
      nels as, 596–597, 598*f*
   unanticipated price level
      channel as, 602
   wealth effects and, 599–600
Transparency, increased by
   inflation targeting, 377–378
TRAPS (Trading Room Automated
   Processing System), 351
Traveler's checks, in M1 mon-
   etary aggregate, 57
Travelers Group, merger with
   Citicorp, 257
Treasury bill rate, 28*b*
Treasury deposits, monetary
   base and, 324
Troubled Asset Relief Program
   (TARP), 282
Truman, Harry S., 306n
Trump, Donald

Dodd-Frank bill and, 287
Fed and, 307*b*
tax cuts under, bond interest
rates and, 124–125
Truth in Lending Act. *See* Con-
sumer Protection Act of 1969
TSLF (Term Securities Lending
Facility), 359*b*

U
UBS, 12
Unanticipated price level channel,
monetary transmission and,
602
Uncertainty, financial crises
and, 270
Undervaluations, purchasing
power parity and, 408–409
Underwriting, 26, 42
Unemployment
coronavirus pandemic and, 472
frictional, 371
during Great Depression, 371
inflation and. *See* Phillips curve
natural rate of, 371, 515–
516, 543
nonaccelerating inflation rate
of, 395
output gap and, 547, 548*f*
structural, 371
Unemployment gap, 543
Unemployment rate, 7
business cycles and, 508–509
in financial news, 510*b*
Unexploited profit opportunities, 151
Unit of account, money as, 51
United, 118
United Kingdom. *See also* Bank
of England
Brexit and, 402, 421–422, 422*f*
British-style universal
banking system in, 258
exchange-rate targeting by, 444
government intervention during 2007–2009 financial
crisis in, 282*b*
inflation targeting in, 375,
376*f*, 377, 379
speculative attack on, 445

United States
British-style universal banking system in, 258
central bank of. *See* Federal
Reserve System (Fed)
foreign banks in, 262–263, 263*t*
low interest rates in, 101–102
negative interest rate in, 76*b*
policy trilemma and, 437
U.S. Bankcorp, 250*t*
U.S. government agency securities, 29*t*, 31
U.S. government securities, 29*t*,
31
U.S. Treasury, foreign exchange
policy and, 426*b*
U.S. Treasury bills, 27*t*, 28
interest rates on, 101, 101*f*
liquidity of, 87
U.S. Treasury bonds
default risk of, 118–120, 119*f*
income taxes and, 123, 124*f*
interest rates on, 117
liquidity of, 122–123
Universal banking, 257–258
Unsecured debt, 167
Unsterilized foreign exchange
interventions, 428–429, 428*f*
US Airways, 118
Uses of funds, 191

V
Value, money as store of, 52
Value-at-risk (VaR) calculations,
226
Vault cash, 191
Velocity of money, 454–456, 455
Venture-capital firms, 177
Vietnam War, buildup for, 482–
483, 483*f*
Virtual banks, 241
Visa, 240
Volcker, Paul
appointment as Fed chair,
306n, 591*b*
disinflation under, 529–530,
530*f*
Great Inflation and, 563
Reagan and Bush's unhappi-
ness with, 307*b*

style as Fed chair, 304
Volcker rule and, 286
Volcker disinflation, 529–530, 530*f*
Volcker rule, 286
critics of, 288

W
Wallace, Neil, 576n
Wealth, 49–50
asset demand and, 87
demand for bonds and, 93,
93*f*, 94*t*, 95
monetary transmission and,
599–600
money demand and, 466
Weiss, Andrew, 170n
Wells Fargo, 241, 250*t*
Wessel, David, 307n
Woodford, Michael, 362
Woodward, Bob, 307n
World Bank, 432
World Trade Organization
(WTO), 432
WorldCom, 172
Wriston, Walter, 204
WTO (World Trade Organiza-
tion), 432

Y
Yellen, Janet, 304, 304*b*–305*b*
on Fed communication, 311*b*
inflation targeting under, 382
Yield curves, 125–126, 125*b*
as forecasting tool for inflation
and the business cycle, 135*b*
interpreting for 1980–2020,
135–137, 136*f*
inverted, 126
Yield to maturity, 64, 68–75
for a coupon bond, 71–74, 72*t*
on a discount bond, 74–75
on a fixed-payment loan, 69–70
on a perpetuity, 73–74
on a simple loan, 68–69

Z
Zero-coupon bonds, 68
yield to maturity on, 74–75
Zimbabwe, hyperinflation in,
369, 462–463
Zingales, Luigi, 182*b*

GUIDE TO COMMONLY USED SYMBOLS

Symbol	Term	Symbol	Term
Δ	change in a variable	M	money supply
π	inflation rate	M^d	demand for money
π^e	expected inflation	M^s	supply of money
π^T	inflation target	$M1$	M1 monetary aggregate
AD	aggregate demand curve	$M2$	M2 monetary aggregate
AS	aggregate supply curve	MB	monetary base (high-powered money)
B^d	demand for bonds	MB_n	nonborrowed monetary base
B^s	supply of bonds	MP	monetary policy curve
BR	borrowed reserves	mpc	marginal propensity to consume
c	currency ratio	NBR	nonborrowed reserves
C	yearly coupon payment	NX	net exports
C	currency	P	price level
C	consumption expenditure	P_s	stock prices
D	demand curve	P_t	price of a security at time t
D	checkable deposits	ρ	price shock
DL	discount loans	r	real interest rate
e	excess reserves ratio	rr	required reserve ratio for checkable deposits
E_t	exchange (spot) rate	R	reserves
E_{par}	par (fixed) exchange rate	R	return
$(E^e_{t+1} - E_t)/E_t$	expected appreciation of domestic currency	R^e	expected return
		R^D	expected return on domestic deposits
EM	equity multiplier	R^F	expected return on foreign deposits
ER	excess reserves	ROA	return on assets
$\bar{f}$	for financial frictions	ROE	return on equity
G	government purchases	RR	required reserves
i	interest rate (yield to maturity)	S	supply curve
i_d	discount rate	T	taxes
i^D	interest rate on domestic assets	V	velocity of money
i^F	interest rate on foreign assets	Y	aggregate output (national income)
i_{oer}	interest rate paid on reserves	Y^{ad}	aggregate demand
I	planned investment spending	Y^P	potential (natural rate level of) output
IS	IS curve		
m	money multiplier		

APPLYING THEORY TO THE REAL WORLD: APPLICATIONS AND BOXES

Applications

Will Bitcoin or Other Cryptocurrencies Become the Money of the Future?, p. 55

Simple Present Value, p. 66

How Much Is That Jackpot Worth?, p. 67

Yield to Maturity on a Simple Loan, p. 68

Yield to Maturity and the Yearly Payment on a Fixed-Payment Loan, p. 70

Yield to Maturity and Bond Price for a Coupon Bond, p. 71

Yield to Maturity on a Perpetuity, p. 73

Yield to Maturity on a Discount Bond, p. 74

Calculating Real Interest Rates, p. 81

Changes in the Interest Rate Due to a Change in Expected Inflation: The Fisher Effect, p. 98

Changes in the Interest Rate Due to a Business Cycle Expansion, p. 100

Explaining Current Low Interest Rates in Europe, Japan, and the United States: Low Inflation and Secular Stagnation, p. 101

Changes in the Equilibrium Interest Rate Due to Changes in Income, the Price Level, or the Money Supply, p. 106

Does a Higher Rate of Growth of the Money Supply Lower Interest Rates?, p. 110

Interpreting Yield Curves, 1980–2020, p. 135

Monetary Policy and Stock Prices, p. 146

The Coronavirus Stock Market Crash of 2020, p. 146

Practical Guide to Investing in the Stock Market, p. 153

What Do Stock Market Crashes Tell Us About the Efficient Market Hypothesis and the Efficiency of Financial Markets?, p. 157

Financial Development and Economic Growth, p. 181

Is China a Counterexample to the Importance of Financial Development?, p. 183

Strategies for Managing Bank Capital, p. 202

How a Capital Crunch Caused a Credit Crunch During the Global Financial Crisis, p. 203

Strategies for Managing Interest-Rate Risk, p. 209

The Mother of All Financial Crises: The Great Depression, p. 272

Could the Coronavirus Pandemic Have Led to a Financial Crisis?, p. 283

Quantitative Easing and the Money Supply During the Global Financial and the Coronavirus Crises, p. 337

How the Federal Reserve's Operating Procedures Limit Fluctuations in the Federal Funds Rate, p. 349

Burgernomics: Big Macs and PPP, p. 407

Effects of Changes in Interest Rates on the Equilibrium Exchange Rate, p. 418

The Global Financial Crisis and the Dollar, p. 420

Brexit and the British Pound, p. 421

The Foreign Exchange Crisis of September 1992, p. 435

How Did China Accumulate $4 Trillion of International Reserves?, p. 438

Testing the Quantity Theory of Money, p. 458

The Zimbabwean Hyperinflation, p. 463

The Vietnam War Buildup, 1964–1969, p. 482

The Fiscal Stimulus Package of 2009, p. 484

Movement Along the *MP* Curve: The Rise in the Federal Funds Rate Target, 2004–2006 and 2015–2019, p. 495

Shift in the *MP* Curve: Autonomous Monetary Easing During the Global Financial and Coronavirus Crises, p. 495

The Volcker Disinflation, 1980–1986, p. 529

Negative Supply Shocks, 1973–1975 and 1978–1980, p. 532

AD/AS Analysis of the Great Recession of 2007–2009, p. 534

An *AD/AS* Analysis of the Covid-19 Recession, p. 535

The Great Inflation, p. 562

Nonconventional Monetary Policy and Quantitative Easing, p. 567

Abenomics and the Shift in Japanese Monetary Policy in 2013, p. 570

The Term Structure of Interest Rates, p. 577

A Tale of Three Oil Price Shocks, p. 586

The Great Recession, p. 604

Applying the Monetary Policy Lessons to Japan's Two Lost Decades, p. 606

Following the Financial News Boxes

Money Market Rates, p. 28

Capital Market Interest Rates, p. 30

Foreign Stock Market Indexes, p. 34

The Monetary Aggregates, p. 57

Yield Curves, p. 125

Foreign Exchange Rates, p. 403

Aggregate Output, Unemployment, and Inflation, p. 510

Global Boxes

Are U.S. Capital Markets Losing Their Edge?, p. 32

The Importance of Financial Intermediaries Relative to Securities Markets: An International Comparison, p. 35

Negative Interest Rates? Japan First, Then the United States, Then Europe, p. 76

Should Foreign Exchange Rates Follow a Random Walk?, p. 153

Barings, Daiwa, Sumitomo, Société Générale, and JP Morgan Chase: Rogue Traders and the Principal–Agent Problem, p. 211

The Spread of Government Deposit Insurance Throughout the World: Is This a Good Thing?, p. 218

Where Is the Basel Accord Heading After the Global Financial Crisis?, p. 223

International Financial Regulation, p. 229

Comparison of Banking Structure in the United States and Abroad, p. 255

Ironic Birth of the Eurodollar Market, p. 261

The European Sovereign Debt Crisis, p. 280

Worldwide Government Bailouts During the 2007–2009 Financial Crisis, p. 282

The European Central Bank's Monetary Policy Strategy, p. 383

Should We Worry About the Large U.S. Current Account Deficit?, p. 431

Will the Euro Survive?, p. 439

Argentina's Currency Board, p. 448

The Demise of Monetary Targeting in Switzerland, p. 581

Ending the Bolivian Hyperinflation: A Successful Anti-Inflation Program, p. 589

Inside the Fed Boxes

Was the Fed to Blame for the Housing Price Bubble?, p. 277

The Political Genius of the Founders of the Federal Reserve System, p. 295

The Special Role of the Federal Reserve Bank of New York, p. 298

The Role of the Research Staff, p. 301

The FOMC Meeting, p. 302

Green, Blue, Teal, and Beige: What Do These Colors Mean at the Fed?, p. 303

Styles of Federal Reserve Chairs: Bernanke, Yellen, and Powell Versus Greenspan, p. 304

Presidential Attacks on the Independence of the Fed, p. 307

The Evolution of the Fed's Communication Strategy, p. 311

A Day at the Trading Desk, p. 352

Using Discount Policy to Prevent a Financial Panic, p. 355

Fed Lending Facilities During the Global Financial and Coronavirus Crises, p. 359

Ben Bernanke's Advocacy of Inflation Targeting, p. 383

The Fed's New Monetary Policy Strategy: Average Inflation Targeting, p. 386

The Fed's Use of the Taylor Rule, p. 396

A Day at the Federal Reserve Bank of New York's Foreign Exchange Desk, p. 426

The Appointment of Paul Volcker, Anti-Inflation Hawk, p. 591

FYI Boxes

Are We Headed for a Cashless Society?, p. 55

Where Are All the U.S. Dollars?, p. 58

Conflicts of Interest at Credit-Rating Agencies and the Global Financial Crisis, p. 121

The Coronavirus Pandemic and the Baa-Treasury Spread, p. 122

Effects of the Trump Tax Cuts on Bond Interest Rates, p. 124

The Yield Curve as a Forecasting Tool for Inflation and the Business Cycle, p. 135

Should You Hire an Ape as Your Investment Adviser?, p. 155

The Enron Implosion, p. 172

The Tyranny of Collateral, p. 182

Bruce Bent and the Money Market Mutual Fund Panic of 2008, p. 246

The Global Financial Crisis and the Demise of Large, Free-Standing Investment Banks, p. 258

Collateralized Debt Obligations (CDOs), p. 275

Was the Fed to Blame for the Housing Price Bubble?, p. 277

Modern Monetary Theory, p. 462

Meaning of the Word *Investment*, p. 474

Deriving the Aggregate Demand Curve Algebraically, p. 497

What Does *Autonomous* Mean?, p. 512

The Phillips Curve Trade-Off and Macroeconomic Policy in the 1960s, p. 543

The Activist/Nonactivist Debate Over the Obama Fiscal Stimulus Package, p. 557

The Political Business Cycle and Richard Nixon, p. 580

Consumers' Balance Sheets and the Great Depression, p. 603

THE SUPREME COURT
OF THE UNITED STATES

A Student Companion

THE SUPREME COURT

COURT

OF THE UNITED STATES

A *Student Companion*

SECOND EDITION

John J. Patrick

OXFORD

UNIVERSITY PRESS

Oxford University Press

Oxford   New York
Athens   Auckland   Bangkok   Bogotá   Buenos Aires   Cape Town
Chennai   Dar es Salaam   Delhi   Florence   Hong Kong   Istanbul   Karachi
Kolkata   Kuala Lumpur   Madrid   Melbourne   Mexico City   Mumbai   Nairobi
Paris   São Paulo   Shanghai   Singapore   Taipei   Tokyo   Toronto   Warsaw

and associated companies in
Berlin   Ibadan

Published by Oxford University Press, Inc.,
198 Madison Avenue, New York, New York 10016
www.oup-usa.org

Oxford is a registered trademark of Oxford University Press

Design: Sandy Kaufman
Consultant: David J. Bodenhamer, Professor of History and Director,
POLIS Research Center, Indiana University–Purdue University at Indianapolis;
author, *Fair Trial: Rights of the Accused in American History*

Library of Congress Cataloging-in-Publication Data

Patrick, John J.
    The Supreme Court of the United States : a student companion / John J. Patrick.—2nd ed.
    p.cm. — (Oxford student companions to American government)
    Rev. ed. of: The young Oxford companion to the Supreme Court of the United States. c1994.
    Includes bibliographical references and index.
    Summary: An alphabetically arranged, illustrated guide to the Supreme Court, including
    biographical articles on all the justices, summaries and analysis of key decisions and
    major cases, and definitions of legal terms.
    ISBN 0-19-515008-2
        1. United States. Supreme Court—Encyclopedias, Juvenile. [1. United States. Supreme Court—
    Encyclopedias.] I. Patrick, John J., Young Oxford companion to the Supreme Court of the
    United States. II. Title. III. Series.

KF8742.A35 P38 2001
347.73'26'03--dc21

9 8 7 6 5 4 3 2

Printed in the United States of America
on acid-free paper.

On the cover: *(top left) The bronze statue of Chief Justice John
Marshall in the Supreme Court Building; (top right) Justice Thurgood
Marshall; (bottom) the Supreme Court Building*

Frontispiece: Authority of Law, *one of two marble statues by James
Earl Fraser that flank the front portico of the Supreme Court Building*

CONTENTS

7

PREFACE TO THE SECOND EDITION

8

PREFACE TO THE FIRST EDITION

9

HOW TO USE THIS BOOK

11

THE SUPREME COURT
OF THE UNITED STATES:
A STUDENT COMPANION

379

APPENDIX 1: TERMS OF THE JUSTICES
OF THE U.S. SUPREME COURT

383

APPENDIX 2: VISITING THE
SUPREME COURT BUILDING

384

APPENDIX 3: WEB SITES

386

FURTHER READING

390

INDEX

PREFACE
TO THE SECOND EDITION

The second edition of this *Companion,* like the first, is dedicated to the principle of liberty. In order for people who enjoy liberty to make choices intelligently, they require knowledge. Therefore, this second edition updates and strengthens the information about the Supreme Court presented in the first edition.

Articles on core concepts such as federalism and separation of powers have been expanded to include the latest relevant Supreme Court decisions. Similarly, articles on controversial topics such as abortion rights, affirmative action, and the relationship of government to religion have been updated. Further, this edition includes eight new full-case treatments of landmark Supreme Court decisions. Finally, there is an annotated guide to web sites on the federal judiciary and decisions of the Supreme Court.

Long ago, James Madison, one of the greatest American political thinkers, raised this question in an essay published in the *National Gazette* on December 20, 1792: "Who are the best keepers of the people's liberties?" His answer, of course, was "the people" in tandem with their institutions of constitutional government, including the Supreme Court of the United States. Without sufficient knowledge and the ability to use it, however, the people cannot and will not be "keepers of their liberties." So this work is designed to contribute to the people's knowledge so that they can be effective and responsible guardians of their rights to liberties.

As I worked to update this book, three young people were constantly in my thoughts: my granddaughters, Rachel Patrick and Abigail May, and my niece, Laurel Ellet. I trust that this work will contribute to the knowledge they need to be keepers of their own liberties.

On the west side of the Supreme Court Building, the inscription beneath the frieze reads "Equal Justice Under Law."

PREFACE
TO THE FIRST EDITION

Liberty, a desired end of constitutional government in the United States, is dependent upon law and justice. This truth is captured by two phrases carved on the marble exterior of the Supreme Court Building: over the east portico, "Justice the Guardian of Liberty," and over the west portico, "Equal Justice Under Law."

According to its framers, the U.S. Constitution was designed to "secure the Blessings of Liberty." The framers knew, however, that this lofty ideal could not be attained without workable instruments of government crafted for this end. The Supreme Court was intended to be a major means of securing the people's liberty.

The Supreme Court has the special duty of guarding the individual's rights to liberty through judicial review, its power to void government actions that violate the supreme law of the Constitution.

James Madison, the major architect of the Constitution, presciently observed that "independent tribunals of justice [headed by the Supreme Court] will consider themselves in a peculiar manner the guardians of those [constitutional] rights; they will be an impenetrable bulwark against every assumption of power in the legislative or executive; they will be naturally led to resist every encroachment upon rights expressly stipulated for in the Constitution."

During the 1830s, a perceptive French visitor to the United States, Alexis de Tocqueville, confirmed the enduring vision of the Constitution's framers about the critical importance of the Supreme Court to the vitality and destiny of their work. "Without [justices of the Supreme Court], the Constitution would be a dead letter," wrote Tocqueville in his classic 1835 commentary about the United States, *Democracy in America.* "Their power is enormous," Tocqueville wrote, "but it is the power of public opinion. [The justices] are all-powerful as long as the people respect the law; but they would be impotent against popular neglect or contempt of the law."

The Court has no power to guard the rights of the people through its rulings about the law unless particular people assume responsibility for bringing cases to the judiciary. Further, the Court's rulings, no matter how wise or just, may practically amount to nothing unless the people are vigilant about their enforcement.

The Supreme Court cannot serve the cause of the people's liberty without popular support. And to be effective, this support depends upon widespread public knowledge of the Court's work and a public commitment, based on reason, to the constitutional values for which it works.

The entries in this volume were written to further the spread of knowledge and understanding about law and its relationship to liberty. The articles introduce the reader to the origins and development of the Supreme Court. They discuss controversies and failures along with the achievements of the justices during different periods of U.S. history. The entries in this book will answer many of your questions about the Court. They are also likely to raise new questions, which can be investigated through use of the many suggestions for further reading.

As I worked on this book two young people, very dear to me, were constantly in my thoughts. And so I dedicate this work to them: my granddaughter, Rachel Patrick, and my niece, Laurel Ellet. I hope that this book will contribute to the education of their generation, the responsible citizens of the future.

HOW TO USE THIS BOOK

The articles in this *Companion* are arranged alphabetically, so you can look up words, ideas, or names as you come across them in other readings. You can then use the SEE ALSO listings at the end of the article to read about related subjects. Sometimes you may find that the *Companion* deals with information under a different article name than what you looked up. The book will then refer you to the proper article. For example, if you look up Judicial Conference of the United States, you will find the notation "SEE Administration of Federal Courts." If you cannot find a separate article on a particular subject, look in the index, which will guide you to the relevant articles. All people are listed alphabetically by last name; for example, the entry for Sandra Day O'Connor is listed as O'Connor, Sandra Day, under O.

You can also use this *Companion* topically, by reading all the articles about a particular aspect of the Supreme Court. Below are several groupings of topics around common themes.

Biographies: There are articles on all the chief justices and associate justices of the Supreme Court, listed by surname. The biographical entries include personal data about each justice, including the place and dates of birth and death, education, previous government experience, and period of service on the Court. The articles emphasize participation in notable Court decisions and significant contributions to constitutional law.

Decisions of the Court: The book contains articles on 100 of the most historically significant cases decided by the Supreme Court. Each article on a case opens with standard information. The name of the case is followed by the official citation from *United States Reports* (for cases since 1875). For example, for *Abington School District* v. *Schempp* the citation is 374 U.S. 203 (1963). This means that the opinion in the case is published in volume 374 of *United States Reports,* beginning on page 203. The year the case was decided follows in parentheses.

Before 1875, official reports of Supreme Court cases were published under the names of the Court reporters. Thus, these names (full or abbreviated) appear in the citations of the Court's decisions before 1875. For example, the citation for *McCulloch* v. *Maryland* is 4 Wheat. 316 (1819). Wheat. is an abbreviation for Henry Wheaton, the Supreme Court Reporter from 1816 to 1827. Thus, this citation indicates that this case can be found in the 4th volume compiled by Wheaton, that it begins on page 316, and that it was decided in 1819.

Each case article in the *Companion* also provides the vote of the justices on the case; who wrote the majority opinion for the Court; who, if anyone, joined with a concurring opinion; and who, if anyone, dissented. Each article on a Supreme Court case also includes background information on the case; the issue or issues before the Court; the Court's opinion and legal reasoning in deciding the case; the dissenting opinions, if any, and reasons for them; and the significance of the case in constitutional law and history.

Core Concepts: Another category includes articles that define and discuss concepts central to the meaning of constitutionalism in the United States and decision making by the Court. There are articles, for example, on the Bill of Rights, Commerce power, Constitutional law, Due process of law, Federalism, Incorporation doctrine, Independent judiciary, Judicial activism and judicial restraint, Judicial review, Jurisdiction, Republicanism, Separation of powers, and Trial by jury.

Ideas and Issues: There are several essays on constitutional ideas and issues that have come before the Court. These essays show how decisions of the U.S. Supreme Court have affected the choices and opportunities of many people throughout American history. These essays include Abortion rights; Affirmative action; Capital punishment; Civil rights; Equality under the Constitution; Freedom of speech and press; Gun control and the right to bear arms; Juvenile justice; Liberty under the Constitution; Privacy, right to; Property rights; Religious issues under the Constitution; Rights of the accused; and Student rights under the Constitution.

Legal Terms and Phrases: The *Companion* contains definitions of many legal terms and phrases involved in the Court's work. For example, you can find definitions of basic technical terms, such as certiorari, writ of; habeas corpus, writ of; precedent; and seditious libel. There are also famous phrases associated with the Court, such as "separate but equal"

(used in *Plessy* v. *Ferguson,* 1896) and Lemon Test (derived from *Lemon* v. *Kurtzman,* 1971).

Procedures, Practices, and Personnel: You can read about the procedures and practices by which the Supreme Court operates. Some examples of these entries are: Administration of federal courts, Conference, Decision days, Discuss list, Opinions, Oral argument, Rules of the Court, and Seniority.

Supreme Court Building: If you visit Washington, D.C., you may want to visit the Supreme Court Building. To learn more about this building, as well as the Court's previous homes, see the article on Buildings, Supreme Court, and Appendix 2, Visiting the Supreme Court Building.

Further Reading: If you want to know more about a specific topic, you can use the FURTHER READING entries at the end of many of the articles as well as the FURTHER READING guide at the end of the book, which lists more general sources.

THE SUPREME COURT OF THE UNITED STATES
A Student Companion

Abington School District v. Schempp

☆ *374 U.S. 203 (1963)*
☆ *Vote: 8–1*
☆ *For the Court: Clark*
☆ *Concurring: Brennan, Douglas, and Goldberg*
☆ *Dissenting: Stewart*

A PENNSYLVANIA law required that each public school day must be started with the reading of at least 10 verses from the Bible, without comment. A student could be excused from this requirement by presenting to school authorities a written request from a parent or guardian. The Schempp family challenged the state law. They refused to request an exception for their child, a student at Abington High School, from the Bible-reading exercise. And they refused to allow their child to attend this exercise. The Schempps brought suit against the Abington School District to block enforcement of the Bible-reading statute.

The Issue Did the Pennsylvania law on Bible reading in public schools violate the 1st Amendment provision against laws "respecting an establishment of religion"?

Opinion of the Court The Court decided in favor of the Schempp family and struck down the state law on Bible reading in public schools. Writing for the Court, Justice Tom Clark concluded that the government may not promote religion in public schools. For the first time, the Court specified a test for determining whether a law violates the establishment clause of the 1st Amendment. Justice Clark wrote:

> The test may be stated as follows: What are the purposes and primary effect of the enactment? If either is the advancement or inhibition of religion then the enactment exceeds the scope of legislative power as circumscribed by the Constitution.... [T]o withstand the strictures of the Establishment Clause there must be a secular legislative purpose and a primary effect that neither advances nor inhibits religion.

According to the Court, the Pennsylvania law on daily Bible reading in public schools failed to pass this establishment clause test. The state law failed

Petitioners work to convince Congress to return Bible reading to public schools. The Abington case had decided that such Bible reading was unconstitutional.

because it advances religion. The Pennsylvania Bible-reading statute was therefore ruled unconstitutional.

Dissent Justice Potter Stewart claimed that the Court had incorrectly applied the 1st Amendment's establishment clause in this case. He emphasized that by striking down the state law, the Court was denying free exercise of religion to the majority of citizens. According to Justice Stewart, this Pennsylvania law was constitutional because it did not force students to participate in a religious exercise. Justice Stewart wrote:

> We err in the first place if we do not recognize, as a matter of history and as a matter of imperatives of our free society, that religion and government must necessarily interact in countless ways....
>
> [T]he central value embodied in the First Amendment... is the safeguarding of an individual's right to free exercise of his religion.... [T]here is involved in these cases a substantial free exercise claim on the part of those who affirmatively desire to have their children's school day open with the reading of passages from the Bible.

Significance This case clearly stated the Court's position that the government cannot foster or promote religious doctrine in public schools through state-legislated religious exercises. By reinforcing the *Engel* v. *Vitale* (1962) decision, the Court in this case seemed to settle the question of state-sponsored religious exercises in public schools. However, public opinion polls from the 1960s to the 1990s have shown that more than 60 percent of Americans disagree with the Court's decisions on the prohibition of prayer in public school–sanctioned programs. Vigorous debate about the separation of church and state continues.

SEE ALSO

Engel v. Vitale; Establishment clause; Religious issues under the Constitution

Abortion rights

ABORTION IS the termination of a pregnancy before the embryo or fetus is capable of survival outside the mother's womb. Should a woman have the right to decide whether or when to have an abortion?

In the United States, the state governments traditionally have regulated the performance of abortions. In 1960 every state government had a law making abortion a crime except when it was done to save the mother's life. By 1973, however, 14 states had passed laws permitting abortions under certain other conditions, such as when the pregnancy resulted from rape or incest, or when the baby, if born, would likely suffer from a severe defect. Alaska, Hawaii, and New York repealed most previous restrictions on the woman's right to an abortion.

In 1973 the U.S. Supreme Court made its landmark ruling on abortion rights in *Roe* v. *Wade*. The Court struck down a Texas law regulating abortion as an unconstitutional infringement of a woman's right to privacy, which had been established in *Griswold* v. *Connecticut* (1965). In *Griswold* the Court invalidated a Connecticut law prohibiting the use of birth control devices by ruling that it violated a person's constitutional right to a zone of privacy based on several provisions of the Bill of Rights and the due process clause of the 14th Amendment. In *Roe* the Court held that the "right of privacy [established in *Griswold*] is broad enough to encompass a woman's decision whether or not to terminate her pregnancy."

Writing for the Court, Justice Harry Blackmun stated that a woman's right to abortion could be limited, however, by "a compelling state interest" to protect her health and life. The Court decided that during the second trimester of a woman's pregnancy (months 4 to 6), the state might intervene to regulate abortion to protect the mother's health and that the state might regulate or prohibit abortion during the third trimester (months 7 to 9). During the first trimester (months 1 to 3) of a pregnancy, however, it seemed unlikely that there would be a reason to restrict abortion rights in order to protect the health and life of the mother.

Writing in dissent, Justice Byron White could not find in the Constitution the right to privacy upon which the *Roe* decision was based. Justice White helped to frame the controversy about abortion rights that has continued since the *Roe* decision. Many critics, like Justice White, have believed that questions about abortion rights should be resolved by state governments, not by the Court, as had been the long-standing practice in the American federal system of government.

Many critics of the *Roe* decision, however, have opposed it on religious or moral grounds. They reject abortion rights because, in their system of belief, abortion is a sin or morally wrong.

Activities to counter or overturn the *Roe* decision have persisted and have led to legal challenges in federal courts. But attempts to erect barriers to abortion rights have mostly failed, as have efforts to overturn *Roe*.

In *Harris* v. *McRae* (1980), however, the Court held that "although government may not place obstacles in the path of a woman's exercise of her freedom of choice [to have an abortion], it need not remove those not of its own creation. Indigency [being poor] falls in the latter category." As a result of this ruling, poor women who could not afford to pay for an abortion were no longer able to use federal Medicaid funds for one, except in cases of rape or incest or when the mother's life is threatened. Further, in *Ohio* v. *Akron Center for Reproductive Health* (1990), the

Court upheld a state law that required minors (those below adult age) seeking an abortion either to notify one parent or get approval from a local court of law.

A major legal challenge to *Roe* emerged in *Webster* v. *Reproductive Health Services* (1989). This case concerned the constitutionality of a 1986 Missouri law that included several provisions for restricting a woman's right to an abortion. The Court upheld only two. One banned the use of public facilities or public employees to carry out an abortion. The other restriction pertained to the performance of an abortion on a woman carrying a fetus thought to be more than 20 weeks old. Before performing such an abortion, the physician must determine, through medical testing, whether the fetus is viable, or capable of living outside the mother's womb. If it is viable, the abortion may be prohibited.

The *Webster* decision thus modified the second-trimester rule in *Roe*, which held that all regulations on abortion rights must be related to protecting the health of the mother. The *Webster* decision, however, stopped short of overturning *Roe*, which antiabortion rights advocates had wanted. And the *Webster* decision held that while government

A protestor holds baby dolls while surrounded by abortion-rights demonstrators in front of the U.S. Supreme Court building after a hearing in April 2000 on partial-birth abortions.

regulation of abortions is permissible, such regulation could not impose "undue burdens" or unreasonable obstacles to a person seeking an abortion.

In 1992, in *Planned Parenthood* v. *Casey,* the Court used the "undue burden" standard to uphold most of the Pennsylvania Control Act. The sustained parts of this law required a woman to wait 24 hours to have an abortion after receiving specific information from a doctor about the procedure, the condition of the fetus, and the possible alternatives to abortion. The one part of the law that the Court found unconstitutional was the requirement that a married woman inform her husband about an intended abortion. As in the *Webster* case, however, the Court's majority refused to overturn the *Roe* decision.

In 2000 (*Stenberg* v. *Carhart*), the Supreme Court struck down a Nebraska law (and, in effect, 30 similar state laws) that banned a procedure called "partial-birth" abortion. Doctors have used this procedure, which they call D&X (dilation and extraction), to terminate late-term pregnancies. Writing for the Court's 5-to-4 majority, Justice Stephen Breyer declared the Nebraska law unconstitutional because it did not provide an exception for cases when the life or health of the mother is in danger. Further, he held the law was written so broadly that it could be used to prohibit abortion procedures other than D&X, which would violate the Court's *Roe* decision. Writing in dissent, Justice Anthony Kennedy deplored the Court's decision and said the 1997 Nebraska law was made "to forbid a procedure many decent and civilized people find so abhorrent as to be among the most serious of crimes against human life."

SEE ALSO
Griswold v. Connecticut; Privacy, right to; Roe v. Wade; Webster v. Reproductive Health Services

FURTHER READING
Garrow, David J. *Liberty and Sexuality: The Right to Privacy and the Making of Roe v. Wade, 1923–1973.* New York: Macmillan, 1993.
Graber, Mark A. *Rethinking Abortion: Equal Choice, the Constitution, and Reproductive Politics.* Princeton, N.J.: Princeton University Press, 1999.
Tribe, Laurence H. *Abortion: The Clash of Absolutes.* New York: Norton, 1990.

Abrams v. United States

☆ *250 U.S. 616 (1919)*
☆ *Vote: 7–2*
☆ *For the Court: Clarke*
☆ *Dissenting: Holmes and Brandeis*

JACOB ABRAMS was arrested in New York City on August 23, 1918. He and several friends had written, printed, and distributed copies of a leaflet that severely criticized President Woodrow Wilson and the U.S. government. The leaflet opposed President Wilson's decision to send a small U.S. military force to Russia during the civil war that followed the communist revolution of 1917. The communists, led by Vladimir Lenin, were fighting against anticommunist Russians and various foreign military forces to retain control of the government. Abrams's leaflet urged American workers to walk off their jobs in protest against President Wilson and the U.S. government and in support of the new communist government in Russia.

Abrams and his friends were arrested for violating the Espionage Act of 1917 and the Sedition Act of 1918. These laws made it a crime to write and publish disloyal or profane statements that were intended to interfere with production of goods necessary to the defense of the United States during wartime. The laws were passed to control antiwar ac-

Jacob Abrams (far right) and these other Russian immigrants dumped leaflets criticizing President Woodrow Wilson from the tops of New York City buildings.

tivity after the United States entered World War I.

The Issue The specific question facing the Court pertained to the constitutionality of the Espionage Act and the Sedition Act. These federal laws were designed to limit freedom of expression in order to protect national security during wartime. However, the 1st Amendment says, "Congress shall make no law... abridging the freedom of speech, or of the press, or the right of the people peaceably to assemble, and to petition the Government for a redress of grievances." Did enforcement of the Espionage Act and the Sedition Act violate the 1st Amendment free speech and press rights of Jacob Abrams?

Opinion of the Court Justice John H. Clarke, writing for the Court, decided against Abrams's claims that his 1st Amendment rights were violated. Clarke based his decision on the "clear and present danger" and "bad tendency" tests stated by Justice Oliver Wendell Holmes in *Schenck* v. *United States* (1919). According to these two tests, which Holmes used interchangeably in *Schenck*, free speech and press could be limited if they were intended to cause an illegal action or if they threatened national security.

Justice Clarke wrote that "men must be held to have intended, and to be accountable for, the effects which their acts were likely to produce." Clarke argued that "the obvious effect" of the leaflet "would be to persuade persons... not to work in ammunition factories, where their work would produce bullets, bayonets, cannons, and other munitions" needed by U.S. military forces in World War I.

Dissent Justice Oliver Wendell Holmes disagreed, for himself and Justice Louis Brandeis, with Justice Clarke's use of the "clear and present danger" test in this case. And he repudiated the "bad tendency" test. Justice Holmes maintained that the government had the right to protect itself against speech that immediately and directly threatens the security and safety of the country. He wrote that the 1st Amendment protected the expression of all opinions "unless they so imminently threaten immediate interference with the lawful and pressing purposes of the law that an immediate check is required to save the country." Justice Holmes denied that Abrams's actions and intentions represented a danger sufficient to justify limitation of his freedom of expression.

Justice Holmes concluded his dissent with a compelling theory of free speech in a constitutional democracy. Arguing for "free trade in ideas," Holmes said: "[T]he best test of truth is the power of the thought to get itself accepted in the competition of the market. . . . That at any rate is the theory of our Constitution. It is an experiment, as all life is an experiment."

Significance The Court's opinion in this case prevailed only in the short run. The dissent of Justice Holmes eventually had more influence on the Court and the American people. Holmes modified the "clear and present danger" test he had stated in *Schenck*, which had been used interchangeably with the "bad tendency" test. In *Abrams*, Holmes rejected the "bad tendency" test, which emphasized a person's intentions to encourage lawless behavior. Instead, Holmes stated in his *Abrams* dissent that a "clear and present danger" exists only when speech can be immediately and directly connected to specific actions that cause illegal behavior threatening the safety or security of the United States. If an imminent danger could not be demonstrated, then speech could not be lawfully limited. The *Abrams* dissent has been called the best defense of free speech ever written by an American.

SEE ALSO

Freedom of speech and press; Schenck v. United States; Seditious libel

FURTHER READING

Polenberg, Richard. *Fighting Faiths: The Abrams Case, the Supreme Court, and Free Speech*. New York: Viking, 1987.

Administration of federal courts

THE SUPREME COURT is in charge of the administration of the federal judicial system. The chief justice and associate justices participate in the work of the Judicial Conference of the United States, the Administrative Office of the United States Courts, and the Federal Judicial Center.

Judicial Conference of the United States

The chief justice presides over the Judicial Conference of the United States, a board of trustees for the federal courts. created by an act of Congress in 1922. The members of the Judicial Conference represent the district or trial courts, the intermediate appellate courts, and the

Supreme Court. By law, the mission of the Judicial Conference of the United States is to oversee the practices and procedures of the federal courts and to recommend changes to improve the functioning of the federal judicial system. The conference meets twice a year at the Supreme Court Building in Washington, D.C.

Administrative Office of the United States Courts

Budgeting services and staff support for the Judicial Conference of the United States are provided by the Administrative Office of the U.S. Courts. The Administrative Office, created in 1939 by an act of Congress, operates under direction of the Judicial Conference to oversee and provide administrative services for the lower federal courts. More than 600 people work for the Administrative Office. The director, appointed by the Supreme Court, reports to the Judicial Conference of the United States.

Federal Judicial Center

In 1967 Congress enacted legislation to create the Federal Judicial Center, which carries out research and training programs to improve the operations of the federal courts. The chief justice presides over the seven-member board of the center, which meets four times each year and oversees the work of the center's staff of more than 100 people. Findings of the center's research projects are reported to the Judicial Conference of the United States.

Admiralty and maritime law

ARTICLE 3, SECTION 2, of the U.S. Constitution says, "The judicial Power shall extend … to all Cases of admiralty and maritime Jurisdiction." Admiralty or maritime law pertains to ships on the sea, including civil and criminal actions. In 1815 Justice Joseph Story, writing for the Court in *De Lovio* v. *Boit,* defined the scope of the Court's admiralty jurisdiction by stating that it extended to all transactions "which relate to the navigation, business, or commerce of the sea."

Advisory opinions

AN ADVISORY OPINION is a legal opinion given before a case is tried. Federal judges do not provide advisory opinions because Article 3 of the U.S. Constitution says their jurisdiction extends only to real cases and controversies "in Law and Equity, arising under this Constitution," and they therefore cannot issue statements about hypothetical cases.

A precedent against advisory opinions was established in 1793, when President George Washington asked Chief Justice John Jay and the Supreme Court to advise him about the federal government's obligations stemming from a 1778 treaty made by the Continental Congress with France. John Jay replied in a letter (August 8, 1793) that it was wrong, under the Constitution, for the Court to provide an advisory opinion to the President or anyone else. Jay's letter explained that the justices should not provide opinions on any matter unless it was brought to the Court through formal legal procedures as a real case.

The letter set a precedent against advisory opinions. It reinforced the principle of separation of powers and judicial independence from the executive branch.

Chief Justice John Jay established the precedent that the Supreme Court would not provide advisory opinions.

Thus, the President turns to the attorney general of the United States or to his own counsel, both of whom are officials of the executive branch, for legal advice.

SEE ALSO
Separation of powers

Affirmative action

DURING THE 1950s and 1960s, the Supreme Court struck down laws that unfairly discriminated against individuals on the basis of race. Through its decisions in cases such as *Brown* v. *Board of Education* (1954) and *Heart of Atlanta Motel* v. *United States* (1964), the Court ruled that African Americans must have "equal protection of the laws," which the 14th Amendment says is a right available to all people in the United States. While lauding this major advance in civil rights for African Americans, many civil rights leaders said it was not sufficient to overcome the negative effects of more than two centuries of racial discrimination in the United States. So, during the 1970s and 1980s, leaders of civil rights organizations, such as the National Association for the Advancement of Colored People (NAACP) and the National Organization of Women (NOW), proposed programs designed to go beyond mere equality of opportunity to provide limited kinds of preferential treatment for victims of long-term racial or gender-based discrimination. These programs are called *affirmative action* because they involve plans designed, through specific actions, to bring about desired outcomes, such as increased job opportunities, job promotions, and admissions to colleges and universities.

Affirmative action plans, as conceived by civil rights leaders, have the following characteristics. First, they may be spon-

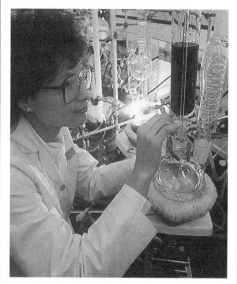

Dr. Yuhpyng Chen, a medical chemist, works in the lab at Pfizer Inc. Large corporations often design affirmative action programs to ensure that members of minority groups have access to job opportunities.

sored or instituted either by government agencies and public educational institutions or by private organizations, such as businesses, labor unions, vocational training schools, or private colleges.

Second, affirmative action plans take into account such personal factors as race, ethnicity, or gender when individuals are under consideration for employment in a job, promotion to a better job, or admission to a school or college. However, individuals must *not* receive education or employment benefits solely on the basis of such factors as race, ethnicity, or gender; rather, these personal factors will determine who receives or does not receive certain opportunities only when minority candidates are otherwise well qualified for the jobs, educational programs, and so forth that they seek to attain.

Third, affirmative action programs are based clearly on the educational or economic need of individuals resulting from unfair treatment in the past of racial, ethnic, or gender groups to which these people belong.

Fourth, affirmative action plans are supposed to be temporary remedies.

Supporters of affirmative action plans have pointed out that most members of certain minority groups, such as African

Americans, lag far behind most white Americans in income, educational attainment, job advancement, and general living standards. They claim that these differences are the result of long-term racial discrimination, rooted in the pre–Civil War institution of slavery. Further, they argue that affirmative action programs, whether required by the government or voluntarily undertaken by private employers and schools, are the best means to overcome the persistent negative consequences of past discrimination against minorities, especially African Americans.

Affirmative action programs have been widely established in education and economic institutions of the United States. These programs have raised a fundamental constitutional question. Does the 14th Amendment's guarantee of "equal protection of the laws" permit certain kinds of preferential treatment of certain categories of individuals, such as African Americans or women, in order to remedy the negative consequences of long-term discrimination against them?

The Supreme Court has upheld some affirmative action practices while striking down extreme versions of this concept. In *Regents of the University of California* v. *Bakke* (1978), for example, the Court ruled that a university could take into account race and ethnicity when making decisions about the admission of students. However, the Court ruled that an affirmative action plan based on rigid racial quotas to boost admission of minority students to a university was unconstitutional. In *United Steelworkers of America* v. *Weber* (1979), the Court permitted an employer's voluntarily imposed and temporary affirmative action program. That program would encourage unskilled black workers to obtain training that would lead to better, more skilled jobs, in which black Americans historically have been underrepresented. Once again, however, the Court rejected rigid, race-based quotas in hiring and job advancement.

In *United States* v. *Paradise* (1987) the Court upheld a temporary and "narrowly tailored" quota system to bring about job promotion for black state troopers in Alabama. The state's affirmative action plan imposed a "one black for one white" promotion quota. This was justified, the Court said, by the "long and shameful record of delay and resistance" to employment opportunities for black Americans in the Alabama state police.

In 1987, in *Johnson* v. *Transportation Agency of Santa Clara County,* the Court endorsed a carefully crafted, temporary, and voluntary affirmative action plan to boost job promotion opportunities for women. The Court held it was permissible to take into account a woman's gender as a positive factor in promotion to a higher-ranking position because women had been systematically denied access to such positions in the past.

In 1995, the Court ruled in *Adarand Constructors, Inc.* v. *Peña* that all public programs that give preferences to minorities should be subjected to the strictest judicial scrutiny. Race-based affirmative action programs would be upheld, the Court declared, only if they were narrowly designed to apply to individuals victimized by past acts of racial discrimination. Thus, the Court emphasized that equal protection of the laws is a right guaranteed by the Constitution to every individual.

In 1996, the Supreme Court let stand a decision of the 5th Circuit Court of Appeals against an affirmative action policy of the University of Texas Law School. The Court of Appeals struck down a policy that allowed admissions officers to consider racial identity as a factor in making decisions about which students to admit to the law school. The policy's purpose was to increase significantly the number of law school students belonging to racial minority groups. In its decision to ban this policy, the Court of Appeals contradicted the Supreme Court's 1978 *Bakke* decision, in which the Court held that colleges or universities could consider race in their admissions policies as long as they did not establish rigid race-based quotas.

In a brief statement about its refusal to hear this University of Texas Law School case, the Court said that the case did not offer a favorable opportunity to decide the issue. Because the University of Texas had abolished the policy at issue in the case, Justice Ruth Bader Ginsburg explained that "we must await a final judgment on a program genuinely in controversy before addressing the important questions raised in this petition."

Due to a last minute settlement, the Court did not hear an affirmative action case during the 1997–1998 term. In 1997 the Court had declined to hear a challenge to a California law banning race- or sex-based preferences in school admissions, public employment, and government contracts. The Court let stand a decision by the Ninth Circuit that the statute at issue, passed by voters in a referendum on Proposition 209, was not unconstitutional. Affirmative action, however, remains a controversial political and legal issue.

SEE ALSO

Brown v. Board of Education; Civil rights; Equality under the Constitution; Heart of Atlanta Motel v. United States; Johnson v. Transportation Agency of Santa Clara County; National Association for the Advancement of Colored People (NAACP); Regents of the University of California v. Bakke; United Steelworkers of America v. Weber

FURTHER READING

Gray, W. Robert. *The Four Faces of Affirmative Action: Fundamental Answers and Actions.* Westport, Conn.: Greenwood, 2001.

Rosenfeld, Michel. *Affirmative Action and Justice.* New Haven: Yale University Press, 1991.

Schwartz, Bernard. *Behind Bakke: Affirmative Action and the Supreme Court*. New York: New York University Press, 1988.

Spann, Girardeau A. *The Law of Affirmative Action: Twenty-Five Years of Supreme Court Decisions on Race and Remedies*. New York: New York University Press, 2000.

African Americans in the Federal Judiciary

In 2000, 10.3 percent of the country's federal judges were African American, while more than 12 percent of the total U.S. population was African American. The Supreme Court included one black justice, Clarence Thomas. Only one other African American had ever sat on the Court: Thurgood Marshall, who served from 1967 to 1991.

Half of the 13 U.S. appellate courts included no one of African-American ancestry in 2000. The Fourth Circuit, which serves Maryland, Virginia, West Virginia, North Carolina, and South Carolina, has never had a black judge, even though 23 percent of the region's population is black. Civil rights organizations, such as the National Association for the Advancement of Colored People (NAACP) have persistently called for the appointment of more African Americans and other minorities to the federal judiciary.

Agostini v. Felton

☆ *521 U.S. 203 (1997)*
☆ *Vote: 5–4*
☆ *For the Court: O'Connor*
☆ *Dissenting: Souter*

Issues involving the relationship of church and state have challenged the Supreme Court throughout the second half of the 20th century. The justices have struggled to determine the extent to which the 1st Amendment's establishment clause requires separation of government and religion.

In *Aguilar* v. *Felton* (1985), the Supreme Court decided for strict separation. It held that New York City could not use government funds to send public school teachers into private religious schools to provide remedial education for disadvantaged children. This program had been authorized by a federal law, Title 1 of the Elementary and Secondary Education Act of 1965. The Court, however, concluded that this New York program led to excessive entanglement of church and state in violation of the U.S. Constitution.

In 1995, the New York City School Board filed a motion in the federal district court to seek reconsideration of the *Aguilar* decision. The petitioners argued that Supreme Court decisions subsequent to *Aguilar* had undermined the Court's ruling in this 1985 case. In *Zobrest* v. *Catalina School District* (1993), for example, the Supreme Court decided that a deaf student in a private religious school could be helped by a sign-language interpreter supported by government funds. The Court explained that this kind of public aid directly helps the student— and not the private religious school or the church that sponsors it—and therefore does not violate the 1st Amendment's establishment clause.

The Issue The 1985 *Aguilar* decision seemed to be contradicted by the 1993 *Zobrest* decision. So the issue in *Aguilar* was raised again: can remedial instruction be provided constitutionally to disadvantaged students in private religious schools through a federal government program?

Opinion of the Court The Supreme Court overturned the decision in *Aguilar* v. *Felton*. By a narrow 5-to-4 majority, the justices repudiated the argument that all government aid to religious schools is unconstitutional. Public funds could be provided to support programs that directly aid students of private religious schools and clearly promote secular purposes that contribute to the public good. The establishment clause is not violated as long as the religious mission of the private school is neither advanced nor obstructed by a government program.

In making this decision, the Court used three criteria, which modified those of the Lemon Test, a set of standards developed by the Court in *Lemon* v. *Kurtzman* (1971). First, does the program of government aid provided to a sectarian school result in religious indoctrination? Second, does it define the recipients of government aid by reference to religion? Third, does it create an excessive entanglement between government and religion? If the answer to these three questions is negative, as it was in the *Agostini* case, then there is no violation of the establishment clause.

Dissent Led by Justice David Souter, the four dissenters argued against overturning the *Aguilar* decision. They predicted that the Court's decision in the *Agostini* case would open the way to direct government aid of religious institutions and thereby to public support of particular religious missions. Thus, the establishment clause of the 1st Amendment would be grossly violated.

Significance The *Agostini* decision buoyed advocates of accommodation between government and religious institutions. It dismayed those in favor of strict separation between church and state.

SEE ALSO
Establishment clause; Lemon Test; Lemon v. Kurtzman; Religious issues under the Constitution

Amendments to the Constitution

THE AUTHORS of the U.S. Constitution realized that this document would have to be revised to meet new needs that would arise as times changed. George Washington expressed the inevitable need for, and value of, constitutional change in a letter to his nephew, Bushrod Washington (Nov. 10, 1787):

> The warmest friends and best supporters the Constitution has do not contend that it is free from imperfections.... I think the People (for it is with them to Judge) can...decide with as much propriety on the alterations and amendments which are necessary [as] ourselves. I do not think we are more inspired, have more wisdom, or possess more virtue than those who will come after us.

The amendment process

George Washington, who presided at the Constitutional Convention of 1787, recognized the importance of Article 5 of the Constitution, which specifies how formal changes, or amendments, may be made. Article 5 says:

> The Congress, whenever two thirds of both Houses shall deem it necessary, shall propose Amendments to this Constitution, or, on the Application

Women voting in New York City after the passage of the 19th Amendment, which guaranteed their right to vote nationwide.

of the Legislatures of two thirds of the several States, shall call a Convention for proposing Amendments, which, in either Case, shall be valid to all Intents and Purposes, as Part of this Constitution, when ratified by the Legislatures of three fourths of the several States, or by Conventions in three fourths thereof, as the one or the other Mode of Ratification may be proposed by the Congress; Provided that no Amendment which may be made prior to the Year One thousand eight hundred and eight shall in any Manner affect the first and fourth Clauses in the Ninth Section of the first Article; and that no State, without its Consent, shall be deprived of its equal Suffrage in the Senate.

The usual procedure for making amendments is for two-thirds of the members of Congress to vote for the proposed amendments. Then the amendment is sent to the legislatures of the 50 states for approval. If three-fourths of the state legislatures ratify, or vote for, the proposal, it becomes an amendment to the U.S. Constitution. Of the 27 constitutional amendments, 26 of them have been made in this way. The 21st Amendment was approved by special conventions in three-fourths of the states, rather than by votes in state legislatures.

There is another method of proposing amendments to the Constitution— a method that has never been used. Congress, upon request of the states, can call for a special constitutional convention to write a proposed amendment. Article 5 states that Congress "shall call a convention for proposing amendments" whenever two-thirds of the states petition for one. This method of proposing amendments is known as an "Article 5 Convention."

The Bill of Rights

The Constitution was first amended in 1791. Amendments 1 through 10, known as the Bill of Rights, were ratified together by the end of 1791. This Bill of Rights limits the power of the federal government in order to protect the civil liberties and rights of individuals. These rights include the freedom of speech, protection against unwarranted searches and seizures, and provision of due process and other rights for people accused of criminal behavior.

A supporter of the Equal Rights Amendment. The ERA failed to win ratification in 1982.

Amendments 11 and 12

The 11th Amendment became part of the Constitution in 1795. It was proposed and ratified in response to an unpopular Supreme Court decision, *Chisholm* v. *Georgia* (1793). The Court decided that the citizens of one state can sue another state in a federal court without the consent of the state being sued. The 11th Amendment reversed the Court's decision by barring citizens of another state or a foreign country from suing a state in a federal court without the state's consent.

Amendment 12 was ratified in 1804 to correct a defect in the procedures for electing the President and Vice President. Article 2, Section 1, of the Constitution said that Presidential electors would vote for two people for President. The person who received the most votes would be the President, provided that he also received a majority of the votes cast. The person who came in second would be the Vice President. If no one received a majority of the electoral votes, then the House of Representatives had to elect the President from among the five candidates with the most votes.

This system broke down in the election of 1800, when Thomas Jefferson and Aaron Burr received an equal number of votes. It was generally understood that Jefferson was the candidate for President and Burr the candidate for Vice President. The Constitution, however, provided only that each elector vote for two people, without specifying which vote was for the Vice Presidential candidate. When Jefferson and Burr received the same number of votes, Burr tried to take advantage of the confusion to win the Presidency. Instead of stepping aside for his partner, Jefferson, he insisted that the contest be decided by the House of Representatives, as provided by the Constitution. Jefferson was the winner in the House election, but it was clear that the Constitution had to be amended to prevent confusion of this kind from happening again. The 12th Amendment provided that electors would cast separate ballots for President and Vice President. If no one receives a majority of votes for President, the House of Representatives selects the President from the three candidates with the largest number of votes. Each state then has one vote, no matter how many representatives it has in the House. If no one receives a majority of the electoral votes for Vice President, then the Senate selects the Vice President from the two candidates with the most votes.

Civil War amendments

Amendments 13, 14, and 15 are known as the Civil War amendments. They were passed in the wake of the Union victory over the slaveholding states of the Confederacy. These three amendments were passed to protect the rights of former slaves.

The 13th Amendment, approved in 1865, prohibits slavery or involuntary servitude. The 14th Amendment, added to the Constitution in 1868, defined citizenship in such a way that state governments could not deny former slaves their rights and privileges as citizens. This amendment says that all people born in the United States are citizens, as are all individuals who are naturalized (foreign-born persons who become citizens through a legal process defined by Congress). According to Amendment 14, all citizens (natural-born and naturalized) have the same legal rights and privileges. This amendment forbids state governments from making and enforcing laws that would deprive any person of life, liberty, or property "without due process of law"; it also says that a state government may not deny to any person under its authority "the equal protection of the laws."

Amendment 15, adopted in 1870, barred the federal and state governments from denying any citizen the right to vote on the basis of race, color, or previous enslavement.

20th-century amendments

The 16th Amendment, passed in 1913, allows the federal government to collect taxes on income earned by citizens. In 1895, the Supreme Court had ruled that a federal income tax law passed in 1894 was unconstitutional. Representatives of the people in Congress and state legislatures overruled the Supreme Court through passage and ratification of this 16th Amendment.

The 17th Amendment was also passed in 1913. It provides for the election of two senators from each state by direct vote of the eligible voters of the state. Before passage of this amendment, two senators were selected by the legislature of each state.

The 18th Amendment, approved in 1919, prohibited the production, sale, or transportation of intoxicating liquors in the United States. The 21st Amendment was passed in 1933 to repeal the 18th Amendment.

Amendments 19, 23, 24, and 26 extended and protected the voting rights of certain groups of people. The 19th Amendment, ratified in 1920, guaranteed the voting rights of women. The 23rd Amendment, adopted in 1961, gave citizens residing in the District of Columbia the right to vote in Presidential elections. The 24th Amendment, ratified in 1964, prohibited state governments from requiring people to pay a tax to qualify to vote, thereby extending the right to vote to people who could not afford to pay a poll tax. The 26th Amendment, added to the Constitution in 1971, required that neither the federal nor state governments could deny to someone 18 years of age or older the right to vote on account of age.

The 20th Amendment, passed in 1933, provided that the term of office of the President and Vice President shall end at noon, January 20, of the year following the last Presidential election. The term of office of senators and representatives shall end at noon, January 3.

The 22nd Amendment was passed in 1951 to prevent a President from serving more than two four-year terms of office. It was passed in response to the four-time election of President Franklin D. Roosevelt. Previously, Presidents had followed a custom begun by George Washington and had retired from office after serving two terms. Many people feared that a President might gain too much power if permitted to hold office for too long. The Constitution was amended to avoid this risk.

The 25th Amendment, passed in 1967, specifies how vacancies are to be filled in the office of Vice President. The President nominates a Vice President to fill a vacancy, but this choice must be approved by a majority of the members of the Senate and House of Representatives. The 25th Amendment also specifies how the Vice President can assume the duties of the President if he is incapacitated. When the President recovers, he can take charge again, but if recovery is not likely to occur, the Vice President can be approved as the new President by a two-thirds vote of both houses of Congress. The 25th Amendment allows a President to resign from office and be replaced by the Vice President. The new President has the power to appoint a new Vice President, subject to approval by a majority of the members of both houses of Congress.

The 27th Amendment, passed in 1992, holds that if members of Congress vote a pay raise for themselves, their constituents must have the opportunity, before the pay raise takes effect, to vote out of office the members who voted for it. This amendment was originally proposed in 1789, along with the amendments that became parts of the Bill of Rights, but it was rejected. In the 18th century, six states ratified the amendment, and one more state ratified it in the 19th century. Thirty-three states approved it between 1978 and May 7, 1992, when Michigan became the final state needed to ratify it.

SEE ALSO
Bill of Rights

FURTHER READING
Bernstein, Richard B., with Jerome Agel. *Amending America: If We Love the Constitution So Much, Why Do We Keep Trying to Change It?* New York: Random House, 1993.
Kyvig, David E. *Explicit and Authentic Acts: Amending the U.S. Constitution.* Lawrence: University Press of Kansas, 1996.
McComas, Maggie. "Amending the Constitution." *Constitution* 4, no. 2 (Spring–Summer 1992): 26–31.

American Bar Association Committee on Federal Judiciary

THE AMERICAN BAR ASSOCIATION (ABA) is the oldest and largest private

Sandra Day O'Connor is sworn in by Chief Justice Warren Burger. O'Connor was rated well qualified by the ABA committee.

organization of lawyers in the United States. In 1946 the ABA established a Standing Committee on Federal Judiciary to advise the government on the selection of Supreme Court justices and judges for federal district and appellate courts.

The committee has 15 members, appointed by the ABA president. Members represent different regions of the country. There is at least one member from each of the geographical areas of the United States in which a circuit court of appeals is located.

The ABA committee's advisory ratings are an important part of the selection of Supreme Court justices. After the President of the United States nominates a person to be a Supreme Court justice, the ABA committee investigates the nominee's background and record of achievement. Then the Committee rates the nominee according to this scale: well qualified, not opposed, or not qualified. These ratings, although advisory, tend to have great influence on the Senate Judiciary Committee and on the Senate as a whole, which has the power to confirm or reject the President's nominations to the Court.

The ABA committee is also involved in the nomination of federal district and appellate court judges. It rates such nominees according to a slightly different scale: well qualified, qualified, qualified/not qualified (indicating a split vote), or not qualified. Its rating is sent to the Senate Judiciary Committee, which has the responsibility of recommending that the Senate approve or reject the nominee. The ABA committee also tries to publicize its ratings through the mass media.

SEE ALSO
Appointment of justices; Rejection of Supreme Court nominees

American Civil Liberties Union (ACLU)

FOUNDED IN 1920, the American Civil Liberties Union (ACLU) is a private organization, supported by dues-paying members, with the mission of defending the rights and liberties of individuals guaranteed by the U.S. Constitution. ACLU staff lawyers offer free legal services to individuals who claim that the government has violated their civil liberties. The ACLU defines civil liberties as those freedoms or rights that the government may not abridge or deny.

The ACLU claims nonpartisan support of the principle of civil liberties, and it has therefore defended the right to free speech of various individuals with conflicting political viewpoints because of its dedication to the idea of free speech for everyone. Moreover, ACLU lawyers have defended the free speech rights of people with whom they personally disagree, such as communists or Nazis, because they are dedicated to protecting the *principle* of free speech, not the *content* of any particular speech.

The ACLU has participated in numerous landmark cases before the U.S. Supreme Court that have greatly expanded the range and reach of the Bill of Rights during the 20th century. For

Roger Baldwin, founder of the American Civil Liberties Union.

example, in *Gitlow* v. *New York* (1925), a case involving 1st Amendment free speech issues, ACLU lawyers served as counsel for Benjamin Gitlow. The ACLU helped to influence the Court to recognize that the due process clause of the 14th Amendment could absorb or incorporate 1st Amendment freedoms. This case laid the foundations for the incorporation doctrine, which has led to the case-by-case application of most of the Bill of Rights to state laws. Lawyers for the ACLU were involved in most of these cases. For example, *Stromberg* v. *California* (1931) involved the 1st Amendment right to freedom of speech; *Engel* v. *Vitale* (1962) dealt with the 1st Amendment prohibition against the establishment of a state religion; and *Miranda* v. *Arizona* (1966) upheld the 5th Amendment right to avoid self-incrimination. The ACLU also cooperated with the National Association for the Advancement of Colored People (NAACP) in landmark civil rights cases, such as *Brown* v. *Board of Education* (1954), which have used the "equal protection of the laws" clause of the 14th Amendment to end racial segregation and discrimination in public facilities and services.

During the 1990s, the ACLU was involved prominently in cases about freedom of expression on the Internet, separation of religion and government in public schools, and the rights of women and minorities.

The ACLU has more than 275,000 members. The national office in Washington, D.C., includes a legal staff, a public education department, and people working on several special projects on legal research and education. The ACLU also has a network of affiliates in all 50 states.

SEE ALSO
Civil rights; Gitlow v. New York; Incorporation doctrine; Miranda v. Arizona; Stromberg v. California

FURTHER READING
Lamson, Peggy. *Roger Baldwin: Founder of the American Civil Liberties Union.* Boston: Houghton Mifflin, 1976.
Walker, Samuel. *In Defense of American Liberties: A History of the ACLU.* New York: Oxford, 1990.

Amicus curiae

AMICUS CURIAE is a Latin term meaning "friend of the court." An amicus curiae brief is a document regarding a case presented by someone who is not a direct party to the legal controversy. A friend of the court brief may be filed voluntarily, or it may be invited by the court. An amicus curiae brief is usually filed by individuals or groups with a special interest in the outcome of a case. However, no one who would benefit or be penalized directly, in a personal way, by the outcome of a case may file an amicus curiae brief.

In *Mapp* v. *Ohio* (1961), for example, the American Civil Liberties Union (ACLU) filed an amicus brief that argued for the exclusion from a criminal trial of evidence seized without a search warrant. Although this issue was not even mentioned by Mapp's own attorneys, the ACLU brief influenced the Supreme Court to apply the exclusionary rule against a state government for the first time.

SEE ALSO
Mapp v. Ohio

Appeal

AN APPEAL is the procedure by which a case is taken to a higher court for its review and possible reversal of the lower

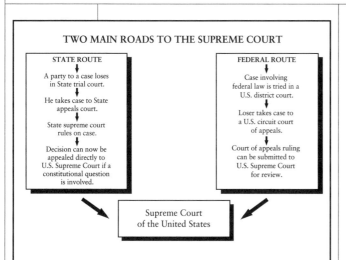

TWO MAIN ROADS TO THE SUPREME COURT

STATE ROUTE

A party to a case loses in State trial court.

He takes case to State appeals court.

State supreme court rules on case.

Decision can now be appealed directly to U.S. Supreme Court if a constitutional question is involved.

FEDERAL ROUTE

Case involving federal law is tried in a U.S. district court.

Loser takes case to a U.S. circuit court of appeals.

Court of appeals ruling can be submitted to U.S. Supreme Court for review.

Supreme Court of the United States

court's decision. The bases for an appeal are claims by the losing party that the lower court made an error or committed an injustice in reaching its decision. In most cases, the U.S. Supreme Court has discretion in deciding whether or not to accept the case for review. However, in some types of cases there is an automatic right of appeal to the U.S. Supreme Court. For example, decisions by the highest court of a state in cases involving federal constitutional issues are always open to appeal by the losing party to the U.S. Supreme Court. However, the Court may decide to let the decision of the lower court stand, without conducting a hearing into the case.

Cases reach the U.S. Supreme Court on appeal after either a lower federal court or a state court has made a decision on them. Decisions by the highest state court can be appealed directly to the U.S. Supreme Court if a constitutional question is involved. The losing party in a case generally has the right to appeal the case to a court of appellate jurisdiction. In the federal judicial system, the U.S. Supreme Court is the appellate court of last resort. It has the final decision, within the judicial system, on cases that come before it.

Courts of appellate jurisdiction give the losing party a new chance to win a

case. This extra chance will be granted if there were errors of legal procedures, interpretation, or evidence in the lower court. Further, cases of great constitutional or national significance are likely to be accepted for determination by the highest appellate court, the U.S. Supreme Court.

SEE ALSO

Circuit Courts of Appeals; Courts of Appeals

Appellant

A PARTY who appeals a lower court decision to a higher court, such as the U.S. Supreme Court, is an appellant.

Appellate jurisdiction

SEE Jurisdiction

Appellee

THE PARTY to an appeal whose position in the case has been upheld by a lower court decision is the appellee. The appellant requires the appellee to respond in the higher court that accepts the case on appeal.

Appointment of justices

SUPREME COURT justices are appointed by the President, with the advice and consent of the Senate, according to Article

2, Section 2, of the Constitution. Although the President alone has the constitutional power to appoint a justice, he seeks advice from various important people and groups. In this way, the President tries to nominate someone for the Court who will have broad support or acceptance. Presidents tend to rely upon advice from the attorney general and the Department of Justice and the White House staff.

The American Bar Association Standing Committee on Federal Judiciary, established in 1946, is generally influential in the selection of justices. This committee rates Supreme Court nominees as well qualified, not opposed, or not qualified.

Many interest groups also express views about the selection of justices. For example, the National Association for the Advancement of Colored People (NAACP) tries to influence selection of justices who will protect and support civil rights for African Americans and other minority groups. Likewise, the National Organization of Women (NOW) pushes for selection of justices who are sympathetic to women's rights.

The Senate Judiciary Committee conducts hearings to investigate the qualifications and merits of a proposed Supreme Court justice. Witnesses are called before the committee to provide information and opinions about the nominee. And the nominee also appears before the committee to answer questions about his or her qualifications to be a justice. Today, these hearings are often broadcast live to large audiences and reported daily in the mass media.

The Senate Judiciary Committee concludes its hearings with a vote to recommend confirmation or rejection of the nomination by the full Senate. A nominee becomes a justice only after a favorable vote by a majority of the U.S. Senate. Of the 148 nominations through 2000, 119 were approved, 13 rejected, and 16 withdrawn. When a President's party controls the Senate, more than 90 percent of the Supreme Court nominations are typically approved; when the opposition controls the Senate, the approval rate for justices drops to 50 percent.

There are no legal requirements for appointment to the U.S. Supreme Court. However, only lawyers have been selected for the Court. And it is unlikely that a nonlawyer could win approval to become a justice. Most justices have been judges on lower courts before becoming members of the Supreme Court. Since 1937, for example, 20 of the 34 justices had prior experience as either a state court judge or as a federal judge. Some of the greatest justices, however, did not serve previously as judges. For example, John Marshall, Joseph Story, Louis Brandeis, Harlan Fiske Stone, and Earl Warren have been rated as great achievers on the Court, but none of them had prior experience as a judge.

Presidents make a strong effort to select justices who will reflect favorably upon them and their administration. Legal scholars have noted the following personal characteristics that are expected of a nominee to the Supreme Court: substantial legal training and knowledge of law, personal integrity and high ethical standards, a strong sense of fair play, high intelligence, capacity for clear and

In June 1986 President Ronald Reagan announces his new Supreme Court appointments—Antonin Scalia (far left) as associate justice and William Rehnquist (third from left) as chief justice. The retiring chief justice, Warren Burger, stands next to Rehnquist.

This 1916 cartoon depicts "conservative" groups crying over the appointment of Louis Brandeis, who is shown walking away with a woman representing the Supreme Court.

cogent written and oral expression, and sound physical and mental health.

Presidents tend to nominate justices whose political and legal views appear to be compatible with their own. They usually do not seek agreement on specific cases or examples. Rather, they tend to want a nominee who shares their general views about constitutional interpretation and the process of making legal judgments.

SEE ALSO

American Bar Association Standing Committee on Federal Judiciary; Rejection of Supreme Court nominees; Senate Judiciary Committee

FURTHER READING

Abraham, Henry J. *Justices, Presidents, and Senators: A History of U.S. Supreme Court Appointments from Washington to Clinton.* Lanham, Md.: Rowman & Littlefield, 1999.

Maltese, John Anthony. *The Selling of Supreme Court Nominees.* Baltimore, Md.: Johns Hopkins University Press, 1998.

Watson, George, and John A. Stookey. *Shaping America: The Politics of Supreme Court Appointments.* New York: Harper-Collins, 1995.

Yalof, David Alistair. *Pursuit of Justices: Presidential Politics and the Selection of Supreme Court Nominees.* Chicago: University of Chicago Press, 1999.

Assembly, association, and petition, rights to

THE 1ST AMENDMENT to the U.S. Constitution guarantees "the right of the people peaceably to assemble, and to petition the Government for a redress of grievances." The constitutional right of peaceful assembly means that people can gather in public to discuss their opinions about government or other concerns. This right to assemble also guarantees the right of association in groups, such as political parties, labor unions, and business organizations.

The right of petition means that individuals, acting alone or as part of a group, can freely send written criticisms or complaints to government officials. The right of petition also provides freedom to circulate documents for people to sign in order to demonstrate mass support for complaints against the government.

These fundamental freedoms of assembly and petition predate the U.S. Constitution, having their origins in the English legal heritage and the colonial governments of British North America. The English Bill of Rights of 1689 affirmed that "it is the right of the subjects to petition the King and all commitments and prosecutions for such petitioning are illegal." Forty-eight years earlier, in 1641, Section 12 of the Massachusetts Body of Liberties guaranteed freedom of speech and petition at public meetings, so that "Every man . . . shall have liberty to . . . present any necessary motion, complaint, petition, Bill or information."

From 1776 to 1783, the freedoms of assembly and petition were included in several of the original state constitutions, including the acclaimed Massachusetts Constitution of 1780, which greatly influenced the U.S. Constitution of 1787. By the 1780s, the twin freedoms of assembly and petition were recognized by Americans as rights of individuals that should be protected. Therefore, it would have been unusual if James Madison had not included them in his proposal to the first federal Congress, dated June 8, 1789, to add "the Great Rights of Mankind" to the Constitution.

In that address, Madison presciently said that "independent tribunals of justice will consider themselves in a peculiar manner the guardians of those rights; they will be an impenetrable bulwark against every assumption of power in the legislative or executive; they will be naturally led to resist every encroachment upon rights expressly stipulated for in the Constitution." Madison's prediction has proved correct, especially in this century, as the freedoms of assembly and petition, along with other fundamental constitutional rights of the people, have been protected by an independent federal judiciary using its power of judicial review.

First Amendment freedoms have been expanded through judicial interpretation throughout 200 years of American constitutional history, and today the rights of assembly and petition and, by extension, the right of association are protected against infringement by the states by the due process clause of the 14th Amendment. The Supreme Court affirmed these rights for the first time in *DeJonge* v. *Oregon* (1937) and *Hague* v. *Congress of Industrial Organizations* (1939). In *DeJonge,* the Court ruled that the Oregon state government could not make it a crime for a member of a radical group, such as the Communist party, merely to conduct and participate in a public meeting. Writing for the Court, Chief Justice Charles Evans Hughes declared, "The right of peaceable assembly is a right cognate to those of free speech and free press and is equally fundamental," and "peaceable assembly for lawful discussion cannot be made a crime."

In *Hague,* the Court struck down a Jersey City, New Jersey, ordinance re-

During the depression, World War I veterans marched in Washington to demand early payment of war bonuses. The Bill of Rights guarantees to all individuals the right to gather peaceably and voice their concerns.

quiring permits from a "director of public safety" in order to hold meetings in public places within the city or to distribute printed material in streets, parks, or other locations.

The freedoms of assembly, association, and petition, like other constitutional rights, have limits. Justice Louis Brandeis wrote in 1927 (*Whitney* v. *California*), "Although the rights of free speech and assembly are fundamental, they are not in their nature absolute. Their exercise is subject to restriction, if the particular restriction proposed is required in order to protect the State from destruction or from serious injury, political, economic or moral." These limits must be justified, as Brandeis emphasized, by a compelling public interest. "Only an emergency can justify repression," said Brandeis. "Such must be the rule if authority is to be reconciled with freedom. Such, in my opinion, is the command of the Constitution. It is therefore always open to Americans to challenge a law abridging free speech [petition] and assembly by showing that there was no emergency justifying it."

Citizens of a constitutional democracy will forever be challenged to decide what constitutes an "emergency justifying" a particular limitation upon freedom of expression. They must respond, case by case, to this broad question: At what point, and under what circumstances, should majority rule be limited by the higher law of the Constitution in order to protect the fundamental freedoms and rights of individuals in the minority, such as their rights of peaceable assembly, association, petition, and speech? Justice Oliver Wendell Holmes reminded us about the occasional difficulty of answering this question, when he wrote, in *United States* v. *Schwimmer* (1929), "If there is any principle of the Constitution that more imperatively calls for attachment than any other, it is the principle of free thought—not free thought for those who agree with us but freedom for the thought that we hate."

An especially poignant example of Justice Holmes's "principle of free thought" was provided in *Collin* v. *Smith* (1978), a case decided by the U.S. Court of Appeals for the Seventh Circuit. In this decision, the federal appellate court decided to permit "followers of Nazism" flaunting the swastika to publicly and peaceably assemble to express their views in the village of Skokie, Illinois. In this decision, the court of appeals appeared to disregard the wishes of the majority in a community, as expressed by their representatives in government, who had passed ordinances prohibiting these American Nazis from publicly assembling to express their "hateful" political and social opinions. Judge Bernard Decker wrote:

> In this case, a small group of zealots, openly professing to be followers of Nazism, have succeeded in exacerbating the emotions of a large segment of the citizens of the Village of Skokie who are bitterly opposed to their views and revolted by the prospect of this public appearance.
>
> When feeling and tensions are at their highest peak, it is a temptation to reach for the exception to the rule announced by Mr. Justice Holmes, . . . freedom for the thought we hate.
>
> Freedom of thought carries with it the freedom to speak and to publicly assemble to express one's thoughts. . . . [I]t is better to allow those who preach racial hate to expend their venom in rhetoric rather than to be panicked into embarking on a dangerous course of permitting the government to decide what its citizens must say and hear.

The U.S. Supreme Court refused to review the lower court decision in *Collin* v. *Smith*. Thus, Judge Decker's decision to overturn the Skokie ordinances was upheld.

This case presaged a heated controversy in the 1980s and 1990s about the limits of 1st Amendment freedoms of speech, press, assembly, association, and petition when these rights are used to assault the beliefs and sensitivities of vulnerable minorities, whether racial, ethnic, sexual, or religious. Exclusion from private organizations on the basis of race, ethnicity, religion, gender, or another category of personal characteristics has also raised questions about the latitude or limits of an individual's rights to association. Do people, for example, have an absolute right of association that permits them to exclude unwanted individuals from their organization? Or can one's right to freedom of association be limited by a state law forbidding discrimination? The Supreme Court ruled in *Boy Scouts of America* v. *Dale* (2000) that the 1st Amendment's protection of the right to freedom of association trumped New Jersey's state law against discrimination in public accommodations. The Boy Scouts, it was decided, have a constitutional right to exclude gay members because to include them would contradict the organization's "expressive message"—that is, its widely known public identity, image, goals, and mission. The Court recognized that private organizations do not have an unlimited right to association and complete freedom from regulation based on compelling public interests, but in this case, the majority concluded that the law did not justify the state's restrictions of the "rights to freedom of expressive association" of the Boy Scouts.

Four members of the Court strongly disagreed with the majority's decision in

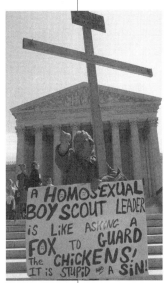

A demonstrator in front of the U.S. Supreme Court expresses his views in the 2000 debate over whether the Boy Scouts had the right to exclude gay members, or whether that would constitute illegal discrimination.

the Boy Scouts case, and the dissent revealed the intensity of current debate about conflicts between private freedoms and public interests. We are challenged today to decide critical questions about how to balance the 1st Amendment rights of various types of individuals, including some who are hateful, with our sense of the public good.

SEE ALSO

Whitney v. California

FURTHER READING

Friendly, Fred W., and Martha J. N. Elliott. "Protecting the Thought That We Hate: Freedom of Speech and the Right of Peaceable Assembly." In *The Constitution: That Delicate Balance.* New York: Random House, 1984.

Attainder, bill of

A BILL of attainder is a law that punishes a person without permitting him a trial or fair hearing in a court of law. It is punishment by legislation. Article 1, Section 9, of the U.S. Constitution forbids Congress to pass a bill of attainder, and Article 1, Section 10, prohibits any state government from enacting one. If the Constitution permitted bills of attainder, government officials could, by law, force the person *attained* or punished by legislative act to forfeit his liberty, property, or income. Using a bill of attainder, government officials could punish an individual who criticizes them or who belongs to an unpopular group. The U.S. Constitution protects the rights of individuals by denying to the government the power to pass a bill of attainder.

"Bad tendency" test

SEE Abrams v. United States; Freedom of speech and press

Bail

BAIL IS a pledge of money given by an accused person as security that he will appear in court for trial when requested. Bail enables the accused person to be out of jail during the period of time between the person's arrest and receipt of charges and the person's trial. Failure of the accused person to appear for trial may result in loss of the bail.

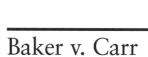

The 8th Amendment to the U.S. Constitution says, "Excessive bail shall not be required," thus assuring an accused person a fair opportunity to be free on bail. Permitting a person to be free on bail allows him to retain employment and income while awaiting trial. It also gives the defendant ample opportunity to prepare a defense to the charges. However, bail is usually denied to those accused of first-degree murder or other heinous crimes.

FURTHER READING

Buranelli, Vincent. *The Eighth Amendment.* Englewood Cliffs, N.J.: Silver Burdett Press, 1991.

Baker v. Carr

☆ *369 U.S. 186 (1962)*
☆ *Vote: 6–2*
☆ *For the Court: Brennan*
☆ *Concurring: Stewart and Clark*
☆ *Dissenting: Frankfurter and Harlan*
☆ *Not participating: Whittaker*

IN 1959, Charles Baker was mayor of Millington, Tennessee, a rapidly growing suburb of Memphis. He requested help from the state government in coping with

A bail bond office in Washington, D.C. Those who cannot afford to pay their own bail often turn to a bondsman, who puts up the bail money in return for a fee.

the problems of urban growth. But he got no satisfaction because the urban areas of Tennessee were underrepresented in the state legislature. By contrast, the rural areas of the state were overrepresented. Approximately 11 percent of the population lived in rural areas of Tennessee, but more than 50 percent of the representatives in the state legislature were elected by the rural areas of the state. The outcome was neglect of the problems and the needs of urban people. The floor leader of the Tennessee House of Representatives said: "I believe in collecting the taxes where the money is—in the cities—and spending it where it's needed—in the country."

Charles Baker decided that the only way to solve the financial problems of Tennessee's cities was to force the government to reapportion the legislature—to draw the legislative districts equally according to population. In this way every citizen of the state, whether living in a rural or urban area, would be represented equally in the legislature—the principle of "one person, one vote." People's votes are equal when each member of the legislature represents about the same number of people. Charles Baker brought suit against Joseph Cordell Carr, the Tennessee secretary of state, to force reapportionment of the legislature. But the federal district court dismissed the suit because the issue was political rather than legal. Thus, according to the trial court, the question should be resolved by the political (legislative and executive) branches of government, not the judicial branch (the courts).

The Issue Baker argued that urban voters in Tennessee were denied the equal protection of the laws guaranteed by the 14th Amendment. He requested that the state be ordered to equalize its legislative districts so that each person's vote was of equal weight. The Court, however, restricted its decision to questions of jurisdiction, standing, and justiciability. Did the court have the jurisdiction (authority) to make decisions about state legislative apportionment? Did Baker have standing (the right) to bring suit in a case of this kind? And was this issue appropriate for judicial decision or should it be left to the political branches of the government to decide?

Opinion of the Court Justice William Brennan, writing for the Court, ruled that the Court had jurisdiction in this case, Baker had standing to bring suit, and the issue was justiciable. He wrote that "the right [to equal districts in the Tennessee legislature] is within the reach of judicial protection under the Fourteenth Amendment."

Although the Court limited its decision to the questions of jurisdiction, standing, and justiciability, Justice Brennan clearly stated that failure to apportion legislative districts of a state equally was a violation of the equal protection clause of the 14th Amendment. He concluded that Baker was entitled to a trial, so the case was sent back to the federal district court.

Dissent Justice Felix Frankfurter and Justice John Marshall Harlan II strongly dissented. Frankfurter argued

Sanders in The Kansas City Star

"Great Scott! We've lost our vote!"

This cartoon satirizes the Baker v. Carr *decision as farm animals, representing rural voters, read about the reapportionment plan in the paper.*

that the issue was essentially political, not judicial, and should be left to the legislative and executive branches to decide. Harlan argued that there was nothing in the U.S. Constitution that required state legislatures to be apportioned so as to equally represent each voter.

Significance This case was the first in a series that led to legislative reapportionment throughout the country. The culminating case was *Reynolds* v. *Sims* (1964), in which the Court decided that states were required to establish equally populated electoral districts for both houses of the state legislature. Within one year of the decision in *Baker* v. *Carr,* 36 states were involved in lawsuits about legislative reapportionment. Eventually, every state of the United States was required to redraw its legislative districts to provide equal representation for all voters of the state.

U.S. Attorney General Robert F. Kennedy called the *Baker* decision "a landmark in the development of representative government." And Chief Justice Earl Warren, near the end of his life, called this case the most important one decided during his 16 years as chief justice.

SEE ALSO

Reynolds v. Sims

FURTHER READING

Cortner, Richard C. *The Apportionment Cases.* Knoxville: University of Tennessee Press, 1970.

Baldwin, Henry

ASSOCIATE JUSTICE, 1830–44

☆ *Born: Jan. 14, 1780, New Haven, Conn.*
☆ *Education: Yale College, LL.D., 1797; studied law under Alexander J. Dallas, Washington, D.C.*
☆ *Previous government service: U.S. representative from Pennsylvania, 1817–22*
☆ *Appointed by President Andrew Jackson Jan. 4, 1830; replaced Bushrod Washington, who died*

☆ *Supreme Court term: confirmed by the Senate Jan. 6, 1830, by a 41–2 vote; served until Apr. 21, 1844*
☆ *Died: Apr. 21, 1844, Philadelphia, Pa.*

HENRY BALDWIN was a strong supporter of Andrew Jackson's 1828 Presidential campaign. In 1830, President Jackson rewarded Baldwin with an appointment to the Supreme Court. Justice Baldwin tended to support states' rights in cases involving conflict between federal power and state sovereignty. However, he argued against extreme positions in support of either state sovereignty or federal supremacy. He claimed to be searching for a middle-of-the-road position between the two extremes.

Justice Baldwin clashed with Chief Justice John Marshall and helped to destroy the unity of the Court. In 1831, for example, he dissented seven times from the majority opinions of the Court. This was a dramatic departure from the tradition of unanimity that Marshall had established.

Justice Baldwin became irritable and erratic as he aged, a striking change from the good humor of the early years of his career. Toward the end of his life, he was often angry and occasionally violent. He was deeply in debt by 1844, when he died of paralysis.

Barbour, Philip Pendleton

ASSOCIATE JUSTICE, 1836–41

☆ *Born: May 25, 1783, Orange County, Va.*
☆ *Education: read law on his own; attended one term, College of William and Mary, 1801*
☆ *Previous government service: Virginia House of Delegates, 1812–14; U.S. representative from Virginia, 1814–25, 1827–30; Speaker of the House of Representatives, 1821–23; state judge, Virginia, 1825–27; presi-*

dent, Virginia Constitutional Convention, 1829–30; U.S. district judge, Court of Eastern Virginia, 1830–36
☆ *Appointed by President Andrew Jackson Feb. 28, 1836; replaced Gabriel Duvall, who resigned*
☆ *Supreme Court term: confirmed by the Senate Mar. 15, 1836, by a 30–11 vote; served until Feb. 25, 1841*
☆ *Died: Feb. 25, 1841, Washington, D.C.*

PHILIP PENDLETON BARBOUR belonged to a prominent family of Virginia landowners. He followed the family tradition to become a wealthy plantation owner and a leader in the state and federal governments. Barbour became an active supporter of Andrew Jackson's Democratic party and backed Jackson's successful campaign for the Presidency in 1828. Two years later, Jackson rewarded him with an appointment to the U.S. District Court for Eastern Virginia. In 1835, Jackson appointed Barbour to the U.S. Supreme Court.

During his brief period on the Court, Justice Barbour strongly supported states' rights and powers and strict limitations on the constitutional powers of the federal government. As a result, proponents of a strong federal government and those who believed in a loose interpretation of the Constitution opposed Justice Barbour. Daniel Webster, for example, wrote in 1837, "His fear, or hatred, of the powers of this [federal] government is so great, his devotion to states' rights so absolute, that perhaps [a case] could hardly arise, in which he would be willing to exercise the power of declaring a state law void."

Bar of the Supreme Court

THE BAR of the Supreme Court consists of lawyers authorized by the Court to argue cases there. During the Supreme Court's first term in 1790, it established two main qualifications for these lawyers. First, the person must have a satisfactory professional and moral character and reputation. Second, the person must have met the standards to practice law before the highest court of one of the states or territories of the United States. The clerk of the Court's office examines all applications and notifies the lawyers whose applications are accepted.

Between 4,000 and 5,000 applicants are admitted each year to practice before the bar of the Court. After receiving notification of acceptance, the applicant is required to pay an admission fee of $100. Each applicant may then be officially admitted to the bar of the Supreme Court by taking an oath of admission either before a notary public or in the open Court. The oath asks the person to "solemnly swear that as an attorney and counselor of this Court, you will conduct yourself uprightly and according to law, and that you will support the Constitution of the United States. So help you God." The applicant replies, "I do."

This certificate authorizes Washington lawyer Pamela Stuart to argue cases before the Supreme Court.

Barron v. Baltimore

☆ *7 Pet. 243 (1833)*
☆ *Vote: 7–0*
☆ *For the Court: Marshall*

JOHN BARRON owned docks and warehouses at the east side of the harbor of Baltimore, Maryland. Barron's wharf was a popular place for ships to tie up for off-loading cargoes into nearby warehouses. Barron and his partners made big profits by renting their wharf to ship owners.

Baltimore Harbor in 1830. John Barron claimed that the city was violating his constitutional right to property by allowing construction projects to interfere with the operation of his docks.

Barron's prosperity was being ruined, however, by construction crews working for the city government of Baltimore. They were digging up land, building streets, and diverting streams. Rainfall caused dirt-laden runoff to flow into the Patapsco River, which deposited the debris under Barron's docks. As a result, the water level at Barron's wharf was lowered to the point of interfering with the safe entry of ships. Barron claimed his profitable business had been severely damaged, and he sued the city of Baltimore to compensate him for the financial losses it had caused.

The Issue Barron claimed that the city of Baltimore had violated his constitutional rights under the 5th Amendment, which says that "private property" shall not "be taken for public use without just compensation." Barron's claim raised this question: Could the 5th Amendment, or any other part of the federal Bill of Rights, be used to limit the powers of a state government? Or does the Bill of Rights restrain only the federal government?

Opinion of the Court Chief Justice John Marshall concluded that the first 10 amendments to the U.S. Constitution applied only to the federal government. This, he said, was the original intention of the framers of the first 10 amend-

ments. Thus, the 5th Amendment could not be used by Barron to require Baltimore to pay him "just compensation" for taking his property. According to Marshall, the Supreme Court had no jurisdiction in the case, and so it was dismissed.

Significance This decision legally established the widely held view that the federal Bill of Rights was intended by its framers in 1789 to bind only the federal government. The constitutional issue of this case was settled until passage of the 14th Amendment in 1868, which was designed to limit the powers of state governments in order to protect the rights of individuals. However, the Supreme Court did not begin to use the 14th Amendment to incorporate, or apply, parts of the federal Bill of Rights to state governments until the second quarter of the 20th century, beginning with *Gitlow* v. *New York* (1925).

SEE ALSO

Incorporation doctrine

FURTHER READING

Friendly, Fred W., and Martha J. H. Elliott. "Barron's Wharf: The First Test of the Bill of Rights." In *The Constitution: That Delicate Balance*. New York: Random House, 1984.

Holmes, Burnham. *The Fifth Amendment.* Englewood Cliffs, N.J.: Silver Burdett Press, 1991.

Benton v. Maryland

☆ *395 U.S. 784 (1969)*
☆ *Vote: 7–2*
☆ *For the Court: Marshall*
☆ *Dissenting: Harlan and Stewart*

BENTON was charged by the state of Maryland with committing two crimes: larceny and burglary. The jury found Benton innocent of larceny and guilty of burglary. Benton appealed his conviction for burglary. This led to the reopening of the larceny charges. In the new trial, Benton was found guilty of both charges—larceny and burglary—and sent to prison.

The Issue The 5th Amendment to the Constitution provides protection against what is known as double jeopardy. It says that no person shall "be subject for the same offense to be twice put in jeopardy of life or limb." However, Benton had been tried twice by the state of Maryland for the same offense. Benton said that the state had violated his 5th Amendment right to protection against double jeopardy.

The state's attorneys pointed to the Court decision in *Palko* v. *Connecticut* (1937), which held that the 5th Amendment right to protection against double jeopardy was not applicable to the states because the due process clause of the 14th Amendment did not apply this right to the state courts. Therefore, this 5th Amendment right, they said, limited only federal government actions, not those of state governments. Was the 5th Amendment ban on double jeopardy applicable to state governments?

Opinion of the Court The Court ruled that the 5th Amendment protection against double jeopardy applied to the states. Justice Thurgood Marshall wrote that this 5th Amendment guarantee "represents a fundamental ideal."

This right, wrote Marshall, is certainly among those rights that are central to the American concept of justice.

Significance The *Benton* decision overruled *Palko* by holding that the double jeopardy prohibition of the 5th Amendment is applicable to the states through the 14th Amendment. This case became part of the gradual process by which the Court, during the 20th century, has applied most parts of the federal Bill of Rights to the states, on a case-by-case basis.

SEE ALSO
Double jeopardy; Palko v. Connecticut

Bethel School District No. 403 v. Fraser

☆ *478 U.S. 675 (1986)*
☆ *Vote: 7–2*
☆ *For the Court: Burger*
☆ *Concurring: Blackmun and Brennan*
☆ *Dissenting: Marshall and Stevens*

MATTHEW FRASER, a 12th-grade student at Bethel High School in Pierce County, Washington, made a brief speech at a school assembly, in support of a friend's candidacy for the student government. The audience included approximately 600 students in grades 9 through 12.

Fraser's speech included no profane or "dirty" words. But it was filled with sexually suggestive comments and gestures. Fraser's performance caused an uproar among many students in the audience, who hooted, cheered, laughed uproariously, and mimicked the sexual activities implied by the suggestive language of the speech. Many other members of the audience, however, appeared to be shocked and upset.

School officials punished Fraser by suspending him from school for three days. Fraser's name was removed from a list of students eligible to speak at graduation exercises. He was charged with violating the school's disruptive conduct rule. According to this rule, "Conduct which materially and substantially interferes with the educational process is prohibited, including the use of obscene, profane language or gestures."

Fraser protested that his 1st Amendment right to freedom of speech had been violated. He sued school district officials.

The Issue Did the public school officials in this case violate a student's constitutional right to free speech by punishing him for violating the school's disruptive conduct rule? Do school officials have authority to impose limits on student speech of the kind specified in the disruptive conduct rule?

Opinion of the Court Writing for the Court, Chief Justice Warren E. Burger decided against Fraser's suit against the Bethel School District. He said, "The First Amendment does not prevent the school officials from determining that to permit a vulgar and lewd speech such as [Fraser's] would undermine the school's mission." Burger noted, "The undoubted freedom to advocate unpopular and controversial views in schools and classrooms must be balanced against the society's countervailing interest in teaching students the boundaries of socially appropriate behavior." The chief justice stressed that "the constitutional rights of students in public schools are not automatically coextensive with the rights of adults in other settings.... Nothing in the Constitution prohibits the states from insisting that certain modes of expression are inappropriate [in schools of the state] and subject to sanctions."

Dissent In a brief dissent, Justice Thurgood Marshall disagreed with the Court majority's conclusion that the student's remarks were disruptive of the school's educational mission. In a separate dissent, Justice John Paul Stevens said that the school district's disruptive conduct rule was too vague to be enforced fairly under the 1st Amendment's guarantee of free speech. He said, "I believe a strong presumption of free speech should apply whenever an issue of this kind is arguable."

Significance The Court's decision contributed to the concept that students in a public school do not necessarily have the same constitutional rights as adults outside of school. This point was also made in *New Jersey* v. *T.L.O.* (1985), which dealt with 4th Amendment protections against unlawful searches, and *Hazelwood School District* v. *Kuhlmeier* (1988), concerning free press rights. However, in *Tinker* v. *Des Moines Independent Community School District* (1969), Justice Abe Fortas, writing for the Court, said, "It can hardly be argued that either students or teachers shed their constitutional rights to freedom of speech or expression at the schoolhouse gate."

SEE ALSO

Freedom of speech and press; Hazelwood School District v. Kuhlmeier; New Jersey v. T.L.O.; Tinker v. Des Moines Independent Community School District

Betts v. Brady

☆ *316 U.S. 455 (1942)*
☆ *Vote: 6–3*
☆ *For the Court: Roberts*
☆ *Dissenting: Black, Douglas, and Murphy*

SMITH BETTS, a 43-year-old unemployed man, was indicted for robbing a store in Carroll County, Maryland. He pleaded not guilty, and because he could not afford to pay for a lawyer, he asked the trial court to appoint an attorney to defend him. The trial judge refused Betts's

request because the courts in Maryland commonly appointed counsel only in special circumstances, such as cases involving mentally incompetent defendants or cases that involved the possibility of the death penalty. Smith Betts represented himself in court and was judged guilty. The judge sentenced him to eight years in the Maryland penitentiary.

While in jail, Betts filed habeas corpus petitions, which required the state either to justify holding him in jail or release him. He demanded to be released on the grounds that he was wrongfully convicted because his constitutional right to a lawyer had been denied. The courts refused his petitions. So Betts appealed his case to the U.S. Supreme Court.

The Issue Smith Betts argued that he had been deprived of the right to a lawyer guaranteed by the 6th Amendment, which says: "In all criminal prosecutions, the accused shall enjoy the right . . . to have the assistance of counsel for his defense." Furthermore, the 14th Amendment says that no state government "shall deprive any person of life, liberty, or property without due process of law."

Did the U.S. Constitution require the state of Maryland to provide a lawyer for a defendant too poor to pay for legal help? Could the right to "assistance of counsel" specified in the 6th Amendment be applied to a state government through the due process clause of the 14th Amendment?

Opinion of the Court The Court decided that "the Sixth Amendment of the Constitution applied only to trials in federal courts." The Court concluded that the Maryland legal system had given Smith Betts ample means to defend himself during his trial. In cases that did not involve capital punishment, a state did not have to provide a lawyer for a defendant too poor to pay for one.

Dissent Justice Hugo Black was joined in dissent by Justices William O. Douglas and Frank Murphy. Black argued that the due process clause of the 14th Amendment "incorporates" those rights spelled out in the federal Bill of Rights, which includes the 6th Amendment guarantee of the right "to have the assistance of counsel." Justice Black therefore concluded that the state of Maryland had denied Smith Betts one of his constitutional rights.

Justice Black wrote that no person should "be deprived of counsel merely because of his poverty. To do so, seems to me to defeat the promise of our democratic society to provide equal justice under the law."

Significance The Court's decision in *Betts* v. *Brady* prevailed until the 1960s. Justice Black's ringing dissent was not forgotten, however. The Court eventually overruled the *Betts* v. *Brady* decision in *Gideon* v. *Wainwright* (1963). And Justice Black, a dissenter in the *Betts* case, wrote the opinion for the Court in the *Gideon* case.

SEE ALSO

Gideon v. Wainwright; Incorporation doctrine; Rights of the accused

FURTHER READING

Force, Eden. *The Sixth Amendment*. Englewood Cliffs, N.J.: Silver Burdett Press, 1991.

Bill of Rights

THE BILL OF RIGHTS consists of Amendments 1 through 10 of the U.S. Constitution. This Bill of Rights sets limits on the power of government in order to protect liberties and rights of individuals from the government's abuse of its power.

Creation of the Bill of Rights

"[A] Bill of Rights is what the people are entitled to against every government on earth, general or particular [that is, federal or state], and what no just government should refuse, or rest on inference," wrote Thomas Jefferson to James Madison on December 20, 1787.

Jefferson was in Paris, serving as U.S. minister to France, when he received a copy of the Constitution drafted at the federal convention in Philadelphia during the summer of 1787 and found that it lacked a bill of rights. Jefferson generally approved of the new Constitution and reported in detail to Madison the many features of the proposed federal government that satisfied him. Then Jefferson declared in his December 20, 1787, letter to Madison that he did not like "the omission of a bill of rights providing clearly and without the aid of sophisms for freedom of religion, freedom of the press, protection against standing armies . . . and trial by jury in all matters of fact triable by the laws of the land."

A bill of rights consists of statements of civil liberties and rights that a government may not take away from the people who live under the government's authority. A bill of rights sets legal limits on the power of government to prevent public officials from denying liberties and rights to individuals, which they possess on the basis of their humanity.

Thomas Jefferson was concerned that the strong powers of government provided for by the U.S. Constitution could be used to destroy inherent civil liberties and rights of the people. He noted with pleasure that the Constitution of 1787 included means to limit the power of government, such as the separation of powers among three branches of government—legislative, executive, and judicial—to prevent any person or group from exercising power tyrannically. However, Jefferson strongly believed that additional guarantees of individual freedoms and rights were needed. He therefore demanded a bill of rights to

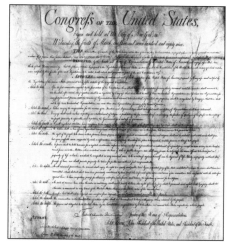

The Bill of Rights was ratified in 1791 to ensure that the fundamental liberties and rights of individuals would not be violated by the federal government.

protect certain liberties of the people, such as freedom to express ideas in public, from infringement by the government. Many Americans agreed with Jefferson, and they supported ratification of the Constitution only on the condition that a bill of rights would be added to it.

James Madison took up this cause at the first federal Congress in 1789. As a member of the Virginia delegation to the House of Representatives, Madison proposed several amendments to the Constitution to place certain liberties and rights of individuals beyond the reach of the government. The Congress approved 12 of these constitutional changes and sent them to the state governments for ratification. In 1791, 10 of these amendments were approved by the states and added to the Constitution. These 10 amendments are known as the Bill of Rights.

Contents of the Bill of Rights

Amendment 1 protects freedom of thought, belief, and expression. Amendment 1 says, for example, that the Congress of the United States is forbidden to pass any law "respecting an establishment of religion" or depriving individuals of certain fundamental civil liberties: religious freedom, the freedom of speech and the press, and the right of the people to gather together peacefully and petition the government to satisfy complaints they have against public policies and officials. The history of the 1st Amendment has involved the expansion of individual freedoms and the separation of church and state. For example, the 1st Amendment has been interpreted to mean that government may not establish an official religion, favor any or all religions, or stop individuals from practicing religion in their own way. Further, the right to assembly has been extended to include the right of association in organizations. Finally, the rights of free speech and press are generally understood to be very broad, if not absolute. There are, however, legal limits concerning the time, place, and manner of speech.

Amendment 2 protects the right of the state governments and the people to maintain militia or armed companies to guard against threats to their social order, safety, and security; and in connection with that state right the federal government may not take away the right of the people to have and use weapons.

Amendment 3 forbids the government, during times of peace, to house soldiers in a private dwelling without the consent of the owner. In a time of war the government may use private dwellings to quarter troops, if this is done lawfully.

Amendment 4 protects individuals against unreasonable and unwarranted searches and seizures of their property. It establishes conditions for the lawful issuing and use of search warrants— official documents authorizing a search —by government officials to protect the right of individuals to security "in their persons, houses, papers, and effects." There must be "probable cause" for issuing a warrant to authorize a search or arrest; and the place to be searched, the objects sought, and the person to be arrested must be precisely described.

Amendment 5 states certain legal and procedural rights of individuals. For example, the government may not act against an individual in the following ways:

• Hold an individual to answer for a serious crime unless the prosecution presents appropriate evidence to a grand jury that indicates the likely guilt of the individual.

• Try an individual more than once for the same offense.

• Force an individual to act as a witness against himself in a criminal case.

• Deprive an individual of life, liberty, or property without due process of law (fair and proper legal proceedings).

• Deprive an individual of his or her private property for public use without compensating the person fairly.

Amendment 6 guarantees individuals suspected or accused of a crime certain protections against the power of government. This amendment provides to individuals:

• The right to a speedy public trial before an unbiased jury picked from the community in which the crime was committed.

• The right to receive information about what the individual has been accused of and why the accusation has been made.

• The right to face, in court, witnesses offering testimony against the individual.

• The right to obtain favorable witnesses to testify for the defendant in court (that is, the right to subpoena witnesses).

• The right to help from a lawyer.

Amendment 7 provides for the right to a trial by jury in civil cases (common lawsuits or cases that do not involve a criminal action) where the value of the item(s) or the demanded settlement involved in the controversy exceeds $20.

Amendment 8 protects individuals from punishments that are too harsh, fines that are too high, and bail (the amount of money required to secure a person's liberty from legal custody) that is too high.

Amendment 9 says that the rights guaranteed in the Constitution are not the only rights that individuals may have. Individuals retain other rights, not mentioned in the Constitution, that the government may not take away.

Amendment 10 says that the state governments and the people of the United States retain any powers the Constitution does not specifically grant to the federal government or prohibit to the state governments, such as the power of the states to establish and manage public school systems.

Expanding the scope of the Bill of Rights

The framers of the first 10 amendments to the U.S. Constitution intended to limit only the powers of the national government, not those of the state governments. Amendment 1, for example, says that Congress may not take away the individual's rights to freedom of religion, speech, press, and so forth. This understanding of the Bill of Rights was supported by the Supreme Court's decision in *Barron* v. *Baltimore* (1833). Writing for a unanimous Court, Chief Justice John Marshall concluded that the Bill of Rights could be used to limit the power only of the federal government, not of the states.

However, the passage of the 14th Amendment in 1868 opened new possibilities. This amendment states that "no state...shall deprive any person of life, liberty, or property, without due process of law."

During the 20th century the Supreme Court has interpreted the due process clause of the 14th Amendment to require state and local governments to comply with most of the provisions of the Bill of Rights. Therefore, state and local governments are now prohibited from encroach-

A BILL OF RIGHTS CHRONOLOGY

June 8, 1789: James Madison, representative from Virginia, presented proposals about constitutional rights to the House of Representatives; he urged that these proposals be added to the Constitution.

September 25, 1789: More than two-thirds of both houses of Congress reacted favorably to most of Madison's proposals about individual rights, and they voted to approve 12 amendments to the Constitution. The amendments were proposed in response to the state ratifying conventions that had called for additional guarantees for civil liberties and rights in the Constitution.

October 2, 1789: President George Washington sent 12 proposed constitutional amendments to the states for their approval. According to Article 5 of the Constitution, three-fourths of the states had to ratify these proposed amendments before they could become part of the Constitution.

November 20, 1789: New Jersey became the first state to ratify 10 of the 12 Amendments, the Bill of Rights.

December 19, 1789: Maryland ratified the Bill of Rights.

December 22, 1789: North Carolina ratified the Bill of Rights.

January 19, 1790: South Carolina ratified the Bill of Rights.

January 25, 1790: New Hampshire ratified the Bill of Rights.

January 28, 1790: Delaware ratified the Bill of Rights.

February 27, 1790: New York ratified the Bill of Rights.

March 10, 1790: Pennsylvania ratified the Bill of Rights.

June 11, 1790: Rhode Island ratified the Bill of Rights.

November 3, 1791: Vermont ratified the Bill of Rights.

December 15, 1791: Virginia ratified the Bill of Rights; these 10 amendments became part of the Constitution of the United States of America.

ing on most of the civil liberties and rights found in the U.S. Constitution. Under provisions of Amendment 14, the federal government has been empowered to act on behalf of individuals against state and local governments or people who would try to abridge other individuals' constitutional rights or liberties.

SEE ALSO

Amendments to the Constitution; Assembly, association, and petition, rights to; Civil rights; Counsel, right to; Freedom of speech and press; Incorporation doctrine; Gun control and the right to bear arms; Liberty under the Constitution; Privacy, right to; Property rights; Religious issues under the Constitution; Rights of the accused; Searches and seizures; Self-incrimination, privilege against; Student rights under the Constitution

FURTHER READING

Bodenhamer, David J., and James W. Ely, Jr. *The Bill of Rights in Modern America after Two-Hundred Years.* Bloomington: Indiana University Press, 1993.

Hall, Kermit L., ed. *By and For the People: Constitutional Rights in American History.* Arlington Heights, Ill.: Harlan Davidson, 1991.

Levy, Leonard. "Why We Have a Bill of Rights." *Constitution* 3, no. 1 (Winter 1991): 6–13.

Levy, Leonard W. *Origins of the Bill of Rights.* New Haven, Conn.: Yale University Press, 1999.

Meltzer, Milton. *The Bill of Rights: How We Got It and What It Means.* New York: Crowell, 1990.

Rakove, Jack. "Inspired Expedient: How James Madison Balanced Principle and Politics in Securing the Adoption of the Bill of Rights." *Constitution* 3, no. 1 (Winter 1991): 19–25.

Black, Hugo Lafayette

ASSOCIATE JUSTICE, 1937–71

☆ *Born: Feb. 27, 1886, Harlan, Ala.*
☆ *Education: Birmingham Medical College, 1903–4; University of Alabama, LL.B., 1906*
☆ *Previous government service: police court judge, Birmingham, 1910–11; solicitor, Jefferson County, Ala.,*

1915–17; U.S. senator from Alabama, 1927–37
☆ *Appointed by President Franklin D. Roosevelt Aug. 12, 1937; replaced Willis Van Devanter, who retired*
☆ *Supreme Court term: confirmed by the Senate Aug. 17, 1937, by a 63–16 vote; retired Sept. 17, 1971*
☆ *Died: Sept. 25, 1971, Bethesda, Md.*

HUGO LAFAYETTE BLACK rose from humble origins to become one of the most highly regarded justices in the Supreme Court's history. He was the eighth child of a farmer and storekeeper in rural Clay County, Alabama. Through hard work and determination, Hugo Black overcame the hardships of his youth to earn a law degree from the University of Alabama and to begin a career as a lawyer and public official in his home state.

In 1926, Black won election to the U.S. Senate, and he was reelected in 1932. During his second term, Senator Black became a strong supporter of President Franklin D. Roosevelt's New Deal policies. Roosevelt responded in 1937 by making Black his first appointment to the U.S. Supreme Court.

Black's membership on the Court became controversial when newspaper reporters revealed that he had been a member of the Ku Klux Klan from 1923 until 1926. The Ku Klux Klan had been organized after the Civil War by white supremacists who wanted to limit the opportunities and rights of black people. Justice Black repudiated his brief association with the racist Ku Klux Klan in a nationwide radio broadcast. "I did join the Klan," said Black. "I later resigned. I have never rejoined.... Before becoming a Senator I dropped the Klan. I have had nothing to do with it since that time." From this controversial beginning on the Court, Justice Black developed into one of its leading members, often taking a strong stand on behalf of the constitutional rights of individuals.

Justice Black favored a strict, literal reading of the Constitution regarding the government's power to infringe individual rights. For example, he wrote that "the First Amendment does not speak equivocally. It prohibits any law 'abridging the freedom of speech, or of the press.' It must be taken as a command of the broadest scope that explicit language . . . will allow" (*Bridges* v. *California,* 1941). In line with this viewpoint, Justice Black joined numerous decisions and wrote several dissents, to advocate virtually unlimited freedom of speech and press. Near the end of his career, however, he dissented from the majority opinions in cases protecting picketing and other nonverbal expression as examples of free speech (*Cox* v. *Louisiana,* 1965, and *Tinker* v. *Des Moines Independent Community School District,* 1969). In the *Tinker* case, for example, Black dissented from the Court's decision to protect the right of students in a secondary school to wear black arm bands to protest U.S. government policy in the Vietnam War. The Court decided that by displaying the arm bands the students were expressing "symbolic speech."

Justice Black was a persistent leader of the Court's use of the federal Bill of Rights to limit the powers of state governments. He interpreted the due process clause of the 14th Amendment, which states, "No state shall . . . deprive any person of life, liberty, or prop-

A political cartoon shows the Ku Klux Klan, in the form of a vulture, hovering over the White House. Soon after he joined the Supreme Court, Hugo Black was severely criticized for his previous membership in the KKK.

erty, without due process of law," to require state governments to comply with all provisions of the Bill of Rights. He stated this "total incorporation" position in his dissent in *Adamson* v. *California* (1947): "My study of the historical events that culminated in the Fourteenth Amendment . . . persuades me that one of the chief objects that the provisions of the Amendment's first section, separately, and as a whole, were intended to accomplish was to make the Bill of Rights applicable to the states."

The Court has not yet agreed with his "total incorporation" doctrine—the application of all provisions of the Bill of Rights to the states. Rather, the Court has continued to "incorporate" particular provisions of the Bill of Rights on a case-by-case basis. Through this process, most parts of the Bill of Rights have been incorporated under the due process clause of the 14th Amendment and applied to the states.

Although Justice Black's total incorporation doctrine has not prevailed, he greatly influenced the gradual application of more and more provisions of the Bill of Rights to the states. Thus, he greatly expanded the constitutional protection of individual rights available to the people of the United States.

Justice Black always carried a well-used copy of the Constitution in his pocket as a sign of his devotion to limited government and the rule of law. This faith in the Constitution lasted for the rest of his life. After 34 years of service on the Court, he retired on September 17, 1971, because of ill health; he died eight days later.

SEE ALSO

Due process of law; Tinker v. Des Moines Independent Community School District

FURTHER READING

Ball, Howard. *Hugo L. Black: Cold Steel Warrior.* New York: Oxford University Press, 1996.

Ball, Howard, and Phillip J. Cooper. *Of Power and Right: Hugo Black, William O. Douglas, and America's Constitutional Revolution.* New York: Oxford University Press, 1992.

Dunne, Gerald T. *Hugo Black and the Judicial Revolution.* New York: Simon & Schuster, 1977.

Newman, Roger. *Hugo Black: A Biography.* New York: Fordham University Press, 1997.

Simon, James F. "The Antagonists: Hugo Black and Felix Frankfurter." *Constitution* 3, no. 1 (Winter 1991): 26–34.

Blackmun, Harry A.

ASSOCIATE JUSTICE, 1970–94

☆ *Born: Nov. 12, 1908, Nashville, Ill.*

☆ *Education: Harvard College, A.B., 1929; Harvard Law School, LL.B., 1932*

☆ *Previous government service: clerk, Eighth Circuit Court of Appeals, 1932–33; judge, Eighth Circuit Court of Appeals, 1959–70*

☆ *Appointed by President Richard M. Nixon Apr. 14, 1970, to replace Abe Fortas, who resigned*

☆ *Supreme Court term: confirmed by the Senate May 12, 1970, by a 94–0 vote; retired Aug. 3, 1994*

☆ *Died: Mar. 4, 1999, Arlington, Va.*

HARRY A. BLACKMUN spent most of his childhood in the Minneapolis–St. Paul area, where he began a lasting friendship with Warren E. Burger, a future chief justice of the United States. After graduation from Harvard Law School in 1932, Blackmun practiced law in Minnesota. In 1959 President Dwight Eisenhower appointed him to the Eighth Circuit Court of Appeals. In 1970 President Richard Nixon appointed him to the U.S. Supreme Court after the Senate had refused to confirm two preceding appointments (Clement F. Haynsworth of South Carolina and G. Harrold Carswell of Florida). The Senate confirmed Blackmun unanimously.

During his early years on the Court, Justice Blackmun tended to vote with his friend, Chief Justice Burger. Their opinions were so similar that news reporters named them "the Minnesota Twins." Later on, however, their views diverged and Blackmun often voted with Justices William Brennan and Thurgood Marshall, who were more liberal in decisions about civil liberties.

Justice Blackmun's most significant opinion was written for the majority in *Roe* v. *Wade* (1973). In this case, the Court defended the right of a pregnant woman to decide whether or not to have an abortion. Criminal penalties against doctors for performing abortions were declared unconstitutional. Justice Blackmun, writing for the Court, based his decision on the division of a pregnancy into three periods, called trimesters. He held that a state government could have no authority to prevent an abortion during the first trimester (the first three months of a pregnancy). During the second trimester, the state could regulate abortion only to protect the mother's well-being. During the third trimester, however, the state could legally prevent a woman from undergoing an abortion.

The *Roe* v. *Wade* decision was controversial. Since 1973, public response has been intense, whether for or against the Court's decision in this case. In the years following *Roe* v. *Wade*, Justice Blackmun has continued to defend the right of a pregnant woman to choose an abortion, in consultation with her doctor, during the first two trimesters of a pregnancy.

SEE ALSO

Privacy, right to; Roe v. Wade

FURTHER READING

Schwartz, Bernard, ed. *The Burger Court: Counter-Revolution or Confirmation?* New York: Oxford University Press, 1998.

Wasby, Stephen L. "Justice Harry A. Blackmun." In *The Burger Court: Political and Judicial Profiles,* edited by Charles M. Lamb and Stephen C. Halpern. Urbana: University of Illinois Press, 1991.

Blair, John, Jr.

ASSOCIATE JUSTICE, 1789–95

☆ Born: 1732, Williamsburg, Va.
☆ Education: College of William and Mary, B.A., 1754; studied law at Middle Temple, London, 1755–56
☆ Previous government service: Virginia House of Burgesses, 1766–70; clerk, Virginia Governor's Council, 1770–75; Virginia Constitutional Convention, 1776; Virginia Governor's Council, 1776; judge, Virginia General Court, 1777–78; chief justice, Virginia General Court, 1779; judge, first Virginia Court of Appeals, 1780–89; Constitutional Convention, 1787; judge, Virginia Supreme Court of Appeals, 1789
☆ Appointed by President George Washington Sept. 24, 1789, as one of the original members of the U.S. Supreme Court
☆ Supreme Court term: confirmed by the Senate Sept. 26, 1789, by a voice vote; resigned Oct. 25, 1795
☆ Died: Aug. 31, 1800, Williamsburg, Va.

JOHN BLAIR, JR., was a member of a prominent Virginia family. He was an outstanding political leader of colonial Virginia and after 1776 continued his career of public service in the new state of Virginia. He participated in the Virginia Constitutional Convention of 1776 and the U.S. Constitutional Convention of 1787. He was one of three Virginians who signed the U.S. Constitution.

In recognition of his outstanding career as a political leader and Virginia state judge, George Washington appointed Blair to be one of the original six members of the U.S. Supreme Court. Blair's most important opinion was written in support of the Court's ruling in *Chisholm v. Georgia* (1793). In this deci-

sion, the Court ruled that Article 3, Section 2, of the U.S. Constitution gave a citizen of one state the right to sue another state in a federal court. This decision was overturned in 1795 by the 11th Amendment to the Constitution.

Justice Blair resigned from the Court on January 27, 1796. He retired to his home in Williamsburg, Virginia, where he died in 1800.

SEE ALSO

Chisholm v. Georgia

Blatchford, Samuel

ASSOCIATE JUSTICE, 1882–93

☆ Born: Mar. 9, 1820, New York, N.Y.
☆ Education: Columbia College, B.A., 1837
☆ Previous government service: judge, Southern District of New York, 1867–72; judge, Second Circuit Court of New York, 1872–82
☆ Appointed by President Chester Alan Arthur Mar. 13, 1882; replaced Ward Hunt, who retired
☆ Supreme Court term: confirmed by the Senate Mar. 27, 1882, by a voice vote; served until July 7, 1893
☆ Died: July 7, 1893, Newport, R.I.

SAMUEL BLATCHFORD entered Columbia College at the age of 13 and graduated four years later at the top of his class. He spent the next four years preparing to become a lawyer by studying with and working for his father's friend New York governor William H. Seward. Samuel Blatchford became a lawyer in 1842 and practiced law first with his father and then with Seward's law firm. Later he established his own law firm.

After serving 15 years as a federal judge in New York (1867–82), Blatchford was appointed to the Supreme Court by President Chester Alan Arthur. Justice Blatchford served on the Supreme Court for 11 years, performing ably but without distinction. During the Court's memorial service for him in 1893, Attorney General Richard Olney said, "If he [Blatchford] was not brilliant, he was safe."

Bradley, Joseph P.

ASSOCIATE JUSTICE, 1870–92

☆ *Born: Mar. 14, 1813, Berne, N.Y.*
☆ *Education: Rutgers University, B.A., 1836*
☆ *Previous government service: none*
☆ *Appointed by President Ulysses S. Grant Feb. 7, 1870; replaced James Wayne, who died in 1867 and whose seat was unoccupied by act of Congress until 1870*
☆ *Supreme Court term: confirmed by the Senate Mar. 21, 1870, by a 46–9 vote; served until Jan. 22, 1892*
☆ *Died: Jan. 22, 1892, Washington, D.C.*

JOSEPH P. BRADLEY was a poor farm boy who became a very successful and wealthy man. He studied hard in school and attracted the attention of a local minister, who recommended him to Rutgers University. After graduating from Rutgers in 1836, Bradley studied law in the office of Arthur Gifford and became a lawyer in 1839. He worked hard and built a rewarding career as a lawyer.

In 1870, President Ulysses Grant appointed Joseph P. Bradley to the Supreme Court. During his 22 years of service on the Court, he was known for his careful research and detailed analysis of constitutional issues. He remained on the Court until the day of his death in 1892.

Brandeis, Louis Dembitz

ASSOCIATE JUSTICE, 1916–39

☆ *Born: Nov. 13, 1856, Louisville, Ky.*

☆ *Education: Harvard Law School, LL.B., 1877*
☆ *Previous government service: attorney, Massachusetts State Board of Trade, 1897–1911; counsel, Ballinger-Pinchot Investigation, 1910; chairman, arbitration board, New York garment workers' labor disputes, 1910–16*
☆ *Appointed by President Woodrow Wilson Jan. 28, 1916; replaced Joseph R. Lamar, who died*
☆ *Supreme Court term: confirmed by the Senate June 1, 1916, by a 47–22 vote; retired Feb. 13, 1939*
☆ *Died: Oct. 5, 1941, Washington, D.C.*

LOUIS DEMBITZ BRANDEIS was the first Jew to serve on the Supreme Court of the United States. His parents, Adolph and Fredericka Dembitz Brandeis, were immigrants from Bohemia who came to the United States in 1848.

The Brandeis family settled in Louisville, Kentucky, where Adolph Brandeis became a successful grain merchant who provided Louis with extraordinary opportunities for education and personal development. Louis completed two years of study at the highly regarded Annen-Realschule in Dresden, Germany. Brandeis returned to the United States to enter Harvard Law School, from which he graduated first in his class in 1877.

Soon after graduation, Brandeis began a law practice in Boston with his close friend and classmate Samuel Warren. By the turn of the century, Brandeis had become a nationally famous lawyer. News reporters called him the "people's attorney" because Brandeis often charged no fee for defending the rights of poor and disadvantaged people. He was also an active supporter of public reforms to bring about equal opportunities and fairness in the operations of businesses and government.

As the defense attorney in *Muller* v. *Oregon* (1908), Brandeis invented a new kind of legal argument, one based on sociological and economic evidence rather than legal precedent. Brandeis argued successfully for an Oregon law that limited the number of hours that women could work in laundries and other businesses. Brandeis's use of social science evidence to support legal reform of workplace conditions became a model for other lawyers, a type of document that they called "the Brandeis brief."

President Woodrow Wilson greatly respected Brandeis and often relied upon his advice. In 1916 Wilson appointed him to the U.S. Supreme Court to fill a vacancy created by the death of Justice Joseph R. Lamar. A vicious public controversy erupted over the nomination.

Many opponents disliked Brandeis because of his record as a political and social reformer. Others were against him because he was a Jew. One of his strongest supporters, Arthur Hill of Harvard Law School, explained the opposition to Brandeis's Supreme Court nomination: "Mr. Brandeis is an outsider, successful and a Jew."

The storm over President Wilson's appointment of Brandeis lasted for more than four months. This was the longest and most bitter battle over confirmation of an associate justice in the history of the Court. The closest example in recent times was the furor over the 1986 nomination of Robert Bork by President Ronald Reagan. Unlike the Bork nomination, however, the Brandeis appointment was eventually supported by the Senate Judiciary Committee, 10 votes to 8. Finally, the full Senate confirmed Brandeis by a vote of 47 to 22.

The new justice's troubles were not over, however. One of his new colleagues, Justice James Clark McReynolds, refused to speak to Brandeis for more than three years. He would leave the conference table whenever Brandeis spoke, revealing his prejudice against the first Jew to serve on the Court.

Brandeis overcame this kind of hostility to become one of the greatest justices of all time. His most important opinions dealt with the constitutional rights of individuals. He sought to protect helpless individuals against oppression by uncaring government officials or an intolerant majority of the people. In *Olmstead* v. *United States* (1928), for example, Brandeis argued in a dissenting opinion for a general constitutional right to privacy. The Court had decided that wiretapping by federal government officials was not a violation of the 4th Amendment. Brandeis disagreed: "The makers of our Constitution. . . sought to protect Americans in their beliefs, their thoughts, their emotions and their sensations. They conferred, as against the Government, the right to be let alone—the most comprehensive of rights and the right most valued by civilized men."

Brandeis's dissent was vindicated in *Katz* v. *United States* (1967), when the Court overturned the *Olmstead* decision. In *Griswold* v. *Connecticut* (1965), the Court recognized a constitutional right to privacy for which Brandeis had argued many years before.

Brandeis was a leader in the movement to apply the federal Bill of Rights to the states through the due process clause of the 14th Amendment, a concept known as the incorporation doctrine. He first stated this idea in *Gilbert* v. *Minnesota* (1920). A few years later, the Court recognized this idea in *Gitlow* v. *New York* (1925). Since then, more and more parts of the Bill of Rights have been used to protect the liberties of individuals against state government violations.

Justice Brandeis was an especially vigorous defender of 1st Amendment freedoms. Through his Supreme Court opinions, he contributed mightily to the gradual expansion of these individual rights. He memorably expressed his commitment to 1st Amendment liberties in *Whitney* v. *California* (1927): "Those who won our independence believed that the final end of the State was to make men free to develop their faculties. . . . They believed liberty to be the secret of happiness."

Louis Brandeis served on the Court for 23 years, retiring in 1939 at the age of 82. A *New York Times* reporter noted: "The storm against him [when he was appointed to the Court] seems almost incredible now." Today, legal experts rate Louis Dembitz Brandeis one of the greatest justices in the history of the Supreme Court.

SEE ALSO

Incorporation doctrine; Muller v. Oregon; Olmstead v. United States; Privacy, right to

FURTHER READING

Baker, Leonard. *Brandeis and Frankfurter: A Dual Biography.* New York: New York University Press, 1984.
Paper, Lewis J. *Brandeis.* Englewood Cliffs, N.J.: Prentice-Hall, 1983.
Purcell, Edward A. *Brandeis and the Progressive Constitution.* New Haven, Conn.: Yale University Press, 2000.
Strum, Phillipa. *Louis D. Brandeis: Justice for the People.* Cambridge: Harvard University Press, 1984.

Brandeis brief

IN 1908 Louis D. Brandeis, as counsel for the state of Oregon in *Muller* v. *Oregon,* prepared a new kind of brief in support of an Oregon law that limited the number of hours that a woman could work each day in laundries and other industries. The brief included only two pages of discussion of the legal issues of the *Muller* case. The other 95 pages of this brief presented evidence about the harmful impact of long hours of strenuous labor on the "health, safety, and morals of women." The sociological evidence presented by Brandeis convinced the Court to support the Oregon law in order to protect public health and safety.

The success of the new kind of brief submitted by Brandeis in the *Muller* case influenced other lawyers to use sociological evidence, when appropriate, to make their arguments. This new kind of brief was named the Brandeis brief in honor of its creator, who later became a highly regarded justice of the U.S. Supreme Court.

SEE ALSO

Brief

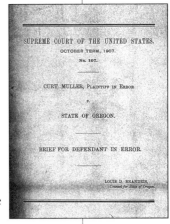

Brandenburg v. Ohio

☆ 395 U.S. 444 (1969)
☆ Vote: Unanimous
☆ For the Court: Per curiam decision

CLARENCE BRANDENBURG, a leader of the Ku Klux Klan, a white supremacist organization, was convicted of violating Ohio's Criminal Syndicalism Act. This state law outlawed speech that advocated violence as a means of achieving social or political reform. Brandenburg had urged violence against black people during a televised Ku Klux Klan rally.

The Issue The Ohio statute used to convict Brandenburg was identical to a California law upheld in *Whitney* v. *California* (1927). Brandenburg, however, claimed that his conviction violated his 1st Amendment free speech rights. What are the limits, if any, to an individual's right to free speech?

Opinion of the Court The Court decided in favor of Brandenburg and struck down as unconstitutional the Ohio Criminal Syndicalism Act. This decision overturned *Whitney* v. *California.*

The first "Brandeis brief," which was submitted by Louis Brandeis in the case of Muller *v.* Oregon. *As counsel for the state of Oregon, Brandeis used sociological evidence to advocate that an Oregon law limiting working hours be upheld.*

Members of the Ku Klux Klan, which promotes white supremacy, have the same right to free speech as other people.

The Court held that the constitutional guarantees of free speech do not permit a state to forbid people from speaking in favor of the use of force or other illegal actions unless it was likely to result in immediate violations of the law. The right to free speech can be limited only when the speech can be directly and immediately connected to specific actions that could result in lawless behavior.

Significance This decision greatly expanded the scope of political speech. The "clear and present danger" test set forth in *Schenck* v. *United States* (1919) and used in subsequent cases allowed restrictions on speech if it had a "bad tendency"—that is, if it appeared to encourage or cause illegal actions. However, the Brandenburg test allows virtually all political speech, unless it is demonstrably linked to immediate lawless behavior.

SEE ALSO

Freedom of speech and press; Schenck v. United States; Whitney v. California

Brennan, William J., Jr.

ASSOCIATE JUSTICE, 1956–90

☆ *Born: Apr. 25, 1906, Newark, N.J.*
☆ *Education: University of Pennsylvania, B.S., 1928; Harvard Law School, LL.B., 1931*
☆ *Previous government service: judge, New Jersey Superior Court, 1949–50; judge, New Jersey Appellate Division, 1950–52; associate judge, New Jersey Supreme Court, 1952–56*
☆ *Appointed by President Dwight D. Eisenhower as a recess appointment Oct. 16, 1956; replaced Sherman Minton, who resigned; nominated by Eisenhower Jan. 14, 1957*
☆ *Supreme Court term: confirmed by the Senate Mar. 19, 1957, by a voice vote; retired July 20, 1990*
☆ *Died: July 24, 1997, Arlington, Va.*

WILLIAM J. BRENNAN was a leader on the Supreme Court during most of his 34 years of service. Chief Justice Earl Warren viewed Brennan as his closest associate and relied upon him for wise advice and strong partnership. After Warren's retirement in 1969, Brennan continued to influence his colleagues, although not as strongly or decisively as before.

William Brennan rose to national prominence through hard work, persistence, and continuous development of his sharp intellect. He was the second of eight children of Roman Catholic immigrants from Ireland. His working-class parents encouraged him to pursue higher education and to achieve excellence in his life. In response to his parents' encouragement, Brennan became a brilliant student at the University of Pennsylvania and Harvard Law School.

After leaving Harvard, Brennan practiced law in Newark, New Jersey, and served in the army during World War II. After the war, he returned to his law practice and became a judge in the state courts of New Jersey.

In 1956, Republican President Dwight Eisenhower appointed Brennan, a Democrat, to the Supreme Court. He immediately joined forces with Chief Justice Warren and wrote several of the Warren Court's landmark decisions between 1956 and 1969.

Brennan wrote the Court's opinion in *Baker* v. *Carr* (1962), which Warren called "the most important case that we decided in my time." In this case, the Court opened the way to a redrawing of voting districts that transferred political power from rural areas to urban ones throughout the United States. Before the *Baker* v. *Carr* decision, rural districts in many states had been unfairly favored over the urban districts to give them more representation in government than was deserved on the basis of population. *Baker* v. *Carr* led to a series of Court decisions (such as *Reynolds* v. *Sims* in 1964) that required state governments to eliminate or redraw voting districts that did not fairly represent various classes of voters.

Another of Brennan's landmark opinions came in *New York Times Co.* v. *Sullivan* (1964), which expanded freedom of the press by making it very difficult for a public official to recover damages for defamatory statements that are untrue. Justice Brennan argued that "debate on public issues should be uninhibited, robust, and wide open." He held that "wide open" freedom of expression is the purpose of the 1st Amendment, which would be undermined if critics of government officials had to conform to "any test of truth." He claimed that "erroneous statement is inevitable in free debate; and it must be protected if the freedoms of expression are to have the breathing space they need." Brennan concluded that all speech about public officials was protected by the Constitution unless it was expressed "with actual malice," that is, expressed "with knowledge that it was false or with reckless disregard of whether it was false or not." Thus, an "actual malice" standard was established as part of constitutional law.

Justice Brennan was a loose constructionist; that is, he gave the Constitution a broad interpretation to promote the rights and opportunities of individuals. He believed in a dynamic Constitution that should be adapted to changing circumstances by judicial interpretation. He wrote in the *South Texas Law Review* (1986) that "the genius of the Constitution rests not in any static meaning it might have had in a world that is dead and gone, but in the adaptability of its great principles to cope with current problems and current needs."

Critics charged that Brennan tried to overextend the powers of the judicial branch to involve federal judges in making policy decisions that belong only to the people's elected representatives in Congress. They accused him and his followers of wanting to make law through their judicial decisions instead of limiting themselves to making judgments in specific cases about the meaning of the Constitution and federal statutes. Critics also said that Brennan was wrong to disregard the intentions of those who wrote the Constitution and its amendments in his broad interpretations of this fundamental document.

Brennan retired in 1990 because of declining health. Both his supporters and his critics recognized Brennan's decisive influence on the development of the Constitution in the latter half of the 20th century.

SEE ALSO

Baker v. Carr; Judicial activism and judicial restraint; New York Times Co. v. Sullivan

FURTHER READING

Friedelbaum, Stanley H. "Justice William J. Brennan." In *The Burger Court: Political and Judicial Profiles*, edited by Charles M. Lamb and Stephen C. Halpern. Urbana: University of Illinois Press, 1991. Michelman, Frank I. *Brennan and Democracy*. Princeton, N.J.: Princeton University Press, 1999.

Brewer, David

ASSOCIATE JUSTICE, 1890–1910

☆ *Born: June 20, 1837, Smyrna, Turkey*

☆ *Education: Wesleyan University, 1852–53; Yale College, B.A., 1856; Albany Law School, LL.B., 1858*

☆ *Previous government service: commissioner, U.S. Circuit Court, Leavenworth, Kans., 1861–62; judge of probate and criminal courts, Leavenworth County, 1863–64; judge, First Judicial District of Kansas, 1865–69; Leavenworth city attorney, 1869–70; justice, Kansas*

Supreme Court, 1870–84; judge, Eighth Federal Circuit Court, 1884–89

☆ *Other government service: president, Venezuela–British Guiana Border Commission, 1895*

☆ *Appointed by President Benjamin Harrison Dec. 4, 1889; replaced Stanley Matthews, who died*

☆ *Supreme Court term: confirmed by the Senate Dec. 18, 1889, by a 53–11 vote; served until Mar. 28, 1910*

☆ *Died: Mar. 28, 1910, Washington, D.C.*

DAVID BREWER was the son of a Congregational missionary who lived in the Anatolian part of the Turkish Empire. The family returned to the United States while Brewer was an infant, and he was raised in Wethersfield, Connecticut.

After graduating from Albany Law School, Brewer went to Kansas, where he served on several state courts, including the Supreme Court of Kansas. During his nearly 21 years as an associate justice of the U.S. Supreme Court, Brewer tended to support decisions to limit government regulation of private businesses. He strongly believed in free enterprise, free markets, and private property rights as foundations of a free government. Brewer also spoke and wrote against acquisition of colonies by the United States after the victorious war against Spain in 1898.

Breyer, Stephen G.

ASSOCIATE JUSTICE, 1994–

☆ *Born: Aug. 15, 1938, San Francisco, Calif.*

☆ *Education: Stanford University, A.B., 1959; Oxford University, B.A., 1961; Harvard Law School, LL.B., 1964*

☆ *Previous government service: law clerk to Justice Arthur Goldberg, 1964–65; assistant to the attorney general, U.S. Department of Justice, 1965–67; assistant special prosecutor of the Watergate Special Prosecution Force, 1973; special counsel of the Senate Judiciary Committee,*

1974–75; chief counsel of the Senate Judiciary Committee, 1979–80; judge, U.S. Court of Appeals for the First Circuit, 1980–94

☆ *Appointed by President Bill Clinton May 17, 1994; replaced Harry A. Blackmun, who resigned*

☆ *Supreme Court term: confirmed by the Senate July 29, 1994, by a 87–9 vote*

STEPHEN G. BREYER showed great promise as a thinker and writer from the beginning of his legal career. As clerk to Associate Justice Arthur Goldberg, he wrote the first draft of Goldberg's landmark opinion on the right to privacy in *Griswold* v. *Connecticut* (1965).

From 1967 to 1981, Breyer moved back and forth between the academic life of Harvard and the civic life of the federal government. He served on the Watergate Special Prosecution Force, which conducted investigations that led to President Richard Nixon's resignation in 1974. During this period, Breyer also served on the faculty of Harvard Law School, where he developed a widely respected theory on government regulation of economic activity. He brought this theory to his subsequent service as a federal judge, from 1980 to 1994.

When President Bill Clinton appointed him to the Supreme Court in 1994, Breyer had earned a reputation as a practical and innovative thinker about fundamental problems of when and how government agencies should regulate various industries. In 1994 he expressed his views on this topic in a series of lectures at Harvard, which were published as *Breaking the Vicious Cycle: Towards Effective Risk and Regulation*.

During his 14-year term as a federal judge, Breyer achieved respect as a consensus builder and as a mediator of conflicting views. His reputation influenced the Senate to confirm his nomination to the Supreme Court in 1994.

During his first term on the Court, Breyer acted forcefully and decisively. He broke Court tradition by participating in the questioning during the first oral argument he heard and by dissenting from the Court's decision in his first written opinion. Further, he wrote a sharp dissent against the Court's decision in *United States* v. *Lopez* (1995). In this case, the Court overturned as unconstitutional a federal law regulating the possession of guns in school zones. The Court's majority decided that under the federal system of the United States, this type of regulation is a power of each state government. Justice Breyer, in his dissent, defended the authority of Congress to regulate this type of gun possession.

Justice Breyer has tended to support concerns of local communities for public order and safety in regard to criminal law issues. For example, he joined the Court's opinion permitting random drug testing of public school athletes in the 1995 case of *Vernonia School District* v. *Acton*.

Brief

A WRITTEN document known as a brief is prepared by the lawyers on each side of a case and submitted to a court. A brief presents the facts of a case and the counsel's legal argument. The term was first used in 1631.

In cases before the U.S. Supreme Court, the attorneys rely upon their written briefs to persuade the Court. Supreme Court rules require that a "brief must be compact, . . . concise, and free from burdensome, irrelevant, immaterial, and scandalous matter." Since 1980 there has been a 50-page limit on all briefs submitted to the Supreme Court.

SEE ALSO
Brandeis brief

Brown, Henry B.
ASSOCIATE JUSTICE, 1891–1906

☆ *Born: Mar. 2, 1836, South Lee, Mass.*
☆ *Education: Yale College, B.A., 1856; studied briefly at Yale Law School and Harvard Law School*
☆ *Previous government service: U.S. deputy marshal, 1861; assistant U.S. attorney, Detroit, Mich., 1863–68; circuit judge, Wayne County, Mich., 1868; federal judge, Eastern District of Michigan, 1875–90*
☆ *Appointed by President Benjamin Harrison Dec. 23, 1890; replaced Samuel Miller, who died*
☆ *Supreme Court term: confirmed by the Senate Dec. 29, 1890, by a voice vote; retired May 28, 1906*
☆ *Died: Sept. 4, 1913, New York, N.Y.*

HENRY B. BROWN became a lawyer in 1860 in Detroit, Michigan, after finishing his formal education at Yale. After a 15-year career as a federal district judge in Michigan, Brown joined the U.S. Supreme Court.

Justice Brown's strong support of property rights and free enterprise, and his tendency to resist strong government regulation of business, reflected the dominant opinions of his time. So did Brown's views about civil rights for black Americans, which were expressed in his opinion for the Court in *Plessy* v. *Ferguson* (1896). The Plessy decision supported a Louisiana state law that required black and white railroad passengers to sit in separate railway cars. Justice Brown, writing for the Court, argued that this Louisiana law did not violate the "equal protection of the laws" clause of the 14th Amendment. Brown used a "separate but equal" doctrine to support the Court's decision. He stated that separate facilities could be required by law for blacks and whites as long as the facilities provided for one group were equal to the facilities provided for the other group. He wrote,

"We consider the underlying fallacy of the plaintiff's argument to consist in the assumption that the enforced separation of the two races stamps the colored race with a badge of inferiority."

The Court's decision in the *Plessy* case led to widespread enactment of state laws to segregate blacks from whites, to keep them apart, in the use of public facilities, such as schools, rest rooms, parks, cemeteries, and so forth.

Justice Brown left the Court in 1906 because of failing eyesight. He was popular then, but is not well regarded today because of his opinion for the Court in the *Plessy* case. Most Americans today strongly reject the legal segregation of blacks and whites, which Justice Brown defended in the 1890s. However, Brown and his Supreme Court colleagues expressed the prevailing view of that era about black-white relationships.

SEE ALSO

Plessy v. Ferguson

Brown v. Board of Education

☆ *347 U.S. 483 (1954)*
☆ *Vote: 9–0*
☆ *For the Court: Warren*

THE 14TH AMENDMENT declares, "No state shall...deny to any person within its jurisdiction the equal protection of the laws." In 1896 the Supreme Court handed down a landmark decision on the meaning of this equal protection clause. In *Plessy* v. *Ferguson*, the Court ruled that the 14th Amendment allowed a state to segregate whites and blacks by providing "separate but equal" facilities for blacks.

For nearly 60 years this doctrine of "separate but equal" served as a constitutional justification for racial segrega-

Thurgood Marshall (center) and two NAACP colleagues after he successfully argued the Brown v. Board of Education *case in favor of school desegregation.*

tion in the United States. This doctrine sanctioned separating blacks and whites in schools, housing, transportation, and recreation.

Not all Americans accepted the view that the Constitution allowed racial discrimination. Those opposed to segregation agreed with Justice John Harlan, who dissented in *Plessy,* declaring, "Our Constitution is color-blind." In 1909 a group of black and white Americans formed the National Association for the Advancement of Colored People (NAACP) to fight segregation and racial injustice. In the 1930s and 1940s, NAACP legal counsel successfully argued a number of Supreme Court cases in which the Court prohibited segregation in public universities, political primaries, and railroads. By 1950 many blacks and whites were ready to challenge the constitutionality of segregated elementary and high schools. In the early 1950s five separate cases—from South Carolina, Virginia, Delaware, Kansas, and Washington, D.C.—made their way through the court system. In each case the parents of black schoolchildren asked lower courts to strike down laws requiring segregated schools. The NAACP provided these parents with legal help. Eventually, the Supreme Court heard these cases together as *Brown* v. *Board of Education*. The case received its name when Mr. and Mrs. Oliver Brown sued the Topeka, Kansas, school board for denying their eight-year-old daughter, Linda, admission to a school only five blocks from their house. She had to leave her home at 7:40 every morning and travel 21 blocks in order to reach her assigned school by 9:00. The school board refused to let Linda attend the school in her own neighborhood solely because she was black and the school nearest to her home was for whites only.

The Issue Thurgood Marshall, later a Supreme Court justice, was director of the NAACP Legal Defense Fund. He provided legal counsel for the Browns and the other plaintiffs. Marshall presented evidence showing that separating black and white students discriminated against blacks, placing them at a severe disadvantage. He argued that segregated schools were not and could never be equal. Such schools, he said, violated the equal protection guarantee of the 14th Amendment.

John W. Davis, a distinguished attorney and a 1924 Presidential candidate, represented the defense. He argued that the authors of the 14th Amendment never intended that article to prevent segregation in the nation's schools. Further, he claimed, the courts did not possess the authority to order the states to desegregate their schools.

Those states with segregated schools claimed that the dual system provided "separate but equal" facilities for whites and blacks. In fact, virtually no black schools were equal to white schools. The South Carolina case, for example, began when the local school board, run by whites, refused to provide school buses

for black children. The board also refused to pay for heating the black schools or to provide them with indoor plumbing—services and facilities provided to white students. In spite of these glaring inequities, the black plaintiffs did not argue that the school systems were separate but *unequal*. Rather, they focused on challenging the "separate but equal" doctrine itself. Did state-supported segregation in public schools, even when black and white schools had equal facilities, violate the equal protection clause of the 14th Amendment?

Opinion of the Court The Supreme Court unanimously struck down the "separate but equal" doctrine as an unconstitutional violation of the 14th Amendment. Chief Justice Earl Warren said that segregation clearly gave black children "a feeling of inferiority as to their status in the community that may affect their hearts and minds in a way unlikely to ever be undone." Even if segregated schools gave blacks access to equal physical facilities, Warren argued, they deprived students of equal educational opportunities.

Warren declared, "We conclude that in the field of public education the doctrine of 'separate but equal' has no place. Separate educational facilities are inherently unequal."

Significance The *Brown* decision overturned *Plessy* v. *Ferguson* (1896). The ruling in this case destroyed the constitutional foundations of all forms of state-supported segregation in the United States. It also prompted massive resistance to school integration in many states. That resistance, in turn, helped spur the growth of the civil rights movement. This movement encouraged the passage of the federal civil rights acts of 1957, 1960, 1964, 1965, and

A 1958 cartoon reveals the continued conflict between the federal government and state governments in the wake of the Brown decision.

1968, which increased black political and civil rights.

Resistance also slowed implementation of the *Brown* decision in schools and led to many additional court cases. For example, Prince Edward County, Virginia, closed all of its public schools— for whites as well as blacks—rather than integrate. The first additional case, *Brown v. Board of Education* (349 U.S. 294), known as *Brown II,* came in 1955.

Brown II came before the Court because, as Chief Justice Warren wrote, "[W]e requested further argument on the question of relief." The Court wanted to consider the issue of how to implement the ruling of *Brown I* to end segregation in public schools. In *Brown II* the Court set forth guidelines that placed the primary responsibility for doing so on local school officials. Federal district courts were to continue their jurisdiction and oversight of school desegregation cases. They could allow school districts to proceed carefully and gradually to complete school desegregation.

Although the Supreme Court ordered school districts to begin desegregation "with all deliberate speed," in reality just the opposite occurred. Fourteen years after *Brown,* less than 20 percent of black students in the South attended integrated schools. Faced with continued resistance, the Supreme Court ruled in 1968, in *Green v. County School Board of New Kent County, Virginia,* that segregation must end "at once." Eventually, lower federal court rulings and the work of the federal executive branch agencies began to change this pattern. By the 1980s most Americans fully accepted the Court's ruling in the *Brown* case as the correct decision. Today, it is hailed as one of the greatest and most important decisions in the history of the Supreme Court.

SEE ALSO

Civil rights; Equality under the Constitution; Marshall, Thurgood; Plessy v. Ferguson

FURTHER READING

Berman, Daniel M. *It Is So Ordered: The Supreme Court Rules on School Segregation.* New York: Norton, 1966.
Kluger, Richard. *Simple Justice.* New York: Knopf, 1976.
Lagemann, Ellen Condliffe, and Lamar P. Miller, eds. *Brown v. Board of Education: The Challenge for Today's Schools.* New York: Teachers College Press, 1996.
Patterson, James T. *Brown v. Board of Education: A Civil Rights Milestone and Its Troubled Legacy.* New York: Oxford University Press, 2000.

Buildings, Supreme Court

THE SUPREME COURT has had several homes since its first meeting, on February 1, 1790, in New York City.

The first federal government of the United States was located in New York from 1789 to 1790. The Supreme Court met, at first, on the second floor of the Royal Exchange Building at the intersection of Broad and Water streets.

In December 1790 the federal government moved to Philadelphia, where the Court occupied a room on the first floor of the State House, known today as Independence Hall. In August 1791, the Court moved to the newly built City Hall, located on the east side of State House Square, where it remained until 1801.

Early Years in Washington

At this time, the Court followed the rest of the federal government to its permanent headquarters, the new city of Washington, in the District of Columbia. Buildings had been constructed especially for the President and the Congress in the new federal city, but there was no new building for the Supreme Court. So Congress permitted the justices to use a small room on the first floor of its still

A plaster relief entitled Justice above the bench in the Old Supreme Court Chamber, in the U.S. Capitol.

unfinished Capitol building. The Court stayed there until 1808, when it moved to another room in the Capitol that also housed the Library of Congress. But the Library was so crowded and inconvenient that the Court often met in a nearby tavern.

From February 1810 until August 1814, the Supreme Court met in a room specially created for it. This courtroom was located in the Capitol basement beneath the new chamber for the U.S. Senate. On the night of August 24, 1814, British troops invaded Washington, during the War of 1812, and burned the Capitol. The Supreme Court was therefore forced to meet in various temporary quarters until its former courtroom was repaired and ready for use in 1819. The Court remained in this location for 41 years. This room, known today as the Old Supreme Court Chamber, is open to visitors. It is furnished as it was when the Court met there long ago. This small courtroom has mahogany desks on a slightly raised platform, behind which the justices sat. There was also a very small room for the clerk of the Court. But there were neither offices nor a library for the justices. So, much of their work was done at home.

By 1860, two wings had been added to the Capitol to provide new, spacious chambers for the House of Representatives and the Senate. The Supreme Court

moved from its cramped basement room to the old Senate chamber on the first floor of the Capitol. This large room, with anterooms for offices and storage, was by far the best home the Court had ever had. And the justices occupied the old Senate chamber for the next 75 years, until 1935.

The Supreme Court Building

The modern Supreme Court Building, opened in 1935, fulfilled the dream of Chief Justice William Howard Taft. He worked for several years to convince Congress to appropriate money to build a suitable, permanent home for the Court. The site chosen for the new Supreme Court Building was a full square block on First Street, across from the Capitol.

In 1928, Chief Justice Taft became chairman of the Supreme Court Building Commission, created by Congress. He picked Cass Gilbert to be the architect for the new Supreme Court Building and worked closely with him in overseeing development of the plans. The cornerstone was laid on October 13, 1932, but Taft was not there to see it, having died on March 8, 1930. Gilbert died in 1934, but his son, Cass Gilbert, Jr., and John Rockart finished the project, under the supervision of David Lynn, Architect of the Capitol. The Court held its first session in its new home on October 7, 1935.

Gilbert, with Taft's approval, used the classical Greek style of architecture as his model. He selected marble to be the primary material for the building, which has four floors and a basement.

The basement contains a garage, laundry, carpentry shop, and police roll-call room. It also has offices and equipment storage rooms for the facilities manager and 32 maintenance workers.

The ground floor houses some of the administrative offices, including the Public Information Office, the clerk's office, the publications office, and police

The courtroom of the Supreme Court Building

offices. It also has exhibit halls, a cafeteria, and a gift shop.

The first floor includes the courtroom, the chambers (offices) of the justices, the robing room, and conference rooms. The courtroom has seating for about 300 people. There is a raised bench along the east wall, where the justices sit to hear oral arguments on cases. The courtroom, at the center of the first floor, is surrounded by the justices' chambers. There is also a robing room, where justices go before sessions of the Court to put on their black judicial robes. Next to the robing room is the Justices' Conference Room, where cases are privately discussed and decided. Two other conference rooms (East and West Conference Rooms) are used for social events and meetings of Supreme Court staff members.

The second floor contains the dining room and library of the justices, the offices of the reporter of decisions and law clerks, and the legal office, which is occupied by the Court counsel and staff who do legal research for the justices.

The third floor is given to the large library. The fourth floor includes a gymnasium with a basketball court and exercise equipment, as well as storage space.

Both the exterior and interior of the Supreme Court Building are decorated with symbols of law and justice, liberty and order. On either side of the steps to the main (west) entrance to the building, for example, are two marble figures: the one at the left is a female symbolizing justice, the one at the right a male representing the authority of law. Also at the main entrance is a pediment with sculptures representing liberty, order, and authority, with an inscription below the panel of sculptures: "Equal Justice Under Law." Panels on the main door feature sculpted scenes in the history of law.

At the building's east side entrance, there is a pediment with a sculpted figure representing the benefits of law and the judicial resolution of conflicts. An inscription below this panel proclaims, "Justice, the Guardian of Liberty."

On the inside, along both sides of the Great Hall, are busts of former chief justices, profiles of great lawgivers in history, and other symbols of law and justice. The Great Hall leads to the Court chamber, or courtroom. Among the various sculpted symbols in this grand room, where the justices hear oral arguments, are figures and objects representing law, government, and the rights and liberty of the people.

SEE ALSO

Appendix 2: Visiting the Supreme Court Building

Burger, Warren E.
CHIEF JUSTICE, 1969–86

☆ *Born: Sept. 17, 1907, St. Paul, Minn.*
☆ *Education: University of Minnesota, 1925–27; St. Paul College of Law, LL.B., 1931*
☆ *Previous government service: assistant U.S. attorney general, Civil Division, 1953–56; judge, U.S. Court of Appeals for the District of Columbia, 1956–69*
☆ *Appointed by President Richard Nixon May 21, 1969; replaced Chief Justice Earl Warren, who retired*
☆ *Supreme Court term: confirmed by the Senate June 9, 1969, by a 74–3 vote; retired Sept. 26, 1986*

☆ *Died: June 25, 1995, Washington, D.C.*

WARREN E. BURGER worked hard to achieve an education. After high school, he worked at part-time jobs while going to college and law school in his home city of St. Paul, Minnesota. From 1931 to 1953, Burger practiced law and participated in Republican party politics in Minnesota. He attracted the attention of national Republican party leaders, and in 1953 President Dwight Eisenhower appointed Burger assistant attorney general of the United States.

In 1956, President Eisenhower named Burger to the U.S. Court of Appeals for the District of Columbia circuit. This position was a stepping-stone to the Supreme Court. In 1969, President Richard Nixon appointed Burger to be the 15th chief justice of the United States. He replaced Earl Warren, the strong leader of the Court during two decades of ground-breaking decisions that greatly expanded the legal opportunities and rights of minorities and individuals accused of crimes.

Chief Justice Burger tended to support the civil rights decisions of the Warren Court. However, in cases regarding the rights of criminal defendants, Burger tended to support the police and prosecutors. He believed that the Court under Earl Warren had moved too far in favor of supporting the rights of accused persons and criminals.

Burger's most important decision was in the case of *United States* v. *Nixon* (1974), when the Court turned down President Nixon's claim of executive privilege as a reason for withholding tape recordings of private White House conversations from criminal investigators. The Court ordered the President to turn over the tapes, a ruling that established an important limitation on the powers of the President. This decision also affirmed the primacy of the Supreme Court in the interpretation of the Constitution.

Chief Justice Burger retired in 1986 to become chairman of the Commission on the Bicentennial of the United States Constitution. His greatest achievements as chief justice were his improvements in the ways in which the federal judicial system carries out its work. He reorganized many procedures for keeping records and for carrying out more efficiently the business of the federal courts. But Chief Justice Burger, unlike his predecessor, Earl Warren, did not exercise a decisive influence on the opinions of his associate justices.

SEE ALSO

Chief justice; United States v. Nixon

FURTHER READING

Lamb, Charles M. "Chief Justice Warren E. Burger." In *The Burger Court: Political and Judicial Profiles*, edited by Charles M. Lamb and Stephen C. Halpern. Urbana: University of Illinois Press, 1991.

Burton, Harold H.
ASSOCIATE JUSTICE, 1945–58

☆ *Born: June 22, 1888, Jamaica Plain, Mass.*
☆ *Education: Bowdoin College, B.A., 1909; Harvard Law School, LL.B., 1912*
☆ *Previous government service: Ohio House of Representatives, 1929; director of law, Cleveland, Ohio, 1929–32; mayor, Cleveland, 1935–40; U.S. senator from Ohio, 1941–45*
☆ *Appointed by President Harry S. Truman Sept. 19, 1945; replaced Owen J. Roberts, who resigned*
☆ *Supreme Court term: confirmed by the Senate Sept. 19, 1945, by a voice vote; retired Oct. 13, 1958*
☆ *Died: Oct. 28, 1964, Washington, D.C.*

HAROLD BURTON, a Republican, was Democratic President Harry Truman's first appointment to the U.S. Supreme Court. He was the only Republican appointed to the Court between 1933 and 1953. Burton achieved an outstanding career in public life before joining the Court. He practiced law in Cleveland, where he had also been the mayor, and served one term in the U.S. Senate.

Justice Burton became a leading advocate of expanding the constitutional rights of African Americans. He spoke strongly against racial segregation and the "separate but equal" doctrine. He participated enthusiastically in the Court's decision in *Brown v. Board of Education* (1954) to end racial segregation in public schools. Burton resigned from the Court in 1958 because of illness; he died in 1964.

FURTHER READING

Berry, Mary F. *Stability, Security, and Continuity: Mr. Justice Burton and Decision-Making in the Supreme Court, 1945–1958.* Westport, Conn.: Greenwood, 1978.

Butler, Pierce

ASSOCIATE JUSTICE, 1923–39

☆ *Born: Mar. 17, 1866, Pine Bend, Minn.*
☆ *Education: Carleton College, B.A., B.S., 1887*
☆ *Previous government service: assistant county attorney, Ramsey County, Minn., 1891–93; state's attorney, Ramsey County, 1893–97*
☆ *Appointed by President Warren G. Harding Nov. 23, 1922; replaced William R. Day, who retired*
☆ *Supreme Court term: confirmed by the Senate Dec. 21, 1922, by a 61–8 vote; served until Nov. 16, 1939*
☆ *Died: Nov. 16, 1939, Washington, D.C.*

PIERCE BUTLER was only the fourth Roman Catholic to be appointed to the Court. He was also a Democrat who was appointed by a Republican President,

Warren G. Harding. Before joining the Court, he had practiced law and served as a prosecuting attorney in Minnesota.

Justice Butler tended to oppose government regulation of businesses. He was a strong opponent of government welfare programs and became a bitter foe of President Franklin D. Roosevelt's New Deal program of the 1930s. He voted against every New Deal policy that came before the Court. He also tended to oppose changes in racial segregation and the "separate but equal" doctrine.

FURTHER READING

Brown, Francis Joseph. *The Social and Economic Philosophy of Pierce Butler.* Washington, D.C.: Catholic University Press, 1945.

Byrnes, James F.

ASSOCIATE JUSTICE, 1941–42

☆ *Born: May 2, 1879, Charleston, S.C.*
☆ *Education: studied law privately*
☆ *Previous government service: court reporter, Second Circuit of South Carolina, 1900–1908; solicitor, Second Circuit of South Carolina, 1908–10; U.S. representative from South Carolina, 1911–25; U.S. senator from South Carolina, 1931–41*
☆ *Appointed by President Franklin D. Roosevelt June 12, 1941; replaced James McReynolds, who retired*
☆ *Supreme Court term: confirmed by the Senate June 12, 1941, by a voice vote; resigned Oct. 3, 1942*
☆ *Subsequent government service: director of the Office of Economic Stabilization, 1942–43; director of the Office of War Mobilization and Reconversion, 1943–45; U.S. secretary of state, 1945–47; governor of South Carolina, 1951–55*
☆ *Died: Apr. 9, 1972, Columbia, S.C.*

JAMES F. BYRNES was the son of Irish immigrants who settled in Charleston, South Carolina. His father died before the younger Byrnes was born. His mother raised the family alone, and James left school to help support himself and his family. He worked as a law clerk and then as a court reporter. These jobs led to an interest in the law, which he studied on his own. He passed the state bar exam in 1903 and began a career as solicitor, or district attorney, for South Carolina's Second Circuit.

In 1910, Byrnes became a Democratic party candidate for a seat in the House of Representatives. His victory launched a spectacular career in the federal government. He became a close friend of President Franklin D. Roosevelt and served in the U.S. Senate during Roosevelt's first two terms. The President rewarded Byrnes for his loyal support by appointing him to the Supreme Court in 1941.

Byrnes's service on the Court lasted less than 14 months. During this time he wrote only 16 opinions. He left the Court to serve President Roosevelt as director of the Office of Economic Stabilization (1942–43) and then as director of the Office of War Mobilization and Reconversion (1943–45). He was secretary of state from 1945 to 1947 under President Harry S. Truman. Byrnes was governor of South Carolina for one term, from 1951 to 1955.

Campbell, John A.

ASSOCIATE JUSTICE, 1853–61

☆ *Born: June 24, 1811, Washington, Ga.*
☆ *Education: University of Georgia, B.A., 1825; U.S. Military Academy, 1825–28*
☆ *Previous government service: Alabama House of Representatives, 1837, 1843*
☆ *Appointed by President Franklin Pierce Mar. 21, 1853; replaced Justice John McKinley, who died*
☆ *Supreme Court term: confirmed by the Senate Mar. 25, 1853, by a voice vote; resigned Apr. 30, 1861*
☆ *Died: Mar. 12, 1889, Baltimore, Md.*

JOHN A. CAMPBELL was a brilliant child who entered college at the age of 11 and graduated three years later. In 1828, he was admitted to the bar by a special act of the Georgia legislature and started his legal career in Alabama two years later. Campbell quickly became one of the best lawyers in Alabama.

Campbell joined the Supreme Court in 1853, during the political crisis that led to the Civil War. Important questions about human rights and property rights faced the Court. In response to these issues, Campbell supported states' rights and slavery. In *Scott* v. *Sandford* (1857), he joined Chief Justice Roger Taney to protect the property rights of slave owners, ruling that Congress could not prohibit slavery in U.S. territories.

When the Civil War started, Campbell left the Court and became assistant secretary of war for the Confederate States of America. After the war, he resumed his career as a lawyer and often represented clients in cases that went to the Supreme Court. For example, he represented the Butchers' Benevolent Association in oral argument in the *Slaughterhouse Cases* (1873).

Capital punishment

THE PENALTY of death for a person convicted of a serious crime, such as intentional murder, is called capital punishment. *Capital* is derived from the Latin word *capitalis*, which means "of the head." Throughout human history, beheading a person has been the most frequent form of killing someone as punishment for a serious crime. Current methods of carrying out capital punish-

An electric chair used in Washington, D.C., before capital punishment there was banned.

ment in the United States are electrocution, firing squad, hanging, poison gas, and lethal injection. The use of lethal injection has become the most common way of carrying out the death penalty in the United States; it is the method used in 17 states.

Capital punishment has been practiced in the United States since the founding of the republic. During the founding period, several crimes were punishable by death in the 13 states: murder, treason, piracy, arson, rape, robbery, burglary, sodomy, counterfeiting, horse theft, and slave rebellion. Today, in the 36 states that permit capital punishment, premeditated murder is virtually the only crime for which the punishment is death. Fourteen states and the District of Columbia have banned the death penalty. The United States government may impose the death penalty for certain federal crimes, such as treason.

In 1972 the U.S. Supreme Court ruled in *Furman* v. *Georgia* that the death penalty could not be imposed without legal guidelines that define precisely the crime and conditions for a sentence of death. A jury in Georgia had convicted William Furman, a black man, of murdering a white man and had sentenced him to death. Under Georgia law, the jury had complete power to decide whether a convicted murderer should receive the death penalty. The Legal Defense Fund of the National Association for the Advancement of Colored People (NAACP) filed an appeal on Furman's behalf. It argued that state laws that gave a jury free rein to impose capital punishment could be unfair. The NAACP lawyers pointed to evidence that blacks convicted of murdering whites were much more likely to be punished by death than whites convicted of murder.

A divided Court (5 to 4) agreed with the NAACP position and, for the first time, nullified a death penalty on the

basis of the 8th Amendment, which forbids "cruel and unusual punishments." Justices William Brennan and Thurgood Marshall argued, in separate concurring opinions, that the death penalty is morally wrong and is always a violation of the "cruel and unusual punishments" clause of the 8th Amendment, as applied to the states through the due process clause of the 14th Amendment. Three other Justices—William O. Douglas, Potter Stewart, and Byron White—wrote separate concurring opinions in which they agreed only that the Georgia system for imposing capital punishment, at issue in this case, was unconstitutional because it led to random and unfair decisions about who should receive the death penalty.

After the *Furman* decision, there was a halt in the use of the death penalty by all 50 state governments. The Georgia government passed a new law regarding capital punishment to address the problems raised by the Court in *Furman*. It created a two-phase procedure for imposing the death penalty in murder cases: the trial phase and the sentencing phase. In the trial phase, a jury would determine a defendant's guilt or innocence. If the defendant was found guilty, the state could request the death penalty. During phase two, there would be a second jury trial with the sole purpose of deciding whether to impose the death penalty. The Georgia law specified mandatory guidelines for determining whether to impose capital punishment. Thus, the law was designed to limit the jury's discretion and eliminate the kind of arbitrary application of the death penalty to which the Court objected in the *Furman* case.

The new Georgia law on capital punishment was tested in *Gregg* v. *Georgia* (1976), in which the Court decided that the death penalty for people convicted of first-degree murder is constitutional. The Court also upheld the

The Passion of Sacco and Vanzetti, *by Ben Shahn. In 1927, Nicola Sacco and Bartolomeo Vanzetti were electrocuted after being convicted of a murder in Massachusetts. Their death was controversial because many believed they were found guilty primarily because they were foreigners and anarchists.*

Georgia law and praised it as a model for other states to follow. Many states have either adopted the Georgia law or created a similar one. The *Gregg* decision appears to have settled the capital punishment issue in favor of the death penalty, as long as it is imposed only in convictions for murder in the first degree and only according to certain clearly spelled out procedures and conditions.

Justices William Brennan and Thurgood Marshall were the two dissenters in the *Gregg* case. They continued to argue that capital punishment is always a violation of the 8th Amendment's "cruel and unusual punishments" clause. By contrast, the defenders of limited uses of capital punishment argue that the U.S. Constitution sanctions the death penalty. They point to the 5th and 14th Amendments, which restrain the government from taking away a person's "life, liberty, or property, without due process of law." These constitutional provisions imply that a person may, under certain conditions, be deprived of life, as long as due process of law is observed. A large majority of Americans have agreed, in public opinion polls, that the death penalty is an acceptable punishment for first-degree murder.

SEE ALSO

Cruel and unusual punishment

FURTHER READING

Bedau, Hugo Adam, ed. *The Death Penalty in America.* New York: Oxford, 1982.
Bigel, Alan I. *Justices William J. Brennan, Jr. and Thurgood Marshall on Capital Punishment.* Lanham, Md.: University Press of America, 1997.
Buranelli, Vincent. *The Eighth Amendment.* Englewood Cliffs, N.J.: Silver Burdett, 1991.

White, Welsh S. *The Death Penalty in the Nineties: An Examination of the Modern System of Capital Punishment.* Ann Arbor: University of Michigan Press, 1991.

Cardozo, Benjamin N.
ASSOCIATE JUSTICE, 1932–38

☆ *Born: May 24, 1870, New York, N.Y.*
☆ *Education: Columbia College, B.A., 1889; M.A., 1890; Columbia Law School, 1891*
☆ *Previous government service: justice, New York State Supreme Court, 1914; judge, New York State Court of Appeals, 1914–32; chief judge, New York State Court of Appeals, 1926–32*
☆ *Appointed by President Herbert Hoover Feb. 15, 1932; replaced Oliver Wendell Holmes, who retired*
☆ *Supreme Court term: confirmed by the Senate Feb. 24, 1932, by a voice vote; served until July 9, 1938*
☆ *Died: July 9, 1938, Port Chester, N.Y.*

BENJAMIN N. CARDOZO was only the second Jew to be appointed to the Supreme Court. He served on the Court with the first Jewish justice, Louis Brandeis.

Benjamin Cardozo was the youngest son of Albert and Rebecca Washington Cardozo, whose ancestors had settled in New York in the 1850s. He was a very bright child and entered Columbia University at age 15, graduating with honors four years later. In 1891, he began to practice law in New York City. Later, he served as a judge of the New York Supreme Court and the New York Court of Appeals.

As a New York State judge, Cardozo achieved a national reputation for his wise decisions and exemplary legal reasoning, which emphasized the effects of law on the lives of people. Cardozo opposed an overemphasis on precedent and tradition as constricting, too formal, and too likely to cause injustice by preventing constitutional changes to fit changing times.

Justice Cardozo served only six years on the U.S. Supreme Court. During this brief period, however, he established the doctrine of "selective incorporation" to guide the Court's use of the 14th Amendment to apply federal Bill of Rights provisions to the states. Cardozo stated this position in *Palko* v. *Connecticut* (1937). He wrote that to be "incorporated" under the due process clause of the 14th Amendment, a provision of the Bill of Rights must be "fundamental"; that is, it must be a right without which "neither liberty nor justice would exist," and the right "must be implicit in the concept of ordered liberty."

Cardozo recommended a case-by-case application of the 14th Amendment to use one or more parts of the Bill of Rights to limit the power of a state government and protect individual rights. This position was opposed by Justice Hugo Black, who wanted "total incorporation" of the Bill of Rights. Cardozo's position has prevailed, and the Court uses it today.

SEE ALSO

Incorporation doctrine; Palko v. Connecticut

FURTHER READING

Cardozo, Benjamin N. *The Nature of the Judicial Process.* New Haven: Yale University Press, 1921.

Kaufman, Andrew L. *Cardozo.* Cambridge: Harvard University Press, 1998.

Polenberg, Richard. *The World of Benjamin Cardozo: Personal Values and the Judicial Process.* Cambridge: Harvard University Press, 1999.

Posner, Richard A. *Cardozo: A Study in Reputation.* Chicago: University of Chicago Press, 1990.

Carroll v. United States

☆ *267 U.S. 132 (1925)*
☆ *Vote: 6–2*
☆ *For the Court: Taft*
☆ *Dissenting: McReynolds and Sutherland*

IN 1923, George Carroll and John Kiro were transporting alcoholic beverages in an automobile. Federal officers suspected they might be carrying liquor, stopped their car, and searched it. They found liquor and arrested Carroll and Kiro, who were charged with violating the Volstead Act (the federal law prohibiting the sale or transportation of alcoholic beverages). Carroll and Kiro were convicted, but they appealed because the federal officers had searched their automobile without a warrant.

The Issue Carroll claimed that the federal officers who searched his automobile had violated the 4th Amendment of the Constitution, which states, "The right of the people to be secure in their persons, houses, papers, and effects, against unreasonable searches and seizures, shall not be violated, and no Warrants shall issue, but upon probable cause, supported by Oath or affirmation, and particularly describing the place to be searched, and the persons or things to be seized." Carroll argued that the federal officers had no legal grounds for searching his car, so the evidence they found should have been excluded from his trial.

Opinion of the Court The Court decided against Carroll. The warrantless search of the car was constitutional, said

New York police arrest bootleggers in 1921. In Carroll v. United States, *the Court decided that police can legally search a car without a warrant.*

Chief Justice William Howard Taft, because the vehicle could be driven away and the people in it could escape before a warrant could be obtained. Thus, an exception to the 4th Amendment warrant requirement could be made.

Dissent Justice George Sutherland joined Justice James McReynolds in dissent. McReynolds argued that no exceptions should be made in cases involving searches of cars to the 4th Amendment requirement of a warrant as protection against unreasonable searches and seizures. He concluded that Carroll had been wrongfully arrested.

Significance This case established a rule about searches of automobiles that has been upheld in subsequent cases such as *United States* v. *Ross* (1982). In *California* v. *Acevedo* (1991), the rule was strengthened by the Court's decision to eliminate a warrant requirement for searches and seizures of closed containers found in an automobile.

SEE ALSO
Searches and seizures; United States v. Ross

Catron, John
ASSOCIATE JUSTICE, 1837–65

☆ *Born: 1786, Pennsylvania*
☆ *Education: self-educated, studied law on his own*
☆ *Previous government service: judge, Tennessee Supreme Court of Errors and Appeals, 1824–31; chief justice of Tennessee, 1831–34*
☆ *Appointed by President Andrew Jackson Mar. 3, 1837, to fill a newly created seat on the Court*
☆ *Supreme Court term: confirmed by the Senate Mar. 8, 1837, by a 28–15 vote; served until May 30, 1865*
☆ *Died: May 30, 1865, Nashville, Tenn.*

JOHN CATRON WAS the son of German immigrants to Pennsylvania. The exact place of his birth is unknown, but the hardships of his childhood in Virginia and Kentucky, and his struggles to overcome them, have been recorded. Although Catron did not have an opportunity to go to school, he educated himself by reading at home.

Catron served under General Andrew Jackson in the War of 1812. His friendship with Jackson worked to his benefit after Jackson became President in 1828. Catron became a loyal Jacksonian Democrat, and the President rewarded him with an appointment to the U.S. Supreme Court in 1837. During his 28 years on the Court, Catron supported states' rights and slavery. But when the Civil War started, he remained loyal to the Union and remained at his job on the Supreme Court.

Certiorari, writ of

THE U.S. SUPREME COURT has the authority, given by Congress (according to Article 3, Section 2, of the Constitution), to issue a writ of certiorari, which is an order to a lower court to prepare the record of a case and submit it to the Supreme Court for review. The Latin term *certiorari* means "to be informed." A party to a case seeking review by the Supreme Court submits a petition to the Court for a writ of certiorari. If at least four justices vote in favor of it, "cert." is granted, and the case comes to the Court for its review and decision.

Each year approximately 5,000 petitions are sent to the Court seeking a writ of certiorari. Less than 5 percent are granted "cert." If the writ of certiorari is denied, the decision of the lower court is sustained. However, a denial of "cert." cannot be used as evidence of the Supreme Court's opinion on the issue in the case.

The rules of the Court provide general guidelines for accepting or rejecting appeals from lower courts. For example, the Court will likely accept a case for review if there appears to be an error in lower court proceedings, if the issue in the case involves an unsettled question of federal law, or if there are conflicting opinions on the case from the highest state court and a federal court of appeals.

According to Rule 10 of the *Rules of the Supreme Court of the United States,* "Review on a writ of certiorari is not a matter of right, but of judicial discretion. A petition for a writ of certiorari will be granted only for compelling reasons." Making decisions about which cases to review, and which ones to reject, is among the most important judgments the Court makes. These decisions go a long way toward setting the agenda of the Court and determining who will and will not have access to it. Although there are other means by which a case comes before the U.S. Supreme Court, the writ of certiorari is the primary means for bringing a case to the Court for its review and disposition.

SEE ALSO

Jurisdiction

Chambers

THE OFFICES of Supreme Court justices are called chambers. Each justice has three connecting rooms on the main floor. One serves as the private office of the justice, and the other two are used by clerks and secretaries.

Charles River Bridge v. Warren Bridge

☆ *11 Pet. 420 (1837)*

☆ *Vote: 4–3*
☆ *For the Court: Taney*
☆ *Dissenting: McLean, Story, and Thompson*

IN 1828, the state government of Massachusetts granted a charter, or permit, for construction of a bridge across the Charles River to connect Boston with Cambridge. This new bridge, the Warren Bridge, was to span the river near an older bridge, the Charles River Bridge. The owners of the Charles River Bridge Company claimed that their charter, which they had obtained in 1785, gave them the right to prevent the construction of a new bridge. They claimed the new bridge would cause them to lose profits by attracting the patronage and the payments of those who had formerly used their bridge. The Charles River Bridge Company earned profits by charging a toll, or fee, to users of their bridge. The owners did not want competition from a new company that would also collect tolls from bridge users. Worse, the new Warren Bridge would become toll-free after six years.

The owners of the Charles River Bridge Company argued that in violating their charter, the new Warren Bridge Company charter violated the contract clause of the U.S. Constitution. They pointed to the Supreme Court's decision in *Dartmouth College* v. *Woodward* (1819), which seemed to support their argument that the state should not violate the terms of a contract. They stated that the Court should not allow the Warren Bridge Company to compete with them.

The Issue Should a contract granted by a state government be interpreted so as to stop the state from granting another charter to build new public facilities that would meet important public needs? Would the granting of such a charter violate the contract clause of Article 1, Section 10, of the Constitution, which provides that no state shall pass a law "impairing the Obligation of Contracts"?

Opinion of the Court The court ruled against the Charles River Bridge Company. Chief Justice Roger Taney wrote the majority opinion, which emphasized that a state must interpret public charters so as to benefit public and community needs. Thus, the state of Massachusetts had the right, under the Constitution, to charter the building of a bridge that would compete with another bridge it had contracted for earlier.

Chief Justice Taney was not ignoring the contract clause of the Constitution. He believed in private property rights and the sanctity of contracts. However, he opposed any interpretation of a contract that infringed upon the rights or needs of the public. The contract granted to the Charles River Bridge Company did not say exactly that no other company could build a bridge nearby. Rather, the company interpreted the contract to give them exclusive rights. Taney and the majority of the Court, however, would not interpret the contract as giving exclusive rights to the older and established Charles River Bridge Company.

Dissent Justice Joseph Story argued for upholding the exclusive contract of the Charles River Bridge Company. He feared that the Court's decision in this case would undermine the faith of property owners in contracts as the means to protect their property rights.

Significance This decision opposed business monopolies (companies having exclusive control of the provision of goods or services) that hurt the public. It encouraged private businesses to compete freely with one another. The Court supported the right of state governments to decide, under the 10th Amendment, whether to grant charters to build new facilities such as highways, railroads, and bridges to serve the public.

SEE ALSO

Contract clause; Dartmouth College v. Woodward

FURTHER READING

Graff, Henry F. "The Charles River Bridge Case." In *Quarrels That Have Shaped the Constitution*, edited by John A. Garraty. New York: Harper & Row, 1987.

Chase, Salmon P.
CHIEF JUSTICE, 1864–73

☆ *Born: Jan. 13, 1808, Cornish, N.H.*
☆ *Education: Dartmouth College, A.B., 1826*
☆ *Previous government service: U.S. senator from Ohio, 1849–55, 1861; governor of Ohio, 1856–60; U.S. secretary of the Treasury, 1861–64*
☆ *Appointed by President Abraham Lincoln Dec. 6, 1864; replaced Chief Justice Roger B. Taney, who died*
☆ *Supreme Court term: confirmed by the Senate Dec. 6, 1864, by a voice vote; served until May 7, 1873*
☆ *Died: May 7, 1873, New York, N.Y.*

SALMON P. CHASE had a lifelong ambition to become President of the United States. He failed to realize his highest goal, but he did become the sixth Chief Justice of the United States.

After graduating from Dartmouth College in 1826, Chase studied law under U.S. Attorney General William Wirt and became a lawyer in Cincinnati. He achieved a national reputation as an opponent of slavery and a defender of escaped slaves who sought refuge in the free Northern states.

His friends and foes called him the "attorney general for runaway Negroes."

In the 1850s, Chase became a leader in the new Republican party and its anti-slavery mission. After an unsuccessful bid to become the Republican party's Presidential candidate in 1860, he backed his party's choice, Abraham Lincoln. The new President appointed Chase to his cabinet as secretary of the Treasury. In 1864, Lincoln chose Chase to be Chief Justice of the United States, even though Chase had tried to take Lincoln's place as the Republican party Presidential candidate in the 1864 election.

As chief justice, Chase continued his concern for the rights of African Americans newly freed from slavery in 1865 by the 13th Amendment. Chief Justice Chase, however, also supported the constitutional rights of a Confederate sympathizer from Indiana in the landmark decision of *Ex parte Milligan* (1866). He joined in the unanimous decision that Lambdin Milligan, who lived in a non–war zone during the Civil War, had been unfairly and illegally tried in a military court, instead of a civilian court, for supposedly committing crimes against the federal government.

Chief Justice Chase presided with dignity and fairness over the 1868 impeachment trial of President Andrew Johnson. And he wrote an enduring opinion for the Court in *Texas* v. *White* (1869) that endorsed the Republican party position that a state did not have a right to secede from the federal Union. Chase argued that Texas's Confederate government had been unlawful and that its acts, therefore, were null and void. Chase argued conclusively that the Constitution created "an indestructible union, composed of indestructible states" and that secession was illegal.

SEE ALSO

Chief Justice; Ex parte Milligan; Texas v. White

FURTHER READING

Blue, Frederick J. *Salmon P. Chase: A Life in Politics*. Kent, Ohio: Kent State University Press, 1987.
Hyman, Harold M. *The Reconstruction of Justice Salmon P. Chase*. Lawrence: University Press of Kansas, 1997.
Niven, John. *Salmon Chase: A Biography*. New York: Oxford University Press, 1995.

Chase, Samuel
ASSOCIATE JUSTICE, 1796–1811

☆ Born: Apr. 17, 1741, Somerset County, Md.
☆ Education: tutored by father; studied law in an Annapolis, Md., law office
☆ Previous government service: Maryland General Assembly, 1764–84; Continental Congress, 1774–78, 1784–85; Maryland Convention and Council of Safety, 1775; judge, Baltimore Criminal Court, 1788–96; chief judge, General Court of Maryland, 1791–96
☆ Appointed by President George Washington Jan. 26, 1796; replaced John Blair, who resigned
☆ Supreme Court term: confirmed by the Senate Jan. 27, 1796, by a voice vote; served until June 19, 1811
☆ Died: June 19, 1811, Baltimore, Md.

SAMUEL CHASE was a patriot in the American revolutionary war. He belonged to the Sons of Liberty and signed the Declaration of Independence.

Justice Chase wrote several important opinions in early key decisions of the Supreme Court. In *Ware* v. *Hylton* (1796), for example, he helped to establish the supremacy of federal treaties over state laws that contradicted them. In *Hylton* v. *United States* (1796), Chase and the Supreme Court made a judgment about whether or not an act of Congress, the carriage tax of 1794, agreed with the Constitution. The Court supported the federal statute, which was its first judgment about the constitutionality of an act of the legislative branch of government. The Court, however, neither asserted nor discussed the power of judicial review, which was established by Chief Justice John Marshall in *Marbury* v. *Madison* (1803).

Justice Chase was a harsh public critic of the Jeffersonian Republicans because he disagreed with their interpretations of the Constitution. When Thomas Jefferson became President in 1801, Chase sharpened his criticism of Jefferson and the Republican majority in Congress. In return, President Jefferson urged that Chase be removed from the Supreme Court. A majority of the House of Representatives voted to impeach Chase. As provided in the Constitution, the case went to the Senate for trial, where two-thirds of the Senators had to vote against Chase to remove him from office. Chase argued that he had done nothing wrong and that a federal judge should not be impeached and removed from office for criticizing the President. Chase was acquitted and remained on the Court until his death in 1811.

SEE ALSO

Hylton v. United States; Impeachment; Ware v. Hylton

FURTHER READING

Haw, James, et al. *Stormy Patriot: The Life of Samuel Chase.* Baltimore: Maryland Historical Society, 1980.

Checks and balances

S E E Separation of powers

Chief justice

THE CHIEF JUSTICE of the United States is the presiding officer of the Supreme Court and the head of the judicial branch of the federal government. The title chief justice is mentioned only once, however, in the U.S. Constitution: Article 1, Section 3, mandates that the chief justice serve as presiding officer of the Senate during an impeachment trial of a President. The office of chief justice is *not* mentioned in Article 3 of the Constitution, which deals with the judicial branch of the federal government.

The office of chief justice was established by the Judiciary Act of 1789. The position has truly been shaped by its occupants, who have established the roles and duties as they performed them. In addition, Congress contributed to development of this office through legislation.

Since 1789, the office of chief justice has developed into a complex and prestigious position. The person occupying this position must serve as Supreme Court leader, judge, administrator, and national symbol of justice under the law.

The chief justice, like the eight associate justices of the Supreme Court, is appointed by the President of the United States "with the Advice and Consent of the Senate," as provided by Article 2, Section 2, of the Constitution. The chief justice, the eight associate justices, and the federal judges of the lower courts "shall hold their Offices during good Behaviour," according to Article 3, Section 1, of the Constitution, which provides lifetime job security for judges who

Chief Justice Earl Warren administers the oath of office to President Lyndon Johnson in 1965.

want it. Further, Article 3, Section 1, says the pay of federal judges "shall not be diminished during their Continuance in Office." Thus, the Constitution provides for the independence of the chief justice, the eight associate justices, and other federal judges.

The chief justice has been called "first among equals" in his relationships with the eight associate justices. He has only one vote, as they do, in deciding cases. The chief justice and the eight associate justices are equal in their virtual lifetime tenure, in their protection against decreases in income, and in their independence as judicial decision makers on cases before the Court. The chief justice also must perform the work of a judge, along with his eight associates. Together, the chief and his associates review and make decisions on all petitions for certiorari (appeals from lower courts for a hearing before the Supreme Court); he must also examine, discuss, and decide, like his associates, all the cases that come to the Court. The chief shares with his associates the work of writing opinions for the Court.

Unlike his associates, however, the chief justice is the sole presiding officer of the Supreme Court. He presides at the conference during which the Court decides which cases to accept from the large number of appeals over which it has discretionary power. He also presides over the public sessions, or hearings of cases, that come before the Court, and he chairs the private conference at which cases are discussed among the nine members of the Court and eventually decided by a vote of the justices. Finally, when the chief justice is in the majority, he has the authority to assign the task of writing the Court's opinion on the case either to himself or to one of the associate justices. Thus, the chief justice is able to influence directly or indirectly the style and sub-

The chief justice's coat hook in the Old Supreme Court Chamber.

CHIEF JUSTICES

Justice	Tenure
John Jay	1789–1795
John Rutledge	1795
Oliver Ellsworth	1796–1800
John Marshall	1801–1835
Roger B. Taney	1836–1864
Salmon P. Chase	1864–1873
Morrison R. Waite	1874–1888
Melville W. Fuller	1888–1910
Edward D. White	1910–1921
William H. Taft	1921–1930
Charles E. Hughes	1930–1940
Harlan F. Stone	1941–1946
Frederick M. Vinson	1946–1952
Earl Warren	1953–1969
Warren E. Burger	1969–1986
William H. Rehnquist	1986–

stance of the Court's written opinion. When the chief justice is not part of the majority decision on a case, the most senior member of the majority assigns the writing of the Court's opinion.

In addition to his duties as presiding officer of the Supreme Court, the chief justice also serves as administrative head of the judicial branch of the federal government. He is chairman of the Judicial Conference of the United States. The conference includes 27 federal judges, who represent all the levels and regions of the federal judiciary. The conference meets twice a year to discuss common problems, to coordinate administrative policies, and to recommend to Congress measures for improving the operation of the federal courts. Administrative and budgetary functions for the conference are carried out by the Administrative Office of the United States Courts. The Administrative Office's director and deputy director are appointed by the Supreme Court and report to the chief justice. The chief justice is also the permanent chairman of the governing board of the Federal Judicial Center, which provides research and training services for the federal judiciary.

The chief justice has several extrajudicial responsibilities. He is manager of the Supreme Court Building. He serves as chancellor of the Smithsonian Institution, a complex of museums and research institutions operated by the federal government. And he is considered the head of the legal profession in the United States.

The chief justice is also the living symbol of the federal judiciary. In this role, the chief administers the oath of office to the President at every inauguration.

Since 1789, there have been 16 chief justices of the United States. The first chief justice was John Jay, who was appointed by President George Washington. President John Adams appointed the chief justice generally acclaimed as the greatest, John Marshall, who served from 1801 until his death in 1835. His tenure as chief justice was the longest. Other chief justices whom scholars and legal experts consider truly great are Roger B. Taney, Charles Evans Hughes, Harlan Fiske Stone, and Earl Warren. Five chief justices, nearly one-third of the total from 1789 to 1993, have performed well enough to receive such excellent ratings.

SEE ALSO
Administration of federal courts; Justices of the Supreme Court

FURTHER READING
Morris, Jeffrey B. *First Among Equals: The Office of the Chief Justice of the United States*. Berkeley: University of California Press, 1993.
Morris, Jeffrey B. "Hail to the Chief Justice." *Constitution* 4, no. 2 (Spring–Summer 1992): 40–50.
Steamer, Robert J. *Chief Justice: Leadership and the Supreme Court*. Columbia: University of South Carolina Press, 1986.

Chisholm v. Georgia

☆ *2 Dall. 419 (1793)*
☆ *Vote: 4–1*
☆ *For the Court: seriatim opinions by Jay, Cushing, Wilson, and Blair*
☆ *Dissenting: Iredell*

DURING THE American War of Independence, agents of the state government of Georgia purchased clothing, blankets, and other goods from Robert Farquhar, a merchant in Charleston, South Carolina. Farquhar died in 1784, and the executor of his estate was Alexander Chisholm. Acting for a minor (non-adult) heir of Farquhar, Chisholm sought payment from the Georgia state government for money that he claimed it owed Farquhar. Georgia officials refused to pay, however, because the state had already paid its agents for the goods. Chisholm was unable to collect the money owed his client from these agents. So he took his case to the newly established federal courts and sued the state of Georgia for the monetary value of the goods supplied by Farquhar.

The Issue The state of Georgia refused to send a representative to the Court. Georgia argued that the Court did not have jurisdiction in this case because a state government could not be sued by a citizen from another state.

Opinion of the Court The Court ruled in favor of Chisholm. This decision was based on Article 3, Section 2, of the U.S. Constitution, which says, "The judicial Power shall extend to all Cases... between a State and Citizens of another State." Chief Justice John Jay wrote, "Any one state in the Union may sue another state in this court, that is, all the people of one state may sue all the people of another state. It is plain, then, that a state may

When the Georgia government refused to pay a South Carolina merchant who had supplied army uniforms during the Revolution, the case went to the Supreme Court.

be sued, and hence it plainly follows that suability and state sovereignty are not incompatible." In other words, a suit brought by citizens of one state against the government of another state does not diminish or threaten the authority or independent power of that state government.

Dissent Justice James Iredell argued that under common law no state could be sued unless it consented to the action. This state right was necessary in order for the state to retain its sovereignty (supreme power within its borders, free of external influences), said Iredell.

Significance This decision caused an uproar in Congress. A large majority in the House of Representatives (81–9) and the Senate (23–2) voted in favor of a proposed constitutional amendment that would effectively overturn the Supreme Court's decision in *Chisholm* v. *Georgia*. The state governments ratified this proposal, which became the 11th Amendment to the Constitution: "The Judicial power of the United States shall not be construed to extend to any suit in law or equity, commenced or prosecuted against one of the United States by citizens of another State, or by Citizens or Subjects of any Foreign State." This was the first time a Supreme Court decision was overturned by constitutional amendment.

What happened to Chisholm's financial claim against Georgia? It succeeded. Robert Farquhar's heir accepted securities in the form of bonds from the Georgia state government in full payment of his claim against the state. These bonds paid interest to the holder and could be exchanged for cash.

FURTHER READING

Orth, John V. *The Judicial Power of the United States: The Eleventh Amendment in American History.* New York: Oxford University Press, 1987.

Circuit Courts of Appeals

THE JUDICIARY ACT of 1789 set up a system of lower federal courts, under the Supreme Court of the United States. At the bottom were federal district courts, one per state except for Massachusetts and Virginia, which had two apiece because of their greater population. Between the Supreme Court and the district courts were three circuit courts of appeals, one for each of three circuits, or districts, each of which included several states. In 1789 the Southern Circuit included South Carolina and Georgia (North Carolina was added in 1790 after it entered the Union). In 1789 the Eastern Circuit contained New York, Connecticut, Massachusetts, and New Hampshire (Rhode Island and Vermont were added when they joined the Union in 1790 and 1791, respectively). The Middle Circuit included Virginia, Maryland, Pennsylvania, Delaware, and New Jersey.

Until 1869 the circuit courts served both as trial courts and appellate courts; both federal district court judges and Supreme Court justices presided in these circuit courts. The judges and justices had to "ride circuit" in order to carry out their circuit court duties; that is, they had to travel from place to place, within the large area of the circuit, to hear cases and make decisions. In the early years of the United States, the judges and justices rode on horseback or in horse-drawn carriages.

Circuit riding was a great hardship, involving long hours of travel. The Supreme Court justices constantly complained to Congress, asking to be relieved of this heavy burden. In the Judiciary Act of 1869, Congress finally responded to their complaints. This law provided for the appointment of nine new circuit court judges, which relieved the Supreme Court justices of their ongoing circuit-riding duties. However, the law did require the justices to participate in circuit court duties once every two years.

The Judiciary Act of 1891 created, for the first time, the U.S. Circuit Courts of Appeals, one for each of nine regions, or circuits, to hear cases on appeal from the lower courts. The old circuit courts were retained, but their duties were merged with the federal district courts. So the federal judiciary consisted of two trial courts (circuit and district courts) and two appellate courts (the Supreme Court and the new Circuit Courts of Appeals). The act eliminated the circuit-riding duties of Supreme Court justices and assigned three judges to each of the nine new Circuit Courts of Appeals. This relieved the burden on the Supreme Court, which until then had carried out most of the federal appellate court work. In 1911 Congress acted to eliminate the old circuit courts because they merely duplicated the work of the district courts, which were retained as the trial courts of the federal judiciary. In 1948 the Circuit Courts of Appeals were given a new name, which they retain today, the Courts of Appeals.

SEE ALSO
Courts of Appeals

Citation

THE WAY in which opinions of the U.S. Supreme Court are identified, or cited, in legal literature is referred to as a citation. A Supreme Court case citation includes the following information, in this order: the names of the parties to the case, separated by "v.," for *versus* (Latin for

"against"); the volume of *United States Reports* in which the case appears (for cases since 1875), or the volume of private reports, for pre-1875 cases; the beginning page number on which the report of the case appears; and the year the decision was made. For example, *Abrams* v. *United States,* 250 U.S. 616 (1919) means that the Supreme Court decision and opinion in this case will be found in Volume 250 of *United States Reports,* beginning on page 616. The case was decided in 1919.

United States Reports, published by the U.S. Government Printing Office, is one of several sources of Supreme Court opinions. Other sources are *Supreme Court Reporter,* published by West Publishing Company, and *United States Supreme Court Reports, Lawyers' Edition,* published by the Lawyers Cooperative Publishing Company.

Before 1875, official reports of Supreme Court cases were cited with the names of the Court reporters. These names (full or abbreviated) appear in the citations for those years. For example, in *Marbury* v. *Madison,* 1 Cr. 137 (1803), "Cr." is an abbreviation for William Cranch, the Supreme Court reporter from 1801 to 1815. The reporters of decisions from 1790 to 1875 were Alexander J. Dallas (1790–1800), William Cranch (1801–15), Henry Wheaton (1816–27), Richard Peters, Jr. (1828–42), Benjamin C. Howard (1843–60), Jeremiah S. Black (1861–62), and John W. Wallace (1863–75).

SEE ALSO
Reporter of decisions

Citizenship

THE 14TH AMENDMENT to the Constitution defines citizenship in the United States as follows: "All persons born or naturalized in the United States, and subject to the jurisdiction thereof, are citizens of the United States and of the state wherein they reside." Citizenship can be acquired by birth; anyone born in any of the 50 states, the District of Columbia, the Commonwealth of Puerto Rico, or the territories of Guam and the Virgin Islands, for example, is a natural-born citizen of the United States. Children born outside the country to at least one American parent are also U.S. citizens by birth. However, before they are 21 years old, they must become residents of the United States or declare their intention to become a U.S. citizen.

A second way to become a U.S. citizen, according to the 14th Amendment, is by naturalization. Article 1, Section 8, of the Constitution provides Congress

Immigrants become naturalized citizens in 1983 in Hawaii. The 14th Amendment guarantees the same protections to naturalized citizens as to the native-born.

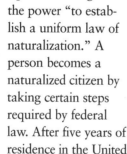

the power "to establish a uniform law of naturalization." A person becomes a naturalized citizen by taking certain steps required by federal law. After five years of residence in the United States (three years if the person is married to an American citizen), a person may file a petition to become a citizen. Two U.S. citizens must testify that the person has fulfilled the residence requirement, exhibits good moral behavior, and believes in the principles of the Constitution. Next, the person completes an examination to prove literacy in English and knowledge of U.S. history and government. Finally, the person pledges an oath of allegiance to the Constitution of the United States and signs a certificate of naturalization.

In *United States* v. *Wong Kim Ark* (1898), the Supreme Court ruled for the first time on a case arising under the 14th Amendment clause that defines citizenship. The Court decided that the race, ethnic identity, or place of birth of a person's parents could not be used to deny citizenship to a person born in the United States. The Court affirmed the fundamental importance of citizenship in *Trop* v. *Dulles* (1958) by refusing to take away a person's citizenship because he had deserted the army during wartime. Writing for the Court, Chief Justice Earl Warren held that such a loss of citizenship would be "cruel and unusual punishment," which is banned by the 8th Amendment.

Naturalized citizens have the same rights and duties as natural-born citizens, with one exception: they are not eligible to become President or Vice President of the United States (Article 2, Section 1, of the Constitution). According to the 14th Amendment, "No state shall make or enforce any law which shall abridge the privileges or immunities of citizens of the United States." Citizenship entitles a person to certain rights, such as the right to vote or to be a federal government official. (The Bill of Rights, however, applies to all individuals living in the United States, both citizens and noncitizens.) In return, all citizens have certain legal responsibilities, such as paying taxes, serving on a jury if called, serving in the country's armed forces if called, serving as a witness in court if summoned, and obeying the laws of the United States. (Noncitizens residing in the United States are also required to pay taxes and obey the law.) In exchange for the privileges and rights of citizenship, all citizens of the United States have the obligation of loyalty and allegiance to their Constitution and their country.

SEE ALSO
United States v. Wong Kim Ark

FURTHER READING
Riesenberg, Peter. *Citizenship in the Western Tradition.* Chapel Hill: University of North Carolina Press, 1992.

City of Boerne, Texas v. Flores

☆ *117 S.Ct. 2157 (1997)*
☆ *Vote: 6–3*
☆ *For the Court: Kennedy*
☆ *Dissenting: O'Connor, Souter, and Breyer*

A ROMAN Catholic priest in a small West Texas city, Boerne, wanted to enlarge the St. Peter's Church. But the city government refused to grant a construction permit for an addition to the small 70-year-old church because it was located in a neighborhood designated by the local government as a historic preservation zone. The purpose of this zoning law was to maintain historic sites by preventing or limiting new construction that would significantly change the appearance of the city's historic district.

Archbishop P. F. Flores of the Roman Catholic Diocese of San Antonio, in which the city of Boerne was located, filed suit to force the city government to permit enlargement of St. Peter's Church. He based his suit on the city's presumed violation of a federal law, the Religious Freedom Restoration Act (RFRA) of 1993.

The RFRA limited the power of federal, state, and local governments to enforce laws that "substantially burden" the free exercise of religion. Such a "burdensome" law could be carried out only if the government could demonstrate a "compelling" public justification for doing so, and if it was "the least restrictive means of furthering that compelling governmental interest." Those whose constitutional rights to free exercise of religion had been "substantially burdened," as Archbishop Flores claimed, could "in a judicial proceeding... obtain appropriate relief against a government."

Using the RFRA to support his case, Archbishop Flores argued that the city of Boerne, through its zoning laws, was illegally interfering with the practices of a religious institution and thereby substantially burdening its constitutionally protected free exercise of religion. The federal district court ruled in favor of the city of Boerne and concluded that the RFRA was unconstitutional. The 5th Circuit Court of Appeals, however, disagreed. It upheld the RFRA as constitutional and reversed the lower court's decision. So the case went to the U.S. Supreme Court for resolution.

The Issue When Congress passed the Religious Freedom Restoration Act, it relied upon the U.S. Constitution's 14th Amendment. Section 1 of the amendment guarantees that a state cannot deprive a person of life, liberty, or property without due process of law, and it cannot deny to any person the equal protection of the laws. Section 5 of the 14th Amendment empowers Congress to enforce these guarantees through enactment of appropriate laws.

In its enactment of the RFRA, Congress claimed that this law was needed to effectively protect a person's 1st Amendment right to free exercise of religion at state and local levels of government. The majority in Congress was concerned about possible state government infringement of rights to religious liberty due to the Supreme Court's decision in *Employment Division Department of Human Resources of Oregon* v. *Smith* (1990). This ruling had overturned a constitutional standard set in *Sherbert* v. *Verner* (1963), which declared that to survive judicial scrutiny, a law restricting the free exercise of religion must advance a compelling public interest of government in the least restrictive manner possible. The RFRA was intended by Congress to restore the "compelling interest" and "least restrictive means" standards of the *Sherbert* v. *Verner* decision.

Counsel for the city of Boerne, Marcia Hamilton, argued that the RFRA, on which Archbishop Flores based his lawsuit against the city, was unconstitutional because it represented an expansion of Congress's authority beyond the scope allowed by the Constitution. Thus, the RFRA violated the constitutional principles of separation of powers and federalism.

Does Congress have power under the 14th Amendment to define rights to religious freedoms more broadly than the U.S. Supreme Court, as it did in the RFRA? And does the RFRA thereby violate the constitutional principles of separation of powers among the three branches of the federal government and the principles of federalism, the division of powers between the federal and state governments?

Opinion of the Court   Writing for the Court, Justice Anthony Kennedy held that Congress went beyond its constitutionally sanctioned power by attempting to substantially interpret the Constitution through legislation. Thus, Congress usurped a power belonging exclusively to the federal courts under the Constitution. This amounts to violation of the constitutional principle of separation of powers. Further, Justice Kennedy concluded that through the RFRA, Congress had unconstitutionally infringed upon the authority of state governments to regulate the health, safety, or general welfare of their citizens. So the RFRA was a violation of the constitutional principle of federalism.

Justice Kennedy wrote, "Congress's discretion is not unlimited...and the courts retain the power, as they have since *Marbury* v. *Madison,* to determine if Congress has exceeded its authority under the Constitution. Broad as the

power of Congress is under the Enforcement Clause of the Fourteenth Amendment, [the] RFRA contradicts vital principles necessary to maintain separation of powers and the federal balance."

Dissent   The dissenters, led by Justice Sandra Day O'Connor, agreed with the Court's majority that Congress cannot redefine or expand the scope of constitutional rights by legislation. However, she disagreed with the Court's majority in its use of the *Smith* decision (1990) as the ruling precedent because she believed the holding in *Smith* had been decided wrongly. She argued for reconsidering the *Smith* decision as bad constitutional law instead of declaring the RFRA unconstitutional.

Significance   Although the city of Boerne won its case, city officials offered a compromise agreement to the local Roman Catholic Church officials. They agreed to allow an enlargement of St. Peter's Church by 850 seats. But 80 percent of the building was to be left intact.

Some public reactions to the Court's decision were not as generous or accommodating as the response of the city of Boerne's government. Senator Orrin Hatch of Utah, for example, said that the Court "once again acted to push religion to the fringes of society." The winning lawyer in this case, Marcia Hamilton, said, "Congress does not have the power to amend the Constitution unilaterally."

Although the *City of Boerne* decision had important consequences for church and state relationships, its primary significance pertained to limitations on Congress's authority to expand its constitutional powers in relationship to the other branches of the federal government and the state governments. The Supreme Court clearly and emphatically served notice to the other branches of government that it has the conclusive power to say what the Constitution means and what it does not mean.

SEE ALSO

Federalism; Religious issues under the Constitution; Separation of powers

Civil law

WITHIN THE legal system of the United States, civil law is a body of law pertaining to noncriminal private disputes among individuals, corporations, and governments. Thus, civil law is distinguished from criminal law, which deals with the enforcement of the laws against those accused of violating them. In a civil action, one private party takes legal action against another private party to seek relief in a court of law for an alleged wrong.

SEE ALSO

Criminal law

Civil rights

CIVIL RIGHTS and civil liberties often mean the same thing. The words are frequently used interchangeably to signify the protection of rights to liberty and equality under the Constitution, such as freedom of speech, protection against "unreasonable searches and seizures," and the right to due process of law. The term *civil rights,* however, is also used to refer to positive actions by the government to protect or extend the rights of people—to provide for individuals or groups opportunities that were previously denied to them. These kinds of civil rights guarantees usually are provided through statutes, such as the Civil Rights Act of 1964, which, for example,

Byzantine emperor Justinian I consolidated Roman civil law into a collection that influenced legal systems of many countries in Europe and other parts of the world.

gives the federal government the power to prevent an employer from denying a job to someone because of the person's race, gender, religion, or ethnic origin.

Civil rights movements are organized efforts to obtain long-denied constitutional rights for individuals and groups such as African Americans, Hispanics, Native Americans, and women. These segments of the American population have not always enjoyed their full rights of citizenship under the U.S. Constitution.

The civil rights movement

The civil rights movement of African Americans, during most of the 20th century, has had a strong impact on the advancement of constitutional rights for all Americans, especially those who had been long-suffering victims of unjust discrimination and unfair treatment under the law. The early leader of this civil rights movement was the National Association for the Advancement of Colored People (NAACP), founded in 1909. After the formation in 1939 of its Legal Defense Fund (LDF), directed by Thurgood Marshall, the NAACP began to have a steady and significant effect on federal court rulings to obtain and expand the civil rights of African Americans with regard to voting and education. In *Smith* v. *Allwright* (1944) the Court ruled that a political party (the Democrats in this case) could not exclude blacks from voting in a primary election to nominate party candidates for a subsequent general election. In *Sweatt* v. *Painter* (1950) the Court decided that a

A taxicab with a sign that says "White Only" in Albany, Georgia, reveals that discrimination was part of everyday life in 1962.

state may not deny admission of qualified blacks to a state law school on the grounds that a separate law school for blacks is available. The biggest breakthrough came with the legal victory, led by Thurgood Marshall and other NAACP attorneys, in *Brown* v. *Board of Education* (1954), which established that racial segregation in public schools is unconstitutional.

After the *Brown* decision, various African-American civil rights organizations, including the NAACP, launched political protest movements to influence enforcement of the *Brown* decision and to demand that the federal government pass laws to protect and promote civil rights for African Americans. Martin Luther King, Jr., and the Southern Christian Leadership Conference (SCLC), which he led, moved to the forefront.

Civil rights legislation

The political protest movement influenced enactment of two legislative milestones: the Civil Rights Act of 1964 and the Voting Rights Act of 1965. The 1964 Civil Rights Act forbids discrimination on the basis of race, color, religion, national origin, and, in employment, sex. The law provides protection from unfair discrimination in employment and in the use of public facilities. It also requires desegregation of public schools and facilities.

The Supreme Court has upheld as constitutional the major provisions of the Civil Rights Act of 1964. And the Court has interpreted this law broadly to expand the opportunities available to racial minorities often victimized by past discriminatory practices. In *Heart of Atlanta Motel* v. *United States* (1964), for example, the Court established beyond challenge that no person can be excluded, because of race or color, from any facility that is open to the general public. Further, the Court has upheld programs of employers to emphasize recruitment of racial minorities that have suffered from the employer's racial discrimination in hiring in the past.

The 1965 Voting Rights Act outlawed discrimination by state governments against African Americans and other minority groups in voter registration and voting in state and federal elections. The Supreme Court upheld the law in *South Carolina* v. *Katzenbach* (1966), ruling that the law is a constitutional use of Congress's power to enforce the 15th Amendment ban on denying a citizen the right to vote because of the person's race or color. Congress renewed and reinforced this voting rights legislation in 1970, 1975, and 1982. The result has been a dramatic increase in the participation of African Americans in public elections as voters and candidates for government offices.

The African-American civil rights movement has become a model for other groups seeking to end legal discrimination against them, such as women, Hispanics, gays, the elderly, and the physically disabled. These groups, too, have tried to bring about favorable legislative acts and judicial decisions.

During the 1980s and 1990s, civil rights advocates have promoted affirmative action programs—the use of preferential treatment of racial, ethnic, or gender groups to provide access to education, employment, and other social benefits. The groups seeking and receiving these

President Lyndon Johnson (center) confers with Martin Luther King, Jr. (left) and other civil rights leaders in 1964. Later that year, Johnson signed the Civil Rights Act, which banned various kinds of discrimination based on race, ethnicity, gender, and religion.

benefits are seen as having been victims of persistent and unfair discrimination. They look to affirmative action as a temporary means to overcome the harmful consequences of systematic discrimination in the past, which has unfairly denied opportunities to some people.

Congress passed the Civil Rights Act of 1991 to amend the Civil Rights Act of 1964. The purpose was to strengthen the scope of federal civil rights protections, which had been weakened by the Supreme Court's decision in *Ward's Cove Packing Company* v. *Atonio* (1989). In the *Ward's Cove* decision, the Court determined that those claiming discrimination by employers had to prove that a specific employment practice had been discriminatory. Even if the plaintiff were to provide the proof required, the employer could still claim that the discriminating practice was necessary to maintain his or her business.

The Civil Rights Act of 1991 overturned the *Ward's Cove* decision by eliminating, as illegal, an employer's claim of "business necessity" as a justification for intentional discrimination against an individual based on race, color, ethnic origin, and gender. Further, the Civil Rights Act of 1991 protects an employee against racial harassment after being hired. Finally, the 1991 law limits the opportunities to legally challenge employers' affirmative action programs.

SEE ALSO

Affirmative action; Brown v. Board of Education; Civil Rights Cases; Equality under the Constitution; Heart of Atlanta Motel v. United States; Johnson v. Transportation Agency of Santa Clara County; Liberty under the Constitution; National Association for the Advancement of Colored People (NAACP); Smith v. Allwright; Sweatt v. Painter

FURTHER READING

Branch, Taylor. *Parting the Waters: America in the King Years, 1954–63.* New York: Simon & Schuster, 1988.

Franklin, John Hope, and Alfred A. Moss, Jr. *From Slavery to Freedom.* New York: Knopf, 1988.

King, Martin Luther, Jr. *Stride Toward Freedom.* New York: Harper & Row, 1958.

King, Martin Luther, Jr. *Why We Can't Wait.* New York: Signet, 1964.

Konvitz, Milton R. *Century of Civil Rights.* New York: Columbia University Press, 1961.

Civil Rights Cases

☆ *109 U.S. 3 (1883)*
☆ *Vote: 8–1*
☆ *For the Court: Bradley*
☆ *Dissenting: Harlan*

The *Civil Rights Cases* were five cases that the Supreme Court decided as a group. In all five situations, the federal Civil Rights Act of 1875 had been enforced by the federal government against private facilities—a railroad company, theater owners, and innkeepers. In each case, a black American had been denied the same accommodations or services enjoyed by white Americans. The Civil Rights Act of 1875 forbade denial of access on the basis of race to theaters, hotels, railroad cars, and other privately owned facilities that served the public. The Civil Rights Act also forbade segregation of blacks and whites in their use of such privately owned facilities as hotels, theaters, and railroad cars. The defendants in these cases argued that the Civil Rights Act of 1875 was an unconstitutional regulation of their management of private property.

The Issue Congress passed the Civil Rights Act of 1875 to implement the "equal protection of the laws" clause of the 14th Amendment. This amendment restricted the power of a state *government* to violate the civil rights of people within its boundaries. But the primary intention of the framers of the 14th Amendment was to secure the rights of black people, which had been at risk. At issue was whether the 14th Amendment enabled Congress to forbid discrimination based on race by owners of *private* facilities used by the public.

Opinion of the Court
The Court ruled that the 14th Amendment banned the violation of individual rights only by state governments. According to Justice Joseph Bradley, the Civil Rights Act of 1875 was unconstitutional because it attempted to regulate the private conduct of individuals with regard to racial discrimination—an action that was beyond the scope of the 14th Amendment. According to Bradley, individuals faced with racial discrimination in their use of privately owned hotels, theaters, railroad cars, and so forth had to seek help from their state government. The federal government, according to the Court, had no constitutional authority to act in these cases.

Dissent Justice John Harlan stood against the Court in this case because its opinion rested "upon grounds entirely narrow and artificial." Harlan argued for a broad interpretation of the 13th and 14th Amendments as a suitable legal basis for the Civil Rights Act of 1875.

Harlan claimed that the federal government had the authority and the responsibility to protect individuals from racial discrimination in their access to privately owned facilities serving the public. He pointed out, for example, that roads and railroads were "established by the authority of these States" and theaters operated under state government licenses. Therefore, Harlan argued, the state's association with these facilities justified federal action to provide all individuals, black and white, equal

This letter from the African M.E. Church praises Justice John Harlan for his dissent in the Civil Rights Cases. *Harlan argued that the 14th Amendment should protect African Americans from discrimination in public facilities even if those facilities are owned by private companies.*

opportunity to use the facilities. Justice Harlan concluded:

> [T]here cannot be, in this republic, any class of human beings in practical subjection to another class, with power in the latter to dole out to the former just such privileges as they may choose to grant. The supreme law of the land has decreed that no authority shall be exercised in this country upon the basis of discrimination, in respect of civil rights, against freemen and citizens because of their race, color, or previous condition of servitude.

Significance Public opinion in the 1880s was solidly in support of the Court's ruling in the *Civil Rights Cases.* However, Harlan's dissent prevailed in the long run in federal legislation such as the Civil Rights Act of 1964 and in Supreme Court decisions such as *Heart of Atlanta Motel* v. *United States* (1964). It is Justice Harlan's dissent that is honored today, not Justice Bradley's opinion for the Court.

SEE ALSO
Heart of Atlanta Motel v. United States

FURTHER READING
Kull, Andrew. "The 14th Amendment That Wasn't." *Constitution* 5, no. 1 (Winter 1993): 68–75.
Westin, Alvin F. "The Case of the Prejudiced Doorkeeper: The Civil Rights Cases." In *Quarrels That Have Shaped the Constitution,* edited by John A. Garraty. New York: Harper & Row, 1987.

Clark, Tom
ASSOCIATE JUSTICE, 1949–67

☆ Born: Sept. 23, 1899, Dallas, Tex.
☆ Education: University of Texas, B.A., 1921; LL.B., 1922
☆ Previous government service: civil district attorney, Dallas County, Tex., 1927–32; special assistant, U.S. Department of Justice, 1937–43; assistant U.S. attorney general, 1943–45; U.S. attorney general,

1945–49
☆ *Appointed by President Harry S. Truman Aug. 2, 1949; replaced Frank Murphy, who died*
☆ *Supreme Court term: confirmed by the Senate Aug. 18, 1949, by a 73–8 vote; retired June 12, 1967*
☆ *Died: June 13, 1977, New York, N.Y.*

TOM CLARK worked in the U.S. Department of Justice and became friendly with Harry Truman, a senator from Missouri. In 1944, Clark supported Truman's bid to become the Democratic candidate for Vice President. When President Franklin D. Roosevelt died in 1945, Truman became President and he appointed Clark to be his attorney general. Four years later, Truman named Clark to the Supreme Court.

Both as attorney general and associate justice, Tom Clark supported government efforts to protect national security against Communist party activity in the United States. He also wrote opinions for the Court on landmark cases that protected individual rights. In *Mapp* v. *Ohio* (1961), for example, Clark declared that evidence seized illegally must be "excluded from" a state government's prosecution of a person accused of a crime. This "exclusionary rule" set forth by Clark in 1961 has endured as a guide to Court decisions.

Clark retired from the Supreme Court in 1967 when his son, Ramsay Clark, was appointed by President Lyndon Johnson to the job of U.S. attorney general, a position that Tom Clark had once filled. Tom Clark left the Court to avoid any possibility of conflict of interest in cases brought to the Court by his son.

He continued to serve the federal government, however, until his death in 1977. He was a founder and the first director of the Federal Judicial Center, which conducts research and training programs to improve operations of the federal courts. He also occasionally served as a judge on various circuits of the U.S. Court of Appeals.

SEE ALSO
Mapp v. Ohio

Clarke, John H.
ASSOCIATE JUSTICE, 1916–22

☆ *Born: Sept. 18, 1857, New Lisbon, Ohio*
☆ *Education: Western Reserve University, B.A., 1877; M.A., 1880*
☆ *Previous government service: federal judge, U.S. District Court for the Northern District of Ohio, 1914–16*
☆ *Appointed by President Woodrow Wilson July 14, 1916; replaced Charles Evans Hughes, who resigned*
☆ *Supreme Court term: confirmed by the Senate July 24, 1916, by a voice vote; resigned Sept. 18, 1922*
☆ *Died: Mar. 22, 1945, San Diego, Calif.*

JOHN H. CLARKE served only six years on the Supreme Court. During this brief period, he often sided with Justice Louis Brandeis. His cooperation with Brandeis brought the hostility of Justice James McReynolds, who was persistently nasty to his two colleagues because he strongly disagreed with their legal ideas. McReynolds also seems to have disliked Brandeis because of a personal prejudice against Jews. McReynolds's ugly behavior was one of the reasons Clarke left the Court. McReynolds refused to sign the official letter expressing regret at Clarke's resignation.

Justice Clarke wrote the Court's opinion in *Abrams* v. *United States* (1919), in which he upheld limitations on free speech under the Espionage Act of 1918. In this opinion Clarke departed from his usual agreement with Brandeis, who joined Oliver Wendell Holmes in a strong dissent against the *Abrams* decision.

After leaving the Supreme Court, Clarke devoted the rest of his life to promoting the cause of world peace. He supported the work of the League of Nations and the creation of the United Nations in 1945.

SEE ALSO

Abrams v. United States

Class action

A LAWSUIT brought to court by one or more individuals on behalf of a category, or *class,* of people is called a *class action.* This type of lawsuit is used when there is a very large number of parties to a dispute who have common interests and stakes in the outcome. In a class action, the case is tried by one or a few parties who represent many others, and the judgment in the case is binding on all members of the class involved in the dispute. Many cases dealing with the civil rights of African Americans were class actions.

Clear and present danger test

SEE Abrams v. United States; Freedom of speech and press; Schenck v. United States

Clerk of the Court

DURING ITS first term, in 1790, the U.S. Supreme Court established the office of the clerk to be responsible for managing the Court's administrative work. The clerk manages the dockets (calendars,

agendas, and schedules of events) of the Court, receives and records all documents filed on the various dockets and distributes these pages to the justices, notifies lower courts of all formal acts and decisions of the Supreme Court, and provides advice to lawyers who need information about the Court's rules and procedures. The clerk has a clerical and administrative staff of 25 people.

SEE ALSO

Staff of the Court, nonjudicial

Clerks of the justices

EACH SUPREME COURT justice may have a staff of four law clerks. Chief Justice William Rehnquist and Justice John Paul Stevens, however, chose to employ only three each. The justices have complete control over the hiring of these legal assistants. Most law clerks work at the job for only one year and use the prestigious position as a stepping stone to important jobs in law firms, on law school faculties, and in government service. Thirty-two former law clerks have become federal judges, and three have become Supreme Court justices: William H. Rehnquist, who clerked for Robert H. Jackson; John Paul Stevens, who clerked for Wiley B. Rutledge; and Byron White, who clerked for Fred M. Vinson.

The law clerks provide valuable research assistance for the justices. They also read, analyze, and write summaries of certiorari petitions, the requests to the Court for review of cases. The justices often depend upon their clerks' summaries and recommendations in deciding which cases to select for review.

Justice Horace Gray was the first member of the Court to employ a law

Sherry Colb, law clerk for Justice Harry Blackmun, working on upcoming Court cases.

clerk. In 1885 Gray hired a recent graduate of Harvard Law School, whom he paid with his own money. In 1922 Congress provided funds for the employment of one law clerk by each justice. In 1924 Congress established permanent law clerk positions at the Supreme Court.

Clifford, Nathan

ASSOCIATE JUSTICE, 1858–81

☆ *Born: Aug. 18, 1803, Rumney, N.H.*
☆ *Education: studied law in the office of Josiah Quincy in Rumney*
☆ *Previous government service: Maine House of Representatives, 1830–34; attorney general of Maine, 1834–38; U.S. representative from Maine, 1839–43; U.S. attorney general, 1846–48; U.S. minister to Mexico, 1848–49*
☆ *Appointed by President James Buchanan Dec. 9, 1857; replaced Benjamin R. Curtis, who resigned*
☆ *Supreme Court term: confirmed by the Senate Jan. 12, 1858, by a 26–23 vote; served until July 25, 1881*
☆ *Died: July 25, 1881, Cornish, Maine*

NATHAN CLIFFORD was a self-educated man who built a successful political career in Maine and in the federal government. He served as attorney general under President James Polk and was appointed by President James Buchanan to the U.S. Supreme Court. He was confirmed in a close vote because Republican senators believed he sympathized with the slave states that were threatening to secede from the Union.

Justice Clifford wrote no major opinions for the Court. He chaired the commission set up to settle the dispute over the Presidential election of 1876. There had been controversy about the correct vote totals and charges of voter fraud in three southern states. Clifford supported the case of Democrat Samuel Tilden but the commission decided in favor of Rutherford B. Hayes, the Republican.

Clinton v. City of New York

☆ *118 S.Ct. 2091 (1998)*
☆ *Vote: 6–3*
☆ *For the Court: Stevens*
☆ *Dissenting: Scalia, O'Connor, and Breyer*

ARTICLE 1, Section 7, of the U.S. Constitution says that bills passed by Congress must be presented to the President, who can either accept or reject any proposal in full. For more than a century, however, Presidents have wanted the power to reject selectively one or more points of a multifaceted bill that they generally approved. President Ulysses S. Grant, for example, asked Congress in 1873 to approve an amendment to the Constitution that would give the chief executive the power to veto particular items of a comprehensive bill enacted by Congress while generally approving the legislation. Congress refused to support the President in his quest for what later came to be called a "line-item veto." In the 20th century, Presidents Franklin Roosevelt and Ronald Reagan unsuccessfully sought the power of the line-item veto. Then in 1996, Congress passed the Line Item Veto Act, and President Bill Clinton signed it.

This new federal statute gave the President the power to "cancel" a particular item on expenditure of funds in an omnibus, or comprehensive, bill that the chief executive otherwise approved. This "cancellation" had to be done within 5 days after the President signed the bill into law. This law also gave Congress the power to restore the item or items "canceled" by the President by passing a new bill within the next 30 days. However, the President could comprehensively sign or veto that bill, and the Congress could overrule the veto by a two-thirds vote.

Six members of Congress, led by Senator Robert C. Byrd of West Virginia, quickly challenged the Line Item Veto Act. They claimed the law violated the "presentment clause" in Article 1, Section 7, of the Constitution. They argued that this clause requires the President comprehensively, not selectively, to sign or veto a bill enacted by Congress and presented intact to the chief executive.

Senator Byrd and his five colleagues filed a suit in a federal district court on January 2, 1997, that asked that the Line Item Veto Act be nullified as unconstitutional. The federal judge agreed with the congressional plaintiffs. The Supreme Court, however, decided in June 1997 (*Raines* v. *Byrd*) that the members of Congress had no legal standing to file the suit because none of them had suffered a personal injury.

In August 1997, President Clinton used his power under the Line Item Veto Act to "cancel" two items from the budget enacted by Congress. And he removed one item from the Taxpayer Relief Act. He had previously signed both bills, which, with the exception of the "canceled" items, became federal law.

Members of Congress from New York opposed President Clinton's cancellation of a budget item that benefited hospitals and health-care workers in New York City. And residents of Idaho objected to the President's veto of a line item giving tax breaks to potato farmers in their state. Representatives of the offended groups in New York City and Idaho filed suits challenging the constitutionality of Clinton's actions under the Line Item Veto Act.

The Issue Did the Line Item Veto Act violate the presentment clause of Article 1, Section 7, of the Constitution? Supporters of the law claimed it was crafted carefully to overcome arguments against its constitutionality. They pointed out, for example, that the President could cancel particular items from an omnibus bill only after he signed it. And, they argued, Congress was empowered by the act to restore canceled items. Opponents of the act argued that it clearly and directly contradicted a specific provision of the Constitution. Thus, it should be nullified.

Opinion of the Court The Court ruled for the plaintiffs and declared the Line Item Veto Act to be unconstitutional. Writing for the Court, Justice John Paul Stevens said that the law at issue violated the presentment clause of the Constitution. He wrote, "This Act gives the President the unilateral power to change the text of duly enacted statutes.... Congress cannot alter the procedures set out in Article 1, Section 7, without amending the Constitution."

Dissent The dissenting opinions defended the constitutionality of the statute at issue. In particular, Justice Antonin Scalia argued that there was no significant difference between a President's cancellation of a line item in an omnibus budget bill and a chief executive's refusal to spend funds that Congress had appropriated because of disapproval of the programs to be supported by the money.

Significance The Federal Office of Budget and Management released all the funds for items the President had vetoed. So the immediate consequence of the decision was the distribution of federal benefits to the plaintiffs and those they represented in New York and Idaho.

The constitutional principle of separation of powers was reinforced. "The Constitution is intact," exclaimed New York Senator Daniel Patrick Moynihan. It appears that the only way to give the President the power of the line-item veto is to amend the Constitution.

Cohens v. Virginia

☆ 6 Wheat. 264 (1821)
☆ Vote: 6–0
☆ For the Court: Marshall

TWO BROTHERS, Philip and Mendes Cohen, were charged with violating a Virginia law by selling lottery tickets within the state. They were tried, convicted, and fined by a local court in Norfolk, Virginia. The Cohens appealed the Virginia court decision to the U.S. Supreme Court under Section 25 of the Judiciary Act of 1789, which provides for review by the U.S. Supreme Court of decisions by state courts that involve issues of constitutional or federal law.

The Cohen brothers said that their lottery had been incorporated in Washington, D.C., according to terms of an act of Congress. Therefore they concluded that their lottery was conducted properly under federal law and could not be restricted by a state law.

The Issue Attorneys for the state of Virginia argued that according to the 11th Amendment to the Constitution, the U.S. Supreme Court could not have jurisdiction in this case. Furthermore, they held that there were no words in the U.S. Constitution that "set up the federal judiciary above the state judiciary." Therefore, they said, Section 25 of the Judiciary Act of 1789 could not be used to justify jurisdiction of the Supreme Court in this case. The issue was: Does the U.S. Supreme Court have jurisdiction in cases originating in state courts when these cases involve questions about federal law and the U.S. Constitution? Is the U.S. Supreme Court the final authority in such cases? Did the state of Virginia wrongfully convict the Cohens for violating a state law against lotteries?

Opinion of the Court Chief Justice John Marshall delivered the unanimous decision of the Court, which upheld the jurisdiction and authority of the U.S. Supreme Court to review decisions of state courts when they involve issues about federal law or the U.S. Constitution. He wrote eloquently in support of Section 25 of the Judiciary Act of 1789 and reaffirmed the Court's decision (written by Justice Joseph Story) in *Martin* v. *Hunter's Lessee* (1816).

Marshall also effectively dismissed Virginia's claim that the 11th Amendment precluded the Supreme Court from having jurisdiction in this case. Finally, after establishing the Court's authority and jurisdiction in this case, Marshall ruled against the Cohen brothers and upheld their conviction under Virginia state law.

Significance Chief Justice Marshall asserted the supremacy of the U.S. Constitution and federal law over state laws that conflicted with them. And he argued compellingly for the ultimate authority of the U.S. Supreme Court over state courts on *all* questions involving the U.S. Constitution and federal law. These views are no longer controversial, but in Marshall's time they were burning constitutional issues. The chief justice, however, framed to these issues and responded to them in a timeless fashion, and his decision undergirds our contemporary conceptions of federal–state relations.

SEE ALSO
Federalism; Judicial review; Jurisdiction; Martin v. Hunter's Lessee

Commerce power

ARTICLE 1, Section 8, of the U.S. Constitution gives Congress the power "to regulate Commerce with foreign Nations and among the several States, and with the Indian Tribes." Commerce

DEVELOPMENT OF THE COMMERCE POWER

Kidd v. Pearson (1888) Manufacturing of goods, such as liquor, is not commerce. Congress cannot regulate such manufacturing as interstate commerce.

Champion v. Ames (1903) Congress may use its power to regulate commerce to outlaw the interstate sale and shipment of lottery tickets.

McCray v. United States (1904) Congress may regulate the sale of oleomargarine (a butter substitute) by placing a high tax on it. This decision, along with *Champion*, strengthened Congress's ability to use the commerce power as a regulatory power for the public good.

Swift and Co. v. United States (1905) The Court announces the "stream of commerce" doctrine. The meat-packing industry is part of a "stream of commerce" from the time an animal is purchased until it is processed and sold as meat. Congress could regulate at any point along that "stream." The "stream of commerce" doctrine became a basic legal concept in the expansion of the federal commerce power.

Adair v. United States (1908) Labor relations do not directly affect interstate commerce. Thus, Congress cannot use the commerce power to prohibit certain kinds of labor contracts.

Shreveport Rate Cases (1914) The Court announces the "Shreveport doctrine." The federal government has power to regulate rail rates within states (intrastate) as well as between states (interstate). This sets the key precedent that whenever intrastate and interstate transactions (such as rail rates) become so related that regulation of one involves control of the other, Congress—not the states—has final authority.

Hammer v. Dagenhart (1918) Congress may not use the commerce power as a police power to regulate working conditions for child laborers or to prohibit the use of children in factories.

Bailey v. Drexel Furniture Co. (1922) Congress may not use its police power to place a high tax on the profits of companies employing child laborers. This decision, along with *Hammer* in 1918, greatly narrowed the federal police power. With these two decisions, the Court frustrated attempts by Congress to end child labor.

Railroad Retirement Board v. Alton Railroad (1935) The commerce clause does not give Congress the power to set up a pension system for railroad workers.

Carter v. Carter Coal Co. (1936) Mining is not commerce and does not affect commerce directly. Thus, Congress may not regulate labor relations in the coal mining industry.

National Labor Relations Board v. Jones & Laughlin Steel Corp. (1937) Congress may regulate labor relations in manufacturing to prevent possible interference with interstate commerce. With this decision, which overturned the *Adair* and *Carter* decisions, the Court gave up the narrow view of Congress's power to regulate commerce it had followed for many years. The Court based its decision on precedents set in the *Swift* and *Shreveport* cases.

Mulford v. Smith (1939) The commerce power gives Congress the authority to regulate market quotas for agricultural production. That is, Congress has the power to limit the amount of a product transported via interstate commerce.

United States v. Darby Lumber Co. (1941) Congress may use its commerce power to prohibit from interstate commerce goods made under substandard labor conditions. This decision overturns the *Hammer* decision.

Wickard v. Filburn (1942) Congress may regulate agricultural production affecting interstate commerce even if the produce is not meant for sale.

Heart of Atlanta Motel v. United States (1964) Congress may use its commerce power to prohibit public hotels and motels from discriminating against customers on the basis of race.

National League of Cities v. Usery (1976) Congress cannot use its commerce power to establish wage and hour standards for state and local government employees.

Garcia v. San Antonio Metropolitan Transit Authority (1985) Neither the 10th Amendment nor any other provision of the Constitution can be interpreted to limit the commerce power of Congress over the state governments. Thus, federal laws on minimum wages and overtime pay can be applied to workers of a transit system owned and operated by the city of San Antonio, Texas. This decision overruled *National League of Cities v. Usery.*

(continued)

DEVELOPMENT OF THE COMMERCE POWER *(continued)*

***United States v. Lopez* (1995)** The Court overturned a federal law banning individuals from carrying a gun near a school. According to a 5–4 majority of the Court, the statute extended beyond the constitutional power of the federal government to regulate interstate commerce.

***Reno v. Condon* (2000)** The Supreme Court upheld the Driver's Privacy Protection Act against a challenge from South Carolina as a constitutional use of Congress's commerce power. This federal law bars states from releasing personal information about licensed motor vehicle drivers without their consent. Thus, federal statutory protection of an individual's privacy rights outweighed states' rights in this case.

refers to the production, selling, and transportation of goods. If these commercial activities affect more than one state, the federal government may use its "commerce power" to regulate them. Ever since the 1820s, the Supreme Court has tended to interpret broadly the meaning of Congress's power to regulate commerce.

The Supreme Court's first major decision to define the meaning of the commerce power involved a controversy over steamboats. In the early 1800s Robert Fulton developed the steamboat as a practical means of travel. Fulton's smoke-belching vessel started a chain of events that led to the case of *Gibbons* v. *Ogden* (1824).

The *Gibbons* case involved two key questions. First, did "commerce" include navigation, and did the commerce clause of the Constitution therefore give Congress the power to regulate navigation?

Workers at the H. J. Heinz Company wash and sort tomatoes. Since the 1820s, the courts have broadly interpreted Congress's power to regulate commercial activities.

Second, did Congress possess exclusive power to regulate interstate commerce or did it share that power with the states?

The *Gibbons* case interpreted the meaning of the term *commerce* to encompass not only "navigation" but also other forms of trade, movement, and business. However, the Court did not spell out exactly what these other forms were. For instance, did commerce include coal mining?

As a result, *Gibbons* v. *Ogden* did not immediately lead to extensive federal regulation of interstate commerce. Yet the decision did open the door for the vast expansion of national control over commerce that we have today. The Court's broad interpretation of the meaning of "commerce" ultimately enabled Congress to regulate manufacturing, child labor, farm production, wages and hours, labor unions, civil rights, and criminal conduct as well as buying and selling. Any activity affecting interstate commerce is now subject to national control. Moreover, the Court's broad interpretation of the commerce power has led to a steady growth of the federal government's power in its relationships with state governments.

Though the *Gibbons* ruling established a precedent, it was left to later courts to determine the scope of the commerce power on a case-by-case basis. The table above lists some of the Court's major decisions on the commerce power made in the years since *Gibbons* v.

Ogden. Through these decisions the Court has further defined Congress's power to regulate commerce in accordance with the commerce clause.

SEE ALSO

Federalism; Gibbons v. Ogden; Hammer v. Dagenhart; Heart of Atlanta Motel v. United States; National Labor Relations Board v. Jones & Laughlin Steel Corp.; United States v. Darby Lumber Co.

FURTHER READING

Corwin, Edward S. *The Commerce Power Versus States' Rights*. Princeton, N.J.: Princeton University Press, 1959.

Common law

LAW MADE by judges through decisions in specific cases is known as the common law. These case-by-case decisions were used again and again in similar cases and thereby became customary, or common to all people living under the authority of the court of law. The common law used in the United States originated in England and was compiled in the 18th century by Sir William Blackstone in his *Commentaries on the Law of England*.

The English common law was taken by emigrants from the Old Country to the American colonies. After the American Revolution, English common law became the foundation of legal procedures in the United States of America. Today, the legal system in every American state, except Louisiana, is based on the Anglo-American common law. In Louisiana, once a French colony, certain French legal customs have been maintained. For instance, the word *parish,* derived from the French, is used instead of *county* to label administrative areas within the state.

Statutory law, the written law passed by a legislature, overrides the common law. Many statutes, however,

are rooted in the common law tradition and are interpreted by judges according to this tradition.

There is no federal common law because the federal government functions on the basis of a written constitution, through which the people delegate power to the government. Federal judges, however, apply the common law to cases involving people from different states when there is no federal law that fits a particular case.

The U.S. Supreme Court's use of precedents in deciding cases is an example of the common law heritage. In its exercise of judicial review in particular cases, the Court sets precedents that apply to future cases. If a statute in a particular state is held unconstitutional, for example, this decision is applicable to similar statutes in all other states. The Supreme Court made this point strongly in *Cooper* v. *Aaron* (1958), in which the Court upheld the application of its decision in *Brown* v. *Board of Education* (1954), which concerned Kansas, to enforce an end to segregation of public schools in Arkansas.

SEE ALSO

Cooper v. Aaron; Precedent

FURTHER READING

Hogue, Arthur R. *Origins of the Common Law.* Indianapolis: Liberty Fund, 1986.
Tribe, Lawrence H. *American Constitutional Law.* Mineola, N.Y.: Foundation Press, 1978.

Concurring opinion

JUSTICES OF the U.S. Supreme Court write concurring opinions on cases when they agree with the outcome of the majority opinion but disagree with the Court's reasons or explanations for the decision. In such a case a justice writes a separate

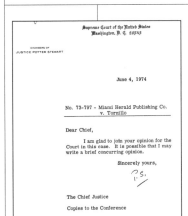

In a memo to the chief justice, Potter Stewart announces that he may write a concurring opinion, but he did not in this case.

concurring opinion, offering his or her own reasons about a decision with which he or she concurs, or agrees. On a few occasions, there have been so many concurring opinions in a case that there was no majority opinion of the Court. For example, in *Regents of the University of California* v. *Bakke* (1978), the Court decided the case by a vote of 5 to 4. However, eight of the justices wrote separate opinions, concurring in part and dissenting in part from the decision. As a result, there was no distinct opinion of the Court in this case. Rather, Justice Lewis Powell wrote an opinion announcing "the judgment of the Court," rather than an opinion for the majority of the Court. Cases decided without a clear-cut majority opinion written for the Court do not establish clear precedents.

SEE ALSO
Majority opinion; Opinions; Plurality opinion

Conference

THE JUSTICES of the Supreme Court meet regularly in the Conference Room of the Supreme Court Building to discuss cases on which they have heard oral arguments. They also use the conference to screen and select petitions for review of new cases and to conduct other Court business. At least six justices must be present for a quorum, the minimum number required for the group to make a decision about a case.

In Wednesday afternoon conferences, the justices discuss cases argued orally before the Court on the previous Monday. The all-day conference on Friday is used to discuss cases argued orally the previous Tuesday and Wednesday.

Unlike the presentation of oral arguments in the Supreme Court chamber (courtroom), which is open to the public, the conference is always private and conducted in complete secrecy. Not even the justices' clerks or secretaries attend. No official records of the conferences are made, and no formal reports of the proceedings are issued. However, justices often make personal notes to help them recall main points or important details of a particular discussion.

Discussion of a case usually begins with the chief justice, who sets the context and reviews key facts and issues. The other justices present their views on the case in order of their seniority, beginning with the most senior. If a formal vote is taken on the case, the justices vote in the opposite order, beginning with the least senior. The chief justice is the last to vote. After everyone has voted, the chief justice announces the vote tally and goes on to the next case. Such a formal vote is often not taken, however, because the justices frequently reveal their votes in the preceding round of discussion.

A justice's views on a case sometimes change in the weeks following the conference, during which opinions are

The Conference Room in the Supreme Court Building. The justices meet here to discuss their cases in private sessions.

written and exchanged and informal discussions of the case continue. Before the final decision and the Court's opinion are announced, justices may modify the positions they expressed during the conference.

Confirmation process

SEE Appointment of justices; Rejection of Supreme Court nominees; Senate Judiciary Committee

Constitutional construction

ONE'S METHOD of interpreting the U.S. Constitution is called constitutional construction. Some interpreters of the Constitution favor a strict or narrow construction of the document. Strict constructionists interpret the Constitution according to their views of the framers' original intentions about the various parts of the document. Strict constructionists also tend to emphasize the literal meaning of the words of the Constitution.

Loose constructionists favor a broad interpretation of the ideas and words of the Constitution. They attempt to apply the purposes and the principles of the Constitution to meet changing circumstances and conditions. Loose constructionists point to the general welfare clause and the necessary and proper clause of Article 1, Section 8, of the Constitution, which grant Congress power "To . . . provide for the . . . general welfare of the United States" and "To make all Laws which shall be necessary and proper for carrying into Execution the foregoing Powers, and all other Powers vested by this Constitution in the

Government of the United States or in any Department or Officer thereof."

Loose constructionists claim that the general welfare clause and the necessary and proper clause are the bases for broad or flexible interpretation of the Constitution to adjust its ideas to changing times. Loose constructionists also emphasize that they abide by the principles of the Constitution and respect precedents and historical developments.

A significant decision on the issue of strict versus broad construction was made in the landmark Supreme Court case of *McCulloch* v. *Maryland* (1819). The Court, under the leadership of Chief Justice John Marshall, argued strongly for loose construction and implied powers (powers not explicitly stated but considered logical extensions of Constitutional language). Since then, the loose constructionist position has prevailed most of the time. Occasionally, however, strict constructionists have exerted influence on the Court's decisions.

SEE ALSO
Marshall, John; McCulloch v. Maryland

Constitutional democracy

THE GOVERNMENT of the United States is called a constitutional democracy. It is a democracy because the government is based on the consent of the people. Further, the government operates according to the principle of majority rule. The people, for example, elect their representatives and senators in Congress by majority vote; and the members of Congress make laws according to majority rule.

The popular and democratic government of the United States, however, is

In a speech delivered to Congress in August 1974, President Gerald Ford stressed that government in the United States is based on the rule of law.

limited by the higher law of the Constitution in order to secure, as the Declaration of Independence says, the "unalienable rights" of every person. These legal limitations on the people's government make the United States a constitutional democracy, not an unlimited democracy.

James Madison and other framers of the Constitution feared the new threat to liberty that could come from a tyrannical majority. In times past, the threat to liberty came from the unrestrained powers of a king or an aristocracy. Madison, however, saw a new danger, which he expressed in a letter to Thomas Jefferson (Oct. 17, 1788):

> Wherever the real power in a Government lies, there is the danger of oppression. In our Governments, the real power lies in the majority of the Community, and the invasion of private rights is *chiefly* to be apprehended, not from acts of Government contrary to the sense of its constituents, but from acts in which the Government is the mere instrument of the major number [majority] of the constituents. This is a truth of great importance, but not yet sufficiently attended to.... Whenever there is an interest and power to do wrong, wrong will generally be done, and not less readily by [a majority of the people] than by a...prince.

Madison wanted government by majority rule of duly elected representatives of the people, but the majority's power must be limited by the higher law of a written constitution. If not, people that the majority disliked could lose basic freedoms and opportunities.

In *The Federalist* Nos. 10 and 51, James Madison argued for constitutional limits on power in government in order to protect the liberty and security of individuals. He opposed equally the absolutism, or total power, of a monarch or military dictator (the tyranny of one), an aristocracy or oligarchy (tyranny of the few over the many), or a majority of the people (tyranny of the many over the few). In a republic or representative democracy (government by elected representatives of the people), the greatest threat to liberty would come from an unrestrained majority. This threat could be overcome by constructing constitutional limits on majority rule in order to protect minority rights.

A constitutional democracy, then, is government by majority rule with protection of minority rights. It is democratic because of its foundations of popular consent and majority rule. It is constitutional because the power of the majority to rule is limited by a supreme law.

In the constitutional democracy of the United States, the Supreme Court uses its power of judicial review to make decisions about issues in specific cases concerning limits on majority rule or on minority rights. In many landmark decisions, such as *West Virginia State Board of Education* v. *Barnette* (1943), the Court has limited the power of majority rule in order to protect the rights to liberty of individuals in the minority. Writing for the Court in the *Barnette* case, Justice Robert Jackson argued that a person's rights to liberty, such as the right to free exercise of religion, "are beyond the reach of majorities." They may not, he wrote, "be submitted to vote," and "they depend on the outcome of no elections."

In other landmark decisions, the Court has limited an individual's rights to liberty in order to maintain the democratic power of majority rule. For example, in *United States* v. *O'Brien* (1968), the Court upheld a federal law that made it a crime for anyone to destroy a draft card, the document that indicates that a person has registered with the government for possible induction into the armed forces. David O'Brien was denied the right to burn his draft card as a protest against the government. According to the Court, this violation of a federal law, enacted by majority rule of Congress, was not a permissible expression of freedom under the 1st Amendment.

SEE ALSO

Constitutionalism; Judicial review; Liberty under the Constitution; *United States* v. *O'Brien; West Virginia State Board of Education* v. *Barnette*

FURTHER READING

Agresto, John. *The Supreme Court and Constitutional Democracy.* Ithaca, N.Y.: Cornell University Press, 1984.
Berns, Walter. *Taking the Constitution Seriously.* Lanham, Md.: Madison Books, 1992.
Elster, Jon, and Rune Slagstad, eds. *Constitutionalism and Democracy.* New York: Cambridge University Press, 1988.

Constitutionalism

LIMITED GOVERNMENT and the rule of law, as embodied in legal documents, institutions, and procedures, are the two essential elements of constitutionalism.

Limited government means that officials cannot act arbitrarily when they make and enforce public decisions. Public officials cannot simply do as they please. Rather, they are guided and limited by laws as they carry out the duties of their government offices. In the United States, the Constitution is the supreme law that guides and limits the exercise of power by government officials. Laws made in conformity with the Constitution also guide and limit the actions of government officials.

The rule of law means that neither government officials nor common citizens are allowed to break the law. Furthermore, people accused of crimes should be treated equally under the law and accorded due process, or fair and proper legal proceedings, in all official actions against them. Law governs the actions of everyone in the system—public officials and the citizenry, from highest to lowest ranks in both government and society. All laws and the actions based on those laws must conform to the highest law of the land, the Constitution.

In the United States, constitutionalism means there is a supreme law by which the people establish and limit the powers of their government. In 1787 representatives of the people of the United States drafted and ratified a Constitution, which stands above all laws made by any legislative body in the United States. Article 6 of the Constitution states this principle: "The Constitution, and the Laws of the United States which shall be made in Pursuance thereof... shall be the supreme Law of the Land." All laws, passed either by Congress or by state legislatures, must conform to the supreme law—the Constitution. As Alexander Hamilton explained in *The Federalist* No. 78: "No legislative act contrary to the Constitution, therefore, can be valid." On the contrary, a legislative or executive action that violates the Constitution can be declared unconstitutional, or unlawful, by the Supreme Court.

James Madison wrote in The Federalist *that limits on the powers of government are necessary to protect the people from abuses.*

In the United States, the ultimate purpose of constitutionalism is stated in the Declaration of Independence: to secure the "unalienable rights" of all people through a government established by "consent of the governed." According to the Declaration, a good constitution limits the power of a government in order to secure the rights of every person, which belong equally to all human beings. If a government fails to secure these rights of individuals, then it is a bad government and the people have the right to alter and replace it.

A continuing problem of constitutionalism, and of constitution makers, is how to establish a government with sufficient power to rule and maintain order yet with sufficient limitations on its power to prevent tyranny. The rights and liberties of individuals are supposed to be protected by law against abuses of power by government officials. However, if constitutional limits on government are too strict, the government will be too weak to carry out its duties effectively. A government that is too limited by law may not even be able to enforce the laws and maintain public order and security. By contrast, if the government is too strong, or unlimited in its use of power, then the liberties of individuals may be lost and tyranny might prevail. An effective constitutional government is neither too powerful nor too weak.

It is difficult to achieve a workable balance between power sufficient to govern effectively and limits on power sufficient to protect the people's liberties and rights. On the eve of the Civil War, Abraham Lincoln asked, "Must a government, of necessity, be too strong for the liberties of its own people, or too weak to maintain its own existence?" During the 1780s, James Madison and Alexander Hamilton argued in *The Federalist* that limited government under the Articles of Confederation (the document that formed the first government of the newly independent states) was too weak to maintain its own existence. The authors of *The Federalist* argued that limited government and the rule of law—principles of government reflected in the 1787 Constitution—would protect the people from abuses of power by would-be tyrants. They feared equally any unrestrained source of power. The power of an unlimited majority of the people, in their view, was just as dangerous to the rights of individuals as the unlimited power of a king. They argued that the best government is both "energetic" (strong enough to act decisively and effectively in the public interest) and "limited by law" to protect individual rights.

The problem of constitutionalism—how to combine the contrary factors of power and restraint, order and liberty, in one constitution—was stated memorably by James Madison in *The Federalist* No. 51:

> But what is government itself but the greatest of all reflections of human nature? If men were angels, no government would be necessary. If angels were to govern men, neither external nor internal controls on government would be necessary. In framing a government which is to be administered by men over men, the great difficulty lies in this: you must first enable the government to control the governed; and in the next place oblige it to control itself. A dependence on the people is, no doubt, the primary control on the government; but experience has taught mankind the necessity of auxiliary precautions [limited government based on the supreme law of a written constitution].

Constitutionalism—limited government and the rule of law—is a means to the elusive end of securing the human rights of all people. This is the ultimate purpose of government under the U.S. Constitution.

SEE ALSO

Constitutional democracy; Constitutional law; Constitution, U.S.; Federalist, The; Judicial review; Liberty under the Constitution

FURTHER READING

Ketchum, Ralph. *Framed for Posterity: The Enduring Philosophy of the Constitution.* Lawrence: University Press of Kansas, 1993.
Lutz, Donald S. *The Origins of American Constitutionalism.* Baton Rouge: Louisiana State University Press, 1988.
Richards, David A. J. *Foundations of American Constitutionalism.* New York: Oxford University Press, 1989.

Constitutional law

DECISIONS BY judges, who interpret and apply the Constitution to specific cases, create constitutional law. For example, judicial interpretation of the meaning of general phrases in the Constitution, such as "due process of law" or "unreasonable searches and seizures" or "interstate commerce," establishes constitutional law. In the United States, the Supreme Court plays a central role in developing constitutional law. In 1982, for instance, the Court decided in *United States* v. *Ross* that the 4th Amendment ban against "unreasonable searches and seizures" did not prevent police, under certain circumstances,

The Taft Court was one of the most distinguished in U.S. history. Seated: James McReynolds, Oliver Wendell Holmes, Chief Justice William Howard Taft, Willis Van Devanter, Louis D. Brandeis. Standing: Edward T. Stanford, George Sutherland, Pierce Butler, Harlan Fiske Stone.

from searching the contents of a car without a search warrant.

Constitutional law in the United States is the product of judicial interpretation of the U.S. Constitution in response to the constitutional issues in cases that come before the courts. Thus, the courts develop a body of case law. The decisions of the courts in these legal cases establish precedents, decisions that serve as models for future decisions. Thus, over time these precedents accumulate to become a body of constitutional law.

The development of American constitutional law is based on the power of the Supreme Court to consider whether particular federal and state laws and executive actions are consistent with the Constitution. If so, the laws or actions at issue are confirmed. If not, they are declared unconstitutional. Thus, the power of judicial review and the principle of constitutionalism are fundamental factors in the development of constitutional law by the judicial branch of government.

SEE ALSO

Constitutionalism; Judicial review; Precedent

FURTHER READING

Lieberman, Jethro K. *The Evolving Constitution: How the Supreme Court Has Ruled on Issues from Abortion to Zoning.* New York: Random House, 1993.

Constitution, U.S.

THE BASIC and supreme law of the land is the Constitution of the United States of America. It consists of 7 articles, which were drafted by the Constitutional Convention of 1787 in Philadelphia, and 27 amendments. More than 200 years old, this document is the oldest written constitution of a national state in use anywhere in the world today. (The oldest written constitution of any

The "Constitutional Centennial March" of 1887 celebrated the adoption of the U.S. Constitution.

sort in use today is the Massachusetts state constitution of 1780.) Most of the national constitutions around the world have existed only since about 1970.

The U.S. Constitution, like other national constitutions, establishes a general framework for organizing and operating a government. It is not a detailed blueprint for governing on a day-to-day basis. The U.S. Constitution consists of only about 7,500 words. It does not attempt to consider the details of how to run the national government. Officials who run the government supply the details that fit the general framework.

As the government's framework, the Constitution must be interpreted as specific problems arise. For example, the 4th Amendment to the Constitution protects people against "unreasonable searches and seizures" by police or other government officials. But what does "unreasonable searches and seizures" mean? The automobile did not exist in 1787, when the Constitution was written. Does the 4th Amendment allow the police to stop and search a car? In the case of *United States* v. *Ross* (1982), the Supreme Court decided that they could.

The Supreme Court is often called upon to answer such questions. Its decisions help to update the Constitution to reflect changing times and circumstances. Decisions by judges who interpret and apply the Constitution to specific cases help to add substance to the general framework of government established by the Constitution. These judicial decisions formulate *constitutional law.*

A constitution delegates powers to various types of public officials who run different parts of the government. For example, Article 1 of the Constitution grants the Congress certain lawmaking powers. Section 8 grants Congress such powers as regulation of commerce among the states, coining money and

regulating its value, and raising and supporting the military forces.

The Constitution also specifies certain powers that the Congress may *not* exercise. According to Article 1, Section 9, Congress may not take money "from the treasury, but in consequence of appropriations made by law." Similarly, Amendment 1 limits the power of Congress: "Congress shall make no law... abridging the freedom of speech, or of the press."

Several other sections of the Constitution assign duties and powers to the public officials heading different branches of the government (Article 1, Section 8, concerns the Congress; Article 2, Section 2, concerns the Presidency; and Article 3, Section 2, deals with the judiciary). For example, the President can dispatch military forces to put down civil disorder or rebellion or to enforce federal laws if necessary. The Constitution also places limits on the powers of officials such as the President, Supreme Court justices, and members of Congress.

Such limitations on the expressed powers granted to the government protect the liberties of the people. For example, although the U.S. Treasury Department collects taxes, an act of Congress must authorize any expenditure of that tax money. More generally, the first 10 amendments to the Constitution, known collectively as the Bill of Rights, protect the liberties of the people.

All government officials must follow the Constitution when carrying out their duties. For example, the Constitution (Article 6) says that "no religious test shall ever be required as a qualification to any office of public trust in the United States." Thus the President may not require any employees of the executive branch of government to attend church services in order to keep their jobs.

The U.S. Constitution grants powers in the name of the people, and the government draws its power from the consent of the governed. The document assumes that government officials will use their powers in the interests of the people. The preamble to the Constitution says, "We the People of the United States . . . do ordain and establish this Constitution for the United States of America."

Representatives of the people wrote and approved the Constitution of the United States. Granting certain powers to government in the name of the people gives legitimacy to the government because most of the people, viewing it as legal and proper, are likely to find it acceptable.

SEE ALSO

Amendments to the Constitution; Bill of Rights; Constitutional democracy; Constitutionalism; Constitutional law

FURTHER READING

Anastaplo, George. *The Constitution of 1787: A Commentary.* Baltimore: Johns Hopkins University Press, 1989.
Currie, David P. *The Constitution of the United States: A Primer for the People.* Chicago: University of Chicago Press, 1988.
Ritchie, Donald A. *The U.S. Constitution.* New York: Chelsea House, 1989.

Contempt power of the courts

THE JUDICIARY ACT of 1789 gives federal courts the power to punish an individual for contempt. A person is deemed in contempt of court when he disobeys a court's order or shows disrespect for its authority.

Contract clause

ARTICLE 1, Section 10, of the U.S. Constitution says, "No State shall . . . pass any . . . Law impairing the Obligation of Contracts." This contract clause prohibits any state government from passing a law that would interfere with contracts made by citizens, either by weakening the obligations assumed by parties to a contract or by making a contract difficult to enforce. The Supreme Court's decisions in *Fletcher* v. *Peck* (1810) and *Dartmouth College* v. *Woodward* (1819) were landmark decisions that used the contract clause to uphold the sanctity of contracts.

The contract clause applies to contracts between private individuals or contracts made by a state government. However, if a contract endangers the health, safety, or welfare of the public, the state may regulate or void it. The state's authority to protect the public in this way is known as its police power. During the 20th century, the Court has often ruled in favor of state regulation or modification of contracts in the public interest.

SEE ALSO

Dartmouth College v. Woodward; Fletcher v. Peck

Cooper v. Aaron

☆ *358 U.S. 1 (1958)*
☆ *Vote: 9–0*
☆ *For the Court: Warren*
☆ *Concurring: Frankfurter*

In *Brown* v. *Board of Education* (1954), the Court ruled against racial segregation in public schools. However, school districts in most southern states were slow to carry out the *Brown* decision.

In the fall of 1957, the people of Little Rock, Arkansas, faced the first phase of the school board's very deliberate school desegregation plan. The day before desegregation was to begin, Governor Orval Faubus placed soldiers of the Arkansas National Guard at Central High School.

When a mob of white people gathered to protest the racial integration of Central High School in Little Rock, Arkansas, President Dwight Eisenhower sent federal troops to protect black students.

The governor said they were there to keep order. But the federal district court ordered the National Guard removed because of a well-founded suspicion that Governor Faubus would use them to stop black students from entering the school.

The National Guard was withdrawn, and white protesters around the school rioted to prevent the black children from entering the high school. President Dwight Eisenhower sent in the 101st Airborne paratroopers to keep order and protect the nine black students at Central High School.

In February 1958 the federal district court gave the Little Rock school board permission for a two-year delay in carrying out school desegregation. In addition, the Arkansas legislature passed a law authorizing the governor to close all public schools required by the federal courts to desegregate. In this way, Governor Faubus and the state legislature directly challenged the supremacy of U.S. constitutional law—specifically, the *Brown* decision—with regard to the issue of school desegregation.

In response to the slow pace and threatened postponement of school desegregation in Little Rock, the National Association for the Advancement of

Colored People (NAACP) filed suit in the federal district court. The suit was filed against William G. Cooper, president of the school board, on behalf of John Aaron and 32 other students.

The federal district and appellate courts had upheld the slow-paced desegregation plan. So the NAACP appealed to the U.S. Supreme Court. Chief Justice Earl Warren convened a special session of the Court in the summer of 1958 to hear this case.

The Issue The NAACP attorneys argued that the slow pace of school desegregation violated the Supreme Court's decision in *Brown* v. *Board of Education* (1954) and *Brown II* (1955) and the black students' rights to equal protection of the laws provided by the 14th Amendment. They pointed to the two-year postponement in implementation of desegregation permitted by the federal district court. Despite the importance of the NAACP's argument about the violation of constitutional rights, an even greater issue was enforcement of U.S. Supreme Court decisions. Could a state government enact and enforce legislation designed to prevent implementation of a Supreme Court decision?

Opinion of the Court The Court ruled against any delay by the Little Rock school board in carrying out its desegregation plan. And the Court strongly rejected the idea that a state government could ignore or actively oppose enforcement of U.S. Supreme Court decisions. Chief Justice Earl Warren wrote that the rights of black students could "neither be nullified openly and directly by state legislatures or state executive officials nor nullified indirectly by them by evasive schemes for segregation."

Significance The *Cooper* case was the Supreme Court's first opportunity to rule on the enforcement of its decision in *Brown* v. *Board of Education* (1954). Further, *Cooper* provided the Court a grand opportunity to assert the supremacy of constitutional law over the states. However, the immediate impact of the *Cooper* decision on school desegregation was slight. Not until the civil rights activities of the 1960s, and especially the passage of the Civil Rights Act of 1964, did school desegregation begin to occur extensively throughout the United States.

SEE ALSO

Brown v. Board of Education; Civil rights

FURTHER READING

Freyer, Tony. *The Little Rock Crisis: A Constitutional Interpretation.* Westport, Conn.: Greenwood Press, 1984.

Counsel, right to

THE 6TH AMENDMENT to the U.S. Constitution provides that "in all criminal prosecutions, the accused shall ... have the assistance of counsel for his defence." This right of an accused person was not applied consistently to state governments until 1963, when the Court ruled in *Gideon* v. *Wainwright* that counsel must be provided for defendants in all state felony cases. If a defendant could not afford to pay for the services of counsel, then the state would be required to provide counsel for him. The guarantee of the right to counsel was extended to all state-level misdemeanor cases in *Argersinger* v. *Hamlin* (1972).

The *Gideon* case applied the right to counsel to the states through the due process clause of the 14th Amendment. This is an example of the Court's use of the incorporation doctrine to extend rights in the federal Bill of Rights to the state level.

SEE ALSO

Due process of law; Gideon v. Wainwright; Incorporation doctrine; Rights of the accused

Court-packing plan

ON FEBRUARY 5, 1937, President Franklin D. Roosevelt sent to Congress his Judicial Reorganization Bill. It called for adding one justice to the Supreme Court for every member over 70 years of age, up to a total of six additional justices.

The President claimed that he wanted to add new justices to increase the Court's efficiency in dealing with a heavy work load. His real motive, however, was to pack the Court with justices favorable to his New Deal political and economic reforms. The Supreme Court had struck down, as unconstitutional, such New Deal programs as the National Industrial Recovery Act, the Railroad Retirement Act, and the Agricultural Adjustment Act.

President Roosevelt's court-packing plan was controversial. Opponents claimed he was trying to destroy the independence of the judiciary to gain political advantage. Roosevelt, however, pushed hard for Congress to pass his bill, and it seemed that he had the votes needed to pass the Judicial Reorganization Bill.

In March 1937 the Court made two decisions favorable to President Roosevelt's New Deal policies in *West Coast Hotel Co.* v. *Parrish* and *National Labor Relations Board* v. *Jones & Laughlin Steel Corp.* Justice Owen Roberts, who had previously voted against

Franklin Roosevelt shows off his plan for an expanded Supreme Court. FDR abandoned his controversial court-packing plan after the Court upheld important New Deal programs in 1937.

New Deal programs, switched his position in these two critical cases. Newspaper writers called Justice Roberts's change in position the "switch in time that saved nine." The momentum for the President's court-packing plan declined in the wake of the two decisions. Further, anti–New Deal justice Willis Van Devanter announced his retirement, giving President Roosevelt the chance to nominate a justice favorable to his views. So the number of Supreme Court justices remained at nine, and the perceived political threat to judicial independence was ended.

SEE ALSO

National Labor Relations Board v. Jones & Laughlin Steel Corp.; West Coast Hotel Co. v. Parrish

FURTHER READING

Baker, Leonard. *Back to Back: The Duel between FDR and the Supreme Court.* New York: Macmillan, 1967.

Leuchtenburg, William. "The Origins of Franklin D. Roosevelt's 'Court-Packing Plan.'" *Supreme Court Review* (1966): 347–400.

Leuchtenburg, William. *The Supreme Court Reborn: The Constitutional Revolution in the Age of Roosevelt.* New York: Oxford University Press, 1996.

Nelson, Michael. "The President and the Court: Reinterpreting the Court-packing Episode of 1937." *Political Science Quarterly* 103, no. 2 (1988): 267–93.

Court reporters

S E E Reporter of decisions

Courts of Appeals

THE U.S. COURTS OF APPEALS are the middle level of the federal judicial system. They stand between the federal district courts at the bottom and the Supreme Court of the United States at the top.

The Courts of Appeals have no original jurisdiction; they do not hear the first trial of a case. They hear only cases on appeal from the lower courts. In turn, cases may be appealed from the Court of Appeal to the highest court, the Supreme Court.

At present, the United States and its territories are divided into 12 circuits, or

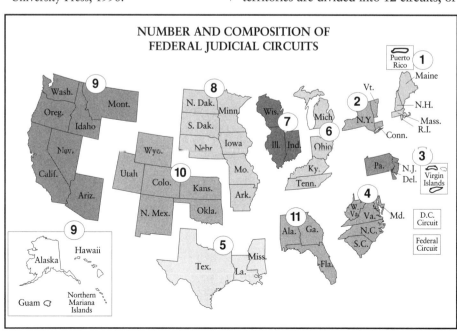

NUMBER AND COMPOSITION OF FEDERAL JUDICIAL CIRCUITS

geographical areas in which a court of appeals is located. There are appellate circuits numbered 1 through 11 plus the Court of Appeals for the District of Columbia. In addition, the Federal Courts Improvement Act of 1982 created the U.S. Court of Appeals for the Federal Circuit, which takes cases on appeal from such specialized lower courts as the Court of Claims, the Court of Customs and Patent Appeals, and the Court of Veterans Appeals. In 2000, 179 judges were authorized to serve on the Courts of Appeals. The U.S. Court of Appeals for the Ninth Circuit (West Coast) has 28 judges, the largest number. The U.S. Court of Appeals for the First Circuit (the New England states) has only 6 judges, the least number. All appellate court judges are appointed by the President with the advice and consent of the Senate, as provided by Article 2, Section 3, of the Constitution.

The U.S. Courts of Appeals have appellate jurisdiction—they review the decisions of lower courts—over two main types of cases. The first type involves civil and criminal case appeals from the federal district courts, including the U.S. territorial courts (in U.S. territories such as Guam and Puerto Rico) and special courts such as the U.S. Tax Court. The second type involves appeals by individuals of decisions made by federal administrative agencies and independent regulatory commissions, such as the National Labor Relations Board. Most cases that come to the Courts of Appeals are of the first type.

The Courts of Appeals are usually organized in three-judge panels to hear cases. They may also sit *en banc* ("with all judges present").

A justice of the U.S. Supreme Court serves as a circuit justice for each federal judicial circuit. The circuit justice has such duties as issuing stays or injunctions and takes responsibility for emer-

gencies that require an immediate response by the Court of Appeals.

SEE ALSO
Circuit Courts of Appeals; Federal judicial system

Criminal law

THE BODY of law that pertains to crimes against public authority—the federal or state governments, for example—is known as criminal law. These are the statutes that executive branch officials have the power to enforce. People who violate these laws may be apprehended by police and tried in a court of law. If convicted, they face the punishment prescribed by the trial court. If the convicted person feels that his constitutional rights have been violated, he may appeal the case to the Supreme Court.

SEE ALSO
Civil law; Rights of the accused

Cruel and unusual punishment

THE 8TH AMENDMENT to the Constitution prohibits the government from inflicting "cruel and unusual punishments." Individuals are protected from inhumane punishments, such as torture, burning at the stake, or crucifixion. Further, any punishment considered too severe in relation to the crime committed has been judged by the Court as "cruel and unusual punishment." In *Weems* v. *United States* (1910), for example, the Court overturned a sentence of 12 to 20

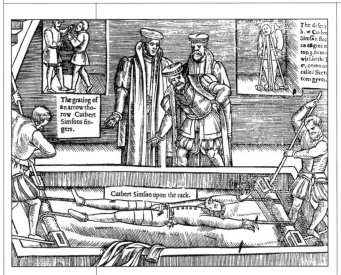

Various torture methods used in the Tower of London in the Middle Ages. The U.S. Constitution prohibits cruel and unusual punishments, such as torture, for crimes.

years in chains for a person convicted of giving false testimony. The Court judged this sentence to be cruel and unusual punishment because the penalty was out of proportion to the crime.

In 1972, in *Furman* v. *Georgia*, the Court decided that the death penalty was cruel and unusual punishment. In 1976, however, the Court held in *Gregg* v. *Georgia* that the death penalty is not necessarily an example of cruel and unusual punishment as long as systematic procedures are followed to eliminate arbitrary or racially discriminatory use of capital punishment.

Chief Justice Earl Warren aptly described the intent of the ban against cruel and unusual punishment in *Trop* v. *Dulles* (1958): "The basic concept underlying the Eighth Amendment is nothing less than the dignity of man. While the State has the power to punish, the Amendment stands to assure that this power be exercised within the limits of civilized standards." Warren also discussed the relationship of the ban on cruel and unusual punishment to community standards: "The Court [has] recognized...that the words of the [Eighth] Amendment are not precise, and that their scope is not static. The Amendment draws its meaning from the evolving standards of decency that mark the progress of a maturing society."

SEE ALSO
Capital punishment; Furman v. Georgia

Curator, Office of the
S E E Staff of the Court, nonjudicial

Curtis, Benjamin R.
ASSOCIATE JUSTICE, 1851–57

☆ *Born: Nov. 4, 1809, Watertown, Mass.*
☆ *Education: Harvard College, A.B., 1829; Harvard Law School, LL.B., 1832*
☆ *Previous government service: Massachusetts state representative, 1849–51*
☆ *Appointed by President Millard Fillmore as a recess appointment Sept. 22, 1851; replaced Levi Woodbury, who died; nominated by Fillmore Dec. 11, 1851*
☆ *Supreme Court term: confirmed by the Senate Dec. 20, 1851, by a voice vote; resigned Sept. 30, 1857*
☆ *Died: Sept. 15, 1874, Newport, R.I.*

BENJAMIN R. CURTIS served only six years as an associate justice of the U.S. Supreme Court. But his dissent in the Dred Scott case is a lasting monument of the struggle for equal rights by African Americans.

Dred Scott, a slave, brought suit against his master, claiming himself a free man because he had lived in areas that banned slavery. The Court decided against Scott and ruled that he had no right to bring a suit to the federal courts.

Justice Curtis disagreed with every major point of the majority opinion in *Scott* v. *Sandford* (1857). He argued that African Americans could be citizens of the United States, although the majority argued that slaves were merely property. If so, they had the right to bring suits to the federal courts. Curtis also held that the federal government had authority under the Constitution to regulate or prevent slavery in territories of the United States. By contrast, Chief Justice Roger Taney's argument for the Court was an attempt to protect slavery against federal government regulation and to deny all constitutional rights to African Americans.

Taney's ideas prevailed in the *Dred Scott* case, but Curtis won in the long run. The 14th Amendment, ratified in 1868, embodies Curtis's ideas about citizenship and constitutional rights. Today, Taney's opinion in the *Dred Scott* case is generally viewed as one of the worst decisions in the history of the Court.

Curtis left the Court a few months after the *Dred Scott* decision. This case caused serious conflict and hostility between Curtis and his associates on the Court. He decided he could no longer work comfortably and cooperatively with Chief Justice Taney and some other justices, and so he resigned.

Curtis returned to the practice of law and continued to attract national attention for his achievements. In 1868, for example, he successfully defended President Andrew Johnson in his impeachment trial. He also argued more than 50 cases before the U.S. Supreme Court.

SEE ALSO
Scott v. Sandford

FURTHER READING
Fehrenbacher, Don E. *The Dred Scott Case.* New York: Oxford University Press, 1978.

Cushing, William

ASSOCIATE JUSTICE, 1790–1810

☆ Born: Mar. 1, 1732, Scituate, Mass.
☆ Education: Harvard College, A.B., 1751, M.A., 1754; Yale University, M.A., 1753; studied law under Jeremiah Gridley, Boston

☆ Previous government service: judge, probate court for Lincoln, Mass. (now Maine), 1760–61; judge, Superior Court of Massachusetts Bay Province, 1772–77; chief justice, Superior Court of the Commonwealth of Massachusetts, 1777–89; Massachusetts Constitutional Convention, 1779; vice president, Massachusetts Ratifying Convention, 1788; delegate to the electoral college, 1788
☆ Appointed by President George Washington Sept. 24, 1789, to fill one of the original six seats on the U.S. Supreme Court
☆ Supreme Court term: confirmed by the Senate Sept. 26, 1789, by a voice vote; served until Sept. 13, 1810
☆ Died: Sept. 13, 1810, Scituate, Mass.

WILLIAM CUSHING was an original member of the U.S. Supreme Court. He was the last judge in the United States to wear a full wig, a traditional adornment for British judges. Cushing did not stop wearing his wig until 1790.

Justice Cushing served 21 years on the Court, the longest term of President George Washington's original appointments, but wrote only 19 opinions. His most important opinion, *Ware* v. *Hylton* (1796), agreed with the Court's majority that a federal treaty cannot be violated by a state law.

SEE ALSO
Ware v. Hylton

Daniel, Peter V.

ASSOCIATE JUSTICE, 1842–60

☆ Born: Apr. 24, 1784, Stafford County, Va.
☆ Education: College of New Jersey (Princeton), 1802–3; studied law with Edmund Randolph in Richmond, Va.
☆ Previous government service: Virginia House of Delegates, 1809–12; Virginia Privy Council, 1812–35; lieutenant governor of Virginia, 1818–35; U.S. district judge, Eastern District of Virginia, 1836–41

☆ *Appointed by President Martin Van Buren Feb. 26, 1841; replaced Philip Barbour, who died*
☆ *Supreme Court term: confirmed by the Senate Mar. 2, 1841, by a 22–5 vote; served until May 31, 1860*
☆ *Died: May 31, 1860, Richmond, Va.*

PETER V. DANIEL was a loyal supporter of Andrew Jackson and the Democratic party. After becoming President, Andrew Jackson rewarded Daniel with an appointment to the federal judiciary in Virginia.

Daniel continued his support of the Democrats and was appointed to the U.S. Supreme Court by President Martin Van Buren. Justice Daniel tended to support the rights and powers of state governments in cases regarding the exercise of power in the federal system.

FURTHER READING

Frank, John P. *Justice Daniel Dissenting.* Cambridge: Harvard University Press, 1964.

Dartmouth College v. Woodward

☆ *4 Wheat. 518 (1819)*
☆ *Vote: 5–1*
☆ *For the Court: Marshall*
☆ *Concurring: Story and Washington*
☆ *Dissenting: Duvall*

DARTMOUTH COLLEGE was established in 1769 by a charter from King George III of England. After the formation of the United States, the agreement with the king became an agreement with the state of New Hampshire. In 1816 that state's legislature passed several amendments to the college's charter. By placing the school under the authority of the state government, these amendments had the effect of changing the private college into a state university.

Officials and friends of Dartmouth College objected. They believed the state legislature should not possess the authority to destroy the private nature of their college.

The Issue Daniel Webster, arguing for the Dartmouth College trustees, maintained that the legislature had violated Article 1, Section 10, of the Constitution, which provides that "no State shall . . . pass any . . . Law impairing the Obligation of Contracts." In an 1810 case (*Fletcher* v. *Peck*), the Supreme Court had ruled that a land grant is a contract. Webster now argued that "a grant of corporate powers and privileges is as much a contract as a grant of land."

Is a charter a contract? Did the Constitution's contract clause protect private corporate charters, such as Dartmouth's?

Opinion of the Court The Court ruled in favor of Dartmouth College. Chief Justice John Marshall's opinion held that the charter of a private corporation was a contract. Thus, the Constitution forbade the state legislature from changing that agreement. For the first time, the Court extended the protection of the Constitution's contract clause to a corporate charter. Marshall intended this ruling to be an important limitation on the powers and rights of state governments within the federal Union.

Dissent Justice Gabriel Duvall dissented in this case. However, he did not file an opinion.

In 1816, the New Hampshire legislature passed several amendments to the charter of Dartmouth College. Claiming that the state had violated its contract, the college took its case to the Supreme Court and won.

Significance The decision increased the power of the federal government over the states. It reaffirmed that the U.S. Supreme Court could invalidate state laws when it found those laws unconstitutional. Further, the case reinforced the practice begun by *Fletcher* v. *Peck* of imposing restrictions upon state legislatures with regard to the regulation of corporations. The national government would not allow state legislatures to void or change existing charters because to do so would violate the contract clause of Article 1, Section 9, of the Constitution.

The *Dartmouth College* decision did not attract the attention of the press at the time. Yet it deserves recognition as one of the early Court's important decisions. Business corporations were just forming in a young nation, and the Court's decision gave these businesses security against unexpected legislative interference.

Such security was vital to those who might invest money in new industries and corporations. Investors could be sure that any rights granted a corporation by one state legislature could not be taken away by some future legislature. Such assurances encouraged investment in railroads and other new industries, which in turn stimulated the country's economic development. The *Dartmouth College* case did not, however, prevent states from regulating corporations. The decision merely held that a state government could not alter corporate charters it had already granted, unless the state reserved the right to do so when it initially granted the charter.

After the resolution of the *Dartmouth College* case, many state legislatures placed restrictions on companies they chartered. These new corporate charters often contained clauses allowing the state, under certain circumstances, to revoke the charters or to buy the companies. Nevertheless, the *Dartmouth Col-* *lege* decision encouraged investors by assuring them that the Supreme Court would regulate state grants and charters and that after the granting of a charter, the grantees could expect the courts to protect their rights.

SEE ALSO

Contract clause; Federalism; Fletcher v. Peck

FURTHER READING

Current, Richard N. "The Dartmouth College Case." In *Quarrels That Have Shaped the Constitution*, edited by John A. Garraty. New York: Harper & Row, 1987.

Data Systems Office

THE DATA SYSTEMS OFFICE maintains technological facilities and equipment, such as computers, printers, and photocopy machines, for the Court. The office electronically transmits (through computers) opinions of the Court to outside agencies. Court documents are processed (typed, printed, and copied) for the justices through the Data Systems Office. In addition, the office works with the Public Information Office to electronically transmit the bench copies of the Court's opinions to organizations outside the Court.

Davis, David
ASSOCIATE JUSTICE, 1862–77

☆ *Born: Mar. 9, 1815, Sassafras Neck, Md.*
☆ *Education: Kenyon College, B.A., 1832; Yale Law School, 1835*
☆ *Previous government service: Illinois House of Representatives, 1845–47; Illinois Constitutional Convention, 1847; Illinois State circuit court judge, 1848–62*
☆ *Appointed by President Abraham Lincoln as a recess appointment Oct.*

17, 1862; replaced John A. Campbell, who resigned; nominated by Lincoln Dec. 1, 1862
☆ Supreme Court term: confirmed by the Senate Dec. 8, 1862, by a voice vote; resigned Mar. 4, 1877
☆ Died: June 26, 1886, Bloomington, Ill.

DAVID DAVIS practiced law in Illinois, where he met Abraham Lincoln. Their friendship had a strong influence on Davis's career. He supported Lincoln's losing 1854 campaign for the U.S. Senate. Davis was Lincoln's campaign manager in 1860, when Lincoln won the Republican nomination for the Presidency and became the 16th President of the United States. In 1862, Lincoln appointed Davis to the Supreme Court.

Davis's outstanding contribution as an associate justice was his opinion for the Court in *Ex parte Milligan* (1866), a landmark decision. In the *Milligan* case, the Court decided that a military court in Indiana, created by order of the President, had illegally tried and convicted a man for the crime of aiding the Confederacy during the Civil War. Justice Davis argued that Indiana had not been a war zone and the civilian courts had remained open. Therefore, it was a denial of Milligan's constitutional rights to try him in a military court. Davis concluded that the Constitution could not be suspended in a national crisis, not even during a civil war, and that the Constitution was "a law for rulers and people, equally in time of war and peace."

SEE ALSO
Ex parte Milligan

Day, William R.
ASSOCIATE JUSTICE, 1903–22

☆ Born: Apr. 17, 1849, Ravenna, Ohio
☆ Education: University of Michigan,

B.A., 1870; University of Michigan Law School, 1871–72
☆ Other government service: judge, Court of Common Pleas, Canton, Ohio, 1886–90; first assistant U.S. secretary of state, 1897–98; U.S. secretary of state, 1898; U.S. delegation, Paris Peace Conference, 1898–99; judge, U.S. Court of Appeals for the Sixth Circuit, 1899–1903; umpire, Mixed Claims Commission, 1922–23
☆ Appointed by President Theodore Roosevelt Feb. 19, 1903; replaced George Shiras, Jr., who resigned
☆ Supreme Court term: confirmed by the Senate Feb. 23, 1903, by a voice vote; resigned Nov. 13, 1922
☆ Died: July 9, 1923, Mackinac Island, Mich.

WILLIAM R. DAY became a prominent lawyer and Republican party leader in Ohio. He developed a close friendship with William McKinley, who relied upon Day for support and advice. After McKinley became President, he appointed Day assistant secretary of state and later secretary of state. In 1899, McKinley further rewarded Day with an appointment to the U.S. Court of Appeals for the Sixth Circuit. McKinley's successor as President, Theodore Roosevelt, named Day to the Supreme Court.

During his 19 years on the Court, Justice Day tended to be an advocate for state powers and rights in the federal system. However, Day did support the power of the federal government to regulate businesses under the Sherman Anti-Trust Act.

FURTHER READING
McLean, Joseph E. *William Rufus Day: Supreme Court Justice from Ohio*. Baltimore: Johns Hopkins University Press, 1946.

Death penalty

SEE Capital punishment

Decision days

THE SUPREME COURT's decisions on cases are announced orally to the public in the Supreme Court chamber (courtroom). The justice who wrote the Court's opinion on the case announces the decision. Justices who wrote concurring or dissenting opinions may also state their position. The writers of the opinions may either briefly summarize their positions or simply state the result.

From 1857 until 1965 the Court followed a tradition of announcing decisions only on Mondays. But on April 15, 1965, the Court announced that it was ending the "Decision Monday" tradition. Now, in weeks when the Court hears oral arguments, opinions are announced on Tuesdays and Wednesdays. During other weeks, decisions are announced on Mondays.

Dennis v. United States

☆ *341 U.S. 494 (1951)*
☆ *Vote: 6–2*
☆ *For the Court: Vinson*
☆ *Concurring: Frankfurter and Jackson*
☆ *Dissenting: Black and Douglas*
☆ *Not participating: Clark*

IN 1940, Congress passed a law banning sedition. It was known as the Smith Act after its sponsor, Representative Howard Smith of Virginia. The Smith Act made it a crime "to knowingly and willfully advocate, abet, advise or teach the duty, necessity, desirability, or propriety of overthrowing or destroying any government in the United States by force or violence." Further, the Smith Act made it a crime for anyone to organize a group with the mission of violently overthrowing the U.S. government.

After World War II, the United States and the Soviet Union—allies during the war—became enemies locked in a cold war. Members of the Communist Party of the United States of America (CPUSA) were suspected of collaborating with the Communist party leaders of the Soviet Union. A central part of the communist ideology was the inevitability of violent revolution to advance the cause of communism throughout the world. Given this perceived threat, many American political leaders urged use of the Smith Act to crack down on American communists.

In 1949 the federal government arrested and convicted 11 members of the CPUSA, including Eugene Dennis, for violating the Smith Act. Dennis appealed on the grounds that the Smith Act was unconstitutional.

The Issue The 1st Amendment of the Constitution says, "Congress shall make no law... abridging the freedom of speech, or of the press." Eugene Dennis was convicted under the Smith Act, however, because of the political ideas he expressed. Did the Smith Act violate the 1st Amendment?

Opinion of the Court The Court voted to uphold the conviction of Dennis and 10 other members of the CPUSA. Chief Justice Fred M. Vinson announced the decision in this case. He argued that protecting the national security of the United States justified use of the Smith Act to limit the free speech of individuals advocating forcible overthrow of the national government.

Vinson wrote, "Overthrow of the government by force and violence... is certainly a substantial enough interest for the Government to limit speech. Indeed this is the ultimate value of any society, for if a society cannot protect its

Eugene Dennis (second from left) and other members of the Communist party were arrested for advocating overthrow of the U.S. government. The Court upheld Dennis's conviction, ruling that free speech could be limited to protect national security.

very structure from armed internal attack, it must follow that no subordinate value can be protected." According to Vinson's opinion, it was reasonable to limit free speech of communists to protect the security of the United States.

Dissent Justices Hugo Black and William O. Douglas believed the Smith Act was unconstitutional. Justice Black wrote:

> I cannot agree that the First Amendment permits us to sustain laws suppressing freedom of speech and press on the basis of Congress's or our own notions of mere "reasonableness." Such a doctrine waters down the First Amendment so that it amounts to little more than an admonition to Congress. The Amendment as so construed is not likely to protect any but those "safe" or orthodox views which rarely need its protection....
>
> Public opinion being what it now is, few will protest the conviction of these Communist petitioners. There is hope, however, that in calmer times when present pressures, passions and fears subside, this or some later Court will restore the First Amendment liberties to the high preferred place where they belong in a free society.

Significance In the short run, the *Dennis* judgment encouraged the U.S. Department of Justice to suppress free speech by Communist party members. In

the long run, however, the Court did fulfill Justice Black's hope. In a similar case, *Yates* v. *United States* (1957), the Court refused to uphold the convictions of Communist party members for violating the Smith Act. From that point on, the Smith Act, though held to be constitutional, was no longer used to suppress political activities of communists or anyone else.

SEE ALSO
Freedom of speech and press; Yates v. United States

Discuss list

THE JUSTICES make decisions at the Court's conference about which cases to hear. However, not all requests for hearings are discussed. The justices make decisions at the conference only on cases that appear on a discuss list, from which many requests have been eliminated. The chief justice is in charge of creating the discuss list. He includes cases that, in his judgment, merit discussion before a decision is made about whether the Court should review the cases.

The discuss list is circulated in advance of the conference to all the justices. Any justice who thinks a case has been wrongly omitted may add it to the list. Each appeal from lower courts for the Supreme Court to hear a case is reviewed by each justice. Only those cases on the discuss list, however, are discussed at the regular conference of the justices.

Only about 30 percent of all the cases sent to the Court for review make the discuss list. The other petitions for review are rejected without further consideration by the Court. The discuss list is a means for reducing the time-consuming work of the Court by greatly reducing the number of cases discussed at conferences.

Dissenting opinion

ONE OR more justices often disagree with the majority of the Court on how to decide a case. Justices who disagree with the majority are dissenters. They interpret the law, as it applies to a case, in a way that differs from the majority's interpretation. A dissenting opinion is different from the concurring opinion, which agrees with the Court's decision but provides an explanation that differs from the majority opinion.

A justice who disagrees with the verdict in a case usually writes a dissenting opinion, though there is no requirement that a dissent be accompanied by an opinion. However, most dissenting justices do write one to explain why they disagree with the majority decision. For example, in *Plessy* v. *Ferguson* (1896), the Court let stand a state law requiring trains to provide "separate but equal" facilities for black and white passengers. Justice John Marshall Harlan wrote a dissenting opinion in which he said that "the Constitution is color-blind, and neither knows nor tolerates classes among citizens."

A dissenting opinion is not an attempt to change the minds of the Court's majority because the Court has already reached a final decision before the dissenting opinion is written. Rather, the dissenter hopes to arouse public opinion against the majority opinion.

Ultimately, the dissenting judge hopes that the Court will reconsider the majority opinion and overrule it and that his opinion will someday become the basis for a majority opinion in a similar case. Chief Justice Charles Evans Hughes wrote: "A dissent in a court of last resort is an appeal to the brooding spirit of the law, to the intelligence of a future day, when a later decision may possibly correct the error into which the dissenting judge believes the court to have been betrayed."

For example, Justice Harlan's 1896 dissent in *Plessy* was vindicated by the majority opinion in *Brown* v. *Board of Education* (1954), in which the Court unanimously rejected the "separate but equal" doctrine and ruled that racially segregated public schools were inherently unequal. Similarly, Justice Hugo Black's dissenting opinion in *Betts* v. *Brady* (1942), in which he wrote that criminal defendants in state courts have the right to counsel, became the majority opinion in *Gideon* v. *Wainwright* (1963).

Over the course of history, however, dissenting opinions have rarely been incorporated into later decisions. Justice Oliver Wendell Holmes, who was known as the Great Dissenter, wrote 173 dissenting opinions during 30 years on the Supreme Court. Yet few of Holmes's dissenting opinions sparked reversals of court decisions.

The Supreme Court does not readily admit errors and overrule past decisions. The principle of *stare decisis* ("Let the decision stand") has a powerful influence on the Court. Justices usually accept precedents established in earlier Court decisions as guides in deciding later cases.

Oliver Wendell Holmes (left) and Louis D. Brandeis were known for their eloquent and frequent dissenting opinions.

SEE ALSO

Concurring opinion; Opinions; Precedent

FURTHER READING

Barth, Alan. *Prophets With Honor: Great Dissents and Great Dissenters on the Supreme Court.* New York: Random House, 1974.

Double jeopardy

THE 5TH AMENDMENT to the U.S. Constitution provides that no person shall "be subject for the same offence to be twice put in jeopardy of life or limb." This provision is known as the double jeopardy clause. It protects individuals against repeated prosecution by the government for a single alleged crime. In *Benton* v. *Maryland* (1969), the Court decided that the 5th Amendment's double jeopardy clause is incorporated by the due process clause of the 14th Amendment and thereby applicable to the states.

The double jeopardy clause protects an individual in three ways. First, it protects a person from being prosecuted a second time for the same offense after being declared innocent of this offense. Second, it protects a person from a second prosecution for the same crime after conviction for this offense. Third, in addition to prohibiting more than one prosecution, the double jeopardy clause protects an individual from being *punished* more than once for the same crime.

The great importance of the double jeopardy clause of the Constitution was emphasized by Justice Hugo L. Black in *Green* v. *United States* (1957): "The underlying idea...is that the State with all its resources and power should not be allowed to make repeated attempts to convict an individual for an alleged offense, thereby subjecting him to embarrassment, expense and ordeal and compelling him to live in a continuing state of anxiety and insecurity; as well as enhancing the possibility that even though innocent he may be found guilty."

SEE ALSO

Benton v. Maryland

Douglas, William O.

ASSOCIATE JUSTICE, 1939–75

☆ *Born: Oct. 16, 1898, Maine, Minn.*
☆ *Education: Whitman College, B.A., 1920; Columbia Law School, LL.B., 1925*
☆ *Previous government service: Securities and Exchange Commission, 1936–39; chairman, 1937–39*
☆ *Appointed by President Franklin D. Roosevelt Mar. 20, 1939; replaced Louis D. Brandeis, who retired*
☆ *Supreme Court term: confirmed by the Senate Apr. 4, 1939, by a 62–4 vote; retired Nov. 12, 1975*
☆ *Died: Jan. 19, 1980, Washington, D.C.*

WILLIAM O. DOUGLAS served on the Supreme Court for 36 years, longer than any other justice. He wrote more opinions than any justice before or since. And he was honored, before his death, with a lasting monument: Congress designated a parkland in Washington as the William O. Douglas National Park to commemorate his concern for the environment.

Douglas overcame crushing poverty and a crippling illness in his childhood to earn the great achievements and honors of his adult life. His father died when Douglas was five years old, leaving his mother with three children and almost no money. Later, he struggled with polio, which seriously weakened his legs. He took long walks in the mountains near his home to build strength in his legs, and his contact with nature influenced him to become a lifelong advocate of environmental causes. His childhood experiences also led Douglas to have sympathy for the "underdog"—a person who copes with poverty, physical handicaps, or racial discrimination.

William Douglas was an outstanding student in school, which opened opportunities for him to become a teacher, lawyer, and government official. His achievements as a lawyer attracted the attention of President Franklin D. Roosevelt, who appointed him to the Securities and Exchange Commission. He became a strong supporter of Roosevelt's New Deal economic recovery programs, and the President appointed him to the Supreme Court in 1939, to fill the seat of Louis Brandeis, who had retired.

Justice Douglas sought to defend the constitutional rights of individuals and professed that the Bill of Rights was meant "to keep government off the backs of people." He joined Justice Hugo Black to extend the limits of free expression and to promote "incorporation" of the Bill of Rights into Section 1 of the 14th Amendment, so that these constitutional rights could be used to protect individuals against abuses by state and local governments. Further, Justice Douglas joined with the majority of the Court under Chief Justice Earl Warren to defend the rights of African Americans, as in *Brown* v. *Board of Education* (1954) and *Cooper* v. *Aaron* (1958).

Douglas's most notable opinion for the Court was *Griswold* v. *Connecticut* (1965), in which he argued for a constitutional right to privacy based on his interpretation of the 1st, 3rd, 4th, 5th, and 9th Amendments. Although this opinion has prevailed, it also has been controversial because a right to privacy is not written specifically into the Constitution.

Douglas was a frequent writer of dissenting opinions, usually in defense of the rights of unpopular persons. He dissented, for example, in *Dennis* v. *United States* (1951), to protest the Court's decision to uphold convictions of American Communist party members for stating and writing that the U.S. government should be overthrown and replaced by a communist form of gov-

ernment. Douglas believed that the 1st Amendment forbade all government limitations upon the content of speech, or what a person could say. According to Justice Douglas, the Constitution gives the government power only to regulate the conduct of the speaker, that is, actions that pose a serious threat to the safety or property of people.

Justice Douglas often spoke and wrote about his beliefs on many topics. Many of his public statements were controversial or in opposition to commonly held viewpoints. As a result, many people disliked Douglas. He faced three attempts to impeach him, the last and most serious occurring in 1970, five years before his retirement from the Court.

Justice Douglas suffered a stroke on Dec. 31, 1974, which partially paralyzed him. Nearly a year later, Douglas left the Court. He died some four years later, a hero to many for his unyielding advocacy of individual rights, especially the rights of persons disliked or neglected by a majority of the people.

SEE ALSO

Griswold v. Connecticut; Incorporation doctrine; Privacy, right to

FURTHER READING

Ball, Howard, and Phillip J. Cooper. *Of Power and Right: Hugo Black, William O. Douglas, and America's Constitutional Revolution.* New York: Oxford University Press, 1992.
Douglas, William O. *The Court Years, 1939–1975: The Autobiography of William O. Douglas.* New York: Vintage, 1981.
Simon, James F. *Independent Journey: The Life of William O. Douglas.* New York: Harper & Row, 1980.
Urofsky, Melvin I. "William O. Douglas, Common-Law Judge." *Constitution* 4, no. 3 (Fall 1992): 48–58.

Dred Scott case

SEE Scott v. Sandford

Due process of law

THE 5TH and 14th Amendments to the U.S. Constitution guarantee individuals the right of due process of law, which is often referred to simply as "due process." The 5th Amendment states, "No person shall be...deprived of life, liberty, or property, without due process of law." The 14th Amendment states, "No state shall...deprive any person of life, liberty, or property, without due process of law."

These two due process clauses provide that the government must act fairly, according to established legal procedures, with regard to a person's rights to life, liberty, and property. Due process means, for example, that an individual accused of a crime is guaranteed certain legal procedural rights, such as the right to know the charges against him, to confront his accusers in court, to have legal counsel, and to have a jury trial. These and other rights of the accused are specified in the 4th, 5th, 6th, and 8th Amendments to the Constitution.

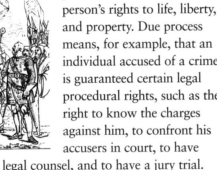

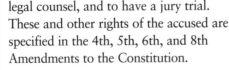

King John of England signs the Magna Carta, which established the concept of the rule of law.

Procedural due process

These rights of the accused are examples of *procedural due process,* and they are constitutional limits on the power of government designed to protect the rights and liberties of individuals.

Procedural due process—the idea that government must follow fair and generally accepted legal procedures in its actions against individuals—has been traced to the great English charter of liberty, the Magna Carta (1215). By signing this document, King John of England agreed to "obey the law of the

land." This idea developed into the legal guarantee of procedural due process of law to protect people against arbitrary or lawless punishments or penalties imposed by the government.

Due process of law was included in an act of the English Parliament in 1354, which affirmed the Magna Carta and specified "that no man...shall be put out of Land or Tenement, nor taken, nor imprisoned, nor disinherited, nor put to death, without being brought to Answer by due Process of Law." This English concept of due process was brought to North America by English colonists and was included in their colonial charters and laws. The Massachusetts Body of Liberties (1641), for example, provided that an individual could not be deprived of life, liberty, and property except by "some express law of the country warranting the same, established by a General Court and sufficiently published." The first American statute to use the words "due process of law" was an act of the colonial government of Massachusetts in 1682.

The original state constitutions, drafted during the founding era of the United States (1776–83), included rights of procedural due process. They typically limited these rights to the traditional "law of the land" idea that stems from the Magna Carta. The Northwest Ordinance, enacted by the U.S. Congress in 1787 to regulate new territories north and west of the Ohio River, also guaranteed procedural due process rights by declaring, "[N]o man shall be deprived of his liberty or property but by the judgment of his peers, or the law of the land."

By 1789, when the federal Bill of Rights was drafted by the first Congress, the concept of due process was an established part of American constitutions and criminal law. Consequently, it was expected that the right of due process would be included in the Bill of Rights.

Substantive due process

During the 20th century, the Supreme Court has reinforced and extended individual rights. This has been done through the development of *substantive due process* and the nationwide application of the federal Bill of Rights through the due process clause of the 14th Amendment.

Substantive due process concerns specific behaviors of individuals that, according to the Court, are generally beyond the reach of government power, such as the free exercise of religion or participation in private organizations that petition the government about public problems and issues. The government may not regulate these actions, not even by the use of the fairest legal procedures, because to do so would violate the most fundamental rights of individuals in a constitutional government, such as rights to liberty, property, and equality under the law. If government officials want to regulate these kinds of usually protected actions, they must demonstrate that they cannot achieve a legitimate public purpose by any other means.

From the 1890s through the 1920s, the Court tended to use substantive due process to protect the property rights of business owners against state government regulations of working conditions, wages paid to employees, and hours of work. Since the 1930s, and especially since the 1960s, the Court has used substantive due process to protect the civil rights of individuals, especially racial minorities and women, against state government actions that threatened these fundamental rights. Thus, the Court has used substantive due process to invalidate hundreds of state laws pertaining to a wide variety of social and economic concerns and civil rights, such as fair conditions of employment.

The Court has, however, permitted state governments to regulate minimum wages and the working hours of employees in private businesses. These state regulations have been upheld, as necessary for the public good, against claims by business owners that they violate private property rights of individuals. This was the Court's ruling in *West Coast Hotel Co. v. Parrish* (1937), an early example of the use of substantive due process to protect and extend the rights of employees.

In the 20th century, the Supreme Court has used the due process clause of the 14th Amendment, which limits the powers of state governments, to apply most of the rights guaranteed by the federal Bill of Rights to the states. This use of the due process clause to protect the individual rights specified in the Bill of Rights against infringement by state and local governments has been referred to as the incorporation doctrine. This process has occurred gradually, on a case-by-case basis.

The Court's use of the incorporation doctrine and substantive due process has been controversial. Critics charge that substantive due process is a distortion of the original meaning of due process, which involved only adherence to formal and fair procedures by government officials in actions against individuals. Further, critics say that substantive due process has been used by judges to interfere in matters that should be left to resolution by majority vote in Congress or state legislatures. Finally, critics claim that substantive due process and the incorporation doctrine have been used by the U.S. Supreme Court to wrongly suppress the authority and power of state governments.

Virtually no one challenges the general value of due process of law as a guarantee of procedural consistency and fairness. Justice Felix Frankfurter expressed a commonly held view about procedural due process in *Malinski* v. *New York* (1945): "The history of American freedom is, in no small measure, the history of procedure." And in *Shaughnessy* v. *United States* (1953), Justice Robert Jackson stressed that controversy about substantive due process does not change the most fundamental and general agreement about procedural fairness, which "is what it [due process] most uncompromisingly requires."

SEE ALSO

Bill of Rights; Incorporation doctrine; West Coast Hotel Co. v. Parrish

FURTHER READING

Graham, Fred. *The Due Process Revolution: The Warren Court's Impact on Criminal Law.* New York: Hayden, 1970. Phillips, Michael J. *The Lochner Court, Myth and Reality: Substantive Due Process from the 1890s to the 1930s.* Westport, Conn.: Praeger, 2001.

Duncan v. Louisiana

☆ *391 U.S. 145 (1968)*
☆ *Vote: 7–2*
☆ *For the Court: White*
☆ *Concurring: Black, Douglas, and Fortas*
☆ *Dissenting: Harlan and Stewart*

GARY DUNCAN was convicted of a misdemeanor—battery—and sentenced to 60 days in jail and a fine of $150. The maximum penalty for this offense was two years in jail and a $300 fine. Duncan had requested a trial by jury. The request was denied because the Louisiana constitution did not require a jury trial in cases involving lesser felonies or misdemeanors. Duncan appealed on the grounds that his rights under the U.S. Constitution had been violated.

The Issue Duncan claimed a 6th Amendment right to a jury trial. However, the Court had not yet used the 14th Amendment to apply this part of the federal Bill of Rights to the states. Was it constitutional for the state of Louisiana to deny Duncan a trial by jury?

Opinion of the Court The Court decided to incorporate the 6th Amendment right to trial by jury under the due process clause of the 14th Amendment, which provides that no state may "deprive any person of life, liberty, or property, without due process of law." Thus, the state of Louisiana had to provide a jury trial in cases like this one. Duncan's conviction was reversed because his right to a jury trial had been unconstitutionally denied. The Court held, however, that prosecutions for certain very minor offenses may not require a jury trial. Since Duncan's case involved a possible maximum imprisonment of two years, the Court decided this case was too serious to be tried without a jury.

Significance This was the first time that the 6th Amendment right to trial by jury was applied to a state through the 14th Amendment. This case, therefore, was part of the gradual process by which the Court has applied most parts of the federal Bill of Rights to the states.

SEE ALSO

Incorporation doctrine; Trial by jury

Duvall, Gabriel

ASSOCIATE JUSTICE, 1811–35

☆ *Born: Dec. 6, 1752, Prince Georges County, Md.*
☆ *Education: studied law privately*
☆ *Previous government service: clerk, Maryland Convention, 1775–76; clerk, Maryland House of Delegates, 1777–87; Maryland State Council, 1782–85; Maryland House of Delegates, 1787–94; U.S. representative from Maryland, 1794–96; chief*

justice, General Court of Maryland, 1796–1802; presidential elector, 1796, 1800; first comptroller of the U.S. Treasury, 1802–11
☆ *Appointed by President James Madison Nov. 15, 1811; replaced Samuel Chase, who died*
☆ *Supreme Court term: confirmed by the Senate Nov. 18, 1811, by a voice vote; resigned Jan. 14, 1835*
☆ *Died: Mar. 6, 1844, Prince Georges County, Md.*

GABRIEL DUVALL served on the Supreme Court for a little more than 23 years. Despite this long period of service, he had a very small impact on the work of the Court and neither wrote significant opinions nor developed ideas to guide the work of his successors.

Duvall's appointment to prominent positions in the federal government, including the Supreme Court, was his reward for many years of loyal service to the Republican party founded by Thomas Jefferson and James Madison. President Jefferson appointed Duvall to be comptroller of the U.S. Treasury in 1802. President Madison appointed Duvall to the Supreme Court in 1811.

During the final 10 years of his Supreme Court service, Duvall was chronically ill and gradually lost his hearing. The infirmities greatly interfered with his ability to do his job, and he was repeatedly asked by his colleagues to resign. Justice Duvall resisted this advice until satisfied that he would be replaced by someone of whom he approved. Duvall resigned in 1835 after President Andrew Jackson promised him that Roger B. Taney, a friend of Duvall's from Maryland, would be named to the Court. In 1835, President Jackson appointed Philip Barbour of Virginia to replace Duvall, and in 1836 he named Taney to replace John Marshall as chief justice.

Ellsworth, Oliver
CHIEF JUSTICE, 1796–1800

☆ *Born: Apr. 29, 1745, Windsor, Conn.*
☆ *Education: College of New Jersey (Princeton), B.A., 1766*
☆ *Other government service: Connecticut General Assembly, 1773–76; state's attorney, Hartford County, Conn., 1777–85; Continental Congress, 1776–83; Connecticut Council of Safety, 1779; Governor's Council, 1780–85, 1801–7; judge, Connecticut Supreme Court, 1785–89; Constitutional Convention, 1787; U.S. senator from Connecticut, 1789–96*
☆ *Appointed by President George Washington Mar. 3, 1796; replaced John Jay, who resigned*
☆ *Supreme Court term: confirmed by the Senate Mar. 4, 1796, by a 21–1 vote; resigned Dec. 15, 1800*
☆ *Died: Nov. 26, 1807, Windsor, Conn.*

OLIVER ELLSWORTH was one of the leading founders of the United States. He played a major role in writing and supporting ratification of the U.S. Constitution. Later, as a senator from Connecticut in the first U.S. Congress, Ellsworth drafted the Judiciary Act of 1789, which set up the federal judicial system in line with Article 3 of the Constitution.

In 1796 President George Washington named Ellsworth chief justice of the United States, a position he held for only three years. Ellsworth had very little influence on development of the Court during his brief term. In 1799, Ellsworth agreed to President John Adams's request that he travel to France to repair broken relationships between the United States and its former ally, with which the United States was fighting an undeclared naval war. Ellsworth helped to resolve the problems with France, but he became ill while overseas and resigned as chief justice before returning to the United States.

FURTHER READING

Casto, William R. *The Supreme Court in the Early Republic: The Chief Justiceships of John Jay and Oliver Ellsworth.* Columbia: University of South Carolina Press, 1995.

Eminent domain

THE GOVERNMENT's power to take land for public use is called eminent domain. According to the 5th Amendment, "No person shall…be deprived of life, liberty, or property, without due process of law; nor shall private property be taken for public use without just compensation."

SEE ALSO
Just compensation

Engel v. Vitale

☆ *370 U.S. 421 (1962)*
☆ *Vote: 7–1*
☆ *For the Court: Black*
☆ *Concurring: Douglas*
☆ *Dissenting: Stewart*
☆ *Not participating: White*

THE BOARD OF REGENTS of the state of New York has the authority to supervise the state's educational system. In 1961, this state education board composed a short prayer: "Almighty God, we acknowledge our dependence upon Thee, and we beg Thy blessings upon us, our parents, our teachers, and our Country." The Board of Regents recommended daily recitation in schools of this nondenominational prayer, on a voluntary basis.

Although the Regents prayer was only a recommendation, the New Hyde Park Board of Education required that this prayer be said aloud at the beginning of each school day by each class of students in the district and in the presence of a teacher. The parents of 10 students objected to this requirement as a violation of the principle of separation of church and state in the 1st Amendment to the Constitution. They took legal action to compel the local board of education to discontinue the use in public schools of an official prayer that was contrary to their beliefs and practices.

The Issue Did the New York Board of Regents and the New Hyde Park Board of Education violate the 1st Amendment ban on laws "respecting an establishment of religion"?

Opinion of the Court The Court decided to strike down the Regents prayer. Justice Hugo Black, writing for the majority, said that the primary concern in this case was the creation of the prayer and the subsequent distribution of it throughout the state by an official agency of the state government. These actions violated the establishment clause of the 1st Amendment, which was applicable to the state of New York through the due process clause of the 14th Amendment. Justice Black concluded, "Neither the fact that the prayer may be denominationally neutral nor the fact that its observance on the part of the students is voluntary [in school districts other than New Hyde

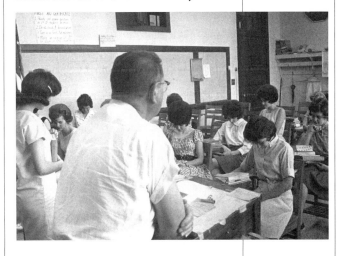

Prayer in public schools was a legal classroom activity before the Supreme Court ruled in Engel v. Vitale that such religious activity violated the separation of church and state.

Park] can serve to free it from the limitations of the Establishment Clause [which] is violated by the enactment of laws which establish an official religion whether those laws operate directly to coerce nonobserving individuals or not."

Dissent Justice Potter Stewart dissented on the grounds that the Regents prayer was nondenominational and voluntary. Justice Stewart wrote: "With all due respect, I think the Court has misapplied a great constitutional principle. I cannot see how an 'official religion' is established by letting those who want to say a prayer say it. On the contrary, I think that to deny the wish of these school children to join in reciting this prayer is to deny them the opportunity of sharing in the spiritual heritage of the Nation."

Significance This case, in combination with the decision in *Abington School District* v. *Schempp* (1963), established a strong position in favor of a strict separation of church and state. However, opponents have continued to challenge this view. In his dissent in *Wallace* v. *Jaffree* (1985), Justice William Rehnquist rejected the idea of strict separation of church and state. Rather, he argued, the establishment clause of the 1st Amendment was meant only to prevent the government from favoring one religion over another.

SEE ALSO
Abington School District v. Schempp; Establishment clause; Religious issues under the Constitution; Wallace v. Jaffree

Equality under the Constitution

THE UNITED STATES was born with a Declaration of Independence that proclaimed, as a self-evident truth, that "all Men are created equal, that they are endowed by their Creator with certain unalienable Rights, that among these are Life, Liberty, and the Pursuit of Happiness—That to secure these Rights, Governments are instituted among Men." According to the founders of the United States of America, all people are equal, by virtue of their humanity, in possession of certain rights (such as rights to liberty) that it is the responsibility of government to protect.

The founders were not claiming that all individuals are equal in their personal attributes, such as physical strength, intelligence, or artistic talent. They were not saying that a government is established to enforce equality or uniformity in the way people think, act, or live. Rather, the founders were committed to establishing a government that would guarantee equally to all individuals the rule of law and security for liberty under the law.

The word *equality,* however, did not appear in the Constitution of 1787 and the Bill of Rights of 1791. Further, the ideal of equal rights for all individuals under a government of laws was contradicted by the existence of slavery and the denial of rights to some people because of race or gender. Although the Constitution and Bill of Rights, as originally written, did not outlaw slavery and discrimination based on race or gender, one of the great early opponents of slavery and racial discrimination, Frederick Douglass, argued in a widely praised Fourth of July speech (1852) that "interpreted as it *ought* to be interpreted, the Constitution is a GLORIOUS LIBERTY DOCUMENT." According to Douglass—and many other opponents of slavery, racial discrimination, and gender discrimination—the Constitution of 1787 was neutral with regard to race and sex, thereby leaving the way open to equal

On the west side of the Supreme Court Building, the inscription beneath the frieze reads "Equal Justice Under Law."

protection under the law for women and racial minorities.

The American ideal of equal rights under law, however, was not explicitly included in the Constitution until after the Civil War, with passage of the three Reconstruction-era amendments. The 13th Amendment (1865) banned slavery. The 14th Amendment (1868) guaranteed equal rights of citizenship to all Americans, with the special intention of protecting the rights of former slaves. The 15th Amendment (1870) provided that voting rights of citizens "shall not be denied or abridged by the United States or by any State on account of race, color, or previous condition of servitude."

The 14th Amendment includes the word *equality* in Section 1, which prohibits a state government from denying "to any person within its jurisdiction the equal protection of the laws." This equal protection clause protects individuals from arbitrary discrimination by government officials. Federal courts have read the equal protection concept into their interpretation of the due process clause of the 5th Amendment,

thereby applying the equal protection limitations to the federal government. Neither federal nor state governments may classify people in ways that violate their liberties or rights under the U.S. Constitution.

The equal protection clause does not require identical treatment in all circumstances. Discrimination is sometimes permitted. For example, laws denying people under 18 years old the right to vote or the right to marry without parental permission are considered reasonable classifications that do not violate the individual's constitutional rights and liberties because a relationship seems to exist between chronological age and the ability to perform in certain ways. However, a law prohibiting redheads from voting would be unreasonable and unconstitutional because no relationship exists between red hair and the ability to vote.

Racial equality and affirmative action

Despite the promise of the 14th Amendment, most black Americans did not enjoy equal protection of the laws until the second half of the 20th century. Indeed, the Supreme Court decision in *Plessy* v. *Ferguson* (1896) exemplified the denial of equality to black Americans in its sanction of "separate but equal" treatment of people based on race. Both before and after *Plessy*, racial segregation was a firmly established fact of American life, with the separate facilities for blacks hardly ever equal to those provided for white Americans.

If *Plessy* was a symbol of the unequal and unjust social conditions of racial segregation, it also contained a seed of social change toward legal equality. In the dissenting opinion, Justice John Marshall Harlan wrote, "Our Constitution is colorblind and neither knows nor tolerates classes among citizens. In respect of civil rights all citizens are equal before the law. . . . It is therefore to be regretted that this high tribunal . . . has reached the conclusion that it is competent for a state to regulate the enjoyment by citizens of their civil rights solely on the basis of race." Justice Harlan's argument for a colorblind Constitution became the rallying cry and goal of the National Association for the Advancement of Colored People (NAACP) and other participants in a civil rights movement committed to equal justice under the law.

The NAACP and its allies achieved several legal victories from the 1930s to the 1950s that advanced the cause of equal protection for the constitutional rights of black Americans. For example, *Smith v. Allwright* (1944) struck down barriers to participation by blacks in Democratic party primary elections. *Missouri ex rel. Gaines* v. *Canada* (1938) and *Sweatt* v. *Painter* (1950) provided access for black students to public law schools previously restricted to white students. The turning point, however, came in *Brown* v. *Board of Education* (1954), which overturned *Plessy* and outlawed state-sanctioned racial segregation in public schools. Several Court decisions after *Brown*, plus the federal Civil Rights Act of 1964, struck down racial segregation laws affecting all facets of American life and advanced the cause of equal security for the constitutional rights of all individuals, regardless of color or race. A key Court decision after *Brown* was *Cooper* v. *Aaron* (1958), which reaffirmed the court's decision in *Brown* against racial segregation in public schools. And *Heart of Atlanta Motel* v. *United States* (1964) buttressed the Civil Rights Act of 1964 in its prohibition of racial discrimination in privately owned accommodations open to the public, such as hotels and restaurants.

In 1967, in *Loving* v. *Virginia*, the Court struck down a state law prohibiting interracial marriages and held that all racial classifications are "inherently suspect classifications." Thus, any legal classification based on race would be subject to "strict scrutiny" by the Court. This means that the suspect classification would be judged unconstitutional unless the government could justify it with a compelling public interest, which is very difficult to do.

Since the 1970s the NAACP and other civil rights organizations have argued for both government-sponsored and private, voluntary affirmative action programs. Such programs are designed to give preferential treatment to racial minorities in order to provide greater access to jobs, competitive college and university programs, promotions to high-level professional and management positions, and government contracts. Advocates of affirmative action have argued that African Americans, for example, lag far behind whites in income, educational achievement, job advancement, and living standards. They claim that these differences are the consequence of many generations of racial discrimination and that affirmative action is the best way to overcome quickly the continuing negative effects of past discrimination.

Opponents of affirmative action view it as "reverse discrimination" based on race and, therefore, a violation of the idea that the Constitution is "color-blind."

The Court has upheld aspects of affirmative action while striking down extreme versions of this concept. In *Regents of the University of California* v. *Bakke* (1978), for example, the Court ruled that a university could take into account race and ethnicity when making decisions about the admission of students. However, the Court ruled that an affirmative action plan based on rigid racial quotas to boost admission of minority students to a university was unconstitutional. In *United Steelworkers of America* v. *Weber* (1979), the Court permitted an employer's voluntarily imposed and temporary affirmative action program. That program would encourage unskilled black workers to obtain training that would lead to better, more skilled jobs, in which black Americans historically have been underrepresented. Once again, however, the Court rejected rigid, race-based quotas in hiring and job advancement.

In *United States* v. *Paradise* (1987), the Court upheld a temporary and "narrowly tailored" quota system to bring about job promotion for black state troopers in Alabama. The state's affirmative action plan imposed a "one black-for-one-white" promotion quota. This was justified, the Court said, by the "long and shameful record of delay and resistance" to employment opportunities for black Americans in the Alabama state police force.

Gender-based issues of equality

Not until the 1970s did the Court extend to women the 14th Amendment's guarantee of "equal protection of the laws." One hundred years earlier, in *Bradwell* v. *Illinois* (1873), the Court had refused to use the equal protection clause to overturn a state government's ruling denying a woman a license to practice law. The denial was based strictly on the person's gender, but the Court ignored this flagrant violation of "equal protection of the laws." Writing for the Court, Justice Joseph P. Bradley justified the decision in *Bradwell* with a paternalistic explanation: "The natural and proper timidity and delicacy which belongs to the female sex evidently unfits it for many of the occupations of civil life [such as being a lawyer]. . . . [T]he domestic sphere [is] that which properly belongs to the domain and functions of womanhood."

The Court's paternalism toward women reflected the general view of the public in the latter half of the 19th century. The late-19th-century Court also ruled that the 14th Amendment did not require state governments to permit women to vote (*Minor* v. *Happersett*, 1875) or to serve on juries (*Strauder* v. *West Virginia*, 1880). It took the 19th Amendment to the Constitution (1920) to overturn the Court's decision against women's voting rights. Not until 1975, in *Taylor* v. *Louisiana*, did the Court overturn *Strauder* and rule against state exclusion of women from jury duty.

Since the 1970s women have successfully challenged restrictions that appear to violate the 14th Amendment's equal protection clause. In *Reed* v. *Reed* (1971), for example, the Court used the 14th Amendment to nullify a state law that discriminated against women in serving as the administrators of the estates of the deceased.

In 1987, in *Johnson* v. *Transportation Agency of Santa Clara County*, the Court endorsed a carefully crafted, temporary, and voluntary affirmative action plan to boost job promotion opportunities for women. The Court held it was permissible to take into account a woman's gender as a positive factor in promotion to a higher-ranking position because women had been systematically denied access to such positions in the past.

In 1996, in *Romer* v. *Evans,* the Supreme Court struck down an amendment to the constitution of Colorado that violated the 14th Amendment's equal protection clause by discriminating against a class of people including homosexuals, lesbians, and bisexuals. Gay people, as a class, had been singled out, said the Court, and denied the right to seek protection from the government against discrimination based on membership in that class.

Continuing controversy

Since the 1970s Americans have tended to agree about the constitutionality and justice of guaranteeing equality of civil rights and liberties to all individuals in the United States, regardless of race, ethnicity, or gender. Also since the 1970s, however, Americans have argued about the issue of affirmative action to remedy the effects of past discrimination against racial minorities and women.

Is any kind of affirmative action plan a violation of the equal protection clause? Or is affirmative action the best short-term and temporary means of reversing many generations of unjust discrimination?

The U.S. Congress endorsed limited uses of affirmative action to redress past injustices in the Civil Rights Act of 1991. However, in *Adarand Constructors, Inc.* v. *Peña* (1995), the Court held that all race-based classifications, including government affirmative action programs, should be subjected to the standard of strict scrutiny. According to Justice Sandra Day O'Connor, all government classifications by race "should be subjected

to detailed judicial inquiry to ensure that the personal right to equal protection of the laws has not been infringed." Policies or programs based on racial classifications—including those designed to boost the opportunities of minorities in an attempt to overcome the negative effects of past discrimination—have to be narrowly defined and designed to advance a compelling government interest. Otherwise, they could be struck down as unconstitutional infringements of the 14th Amendment.

There has been continuous public controversy about the constitutionality and morality of affirmative action programs in education, government, and private enterprise. Citizens and the courts are likely to face tough decisions about modification or termination of policies that sanction unequal treatment of groups in the pursuit of remedies for past injustices.

SEE ALSO

Affirmative action; Brown v. Board of Education; Civil rights; Cooper v. Aaron; Heart of Atlanta Motel v. United States; Johnson v. Transportation Agency of Santa Clara County; Plessy v. Ferguson; Reed v. Reed; Regents of the University of California v. Bakke; Smith v. Allwright; Sweatt v. Painter; United Steelworkers of America v. Weber

FURTHER READING

Baer, Judith A. *Equality under the Constitution.* Ithaca: Cornell University Press, 1983.
Finkelman, Paul. "Race and the Constitution." In *By and for the People: Constitutional Rights in American History,* edited by Kermit L. Hall. Arlington Heights, Ill.: Harlan Davidson, 1991.
Green, Robert P. *Equal Protection and the African American Constitutional Experience.* Westport, Conn.: Greenwood, 2000.
Jackson, Donald W. *Even the Children of Strangers: Equality under the U.S. Constitution.* Lawrence: University Press of Kansas, 1992.
Kull, Andrew. *The Color-Blind Constitution.* Cambridge: Harvard University Press, 1992.
Petrik, Paula. "Women and the Bill of Rights." In *By and for the People: Constitutional Rights in American History,* edited by Kermit L. Hall. Arlington

Heights, Ill.: Harlan Davidson, 1991.
Pole, J. R. *The Pursuit of Equality in American History.* 2nd ed. Berkeley: University of California Press, 1993.
Van Burkleo, Sandra F. "No Rights But Human Rights." *Constitution* 2, no. 2 (Spring–Summer 1990): 4–19.

Equal protection of the laws

THE EQUAL protection clause of the 14th Amendment states, "No state shall... deny to any person within its jurisdiction the equal protection of the laws." The 14th Amendment, ratified in 1868, became part of the U.S. Constitution in the wake of the Civil War, with the direct purpose of protecting the legal rights of African Americans recently emancipated from slavery. The equal protection clause, however, has been applied by the courts to protect the rights of all individuals under the authority of the Constitution.

Until the 1940s, the equal protection clause was rarely used by the Supreme Court to overturn state laws as unconstitutional. Since the 1950s, however, the Court has used the equal protection clause to strike down, as unconstitutional, state laws supporting racial segregation in schools and other public facilities. For example, the Court's decision in *Brown* v. *Board of Education* (1954) was based on the equal protection clause. In *Reed* v. *Reed* (1971) the Court, for the first time, struck down a state law because it discriminated against women, in violation of the 14th Amendment's equal protection clause.

SEE ALSO

Equality under the Constitution

These demonstrators in 1969 claim that women face discrimination and fail to receive equal protection of the laws.

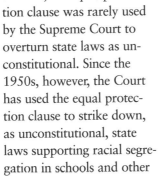

Establishment clause

THE 1ST AMENDMENT to the U.S. Constitution states, "Congress shall make no law respecting an establishment of religion." This establishment clause has been used by the Court to overturn, or declare unconstitutional, state laws involving the government in religious activities, such as prayers or religious programs in public schools. For example, the Court used the establishment clause to strike down state government laws in *Engel* v. *Vitale* (1962) and *Wallace* v. *Jaffree* (1985).

There is general agreement that the establishment clause prohibits an official religion endorsed by the government or preferential support by the government of some religions over others. There have been continuous arguments, however, about whether the establishment clause strictly prohibits all involvement by the government in support of religious activity as long as the involvement is conducted nonpreferentially.

SEE ALSO

Engel v. Vitale; Religious issues under the Constitution; Wallace v. Jaffree

Ethics in the judicial branch

Like members of the legislative and executive branches, federal judges are expected to have high standards of ethics. All federal judges follow the principles outlined in the *Code of Conduct for United States Judges,* which has been adopted by the Judicial Conference of the United States, the federal courts' national policy-making group.

The *Code of Conduct* includes these guidelines:

- A judge should uphold the integrity and independence of the judiciary.
- A judge should avoid impropriety and the appearance of impropriety in all activities.
- A judge should perform the duties of the office impartially and diligently.
- A judge may engage in extrajudicial activities to improve the law, the legal system, and the administration of justice.
- A judge should regulate extrajudicial activities to minimize the risk of conflict with judicial duties.
- A judge should regularly file reports of compensation received for law-related and extrajudicial activities.
- A judge should refrain from political activity.

According to these ethical standards, judges should not hear cases in which they have a financial interest, a personal bias regarding a party to the case, or earlier involvement in the case as a lawyer. Further, judges are expected to participate in activities that contribute to the public good through improvement of the legal and judicial systems, and as a result, many judges are engaged in law-related education activities in schools.

Everson v. Board of Education of Ewing Township

☆ 330 U.S. 1 (1947)
☆ Vote: 5–4
☆ For the Court: Black
☆ Dissenting: Jackson, Frankfurter, Rutledge, and Burton

IN 1941 the New Jersey legislature passed a law that said boards of education could pay the costs of bus transpor-tation, to and from school, of students in public schools and Catholic parochial schools. Arch Everson, a resident of the school district governed by the Ewing Township Board of Education, claimed that this state law violated the 1st Amendment prohibition against the state establishment of religion. Everson claimed that it was unfair and illegal for the state government to use money from taxpayers, like himself, to pay for costs associated with private religious schools.

The Issue The 1st Amendment of the Constitution says, "Congress shall make no law respecting an establishment of religion." Furthermore, the 14th Amendment says, "No state shall... deprive any person of life, liberty, or property without due process of law." Everson argued that the 1st Amendment, which applies only to the U.S. Congress, could also be applied to state governments through the due process clause of the 14th Amendment.

The other constitutional issue was whether the New Jersey law challenged by Arch Everson actually involved the state government in religion in a way that violated the establishment clause of the 1st Amendment.

Opinion of the Court Justice Hugo Black, writing for the Court, argued that the 1st Amendment to the Constitution can be used to limit state governments through the due process clause of the 14th Amendment. On this issue, the Court agreed with Arch Everson. However, the Court disagreed with Everson with regard to the establishment clause and upheld the New Jersey law, which provided bus transportation for Catholic parochial school students at public expense. Justice Black claimed that this New Jersey law did not violate the establishment clause of the 1st Amendment.

Justice Black wrote the following rules to guide decisions about the establishment clause:

Governments are not allowed, under the Constitution, to support or prohibit the practice of religion. In the Everson *case, however, the Court decided that local governments could provide bus transportation for students in Catholic schools.*

Neither a state nor the Federal Government can set up a church. Neither can pass laws which aid one religion, aid all religions, or prefer one religion over another. Neither can force nor influence a person to go to or remain away from church against his will or force him to profess a belief or disbelief in any religion.... In the words of Jefferson, the clause against establishment of religion by law was intended to erect "a wall of separation between Church and State."

Justice Black concluded that the New Jersey statute at issue in this case did not violate the 1st Amendment because public payment for bus transportation of parochial school students had nothing to do with government promoting religion. Rather, this was only a program for moving children safely and easily to and from school, regardless of the religion or school of the children.

Dissent Justice Robert Jackson wrote that he agreed totally with the Court's rules for deciding what is an "establishment of religion." But he disagreed with the Court's conclusion that the *Everson* case did not fit these rules.

Justice Wiley Rutledge wrote a second dissenting opinion that also agreed with Black's rules and held that the New Jersey law *was* an example of an "establishment of religion." He concluded, "The [1st] Amendment's purpose... was to create a complete and permanent separation of the spheres of religious activity and civil authority by comprehensively forbidding every form of public aid or support for religion."

Significance The *Everson* case was the first to apply the establishment clause of the 1st Amendment to the states through the 14th Amendment. And it set standards to guide interpretation of the establishment clause that have been used to resolve later controversies, such as *Engel* v. *Vitale* (1962)

and *Abington School District* v. *Schempp* (1963).

SEE ALSO

Abington School District v. Schempp (1963); Establishment clause; Engel v. Vitale; Religious issues under the Constitution

FURTHER READING

Miller, William Lee. *The First Liberty: Religion and the American Republic*. New York: Paragon House, 1985.

Exclusionary rule

EVIDENCE OBTAINED in violation of a person's constitutional rights cannot be used to prosecute the person. This restriction on the use of evidence obtained illegally is called the exclusionary rule, which was created in *Weeks* v. *United States* (1914). The Court applied the exclusionary rule to a state government for the first time in *Mapp* v. *Ohio* (1961).

The 4th Amendment to the Constitution protects individuals "against unreasonable searches and seizures" by government officials and provides that "no warrants [for searches and seizures] shall issue, but upon probable cause." If government officials seize evidence without a warrant, for example, it usually is excluded, or thrown out, from the legal proceedings against a person accused of a crime. However, in *United States* v. *Leon* (1984), the Court established a "good faith" exception to the exclusionary rule. This means that evidence seized on the basis of a mistakenly issued search warrant can still be used in a trial, if the warrant was issued on good faith—the belief that there were valid reasons for issuing it.

SEE ALSO

Mapp v. Ohio; Searches and seizures; United States v. Leon; Weeks v. United States

President Richard Nixon meets with advisers in the Oval Office. Nixon tape recorded his conversations and later claimed he could withhold the tapes from the courts because of executive privilege.

Executive privilege

FROM TIME to time, Presidents of the United States have claimed the executive privilege of withholding information from Congress, the federal courts, or the general public. Executive privilege has been justified as necessary to protect national security against foreign enemies. President George Washington, for example, kept information on the Jay Treaty from the House of Representatives on behalf of the national interest.

In general, the U.S. Supreme Court has respected executive privilege. But the Court has insisted that executive privilege is not absolute and that the chief executive, under particular circumstances, may be required to disclose information in a judicial or congressional investigation.

In *United States* v. *Nixon* (1974), for instance, the Court ruled that President Richard Nixon was required, despite his claim of executive privilege, to give up to a special prosecutor tape recordings that were sought as evidence against Presidential assistants charged with criminal behavior. Writing for the court, Chief Justice Warren Burger upheld the general claim of executive privilege, while denying its use to President Nixon in this case.

SEE ALSO
United States v. Nixon

Ex parte

WHEN THE Latin phrase *ex parte* (meaning "from the part of") is used in the title of a court case, it means that the action was taken on behalf of the person named in the title of the case. It does not require the notification of or participation by an opposing party. For example, *Ex parte Milligan* (1866) was a legal action taken to the U.S. Supreme Court on behalf of Lambdin P. Milligan by his attorney. Milligan was in jail when the Supreme Court decided his case. He had been sentenced to death by a U.S. military court for treason against the United States during the Civil War. The Supreme Court ruled that the military court had no jurisdiction in this case, and Milligan was released.

Ex parte Milligan

☆ *4 Wall. 2 (1866)*
☆ *Vote: 9–0*
☆ *For the Court: Davis*

IN 1864, the general in command of the military district of Indiana arrested Lambdin P. Milligan. The Civil War still raged in other parts of the country. Federal agents alleged they had evidence of a conspiracy by Milligan and others to release and arm rebel prisoners so they could take part in a Confederate invasion of Indiana.

The army brought Milligan before a special military court instead of before the regular civil courts that were still operating in Indiana. The military court convicted Milligan of conspiracy and sentenced him to death.

Early in the Civil War, President Abraham Lincoln had placed some sections of the country under military rule and replaced civilian courts with military courts to try individuals accused of insurrection. Lincoln also suspended the writ of habeas corpus in such situations. A writ of habeas corpus orders an official who has a person in custody to bring the prisoner to court and explain why he is detaining the person. This basic civil liberty prevents arbitrary arrest and imprisonment.

Article 1, Section 9, of the Constitution says, "The privilege of the writ of habeas corpus shall not be suspended, unless when in cases of rebellion or invasion the public safety may require it." Lincoln believed that his order, later confirmed by Congress, was crucial to the preservation of the Union.

Milligan applied to a civilian court in Indiana for a writ of habeas corpus. He claimed his conviction was unconstitutional and asked for his right to a trial by jury in a civilian court.

The Issue The issue came before the Supreme Court in 1866, a year after the Civil War had ended with the defeat of the Confederacy. The appeal did not involve the question of Milligan's guilt or innocence. Rather, the Court dealt with the constitutional issue of whether the government in wartime could suspend citizens' constitutional rights under the 5th and 6th Amendments and set up military courts in areas that were free from invasion or rebellion and in which the civilian courts were still operating.

Opinion of the Court The Court ruled against the government on this question. It ruled that suspending the right of habeas corpus and trying civilians in military courts when there were civilian courts still operating violated the Constitution.

The Court declared that the civilian courts had been open in Indiana and that the state had been far removed from the battle zone. Thus, neither the President nor Congress could legally deny to an accused person a civilian trial by jury and due process of law as guaranteed by the 5th and 6th Amendments.

Significance The *Milligan* decision represented a great victory for American civil liberties in times of war or internal turmoil. The Court upheld the principle that civilian authorities should control the military even in times of great stress and emergency. Moreover, it reaffirmed that the right of citizens to due process of law remains absolute as long as civilian courts are operating.

SEE ALSO
Habeas corpus, writ of

FURTHER READING
Nevins, Allan. "The Case of the Copperhead Conspirator." In *Quarrels That Have Shaped the Constitution*, edited by John A. Garraty. New York: Harper & Row, 1987.

Ex post facto law

EX POST FACTO is a Latin term meaning "after the fact." Article 1, Section 9, of the Constitution prohibits the federal government from passing an ex post facto law, which is one that makes an action a crime even though it was not a crime when it was committed, or increases the penalty for a crime after it was committed, or changes the rules of evidence to make it easier to convict someone. Similarly, Article 1, Section 10, provides that no state shall pass an ex post facto law. The Constitution protects individuals by denying to the Congress or state legislatures the power to punish people by passing ex post facto laws.

Ex rel

THE TERM *ex rel* is an abbreviation of the Latin phrase *ex relative*, which means "on the relation of." When *ex rel* appears in the title of a case, it means that the legal proceeding was started by a government official in the name of the state or federal government but at the urging of a private individual with an interest in the issue of the case. For example, *Illinois ex rel. McCollum* v. *Board of Education* (1948) was a case brought by the state of Illinois against a local school board at the instigation of a private citizen, Ms. Vashti McCollum.

Federal district courts

THE U.S. DISTRICT COURTS have original jurisdiction in federal criminal cases and civil cases; that is, they are the first to hear these cases. They are the trial courts of the federal judicial system.

There are 94 federal district courts: 90 in the 50 states and the District of Columbia, 1 in the Commonwealth of Puerto Rico, and 3 in the U.S. territories. Each state has at least one federal district court. Three large states—California, New York, and Texas—have four federal district courts each. Nine other states have three federal district courts apiece. In addition, there is a federal district court for each of the three U.S. territories: Guam, the Northern Mariana Islands, and the Virgin Islands.

Approximately 650 federal judges staff the district courts. They are appointed by the President and approved by the Senate, as specified in Article 2, Section 2, of the Constitution.

SEE ALSO
Federal judicial system

Federalism

FEDERALISM REFERS to the division of governmental powers between the national and state governments. The Founding Fathers created a federal system to overcome a tough political obstacle. They needed to convince independent states to join together to create a strong central government. Writing to George Washington before the Constitutional Convention, James Madison considered the dilemma. He said that establishing "one simple republic" that would do away with the states would be "unattainable." Instead, Madison wrote, "I have sought for a middle ground which may at once support a due supremacy of national authority, and not exclude [the states]." Federalism was the answer.

Under federalism, both state and national governments may directly govern through their own officials and laws. Both levels of government derive their legitimacy from the Constitution, which endows each with supreme power over certain areas of government. Both state and federal governments must agree to changes in the Constitution. Both exercise power separately and directly over the people living under their authority, subject to the limits specified in the U.S. Constitution, the supreme law of the country. The Constitution and acts of the national government that conform to it are superior to constitutions, laws, and actions of state and local governments.

In the American federal system, the national (federal) government has certain powers that are granted only to it by the Constitution. The 50 state governments also have powers that the national govern-

The South Carolina State House in Columbia. The balance of power between state governments and the federal government has shifted over the years, as the Supreme Court has tended to make decisions that give the federal government more authority.

ment is not supposed to exercise. For example, only the federal government may coin money or declare war. Only the state government may establish local governments and conduct elections within the state. Some powers are shared by both federal and state governments, such as the power to tax and borrow money. Some powers are denied to the federal and state governments, such as granting titles of nobility and passing bills of attainder.

In the American federal system, the powers of the national government are limited. However, within its field or range of powers, the national government is supreme. The states can neither ignore nor contradict federal laws and the Constitution. The core idea of American federalism is that two levels of government (national and state) exercise power separately and directly on the people at the same time. Under federalism, the state of Indiana has authority over its residents, but so does the federal government based in Washington, D.C. Indiana residents must obey the laws of their state government and their federal government.

Federalism is a central principle of the Constitution, but the balance of power between the state and national governments was not defined exactly at the Constitutional Convention of 1787. Since then, debates about the rights and powers of states in relation to the federal government have continued.

In *The Federalist* No. 45, James Madison gave his vision of how federalism would work:

> The powers delegated by the Constitution to the federal government are few and defined. Those which are to remain in state governments are numerous and indefinite. The former will be exercised principally on external objects, as war, peace, negotiation, and foreign commerce.... The powers reserved to the several states will extend to all objects which, in the ordinary course of affairs, concern the lives, liberties, and properties of the people, and the internal order, improvement, and prosperity of the states.

However, the balance of power within the federal system—between the national government and state governments—has changed steadily since Madison's time. Through constitutional amendments, Supreme Court decisions, federal statutes, and executive actions, the powers of the national government have generally expanded to overshadow those of the states.

The development of national government power within the federal system was advanced initially by decisions of the U.S. Supreme Court under Chief Justice John Marshall. For example, the Court's decisions in *Fletcher* v. *Peck* (1810), *McCulloch* v. *Maryland* (1819), *Cohens* v. *Virginia* (1821), and *Gibbons* v. *Ogden* (1824) struck down state government actions that were judged in violation of federal law and the U.S. Constitution.

The Civil War (1861–65) established, once and for all, that in American federalism a state has no right to secede from the federal Union. In the wake of this war, the U.S. Supreme Court set forth the inviolable terms of federal Union in *Texas* v. *White* (1869): "The Constitution in all its provisions looks to an indestructible Union, composed of indestructible States."

During the 20th century, the Supreme Court has tended to make decisions that have diminished the power of state governments in their relationships with the national government. This trend was advanced strongly after 1937, in cases such as *West Coast Hotel Co. v. Parrish* (1937), when the Supreme Court began to uphold actions of the federal government to regulate economic activities in the states. During the 1950s and 1960s, the Supreme Court under Chief Justice Earl Warren upheld federal civil rights laws that restricted the actions of state governments to deprive racial minorities of individual rights. Further, in numerous landmark decisions the Court used the due process clause of the 14th Amendment to apply most of the federal Bill of Rights to state governments. These kinds of decisions have limited the powers of state governments in regard to the civil rights and liberties of individuals.

From 1995 to 2000, however, the Supreme Court made some decisions that favored the rights and powers of state governments over the federal government. For example, the Court ruled in *United States v. Lopez* (1995) that the federal government's commerce power did not extend to the regulation of gun possession by individuals near schools. Rather, this matter was left to the discretion of state and local governments. In *Printz v. United States* (1997) the Court struck down part of a federal gun control law that required local officials to do a background check on a customer before a gun sale could be completed. The Court held that the Constitution's 10th Amendment prohibits the federal government from controlling or commandeering certain acts of state or local officials that are conducted according to powers reserved to state governments. In *Alden v. Maine* (1999) the Court decided that the 11th Amendment prohibits private individuals from suing a state for violation of a federal law, in this instance the Fair Labor Standards Act of 1938. The Court again used the 11th Amendment in *Kimel v. Florida Board of Regents* (2000) to rule that another federal law, the Age Discrimination in Employment Act, could not be the basis for a private lawsuit against a state. According to the Supreme Court, such issues are to be resolved in state courts according to state laws.

SEE ALSO

Incorporation doctrine; Texas v. White; West Coast Hotel Co. v. Parrish

FURTHER READING

Drake, Frederick D., and Lynn R. Nelson. *States' Rights and American Federalism.* Westport, Conn.: Greenwood, 1999.

Elazar, Daniel J. *American Federalism: A View from the States.* New York: Harper & Row, 1984.

Goldwin, Robert A., and William A. Schambra, eds. *How Federal Is the Constitution?* Washington, D.C.: American Enterprise Institute, 1987.

Kaye, Judith S. "Federalism's Other Tier." *Constitution* 3, no. 1 (Winter 1991): 48–55.

Federalist, The

THE FEDERALIST, a collection of 85 papers, or essays, was written to explain and support ratification of the Constitution of 1787. Seventy-seven essays were first printed in New York City newspapers between October 27, 1787, and April 2, 1788. The complete set of 85 essays was published in May 1788 by McLean and Company of New York City.

Alexander Hamilton, the major author of *The Federalist,* wrote 51 of the 85 papers (Nos. 1, 6–9, 11–13, 15–17, 21–36, 59–61, and 65–85). James Madison wrote 29 essays (Nos. 10, 14, 18–20, 37–58, and 62–63). Illness forced John Jay to withdraw from the project, and he wrote only five essays (Nos. 2–5 and 64).

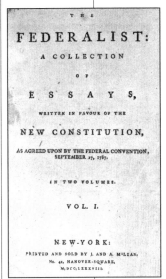

The Federalist *was first published in book form in 1788 after appearing as a series of essays in New York newspapers.*

Each paper was signed with the pseudonym Publius, after Publius Valerius Publicola, a great defender of the Roman Republic of ancient times.

The first objective of *The Federalist* was to persuade the people of New York to ratify the Constitution; each paper was addressed "To the People of the State of New York" and published first in a New York newspaper. A second objective was to influence Americans in all 13 states to approve the Constitution.

The authors submerged their political differences in the overall pursuit of a common goal—ratification of the Constitution. Madison and Jay agreed with Hamilton that the Constitution was "a compromise of... many dissimilar interests and inclinations." It did not exactly reflect the ideas on government of any one of the coauthors, but they agreed that it was the best frame of government achievable under the circumstances and far superior to the Articles of Confederation under which the country had functioned since 1781.

After ratification of the Constitution and formation of the federal government, Madison joined Thomas Jefferson in political clashes with Hamilton that led to the establishment of rival political parties: Federalist (Hamilton) versus Democratic-Republican (Jefferson/Madison). These conflicts, however, lay ahead. In 1787–88, Madison and Hamilton were a formidable team in defense of the Constitution.

Hamilton, Madison, and Jay readily agreed on the name of their projected series of essays, *The Federalist*. With this name, they scored a public relations victory against their opponents, who accepted by default the name of Anti-Federalists. This negative label connoted only opposition, with no constructive ideas to improve the government.

The authors of *The Federalist* agreed on certain fundamental principles of constitutional government: republicanism, federalism, separation of powers, and free government.

A republican government is one "in which the scheme of representation takes place" (*The Federalist* No. 10). It is based on the consent of the governed because power is delegated to a small number of citizens who are elected by the rest of the citizens.

In a federal republic, power is divided between a general (federal) government and several state governments. Two levels of government, each supreme in its own sphere, can exercise powers separately and directly on the people. But state governments can neither ignore nor contradict federal statutes that conform to the supreme law, the Constitution. This conception of federalism departed from traditional forms of government, known today as confederations, in which states retained full sovereignty over their internal affairs.

Publius proclaims in *The Federalist* No. 47: "The accumulation of all powers, legislative, executive, and judiciary, in the same hands... may justly be pronounced the very definition of tyranny." So the Constitution provides for a separation of governmental powers among three branches, according to function. But this separation of powers is not complete. Each branch has various constitutional means to participate in the affairs of the other branches, to check and balance their powers, and to prevent one branch of the government from dominating the others.

Republicanism, federalism, and separation of powers are all characteristics of free government. According to *The Federalist,* free government is popular government, limited by the supreme law of the Constitution, established to protect the security, liberty, and property of individuals. A free government is powerful enough to provide protection against external and internal threats and limited enough to prevent tyranny in any form. In particular, free government is designed to guard against the most insidious danger of government by the people—the tyranny of the majority over minorities. This principle applies equally to constitutional protection of religious, ethnic, racial, or other minority groups.

Since its publication in 1788, *The Federalist* has been viewed as an extraordinary work about the principles and practice of constitutional government. *The Federalist* is "the best commentary on the principles of government which ever was written," wrote Thomas Jefferson to James Madison (Nov. 18, 1788). Chief Justice John Marshall agreed in this instance with Jefferson, his longtime political opponent. In *McCulloch v. Maryland* (1819), John Marshall wrote that *The Federalist* was "entitled to great respect [by courts] expounding the Constitution." Moreover, he wrote in *Cohens v. Virginia* (1821): "[*The Federalist*] is a complete commentary on our Constitution, and it is appealed to by all parties in the questions to which that instrument gave birth." Ever since the founding period, lawyers, judges, politicians, and scholars have used *The Federalist* to guide their decisions about issues of constitutional government.

SEE ALSO

Constitutional democracy; Constitutionalism; Federalism; Republicanism; Separation of powers

FURTHER READING

Carey, George. *The Federalist: Design for a Constitutional Republic.* Urbana: University of Illinois Press, 1989.
Hamilton, Alexander, James Madison, and John Jay. *The Federalist Papers.* Edited by Clinton Rossiter. New York: Mentor, 1999.

Federal Judicial Center

S E E Administration of federal courts

Federal judicial system

THE JUDICIAL SYSTEM of the United States has three levels: the Supreme Court at the top, the 13 Courts of Appeals in the middle, and the 94 district courts and several specialized courts at the bottom.

The district courts are the courts of original jurisdiction, or trial courts. There are from one to four districts in each state, one in the District of Columbia, one in the Commonwealth of Puerto Rico, and one in each of the three U.S. territories.

The lowest level of the federal judicial system also includes specialized courts. For example, the Court of Claims hears cases involving monetary claims against the United States. The Court of Military Appeals hears appeals of courts-martial, or military trials, of people in the U.S. armed forces. The Tax Court hears cases regarding federal taxes. The Court of Customs and Patent Appeals hears cases involving international trade and claims about the legality of patents (legal assurances of ownership rights granted by the government to inventors).

The 13 Courts of Appeals have appellate jurisdiction; that is, they hear cases on appeal from the federal district courts and other lower courts. There is one U.S. Court of Appeals for each of 11 geographical regions (circuits) of the United States. They are numbered 1 through 11. In addition, there is a U.S. Court of Appeals for the District of Columbia and a U.S. Court of Appeals for the Federal Circuit, which hears cases on appeal from specialized lower courts.

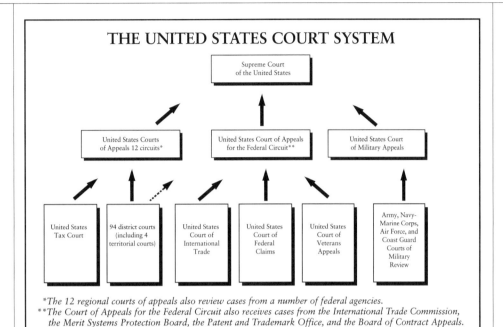

THE UNITED STATES COURT SYSTEM

*The 12 regional courts of appeals also review cases from a number of federal agencies.
**The Court of Appeals for the Federal Circuit also receives cases from the International Trade Commission, the Merit Systems Protection Board, the Patent and Trademark Office, and the Board of Contract Appeals.

The U.S. Supreme Court is primarily an appellate court of last resort. It hears appeals from the federal courts of appeals and the highest state courts in cases involving federal issues or questions, such as claims that a state government action conflicts with the U.S. Constitution or federal law.

SEE ALSO

Circuit Courts of Appeals; Courts of Appeals; Federal district courts

FURTHER READING

Carp, Robert A., and Ronald Stidham. *The Federal Courts.* Washington, D.C.: Congressional Quarterly Press, 1991.

Field, Stephen Johnson

ASSOCIATE JUSTICE, 1863–97

☆ *Born: Nov. 4, 1816, Haddam, Conn.*
☆ *Education: Williams College, B.A., 1837; studied law privately*
☆ *Previous government service: California House of Representatives, 1850–51; justice, California Supreme Court, 1857–63*
☆ *Appointed by President Abraham Lincoln Mar. 6, 1863, to a newly created position on the Court*

☆ *Supreme Court term: confirmed by the Senate Mar. 10, 1863, by a voice vote; retired Dec. 1, 1897*
☆ *Died: Apr. 9, 1899, Washington, D.C.*

STEPHEN FIELD served more than 34 years on the Supreme Court, longer than any other justice except William O. Douglas. During Field's long term, he was a strong supporter of the property rights of individuals.

Justice Field was the Court's leader in using the due process clause of the 14th Amendment to prohibit state governments from regulating or interfering with the property rights of corporations and other businesses or industries. Justice Field viewed a corporation as an individual that could not be deprived of its rights by state governments because of the protection of individual rights guaranteed by Section 1 of the 14th Amendment.

Justice Field and his followers on the Court did not, however, show an equal concern for the rights of people, especially black people, for whose protection the 14th Amendment was drafted and ratified in 1868. They consistently voted as a majority to deny these individual rights to African Americans. Field, for example, voted with the Court's majority in *Plessy* v. *Ferguson* to establish the "separate but equal" doctrine. That doctrine remained the legal basis for racial segregation in the United States until it was overturned in 1954 by the Court's decision in *Brown* v. *Board of Education*. Justice Field argued that the "equal protection of the laws" required by the 14th Amendment required only equal treatment of people, not their freedom of choice.

In the 1890s, Field's ability to work declined as he became disabled by illness and the infirmities of advanced age. His colleagues repeatedly asked him to retire, but Field refused because he wanted to surpass John Marshall's record for length of service on the Court. He finally retired in 1897, but only after barely exceeding Chief Justice Marshall's record of service of 34 years and five months.

FURTHER READING

Kens, Paul. *Justice Stephen Field: Shaping Liberty from the Gold Rush to the Gilded Age.* Lawrence: University Press of Kansas, 1997.

Swisher, Carl B. *Stephen J. Field: Craftsman of the Law.* Washington, D.C.: Brookings Institution, 1930.

First Monday in October

S E E Opening Day

Fletcher v. Peck

☆ *6 Cranch 87 (1810)*
☆ *Vote: 4–1*
☆ *For the Court: Marshall*
☆ *Dissenting: Johnson in part*

IN 1795 the state of Georgia sold 35 million acres in the Yazoo area to four land companies. However, the authorization of the land sales was tainted by fraud and bribery involving important members of the state legislature who were voted out of office in 1796. New members of the Georgia legislature promptly acted to repeal the statute that had authorized the Yazoo land sales. The 1796 legislation invalidated all property rights gained from the Yazoo Land Act of 1795. People who had purchased Yazoo land under the 1795 statute, however, continued to sell this land to third parties. In 1803 John Peck sold 15,000 acres of Yazoo land to Robert Fletcher. Then Fletcher sued Peck for selling him land that was not his to sell.

The Issue Chief Justice John Marshall avoided any discussion of the reasons for the Georgia legislature's action in repealing the 1795 land act. He said that charges of political corruption associated with land titles and sales were a matter for the state government to decide. According to Marshall, the only question before the U.S. Supreme Court was whether the state legislature could deprive investors of land they had acquired under the corrupt grant authorized by the 1795 law. Was depriving investors of this land, by repealing the land grant that had authorized their purchase of it, a violation of the contract clause of Article 1, Section 10, of the U.S. Constitution?

Opinion of the Court Writing for the Court, Chief Justice John Marshall held that the Georgia legislature's act repealing the Yazoo land grant law was unconstitutional because it violated the contract clause of Article 1, Section 10, of the Constitution. That clause says, "No State shall...pass any...Law impairing the Obligation of Contracts." Thus, concluded Marshall, a state government could not make laws that impaired contracts or interfered with land titles acquired in good faith.

Significance This decision was a legal blow against advocates of stronger state powers and rights within the federal system. Chief Justice Marshall emphatically asserted the right of the U.S. Supreme Court to review and strike down a state law as unconstitutional. Further, Marshall established that contracts and property rights would be protected by the federal courts against state government interference. This constitutional protection of an individual's property rights and contracts encouraged large-scale economic development of the nation.

SEE ALSO

Contract clause; Federalism

Fortas, Abe

ASSOCIATE JUSTICE, 1965–69

☆ *Born: June 19, 1910, Memphis, Tenn.*
☆ *Education: Southwestern College, B.A., 1930; Yale Law School, LL.B., 1933*
☆ *Previous government service: assistant director, corporate reorganization study, Securities and Exchange Commission, 1934–37; assistant director, public utilities commission, Securities and Exchange Commission, 1938–39; counsel to the bituminous coal division, Department of the Interior, 1939–41; director, Division of Power, Department of the Interior, 1941–42; undersecretary of the interior, 1942–46*
☆ *Appointed by President Lyndon B. Johnson July 28, 1965; replaced Arthur J. Goldberg, who resigned*
☆ *Supreme Court term: confirmed by the Senate Aug. 11, 1965, by a voice vote; resigned May 14, 1969*
☆ *Died: Apr. 5, 1982, Washington, D.C.*

ABE FORTAS was the son of Jewish immigrants from England who settled in Tennessee. Through his hard work and intelligence, Fortas won scholarships to Southwestern College and Yale Law School and eventually established a very successful legal practice.

In 1948, Fortas successfully defended Lyndon B. Johnson, a member of Congress from Texas. Johnson's election victory had been challenged in court by his opponent, who charged that Johnson won through illegal procedures. Lyndon Johnson never forgot Fortas's help during a critical moment in his political career. After becoming President, Johnson appointed Abe Fortas to the Supreme Court to replace Arthur Goldberg, whom he had encouraged to resign by offering Goldberg the position of U.S. ambassador to the United Nations.

Abe Fortas had won national recognition two years before his appointment to the Supreme Court because he was the winning attorney in the landmark Supreme Court case of *Gideon* v. *Wainwright* (1963). This case established the right of a poor person to be provided with a lawyer by a state government in all criminal cases involving alleged violations of state law. This case reversed the Court's decision in *Betts* v. *Brady* (1942) and was a significant step forward in the gradual "incorporation" of individual rights in the Bill of Rights under the due process clause of the 14th Amendment.

Fortas showed a strong commitment to the rights of individuals during his brief term on the Court. His two most important opinions involved the rights of children: *In re Gault* (1967) and *Tinker* v. *Des Moines Independent Community School District* (1969).

The *Gault* decision extended to juvenile offenders due process rights of the 5th and 14th Amendments that were previously limited to adults. The *Tinker* decision expanded the 1st Amendment freedom of speech right to include "symbolic speech" expressed through the wearing of black arm bands by students in school to protest U.S. participation in the Vietnam War. Fortas argued that a public school's ban on this form of protest was a violation of a student's right to free speech, as long as this form of protest did not disrupt the functioning of the school or violate the rights of other individuals. Fortas wrote, "It can hardly be argued that either students or teachers shed their constitutional rights to freedom of speech or expression at the schoolhouse gate."

In 1968, Fortas's Supreme Court term came to an abrupt and unhappy end. President Johnson nominated Fortas to be chief justice, replacing Earl Warren, who was retiring. But many senators opposed this appointment, and Johnson was pressured to withdraw the nomination. During this controversy, critics of Fortas charged that he had acted improperly in accepting a large fee, raised by donations from friends and former clients, to teach a course at American University. Several months later, a *Life* magazine article claimed that Justice Fortas behaved wrongly in accepting a large fee from a former client in return for serving on a charitable foundation. The *Life* article also reported that Fortas had returned the money.

These charges influenced some members of Congress to discuss the possibility of starting impeachment proceedings against Fortas in order to remove him from the Court. Fortas strongly denied any improper or illegal activity, but he decided to resign from the Court and returned to private law practice. Thus, he was the first justice to leave the Court because of the threat of impeachment.

SEE ALSO

Gideon v. Wainwright; In re Gault; Tinker v. Des Moines Independent Community School District

FURTHER READING

Kalman, Laura. *Abe Fortas: A Biography.* New Haven: Yale University Press, 1990.

Shogan, James F. *A Question of Judgment: The Fortas Case and the Struggle for the Supreme Court.* Indianapolis: Bobbs-Merrill, 1972.

Frankfurter, Felix

ASSOCIATE JUSTICE, 1939–62

☆ *Born: Nov. 15, 1882, Vienna, Austria*
☆ *Education: City College of New York, B.A., 1902; Harvard Law School, LL.B., 1906*
☆ *Previous government service: assistant U.S. attorney, Southern District of New York, 1906–9; law officer, Bureau of Insular Affairs, War Department, 1910–14; assistant to the secretary of war, secretary and counsel, President's Mediation Commission, assistant to the U.S. secretary of labor, 1917–18; chairman, War Labor Policies Board, 1918*
☆ *Appointed by President Franklin D. Roosevelt Jan. 5, 1939; replaced Benjamin Cardozo, who died*
☆ *Supreme Court term: confirmed by the Senate Jan. 17, 1939, by a voice vote; retired Aug. 28, 1962*
☆ *Died: Feb. 21, 1965, Washington, D.C.*

FELIX FRANKFURTER was the only naturalized citizen of the United States to serve on the Supreme Court. He was born into a Jewish family in Vienna, Austria, and came to New York City in 1894, at the age of 12. He was unable to speak English upon his arrival, but he learned the language quickly and thoroughly. He graduated with honors from the City College of New York and Harvard Law School.

Frankfurter served as the U.S. attorney for the southern district of New York (1906–9), as a federal government official from 1910 to 1918, and then as a law professor at Harvard until 1939, when President Franklin D. Roosevelt appointed him to the Supreme Court. During his 23 years on the Court, Justice Frankfurter was an advocate of judicial restraint, the belief that justices should carefully recognize constitutional limitations and defer to legislative decisions, whenever reasonable, as the legitimate expression of the majority of the people. In line with his views on judicial restraint, Justice Frankfurter strongly opposed "total incorporation" of the Bill of Rights under the due process clause of the 14th Amendment, which was promoted by his colleague Justice Hugo Black. He argued, for example, that the framers of the 14th Amendment had not intended state governments to follow exactly the requirements of the federal Bill of Rights in dealing with people accused of violating state laws. In *Adamson* v. *California* (1947), he held that the 14th Amendment was "not the basis of a uniform code of criminal procedure federally imposed. . . . In a federal system it would be a function debilitating to the responsibility of state and local agencies."

Frankfurter was concerned with maintaining the vigor of state and local governments within the federal system. He deplored the trend toward an overwhelming federal government that tended to diminish the functions of state and local governments. He viewed this as a violation of the fundamental constitutional principle of federalism, which originally involved a substantial role for state governments within the Union.

Frankfurter retired from the Court in 1962 after suffering a stroke that greatly weakened him. He died three years later.

SEE ALSO

Federalism; Incorporation doctrine; Judicial activism and judicial restraint

FURTHER READING

Baker, Liva. *Felix Frankfurter.* New York: Coward-McCann, 1969.
Freedman, Max. *Roosevelt and Frankfurter: Their Correspondence.* Boston: Little, Brown, 1967.
Hirsch, Harry N. *The Enigma of Felix Frankfurter.* New York: Basic Books, 1981.
Kurland, Philip B. *Mr. Justice Frankfurter and the Constitution.* Chicago: University of Chicago Press, 1971.
Parrish, Michael E. *Felix Frankfurter and His Times.* New York: Macmillan, 1982.
Simon, James F. "The Antagonists: Hugo Black and Felix Frankfurter." *Constitution* 3, no. 1 (Winter 1991): 26–34.

Freedom of speech and press

THE 1ST AMENDMENT to the Constitution protects free expression through speech or press against suppression by the government: "Congress shall make no law. . . abridging the freedom of speech, or of the press." All 50 state constitutions contain guarantees of free expression similar to those in the U.S. Constitution. An additional protection for the individual's right to free expression comes from Section 1 of the 14th Amendment: "No State shall make or enforce any law which shall abridge the privileges or immunities of citizens of the United States; nor shall any State deprive any person of life, liberty, or property, without due process of law." The Supreme Court has used this section of the 14th Amendment to apply the 1st Amendment guarantee of freedom of speech and press to cases involving state and local governments.

The right to free speech and press means that individuals may publicly express ideas and information—including expressions generally considered to be unwise, untrue, or unpopular—without fear of punishment by the government. In this way, government officials may be criticized and new ways of thinking and behaving may be advanced. Forms of free speech include the use of symbols, orderly public demonstrations, and radio and television broadcasts. Freedom of speech is

The first issue of John Peter Zenger's New-York Weekly Journal *in 1733. The* New York Provincial Council later ordered that the Journal be burned because Zenger had printed criticisms of the New York governor.*

an essential characteristic of a constitutional democracy because by exercising this right, individuals can communicate opinions both to other citizens and to their representatives in the government. Through this free exchange of ideas, government officials may become responsive to the people they are supposed to represent.

The right to free speech stems from the right to freedom of the press established in England during the 17th century. At that time, however, the right to free speech was specifically extended only to members of Parliament. All presses had to be licensed until 1694, when the law requiring licenses lapsed and was not renewed. But controls on the press continued through prosecution for seditious libel, which is speech and writing critical of the government or public officials. In the British colonies of North America, several colonial charters and constitutions explicitly protected freedom of the press, but the right to free speech, as in England, was guaranteed only to members of the legislative branch of government.

The constitutions of most of the original 13 American states protected freedom of the press, but the right of free speech was again extended only to members of the state legislature. An exception was the Pennsylvania Declaration of Rights (1776), which guaranteed freedom of the press and speech to the people.

Proposals for a bill of rights in the U.S. Constitution, advanced in the first session of Congress by James Madison (June 8, 1789), included freedom of speech and press. These rights to freedom of expression became part of the Constitution's 1st Amendment, ratified by the states in 1791.

From 1791 until the early 1900s, the U.S. Supreme Court heard no cases regarding free speech and free press issues. Then, after World War I, the Court decided several cases arising from enforcement of wartime laws to limit freedom of expression that threatened national security. In *Schenck* v. *United States* and *Abrams* v. *United States* (both 1919), the Court upheld such federal laws, basing its decisions on its "clear and present danger" and "bad tendency" tests.

Not until 1925, in *Gitlow* v. *New York,* did the U.S. Supreme Court assert its authority to deal with free speech and press issues originating at the state level of government. Prior to *Gitlow,* the 1st Amendment rights of free speech and press were held to apply only to the federal government (*Barron* v. *Baltimore,* 1833). In *Gitlow,* the Court acknowledged for the first time that the 1st Amendment freedoms of speech and press were tied fundamentally to the ideas of liberty and due process in the 14th Amendment. Thus, the rights of free speech and press were viewed as part of an individual's liberty that, according to the 14th Amendment, could not be taken from any person without due process of law.

Since *Gitlow,* the U.S. Supreme Court has made several landmark decisions that have expanded free speech and press rights through limitations on state government power to restrain or interfere with these rights. Examples of key Court cases on free speech and press issues, originating in the state courts, are listed below.

• *Stromberg* v. *California* (1931): The Court struck down a California statute outlawing the display of a red flag because it symbolized opposition to the government. This state law was held to be a violation of constitutional rights to freedom of expression.

• *Near* v. *Minnesota* (1931): The Court overturned a state law that barred continued publication of a newspaper because it printed articles that

Protesters speak out against the Vietnam War in 1967. The 1st Amendment guarantees individuals the right to express their opinions and criticize government.

insulted racial and religious minorities and said nasty things about certain people. This law was held to be an example of "prior restraint" of the press in violation of the 1st Amendment.

• *New York Times Co. v. Sullivan* (1964): The Court ruled that the 1st Amendment protects the press from libel suits that result from the printing of articles that harm the reputation of a public official.

• *Brandenburg v. Ohio* (1969): The Court ruled that a state may not forbid or limit speech merely because it advocates the use of force against the government or the violation of the law. Rather, government may limit speech only when it is directly and immediately connected to lawless behavior. The Court departed from the "clear and present danger" doctrine used in *Schenck* v. *United States* and *Abrams* v. *United States*, which permitted government prohibition of speech that had a tendency to encourage or cause lawless behavior.

• *Texas* v. *Johnson* (1989): The Court decided that the state of Texas could not convict and punish a person for burning an American flag during a peaceful political protest demonstration. The state's action in this case, said the Court, violated the 1st Amendment's guarantee of freedom of expression.

Since the 1960s, the Supreme Court has also broadened free speech and press rights in cases originating at the federal

level of government. Examples of key cases are *Yates* v. *United States* (1957) and *New York Times Co.* v. *United States* (1971). In *Yates* the court ruled that to prosecute people for violating the Smith Act, which prohibited the advocacy of violent overthrow of the government, there must be proof of overt lawless actions, not just expression of ideas about illegal behavior. In the *New York Times* case, the Court prevented the federal government from exercising "prior restraint" to stop a newspaper from printing information about the Vietnam War that it wanted to withhold from the public.

Supreme Court decisions in cases originating at the state and federal levels of government have protected speech and press from prior restraint by government, from charges of seditious libel by public officials, and from acts by government to ban or restrict unpopular ideas in speech and print—such as antiwar protests, antigovernment protests, and burning of the country's flag.

Americans have great freedom to say and write what they please without fear of government restrictions. But this freedom has limits pertaining to the time, place, and manner of speech. For example, individuals certainly have the right to speak out for or against candidates competing to win government offices. But they may not use amplifiers to broadcast campaign messages so loudly that residents of a community are disturbed late at night, when most people are in bed. This kind of speech is restricted by law because it unreasonably "disturbs the peace" of a community (*Kovacs* v. *Cooper,* 1949). But the government may not make a law restricting freedom of expression because of the content of the speech. In the *Kovacs* case Justice Felix Frankfurter wrote, "So long as a legislature does not prescribe what ideas may be…expressed and what may not be, nor discriminates among those who would make inroads upon the public peace, it is not for us to supervise the limits the legislature may impose."

Further, individuals do not have freedom under the Constitution to provoke a riot or other violent behavior. In times of national crisis, such as war or rebellion, the government could be justified in limiting freedom of expression that would critically threaten national security. The individual's right to freedom of expression must always be weighed against the community's need for stability and security. At issue is the point at which freedom of expression is sufficiently dangerous to the public welfare to justify constitutionally its limitation in speech, the press, television, or radio.

Issues about constitutional limits on freedom of expression have challenged every generation of Americans and will continue to do so. When and how much should the government limit a person's right to freedom of expression?

The answer of some authorities to this question has been an emphatic affirmation of practically unlimited free speech. Justice Hugo Black was an advocate of unfettered free speech. For example, consider this excerpt from his dissent in *Dennis* v. *United States* (1951):

> [A] governmental policy of unfettered communication of ideas does entail dangers. To the Founders of this Nation, however, the benefits derived from free expression were worth the risk. They embodied this philosophy in the First Amendment's command that "Congress shall make no law... abridging the freedom of speech, or of the press...." I have always believed that the First Amendment is the keystone of our government, that the freedoms it guarantees provide the best insurance against destruction of all freedom.... [I] cannot agree that the First Amendment permits us to sustain laws suppressing freedom of speech and press on the basis of

Congress' or our own notions of mere "reasonableness." Such a doctrine waters down the First Amendment so that it amounts to little more than an admonition to Congress. The Amendment as so construed is not likely to protect any but those "safe" or orthodox views which rarely need its protection.

In contrast to Justice Black's view, Chief Justice Fred M. Vinson, in his majority opinion in *Dennis,* stated a more narrow view of free speech and press, which provides more room for restrictions by government in behalf of the public security:

> Overthrow of the Government by force and violence is certainly a substantial enough interest for the Government to limit speech. Indeed, this is the ultimate value of any society, for if a society cannot protect its very structure from armed internal attack, it must follow that no subordinate value can be protected.

An alternative viewpoint, which strongly supports freedom of speech while recognizing the need for limits, was written by Justice Louis Brandeis in *Whitney* v. *California* (1927):

> [A]lthough the rights of free speech and assembly are fundamental, they are not in their nature absolute. Their exercise is subject to restriction, if the particular restriction proposed is required to protect the State from destruction or from serious injury, political, economic or moral....
>
> To justify suppression of free speech there must be reasonable ground to fear that serious evil will result if free speech is practiced....
>
> [N]o danger flowing from speech can be deemed clear and present, unless the incidence of the evil apprehended is so imminent that it may befall before there is opportunity for full discussion. If there be time to expose through discussion the falsehoods and fallacies, to avert the evil

by the processes of education, the remedy to be applied is more speech, not enforced silence. Only an emergency can justify repression.

Brandeis's position—great latitude for free speech, with particular limits associated with the time, manner, and place of that speech—has been the prevalent viewpoint in the United States during most of the 20th century. This viewpoint, however, poses the continuing and complex challenge of making case-by-case judgments about the delicate balance of liberty and order, about the limits on authority and the limits on freedom that in concert sustain a constitutional democracy.

The latitude and limits of free speech are being challenged by new forms of communication, such as e-mail and the Internet. In *Reno* v. *American Civil Liberties Union* (1997), for example, the Supreme Court confronted the issue of federal government regulation of free speech via the Internet. The Court responded by striking down a 1996 federal law, the Communications Decency Act (CDA), which prohibited indecent messages through e-mail or on the Internet in order to shield children from offensive material. In this instance, the right to freedom of expression prevailed over an attempt to regulate it on behalf of the public good.

In *United States* v. *Playboy Entertainment Group* (2000) the Court ruled against a federal law that broadly limited the transmission of sexually explicit programs by cable television operators. The purpose of the regulation was to shield children from images deemed harmful to their healthy development, either by blocking transmission or limiting viewer access to hours when children were unlikely to be watching TV. The Court decided these regulations were too restrictive and thereby in violation of the 1st Amendment's free speech

guarantee. For most of each day, no one in the cable service areas could receive the programs, whether or not a viewer wanted to see them. The Court decided that a system in which viewers could order signal blocking for themselves without restricting others was "an effective, less restrictive alternative" to the federal law at issue.

The question of when and how to limit freedom of expression via new mass communications technologies is likely to persist, and the Court will continue to face challenges about the latitude and limits of free speech and press.

SEE ALSO

Abrams v. United States; Barron v. Baltimore; Brandenburg v. Ohio; Dennis v. United States; Gitlow v. New York; Miami Herald Publishing Co. v. Tornillo; Near v. Minnesota; New York Times Co. v. Sullivan; New York Times Co. v. United States; Prior restraint; American Civil Liberties Union; Schenck v. United States; Stromberg v. California; Texas v. Johnson; Tinker v. Des Moines Independent Community School District; Whitney v. California; Yates v. United States

FURTHER READING

Blanchard, Margaret A. *Revolutionary Sparks: Freedom of Expression in Modern America.* New York: Oxford University Press, 1992.

Curtis, Michael Kent. *Free Speech, "The People's Darling Privilege": Struggles for Freedom of Expression in American History.* Durham, N.C.: Duke University Press, 2000.

Eastland, Terry, ed. *Freedom of Expression in the Supreme Court: The Defining Cases.* Lanham, Md.: Rowman & Littlefield, 2000.

Hemmer, Joseph J. *Communication Law: The Supreme Court and the First Amendment.* Lanham, Md.: University Press of America, 2000.

Hentoff, Nat. *Free Speech for Me—But Not for Thee: How the American Left and Right Relentlessly Censor Each Other.* New York: HarperCollins, 1992.

Kennedy, Sheila Suess. *Free Expression in America.* Westport, Conn.: Greenwood, 1999.

Neuborne, Bert. "Cycles of Censorship." *Constitution* 4, no. 1 (Winter 1992): 22–29.

Powe, Lucas A., Jr. *The Fourth Estate and the Constitution: Freedom of the Press in America.* Berkeley: University of California Press, 1991.

Rosenberg, Norman. "Freedom of Speech" and "Freedom of the Press." In *By and for the People: Constitutional Rights in American History,* edited by Kermit L. Hall. Arlington Heights, Ill.: Harlan Davidson, 1991.

Smolla, Rodney A. *Free Speech in an Open Society.* New York: Knopf, 1992.

Free exercise clause

THE 1ST AMENDMENT to the Constitution states, "Congress shall make no law respecting an establishment of religion, or prohibiting the free exercise thereof." Through its free exercise clause, the 1st Amendment protects the individual's right to freedom of conscience and free expression of religious beliefs.

SEE ALSO

Religious issues under the Constitution

Fuller, Melville W.

CHIEF JUSTICE, 1888–1910

☆ *Born: Feb. 11, 1833, Augusta, Maine*

☆ *Education: Bowdoin College, B.A., 1853; Harvard Law School, 1853–55*

☆ *Previous government service: Illinois Constitutional Convention, 1861; Illinois House of Representatives, 1863–64*

☆ *Appointed by President Grover Cleveland Apr. 30, 1888; replaced Morrison R. Waite, who died*

☆ *Supreme Court term: confirmed by the Senate July 20, 1888, by a 41–20 vote; served until July 4, 1910*

☆ *Died: July 4, 1910, Sorrento, Maine*

MELVILLE W. FULLER was an active and loyal member of the Democratic party. He was also a successful lawyer who regularly represented clients in cases before the U.S. Supreme Court. When Chief Justice Morrison Waite died in 1888, President Grover Cleveland, a Democrat, chose to replace him with Fuller, who seemed to share the President's views about politics and constitutional issues.

During his 22 years as chief justice, Fuller guided Supreme Court decisions that supported racial segregation based on the "separate but equal" doctrine. He opposed government regulation of private businesses and of the uses of private property by individuals. In particular, Fuller believed that government had no right to regulate an employer's dealings with workers, such as setting rules about working conditions, payment of wages, or hours of work. These matters, according to Fuller, should be left to free bargaining between employers and workers. In *Adair* v. *United States* (1908), Fuller wrote, "The employer and the employee have equality of right, and any legislation that disturbs that equality is an arbitrary interference with liberty of contract, which no government can legally justify in a free land."

During his term on the Court, Fuller also served on the Venezuela–British Guiana Border Commission and the Permanent Court of Arbitration in The Hague, Netherlands. In these roles, Fuller worked for the peaceful resolution of international conflicts.

FURTHER READING

Ely, James W. *The Chief Justiceship of Melville Fuller, 1888–1910.* Columbia, S.C.: University of South Carolina Press, 1995.

King, Willard L. *Melville Westin Fuller: Chief Justice of the United States.* Chicago: University of Chicago Press, 1950.

Gibbons v. Ogden

☆ *9 Wheat. 1 (1824)*

☆ *Vote: 6–0*

☆ *For the Court: Marshall*
☆ *Concurring: Johnson*

IN 1807 Robert Fulton made the first successful steamboat run from New York City to Albany. The New York legislature soon granted Fulton and a partner the exclusive right to navigate the waters of New York State. In turn, Fulton and his partner sold Aaron Ogden the right to operate between New York City and the New Jersey shore of the Hudson River.

Meanwhile, Thomas Gibbons secured a license from the U.S. Congress to run two steamships between New York and New Jersey. Competition between Gibbons and Ogden became fierce. Finally, Ogden petitioned a New York state court to order Gibbons to discontinue his business. The state court decided in Ogden's favor, and Gibbons appealed the New York court's decision to the Supreme Court.

The Issue Gibbons argued that under the Constitution, Congress had complete power to regulate interstate commerce. Therefore, his federal license to operate steamboats remained valid despite the ruling of the New York state court. Ogden countered that the congressional commerce power applied only to the transportation and sale of goods, not to navigation. Therefore, he argued, his New York license should prevail and invalidate Gibbons's license. The case raised two issues. First, what did "commerce" include? Did Congress have the power under the commerce clause (Article 1, Section 8) to regulate navigation? Second, did Congress hold an exclusive power or did the states also possess the power to regulate interstate commerce within their boundaries?

Opinion of the Court Chief Justice John Marshall wrote for the Court, which ruled in favor of Gibbons. In doing so, it defined the term *commerce* broadly.

Commerce is more than traffic, the Court said. It includes all kinds of business and trade "between nations and parts of nations [the states]," including navigation.

The Court also ruled that should a state law regulating commerce interfere with a federal law, the federal law was always supreme. Consequently, the New York law giving Ogden his monopoly was invalid because it interfered with the federal law under which Gibbons had acquired his license.

The Court did not, however, resolve the second issue in the case—whether states could regulate areas of commerce Congress had not regulated. Nor did the Court decide whether the states could simultaneously regulate commerce that the Congress was regulating. These issues would have to wait several decades to be settled by additional Court rulings.

Significance The *Gibbons* case established a basic precedent because it paved the way for later federal regulation of transportation, communication, buying and selling, and manufacturing. In the 20th century, for example, the Court ruled that the commerce clause permits Congress to fine a farmer for producing a small amount of wheat for his own use in violation of the quota set by the Department of Agriculture. Little economic activity remains outside the regulatory power of Congress today.

SEE ALSO
Commerce power

FURTHER READING
Baxter, Maurice G. *The Steamboat Monopoly, Gibbons v. Ogden, 1824.* Philadelphia: Philadelphia Book Co., 1972.
Dangerfield, George. "The Steamboat Case." In *Quarrels That Have Shaped the Constitution,* edited by John A. Garraty. New York: Harper & Row, 1987.

Gideon v. Wainwright
☆ *372 U.S. 335 (1963)*
☆ *Vote: 9–0*

☆ For the Court: Black
☆ Concurring: Clark, Douglas, and Harlan

CLARENCE EARL GIDEON, a penniless Florida drifter, was arrested for the burglary of a Florida pool hall. At his trial Gideon asked for a court-appointed attorney because he could not afford a lawyer. The court denied Gideon's request, and he conducted his own defense.

The Florida court convicted Gideon and sentenced him to five years in prison. In his jail cell, using a pencil and pad of paper, Gideon composed a petition asking the Supreme Court to review his case.

"The question is very simple," wrote Gideon. "I requested the [Florida] court to appoint me an attorney and the court refused." He maintained that the state court's refusal to appoint counsel for him denied him rights "guaranteed by the Constitution and the Bill of Rights" in the 6th and 14th Amendments. The Supreme Court decided to review Gideon's case. Unlike the Florida court, however, the Supreme Court did not expect Gideon to argue his own case. Instead, the Court appointed Abe Fortas, a prominent Washington lawyer and a future Supreme Court justice, to argue Gideon's case. Fortas defended Gideon *pro bono publico* (for the good of the public), donating his time and money for the cause of justice.

The Issue The 6th Amendment states that "in all criminal prosecutions the accused shall enjoy the right...to have the assistance of counsel for his defense."

Despite the unmistakably clear meaning of this wording, the Supreme Court had ruled in earlier cases that in state courts, needy defendants had a constitutional right to court-appointed lawyers in only two situations: in cases involving the death penalty (*Powell* v.

Alabama, 1932) and in cases where special circumstances, such as youth or mental incompetence, required furnishing an attorney to assure a fair trial (*Betts* v. *Brady,* 1942).

Does the 6th Amendment right to counsel apply to all criminal cases? Does the due process clause of the 14th Amendment require states to provide lawyers for defendants too poor to hire their own attorneys? Or should the Court continue to follow the precedent set in *Betts* v. *Brady*? The Supreme Court asked the attorneys arguing the *Gideon* case specifically to consider whether it should overrule *Betts* v. *Brady*.

Opinion of the Court The Court ruled unanimously in Gideon's favor and did overrule *Betts* v. *Brady*. The Court held that the right to counsel was so fundamental that the 14th Amendment due process clause extended the 6th Amendment guarantee of counsel to *all* defendants in criminal cases.

Justice Hugo Black, who had written a dissenting opinion in *Betts* v. *Brady* 21 years before, now had the pleasure of writing the Court's opinion to overturn the *Betts* decision.

Significance As a result of the ruling, the state of Florida granted Clarence Earl Gideon a new state trial in August 1963. Represented by a court-appointed lawyer, Gideon was found not guilty. The Supreme Court's decision also caused states throughout the nation to review numerous cases. Defendants too poor to afford attorneys' fees, who had been tried without the benefit of counsel, received retrials. The courts acquitted many and released them from prison.

In this petition to the Supreme Court written from his jail cell, Clarence Gideon claimed that he had been denied his constitutional right to an attorney. The Supreme Court ruled unanimously in his favor.

The *Gideon* case reflected the emergence of a nationwide concern with equal justice for the poor. It recognized that, left without the aid of counsel, even intelligent and educated people have very little chance of successfully defending themselves in criminal trials. Most large cities and some states have public defender offices that provide free legal help to poor people in criminal cases. In other areas, trial court judges appoint private lawyers to represent poor defendants.

SEE ALSO

Betts v. Brady; Powell v. Alabama; Rights of the accused; Counsel, right to

FURTHER READING

Lewis, Anthony. *Gideon's Trumpet.* New York: Random House, 1964.

Ginsburg, Ruth Bader

ASSOCIATE JUSTICE, 1993–

☆ *Born: Mar. 15, 1933, Brooklyn, N.Y.*
☆ *Education: Cornell University, B.A., 1954; Harvard Law School, 1956–58; Columbia University Law School, LL.B., 1959*
☆ *Previous government service: law secretary, U.S. District Court, 1959–61; judge, U.S. Court of Appeals for the District of Columbia Circuit, 1980–93*
☆ *Appointed by President Bill Clinton June 14, 1993, to replace Byron White, who resigned*
☆ *Supreme Court term: confirmed by the Senate Aug. 3, 1993, by a 96–3 vote*

ON JUNE 14, 1993, President Bill Clinton nominated Ruth Bader Ginsburg to replace Justice Byron White on the U.S. Supreme Court. She was the second woman, after Justice Sandra Day O'Connor (appointed in 1981), to be named to the Court. She was the first Jew appointed to the Court since Abe Fortas was nominated by President Lyndon B. Johnson in 1965.

In 1960 Justice Felix Frankfurter rejected Ginsburg's application to serve as his law clerk. She had been an honor student at the law schools of two universities, Harvard and Columbia, and had strong recommendations from her professors. While recognizing her great talent, Justice Frankfurter explained that he did not want a woman as his law clerk. This rebuff inspired Ruth Bader Ginsburg to make her mark on constitutional law.

From 1960 to 1980 Ginsburg moved from a job as a federal district court law clerk to an appointment by President Jimmy Carter as a federal appellate court judge. Judge Ginsburg served for 13 years on the U.S. Court of Appeals for the District of Columbia Circuit.

Before serving as a federal appellate court judge, Ginsburg was a professor of law at Rutgers University (1963–72) and Columbia University (1972–73). From 1973 to 1980 she was an attorney for the American Civil Liberties Union (ACLU), where she started the Women's Rights Project. As an ACLU lawyer, Ginsburg argued six cases before the U.S. Supreme Court and won five of them, including *Reed* v. *Reed*, in which the Court struck down an Idaho law that discriminated against women in the appointment of estate executors. These legal victories greatly advanced the cause of constitutional rights for women.

In nominating Judge Ginsburg for the Supreme Court, President Clinton recognized her outstanding contributions to the development of constitutional law and the rights of women. "Over the course of a lifetime in her pioneering work in behalf of the women of this country," he said, "she has compiled a truly historic record of achievement in the finest traditions of American law and citizenship."

In her opinions for the Court, Justice Ginsburg has taken strong positions in favor of women's rights, civil rights, and 1st Amendment rights to freedom of expression. For example, she wrote the Court's opinion in *United States* v. *Virginia* (1996), which brought an end to the Virginia Military Institute's all-male admissions policy.

Gitlow v. New York

☆ *268 U.S. 652 (1925)*
☆ *Vote: 7–2*
☆ *For the Court: Sanford*
☆ *Dissenting: Holmes and Brandeis*

BENJAMIN GITLOW was a member of the Communist Labor Party of the United States, organized in 1919. He participated in the writing and distribution of a pamphlet published by his party called the *Left Wing Manifesto*. This pamphlet urged the people of the United States to rise up and overthrow their government and bring about a communist revolution. Gitlow was arrested and convicted for violating New York's Criminal Anarchy Law, which made it a crime to advocate violent revolution against the government.

The Issue Gitlow claimed the Criminal Anarchy Law was unconstitutional because it violated his constitutional rights to free speech and press. The 14th Amendment says that a state government cannot deprive a person of liberty without due process of law. Furthermore, Gitlow's lawyers argued that the due process clause of the 14th Amendment could be used to extend 1st Amendment rights of free speech and press to the states. Did New York's Criminal Anarchy Law deprive Gitlow of his constitutional rights to freedom of expression? Could the 14th Amendment's due process clause be used to hold state governments to the free speech and press standards of the 1st Amendment?

Opinion of the Court The Court upheld Gitlow's conviction and concluded that the Criminal Anarchy Law was constitutional. Justice Edward T. Sanford wrote, "[A] state may punish utterances endangering the foundations of organized government and threatening its overthrow by unlawful means." He concluded that Gitlow's pamphlet was not a mere discussion of ideas. Rather, it was "the language of direct incitement" to violent revolution.

The Court agreed, however, that 1st Amendment free speech and press rights could be applied to the states through the 14th Amendment. Justice Sanford wrote that "for present purposes we may and do assume that freedom of speech and of the press—which are protected by the First Amendment from abridgement by Congress—are among the fundamental personal rights and liberties protected by the due process clause of the Fourteenth Amendment from impairment by the states."

Dissent Justice Oliver Wendell Holmes, with Justice Louis Brandeis concurring, disagreed with the Court's decision to uphold the conviction of Gitlow. Holmes argued that the mere expression of ideas, separated from action, could not be punished under the "clear and present danger" doctrine that he had defined in *Schenck* v. *United States* and modified in his dissent in *Abrams* v. *United States* (both 1919). In his *Gitlow* dissent, Holmes followed his line of reasoning in *Abrams,* in which he stated that unless speech could be linked clearly with immediate violent and unlawful action, it should be permitted. Holmes said, "Every idea is an incitement. It offers itself for belief and, if believed it is acted on unless some other belief outweighs it." Further, Holmes said that there was no evidence that Gitlow's pamphlet was likely to incite violent revolution and that it posed only a remote threat to social order.

Benjamin Gitlow, a communist who advocated revolution, claimed that he had a right to free speech. The Court, however, upheld a New York law that made it illegal to call for violent overthrow of the government.

Holmes and Brandeis agreed strongly with the Court's conclusion that the 1st Amendment should apply to the states.

Significance This case was the foundation for the incorporation of the 1st Amendment under the due process clause of the 14th Amendment in order to limit the states' power to restrict the free speech and press rights of individuals. The incorporation doctrine has been used gradually to apply most of the federal Bill of Rights to the states. Furthermore, beginning in the 1960s the Court rejected the narrow interpretation of free speech expressed by Justice Sanford in this case. The broader interpretation of free speech, expressed by Justice Holmes in dissent, has become the prevailing position of the Court. Thus the *Gitlow* case is important because it provided a foundation for the future expansion of free speech and press rights of individuals.

SEE ALSO

Abrams v. United States; Freedom of speech and press; Incorporation doctrine; Schenck v. United States

Goldberg, Arthur J.

ASSOCIATE JUSTICE, 1962–65

☆ *Born: Aug. 8, 1908, Chicago, Ill.*
☆ *Education: Northwestern University, B.S.L., 1929; J.D., 1929*
☆ *Previous government service: U.S. secretary of labor, 1961–62*
☆ *Appointed by President John F. Kennedy Aug. 29, 1962; replaced Felix Frankfurter, who retired*
☆ *Supreme Court term: confirmed by the Senate Sept. 25, 1962, by a voice vote; resigned July 25, 1965*
☆ *Subsequent government service: U.S. ambassador to the United Nations, 1965–68*
☆ *Died: Jan. 19, 1990, Washington, D.C.*

ARTHUR J. GOLDBERG was the youngest child of Russian Jewish parents who settled in Chicago. He served less than three years on the Supreme Court, resigning to become the U.S. ambassador to the United Nations.

After graduating from law school, Goldberg became an expert on the legal concerns of labor unions. He often represented unions in legal disputes with employers. In 1961 President John Kennedy appointed Goldberg to be secretary of labor. One year later, the President named Goldberg to the Supreme Court.

During his brief term on the Court, Justice Goldberg supported the expansion of 1st Amendment freedoms of expression and association. He also backed the rights of individuals accused of crimes. In *Escobedo* v. *Illinois* (1964), for example, Justice Goldberg wrote the Court's opinion that overturned the murder conviction of a man who had been denied the 6th Amendment right to counsel during questioning by the police. Justice Goldberg also argued that the police had not advised Escobedo of his right to remain silent and had therefore violated Escobedo's 5th Amendment protection against self-incrimination.

After leaving the Court, Goldberg served for three years as U.S. ambassador to the United Nations. He then returned to the private practice of law in Washington, D.C.

Good faith exception

S E E Exclusionary rule; United States v. Leon

Grand jury

THE 5TH AMENDMENT to the U.S. Constitution provides that "no person shall be held to answer for a capital, or otherwise infamous crime, unless on a

This 1973 subpoena commands President Richard Nixon to turn over tapes of his private conversations to the grand jury involved in the Watergate investigation.

presentment or indictment of a Grand Jury, except in cases arising in the land or naval forces, or in the Militia, when in actual service in time of War or public danger." A grand jury is a group of 12 to 20 people convened to hear, in private, evidence presented by the prosecutor against a person accused of a crime. If a majority of the jurors agree that the accused person has committed a crime, an indictment, or formal charge, is issued. In this way, the government is empowered to proceed with its legal action against the accused person.

The grand jury is a means of protecting an accused person against hasty and oppressive action by a prosecutor for the government. In *Wood* v. *Georgia* (1962) the U.S. Supreme Court clearly described the value of the grand jury in protecting the rights of an accused person: "[I]t serves the invaluable function of standing between the accuser and the accused... to determine whether a charge is founded upon reason or was dictated by an intimidating power or by malice and personal ill will."

SEE ALSO
Due process of law; Rights of the accused

Gray, Horace

ASSOCIATE JUSTICE,
1882–1902

☆ Born: Mar. 24, 1828, Boston, Mass.
☆ Education: Harvard College, A.B., 1845; Harvard Law School, LL.B., 1849
☆ Previous government service: reporter, Massachusetts Supreme Court, 1853–61; associate justice, 1864–73, Massachusetts Supreme Court; chief justice, Massachusetts Supreme Court, 1873–81
☆ Appointed by Chester A. Arthur Dec. 19, 1881; replaced Nathan Clifford, who died

☆ Supreme Court term: confirmed by the Senate Dec. 20, 1881, by a 51–5 vote; served until Sept. 15, 1902
☆ Died: Sept. 15, 1902, Nahant, Mass.

HORACE GRAY was a notable legal scholar with a reputation for basing decisions on careful research. He believed in the separation of legal decisions from politics.

Justice Gray's most important opinion for the Court was in the case of *United States* v. *Wong Kim Ark* (1898). He interpreted the 14th Amendment to mean that anyone born in the United States, regardless of race or national origin, had a right to U.S. citizenship. Therefore, Wong Kim Ark, who was born in the United States to immigrant parents from China, had a natural right to citizenship that could not be denied by the government.

SEE ALSO
United States v. Wong Kim Ark

Grier, Robert C.

ASSOCIATE JUSTICE,
1846–70

☆ Born: Mar. 5, 1794, Cumberland County, Pa.
☆ Education: Dickinson College, B.A., 1812; studied law privately
☆ Previous government service: judge, Allegheny County District Court, Pa., 1833–46
☆ Appointed by President James K. Polk Aug. 3, 1846; replaced Henry Baldwin, who died
☆ Supreme Court term: confirmed by the Senate Aug. 4, 1846, by a voice vote; retired Jan. 31, 1870
☆ Died: Sept. 25, 1870, Philadelphia, Pa.

ROBERT C. GRIER was a schoolteacher and principal before becoming a lawyer. He was an active supporter of the Jacksonian Democratic party. President James K. Polk appointed Grier to the Supreme Court because of his loyalty to Democratic party ideas on government and law.

Justice Grier's most important opinion for the Court was the *Prize Cases* (1863), which supported President Abraham Lincoln's coastal blockade of Southern ports during the Civil War. Owners of ships and cargoes taken by the federal government as prizes of the war argued that Lincoln's blockade was illegal. Writing for the Court, Justice Grier emphasized the President's duty to preserve the federal union in a time of crisis as justification for the blockade and for the seizure of ships that violated the blockade.

Griswold v. Connecticut

☆ *381 U.S. 479 (1965)*
☆ *Vote: 7–2*
☆ *For the Court: Douglas*
☆ *Concurring: Goldberg, Harlan, and White*
☆ *Dissenting: Black and Stewart*

ESTELLE GRISWOLD, executive director of the Planned Parenthood League of Connecticut, provided information to married people about how to use birth control devices to prevent pregnancy. This behavior violated an 1879 Connecticut law, which banned the use of drugs, materials, or instruments to prevent conception. Griswold was convicted of the crime of giving married couples advice on birth control and contraceptive devices.

The Issue The defendant argued that she had a constitutional right to privacy that was violated by enforcement of the 1879 state law. Is there a constitutional right to privacy that prevents the government from intruding into certain areas of a person's life, such as his or

her choices and actions involving birth control? Could this constitutional right to privacy be applied to the states through the due process clause of the 14th Amendment?

Opinion of the Court
The Court struck down the 1879 Connecticut law as an unconstitutional invasion of the individual's right to privacy in personal relationships between consenting adults. However, the Court offered differing interpretations of the constitutional right to privacy.

Writing for the majority, Justice William O. Douglas said that the 1st, 4th, 5th, and 9th Amendments imply "zones of privacy that are the foundation for a general right to privacy." And, he wrote, the 14th Amendment allows these implications from the federal Bill of Rights to be used to limit state governments. That amendment states, "No State shall make or enforce any law which shall abridge the privileges or immunities of citizens of the United States; nor shall any State deprive any person of life, liberty, or property without due process of law."

Justice Arthur Goldberg argued for a broader view of the right to privacy by using the 9th Amendment: "The enumeration in the Constitution of certain rights shall not be construed to deny or disparage others retained by the people." According to Goldberg, the idea of liberty stated in the 14th Amendment protects personal rights that are not listed in the federal Bill of Rights. These additional rights, protected by the 9th Amendment, are "so rooted in the traditions and conscience of our people as to be ranked fundamental."

Justices Harlan and White presented concurring opinions based solely on the due process clause of the 14th Amendment. Justice Harlan argued that privacy

A couple enters a Planned Parenthood clinic in 1965. That year, the Griswold *case determined that the government cannot ban access to birth control information because that would violate an individual's right to privacy.*

is a fundamental right at the core of due process. There are two conceptions of due process: Procedural due process refers to the necessity of following the rules of the legal process. Substantive due process refers to unspecified rights that are included in the more general definition of due process as legal fairness. Justice Harlan used the idea of substantive due process to justify the protection of an individual's right to privacy from intrusion by the state government.

Dissent The dissenting opinions by Justices Hugo Black and Potter Stewart judged the 1879 Connecticut law to be flawed; Justice Stewart called it "an uncommonly silly law." However, both Black and Stewart argued that the 1879 law did not violate any constitutional right. Stewart wrote, "I can find no such general right of privacy in the Bill of Rights, in any other part of the Constitution, or in any case ever before decided before this Court."

Both Black and Stewart criticized the Court's majority for going beyond the Constitution to use their judicial power willfully to achieve a desired social outcome. Justice Black concluded, "Use of any such broad, unbounded judicial authority would make of this Court's members a day-to-day constitutional convention." According to Stewart, this unrestrained use of judicial power would lead to a "great unconstitutional shift of power to the courts" and away from the legislative and executive branches, the branches directly accountable to the people through regular elections.

Significance The constitutional right to privacy, affirmed in the *Griswold* case, has been used to support the right to an abortion against restrictive state laws, as in the Court's decision in *Roe* v. *Wade* (1973). This right-to-privacy position has, however, remained controversial.
SEE ALSO
Privacy, right to; Roe v. Wade

Gun control and the right to bear arms

THE 2ND AMENDMENT to the U.S. Constitution says, "A well regulated Militia, being necessary to the security of a free State, the right of the people to keep and bear Arms, shall not be infringed." This provision of the federal Bill of Rights was derived from the contents of the original 13 state constitutions. For example, the Virginia Declaration of Rights (1776) stated that "a well-regulated Militia, composed of the body of the people, trained to arms, is the proper, natural, and safe defense of a free State." The Pennsylvania Constitution of 1776 said, "The people have a right to bear arms for the defense of themselves and the state."

The provisions of the 2nd Amendment have raised many issues and arguments about gun control laws and the constitutional limits on the right of individuals to bear arms. Does the 2nd Amendment primarily protect an individual's right to bear arms and prohibit the government from making and enforcing gun control laws? Or does it primarily guarantee to individuals only the right to bear arms in connection with service in a state's militia forces? Does the 2nd Amendment apply only to the federal government, or does it also limit state governments? What has been the Supreme Court's interpretation?

In *Presser* v. *Illinois* (1886) the Court held that the 2nd Amendment applied only to the federal government and did not prohibit state governments from regulating an individual's ownership or use of guns. In 1983 the Court reaffirmed the *Presser* ruling by refusing

This ad, sponsored by Handgun Control Inc., calls for laws banning the sale and use of handguns.

to hear a case about an ordinance in Morton Grove, Illinois, that banned handgun possession within the city. The Court let stand a decision by the Seventh Circuit Court of Appeals, *Quilici* v. *Village of Morton Grove* (1983), which exempts state and local laws from 2nd Amendment restrictions. Thus, the 2nd Amendment remains one of the few provisions of the Bill of Rights that is not "incorporated" under the due process clause of the 14th Amendment and thereby applied to state governments.

The Court has upheld a federal gun control law, the National Firearms Act of 1934. This law required taxation and registration of sawed-off shotguns and automatic weapons. In *United States* v. *Miller* (1939), the Court ruled that the weapons controlled by the National Firearms Act had no "reasonable relationship to the preservation or efficiency of a well-regulated militia."

Since *Miller*, lower-level courts have upheld various gun control laws. Further, the government may regulate the type of weapon individuals keep. For example, individuals do not have the right to own or keep artillery or rockets for their private use. In *United States* v. *Hale* (1992), the U.S. Court of Appeals for the Eighth Circuit held that "it is not sufficient to prove that the weapon in question was susceptible to military use. . . . Rather, the claimant of Second Amendment protection must prove that his or her possession of the weapon was reasonably related to a well-regulated militia."

At present, state governments are not prohibited by the 2nd Amendment from enacting gun control laws. Legal issues about these laws have been left to the state legislatures and state courts to decide. State courts have tended to uphold local ordinances and state laws to regulate or control ownership of guns. In 1968, for example, the New Jersey Supreme Court (*Burton* v. *Sills*) upheld a

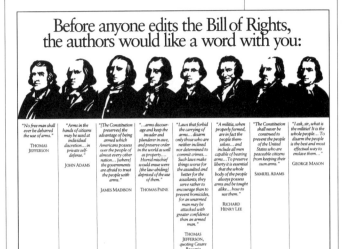

state law that required individuals to obtain permits and licenses for their guns. The New Jersey Supreme Court argued that the 2nd Amendment was "framed in contemplation not of individual rights but of the maintenance of the states' active, organized militia." Further, the federal Seventh Circuit Court of Appeals ruled in the *Quilici* case that the 2nd Amendment "had no other effect than to restrict the power of the National Government" in matters pertaining to "those arms which are necessary to maintain well-regulated militia."

SEE ALSO
Incorporation doctrine

FURTHER READING

Alderman, Ellen, and Caroline Kennedy. "The Right to Keep and Bear Arms." *Constitution* 3, no. 1 (Winter 1991): 66–73.
Cottrol, Robert J., ed. *Gun Control and the Constitution: Sources and Explorations on the Second Amendment.* New York: Garland, 1994.
Cress, Lawrence Delbert. "The Right to Bear Arms." In *By and for the People: Constitutional Rights in American History,* edited by Kermit L. Hall. Arlington Heights, Ill.: Harlan Davidson, 1991.
Halbrook, Stephen P. *That Every Man Be Armed: The Evolution of a Constitutional Right.* Albuquerque: University of New Mexico Press, 1985.
Malcolm, Joyce Lee. *To Keep and Bear Arms: The Origins of an Anglo-American Right.* Cambridge: Harvard University Press, 1996.

An ad from the National Rifle Association uses the 2nd Amendment to claim that government should not limit a person's right to bear arms.

Habeas corpus, writ of

ARTICLE 1, SECTION 9, of the U.S. Constitution states: "The privilege of the Writ of Habeas Corpus shall not be suspended, unless when in Cases of Rebellion or Invasion the public Safety may require it." The Latin term *habeas corpus* means "you shall have the body." A writ is a written order from a court of law that requires the performance of a specific act. A writ of habeas corpus requires officials to bring a person whom they have arrested and held in custody before a judge in a court of law, where they must convince the judge that there are lawful reasons for holding the prisoner. If the judge finds their reasons unlawful, then the court frees the suspect. The writ of habeas corpus is a strong protection for individuals from government officials who might want to jail them merely because they belong to unpopular groups or express criticisms of the government.

The privilege of the writ of habeas corpus is rooted in English common law and was specified in Section 39 of the Magna Carta (1215), through which English aristocrats imposed limits on the power of the king. Parliament enacted a habeas corpus statute in 1641, but because it was not entirely effectual, an amendment act was passed in 1679. The Crown was thus prevented from unjustly holding individuals in prison for personal or political reasons. By the end of the 17th century this individual right was solidly established as the appropriate process for curbing illegal imprisonment.

The English habeas corpus acts were not extended to the Anglo-American colonies. However, the writ was one of the widely recognized common law rights of individuals in the American colonies and was frequently invoked before the Revolution. After the Declaration of Independence, the privilege of the writ of habeas corpus was included in several state constitutions enacted prior to the U.S. Constitution of 1787. The Second Article of Compact of the Northwest Ordinance of 1787 also protected this right. The federal Judiciary Act of 1789 provided power to all federal courts "to grant writs of habeas corpus for the purpose of an inquiry into the cause of commitment." Every state of the United States of America has a similar law providing for writs of habeas corpus.

The U.S. Supreme Court has consistently upheld the individual's habeas corpus right, even when this right has been suspended by the federal government to guard public safety and security. In 1861, after the outbreak of the Civil War, President Abraham Lincoln suspended habeas corpus in parts of Maryland. This action was challenged in *Ex parte Merryman* (1861). Chief Justice Roger Taney, sitting as a circuit judge, ruled that only Congress had the right to suspend the writ, but Lincoln ignored the ruling. In *Ex parte Milligan* (1866) the Supreme Court decided that the writ could not be suspended in states (Indiana, in this case) where public order and safety were not endangered by the Civil War. In 1869 Chief Justice Salmon Chase wrote in *Ex parte Yerger* that the privilege of the writ of habeas corpus is "the best and only sufficient defense of personal freedom." Ever since the founding of the United

The Constitution requires that every prisoner be brought before a judge to determine if there are lawful reasons for holding him.

States, Americans have believed the writ of habeas corpus to be a primary protection of their personal liberties.

SEE ALSO
Ex parte Milligan

FURTHER READING
Yackle, Larry W. "Habeas Corpus." *Constitution* 5, no. 1 (Winter 1993): 61–66.

Hammer v. Dagenhart

☆ *247 U.S. 251 (1918)*
☆ *Vote: 5–4*
☆ *For the Court: Day*
☆ *Dissenting: Holmes, McKenna, Brandeis, and Clarke*

IN 1916 Congress passed the Keating-Owen Child Labor Act, which banned the interstate shipment of products made by child labor. This federal law applied to businesses that employed children younger than 14 years of age or employed children of ages 14 through 16 for more than eight hours a day or more than six days per week.

Roland H. Dagenhart's two sons, Reuben (under 14 years old) and John (between 14 and 16 years old), worked at a cotton mill in Charlotte, North Carolina. He did not want his sons to lose their jobs because of the federal law regulating child labor. So Dagenhart brought suit to prevent the federal government from enforcing the Child Labor Act.

The Issue The Child Labor Act was based on Article 1, Section 8, of the Constitution, which gives Congress power to "regulate commerce among the several states." Dagenhart claimed that the Child Labor Act was not a constitutional regulation of commerce. Rather, it regulated conditions of production at the workplace, a power reserved to the states under the 10th Amendment of the Constitution. Dagenhart also argued that the federal law violated the due process clause of the 5th Amendment by taking away his sons' liberty to work. Did Congress, in passing the Child Labor Act, exceed its power to regulate interstate commerce? Did the Child Labor Act violate the 5th Amendment rights of children desiring employment?

Opinion of the Court Justice William Day agreed with the federal government that child laborers need protection but said the state governments, not the federal government, were the proper source of legal regulation. In his opinion, Justice Day wrote that powers "not expressly delegated to the national government are reserved to the people and the states." This is an incorrect statement of the 10th Amendment, which does not include the word *expressly* but says, "The powers not delegated to the United States by the Constitution, nor prohibited by it to the States, are reserved to the States respectively, or to the people." Inclusion of *expressly* in a restatement of the 10th Amendment implies a narrow interpretation of Congress's commerce power and a broad view of powers reserved to the states, which is the position of the Court in this case. Day concluded that it was North Carolina's right to decide the appropriate age of child laborers or their conditions of work. Congress has no power under the Constitution to

Louisiana children, hired in violation of a state child labor law, shuck oysters for a few cents a day. The Court ruled in the Hammer *case that it was the responsibility of state governments, not the federal government, to regulate child labor.*

force child labor laws on the states. To permit it to do so, wrote Justice Day, would be to destroy the system of federalism established by the Constitution.

Dissent Justice Oliver Wendell Holmes argued for a broad interpretation of the federal government's power to regulate interstate commerce, which, he said, is "given . . . in unqualified terms, [and] the power to regulate [includes] the power to prohibit." Holmes also argued that the Constitution was designed to be adapted to "the felt necessities" and problems of different eras. The Court should interpret the Constitution, said Holmes, to respond to changing times unless the Constitution specifically prevents it from doing so. Holmes concluded: "The public policy of the United States is shaped with a view to the benefit of the nation as a whole. . . . The national welfare understood by Congress may require a different attitude within its sphere from that of some self-seeking state."

Significance The dissent of Justice Holmes eventually prevailed. In *United States v. Darby Lumber Company* (1941), the Court overturned the decision in *Hammer v. Dagenhart*. Justice Holmes's dissent in this case became the basis for the Court's decision in the *Darby* case.

SEE ALSO

Commerce power; Federalism; United States v. Darby Lumber Co.

Harlan, John Marshall
ASSOCIATE JUSTICE, 1877–1911

☆ *Born: June 1, 1833, Boyle County, Ky.*
☆ *Education: Centre College, B.A., 1850; studied law at Transylvania University, 1851–53*
☆ *Previous government service: adjutant general of Kentucky, 1851; county judge, Franklin County, Ky., 1858; attorney general of Kentucky, 1863–67*

☆ *Appointed by President Rutherford B. Hayes Oct. 17, 1877; replaced David Davis, who resigned*
☆ *Supreme Court term: confirmed by the Senate Nov. 29, 1877, by a voice vote; served until Oct. 14, 1911*
☆ *Died: Oct. 14, 1911, Washington, D.C.*

JOHN MARSHALL HARLAN belonged to a wealthy and prominent Kentucky family. They were slaveholders and participants in public affairs.

Harlan joined the Republican party and backed the nomination of Rutherford B. Hayes for President in 1876. President Hayes rewarded Harlan with an appointment to the Supreme Court in 1877. Harlan served on the Court for almost 34 years, one of the longest terms in the Court's history. He was known as the Great Dissenter because of his opposition to several important decisions.

Justice Harlan's most famous dissent was in response to the Court's decision in *Plessy v. Ferguson* (1896). The Court upheld a Louisiana law requiring black railroad passengers to sit in separate cars, apart from white passengers. The Court argued that this state law was in line with the 14th Amendment requirement of "equal protection of the laws" because black passengers were treated equally, though separately. Justice Harlan disagreed: "Our Constitution is color-blind, and neither knows nor tolerates classes among citizens." Harlan's dissenting opinion was vindicated in *Brown v. Board of Education* (1954), which struck down state laws requiring racial segregation in public schools. But at the time of *Plessy,* Harlan was the only member of the Court who had the vision of justice that would prevail later on, in the decisions of the Warren Court in the 1950s and 1960s.

SEE ALSO

Plessy v. Ferguson

Harlan, John Marshall II

ASSOCIATE JUSTICE, 1955–71

☆ *Born: May 20, 1899, Chicago, Ill.*
☆ *Education: Princeton University, B.A., 1920; Oxford University, Rhodes Scholar, B.A., 1923; New York Law School, LL.B., 1925*
☆ *Previous government service: assistant U.S. attorney, Southern District of New York, 1925–27; special assistant attorney general of New York State, 1928–30; chief counsel, New York State Crime Commission, 1951–53; judge, U.S. Court of Appeals for the Second Circuit, 1954–55*
☆ *Appointed by President Dwight D. Eisenhower Nov. 8, 1954; replaced Robert Jackson, who died*
☆ *Supreme Court term: confirmed by the Senate Mar. 16, 1955, by a 71–11 vote; retired Sept. 23, 1971*
☆ *Died: Dec. 29, 1971, Washington, D.C.*

JOHN MARSHALL HARLAN II was the grandson of Justice John Marshall Harlan, who served on the Supreme Court from 1877 to 1911. His family was wealthy and prominent and provided Harlan with the best educational opportunities. He studied hard and made the most of his opportunities, winning a prestigious Rhodes Scholarship to study at Oxford University in England.

A lifelong member of the Republican party, Harlan was appointed to the Supreme Court by Republican President Dwight D. Eisenhower. Two of Justice Harlan's most important opinions were written for *National Association for the Advancement of Colored People* v. *Alabama ex rel. Patterson* (1958) and *Poe* v. *Ullman* (1961).

Justice Harlan's opinion in *NAACP* v. *Alabama* was the first Court decision to include freedom of association within the 1st and 14th Amendment provisions for protection of individual liberties. His dissent in *Poe* v. *Ullman* argued for a right to privacy in marital relationships. Four years later, in *Griswold* v. *Connecticut* (1965), a majority of the Court generally agreed with Justice Harlan's ground-breaking views in the *Poe* case, affirming a constitutional right to privacy.

SEE ALSO

Griswold v. Connecticut; Privacy, right to

FURTHER READING

Przybyszewski, Linda. *The Republic According to John Marshall Harlan.* Chapel Hill: University of North Carolina Press, 1999.
Yarbrough, Tinsley E. *John Marshall Harlan: Great Dissenter of the Warren Court.* New York: Oxford University Press, 1992.
Yarbrough, Tinsley E. *Judicial Enigma: The First Justice Harlan.* New York: Oxford University Press, 1995.

Hazelwood School District v. Kuhlmeier

☆ *484 U.S. 260 (1988)*
☆ *Vote: 6–3*
☆ *For the Court: White*
☆ *Dissenting: Brennan, Marshall, and Stevens*

STUDENTS IN a high school journalism class were involved in the publication of a school-sponsored newspaper. Because the newspaper was produced in the journalism class, it was part of the school curriculum. The journalism students became upset when the school principal deleted two pages from an issue of their newspaper.

The deleted pages contained sensitive information about a student pregnancy and the use of birth control devices and about the divorce of another student's parents. The principal decided that the deleted articles were inappropriate for the intended readers of the school newspaper. But the student journalists claimed that their constitutional

The Supreme Court decided in the Hazelwood *case that school officials have the right to censor the school newspaper if there is a valid educational reason for doing so.*

rights to freedom of expression were violated by the principal.

The Issue Did the school principal violate the student journalists' 1st Amendment right to freedom of the press when he deleted their articles from the school newspaper?

Opinion of the Court The Court held that the students' constitutional rights were *not* violated in this case. Justice Byron White wrote the majority opinion. He argued that "the First Amendment rights of students in the public schools are not automatically coextensive with the rights of adults in other settings." The application of these rights to students in schools, therefore, must be tempered by concern for the special conditions and purposes of the school setting.

White held that a "school need not tolerate student speech that is inconsistent with its basic educational mission, even though the government could not censor similar speech outside the school." The school officials have the authority to regulate the contents of a school newspaper because the student journalists are producing this publication as part of the regular program of studies in the school. Thus, the school officials acted in their capacity as educators of these journalism students when they deleted material from the school newspaper.

Justice White concluded, "It is only when the decision to censor a school-sponsored publication... has no valid educational purpose that the First Amendment is so [involved] as to require judicial intervention to protect students' constitutional rights." In this case, the Court felt that there was a valid educational purpose for limiting the students' freedom of expression.

Dissent Justice William Brennan dissented in this case:

> In my view the principal... violated the First Amendment's prohibitions against censorship of any student expression that neither disrupts classwork nor invades the rights of others....
>
> [E]ducators must accommodate some student expression even if it offends them or offers views or values that contradict those the school wishes to inculcate....
>
> The mere fact of school sponsorship does not, as the court suggests, license such thought control in the high school, whether through school suppression of disfavored viewpoints or through official assessment of topic sensitivity. The former would constitute unabashed and unconstitutional viewpoint discrimination, as well as an impermissible infringement of the students' "right to receive information and ideas."

Significance This decision reinforced the opinion in *Bethel School District No. 403* v. *Fraser* (1986), which held that the 1st Amendment rights of public school students are not exactly the same as the rights of adults in other places. This narrow view of student rights in public schools also prevailed in *New Jersey* v. *T.L.O.* (1985), a case about 4th Amendment rights of protection against unwarranted searches and seizures of an individual's possessions.

SEE ALSO
Bethel School District No. 403 v. Fraser; Student rights under the Constitution; New Jersey v. T.L.O.

Headnotes

SEE Reporter of decisions

Heart of Atlanta Motel v. United States

☆ *379 U.S. 241 (1964)*
☆ *Vote: 9–0*
☆ *For the Court: Clark*
☆ *Concurring: Black, Douglas, and Goldberg*

THE CIVIL RIGHTS ACT of 1964 was the most comprehensive civil rights legislation passed by Congress since 1875. Title II of this law prohibited discrimination on the grounds of race, color, religion, or national origin in public accommodations involved in any way in interstate commerce. Its goal was to end discrimination in facilities such as hotels, motels, restaurants, concert halls, theaters, and sports arenas.

Congress based its power to regulate such businesses on the commerce clause in Article 1, Section 8, of the Constitution, which gives Congress the power to regulate commerce among the states. A case challenging the use of the commerce power by Congress to prevent racial discrimination reached the Supreme Court only a few months after the passage of the 1964 Civil Rights Act.

The Heart of Atlanta Motel in downtown Atlanta, Georgia, defied the new law by refusing to rent rooms to blacks. The motel owner claimed that Congress had exceeded its authority under the commerce clause by enacting Title II to regulate local businesses, such as hotels, that were open to the public.

The owner also argued that Title II violated his 5th Amendment rights. The 5th Amendment says that no person shall be "deprived of life, liberty, or property, without due process of law."

The motel owner claimed the new Civil Rights Act regulated his private property "without due process of law."

The Issue The case represented a major test of a key part of the new Civil Rights Act. The Constitution gave Congress the clear right to regulate interstate commerce. But did this commerce power permit Congress to prohibit discrimination in privately owned accommodations open to the public within a single state?

Opinion of the Court The Supreme Court unanimously upheld Title II of the Civil Rights Act as a legitimate exercise of the commerce power. Justice Tom Clark, a former district attorney from Texas, wrote that the motel did engage in interstate commerce because it sought out-of-state customers by advertising in national publications and 75 percent of its guests were interstate travelers. Citing testimony from the congressional hearing on the act, Justice Clark pointed out that the difficulty blacks encountered in obtaining accommodations frequently discouraged them from traveling. The motel's discrimination therefore obstructed interstate commerce.

Next, Clark defined the meaning of the commerce power of Congress. He declared that Congress's power to regulate interstate commerce also gave it the authority to regulate local business that "might have a substantial and harmful effect" on interstate commerce.

Clark added that the fact that Congress had used its powers under the commerce clause to achieve a moral goal—stopping discrimination—had no bearing on the decision. "Congress was not restricted by the fact that the particular obstruction to interstate commerce with which it was dealing was also deemed a moral and social wrong," he wrote.

Finally, the Court rejected the charge that Title II violated the motel owner's 5th Amendment rights to private property. "In a long line of cases this Court has rejected the claim that the prohibition of racial discrimination in public accommodations interferes with personal liberty," declared the opinion.

Significance The Supreme Court's decision affirmed that Congress has the constitutional power to promote equality of opportunity and to prevent discrimination. The case greatly aided the cause of the civil rights movement of the 1960s, putting a solid constitutional foundation under legislative and political efforts to promote equal rights for African Americans.

SEE ALSO

Civil rights; Commerce power; Equality under the Constitution

Hirabayashi v. United States

☆ *320 U.S. 81 (1943)*
☆ *Vote: 9–0*
☆ *For the Court: Stone*
☆ *Concurring: Douglas, Murphy, and Rutledge*

ON DECEMBER 7, 1941, Japanese aircraft attacked the U.S. naval base at Pearl Harbor, Hawaii, and won a smashing victory against the surprised American defenders. On December 8, the United States declared war on Japan. A few days later, Germany and Italy declared war on the United States. Thus, the United States was drawn into World War II.

The U.S. government feared that the 112,000 people of Japanese ancestry (most of them citizens of the United States) who lived on the West Coast might be a threat to national security in wartime. On February 19, 1942, President Franklin D. Roosevelt issued Executive Order 9066, giving authority to military commanders to establish special zones in U.S. territory threatened by enemy attack. The order invested the military commanders with power to decide who could come, go, or remain in the special military areas. The President issued this executive order on his own authority, under the Constitution, as commander in chief of the nation's armed forces. On March 21, Congress passed a law in support of the President's executive order. On March 24 General John L. DeWitt proclaimed a curfew between the hours of 8:00 P.M. and 6:00 A.M. for all people of Japanese ancestry living on the Pacific Coast.

Gordon Hirabayashi was an American citizen of Japanese ancestry. Born in the United States, he had never seen Japan. He had done nothing to suggest disloyalty to the United States. Hirabayashi was arrested and convicted for violating General DeWitt's curfew order and for failing to register at a control station in preparation for transportation to a relocation camp, which had been established by federal law.

At the time, Hirabayashi was studying at the University of Washington. He was a model citizen and a well-liked student, active in the local YMCA and church organizations. Hirabayashi refused to report to a control center or obey the curfew order because he believed both orders were discriminatory edicts contrary to the very spirit of the United States. He later said: "I must maintain the democratic standards for which this nation lives. . . . I am objecting to the principle of this order which denies the rights of human beings, including citizens."

The Issue Did the U.S. government deprive certain individuals—Americans of Japanese ancestry—of their constitutional rights under the 5th Amendment? The amendment says, "No person shall be . . . deprived of life, liberty, or property, without due process of law." Did the

Japanese Americans on the West Coast read a notice about evacuation to internment camps.

national emergency of World War II permit the U.S. government to suspend the constitutional rights of Japanese Americans?

Opinion of the Court The Court unanimously upheld the curfew law for Japanese Americans living in Military Area No. 1, the Pacific coastal region of the United States. The Court ruled that the President and Congress had used the war powers provided in the Constitution appropriately. The Court also held that the curfew order did not violate the 5th Amendment.

Writing for the Court, Chief Justice Harlan Fiske Stone said that discrimination based only upon race was "odious to a free people whose institutions are founded upon the doctrine of equality." However, in this case, Stone said, the need to protect national security in time of war necessitated consideration of race and ancestry as reasons for confinement of a group of people.

Significance Gordon Hirabayashi spent more than three years in county jails and federal prisons for his refusal to comply with a law that discriminated against people because of their ancestry. However, he never accepted the judgment against him, and he resolved someday to overturn it. His new day in

court came in 1983, when he filed a petition in a federal district court to re-open his case. He eventually won his case, when the Ninth Circuit Court of Appeals ruled in his favor in September 1987. His conviction was overturned on the grounds of misconduct by the law enforcement officials who arrested and detained him.

Throughout his long ordeal, Hirabayashi, like most other Japanese Americans who suffered injustice during World War II, remained a loyal American. After his 1987 legal victory he said: "When my case was before the Supreme Court in 1943, I fully expected that as a citizen the Constitution would protect me. . . . I did not abandon my beliefs and values."

SEE ALSO

Korematsu v. United States

FURTHER READING

Irons, Peter. *The Courage of Their Convictions.* New York: Free Press, 1988.
Irons, Peter. *Justice at War.* New York: Oxford University Press, 1983.
Mydans, Carl. "Internment Remembered." *Constitution* 4, no. 1 (Winter 1992): 43.
Rauch, Rudolph S. "Internment." *Constitution* 4, no. 1 (Winter 1992): 30–42.

Hispanic Americans in the federal judiciary

HISPANIC AMERICANS constituted a mere 5 percent of the total number of federal judges in 2000. By contrast, non-Hispanic whites constituted 83 percent. There has never been a Supreme Court justice of Hispanic origin. In 2000, however, there were 9 Hispanic-American judges among the 179 authorized judicial positions on the U.S. Courts of Appeals. Two were appointed in 2000: Richard A. Paez to the Ninth Circuit and Julio Fuente to the Third Circuit.

Historical Society, Supreme Court

THE SUPREME COURT Historical Society, founded in 1974, is a private, nonprofit membership organization with the goal of promoting public knowledge about the history and current operations of the Supreme Court. One of its primary functions is obtaining grants to support research projects on the history of the Court.

The society has more than 2,600 members who support the organization through dues and additional contributions. The society's publication program also yields income through the sale of books and pamphlets. The society manages a gift shop on the ground floor of the Supreme Court Building, and it maintains the following web site: www.supremecourthistory.org.

Holmes, Oliver Wendell, Jr.

ASSOCIATE JUSTICE, 1902–32

☆ *Born: Mar. 8, 1841, Boston, Mass.*
☆ *Education: Harvard College, A.B., 1861; Harvard Law School, LL.B., 1866*
☆ *Previous government service: associate justice, Supreme Judicial Court of Massachusetts, 1882–99; chief justice, Massachusetts Supreme Court, 1899–1902*
☆ *Appointed by President Theodore Roosevelt as a recess appointment Aug. 11, 1902; nominated by Roosevelt Dec. 2, 1902; replaced Horace Gray, who died*
☆ *Supreme Court term: confirmed by the Senate Dec. 2, 1902, by a voice vote; retired Jan. 12, 1932*
☆ *Died: Mar. 6, 1932, Washington, D.C.*

OLIVER WENDELL HOLMES, JR., was the son and namesake of a famous Boston physician and writer. He, too, won lasting fame. As a young man, Holmes was honored for uncommon courage as a Union soldier in the Civil War. He was seriously wounded in battle three times. As an older man, Holmes became the most important legal thinker and writer of his time.

In 1881 Holmes published *The Common Law,* which has been recognized as one of the greatest works of American legal scholarship. In this book he developed a "realist" view of law and judging that emphasized "the felt necessities of the time." He argued that law is dynamic and adaptable to the changing conditions of people and their society. He wrote, "The life of law has not been logic; it has been experience."

In 1902 President Theodore Roosevelt named Holmes to the Supreme Court, where he served with distinction. During nearly 30 years on the Court, he wrote 873 opinions, more than any other justice. Holmes wrote so gracefully, forcefully, and cogently that many of his opinions continued to influence the Court long after his death, and several of his memorable phrases have often been quoted by judges, legal scholars, and historians from Holmes's time until today.

Justice Holmes's most notable opinions were written in cases about the limits and latitude of free speech. In *Schenck* v. *United States* (1919), Holmes, writing for the Court, said that Congress could restrict speech and writing that threatened the safety and security of the United States. He argued that freedom of speech was not unlimited: a person could be punished for "falsely shouting fire in a theater" and causing a panic. Thus, Congress could make laws to punish speech that posed a "clear and present danger" to the security and safety of people.

In *Abrams* v. *United States* (1919), Holmes wrote in dissent to support honest expression of ideas, including highly unpopular views, that posed "no clear and present danger." He expressed his famous "free market of ideas" viewpoint: "The best test of truth is the power of the thought to get itself accepted in the competition of the market." Thus, political protest and criticism are permissible and even valuable because these dissenting views challenge and test the worth of our most cherished beliefs and practices. Through free and open exchange of ideas, including unusual and unpopular opinions, we seek the truth and find ways to improve our lives.

Throughout his long life, which ended in 1932 at the age of 94, Holmes had faith in law as the best means to settle peacefully and fairly the unavoidable conflicts of human life. And he persistently argued, with considerable influence on judges, lawyers, and scholars, for a dynamic and realistic view of the law. Thus, law would always be molded to fit the changing needs of people and their communities.

SEE ALSO

Abrams v. United States; Schenck v. United States

FURTHER READING

Alschuler, Albert W. *Law without Values: The Life, Work, and Legacy of Justice Holmes.* Chicago: University of Chicago Press, 2000.

Burton, David. *Oliver Wendell Holmes, Jr.* Boston: Twayne, 1980.

Horowitz, Morton J. "The Place of Justice Holmes in American Legal Thought." In *The Transformation of American Law, 1870–1960.* New York: Oxford University Press, 1992.

Novick, Sheldon M. *Honorable Justice: The Life of Oliver Wendell Holmes.* New York: Dell, 1990.

Pohlman, H. L. *Justice Oliver Wendell Holmes: Free Speech and the Living Constitution.* New York: New York University Press, 1991.

Posner, Richard A., ed. *The Essential Holmes: Selections from the Letters, Speeches, Judicial Opinions, and Other Writings of Oliver Wendell Holmes, Jr.* Chicago: University of Chicago Press, 1992.

White, G. Edward. *Justice Oliver Wendell Holmes: Law and the Inner Self.* New York: Oxford University Press, 1993.

Hughes, Charles Evans

ASSOCIATE JUSTICE, 1910–16

CHIEF JUSTICE, 1930–41

☆ *Born: Apr. 11, 1862, Glens Falls, N.Y.*

☆ *Education: Colgate University, 1876–78; Brown University, B.A., 1881; M.A., 1884; Columbia Law School, LL.B., 1884*

☆ *Other government service: special counsel, New York State Investigating Commissions, 1905–6; governor of New York, 1907–11; U.S. secretary of state, 1921–25; U.S. delegate, Washington Armament Conference, 1921; U.S. member, Permanent Court of Arbitration, 1926–30; judge, Permanent Court of International Justice, 1928–30*

☆ *Appointed by President William Howard Taft to be associate justice Apr. 25, 1910; replaced David Brewer, who died; appointed by President Herbert Hoover to be chief justice Feb. 3, 1930; replaced Chief Justice William Howard Taft, who retired*

☆ *Supreme Court term: confirmed as associate justice by the Senate May 2, 1910, by a voice vote; resigned June 10, 1916, to become Republican party candidate for President; confirmed by the Senate as chief justice Feb. 13, 1930, by a 52–26 vote; retired July 1, 1941*

☆ *Died: Aug. 27, 1948, Cape Cod, Mass.*

CHARLES EVANS HUGHES served two terms on the Supreme Court, first as an associate justice (1910–16) and then as the chief justice (1930–41). He resigned from his first Court term to become the Republican party candidate for President. He lost to his Democratic party opponent, President Woodrow Wilson, by only 23 electoral votes.

Hughes served two Republican Presidents, Harding and Coolidge, as secretary of state. In this role, he negotiated several important treaties to limit international weapons buildups and promote world peace. He was a judge on the Permanent Court of International Justice when President Herbert Hoover appointed him to succeed William Howard Taft as chief justice of the United States.

Under Hughes's leadership, the Supreme Court actively protected the constitutional rights of individuals. In *Stromberg* v. *California* (1931), *Near* v. *Minnesota* (1931), and *DeJonge* v. *Oregon* (1937), Hughes used the due process clause of the 14th Amendment to deny state governments the power to abridge 1st Amendment freedoms of speech, press, and assembly. He also weakened the "separate but equal" doctrine on racial segregation. In his opinion for the Court in *Missouri ex rel. Gaines* v. *Canada* (1938), Hughes wrote that a state university had violated the 14th Amendment's equal protection clause by its refusal to admit a qualified African-American student to its law school.

During President Franklin D. Roosevelt's first term (1933–37), Hughes influenced the Court to reject key parts of the President's New Deal program that, according to the Court's majority, gave the federal government too much power to regulate or direct private businesses in their relationships with workers and consumers. Hughes also successfully resisted Roosevelt's court-packing plan, by which the President had hoped to add justices to the Court who would support his New Deal.

After 1937, however, Hughes began to support important New Deal legislation, to the delight of President Roosevelt and his supporters. It seems that Hughes recognized that the vast majority of the American people supported Roosevelt's

programs. They had voted overwhelmingly for his reelection in 1936. Hughes thus bowed to the election returns and ceased to be a major obstacle to the President's program.

Upon his retirement in 1941, Hughes was hailed as a great chief justice. In 1942 the American Bar Association honored Hughes with its medal for distinguished contributions to the law.

SEE ALSO

Court-packing plan; Near v. Minnesota; Stromberg v. California

FURTHER READING

Pusey, Merlo. *Charles Evans Hughes.* 2 vols. New York: Macmillan, 1951.

Hunt, Ward

ASSOCIATE JUSTICE, 1873–82

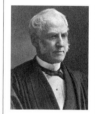

☆ *Born: June 14, 1810, Utica, N.Y.*
☆ *Education: Union College, B.A., 1828; Litchfield Law School, 1829*
☆ *Previous government service: New York Assembly, 1839; mayor, Utica, N.Y., 1844; judge, New York State Court of Appeals, 1866–69; New York State commissioner of appeals, 1869–73*
☆ *Appointed by President Ulysses S. Grant Dec. 3, 1872; replaced Samuel Nelson, who retired*
☆ *Supreme Court term: confirmed by the Senate Dec. 11, 1872, by a voice vote; retired Jan. 27, 1882*
☆ *Died: Mar. 24, 1886, Washington, D.C.*

WARD HUNT served only nine years on the Supreme Court. He regularly sided with the Court's majority, led by Chief Justice Morrison R. Waite. Hunt tended to oppose claims by African Americans for equal protection of the laws under the 14th Amendment. He also opposed extension of voting rights for women.

Justice Hunt departed from his usual position to be the lone dissenter in *United States* v. *Reese* (1876), arguing that the federal government had the power to coerce state governments to recognize the voting rights of African Americans guaranteed by the 15th Amendment. However, he returned to his usual position in *United States* v. *Cruikshank* (1876) and went along with the Court's position of indifference to the voting rights of African Americans.

Hylton v. United States

☆ *3 Dall. 171 (1796)*
☆ *Vote: 3–0*
☆ *For the Court: Seriatim opinions by Iredell, Paterson, and Chase*
☆ *Not participating: Cushing, Wilson, and Ellsworth*

IN 1794 Congress passed a law to tax carriages used as passenger vehicles. Daniel Hylton of Virginia refused to pay the tax, and the U.S. government sued Hylton for nonpayment of taxes.

The Issue Daniel Hylton said that the federal carriage tax was a direct tax of the kind prohibited by Article 1, Section 9, of the Constitution. Did Congress have the power to levy a carriage tax on passenger vehicles?

Opinion of the Court The Court upheld Congress's power to tax carriages used as passenger vehicles. The carriage tax law was an *indirect* tax, said the Court, and was not prohibited by Article 1, Section 9, of the Constitution. Justice Paterson wrote, "All taxes on expenses or consumptions are indirect taxes."

Significance This was the first time that the Supreme Court made a judgment about whether an act of Congress was constitutional. By upholding the federal carriage tax, the Court implied that it had the power to overturn it. The justices did not directly discuss the power of judicial review—the power of the Court

to declare an act of Congress unconstitutional, or in violation of the Constitution, and therefore void. However, they seemed to believe that they had the power to nullify acts of Congress that conflicted with the higher law of the Constitution. Justice Samuel Chase wrote that he would use this power of judicial review only "in a very clear case."

In 1803 Chief Justice John Marshall used the case of *Marbury* v. *Madison* to explain and justify the Court's power of judicial review of acts of Congress.

SEE ALSO

Judicial power; Judicial review; Marbury v. Madison

Impeachment

IMPEACHMENT IS the procedure, specified in the U.S. Constitution, by which members of the federal executive or judicial branches can be formally accused of wrongful behavior. The investigation of such accusations may result in their removal from office. According to Article 1, Section 2, of the Constitution, "The House of Representatives . . . shall have the sole Power of Impeachment"; that is, only the House can bring charges of wrongful behavior against a federal judicial or executive officer, such as the President of the United States or a justice of the U.S. Supreme Court.

According to Article 1, Section 3, "The Senate shall have the sole Power to try all Impeachments. . . . And no Person shall be convicted without the Concurrence of two thirds of the Members present." Only the Senate has the power to try the case of any person who has been impeached, or formally accused, by the House of Representatives. Conviction of the impeached person can be achieved only by a two-thirds vote of the senators present at the impeachment trial.

Article 1, Section 3, of the Constitution states, "Judgment in Cases of Impeachment shall not extend further than to removal from Office, and disqualification to hold and enjoy any Office of honor, Trust or Profit under the United States; but the Party convicted shall nevertheless be liable and subject to Indictment, Trial, Judgment and Punishment, according to Law." So, if a person is impeached by the House of Representatives and convicted by the Senate, that person will be removed from federal office and prevented from holding another federal office at any time in the future.

Only one Supreme Court justice has been impeached: Samuel Chase, in 1805, for behaving in a partisan manner. Justice Chase was an outspoken promoter of the Federalist party and an acid critic of the Jeffersonian Republican party. In 1801 Thomas Jefferson became President and the majority in Congress was made up of Jeffersonian Republicans. Justice Chase's flagrant anti-Republican behavior vexed many of the Jeffersonian Republicans, who were determined to strike back at him. The proper moment came in 1805, they believed, after the reelection of Jefferson and a Republican party majority in Congress. The House of Representatives voted to impeach Justice Chase. But the Senate voted not to convict him, and he remained a justice of the Supreme Court until his death in 1811.

The impeachment proceedings against Justice Chase set a precedent that a person should not be impeached and removed from office because of his political opinions. Article 3, Section 1, of the U.S. Constitution says, "The Judges, both of the supreme and inferior Courts, shall hold their Offices during good Behaviour." The key issue in Jus-

tice Chase's impeachment trial was whether expression of political opinions was a violation of the constitutional provision for holding office "during good Behaviour."

Was free expression of unpopular political opinions a legitimate reason for removing a justice from office? From Justice Chase's time until today, the answer has been a strong "no." Thus, the independence of Supreme Court justices has been protected against the changing tides of majority political opinion.

SEE ALSO

Chase, Samuel; Independent judiciary; Separation of powers

FURTHER READING

Berger, Raoul. *Impeachment: The Constitutional Problems.* 2nd ed. Cambridge: Harvard University Press, 1999.
Rehnquist, William H., and Cynthia Adams Phillips. *Grand Inquests: The Historic Impeachments of Justice Samuel Chase and President Andrew Johnson.* New York: Quill, 1999.

There were three unsuccessful attempts to impeach Justice William O. Douglas. This 1969 cartoon suggests that some members of Congress were upset with the judicial behavior of Justice Douglas.

Implied powers

THE CONSTITUTION of the United States delegates various powers to the three branches of government. For example, Article 1, Section 8, is a list, or enumeration, of powers that Congress may exercise. The final item in this list gives Congress the power "To make all Laws which shall be necessary and proper for carrying into Execution the foregoing powers, and all other Powers vested by this Constitution in the Government of the United States, or in any Department or Officer thereof."

This necessary and proper clause permits Congress to exercise *implied powers;* that is, to identify and use powers that are logical extensions or implications of the other powers delegated in the Constitution. For example, the doctrine of implied powers gave Congress justification for making a law to charter a national bank in 1791, even though this power is not specifically listed in the Constitution as one delegated to Congress. This power was implied as "necessary and proper" for the federal government to carry out its enumerated powers, such as borrowing money, regulating currency, and providing for the general welfare of the country.

The issue of the scope of implied powers under the Constitution was first confronted by the Supreme Court in *McCulloch* v. *Maryland* (1819). This case raised the issue of whether Congress had the power to charter a bank under authority of the necessary and proper clause. Writing for a unanimous Court, Chief Justice John Marshall favored a broad construction of Congress's implied powers that clearly included the power to charter a national bank. Marshall wrote, "Let the end

Regulating the airline industry is a government activity that the Founding Fathers could not have envisioned. Congress assumes this responsibility, however, as an implied power.

be legitimate, let it be within the scope of the Constitution, and all means which are appropriate, which are plainly adapted to that end, which are not prohibited, but consistent with the letter and spirit of the Constitution, are constitutional."

Chief Justice Marshall's viewpoint agreed with ideas expressed earlier by Alexander Hamilton in *The Federalist* No. 23. Hamilton wrote: "[I]t is both unwise and dangerous to deny the federal government an unconfirmed authority in respect to all those objects which are entrusted to its management [grants of power enumerated in the Constitution]." In *The Federalist* No. 44, James Madison wrote that the necessary and proper clause was essential to the effective operation of the federal government. He said, "Without the substance of this power, the whole Constitution would be a dead letter."

Ever since the founding of the United States, scholars, lawyers, judges, and political leaders have argued about the scope of implied powers under the Constitution. Since the decisive opinions of Chief Justice John Marshall, however, the doctrine of implied powers has been solidly established as an important source of federal government power under the Constitution.

SEE ALSO
Constitutional construction; McCulloch v. Maryland

Incorporation doctrine

THE PASSAGE of the 14th Amendment in 1868 established new restrictions on the power of state governments to deprive individuals of civil rights and liberties. Over the course of the 20th century, the Supreme Court has decided that the 14th Amendment incorporates or absorbs most provisions of the federal Bill of Rights, thereby applying these rights to the states.

Prior to the passage of the 14th Amendment, the federal Bill of Rights (Amendments 1 through 10 to the Constitution) was understood to restrict only the actions of the federal government. This common understanding was confirmed by the Supreme Court's decision in *Barron* v. *Baltimore* (1833), which held that the 5th Amendment could not be used to restrict a state or local government from taking private property for public use without providing "just compensation." Thus, following *Barron,* the 1st Amendment freedoms of religion, speech, press, assembly, and petition, for example, checked only the federal government, not the state governments, which retained power to deal with these matters according to their own constitutions and statutes.

In 1868 the 14th Amendment was passed, primarily to protect the civil rights and liberties of former slaves, who had been freed by the Civil War and the 13th Amendment, against state governments that might try to discriminate unfairly against them. Section 1 of the 14th Amendment says, "No State shall make or enforce any law which shall abridge the privileges or immunities of citizens of the United States; nor shall any State deprive any person of life, liberty, or property, without due process of law; nor deny to any person within its jurisdiction the equal protection of the laws." However, during the remainder of the 19th century and the first quarter of the 20th century, the Supreme Court tended to interpret the 14th Amendment narrowly and thus did not use it to enhance significantly the constitutional rights of former slaves or anyone else.

The first departure from this narrow view of the 14th Amendment came in 1897 with the decision in *Chicago,*

Burlington & Quincy Railroad Co. v. *Chicago.* The Supreme Court decided that the due process clause of the 14th Amendment required the states, when taking private property for public use, to give the property owners fair compensation. This right is also provided by the just compensation clause of the 5th Amendment to the Constitution. Thus, for the first time, a provision of the Bill of Rights (Amendment 5 in this instance) had been used to limit the power of a state government via the due process clause of the 14th Amendment.

The next opening for the application of the Bill of Rights to the states came in 1908 with the decision in *Twining* v. *New Jersey.* The court decided against application of the self-incrimination clause of the 5th Amendment to the states via the due process clause of the 14th Amendment. The Court stipulated, however, that the due process clause could in principle *incorporate* some rights similar to those in the federal Bill of Rights because they were essential to the idea of due process of law. The Court provided this guideline for future decisions about which rights were due each individual: "Is it [the right in question] a fundamental principle of liberty and justice which inheres in the very idea of free government and is the inalienable right of a citizen of such a government?" With this guideline, *Twining* v. *New Jersey* opened the way to future applications to the states of rights in the federal Bill of Rights via the incorporation doctrine.

In 1925 the door to application of the federal Bill of Rights to the states was opened wider in the case of *Gitlow* v. *New York.* Benjamin Gitlow had been convicted for violating New York's Criminal Anarchy Law, which made it a crime to advocate violent revolution against the government. He claimed that the state of New York had unlawfully denied his 1st

Amendment right to free expression under the due process clause of the 14th Amendment. The Court upheld Gitlow's conviction but acknowledged the doctrine of incorporation of 1st Amendment freedoms in the due process clause of the 14th Amendment and their application to the states. The Court asserted that for "present purposes we may and do assume that freedom of speech and of the press—which are protected by the First Amendment from abridgement by Congress—are among the fundamental personal rights and 'liberties' protected by the due process clause of the Fourteenth Amendment from impairment by the states." This idea was reinforced in *Fiske* v. *Kansas* (1927), in which the Court used the 14th Amendment to protect the free speech rights of individuals against a state law.

In 1931, the Court ruled again (in *Near* v. *Minnesota* and *Stromberg* v. *California*) that the 14th Amendment due process clause guaranteed the 1st Amendment rights of freedom of speech (*Stromberg*) and freedom of the press (*Near*) against the power of state governments. Chief Justice Charles Evans Hughes wrote (*Near*), "It is no longer open to doubt that the liberty of the press and of speech is within the liberty safeguarded by the due process clause of the Fourteenth Amendment. It was found impossible to conclude that this essential liberty of the citizen was left unprotected by the general guaranty of fundamental rights of person and property."

Thus the Supreme Court, through its power of judicial review, had extended to all the states beyond doubt the 1st Amendment freedoms of speech and press. What about the other rights in the Bill of Rights? Were they also applicable to the states through the due process clause of the 14th Amendment?

These questions were answered slowly, on a case-by-case basis, from the 1930s through the 1980s. At present, most provisions in the Bill of Rights have been extended nationwide through decisions of the Supreme Court and are generally accepted as legitimate limitations on the powers of state governments. The exceptions are Amendment 2 (the right to bear arms), Amendment 3 (restrictions on the quartering of soldiers), the grand jury indictment clause of Amendment 5, Amendment 7 (requirement of jury trials in civil cases), and the excessive fines and bail clause of Amendment 8.

James Madison, primary author of the Bill of Rights, had wanted to restrict the powers of state governments to interfere with the individual's rights to freedom of speech, press, and religion and to trial by jury in criminal cases. He had proposed to the first federal Congress, in the summer of 1789, that "No state shall infringe the equal rights of conscience, nor the freedom of speech, or of the press, nor of the right to trial by jury in criminal cases." However, this proposal was voted down in Congress, and the principle inherent in it was not revived until ratification of the 14th Amendment in 1868. According to the records of the first Congress, "Mr. Madison conceived this to be the most valuable amendment on the whole list [of amendments that constituted the Bill of Rights]; if there was any reason to restrain the government of the United States from infringing upon these essential rights, it was equally necessary that they should be secured against the state governments."

The Supreme Court, in developing the incorporation doctrine to extend rights in the Bill of Rights to the states, has gradually and securely fulfilled Madison's great hope that the law would be used to limit the power of both federal and state governments in order to protect the inherent rights and liberties of individuals.

THE DEVELOPMENT OF THE INCORPORATION DOCTRINE

The cases listed below established the incorporation of particular rights in the Bill of Rights into the due process clause of the 14th Amendment. Thus these rights were extended to the states.

YEAR	CASE	AMENDMENT	RIGHT
1897	*Chicago, Burlington & Quincy Railroad* v. *Chicago*	5	just compensation
1925	*Gitlow* v. *New York*	1	freedom of speech
1927	*Fiske* v. *Kansas*	1	freedom of speech
1931	*Stromberg* v. *California*	1	freedom of speech
1931	*Near* v. *Minnesota*	1	freedom of press
1937	*DeJonge* v. *Oregon*	1	right to assembly
1939	*Hague* v. *Congress of Industrial Organizations*	1	right to petition
1940	*Cantwell* v. *Connecticut*	1	free exercise of religion
1947	*Everson* v. *Board of Education of Ewing Township*	1	no establishment of religion
1947	*Cole* v. *Arkansas*	6	notice of accusation
1948	*In re Oliver*	6	right to public trial
1949	*Wolf* v. *Colorado*	4	no unreasonable searches and seizures
1961	*Mapp* v. *Ohio*	4	exclusion from trials of illegally seized evidence
1962	*Robinson* v. *California*	8	no cruel and unusual punishment
1963	*Gideon* v. *Wainwright*	6	right to counsel
1964	*Malloy* v. *Hogan*	5	no self-incrimination
1965	*Pointer* v. *Texas*	6	right to confront witnesses
1966	*Parker* v. *Gladden*	6	right to impartial jury
1967	*Klopfer* v. *North Carolina*	6	right to speedy trial
1967	*Washington* v. *Texas*	6	right to compulsory process for obtaining witnesses
1968	*Duncan* v. *Louisiana*	6	right to jury trial in criminal prosecutions
1969	*Benton* v. *Maryland*	5	no double jeopardy

SEE ALSO

Barron v. Baltimore; Benton v. Maryland; Bill of Rights; Constitutional law; Due process of law; Duncan v. Louisiana; Everson v. Board of Education of Ewing Township; Gideon v. Wainwright; Gitlow v. New York; Mapp v. Ohio; Near v. Minnesota; Stromberg v. California; Wolf v. Colorado

FURTHER READING

Cortner, Richard. *The Supreme Court and the Second Bill of Rights: The Fourteenth Amendment and the Nationalization of the Bill of Rights.* Madison: University of Wisconsin Press, 1981.

Perry, Michael J. *We the People: The Fourteenth Amendment and the Supreme Court.* New York: Oxford University Press, 1999.

Independent judiciary

THE INDEPENDENCE of the federal judicial branch is based on the insulation of its members, once appointed and confirmed in their positions, from punitive actions by the legislative and executive branches. According to Article 3 of the Constitution, federal judges may hold their positions "during good Behaviour"; in effect, they have lifetime appointments as long as they satisfy the ethical and legal standards of their judicial offices. Furthermore, Article 3 provides that the legislative and executive branches may not combine to punish federal judges by decreasing payments for their services. The intention of these constitutional provisions is to guard the federal judges against undue influence from the legislative and executive branches in the exercise of their judicial power.

When President Lyndon Johnson (right) nominated Abe Fortas to be chief justice, critics accused Fortas of unethical behavior, and his nomination was withdrawn.

Alexander Hamilton argued for an independent judiciary in *The Federalist* No. 78. He wrote, "The complete independence of the courts of justice is peculiarly essential in a limited Constitution." Hamilton claimed that only an independent judicial branch of government would be able to impartially check excessive exercise of power by the other branches of government.

SEE ALSO
Separation of powers

Individual rights

S E E Bill of Rights; Civil rights; Liberty under the Constitution

In forma pauperis

THE LATIN phrase *in forma pauperis* means "in the manner of a pauper." Appeals for a hearing before the U.S. Supreme Court that are brought by individuals unable to pay court costs are known as *in forma pauperis* petitions. Appellants in such cases are not required to pay the filing fee.

Injunction

AN INJUNCTION is a court order requiring a person to do, or not to do, something in order to protect another's personal or property rights. A person who violates an injunction is in contempt of court and the court may fine or imprison him. An injunction usually is issued to prohibit an action. When it is used to command a positive action, it is called a mandatory injunction.

During the 20th century, courts have used injunctions to protect and promote the civil rights of minorities, especially African Americans. For example, federal courts used injunctions to stop school district officials from continuing racial segregation in schools after the decision in *Brown* v. *Board of Education* (1954). Courts also used injunctions to take positive actions, such as redrawing school district boundaries and ordering the busing of students between districts to achieve racially mixed schools. Thus, federal injunctions have become an important way of protecting the constitutional rights of individuals against infringement by state governments.

SEE ALSO
Brown v. Board of Education

In re

IN RE is a Latin phrase meaning "in the matter of." When *in re* appears in the title of a case, it means that the case does *not* have formal opposing parties. The use of *in re* refers to the object or person that is the primary subject of the case. For example, *In re Winship* (1970) was a case without adversaries. The state did not oppose the person to whom the title refers, Samuel Winship. Thus, Winship was not required in this case to defend himself in any way. Rather, this case dealt only with the standard of proof necessary to incarcerate a 12-year-old boy who had been sentenced and committed to a training school for juvenile offenders. The phrase *in re* is often used in cases involving preadult offenders, which are handled by the juvenile justice system.

SEE ALSO
In re Winship; Juvenile justice

In re Gault

☆ *387 U.S. 1 (1967)*
☆ *Vote: 8–1*
☆ *For the Court: Fortas*
☆ *Concurring: Black, White, and Harlan*
☆ *Dissenting: Stewart*

GERALD GAULT, a 15-year-old boy, made obscene telephone calls to a neighbor. At the time, he was on court-ordered probation for a different act of juvenile delinquency.

As a juvenile, Gault did not have the standard constitutional guarantees of due process, such as the right to counsel, the right to confront or cross-examine one's accuser, the privilege of protection from self-incrimination, and the right to notice of a legal hearing. The juvenile justice system was separated from the usual criminal processes applied to adults. The intention had been to protect juvenile offenders from the harshness of adult criminal law. But these good intentions could in some cases lead to injustice, which is what Gault's advocates claimed.

If Gault had been tried as an adult, his punishment would have been a $50 fine or two months in jail. As a juvenile offender, he was sentenced to the Arizona State Industrial School until the age of 21, a six-year sentence. Further, Arizona law provided juvenile offenders virtually no due process rights, such as those set out in the 5th and 6th Amendments to the U.S. Constitution.

A state juvenile court judge convicted and sentenced Gerald Gault after two hearings. Gault's father sought his son's release from state-imposed detention on the grounds that he had been denied due process rights guaranteed by the U.S. Constitution.

The Issue Do the due process rights of individuals, specified in the

In 1967 the Supreme Court decided in In re Gault *that juveniles deserve some of the same due process rights as adults.*

5th, 6th, and 14th Amendments, apply to juveniles, just as they do to adults accused of crimes?

Opinion of the Court The Court decided that Gerald Gault had been denied his constitutional rights of due process. Justice Abe Fortas declared that "neither the Fourteenth Amendment nor the Bill of Rights is for adults alone.... Under our Constitution, the condition of being a boy does not justify a kangaroo court.... The essential difference between Gerald's case and a normal criminal case is that safeguards available to adults were discarded in Gerald's case."

Justice Fortas held that due process of law for juveniles required at least four procedural protections of individual rights: written notification of specific charges to the juvenile and his parents, assistance of a lawyer, confrontation and cross-examination of witnesses, and protection against self-incrimination.

Justice Fortas argued that the guarantee of these four due process rights for juveniles would not require the state to treat a juvenile accused of delinquency exactly like an adult accused of crime. Rather, these safeguards would protect a juvenile against injustices that otherwise might occur.

Significance This is the Court's most important decision about the rights of juveniles accused of illegal actions. It established that juveniles have certain constitutional rights that cannot be taken away solely because of age. However, the *Gault* decision did not abolish distinctive qualities of a separate juvenile court system. In particular, the due process requirements of *Gault* apply only to the adjudication (hearing and deciding) phase of legal proceedings and not to the conviction phase. Thus, *Gault* does not interfere with the emphasis that juvenile courts have traditionally placed on personalized treatment for rehabilitation of the individual.

SEE ALSO

Due process of law; Juvenile justice

FURTHER READING

Bernard, Thomas J. *The Cycle of Juvenile Justice.* New York: Oxford University Press, 1992.

In re Winship

☆ *397 U.S. 358 (1970)*
☆ *Vote: 6–3*
☆ *For the Court: Brennan*
☆ *Concurring: Harlan*
☆ *Dissenting: Burger, Stewart, and Black*

A 12-YEAR-OLD boy, Samuel Winship, was charged with an act of juvenile delinquency that, if committed by an adult, would be considered larceny. The boy was convicted by a family court judge according to the prevailing New York statute, which required only a "preponderance of the evidence" to justify juvenile detention. Advocates for the convicted juvenile claimed that a higher standard of proof—guilt "beyond a reasonable doubt"—should have been used in this case. That higher standard of proof had historically been the one accepted by the Court in adult criminal proceedings.

The Issue What standard of proof should be necessary to convict a juvenile for an act that would be considered a serious crime if committed by an adult? Should the due process clauses of the 5th and 14th Amendments be interpreted to require proof beyond a reasonable doubt as the standard for conviction of an accused juvenile?

Opinion of the Court Justice William J. Brennan decided that defendants in juvenile proceedings have the constitutional right to the higher standard of proof—"beyond a reasonable doubt." Brennan wrote, "We explicitly hold that the Due Process Clause protects the accused against conviction except upon proof beyond a reasonable doubt of every fact necessary to constitute the crime with which he is charged." Brennan based his opinion on common law and precedent because the "beyond a reasonable doubt" standard is not specifically stated in the U.S. Constitution.

Dissent Justice Hugo Black criticized the Court's majority in this case for stepping beyond the boundaries of its power in order to amend the Bill of Rights. He wrote, "Nowhere in that document is there any statement that conviction of crime requires proof of guilt beyond a reasonable doubt."

Significance The *Winship* decision provided juveniles accused of unlawful behavior with new constitutional protection. As stated by the Court, this higher standard of proof was also legally established for adults accused of criminal behavior.

SEE ALSO

Juvenile justice

FURTHER READING

Bernard, Thomas J. *The Cycle of Juvenile Justice.* New York: Oxford University Press, 1992.

Iredell, James

ASSOCIATE JUSTICE, 1790–99

☆ *Born: Oct. 5, 1751, Lewes, England*
☆ *Education: read law under Samuel Johnston of North Carolina*
☆ *Previous government service: comptroller of customs, Edenton, N.C.,* 1768–74; *collector of customs, Port of North Carolina, 1774–76; judge, Superior Court of North Carolina, 1778; attorney general of North Carolina, 1779–81; North Carolina Council of State, 1787; North Carolina Ratifying Convention, 1788*
☆ *Appointed by President George Washington Feb. 8, 1790*
☆ *Supreme Court term: confirmed by the Senate Feb. 10, 1790, by a voice vote; served until Oct. 20, 1799*
☆ *Died: Oct. 20, 1799, Edenton, N.C.*

JAMES IREDELL was an original member of the Supreme Court. President Washington decided to appoint Iredell because of his good reputation as a legal expert and his skill as a political leader in North Carolina, where he had argued decisively against opponents of the 1787 Constitution.

Iredell had attracted Washington's attention during the debates about ratification of the Constitution. Iredell published a pamphlet opposing the "Objections to the New Constitution" by George Mason, a delegate from Virginia. Iredell also stood firm against the majority of citizens in North Carolina who at first opposed the Constitution of 1787. He eventually helped to persuade North Carolinians to ratify the federal Constitution in 1789.

In dissent from the Court's decision in *Chisholm* v. *Georgia* (1793), Justice Iredell held that a state government could not be sued in a federal court by a person from another state. This position became part of the Constitution in 1795 with ratification of the 11th Amendment.

In *Calder* v. *Bull* (1798), Iredell argued that the Court had authority to declare laws null and void if they violated the Constitution of the United States, the supreme law. This position on the power of judicial review was also implied by the Court, including Iredell, in *Hylton* v. *United States* (1796). In the *Hylton* case, the Court upheld the constitutionality of a federal tax law, and the decision implied that the Court could have ruled this federal law unconstitutional. However, the Court did not discuss the power of judicial review in this case. A few years later, in *Marbury* v. *Madison* (1803), Chief Justice John Marshall argued compellingly for the Court's power of judicial review to strike down acts of Congress that were in violation of the U.S. Constitution.

SEE ALSO

Hylton v. United States; Judicial review

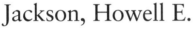

Jackson, Howell E.

ASSOCIATE JUSTICE, 1893–95

☆ *Born: Apr. 8, 1832, Paris, Tenn.*
☆ *Education: West Tennessee College, B.A., 1849; University of Virginia, 1851–52; Cumberland University, 1856*
☆ *Previous government service: judge, Court of Arbitration for Western Tennessee, 1875–79; Tennessee House of Representatives, 1880; U.S. senator from Tennessee, 1881–86; judge, Sixth Federal Circuit Court, 1886–91; judge, Circuit Court of Appeals, 1891–93*
☆ *Appointed by President Benjamin Harrison Feb. 2, 1893; replaced Lucius Q. C. Lamar, who died*
☆ *Supreme Court term: confirmed by the Senate Feb. 18, 1893, by a voice vote; served until Aug. 8, 1895*
☆ *Died: Aug. 8, 1895, Nashville, Tenn.*

HOWELL E. JACKSON achieved an outstanding record of public service in his home state, Tennessee. He was rewarded in 1881 by election to the U.S. Senate, where he developed a close friendship with a senator from Indiana, Benjamin Harrison, and with President Grover Cleveland. In 1886, Jackson left the Senate to accept President Cleveland's appointment to the U.S. Court of Appeals for the Sixth Circuit. In 1893,

Jackson was appointed to the Supreme Court by his old friend from the Senate, President Benjamin Harrison.

Jackson served less than two years on the Court because of poor health. In fact, during this time his illness prevented him from participating in several important decisions of the Court.

Jackson's most notable opinion was his dissent in *Pollock* v. *Farmers' Loan and Trust Co.* (1895). The Court decided that the 1894 federal income tax law was unconstitutional. Jackson strongly disagreed, and his position was confirmed in 1913 with passage of the 16th Amendment to the Constitution, which grants power to the federal government to tax incomes "from whatever source derived."

Jackson, Robert H.

ASSOCIATE JUSTICE, 1941–54

☆ *Born: Feb. 13, 1842, Spring Creek, Pa.*
☆ *Education: Albany Law School, 1912*
☆ *Previous government service: general counsel, Internal Revenue Bureau, 1934–36; special counsel, Securities and Exchange Commission, 1935; assistant U.S. attorney general, 1936–38; U.S. solicitor general, 1938–39; U.S. attorney general, 1940–41*
☆ *Appointed by President Franklin D. Roosevelt June 12, 1941; replaced Harlan F. Stone, who became chief justice*
☆ *Supreme Court term: confirmed by the Senate July 7, 1941, by a voice vote; served until Oct. 9, 1954*
☆ *Died: Oct. 9, 1954, Washington, D.C.*

ROBERT H. JACKSON was a Democratic party activist before he became a lawyer. After completing law school, he continued his involvement in the Democratic party of New York and became an ally and close friend of Franklin D. Roosevelt. In 1934 Jackson went to Washington, D.C., to work in the

federal government led by President Roosevelt. He eventually became solicitor general in 1938 and attorney general in 1940, and he was also an important adviser to the President. In 1941 President Roosevelt named Jackson to fill a vacancy on the Supreme Court.

Justice Jackson tended to defend the individual against threats of oppression by government officials or by an intolerant majority of the people. In *West Virginia State Board of Education* v. *Barnette* (1943), Jackson upheld the rights of a religious minority, Jehovah's Witnesses, to refrain from participating in a public exercise, saluting the flag and reciting the pledge of allegiance. He wrote: "If there is any fixed star in our constitutional constellation, it is that no official, high or petty, can prescribe what shall be orthodox in politics, nationalism, religion, or other matters of opinion or force citizens to confess by word or act their faith therein."

Jackson, however, also recognized the need for public safety and social order, which could be threatened by unlimited or extreme expressions of individual liberty. He therefore voted with the Court's majority in *Dennis* v. *United States* (1951) to uphold the convictions of American Communist party leaders who promoted the violent overthrow of the U.S. government.

In May 1945, at the end of World War II, President Harry Truman asked Jackson to serve as chief counsel for the United States in the prosecution of Nazi war criminals at the Nuremberg (Germany) war crimes trials. In this role, Jackson developed the legal principles and procedures by which leading Nazis were tried and convicted of war crimes against humanity.

SEE ALSO

West Virginia State Board of Education v. Barnette

FURTHER READING

Gerhart, Eugene C. *America's Advocate: Robert H. Jackson*. Indianapolis: Bobbs-Merrill, 1958.

Jay, John
CHIEF JUSTICE, 1789–95

☆ *Born: Dec. 12, 1745, New York, N.Y.*
☆ *Education: King's College (Columbia University), B.A., 1764; read law with Benjamin Kissam in New York, N.Y.*
☆ *Previous government service: secretary, Royal Boundary Commission, 1773; Continental Congress, 1774, 1775, 1777, president, 1778–79; New York Provincial Congress, 1776–77; chief justice, New York State, 1777–78; U.S. minister to Spain, 1779; U.S. secretary of foreign affairs, 1784–89*
☆ *Appointed by President George Washington Sept. 24, 1789, to be the first chief justice of the United States*
☆ *Supreme Court term: confirmed by the Senate Sept. 26, 1789, by a voice vote; resigned June 29, 1795*
☆ *Subsequent government service: governor of New York, 1795–1801*
☆ *Died: May 17, 1829, Bedford, N.Y.*

JOHN JAY was one of the great founders of the United States. Jay was elected to the First Continental Congress in 1774 and at first resisted independence from Great Britain, but he became a fervent patriot in 1776, after the Declaration of Independence.

Jay was the main author of the New York state constitution of 1777. In 1778, he was elected president of the Continental Congress. During the 1780s he was involved in making and conducting foreign policy for the United States.

Although Jay did not attend the Constitutional Convention of 1787, he worked effectively for ratification of the federal Constitution. Toward this end, he wrote five of *The Federalist Papers* (Nos. 2, 3, 4, 5, and 64), which were originally printed in New York newspapers to support the ratification of the U.S. Constitution. Other authors were James Madison and Alexander Hamilton, who were leaders in the movement to write and ratify the Constitution. Later, Hamilton became U.S. secretary of the Treasury under President George Washington, and Madison served as a Virginia member of the House of Representatives in the first federal Congress. Madison became the fourth President of the United States in 1809.

President George Washington appointed Jay the first chief justice of the United States. The most important decision over which Jay presided was *Chisholm v. Georgia* (1793), in which the Court ruled that citizens of one state could bring suit in a federal court against another state.

Overall, however, Jay was disappointed at the apparent weaknesses and insignificance of the Court in comparison to the executive and legislative branches of the federal government. Political leaders seemed to pay slight attention to the Court, and few cases were taken to it. For this reason, Jay resigned as chief justice in 1795 to become governor of New York, a position for which he was elected while serving as chief justice.

President John Adams wanted to reappoint Jay as chief justice in 1800, but Jay refused because he believed the Court lacked "the energy, weight and dignity which are essential to its affording due support to the national government." In 1801, he retired from public life.

SEE ALSO

Chisholm v. Georgia

FURTHER READING

Casto, William R. *The Supreme Court in the Early Republic: The Chief Justiceships of John Jay and Oliver Ellsworth*. Columbia: University of South Carolina Press, 1995.

Morris, Richard B. *John Jay, the Nation and the Court*. Boston: Boston University Press, 1967.

Johnson, Thomas

ASSOCIATE JUSTICE, 1791–93

☆ Born: Nov. 4, 1732, Calvert County, Md.
☆ Education: Studied law under Stephen Bordley, Annapolis, Md.
☆ Previous government service: Maryland Provincial Assembly, 1762; Annapolis Convention, 1774; Continental Congress, 1774–77; governor of Maryland, 1777–80; Maryland House of Delegates, 1780, 1786–88; Maryland Ratifying Convention, 1788; chief judge, General Court of Maryland, 1790–91
☆ Appointed by President George Washington as a recess appointment Aug. 5, 1791; replaced John Rutledge, who resigned; nominated by Washington Oct. 31, 1791
☆ Supreme Court term: confirmed by the Senate Nov. 7, 1791, by a voice vote; resigned Jan. 16, 1793
☆ Died: Oct. 26, 1819, Frederick, Md.

THOMAS JOHNSON was an American patriot who fought for the United States in the War of Independence. He became a friend of George Washington, who appointed him to the Supreme Court in 1791.

Johnson served on the Court for only 14 months and wrote only one opinion for the Court. President Washington later appointed Johnson to the committee that planned the new federal city. In 1795, Johnson refused Washington's offer to become secretary of state, and he retired from public life.

Johnson, William

ASSOCIATE JUSTICE, 1804–34

☆ Born: Dec. 27, 1771, Charleston, S.C.
☆ Education: College of New Jersey (Princeton), B.A., 1790; studied law with Charles Cotesworth Pinckney in Charleston

☆ *Previous government service: South Carolina House of Representatives, 1794–98, Speaker, 1798; judge, South Carolina Constitutional Court, 1799–1804*

☆ *Appointed by President Thomas Jefferson Mar. 22, 1804; replaced Alfred Moore, who resigned*

☆ *Supreme Court term: confirmed by the Senate Mar. 24, 1804, by a voice vote; served until Aug. 4, 1834*

☆ *Died: Aug. 4, 1834, Brooklyn, N.Y.*

WILLIAM JOHNSON was President Thomas Jefferson's first appointee to the Supreme Court. Of all the justices of the Court under John Marshall, Johnson was the one most likely to disagree with the dominating chief justice. He has been remembered as the first great dissenter of the Supreme Court.

Justice Johnson was a hardworking member of the Court who wrote 112 majority opinions, 21 concurrences, and 34 dissents during 29 years on the Court. Only John Marshall and Joseph Story produced more opinions during Johnson's tenure on the Court.

FURTHER READING

Morgan, Donald G. *Justice William Johnson: The First Dissenter.* Columbia: University of South Carolina Press, 1954.

Johnson v. Transportation Agency of Santa Clara County

☆ *480 U.S. 616 (1987)*
☆ *Vote: 6–3*
☆ *For the Court: Brennan*
☆ *Concurring: O'Connor and Stevens*
☆ *Dissenting: White, Scalia, and Rehnquist*

IN 1978 the Transportation Agency of Santa Clara County, California, created an affirmative action plan to bring about fair representation in its work force of women, minorities, and disabled people. Affirmative action refers to programs or policies to provide opportunities to individuals on the basis of membership in certain groups, such as racial, ethnic, or gender categories that have been discriminated against in the past. The Santa Clara plan did not set aside a certain number of jobs for minorities, women, or the disabled. Rather, it set annual goals as guidelines for decisions about hiring and promoting workers so that eventually there would be "a work force whose composition reflected the proportion of minorities and women in the labor force."

In 1979 the Santa Clara County Transportation Agency gave notice of a vacancy for the job of road dispatcher. This was a craftworker position, a high-level, skilled job category. None of the 238 jobs in the agency's craftworker category was held by a woman. Paul Johnson and Diana Joyce were the leading candidates, among 12 applicants, for the vacant position.

The interviewers rated both Johnson and Joyce as well qualified. Johnson, however, had a slightly higher job interview score than Joyce did, and the selection panel recommended that he get the position. Nevertheless, Diana Joyce got the job. So Johnson filed a complaint under the federal Civil Rights Act of 1964. He claimed that he was denied the job because of his sex.

The Issue This was the first case to test the legality of sex-based affirmative action plans under Title VII of the Civil Rights Act of 1964. Did the Santa Clara affirmative action plan violate Title VII of the 1964 Civil Rights Act, which prohibits an employer from depriving "any individual of employment opportunities... because of such individual's race, color, religion, sex, or national origin"?

Did Santa Clara's voluntary sex-based affirmative action plan deprive Johnson of his 14th Amendment right to "equal protection of the laws"?

Opinion of the Court The Court upheld the Santa Clara Transportation Agency's affirmative action plan. Justice William Brennan wrote that it could be legal under Title VII of the 1964 Civil Rights Act to remedy imbalances of female and male workers in a skilled job category. This affirmative action plan was legal, Brennan wrote, because it merely set goals but did not establish quotas for hiring female employees. Further, this plan recognized gender as only one of several factors in decisions about hiring and promotion. Finally, the plan was acceptable because it was only a temporary means to overcome past discrimination against workers based on sex.

Dissent Justice Antonin Scalia argued that this sex-based affirmative action plan was in conflict with the specific words of Title VII of the 1964 Civil Rights Act. He wrote, "The court today completes the process of converting this [Civil Rights Act of 1964] from a guarantee that race or sex will *not* be the basis for employment discrimination, to a guarantee that it often *will*. [W]e effectively replace the goal of a discrimination-free society with the

quite incompatible goal of proportionate representation by race and by sex in the workplace."

Significance For the first time, the Court decided that a voluntary sex-based affirmative action plan can be used to overcome the effects of past job discrimination based on gender. Further, the *Johnson* decision clearly endorsed affirmative action as a remedy for past discrimination, as long as it is temporary.

SEE ALSO

Affirmative action; Equality under the Constitution

FURTHER READING

Urofsky, Melvin I. *Affirmative Action on Trial: Sex Discrimination in Johnson v. Santa Clara.* Lawrence: University Press of Kansas, 1997.
Urofsky, Melvin I. *A Conflict of Rights: The Supreme Court and Affirmative Action.* New York: Scribners, 1991.

Judicial activism and judicial restraint

ARTICLE 3, SECTION 1, of the U.S. Constitution says, "The judicial Power of the United States, shall be vested in one supreme Court, and in such inferior Courts as the Congress may from time to time ordain and establish." Article 3, Section 2, provides that the "judicial Power shall extend to all Cases in Law and Equity, arising under this Constitution, the Laws of the United States, and Treaties made, or which shall be made, under their Authority." Thus, the justices of the U.S. Supreme Court have the power to interpret the Constitution, and laws and treaties of the United States, in response to cases that come before the Court.

In 1796, in *Ware* v. *Hylton*, the Supreme Court held a Virginia statute void because it violated a 1783 peace treaty

In 1987 the Supreme Court upheld an affirmative action plan used by the Transportation Agency of Santa Clara County, California, designed to give more opportunities for skilled jobs to women and minorities.

with Great Britain. In *Marbury* v. *Madison* (1803) the Supreme Court declared a federal law unconstitutional. These cases established the power of judicial review in the Supreme Court—the power to declare acts of the state governments and of the legislative and executive branches of the federal government null and void if they violate provisions of the Constitution. Since the early 19th century, debate has continued over how federal judges should use their powers. Should they practice restraint, or should they actively expand the scope of the Constitution in their interpretations of law, treaties, and constitutional provisions?

Judicial restraint

Those who advocate judicial restraint believe the courts should uphold all acts of Congress and state legislatures unless they clearly violate a specific section of the Constitution. In practicing judicial restraint, the courts should defer to the constitutional interpretations of Congress, the President, and others whenever possible. The courts should hesitate to use judicial review to promote new ideas or policy preferences. In short, the courts should interpret the law, not intervene in policy-making.

Over the years, eminent Supreme Court Justices such as Felix Frankfurter have called for judicial self-restraint. In *West Virginia State Board of Education* v. *Barnette* (1943), Frankfurter said, "As a member of this Court I am not justified in writing my opinions into the Constitution, no matter how deeply I may cherish them. . . . It can never be emphasized too much that one's own opinion about the wisdom or evil of a law should be excluded altogether when one is doing one's duty on the bench."

Judicial activism

Sometimes judges appear to exceed their power in deciding cases before the Court. They are supposed to exercise judgment in interpreting the law, according to the Constitution. Judicial activists, however, seem to exercise their will to *make* law in response to legal issues before the Court.

According to the idea of judicial activism, judges should use their powers to correct injustices, especially when the other branches of government do not act to do so. In short, the courts should play an active role in shaping social policy on such issues as civil rights, protection of individual rights, political unfairness, and public morality.

Chief Justice Earl Warren (who served from 1954 to 1969) and many members of the Warren Court, such as William O. Douglas, practiced judicial activism when they boldly used the Constitution to make sweeping social changes promoting such policies as school desegregation and to ensure that all Americans had the opportunity to vote and to participate in U.S. society. In 1956 Justice Douglas wrote, "[T]he judiciary must do more than dispense justice in cases and controversies. It must also keep the charter of government current with the times and not allow it to become archaic or out of tune with the needs of the day."

Arguments against judicial activism

Opponents of judicial activism argue that activist judges make laws, not just interpret them, which is an abuse of their constitutional power. The issue, they claim, is not whether social problems need to be solved but whether the courts should involve themselves in such problem solving. By making decisions about how to run prisons or schools, argue the critics of judicial activism, the courts assume responsibilities that belong exclusively to the legislative and executive branches of government.

Critics of judicial activism worry that court decisions that so freely "inter-

The racial integration of college campuses in some parts of the country was largely the result of judicial activism, the principle that the Supreme Court should use its power to correct social injustices such as racial segregation.

pret" the meaning of the Constitution will undermine public confidence in and respect for the courts. Justice Byron R. White wrote in *Bowers* v. *Hardwick* (1986), "The Court is most vulnerable and comes nearest to illegitimacy when it deals with judge-made constitutional law having little or no cognizable [knowable] roots in the language or design of the Constitution."

In addition, critics point out that federal judges are not elected; they are appointed for life terms. As a result, when judges begin making policy decisions about social or political changes society should make, they become unelected legislators. Consequently, the people lose control of the right to govern themselves. Further, unlike legislatures, courts are not supposed to be open to influence from interest groups. As a result, the courts may not hear different points of view on complex social issues. In legislatures, by contrast, elected officials are responsive to such interests.

Finally, opponents of judicial activism argue that judges lack special expertise in handling such complex tasks as running prisons, administering schools, or determining hiring policies for businesses. Judges are experts in the law, not in managing social institutions.

Opponents of judicial activism point to the constitutional principle of separation of powers (the division of power

among the executive, legislative, and judicial branches of the federal government) and federalism (the division of power between the states and the federal government) to justify judicial restraint. They claim that judicial activism leads to unconstitutional intrusions of federal judicial power into the duties and powers of the executive and legislative branches of government and into the state governments. In *Griswold* v. *Connecticut* (1965), Justice John M. Harlan wrote, "Judicial self-restraint...will be achieved...only by continual insistence upon...the great roles that the doctrines of federalism and separation of powers have played in establishing and preserving American freedoms."

Arguments for judicial activism

Supporters of judicial activism argue that it is necessary to correct injustices and promote needed social changes. They view the courts as institutions of last resort for those in society who lack the political power to influence the other branches of government.

Supporters of judicial activism point out that the courts often step in only after governors and state legislatures have refused to do anything about a problem. For example, neither state legislatures nor Congress acted to ban racially segregated schools, trains, city buses, parks, and other public facilities for decades. Segregation might still exist legally if the Supreme Court had not declared it unconstitutional in 1954.

Supporters of judicial activism also mention that local courts and judges are uniquely qualified to ensure that local officials uphold the guarantees of the Constitution. In fact, with a few exceptions, district court judges have written most of the decisions affecting local institutions. For example, an Alabama judge took over the administration of the prison system in that state because he decided that the conditions in the prisons violated the Constitution's prohibition of "cruel and unusual punishments." Similarly, a Texas judge, a man born and raised in the Lone Star State, ordered sweeping changes in the Texas prison system. And a Massachusetts judge, himself a Boston resident, ordered massive school desegregation in that northern city. In each case, the district judge adopted an activist solution to a problem. But each pursued an activist course because he felt that only such measures would enforce the dictates of the Constitution.

Judicial activists argue that the courts do not create policy as legislatures do. Judges inevitably shape policy, however, as they interpret the law. And, they argue, interpreting the law is the job of the courts. Chief Justice Earl Warren put it this way: "When two [people] come into Court, one may say: 'an act of Congress means this.' The other says it means the opposite. We [the Court] then say it means one of the two or something else in between. In that way we *are* making the law, aren't we?"

Finally, judicial activists argue that the framers of the Constitution expected the courts to interpret the Constitution actively in order to react to new conditions. As Justice Frank Murphy wrote in *Schneiderman* v. *United States* (1943), "The constitutional fathers, fresh from a revolution, did not forge a political strait-jacket for the generations to come."

SEE ALSO
Constitutional construction; Judicial power; Judicial review; Separation of powers

FURTHER READING
Lewis, Frederick P. *The Context of Judicial Activism.* Lanham, Md.: Rowman & Littlefield, 1999.
Peretti, Terri Jennings. *In Defense of a Political Court.* Princeton, N.J.: Princeton University Press, 1999.
Wellington, Harry H. *Interpreting the Constitution: The Supreme Court and the Process of Adjudication.* New Haven: Yale University Press, 1991.

Judicial Conference of the United States

SEE Administration of federal courts

Judicial power

ARTICLE 3, Section 1, of the U.S. Constitution says, "The judicial Power of the United States shall be vested in one supreme Court, and in such inferior Courts as the Congress may from time to time ordain and establish." Section 2 says, "The judicial Power shall extend to all Cases, in Law and Equity, arising under this Constitution, the laws of the United States, and Treaties made, or which shall be made, under their Authority."

The judicial power specified in the Constitution is the capacity and authority of the U.S. Supreme Court and lower federal courts to hear and decide cases brought before them on the basis of the supreme law—the Constitution—and federal statutes and treaties that conform to the Constitution. The judicial power of the Supreme Court therefore involves interpretation of the law to make decisions in actual controversies that adversaries bring to the Court. Hypothetical cases are not subjects for Supreme Court decisions.

Article 3, Section 2, of the Constitution says that the judicial power of the federal courts can be exercised in two categories of cases: cases defined by the parties to the controversy and cases defined by their substance. The first category includes legal disputes in which the United States is a party, in which the opposing parties are different states of the

Chief Justice John Marshall wrote that judicial power involved the review of laws passed by Congress in cases before the Court.

federal system, or in which the parties are citizens of different states. The second category includes cases about the meaning or application of provisions of the Constitution, federal statutes, or treaties. It also includes cases pertaining to admiralty and maritime law and to ambassadors and officials from other countries.

Judicial review, although not mentioned in the Constitution, has become an important power of the federal judiciary. Judicial review is the power of a court to declare an act of the federal or state government unconstitutional, or unlawful and void. According to this concept, judges in courts of law appraise acts of the legislative and executive branches of federal and state governments to decide whether they are in conflict with the Constitution. All courts, federal and state, may practice judicial review. The Supreme Court of the United States, however, has final say within the judicial system on whether laws or actions violate or are in accord with the U.S. Constitution.

Judicial review is based on three ideas: that the Constitution is the supreme law, that acts contrary to the Constitution are null and void, and that judges in courts of law are responsible for determining if acts violate or agree with the Constitution.

The judicial power, including the power of judicial review, is one of three coordinate and separate powers of government in the United States: legislative, executive, and judicial. Chief Justice John Marshall, in *Osborn* v. *Bank of the United States* (1824), summarized the relationships of the three branches of government: "[T]he legislative, executive, and judicial powers, of every well constructed government, are co-extensive with each other. . . . The executive department may constitutionally execute every law which the Legislative may constitutionally make, and the judicial

department [has] . . . the power of construing every such law." As Marshall wrote in *Marbury* v. *Madison* (1803), "It is emphatically, the province and duty of the judicial department, to say what the law is." The federal judicial power, then, has the authority and capacity to interpret the Constitution and laws and treaties made under it; to apply the law to decisions about cases brought before the courts; and to declare laws unconstitutional if they do not conform to the supreme law, the U.S. Constitution.

The disputed Presidential election of 2000 provided a dramatic example of the Supreme Court's authority and legitimacy in exercising the judicial power under the Constitution. More than one month after Election Day, the contest between Republican party candidate George W. Bush and Democratic party candidate Albert Gore was still unsettled. At issue were several thousand disputed ballots in Florida. Gore demanded a recount, and the Florida Supreme Court agreed with him. Bush appealed to the U.S. Supreme Court. He claimed that the procedures for conducting a recount violated the due process and equal protection clauses of the U.S. Constitution's 14th Amendment. In *Bush* v. *Gore*, the U.S. Supreme Court agreed with Bush, reversed the Florida Supreme Court's decision, and ordered an end to the recount of ballots, holding that such a recount will not satisfy "minimal constitutional standards." The consequence of the Court's decision was that Bush maintained a slim lead in the Florida popular vote and thereby gained the state's 25 electoral votes, which brought him victory in the Presidential election.

Bush v. *Gore* was the first case the Court had ever taken that would decide the outcome of a Presidential election, and the justices took it up reluctantly. Like the public they serve, the justices prefer elections to be decided by the voters through the political process. In *Bush* v. *Gore* the Court's *per curiam* (by the court) opinion said, "When contending parties invoke the process of the courts, however, it becomes our unsought responsibility to resolve the federal and constitutional issues the judicial system has been forced to confront." The public tended to agree with the necessity and finality of the Court's action, even though its decision was controversial. Thus, at a time of impending political crisis, the Supreme Court, authoritatively exercising its judicial power, was the publicly sanctioned vehicle for legitimately resolving a critical public issue.

SEE ALSO

Judicial review; Jurisdiction; Marbury v. Madison; Separation of powers

FURTHER READING

Abraham, Henry J. *The Judicial Process.* New York: Oxford University Press, 1993.

Judicial review

JUDICIAL REVIEW is the power of the judiciary, or the courts, to determine whether the acts of other branches of government are in accordance with the Constitution. All courts, federal and state, may exercise the power of judicial review, but the Supreme Court of the United States has the final judicial decision on whether laws or actions of local, state, or federal governments violate or conform to the U.S. Constitution, the highest law of the land.

Judges use their power of judicial review only in cases brought before the courts. They consider only actual controversies, not hypothetical questions about the Constitution. Congress cannot, for example, ask the Supreme Court for its advice about whether a bill is constitu-

tional. The Court would make this kind of decision only if the bill became a law and someone challenged it.

Judicial review is not mentioned in the Constitution. However, before 1787 this power was used by courts in several of the American states to overturn laws that conflicted with the state constitution.

Judicial review of state laws

The federal judiciary's power to review state laws is implied in Articles 3 and 6 of the U.S. Constitution. Article 3 says that the federal courts have power to make judgments in all cases pertaining to the Constitution, statutes, and treaties of the United States.

Article 6 implies that the judicial power must be used to protect and defend the authority of the U.S. Constitution with respect to the laws and constitutions of the states: "This Constitution, and the Laws of the United States which shall be made in Pursuance thereof; and all Treaties made, or which shall be made under the authority of the United States, shall be the supreme Law of the Land; and the Judges in every State shall be bound thereby, any Thing in the Constitution or Laws of any State to the Contrary notwithstanding." Furthermore, Article 6 declares that all officials of the federal and state governments, including all "judicial Officers, both of the United States and of the several States, shall be bound by Oath or Affirmation, to support this Constitution."

To establish a judicial system for the United States, Congress enacted the Judiciary Act of 1789. Section 25 of this statute provided for review by the U.S. Supreme Court of decisions by state courts that involved issues of federal law.

On the basis of Articles 3 and 6 of the U.S. Constitution and Section 25 of the Judiciary Act of 1789, the Supreme Court in 1796 (*Ware* v. *Hylton*) exercised the power of judicial review to

The Supreme Court threw out the Agricultural Adjustment Act in 1936 on the grounds that agriculture is not an interstate activity and cannot be regulated by the federal government.

strike down a law of the state government of Virginia. According to the Supreme Court, the Virginia law, which protected Virginia citizens with debts to British creditors from having to pay, was unconstitutional because it violated the 1783 Treaty of Paris, which guaranteed that prewar debts owed to the British would be paid. This judicial decision was generally viewed as consistent with the words of the U.S. Constitution and the intentions of its framers.

Judicial review of federal laws and actions

An open-ended and troublesome question of the founding period was whether the power of judicial review could be used to nullify acts of the legislative or executive branches of the federal government.

In 1788 Alexander Hamilton argued in *The Federalist* No. 78 for judicial review as a means to void all governmental actions contrary to the Constitution. He maintained that limitations on the power of the federal legislative and executive branches in order to protect the rights of individuals "can be preserved in practice no other way than through . . . courts of justice, whose duty it must be to declare all acts contrary

to . . . the Constitution void. Without this [power of judicial review], all the reservations of particular rights or privileges would amount to nothing."

Hamilton concluded, "No legislative act, therefore, contrary to the Constitution, can be valid. . . . [T]he interpretation of the laws is the proper and peculiar province of the courts. A constitution is . . . a fundamental law. It therefore belongs to [judges] to ascertain its meaning as well as the meaning of any particular act proceeding from the legislative body."

Marbury v. Madison

The ideas on judicial review in *The Federalist* No. 78 were applied by John Marshall, chief justice of the United States, in *Marbury* v. *Madison* (1803). The specific issue and decision in this case are of little interest or consequence today. However, Chief Justice Marshall's argument for judicial review, which firmly established this power in the federal government's system of checks and balances, has become a strong instrument of the federal courts in securing the constitutional rights of individuals.

In *Marbury* v. *Madison*, the Supreme Court was confronted with an act of Congress that conflicted with a provision of the United States Constitution. The question, in Marshall's words, was "whether an act, repugnant to the constitution, can become the law of the land." He answered that the Constitution is "the fundamental and paramount law of the nation, and consequently, . . . an act of the legislature repugnant to the constitution is void." Marshall argued, from the supremacy clause of Article 6, that *no* act of Congress that violates any part of the Constitution can be valid. Rather, he wrote, it must be declared unconstitutional and repealed.

Marshall concluded with his justification for the Supreme Court's power of judicial review:

It is, emphatically, the province and duty of the judicial department, to say what the law is. . . . So, if a law be in opposition to the constitution; if both the law and the constitution apply to a particular case, so that the court must either decide that case, conformable to the law, disregarding the constitution; or conformable to the constitution, disregarding the law; the court must determine which of these conflicting rules governs the case; this is of the very essence of judicial duty. If then, the courts are to regard the constitution, and the constitution is superior to any ordinary act of the legislature, the constitution, and not such ordinary act, must govern the case to which both apply.

Marshall used three provisions of the Constitution to justify his arguments for judicial review. The first was Article 3, Section 2, which extends the judicial power to "all Cases, in Law and Equity, arising under this Constitution." Marshall argued, "Could it be the intention of those who gave this power, to say, that in using it, the constitution should not be looked into? That a case arising under the constitution should be decided, without examining the instrument under which it arises? This is too extravagant to be maintained."

Second, Article 6 requires judges to pledge "to support this Constitution." Marshall wrote, "How immoral to impose [this oath] on them, if they were to be used as the instruments... for violating what they swear to support!"

Third, Marshall pointed out "that in declaring what shall be the supreme law of the land [Article 6], the constitution itself is first mentioned; and not the laws of the United States, generally, but those only which shall be made in pursuance of the constitution, have that rank."

Finally, Chief Justice Marshall stated "the principle, supposed to be essential to all written constitutions, that a law repugnant to the constitution is void; and that courts, as well as other departments [of the government], are bound by that instrument."

Significance of judicial review

James Madison spoke with foresight during the first federal Congress when, on June 8, 1789, he predicted that the "independent tribunals of justice [federal courts] will consider themselves in a peculiar manner the guardians of those [constitutional] rights... [and] resist every encroachment upon rights expressly stipulated... by the declaration [bill] of rights."

During the more than 200 years of its existence, the Supreme Court has used its power of judicial review to overturn more than 150 acts of Congress and more than 1,200 state laws. The great majority of these invalidations of federal and state acts have occurred during the 20th century. The Supreme Court declared only 3 federal acts and 53 state laws unconstitutional from 1789 until 1868. Most of the laws declared unconstitutional since 1925 have involved civil liberties guaranteed by the Bill of Rights and subsequent amendments concerned with the rights of individuals. Thus, the Supreme Court has become the guardian of the people's liberties that James Madison said it would be at the inception of the republic.

SEE ALSO

Constitutional democracy; Constitutionalism; Judicial power; Marbury v. Madison; Separation of powers; Ware v. Hylton

FURTHER READING

Clinton, Robert Lowry. *Marbury v. Madison and Judicial Review.* Lawrence: University Press of Kansas, 1989.

Ely, John H. *Democracy and Distrust: A Theory of Judicial Review.* Cambridge: Harvard University Press, 1980.

Hall, Kermit L. *The Supreme Court and Judicial Review in American History.* Washington, D.C.: American Historical Association, 1985.

Keynes, Edward, with Randall K. Miller. *The Court vs. Congress: Prayer, Busing, and Abortion.* Durham, N.C.: Duke University Press, 1989.

Wolfe, Christopher. *The Rise of Modern Judicial Review.* New York: Basic Books, 1986.

Judiciary Act of 1789

ARTICLE 3 of the U.S. Constitution provides for a Supreme Court to exercise the "judicial Power of the United States." It also empowers Congress to provide through legislation "such inferior Courts as [it] may from time to time ordain and establish." The first federal Congress passed the Judiciary Act of 1789 to establish the structure of the federal court system under the Supreme Court of the United States.

An 1890 banquet celebrated the centennial of the federal judiciary, which was established by the Judiciary Act of 1789. The invitation bore the portraits of the first chief justice, John Jay, and the current one, Melville Fuller.

This 1789 law created two lower levels of federal courts. At the lowest level, it created 13 federal district courts, one for each of the 13 states. At the next level, it established three circuit courts to hear appeals from the district courts. At the top of the three-level federal judiciary was the Supreme Court, consisting of the chief justice of the United States and five associate justices.

The Judiciary Act of 1789 stipulated that the Supreme Court, as the court of last resort, would hear questions of law on appeal from lower federal courts. Section 25 of this law gave the Supreme Court the power to exercise judicial review over the highest state courts when they made decisions that involved issues of federal law or the U.S. Constitution.

SEE ALSO

Federal judicial system

FURTHER READING

Marcus, Maeva, ed. *Origins of the Federal Judiciary: Essays on the Judiciary Act of 1789.* New York: Oxford University Press, 1992.

Judiciary Act of 1869

THIS FEDERAL law set the number of Supreme Court justices at nine, the number that sits on the Court today. It also reformed the circuit courts by establishing a separate circuit court judiciary of nine members, one for each of nine new circuits or regions of the United States. Justices of the Supreme Court still had circuit-riding duties, but they were greatly decreased by the law; now they had to attend circuit court proceedings only once every two years.

SEE ALSO

Circuit Courts of Appeals

Judiciary Act of 1891

THIS FEDERAL law created a new intermediate level for the federal judiciary —nine U.S. Circuit Courts of Appeals (renamed Courts of Appeals in 1948). It eliminated the need for Supreme Court justices to participate in deciding circuit court cases. However, it retained the old circuit courts, which were not eliminated until 1911, when their work was assigned to the federal district courts, the lowest level of the federal judicial system.

The nine Courts of Appeals were staffed with three judges each. Since 1891

An 1885 cartoon depicts an over-worked Supreme Court. In 1891 the Judiciary Act relieved the Court's burden of deciding circuit court cases by establishing a new level of federal courts.

the number of the Courts of Appeals has increased to 13, one for each of 11 circuits or regions of the United States. In addition, there is the Court of Appeals for the District of Columbia Circuit and the Court of Appeals for the Federal Circuit. The basic structure of the federal judiciary today, however, was put in place by the Judiciary Act of 1891.

SEE ALSO
Courts of Appeals; Federal judicial system

Judiciary Act of 1925

THIS JUDICIARY Act gave the U.S. Supreme Court expanded power to decide which cases it would accept or reject from lower courts. By limiting the number of cases the Court was required to accept, the Judiciary Act left the Court free to concentrate on cases of great national and constitutional significance.

By sharply limiting the number of cases that would go to the Supreme Court, the 1925 act enhanced the authority and prestige of the Courts of Appeals. These appellate courts became the final review courts for the great majority of appellate cases.

Jurisdiction

THE EXTENT or scope of a court's authority to hear and decide a case properly brought to it is its jurisdiction. There are two types of jurisdiction: original and appellate.

Original jurisdiction is the authority of a court to hear and decide a case for the first time. In general, courts of original jurisdiction are minor courts or trial courts. Federal district courts, for example, are courts of original jurisdiction. Article 3, Section 2, of the U.S. Constitution states that the U.S. Supreme Court has original jurisdiction only in suits involving ambassadors from other countries and in suits to which a state of the United States is a party. For instance, the Court had original jurisdiction in *Georgia* v. *South Carolina* (1990), a case involving the correct location of a boundary between the two states. In all cases except the types listed above, the U.S. Supreme Court has appellate jurisdiction, which is the authority of a court to hear and decide cases brought on appeal from a lower court.

Indeed, the U.S. Supreme Court is primarily an appellate court. Throughout its history, the Court has exercised original jurisdiction in fewer than 160 cases. Article 3, Section 2, of the Constitution provides that "the Supreme Court shall have appellate Jurisdiction, both as to law and fact" with only a few exceptions. However, Article 3 also says that Congress has the power to regulate the nature and scope of the Supreme Court's power of appellate jurisdiction. Using this power, Congress passed the Judiciary Act of 1925 to give greater authority to the Court to decide which cases it would accept or reject on appeal from lower courts. The result was to greatly reduce the number of cases in the Court's caseload.

SEE ALSO
Judicial power

Just compensation

THE 5TH AMENDMENT to the U.S. Constitution states, "No person shall be...deprived of life, liberty, or property, without due process of law; nor shall private property be taken for public use without just compensation." The 5th Amendment recognizes the property rights of individuals and guarantees that the government must provide fair payment to a person whose property is taken for public use. Just compensation is determined by the market value of the property—the amount of money a willing buyer would pay a willing seller for the property in an open and free marketplace. In *Chicago, Burlington & Quincy Railroad Co.* v. *Chicago* (1897) the Supreme Court ruled that state and local governments are required to pay "just compensation" when taking private property for public use. In this case a public street in Chicago was opened across a privately owned railroad track.

SEE ALSO
Eminent domain

Justices of the Supreme Court

THERE ARE nine seats on the U.S. Supreme Court: one chief justice and eight associate justices. The number of justices is set by Congress. The Judiciary Act of 1789 created a Supreme Court of six members: five associate justices and a chief justice.

The size of the Court remained at six members until the Judiciary Act of 1801 reduced the number to five. A year later, however, the Judiciary Act of 1802 restored the six-member Court. Congress added a seventh justice in 1807, eighth and ninth justices in 1837, and a tenth justice in 1863.

In 1866, however, Congress reduced the Court to seven members. Through this measure, the Republican party majority in Congress deprived President Andrew Johnson, whom it opposed, of an opportunity to appoint new justices to the Court. After the election of the popular Ulysses S. Grant to the Presidency, Congress passed the Judiciary Act of 1869, which set the Court's membership at nine. This number has remained the same ever since. In 1937, President Franklin Roosevelt attempted unsuccessfully to expand the membership of the court to gain support on the Court for his New Deal programs. He proposed adding one justice to the Supreme Court for every member over 70 years of age, up to a total of six additional justices.

Duties and powers

The chief justice of the United States is the presiding officer of the Supreme Court and the head of the federal judiciary. The eight associate justices work with the chief justice to decide cases that come before the Court. They are expected to make and justify these decisions within the framework of the Constitution and the system of law based on it. The associate justices also collaborate with each other and the chief justice to review all petitions for certiorari (appeals from lower courts for a hearing before the Supreme Court) and decide which of these appeals will be accepted for Supreme Court review.

The U.S. Supreme Court during the Clinton administration. Seated, left to right, are Associate Justices Antonin Scalia and John Paul Stevens, Chief Justice William H. Rehnquist, Associate Justices Sandra Day O'Connor and Anthony M. Kennedy; standing, left to right, are Associate Justices Ruth Bader Ginsburg, David H. Souter, Clarence Thomas, and Stephen Breyer.

All associate justices are equal in their formal power. Each associate justice has one vote, and each vote has the same weight. Some justices, however, tend to have more influence than others on Court decisions because they have more skill in reasoning and arguing about legal issues. Some are better at managing human relationships and leading their peers. The justices with more ability to persuade through the force of intellect or personal style are likely to have a greater impact on the deliberations and decisions of the Court. For example, Justice William Brennan, who served on the Court from 1956 to 1990, had great ability to influence other justices. His colleague Thurgood Marshall said, "There's nobody here that can persuade the way Brennan can persuade."

The chief justice has more authority and power than the associate justices, even though he, too, has only one vote. The chief justice, in presiding over the Court in conference, is able to direct and structure the discussion of cases and thereby to influence the outcome. Further, the chief justice has authority to make up the first version of the discuss list, which is the list of petitions for Su-

preme Court review that will be considered. By carrying out this task, the chief justice has great power in determining which cases are to be denied a hearing by the Court. Another example of the special role of the chief justice is his power to assign the task of writing the Court's opinion on a case, whenever he is part of the majority in the initial vote in conference. When the chief justice is not part of the majority, the senior justice in the majority makes the assignment. The chief justice tends to make most of the assignments and is thereby able to influence the contents and style of the Court's opinion. For example, the chief may decide to write the opinion of the Court in very important cases, or he may choose an associate justice who tends to agree with him.

Appointment and terms

Both the chief justice and associate justices are appointed by the President of the United States "with the Advice and Consent of the Senate," as provided by Article 2, Section 2, of the U.S. Constitution. They "hold their Offices during good Behaviour," as prescribed by Article 3, Section 1, of the Constitution. This clause practically guarantees appointment for life for those who desire it. Fifty justices have died in office. The justice who served the longest on the Court was William O. Douglas, whose tenure was 36 years and 7 months (1939–75). Justice Oliver Wendell Holmes was the oldest person to serve on the Court. He retired in 1932 at age 90, after 30 years on the Court. By contrast, two associate justices served less than two years. Thomas Johnson had served less than 14 months when he died in 1793, the shortest tenure in the history of the Court. Justice James F. Byrnes served only 16 months before resigning in 1942 to take another job in the federal government.

Salaries of the justices

Article 3, Section 1, of the Constitution says, "The Judges, both of the supreme and inferior Courts, shall... at stated Times, receive for their Services, a Compensation, which shall not be diminished during their Continuance in Office." This provision was designed to keep the judiciary independent by protecting federal judges from threats of pay cuts that might influence their decisions.

The Judiciary Act of 1789 set the chief justice's annual salary at $4,000 and an associate justice's salary at $3,500. Since then, Congress has appropriated larger amounts for judicial salaries. The 1989 Ethics Reform Act provided an annual salary of $124,000 for the chief justice and $118,600 for the associate justices. In 2000 the associate justices received an annual salary of $173,600, and the chief justice was paid $181,400.

Membership of the Court

Since 1789, 96 people have served as associate justices of the U.S. Supreme Court. Five of the 16 chief justices served as associate justices before becoming chief justice: John Rutledge, Edward D. White, Charles Evans Hughes, Harlan F. Stone, and William H. Rehnquist. The overwhelming majority of the justices, including 14 of 16 chief justices, have been white men affiliated with Protestant religions.

The first woman associate justice is Sandra Day O'Connor, who was appointed in 1981 by President Ronald Reagan. Ruth Bader Ginsburg, appointed by President Bill Clinton in 1993, is the second woman to become an associate justice. Two associate justices have been African Americans: Thurgood Marshall, who served from 1967 to 1991, and Clarence Thomas, who was appointed in 1991 to replace Justice Marshall.

Six associate justices have been Jewish: Louis D. Brandeis, Benjamin Cardozo, Felix Frankfurter, Arthur Goldberg, Abe Fortas, and Ruth Bader Ginsburg.

Eight associate justices have been Roman Catholics: Edward D. White, Joseph McKenna, Pierce Butler, Frank Murphy, William Brennan, Antonin Scalia, Anthony Kennedy, and Clarence Thomas. White also served as chief justice. Another Roman Catholic, Roger B. Taney, served only as chief justice.

SEE ALSO

Chief justice; Court-packing plan; Judiciary Act of 1789; Judiciary Act of 1869; Opinions; Seniority

Justiciable questions

THE U.S. SUPREME COURT has held that federal courts may deal only with cases or questions that are justiciable, that is, questions "appropriate for judicial determination" (*Aetna Life Insurance Co.* v. *Haworth,* 1937). In the *Aetna* case Chief Justice Charles Evans Hughes discussed the differences between justiciable questions or issues and those not justiciable. He emphasized that justiciable questions involve a "real and substantial controversy" that can be resolved by a conclusive decision of a court of law.

The U.S. Supreme Court does not provide advisory opinions because they do not pertain to justiciable questions: real cases that are appropriate for a judicial decision. The Court also does not accept cases that require decisions on political questions because they cannot, in the Court's opinion, be resolved on legal or constitutional grounds. Rather, political questions are those appropriate for resolution by the legislative and executive branches of government. For instance, the President, not the Court, decides whether the United States should recognize and maintain diplomatic relations with foreign governments. The Congress, not the Court, decides political questions such as how much federal money should be appropriated to maintain the U.S. armed forces.

SEE ALSO

Advisory opinions; Jurisdiction; Political questions

Juvenile justice

PEOPLE WHO have not reached the legal age of adulthood (usually 18 years old) are considered juveniles under the law. There are special courts of law throughout the United States designed to meet the presumed needs of preadult lawbreakers. These juvenile courts are the core of a system of juvenile justice, with legal procedures that specify what can and cannot be done with, to, and for juveniles by various public officials, including police, prosecutors, judges, and probation officers. The juvenile justice system is separate from the adult criminal justice system.

Juveniles are required to obey the same federal, state, and local laws that adults must obey. Both juveniles and adults, for example, are required to obey laws forbidding such criminal offenses as burglary, arson, rape, and murder. Juveniles also are required to obey laws that adults do not have to obey, such as laws against running away from home, disobeying parents, refusing to attend school (truancy), drinking alcoholic beverages, or participating in consensual sexual activity. Such laws pertain to *status offenses,* so called because they apply only to those with the status of a juvenile.

In most states, people under 18 years old are sent to a juvenile court when they break the law. In a few states, such as New York, those older than 15 who commit criminal offenses are sent to an adult criminal court. In general, juveniles may be tried in an adult court when they commit serious or frequent crimes.

In a few states, such as Pennsylvania, all juveniles accused of homicide (no matter what their age) are sent directly to an adult criminal court. There, the juvenile's lawyer can try to persuade the judge that the accused youth should be transferred to a juvenile court. If the judge agrees, the case can be sent to a juvenile court.

The original purpose of juvenile courts was to provide special care and treatment for preadult offenders, with the intention of rehabilitating the offender in order to prevent repeated illegal behavior. A symbol of the special concern for preadult offenders in juvenile courts is the manner of naming the cases. The typical title of a juvenile court case is *In re Joe Dokes,* which means "in the matter of..." By contrast, the usual title of a criminal court case is *State* v. *Joe Dokes,* which implies that the defendant is involved in a legal contest with the state. There usually is no suggestion in the name of a juvenile court case that the

The Juvenile Rights Division of the Legal Aid Society recruits students at New York University law school. The juvenile justice system is separate from the adult system so that rehabilitation may be offered to preadult offenders where possible.

preadult (Joe Dokes) must defend himself against the state. In return for the special care provided to offenders in the juvenile justice system, juveniles did not have the constitutional rights to due process of law guaranteed to adults in criminal courts, such as the right to counsel, the right to confront and cross-examine witnesses, and the protection against self-incrimination.

During the 1950s critics pointed out that juvenile courts often did not provide special concern for preadult offenders or act in their best interests. Rather, the juvenile justice system often appeared only to punish juveniles for their offenses and not to remedy their problems or address their particular needs. So the critics recommended that juveniles accused of criminal offenses should have the constitutional rights of due process, just like adults in criminal courts.

In the case of *In re Gault* (1967), the Supreme Court for the first time confronted the issue of due process rights for juvenile offenders. The Court rejected the traditional claim that a juvenile's rights are sufficiently protected by judges in juvenile courts, who act as substitute parents. Rather, the Court held that juvenile courts must provide the same basic due process rights that the U.S. Constitution guarantees to

adults. Writing for the Court, Justice Abe Fortas specified four due process rights that must be provided: written notification of specific charges to the juvenile and his or her parents, assistance of a lawyer, confrontational cross-examination of witnesses, and protection against self-incrimination (the right to remain silent when questioned by prosecutors).

The constitutional rights of preadults in juvenile courts were expanded by the Court in the case of *In re Winship* (1970). The offender, Samuel Winship, was convicted of theft by a juvenile court judge. However, the evidence used to convict Winship was slight. It would not have met the standard of proof typically used in an adult criminal case, which is referred to as proof "beyond a reasonable doubt." This means that the evidence against the accused person is so great that there can be little or no doubt that the person committed the crime. The Court decided that preadults in a juvenile court should have the right to the higher standard of proof available in criminal court proceedings.

In *McKeiver* v. *Pennsylvania* (1971), a juvenile was charged with robbery, larceny, and receiving stolen goods. The defendant's lawyer requested a trial by jury because punishment for these serious offenses could be as much as five years of detention. The state refused the lawyer's request and the defendant was convicted and sentenced without a jury trial. He appealed on the grounds that the right to trial by jury, granted to adults accused of criminal offenses, was unconstitutionally denied to him.

The Supreme Court decided that due process of law for juveniles does not require a trial by jury. Writing for the Court, Justice Harry Blackmun argued that a jury trial would subject juveniles to unnecessary and disruptive adversarial proceedings without the compensating benefits of greater accuracy in fact-finding or determination of guilt or innocence. The *McKeiver* decision indicated that the Court was unwilling to extend all the rights of the criminally accused to juveniles charged with criminal offenses.

In *Schall* v. *Martin* (1984) the Court made another decision that limits the due process rights of juveniles. The Court upheld a New York law that permits a judge to order pretrial confinement for up to 17 days of a juvenile accused of a criminal offense, when there is a significant risk that the juvenile may commit a serious crime before the trial. Justice William Rehnquist emphasized that it is the state's duty to protect the community against criminal acts. The *Schall* decision has influenced other states to enact preventive detention laws similar to the New York law upheld by the Court. Justice Thurgood Marshall dissented from the Court's opinion in *Schall* v. *Martin*. He argued that preventive detention laws give power to judges to treat different juveniles unequally and unfairly.

The *McKeiver* and *Schall* decisions put certain limitations on due process rights in the juvenile justice system. The due process protections provided by the *Gault* and *Winship* decisions, however, have been firmly established. They have profoundly changed the juvenile justice system in the United States.

Before the *Gault* decision, juveniles had no due process rights. But in exchange for the lack of legal protection from the state, juveniles were supposed to receive benevolent treatment from officials. This pre-*Gault* juvenile justice system permitted competent, caring officials to readily help children. There were no complex due process procedures to get in the way of direct, discreet, and benign behavior on the part of good officials to assist troubled youths. The

problem with the pre-*Gault* system was that bad or stupid officials could hurt juveniles, who had no recourse to due process procedures to protect them from abuses of the system.

The post-*Gault* juvenile justice system is concerned more with punishment and prevention of crime than with treatment and reform of troubled youth. Thus, it has become more like the adult criminal justice system, with its adversarial proceedings and guarantees of constitutional due process rights to protect the accused person against the power of the state. Older juveniles accused of serious criminal offenses are likely to be transferred to the criminal courts. Status offenses, such as truancy or disobedience, are still handled by juvenile courts in the traditional paternal and caring manner, with an emphasis on diagnosis and treatment of the psychological and social problems of the offenders.

SEE ALSO

Due process of law; In re Gault; In re Winship; McKeiver v. Pennsylvania

FURTHER READING

Bernard, Thomas J. *The Cycle of Juvenile Justice*. New York: Oxford University Press, 1992.
Manfredi, Christopher P. *The Supreme Court and Juvenile Justice*. Lawrence: University Press of Kansas, 2000.

Katz v. United States

☆ *389 U.S. 347 (1967)*
☆ *Vote: 7–1*
☆ *For the Court: Stewart*
☆ *Concurring: Harlan and White*
☆ *Dissenting: Black*
☆ *Not Participating: Marshall*

CHARLES KATZ was known to be a gambler, and the Federal Bureau of Investigation (FBI) suspected him of engaging in illegal activities in making bets. In particular, the FBI believed he

was using a public telephone booth to transmit information about wagers from Los Angeles to Miami and Boston. So FBI agents placed electronic devices outside a telephone booth regularly used by Katz to make his calls. The agents recorded Katz's telephone conversations in order to gather evidence of his illegal gambling activity.

At Katz's trial, the federal government used evidence of his telephone conversations to win a conviction. Katz appealed his conviction on grounds that the evidence introduced against him had been obtained illegally.

The Issue Charles Katz argued that the government had violated his 4th Amendment rights—"The right of the people to be secure in their persons, houses, papers, and effects, against unreasonable searches and seizures." Katz said that the illegally gathered evidence against him should have been excluded from his trial.

Lawyers for the federal government argued that placing a tap on the outside of a public telephone booth was not a violation of the 4th Amendment. They based their argument on the case of *Olmstead* v. *United States* (1928), which had permitted federal government use of electronic surveillance and wiretapping on the grounds that those actions outside a person's home fell outside the scope of the 4th Amendment.

Opinion of the Court In *Katz,* the Court overturned the decision in *Olmstead* v. *United States.* Justice Potter Stewart argued that the 4th Amendment protects people, not places. It protects an individual's right even in a place accessible to the public, such as a telephone booth on a street corner. Justice Stewart wrote, "[T]he Government's activities in electronically listening to and recording [Katz's] words violated the privacy upon which he justifiably relied while using the telephone booth

and thus constituted a 'search and seizure' within the meaning of the Fourth Amendment."

Significance The *Katz* case expanded the scope of 4th Amendment rights to include protection against certain kinds of electronic invasions of an individual's privacy. Since the *Katz* decision, the 4th Amendment has been a means to protect individual privacy in places open to the public.

SEE ALSO

Olmstead v. United States; Searches and seizures

FURTHER READING

Westin, Alvin F. "Civil Liberties in the Technology Age." *Constitution* 3, no. 1 (Winter 1991): 56–64.

In the Katz *case, the Court decided an FBI wiretap of a public phone is illegal. The 4th Amendment, according to the Court, protects people from invasions of their privacy, even in public places.*

Kennedy, Anthony M.

ASSOCIATE JUSTICE, 1988–

☆ *Born: July 23, 1936, Sacramento, Calif.*

☆ *Education: Stanford University, B.A., 1958; London School of Economics, 1957–58; Harvard Law School, LL.B., 1961*

☆ *Previous government service: judge, Ninth Circuit Court of Appeals, 1975–88*

☆ *Appointed by President Ronald Reagan Nov. 30, 1987; replaced Louis F. Powell, Jr., who retired*

☆ Supreme Court term: confirmed by the Senate Feb. 3, 1988, by a 97–0 vote

ANTHONY M. KENNEDY was, for most of his career, a partner in a law firm and a teacher at the McGeorge School of Law of the University of the Pacific in Sacramento, California. President Gerald Ford appointed Kennedy to be a federal appellate court judge, and between 1975 and 1988, Kennedy wrote more than 400 opinions as a federal judge on the Ninth Circuit Court of Appeals.

After his appointment to the Supreme Court in 1988, Justice Kennedy, as a moderate conservative, tended to vote in agreement with Chief Justice William Rehnquist during the 1988–89 term. In 90 percent of the cases, he voted in agreement with the chief justice. Since then, he has shown more independence.

In *Church of the Lukumi Babalu Aye* v. *City of Hialeah* (1993), Kennedy wrote the decision for the Court to strike down a city's ban on ritual animal sacrifice, practiced by the followers of the Santería religion. Kennedy held that the city government of Hialeah, Florida, had violated the 1st Amendment right to free exercise of religion. In *Romer* v. *Evans* (1996), he wrote the Court's opinion to strike down an amendment to the Colorado constitution that prohibited legislation created specifically to protect the rights of homosexuals.

Korematsu v. United States

☆ *323 U.S. 214 (1944)*
☆ *Vote: 6–3*
☆ *For the Court: Black*
☆ *Concurring: Frankfurter*
☆ *Dissenting: Roberts, Murphy, and Jackson*

AFTER JAPAN'S attack on Pearl Harbor, Hawaii, on December 7, 1941, more than 100,000 Americans of Japanese ancestry were removed from their homes on the Pacific Coast of the United States and sent to internment camps in the interior of the country. Most of them spent the duration of the war, until August 1945, confined in one of these camps, even though they were loyal U.S. citizens who had done nothing to harm their homeland, the United States.

One such U.S. citizen was Fred Korematsu, born and raised in Alameda County, California. He had never visited Japan and knew little or nothing about the Japanese way of life.

In June 1941, before the official U.S. declaration of war, Fred Korematsu had tried to enlist in the navy. Although the navy was actively recruiting men in anticipation of the U.S. entry into the war, the service did not allow Korematsu to enlist because of poor health. He then went to work in a shipyard as a welder. When the war began, he lost his job because of his Japanese heritage.

On May 9, 1942, General John L. DeWitt ordered all people of Japanese background or ancestry excluded from Military Area No. 1, the Pacific coastal region of the United States. This military order was authorized by an executive order of President Franklin D. Roosevelt (issued on February 19) and an act of Congress (passed on March 21).

Hoping to move to Nevada with his fiancée, who was not of Japanese ancestry, Korematsu ignored the evacuation orders when they came. As a U.S. citizen, he felt the orders should not apply to him in any event. The FBI arrested Korematsu, and he was convicted of violating the orders of the commander of Military Area No. 1.

The Issue   The U.S. government justified the internment in two ways. The government claimed that American citizens of Japanese ancestry were more loyal to Japan than to their own country and would spy for Japan. Second, the government claimed that because Japan had attacked the U.S. territory of Hawaii, those Americans of Japanese ancestry might have helped Japan.

Korematsu claimed that military commanders, acting under authority granted by the President and Congress, had denied more than 75,000 U.S. citizens their constitutional rights of due process. The 5th Amendment says, "No person shall be . . . deprived of life, liberty, or property, without due process of law." Had the government wrongly taken away the constitutional rights of Japanese Americans?

Opinion of the Court   The Court upheld the exclusion of Japanese Americans from the Pacific coastal region. The needs of national security in a time of crisis, it said, justified the exclusion orders. The war powers of the President and Congress, specified by the Constitution, provided the legal basis for the majority decision.

Justice Hugo Black admitted that the exclusion orders forced citizens of Japanese ancestry to endure severe hardships. "But hardships are a part of war," said Black, "and war is an aggregation of hardships."

Justice Black maintained that the orders had not excluded Korematsu primarily for reasons of race but for reasons of military security. The majority ruling really did not say whether the relocation of Japanese Americans was constitutional. Rather, the Court sidestepped that touchy issue, emphasizing instead the national crisis caused by the war.

Dissent   Three justices—Frank Murphy, Robert Jackson, and Owen Roberts—disagreed with the majority.

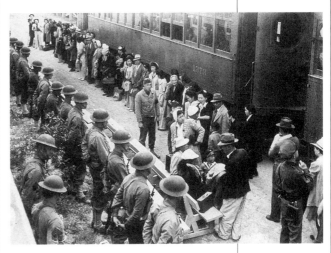

Justice Roberts thought it a plain "case of convicting a citizen as punishment for not submitting to imprisonment in a concentration camp solely because of his ancestry," without evidence concerning his loyalty to the United States.

Justice Murphy said that the exclusion orders violated the right of citizens to due process of law. Furthermore, Murphy protested that the decision of the Court's majority amounted to the "legalization of racism. Racial discrimination in any form and in any degree has no justifiable part whatever in our democratic way of life."

Murphy admitted that the argument citing military necessity carried weight, but he insisted that such a claim must "subject itself to the judicial process" to determine "whether the deprivation is reasonably related to a public danger that is so 'immediate, imminent, and impending.' "

Finally, Murphy concluded that "individuals must not be left impoverished in their constitutional rights on a plea of military necessity that has neither substance nor support."

Justice Jackson expressed grave concern about the future uses of the precedent set in this case. He wrote:

A military order, however unconstitutional, is not apt to last longer than the military emergency. . . . But once a judi-

U.S. citizens of Japanese ancestry arrive at a relocation center in Santa Anita, California, before being moved to camps farther inland.

cial opinion rationalizes such an order to show that it conforms to the Constitution…the Court for all time has validated the principle of racial discrimination in criminal procedures and of transplanting American citizens. The principle then lies about like a loaded weapon ready for the hand of any authority that can bring forward a plausible claim of an urgent need.

Significance The *Korematsu* ruling has never been revoked by law or Supreme Court ruling. In 1980, however, Congress reopened investigations into the treatment of Japanese Americans during World War II and created the Commission on Wartime Relocation and Internment of Civilians. After nearly three years of careful examination of the evidence, which included testimony from 750 witnesses, the commission issued a report on February 25, 1983. The report concluded: "A grave injustice was done to American citizens and resident aliens of Japanese ancestry who, without individual review or any probative evidence against them, were excluded, removed, and detained by the United States during World War II."

In 1988, on the basis of the 1983 report, Congress officially recognized the "grave injustice" of the relocation and internment experience and offered payments of $20,000 as compensation to each person still living who had been detained in a relocation center.

SEE ALSO
Hirabayashi v. United States

FURTHER READING
Irons, Peter. *Justice at War.* New York: Oxford University Press, 1983.
Mydans, Carl. "Internment Remembered." *Constitution* 4, no. 1 (Winter 1992): 43.
Rauch, Rudolph S. "Internment." *Constitution* 4, no. 1 (Winter 1992): 30–42.

Kunz v. New York

☆ *340 U.S. 290 (1951)*
☆ *Vote: 8–1*

☆ *For the Court: Vinson*
☆ *Concurring: Black and Frankfurter*
☆ *Dissenting: Jackson*

A BAPTIST MINISTER, Carl J. Kunz, was denied a permit to preach on the streets of New York City by the city police commissioner. A city ordinance prohibited religious services on public streets without a permit from the city government. The ordinance did not spell out the reasons for denying someone a permit. The Reverend Mr. Kunz was denied a permit because he had a reputation for using obscene words in his speeches to denounce Catholics and Jews. Kunz defied the city ordinance and preached on a street corner without a permit. He was arrested and convicted for violating the city ordinance.

The Issue Were Carl Kunz's rights to freedom of speech and free exercise of religion, guaranteed by the 1st and 14th Amendments, violated by the New York City ordinance that was used to deny him a permit to preach in public?

Opinion of the Court The Court struck down as unconstitutional the New York City ordinance that barred worship services on public streets without a permit. Chief Justice Fred Vinson said that enforcement of the ordinance was an unconstitutional "prior restraint" (advance censorship) on an individual's rights to free speech and free exercise of religion. Vinson ruled that New York could not legally give an administrative official control over the right to speak on religious subjects without "appropriate standards to guide his action."

Dissent Justice Robert Jackson defended the restrictions on Kunz's freedom of expression because the reverend had used "fighting words." Justice Jackson based his dissenting opinion on the "fighting words" doctrine used by the

Court in *Chaplinski* v. *New Hampshire* (1942), which held that "the lewd and obscene, the profane, the libelous" and insulting or "fighting words" did not have any "social value" in the search for truth, public order, and safety. Therefore, the Court had ruled that "fighting words" are outside the protection of 1st Amendment guarantees of free speech.

Significance The *Kunz* case established that any broadly worded law restricting freedom of expression in public places is an unconstitutional exercise of prior restraint. The "fighting words" doctrine, employed in the dissenting opinion, has subsequently declined as an argument for restrictions on speech. The only prevailing justification for restricting speech is to prevent direct, immediate, and substantial harm to a vital social interest, such as national security, public order, and the safety of individuals.

SEE ALSO
Freedom of speech and press

Lamar, Joseph R.

ASSOCIATE JUSTICE,
1911–16

☆ *Born: Oct. 14, 1857, Ruckersville, Ga.*
☆ *Education: University of Georgia, 1874–75; Bethany College, B.A., 1877; Washington and Lee University, 1877*
☆ *Previous government service: Georgia House of Representatives, 1886–89; commissioner to codify Georgia laws, 1893; associate justice, Georgia Supreme Court, 1903–5*
☆ *Appointed by President William Howard Taft Dec. 12, 1910; replaced William Henry Moody, who retired*
☆ *Supreme Court term: confirmed by the Senate Dec. 15, 1910, by a voice vote; served until Jan. 2, 1916*
☆ *Died: Jan. 2, 1916, Washington, D.C.*

JOSEPH R. LAMAR belonged to a socially prominent family in Georgia. His

ardent studies of law and legal history led to his appointment to a state commission to codify the laws of Georgia. He alone wrote the resulting volume on civil law in Georgia. He later wrote several books on the history of law in Georgia.

During his brief term on the Court, Justice Lamar tended to vote with the majority. He wrote only eight dissents. His only notable opinion for the Court was in a 1911 case, *United States* v. *Grimaud*, which upheld a federal law, the Forest Reserve Act of 1911. This decision gave leeway to federal administrations to "fill in details" when carrying out laws.

Lamar, Lucius Q.C.

ASSOCIATE JUSTICE,
1888–93

☆ *Born: Sept. 17, 1825, Eatonton, Ga.*
☆ *Education: Emory College, B.A., 1845*
☆ *Previous government service: Georgia House of Representatives, 1853; U.S. representative from Mississippi, 1857–60, 1873–77; U.S. senator from Mississippi, 1877–85; U.S. secretary of the interior, 1885–88*
☆ *Appointed by President Grover Cleveland Dec. 6, 1887; replaced William Woods, who died*
☆ *Supreme Court term: confirmed by the Senate Jan. 16, 1888, by a 42–38 vote; served until Jan. 23, 1893*
☆ *Died: Jan. 23, 1893, Macon, Ga.*

LUCIUS LAMAR was a prominent leader of the Confederate States of America and wrote the state of Mississippi's ordinance of secession from the United States. In 1861 he resigned from the U.S. Congress to become a colonel in the Confederate army and fight against the Union in the Civil War. Years later, Lucius Lamar was called the "Great Pacificator" because of his efforts to reconcile the differences

between Americans who had fought on opposing sides in the Civil War.

During the latter half of the 1800s, Lamar served in all three branches of the federal government: as a member of Congress, as the secretary of the interior, and as an associate justice of the Supreme Court. His nomination to the Court by President Grover Cleveland was bitterly opposed by die-hard foes of anyone associated with the Confederate cause. As a result, Lamar was narrowly confirmed by a Senate vote of 42 to 38. He was the first Southerner to take a seat on the Court since his own cousin, John A. Campbell, in 1853. During his brief term on the Court, Lamar tended to vote with the Court majority in opposition to strong state regulation of economic activity.

FURTHER READING

Murphy, James B. *L. Q. C. Lamar, Pragmatic Patriot.* Baton Rouge: Louisiana State University Press, 1973.

Lawyers' Edition

ONE OF the unofficial publications of U.S. Supreme Court decisions is *United States Supreme Court Reports,* Lawyers' Edition, which began in 1882. It is commonly referred to as the *Lawyers' Edition.* Special features of this publication are summaries of briefs in selected cases and annotations of key ideas and arguments in some very significant cases.

The single official version of all U.S. Supreme Court decisions is *United States Reports,* which is published by the U.S. Government Printing Office.

SEE ALSO

Supreme Court Reporter; United States Reports; Appendix 3: Web Sites

Legal Counsel, Office of the

S E E Staff of the Court, nonjudicial

Lemon Test

IN LEMON V. KURTZMAN (1971), the Supreme Court stated three standards, or criteria, by which to decide cases involving disputes about the meaning of the 1st Amendment's establishment clause, which concerns government involvement with religion. These three standards are known as the Lemon Test. In order for a statute *not* to violate the establishment clause, it must meet these three conditions: First, it must have a secular or nonreligious purpose. Second, it must neither promote nor restrict religion in its primary effects. Third, it must not bring about an excessive entanglement with religion.

SEE ALSO

Establishment clause; Lemon v. Kurtzman; Religious issues under the Constitution

Lemon v. Kurtzman

☆ *403 U.S. 602 (1971)*
☆ *Vote: 8–0*
☆ *For the Court: Burger*
☆ *Concurring: Brennan and White*
☆ *Not participating: Marshall*

ACCORDING TO Pennsylvania's Non-Public Elementary and Secondary Education Act of 1968, the state could directly support salaries of teachers of secular (nonreligious) subjects in parochial (church-run) and other private schools. The state could also reimburse the non-public schools for the purchase of textbooks and other instructional materials used to teach secular subjects. Alton Lemon, a taxpayer and resident of Pennsylvania, believed these state government payments of expenses for parochial schools, which had the primary mission of promoting particular religious beliefs, were unconstitutional. So Lemon brought suit against David Kurtzman, the state superintendent of schools, to stop state payments to parochial schools.

The Issue Did the Pennsylvania law, which authorized state payments to Roman Catholic schools and other private schools with a religious mission, violate the 1st Amendment's religious freedom clause, which said, "Congress shall make no law respecting an establishment of religion, or prohibiting the free exercise thereof"?

Opinion of the Court The Court struck down the Pennsylvania law at issue in this case because it provided for an "excessive entanglement" of the state with institutions (parochial schools) set up for the purpose of promoting religious doctrine. Chief Justice Warren Burger wrote, "The Constitution decrees that religion must be a private matter for the individual, the family, and the institutions of private choice, and that while some involvement and entanglements are inevitable, lines must be drawn."

The Court drew three lines, known ever since as the Lemon Test, to guide decisions in similar cases. For a statute to be constitutional under the establishment clause of the 1st Amendment, it had to meet these three standards of the Lemon Test: it must have a secular or nonreligious purpose; it must neither promote nor interfere with religion; and it cannot cause an excessive entanglement of government with religion.

Although the Court had maintained a barrier between church and state, Chief Justice Burger said it was "far

from being a wall." He was referring to Thomas Jefferson's famous phrase— "a wall of separation between church and state"—which the Court had used previously to interpret the establishment clause of the 1st Amendment. Burger claimed that separation of church and state is "a blurred, indistinct, and a variable barrier depending on all the circumstances of a particular relationship."

Significance The Court maintained a separation of church and state, as it had in several other cases since the 1940s, such as *Everson* v. *Board of Education of Ewing Township* (1947), *Engel* v. *Vitale* (1962), and *Abington School District* v. *Schempp* (1963). Further, the Court attempted to clarify the meaning of the separation of church and state through its three-part Lemon Test. However, the Court, through the opinion of Chief Justice Burger, exhibited uncertainty about when or how this "variable barrier" of separation between church and state might be lowered.

In 1993 the Court upheld student led prayers at graduation ceremonies when it let stand the Fifth Circuit Court of Appeals decision in *Jones* v. *Clear Creek Independent School District*. But in *Lee* v. *Weisman* (1992), the Court struck down a Rhode Island policy that permitted school officials to include prayers in public high school graduation

In Lemon *v.* Kurtzman, *the Court ruled that a state cannot pay the salaries of teachers of secular subjects in religious schools. The Court also established a series of guidelines known as the Lemon Test to determine if government involvement with religious schools is constitutional.*

ceremonies. Further, in *Zobrest* v. *Catalina School District* (1993), the court ruled that government funds can be used to pay for a sign-language interpreter to assist a deaf student in a Catholic school.

SEE ALSO

Abington School District v. Schempp; Engel v. Vitale; Everson v. Board of Education of Ewing Township; Lemon Test; Religious issues under the Constitution

LEXIS

LEXIS IS a computerized legal research service operated by a private corporation. It contains the full text of all Supreme Court decisions from 1790 to the present. The Court electronically transmits its decisions to the LEXIS database on the same day they are made. LEXIS users can access either the citations or the full text of particular Supreme Court decisions and print them out.

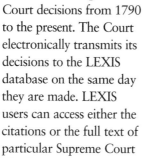

The LEXIS database allows lawyers instant electronic access to Supreme Court opinions.

SEE ALSO

WESTLAW; Appendix 3: Web Sites

Liberty under the Constitution

LIBERTY MEANS that a person is free to make choices about, for example, what to say or to do. A primary purpose of constitutional government in the United States is to make the liberty of individuals secure. The preamble to the Constitution proclaims that a principal reason for establishing the federal gov-

ernment is to "secure the Blessings of Liberty to ourselves and our Posterity."

The Bill of Rights, Amendments 1 to 10 of the Constitution, protects the individual's rights to liberty from the power of government. The 1st Amendment, for example, says that Congress shall not take away a person's freedoms of religion, speech, press, assembly, and petition. The 4th Amendment protects personal liberty; it guarantees the right of the people to be secure against unwarranted intrusions into their private lives by forbidding "unreasonable searches and seizures" by government officials. The 5th Amendment prohibits the federal government from taking away a person's "life, liberty, or property, without due process of law." And the 14th Amendment applies the same prohibition against abuses of a person's liberty by state governments.

The freedoms spelled out in the U.S. Constitution are called civil liberties. However, these civil liberties are not granted by government to individuals. Rather, the Constitution assumes that all people automatically have these civil liberties and therefore restrains the government from using its power to abuse individuals. Thus, there is a private realm of life, which government officials cannot invade without violating the Constitution. Within this domain of privacy, individuals have certain liberties of thought, belief, and action.

The Constitution also guarantees liberty for the people to participate publicly in the political life of their society. The 1st Amendment freedoms, for example, protect a person's right to participate freely in activities to elect representatives in government and to influence public decisions of elected and appointed government officials.

Liberty under the Constitution, then, is secured by limiting the power of government in order to protect the

"Justice the Guardian of Liberty" is the inscription on the rear of the Supreme Court Building.

people's rights to freedom. But if the government has too little power, so that law and order break down, then the people's liberties may be lost. Neither freedom of thought nor action is secure in a lawless and disorderly society, where there are no law enforcement officers to protect people against criminals who would abuse them.

So an overriding purpose of constitutional government in the United States has been to provide for the use of sufficient power to maintain order, stability, and security for the liberties of the people. The American Declaration of Independence (1776), for example, clearly and emphatically states, "That to secure these Rights [to Life, Liberty, and the Pursuit of Happiness] Governments are instituted among Men."

Ordered liberty is the desirable condition whereby both public order and personal liberty are secured for the individuals in a society. How can liberty and authority, freedom and power, be combined and balanced? This was the basic political problem of the founding period in the United States, and it continues to challenge Americans today. During the debate on ratification of the Constitution, for example, James Madison wrote to Thomas Jefferson in 1788, "It is a melancholy reflection that liberty should

be equally exposed to danger whether the Government have too much or too little power; and that the line which divides these extremes should be so inaccurately defined by experience."

Madison noted the standing threat to liberty posed by insufficient constitutional limits on government. He also recognized that liberty carried to the extreme of license, as in a riot, is equally dangerous to the freedom and rights of individuals. A good constitution is a source of liberty and order, but the right mix of these two factors is sometimes difficult to find and maintain. The challenging questions, of course, are these two: At what point, and under what conditions, should the power of government be limited to protect the rights to liberty of individuals? At what point, and under what conditions, should limits be placed on the freedoms and rights of individuals to protect public order, upon which the security for liberty depends?

In the United States, the Supreme Court has the power and the constitutional responsibility to address authoritatively these broad questions and to resolve disputes about them on a case-by-case basis. Through its power of judicial review, the Court can uphold or overturn, as violations of the Constitution, acts of federal and state governments pertaining to questions of liberty and order. But the questions are never answered for all time. They remain as challenges of a constitutional democracy.

In many of its landmark decisions, the Supreme Court has decided to protect the individual's rights to liberty under the Constitution from an unconstitutional exercise of power by government officials. In *Katz* v. *United States* (1967), for example, the Court prohibited federal law enforcement officials from using evidence against a defendant gained by electronic surveillance (listening in) of his telephone conversations. According to the Court, the federal agents had violated the 4th Amendment guarantee of security "against unreasonable searches and seizures." And in *Texas* v. *Johnson* (1989) the Court struck down, as an unconstitutional violation of 1st Amendment rights to freedom of expression, a state law that banned public protest involving the burning of the American flag.

In other significant decisions, the Court has upheld the constitutional exercise of government power and thereby restricted the rights to liberty of individuals. In *United States* v. *Ross* (1982) the Court upheld the authority of police officers to search an entire automobile they have stopped, without obtaining a warrant (required by the 4th Amendment), if they have "probable cause" to suspect that drugs or other illegally possessed objects are in the vehicle. And in *Kovacs* v. *Cooper* (1949) the Court upheld as constitutional a local law that banned the use of sound-amplifying equipment on city streets to transmit information. In this case, the Court favored the community's desire to avoid noisy disturbances over the individual's presumed constitutional right to freedom of expression.

SEE ALSO

Bill of Rights; Civil rights; Constitutional democracy; Constitutionalism; Judicial review; Katz v. United States; Texas v. Johnson; United States v. Ross

FURTHER READING

Barnett, Randy E. *The Structure of Liberty: Justice and the Rule of Law.* New York: Oxford University Press, 1998.
Dinan, John J. *Keeping the People's Liberties: Legislators, Citizens, and Judges as Guardians of Rights.* Lawrence: University Press of Kansas, 1998.
Hand, Learned. *The Spirit of Liberty.* New York: Knopf, 1960.
Kammen, Michael. *Spheres of Liberty: Changing Perceptions of Liberty in American Culture.* Ithaca, N.Y.: Cornell University Press, 1986.
Muller, Herbert J. *Freedom in the Western World.* New York: Harper & Row, 1963.
Patterson, Orlando. *Freedom in the Making of Western Culture.* New York: Basic Books, 1991.
Sandoz, Ellis, ed. *The Roots of Liberty.* Columbia: University of Missouri Press, 1993.

Librarian, Supreme Court

S E E Staff of the Court, nonjudicial

Limited government

S E E Constitutional democracy; Constitutionalism; Separation of powers

Livingston, Henry Brockholst

ASSOCIATE JUSTICE, 1807–23

☆ Born: Nov. 25, 1757, New York, N.Y.
☆ Education: College of New Jersey (Princeton), B.A., 1774; studied law with Peter Yates in New York, N.Y.
☆ Previous government service: New York Assembly, 1786, 1798–99; judge, New York State Supreme Court, 1802–7
☆ Appointed by President Thomas Jefferson as a recess appointment Nov. 10, 1806; replaced William Paterson, who died; nominated by Jefferson Dec. 13, 1806
☆ Supreme Court term: confirmed by the Senate Dec. 17, 1806, by a voice vote; served until Mar. 18, 1823
☆ Died: Mar. 18, 1823, Washington, D.C.

HENRY BROCKHOLST LIVINGSTON was a patriot who served in the Continental Army during the American War of Independence. After the war, he practiced law in New York and became a leading judge of the New York State Supreme Court.

Justice Livingston was a minor figure on the U.S. Supreme Court, which was dominated at that time by Chief Justice John Marshall. However, he was considered an expert on commercial law.

Lochner v. New York

☆ *198 U.S. 45 (1905)*
☆ *Vote: 5–4*
☆ *For the Court: Peckham*
☆ *Dissenting: Harlan, White, Day, and Holmes*

JOSEPH LOCHNER owned a small bakery shop in Utica, New York. In 1901 the state charged him with violating the Bakeshop Act, a New York law that banned bakers from working more than 10 hours a day or 60 hours a week. Lochner had required an employee, Aman Schmitter, to work more than the 60 hours per week permitted by the state law. The Oneida County Court convicted Lochner, and he appealed his case. After losing in the New York State appellate courts, Lochner appealed to the U.S. Supreme Court.

The Issue Lochner said that the Bakeshop Act violated the 14th Amendment because it deprived him of "life, liberty, or property, without due process of law." Lochner claimed that the Bakeshop Act unconstitutionally interfered with his freedom to make a contract with his workers about pay and hours of work. State officials countered that the Bakeshop Act was intended to protect the health and well-being of workers against employers who might otherwise exploit them.

Opinion of the Court Justice Rufus Peckham, writing for the Court, said the Bakeshop Act was unconstitutional because it took away "the right of the individual to liberty of person and freedom of contract." Under the 14th Amend-

ment, Peckham argued, individuals were free to purchase and sell labor. Therefore, any state law interfering with this "liberty of contract" would be unconstitutional "unless there are circumstances which exclude that right."

This right was not stated in the Constitution. Rather, the Court "found" this right through its interpretation of the due process clause of the 14th Amendment, which says that no state government shall "deprive any person of life, liberty, or property without due process of law." Thus, the Court developed the doctrine of substantive due process, by which it claimed the power to examine the content of laws to determine their fairness. In this way, the Court decides whether laws violate any fundamental rights of individuals, such as rights the Court believes to be associated with "life, liberty, or property." This doctrine of substantive due process was a departure from the traditional understanding of due process solely as government procedures that follow rules of fairness.

Dissent Justice Oliver Wendell Holmes sharply disagreed with the *Lochner* decision and the doctrine of substantive due process upon which it

The bakery owned by Joseph Lochner in Utica, New York. In Lochner v. New York, *the Court struck down a state law limiting the number of hours an employee could work.*

was based. He argued that the Bakeshop Act was a "reasonable" regulation of private business in behalf of a compelling public interest, as determined by a majority of the people's representatives in the state government.

According to Holmes, the Court had no authority to strike down laws made by legislative majorities on the basis of the personal opinions of the justices, which they read into the Constitution through the specious doctrine of substantive due process. Holmes believed that "liberty in the Fourteenth Amendment" was "perverted" when "held to prevent the natural outcome of a dominant opinion" (the legislative majority) unless a "rational and fair man" would conclude that the law violated "fundamental principles" of law and tradition. Holmes charged that the Court overstepped the boundaries of its judicial powers by using substantive due process to substitute its opinion of wise social policy for that of the popularly elected state legislature.

Significance The *Lochner* decision did not stop the movement for legal regulation of the workplace to protect employees. In *Muller* v. *Oregon* (1908), for example, the Court upheld a state law limiting the number of hours per day that women could work. And in *Bunting* v. *Oregon* (1917), the Court sustained a 10-hour workday limit for male workers. However, the Court continued to use the *Lochner* decision as the basis for overseeing legislative regulations of businesses. In 1937, however, the Court overruled *Lochner* v. *New York* with its decision in *West Coast Hotel Co.* v. *Parrish* (1937). In this case, the Court upheld a state law regulating minimum wages for children and women workers.

SEE ALSO

Due process of law; Muller v. Oregon; West Coast Hotel Co. v. Parrish

FURTHER READING

Kens, Paul. *Lochner v. New York: Economic Regulation on Trial.* Lawrence: University Press of Kansas, 1998.

Lurton, Horace H.
ASSOCIATE JUSTICE, 1910–14

☆ *Born: Feb. 26, 1844, Newport, Ky.*
☆ *Education: Douglas University, 1860; Cumberland Law School, LL.B., 1867*
☆ *Previous government service: judge, Tennessee Supreme Court, 1886–93; judge, U.S. Court of Appeals for the Sixth Circuit, 1893–1909*
☆ *Appointed by President William Howard Taft Dec. 13, 1909; replaced Rufus W. Peckham, who died*
☆ *Supreme Court term: confirmed by the Senate Dec. 20, 1909, by a voice vote; served until July 12, 1914*
☆ *Died: July 12, 1914, Atlantic City, N.J.*

HORACE H. LURTON served in the Confederate Army during the Civil War. He was captured by Union forces and kept in a camp for prisoners of war. After the war, Lurton studied law and set up a private law practice in Clarksville, Tennessee.

During his brief term on the Court, Justice Lurton wrote few opinions. Instead, he usually went along with the Court's majority in deciding cases. He tended to support a strict construction of the Constitution and judicial restraint. Justice Lurton strongly opposed the use of judicial power to overcome social problems. In 1911 he wrote in *North American Review,* "The contention that...the Constitution is to be disregarded if it stands in the way of that which is deemed of public advantage... is destructive of the whole theory upon which our American Commonwealths have been founded."

Majority opinion

THE OPINION of the U.S. Supreme Court in cases that it decides is usually a majority opinion. A majority is one more than half of the justices participating in a decision. When five of the nine justices agree with the opinion of the Court, there is a majority opinion of the Court. When four of seven justices agree (with two justices not participating), there is a majority opinion. All decisions of the Court are by majority vote. In some cases, however, there is not a majority opinion because too many justices write their own concurring opinions. These justices vote with the majority to reach a decision on a case, but they write separate concurring opinions. For example, in 1989 the Court decided *Webster* v. *Reproductive Health Services* by a 5 to 4 vote. However, two justices voting with the majority wrote separate concurring opinions. Only three justices joined the opinion announced by the Court. As a result, there was a plurality opinion in the case, not a majority opinion.

SEE ALSO

Concurring opinion; Dissenting opinion; Opinions; Plurality opinion

Mapp v. Ohio

☆ *367 U.S. 643 (1961)*
☆ *Vote: 6–3*
☆ *For the Court: Clark*
☆ *Concurring: Black, Douglas, and Stewart*
☆ *Dissenting: Harlan, Frankfurter, and Whittaker*

ON MAY 23, 1957, police officers forced their way into the home of Dollree Mapp, whom they suspected of

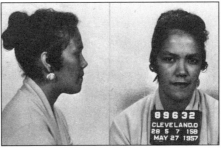

Dollree Mapp's mug shot, taken after she was arrested for possession of obscene pictures. The Supreme Court reversed her conviction because police officers had found these pictures during an illegal search of her house.

criminal activities. The police claimed they had a search warrant, which is required under the 4th Amendment to the Constitution, but they never proved it. During their unwarranted search of Mapp's house, the police seized obscene pictures, which under an Ohio law were illegal objects for someone to have. Mapp was convicted of possessing obscene pictures and sentenced to prison. Her lawyer appealed to the U.S. Supreme Court.

The Issue The police obtained evidence of Dollree Mapp's illegal behavior through actions that violated the 4th Amendment guarantee against unreasonable searches and seizures. Can evidence obtained through an illegally conducted search be used to convict a person of violating a state law?

Opinion of the Court The Court overturned Dollree Mapp's conviction. Justice Tom Clark wrote that evidence obtained in violation of the 4th Amendment of the U.S. Constitution must be excluded from use in state as well as federal criminal trials. The Court thus applied the exclusionary rule for the first time in ruling against a state government.

Dissent The dissenting opinions were based on opposition to the incorporation doctrine, by which the exclusionary rule associated with the 4th Amendment was applied to a state government through the due process clause of the 14th Amendment. The dissenting justices believed that the 4th Amendment guarantees of individual rights were applicable only to the federal government.

Significance The exclusionary rule was created by the Court in *Weeks* v. *United States* (1914). Before the *Mapp* case, however, this rule had never been used against a state government. During the 1980s the Court recognized certain exceptions to the exclusionary rule as used in the *Mapp* case. For example, in *United States* v. *Leon* (1984), the Court ruled that evidence seized on the basis of a mistakenly issued search warrant can be used in a trial, if the warrant was issued in good faith—that is, on presumption that there were valid reasons for issuing the warrant. As a result, the exclusionary rule has been narrowed by this "good faith" exception.

SEE ALSO

Exclusionary rule; Incorporation doctrine; Searches and seizures; United States v. Leon; Weeks v. United States

FURTHER READING

Friendly, Fred W., and Martha J. H. Elliott. "A Knock at the Door: How the Supreme Court Created a Rule to Enforce the Fourth Amendment." In *The Constitution: That Delicate Balance.* New York: Random House, 1984.

Marbury v. Madison

☆ *1 Cranch 137 (1803)*
☆ *Vote: 6–0*
☆ *For the Court: Marshall*

IN THE PRESIDENTIAL election of 1800, Thomas Jefferson, the candidate of the Democratic-Republican party, defeated the Federalist candidate, John Adams. Not only had Adams lost the Presidency but the Federalists had lost control of Congress. Adams and his party feared that Jefferson would ruin the country by undoing everything the Federalists had accomplished in the previous 12 years. Between the November election and the March inauguration, the

Federalists tried to ensure that they would continue to play a role in the U.S. government.

On January 20, 1801, Adams appointed Secretary of State John Marshall to be chief justice of the United States. Although the Senate confirmed this nomination in less than two weeks, Marshall remained secretary of state until Jefferson took office.

Throughout February the Federalists, who controlled Congress, created offices for Adams to fill with loyal supporters. During his last month as President, Adams nominated more than 200 men to new offices. These nominations included 42 justices of the peace for the new national capital at Washington, D.C. Adams appointed William Marbury as one of these justices of the peace.

The Senate received the nominations of the new justices of the peace on March 2 and confirmed them on March 3, Adams's last day in office. In order for the confirmed appointees to assume office, the executive had to complete one more procedure: the President had to sign commissions empowering each man to hold office, and the secretary of state had to place the official seal of the U.S. government on those commissions and supervise their delivery. In those days, officials prepared the commissions by hand. Thus, Adams spent his last evening as President signing commissions. The secretary of state, John Marshall, worked well into the night, affixing the Great Seal of the United States to the commissions and sending them off for delivery. However, in the chaos of Adams's last day in office, a number of commissions, including William Marbury's, though signed and sealed, remained undelivered.

On March 4, 1801, Jefferson became President. Soon after, Marbury asked the new secretary of state, James Madison, for his commission. Madison, after consulting with Jefferson, refused

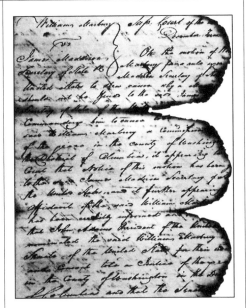

A fragment of the order given to Secretary of State James Madison requiring him to deliver William Marbury's commission to serve as justice of the peace in Washington, D.C.

to give Marbury the commission. Marbury then appealed to the Supreme Court for help.

Marbury asked the Court to issue a writ of mandamus directed to Secretary of State James Madison. A writ of mandamus orders a public official to carry out his duties. Marbury argued that he was legally entitled to his commission and that Madison should give it to him. Madison ignored these legal proceedings. Neither he nor Jefferson believed that the Supreme Court could give orders to the other two branches of government. Thus, the Court had to rule on Marbury's case with the knowledge that Madison might ignore the ruling. The man responsible for making the ruling was John Marshall, who as secretary of state had failed to send Marbury his commission in the first place.

The Issue   Marbury argued that Section 13 of the Judiciary Act of 1789 gave the Supreme Court authority to issue a writ of mandamus under its original jurisdiction, its power to hear and decide such a case for the first time. The writ would require Secretary of State Madison to deliver Marbury's commission. Marbury pointed out that an act of Congress had created the office and the Senate had confirmed his Presidential appointment. With the commission legally signed and sealed, delivery of the commission was not, in Marbury's view, a discretionary act on the part of the secretary of state. Madison did not, Marbury claimed, have the authority to choose whether to deliver the commission. Rather, his job required him to deliver it.

Did Marbury have a right to the commission, and did the law provide him a means to obtain it? These were the apparent issues of the case. Chief Justice Marshall, however, asserted another issue: Could the Supreme Court, under the U.S. Constitution, have original jurisdiction in this case? Or, to put it another way, did Section 13 of the Judiciary Act of 1789 contradict or violate the U.S. Constitution?

Opinion of the Court   The Court ruled that Marbury was due his commission. Chief Justice John Marshall said, "To withhold his commission is an act" that violates the law.

Marshall held that the writ of mandamus was the proper legal procedure to require a public official to do his duty. Marshall also acknowledged that the Judiciary Act of 1789 authorized the Supreme Court to issue such a writ.

Marshall knew, however, that if he ruled in favor of Marbury, Madison would probably ignore the Court's order to deliver the commission and cause a constitutional crisis. Above all else, Marshall hoped to avoid such a controversy. So one more question remained for Marshall to answer. Could the Supreme Court actually issue the writ of mandamus? If it could, then Marshall had backed himself into a corner. Having admitted that Marbury deserved the writ, he would then have to issue one. But Marshall had an out.

Marbury had directed his request for a writ of mandamus to the Supreme Court. By asking the Supreme Court to issue the writ, Marbury had asked the Court to take original jurisdiction in the case, to be the first court to consider the request. In complying with such a request, the Supreme Court would act as a trial court. However, the founders of the Supreme Court had designed the Supreme Court as an appellate court—a court to hear appeals from other federal courts and from the state courts. The Constitution, in Article 3, Section 2, Clause 2, spelled out the few types of cases over which the Supreme Court would exercise original jurisdiction. Marshall examined that clause of the Constitution and concluded it did not authorize the Supreme Court to issue a writ of mandamus. Such a writ, he decided, could come only from a lower court.

Thus, Marshall concluded that Section 13 of the Judiciary Act of 1789, which authorized the Court to issue a writ of mandamus, violated the Constitution. Because the Supreme Court could not enforce an unconstitutional law, Marbury did not get his writ.

Marshall's opinion avoided generating a confrontation with Madison and Jefferson. He did not order Madison to give Marbury his commission. Marshall also succeeded in lecturing Madison and Jefferson on their respective responsibilities as secretary of state and President. In addition, by his opinion Marshall successfully asserted the Supreme Court's power to declare acts of Congress unconstitutional. This power is known as judicial review.

Marshall used three provisions of the Constitution to justify his arguments for judicial review. The first was Article 3, Section 2, which extends the judicial power to "all Cases, in Law and Equity, arising under this Constitution." Marshall argued: "Could it be the intention of those who gave this power, to say, that in using it, the constitution should not be looked into? That a case arising under the constitution should be decided, without examining the instrument under which it arises? This is too extravagant to be maintained."

Second, Article 6 requires judges to pledge "to support this Constitution." Marshall wrote, "How immoral to impose [this oath] on them, if they were to be used as the instruments...for violating what they swear to support!"

Third, Marshall pointed out that "in declaring what shall be the supreme law of the land [Article 6], the constitution itself is first mentioned; and not the laws of the United States, generally, but those only which shall be made in pursuance of the constitution, have that rank." Marshall argued from the supremacy clause of Article 6 that no act of Congress that violates any part of the Constitution, the highest law, can be valid. Rather, it must be declared unconstitutional and repealed.

Marshall memorably defined the Supreme Court's duty under the U.S. Constitution:

> It is, emphatically, the province and duty of the judicial department, to say what the law is.... So, if a law be in opposition to the constitution; if both the law and the constitution apply to a particular case, so that the court must either decide that case, conformable to the law, disregarding the constitution; or conformable to the constitution, disregarding the law; the court must determine which of these conflicting rules governs the case; this is of the very essence of judicial duty. If then, the courts are to regard the constitution, and the constitution is superior to any ordinary act of the legislature, the constitution, and not such ordinary act, must govern the case to which both apply.

Significance The *Marbury* decision provided the constitutional basis for the Supreme Court's power of judicial review of the actions and laws of the federal government. This decision asserted the Court's power to declare invalid those federal laws it finds in conflict with the Constitution. The Court's decision laid the foundation on which the Supreme Court eventually developed into an important branch of the federal government.

Full acceptance of judicial review would not happen until after the Civil War. Regardless, this case established the principle that the courts and government should not enforce unconstitutional federal laws.

SEE ALSO

Judicial power; Judicial review; Judiciary Act of 1789

FURTHER READING

Clinton, Robert Lowry. *Marbury v. Madison and Judicial Review.* Lawrence: University Press of Kansas, 1989.
Garraty, John A. "The Case of the Missing Commissions." In *Quarrels That Have Shaped the Constitution,* edited by John A. Garraty. New York: Harper & Row, 1987.

Marshal, Supreme Court

SEE Staff of the Court, nonjudicial

Marshall, John

CHIEF JUSTICE, 1801–35

☆ *Born: Sept. 24, 1755, Germantown, Va.*
☆ *Education: taught at home by his father and two clergymen; self-educated in law; attended one course on law, College of William and Mary, 1780*
☆ *Previous government service: Virginia House of Delegates, 1782–85, 1787–90, 1795–96; Executive Council of State, Virginia, 1782–84; recorder, Richmond City Hustings Court, Virginia, 1785–88; U.S. minister to France, 1797–98; Virginia Ratifying Convention, 1788; U.S. representative from Virginia, 1799–1800; U.S. secretary of state, 1800–1801*

☆ *Appointed by President John Adams Jan. 20, 1801; replaced Oliver Ellsworth, who resigned*
☆ *Supreme Court term: confirmed by the Senate Jan. 27, 1801, by a voice vote; served until July 6, 1835*
☆ *Died: July 6, 1835, Philadelphia, Pa.*

JOHN MARSHALL was the fourth chief justice of the United States. From his time to ours, he has been called the Great Chief Justice.

Born and raised in the backcountry of Virginia, Marshall was educated mostly at home, with his father as the main teacher. His formal education in the law consisted of one course of lectures by George Wythe, a leading Virginia political leader and legal authority at the College of William and Mary. Marshall, however, had a keen mind that he filled with knowledge through a lifetime of reading, thinking, and interacting with political leaders in the public affairs of Virginia and the United States.

Participation in the American Revolution shaped John Marshall's lifetime loyalty to the United States. He later expressed this loyalty decisively during his tenure on the Supreme Court through opinions that reinforced the power and authority of the federal government over the states. He served in the Continental Army for nearly six years, fought in the battles of Great Bridge, Brandywine, Germantown, and Monmouth and spent the grueling winter with George Washington's forces at Valley Forge. He left the Continental Army in 1781 with the rank of captain. Marshall exhibited intense patriotism and had great admiration for George Washington, which he expressed later in his five-volume biography *Life of George Washington,* published in 1804–7.

President John Adams appointed Marshall to be chief justice in 1801 as one of his final actions before leaving office. Adams's first choice for the job was John Jay, who had been the first chief justice. Jay, however, declined because in his view, widely shared at the time, the Supreme Court was too weak and unimportant; he said that he would not be head of "a system so defective." So John Marshall took the job that Jay refused and transformed it into the most powerful and prominent judicial position in the world.

Marshall brought unity and order to the Court by practically ending *seriatim* opinions (the writing of opinions by various justices). Before Chief Justice Marshall, the Court did not issue a single majority opinion. He, however, influenced the Court's majority to speak with one voice, through an opinion for the Court on each case before it. Of course, members of the Court occasionally wrote concurring or dissenting opinions, as they do today.

Often the Court's voice was John Marshall's. During his 34 years on the Court, the longest tenure of any chief justice, Marshall wrote 519 of the 1,100 opinions issued during that period, and he dissented only eight times.

Chief Justice Marshall's greatest opinions were masterworks of legal reasoning and graceful writing. They stand today as an authoritative commentary on the core principles of the U.S. Constitution.

Marshall's first great decision came in *Marbury* v. *Madison* (1803), in which he ruled that Section 13 of the Judiciary Act of 1789 was void because it violated Article 3 of the Constitution. In this opinion, Marshall made a compelling argument for judicial review, the Court's power to decide whether an act of Congress violates the Constitution. If it does, Marshall wrote, then the legislative act contrary to the Constitution is unconstitutional, or illegal, and could not be enforced. Marshall wrote, "It is emphatically the province and duty of the judicial department to say what the law is. . . . So if a law be in opposition to the constitution . . . the constitution and not such ordinary Act, must govern the case to which they both apply."

In a series of great decisions, Marshall also established, beyond legal challenge, the Court's power of judicial review over acts of state government. In *Fletcher* v. *Peck* (1810), *Dartmouth College* v. *Woodward* (1819), *McCulloch* v. *Maryland* (1819), and *Cohens* v. *Virginia* (1821), Marshall wrote for the Court that acts of state government in violation of federal statutes or the federal Constitution were unconstitutional or void.

The Marshall Court's decisions also defended the sanctity of contracts and private property rights against would-be violators in the cases of *Fletcher* v. *Peck* and *Dartmouth College* v. *Woodward*. In *Gibbons* v. *Ogden* (1824), Marshall broadly interpreted Congress's power to regulate commerce (Article 1, Section 8, of the Constitution) and prohibited states from passing laws to interfere with the flow of goods and transportation across state lines.

Chief Justice Marshall's greatest opinions protected private property rights as a foundation of individual liberty. They also rejected claims of state sovereignty in favor of a federal Constitution based on the sovereignty of the people of the United States. Finally, Marshall clearly and convincingly argued for the Constitution as a permanent supreme law that the Supreme Court was established to interpret and defend. "Ours is a Constitution," Marshall wrote in 1819 (*McCulloch* v. *Maryland*), "intended to endure for ages to come, and consequently, to be adapted to the various crises of human affairs."

Only through broad construction of the federal government's powers could the Constitution of 1787 be "adapted" to meet changing times. And only through strict limits on excessive use of the government's powers could the Constitution endure as a guardian of individual rights. The special duty of the Supreme Court, according to Marshall, was to make the difficult judgments, based on the Constitution, about when to impose limits or to permit broad exercise of the federal government's powers.

In 1833, near the end of John Marshall's career, his associate on the Supreme Court, Justice Joseph Story, wrote a "Dedication to John Marshall" that included these words of high praise: "Your expositions of constitutional law . . . constitute a monument of fame far beyond the ordinary memorials of political or military glory. They are destined to enlighten, instruct and convince future generations; and can scarcely perish but with the memory of the Constitution itself." And so it has been, from Marshall's time until our own, that his judgments and commentaries on the Constitution have instructed and inspired Americans.

SEE ALSO

Cohens v. Virginia; Dartmouth College v. Woodward; Fletcher v. Peck; Judicial review; Marbury v. Madison; McCulloch v. Maryland

FURTHER READING

Baker, Leonard. *John Marshall: A Life in Law.* New York: Macmillan, 1974.

Hobson, Charles F. *The Great Chief Justice: John Marshall and the Rule of Law.* Lawrence: University Press of Kansas, 1996.

Johnson, Herbert. *The Chief Justiceship of John Marshall, 1801 1835.* Columbia: University of South Carolina Press, 1998.

Rudko, Frances H. *John Marshall, Statesman and Chief Justice.* Westport, Conn.: Greenwood Press, 1991.

Smith, Jean E. *John Marshall: Definer of a Nation.* New York: Henry Holt, 1996.

Stites, Francis N. *John Marshall: Defender of the Constitution.* Boston: Little, Brown, 1981.

White, G. Edward. *The Marshall Court and Cultural Change.* New York: Oxford University Press, 1991.

Marshall, Thurgood

ASSOCIATE JUSTICE, 1967–91

☆ Born: July 2, 1908, Baltimore, Md.
☆ Education: Lincoln University, B.A., 1930; Howard University Law School, LL.B., 1933
☆ Previous government service: judge, Second Circuit Court of Appeals, 1961–65; U.S. solicitor general, 1965–67
☆ Appointed by President Lyndon B. Johnson June 13, 1967; replaced Tom C. Clark, who retired
☆ Supreme Court term: confirmed by the Senate Aug. 30, 1967, by a 69–11 vote; retired Oct. 1, 1991
☆ Died: Jan. 24, 1993, Bethesda, Md.

THURGOOD MARSHALL, the great-grandson of a slave, was the first African-American justice of the Supreme Court. He began his historic career in 1933, as a civil rights lawyer for the National Association for the Advancement of Colored People (NAACP). In 1940 Marshall became head of the NAACP Legal Defense Fund. In this position, he led the NAACP's legal fight against racial segregation and denial of individual rights of black people. Marshall successfully argued 29 out of 32 cases before the U.S. Supreme Court.

In 1954 Thurgood Marshall achieved his biggest victory for the NAACP in *Brown* v. *Board of Education.* In this landmark case, Marshall convinced the Supreme Court to decide that racial segregation in public schools was unconstitutional. This was the beginning of the eventual ending of state government laws that denied equal rights to black people.

In 1961 President John F. Kennedy appointed Marshall to the U.S. Court of Appeals for the Second Circuit. In 1965 President Lyndon B. Johnson selected Marshall to be solicitor general of the United States, the top lawyer for the U.S.

government in federal court cases. Mar-shall was the first African American to serve as the solicitor general and to argue cases for the government at the Supreme Court.

During his 24 years on the Court, Justice Marshall wrote many opinions on various issues pertaining to federal jurisdiction, antitrust laws, and civil rights. He wrote numerous dissenting opinions about equal protection of the laws, the rights of minorities, and capital punishment. He strongly opposed the death penalty, which in his opinion was a violation of the 8th Amendment prohibition of "cruel and unusual punishment." Throughout his long career in law, Thurgood Marshall was an outspoken advocate for the rights and opportunities of minorities, especially for African Americans and poor people.

During his final years on the Court, Justice Marshall often wrote strong dissents to call attention to his views about unmet needs for social justice. He opposed the conservative tendencies of the Court during the 1980s and was a staunch ally of Justice William Brennan in arguing for liberal positions. He remained on the Court only one term after Brennan retired, citing declining health as a major reason for his retirement. Marshall's death in 1993 brought an outpouring of praise for his remarkable career.

SEE ALSO

Brown v. Board of Education; Civil rights; National Association for the Advancement of Colored People (NAACP)

FURTHER READING

Aldred, Lisa. *Thurgood Marshall.* New York: Chelsea House, 1990.

Rowan, Carl T. *Dream Makers, Dream Breakers: The World of Thurgood Marshall.* Boston: Little, Brown, 1993.

Tushnet, Mark V. *Making Civil Rights Law: Thurgood Marshall and the Supreme Court, 1936–1961.* New York: Oxford University Press, 1994.

Tushnet, Mark V. *Making Constitutional Law: Thurgood Marshall and the Supreme Court, 1961–1991.* New York: Oxford University Press, 1997.

Williams, Juan. *Thurgood Marshall: American Revolutionary.* New York: Times Books, 2000.

Martin v. Hunter's Lessee

☆ *1 Wheat. 304 (1816)*
☆ *Vote: 6–0*
☆ *For the Court: Story*
☆ *Not participating: Marshall*

THOMAS, SIXTH LORD FAIRFAX, owned more than 5 million acres of valuable land in the northern area of western Virginia. In 1781 Lord Fairfax died and left his property to a nephew, Denny Martin, a British subject. However, during the War of Independence, Virginia had passed laws confiscating the property of Loyalists, such as Lord Fairfax, who supported Great Britain. The state sold the land to private owners, including David Hunter, who denied Denny Martin's claim to his uncle's property. Martin challenged Hunter's right to this property and filed a lawsuit against him.

Lord Fairfax owned land in the northern neck of Virginia. When his nephew inherited the land, the state of Virginia tried to deny the claim but the Supreme Court decided that the inheritance was protected by a U.S. treaty with Great Britain.

The state courts of Virginia decided in favor of Hunter, so Martin took his case to the U.S. Supreme Court. In *Fairfax's Devisee* v. *Hunter's Lessee* (1813), the Court decided in favor of Martin. (Chief Justice John Marshall did not participate in this decision because of financial interests in the land at issue.)

Writing for the Court, Justice Joseph Story overturned the Virginia laws used to take the Fairfax lands, reasoning that Martin's inheritance was protected by the Treaty of Paris (1783) and Jay's Treaty (1794). Both of these treaties between the United States and Great Britain pledged that the property of Loyalists in the United States would be protected by the federal government. Justice Story pointed to Article 6 of the Constitution, which included treaties of the United States as part of the "supreme Law of the Land." Further, Article 6 said that "the Judges in every State shall be bound thereby, any thing in the Constitution or Laws of any State to the Contrary notwithstanding." Finally, Justice Story referred to Section 25 of the Judiciary Act of 1789, which provided for review by the U.S. Supreme Court of decisions by state courts that involved the U.S. Constitution, federal laws, and treaties.

Justice Story ordered the Virginia Court of Appeals to carry out the decision of the U.S. Supreme Court. The Virginia judges refused to obey the order, however. They claimed that Section 25 of the Judiciary Act of 1789 was not valid because it violated the powers and rights of state governments in the federal Union.

The Issue Virginia's refusal to comply with Justice Story's ruling brought the case back to the U.S. Supreme Court. The issue cut to the heart of the federal Union. Did the Supreme Court have authority over all state laws and state judicial decisions that involved the U.S. Constitution, federal laws, and treaties? Or did each state have authority under the U.S. Constitution to defy certain kinds of federal treaties or decisions if it did not approve of them?

Opinion of the Court Once again, Joseph Story wrote for the Court. (Chief Justice Marshall again declined to participate because of a possible conflict of interest.) Justice Story decided that the U.S. Supreme Court had jurisdiction in this case, and he rebuked the Virginia judges who had refused to comply with the Court's orders. Contrary to the views of the Virginia judges, Story argued that the U.S. Supreme Court's appellate jurisdiction extended to all cases involving federal issues, not merely to cases coming to it from lower federal courts.

Story asserted that Article 25 of the Judiciary Act of 1789 was constitutional and was necessary to the enforcement of federal laws and treaties as part of the supreme law of the land, as defined by Article 6 of the Constitution. He rejected Virginia's claim to equal sovereignty with the United States and argued that the American people, not the states, had created the federal Union.

Finally, Justice Story insisted that to enforce the supremacy clause of Article 6, the U.S. Supreme Court had the final power to interpret the U.S. Constitution. Without this power over state governments, Story insisted, there could be no enduring federal Union.

Significance The Court's judgment, expressed by Justice Story, has been called the greatest argument ever made for judicial review of state laws and court decisions by the U.S. Supreme Court. Story's opinion also gave great strength to the nationalists' side of the ongoing argument about state powers and rights in the federal system of the United States. The claims of extreme states' rights advocates, however, were not subdued until after the Civil War.

SEE ALSO

Federalism; Judicial power; Judicial review; Jurisdiction

Matthews, Stanley

ASSOCIATE JUSTICE, 1881–89

☆ Born: July 21, 1824, Cincinnati, Ohio
☆ Education: Kenyon College, B.A., 1840
☆ Previous government service: assistant prosecuting attorney, Hamilton County, Ohio, 1845; clerk, Ohio House of Representatives, 1848–49; judge, Hamilton County Court of Common Pleas, 1851–53; Ohio Senate, 1855–58; U.S. attorney for the Southern District of Ohio, 1858–61; judge, Superior Court of Cincinnati, 1863–65; counsel, Hayes-Tilden electoral commission, 1877; U.S. senator from Ohio, 1877–79
☆ Appointed by President James A. Garfield Mar. 14, 1881; replaced Noah Swayne, who retired
☆ Supreme Court term: confirmed by the Senate May 12, 1881, by a 24–23 vote; served until Mar. 22, 1889
☆ Died: Mar. 22, 1889, Washington, D.C.

STANLEY MATTHEWS's political connections led to his appointment to the Supreme Court. He campaigned for Presidential candidate Rutherford B. Hayes in 1876. Then he served as a lawyer for Hayes at the 1877 electoral commission that decided the contested Presidential election in favor of Hayes. Consequently, Hayes appointed Matthews to fill a vacancy on the Court, but the Senate blocked the nomination. They recalled his involvement in a controversial federal case in 1859, when Matthews served as the U.S. attorney for southern Ohio. Although Matthews had sided publicly with the cause of abolishing slavery, he vigorously prosecuted an abolitionist for helping two fugitive slaves to escape to freedom. Many senators objected to Matthews because of his role as prosecuting attorney in this case. Matthews was renominated by President Hayes's successor, James A. Garfield, but he was still opposed by many senators and was barely confirmed, by a vote of 24–23.

The controversy about Matthews's appointment to the Court eventually died down and he served satisfactorily as an associate justice. He wrote 232 opinions for the Court and 5 dissents in a Supreme Court career of less than eight years.

McCulloch v. Maryland

☆ 4 Wheat. 316 (1819)
☆ Vote: 7–0
☆ For the Court: Marshall

CONGRESS CHARTERED the Second Bank of the United States in 1816 to provide a sound national currency. But the bank soon proved very unpopular in many states. Maryland passed a law that levied an extremely high tax on any bank in the state without a state charter. At the time, the Second Bank of the United States was the only bank operating in Maryland that was not chartered by the state. McCulloch, the cashier of the Baltimore branch of the Bank of the United States, refused to pay the tax. Maryland sued McCulloch and won in the Maryland courts.

Officials of the bank appealed to the U.S. Supreme Court. They claimed the state tax interfered unconstitutionally with the federally chartered bank. Maryland argued that Congress had no power to charter the bank and that the state had the power to tax the bank.

The Issue The Constitution did not expressly give Congress the power to charter a national bank. However, Article 1, Section 8, Clause 18, did grant Congress the power to "make all laws which shall be necessary and proper for carrying into Execution the foregoing Powers." Did this "necessary and proper" clause give Congress adequate power only to do those few things indispensable for carrying out its listed, or delegated, powers? Or did it ensure that

Congress could do nearly anything it wanted, such as chartering a national bank, to exercise its delegated powers?

In addition, did states have the power to tax a national bank? Was national law or state law supreme in this case?

Opinion of the Court The Court upheld the power of Congress to create a national bank. Chief Justice John Marshall wrote that the Constitution did not need to expressly authorize Congress to establish a bank. Such expressly listed congressional powers as the power to tax, to spend money, to borrow money, and to support the army and navy implied that Congress had the power to establish a bank.

At the same time, the Court ruled that the states could not tax the bank. Marshall declared that allowing states to tax part of the national government would interfere with national supremacy: "The power to tax involves the power to destroy."

Thus, the Court established two important constitutional principles. The first, the implied powers doctrine, stated that the legal system should interpret broadly the necessary and proper clause of the Constitution to let Congress choose the means it wished to employ to carry out the powers the Constitution expressly gave it. Marshall wrote, "Let the end be legitimate, let it be within the scope of the Constitution, and all means which are appropriate, which are plainly adapted to that end, which are not prohibited, but

consist with the letter and spirit of the Constitution, are constitutional."

The second principle, national supremacy, forbids the states to intrude into the constitutional operations of the federal government. It reinforced the supremacy of the Constitution and federal laws over state laws that conflict with them.

Significance The *McCulloch* decision has been used to support a broad construction of the Constitution that enables the federal government to apply the supreme law flexibly to meet the new problems of changing times. In the *McCulloch* case Chief Justice Marshall made a memorable statement, which is often quoted to support a broad interpretation of the federal government's constitutional powers: "This . . . is . . . a constitution we are expounding, intended to endure for ages to come, and consequently, to be adapted to the various crises of human affairs."

Today, many bills Congress passes draw their legitimacy to some extent from the necessary and proper clause and the broad construction of the Constitution exemplified in Marshall's *McCulloch* opinion. For example, federal laws pertaining to the regulation of airlines or broadcasting are based on the necessary and proper clause, not on express powers of Congress specified in the Constitution.

The *McCulloch* decision also strengthened the Court's powers of judicial review over acts of state governments. Thus, it pleased advocates of federal supremacy and infuriated supporters of state powers and rights. The vision of national supremacy under the Constitution, expressed in Chief Justice Marshall's *McCulloch* opinion, has prevailed in the 20th century.

SEE ALSO
Constitutional construction; Federalism; Implied powers

The Bank of the United States in Philadelphia. The Supreme Court decided that the necessary and proper clause of the Constitution gave Congress the power to establish a national bank.

FURTHER READING
Gunther, Gerald. *John Marshall's Defense of McCulloch v. Maryland.* Stanford, Calif.: Stanford University Press, 1969.
Hammond, Bray. "The Bank Cases." In *Quarrels That Have Shaped the Constitution,* edited by John A. Garraty. New York: Harper & Row, 1987.

McKeiver v. Pennsylvania

☆ *403 U.S. 528 (1971)*
☆ *Vote: 6–3*
☆ *For the Court: Blackmun*
☆ *Concurring: White, Harlan, and Brennan*
☆ *Dissenting: Douglas, Black, and Marshall*

JOSEPH McKEIVER, 16 years old, was a juvenile defendant who had been accused of serious acts of delinquency—robbery and receiving stolen goods. He faced the possible punishment of detention for five years. McKeiver asked for a trial by jury, but the state of Pennsylvania denied his request. McKeiver was convicted and sentenced without a jury trial. He appealed his conviction on the grounds that his constitutional right to a trial by jury had been violated.

The Issue Adults accused of crimes have a constitutional right to trial by jury. This right is included in the 6th Amendment, and it is applicable to the states through the due process clause of the 14th Amendment. Is this right to trial by jury required in state proceedings against a juvenile accused of unlawful behavior?

Opinion of the Court The Court decided that due process of law for juveniles does not require a trial by jury. Justice Harry Blackmun stated a standard of "fundamental fairness" for due process in juvenile cases. Thus, a right to trial by jury in juvenile cases had to be balanced against the special requirements of juvenile justice. Justice Blackmun feared that a jury trial would subject juveniles to unnecessary and disruptive adversarial proceedings without providing compensating benefits of greater accuracy in fact-finding or determination of guilt.

Significance The Court decided in another case about a juvenile offender, *In re Gault* (1967), to extend constitutional rights of due process to juvenile court proceedings. The McKeiver decision, however, indicated that the Court was unwilling to extend all the rights of the criminally accused to juveniles accused of serious crimes. According to this decision, states are not required to provide a jury trial for a juvenile, but they may choose to do so. To date, none has done so.

SEE ALSO

In re Gault; Juvenile justice; Trial by jury

FURTHER READING
Bernard, Thomas J. *The Cycle of Juvenile Justice.* New York: Oxford University Press, 1992.

McKenna, Joseph

ASSOCIATE JUSTICE, 1898–1925

☆ *Born: Aug. 10, 1843, Philadelphia, Pa.*
☆ *Education: Benicia Collegiate Institute, 1865*
☆ *Previous government service: district attorney, Solano County, Calif., 1866–70; California Assembly, 1875–76; U.S. representative from California, 1885–92; judge, U.S. Court of Appeals for the Ninth Circuit, 1892–97; U.S. attorney general, 1897*
☆ *Appointed by President William McKinley Dec. 16, 1897; replaced Stephen J. Field, who retired*
☆ *Supreme Court term: confirmed by the Senate Jan. 21, 1898, by a voice vote; retired Jan. 5, 1925*
☆ *Died: Nov. 21, 1926, Washington, D.C.*

JOSEPH MCKENNA was the son of immigrants from Ireland. He was a successful politician who served seven years in the U.S. House of Representatives, where he became a friend of William McKinley. When McKinley became President, he appointed his old friend to fill a vacancy on the Supreme Court.

Justice McKenna served on the Court for 27 years. He joined in the Court's opinions to regulate various kinds of economic activity under the "commerce clause" of Article 1, Section 8, of the Constitution. He also supported regulation of businesses under the Pure Food and Drug Act.

During his later years on the Court, McKenna's reasoning powers seemed to decline. His associates urged him to resign, which he did in 1925, at age 83.

FURTHER READING

McDevitt, Matthew. *Joseph McKenna.* 1946. Reprint. New York: Da Capo, 1974.

McKinley, John

ASSOCIATE JUSTICE, 1837–52

☆ *Born: May 1, 1780, Culpeper County, Va.*
☆ *Education: self-educated in the law*
☆ *Previous government service: Alabama House of Representatives, 1820, 1831, 1836; U.S. senator from Alabama, 1826–31; U.S. representative from Alabama, 1833–35*
☆ *Appointed by President Martin Van Buren as a recess appointment Apr. 22, 1837, to a newly created position on the Supreme Court; nominated by Van Buren Sept. 18, 1837*
☆ *Supreme Court term: confirmed by the Senate Sept. 25, 1837, by a voice vote; served until July 19, 1852*
☆ *Died: July 19, 1852, Lexington, Ky.*

JOHN MCKINLEY was a loyal supporter of the Jacksonian Democrats, who backed the Presidential candidacies of Andrew Jackson and Martin Van Buren. After Van Buren became President, he rewarded McKinley with an appointment to the Supreme Court.

Justice McKinley was a strong supporter of states' rights and slavery. However, he was an unproductive and mediocre associate justice who wrote only 20 opinions for the Court during his 15 years of service. He usually voted with the Court's majority and dissented only when joined by at least one other justice. He wrote no opinions that contributed significantly to the development of constitutional law.

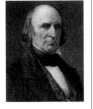

McLean, John

ASSOCIATE JUSTICE, 1830–61

☆ *Born: Mar. 11, 1785, Morris County, N.J.*
☆ *Education: studied at home with private tutors; read law in the office of Arthur St. Clair, Jr., in Cincinnati*
☆ *Previous government service: examiner, U.S. Land Office, Cincinnati, Ohio, 1811–12; U.S. representative from Ohio, 1813–16; judge, Ohio Supreme Court, 1816–22; commissioner, General Land Office, 1822–23; U.S. postmaster general, 1823–29*
☆ *Appointed by President Andrew Jackson Mar. 6, 1829; replaced Robert Trimble, who died*
☆ *Supreme Court term: confirmed by the Senate Mar. 7, 1829, by a voice vote; served until Apr. 4, 1861*
☆ *Died: Apr. 4, 1861, Cincinnati, Ohio*

JOHN MCLEAN was President Andrew Jackson's first appointment to the Supreme Court. During his 32 years on the Court, however, Justice McLean moved away from Jacksonian views, which favored states' rights, to support nationalism and the federal government's power to regulate foreign and interstate commerce.

Justice McLean's dislike of slavery and states' rights was expressed in his famous dissent in the Dred Scott case (*Scott* v. *Sandford*, 1857). In opposition to the Court's majority, he argued that Congress could ban slavery in the territories of the United States, that blacks could be citizens, and that Dred Scott was a free man because he had lived in a free state and a free territory. This dissent was vindicated by ratification of the 13th and 14th Amendments, which overturned the *Dred Scott* decision.

SEE ALSO

Scott v. Sandford

FURTHER READING

Weisenburger, Francis P. *The Life of John McLean*. 1937. Reprint. New York: Da Capo, 1971.

McReynolds, James Clark

ASSOCIATE JUSTICE, 1914–41

☆ *Born: Feb. 3, 1862, Elkton, Ky.*
☆ *Education: Vanderbilt University, B.S., 1882; University of Virginia, LL.B., 1884*
☆ *Previous government service: assistant U.S. attorney, 1903–7; U.S. attorney general, 1913–14*
☆ *Appointed by President Woodrow Wilson Aug. 19, 1914; replaced Horace H. Lurton, who died*
☆ *Supreme Court term: confirmed by the Senate Aug. 29, 1914, by a 44–6 vote; retired Jan. 31, 1941*
☆ *Died: Aug. 24, 1946, Washington, D.C.*

JAMES McREYNOLDS was an outspoken man with strong views and a disagreeable personality. He was intolerant of colleagues with opposing views and expressed his feelings through rude behavior. He disliked Associate Justices Louis Brandeis and Benjamin Cardozo so much that he would not speak to them. Brandeis and Cardozo were Jews and critics accused McReynolds of anti-Semitism. He also seemed to favor racial segregation and to be prejudiced against female attorneys.

Justice McReynolds was a harsh critic of President Franklin D. Roosevelt's New Deal programs and joined several majority opinions to strike down New Deal legislation between 1934 and 1936. During President Roosevelt's second term, however, the Court shifted to majority support of New Deal enactments. Justice McReynolds therefore became a bitter dissenter during his last years on the Court.

Miami Herald Publishing Co. v. Tornillo

☆ *418 U.S. 241 (1974)*
☆ *Vote: 9–0*
☆ *For the Court: Burger*
☆ *Concurring: Brennan, Rehnquist, and White*

IN SEPTEMBER 1972, the *Miami Herald* printed editorials that were highly critical of Pat Tornillo, a candidate for the Florida House of Representatives. The editorials faulted Tornillo's judgment and character and advised voters not to support him.

Tornillo demanded that the *Miami Herald* print his response to its critical editorials. When the newspaper's publisher refused, Tornillo pointed to a 1913 Florida law that provided that "if a candidate for nomination in election is assailed regarding his personal character or official record by any newspaper, the candidate has a right to demand that the newspaper print...any reply the candidate may make to the newspaper's charges."

The *Miami Herald*'s publisher continued to ignore Tornillo's request, so Tornillo filed suit, asking that the Florida "right to reply" law be enforced in his behalf.

The Florida Supreme Court upheld the "right to reply" law as furthering the "broad societal interest in the free flow of information to the public." The *Miami Herald* appealed to the U.S. Supreme Court.

The Issue The 1st Amendment to the U.S. Constitution says, "Congress shall make no law... abridging the freedom of speech, or of the press." The 1st Amendment freedoms of speech and press have been applied by the Court to the states through the due process clause of the 14th Amendment. Did the Florida "right to reply" law violate the *Miami Herald*'s constitutional right to freedom of the press?

Opinion of the Court The Court reversed the Florida Supreme Court judgment and declared the "right to reply" law unconstitutional. Chief Justice Warren Burger concluded that the 1913 Florida statute was a clear violation of the 1st Amendment guarantee of a free press. Burger wrote, "The choice of material to go into a newspaper, and the decisions made as to... treatment of public issues and public officials—whether fair or unfair—constitute the exercise of editorial control and judgment."

Significance This case established that the government cannot force a

The second draft of the Supreme Court's decision in Miami Herald Publishing Co. v. Tornillo. *This copy belonged to Justice Thurgood Marshall.*

newspaper publisher to print and distribute particular information. However, the Court has upheld government "right to reply" regulations with regard to news broadcasting, as in *Red Lion Broadcasting Co., Inc.* v. *Federal Communications Commission* (1969). That is because the broadcast media, unlike print media, have a limited number of frequencies or channels available, so the only way to provide for access to different points of view is a "right to reply" regulation that can be imposed by the Federal Communications Commission.

SEE ALSO

Freedom of speech and press; Incorporation doctrine

FURTHER READING

Powe, Lucas A., Jr. *American Broadcasting and the First Amendment.* Berkeley: University of California Press, 1987.

Miller, Samuel Freeman

ASSOCIATE JUSTICE,
1862–90

☆ Born: Apr. 5, 1816, Richmond, Ky.
☆ Education: Transylvania University, M.D., 1838; studied law privately
☆ Previous government service: justice of the peace and member of the Knox County Court, Ky., 1840s
☆ Appointed by President Abraham Lincoln July 6, 1862; replaced Peter V. Daniel, who died
☆ Supreme Court term: confirmed by the Senate July 16, 1862, by voice vote; served until Oct. 13, 1890
☆ Died: Oct. 13, 1890, Washington, D.C.

SAMUEL MILLER participated in more than 5,000 decisions of the Supreme Court during his 28 years of service. Before Justice Miller, no other member of the Court had written as many opinions.

During and after the Civil War, Miller voted to sustain President Abraham Lincoln's actions to suspend habeas corpus and to try civilians in military courts in cases involving charges of disloyalty to the Union. A writ of habeas corpus requires officials to bring a person whom they have arrested and held in custody before a judge in a court of law. If a judge finds their reasons for holding the person unlawful, then the court frees the suspect.

However, Justice Miller's greatest influence on constitutional law was in his decision to support state government rights and powers. Thus, he opposed a broad interpretation of the 14th Amendment that would involve the Court as "a perpetual censor upon all legislation of the states." He asserted this opinion for the Court in the *Slaughterhouse Cases* (1873). In this decision, Justice Miller advanced a narrow interpretation of the 14th Amendment that supported state government authority over the privileges and immunities of citizenship instead of emphasizing the federal government's power in these matters. Justice Miller concluded that it would be a violation of the Constitution to bring protection of all civil rights under the authority of the federal government. This would, he wrote, "fetter and degrade the state governments by subjecting them to the control of Congress."

Justice Miller and his supporters on the Court effectively blocked the use of the 14th Amendment to protect black Americans from state government acts that would restrict their civil rights, especially their right to "equal protection of the laws." This narrow interpretation of the 14th Amendment persisted until the middle of the 20th century.

SEE ALSO

Slaughterhouse Cases

FURTHER READING

Fairman, Charles. *Mr. Justice Miller and the Supreme Court.* Cambridge: Harvard University Press, 1938.

Minersville School District v. Gobitis

☆ *310 U.S. 586 (1940)*
☆ *Vote: 8–1*
☆ *For the Court: Frankfurter*
☆ *Dissenting: Stone*

ONE DAY in 1936, Lillian Gobitis, age 12, and her brother William, age 10, came home from school with news that distressed their parents. They had been expelled from their Minersville, Pennsylvania, school for refusing to salute the American flag during the morning patriotic exercises.

The Gobitis family belonged to the Jehovah's Witnesses faith. This religion taught that saluting the flag was like worshiping a graven image (an idol), an offense against God's law.

Lillian and William's parents asked the Minersville school board to excuse their children from the flag salute requirement. The board refused, and the Gobitises placed their children in a private school. Mr. Gobitis then sued the school board to stop it from requiring children attending the public schools to salute the flag. Federal district and appellate judges upheld Gobitis's suit. The Minersville school board then appealed to the Supreme Court.

The Issue Could public school officials force Jehovah's Witnesses to salute the American flag even though doing so contradicted their religious beliefs? The Witnesses claimed the Minersville school board's regulation violated their 1st Amendment right to the "free exercise" of religion.

Opinion of the Court The Court voted to sustain the lower courts' rulings and uphold the flag salute requirement. Justice Felix Frankfurter wrote the majority opinion. He argued that religious

Walter Gobitis and his children, William and Lillian, after they were expelled from school for refusing to salute the American flag. As Jehovah's Witnesses, they claimed that saluting the flag violated their religious beliefs.

liberty had to give way to state authority as long as the state did not directly promote or restrict religion. Because it met this requirement, the school board's flag salute requirement was constitutional.

Frankfurter called the controversy a "tragic issue" that defied the Court to find a clear-cut solution. However, he argued that national unity is the basis for national security. If a local school board believed that a compulsory flag salute promoted national unity, then the Court should not prevent it from requiring students to salute the flag.

Dissent Justice Harlan Fiske Stone was the lone dissenter in the *Gobitis* case. He considered religious freedom to be outside the jurisdiction of political authority. Stone argued that when the state attempts to force children to express a belief they do not really hold, it violates their 1st Amendment rights to freedom of speech and free exercise of religion. Furthermore, he suggested that there were other ways to instill patriotism in students.

Significance Within three years, the majority of the Court would come to agree with Stone's opposition to the *Gobitis* decision. *Gobitis* established a precedent, but that precedent did not last. Two factors influenced the Court's determination to overrule it: the reaction of the public and the legal community and changes in the Court's membership.

To Justice Frankfurter's surprise, a substantial public outburst greeted the *Gobitis* decision. More than 170 newspapers opposed the decision. The stance of the *St. Louis Post-Dispatch* typified the nationwide criticism. "We think this decision of the United States Supreme Court is dead wrong," declared its editorial. Members of the legal profession, exerting

influence on the justices, strongly condemned the decision. Articles in legal journals opposed the decision nearly unanimously and agreed with the dissent of Justice Stone.

Over a three-year period the membership of the Court changed. This change proved a second factor leading to the overruling of *Gobitis*. The first new member was Robert H. Jackson, an advocate of civil liberties for minorities. Then Wiley B. Rutledge, known for strong views in favor of freedom of religion, joined the Court. In addition, Justice Stone, who had stood alone against the *Gobitis* decision, became chief justice. A new point of view prevailed on the Court after these changes in membership.

The Court reversed the *Gobitis* decision in 1943 in the case of *West Virginia State Board of Education v. Barnette,* which said that Jehovah's Witnesses in public schools had the right to refuse to participate in required flag salute ceremonies.

SEE ALSO

Religious issues under the Constitution; West Virginia State Board of Education v. Barnette

FURTHER READING

Irons, Peter. *The Courage of Their Convictions.* New York: Free Press, 1988.

Minority rights

S E E Affirmative action; Constitutional democracy; Civil rights; Equality under the Constitution; Liberty under the Constitution

Minton, Sherman

ASSOCIATE JUSTICE, 1949–56

☆ *Born: Oct. 20, 1890, Georgetown, Ind.*
☆ *Education: Indiana University, LL.B., 1925; Yale University, LL.M., 1927*

☆ *Previous government service: Indiana public counselor, 1933–34; U.S. senator from Indiana, 1935–41; administrative assistant to the President, 1941; federal judge, Seventh Circuit Court of Appeals, 1941–49*
☆ *Appointed by President Harry S. Truman Sept. 15, 1949; replaced Wiley B. Rutledge, who died*
☆ *Supreme Court term: confirmed by the Senate Oct. 4, 1949, by a 48–16 vote; retired Oct. 15, 1956*
☆ *Died: Apr. 9, 1965, New Albany, Ind.*

SHERMAN MINTON graduated from Indiana University, where he excelled as a scholar and a varsity athlete in football and basketball. After holding a minor position in the state government, he entered national politics in 1934, winning a seat in the U.S. Senate. A Democrat, he strongly supported the New Deal programs of President Franklin D. Roosevelt.

Justice Minton supported the authority of the executive and legislative branches to make policies without interference from the judiciary. So he tended to favor a broad interpretation of the constitutional powers of the federal government.

Minton's term on the Court was cut short by a severe case of anemia that caused physical weakness and exhaustion. This condition forced him to retire after only seven years of service. As a result, his impact on constitutional law was minimal. He tended to favor government regulations over the civil liberties and rights of individuals. Justice Minton was an avid supporter of national security objectives, which he expressed as the writer of the Court's opinion in *Adler v. Board of Education*. This ruling upheld a New York law that banned members of subversive organizations, such as the Communist party, from teaching in public schools.

FURTHER READING

Gugin, Linda C., and James E. St. Clair. *Sherman Minton: New Deal Senator, Cold War Justice*. Indianapolis: Indiana Historical Society, 1997.

Miranda v. Arizona

☆ *384 U.S. 436 (1966)*
☆ *Vote: 5–4*
☆ *For the Court: Warren*
☆ *Dissenting: Clark, Harlan, White, and Stewart*

IN 1963 Ernesto Miranda was arrested for kidnapping and attacking a young woman near Phoenix. The woman identified him at the police station and the police questioned him for two hours. No one told him that he had the right to refuse to answer questions or to see a lawyer. Miranda confessed. He was tried and convicted on the basis of his confession.

Miranda appealed his conviction to the U.S. Supreme Court. His lawyer claimed the police violated Miranda's 5th Amendment protection against self-incrimination. The 5th Amendment says, "No person . . . shall be compelled in any criminal case to be a witness against himself."

Arizona's lawyers argued that Miranda could have asked for a lawyer at any time during questioning. He had not done so. They also said no one had forced him to confess. Because he had given his confession voluntarily, the prosecution could use it in court.

The Issue Does the 5th Amendment require the police to inform suspects of their right to remain silent and that anything they say can be held against them? Could the police use evidence obtained without such warnings in court?

Opinion of the Court The Court struck down Miranda's conviction, ruling that the 5th Amendment requires police to inform suspects in their custody that they have the right to remain silent, that anything they say can be held against them, and that they have a right to consult a lawyer. The police must give these warnings, the Court said, before any questioning of a suspect can take place. A defendant can then voluntarily waive these rights.

The Court added that if a suspect wants to remain silent or to contact a lawyer, police interrogation must stop until the suspect is ready to talk again or a lawyer is present. The prosecution cannot use any confessions obtained in violation of this rule in court.

Chief Justice Earl Warren argued that the U.S. system of justice is based on the idea that an individual is innocent until proved guilty. The government, he claimed, must produce evidence against an accused person. It cannot resort to forcing suspects to prove themselves guilty.

Dissent In a strong dissent, Justice John Harlan argued: "It's obviously going to mean the disappearance of confessions as a legitimate tool of law enforcement." He concluded, "[T]he thrust of the new rule is to negate all pressures, to reinforce the nervous or ignorant suspect, and ultimately to discourage any confession at all."

Significance The *Miranda* decision was controversial. Many law enforcement officials complained the decision "handcuffed the police." However, in 1986, in *Moran v. Burbine,* the Court referred to the *Miranda* case as a decision that "embodies a carefully crafted balance designed to fully protect both the defendant's and society's interests."

Ever since the *Miranda* decision, police have carried cards that they use to read suspects their rights. This message has become known as the Miranda warnings, which consist of four points: the right to remain silent, the reminder that anything said by the suspect can be used against him, the right to a lawyer,

---

WARNING AS TO YOUR RIGHTS

You are under arrest. Before we ask you any questions, you must understand what your rights are.

You have the right to remain silent. You are not required to say anything to us at any time or to answer any questions. Anything you say can be used against you in court.

You have the right to talk to a lawyer for advice before we question you and to have him with you during questioning.

If you cannot afford a lawyer and want one, a lawyer will be provided for you.

If you want to answer questions now without a lawyer present you will still have the right to stop answering at any time. You also have the right to stop answering at any time until you talk to a lawyer. P-4475

Police officers must read the Miranda warning to all suspects to notify them of their constitutional rights.

---

and the reminder that a lawyer will be provided free if the suspect cannot afford to hire one.

The Court reaffirmed, by a 7-to-2 vote, the Miranda rights of suspects in *Dickerson v. United States* (2000). At issue was a 1968 federal law that held it was not always necessary to read Miranda warnings to suspects before they confessed voluntarily to crimes. In striking down this statute, Chief Justice William Rehnquist, in his opinion for the Court, said, "Miranda has become embedded in routine police practice to the point where the warnings have become part of our national culture." The police must continue to give the Miranda warnings or risk having a suspect's confession excluded as evidence against him.

SEE ALSO

Counsel, right to; Rights of the accused

FURTHER READING

Baker, Liva. *Miranda: Crime, Law and Politics.* New York: Atheneum, 1983.

Mitchell v. Helms

☆ *530 U.S. 793 (2000)*
☆ *Vote: 6–3*
☆ *For the Court: Thomas*
☆ *Concurring: O'Connor*
☆ *Dissenting: Souter*

IN 1981, the U.S. Congress passed the Education Consolidation and Improvement Act. Chapter 2 of this statute provided federal funds to education agencies or departments of the 50 states for the purpose of distributing instructional material and equipment, including computer hardware and software, to local education agencies. The federal law required such agencies to include both public and private schools, including religiously affiliated schools.

In 1985, Mary Helms and other parents in Jefferson Parish, Louisiana, sued the local education agency of their school district to stop it from providing federal aid to Catholic schools under the terms of Chapter 2 of the federal program. (In Louisiana a parish is a civil jurisdiction, equivalent to a county in other states.)

In a typical year, about 30 percent of Chapter 2 funds spent in Jefferson Parish were allocated to private schools; most of those were Catholic schools. The suit that Helms and others brought to the federal district court claimed that the administration of Chapter 2 funds in Jefferson Parish violated the establishment clause of the U.S. Constitution's 1st Amendment.

A federal district judge upheld the Chapter 2 program, but the 5th Circuit Court of Appeals overruled the lower court's decision. The appellate court judges based their decision on two related cases of the 1970s: *Meek* v. *Pittenger* (1975) and *Wolman* v. *Walter* (1977), which held that the government could provide textbooks to religiously affiliated schools but not other instructional materials and equipment. The decisions in these two cases were based on the Lemon Test, developed in the case of *Lemon* v. *Kurtzman* (1971), which prohibited government support that promotes or impedes a religious mission. Textbooks can be provided to religious schools through government funds, according to the Court, because their contents can be screened in advance to prevent distribution of materials that would violate the Lemon Test.

Before the 5th Circuit Court of Appeals announced its decision on the Jefferson Parish case, the U.S. Supreme Court decided *Agostini* v. *Felton* (1997). In this decision, the Court modified the Lemon Test and thereby cast doubt on its applicability to the Jefferson Parish case

by way of the decisions in *Meek* v. *Pittenger* and *Wolman* v. *Walter*. Regardless, the appellate court judges concluded that *Agostini* had not directly overturned *Meek* and *Wolman*. Further, it had not rejected the distinction between textbooks and other kinds of instructional materials or equipment support, which the 5th Circuit Court of Appeals had used to declare unconstitutional the Chapter 2 federal program in Jefferson Parish. This appellate court decision was appealed to the U.S. Supreme Court.

The Issue   The central issue before the Court pertained to the federal government program known as Chapter 2, which is a block grant to states administered under the Elementary and Secondary Education Act. This program, as administered in Jefferson Parish, Louisiana, distributed computers and library materials to religious schools. Did this program violate the establishment clause of the U.S. Constitution's 1st Amendment?

Opinion of the Court   The Court upheld the program for administration of federal aid to religious schools in Jefferson Parish. A majority of the justices ruled that the federally funded program did not violate the 1st Amendment's prohibition of an establishment of religion. A four-judge plurality opinion was written by Clarence Thomas and joined by Chief Justice William Rehnquist, Anthony Kennedy, and Antonin Scalia. A concurring opinion was written by Sandra Day O'Connor and joined by Stephen Breyer.

The plurality opinion held that government provision of instructional resources is constitutional as long as the resources are not unsuitable for public schools because of religious content and as long as they are provided neutrally and equally to schools of various religious affiliations. Justice Thomas wrote, "Where the aid would be suitable for use in a public school, it is also suitable for use in any private school." Further, he argued that "the religious nature of a recipient should not matter to the constitutional analysis, so long as the recipient adequately furthers the government's secular purpose."

Thomas concluded that "hostility to aid to pervasively sectarian [Catholic] schools has a shameful pedigree that we do not hesitate to disavow. . . . In short, nothing in the Establishment Clause requires the exclusion of pervasively sectarian [Catholic] schools from otherwise permissible aid programs, and other Doctrines of this Court bar it [*Zobrest v. Catalina School District* (1993) and *Agostini v. Felton* (1997)]. This doctrine [of exclusion based on religious affiliation] was born of bigotry [against Catholicism] and should be buried now."

The Court's plurality opinion emphasized that government aid programs involving religious schools should be ruled constitutional on "the principles of neutrality and private choice." Thus, if the government program "offers aid on the same terms without regard to religion," then no unconstitutional religious purpose or intention could be attributed to the government aid program. Further, if individuals make their own private choices about how to use government-provided resources, then the government cannot be charged with advancing an impermissible religious purpose.

The plurality opinion of the Court by Justice Thomas and the concurring opinion by Justice O'Connor held that the federal program at issue in this case was constitutional because it satisfied the three criteria used by the Court in *Agostini v. Felton* (1997), which modified the Lemon Test. The *Agostini* decision consolidated the third part of the Lemon Test (the requirement for no excessive entanglement with religion) with the second part (no primary effect of promoting or obstructing religion).

Three criteria were used to determine whether government aid has the impermissible primary effect of promoting religion. First, does it result in religious indoctrination by the government? Second, does it define recipients of the government aid by reference to religion? Third, does it create an excessive entanglement between government and religion? If "no" is the answer to these questions, then the government aid program is constitutional. Justice O'Connor's concurring opinion also agreed with the Court's plurality that the *Meek* and *Wolman* decisions, by which the 5th Circuit Court of Appeals had held the federal aid to religious schools to be unconstitutional, "should be overruled."

The concurring opinion, however, departed from the plurality opinion concerning "neutrality." O'Connor argued that the plurality opinion's principle of neutrality was stated too broadly and emphatically. She disagreed with Thomas's claim that "neutrality" is determined by whether or not government aid is equally available to students no matter where they go to school. O'Connor particularly objected to this statement by Thomas: "If the religious, irreligious, and areligious are all alike eligible for governmental aid, no one would conclude that any indoctrination that any particular recipient conducts has been done at the behest of the government." The concurring opinion also made a sharp distinction between permissible government aid to religiously affiliated schools for instructional materials and equipment, such as library books and computers, and broader forms of aid, which may not be permissible.

Dissent Justice David Souter (joined by Ruth Bader Ginsburg and John Paul Stevens) disagreed sharply with Justice Thomas's opinion. Souter argued that the plurality opinion unwisely departed from the Court's precedents. Further, he claimed that Thomas's opinion opened the way to government aid to further a sectarian school's religious mission. Thus, Justice Souter contended, "The Court has no choice but to hold that the program as applied violated the Establishment Clause."

In conclusion, Souter wrote, "The plurality would break with the law. The majority [concurring opinion] misapplies it. That misapplication is, however, the only consolation in the case, which reaches an erroneous result but does not stage a doctrinal coup. But there is no mistaking the abandonment of doctrine that would occur if the plurality were to become a majority."

Significance The Court's decision was hailed by leaders of religiously affiliated schools. Archbishop Francis B. Schulte of New Orleans said, "This decision brightens our educational future." Mark Chopko, general counsel of the U.S. Catholic Conference, said the decision "has nationwide ramifications because children attending religious schools throughout the country are eligible to receive [specific federal government] services."

Supporters of a strict separation between church and state were dismayed. They feared that the Court's plurality opinion might open the way to increased accommodation of government and religion, which might include use of public money to offset or pay tuition for students in religiously affiliated schools. The concurring opinion, however, seemed to oppose such an excessively broad application of federal aid for students in religious schools (referred to as "school voucher programs"). Thus, Marc D. Stern, a lawyer for the American Jewish Congress, which supports separation of church and state, said, "Had Thomas gathered five votes for his opinion, vouchers would be constitutional. Since he didn't, it leads me to think that vouchers are unconstitutional."

The Court's plurality decision, and the public's divided reaction to it, reflect the sharp controversy associated with issues about the relationship between government and religion in the United States. Clearly, the Court has strengthened the accommodationist position with regard to government aid for students in religious schools.

SEE ALSO

Agostini v. Felton; Lemon Test; Lemon v. Kurtzman; Religious issues under the Constitution

Moody, William Henry
ASSOCIATE JUSTICE, 1906–10

☆ Born: Dec. 23, 1853, Newbury, Mass.
☆ Education: Harvard College, A.B., 1876; Harvard Law School, 1876–77
☆ Previous government service: city solicitor, Haverhill, Mass., 1888–90; district attorney, Eastern District of Massachusetts, 1890–95; U.S. representative from Massachusetts, 1895–1902; U.S. secretary of the navy, 1902–4; U.S. attorney general, 1904–6
☆ Appointed by President Theodore Roosevelt Dec. 3, 1906; replaced Henry B. Brown, who retired
☆ Supreme Court term: confirmed by the Senate Dec. 12, 1906, by a voice vote; retired Nov. 20, 1910
☆ Died: July 2, 1917, Haverhill, Mass.

WILLIAM MOODY became a friend of Theodore Roosevelt in 1895. The two men shared similar interests and ideas; when Roosevelt became President, he appointed Moody as secretary of the navy. In 1904, President Roosevelt chose Moody to be the U.S. attorney general. In 1906, he named Moody an associate justice of the Supreme Court.

Justice Moody's most important opinion for the Court came in *Twining v. New Jersey* (1908). Moody, writing for the Court, refused to apply to a state government the 5th Amendment right of an accused person to refuse to testify against himself, to avoid self-incrimination. He argued that this right of the individual, as granted in the federal Bill of Rights, could not be used to restrict state governments because the Bill of Rights applies only to the federal government. This decision was later overturned, but it had force and influence for many years.

Justice Moody's impact on constitutional law was limited by his very short term of service on the Court. He was forced to retire because of the crippling disease of rheumatism.

SEE ALSO
Twining v. New Jersey

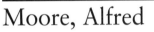

Moore, Alfred
ASSOCIATE JUSTICE, 1800–1804

☆ Born: May 21, 1755, New Hanover County, N.C.
☆ Education: studied law under his father
☆ Previous government service: North Carolina General Assembly, 1782, 1792; attorney general of North Carolina, 1782–91; judge, North Carolina Superior Court, 1799
☆ Appointed by President John Adams Dec. 6, 1799; replaced James Iredell, who died
☆ Supreme Court term: confirmed by the Senate Dec. 10, 1799, by a voice vote; resigned Jan. 26, 1804
☆ Died: Oct. 15, 1810, Bladen County, N.C.

ALFRED MOORE was a strong supporter of an independent United States of America during the 1770s conflict with the British. He served in the First North Carolina Regiment in the War of Independence and was recognized for his courage and ability as a military leader.

During the 1780s, Moore backed the movement for a strong federal gov-

ernment, which resulted in the framing of the Constitution of 1787. He helped to achieve ratification of the Constitution in North Carolina.

Moore served briefly on the Supreme Court because of ill health. In 1800, he wrote his only opinion for the Court in a case involving the capture of a French vessel by the U.S. navy during the undeclared naval war with France in 1798. The vessel had been owned by an American before its capture by the French. The court ruled that the former owner had to pay one-half the value of the ship in order to reclaim it from the U.S. government.

Muller v. Oregon
☆ 208 U.S. 412 (1908)
☆ Vote: 9–0
☆ For the Court: Brewer

IN THE EARLY 1900s state legislatures began passing laws aimed at reforming working conditions. Employers soon challenged the new laws. As a result, the Supreme Court began to face questions regarding the constitutionality of these reform laws.

A case arose in 1907 that dramatically changed how the Supreme Court made decisions about such social reform legislation. That year, Curt Muller, a Portland, Oregon, laundry owner, was charged with violating an Oregon law that set a maximum 10-hour workday for women working in laundries. Muller challenged the law as a violation of his "liberty to contract," which he claimed was guaranteed by the 14th Amendment.

Muller argued that the due process clause of the 14th Amendment prevented the state from interfering with his liberty to enter into any contracts, including those setting wages and hours for workers,

Workers at the laundry of Curt Muller, who challenged an Oregon law that limited the workday for women to 10 hours. The Supreme Court upheld the Oregon law.

necessary for running his business. (The amendment states, in part, "nor shall any State deprive any person of life, liberty, or property, without due process of law.") The Supreme Court had supported this interpretation of the 14th Amendment in several earlier cases.

Louis D. Brandeis, a brilliant lawyer who later became a distinguished Supreme Court justice, argued the case for Oregon. Brandeis took a startling new approach. He presented sociological, medical, and statistical information to show that long hours of hard labor had a harmful effect upon women's health. He claimed the Court must consider whether the Oregon law was a reasonable attempt to protect public health and safety. A state law might be allowed to interfere with the 14th Amendment's presumed guarantee of liberty of contract if it could be justified as protecting public health against real dangers.

How could the Court decide when a state law met such a standard? Brandeis argued that the Court could not rely merely on legal precedents and the vague words of the Constitution in judging such cases. It also had to consider relevant facts about the social conditions that led to the law in the first place.

The Issue Brandeis defined the question before the Court: Did the consideration of social conditions justify the Oregon law's interference with the 14th Amendment's supposed guarantee of liberty of contract?

Would the Court accept Brandeis's novel thesis that it should consider relevant social facts in deciding the case? Or would the Court, as it had in the past, decide the case strictly through reference to legal arguments?

Opinion of the Court The Court accepted Brandeis's argument, ruling unanimously to uphold Oregon's law. The factual evidence Brandeis supplied proved convincing. The Court ruled that longer working hours might harm women's ability to bear children. Thus, the state's limitation of those hours was a justified interference with liberty of contract and property and within the state's regulatory power.

Significance The *Muller* case established that lawyers could use social facts and statistics as well as strictly legal arguments in the briefs they presented to the Supreme Court. A brief is a document summarizing the facts and legal arguments that a lawyer gives to a court when appealing a case. Today we call a brief that contains substantial nonlegal data a *Brandeis brief*. Ever since the *Muller* case, lawyers have used relevant social data in their arguments before the Court. When deciding subsequent cases—*Brown* v. *Board of Education* (1954), for example—the Supreme Court has recognized that information about social conditions could appropriately supplement legal principles.

SEE ALSO
Brandeis brief

FURTHER READING
Mason, Alpheus Thomas. "The Case of the Overworked Laundress." In *Quarrels That Have Shaped the Constitution,* edited by John A. Garraty. New York: Harper & Row, 1987.
Woloch, Nancy. *Muller v. Oregon: A Brief History with Documents.* Boston: Bedford Books, 1996.

Munn v. Illinois

☆ 94 U.S. 113 (1877)
☆ Vote: 7–2
☆ For the Court: Waite
☆ Dissenting: Field and Strong

MUNN V. ILLINOIS was the first of a famous series of cases known as the *Granger Cases*. These cases dealt with issues resulting from the rapid growth of manufacturing and transportation companies that began after the Civil War ended in 1865.

Many of these companies, particularly those formed by railroad concerns and operators of huge grain warehouses, began to abuse the nearly complete control they had over hauling and storing farm products, especially grain. The railroads and grain warehouses charged farmers very high prices and often tried to cheat them. By the 1870s, the situation had deteriorated so much that even the *Chicago Tribune*, a newspaper known for its pro-business sympathies, called the grain warehouses "blood-sucking insects."

In response to such conditions, a large, politically powerful farm group, the Grange, developed. Farmers in the Granger movement influenced state legislatures in the Midwest to pass laws regulating the prices railroads, warehouses, and public utilities charged for hauling freight and storing grain.

The Issue The railroads and grain warehouses fought against state regulation of their businesses in the courts. They claimed the states' Granger laws violated the Constitution in three ways: they infringed on Congress's right to regulate interstate commerce, they violated the Constitution's prohibition against interfering with contracts, and they violated the 14th Amendment by depriving businesses of their liberty and property without due process of law.

The *Munn* case posed a clear and important question for a nation with rapidly developing industries. Did the Constitution permit a state to regulate privately owned businesses?

Opinion of the Court The Court ruled in favor of the states. It said the Illinois state legislature could fix maximum rates for grain storage in Chicago and other places in the state. Chief Justice Morrison R. Waite set forth a doctrine that both Congress and state legislatures still use to regulate many private business activities—the doctrine of "business affected with a public interest."

Waite said that when the activity of a company "has public consequences and affect(s) the community at large," it is a "business affected with a public interest." Under the Constitution the states can regulate such a business, and the owner of such a business "must submit to be controlled by the public for the common good."

Dissent Justice Stephen J. Field argued against the *Munn* opinion as an invasion of private property rights, which he said were protected against state power by the due process clause of the 14th Amendment. Justice Field wanted to limit the use of state "police power" to regulate businesses.

Significance The Court's decision established the power of state government to regulate businesses other than public

Ira Munn's grain warehouse was on the right side of the Chicago River. When Munn ignored state laws regulating the rates he could charge for storage, the case went to the Supreme Court. The Court ruled that states could regulate privately owned businesses.

utilities. Today, state legislatures exercise tremendous regulatory powers over such matters as working conditions, transportation of goods and people, and manufacturing of products for sale to the public. The constitutional basis for much of this activity rests directly on the Court's decision in *Munn* v. *Illinois*.

Murphy, Frank

ASSOCIATE JUSTICE, 1940–49

☆ Born: Apr. 13, 1890, Harbor Beach, Mich.
☆ Education: University of Michigan, B.A., 1912; LL.B., 1914
☆ Previous government service: chief assistant attorney general, Eastern District of Michigan, 1919–20; judge, Recorder's Court, Detroit, Mich., 1923–30; mayor of Detroit, 1930–33; governor general of the Philippines, 1933–35; U.S. high commissioner to the Philippines, 1935–36; governor of Michigan, 1937–39; U.S. attorney general, 1939–40
☆ Appointed by President Franklin D. Roosevelt Jan. 4, 1940; replaced Pierce Butler, who died
☆ Supreme Court term: confirmed by the Senate Jan. 15, 1940, by a voice vote; served until July 19, 1949
☆ Died: July 19, 1949, Detroit, Mich.

FRANK MURPHY was a strong supporter of Franklin D. Roosevelt's 1932 campaign for the Presidency. After serving as an administrator of the U.S. territory of the Philippines and as U.S. attorney general, Murphy was appointed by President Roosevelt to the Supreme Court.

As an associate justice, Murphy was a strong defender of minority rights. His most notable opinions were written in dissent of the Court's decisions to favor federal or state government interests above the rights of individuals.

Justice Murphy's dissent in *Korematsu* v. *United States* (1944) has been regarded as an example of the best opinions to be found in the Supreme Court literature. In this wartime case, the Court upheld the right of the government to relocate and confine all persons of Japanese ancestry living on the Pacific coast of the United States. The Court's majority argued that this action was necessary to protect national security during the war against Japan. Justice Murphy disagreed and said the relocation was "utterly revolting among a free people who have embraced the principles set forth in the Constitution of the United States."

Murphy's dissent in the *Korematsu* case is honored today as a courageous and correct view of the case. And the majority opinion in that case tends to be criticized, in Murphy's terms, as "legalization of racism."

SEE ALSO

Korematsu v. United States

FURTHER READING

Fine, Sidney. *Frank Murphy: The Washington Years.* Ann Arbor: University of Michigan Press, 1984.
Howard, J. Woodford. *Mr. Justice Murphy: A Political Biography.* Princeton, N.J.: Princeton University Press, 1968.

National Association for the Advancement of Colored People (NAACP)

THE NATIONAL ASSOCIATION for the Advancement of Colored People (NAACP) is a private, not-for-profit organization founded in 1909 to protect and expand the civil rights of African Americans. The NAACP has used both political and legal strategies to carry out its mission. In 1939 the NAACP Legal

Thurgood Marshall (sitting on the table) with his staff at the NAACP. Under Marshall's leadership, the Legal Defense Fund successfully argued cases before the Supreme Court to secure civil rights for African Americans.

Defense Fund (LDF) was created to support legal strategies on behalf of civil rights for African Americans. From 1940 to 1961 Thurgood Marshall was the director of the LDF. He was primarily responsible for winning 29 victories for the LDF in cases before the Supreme Court. Marshall and the LDF helped the NAACP to win its greatest legal victory, the Supreme Court decision in *Brown* v. *Board of Education* (1954), which outlawed racial segregation in public schools. Marshall went on to become an associate justice of the Supreme Court.

The NAACP carefully monitors the President's nominations of Supreme Court justices and other federal judges. The purpose is to encourage the appointment of people who are likely to agree with the organization's views on civil rights.

SEE ALSO
Brown v. Board of Education; Civil rights

National Labor Relations Board v. Jones & Laughlin Steel Corp.

☆ *301 U.S. 1 (1937)*
☆ *Vote: 5–4*
☆ *For the Court: Hughes*
☆ *Dissenting: Sutherland, Van Devanter, McReynolds, and Butler*

IN JULY 1935 the Jones & Laughlin Steel Corporation fired 10 workers at its Aliquippa, Pennsylvania, plant. They were leaders of a local unit of the American Federation of Labor (AFL), a national labor union. The managers of the steel company wanted to stop their workers from joining the labor union.

On July 5, 1935, four days before Jones & Laughlin dismissed the 10 labor union leaders, President Franklin D. Roosevelt signed into law the National Labor Relations Act, often called the Wagner Act after New York senator Robert Wagner, the law's major sponsor in Congress. This new federal law made it illegal for an employer to fire or otherwise harass a worker because he belonged to a labor union. The law also protected the right of workers at a company to designate, by majority vote, a labor union to represent them as their sole bargaining agent with their employer.

The Wagner Act applied to all businesses either engaged directly in interstate commerce or whose operations affected interstate commerce. Thus, the law could be applied to a business such as Jones & Laughlin Steel Corporation, which shipped steel across state lines.

The government set up the National Labor Relations Board (NLRB) to enforce the Wagner Act. On April 9, 1936, the NLRB charged Jones & Laughlin with violating the Wagner Act by discharging the 10 workers because they were labor union leaders. The company was ordered to reinstate the men and to give them back pay for the period they were not permitted to work. Jones & Laughlin's response was to challenge the NLRB and the Wagner Act as unconstitutional.

The Issue   Lawyers for Jones & Laughlin argued that the Wagner Act was based on an excessively broad interpretation of the commerce powers of Congress specified in Article 1, Section 8, of the U.S. Constitution. According to Jones & Laughlin, Congress did not have power under the commerce clause to regulate the relationships of managers and workers of a private corporation. Furthermore, the company claimed, the Wagner Act violated the due process clause of the 5th Amendment, which had been held in previous decisions of the Court to protect the "liberty of contract" between employers and employees. The federal government had no power, said the Jones & Laughlin lawyers, to interfere with the rights of private property owners and workers to bargain about wages, hours of work, and working conditions.

Opinion of the Court   The Court sustained the Wagner Act as a constitutional exercise of Congress's commerce power and ruled that it did not violate the 5th Amendment's due process clause. Chief Justice Charles Evans Hughes wrote that the Wagner Act's purpose was to reduce the possibility of strikes, which could disrupt the production and distribution of products and thereby increase the bargaining power to achieve satisfactory working conditions. Strikes could be prevented, Hughes said, by protecting the right of workers to organize labor unions. Hughes also rejected the "liberty of contract" argument based on the due process clause of the 5th Amendment. He emphasized that the Wagner Act in fact *enhanced* workers' power to bargain through a democratically elected representative of a labor union.

Significance   In this decision, the Court affirmed President Roosevelt's position that the federal government has the power under the Constitution to regulate the economic system. The *Jones & Laughlin* decision was a departure from several decisions between 1933 and 1937 in which the Court had firmly rejected President Roosevelt's New Deal programs.

The Court's opposition had so angered the President that, following his landslide victory in the 1936 election, he threatened to change the membership of the Court in his favor. On February 5, 1937, Roosevelt announced that he would ask Congress to enact legislation to enable the President to add up to six additional justices to the Court. With such a law, he could immediately add new justices to the Court who would be likely to vote for his economic regulation policies. This Court-packing plan was abandoned by President Roosevelt after the Court made decisions he agreed with in *Jones & Laughlin* and other 1937 cases.

The upholding of the Wagner Act by the Court greatly changed labor-management relations throughout the United States. It led to an enormous growth in the membership and power of labor unions, which were influential in improving wages, hours of work, and working conditions.

SEE ALSO
Commerce power; Court-packing plan

FURTHER READING
Cortner, Richard C. *The Jones & Laughlin Case.* New York: Knopf, 1970.

Natural law

THE THEORY of natural law holds that there is a certain order in nature from which humans, by use of their reason, can derive standards for human conduct. For example, Saint Thomas Aquinas (a 13th-century European scholar and Roman Catholic priest), in his *Summa Theologica*, attempted to derive natural law from his understanding of the divine law revealed by God.

By contrast, philosophers of the European Age of Enlightenment (from the 1680s through the 1700s) such as John Locke in his *Two Treatises of Government* (1690) ignored the idea of divine law and based their concept of natural law on the fundamental human desire for self-preservation and fulfillment. Accordingly, Locke and other Enlightenment thinkers held that the laws of nature imply government based on consent of the governed as the way to secure natural rights of individuals to life, liberty, and property. The natural law standard for judging the worth of government was the effectiveness of the government in securing the natural rights of individuals. These rights were thought to exist prior to the people's establishment of their government, and all people were entitled to these rights by virtue of their humanity. All were bound to respect and abide by these natural rights because of their capacity to know and justify them through human reason.

British philosopher John Locke based his concept of natural law on the universal human desires for life, liberty, and property.

The Enlightenment conception of natural law and natural rights influenced the founders of constitutional government in the United States. This influence is evident in the text of the Declaration of Independence and the preambles to the first state constitutions of the original 13 states. However, there were other important influences on the constitutional thought of the founders, such as the political and legal ideas brought to America from England and the experiences in establishing and developing their colonial governments.

The idea of natural law was used from time to time in debates about constitutional issues. For example, both sides in the slavery controversy, from the 1780s to the 1860s, appealed to natural law as justification for their views. Nineteenth-century opponents of strong government regulation of private business also appealed to natural law to support their constitutional arguments. However, during the 20th century, natural law theories had little influence on the decisions of Supreme Court justices or the thoughts of most legal scholars. Legal protection of individual rights has not been based on natural law doctrines but on the principles and precedents stemming from interpretation of the U.S. Constitution and federal statutes.

SEE ALSO
Constitutional democracy; Constitutionalism; Constitutional law

FURTHER READING
Arkes, Hadley. "Natural Law." *Constitution* 4, no. 1 (Winter 1992): 13–20.
Finnis, John. *Natural Law and Natural Rights.* New York: Oxford University Press, 1996.
George, Robert P. *In Defense of Natural Law.* New York: Oxford University Press, 1999.

Near v. Minnesota

☆ *283 U.S. 697 (1931)*
☆ *Vote: 5–4*
☆ *For the Court: Hughes*
☆ *Dissenting: Butler, Van Devanter,*
  Sutherland, and McReynolds

IN 1927 Jay Near and Howard Guilford established the *Saturday Press* in Minneapolis. Near, an experienced journalist, was known for his bigotry against Catholics, blacks, Jews, and organized labor. He specialized in reporting scandals in a sensational manner.

From its first issue, the *Saturday Press* hammered away at alleged ties between gangsters and police in a series of sensational stories. The paper proved especially tough on city and county government officials.

The *Saturday Press* attacked, among others, county prosecutor Floyd Olson, who later became a three-term Minnesota governor. The *Saturday Press* called him "Jew lover" Olson and accused him of dragging his feet in the investigation of organized crime. Olson was enraged. On November 21, 1927, he filed a complaint under Minnesota's Public Nuisance Abatement Law with the county district judge. Olson charged that the *Saturday Press* had defamed various politicians, the county grand jury, and the entire Jewish community.

The county judge issued a temporary restraining order against the *Saturday Press* prohibiting publication of the paper under the Public Nuisance Abatement Law. That law was known as a "gag law" because it authorized a form of censorship called prior restraint. Prior

The state of Minnesota issued an injunction banning publication of the Saturday Press, but the Supreme Court ruled in Near v. Minnesota *that such prior restraint of the newspaper was illegal.*

restraint allows government officials to restrict a newspaper or magazine *in advance* from publishing materials of which they disapprove.

Near and Guilford obeyed the restraining order issued against them. They claimed, however, that it was unconstitutional. As the Minnesota courts dealt with this case, Howard Guilford withdrew from the legal battle. More important, Near recruited a rich and powerful ally. Robert McCormick, the publisher of the *Chicago Tribune,* sympathized with Near for a number of reasons. Like Near, the bigoted McCormick disliked blacks, Jews, and other minorities. McCormick had also fought numerous legal battles over articles published in his paper. These struggles had taught McCormick the importance of defending the 1st Amendment. He did not want the Illinois legislature to copy the Minnesota gag law. And so the interests of the rich publisher in Chicago and those of the poor scandalmonger in Minnesota coincided. Near wanted his little paper back in business; McCormick wanted a free press. McCormick committed the *Tribune*'s full resources to the case. His lawyers represented Near in future legal proceedings.

The Minnesota Supreme Court decided against Near and upheld the Public Nuisance Abatement Law. Near, with McCormick's support, appealed to the U.S. Supreme Court.

The Issue Near's attorney claimed that the Minnesota Public Nuisance Abatement Law allowed prior restraint and thus violated the 1st Amendment, which guarantees freedom of speech and press, and the 14th Amendment, which forbids the states to "deprive any person of life, liberty, or property, without due process of law." He argued that the Constitution guaranteed freedom of the press as a fundamental right. No state could take the right away through prior restraint.

Near's attorney admitted that the *Saturday Press* article was "defamatory" of government officials. But, he added, "So long as men do evil, so long will newspapers publish defamation." The attorney argued, "Every person does have a constitutional right to publish malicious, scandalous and defamatory matter, though untrue and with bad motives, and for unjustifiable ends." Such a person could be punished afterward. The remedy, then, was not censorship of an offending newspaper by prior restraint. Rather, the state should bring specific criminal charges against such a newspaper after it published the material.

Minnesota argued that the Public Nuisance Abatement Law was constitutional and that the injunction against the *Saturday Press* was not prior restraint. The injunction was issued only after the *Saturday Press* had attacked the reputations of public officials. Thus, the law punished an offense already committed. The Constitution was designed to protect individual freedoms, not serve the purposes of wrongdoers, such as Near and his scandalous *Saturday Press*.

Opinion of the Court The Court ruled in favor of Jay Near and held that the Minnesota Public Nuisance Abatement Law was a prior restraint on the press that violated both the 1st Amendment and the due process clause of the 14th Amendment.

Chief Justice Charles Evans Hughes, in the majority opinion, declared the Minnesota law "the essence of censorship." He stated that libel laws, not newspaper closures, should counter false charges and character assassinations. He emphasized that the right to criticize government officials was one of the foundations of the American nation.

Hughes stressed that "this statute [the Public Nuisance Abatement Law] raises questions of grave importance transcending the local interests involved in the particular action. It is no longer open to doubt that the liberty of the press... is within the liberty safeguarded by the due process clause of the Fourteenth Amendment from invasion by state action."

Dissent Justice Pierce Butler argued that the Minnesota law was not an example of prior restraint. Rather, it allowed public officials to control unacceptable publications after reading the published material. Butler also argued that the U.S. Supreme Court had imposed on a state government "a federal restriction that is without precedent." He was referring to the fact that this decision was the first time that the Court used the due process clause of the 14th Amendment to apply the 1st Amendment right to freedom of the press to a state. Butler and his colleagues in dissent said this should not be done.

Significance Jay Near was triumphant when he learned of the Court's verdict. In October 1932 Near again began to publish the *Saturday Press*. The paper did not survive, however, and in April 1936 Near died in obscurity.

The Court's ruling also pleased Colonel McCormick. He wrote Chief Justice Hughes: "I think your decision in the Gag Law case will forever remain one of the buttresses of free government."

As a result of *Near* v. *Minnesota*, the United States has built a tradition against prior restraints unlike any other in the world. This tradition has helped keep the free press from censorship by government officials merely because it is critical of them.

In 1971 the Supreme Court relied on the *Near* precedent in the Pentagon Papers case (*New York Times Co.* v. *United States*). In that case the federal government attempted to stop the *New York Times* from publishing secret documents describing the history of U.S. involvement in the Vietnam War.

The Court ruled against the government and permitted publication of the documents.

SEE ALSO

Freedom of press and speech; Incorporation doctrine; New York Times Co. v. United States; Prior restraint

FURTHER READING

Friendly, Fred W. *Minnesota Rag: The Dramatic Story of the Landmark Court Case That Gave New Meaning to Freedom of the Press.* New York: Random House, 1981.
Murphy, Paul L. "The Case of the Miscreant Purveyor of Scandal." In *Quarrels That Have Shaped the Constitution,* edited by John A. Garraty. New York: Harper & Row, 1987.

Necessary and proper clause

SEE Constitutional construction; Implied powers

Nelson, Samuel

ASSOCIATE JUSTICE, 1845–72

☆ *Born: Nov. 10, 1792, Hebron, N.Y.*
☆ *Education: Middlebury College, B.A., 1813*
☆ *Previous government service: postmaster, Cortland, N.Y., 1820–23; New York State Constitutional Convention, 1821; Presidential elector, 1820; judge, Sixth Circuit Court of New York, 1823–31; associate justice, New York Supreme Court, 1831–37; chief justice, New York Supreme Court, 1837–45*
☆ *Appointed by President John Tyler Feb. 4, 1845; replaced Smith Thompson, who died*
☆ *Supreme Court term: confirmed by the Senate Feb. 14, 1845, by a voice vote; retired Nov. 28, 1872*
☆ *Died: Dec. 13, 1873, Cooperstown, N.Y.*

SAMUEL NELSON was the son of Scotch-Irish parents who came to North America in the 1760s. After admission to the New York bar in 1817, he began a career in law and politics. In 1823 he was appointed to the position of judge on the Sixth Circuit Court of New York. For nearly the rest of his life, Nelson occupied judicial positions in the state of New York and on the U.S. Supreme Court.

During his 27 years on the Supreme Court, Nelson performed satisfactorily but without distinction. His decisions tended to favor states' rights and judicial self-restraint. In his opinion for the Court in *Georgia* v. *Stanton* (1868), Justice Nelson showed his strong belief in judicial restraint to the point of deciding against states' rights. He decided against the attempts of two Southern states to obstruct Reconstruction policies of the federal government. He held that the case presented by the Southern states should be dismissed because it involved "political questions" that the Supreme Court could not decide.

New Jersey v. T.L.O.

☆ *469 U.S. 325 (1985)*
☆ *Vote: 6–3*
☆ *For the Court: White*
☆ *Dissenting: Stevens, Brennan, and Marshall*

A TEACHER at a New Jersey high school discovered a student smoking cigarettes in a school bathroom, which was a violation of school rules. The teacher took the student to the principal's office. The assistant principal questioned the student, who denied she had been smoking in the bathroom. The school official then demanded to see her purse. After opening it, he found cigarettes, cigarette rolling papers that are commonly associated with the use of marijuana, a pipe, plastic bags, money, a list of students who owed her money, and two letters that contained evidence that she had been involved in marijuana dealings.

As a result of this search of the student's purse and the seizure of items in it, the state brought delinquency charges against the student in New Jersey Juvenile Court. The student (identified in the case only by her initials, T.L.O.) countered with a motion to suppress evidence found in her purse as a violation of her constitutional rights against unreasonable and unwarranted searches and seizures.

The Issue Is the 4th Amendment prohibition of unreasonable and unwarranted searches and seizures applicable to officials in a public school with regard to its students?

Opinion of the Court The Supreme Court decided that the 4th Amendment prohibition of *unreasonable* searches and seizures is applicable to searches conducted by public school officials, but that in this case a warrantless search of the student's purse *was* reasonable and permissible.

Justice Byron White wrote the opinion of the Court. He said that school officials may search a student in school as long as "there are reasonable grounds for suspecting that the search will turn up evidence that the student has violated or is violating either the law or the rules of the school."

Dissent Justice John Paul Stevens wrote in dissent:

> The search of a young woman's purse by a school administrator is a serious invasion of her legitimate expectations of privacy.... Because [the student's] conduct was neither unlawful nor significantly disruptive of school order or the educational process, the invasion of privacy associated with the forcible opening of T.L.O.'s purse was entirely unjustified at its inception....
>
> The rule the Court adopts today is so open-ended that it may make the Fourth Amendment virtually

meaningless in the school context. Although I agree that school administrators must have broad latitude to maintain order and discipline in our classrooms, that authority is not unlimited.

Significance This decision indicated that the Court did not view the rights of students in a public school as equivalent to the rights of adults in a nonschool setting. Police need to demonstrate "probable cause" that individuals they search have violated or are violating a law. School officials, by contrast, need to have only "reasonable suspicion" of unlawful conduct to justify a search of students in school. School authorities, in this view, may restrict the rights of students in behalf of the school's compelling educational purpose.

SEE ALSO

Searches and seizures; Student rights under the Constitution

New York Times Co. v. Sullivan

☆ *376 U.S. 254 (1964)*
☆ *Vote: 9–0*
☆ *For the Court: Brennan*

ON MARCH 29, 1960, the *New York Times* printed a full-page advertisement paid for by two black civil rights organizations. L. B. Sullivan, an elected city commissioner of Montgomery, Alabama, read the advertisement and decided to bring a libel suit against the *New York Times* and the sponsors of the advertisement. Libel is the act of slandering, or hurting a person's reputation by saying negative things about him that are untrue or misleading.

Sullivan was upset about the advertisement because it described civil rights

Police Commissioner L. B. Sullivan (right) in court during his libel suit against the New York Times.

activities in southern states, including Alabama, and appealed for donations of money to support the programs of the ad's two sponsors. The ad also included an eight-line description of events in Montgomery, Alabama, that criticized the city police for abuses against black demonstrators. Sullivan's name was not mentioned, but he was offended because he was in charge of the Montgomery police department. So he claimed that false and exaggerated charges against the city police were slanders against him in his role as police commissioner.

State courts in Alabama decided in favor of Sullivan. Sullivan proved that there were several errors about details, but not main points, in the advertisement. The state courts concluded that he had been libeled and awarded him $500,000 in damages. The *New York Times* appealed this decision to the U.S. Supreme Court.

The Issue L. B. Sullivan argued that the advertisement in this case was libelous because it contained untrue statements. He claimed that the Constitution does not protect speech that is false or misleading about the actions of a person. The *New York Times* argued that the libel law of Alabama, which permitted restrictions on untrue speech, was an infringement on 1st Amendment freedoms to express criticisms of public officials. To what extent do constitutional protections of free speech limit a state government's power to award damages in a libel action brought by a government official against his critics?

Opinion of the Court The U.S. Supreme Court reversed the decision of the Alabama Supreme Court. Justice William Brennan argued that the Alabama libel law threatened 1st Amendment freedoms of speech and press by "raising…the possibility that a good-faith critic of government will be penalized for his criticism." Brennan said that "debate on public issues should be uninhibited, robust, and wide-open, and that it may well include vehement, caustic, and sometimes unpleasantly sharp attacks on government and public officials."

Brennan maintained that "erroneous statement is inevitable in free debate." Therefore, even false statements about public officials must be protected if citizens and the media are to act effectively as critics of their government. Therefore, the Court concluded, public officials may not be awarded damages for defamatory statements about their official conduct merely because the statements are false. Rather, the offended public official must prove actual malice. That is, he must demonstrate that "the statement was made with…knowledge that it was false or with reckless disregard of whether it was false or not."

Significance This decision has made it very difficult for public officials to bring libel actions against the media. As a result, freedom of expression about the actions of government has been greatly expanded. The media have been encouraged to play the role of watchdog and exposer of questionable or improper actions by public officials, such as corrupt or foolish behavior.

SEE ALSO

Freedom of speech and press

FURTHER READING

Lewis, Anthony. *Make No Law: The Sullivan Case and the First Amendment.* New York: Random House, 1991.

New York Times Co. v. United States

☆ *403 U.S. 713 (1971)*

☆ *Vote: 6–3*

☆ *For the Court: per curiam opinion; Douglas, Stewart, White, Marshall, Black, and Brennan writing separately*

☆ *Dissenting: Burger, Blackmun, and Harlan*

Federal judge Gerhard Gesell hears arguments in the Pentagon Papers case. The Supreme Court ruled that publication of the Pentagon Papers was not a sufficient threat to national security to justify prior restraint.

IN JUNE 1971, the *New York Times* and the *Washington Post* started to publish a series of articles based on U.S. government documents that became known as the Pentagon Papers. The Pentagon is the headquarters of the U.S. Department of Defense, the compiler of these documents, which included information about U.S. military involvement in Vietnam and federal government policies on the Vietnam War that was classified as top secret. Federal officials did not want the Pentagon Papers released to the public and printed only 15 copies. Daniel Ellsberg, a researcher involved in compiling and editing the Pentagon Papers, made a photocopy of these documents and gave most of them to Neil Sheehan of the *New York Times.*

A team of *Times* reporters wrote a series of articles on U.S. involvement in the Vietnam War based on the top secret information in the Pentagon Papers. A short time later, Daniel Ellsberg also provided materials from the Pentagon Papers to the *Washington Post,* and articles based on these documents began to appear in that paper, too.

The federal government objected to the publication in daily newspapers of information it classified as top secret. Government officials claimed that wide distribution of information in the Pentagon Papers would be damaging to national security. So the government brought legal action against the *New York Times* and the *Washington Post* to stop them, and other newspapers, from publishing articles about the Pentagon Papers.

The Issue Representatives of the *New York Times* said the federal government's attempt to stop publication of articles about the Pentagon Papers was an example of prior restraint—when the government restricts a publication in advance from publishing certain information—and a violation of freedom of the press guaranteed in the 1st Amendment. The federal government argued that publication of this top secret information would put the lives of soldiers in danger and give assistance during wartime to enemies of the United States. Do the needs of national security during wartime outweigh the value of free and open communication of information? Does the President's constitutional duty as commander in chief of the armed forces require that he have power to restrict publication of military secrets? What are the constitutional limits on a free press during wartime?

Opinion of the Court The Court rejected the federal government's arguments for prior restraint on the publication of information from the Pentagon Papers. The Court concluded that the government failed to show that publication of this information about the Vietnam War would cause such serious harm as to outweigh the value of free expression of information.

Dissent Chief Justice Warren Burger emphasized the complexity of this kind of case. He agreed in principle with constitutional limits on prior restraint. But he also argued that there are limits on 1st Amendment freedoms. He said, "[T]he imperative of a free and unfettered press comes into collision with another imperative, the effective functioning of a complex modern government and specifically the effective exercise of certain constitutional powers of the Executive." He referred to the constitutional powers of the President pertaining to conduct of foreign policy and command of military forces.

Significance The Supreme Court decision in this case was a clear defeat for advocates of prior restraint under conditions of wartime or other national crises. The decision also encouraged the media in their efforts to check federal government officials or hold them accountable by obtaining and publishing information that the government wants to keep from public view.

SEE ALSO
Freedom of speech and press; Prior restraint

FURTHER READING
The Pentagon Papers as Published by the New York Times. New York: Bantam, 1971.
Rudenstine, David. *The Day the Presses Stopped: A History of the Pentagon Papers Case.* Berkeley: University of California Press, 1998.
Unger, S. J. *The Papers and the Papers: An Account of the Legal and Political Battles over the Pentagon Papers.* New York: Dutton, 1972.

Nomination of justices

S E E Appointment of justices; Rejection of Supreme Court nominees

Northern Securities Co. v. United States

☆ *193 U.S. 197 (1904)*
☆ *Vote: 5–4*
☆ *For the Court: Harlan*
☆ *Concurring: Brewer*
☆ *Dissenting: White, Holmes, Fuller, and Peckham*

J. P. MORGAN, James J. Hill, and Edward H. Harriman were powerful stock market speculators and investors who were interested mainly in railroads. Each desperately desired to control the three leading railroads linking the Great Lakes and the Pacific Northwest. In 1901 they battled fiercely on the stock exchange to gain control of the railroads. None of the three succeeded, so they settled their differences and joined together to form the Northern Securities Company to control the three railroads. They chartered their company under New Jersey laws.

In 1890, however, Congress had passed the Sherman Antitrust Act in an effort to prevent the growth of business monopolies. (A monopoly is the exclusive control of an industry by a single owner or company.) This law prohibited trusts, or business combinations "in restraint of trade or commerce among the several States." Congress had the power to pass that law under the commerce clause of the Constitution (Article 1, Section 8), which had been defined broadly in the Supreme Court case *Gibbons* v. *Ogden* (1824). But the Sherman Antitrust Act was vague. What did "restraint of trade and commerce" mean?

The government argued that the Northern Securities Company was guilty of the very thing the law forbade. The Sherman Act aimed to prevent monopolies from taking over an industry or an aspect of an industry. The Northern Securities Company controlled *all* of the major railroads throughout a huge section of the country. If the Court allowed the three competing railroads to merge into one giant company, competition in the area would disappear. Because people had no alternative method of transportation, the Northern Securities Company would have been able to charge them exorbitant fees. Serving only the narrow interests of Morgan, Hill, and Harriman, this monopoly would harm the public and nation.

The Northern Securities Company argued that the federal government could not interfere with its affairs because it was merely a holding company created by a stock transaction. (A holding company is created solely to hold the ownership rights to two or more companies. But the holding company, as an administrative convenience, does not by itself deal in commerce.) Legally, under New Jersey laws, the corporation therefore did not deal in commerce. Federal government interference would violate state powers as protected by the 10th Amendment.

The Issue   Did the combination of railroads under the Northern Securities Company represent a "restraint of trade or commerce" covered by the Sherman Antitrust Act? Or was the combination just a stock transaction, not commerce? If it was the latter, it merited legal recognition under New Jersey law and 10th Amendment protection.

As often happens in Supreme Court cases, however, this specific question reflected a larger, more general issue. Could the national government regulate the activities of the huge, powerful businesses that were developing in the nation? A decision in favor of the Northern Securities Company would greatly limit the effectiveness of the Sherman Antitrust Act and the ability of the government to gain some control over business.

Opinion of the Court   The Court ruled in favor of the government. It found that the Northern Securities Company intended to eliminate competition among the railroads involved. Hence, the company was "a combination in restraint of interstate commerce" and was illegal under the Sherman Antitrust Act.

The Court interpreted the act broadly. Justice John Harlan wrote that a combination of businesses, a trust, did not need to engage directly in commerce to violate the act. If it restrained commerce in any way, a trust was illegal.

Dismissing the argument that the Sherman Act violated state powers under the Constitution, Harlan said a state law could not confer immunity from federal law. In regulating interstate commerce, Congress superseded the states' power to create corporations. Acting within its legitimate sphere, such as regulating commerce, the national government was supreme.

Dissent   Chief Justice Edward D. White argued that Congress could not regulate the ownership of stock through laws such as the Sherman Antitrust Act because this was a violation of powers reserved to the states by the 10th Amendment. He also claimed that a broad interpretation of the Sherman Act would have a negative effect on business.

Significance   The Court's decision helped establish increased government control of trusts and monopolies. The *Northern Securities* case symbolized the federal government's right and duty to regulate the national economy for the public good. The Court's ruling gave the federal government the authority to begin to exercise stricter supervision of the growing number of large American corporations. For example, the Federal Trade Commission Act of 1914 provided for regulation of businesses to prevent activities that would reduce competition in the marketplace or cheat consumers.

SEE ALSO

Commerce power

FURTHER READING

Apple, R. W., Jr. "The Case of the Monopolistic Railroadmen." In *Quarrels That Have Shaped the Constitution,* edited by John A. Garraty. New York: Harper & Row, 1987.

Nullification

IN THE YEARS preceding the Civil War, some supporters of state powers and rights developed the doctrine of nullification. Advocates of nullification claimed that state governments had the power, under the U.S. Constitution, to declare a federal law unconstitutional, or unlawful and void.

John C. Calhoun of South Carolina, then Vice President of the United States, was the leading proponent of nullification. In the essay *South Carolina Exposition and Protest* (1828), Calhoun argued that the Constitution and federal Union were established by sovereign states, not by the people of the United States. Thus, the state governments have authority to decide whether acts of the federal government are constitutional or not.

If a state government decided that the federal government had exceeded constitutional limits on its powers, then the state could call a special convention to nullify the law, thereby declaring that the law would *not* be enforced in the state. The nullification doctrine was linked to the claim that a state had a right to secede from, or leave, the federal Union.

In 1832, during a controversy about a federal tariff law, South Carolina attempted to use Calhoun's nullification

John Calhoun believed each state had the power to nullify federal laws.

doctrine to declare the federal statute unconstitutional. There was talk of secession. President Andrew Jackson responded with the threat of military force to suppress actions that he viewed as rebellious violations of the U.S. Constitution. The crisis ended with a compromise about the terms of the disputed federal tariff law.

Arguments about the nullification doctrine and the right of secession were settled, once and for all, by the Civil War (1861–65). After the Union victory over the Confederate states, there was no more serious advocacy of a state's right to nullify a federal law or to secede from the federal Union. The Supreme Court, in *Texas v. White* (1869), concluded that the Constitution created "an indestructible Union, composed of indestructible states."

SEE ALSO

Constitutionalism; Federalism; Implied powers; Texas v. White

FURTHER READING

Lence, Ross M., ed. *Union and Liberty: The Political Philosophy of John C. Calhoun.* Indianapolis: Liberty Fund, 1992.

Oath of office

THE CONSTITUTION says in Article 6 that "judicial officers, both of the United States and of the several states, shall be bound by oath or affirmation, to support this Constitution." In line with this clause, the federal Judiciary Act of 1789 specifies an oath of office to be taken by all federal judges before they assume their official duties: "I, [judge's name], do solemnly swear or affirm, that I will administer justice without respect to persons, and do equal right to the poor and to the rich, and that I will faithfully and impartially discharge and perform all the duties incumbent on me as [title or position], according to the best of my abilities and understanding, agreeably to the Constitution and laws of the United States. So help me God."

Obiter dictum

IN WRITING an opinion, justices of the Supreme Court or judges of a lower court sometimes make statements that are not necessary to the legal reasoning of the decision in the case. Such a statement is called *obiter dictum,* which is Latin for "said in passing." Occasionally, obiter dicta (the plural of the term) have become important in the development of constitutional law. Justice Edward T. Sanford, for example, made a statement in passing (obiter dictum) in *Gitlow* v. *New York* (1925) that greatly influenced the incorporation of 1st Amendment free speech and press rights under the due process clause of the 14th Amendment. Justice Sanford wrote, "[W]e may act to assume that freedom of speech and of the press... are among the fundamental personal rights and liberties protected by the due process clause of the Fourteenth Amendment from impairment by the States."

Justice Sanford's statement was not part of his reasoning in the decision of this case. Nevertheless, it soon influenced decisions of the Court in two important cases: *Near* v. *Minnesota* and *Stromberg* v. *California* (both 1931), which applied the 1st Amendment freedoms of speech (*Stromberg*) and the press (*Near*) to the states through the due process clause of the 14th Amendment.

SEE ALSO

Gitlow v. New York; Near v. Minnesota; Stromberg v. California

O'Connor, Sandra Day

ASSOCIATE JUSTICE, 1981–

☆ *Born: Mar. 26, 1930, El Paso, Tex.*
☆ *Education: Stanford College, B.A., 1950; Stanford University Law School, LL.B., 1952*
☆ *Previous government service: assistant attorney general, Arizona, 1965–69; Arizona Senate, 1969–75, majority leader of the Arizona Senate, 1973–74; judge, Maricopa County Superior Court, Arizona, 1975–79; judge, Arizona Court of Appeals, 1979–81*
☆ *Appointed by President Ronald Reagan Aug. 19, 1981; replaced Potter Stewart, who retired*
☆ *Supreme Court term: confirmed by the Senate Sept. 21, 1981, by a 99–0 vote*

SANDRA DAY O'CONNOR was the first woman to be appointed and confirmed to the U.S. Supreme Court. She was a brilliant student, and her record at Stanford University Law School was outstanding. However, she had difficulty, at first, in pursuing a career in the law because of her gender. She was an outstanding woman in a profession traditionally dominated by men. Many male lawyers did not want to work with women, and O'Connor had a hard time getting a job she wanted. One prominent law firm offered her a job as a secretary.

Through persistence and competence, O'Connor earned recognition as a lawyer, as a state senator in Arizona, and as a judge in the Arizona state court system. She also found time to raise three sons with her husband, John O'Connor.

In 1981, President Ronald Reagan appointed Sandra Day O'Connor to the U.S. Supreme Court. Justice O'Connor has appeared to resist overturning *Roe* v. *Wade* (1973), which granted women the right to have an abortion, although she has tended to narrow the scope of that decision by upholding state-level regulations "not unduly burdensome" to the woman. She has also shaped Supreme Court rulings on affirmative action and separation of church and state with regard to state government actions. She appears to favor strict neutrality over strict separation in the state's treatment of religion. And in response to state-level affirmative action cases, she has tended to favor a strict scrutiny test that would permit programs to rectify prior discrimination by the state government.

Justice O'Connor wrote the Court's first opinion to restrict the use of race as a category in determining the boundaries of state legislative and congressional districts (*Shaw* v. *Reno*, 1998). She has, however, expressed opposition to the complete removal of the consideration of race in redistricting cases, as long as it is not the primary factor in drawing boundaries of election districts (*Bush* v. *Vera*, 1996).

FURTHER READING

Cook, Beverly B. "Justice Sandra Day O'Connor: Transition to a Republican Court Agenda." In *The Burger Court: Political and Judicial Profiles*, edited by Charles M. Lamb and Stephen C. Halpern, 238–75. Urbana: University of Illinois Press, 1991.

Gherman, Beverly. S*andra Day O'Connor: Justice for All.* New York: Viking, 1991.

Huber, Peter. *Sandra Day O'Connor.* New York: Chelsea House, 1990.

Maveety, Nancy. *Justice Sandra Day O'Connor: Strategist on the Supreme Court.* Lanham, Md.: Rowman & Littlefield, 1996.

Olmstead v. United States

☆ *277 U.S. 438 (1928)*
☆ *Vote: 5–4*
☆ *For the Court: Taft*
☆ *Dissenting: Holmes, Brandeis, Butler, and Stone*

IN 1919, the 18th Amendment to the U.S. Constitution was ratified. It banned the sale, transportation, and importation of alcoholic beverages. Congress passed the National Prohibition Act to implement the 18th Amendment. Roy Olmstead, however, defied the National Prohibition Act by conducting a large-scale business to transport liquor throughout the state of Washington and British Columbia in Canada.

Federal agents gained evidence of Olmstead's illegal business by tapping the telephone line in one of his company's offices and the telephone lines into the homes of four of his workers. The agents listened to his telephone conversations and took notes about illegal activities.

Roy Olmstead and several others were convicted of conspiracy to violate the National Prohibition Act. Olmstead appealed his conviction to the Supreme Court. He claimed that the wiretap violated his rights under the 4th Amendment, which says, "The right of the people to be secure in their persons, houses, papers, and effects, against unreasonable searches and seizures, shall not be violated." Further, he argued that searches and seizures are unreasonable unless officials conducting them have obtained warrants only for "probable cause" that the person to be searched has violated or is violating the law. He also pointed to the 5th Amendment right that "no person... shall be compelled in any criminal case to be a witness against himself."

The Issue Was the use of evidence obtained through a telephone wiretap a violation of an individual's 4th and 5th Amendment rights? Should evidence obtained through a telephone wiretap be excluded from the trial of a person accused of a crime?

Opinion of the Court The Court upheld Olmstead's conviction. Chief Justice William Howard Taft wrote that conversations were not protected by the

Louis Brandeis dissented in the Olmstead *case, claiming that a federal wiretap of a person's phone is an illegal invasion of privacy. Later, using Brandeis's dissent, the Court overturned the* Olmstead *decision.*

4th Amendment and that the wiretaps on the telephone lines were not an invasion of the defendant's house or office. Taft agreed with the decision in *Weeks* v. *United States* (1914) that evidence obtained illegally must be excluded from a defendant's trial. However, he concluded that the evidence against Roy Olmstead was gathered legally.

Dissent Justice Louis D. Brandeis wrote an eloquent dissent that took account of the new technologies involved in this case; the electronic devices involved in the case did not exist when the 4th Amendment was written and ratified.

The wiretaps by federal agents, said Brandeis, were an invasion of privacy, which violated the intention of those who wrote and ratified the Constitution. According to Brandeis, they "sought to protect Americans in their beliefs, their thoughts, their emotions and their sensations. They conferred, as against the government, the right to be let alone—the most comprehensive of rights and the right most valued by civilized men." He asserted that to protect the person's right to privacy, every "unjustifiable intrusion by the government... whatever the means employed" must be viewed as a violation of the 4th Amendment. In addition, he said, use of evidence gathered illegally, such as through telephone wiretaps, violates the 5th Amendment.

Significance The *Olmstead* case was the first one in which the Court considered the impact of new electronic technology on the constitutional rights of individuals accused of criminal activity. It was also the first case in which a general right to privacy was asserted as a fundamental right—the basis of the dissenting opinion by Justice Brandeis.

The Court's decision in *Olmstead* was overturned in *Katz* v. *United States* (1967), which concluded that wiretaps and other forms of electronic surveillance are violations of the 4th Amendment. In

Title III of the Crime Control and Safe Streets Act of 1968, Congress banned wiretapping to gain evidence against individuals in the United States except when it was approved in advance by a federal judge according to guidelines in the 1968 act. In the long run the dissenting views of Justice Brandeis prevailed concerning the use of wiretapping to gather evidence of criminal behavior. Brandeis's views about privacy as a general constitutional right are still controversial, although this idea has influenced opinions in several key cases. These include *Griswold* v. *Connecticut* (1965) and *Roe* v. *Wade* (1973), which dealt with the issues of birth control and abortion.

SEE ALSO

Griswold v. Connecticut; Katz v. United States; Privacy, right to; Roe v. Wade; Searches and seizures

FURTHER READING

Murphy, Walter F. *Wiretapping on Trial: A Case Study in the Judicial Process.* New York: Random House, 1965.

One person, one vote

S E E Baker v. Carr; Reynolds v. Sims

Opening day

SINCE 1917 the first Monday in October has been the official opening day of the annual term of the Supreme Court. The chief justice ceremoniously opens the session at 10:00 A.M. New justices, if any, take their oath of office, and attorneys are admitted to the bar of the Supreme Court. The Court shows its respect to retired and deceased colleagues and Supreme Court officers through brief state-

This 1978 play, which accurately foreshadowed the appointment of the first woman to the Court, took its title from the Court's traditional opening day. Fifteen years later, the first woman justice, Sandra Day O'Connor, swore in actress Jane Alexander as head of the National Endowment for the Arts.

ments of tribute. Since 1975 the opening day has also included oral arguments.

Opinions

THE SUPREME COURT presents its decisions on cases to the public through written opinions. The opinions announce the outcomes of cases decided by the Court and provide the legal reasoning in support of the decisions.

When the chief justice is part of the majority opinion on a case, he may either write the Court's opinion himself or assign it to another justice in the majority group. When the chief justice is not part of the Court's majority, the most senior associate justice in the majority group assigns the task of writing the opinion. The writing of minority or dissenting opinions is not assigned. The justices who wish to write them merely assume this responsibility voluntarily.

The first page of a Supreme Court opinion.

> NOTICE: This opinion is subject to formal revision before publication in the preliminary print of the United States Reports. Readers are requested to notify the Reporter of Decisions, Supreme Court of the United States, Washington, D.C. 20543, of any typographical or other formal errors, in order that corrections may be made before the preliminary print goes to press.
>
> **SUPREME COURT OF THE UNITED STATES**
>
> No. 91–2024
>
> LAMB'S CHAPEL AND JOHN STEIGERWALD, PETITIONERS v. CENTER MORICHES UNION FREE SCHOOL DISTRICT ET AL.
>
> ON WRIT OF CERTIORARI TO THE UNITED STATES COURT OF APPEALS FOR THE SECOND CIRCUIT
>
> [June 7, 1993]
>
> JUSTICE WHITE delivered the opinion of the Court.
>
> Section 414 of the New York Education Law (McKinney 1988 and Supp. 1993), authorizes local school boards to adopt reasonable regulations for the use of school property for 10 specified purposes when the property is not in use for school purposes. Among the permitted uses is the holding of "social, civic and recreational meetings and entertainments, and other uses pertaining to the welfare of the community; but such meetings, entertainment and uses shall be non-exclusive and open to the general public." § 414(c).[1] The list of permitted uses does not include meetings for religious purposes, and a New York appellate court in *Trietley* v. *Board of Ed. of Buffalo,* 409 N. Y. S. 2d 912, 915 (App. Div. 1978), ruled that local boards could not allow student bible clubs to meet on school property because "[r]eligious purposes are not included in the enumerated purposes for which a school
>
> [1] Section 414(e) authorizes the use of school property "[f]or polling places for holding primaries and elections and for the registration of voters and for holding political meetings. But no meetings sponsored by political organizations shall be permitted unless authorized by a vote of a district meeting, held as provided by law, or, in cities by the board of education thereof."

When the justice assigned to write the Court's opinion completes a first draft, the opinion is distributed to the other eight justices, who may join the opinion. Sometimes, the opinion is modified to satisfy one or more justices, who otherwise will not sign it. These differences and compromises are discussed among the justices in meetings and in written messages in response to drafts of opinions that have been circulated.

If a justice agrees with the Court's decision but disagrees somewhat with the written opinion of the Court, he or she may write a concurring opinion, one that reaches the same conclusion but using different legal reasoning. Justices who disagree with the Court's decision on a case may write a dissenting opinion.

SEE ALSO

Concurring opinion; Dissenting opinion; Majority opinion; Per curiam; Plurality opinion; Seriatim opinions

Oral argument

AFTER THE COURT decides to hear a case, the clerk of the Court schedules the oral argument on the case. At this time, attorneys for both sides of the case speak before the justices in the Supreme Court chamber, or courtroom. Each side is limited to a 30-minute oral presentation. The attorneys may not read a set speech. They usually interact with the justices, who ask them questions. The justices may interrupt an advocate with questions or comments whenever they wish. About one-third of the counsel's 30-minute presentation is taken up with questions or remarks by justices. The effective advocate makes skillful responses to the questions of the justices. Those who stumble in responding or try to evade the question are likely to make a bad impression on the Court. During oral arguments, passionate exchanges at times occur between advocate and justices or between different justices who take exception to the reasoning or style of the commentary.

In presenting their oral arguments before the Supreme Court, 19th-century lawyers delivered eloquent speeches that sometimes lasted for days. Today, lawyers still must present a compelling speech even though they are not allowed to read their remarks and are limited to 30 minutes.

The justices read briefs, which are the lawyers' summaries of their arguments, and other documents regarding each case, such as memoranda about the case prepared by their law clerks and records from the trial court, before the day of the oral argument. As a result, they are likely to bring questions and concerns about the issues to the oral argument. This hearing gives the justices an opportunity to test the worth of the arguments on both sides of the case. Moreover, through this open hearing the justices demonstrate to the public that arguments on both sides of the case will be considered and challenged before a decision is made.

Orders list

THE CLERK of the Supreme Court prepares orders lists that appear near the end of volumes of the *United States Reports,* the official record of the Court's opinions. Each orders list is made up of brief summaries of the Court's actions on a particular day regarding certain cases under review but does not include opinions. For example, the Court may decide to refuse or accept a writ of appeal; it may deny or accept petitions for a writ of certiorari (an order for a lower court to send the official record of a case to the Supreme Court). Orders may treat such matters as stays of execution for a person scheduled for capital punishment, permissions to file amicus curiae briefs (which are filed by individuals or organizations not involved in a particular case but who have a special interest in the issue under review), or actions on disbarment of attorneys (expulsion from the legal profession).

SEE ALSO
United States Reports

Original intent

THE METHOD of interpreting the U.S. Constitution according to the literal intentions of its authors is known as original intent. Advocates of this method of constitutional interpretation claim that judges are obligated to find out what the framers intended by the words they used in writing the Constitution. Robert H. Bork, a legal scholar who favors original intent, stated in 1984, "It is necessary to establish the proposition that the framers' intentions . . . are the sole premise from which constitutional analysis may proceed."

Critics of the original intent method say that most of the framers did not expect those who came after them to be bound strictly by their work. Rather, they claim, the framers expected that the basic principles of the Constitution would be retained but details would be adapted to meet the changing and unforeseen circumstances of the future.

Justice William J. Brennan, for example, opposed the doctrine of original intent. He said in a 1985 speech, "We current Justices read the Constitution in the only way we can: as Twentieth Century Americans. We look to the history of the time of framing and to the intervening history of interpretation. But the ultimate question must be, what do the words of the text mean in our time. For the genius of the Constitution rests not in any static meaning it might have had in a world that is dead and gone, but in the adaptability of its great principles to cope with current problems and current needs."

Defenders of original intent, however, argue that the rule of law cannot be maintained unless judges apply the Con-

The 1787 Constitutional Convention in Philadelphia. Some legal scholars today believe that courts should try to determine the original intent of the founders when applying the law.

stitution to current controversies as the framers intended it to be applied. If original intent is ignored, they claim, then judges become lawmakers, not law interpreters, as they are supposed to be. Robert H. Bork, for example, told the Senate Judiciary Committee in 1987, "How should a judge go about finding the law? The only legitimate way, in my opinion, is by attempting to discern what those who made the law intended.... If a judge abandons intention as his guide, there is no law available to him and he begins to legislate a social agenda for the American people. That goes way beyond his legitimate power."

Is it the duty of the judges to keep the Constitution in tune with the times? No, say the advocates of original intent. Rather, they argue, it is the duty of judges to maintain an unbroken continuity of constitutional meaning from the founding era to their own times.

SEE ALSO

Constitutional construction; Judicial activism and judicial restraint

FURTHER READING

Belz, Herman. *A Living Constitution or Fundamental Law.* Lanham, Md.: Rowman & Littlefield, 1998.
Lynch, Joseph M. *Negotiating the Constitution: The Earliest Debates over Original Intent.* Ithaca, N.Y.: Cornell University Press, 1999.
Rackove, Jack N. *Original Meanings: Politics and Ideas in the Making of the Constitution.* New York: Knopf, 1996.

Original jurisdiction

SEE Jurisdiction

Palko v. Connecticut

☆ *302 U.S. 319 (1937)*
☆ *Vote: 8–1*
☆ *For the Court: Cardozo*
☆ *Dissenting: Butler*

FRANK PALKO robbed a store in Connecticut and shot and killed two police officers. He was tried for first-degree murder. The jury, however, found Palko guilty of the lesser crime of second-degree murder. He was sentenced to life in prison. The state prosecutors appealed this conviction and won a second trial, at which new evidence against Palko was introduced.

The judge at the first trial had refused to allow Palko's confession to be used as evidence against him. The absence of this evidence led to a lesser sentence for the defendant. At the second trial, however, all available evidence was used. As a result, Palko was convicted of the more serious charge of first-degree murder and sentenced to death.

Frank Palko appealed to the U.S. Supreme Court. His appeal was based on the 5th Amendment, which guarantees that no one should endure double jeopardy—that is, be put on trial twice for the same crime. The 5th Amendment, however, applies only to actions of the federal government. So Palko also pointed to the 14th Amendment provision that no state can "deprive any person of life, liberty, or property, without due process of law." Palko claimed that the 5th Amendment protection against double jeopardy could be applied to a state government through the due process clause of the 14th Amendment.

The Issue There was no question about Palko's guilt or innocence. The issue was whether he had been unconstitutionally subjected to double jeopardy. Does the 14th Amendment's due process clause encompass the 5th Amendment's prohibition of double jeopardy? Or does

Writing in the Palko case, Benjamin Cardozo outlined the process by which certain "fundamental rights" in the Bill of Rights should be applied to state governments.

the 5th Amendment apply only to actions of the federal government?

Opinion of the Court Palko's appeal was denied. His basic argument—"[W]hatever is forbidden by the Fifth Amendment is forbidden by the Fourteenth also"—was rejected. In reaching this conclusion, the Court proposed a new test to determine which rights of an accused person, as stated in the federal Bill of Rights, are so fundamental that they apply equally to the state and federal governments. Justice Benjamin Cardozo wrote that fundamental rights are "the very essence of a scheme of ordered liberty," without which justice is not possible. To deprive an individual of these rights is "a hardship so acute and shocking that our polity will not endure it."

According to Cardozo, the 5th Amendment rights claimed by Palko in this case were important but were not "principles of justice so rooted in the traditions and conscience of our people as to be ranked fundamental." Thus, the Court would not apply to the states in this case the 5th Amendment right of protection against double jeopardy.

Significance The *Palko* case was an important contribution in creating an acceptable test to guide the Court's use of the 14th Amendment's due process clause in limiting the actions of state governments. Justice Cardozo created the "fundamental rights" test in the *Palko* opinion. According to this test, the 14th Amendment's due process clause does not necessarily incorporate the federal Bill of Rights. However, it does open the way for a case-by-case consideration of what and how to select parts of the federal Bill of Rights to apply them to the states. In 1969 the Court overruled *Palko* in *Benton* v. *Maryland*. Double jeopardy became one of the provisions of the federal Bill of Rights to be selectively incorporated into the 14th Amendment and applied to the states.

SEE ALSO
Benton v. Maryland; Double jeopardy; Incorporation doctrine

Pardon power

ARTICLE 2, SECTION 2, of the U.S. Constitution states, "The President... shall have Power to grant Reprieves and Pardons for Offenses against the United States, except in cases of Impeachment." President Jimmy Carter, for example, used this pardon power to officially forgive all individuals who had illegally evaded the military draft during the Vietnam War. The men who were pardoned were forever exempt from criminal prosecutions or other penalties for breaking this federal law.

The specter of those who died in the Vietnam War hovers over President Jimmy Carter as he contemplates pardoning draft dodgers. Carter did issue the pardon.

Paterson, William
ASSOCIATE JUSTICE, 1793–1806

☆ Born: Dec. 24, 1745, County Antrim, Ireland
☆ Education: College of New Jersey (Princeton), B.A., 1763, M.A., 1766; studied law under Richard Stockton
☆ Previous government service: New Jersey Provincial Congress, 1775–76; New Jersey State Constitutional Convention, 1776; attorney general of New Jersey, 1776–83; Constitutional Convention, 1787; U.S. senator from New Jersey, 1789–90; governor of New Jersey, 1790–93
☆ Appointed by President George

Washington Mar. 4, 1793; replaced Thomas Johnson, who resigned
☆ *Supreme Court term: confirmed by the Senate Mar. 4, 1793, by a voice vote; served until Sept. 9, 1806*
☆ *Died: Sept. 9, 1806, Albany, N.Y.*

WILLIAM PATERSON, born in Ireland, was one of the founders of the United States of America. He helped to draft the first constitution of New Jersey in 1776 and the U.S. Constitution in 1787. At the Constitutional Convention, Paterson was the main author of the New Jersey Plan, an outline of how the government should be set up that he introduced as an alternative to the Virginia Plan of James Madison and Edmund Randolph. Several parts of the New Jersey Plan were combined with the Virginia Plan to create the foundation of the U.S. Constitution.

Paterson participated in the 1st Congress of the United States as a senator from New Jersey. He worked with Oliver Ellsworth of Connecticut to draft the Judiciary Act of 1789, which created the federal judicial system.

President George Washington appointed Paterson to the Supreme Court in 1793. Justice Paterson consistently argued for the supremacy of the federal government in cases about state powers and rights. For example, in *Ware* v. *Hylton* (1796), he decided that an act of the Virginia state government was unconstitutional because it violated the U.S. government's treaty of peace with Great Britain. According to Article 6 of the U.S. Constitution, valid treaties of the United States are part of the supreme law of the land, which all state governments are bound to obey.

William Paterson was injured critically in 1804 while riding circuit for the Court. In those days, justices of the Supreme Court were responsible also for duties on the federal Circuit Courts of

Appeals. Each circuit court encompassed a certain region of the United States. Riding circuit involved traveling from place to place to hear cases on appeal from lower courts. During one of those trips in 1804, the horses pulling Justice Paterson's carriage bolted, overturning the vehicle and severely injuring Paterson. He never recovered and died in 1806. The city of Paterson, New Jersey, which he helped to plan, is named after him.

SEE ALSO
Ware v. Hylton

FURTHER READING
O'Connor, John E. *William Paterson: Lawyer and Statesman.* New Brunswick, N.J.: Rutgers University Press, 1979.

Peckham, Rufus W.
ASSOCIATE JUSTICE, 1896–1909

☆ *Born: Nov. 8, 1838, Albany, N.Y.*
☆ *Education: studied law in his father's law firm*
☆ *Previous government service: district attorney, Albany County, N.Y., 1869–72; judge, New York Supreme Court, 1883–86; judge, New York Court of Appeals, 1886–95*
☆ *Appointed by President Grover Cleveland Dec. 3, 1895; replaced Howell Jackson, who died*
☆ *Supreme Court term: confirmed by the Senate Dec. 9, 1895, by a voice vote; served until Oct. 24, 1909*
☆ *Died: Oct. 24, 1909, Altamont, N.Y.*

RUFUS W. PECKHAM was named to the Supreme Court in 1895. In the previous year, his brother, Wheeler H. Peckham, had been nominated by President Grover Cleveland and rejected by the Senate. The Senate, however, readily confirmed Rufus Peckham's nomination.

During his 13 years on the Court, Justice Peckham favored property rights and contract rights of individuals. He usually opposed state government regulation of businesses and working conditions in favor of economic liberty. His most notable opinion for the Court was in *Lochner* v. *New York* (1905). He ruled that a New York law limiting the length of the workday for bakers was unconstitutional because it violated the rights of workers and employers to freely make contracts.

SEE ALSO

Lochner v. New York

Per curiam

PER CURIAM is Latin for "by the court." An opinion designated "by the Court," as a body, instead of by one member, is called a *per curiam* decision. In *Brandenburg* v. *Ohio* (1969), for example, the opinion of the court was not attributed to a particular justice. Instead, it was announced as a *per curiam* decision. This kind of opinion is used to summarily deal with an issue in a concise and unsigned opinion that signifies the general authority of the Court.

In *Bush* v. *Gore* (2000), the Supreme Court issued an unsigned per curiam opinion to reverse a decision by the Florida Supreme Court on the recounting of disputed ballots in the Presidential election contest between the Republican party candidate, George W. Bush, and the Democratic party candidate, Albert Gore. The result of this decision was that Bush maintained a slim lead in the Florida popular vote and thereby gained the state's 25 electoral votes, which brought him victory in the Presidential election.

Pitney, Mahlon

ASSOCIATE JUSTICE, 1912–22

☆ *Born: Feb. 5, 1858, Morristown, N.J.*
☆ *Education: College of New Jersey (Princeton), B.A., 1879, M.A., 1882*
☆ *Previous government service: U.S. representative from New Jersey, 1895–99; New Jersey Senate, 1899–1901; president, New Jersey Senate, 1901; associate justice, New Jersey Supreme Court, 1901–8; chancellor of New Jersey, 1908–12*
☆ *Appointed by President William Howard Taft Feb. 19, 1912; replaced John Marshall Harlan, who died*
☆ *Supreme Court term: confirmed by the Senate Mar. 13, 1912, by a 50–26 vote; retired Dec. 31, 1922*
☆ *Died: Dec. 9, 1924, Washington, D.C.*

MAHLON PITNEY was a strong supporter of individual rights, especially economic liberty and property rights. He tended to oppose strong government regulation of economic activities.

Pitney, however, tended to support limits on freedom of expression when it appeared to threaten national security. In *Pierce* v. *United States* (1920), for example, Justice Pitney upheld the prosecution of individuals under the Espionage Act of 1917 because their freedom of expression, he argued, threatened the security of the U.S. government.

Justice Pitney believed that the individual's right to contract was the most important constitutional right. He, therefore, tended to oppose the interests of labor unions as a threat to the economic liberty of individuals. However, he showed great concern for compensation of workers injured at the workplace. In *New York Railroad Company* v. *White* (1917) and several subsequent cases, Justice Pitney upheld state government laws that required employers to compensate workers for injuries suffered during their employment.

When a defendant consents to a plea bargain, he gives up his right to trial by jury and deals directly with the prosecutor and judge.

Plea bargaining

PLEA BARGAINING is the process by which a person accused of a crime may bargain with the prosecutor to receive a lesser punishment. Typically, the accused person will plead guilty, sometimes to a lesser charge than the original one (to manslaughter rather than murder, for example). This process saves the government the time and cost of a jury trial in exchange for a reduced sentence.

Defendants who plead guilty as part of a plea bargain give up three constitutional rights: the right of trial by jury, the right to confront and question one's accusers, and the right to refuse to incriminate oneself. In *Boykin v. Alabama* (1969) the Court ruled that plea bargaining is constitutional as long as the defendant gives up his constitutional rights voluntarily and with full comprehension of the trade-offs of the deal.

Plessy v. Ferguson

☆ *163 U.S. 537 (1896)*
☆ *Vote: 7–1*
☆ *For the Court: Brown*
☆ *Dissenting: Harlan*
☆ *Not participating: Brewer*

THE RATIFICATION of the 13th Amendment in 1865, shortly after the end of the Civil War, abolished slavery in the United States. However, prejudices against blacks remained strong. Southern states began to pass laws to keep blacks separated from whites. A group of black leaders in Louisiana formed a Citizens' Committee to deliberately test the constitutionality of one such law, the Separate Car Law.

Acting for the Citizens' Committee, Homer Plessy, a Louisiana resident who was one-eighth black, bought a first-class ticket for a train in Louisiana. Plessy took a seat in the railroad car reserved for whites only, ignoring the coach marked "colored only." When Plessy refused to move to the coach reserved for "colored," he was arrested. He had violated the Louisiana law requiring separate railroad accommodations for blacks and whites.

The Citizens' Committee and Plessy claimed the Louisiana law denied him the "equal protection of the laws" guaranteed by the 14th Amendment. Plessy's lawyers also claimed the law violated the 13th Amendment ban on slavery by destroying the legal equality of the races and, in effect, reintroducing slavery.

The Issue Did a state law requiring segregation of the races violate the 13th Amendment ban on slavery or the 14th Amendment guarantee of equal protection of the laws for all citizens?

Opinion of the Court The Supreme Court ruled against Plessy. The Court held that the "equal protection of the laws" clause of the 14th Amendment allowed a state to provide "separate but equal" facilities for blacks. Justice Henry Brown wrote that the 14th Amendment aimed "to enforce the absolute equality of the two races before the law, but in the nature of things it could not have been intended to abolish distinctions based upon color, or to enforce social...equality."

The Court also ruled that the Louisiana law did not violate the 13th Amendment ban on slavery. Brown said a law "which implies merely a legal distinction between the white and colored races… has no tendency to…reestablish a state of involuntary servitude [slavery]."

Dissent Justice John M. Harlan dissented in the *Plessy* decision. Harlan, a native of Kentucky and a former slaveholder, argued strongly against dividing people by race. He declared, "[I]n the eye of the law there is in this country no superior, dominant, ruling class of citizens. There is no caste here. Our Constitution is color-blind and neither knows nor tolerates classes among citizens." Justice Harlan's view finally prevailed in 1954, when the Supreme Court overruled the *Plessy* decision in the case of *Brown* v. *Board of Education.*

Significance The "separate but equal" doctrine established by the Court served to justify segregation in many states for the next half century. The *Plessy* decision reinforced state-ordered segregation, which had become a fact of life in the southern states. State laws required blacks to use separate toilets, water fountains, streetcars, and waiting rooms. Blacks had to attend different schools and remained separated from whites in prisons, hospitals, parks, theaters, and other public facilities. By 1920 segregation regulated every facet of life in the South. Blacks and whites could not eat at the same restaurants, stay in the same hotels, use the same elevators, or visit the same beaches, swimming pools, or amusement parks. Blacks and whites attended separate public schools, and in some states at the end of each school year the school board had to store the books from black schools separately from the books from white schools. One state required the segregation of public telephones, while another prohibited blacks and whites from playing checkers together.

Born in segregated hospitals, educated in segregated schools, employed at workplaces that kept blacks and whites separated, and buried in the segregated cemeteries of segregated churches, the people of the South endured the all-pervasive influence of segregation. The separation of the races was one of the most important aspects of southern life. *Plessy* v. *Ferguson* gave this entire system legitimacy. Although that decision established the well-known doctrine of "separate but equal," in actual practice separate but *unequal* was the rule throughout the South.

The "separate but equal" doctrine was upheld by Supreme Court rulings for the next 50 years. For decades, however, the Court refused to examine the actual conditions in the South to determine if equality existed along with separateness. Not until the 1930s and 1940s did the Supreme Court begin to enforce the "equal" part of the doctrine. And not until 1954 did the Court directly face the more basic question of whether separating whites and blacks was an inherently discriminating act that by nature ensured unequal treatment. In *Brown* v. *Board of Education* (1954), the Court overturned the *Plessy* decision,

In the early 20th century, public facilities such as railroad waiting rooms were usually segregated in southern states. The Court ruled in Plessy v. Ferguson that segregation was legal as long as the separate facilities were equal.

declaring in a now-famous phrase that "Separate educational facilities are inherently unequal."

SEE ALSO

Brown v. Board of Education; Civil rights; Equality under the Constitution; Segregation, de facto and de jure

FURTHER READING

Kull, Andrew. "The 14th Amendment That Wasn't." *Constitution 5*, no. 1 (Winter 1993): 68–75.

Thomas, Brook, ed. *Plessy v. Ferguson: A Brief History with Documents.* Boston: Bedford Books, 1997.

Woodward, C. Vann. "The Case of the Louisiana Traveler." In *Quarrels That Have Shaped the Constitution,* edited by John A. Garraty. New York: Harper & Row, 1987.

Plurality opinion

The U.S. Supreme Court decides cases by majority vote; more than half of the justices participating must vote in favor of the decision. If the justices in the majority agree to sign a single opinion, they produce a majority opinion for the Court. Now and then, however, there are so many individual concurring opinions that the opinion that garners the most votes is called not a majority opinion but a plurality opinion.

For example, in *Dennis* v. *United States* (1951), the Court decided the case by a vote of 6 to 2 (one justice did not participate). Two justices wrote separate concurring opinions and thereby made it impossible for there to be a single majority opinion for the Court. Instead, there was a plurality opinion (signed by four justices), supported in many respects by two justices' concurring opinions, and opposed by the other two justices' dissenting opinions. Thus, Chief Justice Vinson announced the decision of the Court based on a plurality opinion.

SEE ALSO

Concurring opinion; Dissenting opinion; Majority opinion; Opinions

Political questions

THE SUPREME COURT may decide not to accept a case because it involves what it considers to be political questions, which are outside the scope of the Court's authority. Political questions may include problems clearly in the domain of Congress or the President. These are questions that, in the Court's opinion, defy resolution on legal or constitutional grounds. For example, the Court has ruled that the President, not the Court, should determine whether the United States should recognize a certain foreign government.

The political questions doctrine is a limitation that the Court has imposed upon its own powers of judicial review. Only the Supreme Court itself decides which cases involve political questions, thereby disqualifying them for review and judgment by the Court. Such political questions are referred to as non-

In 1912 Oregon passed a law taxing telephone companies. One company claimed that the state was violating the Constitution because the law had been passed by popular election, not by the legislature. The Supreme Court claimed that this was a political question, not subject to its review.

justiciable. Justiciable questions, by contrast, are those the Supreme Court accepts as appropriate for its review and judgment.

In *Pacific States Telephone & Telegraph* v. *Oregon* (1912), the Court faced an issue that it decided was outside the scope of judicial review. The issue pertained to Article 4, Section 4, of the Constitution, which says, "The United States shall guarantee to every State in the Union a Republican Form of Government. . . . " The Pacific States Telephone & Telegraph Company argued that the state of Oregon was enacting laws in a nonrepublican manner, which violated Article 4, Section 4. The state had passed a tax of 2 percent on the income of all telephone and telegraph companies in the state. This tax law was passed through a popular initiative and referendum, not strictly and exclusively by the state legislature. The people of the state used an initiative to petition the government to pass the tax law; in response to this initiative, the voters of Oregon were permitted to decide in a public election (a referendum, which was also called for by the voters) whether to pass the law.

SEE ALSO

Judicial power; Judicial review; Justiciable questions

Popular sovereignty

POPULAR SOVEREIGNTY is government based on the consent of the people. Government, established by free choice of the people, is expected to serve the people, who have sovereignty, or supreme power.

Popular sovereignty is the basis of constitutional government in the United States. The U.S. Constitution clearly establishes government in the name of

POGHKEEPSIE,
July 2d, 1788.

JUST ARRIVED

BY EXPRESS,

The Ratification of the New Constitution by the Convention of the State of Virginia, on Wednesday the 25th June, by a majority of 10 ; 88 agreeing, and 78 dissenting to its adoption.

"WE the Delegates of the People of Virginia, duly elected in Pursuance of a Recommendation of the General Assembly; and now met in Convention, having fully and fairly investigated and discussed the Proceedings of the Federal Convention, and being

With these Impressions, with a solemn Appeal to the Searcher of Hearts for the Purity of our Intentions, and under the Conviction, that whatsoever Imperfections may exist in the Constitution, ought rather to be examined in the Mode prescribed therein, than to bring the Uni-

the people. The preamble says: "We the people of the United States . . . do ordain and establish this Constitution for the United States of America."

Popular sovereignty was exercised according to Article 7 of the Constitution, which required that nine states approve the proposed frame of government before it could become the supreme law of the United States. The people chose representatives to ratification conventions who freely decided to approve the Constitution in the name of those who elected them. Popular sovereignty was also recognized in Article 5 of the Constitution, which provides for amendments to the Constitution through decisions by elected representatives of the people. Finally, popular sovereignty is reflected in Article 1, which requires that representatives to Congress be elected by the people.

Popular sovereignty, or government by the people, implies majority rule. People elect representatives in government by majority vote, and these representatives of the people make laws by majority vote.

SEE ALSO

Constitutional democracy; Constitutionalism; Republicanism

FURTHER READING

McAffee, Thomas B. *Inherent Rights, the Written Constitution, and Popular*

The ratification of the U.S. Constitution by the people of individual states was an example of popular sovereignty, or government based on the consent of the people.

Sovereignty: The Founders' Understanding. Westport, Conn.: Greenwood, 2000.
Morgan, Edmund S. Inventing the People: The Rise of Popular Sovereignty in England and America. New York: Norton, 1988.

Powell, Lewis F., Jr.

ASSOCIATE JUSTICE, 1972–87

☆ Born: Sept. 19, 1907, Suffolk, Va.
☆ Education: Washington and Lee University, B.S., 1929; Washington and Lee University Law School, LL.B., 1931; Harvard Law School, LL.M., 1932
☆ Previous government service: chairman, Richmond School Board, Va., 1952–61; Virginia State Board of Education, 1961–69; president, Virginia State Board of Education, 1968–69
☆ Appointed by President Richard Nixon Oct. 21, 1971; replaced Hugo L. Black, who retired
☆ Supreme Court term: confirmed by the Senate Dec. 6, 1971, by an 89–1 vote; retired June 26, 1987
☆ Died: Aug. 25, 1998, Richmond, Va.

LEWIS F. POWELL, JR., belonged to a respected family with deep roots in Virginia. The first American Powell was one of the original settlers of Jamestown in 1607.

Though a member of the Virginia establishment, Powell opposed the long-established practice of racial segregation in the public schools. As chairman of the Richmond School Board, he presided over the peaceful integration of the city's schools in the wake of the *Brown v. Board of Education* (1954) decision. He also stood up to leading Virginians who resisted statewide integration of schools. As a member of the Virginia State Board of Education, he led the successful racial integration of the state's public schools.

As a justice of the Supreme Court, Powell tried to balance the needs of society against the rights of individuals. His most famous opinion for the Court was *Regents of the University of California v. Bakke* (1978), a case about the legality of a plan that provided special opportunities for minority group applicants (such as African Americans) to gain admission to the university. Powell characteristically sought the middle ground between competing claims for preferences based on race and equality of individual rights in decisions about whom to admit to the state university. Powell decided against the establishment of rigid racial quotas for minorities seeking admission to the university. However, he also upheld the principle of "affirmative action" as one factor, among others, that could be considered in making decisions about admitting students to the university. Affirmative action means making a special effort to provide opportunities for members of groups that had been discriminated against in the past. Considering the racial identity of an applicant as a positive factor in making a decision about student admissions could be done to compensate for the negative effects of past discrimination.

SEE ALSO

Regents of the University of California v. Bakke

FURTHER READING

Haupt, Donna. "A Justice Reflects." *Constitution* 2, no. 3 (Fall 1990): 16–25.
Landynski, Jacob W. "Justice Lewis F. Powell, Jr.: Balance Wheel of the Court." In *The Burger Court: Political and Judicial Profiles,* edited by Charles M. Lamb and Stephen C. Halpern. Urbana: University of Illinois Press, 1991: 276–314.

Powell v. Alabama

☆ 287 U.S. 45 (1932)
☆ Vote: 7–2
☆ For the Court: Sutherland
☆ Dissenting: Butler and McReynolds

ON MARCH 25, 1931, nine African-American youths, ranging in age from 12 to 20, were arrested near Scottsboro, Alabama. They were accused of having raped two white women. A hostile crowd gathered outside the jail in Scottsboro and shouted insults at the young men.

The nine youths were quickly indicted and a trial date was set for six days later. The nine defendants were too poor to hire an attorney to represent them. According to Alabama law, the judge was required to appoint counsel to assist them because they were accused of a capital offense (a crime punishable by death). The judge responded to this legal requirement by declaring that every licensed lawyer in Scottsboro was assigned to represent the nine men. No one attorney, however, took personal responsibility for their defense.

On the day of the trial, two attorneys did show up to defend the accused youths. They asked the judge to postpone the trial so they could have time to prepare their defense. But the judge refused, and the lawyers had only 30 minutes before the trial started to consult with the defendants.

The trial was conducted quickly. Eight of the nine defendants were found guilty and sentenced to death. The jury was unable to reach a decision about one of the defendants.

The decision was appealed to the Alabama Supreme Court, which upheld the conviction of seven of the defendants. The conviction of one defendant was reversed because he was a juvenile (only 12 years old). The Alabama Supreme Court ruling with regard to the other seven was appealed to the U.S. Supreme Court.

The Issue The defendants, too poor to hire a lawyer, were tried, convicted, and sentenced to death without effective assistance of an attorney. However, the 14th Amendment to the U.S. Constitution says, "No state shall... deprive any person of life, liberty, or property, without due process of law."

Were due process rights denied to the defendants in this case? Do people without means to obtain a lawyer have the right to counsel at the government's expense?

Opinion of the Court Writing for the Court, Justice George Sutherland overturned the convictions of the defendants. This decision was based on the due process clause of the 14th Amendment. Justice Sutherland argued that the right to counsel is an essential element of due process. Further, he rejected claims by the prosecutors that the defendants

The nine "Scottsboro boys" are guarded by the Alabama militia on their way to court. When eight of the defendants were found guilty of rape and sentenced to death, the case was appealed to the Supreme Court because they had been denied adequate counsel.

were given effective legal assistance. He pointed to the last-minute assignment of counsel for the defense as inadequate.

Justice Sutherland wrote about the critical importance of effective legal counsel, without which a fair trial is impossible. A defendant, he said, "lacks both the skill and knowledge adequately to prepare his defense, even though he has a perfect one. He requires the guiding hand of counsel at every step in the proceedings against him. Without it, though he be not guilty, he faces the danger of conviction because he does not know how to establish his innocence."

Dissent Justice Pierce Butler, joined in dissent by Justice James McReynolds, argued that the defendants had received adequate legal assistance. Further, they said that the Court's reversal of the convictions was unjustified interference with the operations of a state court system.

Significance In the *Powell* case the Court decided for the first time that the 14th Amendment required states to provide legal help for poor defendants in order to guarantee a fair trial. After *Powell,* state governments were required to provide counsel for poor defendants in all capital cases.

By contrast, the assistance of counsel clause of the 6th Amendment to the Constitution required the federal government to provide counsel for indigent defendants in both capital and noncapital cases. Federal and state government requirements regarding the assistance of counsel were not brought into conformity until 1963 with the decision in *Gideon* v. *Wainwright.* In this landmark case, the Court ruled for the first time that the 6th Amendment assistance of counsel clause applied to state governments. The Court incorporated the 6th Amendment right to an attorney under the due process clause of the 14th Amendment. The states have to provide legal assistance to indigent defendants, in both capital and noncapital cases, in order to guarantee that the defendant receives the constitutional right to due process in criminal justice proceedings.

Following the Court's decision in *Powell,* the case was returned to Alabama for retrial of the seven youths on rape charges. This time, the defendants were represented by counsel, as required by the Supreme Court decision. However, they were again convicted and sentenced to death. Once again, they appealed their conviction and the case returned to the U.S. Supreme Court as *Norris* v. *Alabama* (1935). This appeal was based on the exclusion of blacks from the jury pool for the trial. The Court again overturned the convictions on the grounds that the 14th Amendment due process rights of the defendants were violated by systematic exclusion of jurors because of race.

The case was returned once more to Alabama for a jury trial. In subsequent state trials, the defendants were convicted again. However, none of them was sentenced to the death penalty. After several years of very complicated proceedings, all of the defendants were released from prison on parole, the last one in 1950.

SEE ALSO

Counsel, right to; Due process of law; Gideon v. Wainwright; Incorporation doctrine

FURTHER READING

Carter, Dan T. *Scottsboro—A Tragedy of the American South.* Rev. ed. Baton Rouge: Louisiana State University Press, 1979.

Precedent

APPEALS COURTS in the United States, including the Supreme Court, follow precedent, or past decisions, in making

new ones. Once a case has been decided, similar cases are supposed to be decided in the same way. This practice is based on the doctrine of *stare decisis,* a Latin phrase meaning "Let the decision stand." The principle of *stare decisis* gives stability and predictability to the law. Decisions of the Supreme Court are binding on all lower courts in the United States, and they also serve as guidelines for subsequent Supreme Court decisions.

Occasionally, however, the Court departs from precedent to decide a case in a new way. Its decision in *Brown* v. *Board of Education* (1954), for example, rejected the precedent of "separate but equal" that had been established in *Plessy* v. *Ferguson* (1896) to support racial segregation.

SEE ALSO
Constitutional law; Dissenting opinion; Judicial review

Prior restraint

PRIOR RESTRAINT is a form of censorship in which government officials restrict a newspaper or magazine in advance from publishing materials of which they disapprove. The 1st Amendment guarantee of a free press precludes the government's use of prior restraint to control the content of a publication. This 1st Amendment ban on prior restraint was applied to state governments through the due process clause of the 14th Amendment in *Near* v. *Minnesota* (1931). In this landmark decision, the Court ruled that an injunction to stop publication of a newspaper with objectionable content was an example of prior restraint and therefore unconstitutional. The Court did not rule, however, that a publisher was protected from legal action *after* publishing questionable material.

SEE ALSO
Freedom of speech and press; Near v. Minnesota; New York Times Co. v. United States

Privacy, right to

THE WORD *privacy* cannot be found in the Constitution of the United States. Yet Americans have tended to believe in a constitutional right to privacy—the right to be secure against unlawful intrusions by government into certain protected areas of life. Ever since the founding era, most Americans have recognized public and private domains of society. The public domain is open to regulation by government. For example, the people expect their police officers to keep order on the streets of a community, a function that involves certain limits on the free movement of people. The private domain, by contrast, is generally closed to invasion and control by government and can be entered and regulated by police officers only for a compelling public purpose and according to due process of law.

There are continuing legal issues about the boundaries between the public and private domains of society because these two realms of life are inextricably bound together. Thus, for example, the government can constitutionally justify certain regulations of private property owners to protect the public against abuses, such as pollution of the environment. Further, the government may constitutionally enter a person's home to prevent individuals from conducting activities that violate the public interest, such as molesting children. When, and under what circumstances, does a person's right to privacy end and the public's authority to regulate behavior in the public interest begin? This is an ongoing problem in the courts.

THE DECISION TO HAVE A BABY COULD SOON BE BETWEEN YOU, YOUR HUSBAND AND YOUR SENATOR.

A pro-choice advertisement from Planned Parenthood. A woman's right to have an abortion, established in the Roe v. Wade *decision in 1973, is based on an implied constitutional right to privacy.*

Justice Louis D. Brandeis argued for a general constitutional right to privacy in a famous dissent in *Olmstead* v. *United States* (1928): "The makers of our Constitution undertook to secure conditions favorable to the pursuit of happiness.... They conferred, as against the Government, the right to be let alone—the most comprehensive of rights and the right most valued by civilized men." Justice Brandeis pointed to the 4th Amendment protections against "unreasonable searches and seizures" and the 5th Amendment guarantees against self-incrimination as examples of constitutional protection against "unjustifiable intrusion by the Government upon the privacy of the individual."

For more than 30 years after the *Olmstead* case, the Court avoided serious discussions of a constitutional right to privacy. Then, in *Poe* v. *Ullman* (1961), Justices John Marshall Harlan and William O. Douglas argued in dissent for the individual's right to privacy against a Connecticut law banning the use of birth control devices, even by married couples. Harlan pointed to the 14th Amendment's provision that "no State shall make or enforce any law which shall... deprive any person of life, liberty, or property, without due process of law." According to Harlan, the state law at issue unconstitutionally deprived individuals of their liberty, without due process of law, to use birth control devices, which was "an intolerable and unjustifiable invasion of privacy." Thus, Harlan linked the 14th Amendment's guarantee of liberty to the right to privacy.

In *Griswold* v. *Connecticut* (1965), the Court overturned the decision in *Poe* v. *Ullman* (1961). The Court decided that the Connecticut law against contraception was unconstitutional and based its decision on a constitutional right to privacy. However, the justices disagreed about where in the Constitution this right to privacy could be found.

Justice William O. Douglas found a general right to privacy which, he believed, can be interpreted from the words of parts of the Bill of Rights (the 1st, 3rd, 4th, and 5th Amendments). He argued that the state of Connecticut had specifically violated the right to marital privacy, which fits within the "zone of privacy" one can infer from the text of the Bill of Rights.

Justice Arthur Goldberg's concurring opinion in *Griswold* emphasized the 9th Amendment: "The enumeration in the Constitution of certain rights shall not be construed to deny or disparage others retained by the people." Justice Goldberg held that the right to privacy in marital relationships was one of those rights not written in the Constitution that was nonetheless "retained by the people." Justice Goldberg wrote, "To hold that a right so basic and fundamental and so deep-rooted in our society as the right to privacy in marriage may be infringed because the right is not guaranteed in so many words by the first eight amendments to the Constitution is to ignore the Ninth Amendment and to give it no effect whatsoever."

Justice John Marshall Harlan also concurred with the Court's opinion in the *Griswold* case. However, Harlan based his decision on the due process clause of the 14th Amendment, as he had done in his dissent in the *Poe* case four years earlier.

Justices Hugo L. Black and Potter Stewart dissented from the Court's opinion in *Griswold*. They argued that a general right to privacy cannot be inferred from any part of the Constitution. Further, they criticized the Court's majority for deciding this case according to personal opinion instead of following the text of the Constitution. Justice Black wrote, "I like my privacy as well as the next one, but I am nevertheless compelled to admit that government has a right to invade it unless prohibited by some specific constitutional provision." In *Griswold,* Black found no "specific constitutional provision" that prohibited the state government's regulation of the private behavior at issue in this case.

Support for a right to privacy has continued since the *Griswold* decision. In *Katz* v. *United States* (1967), the Court overturned the decision in *Olmstead* v. *United States* (1928). The Court held that the 4th and 5th Amendments protect an individual's right to privacy against electronic surveillance and wiretapping by government agents, even in a place open to the public, such as a telephone booth on a city street. In *Roe* v. *Wade* (1973), the Court ruled that the right to privacy included a woman's choice to have an abortion during the first three months of pregnancy.

While continuing to recognize a constitutional right to privacy, the Court has acted recently to set limits on it. In *Skinner* v. *Railway Labor Executives Association* (1989) and *National Treasury Employees Union* v. *Von Raab* (1989), the Court has upheld federal regulations that provide for drug testing of railroad and customs workers, even without warrants or reasonable suspicion of drug use. In these cases, the Court decided that the need for public safety was a compelling reason for limiting the individual's right to privacy against government regulation.

Since the 1960s the often-contested right to privacy has been established in a line of Supreme Court decisions. As Justice Harry A. Blackmun wrote in *Thornburgh* v. *American College of Obstetricians and Gynecologists* (1986), "Our cases long have recognized that the Constitution embodies a promise that a certain private sphere of individual liberty will be kept largely beyond the reach of government."

An individual's right to privacy was reinforced in *Reno* v. *Condon* (2000), in which South Carolina challenged a federal law, the Driver's Privacy Protection Act (DPPA). This statute prevents states from releasing personal information in motor vehicle records without consent. The South Carolina attorney general claimed that the DPPA violated the constitutional powers and rights of a state within the federal system of the United States. The Court rejected the claim and upheld the DPPA as a constitutional means of protecting the privacy of licensed drivers. In this case, an individual's privacy rights were upheld over states' rights.

The exact meaning and limits of this widely recognized right to privacy, however, will continue to be controversial. Every extension of the right to privacy limits the power of government to regulate behavior for the public good, which citizens of a constitutional democracy expect. By contrast, every expansion of government's power to regulate the behavior of individuals diminishes the "private sphere of individual liberty" cherished by citizens of a constitutional democracy. How to justly balance and blend these contending factors, so that both are addressed but neither one is sacrificed to the other, is an ongoing issue of the Supreme Court and the citizenry of the United States.

SEE ALSO

Griswold v. Connecticut; Katz v. United States; Olmstead v. United States; Roe v. Wade

FURTHER READING

Alderman, Ellen, and Caroline Kennedy. *The Right to Privacy.* 1995. Reprint, New York: Vintage, 1997.

Barnett, Randy, ed. *The Rights Retained by the People: The History and Meaning of the Ninth Amendment.* Fairfax, Va.: George Mason University Press, 1989.

Van Burkleo, Sandra F. "The Right to Privacy." In *By and for the People: Constitutional Rights in American History,* edited by Kermit L. Hall. Arlington Heights, Ill.: Harlan Davidson, 1991.

Westin, Alan F. *Privacy and Freedom.* New York: Atheneum, 1968.

Probable cause

THE 4TH AMENDMENT to the U.S. Constitution requires that "no [search or arrest] warrants shall issue, but upon probable cause." Thus, government officials may not obtain a warrant to search or arrest someone unless they have probable cause, or good reasons, to believe that the person may be involved in criminal behavior of some kind. Judges, not law enforcement officers, have the authority to decide if there is probable cause for issuing a warrant to search or arrest someone. In *Terry* v. *Ohio* (1968), however, the Court adjusted this standard to allow police officers to stop and frisk suspects if they consider it necessary to protect themselves, even without probable cause for arrest.

SEE ALSO

Searches and seizures; Terry v. Ohio

Property rights

THE FOUNDERS of the United States believed that the right to acquire, own, and use private property was an essential element of a free society. John Adams expressed a prevailing opinion of his times when he wrote in 1790, "Property must be secured or liberty cannot exist."

Land ownership was one kind of property right the founders wanted to protect. They were also concerned about rights to other kinds of property, such as personal goods (clothing, tools, houses, and animals, for instance), ideas, inventions, and money. Property takes many forms that represent both wealth and the means of creating or producing wealth.

A main purpose of the U.S. Constitution of 1787 was to limit the power of government in order to protect individual rights, including property rights. The framers used separation of powers, with checks and balances, to constitutionally limit the government for the purpose of guarding individual property rights and other fundamental rights. The framers of the Constitution and of the Bill of Rights also provided protections for property rights in specific clauses.

For example, Article 1, Section 10, states, "No State shall...pass any Bill of Attainder...or Law impairing the Obligation of Contracts." By prohibiting bills of attainder, or the punishment of a person by a legislative act (rather than by a court of law), the Constitution protects individuals from legislative actions to arbitrarily deprive them of property or punish them in some other way. By prohibiting legislative actions interfering with the terms of a contract, the Constitution protects property rights involved in the contract. Further, in Article 1, Section 8, Congress is granted the power to

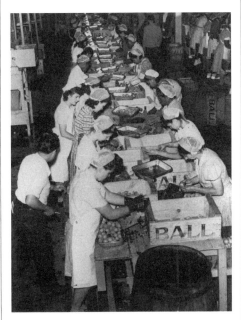

The Supreme Court has recognized limits on the rights of property owners in favor of government regulations that promote the public good, such as regulations establishing minimum wages and maximum hours of work.

protect the property rights of inventors and writers to their ideas and creations "by securing for limited Times to Authors and Inventors the exclusive Right to their respective Writings and Discoveries." Finally, Article 1, Section 9, prohibits Congress from levying direct taxes on individuals unless they are apportioned according to population. This constitutional provision limited the Congress's power to impose land taxes, thereby protecting a person's private property from acquisition by the federal government. (The 16th Amendment, passed in 1913, permits the federal government to levy taxes on the income of individuals, whatever the source.)

The 5th Amendment to the U.S. Constitution (ratified in 1791 as part of the Bill of Rights) says, "No person shall be...deprived of life, liberty, or property, without due process of law; nor shall private property be taken for public use without just compensation." The 14th Amendment (ratified in 1868) provides protection for private property rights by prohibiting any state government from taking a person's property "without due process of law." The 5th and 14th Amendments limit the power

of the federal and state governments to abuse the property rights of individuals.

Chief Justice John Marshall strongly supported private property rights of individuals as a bulwark of personal liberty and as a stimulus to productive use of resources. Marshall believed, as did most other leaders of his time, that security in the ownership of property helped a person to resist domination by others, especially government officials. Chief Justice Marshall's opinions in *Fletcher* v. *Peck* (1810) and *Dartmouth College* v. *Woodward* (1819) bolstered the "Obligation of Contracts" cited in Article 1, Section 10, of the Constitution as a guarantee of private property rights.

If the Constitution set limits on the power of government to violate property rights, it also implied that there are limits on the rights of individuals in behalf of the public good. For example, Chief Justice Roger Taney was a strong supporter of private property rights. In *Charles River Bridge* v. *Warren Bridge* (1837), however, Taney held that property rights in a contract could sometimes be overridden to permit development of innovations or improvements to benefit the public. In *West River Bridge Co.* v. *Dix* (1848), the Taney Court held that the contract clause of the Constitution did not protect a corporation from the state's right of eminent domain—its power to take private property, with fair compensation, to use for the public good.

There has been persistent tension between the private property rights of individuals and the public's need for limitations or regulations on private property rights. Justice John M. Harlan stressed in *Chicago, Burlington & Quincy Railroad Company* v. *Chicago* (1897), "Due protection of the rights of property has been regarded as a vital principle of republican institutions." Justice Harlan also wrote (*Mugler* v. *Kansas*, 1887), "All property in this country is held under the implied obligation that the owner's use of it shall not be injurious to the community." However, he qualified this recognition of the government's authority to regulate property rights by insisting that there were "limits beyond which legislation cannot rightfully go."

At times the Court has tilted to the government-regulation side of the debate on property rights. In *Munn* v. *Illinois* (1877), for instance, the Court upheld an Illinois law regulating the price for storing grain in privately owned storage elevators. Chief Justice Morrison R. Waite wrote, "When private property is devoted to a public use, it is subject to public regulation."

More often, however, from the 1870s until the 1930s the Court seemed to oppose any government laws that interfered with the free market, such as state laws regulating wages or working conditions of employees. In *Lochner* v. *New York* (1905), for example, the Court overturned a New York law that restricted hours of work in bakeries. Writing for the Court, Justice Rufus W. Peckham argued that the New York law violated the "liberty of contract" protected by the 14th Amendment.

The *Lochner* decision set the trend for Court rulings on state regulation of private property rights for the next 30 years. Not until 1937, when the Court upheld federal laws regulating the economy for the public good (in *National Labor Relations Board* v. *Jones & Laughlin Steel Corp.* and *West Coast Hotel Co.* v. *Parrish*), did the trend shift away from the resistance to many kinds of public regulations of private property rights. In the *Parrish* case, Chief Justice Charles Evans Hughes rejected the "liberty of contract" idea that had prevailed in the *Lochner* decision and other subsequent decisions. He wrote for the Court, "Liberty under the Constitution is . . . necessarily subject to the restraints of due process, and regulation [of a private business by a state government to protect the health, welfare, and personal rights of workers] which is adopted in the interests of the community is due process."

During the middle years of the 20th century, from 1937 until the 1960s, the Court tilted strongly toward public regulation of private property for the public good and away from 19th-century views on the connection of private property rights to personal liberty. For example, Justice Hugo Black wrote in *Marsh* v. *Alabama* (1946), "Ownership does not always mean absolute domination. The more an owner, for his advantage, opens up his property for use by the public in general, the more do his rights become circumscribed by the statutory and constitutional rights of those who use it. . . . Thus, the owners of privately held bridges, ferries, turnpikes, and railroads may not operate them as freely as a farmer does his farm. Since these facilities are built and operated primarily to benefit the public and since their operation is essentially a public function, it is subject to state regulation."

Since the 1970s, however, the Court has tended to reemphasize private property rights in a continuing quest for a just balance between private property rights and the public good. Justice Potter Stewart expressed in *Lynch* v. *Household Finance Corporation* (1972) the Court's renewed emphasis on property rights as a key to liberty and a free society: "In fact, a fundamental interdependence exists between the personal right to liberty and the personal right in property. Neither could have meaning without the other."

SEE ALSO

Charles River Bridge v. Warren Bridge; Contract clause; Dartmouth College v. Woodward; Fletcher v. Peck; Lochner v. New York; Munn v. Illinois; National Labor Relations Board v. Jones & Laughlin Steel Corp.; West Coast Hotel Co. v. Parrish

FURTHER READING

Bakken, Gordon Morris. "Property Rights." In *By and for the People: Constitutional Rights in American History*, edited by Kermit L. Hall. Arlington Heights, Ill.: Harlan Davidson, 1991.

Ely, James W., Jr. *The Guardian of Every Other Right: A Constitutional History of Property Rights*. New York: Oxford University Press, 1992.

Epstein, Richard. *Takings: Private Property and the Power of Eminent Domain*. Cambridge: Harvard University Press, 1985.

Public Information Office

S E E Staff of the Court, nonjudicial

Recusal

A JUDGE may recuse himself or herself, or refuse to participate in deciding a case, because of a special interest in the outcome that could influence his or her decision. The term *recuse* is derived from the Latin word *recusare*, which means "to refuse." Chief Justice John Marshall, for example, recused himself in the case of *Martin* v. *Hunter's Lessee* (1816) because he had served as attorney to one of the parties (Martin) in an earlier phase of the case. In addition, he had a financial stake in the outcome of the case.

Reed, Stanley F.

ASSOCIATE JUSTICE, 1938–57

☆ Born: Dec. 31, 1884, Minerva, Ky.
☆ Education: Kentucky Wesleyan College, B.A., 1902; Yale College, B.A., 1906; legal studies at University of Virginia and Columbia University
☆ Previous government service: Kentucky General Assembly, 1912–16;

general counsel, Federal Farm Board, 1929–32; general counsel, Reconstruction Finance Corporation, 1932–35; special assistant to the U.S. attorney general, 1935; U.S. solicitor general, 1935–38
☆ Appointed by President Franklin D. Roosevelt Jan. 15, 1938; replaced George Sutherland, who retired
☆ Supreme Court term: confirmed by the Senate Jan. 25, 1938, by a voice vote; retired Feb. 25, 1957
☆ Died: Apr. 2, 1980, Huntington, N.Y.

STANLEY REED was a prominent defender of the New Deal policies of President Franklin D. Roosevelt. As a lawyer for the federal government, he defended New Deal programs in several important Supreme Court cases. His reward was appointment in 1938 by President Roosevelt to a vacancy on the Supreme Court.

Justice Reed continued to support the economic programs of President Roosevelt's New Deal. He tended to favor broad exercise of the federal government's power to regulate commerce or trade among the states (Article 1, Section 8, of the Constitution). However, Justice Reed tended to have a narrow view of freedom of expression when he thought it threatened national security or public order.

Reed retired from the Court in 1957, but he continued to assist the Court of Claims and the Court of Appeals for the District of Columbia. In 1980, he died at the age of 95, having lived longer than any other justice of the Supreme Court.

Reed v. Reed

☆ 404 U.S. 71 (1971)
☆ Vote: 7–0
☆ For the Court: Burger

SALLY AND CECIL REED were the separated parents of a deceased son,

Richard Reed. Both parents petitioned an Idaho court for appointment as the administrator of their son's estate. The Court denied Sally Reed's petition in favor of Cecil Reed, based on an Idaho statute that preferred males to females in choosing administrators of estates.

Sally Reed sued Cecil for the right to administer Richard's estate, which was valued at less than $1,000. She claimed that the Idaho law giving preference to a male over a female violated the 14th Amendment guarantee of "equal protection of the laws." Ruth Bader Ginsburg, as a lawyer for the American Civil Liberties Union, argued Sally Reed's case before the Supreme Court.

The Issue The 14th Amendment says, "No State shall... deny to any person within its jurisdiction the equal protection of the laws." However, in past cases the Court had not used the "equal protection" clause of the 14th Amendment to overturn laws that discriminated against individuals on the basis of gender. The Court had used what it called a rational basis test to uphold sex-based laws. According to this test, such laws were constitutional unless one could prove they were not reasonably connected to a compelling public interest. Did the Idaho law in this case violate the equal protection clause of the 14th Amendment? Was there any compelling public reason for sustaining this law?

Opinion of the Court The Court decided this case in favor of Sally Reed, ruling that the Idaho statute did not meet the rational basis test. Chief Justice Warren E. Burger wrote, "To give a mandatory preference to members of either sex... merely to accomplish the elimination of hearings on the merits, is to make the very kind of arbitrary legislative choice forbidden by the Equal Protection Clause of the Fourteenth Amendment."

Significance This case was the first to rule that laws mandating gender dis-

crimination are violations of the 14th Amendment. The Court has used the precedent established in the *Reed* case to strike down many laws that unfairly discriminated against women. For instance, in *Kahn* v. *Shevin* (1974) it ruled that a Florida law that gave a property tax exemption to widowers (males), but not to widows (females) was unconstitutional.

SEE ALSO
Equality under the Constitution

Regents of the University of California v. Bakke

☆ *438 U.S. 265 (1978)*
☆ *Vote: 5–4*
☆ *For the Court: Powell*
☆ *Concurring: Burger, Rehnquist, Stevens, and Stewart*
☆ *Dissenting: Blackmun, Brennan, Marshall, and White*

IN 1972 there were 2,664 applicants for admission to the medical school of the University of California at Davis. From this large pool of applicants, the medical school intended to select 100 students. Eighty-four of the 100 openings were to be filled according to usual procedures of the standard admissions program. Sixteen of the 100 places were to be filled through a special affirmative action program designed to increase the number of disadvantaged students from certain minority groups, such as African Americans, Latinos, and Native Americans.

Students applying for admission through the affirmative action program did not have to meet the same standards as students applying through the regular admissions program. For example, requirements for grade point averages and scores on standardized tests of scholastic aptitude and achievement were lower

White protesters call for an end to racial discrimination—against whites. Allan Bakke, rejected by a University of California medical school, had charged that black applicants did not have to meet the same requirements that he did.

for those seeking admission through the special program.

Allan Bakke, a white male, wanted to become a doctor. In 1972 he applied through the regular program for admission to the Davis medical school. He was rejected even though his grade point average and standardized test scores were higher than those of several students admitted to the medical school through the affirmative action program.

In 1973 Bakke again tried to gain admission to the Davis medical school. This time he was one of 3,737 applicants for 100 vacancies. Once again, 16 places were set aside for applicants through the special affirmative action program. Bakke was rejected a second time, even though he appeared to be more qualified, based on certain statistical indicators, than several applicants admitted through both the affirmative action program and the regular process.

Bakke claimed he was a victim of unequal and unfair treatment. He sued for admission to the state medical school.

The Issue Bakke argued that the medical school's admissions program violated the "equal protection of the laws" guarantee of the 14th Amendment.

Bakke also claimed that the university's affirmative action admissions program conflicted with Title VI of the Civil Rights Act of 1964, which forbids discrimination based on race or ethnicity in programs supported by federal funds.

The University of California defended its special admissions program as necessary to compensate for past injustices suffered by members of certain disadvantaged groups. The special admissions program, university officials said, was one way to open new opportunities for individual members of groups that in the past had not enjoyed these opportunities to the same degree as other members of society.

Allan Bakke, however, questioned whether the affirmative action admissions program went too far in trying to provide new opportunities for members of certain disadvantaged groups. To Bakke, the medical school's affirmative action admissions program seemed to be "reverse discrimination" based on race or ethnicity. Therefore, he asserted, it violated federal statutes and the U.S. Constitution.

Opinion of the Court The Court was so sharply divided in its response to this case that the majority could not agree on a common opinion for the Court. Lewis F. Powell was designated to announce the decision, but the four concurring justices wrote separate opinions, which were mixed in their reasons for supporting or opposing different aspects of the Court's decision.

A majority decided that Allan Bakke must be admitted to the University of California Medical School at Davis. Justice Powell noted that Bakke had been excluded from competition for one of the 16 positions reserved for individuals seeking admission through the special affirmative action program. Therefore, Powell concluded, Bakke had been denied "equal protection of the laws" as required by the 14th Amendment.

Justice Powell wrote, "The guarantees of the Fourteenth Amendment extend to all persons. . . . The guarantee of equal protection cannot mean one thing when applied to one individual and something else when applied to a person of another color. If both are not accorded the same protection, then it is not equal."

The Court held that a university may use admissions standards involving race or ethnicity as one part of a complex admissions process. But "fixed quotas"—guaranteeing a certain number of positions for students of a particular race or ethnicity—cannot be used. Race and ethnic background may be viewed favorably in making decisions about when to admit a person to a university program. But they cannot be the sole factor in determining whether to admit or reject someone.

Dissent Justices William Brennan, Byron White, Thurgood Marshall, and Harry Blackmun voted against admission of Bakke to the medical school. And they would have upheld the quota-based admissions system of the medical school. However, they joined with Justice Powell to permit "race conscious programs in the future," as long as they are only one factor considered in a multifactor admissions process. Thus, the four dissenters from the decision to admit Bakke to the medical school blocked the other four justices (Warren Burger, William Rehnquist, John Paul Stevens, and Potter Stewart), who would have prohibited any use of a person's race as a factor in deciding whom to admit to a university program.

The four dissenters defended the affirmative action admissions program of the medical school:

> The Davis program does not simply advance less qualified applicants; rather it compensates applicants, who it is uncontested are fully qualified to study medicine, for educational disadvantages that it was reasonable to conclude were a product of state-fostered discrimination. Once admit-

ted, these students must satisfy the same degree requirements as regularly admitted students.

Significance This case was the Court's first major statement on whether affirmative action programs are constitutional. And the results were mixed. The rejection of Allan Bakke as a result of the medical school's special admissions program was declared in violation of the U.S. Constitution. However, race could be an important factor in admissions programs, as long as it was not the sole or dominating factor in making an admissions decision.

Allan Bakke certainly benefited from the Court's decision. He graduated in 1982 from the University of California Medical School at Davis and later served as a resident at the prestigious Mayo Clinic in Rochester, Minnesota. However, the *Bakke* decision has had only slight impact on university admissions programs, which shun explicitly stated quotas but tend to consider race and ethnicity as important factors in admissions decisions. This matter remains complex and controversial.

SEE ALSO

Affirmative action

FURTHER READING

Friendly, Fred W., and Martha J. H. Elliott. "Bakke and the Equal Protection Clause." In *The Constitution: That Delicate Balance.* New York: Random House, 1984.
Wilkinson, J. Harvie. *From Brown to Bakke: The Supreme Court and School Integration, 1954–1978.* New York: Oxford University Press, 1979.

Rehnquist, William H.

ASSOCIATE JUSTICE, 1972–86

CHIEF JUSTICE, 1986–

☆ Born: Oct. 1, 1924, Milwaukee, Wis.
☆ Education: Stanford University, B.A., 1948, M.A., 1949; Harvard

University, M.A., 1950; Stanford University Law School, LL.B., 1951

☆ *Previous government service: law clerk to Justice Robert H. Jackson of the Supreme Court, 1952–53; assistant U.S. attorney general, 1969–71*

☆ *Appointed by President Richard Nixon to the position of associate justice Oct. 21, 1971; replaced John Marshall Harlan II, who retired; appointed chief justice by President Ronald Reagan June 20, 1986; replaced Chief Justice Warren E. Burger, who retired*

☆ *Supreme Court term: confirmed by the Senate as associate justice Dec. 10, 1971, by a 68–26 vote; confirmed by the Senate as chief justice Sept. 17, 1986, by a 65–33 vote*

WILLIAM H. REHNQUIST ranked first in his class at Stanford Law School, which also included Justice Sandra Day O'Connor. And he was a distinctive member of the Supreme Court under Chief Justice Warren Burger. Justice Rehnquist dissented more than any other member of that Court. In 1986, President Reagan named Rehnquist the Chief Justice of the United States.

Rehnquist has tended to support the rights and powers of state governments within the federal system. He strongly believes that the Constitution limits the federal government so that the state governments have substantial powers in many areas. He has favored state law enforcement powers over the rights of accused persons, as in *New York* v. *Quarles* (1984) and *United States* v. *Leon* (1984). He also has upheld state rules that restrict abortion rights but has stopped short of total opposition to *Roe* v. *Wade* (1973), the landmark case restricting states from taking away the abortion rights of women.

Rehnquist emphasizes limitations of judicial power and tries to avoid judicial infringement of the legitimate powers of the legislative and executive branches of government. The judicial branch,

according to Rehnquist, should scrupulously avoid political questions and restrict itself to exercising judgment according to the words of the Constitution and the intentions of the framers.

In 1999 Chief Justice Rehnquist presided at the Senate's impeachment trial of President Bill Clinton, as required by the Constitution. The Senate voted against conviction of the President.

FURTHER READING

Davis, Sue. "Justice William H. Rehnquist: Right-Wing Ideologue or Majoritarian Democrat?" In *The Burger Court: Political and Judicial Profiles*, edited by Charles M. Lamb and Stephen C. Halpern, Urbana: University of Illinois Press, 1991: 315–42.

Davis, Sue. *Justice Rehnquist and the Constitution*. Princeton, N.J.: Princeton University Press, 1989.

Rehnquist, William H. *The Supreme Court—How It Was—How It Is*. New York: Morrow, 1987.

Savage, David G. *Turning Right: The Making of the Rehnquist Supreme Court*. New York: Wiley, 1992.

Yarbrough, Tinsley E. *The Rehnquist Court and the Constitution*. New York: Oxford University Press, 2000.

Rejection of Supreme Court nominees

ACCORDING TO Article 2, Section 2, of the Constitution, the President "shall nominate, and by and with the Advice and Consent of the Senate, shall appoint . . . Judges of the Supreme Court." The President's nominees for seats on the Supreme Court must be approved by a majority vote of the Senate. Thus, one part of the legislative branch has the power to check the power of appointment of the executive branch.

From 1789 to 2000 the Senate either rejected by formal vote, or informally turned away, 28 Presidential nominees to the Supreme Court. The Senate officially rejected 11 nominees by majority vote. Seventeen nominations were either withdrawn by the President before a formal vote or no action was taken by the Senate on the nomination, thereby defeating it.

The Senate first formally voted to reject a nominee in 1811, when it refused to confirm President James Madison's nomination of Alexander Wolcott. The vote was 9 senators for Wolcott and 24 against him. The main reason for rejection was doubt about his competence.

Four nominees were voted down by the Senate during the period from 1900 to 1993: John Parker, nominated by President Herbert Hoover in 1930 (by a vote of 39 to 41); Clement Haynsworth, nominated by President Richard Nixon in 1969 (by a vote of 45 to 55); G. Harrold Carswell in 1970, nominated by Nixon (by a vote of 45 to 51); and Robert H. Bork, nominated by President Ronald Reagan in 1987 (by a vote of 42 to 58).

Both John Parker and Robert Bork

REJECTION OR WITHDRAWAL OF SUPREME COURT NOMINATIONS

NOMINEE	YEAR	NOMINATED BY	ACTION
William Paterson*	1793	George Washington	Withdrawn
John Rutledge	1795	George Washington	Withdrawn
Alexander Wolcott	1811	James Madison	Rejected
John Crittenden	1828	John Quincy Adams	None
Roger B. Taney*	1835	Andrew Jackson	None
John Spencer	1844	John Tyler	Rejected
Reuben Walworth	1844	John Tyler	Withdrawn
Edward King	1844	John Tyler	None
Edward King	1845	John Tyler	Withdrawn
John Read	1845	John Tyler	None
George Woodward	1845	James K. Polk	Rejected
Edward Bradford	1852	Millard Fillmore	None
George Badger	1853	Millard Fillmore	None
William Micou	1853	Millard Fillmore	None
Jeremiah Black	1861	James Buchanan	Rejected
Henry Stanbery	1866	Andrew Johnson	None
Ebenezer Hoar	1869	Ulysses S. Grant	Rejected
George Williams	1873	Ulysses S. Grant	Withdrawn
Caleb Cushing	1874	Ulysses S. Grant	Withdrawn
Stanley Matthews*	1881	Rutherford B. Hayes	None
William Hornblower	1893	Grover Cleveland	Rejected
Wheeler Peckham	1894	Grover Cleveland	Rejected
John Parker	1930	Herbert C. Hoover	Rejected
Abe Fortas*	1968	Lyndon B. Johnson	Withdrawn
Homer Thornberry	1968	Lyndon B. Johnson	None
Clement Haynsworth	1969	Richard M. Nixon	Rejected
G. Harrold Carswell	1970	Richard M. Nixon	Rejected
Robert Bork	1987	Ronald Reagan	Rejected

*William Paterson was nominated a second time and confirmed. Roger Taney was nominated twice, the second time for the office of chief justice, and was confirmed. Stanley Matthews was nominated a second time and confirmed. Abe Fortas was a sitting justice when President Johnson nominated him for the office of chief justice; a controversy ensued, leading to withdrawal of the nomination and the resignation of Fortas from the Supreme Court.

Judge Robert Bork testifies before the Senate Judiciary Committee in 1987. The committee rejected his nomination because of his conservative philosophy.

were defeated because important interest groups opposed them. Parker, for example, was defeated by two votes in the Senate because of pressure exerted by labor unions, whose leaders believed him to be opposed to more federal regulation of businesses to improve wages and working conditions. Bork's defeat in the Senate was influenced by civil rights and feminist groups, who disliked his conservative ideas about a woman's right to an abortion and government programs to advance opportunities of minorities and women. Furthermore, some senators opposed Bork because they disagreed with his conservative legal philosophy, which emphasized judicial restraint and a strict construction of the Constitution. For example, Bork could find no justification in the Constitution for the Court's decision in *Roe* v. *Wade* (1973), which affirmed a woman's right to an abortion during a certain period of pregnancy. He believed that the issue of abortion rights should be decided by state legislatures, not by the federal judiciary. Despite disagreements with his legal and political ideas, most of Robert Bork's opponents respected the high quality of his intellect, legal work, and personal integrity.

By contrast, President Nixon's nomination of Clement Haynsworth in 1969 failed largely because most senators had doubts about his competence and character. The Senate also rejected Nixon's nomination of G. Harrold Carswell the following year because of doubts about Judge Carswell's ability to do the job.

In general, reasons for the Senate's rejection of the President's nominees to the Court have included political opposition to the President making the nomination, rather than strong dislike of the nominee; disagreement with the nominee's views on controversial public issues; lack of confidence in the nominee's qualifications; doubts about the judicial ethics or the personal morality of the nominee; and strong opposition to the nominee by large or influential special interest groups.

SEE ALSO

Appointment of justices; Senate Judiciary Committee

FURTHER READING

Abraham, Henry J. *Justices and Presidents: A Political History of Appointments to the Supreme Court.* New York: Oxford University Press, 1992.

Religious issues under the Constitution

THE 1ST AMENDMENT to the U.S. Constitution requires that "Congress shall make no law respecting an establishment of religion, or prohibiting the free exercise thereof." There are two parts to this constitutional provision about religion: the establishment clause and the free exercise clause.

Establishment clause

Americans have always agreed that the establishment clause bans government actions establishing or promoting an official religion. Americans have argued vehemently, however, about whether the establishment clause strictly prohibits all government involvement in support of religion.

Thomas Jefferson wrote in 1802 that the intent of the 1st Amendment was to build "a wall of separation between church and state." Justice Hugo Black agreed with Jefferson in writing for the Court in *Everson* v. *Board of Education of Ewing Township* (1947), the case that began the ongoing contemporary debate about the meaning of the establishment clause. Justice Black wrote that neither federal nor state governments can act to "aid one religion, aid all religions, or prefer one religion over another." The *Everson* decision was the first time the Court applied the 1st Amendment's establishment clause to the states through the due process clause of the 14th Amendment.

Justice Black, like Thomas Jefferson, held an *absolutist* position on the meaning of the establishment clause. Absolutists argue for complete separation of government from religious activity. According to the absolutists, religious activity should be carried out solely in the private sphere of society, free of both government interference and government support.

Since the earliest years of the republic, many Americans have disagreed with the absolutist position on church-state relations. For example, Justice William O. Douglas, writing for the Court in *Zorach* v. *Clauson* (1952), argued that the 1st Amendment "does not say that in every and all respect there shall be a separation of church and state." In *Zorach,* the Court approved a program whereby public school students could be released during school hours to receive religious instruction, but not within the public school facilities. The *Zorach* decision was the first in which the Court accommodated a relationship between church and state in a nonpreferential and voluntary program of religious education. However, *Zorach* was a very small breach in the "wall of separation"

supported by the *Everson* case and later Court rulings.

Since the *Everson* decision in 1947, the Court has for the most part rejected the nonpreferentialist interpretation of the establishment clause, in which minimal government support of religion is permitted as long as it does not give preference to a particular religious denomination. Other key cases supporting strict separation of church and state are *Engel* v. *Vitale* (1962), *Abington School District* v. *Schempp* (1963), and *Wallace* v. *Jaffree* (1985). With these decisions, the Court has overturned state laws that require or sanction prayer and Bible-reading activities in public schools. These prohibitions apply even when the prayers or religious activities at issue are nondenominational, nonpreferential, and voluntary.

In *Lee* v. *Weisman* (1992) the Court prohibited prayers as part of a public school's formal graduation ceremony. A major factor in the case was the direction of the ceremony by school officials. The Court stressed that under the establishment clause, public authorities are forbidden to sanction even nondenominational or supposedly voluntary prayers. Finally, in this case, as in others of its type, the Court emphasized the importance of protecting the rights of individuals in the minority against the control or coercion of majority rule and peer pressure. However, students remain free to organize, on their own and without school support, voluntary religious programs associated with graduation from school. In 1993 the Supreme Court let stand, without comment, a decision of the U.S. Court of Appeals for the Fifth Circuit that upheld a Texas public school district's policy of permitting students to lead voluntary prayers at graduation ceremonies.

In *Santa Fe Independent School District* v. *Doe* (2000), the Court main-

In this cartoon, the Supreme Court tries to balance the scales of justice with a Bible on one side and the Constitution on the other. The separation between church and state is an essential part of the Constitution.

tained a long-standing prohibition against prayer at public school events and ruled that student-led prayer at public high school football games was unconstitutional. Chief Justice William Rehnquist dissented, as did Antonin Scalia and Clarence Thomas, and continued in his opposition to the strict separation of government and religion.

In 1985 Rehnquist had expressed strong opposition to the absolutist position developed by the Court since the *Everson* decision. In his dissent in *Wallace* v. *Jaffree*, Rehnquist wrote, "The establishment clause did not require government neutrality between religion and irreligion nor did it prohibit the federal government from providing nondiscriminatory aid to religions."

Justice Rehnquist and others support a position referred to as *nonpreferentialist*. The position rejects Jefferson's "wall of separation" viewpoint. Nonpreferentialists assert that government should be able to aid religious activity, as long as the support would be provided equally to all religions. That is, no religious denomination would be favored or preferred over others.

The Lemon Test, developed by the Court in *Lemon* v. *Kurtzman* (1971), was an attempt to accommodate some modest relationships between church and state. The test involves three standards for deciding whether federal or state aid to religious schools or programs is constitutional. The Lemon Test says that a statute does not violate the establishment clause if its purpose is secular or nonreligious, if it neither promotes nor restricts religion in its primary effects, and if it does not bring about excessive government entanglement with religion.

During the 1980s the Supreme Court moved slightly in the direction of accommodation between church and state. In *Marsh* v. *Chambers* (1983), the Court held that the Nebraska legislature could begin its sessions with prayers led by a paid chaplain. In *Lynch* v. *Donnelly* (1984) the Court upheld the placing of a crèche, a Christian nativity scene, at public expense on public property in front of a city hall at Christmastime. The display, the Court held, was permissible because it was within the context of a larger exhibit that emphasized secular or nonreligious objects, such as a Santa Claus, reindeers, and talking wishing wells. However, in *Allegheny County* v. *American Civil Liberties Union, Greater Pittsburgh Chapter* (1989), the Court ruled that an exclusively religious exhibit, a Jewish menorah and a crèche, could not be displayed in a government building because this kind of religious exhibit violated the establishment clause.

Another move toward accommodation of church and state was made by the Court in *Westside Community Board of Education* v. *Mergens* (1990). The Court held that the Equal Access Act, passed by Congress in 1984, did not violate the establishment clause. This law requires schools that receive federal funds to permit student organizations, not related to the curriculum, to meet within the school on equal terms. For example, if a chess club could meet at the school, so could a student-led Bible club. The federal law forbade schools to deny access to student organizations "on the basis of the religious, political, philosophical or other content of the speech at such meetings." In the *Mergens* case, the Court ruled that the Westside Community Board of Education could not prevent a student-initiated Christian club from meeting at the school as an extracurricular activity. Further, in *Zobrest* v. *Catalina School District* (1993), the Court ruled that a deaf student at a private parochial school (run by the Catholic church) could be assisted by a publicly funded sign-language interpreter. This kind of aid helps the student, not the Church, said the Court. It therefore does not violate the 1st Amendment's establishment clause.

Free exercise clause

The free exercise clause of the 1st Amendment has not provoked as much controversy as the establishment clause. This clause clearly indicates that government must neither interfere with religious practices of individuals nor prescribe their religious beliefs. From the founding era of the United States until today, most Americans have heartily agreed that individuals have the right to freely express their religious beliefs in the private sphere of society.

The Court has protected the free-exercise rights of religious minorities since the 1940s. In *Cantwell* v. *Connecticut* (1940) the free exercise clause was for the first time "incorporated" by the Court under the due process clause of the 14th Amendment and applied to state governments. The outcome was the protection of the right of Jehovah's Witnesses, a minority religion, to peacefully distribute religious information to people in their neighborhoods with the aim of winning converts.

In *West Virginia State Board of Education* v. *Barnette* (1943) the Court struck down a state flag-salute law because it forced some students, who were

Jehovah's Witnesses, to violate their religious beliefs. Writing for the Court, Justice Robert Jackson emphasized that the individual's right to free exercise of religion was placed by the 1st Amendment "beyond the reach of majorities and officials." He emphasized that it was the Court's responsibility to protect this constitutional right of individuals against the power of majority rule, whenever the majority, acting through representatives in government, might try to deny that right to unpopular minority groups.

Like freedom of speech, the individual's free exercise of religion is not absolute. The Court has ruled that in some instances religious expression may be limited on behalf of the public good.

In *Reynolds* v. *United States* (1879), for example, the Supreme Court upheld a federal law against the practice of polygamy—having multiple spouses—in federal territories. The Court ruled that the anti-polygamy law did not violate the right to free exercise of religion of a member of the Church of Jesus Christ of Latter-Day Saints (Mormons), who claimed it was his religious obligation to have more than one wife. Writing for the Court, Chief Justice Morrison Waite argued that the federal law prohibiting polygamy, even when practiced for religious reasons, was necessary for the good of the community.

Jehovah's Witnesses gather for a convention in 1950 in New York City. The 1st Amendment guarantees that people will not be prohibited from practicing the religion of their choice.

In order to restrict an individual's free exercise of religion, the government must demonstrate a compelling public interest. In *Sherbert* v. *Verner* (1963), the Court ruled that a state could not refuse unemployment benefits to a worker who would not make herself available for employment on Saturday because this was her special day of worship (she was a Seventh-Day Adventist). An entitlement such as state unemployment benefits cannot be denied to someone because of her religious practices.

By contrast, in *Employment Division, Department of Human Resources of Oregon* v. *Smith* (1990), the Court ruled against state employees who were denied unemployment benefits after being dismissed from their jobs for religion-related reasons. The employees, who were Native Americans, practiced a religion with rituals involving the smoking of peyote, an illegal substance under state law. Because they were dismissed for violating a state law, the Court upheld the denial of unemployment compensation.

In 1993, however, the Court struck down a city ordinance that banned ritual animal sacrifice by a religious group. The Court held in *Church of the Lukumi Babalu Aye* v. *City of Hialeah* (1993) that the ordinance violated the 1st Amendment's free exercise clause because it suppressed, without a compelling argument on behalf of the public good, a religious ceremony fundamental to members of a church.

Deciding when the free exercise of religion needs protection, however, is not always a straightforward task. When the city of Boerne, Texas, refused a Roman Catholic church's request to build a larger sanctuary, the Supreme Court ruled for the city. In *City of Boerne, Texas* v. *Flores* (1997), speaking for the majority, Justice Anthony Kennedy struck down the Religious Freedom Restoration Act, a federal law passed in 1993 that limited the power of federal, state, and local governments to enforce laws that "substantially burden" the free exercise of religion. Kennedy emphasized that the power to determine violations of the Constitution is reserved for government's judicial branch.

Continuing controversies

The fiercest arguments today about religion-related constitutional rights pertain to the establishment clause, not the free exercise clause. The absolutists and the nonpreferentialists strongly disagree about such issues as state-sponsored prayer in schools and neutral or nonpreferential support for religious practices in public places or with public funds. Public opinion polls have revealed more than 70 percent of Americans to be against the absolutist, or strict separation, position.

Recent Court decisions indicate a movement toward more accommodation and less separation of religion from the state. In *Capitol Square Review and Advisory Board* v. *Pinette* (1995), the Court ruled that a private group may put religious symbols on government property if there is no appearance of government support for the religious message. And the Court decided in 1995 that a state university cannot discriminate against a student religious publication by denying it financial support on equal terms with other student publications (*Rosenberger* v. *Rector and Visitors of University of Virginia*).

The Supreme Court's movement toward accommodation between government and religion continued in *Agostini* v. *Felton* (1997). This decision, which overturned *Aguilar* v. *Felton* (1985), held that government funds can be used to provide remedial education for disadvantaged students in private religious schools. As long as the public funds aid students directly and do not promote religion or excessively entangle government with a religious institution, then the government-funded program is constitutional.

In *Mitchell* v. *Helms* (2000) the Court upheld a federal program that provided computer equipment and software and other media materials to religiously affiliated schools. In a plurality opinion, Justice Clarence Thomas, joined by Rehnquist, Scalia, and Kennedy, held that federal programs in agreement with "the principles of neutrality and private choice" are not in violation of the 1st Amendment's establishment clause. Justices Sandra Day O'Connor and Stephen Breyer concurred that the federal program at issue was constitutional, but they did not agree with Thomas's "neutrality principle." The Supreme Court clearly has moved strikingly toward an accommodationist position in church-state relationships. How far this accommodation may go, however, is the subject of a lively debate.

SEE ALSO

Abington School District v. Schempp; City of Boerne, Texas v. Flores; Engel v. Vitale; Establishment clause; Everson v. Board of Education of Ewing Township; Free exercise clause; Lemon Test; Lemon v. Kurtzman; Wallace v. Jaffree; West Virginia State Board of Education v. Barnette; Zorach v. Clauson

FURTHER READING

Alley, Robert S., ed. *James Madison on Religious Liberty.* Buffalo, N.Y.: Prometheus Books, 1985.

Alley, Robert S., ed. *The Supreme Court on Church and State.* New York: Oxford University Press, 1988.

Curry, Thomas J. *The First Freedoms: Church and State in America to the Passage of the First Amendment.* New York: Oxford University Press, 1986.

Gaustad, Edwin S. *Church and State in America.* New York: Oxford University Press, 1999.

Levy, Leonard W. *The Establishment Clause: Religion and the First Amendment.* New York: Macmillan, 1986.

Miller, William Lee. *The First Liberty: Religion and the American Republic.* New York: Paragon House, 1985.

Patrick, John J., and Gerald P. Long. *Constitutional Debates on Freedom of Religion.* Westport, Conn.: Greenwood, 1999.

Urofsky, Melvin I. "The Religion Clauses." In *By and for the People: Constitutional Rights in American History,* edited by Kermit L. Hall. Arlington Heights, Ill.: Harlan Davidson, 1991.

Reno v. American Civil Liberties Union

☆ *117 S. Ct. 2329 (1997)*
☆ *Vote: 9–0*
☆ *For the Court: Stevens*
☆ *Concurring: O'Connor and Rehnquist*

IN 1996 CONGRESS, with the strong support of President Bill Clinton, passed the Communications Decency Act (CDA) to prohibit the transmission of indecent or pornographic messages via e-mail or the Internet. The law made it a crime for a person to send indecent messages by way of an interactive computer network to anyone younger than 18. It also banned Internet displays of pornography that would be accessible to someone under 18. The law did not clearly or precisely define the material to be banned. Rather the act referred to "patently offensive" and "indecent" portrayals of sexual or excretory activities. Convicted violators of the CDA could be fined $25,000, sentenced to two years in prison, or both.

Supporters of the CDA argued that the law served a compelling public interest—the common good of protecting the moral development of preadults. Opponents, however, denounced the CDA as an unconstitutional limitation on 1st Amendment rights to freedom of expression.

The American Civil Liberties Union (ACLU), in concert with other groups including the American Library Association (ALA), filed suit against enforcement of the CDA by the attorney general of the United States, Janet Reno. A three-judge panel of a federal district court agreed with the plaintiffs and ruled that the CDA was unconstitutional. Then the case was appealed to the U.S. Supreme Court.

The Issue This case raised questions about the extent to which the federal government may regulate the transmission of messages via the new electronically driven mass media, such as the Internet. Should the Court view the Internet as similar to newspapers and books and provide the highest level of constitutional protection to freedom of expression? Or should it treat the Internet the way it has responded to broadcast and cable television and permit greater regulation by government on behalf of the public good? Can all communication on the Internet be limited by federal law for the purpose of protecting children against exposure to indecent messages? Or is the Constitution's 1st Amendment violated by a federal law that would limit all speech on the Internet to the level of a child?

Opinion of the Court Justice John Paul Stevens wrote, "Notwithstanding the legitimacy and importance of the congressional goal of protecting children from harmful materials, we agree . . . that the statute abridges the freedom of speech protected by the First Amendment. . . . The interest in encouraging freedom of expression in a democratic society outweighs any theoretical but unproven benefit of censorship." So the Communications Decency Act's prohibition of indecent material on the Internet was declared unconstitutional.

Justice Sandra Day O'Connor was joined by Chief Justice William Rehnquist in a concurring opinion. She argued that a federal law, such as the CDA, could be upheld only in cases where it is clear that the transmitter of the material intended the messages exclusively for preadults. She also agreed with Justice Stevens that the CDA was flawed

because it did not clearly define or specify the material to be excluded.

Significance The Court's decision left the Internet to expand freely without strict regulation by government of its content. The executive director of the Center for Democracy and Technology applauded the ruling and claimed, "The Supreme Court has written the Bill of Rights for the 21st century." Many others, however, sided with Indiana Senator Dan Coats, who regretted that "the Court was telling families to fend for themselves on an Internet of raw indecency." So parents and other private guardians of the moral development of youth were left with the responsibility of regulating the Internet access of children and teenagers.

Reporter of decisions

IN 1816 Congress officially created the office of reporter of decisions of the Supreme Court. The reporter, with a staff of nine, records and edits all the Court's case decisions. Since 1955 audio tapes have been made of oral arguments before the Court. These recordings are stored at the National Archives. The reporter oversees the process of printing and publishing the record of the Court's decisions in *United States Reports*, the official publication of the Court's decisions.

The reporter also supervises the printing of a headnote for each decision of the Court. The headnote is a summary of the case that includes background facts, the legal reasoning used in the decision, and the voting record of the justices on the case. The headnote also tells whether the lower court's ruling has been affirmed or overturned by the Supreme Court's decision. Each headnote contains this statement: "The syllabus [headnote] constitutes no part of the opinion of the Court but has been prepared by the Reporter of Decisions for the convenience of the reader."

The first reporter of decisions was Alexander Dallas, who served unofficially on the job from 1790 to 1800. He was self-appointed, but the Court gave its approval to his work. He was not paid by the federal government, but he tried to make a profit through sales of his published reports. William Cranch, the second reporter, also worked unofficially at this job from 1801 to 1815. Henry Wheaton, who served from 1816 to 1827, was the first official reporter of the Supreme Court. The early reporters of decisions did their work laboriously by hand. Today, the reporter and his staff use audiotape and recorders, photocopy machines, and high-speed computers and printers to process information and produce the formal record of the Court's work.

SEE ALSO

Staff of the Court, nonjudicial; United States Reports

Republicanism

REPUBLICANISM IS the belief in the worth of a republic, a type of government that is based on the consent of the governed and is conducted by elected representatives of the people. In a republican government, the people are sovereign, or supreme, because their representatives serve at their pleasure for the common good. Today, people tend to use the terms *republic* and *representative democracy* interchangeably. In contrast to a republic, a *pure* or *direct democracy* is a form of government in which the people govern directly—in a town meeting, for example—instead of through representatives whom they elect.

In *The Federalist* No. 39, James Madison presented the idea of republicanism that is embodied in the U.S. Constitution:

What, then, are the distinctive characters of the republican form?...

If we resort for a criterion...we may define a republic to be...a government which derives all its powers directly or indirectly from the great body of the people, and is administered by persons holding their offices during pleasure for a limited period, or during good behavior. It is essential to such a government that it be derived from the great body of the society, not from an inconsiderable proportion or a favored class of it... is *sufficient* for such a government that the persons administering it be appointed, either directly or indirectly, by the people; and that they hold their appointments by either of the tenures just specified.

In the world of the 1780s, the republican form of government was rare; monarchies and aristocracies prevailed. These nonrepublican forms of government function without representation of or participation by the common people. In an absolute monarchy, the monarch (the king or queen or both) rules; and in an aristocracy, a small elite group of aristocrats or nobles exercises power in government. Power usually is based on heredity in a monarchy or aristocracy; titles are passed from father to children (usually sons).

Americans in the 1780s were committed to republicanism, rather than a monarchy, aristocracy, or other nonrepublican form of government. They agreed that the rights and liberty of individuals could best be secured through a republican form of government. As a result, they built republicanism into the U.S. Constitution. Article 4, Section 4, says, "The United States [federal government] shall guarantee to every State in this Union a Republican Form of Government."

SEE ALSO

Constitutional democracy; Constitutionalism; Liberty under the Constitution

FURTHER READING

Rahe, Paul. *Republics Ancient and Modern.* Chapel Hill: University of North Carolina Press, 1992.

Reversals of Supreme Court decisions

THE SUPREME COURT has the last word, within the American judicial system, on questions of constitutional interpretation. However, a Supreme Court decision regarding interpretation of the Constitution can be overturned by a constitutional amendment. A Court decision on interpretation of federal laws can be overturned by Congressional enactment of a new law.

Reversals by Constitutional amendment

The people, through their representatives in government, can use Article 5 of the Constitution to overturn the Court's decisions. Article 5 provides that constitutional amendments can be proposed by a two-thirds vote of the members of each house of Congress or by a special convention that Congress calls after two-thirds of the state legislatures have voted to request it. For a proposed amendment to be ratified, three-fourths of the states must approve it, either by their legislatures or by conventions especially convened for this purpose. To date, all amendments have been proposed by Congress, and all but one (the 21st) have been ratified by state legislatures. The 21st Amendment was ratified by state conventions.

Of the 27 amendments to the Constitution, 4 clearly were enacted to overturn unpopular Supreme Court decisions. The 11th Amendment overturned *Chisholm* v. *Georgia* (1793) by guaranteeing the immunity of states from lawsuits by citizens of another state or a foreign country. The 14th Amendment nullified *Scott* v. *Sandford* (1857) by guaranteeing the civil rights and citizenship of African Americans. The 16th Amendment overrode *Pollock* v. *Farmers' Loan and Trust Co.* (1895) by giving Congress the power to levy an income tax. The 26th Amendment negated *Oregon* v. *Mitchell* (1970) by permitting 18-year-olds to vote in state elections. Many other attempts to enact constitutional amendments to override Supreme Court decisions have failed.

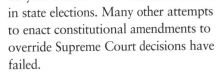

Reversals of Court decisions by Congress

Congress has a rather simple and direct way to negate unpopular decisions of the Court that have nullified federal statutes: It can pass a new law. For example, Congress passed the Civil Rights Act of 1991 to overturn the Court's decision in *Ward's Cove Packing Company* v. *Atonio* (1989). In *Ward's Cove,* the Court decided that an individual proving discrimination by an employer could still be dismissed or demoted from a desired job as long as the employer could prove that the discriminating practice was necessary to maintain his business. The Civil Rights Act of 1991 makes it illegal for an employer to claim "business necessity" as a reason for

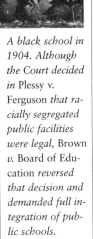

A black school in 1904. Although the Court decided in Plessy v. Ferguson *that racially segregated public facilities were legal,* Brown v. Board of Education *reversed that decision and demanded full integration of public schools.*

intentional job discrimination against an individual based on race, color, ethnic origin, and gender.

Although most bills that have been introduced to overturn Supreme Court decisions have *not* been passed, the power of Congress to negate certain kinds of Court decisions is an important part of the American constitutional system of separation of powers and checks and balances.

SEE ALSO

Amendments to the Constitution; Precedent; Separation of powers

Reynolds v. Sims

☆ *377 U.S. 533 (1964)*
☆ *Vote: 8–1*
☆ *For the Court: Warren*
☆ *Concurring: Stewart and Clark*
☆ *Dissenting: Harlan*

BY THE EARLY 1920s the distribution of the U.S. population had clearly changed since the 19th century. For the first time, more Americans were living in cities than in rural areas. This change created inequities between the populations of urban and rural state legislative districts.

By 1960 nearly every state had some urban legislative districts populated by at least twice as many people as rural districts in the state. In Alabama, for example, the smallest congressional district had a population of 6,700 and the largest had a population of 104,000. In a representative democracy people's votes possess equal value only when each member of a legislative body represents the same number of people. Clearly, the people in more populous urban districts and the people in less populous rural districts were not represented equally. As a result, city and suburban problems did not receive appropriate attention in state

legislatures dominated by representatives from farming and rural districts.

The domination by rural interests also meant that state legislatures refused to redistrict to ensure that each member of the legislature would represent roughly the same number of people. Some simply ignored sections in their state constitutions requiring redistricting every 10 years. Others merely redistricted in ways that continued to favor rural interests. There was little voters could do to change things through the ballot box.

During the 1960s the Supreme Court heard a series of cases challenging the apportionment (distribution) of state legislative districts. In *Reynolds* v. *Sims*, voters in Jefferson County, Alabama, claimed that the unequal representation of citizens in Alabama districts violated the equal protection clause of the 14th Amendment.

The Issue The 14th Amendment declares: "No state. . . shall deny to any person within its jurisdiction the equal protection of the laws." Did Alabama and other states violate the equal protection rights of voters by setting up legislative districts that contained unequal numbers of people?

Opinion of the Court The Supreme Court ruled that the 14th Amendment required states to establish equally populated electoral districts for both houses of state legislatures. Chief Justice Earl Warren declared that plans for setting up legislative districts could not discriminate against people on the basis of where they live (city versus country, in this case) any more than they could on the basis of race or economic status.

The Court rejected the idea that state legislatures, like Congress, could create senate districts on the basis of area rather than population. The Constitution, which allotted equal representation to states in the U.S. Senate no matter what their size, recognized the states as

Birmingham, Alabama, in 1963. In Reynolds v. Sims, *the Supreme Court ruled that Alabama had to reapportion its legislative districts so that people living in urban areas had the same representation as rural voters.*

"sovereign entities." Political subdivisions within a state (such as counties or regions), however, did not possess the status of sovereign entities. Thus, Warren argued, the people of a state must benefit from equal representation in *both* houses of a state legislature. "Legislators represent people, not trees or acres," Warren declared.

The Court ruled that state legislatures did not have to draw legislative districts with "mathematical exactness or precision." However, such districts did have to be based "substantially" on equal population. The Court thus established the key principle of "one person, one vote."

Dissent Justice John Marshall Harlan argued that this case did not pertain to violation of constitutional rights. Rather, he said, it involved a political question that should be decided by elected representatives of the people, not by the Court.

Significance The *Reynolds* decision had a major impact on state legislatures. After the decision, 49 state legislatures reapportioned their legislative districts on the basis of equal population. Oregon had already done so in 1961. The decision caused a fundamental shift in American politics by declaring unconstitutional the practices that enabled rural minorities to control state legislatures. The decision also affected national politics because state legislatures draw the lines for U.S. congressional districts.

FURTHER READING
Cortner, Richard C. *The Apportionment Cases.* Knoxville: University of Tennessee Press, 1970.

Rights of the accused

A PRIMARY PURPOSE of government is to enforce law and order. The federal and state constitutions of the United States, for example, grant certain powers to government officials so they can maintain an orderly society and protect the lives, property, and rights of the people. Federal and state government officials have the duty of preventing some individuals from harming others through criminal acts such as theft, assault, rape, and murder. Nevertheless, criminal behavior has become a serious threat to many American communities where violence, theft, and illegal drug use are rampant. Most Americans, therefore, want law enforcement officials to be tough on criminals, to apprehend and punish them.

There are, however, constitutional limits on the power of government officials in order to prevent them from abusing the rights of individuals, including those accused of criminal behavior. From colonial times until the present, Americans have believed in an old English saying: "It is better for 99 guilty persons to go free than for one innocent person to be punished." In the United States, a person accused of a crime is presumed innocent until proved guilty. The burden of proving the suspect guilty is upon the government prosecutors.

Americans want their federal and state governments to be both powerful and limited, so that freedom and order are balanced. On the one side, government officials should have enough power to keep order so that people are safe and secure. On the other side, the power of government officials to enforce law and order should be sufficiently limited so that they cannot oppress anyone.

Constitutional rights of the accused

The U.S. Constitution, especially the Bill of Rights (Amendments 1 to 10), protects individuals from wrong or unjust accusations and punishments by law enforcement officials.

Amendment 4 protects individuals against unreasonable and unwarranted searches and seizures of their property. It establishes conditions for the lawful issuing and use of search warrants by government officials in order to protect the right of individuals to security "in their persons, houses, papers and effects." There must be a "probable cause" for issuing a warrant to authorize a search or arrest, and the place to be searched, the objects sought, and the person to be arrested must be precisely described.

Amendment 5 states certain legal and procedural rights of individuals. For example, the government may not act against an individual in the following ways:

• Hold an individual to answer for a serious crime unless the prosecution presents appropriate evidence to a grand jury that indicates the likely guilt of the individual.

• Try an individual more than once for the same offense.

• Force an individual to act as a witness against himself in a criminal case.

• Deprive an individual of life, liberty or property without due process of law (fair and proper legal proceedings).

Amendment 6 guarantees people suspected or accused of a crime certain protections against the power of government. It provides these rights to individuals:

• A speedy public trial before an unbiased jury picked from the state and community in which the crime was committed.

• Information about what the individual has been accused of and why the accusation has been made.

• A meeting with witnesses offering testimony against the individual.

• Means of obtaining favorable witnesses, including the right to subpoena, or legally compel, witnesses to testify in court.

• Help from a lawyer.

Amendment 8 protects individuals from overly harsh punishments and excessive fines and bail (the amount of money required to secure a person's release from custody while awaiting trial).

Amendment 14 provides general protection for the rights of the accused against the powers of state governments. This amendment forbids state governments from making and enforcing laws that will deprive any individual of life, liberty, or property "without due process of law"; it also says that a state government may not deny to any person under its authority "the equal protection of the laws."

The U.S. Constitution includes other protections of individual rights that are not in the Bill of Rights or subsequent amendments. For example, Article 1, Section 9, prohibits government from suspending the privilege of the writ of habeas corpus. A writ of habeas corpus requires officials to bring a person whom they have arrested and held in custody before a judge in a court of law. The officials must convince the judge that there are lawful reasons for holding the person. If the judge finds their reasons unlawful, then the court frees the suspect. Thus, the writ of habeas corpus protects individuals from government officials who might want to jail them arbitrarily—because they belong to unpopular groups or express criticisms of the government, for instance.

Article 1, Section 9, also prohibits enactment by the federal government of bills of attainder and ex post facto laws. A bill of attainder is a law that punishes an individual solely by means of legislation, without a trial or fair hearing in a court of law. An ex post facto (literally, "after the fact") law makes an action a crime after it was committed.

Article 1, Section 10, prohibits state governments from enacting bills of attainder and ex post facto laws.

Article 3, Section 2, provides individuals accused of a crime the right to trial by jury.

Article 3, Section 3, protects individuals against arbitrary accusations of treason—an attempt to overthrow the government or to give aid and support to enemies of the United States, such as countries waging war against it. This article also establishes rigorous standards for convicting a person of treason.

Sources of rights of the accused

American ideas about the rights of the accused—criminal defendants—can be traced to the great English documents of liberty, such as the Magna Carta (1215), the Petition of Right (1628), and the English Bill of Rights (1689). These documents embodied the principles of limited government and the rule of law, which all were bound to obey, even the king. For example, Section 39 of the Magna Carta said that no "freeman" could be put in prison except "by the lawful judgment of peers or the law of the land." This was the beginning of due process of law and rights for individuals accused of crimes. These ideas were developed in England and brought to the North American colonies in the 1600s.

American colonists expanded their English legal heritage to provide new and higher levels of protection for the rights of the accused. The Massachusetts Body of Liberties (1641), for example, established many provisions that appeared later in the federal Bill of Rights, such as the rights to trial by jury, to challenge jurors, to have assistance of counsel, to know the charges of criminal behavior, to

reasonable bail, and to protection against cruel or unusual punishment.

By the time of the American Revolution, legal protections for those accused of crimes were a generally accepted part of government. The Declaration of Independence (1776) accused the British king of, among other charges, violating the due process rights of Americans, such as "depriving us, in many cases, of the Benefits of Trial by Jury."

The new constitutions of the first 13 states of the United States, written between 1776 and 1783, included ample provisions for the rights of the accused. These state constitutions reflected an American consensus about the general importance of due process of law in criminal proceedings and about specific protections for the rights of accused persons. The rights of the accused expressed in the U.S. Constitution (1787) and Bill of Rights (1791) were drawn from the provisions in the original 13 state constitutions.

Rights of the accused under Constitutional law

Throughout most of U.S. history, the federal Bill of Rights had little impact on individuals accused of crimes. Most criminal cases in the American federal system were (and will be) within the jurisdiction of state governments. And the U.S. Supreme Court ruled in Barron v. Baltimore (1833) that the federal Bill of Rights restrained only the federal government. As a result, the rights of the accused guaranteed by Amendments 4, 5, 6, and 8 of the U.S. Constitution were not applicable to law enforcement activi-

The Constitution guarantees specific rights, such as the right to a speedy trial, to those accused of crimes in order to prevent the abuse of power by officials.

ties of state governments. Most defendants, therefore, could look only to their state constitutions and bills of rights for legal protection against police power.

The 14th Amendment, ratified in 1868, appeared to impose certain legal restrictions on the states in criminal proceedings. This amendment stated, "No state shall... deprive any person of life, liberty, or property, without due process of law, nor deny to any person within its jurisdiction the equal protection of the laws."

In *Hurtado* v. *California* (1884), the U.S. Supreme Court faced the question of whether the due process clause of the 14th Amendment required a state government to provide the 5th amendment guarantee of a grand jury indictment in criminal proceedings. The Court ruled that the 14th Amendment did not incorporate, or include, any part of the 5th Amendment and thereby make it binding on state governments. *Hurtado,* like *Barron* v. *Baltimore,* implied that the federal Bill of Rights could be used only to limit the federal government.

Justice John Marshall Harlan dissented from the Court's opinion in *Hurtado* v. *California.* He argued that the intent of the 14th Amendment was "to impose upon the States the same restrictions, in respect of proceedings involving life, liberty, and property, which had been imposed upon the general government." Harlan concluded that the rights of the accused in the federal Bill of Rights could be applied to the states through the 14th Amendment's due process clause.

Justice Harlan's dissent in *Hurtado* prevailed in the long run. In *Powell* v. *Alabama* (1932) the U.S. Supreme Court ruled that the due process clause of the 14th Amendment required assistance of a lawyer for defendants charged in a state court with a crime punishable by death. In *Cole* v. *Arkansas* (1947) the Court used the 14th Amendment's due process clause to apply to a state the 6th Amendment's requirement of notice of accusation to a defendant. And in *In re Oliver* (1948), the 6th Amendment requirement of a public trial was imposed upon the states through the 14th Amendment. Further, in *Wolf* v. *Colorado* (1949), the Court incorporated the 4th Amendment's protections against unreasonable searches and seizures into the 14th Amendment.

The Supreme Court's case-by-case application of the rights of the accused listed in the federal Bill of Rights to the states moved ahead dramatically during the 1960s. This rapid change, often called a "due process revolution," took place under the leadership of Chief Justice Earl Warren. The following cases applied virtually all of the 4th, 5th, 6th, and 8th Amendment rights of the accused to the states through the due process clause of the 14th Amendment:

• *Mapp* v. *Ohio* (1961): Evidence obtained in violation of 4th Amendment rights must be excluded from the state's prosecution of criminal defendants.

• *Robinson* v. *California* (1962): State governments cannot use cruel and unusual punishments in violation of the 8th Amendment.

• *Gideon* v. *Wainwright* (1963): The 6th Amendment right to counsel must be provided to all defendants.

• *Malloy* v. *Hogan* (1964): Defendants in state courts have the 5th Amendment right of protection against self-incrimination.

• *Pointer* v. *Texas* (1965): States must observe the 6th Amendment right of defendants to confront witnesses against them.

• *Parker* v. *Gladden* (1966): Defendants in state courts have the 6th Amendment right to an impartial jury.

• *Miranda* v. *Arizona* (1966): Police

are required to advise suspects of their 5th Amendment right of protection against self-incrimination and 6th Amendment right to an attorney.

• *Klopfer* v. *North Carolina* (1967): Defendants in state courts have the 6th Amendment right to a speedy trial.

• *Washington* v. *Texas* (1967): Defendants in state courts have the 6th Amendment right to subpoena witnesses to testify in their favor.

• *Duncan* v. *Louisiana* (1968): States must guarantee the defendant's 6th Amendment right to a jury trial in criminal cases.

• *Benton* v. *Maryland* (1969): State law enforcers cannot subject a person to double jeopardy; that is, they cannot deprive individuals of their 5th Amendment right not to be tried twice for the same crime.

Controversies about rights of the accused

The Warren Court's due process revolution nationalized the rights of the accused in the federal Bill of Rights; that is, people accused of crimes anywhere in the United States could expect the same legal protections.

Many Americans hailed the due process revolution. Others, however, criticized it for caring too much for the rights of accused criminals and too little for the victims of crime and the law-abiding majority of the people. The critics claimed that such decisions as *Mapp*, *Malloy*, and *Miranda* restricted police too much and made it too easy for criminals to evade punishment.

During his 1968 Presidential campaign, Richard Nixon sided with the critics when he said, "Let us always respect, as I do, our courts and those who serve on them, but let us also recognize that some of our courts have gone too far in weakening the peace forces as against the criminal forces in this country." After

winning the Presidency, Nixon appointed a new chief justice, Warren Burger, who agreed with him about issues of law, order, and the rights of the accused. From 1970 to 1971 President Nixon appointed three more justices: Harry Blackmun, Lewis Powell, and William Rehnquist. Later, Presidents Ronald Reagan and George Bush also expressed strong concern for the rights of crime victims and criticized what they saw as an overemphasis on the rights of criminal suspects.

Despite high-level objections to some aspects of the due process revolution of the Warren Court, none of the Court's rulings on the rights of the accused has been overruled. Only minor modifications have been made in the *Mapp* and *Miranda* decisions about certain 4th and 5th Amendment rights. In *New York* v. *Quarles* (1984), the Court decided that police officers could, in order to protect themselves against harm, question a suspect about possession of weapons before advising the suspect of his Miranda rights to remain silent and obtain counsel. In *United States* v. *Leon* (1984) the Court adopted a "good faith exception" to the exclusionary rule established by the *Mapp* decision. This means that evidence obtained illegally may be used to prosecute a defendant if the police who obtained it thought they were acting legally at the time. In *Dickerson* v. *United States* (2000), however, the Court acted to reinforce the rights of a suspect by deciding that Congress cannot enact legislation to overrule the long-standing Miranda warnings requirement.

In a free society, there will always be arguments about the proper balance between liberty and order, between the rights of criminal suspects and the public's need for safety and security against crime. The exact meaning and practical applications of due process of law will continue to be debated in public forums and courts of law. Such constructive controversies are signs of a healthy constitutional democracy.

SEE ALSO

Benton v. Maryland; Bill of Rights; Counsel, right to; Double jeopardy; Due process of law; Duncan v. Louisiana; Exclusionary rule; Gideon v. Wainwright; Grand jury; Habeas corpus, writ of; Incorporation doctrine; Juvenile justice; Mapp v. Ohio; Miranda v. Arizona; Powell v. Alabama; Searches and seizures; Trial by jury; United States v. Leon; Wolf v. Colorado

FURTHER READING

Bodenhamer, David J. *Fair Trial: Rights of the Accused in American History.* New York: Oxford University Press, 1992.

Bodenhamer, David J. "Trial Rights of the Accused." In *By and for the People: Constitutional Rights in American History,* edited by Kermit L. Hall. Arlington Heights, Ill.: Harlan Davidson, 1991.

Bodenhamer, David J., and James W. Ely, Jr. *The Bill of Rights in Modern America after Two Hundred Years.* Bloomington: Indiana University Press, 1993.

Graham, Fred. *The Due Process Revolution: The Warren Court's Impact on Criminal Law.* New York: Hayden, 1970.

Walker, Samuel. *Popular Justice: A History of American Criminal Law.* New York: Oxford University Press, 1980.

Walker, Samuel. "Rights Before Trial." In *By and for the People: Constitutional Rights in American History,* edited by Kermit L. Hall. Arlington Heights, Ill.: Harlan Davidson, 1991.

Roberts, Owen J.

ASSOCIATE JUSTICE, 1930–1945

☆ *Born: May 2, 1875, Germantown, Pa.*
☆ *Education: University of Pennsylvania, A.B., 1895, LL.B., 1898*
☆ *Previous government service: special deputy attorney general, Eastern District of Pennsylvania, 1918; special U.S. attorney, 1924–30*
☆ *Appointed by President Herbert Hoover May 9, 1930; replaced Justice Edward Terry Sanford, who died*
☆ *Supreme Court term: confirmed by the Senate May 20, 1930, by a voice vote; resigned July 31, 1945*

☆ *Died: May 17, 1955, West Vincent Township, Pa.*

OWEN J. ROBERTS served on the Supreme Court during an era of crisis and controversy, which included the Great Depression and World War II. He initially participated with the Court's majority in opposing President Franklin Roosevelt's New Deal programs. Later, he switched his position to join the Court's majority in favor of New Deal programs and laws. His change in position seemed to reflect a great change in popular opinion signaled by President Roosevelt's landslide victory in the 1936 election.

Justice Roberts's most notable Supreme Court opinion came in dissent in *Korematsu* v. *United States* (1944). The Court upheld the compulsory movement of Japanese Americans during World War II to internment centers because they were viewed as a threat to national security following Japan's attack on Pearl Harbor in Hawaii. Roberts, however, disagreed and wrote: "[This] is the case of convicting a citizen as a punishment for not submitting to imprisonment in a concentration camp, based on his ancestry... without evidence or inquiry concerning his loyalty and good disposition towards the United States.... I need hardly labor the conclusion that constitutional rights have been violated." Justice Roberts's dissent in the *Korematsu* case is viewed by most Americans today as the correct opinion.

SEE ALSO

Korematsu v. United States

Robing room

BEFORE EACH session of the Court, the justices go to the robing room on the

main floor of the Supreme Court Building, next to the Conference Room. The robing room contains nine closets, one for each justice, which hold the judicial robes. In this room, the justices put on their robes before appearing in public for a session of the Court.

Roe v. Wade

☆ *410 U.S. 113 (1973)*
☆ *Vote: 7–2*
☆ *For the Court: Blackmun*
☆ *Concurring: Douglas, Stewart, and Burger*
☆ *Dissenting: White and Rehnquist*

IN AUGUST 1969 an unmarried pregnant woman living in Texas wanted to terminate her pregnancy by having an abortion. Her doctor refused this request because Texas law made it a crime to have an abortion unless the operation was necessary to save the mother's life. So the woman sought legal help and filed suit against Henry Wade, district attorney for Dallas County, Texas. Throughout the legal proceedings, the woman was identified as Jane Roe to protect her anonymity. The plaintiff later was identified by the media as Norma McCorvey.

Jane Roe argued that the Texas abortion laws were unconstitutional. So she requested an injunction to restrain Henry Wade from enforcing them.

The Issue Roe's lawyers claimed that the Texas abortion laws violated her rights under the due process clause of the 14th Amendment, which prohibited states from depriving their citizens of life, liberty, or property without due process of law. Does the 14th Amendment protect the right of a woman to have an abortion? Are state laws prohibiting abortion unconstitutional?

Opinion of the Court The Court ruled that the Texas statutes on abortion

Sarah Weddington argued Jane Roe's case before the Supreme Court and claimed that a Texas law banning abortion was unconstitutional.

were unconstitutional and that a woman did have the right to terminate her pregnancy. Justice Harry Blackmun wrote, "The right of privacy... whether it is to be found in the Fourteenth Amendment's concept of personal liberty ... or... in the Ninth Amendment's reservation of rights to the people, is broad enough to encompass a woman's decision whether or not to terminate her pregnancy."

Justice Blackmun recognized that a woman's right to an abortion could be limited by "a compelling state interest" to protect her health and life. Based on medical evidence, Justice Blackmun concluded that during the "second trimester" of a woman's pregnancy (months 4 to 6), the state might intervene to regulate abortion to protect the mother's well-being. And the state could regulate or prohibit abortion during the third trimester (months 7 to 9). However, during the first trimester (months 1 to 3) of a pregnancy, it seemed unlikely that there would be "a compelling state interest" to restrict abortion rights to protect the health and life of the mother.

Dissent Justice Byron White could not find in the Constitution the right to privacy upon which the *Roe* decision was based. He wrote, "I find nothing in the language or history of the Constitution to support the Court's judgment.... This issue, for the most part, should be left with the people and the political processes the people have devised to govern their affairs." Justices White and William Rehnquist both objected to the Court's involvement in a question they believed

In 1989, 16 years after the Roe decision, the debate between pro-abortion and anti-abortion forces was still strong. At a demonstration in Texas, Planned Parenthood banners assert women's right to abortion.

should be left to state governments to decide, without interference from the federal courts. They also believed that the *Roe* decision unjustly disregarded the protection due to the life of the fetus.

Significance The *Roe* decision has generated continuing controversy. Women's rights advocates have hailed *Roe* as a landmark victory. Its critics can be roughly divided into two groups: those who oppose the decision because they believe abortion is murder and those who believe that the Court improperly substituted its policy preference for the will of the people as expressed through their elected representatives in state governments.

Justice Byron White accurately remarked in his dissent that the right to an abortion is an issue about which "reasonable men may easily and heatedly differ." And so it has been since 1973, when the *Roe* case was decided.

Efforts to modify or overturn the *Roe* decision have continued. In *Webster v. Reproductive Health Services* (1989), for example, the court upheld provisions of a Missouri law that restricted the right to an abortion, a retreat from the *Roe* decision that stopped short of overturning it. *Rust v. Sullivan* (1991) limited the access of poor women to abortions by forbidding federally funded clinics, such as those run by Planned Parenthood, to advise patients about abortion. In *Stenberg v. Carhart* (2000), the Court ruled against state laws banning a type of late-term abortion known as "partial-birth" abortion.

SEE ALSO
Abortion rights; Privacy, right to; Webster v. Reproductive Health Services

FURTHER READING
Faux, Marian. *Roe v. Wade.* New York: Macmillan, 1988.
Garrow, David J. *Liberty and Sexuality: The Right to Privacy and the Making of Roe v. Wade, 1923–1973.* New York: Macmillan, 1993.
Rosenberg, Rosalind. "The Abortion Case." In *Quarrels That Have Shaped the Constitution*, edited by John A. Garraty. New York: Harper & Row, 1987.
Tribe, Laurence H. *Abortion: The Clash of Absolutes.* New York: Norton, 1990.
Weddington, Sarah. *A Question of Choice.* New York: Putnam, 1992.

Rule of Four

PETITIONERS SEEKING review of a case by the Supreme Court will petition the Court for a writ of certiorari, an order from the Supreme Court to a lower court requiring that a record of a case be sent to the Court for review. If at least four of the nine justices vote in favor of this action, the Court will grant a petition for certiorari. This procedure is known as the Rule of Four.

SEE ALSO
Certiorari, writ of

Rule of law

SEE Constitutionalism

Rules of the Court

DURING ITS first term, in 1790, the Supreme Court established rules for its activities. Since then, the Court has occasionally revised the rules. The rules and revisions are published in the *United States Reports.*

Changes in the rules may be proposed by one or more of the justices, by members of the bar, or by committees of lawyers and members of the federal judiciary that the Court creates to review the rules. By tradition, the justices agree upon revisions of the rules by consensus, not by a formal majority vote.

The rules cover various aspects of the Court's work. For example, there are rules to be followed by attorneys in Court proceedings. Rule 38 regulates an advocate's behavior during the oral argument, when a case is heard by the Court. The attorney presenting an oral argument may speak no longer than 30 minutes and may not read the oral argument. The rule says, "The Court looks with disfavor on any oral argument that is read from a prepared text." There are rules on the format, content, and length of certain documents involved in Court proceedings. For example, Rule 33 says that a lawyer's brief, submitted to the Court in advance of the oral argument in a case, must not be more than 50 typeset pages in length. Rule 34 specifies the contents and format of a brief and states, "Briefs must be compact, logically arranged with proper headings, concise, and free from burdensome, irrelevant, immaterial, or scandalous matter." One group of rules specifies the duties of the Court's officers, such as the clerk, librarian, and reporter of decisions. Another category of rules pertains to the Court's jurisdiction, or the types of cases it has the authority to review and hear. As of 2001, there were 48 rules of the Court.

Rutledge, John

ASSOCIATE JUSTICE, 1790–91

CHIEF JUSTICE (UNCON-FIRMED), 1795

☆ *Born: Sept. 1739, Charleston, S.C.*
☆ *Education: privately tutored at home; studied law at the Middle Temple, London*
☆ *Other government service: South Carolina Commons House of Assem-*

bly, 1761–76; attorney general of South Carolina, 1764–65; Stamp Act Congress, 1765; Continental Congress, 1774–76, 1776–78; governor of South Carolina, 1779–82; judge of the Court of Chancery of South Carolina, 1784–91; chief, South Carolina delegation to the Constitutional Convention, 1787; South Carolina Ratifying Convention, 1788; chief justice, South Carolina Court of Common Pleas, 1791

☆ *Appointed by President George Washington to be an associate justice Sept. 24, 1789, as one of the original members of the U.S. Supreme Court; appointed by Washington as a recess appointment July 1, 1795, to be chief justice; replaced Chief Justice John Jay, who resigned*

☆ *Supreme Court term: confirmed by the Senate as an associate justice Sept. 26, 1789, by a voice vote; resigned Mar. 5, 1791; sworn in as recess appointment to position of chief justice Aug. 12, 1795; the Senate rejected his appointment as chief justice by a vote of 14 to 10 and his service was terminated on Dec. 15, 1795*

☆ *Died: June 21, 1800, Charleston, S.C.*

JOHN RUTLEDGE was one of the founders of the United States. He was a member of the Continental Congress and the Constitutional Convention of 1787. He was also a member of the committee that wrote the first constitution of South Carolina in 1776.

In 1789 President George Washington appointed Rutledge to be one of the original associate justices of the U.S. Supreme Court. Rutledge resigned in 1791, having written no opinions for the Supreme Court. He left the Supreme Court to become chief justice of South Carolina, which at that time was considered a more important position.

In 1795 President Washington appointed Rutledge to replace John Jay as chief justice of the United States. Jay had resigned to become governor of New York. Rutledge presided over the Court (without Senate confirmation) from August 12 to December 15, 1795, while the

Congress was in recess. However, the Senate refused to confirm his nomination because of political disagreements with Rutledge, who had spoken publicly against a treaty negotiated by John Jay with the British government. The Senate had ratified the Jay Treaty in 1794 and many members were angered by Rutledge's promotion of public criticism of the Senate about the matter. So President Washington named Oliver Ellsworth to be the chief justice, and the Senate confirmed this appointment.

Rutledge was so shaken by the Senate's rejection of his nomination that he tried to drown himself. He recovered from this suicide attempt but spent the rest of his life in seclusion. He died at the age of 60 in Charleston, South Carolina.

SEE ALSO
Rejection of Supreme Court nominees

Rutledge, Wiley B.

ASSOCIATE JUSTICE, 1943–49

☆ *Born: July 20, 1894, Cloverport, Ky.*
☆ *Education: University of Wisconsin, B.A., 1914; University of Colorado, LL.B., 1922*
☆ *Previous government service: judge, U.S. Court of Appeals for the District of Columbia, 1939–43*
☆ *Appointed by President Franklin D. Roosevelt Jan. 11, 1943; replaced James F. Byrnes, who resigned*
☆ *Supreme Court term: confirmed by the Senate Feb. 8, 1943, by a voice vote; served until Sept. 10, 1949*
☆ *Died: Sept. 10, 1949, York, Maine*

WILEY B. RUTLEDGE was a strong supporter of President Franklin Roosevelt's New Deal. As dean of the University of Iowa Law School, Rutledge spoke against the Supreme Court majority that opposed President Roosevelt's policies in key Court cases. The President rewarded Rutledge with an appointment to the U.S. Court of Appeals for the District of Columbia. As an appellate court judge, Rutledge consistently supported the President's New Deal. When James F. Byrnes retired from the Court in 1942, President Roosevelt picked Rutledge to replace him.

During his six years on the Court, Justice Rutledge was a strong defender of 1st Amendment freedoms. His only lapses from this position were his votes with the majority in the Japanese-American internment cases of World War II (e.g., *Korematsu* v. *United States* and *Hirabayashi* v. *United States*), in which he supported the government's right to detain Japanese Americans on the basis that they might be a threat to national security.

FURTHER READING
Harper, Fowler. *Justice Rutledge and the Bright Constellation.* Indianapolis: Bobbs-Merrill, 1965.

San Antonio Independent School District v. Rodriguez

☆ *411 U.S. 1 (1973)*
☆ *Vote: 5–4*
☆ *For the Court: Powell*
☆ *Concurring: Stewart*
☆ *Dissenting: Douglas, Brennan, White, and Marshall*

DEMETRIO RODRIGUEZ was a Mexican American living in San Antonio, Texas. His children, along with many other Mexican-American students, attended the Edgewood Independent Schools. Rodriguez and other Mexican-American parents were upset about the poor educational facilities and programs provided in their school district. They believed that public funds for schools were administered unfairly in Texas. It seemed to them that school districts with mostly higher-income families received more resources than those with mostly Mexican-American students or students of lower economic status.

Demetrio Rodriguez complained to leaders of the Mexican American Legal Defense and Education Fund (MALDEF) about unequal funding of Texas schools that deprived the Mexican-American students and other students from low-income families of fair educational opportunities. MALDEF filed suit against Texas on behalf of Rodriguez and several other San Antonio parents. The suit charged that the Texas system for financing schools was unconstitutional because it violated the "equal protection of the laws" provision of the 14th Amendment.

The Issue MALDEF argued that a high-quality education is a fundamental constitutional right of individuals. This right, acording to MALDEF, was denied to Mexican-American children and others from low-income families who were required to attend public schools with few resources and poor facilities. At fault was the Texas school finance system, which distributed funds unequally —providing much more for some public schools than others. Was this system, as MALDEF claimed, a violation of the 14th Amendment?

Opinion of the Court The right to an education, the Court decided, is not a fundamental right guaranteed by the Constitution. Justice Lewis Powell wrote, "[A]t least where wealth is concerned the Equal Protection Clause does not require absolute equality or precisely equal advantages. So, the Texas system for financing public schools does not violate the Fourteenth Amendment."

Dissent Justice Thurgood Marshall disagreed with the Supreme Court's opinion. He wrote, "[T]he majority's holding can only be seen as a retreat from our historic commitment to equality of educational opportunity and as unsupportable acquiescence in a system which deprives children in their earliest years of the chance to reach their full potential as citizens."

Significance The *Rodriguez* decision seemed to impede attempts to fundamentally reform distribution of funds to public schools within a state. The Court appeared to validate state funding systems designed to maintain grossly unequal and unfair distributions of resources to public schools. Since the *Rodriguez* decision, however, several states have decided, without the coercion of a U.S. Supreme Court decision, to reform and equalize their school funding systems.

Sanford, Edward Terry

ASSOCIATE JUSTICE, 1923–30

☆ *Born: July 23, 1865, Knoxville, Tenn.*
☆ *Education: University of Tennessee, B.A., 1883; Harvard, A.B., 1884, M.A., 1889; Harvard Law School, LL.B., 1889*
☆ *Previous government service: special assistant to the U.S. attorney general, 1906–7; assistant U.S. attorney general, 1907–8; federal judge, U.S. District Court for the Middle and Eastern Districts of Tennessee, 1908–23*
☆ *Appointed by President Warren G. Harding Jan. 24, 1923; replaced Mahlon Pitney, who retired*
☆ *Supreme Court term: confirmed by the Senate Jan. 29, 1923, by a voice vote; served until Mar. 8, 1930*
☆ *Died: Mar. 8, 1930, Washington, D.C.*

EDWARD TERRY SANFORD served only seven years on the Supreme Court, after 15 years of service as a federal district judge in Tennessee. His one notable achievement came in the area of constitutional rights. Writing for the Court in *Gitlow* v. *New York* (1925), Justice

Sanford denied free speech and press rights to a publisher who advocated violent overthrow of the government. However, he also wrote that the 1st Amendment freedoms of speech and press "are among the fundamental personal rights and liberties protected by the due process clause of the Fourteenth Amendment from impairment by the states."

Two years later, in *Fiske* v. *Kansas* (1927), Justice Sanford wrote the opinion for the Court when it overturned, for the first time, a state law on grounds that it violated the 1st and 14th Amendments to the Constitution in denying an individual his freedom of speech. Thus, Justice Sanford laid the foundation for the later Court decisions to "incorporate" most of the Bill of Rights into the due process clause of the 14th Amendment, thereby prohibiting state governments from violating the Bill of Rights.

SEE ALSO

Gitlow v. New York; Incorporation doctrine

Santa Clara County v. Southern Pacific Railroad Co.

☆ *118 U.S. 394 (1886)*
☆ *Vote: 9–0*
☆ *For the Court: Harlan*

THE STATE of California tried to collect taxes owed by the Southern Pacific and Central Pacific railroads. Advocates for the railroad companies claimed that the due process clause of the 14th Amendment made the state tax levy against them unconstitutional. The 14th Amendment says that no state shall "deprive any person of life, liberty, or property without due process of law." The railroad company advocates argued that

the state tax levy was an unconstitutional denial of their rights to property.

The Issue Was a corporation protected against state interference with its rights in the same way that a person was protected? If not, the California taxes on the railroads should be enforced. If so, the taxes could be declared invalid.

Opinion of the Court The Court did not directly address the 14th Amendment issue in its opinion. Indeed, Chief Justice Morrison Waite announced, even before the Court heard oral arguments, that the Court would not deal with the question of "whether the provision in the Fourteenth Amendment to the Constitution which forbade a state to deny to any person within its jurisdiction the equal protection of the Constitution, applied to these corporations. We are all of the opinion that it does."

Having established that the Court would apply the 14th Amendment protection of constitutional rights to corporations in the same way as it did to individuals, the Court focused on the narrow issue of whether the state of California could tax fences on the railroad companies' property. The Court decided against the state of California, ruling that the state tax law was a violation of the 14th Amendment due process rights of the corporation, defined by the Court as a person.

Significance Corporations were established in constitutional law as "persons" within the meaning of the 14th

When the Southern Pacific Railroad Company objected to taxes imposed by the state of California, the Court sided with the railroad. It ruled that the company had the same rights to liberty and property as a person.

Amendment. By using the due process guarantees of the 14th Amendment, corporation lawyers were able to protect businesses from many kinds of state government regulations put forward in behalf of the public good. This view of corporations as persons protected by the 14th Amendment was not fully overturned until the 1930s. In *West Coast Hotel Co. v. Parrish* (1937), for example, the Court upheld a state law regulating wages of women workers of a private business. The Court refused to protect the rights of the business as a person under the 14th Amendment.

SEE ALSO

West Coast Hotel Co. v. Parrish

Scalia, Antonin

ASSOCIATE JUSTICE,
1986–

☆ *Born: Mar. 11, 1936, Trenton, N.J.*
☆ *Education: Georgetown University, B.A., 1957; Harvard Law School, LL.B., 1960*
☆ *Previous government service: general counsel, White House Office of Tele-communications Policy, 1971–72; chairman, Administrative Conference of the United States, 1972–74; assistant U.S. attorney general, Office of Legal Counsel, 1974–77; judge, U.S. Court of Appeals for the District of Columbia Circuit, 1982–86*
☆ *Appointed by President Ronald Reagan June 24, 1986; replaced William H. Rehnquist, who became chief justice*
☆ *Supreme Court term: confirmed by the Senate Sept. 17, 1986, by a 98–0 vote*

ANTONIN SCALIA is the first American of Italian ancestry to become a Supreme Court Justice. He is one of seven children of Eugene and Catherine Scalia, who came to the United States from Italy. Scalia is the first Roman Catholic to be appointed to the Court since William Brennan in 1957.

Justice Scalia has been a strong force on the Court in decisions protecting the constitutional rights of individuals and demanding equal protection of the laws. He has also favored government regulations that protect the safety and security of the community, even if this would mean limitations on the rights of certain individuals. For example, he wrote the opinion for the Court in *Vernonia School District* v. *Acton* (1995), which permitted a drug-testing program for student athletes and restricted, in the context of school, their 4th Amendment rights to freedom from unreasonable searches and seizures.

Scalia often argues for an "original intent" method of interpreting the Constitution. For example, in cases about individual rights, he urges reliance on the intentions of the Constitution's framers as guides to the Court's decisions.

SEE ALSO

Vernonia School District v. Acton

FURTHER READING

Brisbin, Richard A., Jr. *Justice Antonin Scalia and the Conservative Revival.* Baltimore, Md.: Johns Hopkins University Press, 1997.
Schultz, David, and Christopher E. Smith. *The Jurisprudential Vision of Justice Antonin Scalia.* Lanham, Md.: Rowman & Littlefield, 1996.

Schechter Poultry Corp. v. United States

☆ *295 U.S. 495 (1935)*
☆ *Vote: 9–0*
☆ *For the Court: Hughes*

DURING THE early 1930s President Franklin D. Roosevelt fought the Great Depression by proposing many economic recovery programs. The centerpiece of his efforts was the National Industrial Recovery Act (NIRA) of 1933, managed

by the National Recovery Administration (NRA).

Under that law, Congress granted the President authority to approve codes of fair competition for different industries. Drawn up by trade and industry groups themselves, each of these codes included standards of minimum wages and maximum hours of work. Presidential approval of the code for an industry gave that code the force of law.

By 1935 many industries had started to ignore the NIRA. The government decided to bring a test case before the Supreme Court in the hope that a ruling in favor of NIRA codes would encourage industries to accept the codes.

A case involving four brothers who ran a poultry business became a key test of Roosevelt's program. The Schechters bought live poultry outside New York State and sold it in New York City. The government convicted the brothers of violating several provisions of the NIRA live poultry code in order to keep their prices below those of competitors. Prosecutors also charged them with selling thousands of pounds of diseased chickens to a local butcher. The Schechters appealed to the Supreme Court. The press called the suit the "sick chicken case."

The Issue   The case involved three questions: Did the economic crisis facing the nation justify resorting to the NIRA? Did the Constitution allow Congress to delegate so much power to the President? And did the law come under Congress's

power to regulate interstate commerce?

Opinion of the Court   The NIRA lost on all counts. The Supreme Court ruled that the economic problems of the nation did not justify the NIRA. Chief Justice Charles Evans Hughes wrote that "extraordinary conditions do not create or enlarge constitutional power."

Second, the Court said that under the Constitution only Congress has the power to make laws. If Congress wanted to delegate any of this power to the President, it had to set clear standards to guide the executive branch in making detailed applications of the general law. The NIRA was unconstitutional because, in effect, it gave trade and industry groups unregulated power to create any laws they wanted.

Finally, the Court recognized that although the Schechters bought their poultry in many states, they processed and sold it only in New York. Thus, the Schechters' operation was a local concern not directly affecting interstate commerce, and so it was beyond federal control.

Significance   The decision at first appeared to devastate President Roosevelt's New Deal economic recovery program. But by 1937 the Supreme Court began upholding new laws passed to fulfill New Deal objectives. The National Labor Relations Act of 1935, for example, was upheld by the Court in *National Labor Relations Board* v. *Jones & Laughlin Steel Corp.* (1937).

The *Schechter* case established the principle that in domestic affairs Congress may not delegate broad legislative powers to the President without also outlining clear standards to guide the President in employing these powers. This principle stands today.

FURTHER READING
Freidel, Frank. "The Sick Chicken Case." In *Quarrels That Have Shaped the Constitution*, edited by John A. Garraty. New York: Harper & Row, 1987.

Schenck v. United States

☆ *249 U.S. 47 (1919)*
☆ *Vote: 9–0*
☆ *For the Court: Holmes*

DURING WORLD WAR I, Congress passed the Espionage Act of 1917. This law made it illegal to encourage insubordination in the armed forces or to use the mails to distribute materials urging resistance to the government.

Charles Schenck, general secretary of the Socialist party in the United States, was an outspoken critic of America's role in the war. Schenck printed and mailed about 15,000 leaflets to men eligible for the draft. The leaflets denounced the draft as involuntary servitude (slavery) and therefore a violation of the 13th Amendment. The pamphlets also argued that participation in World War I did not serve the best interests of the American people.

Schenck was arrested and convicted of violating the Espionage Act of 1917. At his trial, Schenck claimed his 1st Amendment right to free speech had been violated. The 1st Amendment states: "Congress shall make no law... abridging the freedom of speech, or of the press."

The Issue Did the Espionage Act of 1917, under which Schenck was arrested, violate the 1st Amendment protection of free speech? The *Schenck* case also posed a larger question about potential limitations on free speech. For the first time in its history, the Supreme Court faced directly the question of whether the government might limit speech under special circumstances.

Opinion of the Court The Court decided against Schenck, ruling that the Espionage Act of 1917 did not violate the 1st Amendment rights of free speech and free press.

Justice Oliver Wendell Holmes wrote the Court's opinion. He set forth a test to determine when government might limit free speech. Holmes said, "The most stringent protection of free speech would not protect a man in falsely shouting fire in a theatre and causing a panic." When spoken or written words "create a clear and present danger" of bringing about evils that Congress has the authority to prevent, the government may limit speech.

Holmes reasoned that during peacetime the 1st Amendment would have protected Schenck's ideas. During a wartime emergency, however, urging men to resist the draft presented a "clear and present danger" to the nation. Holmes declared: "When a nation is at war, many things that might be said in time of peace are such a hindrance to its efforts that their utterance will not be... protected by any constitutional right."

Significance The *Schenck* decision established important precedents. First, it set up the "clear and present danger" test. This formula was applied to many subsequent free speech cases. In addition, the decision announced that certain speech may be permissible in peacetime but not in wartime. Thus, the *Schenck* case established that the 1st Amendment protection of free speech is not an absolute guarantee. Under conditions such as those Holmes described, the government may constrain speech.

Police in Cambridge, Massachusetts, load communist propaganda into a wagon in 1919. That year the Supreme Court upheld the conviction of Charles Schenck, who had been arrested for distributing Socialist party leaflets criticizing the U.S. role in World War I.

Later, in another free speech case, *Abrams* v. *United States,* 1919, Holmes wrote a dissenting opinion that modified the "clear and present danger" test set forth in *Schenck*. In his *Abrams* dissent, Holmes emphasized that a "clear and present danger" must be directly connected to specific actions that would bring about evil consequences. If the imminent danger could not be demonstrated, then speech could not be lawfully limited. In the 1950s and 1960s, the modified version of Holmes's "clear and present danger" test prevailed in the Court's opinions. In *Yates* v. *United States* (1957), for example, the Court protected the freedom of expression of Communist party members. And in *Brandenburg* v. *Ohio* (1969), the Court protected free speech by a racist Ku Klux Klan leader.

SEE ALSO

Abrams v. United States; Brandenburg v. Ohio; Freedom of speech and press; Seditious libel; Yates v. United Staes

Scott v. Sandford

☆ *19 How. 393 (1857)*
☆ *Vote: 7–2*
☆ *For the Court: Taney*
☆ *Dissenting: Curtis and McLean*

WHEN THE Constitution was written in 1787, it permitted slavery. Many of the framers owned slaves; others opposed slavery. During the Constitutional Convention they hotly debated the issue of how to deal with slavery, and the problem continued to plague the new nation. By the 1850s some states had forbidden slavery, while others still protected it.

In 1854 Dred Scott, a slave, was taken by his master to Rock Island, Illinois, a town in a free state. His master later took him to the Wisconsin Territory (an area that is now part of Minnesota), where the Missouri Compromise of 1820, a federal law, had forbidden slavery. His master then brought Scott back to Missouri, a slave state. Scott brought suit against his master, claiming that he was a free man because he had resided in areas that had banned slavery.

The Issue The case involved three issues: (1) Scott had lived in the free state of Illinois. Had he become free while living there? Should Missouri have to recognize that freedom? (2) Scott had traveled to a federal territory that Congress had declared a free territory in the Missouri Compromise of 1820. Had he become free while living there, and should Missouri have to recognize that freedom? (3) Did the Supreme Court have the jurisdiction, or power, to hear this case?

Scott claimed that his master had freed him by taking him to Illinois, where slavery was not allowed. Therefore, any slave taken there became free. Once Scott became free in Illinois, no Missouri law could turn him into a slave again. Scott's lawyers further argued that Missouri must recognize the laws of any other state in the Union.

Scott also claimed that he was free under the Missouri Compromise. Passed by Congress and recognized as the law of the land since 1820, the Missouri Compromise prohibited slavery in all the federal territories north of Missouri. When Scott's master took him to Fort Snelling in the Wisconsin Territory, Scott had also become free there. Even if Missouri chose not to recognize the laws of Illinois, the Constitution required all states to recognize the laws of Congress, as the supremacy clause of the Constitution (Article 6, Clause 2) clearly stated.

Finally, Scott's lawyers argued that

When Dred Scott, a slave, sued for his freedom because he had traveled with his owner to a state that banned slavery, the Supreme Court denied his claim and stated that black people, whether enslaved or free, had no rights as citizens.

the Supreme Court did have the power to hear this case. Article 3, Section 2, of the Constitution established the jurisdiction, the authority to hear cases, of the federal courts. This jurisdiction extended to cases "between citizens of different states." Scott's master was now dead, leaving Scott technically under the control of his dead master's brother-in-law, John F. A. Sanford, who lived in New York. (The case is called *Scott* v. *Sandford* because a court clerk misspelled the name of the defendant.) Scott claimed that if he was free, then he had to be a citizen of Missouri. As such, he could sue a citizen of New York in federal court.

Opinion of the Court The Supreme Court ruled against Scott on all three issues. In an extraordinary decision, all nine judges wrote opinions that totaled 248 pages. Chief Justice Roger B. Taney's 55-page opinion of the court expressed the collective view of the majority.

Taney first argued that Scott could not sue in a federal court because he was not a citizen of the United States. Taney said that no black person, slave or free, could be a citizen. Taney wrote, "The question is simply this: Can a negro, whose ancestors were imported into this country and sold as slaves, become a member of the political community formed and brought into existence by the Constitution of the United States?" Taney answered his own question: "We think they are not... included, and were not intended to be included, under the word 'citizens' in the Constitution." Rather, Taney asserted that at the time the Constitution was written, blacks were "considered as a subordinate and inferior class of beings, who had been subjugated by the dominant race, and whether emancipated or not... had no rights or privileges but such as those who held the power and the Government might choose to grant them."

Having concluded that Scott had no right to sue in a federal court, Taney might have stopped. However, the issue of slavery in the federal territories was an important political question, and Taney wanted to let the nation know where the Court stood on it. So he examined Scott's other claims.

The Court easily disposed of the claim to freedom based on Illinois law. Taney held that Scott lost whatever claim to freedom he had while in Illinois when he left the state, and no law or precedent obligated Missouri to enforce the Illinois law.

Scott's claim based on the Missouri Compromise presented more complications. Considering the Missouri Compromise, passed by Congress in 1820, as the law of the land would obligate the state of Missouri to recognize it. Taney, however, decided that the ban on slavery in the Missouri Compromise was unconstitutional. He reasoned that the territories belonged to all the citizens of the United States. Under the Constitution's 5th Amendment, no one could deprive a person of his property without "due process of law" and "just compensation." But the Missouri Compromise would deprive men like Scott's owner of their property simply for entering federal territories. Thus, the Court held that the Missouri Compromise was unconstitutional. For only the second time, the Supreme Court declared an act of Congress unconstitutional. This power of judicial review of acts of Congress had first been used by the Court in *Marbury v. Madison* (1803)

Dissent In a 69-page dissent, Justice Benjamin R. Curtis took Taney to task at every point. Curtis pointed out that at the time of the ratification of the Constitution blacks voted in a number of states, including Massachusetts, New Hampshire, and New York. Thus, Curtis argued, free blacks had always been citizens in the nation, and if Scott was free the Court had jurisdiction to hear his case. Curtis also argued in favor of the constitutionality of the Missouri Compromise, which he pointed out had existed as accepted law for more than three decades and served as the basis of the sectional understanding that had kept the North and South together in one Union.

Significance Taney had hoped to settle the issue of slavery in the territories through the *Scott* verdict. Instead, Taney's decision itself became a political issue. Abraham Lincoln and Stephen A. Douglas argued over its merits in their famous debates of 1858. Instead of lessening sectional tensions, Taney's decision exacerbated them and helped bring on the Civil War.

When the Civil War was finally over, the 13th Amendment (1865) ended slavery. The 14th Amendment (1868) gave blacks citizenship. Thus, by amending the Constitution, the people overturned the *Scott* decision.

SEE ALSO
Jurisdiction

FURTHER READING

Fehrenbacher, Don E. *The Dred Scott Case: Its Significance in American Law and Politics.* New York: Oxford University Press, 1978.

Fehrenbacher, Don E. "The Dred Scott Case." In *Quarrels That Have Shaped the Constitution,* edited by John A. Garraty. New York: Harper & Row, 1987.

Finkelman, Paul. *Dred Scott v. Sandford: A Brief History with Documents.* Boston: Bedford Books, 1997.

Searches and seizures

THE 4TH AMENDMENT to the U.S. Constitution says, "The right of the people to be secure in their persons, houses, papers, and effects, against unreasonable searches and seizures, shall not be violated, and no Warrants shall

issue, but upon probable cause, supported by Oath or affirmation, and particularly describing the place to be searched, and the persons or things to be seized."

An agent of the Drug Enforcement Agency aims at a suspect in a car. The Supreme Court has ruled that police can search a car without a warrant.

The principle in the 4th Amendment is clear: the privacy of the individual is protected against arbitrary intrusion by agents of the government. In 1949 Justice Felix Frankfurter wrote (*Wolf* v. *Colorado*): "The security of one's privacy against arbitrary intrusion by the police is basic to a free society. The knock at the door, whether by day or by night, as a prelude to a search, without authority of law but solely on the authority of the police, did not need the commentary of recent history to be condemned as inconsistent with the conception of human rights enshrined in the history and the basic constitutional documents of English-speaking peoples."

The 4th Amendment protection against unreasonable searches and seizures is reinforced by the clause that requires a warrant, or court authorization, for such searches and seizures. A warrant should not be issued, of course, unless there is a finding of "probable cause" by a neutral magistrate or judge.

The 4th Amendment principle of personal security against unlawful intrusion is clear enough. But the exact meaning of the key phrases and their precise application in specific cases requires interpretation and judgment—the duties of the federal courts. What constitutes "unreasonable searches and seizures"? What exactly is the meaning of "probable

THE EVOLUTION OF 4TH AMENDMENT RIGHTS

Weeks **v.** *United States* (1914) A person may require that evidence obtained in a search shall be excluded from use against him in a federal court if the evidence was seized illegally—without probable cause or a search warrant.

Carroll **v.** *United States* (1925) Federal agents can conduct searches of automobiles without a warrant whenever they have a reasonable suspicion of illegal actions.

Olmstead **v.** *United States* (1928) Wiretaps by federal agents are permissible where no entry of private premises has occurred.

Wolf **v.** *Colorado* (1949) The 4th Amendment protections apply to searches by state officials as well as federal agents. However, state judges are not required to exclude evidence obtained by searches in violation of 4th Amendment rights.

Mapp **v.** *Ohio* (1961) Evidence obtained in violation of 4th Amendment rights must be excluded from use in state and federal trials.

Katz **v.** *United States* (1967) Electronic surveillance and wiretapping are within the scope of the 4th Amendment because it protects whatever an individual wants to preserve as private, including conversations and behavior, even in a place open to the public.

Terry **v.** *Ohio* (1968) The police may stop and frisk, or search, a suspect's outer clothing for dangerous weapons without first obtaining a warrant if they suspect that a crime is about to be committed.

Chimel **v.** *California* (1969) Police may search without a warrant only the immediate area around the suspect from which he could obtain a weapon or destroy evidence. But a person's entire dwelling cannot be searched merely because he is arrested there.

Marshall **v.** *Barlow's, Inc.* (1978) Federal laws cannot provide for warrantless inspections of businesses that are otherwise legally regulated by a federal agency. A federal inspector must obtain a search warrant when the owner of the business to be inspected objects to a warrantless search.

United States **v.** *Ross* (1982) Police officers may search an entire vehicle they have stopped without obtaining a warrant if they have probable cause to suspect that drugs or other contraband is in the vehicle.

United States **v.** *Leon* (1984) Evidence seized on the basis of a mistakenly issued search warrant can be introduced in a trial if the warrant was issued in good faith— that is, on presumption that there were valid grounds for issuing the warrant.

New Jersey **v.** *T.L.O.* (1985) School officials do not need a search warrant or probable cause to conduct a reasonable search of a student. The school officials may search a student if there are reasonable grounds for suspecting that the search will uncover evidence that the student has violated or is violating either the law or the rules of the school.

California **v.** *Greenwood* (1988) The police may search through garbage bags and other trash containers that people leave outside their houses in order to obtain evidence of criminal activity. This evidence may subsequently be used as the basis for obtaining a warrant to search a person's house.

Michigan **v.** *Sitz* (1990) The police may stop automobiles at roadside checkpoints and examine the drivers for signs of intoxication. Evidence obtained in this manner may be used to bring criminal charges against the driver.

Minnesota **v.** *Dickerson* (1993) Police do not need a warrant to seize narcotics that were found when frisking or quickly searching a suspect for concealed weapons. Evidence seized in this way can be used to bring criminal charges against a suspect.

(continued)

THE EVOLUTION OF 4TH AMENDMENT RIGHTS *(continued)*

Vernonia School District v. *Acton* (1995) Public school officials may carry out a policy of drug testing for students involved in interschool athletic programs.

Wilson v. *Arkansas* (1995) Police must announce themselves before entering a premises. If the knock-and-announce rule is violated, then an otherwise warranted search is invalidated.

Chandler v. *Miller* (1997) State laws cannot require candidates for public offices to be tested for drugs. This requirement constitutes an unreasonable search.

Maryland v. *Wilson* (1997) When making a traffic stop, police may order a passenger as well as a driver out of the vehicle without requiring either probable cause or reasonable suspicion.

Illinois v. *Wardlow* (2000) Unprovoked flight by a suspect at the mere sight of a police officer may, in the context of other compelling factors, provide the "reasonable suspicion" necessary to justify a "stop and frisk" search of the person.

Bond v. *United States* (2000) Without "reasonable suspicion" of illegal behavior, law enforcement officers cannot move down the aisle of a bus and squeeze baggage stored in overhead racks to find out if any contain illegal contents. Such behavior violates a passenger's 4th Amendment rights.

cause"? Are there any situations that justify a warrantless search by government officials? If so, what are they, and what are the justifications?

In making judgments about 4th Amendment rights, the federal courts attempt to balance liberty and order—the rights of the individual to freedom from tyranny and the needs of the community for stability, security, and safety. Judges must decide when to provide more or less latitude for the rights of individuals suspected of criminal behavior.

The Supreme Court ruled on what is "unreasonable" in *Weeks* v. *United States* (1914). Evidence seized illegally by federal government agents—without probable cause or a search warrant— must be excluded from a defendant's trial, according to the Court. This exclusionary rule applied, however, only to federal government officials. The Court did not establish the exclusionary rule as a limitation on state governments until 1961, in *Mapp* v. *Ohio*.

The Supreme Court established a "good faith" exception to the exclusionary rule in *United States* v. *Leon* (1984). The Court ruled that evidence seized as the result of a mistakenly issued search warrant can be used in a trial as long as the warrant was issued on good faith that there was probable cause for issuing it.

Judges, not law enforcement officers, are supposed to determine whether or not there is probable cause for issuing a search warrant. Evidence seized by police with a valid search warrant can, of course, be used against the defendant in a trial. There are, however, exceptions to the requirement of a warrant to justify a search and seizure of evidence. The Supreme Court ruled, for example, in *Terry* v. *Ohio* (1968) that police may stop and search a suspect's outer clothing for a gun or other weapons without a warrant if they suspect a crime is about to be committed. Further, police may stop and search automobiles without first obtaining a warrant if they have a reasonable suspicion that illegal goods are inside or that illegal actions are about to take place.

The above table of cases on 4th Amendment rights demonstrates the evolution of constitutional rights in the 20th century. As it shows, the incorporation of the 4th Amendment into the due process clause of the 14th Amendment did not occur until 1949, in the case of *Wolf* v. *Colorado*. Since that time, however, most of the 4th Amendment cases have involved actions at the state level of government. On balance, decisions in these cases have gradually enhanced the rights of individuals against the power of government.

SEE ALSO

Bill of Rights; Exclusionary rule; Incorporation doctrine; Katz v. United States; Mapp v. Ohio; New Jersey v. T.L.O.; Olmstead v. United States; Probable cause; Terry v. Ohio; United States v. Leon; United States v. Ross; Weeks v. United States; Wolf v. Colorado

Seditious libel

SEDITIOUS LIBEL is the crime of making public statements that threaten to undermine respect for the government, laws, or public officials. The Sedition Act of 1798 made it a crime to criticize, ridicule, or erode the authority of the federal government, the President, or other federal officials. This law was used by government officials to prosecute members of the Republican party, headed by Thomas Jefferson, who were rivals to the ruling Federalist party, headed by President John Adams. After Jefferson's victory in the Presidential election of 1800, the Sedition Act of 1798 was allowed to expire.

Controversy about seditious libel emerged during World War I, with passage of the Sedition Act of 1918. In *Abrams* v. *United States* (1919) the court upheld the federal government's use of this law to convict Jacob Abrams of distributing leaflets that severely criticized President Woodrow Wilson and the U.S. government. The Court's decision in *Abrams* was based on the "clear and present danger" test stated by Justice Oliver Wendell Holmes in *Schenck* v. *United States* (1919). Justice Holmes,

however, wrote a stinging dissent against the Court's use of the "clear and present danger" test in *Abrams* to limit freedom of speech and press. Holmes stressed that a "clear and present danger" exists only when speech can be connected immediately and directly to specific acts of lawless behavior threatening the security of the United States. If the imminent danger could not be demonstrated, said Holmes, then speech could not be lawfully limited.

Arguments about the constitutionality of seditious libel laws under the 1st Amendment, however, continued until the 1960s, when the U.S. Supreme Court made landmark decisions about this traditional limitation on freedom of speech and press.

In *New York Times Co.* v. *Sullivan* (1964) the Court ruled against a civil libel suit by a public official who tried to collect damages from critics who had denounced him in a newspaper advertisement. In rejecting the suit, the Court compared it to seditious libel prosecutions undertaken to prevent negative speech about the government. The Court concluded that such efforts to limit freedom of speech and press were not permitted by the U.S. Constitution.

In *Garrison* v. *Louisiana* (1964) the Supreme Court overturned a criminal libel conviction. And in *Brandenburg* v. *Ohio* (1969) the court used ideas from Justice Holmes's dissent in *Abrams* to strike down a state law on seditious libel. Thus, the Court acted against seditious libel prosecutions, civil or criminal, and thereby protected the freedom to criticize or otherwise speak out against government actions or officials.

SEE ALSO

Abrams v. United States; Brandenburg v. Ohio; Freedom of speech and press; New York Times Co. v. Sullivan; Schenck v. United States

The sign in this Atlanta park indicates that by city regulation blacks were allowed to enter only as servants. The Court has ruled that such de jure *segregation is unconstitutional.*

Segregation, de facto and de jure

DE JURE (Latin for "from the law") segregation is the separation of people on the basis of race as required by law. For example, after the Civil War and the ending of slavery by the 13th Amendment to the Constitution (1865), the governments of the former slave states found new ways to discriminate against black Americans. They enacted laws to require separate public facilities for blacks and whites. Blacks were required, for example, to attend separate schools, to use separate public rest rooms, and to use separate public drinking fountains. The separate facilities for blacks were supposed to be equal to the facilities provided for whites. This "separate but equal" doctrine was endorsed by the Supreme Court decision in *Plessy* v. *Ferguson* (1896). In reality, however, the facilities for black people were rarely, if ever, equal in quality to those provided for whites.

Racial separation that exists as a matter of custom rather than as a legal requirement is known as *de facto* (Latin for "in fact") segregation. For example, one neighborhood may include only white families, and another nearby neighborhood may include only black families. However, this racial segregation may have developed informally in response to social and economic factors, not as a requirement of the law.

De jure segregation has been declared unconstitutional by the U.S. Supreme Court. In *Brown* v. *Board of Education* (1954) the Court ruled against de jure racial segregation in public schools. In subsequent cases the Court outlawed racial discrimination in other areas of public life. In 1964 Congress passed the Civil Rights Act, which outlawed de jure segregation.

The Court has ruled in *Milliken* v. *Bradley* (1974) that courts of law can remedy de facto segregation only if it was caused by specific acts of government. In *Washington* v. *Seattle School District No. 1* (1982) the Court upheld voluntary acts by state agencies to overcome de facto segregation.

SEE ALSO

Brown v. Board of Education; Civil rights; Equality under the Constitution; Plessy v. Ferguson

Selection of justices

SEE Appointment of justices; Rejection of Supreme Court nominees

Self-incrimination, privilege against

THE 5TH AMENDMENT to the U.S. Constitution guarantees that "no person ... shall be compelled in any criminal case to be a witness against himself." Thus, a criminal defendant has the right to refuse to answer questions that could result in a conviction for a crime.

The 5th Amendment right to avoid self-incrimination was extended to the states when the U.S. Supreme Court incorporated this right into the due process clause of the 14th Amendment in *Malloy* v. *Hogan* (1964). In *Miranda* v. *Arizona* (1966) the Court required law enforcement officers to inform suspects of their 5th Amendment right to remain silent.

Critics have complained that the Court's decision in the *Miranda* case helps criminals resist prosecution. Justice Arthur Goldberg, however, saw the 5th Amendment as a great guarantee of individual rights. In *Murphy* v. *Waterfront Commission of New York* (1964) Goldberg wrote, "[T]he privilege [of avoiding self-incrimination] while sometimes a shelter to the guilty, is often a protection to the innocent."

SEE ALSO

Incorporation doctrine; Miranda v. Arizona; Rights of the accused

Senate Judiciary Committee

ESTABLISHED IN 1816, the Judiciary Committee is one of the standing, or permanent, committees of the U.S. Senate. In 1868 the Senate directed the Judiciary Committee to examine and screen, for the full Senate, all Presidential nominations to the Supreme Court. Since then, one of the highly visible and very important duties of the committee is its investigations and recommendations about Presidential nominations to the Supreme Court.

The full Senate sends the President's judicial nominations to the Judiciary Committee for review. The committee holds public hearings to consider the merits of each person nominated to fill a vacancy on the Supreme Court. The nominee is invited to appear before the committee to answer questions about his or her background, qualifications, and ideas about law and the U.S. Constitution.

In 1925 Harlan F. Stone became the first nominee to appear before the committee for a hearing. He was subsequently confirmed by the Senate. Since 1955, when John Marshall Harlan II appeared before the Senate Judiciary Committee, all nominees have participated in formal committee hearings.

The committee concludes its hearings on Supreme Court nominations with a vote and a recommendation to the full Senate. The committee's recommendation tends to be decisive. A likely negative committee vote sometimes influences the nominee to withdraw from the process. In 1968 President Lyndon Johnson withdrew his nomination of Abe Fortas for the office of chief justice when it became clear during the confirmation hearings that the Senate Judiciary Committee would vote against Fortas. A negative recommendation sent by the committee to the full Senate for discussion and vote usually ends in the defeat of the nominee.

SEE ALSO

Appointment of justices; Rejection of Supreme Court nominees

Seniority

SENIORITY REFERS to the length of time each justice has served on the Court. Certain rules and procedures of the Court are based on seniority. Only the chief justice is exempt from considerations of seniority.

The senior associate justices, those with the longest periods of service, may choose to occupy the larger chambers, or offices, in the Supreme Court Building. The four senior justices also get the better (more spacious) places around the Court's conference table. The most junior justice

The seating of the justices is arranged by seniority, with the newest justices sitting on the ends.

serves as the doorkeeper during the Court's private conferences. He or she is also the designated receiver and sender of messages during the conferences.

In the Courtroom, the chief justice is seated at the center. The senior associate justice sits to the right of the chief, and the second most senior to his left. The other justices take their places in alternating order of seniority, with the most junior associate justice at the far left of the bench.

During the conferences, the justices speak in order of seniority, from the most senior to the most junior. By speaking first, the senior justices are able to shape the terms of arguments on issues. And, in any case in which the chief justice is not part of the Court's majority, the senior associate justice in the majority has the duty of assigning the writing of the Court's opinion. (If the chief justice is part of the majority, he assigns the writing of the opinion.)

Separate but equal doctrine

IN 1896 in *Plessy* v. *Ferguson*, the Supreme Court ruled that a state law requiring racial segregation in public transportation was constitutional as long as the separate facilities were equal. This "separate but equal" doctrine was used to justify racial segregation in public schools and a wide variety of other public facilities. In 1954 the Court over-

turned the "separate but equal" doctrine in *Brown* v. *Board of Education.*

SEE ALSO

Brown v. Board of Education; Civil rights; Equality under the Constitution; Plessy v. Ferguson; Segregation, de facto and de jure

Separation of powers

SEPARATION OF powers, a major principle of the U.S. Constitution, is the distribution of power among three branches of government: the legislative, the executive, and the judicial. The legislative branch (Congress) has the power, according to Article 1 of the Constitution, to make certain kinds of laws. In Article 2, the Constitution says that the executive branch (headed by the President) has the power to enforce or carry out laws. The judicial branch (headed by the Supreme Court) is established in Article 3 of the Constitution to interpret and apply the law in federal court cases.

Further, legislative power is divided between the two houses of Congress: the Senate and the House of Representatives. Both houses must pass a bill for it to become law.

Separation of powers among the three branches of the federal government is the fundamental constitutional means for achieving limited government and protecting the people against abuses of power. Limited government means that officials cannot act arbitrarily. Rather, they are bound by the higher law of the Constitution, which guides and limits their use of power in order to protect the liberties of the people and prevent tyranny. James Madison summarized this view of the need for separation of powers in *The Federalist* No. 47: "The accumulation of all powers, legislative, executive, and judiciary, in the same hands, whether of one, a few, or many, and whether hereditary, self-appointed, or elected, may justly be pronounced the very definition of tyranny."

In *The Federalist* No. 48, Madison emphasized that the separation of powers in the U.S. Constitution is complemented by a system of checks and balances, whereby one branch can block or check an action of another branch in order to maintain a balance of power in the government. Madison said that unless the separate branches of government "be so far connected and blended [balanced] as to give each a constitutional control [check] over the others the degree of separation... essential to a free government can never in practice be duly maintained."

In this cartoon, the legislative branch marches with President Franklin Roosevelt, representing the executive branch. However, the Supreme Court, headed by Chief Justice Charles Evans Hughes, maintained the separation of powers as it overruled much of Roosevelt's New Deal legislation.

There are many examples of ways that one branch of the government checks the actions of another branch to maintain a balance of powers so that no branch can continually dominate the others. The President, for example, can check Congress by vetoing bills it has passed. But the President's veto can be overturned by a subsequent two-thirds vote of Congress. The President can appoint executive branch officials and federal judges, including justices of the Supreme Court. The Senate, however, must approve these appointments by majority vote. The President is commander in chief of the armed forces. But only Congress can enact legislation to provide funds needed by the armed forces and their commander to carry out missions. The President makes treaties with foreign governments, but the Senate has the power to confirm or reject them.

Additional examples of the checks and balances system are listed in Articles 1, 2, and 3 of the Constitution.

Judicial review

The Supreme Court uses the power of judicial review to check the executive and legislative branches of government and to maintain the separation of powers. This power enables the Court to declare acts of the executive or legislative branches unconstitutional (in violation of some part of the Constitution). Thus, the Court can declare null and void actions of the other branches that exceed or contradict their powers as expressed in the Constitution.

The Court established its power of judicial review of the federal legislative and executive branches in *Marbury* v. *Madison* (1803). Since that time, the Court has exercised the power of judicial review to declare more than 150 acts of Congress and the President unconstitutional. In *Youngstown Sheet & Tube* Co. v. *Sawyer* (1952), for example, the Court ruled that President Harry Truman's use of an executive order to temporarily take control of privately owned steel mills was unconstitutional. Writing for the Court, Justice Hugo Black explained: "In the framework of our Constitution, the President's power to see that the laws are faithfully executed refutes the idea that he is to be a lawmaker. The Constitution limits his functions in the lawmaking process to the recommending of laws he thinks wise and the vetoing of laws he thinks bad."

In *Clinton* v. *City of New York* (1998) the Court struck down the Line Item Veto Act, which Congress had passed and President Bill Clinton had signed in 1996. This federal statute gave the President the power to "cancel" an item in an appropriations bill passed by Congress and of which he otherwise approved. Clinton's use of the line-item veto was challenged by some members of Congress who protested when he used it to veto their projects. The Court ruled that the law at issue violated Article 1, Section 7, of the Constitution. The principle of the separation of powers was maintained against an act to extend the chief executive's power into an area of government reserved by the Constitution for Congress.

As the preceding examples indicate, each branch of the government has some influence over the actions of the others, but no branch can exercise its powers without cooperation from the others. Each branch has some say in the work of the others as a way to check and limit the power of the others, but no branch may encroach unconstitutionally upon the domains of the other branches.

In this system of separation of powers, with its checks and balances, no branch of the government can accumulate too much power. But each branch, and the government generally, is supposed to have enough power to do what the people expect of it. So the government is supposed to be both limited and strong; neither too strong for the liberty of the people nor too limited to be effective in maintaining order, stability, and security for the people. This is the theory of separation of powers as a means to a limited but effective government.

Justice Louis D. Brandeis nicely summed up the founders' purposes and reasons for separation of powers in a dissenting opinion in *Myers* v. *United States* (1926): "The doctrine of the separation of powers was adopted by the Convention of 1787, not to promote efficiency but to preclude the exercise of arbitrary power. The purpose was not to avoid friction but, by means of the inevitable friction incident to the distribution of the governmental powers among three departments, to save the people from autocracy."

SEE ALSO

Constitutional democracy; Constitutionalism; Federalist, The; Impeachment; Independent judiciary; Judicial activism and judicial restraint; Judicial power; Judicial review; Marbury v. Madison; Reversals of Supreme Court decisions; Youngstown Sheet & Tube Co. v. Sawyer

FURTHER READING

Carey, George. *The Federalist: Design for a Constitutional Republic.* Urbana: University of Illinois Press, 1991.
Diamond, Martin. *The Founding of the Democratic Republic.* Itasca, Ill.: F. E. Peacock, 1981.
Fisher, Louis. *Constitutional Conflicts between Congress and the President.* Princeton, N.J.: Princeton University Press, 1985.
Fisher, Louis. *Constitutional Dialogues.* Princeton, N.J.: Princeton University Press, 1988.
Pious, Richard M. "A Prime Minister for America." *Constitution* 4, no. 3 (Fall 1992): 4–14.
Vile, M. J. C. *Constitutionalism and the Separation of Powers.* New York: Oxford University Press, 1967.

Seriatim opinions

SERIATIM is the Latin word for "severally," or "in a series." When appellate court judges render seriatim opinions, each one presents a separate judgment on a case; no one writes an opinion for the court as a whole. From its origin until 1803, the U.S. Supreme Court followed the practice of writing seriatim opinions. But under Chief Justice John Marshall this practice stopped and the Court began the practice, which is nearly always employed today, of having one justice write a majority opinion for each case decided by the Court.

SEE ALSO

Concurring opinion; Dissenting opinion; Majority opinion; Opinions; Plurality opinion

Shiras, George, Jr.

ASSOCIATE JUSTICE, 1892–1903

☆ *Born: Jan. 26, 1832, Pittsburgh, Pa.*
☆ *Education: Ohio University, 1849–51; Yale College, B.A., 1853; studied law at Yale and privately*
☆ *Previous government service: none*
☆ *Appointed by President Benjamin Harrison July 19, 1892; replaced Joseph P. Bradley, who died*
☆ *Supreme Court term: confirmed by the Senate July 26, 1892, by a voice vote; retired Feb. 23, 1903*
☆ *Died: Aug. 2, 1924, Pittsburgh, Pa.*

GEORGE SHIRAS, JR., was a successful lawyer before his appointment to the Supreme Court. However, he had no prior experience in government service, unlike all other Supreme Court justices.

Justice Shiras strongly supported property rights and economic liberty. Thus, he voted to strike down or limit federal and state regulations of businesses in the cases of *United States* v. *E. C. Knight* (1895) and *Allgeyer* v. *Louisiana* (1897). In *Wong Wing* v. *United States* (1896), however, Justice Shiras wrote for the Court in protecting the rights of illegal aliens against unduly harsh punishments that disregarded 5th and 6th Amendment rights of due process and trial by jury.

FURTHER READING

Shiras, Winfield. *Justice George Shiras, Jr. of Pittsburgh*. Pittsburgh: University of Pittsburgh Press, 1953.

Slaughterhouse Cases

☆ *16 Wall. 36 (1873)*
☆ *Vote: 5–4*
☆ *For the Court: Miller*
☆ *Dissenting: Field, Bradley, Chase, and Swayne*

IN 1869 the Louisiana legislature passed a law incorporating the Crescent City Live-Stock Landing and Slaughter House Company. This law required that all butchering of animals in New Orleans had to be done at the facilities of the new Crescent City Company. According to state officials, the reason for passing this law was to protect the health and safety of the community. They claimed that local butchers were causing pollution and spreading diseases by using unsanitary procedures when they slaughtered animals to be processed into food products. By combining all butchering work in one place, the state officials claimed they could regulate this work in order to reduce health risks.

The local butchers were outraged. The new law forced them to take their business to one location and pay high fees for slaughtering their animals there. They argued that the new law was passed primarily to benefit the owners of the Crescent City Company, not the public good.

The local butchers formed their own organization, the Butchers' Benevolent Association, and hired a lawyer, John A. Campbell, who had been a U.S. Supreme Court justice. Campbell sued the Crescent City Company for depriving the local butchers of their right to property. He argued that this is a basic right of individuals, protected by the privileges and immunities clause of the 14th Amendment, which says, "No state shall make or enforce any law which shall abridge the privileges or immunities of citizens of the United States." Further, Campbell argued that the state law at issue deprived the local butchers of their property rights primarily for the private profit of the Crescent City Company and not for the good of the community, as had been claimed.

New Orleans slaughterhouses in the 1860s. In the Slaughterhouse Cases, *the Court decided that a company's right to property was subject to state regulation.*

In 1870 the issue went to the Louisiana Supreme Court, which upheld the state law and rejected the suit of the Butchers' Benevolent Association. The butchers appealed to the U.S. Supreme Court.

The Issue Did the Louisiana law creating the Crescent City Live-Stock Landing and Slaughter House Company violate the property rights of local butchers under the privileges and immunities clause of the 14th Amendment?

Opinion of the Court In a close vote (5 to 4), the Court upheld the Louisiana law at issue and decided against the suit brought by the Butchers' Benevolent Association. Writing for the Court, Justice Samuel F. Miller held that the Louisiana state government had not violated the 14th Amendment by creating the Crescent City Company and giving it control of the slaughterhouse business in New Orleans.

Justice Miller argued that the 14th Amendment's privileges and immunities clause did not protect the butchers' property rights or their right to work. Further, he narrowly interpreted the privileges and immunities clause to pertain only to very few rights of national citizenship that states could not abridge or take away. According to Justice Miller, rights of property and labor were not among these few fundamental rights protected by the 14th Amendment from

abridgment by state governments. Rather, these rights were subject to state regulation for the good of the community, said Justice Miller. He also argued that the primary purpose of the 14th Amendment (which was enacted after the Civil War) was to protect the rights of African Americans and not to expand or add to the rights of white people.

Dissent Justice Stephen J. Field argued that property rights and the right to labor *were* among the privileges and immunities protected from state interference by the 14th Amendment. Justices Joseph Bradley and Noah Swayne also contended that the Louisiana law violated the 14th Amendment by depriving the butchers of property without due process of law. Finally, all of the dissenting justices rejected the Court's argument that the 14th Amendment was designed to protect the rights only of black Americans.

Significance Justice Miller's opinion for the Court strictly limited future applications of the privileges and immunities clause of the 14th Amendment. This clause might have been used to allow federal government protection for a wide range of fundamental rights, including the federal Bill of Rights, against infringement by state governments. The *Slaughterhouse* decision, by rejecting a broad interpretation of the privileges and immunities clause, made this constitutional provision virtually useless as a guarantee of the most important individual rights. Individuals therefore had to depend upon their state constitutions and governments for protection of their basic rights. This put black people, newly freed from slavery, at a disadvantage in seeking such protection from southern state governments dominated by former slaveholders. One positive outcome of the *Slaughterhouse* decision, however, was the encouragement given to states in the 1870s and 1880s to regulate economic activities for the good of the community; that is, to protect public health, safety, or morals.

SEE ALSO
Property rights

Smith v. Allwright

☆ *321 U.S. 649 (1944)*
☆ *Vote: 8–1*
☆ *For the Court: Reed*
☆ *Dissenting: Roberts*

LONNIE SMITH, an African American, lived in Harris County, Texas. On July 27, 1940, Smith was stopped from voting in the Democratic party's primary election for selecting the party's nominees for U.S. senator, representative to Congress, and several state offices. Smith met all the Texas qualifications for eligibility to vote. He was denied the ballot by Democratic party election officials only because of his race.

Smith sought help from the National Association for the Advancement of Colored People (NAACP). One of the NAACP lawyers who helped him was Thurgood Marshall, a future justice of the U.S. Supreme Court. Lonnie Smith sued S. E. Allwright, a Democratic party election judge, for illegally denying him the right to vote.

The Issue The 15th Amendment to the Constitution clearly protected Lonnie Smith's right to vote: "The right of citizens of the United States to vote shall not be denied or abridged by the United States or any State on account of race, color, or previous condition of servitude." In addition, Section 1 of the 14th Amendment protected Smith's rights against state government interference.

However, the Democratic party was a private organization, not part of the Texas state government. So party officials

claimed they could deny Smith the right to participate in a Democratic party primary election without violating the 14th and 15th Amendments, which limited only the federal and state governments, not private associations. They argued that as long as Smith was allowed to vote in the final general election, where he could choose between the Democratic and Republican candidates, his constitutional right to vote was protected.

Smith and his lawyers disagreed. They pointed out that the Democratic party dominated politics and government in Texas. The candidates who won the Democratic party primary election almost always won the subsequent general election. So, by denying Smith and other black citizens the right to vote in the primary election, the Democratic party was preventing them from effectively participating in electing their representatives in government.

Did the 14th and 15th Amendment protections of the right to vote apply to the primary elections of a political party?

Opinion of the Court Lonnie Smith and the NAACP won this case. The Court held that political party primary elections are operated in association with state government machinery set up to choose state and federal officials. Thus, the 14th and 15th Amendments to the U.S. Constitution could be used to

In 1942, Maryland election officials show a black man how to vote. Not until 1944, however, did the Supreme Court rule that blacks must be allowed to vote in primary elections as well as general elections.

protect Smith's right to vote in the Democratic party primary election.

Justice Stanley Reed wrote:

The United States is a constitutional democracy. Its organic law grants to all citizens a right to participate in the choice of elected officials without restriction by any State because of race. This grant to the people of the opportunity for choice is not to be nullified by a state through casting its electoral process in a form which permits a private organization to practice racial discrimination in the election. Constitutional rights would be of little value if they could be thus indirectly denied.

Significance This decision overturned *Grovey* v. *Townsend* (1935), which had permitted racial discrimination in the conduct of a party primary election. *Smith* v. *Allwright* was the beginning of legal developments that culminated in the 1960s in full voting rights for African Americans through the passage of the Voting Rights Act of 1965. This federal law was affirmed by the Court in *South Carolina* v. *Katzenbach* (1966) as constitutional under the 15th Amendment.

SEE ALSO

Civil rights; Equality under the Constitution

FURTHER READING

Rogers, Donald W., ed. *Voting and the Spirit of Democracy: Essays in the History of Voting and Voting Rights in America.* Urbana: University of Illinois Press, 1992.

Solicitor general

THE PRESIDENT of the United States appoints the solicitor general to represent the federal executive department before the Supreme Court. Congress created the position of solicitor general in

Thurgood Marshall is sworn in as solicitor general in 1965. President Lyndon Johnson stands to the left of Marshall.

1870 as part of the Department of Justice. The solicitor general assists the attorney general of the United States, who heads the Department of Justice.

The main duty of the solicitor general is to argue the executive branch's position in cases being heard by the Supreme Court. The solicitor general maintains offices at both the Justice Department headquarters and the Supreme Court building. As a result, a close working relationship has developed between the solicitor general and the justices of the Court.

Thurgood Marshall, an associate justice from 1967 to 1991, served as solicitor general from 1965 to 1967. In this role, he won the Supreme Court's affirmation of the Voting Rights Act of 1965 in *South Carolina* v. *Katzenbach* (1966).

FURTHER READING

Sachs, Andrea. "The Government's Advocate." *Constitution* 3, no. 3 (Fall 1991): 4–14.

Salokar, Rebecca Mae. *The Solicitor General: The Politics of Law.* Philadelphia: Temple University Press, 1992.

Souter, David H.

ASSOCIATE JUSTICE, 1990–

☆ *Born: Sept. 17, 1939, Melrose, Mass.*
☆ *Education: Harvard College, A.B., 1961; Harvard Law School, LL.B., 1965*
☆ *Previous government service: attorney general of New Hampshire, 1976–78;*

superior judge, New Hampshire, 1978–83; justice, New Hampshire Supreme Court, 1983–90; judge, Federal Court of Appeals of the First Circuit, 1990

☆ *Appointed by President George Bush July 25, 1990; replaced Justice William Brennan, who retired*

☆ *Supreme Court term: confirmed by the Senate Oct. 2, 1990, by a vote of 90–9*

DAVID H. SOUTER was President George Bush's first appointment to the Supreme Court. President Bush was determined to nominate a noncontroversial person who would be readily confirmed by the Senate, without conflict and acrimony. The President also wanted a justice who favored judicial restraint and policy-making only by the legislative and the executive branches of government. Souter clearly was the President's man. He had neither written nor publicly said anything controversial enough that could be used to deny his confirmation. Further, he seemed to agree with the President about judicial self-restraint in interpreting the Constitution.

During his confirmation hearings before the Senate Judiciary Committee, Souter performed cautiously and competently. He was confirmed by the Senate and took his seat as the 105th justice of the U.S. Supreme Court.

During his first few years on the Court, Justice Souter has been a capable justice. He has tended to side with the Court's conservative majority, but he clearly has demonstrated intellectual flexibility and independence. For example, he joined the Court's 1993 decision in *Church of the Lukumi Babalu Aye* v. *City of Hialeah,* which struck down a local law banning animal sacrifice as part of a religious ritual. Souter wrote a concurring opinion that protected the 1st Amendment right of free exercise of religion. Souter's concurring opinion, however, was more strongly and broadly stated than the opinion of the Court, written by Justice Anthony Kennedy. Justice Souter has also been a frequent dissenter from the Court majority. For example, he joined with liberals on the Court in dissenting opinions against decisions that restricted the use of race as a factor in drawing boundaries for congressional districts, as in *Bush* v. *Vera* (1996).

Staff of the Court, nonjudicial

MORE THAN 319 permanent staff members assist the justices in carrying out the business of the U.S. Supreme Court. Most of these employees of the Court work for one of the five officers, whose jobs were established by law: administrative assistant to the chief justice, clerk of the Court, reporter of decisions, marshal, and librarian.

Administrative assistant to the chief justice

The administrative assistant, with a staff of three, assists the chief justice in management of nonjudicial business, such as the administration of the Judicial Conference of the United States, the Federal Judicial Center, and the Administrative Office of the United States Courts. The administrative assistant also supervises personnel matters and budgets of the Court.

Clerk of the Court

The clerk of the court oversees a staff of 25 people. Among other duties, they manage dockets (agendas) and calendars of the Court, keep track of petitions and briefs that are submitted to the Court, notify lower courts of Supreme Court actions and decisions, and advise lawyers, upon request, about rules and procedures of the Court.

Reporter of decisions

The reporter supervises a staff of nine people who are responsible for recording, editing, and printing the opinions of the Court. The reporter of decisions oversees the official publication of the Supreme Court case decisions in *United States Reports,* which is printed by the U.S. Government Printing Office.

Marshal

With a staff of more than 200 people, the marshal of the Supreme Court manages the security, physical facilities, and payroll of the Court. The marshal receives all important visitors to the Supreme Court Building. He also takes charge of the safety of justices when they carry out formal duties outside the Supreme Court Building.

The marshal declares the beginning of each public session of the Court. He stands at one side of the bench and announces, "The Honorable, the chief justice and the associate justices of the Supreme Court of the United States." As the justices file into the courtroom, the marshal declares, "Oyez, oyez, oyez [Hear ye]: All persons having business before the Honorable, the Supreme Court of the United States, are admonished to draw near and give their attention, for the Court is now sitting. God save the United States and this honorable Court."

Librarian

A staff of 25 helps the librarian of the Supreme Court manage more than 250,000 books and several computerized databases. The librarian supervises the library in the Supreme Court Building and arranges for interlibrary loans.

Besides these officers, other employees work for the Office of the Curator, Office of the Legal Counsel, Public Information Office, and Data Systems Office.

Office of the Curator

The curator of the Supreme Court has the duty of recording and preserving the history of the Court. Chief Justice Warren Burger established the Office of the Curator in 1973. The office collects and preserves memorabilia, such as photographs, prints, manuscripts, and videotapes, that are related to the lives and work of the justices.

Items from the collections of the curator are used in the two exhibits the curator's staff prepares each year. These exhibits are presented in the lower Great Hall of the Supreme Court Building.

The curator's staff responds regularly to requests for information about the Supreme Court from scholars, the justices, other federal judges, and the general public. The staff also conducts hourly lectures and tours for the thousands of visitors who annually visit the Supreme Court Building.

Office of the Legal Counsel

Two attorneys assist the Court with legal research. The attorneys prepare for the justices summaries and analyses of the cases in which the Court has original jurisdiction (cases not on appeal from lower courts, but heard for the first time by the Supreme Court). This office serves as a general counsel for the Court; that is, it provides legal information for the justices upon request. Unlike the justices' law clerks, who serve short terms, the Office of the Legal Counsel provides the continuous legal research services of experienced attorneys.

Public Information Office

A staff of four people works for the Public Information Office. This office distributes 4,000 slip opinions on Supreme Court cases—preliminary, unedited full-text reports on opinions that are circulated within three days of decisions. The slip opinions help newspaper reporters and broadcasters to publicize news of Supreme Court opinions quickly; without the slip opinions, they would have to wait for the fully edited and official publication of the Court opinions. The Public Information Office maintains a press room and broadcast booths for the use of journalists. One hundred seventy-five bench copies of the Court's opinions, preliminary full-text reports, are provided to reporters on the day the opinion is announced by the Court. The Public Information Office also transmits the bench copies of opinions electronically to legal database services, such as LEXIS and WESTLAW.

SEE ALSO
Clerk of the Court; Clerks of the justices; Reporter of decisions

Standing to sue

A PERSON who has the right to bring legal action against another party has standing to sue that party. A party who is injured by another party has standing to sue that party, if the injured one can show that his rights were violated. A party has standing to sue the government only if that party has been injured by the government. For example, if local police conduct an illegal search of a person's home, the person has standing to sue the government under the 4th and 14th Amendments to the Constitution.

By contrast, if a person has no justifiable connection to an alleged wrongful action by the government, then the person has no standing to sue in that regard. For example, a citizen of the United States does not have standing to sue the federal government for recognizing a foreign government that has been charged with violations of international law.

Stare decisis
SEE Precedent

State courts

SOME CASES that go to the Supreme Court originated in the courts of the 50 states. The direct line of appeal, however, is only from the highest appellate court of a state. For example, a case originating in a trial court in Indiana must be appealed first to the Indiana Supreme Court before it can be heard by the U.S. Supreme Court.

In addition, state-level cases may be appealed to the U.S. Supreme Court only if they involve federal questions—issues pertaining to the U.S. Constitution, federal treaties, or federal laws. State courts are required to act in accordance with the Constitution, as well as federal statutes and treaties made under the Constitution. They must recognize the supremacy of federal law—acts of Congress as well as the Constitution—over state law. And they must interpret federal law in accordance with prevailing decisions of the U.S. Supreme Court.

SEE ALSO
Federalism; Judicial review

Statute

A STATUTE is a written law enacted by a legislature. A federal statute is a law enacted by Congress. State statutes are enacted by state legislatures; those that violate the U.S. Constitution may be struck down by the Supreme Court if the issue is appealed to the Court.

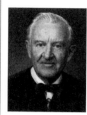

Stevens, John Paul

ASSOCIATE JUSTICE, 1975–

☆ Born: Apr. 20, 1920, Chicago, Ill.
☆ Education: University of Chicago, B.A., 1941; Northwestern University School of Law, J.D., 1947
☆ Previous government service: law clerk to Justice Wiley B. Rutledge, 1947–48; associate counsel, Subcommittee on the Study of Monopoly Power, House Judiciary Committee, 1951; U.S. Attorney General's National Committee to Study the Antitrust Laws, 1953–55; judge, Seventh Circuit Court of Appeals, 1970–75
☆ Appointed by President Gerald R. Ford Nov. 28, 1975; replaced William O. Douglas, who retired
☆ Supreme Court term: confirmed by the Senate Dec. 17, 1975, by a 98–0 vote

JOHN PAUL STEVENS has been an independent thinker on the Court. He has often written separate concurring opinions and dissenting opinions.

Justice Stevens has tended to support national government authority in cases on federalism, which has restricted the powers and independent activities of state governments. In particular, he has favored broad interpretations of the Constitution's "commerce clause" (Article 1, Section 8), which grants power to Congress to regulate trade among the states.

Justice Stevens has tended to support protection of individual rights, especially 1st Amendment freedoms of religion, speech, and assembly. He wrote notably for the Court, for example, in *Wallace* v. *Jaffree* (1985) to defend strict separation of church and state. In 1997, he led the Court in striking down a federal law designed to ban "indecent" materials from the Internet in the case of *Reno* v. *American Civil Liberties Union.*

SEE ALSO
Reno v. American Civil Liberties Union; Wallace v. Jaffree

FURTHER READING
Canon, Bradley C. "Justice John Paul Stevens: The Lone Ranger in a Black Robe." In *The Burger Court: Political and Judicial Profiles,* edited by Charles M. Lamb and Stephen C. Halpern, 343–74. Urbana: University of Illinois Press, 1991.

Stewart, Potter

ASSOCIATE JUSTICE, 1958–81

☆ Born: Jan. 23, 1915, Jackson, Mich.
☆ Education: Yale College, B.A., 1937; fellow, Cambridge University, 1937–38; Yale Law School, LL.B., 1941
☆ Previous government service: Cincinnati City Council, Ohio, 1950–53; vice mayor of Cincinnati, 1952–53; judge, Sixth Circuit Court of Appeals, 1954–58
☆ Appointed by President Dwight D. Eisenhower as a recess appointment Oct. 14, 1958; replaced Harold H. Burton, who retired; nominated by Eisenhower Jan. 17, 1959
☆ Supreme Court term: confirmed by the Senate May 5, 1959, by a 70–17 vote; retired July 3, 1981
☆ Died: Dec. 7, 1985, Hanover, N.H.

POTTER STEWART was an especially strong defender of individual rights protected by the 1st, 4th, and 14th Amendments. For example, in *Katz* v. *United States* (1967), Stewart strengthened the protection of the 4th Amendment against government's invasion of an individual's privacy. He argued that private conversations must be protected against police interception no matter where the conversation takes place. Stewart wrote: "The Fourth Amendment protects people not places." Thus, a microphone placed against the wall of a telephone booth by federal investigators was held to be a violation of the

4th Amendment's ban on "unwarranted searches and seizures" and a violation of the right of privacy.

Justice Stewart had a way with words and many of his statements in Supreme Court opinions have become famous quotations. For example, he admitted his difficulty in stating an exact definition of pornography in *Jacobellis* v. *Ohio* (1964); Stewart wrote this often-quoted statement about pornography: "I know it when I see it."

SEE ALSO

Katz v. United States

FURTHER READING

Yarbrough, Tinsley E. "Justice Potter Stewart: Decisional Patterns in Search of Doctrinal Moorings." In *The Burger Court: Political and Judicial Profiles,* edited by Charles M. Lamb and Stephen C. Halpern, 375–406. Urbana: University of Illinois Press, 1991.

Stone, Harlan Fiske

ASSOCIATE JUSTICE, 1925–41

CHIEF JUSTICE, 1941–46

☆ *Born: Oct. 11, 1872, Chesterfield, N.H.*
☆ *Education: Amherst College, B.A., 1894, M.A., 1897, LL.D., 1913; Columbia University Law School, LL.B., 1898*
☆ *Previous government service: U.S. attorney general, 1924–25*
☆ *Appointed by President Calvin Coolidge to be an associate justice Jan. 5, 1925; replaced Joseph McKenna, who retired; appointed chief justice by President Franklin D. Roosevelt June 12, 1941; replaced Chief Justice Charles Evans Hughes, who retired*
☆ *Supreme Court term: confirmed as an associate justice by the Senate Feb. 5, 1925, by a 71–6 vote; confirmed by the Senate as chief justice June 27, 1941, by a voice vote; served until Apr. 22, 1946*
☆ *Died: Apr. 22, 1946, Washington, D.C.*

HARLAN FISKE STONE was the only university professor ever to become chief justice of the United States. As a Republican appointed by Democratic President Franklin Roosevelt, Stone is one of only two chief justices nominated by a President from a different political party. (Chief Justice Edward White was the other one.)

Before entering federal government service, Stone was a professor and dean of the Columbia University School of Law (1910–23). He served under President Calvin Coolidge as attorney general of the United States before Coolidge named Stone as associate justice of the Supreme Court. The great respect among the other justices for Stone led President Roosevelt to appoint him to the office of chief justice in 1941.

Throughout his term on the Supreme Court, Harlan Fiske Stone followed the principle of judicial self-restraint, which he stated in a dissenting opinion in *United States* v. *Butler* (1936). In this case, the Court struck down as unconstitutional the Agricultural Adjustment Act, which was part of the New Deal. Justice Stone could find no constitutional basis for this decision and claimed it was based on the anti–New Deal policy preferences of the Court's majority, which were used to override the policymaking majority in Congress. Justice Stone wrote that the President and Congress are restrained by the "ballot box and the processes of democratic government. . . . The only check on our own exercise of power is our own sense of [judicial] self-restraint."

According to Justice Stone, the Court should leave the making of policies and laws to the executive and legislative branches. The Court should not substitute its policy preferences for those of the democratically elected Congress and President because this would be an unconstitutional overextension of the Court's power.

Justice Stone opposed the judicial activism of the justices who opposed, for conservative political reasons, the New Deal programs of President Roosevelt. Later, as chief justice, Stone opposed the judicial activism of liberal justices who wanted to expand the power and benefits of organized labor.

Chief Justice Stone acted strongly to support 1st Amendment freedoms in the "flag salute cases" of 1940 and 1943; he dissented against the Court's majority in *Minersville School District* v. *Gobitis* (1940), which upheld a state law requiring students in public schools to salute the U.S. flag and pledge allegiance to the United States. Three years later, Chief Justice Stone was instrumental in organizing the Court's majority in *West Virginia State Board of Education* v. *Barnette* (1943), which overturned the *Gobitis* decision. Thus, a state law requiring students in public schools to salute the flag was struck down as a violation of the free exercise of religion by Jehovah's Witnesses.

Chief Justice Stone, however, led the majority in the Japanese-American internment cases, which restricted individual rights of Japanese Americans in favor of national security concerns during World War II. For example, in the cases of *Korematsu* v. *United States* (1944) and *Hirabayashi* v. *United States* (1943), Chief Justice Stone voted to uphold federal laws restricting the freedom of Japanese Americans on the presumption, without evidence, that they might aid Japan, a World War II enemy of the United States. Most Americans today believe these cases were decided unjustly.

SEE ALSO
Hirabayashi v. United States; Judicial activism and judicial restraint; Korematsu v. United States; Minersville School District v. Gobitis; West Virginia State Board of Education v. Barnette

FURTHER READING
Konefsky, S. J. *Chief Justice Stone and the Supreme Court.* New York: Macmillan, 1946.
Mason, Alpheus Thomas. *Harlan Fiske Stone: Pillar of the Law.* New York: Viking Press, 1956.
Urofsky, Melvin I. *Division and Discord: The Supreme Court under Stone and Vinson, 1941–1953.* Columbia: University of South Carolina Press, 1999.

Story, Joseph
ASSOCIATE JUSTICE, 1812–45

☆ *Born: Sept. 18, 1779, Marblehead, Mass.*
☆ *Education: Harvard College, A.B., 1798; read law with Samuel Sewall and Samuel Putnam in Boston, 1799–1801*
☆ *Previous government service: Massachusetts House of Representatives, 1805–8, Speaker, 1811; U.S. representative from Massachusetts, 1808–9*
☆ *Appointed by President James Madison Nov. 15, 1811; replaced William Cushing, who died*
☆ *Supreme Court term: confirmed by the Senate Nov. 18, 1811, by a voice vote; served until Sept. 10, 1845*
☆ *Died: Sept. 10, 1845, Cambridge, Mass.*

JOSEPH STORY was one of the greatest justices of the Supreme Court. He worked in close partnership with Chief Justice John Marshall to establish the supremacy of the U.S. Constitution and the federal government over state constitutions and governments. He also acted with Marshall to uphold private property rights and economic liberty as fundamental principles of the Constitution. Finally, his peers generally agreed that Story was the greatest legal scholar and educator of his time.

Justice Story's greatest opinion for the Court was *Martin* v. *Hunter's Lessee* (1816), in which he upheld the constitutionality of Section 25 of the Judiciary Act of 1789. The constitutional question was whether or not the U.S. Supreme Court should have the power of judicial review over decisions of state courts, as specified in Section 25 of the Judiciary Act of 1789. Justice Story successfully argued for the constitutionality of Section 25, which bolstered the supremacy of the federal government in its relationships with the states. This decision was vindicated, once and for all, by Chief Justice John Marshall (with Story's support) in *Cohens* v. *Virginia* (1821).

Most of Chief Justice Marshall's great decisions were products of close collaboration with Justice Story. He endorsed and helped to develop John Marshall's broad construction of the Constitution. Likewise, Justice Story provided substance and technical precision for Chief Justice Marshall's great opinions about commercial law, contracts, and private property. Like Marshall, Story believed that protection of private property rights was necessary for the preservation of free government.

Throughout his long tenure on the Court, Justice Story found time to be a scholar and educator. He reorganized legal education at the Harvard Law School and served there as a distinguished professor of law. He also wrote several volumes that have become classics of legal scholarship. For example, his *Commentaries on the Constitution* (originally published in 1833) influenced constitutional thought throughout the 19th century. Story's achievements as a teacher and scholar made the Harvard Law School the biggest and best in the United States.

Justice Story's influence on the Court declined after the death of John Marshall in 1835, who was replaced as chief justice by Roger B. Taney. Under Taney's leadership, the Court reflected the ideas of Jacksonian democracy, not Marshall's federalism. The Jacksonians, unlike Marshall, tended to resist strong emphasis on federal government power. States' rights and powers were favored more than before, causing Justice Story to become a dissenter on the Court. Despite Story's declining status on the Taney Court, his influence outside the Court remained strong. His published commentaries on various aspects of the law shaped legal thinking long after his death.

SEE ALSO

Cohens v. Virginia; Martin v. Hunter's Lessee

FURTHER READING

Dunne, Gerald T. *Justice Joseph Story and the Rise of the Supreme Court.* New York: Simon & Schuster, 1970.
McClellan, James. *Joseph Story and the American Constitution: A Study in Political and Legal Thought.* Norman: University of Oklahoma Press, 1990.
Newmyer, R. Kent. "The Lost Legal World of Joseph Story." *Constitution* 4, no. 1 (Winter 1992): 58–65.
Newmyer, R. Kent. *Supreme Court Justice Joseph Story: Statesman of the Old Republic.* Chapel Hill: University of North Carolina Press, 1985.

Strict scrutiny

SEE Equality under the Constitution; Suspect classifications; Time, place, and manner rule

Stromberg v. California

☆ *283 U.S. 359 (1931)*
☆ *Vote: 7–2*
☆ *For the Court: Hughes*
☆ *Dissenting: Butler and McReynolds*

YETTA STROMBERG was a 19-year-old counselor at a summer camp for children in California. She was also an

active member of the Young Communist League. Stromberg taught the children about communist ideas and praised the communist government of the Soviet Union. In teaching one of her lessons, Stromberg had the children make a replica of the red flag of the U.S.S.R. She and the children raised the banner and recited a pledge of allegiance to it.

The sheriff of San Bernardino County arrested Yetta Stromberg for teaching activities that violated a 1919 state law prohibiting the display of a red flag "as an emblem of opposition to organized government." After her conviction under the California law, Stromberg appealed to the U.S. Supreme Court.

The Issue Stromberg argued that the state of California had denied her right to freedom of speech guaranteed by the 1st and 14th Amendments to the U.S. Constitution. California attorneys claimed that the state law used to convict Stromberg was within the state's power to maintain order and safety.

Opinion of the Court Chief Justice Charles Evans Hughes, writing for the Court, overturned the conviction of Yetta Stromberg. The California "red flag law" was declared unconstitutional because it violated "the conception of liberty under the due process clause of the Fourteenth Amendment [which] embraces the right of free speech [in the First Amendment]."

Significance The *Stromberg* case was one of the Court's early uses of the 14th Amendment to incorporate the 1st Amendment's right to free speech—that is, to protect this right from infringement by a state government. The 14th Amendment states, "No State shall . . . deprive any person of life, liberty, or property, without due process of law."

In addition, in *Stromberg* the Court for the first time protected the substance of symbolic speech (a flag display) against state government restriction.

SEE ALSO

Freedom of speech and press; Gitlow v. New York; Incorporation doctrine; Near v. Minnesota

FURTHER READING

Murphy, Paul L. *The Meaning of Freedom of Speech*. Westport, Conn.: Greenwood, 1972.
Smolla, Rodney. *Free Speech in an Open Society*. New York: Knopf, 1992.

Strong, William
ASSOCIATE JUSTICE, 1870–80

☆ *Born: May 6, 1808, Somers, Conn.*
☆ *Education: Yale University, B.A., 1828, M.A., 1831*
☆ *Previous government service: U.S. representative from Pennsylvania, 1847–51; justice, Pennsylvania Supreme Court, 1857–68*
☆ *Appointed by President Ulysses Grant Feb. 7, 1870; replaced Robert C. Grier, who retired*
☆ *Supreme Court term: confirmed by the Senate Feb. 18, 1870, by a voice vote; retired Dec. 14, 1880*
☆ *Died: Aug. 19, 1895, Lake Minnewaska, N.Y.*

WILLIAM STRONG rarely wrote opinions for the Court during his 10-year term as an associate justice. He tended to side with the majority in decisions supporting property and contractual rights.

Justice Strong had a mixed record in civil rights cases. He joined the Court's majority in the *Slaughterhouse Cases* (1873) to restrict the rights of individuals under the 14th Amendment. However, he wrote for the Court in *Strauder* v. *West Virginia* (1880), the decision to strike down a state law excluding black people from juries. In a related case, *Ex parte Virginia* (1880), Justice Strong upheld a section of the Civil Rights Act of 1875 that banned racial discrimination in jury selection.

Justice Strong retired from the Court in robust health at the age of 72. He wanted to set an example for three colleagues on the Court who continued to serve despite age-related health problems that interfered with their performance. Within two years, the three resigned.

Student rights under the Constitution

JUSTICE ABE FORTAS, writing for the U.S. Supreme Court in *Tinker* v. *Des Moines Independent Community School District* (1969), stated, "It can hardly be argued that either students or teachers shed their constitutional rights to freedom of speech or expression at the schoolhouse gate." The Supreme Court has ruled that some constitutional rights of students in public schools are the same as those of other people in the United States. Other constitutional rights, how- ever, are not the same for children and adults. For example, people younger than 18 years old are not eligible to vote in public elections. Further, state governments may constitutionally deny to children certain privileges available to adults, such as licenses to drive automobiles or to marry.

The Supreme Court has also held that certain constitutional rights of adults or students outside of school are not necessarily the same for students in a public school. During the 20th century, the U.S. Supreme Court has decided cases about such constitutional rights of students as freedom of speech and press, religious freedom, freedom of assembly and association, protection against unreasonable searches and seizures, and due process of law.

Free speech and press

In 1969, the Supreme Court upheld student rights to free speech in a landmark decision, *Tinker* v. *Des Moines Independent Community School District*. The Court ruled that students who wore black armbands to school to protest U.S. involvement in the Vietnam War had a constitutional right to such freedom of expression. In this case and others, however, the Court has affirmed the authority of school officials to regulate freedom of expression with regard to the time, place, and manner of the spoken or written messages. School officials may therefore limit student speech in order to prevent serious disruption of the teaching and learning processes of the school.

For example, in *Bethel School District No. 403* v. *Fraser* (1986), the Court upheld the restriction of a student's speech by school officials because the speech was obscene and therefore disrupted the educational process. Chief Justice Warren Burger, writing for the Court, declared, "The undoubted free-

In a school setting, students do not have all the constitutional rights that they have outside of school. Free speech, for example, may be limited if it disrupts the educational process.

dom to advocate unpopular and controversial views in schools and classrooms must be balanced against the society's countervailing interest in teaching students the boundaries of socially appropriate behavior."

In *Hazelwood School District* v. *Kuhlmeier* (1988) the Court upheld restrictions by school officials on the content of articles printed in a school newspaper. The students' writing for this publication was viewed by the Court as part of the school curriculum and therefore subject to regulation by school authorities. Justice Byron White, writing for the Court, argued, "A school need not tolerate student speech that is inconsistent with its basic educational mission, even though the government could not censor similar speech outside the school." The Court in this case emphasized that the constitutional rights of students in public schools are not necessarily and always the same as the rights of individuals in other places. The Court also stressed that the rights of students in extracurricular activities of the school are broader than their rights in activities of the school's formal program of studies. Thus, Justice White concluded, "It is only when the decision to censor a school sponsored publication...has no valid educational purpose [or is not part of the school curriculum] that the First Amendment [can be used] to protect students' constitutional rights."

Protection against unreasonable searches and seizures

The Court has ruled (*New Jersey* v. *T.L.O.*, 1985) that the 4th Amendment rights of public school students are not exactly the same as the rights of adults in nonschool settings. In the *T.L.O.* case, the Court permitted school officials to conduct a search of a student's purse without a warrant, on the grounds that this action was reasonable under the circumstances. There was reason to suspect that the search would turn up evidence of violation of either the law or school rules, so the warrantless search was upheld even though a similar search outside of school would have been ruled unconstitutional.

In line with the *T.L.O.* decision, federal courts have upheld warrantless searches of student lockers when there is a reasonable suspicion of uncovering evidence of actions violating laws or school rules. School authorities may suspend or expel students from school for possession of illegal drugs, alcohol, or weapons uncovered by warrantless searches of lockers or purses. In 1995 (*Vernonia School District* v. *Acton*), the Supreme Court sanctioned school-based drug testing of student athletes.

Due process rights

The 5th and 14th Amendments to the Constitution guarantee due process of law—certain legal procedural rights—to individuals charged with breaking the law and to those facing deprivation of life, liberty, or property by the government. In *Goss* v. *Lopez* (1975) the Supreme Court considered the due process rights of students suspended from school for violating school rules. The Court held that public school officials must follow minimal due process procedures when suspending a student from school for 10 days or less. Students facing such suspension, ruled the Court, must at least receive oral or written notice of charges against them and an opportunity for a hearing to present their side regarding the charges. However, the Court said that due process rights for short-term suspensions do not require that the students charged with wrongdoing have the rights to assistance of legal counsel, to question witnesses against them, and to call their own witnesses to refute the charges against them, which are due process rights specified in the 6th Amendment to the Constitution. Further, the Court said that notice of charges and a hearing should be provided before suspension, unless a student's presence in school threatens the safety, property, or educational opportunities of others.

In its *Goss* ruling, the Court emphasized that it was responding only to an issue about suspensions of 10 days or less. It advised school officials that "longer suspensions or expulsion for the remainder of the school term, or permanently, may require more formal procedures."

In *Honig* v. *Doe* (1988) the Supreme Court ruled on the due process rights of disabled students. Before school officials expel a disabled student from school, they must determine whether the offending behavior was caused by the student's disability. If so, the student cannot be expelled from school. However, the disabled student may be suspended from school, for no more than 10 days, even if the offending behavior stemmed from the disability. If the offending behavior was not caused by the student's disability, the student may be expelled, following careful observance of due process rights, just like a student without a disability. However, a disabled student expelled from school may not be totally deprived of educational services by the public school system.

The Supreme Court in *Ingraham* v. *Wright* (1977) decided that school officials may carry out corporal (physical) punishment as a means of disciplining students without providing due process rights to the student. Lower federal courts have, however, spelled out minimal due process procedures for corporal punishment, which involve prior notice to students about the kinds of misbehavior that could result in corporal punishment and administration of such punishment by one school official in the presence of another school official. Even though the Supreme Court has neither banned nor strictly limited corporal punishment in schools, many school districts and some state legislatures have regulated or eliminated this kind of punishment.

Student rights to religious liberty

The Supreme Court has upheld the right of students in public schools to free exercise of religious belief. In *West Virginia State Board of Education* v. *Barnette* (1943), the Court overturned a state flag-salute law. The Court held that the state law forced some students (Jehovah's Witnesses) to salute the flag even though this action violated their religious beliefs.

The Supreme Court has consistently opposed state and local laws that require public school students to pray or otherwise engage in religious activities during the school day or in school-sponsored extracurricular activities. This restriction has been maintained even when the religious content of the prayers or other activities has been nondenominational, nonpreferential, and voluntary, as long as the government has sanctioned the activity. The Court has held (in *Engel* v. *Vitale*, 1962; *Abington School District* v. *Schempp*, 1963; and *Wallace* v. *Jaffree*, 1985) that these kinds of public school–sanctioned religious activities violate the establishment clause of the 1st Amendment to the Constitution.

Further, in *Stone* v. *Graham* (1980) the Court ruled unconstitutional a state law that required copies of the Ten Commandments to be displayed in public school classrooms because it violated the 1st Amendment's establishment clause. And in 1992 (*Lee* v. *Weisman*) the Court prohibited prayers as part of an official public school graduation ceremony. However, students are free to organize, on their own and without school support, voluntary religious programs associated with graduation. In 1993, the Court let stand a decision of the Court of Appeals for the Fifth Circuit (*Jones v. Clear Creek Independent School District*) that ruled that a Texas school district's policy allowing students to voluntarily lead prayers at public school graduation ceremonies does not violate the 1st Amendment's establishment clause.

The Supreme Court rulings on prayer and religious programs in public schools do not prohibit individuals from quietly praying, on their own, during the school day or in school-sponsored extracurricular activities. And students may participate voluntarily in religious events before or after class on school grounds, such as "see you at the flag-pole" prayer programs. School officials may neither promote nor prevent such activities. Further, the Court's rulings do not prohibit teaching and learning about religious beliefs in history or literature courses, as long as teachers refrain from the indoctrination of particular religions.

The Court has supported student rights to free speech and free exercise of religion by upholding the federal Equal Access Act in *Westside Community Board of Education* v. *Mergens* (1990). This federal law states that it is unlawful for "any public secondary school which receives Federal financial assistance and which has a limited open forum to deny equal access or a fair opportunity to, or discriminate against, any students who wish to conduct a meeting within the limited open forum on the basis of the religious, political, philosophical, or other content of the speech at such meetings." The Court has ruled that the federal Equal Access Act does not violate the establishment clause and does provide opportunity for students to voluntarily form a religious club and hold meetings of their organization on school premises after school hours.

In *Lamb's Chapel* v. *Center Moriches Union Free School District* (1993) the Supreme Court held that a New York public school district had violated the freedom of expression and free exercise of religion rights of a church-supported group by not letting it use school facilities to hold a meeting after completion of the formal school day. The public school officials had opened school buildings to other community groups for meetings. Thus, it was unlawful, said the Court, for them to deny access to a church group because the group wanted to exhibit and discuss films about their religious beliefs.

Issues on the religious rights of students in public schools have persisted. In *Santa Fe Independent School District* v. *Doe* (2000), for example, the Supreme Court ruled that organized, student-led prayer at a public high school athletic event, such as a football game, is a violation of the 1st Amendment's prohibition against an establishment of religion.

SEE ALSO

Abington School District v. Schempp; Bethel School District No. 403 v. Fraser; Engel v. Vitale; Hazelwood School District v. Kuhlmeier; New Jersey v. T.L.O.; Tinker v. Des Moines Independent Community School District; Westside Community Board of Education v. Mergens; West Virginia State Board of Education v. Barnette; Wallace v. Jaffree

FURTHER READING

Hempelman, Kathleen A. *Teen Legal Rights*. Westport, Conn.: Greenwood, 2000.

Irons, Peter, ed. *May It Please the Court: Courts, Kids, and the Constitution*. New York: New Press, 2000.

Raskin, Jamin B. *We the Students: Supreme Court Cases for and about Students*. Washington, D.C.: Congressional Quarterly, 2000.

Weeks, J. Devereux. *Student Rights under the Constitution*. Athens: Carl Vinson Institute of Government, University of Georgia, 1992.

Supreme Court Reporter

SINCE 1883 the West Publishing Company has regularly issued the *Supreme Court Reporter,* an unofficial record of U.S. Supreme Court decisions. The contents of the decisions in the *Supreme Court Reporter* are the same as in the official edition, *United States Reports,* which is issued by the U.S. Government Printing Office. Summaries of all cases are prepared by West. In addition, tables of key words, phrases, and statutes are developed to help readers interpret information in the full-text reports of the Court's opinions.

SEE ALSO
United States Reports; Appendix 3: Web Sites

Suspect classifications

THE EQUAL protection clause of the 14th Amendment and the due process clause of the 5th Amendment restrict state and federal governments from discriminating against individuals. Not all discrimination by the government, however, is unconstitutional. The law may treat classes of individuals differently if it is reasonable to do so and there is a compelling government interest. A state government may, for example, discriminate on the basis of age in determining who is eligible to obtain a driver's license because such discrimination is reasonable and serves the compelling government interest of promoting public safety.

Suspect classifications, by contrast, are assumed to be unreasonable and cannot be justified as necessary to achieve a compelling government interest. Government discrimination against suspect classifications of individuals has been judged by the Supreme Court to be unconstitutional. It considers both race and religion to be suspect classifications; therefore, any government discrimination against racial or religious groups is unlikely to be upheld. When discrimination involving suspect classifications is challenged in court, the government has the very difficult, if not impossible, task of demonstrating that the discrimination is necessary to achieve a compelling state interest. This heavy burden of proof is known as the test of strict scrutiny.

In contrast to the ordinary scrutiny of the Court, strict scrutiny is undertaken on the assumption that the challenged government act is unconstitutional. Only in very few cases has a challenged government act passed the test of strict scrutiny.

Sutherland, George

ASSOCIATE JUSTICE,
1922–38

☆ *Born: Mar. 25, 1862,*
  Buckinghamshire, England
☆ *Education: University of Michigan*
  Law School, 1883
☆ *Previous government service: Utah*
  Senate, 1896–1900; U.S. representative
  from Utah, 1901–3; U.S. senator from
  Utah, 1905–17; chairman, advisory
  committee to the Washington Confer-
  ence for the Limitation of Naval
  Armaments, 1921; U.S. counsel,
  Norway–United States arbitrations,
  The Hague, Netherlands, 1921–22
☆ *Appointed by President Warren G.*
  Harding Sept. 5, 1922; replaced Justice
  John H. Clarke, who resigned
☆ *Supreme Court term: confirmed by*
  the Senate Sept. 5, 1922, by a voice
  vote; retired Jan. 17, 1938
☆ *Died: July 18, 1942, Stockbridge, Mass.*

GEORGE SUTHERLAND was a strong advocate of private rights and limited government. He opposed extensive government regulation of businesses as an invasion of property rights and contractual rights. For example, he wrote for the Court in *Adkins* v. *Children's Hospital* (1923), the decision that struck down a minimum wage law for female workers. Justice Sutherland argued that this law interfered unconstitutionally with a woman's right to negotiate a contract.

Justice Sutherland was capable of defending the civil rights of accused people as vigorously as property rights. In *Powell* v. *Alabama* (1932), he overturned the conviction of black youths sentenced to death for an assault on a white girl because they had been denied their constitutional right to legal counsel (provided by Amendment 6).

Justice Sutherland's views in support of economic liberty and against heavy-handed government regulation of businesses put him at odds with President Franklin Roosevelt's New Deal programs. He was known as one of the Court's "Four Horsemen"—the hard-line opponents of the New Deal. The Court's movement in 1937 toward acceptance of the New Deal influenced Sutherland to retire from the Court in 1938.

SEE ALSO

Powell v. Alabama

FURTHER READING

Arkes, Hadley. *The Return of George Sutherland: Restoring a Jurisprudence of Natural Rights.* Princeton: N.J.: Princeton University Press, 1994.

Swayne, Noah H.

ASSOCIATE JUSTICE, 1862–81

☆ Born: Dec. 7, 1804, Frederick County, Va.
☆ Education: studied law privately
☆ Previous government service: Coshocton County, Va., prosecuting attorney, 1826–29; Ohio House of

Representatives, 1830, 1836; U.S. attorney for Ohio, 1830–41; Columbus City councilman, Ohio, 1834
☆ Appointed by President Abraham Lincoln Jan. 22, 1862; replaced John McLean, who died
☆ Supreme Court term: confirmed by the Senate Jan. 24, 1862, by a 38–1 vote; retired Jan. 24, 1881
☆ Died: June 8, 1884, New York, N.Y.

NOAH H. SWAYNE was a zealous foe of slavery, which led him to join the Republican party and support Abraham Lincoln for the presidency. He became President Lincoln's first Supreme Court appointment.

Justice Swayne readily supported Lincoln's Civil War policies. For example, he backed the President's blockade of southern ports in the *Prize Cases* (1863), and he sustained the use of military trials for civilian defendants in *Ex parte Vallandigham* (1864). After the war, Justice Swayne continued to back Republican party programs.

Sweatt v. Painter

☆ *339 U.S. 629 (1950)*
☆ *Vote: 9–0*
☆ *For the Court: Vinson*

HERMAN MARION SWEATT was a post office worker in Houston, Texas, who wanted to become a lawyer. He applied for admission to the law school of the University of Texas. Sweatt's application to this racially segregated law school was turned down solely because he was black.

Sweatt turned for help to the National Association for the Advancement of Colored People (NAACP) and its chief legal counsel, Thurgood Marshall, who would later become an associate justice of the U.S. Supreme Court.

The NAACP and Sweatt filed suit to demand his admission to the University of Texas. The trial court judge continued, or postponed, the case for six months to give the state government time to set up a law school for black people that could admit Herman Sweatt. At the end of the six-month period, the judge dismissed Sweatt's suit because the state was setting up a law school to which he could be admitted.

Sweatt, however, was not satisfied. He claimed that the new law school for blacks would be greatly inferior to the University of Texas law school. But the Texas courts decided that the two law schools—one for whites and the other for blacks—were "substantially equivalent." Sweatt and the NAACP appealed to the U.S. Supreme Court.

The Issue This case was a test of the "separate but equal" doctrine established by the Court in *Plessy* v. *Ferguson* (1896). Did the separate Texas law schools—one for white students and the other for blacks—satisfy the 14th Amendment requirement that "No state shall...deny to any person within its jurisdiction the equal protection of the laws"?

Opinion of the Court The Court decided in favor of Sweatt. Chief Justice Fred M. Vinson concluded that the new law school for black students could not be equal to the University of Texas law school, which had a long tradition, a highly regarded faculty, and ample resources. The racially segregated law schools of Texas violated the equal protection clause of the 14th Amendment.

Significance This decision was a clear rejection of the long-standing "separate but equal" doctrine set forth in *Plessy* v. *Ferguson* (1896), and it pointed the way to a more sweeping decision against that doctrine that occurred four years later in *Brown* v. *Board of Education* (1954).

SEE ALSO

Brown v. Board of Education; Civil rights; Equality under the Constitution; National Association for the Advancement of Colored People (NAACP), Plessy v. Ferguson; Segregation, de facto and de jure

Taft, William Howard
CHIEF JUSTICE, 1921–30

☆ Born: Sept. 15, 1857, Cincinnati, Ohio
☆ Education: Yale College, B.A., 1878; University of Cincinnati Law School, LL.B., 1880
☆ Previous government service: assistant prosecuting attorney, Hamilton County, Ohio, 1881–82; assistant county solicitor, Hamilton County, 1885–87; judge, Ohio Superior Court, 1887–90; U.S. solicitor general, 1890–91; federal judge, Sixth Circuit, 1892–1900; chairman, Philippine Commission, 1900–1901; civil governor of the Philippines, 1901–4; U.S. secretary of war, 1904–8; President of the United States, 1909–13; joint chairman, National War Labor Board, 1918–19
☆ Appointed by President Warren G. Harding June 30, 1921; replaced Chief Justice Edward D. White, who died
☆ Supreme Court term: confirmed by the Senate June 30, 1921, by a voice vote; retired Feb. 3, 1930
☆ Died: Mar. 8, 1930, Washington, D.C.

WILLIAM HOWARD TAFT is the only President of the United States to also serve as chief justice of the United States. Of the two positions, chief justice was the one to which he most strongly aspired. From his youth to old age, Taft ardently desired to sit on the Supreme Court. When he was 63 years old, his ambition was fulfilled when President Warren G. Harding appointed him to the Court.

Taft's opportunity to achieve his ambition was affected by one of his decisions as President. When Chief Justice Melville Fuller died in 1910, President Taft had considered two men as his replacement: Charles Evans Hughes and Edward D. White. Hughes was 17 years younger than White, whom Taft appointed to be the new chief justice. If

President Taft had picked Hughes instead of White, his lifelong dream might not have been attained.

Chief Justice Taft was a great judicial administrator. He influenced Congress to pass the Judiciary Act of 1925, which gave the Court almost total authority to choose what cases it would decide. And Taft influenced Congress to appropriate money for construction of the magnificent Supreme Court Building in which the Court conducts its work today. (Since 1860, the Court had been conducting its business on the first floor of the Capitol, in the old Senate chamber.) Chief Justice Taft was also known as a skillful manager of the Court's work load and an adept mediator among his colleagues.

Chief Justice Taft was a great administrator, but he was not as accomplished at formulating doctrine or writing opinions. Though he wrote 249 opinions for the Court, he left no landmark decisions or enduring interpretations of the Constitution. His most significant opinion was in *Myers* v. *United States* (1926). The Court ruled that the President had the power to remove an executive appointee, a postmaster, without the consent of the Senate. Taft said: "I never wrote an opinion I felt to be so important in its effect."

SEE ALSO

Buildings, Supreme Court

FURTHER READING

Mason, Alpheus Thomas. *William Howard Taft: Chief Justice.* New York: Simon & Schuster, 1964.

Taney, Roger Brooke
CHIEF JUSTICE, 1836–64

☆ *Born: Mar. 17, 1777, Calvert County, Md.*
☆ *Education: Dickinson College, B.A., 1795; read law in the office of Judge Jeremiah Chase in Annapolis, Md.*

☆ *Previous government service: Maryland House of Delegates, 1799–1800; Maryland Senate, 1816–21; attorney general of Maryland, 1827–31; U.S. attorney general, 1831–33; acting U.S. secretary of war, 1831; U.S. secretary of the Treasury, 1833–34 (appointment rejected by the Senate)*
☆ *Appointed by President Andrew Jackson Dec. 28, 1835; replaced John Marshall, who died*
☆ *Supreme Court term: confirmed by the Senate Mar. 15, 1836, by a 29–15 vote; served until Oct. 12, 1864*
☆ *Died: Oct. 12, 1864, Washington, D.C.*

CHIEF JUSTICE Roger Brooke Taney is linked inseparably with his infamous opinion in *Scott* v. *Sandford* (1857), which sanctioned slavery and denied the rights of black Americans. Yet Taney freed his own slaves, whom he inherited. He also has been ranked by legal scholars as one of the great justices in Supreme Court history.

Roger Taney began his career in the federal government as a staunch Jacksonian Democrat. He served President Andrew Jackson's interests ably as U.S. attorney general, acting secretary of war, and secretary of the Treasury.

In 1835, President Jackson appointed Taney to fill a vacancy on the Supreme Court. The Senate, however, rejected the appointment because of disagreements with Taney's performance as secretary of the Treasury. A few months later, Chief Justice John Marshall died, and President Jackson turned again to Taney. This time the Senate confirmed the President's appointment, after a bitter debate, and Roger Taney succeeded John Marshall as chief justice of the United States.

Chief Justice Taney's greatest opinion was *Charles River Bridge* v. *Warren Bridge* (1837). Writing for the Court, Taney rejected the claim of owners of the Charles River Bridge that their charter, granted by the state of Massachusetts, implicitly gave them a monopoly and thereby prevented the state from granting rights to another company to build a second bridge over the same river. The Charles River Bridge Company, which charged passengers a toll for crossing its bridge, did not want any competition from a second company. In deciding against the monopoly claims of the Charles River Bridge Company, Taney sought to balance private property rights with the public good. He wrote: "The object and end of government is to promote the happiness and prosperity of the community. . . . While the rights of private property are sacredly guarded, we must not forget that the community also has rights, and that the happiness and well-being of every citizen depends on their faithful preservation."

With this decision, Chief Justice Taney defined a major, continuing issue of American constitutional law. From Taney's time until today, jurists have tried, as he did, to balance the sometimes competing claims of private property rights and the community's rights.

Taney's tenure on the Court was marked by growing concerns to protect state government powers and rights within the federal system. This trend was in sharp contrast to the Marshall Court's persistent concern with establishing federal government supremacy over the states. The Taney Court emphasized the sovereignty of the states over matters within their jurisdiction, as provided by the U.S. Constitution, such as maintaining public order, building public facilities, and regulating local businesses.

Taney's conception of states' rights shaped his decisions about slavery. He held that the power to maintain slavery or to free slaves belonged solely to the state governments. His views were expressed memorably and disastrously in *Scott* v. *Sandford* (1857). In this decision, Taney asserted that black Americans could not be citizens of the United States;

that the U.S. Constitution protected private property rights, including the right to own slaves; that each state had exclusive power to make decisions about slavery or emancipation of slaves; and that the federal government had no power to ban slavery in the territories of the United States. The *Dred Scott* decision fanned the flames of conflict between the so-called slave states and free states and was one important cause of the Civil War.

SEE ALSO

Charles River Bridge v. Warren Bridge; Federalism; Scott v. Sandford

FURTHER READING

Lewis, Walker. *Without Fear or Favor: A Biography of Chief Justice Roger Brooke Taney.* Boston: Houghton Mifflin, 1965.
Newmyer, R. Kent. *The Supreme Court Under Marshall and Taney.* Arlington Heights, Ill.: Harlan Davidson, 1986.
Swisher, Carl B. *Roger B. Taney.* New York: Macmillan, 1974.

Terms of the Supreme Court

A TERM of the U.S. Supreme Court is the period of time when the Court is in session. The Judiciary Act of 1789 required that the Court terms begin on the first Monday in February and August. The terms of the Court have been changed, from time to time, by Congress. In 1979 the Court began its current practice of holding sessions throughout the year with periodic recesses. According to law, the Supreme Court begins each annual term on the first Monday in October. This practice was started in 1917.

The Court is in session to hear oral arguments on Monday, Tuesday, and Wednesday for two weeks of each month from October until the end of April. A session may also be held on Monday of the third week of the month. During

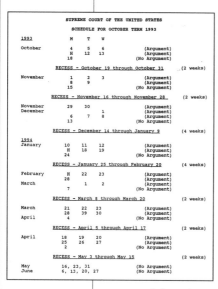

This schedule shows which days the Supreme Court will be in session and when it will hear arguments during the 1993 term.

May and June, the Court is in session to deliver opinions on cases heard during the term. However, some opinions are announced earlier in the term. The justices spend time away from the Court during the summer. But they also continue their work on petitions for hearing cases on appeal from lower courts. The justices meet in late September to take care of unfinished business and to prepare for the new term beginning in October.

SEE ALSO
Decision days; Opening day

Terry v. Ohio

☆ *392 U.S. 1 (1968)*
☆ *Vote: 8–1*
☆ *For the Court: Warren*
☆ *Concurring: Harlan, Black, and White*
☆ *Dissenting: Douglas*

A POLICE OFFICER in plain clothes, Martin McFadden, was patrolling downtown Cleveland when he observed two men acting suspiciously. They were walking back and forth in front of a store, pausing to look into the window. They soon were joined by a third man, who talked with them.

Officer McFadden thought the three men were preparing to rob the store. He confronted the three men, identified himself as a police officer, and frisked them to see if they were armed. He found that one of the men, John Terry, was carrying a pistol. A second man also had a con-

cealed weapon. So McFadden arrested them on concealed weapons charges.

Terry and his companions were convicted. Terry, however, appealed to the U.S. Supreme Court. He claimed that his 4th Amendment and 14th Amendment rights had been violated because Officer McFadden had searched him without a warrant.

The Issue Was the warrantless search of Terry a violation of the 4th Amendment protection against unreasonable searches and seizures and the 14th Amendment guarantee of due process of law in state proceedings?

Opinion of the Court The Court decided against Terry. The policeman's "stop and frisk" action in this case was constitutional because it was reasonable under the circumstances. The Court made its decision "by balancing the need to search against the invasion which the search entails."

Chief Justice Earl Warren concluded, "[W]here a police officer observes unusual conduct which leads him reasonably to conclude...that criminal activity may be afoot and that the person...may be armed and presently dangerous...he is entitled for the protection of himself and others in the area to conduct a carefully limited search of the outer clothing of such persons in an attempt to discover weapons which might be used to assault him."

Significance *Terry* was the first case to recognize "stop and frisk" as a legal practice by police officers under certain conditions. It has become an established exception to the standard requirement of a search warrant. However, police can stop and frisk a person only when they have reason to believe their lives are in danger. The search must be limited to the area of the body in which the police suspect the presence of weapons.

SEE ALSO
Searches and seizures

Test cases

A TEST CASE is one in which an individual or a group intentionally violates a law in order to bring a case to court. The purpose is to test the constitutionality of the law. For example, in 1989 Congress passed a law against flag burning. Soon afterward, protesters broke this law because they wanted to bring a test case to the courts. Thus, the case of *United States* v. *Eichman* (1990) was tried and eventually taken to the U.S. Supreme Court. The Court decided that the federal flag-burning law was unconstitutional and overturned it—exactly the outcome desired by those who initiated the test case.

Texas v. Johnson

☆ *491 U.S. 397 (1989)*
☆ *Vote: 5–4*
☆ *For the Court: Brennan*
☆ *Concurring: Kennedy*
☆ *Dissenting: Rehnquist, White, O'Connor, and Stevens*

THE REPUBLICAN PARTY held its 1984 convention in Dallas, Texas. During one of the convention sessions, a group of demonstrators marched through the streets nearby to protest the policies of President Ronald Reagan, a Republican, who was overwhelmingly supported by delegates at the convention.

When the protest march ended, one of the demonstrators, Gregory Johnson, displayed the American flag, soaked it with kerosene, and set it on fire. As the flag burned, the demonstrators cheered. Some of them chanted, "America, the red, white, and blue, we spit on you."

Police officers arrested Johnson and charged him with violating the flag dese-

cration law of the state of Texas. He was convicted and sentenced to one year in jail and a fine of $2,000. The Texas Court of Criminal Appeals reversed the decision, on the grounds that the decision was a violation of his free speech rights and the Texas and U.S. Constitutions, and the state appealed to the U.S. Supreme Court.

The Issue Advocates for Texas argued that its flag desecration law was a constitutional means to preserve the flag as a symbol of national unity. Further, this state law could be used to stop behavior that threatened to disrupt public order. Johnson argued that his conviction under Texas state law was a violation of 1st Amendment guarantees of freedom of expression as extended to the state through the due process clause of the 14th Amendment. Is flag burning, in the circumstances of this case, protected by the U.S. Constitution? Was the Texas statute on flag desecration constitutional?

Opinion of the Court The Court ruled in favor of Johnson. Justice William Brennan based his opinion on the prevailing free speech doctrine that justifies limitations only when the speech in question incites others directly and imminently to violence or other unlawful behavior. But there was no evidence that Johnson's "symbolic speech" (expression of an idea through an action, such as burning a flag) was an immediate threat to public order and safety. Brennan concluded, "If there is a bedrock principle underlying the First Amendment, it is that Government may not prohibit the expression of an idea simply because society finds the idea itself offensive or disagreeable."

Dissent Chief Justice William Rehnquist emphasized that freedom of expression may be limited in behalf of a legitimate government interest, such as preventing incitement of a riot or the

The Supreme Court ruled in Texas v. Johnson *that flag burning, as an example of symbolic speech, is protected by the 1st Amendment right to freedom of speech.*

MONUMENT TO THE FIRST AMENDMENT

desecration of a revered national symbol. Rehnquist wrote that the American flag is a "visible symbol embodying our Nation." It is not just "another symbol" and therefore deserves special protection against desecration.

Justice John Paul Stevens wrote that the American flag represents values, such as liberty and equality, that "are worth fighting for." Thus, it cannot be "true that the flag . . . is not itself worthy of protection from unnecessary desecration."

Significance This decision was very controversial. Public opinion polls showed that more than 80 percent of Americans opposed it and wanted a constitutional amendment or a federal law to reverse the *Johnson* decision. President George Bush also condemned the Court's decision.

Congress subsequently passed the Flag Protection Act of 1989, which provided penalties of one year in jail and a $1,000 fine for desecration of the American flag. This federal law had a very short life. The Court declared it unconstitutional in *United States* v. *Eichman* (1990). Thus, the Court's position in the *Johnson* case has prevailed.

SEE ALSO
Freedom of speech and press

Texas v. White

☆ *7 Wall. 700 (1869)*
☆ *Vote: 6–3*
☆ *For the Court: Chase*
☆ *Dissenting: Grier, Miller, and Wayne*

IN 1861, early in the Civil War, Texas seceded from the Union to join the Confederate States of America. After the war, Texas was temporarily governed under the Reconstruction policies of the federal government. This Reconstruction government of Texas brought suit to recover state-owned bonds (certificates of debt) that the state's Confederate government had sold.

Buyers of these bonds, such as George White, argued that Texas was at that time not a state and therefore could not sue anyone in a federal court. White based his claim on the fact that Texas had not yet been fully restored to the Union.

The Issue Was Texas able to file a suit in the U.S. Supreme Court, given the facts of its secession, its status as a Confederate state during the Civil War, and its current status under Reconstruction policies? Did the U.S. Supreme Court have jurisdiction in this case?

Opinion of the Court The Court ruled against White, and Texas was able to get back its bonds. In his opinion, Chief Justice Salmon Chase set forth enduring ideas about the nature of the federal Union. He stated that the Constitution created "an indestructible Union, composed of indestructible States." Thus, secession was illegal, and in a legal sense Texas had never left the Union. Therefore, as a full-fledged state of the federal Union, Texas could file suit in the federal courts.

Significance Chief Justice Chase's decision established that secession was not valid under the U.S. Constitution. A constitutional argument that had persisted from the founding of the United States through the Civil War was finally settled.

Thomas, Clarence

ASSOCIATE JUSTICE, 1991–

☆ *Born: June 23, 1948, Savannah, Ga.*

☆ *Education: Holy Cross College, B.A., 1970; Yale Law School, LL.B., 1973*

☆ *Previous government service: assistant to the Missouri attorney general, 1973–77; legislative assistant to U.S. Senator John Danforth, 1979–81; assistant secretary of education, Civil Rights Division, 1981–82; chairman, Equal Employment Opportunity Commission, 1982–90; judge, U.S. Court of Appeals for the District of Columbia Circuit, 1990–91*

☆ *Appointed by President George Bush July 1, 1991; replaced Thurgood Marshall, who retired*

☆ *Supreme Court term: confirmed by the Senate Oct. 15, 1991, by a vote of 52–48*

CLARENCE THOMAS became, at the age of 43, the second black associate justice of the Supreme Court of the United States. He replaced Thurgood Marshall, the first African American on the Court. Thomas's road to the pinnacle of judicial power, however, was filled with obstacles.

Clarence Thomas rose to prominence from humble origins. He was raised by his grandfather, Myers Anderson, after his father abandoned him. Although poor, Anderson was a proud man with high hopes for his grandson. He pushed Thomas to excel in school and provided discipline and stability for his grandson. Thomas responded with high achievement in school that led him eventually to graduate from Yale Law School in 1973.

Thomas's first job as a lawyer was in Missouri, where he worked for the attorney general, John Danforth. Later, Danforth was elected to the U.S. Senate as a Republican, and Thomas went to Washington as the Senator's legislative assistant. During the 1980s, Thomas, with support from Senator Danforth,

achieved top-level jobs in the U.S. Department of Education and the Equal Employment Opportunity Commission.

In 1990, President George Bush appointed Thomas to the U.S. Court of Appeals for the District of Columbia Circuit. Eighteen months later, Thurgood Marshall resigned from the Supreme Court at the age of 82. On July 1, 1991, President Bush nominated Thomas to replace Justice Marshall. The President said: "If credit accrues to him for coming up through a tough life as a minority in this country, so much the better. It proves he can do it, get the job done. And so that does nothing but enhance the Court, in my view."

Standing next to the President, Clarence Thomas replied: "In my view, only in America could this have been possible. . . . As a child I could not dare dream that I would ever see the Supreme Court, not to mention be nominated to it."

The move from nomination to Senate confirmation was difficult for Thomas and the President. After several days of hearings, the Senate Judiciary Committee was sharply divided along partisan lines in its evaluation of Thomas. The Democrats, with one exception, clearly opposed his nomination, and the Republican members of the committee favored it. The committee vote was deadlocked, seven members for Thomas and seven against him.

Suddenly, the confirmation process became embroiled in controversy. Anita Hill, a former employee of Thomas at the U.S. Department of Education and the Equal Employment Opportunity Commission, charged him with sexual harassment. The Senate Judiciary Committee conducted special sessions to examine these charges by Hill. After three days of intense and acrimonious discussion of this issue, the Senate Judiciary Committee concluded its work and sent Thomas's nomination to the Senate for a final decision. The Senate committee vote remained at seven for Thomas and seven against him.

The Senate voted to confirm Justice Thomas by a vote of 52 to 48. This was the closest vote of approval for a Supreme Court appointment in more than 100 years. Eleven Democrats joined 41 Republicans to vote for Justice Thomas.

Justice Thomas has performed carefully and competently. At first, he usually joined with Antonin Scalia when presenting concurring or dissenting opinions. Since 1994, however, Thomas has often acted independently to challenge conventional legal positions. For example, he wrote the Court's opinion in *Wilson v. Arkansas* (1995), which revived the old English common law "knock and announce" rule to augment the 4th Amendment's protection against unwarranted searches and seizures. This common law rule requires law-enforcement officers to announce their presence before entering a home or place of business.

FURTHER READING

Flax, Jane. *The American Dream in Black & White: The Clarence Thomas Hearings.* Ithaca, N.Y.: Cornell University Press, 1998.

Gerber, Scott Douglas. *First Principles: The Jurisprudence of Clarence Thomas.* New York: New York University Press, 1999.

Thompson, Smith

ASSOCIATE JUSTICE, 1823–43

☆ Born: Jan. 17, 1768, Amenia, N.Y.
☆ Education: College of New Jersey (Princeton), B.A., 1788; read law with James Kent in Poughkeepsie, N.Y.
☆ Previous government service: New York Assembly, 1800; New York Constitutional Convention, 1801; associate justice, New York Supreme Court, 1802–14; New York State Board of Regents, 1813; chief justice, New York Supreme Court, 1814–18; U.S. secretary of the navy, 1819–23

☆ Appointed by President James Monroe as a recess appointment Sept. 1, 1823; replaced Henry Brockholst Livingston, who died; nominated by Monroe Dec. 8, 1823
☆ Supreme Court term: confirmed by the Senate Dec. 19, 1823, by a voice vote; served until Dec. 18, 1843
☆ Died: Dec. 18, 1843, Poughkeepsie, N.Y.

SMITH THOMPSON served on the Supreme Court for 20 years. During this lengthy period of service, however, he had only a slight impact on constitutional law. He developed a position on regulation of commerce at odds with the prevailing view of the Court, which gave broad powers of commercial regulation to the federal government. By contrast, Justice Thompson held that states could regulate commerce in all cases except those that conflicted with a federal law. This position was known as the doctrine of concurrent commerce powers; that is, the federal government and the state government could act jointly in most cases to regulate commerce. Thompson's position influenced the judicial thought of Roger B. Taney, John Marshall's successor as chief justice.

Justice Thompson's most significant opinion was his dissent in *Cherokee Nation v. Georgia* (1831). The state of Georgia asserted control over Cherokee lands within the state that had been granted to the Native Americans by a treaty with the federal government. Thompson argued that the Cherokee were an independent and sovereign nation, despite their status as a conquered people, and must be treated like other sovereign nations in legal dealings with the U.S. government. This dissenting opinion became the majority position, expressed by John Marshall, in *Worcester v. Georgia* (1832).

Time, place, and manner rule

THE U.S. SUPREME COURT has developed the time, place, and manner rule to determine whether government regulations or limitations of free speech are legal. According to this guideline, regulations about free speech may be constitutional if they are neutral concerning the content of the speech and deal only with the time, place, and manner of speech.

For example, people may talk freely to each other in public, but they may not talk at a time or place that would block traffic. Individuals may freely criticize government officials, but they may not express themselves in a manner that would interfere with the necessary work of the government. Individuals have the right to speak in favor of candidates for election to government offices. But they may not use a loudspeaker in a residential neighborhood at three o'clock in the morning to broadcast their messages because this would unfairly disturb sleeping residents of the community. In *Kovacs* v. *Cooper* (1949), for example, the Court upheld a local law restricting the use of sound-amplifying equipment on public streets.

When a free-speech regulation is challenged in court, the judges always inquire whether the regulation is neutral with regard to the content of the speech. If not, the Court will apply the test of strict scrutiny; that is, a compelling public interest must be demonstrated as justification for regulating the content of speech. Otherwise, the regulation will be overturned as unconstitutional. An example of a compelling public interest that could pass the strict scrutiny test is protecting the safety of individuals who might be endangered by the unregulated speech.

SEE ALSO
Freedom of speech and press

Tinker v. Des Moines Independent Community School District

☆ *393 U.S. 503 (1969)*
☆ *Vote: 7–2*
☆ *For the Court: Fortas*
☆ *Concurring: Stewart and White*
☆ *Dissenting: Black and Harlan*

IN DECEMBER 1965 some students in Des Moines, Iowa, decided to publicly express their opposition to the war in Vietnam by wearing black armbands. Des Moines school administrators, however, decided upon a policy that forbade the wearing of a black armband in school. Students who violated the policy would be suspended from school until they agreed to comply with the policy.

On December 16, Mary Beth Tinker and Christopher Eckhardt wore armbands to school. John Tinker did the same thing the next day. As a consequence, the three students were suspended from school and told not to return unless they removed their armbands. They stayed away from school until the early part of January 1966.

The three students filed a complaint, through their parents, against the school

Mary Beth and John Tinker wore black armbands to protest the Vietnam War. Their school suspended them for wearing the armbands, but the Supreme Court ruled that the school's action violated the students' right to free speech.

officials. They sought an injunction to prevent the officials from punishing them for wearing black armbands to school.

The Issue Did the school district's policy of prohibiting the wearing of black armbands in school violate the students' 1st Amendment right to free speech, as extended to the states through the due process clause of the 14th Amendment?

Opinion of the Court The Court decided by a vote of 7 to 2 that the school district had violated the students' right to free speech under the 1st and 14th Amendments to the Constitution. In previous cases, such as *Stromberg* v. *California,* the Court had ruled that 1st Amendment free speech rights were incorporated by the due process clause of the 14th Amendment, which provides that no state shall "deprive any person of life, liberty [such as free speech], or property, without due process of law."

Justice Abe Fortas wrote the majority opinion, in which he stated that the wearing of black armbands to protest the Vietnam War was a form of "symbolic speech" protected by the 1st Amendment. Therefore, a public school ban on this form of protest was a violation of the students' right to free speech, as long as the protest did not disrupt the functioning of the school or violate the rights of other individuals. Justice Fortas wrote, "First Amendment rights applied in light of the special characteristics of the school environment or are available to teachers and students. It can hardly be argued that either students or teachers shed their constitutional rights to freedom of speech or expression at the schoolhouse gate."

Dissent Justice Hugo Black was one of the two dissenters in this case. He wrote:

> While I have always believed that under the First and Fourteenth Amendments neither the State nor the Federal Government has any authority to regulate or censor the content of speech, I have never believed that any person has a right to give speeches or engage in demonstrations where he pleases and when he pleases. This Court has already rejected such a notion....
>
> One does not need to be a prophet or the son of a prophet to know that after the Court's holding today some students in Iowa schools and indeed in all schools will be ready, able, and willing to defy their teachers on practically all orders....
>
> This case, therefore, wholly without constitutional reasons in my judgment, subjects all the public schools in the country to the whims and caprices of their loudest-mouthed, but maybe not their brightest students.

Significance *Tinker* is one of the most important cases on the constitutional rights of students in public schools. It supports a protection of free expression that does not disrupt the educational purposes of the school or violate the rights of other students.

In subsequent cases involving students in public schools, such as *Bethel School District No. 403* v. *Fraser* (1986) and *Hazelwood School District* v. *Kuhlmeier* (1988), the Court supported the power of public school officials to limit freedom of expression by students if such expression—in these cases, a vulgar speech and the publication of sensitive material in the student newspaper—disrupted the schools' educational mission.

SEE ALSO

Bethel School District No. 403 v. Fraser; Freedom of speech and press; Hazelwood School District v. Kuhlmeier; Student rights under the Constitution

FURTHER READING

Johnson, John W. *The Struggle for Student Rights: Tinker v. Des Moines and the 1960s.* Lawrence: University Press of Kansas, 1997.

Irons, Peter. *The Courage of Their Convictions.* New York: Free Press, 1988.

Todd, Thomas

ASSOCIATE JUSTICE, 1807–26

☆ *Born: Jan. 23, 1765, King and Queen County, Va.*

☆ *Education: Liberty Hall (Washington and Lee University), B.A., 1783; read law under Harry Innes, Bedford County, Va.*

☆ *Previous government service: clerk, federal district for Kentucky, 1789–92; clerk, Kentucky House of Representatives, 1792–1801; clerk, Kentucky Court of Appeals, 1799–1801; judge, Kentucky Court of Appeals, 1801–6; chief justice of Kentucky, 1806–7*

☆ *Appointed by President Thomas Jefferson Feb. 28, 1807, to occupy a new seat on the Court*

☆ *Supreme Court term: confirmed by the Senate Mar. 3, 1807, by a voice vote; served until Feb. 7, 1826*

☆ *Died: Feb. 7, 1826, Frankfort, Ky.*

THOMAS TODD was a veteran of the American War of Independence. At the age of 16, he served in the Continental Army. Before the war was over, Todd went to college and prepared to become a lawyer. In 1783, Todd moved to the western frontier in Kentucky, where he practiced law and served as a clerk in the government.

During his nearly 19 years on the Supreme Court, Justice Todd wrote only 14 opinions. He mostly followed the leadership of Chief Justice John Marshall, even though he was appointed by President Thomas Jefferson, a political foe of Marshall.

Tort

A TORT is a civil wrong, other than a contract violation, done by one party to another party. By contrast, a crime is a violation of a government's laws; these are the statutes that pertain to wrongs against society, which the government has authority to punish through its law enforcement powers.

Torts involve violations of civil law, not criminal law. They usually are the responsibility of state courts, but the U.S. Supreme Court sometimes becomes involved when the tort law of a state conflicts with the Constitution or federal laws.

Trial by jury

A TRIAL involves public examination of a legal issue in a court of law. A jury is a group of supposedly impartial citizens selected to determine the facts and sit in judgment of a defendant in a trial. The jury, at the end of the trial, reaches a verdict of guilty or innocent, which determines whether the defendant is freed or punished.

The right of an individual to a trial by jury is provided in three parts of the U.S. Constitution. Article 3, Section 2, says, "The Trial of all Crime, except in Cases of Impeachment, shall be by Jury." Amendment 6 says, "In all criminal prosecutions, the accused shall enjoy the right to a speedy and public trial." Amendment 7 says, "In Suits at common law, where the value in controversy shall exceed twenty dollars, the right to trial by jury shall be preserved."

The Supreme Court ruled in *Baldwin* v. *New York* (1970) that the right to a trial by jury is provided to any adult accused of a crime if the potential punishment is incarceration for more than six months. And, according to the 7th Amendment, a trial by jury is available to those involved in a common lawsuit (federal civil, or noncriminal, case) if the controversy involves more than $20.

In a trial by jury of a criminal case, the jury has the power to decide whether the accused person is guilty or innocent. The jury also may make decisions, within legally prescribed limits, about degrees of criminal behavior (for example, whether a person is guilty of murder or merely manslaughter) and the severity of punishment for a guilty person.

The traditional size of a jury, 12 people, is based on English legal traditions that were brought to America during the colonial era. However, some states have experimented with smaller juries, especially in trials of less serious crimes. The U.S. Supreme Court ruled in *Williams* v. *Florida* (1970) that a six-person jury is not necessarily a violation of the constitutional guarantee of due process of law. Further, Section 48 of the Federal Rules of Civil Procedure permits the parties in a dispute to agree to a jury of less than 12 members.

Another tradition has been the requirement of a unanimous decision by a jury in reaching a verdict. Some states, however, have experimented with rules that permit verdicts by juries that are less than unanimous. Usually, these rules have required large majorities, such as 9 or 10 jurors, in reaching a verdict.

The Supreme Court decided in *Minneapolis and St. Louis Railway Company* v. *Bombolis* (1916) that jury verdicts in state court proceedings based on less than a unanimous vote were not denials of the fair legal procedures required by the due process clause in the Constitution. Later, however, in *Burch* v. *Louisiana* (1979), the Court overturned a Louisiana law that permitted verdicts to be reached by a 5-to-1 vote of a six-person jury. In contrast to some state court practices, the unanimous verdict rule remains the standard in federal cases involving a jury trial.

SEE ALSO

Bill of Rights; Rights of the accused

FURTHER READING

Bodenhamer, David J. *Fair Trial: Rights of the Accused in American History.* New York: Oxford University Press, 1992.

Trimble, Robert

ASSOCIATE JUSTICE, 1826–28

☆ Born: Nov. 17, 1776, Berkeley County, Va.
☆ Education: read law under George Nicholas and James Brown, Lexington, Ky.
☆ Previous government service: Kentucky House of Representatives, 1802; judge, Kentucky Court of Appeals, 1807–9, 1810; U.S. district attorney for Kentucky, 1813–17; U.S. district judge for Kentucky, 1817–26
☆ Appointed by President John Quincy Adams Apr. 11, 1826; replaced Thomas Todd, who died
☆ Supreme Court term: confirmed by the Senate May 9, 1826, by a voice vote; served until Aug. 25, 1828
☆ Died: Aug. 25, 1828, Paris, Ky.

ROBERT TRIMBLE was the son of pioneers who arrived in the territory of Kentucky in 1780. Trimble took advantage of an opportunity to go to school and attended the Bourbon Academy. Later, he prepared for a career in law by studying with two local attorneys. Trimble became a successful lawyer and judge in Kentucky.

Trimble was the only Supreme Court appointment of President John Quincy Adams. He was the first federal district judge to become a justice of the Supreme Court. Like President Adams, he favored a strong federal government. Justice Trimble served briefly on the Court and wrote only 16 opinions before his sudden death from an undiagnosed illness.

Twining v. New Jersey

☆ *211 U.S. 78 (1908)*
☆ *Vote: 8–1*
☆ *For the Court: Moody*
☆ *Dissenting: Harlan*

NEW JERSEY charged Albert Twining with the crime of reporting false information to a state government bank examiner. Twining refused to testify at his state court trial, an action that the judge interpreted, in his charge to the jury, as an admission of guilt. Under New Jersey law, the judge could make such an interpretation.

Twining was convicted and the New Jersey Supreme Court upheld the conviction. Twining, however, argued that he had a constitutional right to protection against giving evidence against himself. He pointed to the 5th Amendment to the U.S. Constitution, which says, "No person shall be . . . compelled in any criminal case to be a witness against himself." Twining appealed to the U.S. Supreme Court.

The Issue Did the New Jersey trial court judge's instructions to the jury violate the 5th Amendment guarantee of protection against self-incrimination? If so, could this part of the federal Bill of Rights be applied to a state government through the due process clause of the 14th Amendment, which says, "No state shall . . . deprive any person of life, liberty, or property, without due process of law"?

Opinion of the Court Justice William H. Moody recognized that the trial judge violated the self-incrimination clause of the 5th Amendment. However, he upheld the conviction of Twining because, in the Court's view, the self-incrimination clause in the federal Bill of Rights could not be applied to a state government via the due process clause of the 14th Amendment. However, the Court stated that this due process clause could in principle incorporate some fundamental rights in the federal Bill of Rights if these rights were judged essential to the idea of fairness in due process of law. Justice Moody provided this guideline for future decisions about which rights could be incorporated and applied to state governments: "Is it [the right in question] a fundamental principle of liberty and justice which inheres in the very idea of free government and is the inalienable right of a citizen of such a government?"

The Court decided that the 5th Amendment's self-incrimination clause was not one of the "fundamental principles" of the federal Bill of Rights that could be applied to state governments through the 14th Amendment. But Justice Moody's guidelines did open the way for future applications to the states of selected rights in the federal Bill of Rights.

Dissent Justice John Marshall Harlan concluded that the 5th Amendment's self-incrimination clause did apply to the states through the 14th Amendment. In his opinion, this right to remain silent was a fundamental part of the principle of liberty embedded in the Constitution.

Significance The Court rejected *total incorporation*—the idea that Amendments 1 to 8 of the federal Bill of Rights could be completely applied to the states through the due process clause of the 14th Amendment. However, the Court did provide an opening for *selective incorporation*—the idea that certain parts of the federal Bill of Rights could be applied to the states on a case-by-case basis. During the 20th century, the Court has selectively incorporated most provisions of the federal Bill of Rights through the due process clause of the 14th Amendment, thereby applying these fundamental rights to the states.

SEE ALSO

Incorporation doctrine; Rights of the accused; Self-incrimination, privilege against

United States Reports

ALL DECISIONS of the Supreme Court of the United States are recorded in an authorized publication, the *United States Reports*. This series of volumes was initially compiled by Alexander J. Dallas, the Court's first reporter (1790–1800). Dallas's work was approved by the Court, although he held no official position and sold the publication of his work for profit. The position of reporter of the Supreme Court was not established by Congress until 1816.

Private publishers issued the *United States Reports* until 1922. Since then, the U.S. Government Printing Office has been the publisher.

The Court's decisions are not reported exclusively in the *United States Reports*. They also appear, for example, in *Supreme Court Reporter; United States Law Week,* a weekly publication that covers Supreme Court news and proceedings, including the full text of all Court decisions on cases; and the legal databases LEXIS and WESTLAW. However, the only official report of the Court's decisions is in *United States Reports.* This is the version that must be cited in all briefs and memoranda to the Court, and it should be listed first in any multiple listing of sources of a citation.

SEE ALSO
Reporter of decisions; Appendix 3: Web Sites

United States v. Curtiss-Wright Export Corp.

☆ *299 U.S. 304 (1936)*
☆ *Vote: 7–1*
☆ *For the Court: Sutherland*
☆ *Dissenting: McReynolds*
☆ *Not participating: Stone*

IN 1934, Bolivia and Paraguay were at war with each other. Both countries needed military weapons from abroad, and American weapons makers were eager to sell to them. At the same time, the American public and Great Britain wanted the United States to help end the war by stopping all arms sales to the two nations.

On May 28, 1934, Congress passed a joint resolution giving President Franklin Delano Roosevelt authority to place an embargo, or ban, on selling weapons to Bolivia and Paraguay. Four days later, Roosevelt declared the embargo in effect because he believed it would help restore peace. The federal government later indicted the Curtiss-Wright Corporation for violating the embargo by selling armed aircraft to Bolivia. Curtiss-Wright claimed that the Constitution did not allow Congress to give the President power to declare an embargo.

The Issue Did Congress's joint resolution unconstitutionally delegate legislative power to the executive branch? Or did Congress have the authority to delegate broad discretionary powers in foreign affairs to the President?

Opinion of the Court The Supreme Court ruled to uphold the President's embargo. The Court distinguished between the powers exercised by Congress and the President in "external" (foreign) affairs and "internal" (domestic) affairs. The Court said that the national government could take action in conducting foreign affairs that might exceed its authority to direct domestic policy.

Writing for the majority, Justice George Sutherland reasoned that since the United States had existed as a sovereign nation before the adoption of the Constitution, it retained powers to influence international affairs that were neither implied nor listed in the Constitution.

These powers stemmed from the simple unspoken reality that the United States existed in a world of nations and must have powers to meet its international responsibilities just as other sovereign nations did. This idea established a new precedent, the doctrine of inherent powers.

Further, the Court ruled that Congress could delegate broad discretionary powers to the President to cope with foreign affairs issues. This verdict contrasted with the Court's ruling on domestic affairs, which limited Congress to delegating legislative powers to the President only if it also set clear guidelines for using those delegated powers.

Dissent Although Justice James McReynolds dissented in this case, he filed no opinion.

Significance The *Curtiss-Wright* decision recognized the broad responsibility of the executive branch of the national government for foreign affairs, giving the President great freedom in directing the nation's foreign policy. Justice Sutherland wrote: "[T]he President alone has the power to speak as a representative of the nation." He described the President's power in foreign affairs as "plenary [full] and exclusive." The President is "the sole organ of the federal government in... international relations." This decision thereby provided the foundations for strong and decisive Presidential leadership in world affairs.

FURTHER READING

Divine, Robert A. "The Case of the Smuggled Bombers." In *Quarrels That Have Shaped the Constitution*, edited by John A. Garraty. New York: Harper & Row, 1987.

United States v. Darby Lumber Co.

☆ *312 U.S. 100 (1941)*
☆ *Vote: 9–0*
☆ *For the Court: Stone*

IN 1938, the U.S. Congress passed the Fair Labor Standards Act, which set minimum wages, maximum hours, and overtime pay regulations for workers in businesses involved in interstate commerce—that is, in shipping their products across state lines. Enactment of this federal law was based on Congress's power "to regulate Commerce... among the several States" (Article 1, Section 8, of the Constitution).

The Darby Lumber Company claimed that the Fair Labor Standards Act was unconstitutional, so it filed suit to prevent enforcement of this federal law.

The Issue The Darby Lumber Company argued that Congress exceeded its powers under the commerce clause of the Constitution when it passed the Fair Labor Standards Act. It claimed that, according to the 10th Amendment to the Constitution, the power to regulate wages, hours of work, working conditions, and so forth belongs to the states. (The amendment states, "The powers not delegated to the United States by the Constitution, nor prohibited by it to the States, are reserved to the States respectively, or to the people.") This claim was based on the Supreme Court's decision in *Hammer v. Dagenhart* (1918). Was enactment of the Fair Labor Standards Act a constitutional exercise of the commerce power, or did this federal law violate the 10th Amendment of the Constitution? Further, did the Fair Labor Standards Act violate the due process clause of the 5th Amendment by taking away the right of employers and workers to bargain freely about wages and working conditions?

Opinion of the Court The Court upheld the Fair Labor Standards Act.

Women can peaches in California for shipment around the country. In 1941 the Supreme Court upheld the Fair Labor Standards Act, which set minimum wages and maximum hours for workers in industries involved with interstate commerce.

Writing for the Court, Justice Harlan F. Stone based his opinion on the dissent of Justice Oliver Wendell Holmes in *Hammer v. Dagenhart* (1918). Agreeing with Holmes, Stone argued that the federal government's power to regulate commerce among the states should be interpreted broadly. Thus, the power to regulate wages and working conditions can, said Justice Stone, be tied to the power to regulate interstate commerce. Stone wrote, "The conclusion is inescapable that *Hammer v. Dagenhart*... should be and now is overruled."

Significance This decision expanded the federal government's power to regulate national economic affairs. Further, this opinion rejected the argument, advanced in *Hammer v. Dagenhart,* that the 10th Amendment strictly limits the enumerated, or specifically listed, powers of Congress. Instead, it established a broad interpretation of the Congress's commerce power.

SEE ALSO
Commerce power; Federalism; Hammer v. Dagenhart

United States v. E. C. Knight Co.

☆ *156 U.S. 1 (1895)*
☆ *Vote: 8–1*
☆ *For the Court: Fuller*
☆ *Dissenting: Harlan*

IN 1890 Congress passed the Sherman Antitrust Act, which seemed to outlaw business monopolies. A monopoly has control over the means of producing and selling a product or service. The Sherman Antitrust Act provided that "every contract, combination in the form of trust or otherwise, or conspiracy, in restraint of trade or commerce among the several states, or with foreign nations, is hereby declared to be illegal." So, according to this federal law, any business that acted to restrain trade by controlling most or all of a particular business activity would seem to be illegal.

In the late 19th century the American Sugar Refining Company was the dominant maker of sugar in the United States. It was known as the Sugar Trust. In 1892 the Sugar Trust acquired four Philadelphia sugar refineries, including the E. C. Knight Company. As a result, the American Sugar Refining Company controlled 98 percent of sugar manufacturing in the United States. The federal government filed suit under the Sherman Antitrust Act to prevent the "restraint of trade or commerce among the several states" by the American Sugar Refining Company's takeover of nearly all the sugar refining businesses in the United States.

The Issue Was the Sugar Trust in violation of the Sherman Antitrust Act? Did its control of 98 percent of the sugar refining business in the United States constitute an illegal restraint of trade or commerce?

Opinion of the Court In its first interpretation of the Sherman Antitrust Act, the Court decided against the federal government. It upheld the lower court's dismissal of the government's suit. The Sherman Antitrust Act, according to the Court, did not apply to a trust that refined 98 percent of the sugar sold throughout the United States.

Writing for the Court, Chief Justice Melville Fuller argued that a monopoly of the production of refined sugar did not necessarily lead to an illegal restraint of trade, which was what the Sherman Antitrust Act prohibited. Fuller said that production and commerce were two very different kinds of business activity. He wrote that only the distribution or sale of a product (such as refined sugar) was subject to federal regulation under the commerce clause of the Constitution (Article 1, Section 8). By contrast, Congress did not have the power under the Constitution to regulate the manufacturing of a product that occurred within the boundaries of a state. This power, according to Fuller, belonged to the government of the state in which a manufacturing company was located. So the federal government suit against the Sugar Trust exceeded the scope of the Sherman

Antitrust Act, and it could not be applied to E. C. Knight.

Dissent Justice John Marshall Harlan argued that the Sugar Trust's near monopoly of the production of refined sugar gave it power to dominate the distribution and sale of this product. For example, the Sugar Trust could control the market price of refined sugar. Therefore, the Sugar Trust was in violation of the Sherman Antitrust Act.

Justice Harlan argued for a broad interpretation of the federal government's commerce power. He believed that Congress had the authority to regulate business to prevent any interference with free trade among the states. He wrote, "The general [federal] government is not placed by the Constitution in such a condition of helplessness that it must fold its arms and remain inactive while capital combines... to destroy competition."

Significance The *E. C. Knight* decision opened the way to large-scale combinations of manufacturing businesses whose production activities had been ruled beyond the scope of the Sherman Antitrust Act. Further, this decision diminished the power of the federal government to regulate economic activity.

The Sugar Trust (second from right) marches with other major trusts in a triumphant parade. When the federal government filed suit against the Sugar Trust for violating the Sherman Antitrust Act, the Supreme Court ruled in favor of the trust, even though it controlled 90 percent of the sugar refining business in the country.

The *E. C. Knight* ruling prevailed until the end of the 1930s, when the Court took a different position on the federal government's power, under the commerce clause, to regulate the economy. For example, in *National Labor Relations Board* v. *Jones & Laughlin Steel Corp.* (1937) and *West Coast Hotel Co. v. Parrish* (1937), the Court upheld federal and state laws regulating wages and working conditions of private businesses. These decisions emphasized a broad interpretation of the federal government's commerce power, which could include the interrelated issues of production and distribution of goods and services. After the erosion of the *Knight* decision in 1937, the federal government exercised broad authority to regulate economic activity for the public good.

SEE ALSO

Commerce power; National Labor Relations Board v. Jones & Laughlin Steel Corp.; West Coast Hotel Co. v. Parrish

United States v. Leon

☆ *468 U.S. 897 (1984)*
☆ *Vote: 6–3*
☆ *For the Court: White*
☆ *Concurring: Blackmun*
☆ *Dissenting: Brennan, Marshall, and Stevens*

IN 1981 the police in Burbank, California, received information about drug dealing by two residents of their city. So the police began to regularly watch the Burbank home of the two suspects, where they spotted an automobile owned by Alberto Leon, another suspected drug dealer.

The Burbank police obtained a search warrant from a local judge, searched the residence, and found illegal drugs belonging to Alberto Leon. This evidence led to Leon's arrest and conviction.

The Issue Leon's lawyer argued that the search warrant used by the Burbank police was not valid because there was no "probable cause" for the police to request it or for the judge to issue it. As a result, the evidence against Leon gathered by the police should have been thrown out under the exclusionary rule established in *Mapp v. Ohio* (1961), according to which evidence obtained in violation of a person's constitutional rights cannot be used to prosecute the person. Should the evidence against Leon be excluded because it was obtained through procedures that violated the 4th Amendment guarantee to "the right of the people to be secure in their persons, houses, papers, and effects, against unreasonable searches and seizures"? Or should the Court permit an exception to the exclusionary rule when the police make a "good faith" mistake in obtaining and using a search warrant?

Opinion of the Court The Court acknowledged that the police used an invalid search warrant to obtain evidence against Leon. Nonetheless, the Court ruled against Leon and permitted a "good faith" exception to the exclusionary rule. The exclusionary rule is not a constitutional right, said Justice Byron White, but merely serves to limit oppressive police actions. However, when police act on "good faith" to obtain valid evidence of criminal behavior, the exclusionary rule does not apply to the case.

Dissent Justice William Brennan, who had established the exclusionary rule in *Mapp v. Ohio*, opposed any "good faith" exception to this rule. He feared that this exception would lead to an increase in illegal police behavior in gathering evidence against people suspected of criminal behavior.

Significance The *Leon* decision narrowed the exclusionary rule protections under the 4th Amendment of the Constitution. This outcome was hailed

In the Leon *case, the Court ruled that even if police or federal agents search a house with an invalid warrant, any evidence found can be used in a trial if the officers were acting in "good faith" when they sought the warrant.*

by many law enforcement officials, who often felt frustrated by judicial decisions that permitted a criminal to avoid conviction because of a technical error by the police. However, defenders of the exclusionary rule argued against any exceptions to it because of their strong commitment to 4th Amendment rights.

SEE ALSO
Exclusionary rule; Mapp v. Ohio; Searches and seizures

United States v. Nixon

☆ *418 U.S. 683 (1974)*
☆ *Vote: 8–0*
☆ *For the Court: Burger*
☆ *Not participating: Rehnquist*

BEGINNING WITH George Washington, several Presidents have asserted the right to withhold information from Congress or from a court. The right of the President to do this has come to be called *executive privilege*. Presidents have often made such claims in the area of foreign affairs. In 1974, however, President Richard Nixon claimed executive privilege for another reason.

In the spring of 1972, employees of President Nixon's reelection committee burglarized the Democratic party headquarters in the Watergate office complex in Washington and planted illegal elec-

tronic bugging equipment. Eventually, seven of President Nixon's top aides, including former attorney general John Mitchell, were indicted for their role in planning the Watergate break-in, as it came to be known, and for obstructing justice by trying to cover up their actions. During Senate hearings on the break-in and the cover-up, a Nixon aide admitted that there were secretly recorded tapes of Nixon's conversations with his aides. A special prosecutor investigating the Watergate break-in subpoenaed the tapes for use as evidence in the criminal investigations.

President Nixon refused to surrender the tapes. He claimed that the principle of executive privilege protected the record of his private conversations from such a subpoena. He argued that the actions of many past Presidents clearly established the tradition of executive privilege. He also claimed that to allow another branch of government, the courts, to obtain the tapes would destroy the separation of powers established by the Constitution and would weaken the Presidency.

The Issue Did the constitutional principle of separation of powers and the tradition of executive privilege prevent the courts from requiring the President to turn over material needed as evidence in a criminal trial?

Opinion of the Court The Court ordered President Nixon to turn over the tapes and other documents to the trial court for use as evidence. The Supreme Court rejected the claim that either separation of powers or executive privilege could make the President immune from the judicial process. The Court's ruling established the precedent that unless important military or diplomatic secrets affecting national security were involved, the need to ensure a fair trial outweighed the principle of executive privilege. The decision limited the concept of executive privilege by determining that a President could not use it to prohibit disclosure of criminal conduct.

At the same time, the Court's decision acknowledged the constitutionality of executive privilege in certain other situations. The Constitution does not mention executive privilege, and until the Court reached this decision, legal scholars had frequently debated whether any real constitutional basis supported the doctrine.

In *United States* v. *Nixon,* Chief Justice Warren Burger, a Nixon appointee, said that Presidents and their aides must be free to consider alternatives as they make decisions. In order to do so, they must possess the confidence to express themselves freely without fear that the public will gain access to their ideas. Thus, Burger wrote, "[Executive] privilege is fundamental to the operation of government and inextricably rooted in the separation of powers under the Constitution."

Significance President Nixon obeyed the Court's decision and turned over the tapes to the special prosecutor. Nixon claimed the demand for the tapes was a political maneuver by his enemies. However, this claim could not stand up in the face of a unanimous Court decision written by a Nixon appointee and supported by two other Nixon appointees. The tapes revealed that Nixon had participated in the cover-up. When the contents of these tapes became public knowledge, even Nixon's strongest supporters in Congress believed that he could no longer remain in office. Some Republican congressmen said they would have to vote for his impeachment, and leading Republican senators publicly announced that they saw no way he could avoid conviction. Nixon became the first U.S. President to resign from office.

SEE ALSO

Executive privilege; Separation of powers

United States v. O'Brien

☆ *391 U.S. 367 (1968)*
☆ *Vote: 7–1*
☆ *For the Court: Warren*
☆ *Concurring: Harlan*
☆ *Dissenting: Douglas*
☆ *Not participating: Marshall*

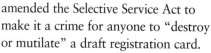

IN THE 1960s, the United States was fighting a war in Vietnam. The war was controversial, and many Americans protested against the selective service system, which drafted young men into the armed forces of the United States. Some of the antiwar protests involved the destruction of draft registration cards, which were issued to all men eligible for induction into the U.S. military. Congress in 1965 amended the Selective Service Act to make it a crime for anyone to "destroy or mutilate" a draft registration card.

On March 31, 1966, David O'Brien burned his draft card during an antiwar demonstration at an entrance to a South Boston courthouse. Agents of the Federal Bureau of Investigation (FBI) saw O'Brien burn his draft card and arrested him for violating the Selective Service Act, as amended in 1965.

The Issue David O'Brien claimed that he had publicly burned his draft card to express his opposition to the Vietnam War. This "symbolic speech" was, in his opinion, permissible because of his 1st Amendment right to free speech. His attorney pointed to the Court's opinion in *Stromberg* v. *Califor-*

A protester burns a draft card in a demonstration against the Vietnam War. In the O'Brien case, the Supreme Court upheld the law that prohibited the burning of draft cards, ruling that it was not "symbolic speech" protected by the 1st Amendment.

nia (1931), which ruled that symbolic speech was protected from government prohibition by the 1st Amendment.

The federal government's attorney argued that O'Brien's actions seriously interfered with its legitimate business because he wanted "to influence others to adopt his anti-war beliefs" and thwart the government's ability to conduct the war. The government argued that the requirements of national security justified limitations on symbolic speech.

Was the 1965 amendment to the Selective Service Act, which banned destruction of draft cards, a valid limitation on free speech? Or was this federal statute an unconstitutional violation of the 1st Amendment?

Opinion of the Court The Court upheld the 1965 law and rejected David O'Brien's claims that it violated his right to free speech. Chief Justice Earl Warren wrote:

> We cannot accept the view that an apparently limitless variety of conduct can be labeled "speech" whenever the person engaging in the conduct intends thereby to express an idea. However, even on the assumption that the alleged communicative element in O'Brien's conduct is sufficient to bring into play the First Amendment, it does not necessarily follow that the destruction of a registration certificate is a constitutionally protected activity. This Court has held that when "speech" and "nonspeech" elements are combined in the same course of conduct, a sufficiently important governmental interest in regulating the nonspeech element can justify incidental limitations on First Amendment freedoms. . . . [W]e think it clear that a government regulation is sufficiently justified if it is within the constitutional power of the Government; if it furthers an important or substantial governmental interest; if the governmental interest is unrelated to the suppression of free

expression; and if the incidental restriction on alleged First Amendment freedoms is no greater than is essential to the furtherance of that interest.

Significance The Court provided guidelines for subsequent decisions about when the government could regulate symbolic speech. These guidelines required the government to have a valid, compelling interest, such as the necessity for a military draft, unrelated to the purpose of suppressing free speech. Moreover, any restrictions on free speech could be no broader than was necessary to carry out that valid interest. The *O'Brien* guidelines, or tests, for deciding permissible limits on free speech are now an established part of constitutional law.

SEE ALSO

Freedom of speech and press; Stromberg v. California

United States v. Ross

☆ *456 U.S. 798 (1982)*
☆ *Vote: 6–3*
☆ *For the Court: Stevens*
☆ *Concurring: Blackmun and Powell*
☆ *Dissenting: White, Marshall, and Brennan*

DETECTIVE MARCUM of the Washington, D.C., Metropolitan Police received a telephone call about criminal activity in a local neighborhood. The caller reported that a man was selling drugs in the vicinity of 439 Ridge Street. The informer described the drug seller and his automobile in detail.

Marcum and two other police officers, Detective Cassidy and Sergeant Gonzales, quickly went to check out the reported drug dealing on the city streets. They found the car of the alleged drug dealer and used the license plate number to obtain information about the owner, Albert Ross.

In 1982 the Supreme Court ruled that police officers could search compartments of a car and containers inside a car without first obtaining a search warrant. The general right to search a car without a warrant had been established in 1925.

The police officers stopped Albert Ross's car, asked him to step outside, and searched him. Sergeant Gonzales, looking through the automobile window, noticed a bullet on the front seat. He entered the car, searched it for weapons, and found a pistol in the glove compartment. The officers arrested Ross for violating the local firearms code.

The officers unlocked the trunk of the car and found a bag and a small pouch. Plastic envelopes in the bag contained white powder, which later proved to be heroin. The pouch contained $3,200 in cash.

Ross was charged with possession of an illegal substance, heroin, with intent to sell it. He, in turn, accused the police of violating his constitutional rights by searching his car and containers in the car without first obtaining a search warrant. His attorney filed a motion asking that the evidence obtained without a warrant be excluded from Ross's trial. Ross's motion was denied, and he was convicted. His attorney appealed and the case eventually went to the U.S. Supreme Court.

The Issue The 4th Amendment to the Constitution guarantees the "right of the people to be secure in their persons, houses, papers, and effects against unrea-

sonable searches and seizures . . . and no warrants shall issue, but upon probable cause." However, cars have been treated differently from houses ever since *Carroll v. United States* (1925), when the Court held that police could search an automobile without a warrant when they had a reasonable suspicion of criminal activity. The justification for this exception to the usual 4th Amendment requirements was that a car can be quickly driven away while police take time to obtain a search warrant. The opportunity to obtain evidence of illegal activity would then be lost.

If cars could be stopped by police and searched without a warrant, legal questions still remained about how far such a search could extend. Was it legal for police to search a car's glove compartment or trunk without a warrant? Can police examine containers spotted in a car, such as boxes or pouches, without obtaining a warrant from a magistrate?

Opinion of the Court Justice John Paul Stevens held that police officers do not need to obtain a warrant before they search compartments of a car or containers found in the vehicle. They can conduct such searches as long as they can demonstrate "probable cause" to believe that they will find evidence of illegal activity. This is the same standard needed to obtain a search warrant prior to conducting a search and seizing evidence.

Justice Stevens wrote, "If probable cause justifies the search of a lawfully stopped vehicle, it justifies the search of every part of the vehicle and its contents that may conceal the object of the search."

Dissent Justices Thurgood Marshall, William Brennan, and Byron White argued that the Court's decision gave a police officer the same authority as a judge to determine probable cause. They said that this was a wrongful blurring of the constitutional separation of judicial powers and executive or law enforcement powers. Justice Marshall feared that the Court's opinion was "a first step toward an unprecedented 'probable cause' exception to the warrant requirement." If this exception were to occur, Marshall said, the constitutional rights of individuals would be unjustly limited.

Significance The Court's decision in *Ross* extended the automobile exception to 4th Amendment requirements established in *Carroll v. United States* (1925). In effect, the *Ross* decision gave the power to determine "probable cause" to police officers rather than to a court.

Since the *Ross* case, the Court has continued to support the automobile exception to usual search and seizure standards. As a result, the 4th Amendment protections against automobile searches are minimal.

SEE ALSO

Carroll v. United States; Probable cause; Searches and seizures; Terry v. Ohio

---

United States v. United States District Court

☆ *407 U.S. 297 (1972)*
☆ *Vote: 8–0*
☆ *For the Court: Powell*
☆ *Concurring: Burger, Douglas, and White*
☆ *Not participating: Rehnquist*

IN 1968 Congress passed the Omnibus Crime Control and Safe Streets Act, which provided for court-approved electronic surveillance to fight certain kinds of crimes. This law also provided that "nothing contained [in the section about electronic surveillance] shall limit the constitutional power of the President to take such measures as he deems necessary to protect the United States against the overthrow of the Government."

President Richard Nixon used this section of the act to use electronic surveillance (telephone wiretaps, for exam-

ple) to monitor American citizens suspected of activities dangerous to the security of the United States. The Nixon administration did so without first showing "probable cause" and obtaining a warrant, or permission, from a court, as required by the 4th Amendment.

Electronic surveillance had been used by the Nixon administration against defendants accused of bombing a Central Intelligence Agency office in Ann Arbor, Michigan. Before their trial, the defendants petitioned the U.S. District Court for the Eastern District of Michigan to require the federal government to produce any information about them obtained from electronic surveillance. The U.S. attorney general, John Mitchell, said that such information existed, but he refused to release it. The district court, however, ruled that the Nixon administration's use of electronic surveillance violated the 4th Amendment and ordered the federal government to turn over the requested information. The federal government appealed this ruling to the U.S. Supreme Court.

The Issue The Nixon administration argued that disclosure of the requested information "would prejudice the national interest." Further, the Nixon administration held that Article 2 of the Constitution implied that the President had power to use electronic surveillance or any other means necessary to gather information to protect the federal government from destruction. Did the needs of national security, for which

President Richard Nixon and Attorney General John Mitchell argued that they should not have to turn over to the courts information gained through electronic surveillance of defendants accused of bombing a CIA office.

the President is responsible under the U.S. Constitution, outweigh the protection of individual rights guaranteed by the U.S. Constitution, such as the 4th Amendment right to protection against unwarranted governmental searches and seizures of one's private possessions? Was the federal government required to obey the district court's order to disclose certain information obtained through electronic surveillance conducted without a warrant?

Opinion of the Court The Supreme court upheld the federal district court's order. The Court stressed that this case involved protection of 1st and 4th Amendment rights. It viewed the electronic surveillance project of the Nixon administration as a discouragement to free and open exchange of information by individuals critical of the government.

Significance The decision in this case was a strong statement about the primary importance of constitutional rights. Not even pervasive social upheavals and threats to national security could justify denial of fundamental rights of liberty and justice for all individuals.

FURTHER READING

Westin, Alvin F. "Civil Liberties in the Technology Age." *Constitution* 3, no. 1 (Winter 1991): 56–64.

United States v. Virginia

☆ *518 U.S. 515 (1996)*
☆ *Vote: 7–1*
☆ *For the Court: Ginsburg*
☆ *Dissent: Scalia*
☆ *Not participating: Thomas*

In 1990, a female student (never identified) in a Virginia public high school filed a complaint with the U.S. Department of Justice. She charged the Virginia Military Institute (VMI), a state-supported institution of higher education, with illegal sex discrimination in violation of the 14th Amendment's equal protection clause.

In 1990, VMI and the Citadel in South Carolina were the only government-supported all-male military colleges in the United States. Both institutions had long, proud records of distinguished service and achievement. And they were committed to the preservation of their venerable traditions, especially their men-only admissions policies. The time-honored principles and practices of VMI and the Citadel were suddenly and critically threatened by the legal complaint of an anonymous high school senior who charged that the VMI office of admissions failed to acknowledge or respond to her application to attend the college. The case initiated by the 1990 complaint against VMI reached the U.S. Supreme Court after more than five years in lower federal courts.

After losing the first round in the federal district court, the U.S. Department of Justice took the case to the 4th U.S. Circuit Court of Appeals, which decided that the all-male policy violated the 14th Amendment's guarantee of "equal protection of the laws." Instead of ordering immediate admission of women to VMI, however, the appeals court remanded the case to the district court of original jurisdiction to explore alternative remedies to the nullified admissions policy. In response, VMI created a plan to offer state-supported military education for women in the Virginia Women's Institute for Leadership (VWIL), which it established at nearby Mary Baldwin College. The U.S. government appealed this outcome of the appellate court's decision to the U.S. Supreme Court.

The federal government's lawyers charged that the VWIL plan did not satisfy the 14th Amendment's guarantee of equal protection. Further, they claimed it did not even meet the now discredited standard of *Plessy* v. *Ferguson* (1896)—"separate but equal"—and thereby was a disgraceful attempt to avoid compliance with constitutional law.

Advocates for the state of Virginia defended the VWIL plan as an equitable alternative that provided new opportunities for women. At the same time, it preserved a hallowed and publicly useful tradition of all-male military education that had demonstrated its worth by producing leaders who, generation after generation, served the common good in Virginia and the United States. Further, the counsel for Virginia claimed that women were not capable of performing competently under the physically and psychologically stressful "adversative" method of training used at VMI.

The Issue Does the 14th Amendment's guarantee of "equal protection of the laws" prohibit a state government from maintaining an all-male military college? Or is such a policy justified by serving important governmental objectives that contribute uniquely and compellingly to the common good?

Opinion of the Court Justice Ruth Bader Ginsburg's opinion ended the 157-year tradition of all-male education at VMI, and by extension at the Citadel in South Carolina. Justice Ginsburg wrote, "While Virginia serves the state's sons [at VMI] it makes no provision whatever for her daughters. That is not equal protection" as guaranteed by the U.S. Constitution. Ginsburg's opinion rejected Virginia's claim that the VWIL program at Mary Baldwin College provided an equal opportunity for the state's women. Further, the justice pointed out that women successfully attended and graduated from the United States Military Academy. This repudiated the Virginia counsel's claim that women could not meet standards at VMI suitable only for males. Justice Ginsburg concluded, "Women seeking

and fit for a VMI-quality education cannot be offered anything else." (Justice Thomas did not participate in the Court's decision because his son, Jamal, was a student at VMI.)

Dissent Justice Antonin Scalia objected strongly to the Court's decision. He lamented, "Today the Court shuts down an institution that has served the people of the Commonwealth of Virginia with pride and distinction for over a century and a half." He argued that single-sex public schools should and could be constitutionally permitted for those who wanted them.

Significance The Court's opinion in the VMI case requires government to make an "exceedingly persuasive justification" based on a compelling public interest for the maintenance of a single-sex public school or even private school that receives public funds.

Both VMI and the Citadel complied with the Court's decision. VMI, however, did it reluctantly at first. The school's superintendent called the decision "a savage disappointment" and proposed that VMI should become a private school without obligation to comply with the Court's ruling in this case. But the VMI Board of Visitors rejected this proposal and approved the admission of women beginning in 1997.

United States v. Wong Kim Ark

☆ *169 U.S. 649 (1898)*
☆ *Vote: 6–2*
☆ *For the Court: Gray*
☆ *Dissenting: Fuller and Harlan*
☆ *Not participating: McKenna*

WONG KIM ARK was born in San Francisco, California, in 1873. His parents had gone to California from China.

A scene from San Francisco's Chinatown at the turn of the century. In 1898 the Supreme Court ruled that anyone born in the United States, regardless of ancestry, has the rights of a U.S. citizen.

They were not citizens of the United States but retained their status as subjects of the emperor of China.

Wong Kim Ark traveled to China in 1894. When he returned to California one year later, federal agents refused him admission to the United States because, they said, he was Chinese and not a citizen of the United States. Wong Kim Ark claimed U.S. citizenship because he was born in the United States.

The Issue The 14th Amendment says, "All persons born or naturalized in the United States, and subject to the jurisdiction thereof, are citizens of the United States and of the State wherein they reside." The federal government argued that Wong Kim Ark was not a citizen of the United States because his parents were Chinese. Thus, neither Wong Kim Ark nor his parents were "subject to the jurisdiction" of the United States. Rather, claimed the federal government, they were subject to the jurisdiction of China. Did a person of Chinese descent, born in the United States, have the right of U.S. citizenship?

Opinion of the Court The decision favored Wong Kim Ark. Justice Horace Gray held that the common law tradition and the 14th Amendment clearly guaranteed U.S. citizenship to all people born in the country. The ethnic identity or place of birth of the person's parents could not be used to deny citizenship to a person born in the United States.

Significance This case immediately established the citizenship rights of people of Asian descent born in the United States. It also established the general rule of *jus soli* (a Latin term meaning the "right based on soil")—the determination of citizenship by place of birth. The *Wong Kim Ark* case rejected the general rule of *jus sanguinis* (a Latin term meaning the "right based on blood")—the determination of citizenship by the ethnicity of the parents. Given the rule of *jus soli*—embodied in the 14th Amendment—Wong Kim Ark was entitled to all privileges and rights of U.S. citizenship on equal terms with any other citizen, whether naturalized (by legal procedure) or natural born, as he was.

SEE ALSO
Citizenship

United Steelworkers of America v. Weber

☆ *443 U.S. 193 (1979)*
☆ *Vote: 5–2*
☆ *For the Court: Brennan*
☆ *Dissenting: Burger and Rehnquist*
☆ *Not participating: Powell and Stevens*

THE UNITED Steelworkers of America, a labor union, made an agreement with the Kaiser Aluminum and Chemical Company to set up a training program to develop the skills of workers at a Kaiser plant in Gramercy, Louisiana. Half of the places in the program were reserved for black workers. In the past, black workers in this region had been denied opportunities to become highly

An apprentice steelworker on the job. The Supreme Court ruled in 1979 that companies can establish affirmative action plans to choose workers for their training programs.

skilled craftworkers, and most of them worked at low-paying, menial jobs. The company's voluntary and temporary plan was designed to overcome past job discrimination and to create new opportunities for black workers.

Brian Weber, a white unskilled worker and a member of the union, applied for a position in the new job training program. He was rejected. However, black workers with less seniority than Weber were selected in order to fill the 50 percent quota reserved for black workers in the new training program.

Seniority refers to the amount of time a worker has been employed in a job. Labor unions often use seniority as a standard for distributing benefits of one kind or another; those with more years of service get preference in promotions to better jobs or positions in job training programs.

Weber charged that his rejection for admission to the job training program was unfair because it was based on race, not the usual standard of seniority. He claimed this was a violation of Title VII of the Civil Rights Act of 1964, which forbids an employer to discriminate against an employee "because of such individual's race, color, religion, sex, or national origin." Weber sued the union and his employer.

The Issue Was the plan for selecting applicants to the job training program, set up by the United Steelworkers of America in agreement with the Kaiser plant, a violation of Title VII of the Civil Rights Act of 1964? Was Brian Weber illegally denied admission to the new job training program at the Kaiser plant in Gramercy, Louisiana?

Opinion of the Court The Court held that the plan for selecting applicants to the job training program did not violate the Civil Rights Act of 1964. Justice William Brennan wrote that the plan for selecting applicants was in line with the intent of the Civil Rights Act to "break down old patterns of racial segregation and hierarchy."

Brennan emphasized that the race-based quota in the plan was temporary and resulted from a voluntary agreement between a labor union and an employer. Further, he said, the purpose was not to maintain a racial balance but to overcome a long-standing racial imbalance in employment opportunity.

Dissent Chief Justice Warren Burger and Justice William Rehnquist argued that the plan for admission to the job training program conflicted with the words and the intent of the 1964 Civil Rights Act. According to the dissenters, the federal law clearly prohibits discrimination on the basis of race in selecting participants for a job training program.

Significance This was the first case in which the Court decided an issue about an employer's affirmative action plan—a program that gives favored treatment to members of certain groups supposed to have suffered from past discrimination in employment opportunities. The decision encouraged private employers to experiment with temporary and voluntary affirmative action plans.

SEE ALSO
Affirmative action

Van Devanter, Willis

ASSOCIATE JUSTICE, 1911–37

☆ *Born: Apr. 17, 1859, Marion, Ind.*
☆ *Education: Indiana Asbury University (DePauw University), B.A., 1878; University of Cincinnati Law School, LL.B., 1881*
☆ *Previous government service: city attorney, Cheyenne, Wyo., 1887–88; Wyoming Territorial Legislature, 1888; chief justice, Wyoming Territory Supreme Court, 1889–90; assistant U.S. attorney general, 1897–1903;*

judge, U.S. Court of Appeals for the Eighth Circuit, 1903–1910
☆*Appointed by President William Howard Taft Dec. 12, 1910; replaced William Moody, who retired*
☆ *Supreme Court term: confirmed by the Senate Dec. 15, 1910, by a voice vote; retired June 2, 1937*
☆ *Died: Feb. 8, 1941, Washington, D.C.*

WILLIS VAN DEVANTER moved, as a young man, from his settled community in Indiana to Cheyenne in the Wyoming Territory. On the last western frontier, he built a successful career in law and politics that led him back east to federal government service in Washington, D.C.

Van Devanter served 26 years on the Supreme Court, where he exercised great influence on his colleagues during most of his long term. He rarely wrote opinions; his average number of opinions per year was only 14. (Most justices wrote more than 30 per year.) Justice Van Devanter influenced the other justices through face-to-face discussions about the cases before the Court. He often influenced the direction and substance of opinions written by others.

Justice Van Devanter argued persistently for limited government and against the expansion of the federal government's power to regulate businesses and the relationships between employers and workers. Accordingly, he reacted strongly against the New Deal programs of President Franklin D. Roosevelt. He succeeded in influencing the Court to strike down several New Deal laws during President Roosevelt's first term of office. However, by 1936 the tide had turned against him. Public opinion was strongly on the side of Roosevelt's New Deal. The President's new appointments to the Court reflected this public mood and Roosevelt's views. As a result, Van Devanter decided to retire from the Court in 1937.

Vernonia School District v. Acton

☆ *515 U.S. 646 (1995)*
☆ *Vote: 6–3*
☆ *For the Court: Scalia*
☆ *Concurring: Ginsburg*
☆ *Dissent: O'Connor, Stevens, and Souter*

VERNONIA, OREGON, a small community of about 3,000 people, faced a serious problem of drug use among students of the local public schools. So the Vernonia School Board approved an antidrug policy, which required random drug testing of students wanting to participate in interschool athletics.

Vernonia's drug-testing program required all middle-school and high-school student athletes to provide a urine sample at the beginning of their team's season. During the remainder of the season, on a weekly basis, 10 percent of the team members would be chosen at random for a new test. Athletes refusing to take the test would be prevented from participating in interschool sports activities for two years. Students with a positive test result would be suspended from participating in the school's sports program for an unspecified period while undergoing counseling to remedy their problems.

The drug-testing policy seemed to be acceptable among parents in Vernonia. No one objected to the policy when the school board approved it in 1989. However, when James Acton wanted to join his school's seventh-grade football team, his parents challenged the drug-testing policy. They refused to sign a urinalysis consent form to permit their son to take the test. And they filed suit in the federal district court in 1991 to stop the drug-testing policy because, in their opinion, it

James Acton (center) leaves the Supreme Court with his parents (right) and supporters. The Actons argued that their school district's drug testing policy constituted "unreasonable" search.

violated the 4th Amendment's prohibition against "unreasonable" searches.

The federal district court in Oregon dismissed the Actons' suit. They appealed to the Court of Appeals for the 9th District, which favored the Actons' complaint and voided the Vernonia drug-testing program. However, this decision conflicted with a 1988 ruling of the 5th Circuit Court of Appeals that permitted random drug testing in public schools of Indiana, Illinois, and Wisconsin. So the Acton case went on appeal to the U.S. Supreme Court, which was called upon to resolve the conflicting appellate court opinions.

The Issue Did the Vernonia School District's mandatory drug-testing policy violate the 4th Amendment rights of students? The Acton family claimed it called for unreasonable searches of a student's body and thereby violated the person's rights under the Constitution's 4th Amendment. The school district's lawyers argued that a compelling public interest—preventing illegal drug use among preadults—justified limitations on the 4th Amendment rights of students in public schools.

Opinion of the Court The Supreme Court upheld the Vernonia drug-testing policy. The Court concluded that the school board's objective on behalf of the community to protect the public against drug abuse, a rampant problem, outweighed the minimal limitations of an individual's 4th Amendment rights associated with the drug-testing regulations. The Court pointed out that only members of sports teams were subjected to drug-testing and that participation in interschool athletics was voluntary.

Writing for the Court, Justice Antonin Scalia said, "The most significant element in this case is...that the Policy was undertaken in furtherance of the government's responsibilities, under a public school system, as guardian and tutor for children entrusted to its care." He pointed out that "when the government acts as a guardian and tutor the relevant question is whether the search is one that a reasonable guardian and tutor might undertake." And he concluded that given the mission of public schools, and the circumstances of this case, the searches required by the school board's policy were "reasonable" and thereby permissible under the Constitution's 4th Amendment.

Dissent According to Justice Sandra Day O'Connor, the Vernonia School Board's policy permitted "suspicionless searches" of students, and this violated their 4th Amendment rights. She wrote that innocent students could be "open to an intrusive bodily search" [even though most of them] have given school officials no reason whatsoever to suspect they use drugs at school." Justice O'Connor concluded that it would be "far more reasonable" to restrict drug testing to students who caused disciplinary problems at school.

Significance Federal government officials praised the Court's decision as supportive of their war against illegal drug use. Lee Brown, President Bill Clinton's adviser on drug policy, called the ruling "a victory for kids." But a leader of the American Civil Liberties

Union criticized the Court for failing to protect the rights of students in schools. He said, "It makes students second-class citizens." The Acton case is a prime example of the ongoing controversy in a free society about how to balance the community's legitimate needs for order and safety against the individual's constitutional rights to liberty.

Vinson, Fred M.

CHIEF JUSTICE, 1946–53

☆ *Born: Jan. 22, 1890, Louisa, Ky.*
☆ *Education: Centre College, B.A., 1909, LL.B., 1911*
☆ *Previous government service: commonwealth's attorney, 32nd District of Kentucky, 1921–24; U.S. Representative from Kentucky, 1924–29, 1931–38; judge, U.S. Court of Appeals for the District of Columbia Circuit, 1938–43; director, U.S. Office of Economic Stabilization, 1943–45; administrator, Federal Loan Agency, 1945; director, U.S. Office of War Mobilization and Reconversion, 1945; U.S. secretary of the Treasury, 1945–46*
☆ *Appointed by President Harry S. Truman June 6, 1946; replaced Harlan Fiske Stone, who died*
☆ *Supreme Court term: confirmed by the Senate June 20, 1946, by a voice vote; served until Sept. 8, 1953*
☆ *Died: Sept. 8, 1953, Washington, D.C.*

FRED M. VINSON became the 13th chief justice of the United States in 1946. This was the capstone of a long and meritorious career in all three branches of the federal government. Chief Justice Vinson served only seven years, until his death in 1953, as chief justice. These were years of tumult and controversy involving the Court in issues of patriotism and loyalty to the United States and issues of civil liberties and equal protection against racial discrimination.

Chief Justice Vinson acted strongly against individuals he viewed as a threat to the government of the United States. In *Dennis* v. *United States* (1951), for example, he upheld the Smith Act, which provided for criminal convictions of anyone advocating violent overthrow of the U.S. government. In the *Dennis* case, several leaders of the American Communist party were punished.

Chief Justice Vinson supported equal rights for black Americans in several opinions. For example, he led the Court in overturning state laws that unfairly discriminated against black people in *Sweatt* v. *Painter* (1950) and *McLaurin* v. *Board of Regents* (1950). These rulings helped to set the stage for the Court's landmark decision in *Brown* v. *Board of Education* (1954), which marked the beginning of the end of racial segregation in public schools and other institutions.

SEE ALSO

Dennis v. United States; Sweatt v. Painter

FURTHER READING

Palmer, Jan S. *The Vinson Court Era.* New York: AMS Press, 1990.
Pritchett, C. Herman. *Civil Liberties and the Vinson Court.* Chicago: University of Chicago Press, 1954.
Urofsky, Melvin I. *Division and Discord: The Supreme Court under Stone and Vinson, 1941–1953.* Columbia: University of South Carolina Press, 1999.

Waite, Morrison R.

CHIEF JUSTICE, 1874–88

☆ *Born: Nov. 29, 1816, Lyme, Conn.*
☆ *Education: Yale College, B.A., 1837*
☆ *Previous government service: Ohio House of Representatives, 1850–52; president, Ohio Constitutional Convention, 1873–74*
☆ *Appointed by President Ulysses S. Grant Jan. 19, 1874; replaced Salmon P. Chase, who died*

☆ *Supreme Court term: confirmed by the Senate Jan. 21, 1874, by a 63–0 vote; served until Mar. 23, 1888*

☆ *Died: Mar. 23, 1888, Washington, D.C.*

MORRISON R. WAITE had no judicial experience before his appointment as chief justice, and he had never presented a case before the Supreme Court. President Ulysses S. Grant appointed Waite to head the Supreme Court because of his effectiveness in representing the United States in an international arbitration case in Geneva.

At first, Chief Justice Waite was not respected by other members of the Supreme Court because of his lack of experience. He eventually won their acceptance and respect for his hard work and leadership of the Court.

Chief Justice Waite often decided in favor of the power and rights of state governments. For example, in his most notable opinion, *Munn* v. *Illinois* (1877), Chief Justice Waite upheld an Illinois law that set maximum rates that could be charged by grain elevator owners. He supported the power of the state of Illinois to regulate the use of private property "when such regulation becomes necessary for the public good."

In the *Munn* case, and similar cases involving state laws, Waite believed that the political process, not the Courts, was the correct avenue for opponents of the laws. In *Munn* v. *Illinois*, Waite wrote: "For protection against abuse by legislatures, the people must resort to the polls, not to the courts." Waite believed that the legislative branch of government, not the judicial branch, should always take the lead in making public policy. The judiciary, he argued, should limit itself to questions of legal interpretation.

Under Waite's leadership, the Court tended to narrowly interpret the rights of black Americans under the 14th and 15th Amendments to the U.S. Constitution. Waite argued that most civil rights were associated with state citizenship, which should be guaranteed by the state governments, not the federal government. This viewpoint, which often prevailed on the Court at this time, meant that the civil rights of black Americans varied considerably depending upon the state in which they lived. In many states, their rights were not equal to those of white Americans, and the Supreme Court, under Waite, was reluctant to intervene into the states' affairs to secure these rights.

SEE ALSO

Judicial activism and judicial restraint; Munn v. Illinois

FURTHER READING

Magrath, Peter C. *Morrison R. Waite: The Triumph of Character*. New York: Macmillan, 1963.

Wallace v. Jaffree

☆ *472 U.S. 38 (1985)*

☆ *Vote: 6–3*

☆ *For the Court: Stevens*

☆ *Concurring: Powell and O'Connor*

☆ *Dissenting: Burger, White, and Rehnquist*

FROM 1978 TO 1982 the Alabama legislature passed three laws pertaining to prayer in public schools. The 1978 law authorized schools to provide a daily minute of silence for meditation. A 1981 law provided for a similar period "for meditation or voluntary prayer." A third law, enacted in 1982, allowed teachers to lead "willing students" in a prescribed prayer.

In 1982 Ishmael Jaffree filed suit against the school board of Mobile County to challenge the 1981 and 1982 Alabama laws permitting a period of

Ishmael Jaffree on the steps of the Supreme Court. When Jaffree's children reported that their teachers were leading prayers in school, he filed suit against the state for violating the constitutional separation of church and state.

silence and prayer in public schools. Jaffree decided to file this suit after his three children reported that their teachers had led prayers in school. Jaffree claimed that the 1981 and 1982 Alabama statutes on prayer in public schools violated the establishment clause of the 1st Amendment to the U.S. Constitution, which prohibited the states from making laws regarding the establishment of religion. He cited Supreme Court decisions such as *Engel* v. *Vitale* (1962) and *Abington School District* v. *Schempp* (1963) to support his argument. In both cases, the Court found that state-mandated religious activities in public schools were unconstitutional.

A federal district court ruled against Jaffree, stating that the *Engel* and *Schempp* cases were decided incorrectly. This district court ruling was overturned by the U.S. Court of Appeals for the 11th Circuit. The Court of Appeals followed the precedents of the *Engel* and *Schempp* cases and held that the 1981 and 1982 Alabama laws violated the establishment clause of the 1st Amendment as applied to the states through the 14th Amendment. The state of Alabama appealed the federal appellate court's decision to the U.S. Supreme Court.

The Issue The Supreme Court summarily upheld the appellate court's decision to strike down the 1982 statute, which clearly authorized teachers and students to set aside time for expression of prayer in public schools. According to the Court, this was a clear violation of the 1st Amendment's establishment clause. Therefore, the Court agreed to hear oral arguments only about the

1981 statute, which authorized the moment of silence for "meditation or voluntary prayer." Does a state law authorizing a moment of silence in a public school, for the express purpose of prayer, violate the 1st Amendment provisions on religion: "Congress shall make no law respecting an establishment of religion, or prohibiting the free exercise thereof"?

Opinion of the Court The Court decided for Jaffree and overturned the Alabama law at issue in this case because of the law's religious purpose and intentions. Justice John Paul Stevens relied upon the Court's previous rulings in *Abington School District* v. *Schempp* (1963) and *Lemon* v. *Kurtzman* (1971) to justify the *Jaffree* decision.

Dissent Justice William Rehnquist argued for a totally new interpretation of the 1st Amendment's establishment clause. He rejected the idea of a "wall of separation" between church and state. And he opposed the precedents of *Schempp* and *Lemon* as bases for making decisions about establishment clause issues. Instead, Rehnquist claimed that the 1st Amendment was designed only to prevent the government from favoring one religion over another. As long as all religions were treated neutrally or equally (nonpreferentially), said Rehnquist, the government could provide support for religion in public schools.

Significance This case is notable for what it did not decide. The question of a legislated moment of silence without specific provision for prayer was not addressed. As a result, moments of silence continue to be observed in the public schools of more than 25 states, including Alabama.

SEE ALSO

Abington School District v. Schempp; Engel v. Vitale; Establishment clause; Lemon v. Kurtzman; Religious issues under the Constitution

FURTHER READING

Irons, Peter. *The Courage of Their Convictions.* New York: Free Press, 1988.

Ware v. Hylton

☆ *3 Dall. 199 (1796)*
☆ *Vote: 4–0*
☆ *For the Court: seriatim opinions by Chase, Paterson, Wilson, and Cushing*
☆ *Not participating: Ellsworth and Iredell*

THE TREATY OF PARIS (1783), which ended the American War of Independence, guaranteed that prewar debts owed by Americans to British subjects would be recoverable. The state of Virginia, however, had passed legislation during the war to protect citizens of Virginia who had debts to British creditors against demands for repayment of the debts. Ware, the financial agent of a British subject, sought payment of a debt owed his client by Daniel Hylton, a Virginia citizen, so Ware took his case to a federal court.

The Issue Article 6 of the Constitution says that "all Treaties made, or which shall be made, under the Authority of the United States, shall be the supreme Law of the Land; and the Judges in every State shall be bound thereby, any Thing in the Constitution or Laws of any State to the Contrary notwithstanding." Given the precise wording of the Constitution about treaties as supreme law, was it possible for Virginia to violate a provision of the 1783 Treaty of Paris about payment of debts to British subjects?

Hylton's attorney was John Marshall, a future chief justice of the United States. Marshall argued that a U.S. treaty could not override a state law enacted before the Constitution was written in 1787 and before the Treaty of Paris was ratified. Ware argued that the Virginia law at issue violated the U.S. Constitution and, therefore, should be struck down by the Court.

Opinion of the Court The Supreme Court decided against Hylton and the state of Virginia. It ruled that the Treaty of Paris was part of the supreme law of the United States and its provisions took precedence over any state law that conflicted with it. The Court declared the state law unconstitutional and therefore null and void. Justice Samuel Chase wrote, "A treaty cannot be the supreme law of the land... if any act of a state legislature can stand in its way.... [L]aws of any states, contrary to a treaty shall be disregarded [as]... null and void."

Significance John Marshall lost the only case he argued before the Supreme Court, which he later dominated for 34 years. Ironically, the Court's sweeping defense of federal supremacy over conflicting state laws was in keeping with Marshall's subsequent opinions for the Court.

This case marks the Court's first use of judicial review to strike down a state action because it violated the U.S. Constitution. This power, implied by Article 6 of the U.S. Constitution, is spelled out in Section 25 of the Judiciary Act of 1789.

SEE ALSO
Federalism; Judicial review

Warren, Earl
CHIEF JUSTICE, 1953–69

☆ *Born: Mar. 19, 1891, Los Angeles, Calif.*
☆ *Education: University of California at Berkeley, B.L., 1912, J.D., 1914*
☆ *Previous government service: deputy city attorney, Oakland, Calif., 1919–20; deputy assistant district attorney, Alameda County, Calif., 1920–23;*

chief deputy district attorney, Alameda County, 1923–25; district attorney, Alameda County, 1925–39; attorney general of California, 1939–43; governor of California, 1943–53

☆ *Appointed by President Dwight D. Eisenhower as a recess appointment Oct. 2, 1953; replaced Chief Justice Fred M. Vinson, who died; nominated by Eisenhower Jan. 11, 1954*

☆ *Supreme Court term: confirmed by the Senate Mar. 1, 1954, by a voice vote; retired June 23, 1969*

☆ *Died: July 9, 1974, Washington, D.C.*

EARL WARREN, the son of immigrants from Norway, had a profound influence on constitutional law in the United States. As the 14th chief justice of the United States, he presided over a judicial revolution in the 1950s and 1960s.

Warren's public life before becoming chief justice gave little hint of what he would do on the Court. His career was conducted exclusively in California local and state politics from 1919 until 1953, when he joined the Supreme Court. During World War II, as attorney general and governor of California, Warren vigorously supported the federal order removing people of Japanese ancestry from the Pacific Coast of the United States and confining them in grim camps. He believed, without any evidence, that these people could threaten the national security of the United States during its war with Japan. At the end of his life, Warren expressed remorse: "I have since deeply regretted the removal order and my own testimony advocating it, because it was not in keeping with our American concept of freedom and the rights of citizens."

Governor Warren moved to the Supreme Court through his participation in the Presidential election of 1952, when he helped Dwight D. Eisenhower win the Republican party nomination for President. After winning the Presidency,

Eisenhower rewarded Earl Warren with the appointment to the office of chief justice.

Eisenhower later said this appointment was "the biggest damn-fool mistake I ever made." Supreme Court scholars, however, have lauded Warren as one of the Court's all-time great justices. What did Warren do to disappoint Eisenhower and win the acclaim of scholars?

Earl Warren presided over the Supreme Court during a period of great controversy and change. Under his leadership, the Court stated new ideas on equal protection of the laws, the rights of persons accused of crime, freedom of expression, and representation in government.

Chief Justice Warren's greatest opinion was written in 1954, at the beginning of his 16-year term. In *Brown* v. *Board of Education*, Chief Justice Warren skillfully influenced the Court's unanimous decision to strike down state laws that required separate schools to be provided for black and white students. This decision overturned the 1896 ruling in *Plessy* v. *Ferguson* that had sanctioned racial segregation in public facilities.

Several decisions of the Warren Court greatly expanded the constitutional rights of those suspected or accused of crime. For example, state law enforcement officials were required to exclude illegally obtained evidence in criminal proceedings (*Mapp* v. *Ohio*, 1961), to guarantee the right to competent legal assistance for an accused person (*Gideon* v. *Wainwright*, 1963), and to inform people of their right against self-incrimination (*Griffin* v. *California*, 1965, and *Miranda* v. *Arizona*, 1966). These decisions overruled earlier Court rulings that had allowed the states to deviate from strict observance of the federal Bill of Rights. The Warren Court moved decisively to apply the rights of an accused person, as outlined in the federal Bill of Rights, to all of the states under the due process clause of the 14th Amendment to the U.S. Constitution.

The Warren Court's most significant ruling on freedom of expression came in *New York Times Co. v. Sullivan* (1964). The Court held that a public official may not sue and recover damages for libel against a person who has written untrue statements about him unless there was a complete and reckless disregard for truth. The Court's intention was to remove barriers to the free flow of information about government officials that is a necessary part of the democratic process.

Chief Justice Warren considered the Court's rulings on a series of "reapportionment cases" to be its most important contribution to constitutional law. These decisions, beginning with *Baker v. Carr* (1962) and culminating in *Reynolds* v. *Sims* (1964), established the principle of "one person, one vote" in state and federal elections. State governments were required to apportion, or divide, the state, for purposes of political representation, into districts based solely on population, with the districts as nearly equal in population as was possible. This decision ended the practice of creating districts to unfairly inflate representation in government of some groups at the expense of other groups.

Chief Justice Warren believed it was the Court's responsibility to protect the civil liberties and rights of individuals against overbearing majorities acting privately or through their representatives in government. Warren also believed that the Court should be an active partner with the other branches of government in achieving social justice and protection of the individual against the powers of the state.

SEE ALSO

Brown v. Board of Education; Incorporation doctrine; Judicial activism and judicial restraint; Miranda v. Arizona; Reynolds v. Sims

FURTHER READING

Cray, Ed. *Chief Justice: A Biography of Earl Warren.* New York: Simon & Schuster, 1997.
Powe, Lucas A. *The Warren Court and American Politics.* Cambridge: Harvard University Press, 2000.
Schwartz, Bernard. *Superchief: Earl Warren and His Supreme Court.* New York: New York University Press, 1983.
Schwartz, Bernard. *The Warren Court: A Retrospective.* New York: Oxford University Press, 1996.
White, G. Edward. *Earl Warren: A Public Life.* New York: Oxford University Press, 1982.

Washington, Bushrod

ASSOCIATE JUSTICE, 1798–1829

☆ *Born: June 5, 1762, Westmoreland County, Va.*
☆ *Education: College of William and Mary, B.A., 1778; read law with James Wilson in Philadelphia, Pa.*
☆ *Previous government service: Virginia House of Delegates, 1787; Virginia Ratifying Convention, 1788*
☆ *Appointed by President John Adams as a recess appointment Sept. 29, 1798; replaced James Wilson, who died; nominated by Adams Dec. 19, 1798*
☆ *Supreme Court term: confirmed by the Senate Dec. 20, 1798, by a voice vote; served until Nov. 26, 1829*
☆ *Died: Nov. 26, 1829, Philadelphia, Pa.*

BUSHROD WASHINGTON was George Washington's favorite nephew, who inherited his uncle's property at Mount Vernon. He served in the Continental Army under his Uncle George during the War of Independence. He studied law under James Wilson, whom Bushrod Washington succeeded on the Supreme Court.

Bushrod Washington served on the Supreme Court for 31 years, but he wrote no important decisions. Rather, his contributions came as an ardent supporter of Chief Justice Marshall's opinions.

His ties to John Marshall were so close that another associate justice, William Johnson, said that they "are commonly estimated as a single judge."

Justice Washington and Chief Justice Marshall were together on the Supreme Court for 29 years. They disagreed only three times.

Wayne, James M.

ASSOCIATE JUSTICE, 1835–67

☆ Born: 1790, Savannah, Ga.
☆ Education: College of New Jersey (Princeton), B.A., 1808; read law under Charles Chauncey in New Haven, Conn.
☆ Previous government service: Georgia House of Representatives, 1815–16; mayor of Savannah, 1817–19; judge, Savannah Court of Common Pleas, 1820–22; judge, Georgia Superior Court, 1822–28; U.S. Representative from Georgia, 1829–35
☆ Appointed by President Andrew Jackson Jan. 7, 1835; replaced William Johnson, who died
☆ Supreme Court term: confirmed by the Senate Jan. 9, 1835, by a voice vote; served until July 5, 1867
☆ Died: July 5, 1867, Washington, D.C.

JAMES M. WAYNE served 32 years as an associate justice of the U.S. Supreme Court. During this time he was torn by his conflicting loyalties to the South and to the federal Union. He was a slaveholder from Georgia who believed in the power and right of each state to decide, without federal interference, about the institution of slavery. He was also committed to the preservation of the United States of America.

When the Civil War erupted, Justice Wayne remained loyal to the Union and remained on the Supreme Court. His son, by contrast, resigned from the U.S. Army and became the adjutant general of the Confederate state of Georgia. In 1861, Georgia declared Justice Wayne an "enemy alien" and confiscated his property.

During the Civil War, Justice Wayne supported President Abraham Lincoln's policies in the *Prize Cases* (1863), upholding Lincoln's blockade of Southern ports, and in *Ex parte Vallandigham* (1864), which permitted the conviction of a civilian Confederate sympathizer in a military court.

FURTHER READING

Lawrence, Alexander A. *James Moore Wayne: Southern Unionist.* Chapel Hill: University of North Carolina Press, 1943.

Webster v. Reproductive Health Services

☆ *492 U.S. 490 (1989)*
☆ *Vote: 5–4*
☆ *For the Court: Rehnquist*
☆ *Concurring: Scalia and O'Connor*
☆ *Dissenting: Blackmun, Brennan, Marshall, and Stevens*

IN 1986 the state of Missouri passed a law that placed certain restrictions on the performance of abortions. This law was challenged as an unconstitutional violation of women's rights by Reproductive Health Services, a federal organization providing assistance for women seeking abortions. A district court and circuit court of appeals struck down the Missouri law because it placed restrictions on a woman's right to choose an abortion, which was established in *Roe v. Wade* (1973). The state of Missouri appealed to the U.S. Supreme Court.

The Issue At issue was the constitutionality of the Missouri law restricting a woman's right to an abortion, which violated the precedent established by the Court in *Roe v. Wade*.

Opinion of the Court Chief Justice William Rehnquist reported the opinion of a divided Court. A bare majority upheld two of several provisions of the Missouri law: "[W]e uphold the Act's restrictions on the use of public employees and facilities for the performance or assistance of non-therapeutic abortions [those not necessary to save a mother's life]." The other provision of the Missouri law upheld by the Court was a requirement that "before a physician performs an abortion on a woman he has reason to believe is carrying an unborn child of twenty or more weeks… the physician shall first determine if the unborn child is viable [capable of life outside the womb]." Thus, the *Webster* decision modified the second-trimester rule in *Roe* v. *Wade,* which held that all regulations on abortion rights during the fourth through sixth months of pregnancy must be related to protecting the health of the mother. The *Webster* decision, however, stopped short of overturning *Roe,* which antiabortion advocates had wanted.

Dissent Justice Harry Blackmun, author of the Court's opinion in *Roe* v. *Wade,* wrote a passionate dissent. He wrote, "Today, *Roe* v. *Wade* (1973) and the fundamental right of women to decide whether to terminate a pregnancy survive but are not secure." According to Justice Blackmun, the Court's decision in the *Webster* case "implicitly invites every state legislature to enact more and more restrictive abortion regulations in order to provoke more and more test cases, in the hope that sometime down the line the Court will return the law of procreative freedom to the severe limitations that generally prevailed in this country before January 22, 1973."

Significance This case fueled the heated public controversy about the abortion rights issue. Pro-choice groups, who favored abortion rights, saw the Court's decision as an assault on their position. Their opponents cheered it as the beginning of the end for *Roe* v. *Wade.* Both sides increased their attempts to influence state government officials to support their views in this ongoing dispute.

SEE ALSO

Abortion rights; Roe v. Wade

Weeks v. United States

☆ *232 U.S. 383 (1914)*
☆ *Vote: 9–0*
☆ *For the Court: Day*

LOCAL POLICE and U.S. marshals suspected Weeks of criminal behavior. His house was searched twice, first by local police and then by a U.S. marshal. Incriminating evidence was found and used to charge Weeks with the crime of sending lottery tickets through the mail.

Neither search of Weeks's home was authorized by a search warrant. So Weeks petitioned a federal court for the return of his property because it had been taken in violation of the 4th and 5th Amendments to the Constitution. The 4th Amendment requires government officials to obtain a warrant before they can search a person's home. The 5th Amendment says that no person can be "deprived of life, liberty, or property, without due process of law." Weeks's petition for return of his property went to the U.S. Supreme Court.

The Issue Did the warrantless search of Weeks's house by a federal officer violate his constitutional rights? Could Weeks's property, taken in a warrantless search, be kept by the government and used against Weeks in court?

Opinion of the Court Justice William R. Day narrowed the case to the consideration of Weeks's 4th Amendment rights, which clearly were violated by the federal marshal's warrantless search of his home. The judgment against Weeks was reversed because the evidence used against him was obtained illegally. His illegally seized property was returned to him and could not be used in any trial.

Significance This case was the origin of the exclusionary rule, which requires that evidence obtained in violation of a person's constitutional rights must be excluded from any legal proceedings against him. Prior to the *Weeks* case, courts admitted illegally seized evidence because the rights of the individual were considered secondary to society's need for the punishment of criminal behavior.

SEE ALSO
Exclusionary rule; Searches and seizures

West Coast Hotel Co. v. Parrish

☆ *300 U.S. 379 (1937)*
☆ *Vote: 5–4*
☆ *For the Court: Hughes*
☆ *Dissenting: Sutherland, Butler, McReynolds, and Van Devanter*

ELSIE PARRISH worked as a chambermaid at the Cascadian Hotel in Wenatchee, Washington. Her pay was $12 for a 48-hour week. This was less than the amount required by the state of Washington's minimum wage law. So Elsie Parrish brought suit against her employer. The state supreme court decided in favor of Parrish, but the hotel owners appealed to the U.S. Supreme Court.

The Issue One year earlier, in *Morehead* v. *New York ex rel. Tipaldo* (1936), the Court ruled a New York State minimum wage law unconstitu-

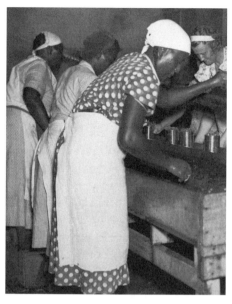

In 1937 the Supreme Court ruled that a Washington State minimum wage law, which protected workers from exploitation by employers, was constitutional.

tional. The Court argued for liberty of contract between employer and employee to decide without government regulation about wages and hours of work. This liberty of contract was held to be protected from state government regulations by the due process clause of the 14th Amendment. Did the state of Washington's minimum wage law violate the 14th Amendment?

Opinion of the Court The Court upheld the state minimum wage law and reversed the decisions in *Morehead* v. *New York ex rel. Tipaldo* (1936) and *Adkins* v. *Children's Hospital* (1923), upon which the *Morehead* decision was based. In *Adkins,* the Court declared unconstitutional an act of Congress that established a minimum wage for children and women workers in the District of Columbia. The dissenting view in *Morehead*—by Chief Justice Charles Evans Hughes and Justices Louis Brandeis, Benjamin Cardozo, and Harlan Fiske Stone—was the foundation for the Court's opinion in this case, written by Hughes. Justice Owen Roberts joined the four *Morehead* dissenters to form the Court majority in this case.

Chief Justice Hughes rejected the idea of liberty of contract set forth in the

Adkins and *Morehead* cases. He wrote:

> The Constitution does not speak of freedom of contract. It speaks of liberty and prohibits the deprivation of liberty without due process of law. In prohibiting that deprivation the Constitution does not recognize an absolute and uncontrollable liberty. ... The liberty safeguarded is liberty in a social organization which requires the protection of law against the evils which menace the health, safety, morals, and welfare of the people. Liberty under the Constitution is thus necessarily subject to the restraints of due process, and regulation which is adopted in the interests of the community is due process.

Significance Justice Roberts's vote in support of the Washington State minimum wage law was a complete change from his vote in the *Morehead* case, and it made the difference in the *Parrish* case. Reporters called it "the switch in time that saved nine." This reference was to the court-packing plan of President Franklin D. Roosevelt. He had been frustrated by several of the Court's decisions against his New Deal programs involving government regulation of businesses on behalf of the public good. So the President had proposed that Congress enact legislation to enable him to appoint six new justices to the Supreme Court. After the *Parrish* decision, however, the President backed away from his plan to alter the membership of the Court.

The *Parrish* decision provided legal support for Congress to pass the Fair Labor Standards Act in 1938, which included a minimum wage provision for businesses involved in interstate commerce. The *Parrish* decision also provided a precedent for federal court decisions against liberty of contract claims that would endanger important community interests and the public good.

SEE ALSO

Court-packing plan

WESTLAW

WEST PUBLISHING COMPANY has a computerized research service—WESTLAW—that contains a database of all Supreme Court decisions since 1790. Data on current decisions are sent electronically to the WESTLAW database from the Court and can be accessed via computer on the same day the decision is made. The database contains the full text of all decisions of the Court, summaries of recent decisions, and reports about changes in Supreme Court rules. The WESTLAW database also contains information about orders, such as the schedule for oral arguments, stays of execution, and invitations or permissions to file amicus curiae (friend of the court) briefs on cases scheduled to be heard by the Court, and cases accepted on appeal or denied review by the Court.

SEE ALSO

LEXIS; Appendix 3: Web Sites

Westside Community Board of Education v. Mergens

☆ *496 U.S. 226 (1990)*
☆ *Vote: 8–1*
☆ *For the Court: O'Connor*
☆ *Concurring: Brennan, Kennedy, Marshall, Scalia*
☆ *Dissenting: Stevens*

BRIDGET MERGENS, a student at Westside High School in Omaha, Nebraska, wanted to organize a Christian student club. This voluntary, student-led organization, which she proposed to the school principal, would meet at the school, but after the school day had ended, to discuss the Bible and pray. The club would be open to all students of the high school, regardless of their religious affiliation.

The principal refused this proposal because, in his view, it would violate the establishment clause of the U.S. Constitution's 1st Amendment. The Board of Education supported the principal's denial of Bridget Mergens's request.

Mergens and several other students sued the Board of Education for violation of their rights under a federal statute, the Equal Access Act (1984), which specifies the conditions by which public secondary schools are required to permit student religious organizations to use school facilities for their meetings.

First, it is "unlawful for any public secondary school which receives Federal financial assistance and which has a limited open forum to deny equal access or a fair opportunity to . . . any students who wish to conduct a meeting within that limited open forum on the basis of the religious . . . content of the speech at such meetings."

Second, there is a "limited open forum" in a public secondary school whenever it "grants an offering to or opportunity for one or more noncurriculum student groups to meet on school premises during noninstructional time."

Third, a school offers to students a "fair opportunity" to hold religion-based meetings within the school's "limited open forum" if the school equally and pervasively provides that meetings are initiated voluntarily by students; meetings are not sponsored by "the school, the government, or its agents or employees"; meetings may include the presence of "employees or agents of the school or government" only if they are not participants in the

activities; meetings may not "materially and substantially interfere with the orderly conduct of educational activities" of the school; and meetings may not be directed or controlled by "nonschool persons" and such persons may not regularly attend activities of the voluntary student organization.

Fourth, the government of the United States or any state government may not promote or support any religious activity beyond "the incidental cost of providing the space for student-initiated meetings."

Lawyers for Bridget Mergens brought her case to the U.S. District Court in Nebraska, where they argued that school officials had violated the Equal Access Act. They presented evidence that Westside High School had 30 student clubs, including several noncurriculum-related organizations. Thus, the school officials had created "a limited open forum" and were thereby obligated, as recipients of federal funds, to follow the provisions of the Equal Access Act. Further, Mergens claimed that her constitutional rights to freedom of speech, assembly, association, and free exercise of religion had been denied by school officials.

The federal district court denied relief to Bridget Mergens. This decision, however, was reversed by the U.S. Court of Appeals for the 8th Circuit. The Board of Education of the Westside Community Schools appealed to the U.S. Supreme Court to overturn the decision of the U.S. Court of Appeals.

The Issue At issue was the constitutionality of the Equal Access Act. This federal law was made to buttress the 1st Amendment's clause on free exercise of religion. But did it unconstitutionally undermine or compromise the 1st Amendment's prohibition of an establishment of religion?

The Westside Community Board of

Education had refused to permit students to organize a Christian club with the same privileges as other after-school student clubs. They claimed their decision was consistent with the establishment clause of the U.S. Constitution's 1st Amendment. Thus, the Equal Access Act should be judged an unconstitutional violation of the establishment clause.

Opinion of the Court The Supreme Court disagreed with the Westside Community Board of Education. The Court upheld the constitutionality of the Equal Access Act and ruled that the public school officials had violated this federal law by refusing recognition to the student-initiated Christian club. Writing for the Court, Justice Sandra Day O'Connor said:

> [T]here is a crucial difference between government speech endorsing religion, which the Establishment Clause forbids, and private speech endorsing religion, which the Free Speech and Free Exercise Clauses protect. We think that secondary school students are mature enough and are likely to understand that a school does not endorse or support student speech that it merely permits on a nondiscriminatory basis.... Although a school may not itself lead or direct a religious club, a school that permits a student-initiated and student-led religious club to meet after school, just as it permits any other student group to do, does not convey a message of state approval or endorsement of the particular religion.... To the extent that a religious club is merely one of many different student-initiated voluntary clubs, students should perceive no message of government endorsement of religion. Thus, we conclude that the Act does not, at least on its face and as applied to Westside, have the primary effect of advancing religion.

Justice O'Connor emphasized that the Equal Access Act, as applied to the case at Westside High School, did not violate the three-part Lemon Test set forth by the Court in the landmark decision of *Lemon* v. *Kurtzman* (1971). First, she held that the purpose of the Equal Access Act is "undeniably, secular." Second, she pointed out that the act's purpose was not to "endorse or disapprove of religion." Third, it did not bring about "an excessive entanglement with religion." Further, Justice O'Connor stressed that "if a State refused to let religious groups use facilities open to others, then it would demonstrate not neutrality but hostility toward religion." She maintained that the 1st Amendment's prohibition of an establishment of religion does not require or encourage government officials to act negatively toward religion.

Dissent Justice John Paul Stevens wrote the sole dissenting opinion in this case. He argued that the Court's interpretation of the Equal Access Act tended toward the constitutionally prohibited outcome of an excessive entanglement of government and religion. He wrote, "The Act, as construed by the majority, comes perilously close to an outright command to allow organized prayer... and religious ceremonies... on school premises."

Significance The Court's decision has strengthened the accommodationist position regarding relationships between government and religion under the Constitution. It has affected public schools throughout the United States by encouraging students to use their rights to free exercise of religion in ways that are consistent with constitutional law.

SEE ALSO

Establishment clause, Free exercise clause; Lemon Test; Lemon v. Kurtzman; Religious issues under the Constitution; Student rights under the Constitution

West Virginia State Board of Education v. Barnette

☆ *319 U.S. 624 (1943)*
☆ *Vote: 6–3*
☆ *For the Court: Jackson*
☆ *Concurring: Black, Douglas, and Murphy*
☆ *Dissenting: Frankfurter, Roberts, and Reed*

THE GOVERNMENT of West Virginia made a law that required students in public schools to salute the flag and pledge allegiance to it. Refusal to comply with this act would be considered insubordination punishable by expulsion from school. Readmission to school would be granted only on condition that the student comply with the flag-salute law. Furthermore, expelled students would be considered unlawfully absent from school, and their parents or guardians would be liable to prosecution.

Some children and their parents, who were Jehovah's Witnesses, refused to obey the flag-salute law on the grounds that it violated their religious beliefs. They viewed the flag of the United States as a "graven image," and their religion forbade them to "bow down to" or "worship a graven image." They argued that God's law was superior to the laws of the state. In turn, the local school authorities, backed by the West Virginia Board of Education, moved to punish the children and parents who would not obey the law. Thus, several West Virginia Jehovah's Witnesses families, including the family of Walter Barnette, sued for an injunction to stop enforcement of the flag-salute law.

The Issue Did the West Virginia flag-salute law violate the constitutional right to religious freedom of children

professing the religion of Jehovah's Witnesses?

Opinion of the Court The Court ruled that the West Virginia flag-salute requirement was unconstitutional. Justice Robert H. Jackson said that public officials could act to promote national unity through patriotic ceremonies. However, they could not use compulsion of the kind employed in this case to enforce compliance. In particular, the 1st Amendment to the Constitution (applied to the state government through the due process clause of the 14th Amendment) prohibited public officials from forcing students to salute the flag against their religious beliefs. Justice Jackson concluded with one of the most quoted statements in the annals of the Supreme Court:

> The very purpose of a Bill of Rights was to withdraw certain subjects from the vicissitudes of political controversy, to place them beyond the reach of majorities and officials and to establish them as legal principles to be applied by the courts. One's right to life, liberty, and property, to free speech, a free press, freedom of worship and assembly, and other fundamental rights may not be submitted to vote; they depend on the outcome of no elections. . . .
>
> If there is any fixed star in our constitutional constellation, it is that no official, high or petty, can pre-

In 1943 the Supreme Court ruled that a West Virginia law requiring students to salute the American flag was unconstitutional.

scribe what shall be orthodox in politics, nationalism, religion, or other matters of opinion or force citizens to confess by word or act their faith therein. If there are any circumstances which permit an exception, they do not now occur to us.

Dissent Justice Felix Frankfurter concluded that the state school board had the constitutional authority to require public school students to salute the flag. He wrote that by not complying with the law, minorities can disrupt government and civil society, and therefore the Court should support the duly enacted legislation at issue in this case, which clearly reflected the will of the majority in West Virginia. If citizens of West Virginia dislike laws enacted by their representatives in the state legislature, then they should try to influence the legislature to change the laws. According to Justice Frankfurter, the Supreme Court had overstepped its authority in placing its judgment above that of the elected legislature and school boards in West Virginia. "The courts ought to stand aloof from this type of controversy," he concluded.

Frankfurter especially objected to Jackson's argument that questions associated with the Bill of Rights should be beyond the reach of local officials and legislatures. Frankfurter believed judges had a duty to respect and give in to the discretion of legislatures and the laws they passed.

Significance The *Barnette* decision overturned the Court's ruling, only three years earlier, in *Minersville School District* v. *Gobitis*, which had upheld a Pennsylvania law requiring students in public schools to pledge allegiance to the American flag. The two flag-salute cases show how the Supreme Court can change its mind about the meaning of the Constitution. Applications of the doctrine of *stare decisis*—the use of pre-

cedent, or previously decided cases, to decide new cases—create stability in the law. However, allowing for exceptions to *stare decisis* and overruling precedents are ways the Court adapts the Constitution to changing conditions.

The *Barnette* case set a new precedent that the legal system has followed to this day. Federal courts applying the *Barnette* precedent have turned back several attempts by officials to establish new flag-salute requirements.

SEE ALSO

Free exercise clause; Minersville School District v. Gobitis; Religious issues under the Constitution; Student rights under the Constitution

FURTHER READING

Dillard, Irving. "The Flag-Salute Cases." In *Quarrels That Have Shaped the Constitution,* edited by John A. Garraty. New York: Harper & Row, 1987.

White, Byron R.
ASSOCIATE JUSTICE,
1962–93

☆ *Born: June 8, 1917, Fort Collins, Colo.*
☆ *Education: University of Colorado, B.A., 1938; Rhodes Scholar, Oxford University, 1939; Yale Law School, LL.B., 1946*
☆ *Previous government service: law clerk to Chief Justice Fred M. Vinson, 1946–47; deputy U.S. attorney general, 1961–62*
☆ *Appointed by President John F. Kennedy Mar. 30 , 1962; replaced Charles E. Whittaker, who retired*
☆ *Supreme Court term: confirmed by the Senate Apr. 11, 1962, by a voice vote; retired June 28, 1993*
☆ *Died: Apr. 15, 2002, Denver, Colo.*

BYRON R. WHITE was an excellent scholar-athlete at the University of Colorado. He ranked first in his class as a scholar, and he was a star on the varsity teams in football, basketball, and baseball. His prowess as a running back in football brought him national fame as an All American and earned him the nickname of Whizzer.

After graduation from college Whizzer White played one season for the Pittsburgh Steelers and led the National Football League in yards gained as a running back. Then he went to England as a Rhodes Scholar to study at Oxford. There he met John F. Kennedy, a future President of the United States.

During World War II, White joined the navy and served in the Pacific theater of the war, where he again met John Kennedy, an officer in the navy. Later, when Kennedy campaigned for President, Byron White supported him, which led to his appointment to the Supreme Court by Kennedy.

Justice White consistently supported equal protection of the law and civil rights of minorities, especially black Americans. However, he was cautious about expanding the rights of people suspected of criminal activity. For example, he dissented from the Warren Court majority in *Miranda* v. *Arizona* (1966) to argue that the Court's decision would unduly hamper efforts by police to obtain a confession from those suspected of criminal behavior. And he wrote for the Burger Court majority in *United States* v. *Leon* (1984) to establish a "good faith" exception to the exclusionary rule established by the Warren Court in *Mapp* v. *Ohio* (1961). The *Leon* case established that when police act on good faith to obtain evidence of criminal behavior without a valid search warrant, the evidence does not have to be excluded from the trial. Justice White also wrote for the Court in *New Jersey* v. *T.L.O.* (1985), which permitted public school officials to disregard the 4th Amendment protection against "unwarranted searches and seizures" when inspecting the personal belongings of stu-

dents in school who are presumed to be hiding evidence of unlawful behavior.

SEE ALSO

New Jersey v. T.L.O.; United States v. Leon

FURTHER READING

Hutchinson, Dennis J. *The Man Who Once Was Whizzer White: A Portrait of Justice Byron R. White.* New York: Free Press, 1998.

Kramer, Daniel C. "Justice Byron R. White: Good Friend to Polity and Solon." In *The Burger Court: Political and Judicial Profiles,* edited by Charles M. Lamb and Stephen C. Halpern, 407–32. Urbana: University of Illinois Press, 1991.

White, Edward D.

ASSOCIATE JUSTICE, 1894–1910

CHIEF JUSTICE, 1910–21

☆ Born: Nov. 3, 1845, Lafourche Parish, La.

☆ Education: Mount St. Mary's College, 1856; Georgetown University, B.A., 1861; studied law under Edward Bermudez in New Orleans

☆ Previous government service: Louisiana Senate, 1874; associate justice, Louisiana Supreme Court, 1878–1880; U.S. senator from Louisiana, 1891–94

☆ Appointed by President Grover Cleveland to be an associate justice Feb. 19, 1894; replaced Samuel Blatchford, who died; appointed by President William Howard Taft to be chief justice Dec. 12, 1910; replaced Melville Fuller, who died

☆ Supreme Court term: confirmed by the Senate as associate justice Feb. 19, 1894, by a voice vote; confirmed by the Senate as chief justice Dec. 12, 1910, by a voice vote; served until May 19, 1921

☆ Died: May 19, 1921, Washington, D.C.

EDWARD D. WHITE was the first associate justice to be promoted to chief justice of the U.S. Supreme Court. It seems that President William Howard Taft appointed him, instead of a much younger

man, in order to keep open the possibility that Taft himself might become chief justice after retirement from the Presidency.

During his 27 years on the Court, White's single major contribution to legal doctrine was his controversial "rule of reason" used to interpret the Sherman Antitrust Act. This federal law was written to outlaw all combinations of businesses for the purpose of restraining trade. White, however, argued that only "unreasonable" restraints were banned by the Sherman Antitrust Act. Of course, what is "reasonable" or "unreasonable" is a matter of interpretation that may vary from one person to another. Chief Justice White's "rule of reason" doctrine gained a majority in *Standard Oil* v. *United States* (1911), which decided that the Standard Oil monopoly had to be broken up.

White was succeeded as chief justice by William Howard Taft in 1921. The former President's long-standing ambition to be chief justice was fulfilled at last.

FURTHER READING

Highsan, Robert B. *Edward Douglass White: Defender of the Conservative Faith*. Baton Rouge: Louisiana State University Press, 1981.

Whitney v. California

☆ *274 U.S. 357 (1927)*
☆ *Vote: 9–0*
☆ *For the Court: Sanford*
☆ *Concurring: Brandeis and Holmes*

CHARLOTTE ANITA WHITNEY was a socialist who helped to found the Communist Labor Party (CLP), an organization dedicated to bringing about fundamental changes in the political and economic systems of the United States, by violent means if necessary. The ultimate goal of the CLP was public ownership of the means of production of goods

and services and a redistribution of wealth to benefit the masses of workers. California police arrested Whitney because of her socialist and CLP activities.

The state charged Whitney with violating the California Criminal Syndicalism Act of 1919. According to this law, criminal syndicalism was defined as "advocating, teaching or aiding... sabotage ... or unlawful acts of force and violence... as a means of accomplishing a change in industrial ownership or control, or effecting any political change."

Whitney was tried and convicted solely on the basis of her involvement with the CLP, an organization that advocated the use of violent revolution to bring about social changes.

The Issue At first, the Court refused to hear the *Whitney* case on the grounds that no federal issue was involved. But Whitney's attorneys proved that in the California Court of Appeals, questions had been raised about possible conflicts of the California Criminal Syndicalism Act with the due process and equal protection clauses of the 14th Amendment. So the Supreme Court accepted the case.

Did the California law used to convict Charlotte Anita Whitney violate her 14th Amendment rights? Moreover, did it also violate her 1st Amendment right of free speech as applied to the states through the due process clause of the 14th Amendment?

Opinion of the Court The Court upheld the California Criminal Syndicalism Act. Justice Edward Sanford concluded that the state's power and duty to maintain public safety and order outweighed the claims of the defendant about protection of her individual rights.

In his concurring opinion, Justice Louis D. Brandeis argued that Whitney's attorneys should have used the "clear and present danger" doctrine, developed in preceding cases by Brandeis and

Oliver Wendell Holmes, to distinguish between mere expression of ideas and ideas that would result in actions that would endanger public safety and order. Whitney had claimed that the California law violated the U.S. Constitution, but, said Brandeis, "she did not claim that it was void because there was no clear and present danger of serious evil" that would result from her speech and actions. This version of the "clear and present danger" doctrine had been expressed by Justice Oliver Wendell Holmes in *Abrams* v. *United States* (1919).

Justice Brandeis set forth an often-quoted statement about the latitude and limits of free speech:

> [A]lthough the rights of free speech and assembly are fundamental, they are not in their nature absolute. Their exercise is subject to restriction, if the particular restriction proposed is required to protect the State from destruction or from serious injury, political, economic, or moral....
>
> [T]o justify suppression of free speech there must be reasonable ground to fear that serious evil will result if free speech is practiced....
>
> [N]o danger flowing from speech can be deemed clear and present unless the incidence of the evil apprehended is so imminent that it may befall before there is opportunity for full discussion. If there be time to expose through discussion the falsehoods and fallacies, to avert the evil by the process of education, the remedy to be applied is more speech, not enforced silence. Only an emergency can justify repression. Such must be the rule if authority is to be reconciled with freedom. Such, in my opinion, is the command of the Constitution. It is therefore always open to Americans to challenge a law abridging free speech and assembly by showing that there was no emergency justifying it.

Significance Justice Brandeis's concurring opinion has the tone of a dissent. It immediately influenced the life of Charlotte Anita Whitney. The California governor, C. C. Young, pardoned her only a few months after the Supreme Court decision; he gave reasons similar to the ideas in Justice Brandeis's opinion.

In 1969 the Supreme Court overturned the *Whitney* decision in its ruling in *Brandenburg* v. *Ohio*. The ideas of Justice Brandeis influenced the Court's reasoning in this case; it pointed out a defense of free speech rights that could have prevailed for Whitney, if only she and her attorney had used this line of reasoning to support her case.

SEE ALSO

Abrams v. United States; Brandenburg v. Ohio; Freedom of speech and press

Whittaker, Charles E.

ASSOCIATE JUSTICE, 1957–62

☆ *Born: Feb. 22, 1901, Troy, Kans.*
☆ *Education: University of Kansas City Law School, LL.B., 1924*
☆ *Previous government service: federal judge, U.S. District Court for Western Missouri, 1954–56; judge, U.S. Eighth Circuit Court of Appeals, 1956–57*
☆ *Appointed by President Dwight D. Eisenhower Mar. 2, 1957; replaced Stanley Reed, who retired*
☆ *Supreme Court term: confirmed by the Senate Mar. 19, 1957, by a voice vote; retired Mar. 31, 1962*
☆ *Died: Nov. 26, 1973, Kansas City, Mo.*

CHARLES E. WHITTAKER was appointed to the Supreme Court in 1957, after serving briefly as a federal district court judge in Missouri and as a judge of the U.S. Eighth Circuit Court of Appeals. He had risen to these distinguished positions through hard work and persistence.

Justice Whittaker's brief term on the Court was undistinguished. He wrote few opinions, none of them memorable, and he was generally viewed as the weakest thinker on the Court. He retired because of poor health.

Wilson, James

ASSOCIATE JUSTICE, 1789–98

☆ *Born: Sept. 14, 1742, Fifeshire, Scotland*
☆ *Education: University of St. Andrews, Scotland; read law in the office of John Dickinson, Philadelphia, Pa.*
☆ *Previous government service: first Provincial Convention at Philadelphia, 1774; Continental Congress, 1775–77, 1783, 1785–87; Constitutional Convention, 1787; Pennsylvania Ratifying Convention, 1787*
☆ *Appointed by President George Washington Sept. 24, 1789, as one of the original members of the U.S. Supreme Court*
☆ *Supreme Court term: confirmed by the Senate Sept. 26, 1789, by a voice vote; served until Aug. 21, 1798*
☆ *Died: Aug. 21, 1798, Edenton, N.C.*

JAMES WILSON traveled to the British colony of Pennsylvania from rural Scotland and helped to found a new nation, the United States of America. He served in the Continental Congress during the American War of Independence and participated influentially in the Constitutional Convention of 1787. Historians have rated him as one of the most important framers of the Constitution because many of his ideas were included in the final draft of this document.

In 1789, President George Washington appointed Wilson to the first Supreme Court of the United States. He was generally viewed as the best legal scholar among the original appointments to the Court. However, Justice Wilson's performance did not match his potential, and he contributed little of lasting significance as a Supreme Court justice.

His brief term on the Court was marred by heavy personal problems, including great indebtedness. Wilson's worries led to illness and death, in poverty, at the age of 55.

FURTHER READING

Smith, Page. *James Wilson: Founding Father.* Chapel Hill: University of North Carolina Press, 1956.

Wolf v. Colorado

☆ *338 U.S. 25 (1949)*
☆ *Vote: 6–3*
☆ *For the Court: Frankfurter*
☆ *Dissenting: Douglas, Murphy, and Rutledge*

DR. WOLF, a Colorado physician, was suspected of performing abortions secretly, in violation of state laws. But the police were unable to obtain evidence to prove their suspicions. A deputy sheriff assigned to the case took Dr. Wolf's appointment book from his office, without the doctor's knowledge. The police contacted people listed in this appointment book about Dr. Wolf's medical practice. Through these interviews the police gained enough evidence to convict Wolf of conspiracy to commit abortions.

The Issue Wolf said his constitutional rights had been violated. He pointed to the 4th Amendment to the U.S. Constitution: "The right of the people to be secure in their persons, houses, papers, and effects, against unreasonable searches and seizures, shall not be violated." He also pointed to the 14th Amendment: "No state…shall deprive any person of life, liberty, or property, without due process of law."

Wolf's attorney asked the Court to overturn his client's conviction because it was based on illegally obtained evidence. He cited the Court's decision in *Weeks* v. *United States* (1914). In that case, evidence obtained in violation of the 4th Amendment was excluded from consideration by prosecutors.

Were Wolf's 4th Amendment rights violated? Are the 4th Amendment guarantees against unreasonable searches and seizures incorporated by the due process clause of the 14th Amendment and thus applicable to the states? Should evidence obtained in violation of the 4th Amendment be excluded by judges from consideration at the trial of a defendant?

Felix Frankfurter ruled in the Wolf *case that individuals must be secure in their homes and businesses against unreasonable invasions of their privacy.*

Opinion of the Court Justice Felix Frankfurter agreed that the 4th Amendment was applicable to the states through the 14th Amendment. He wrote eloquently about the fundamental right of the individual to be secure against arbitrary intrusion by agents of the government. Frankfurter said, "The security of one's privacy against arbitrary intrusion by the police is basic to a free society. The knock on the door, whether by day or by night, as a prelude to a search, without authority of law but solely on the authority of the police [is] inconsistent with the conception of human rights enshrined in the history and basic constitutional documents of English-speaking peoples."

The Court held that 4th Amendment protection applies to searches by state officials as well as by federal agents. However, the exclusionary rule established in the *Weeks* case was not applied to the states. State judges were not required to exclude evidence obtained by searches in violation of 4th Amendment rights, so Wolf's conviction was upheld.

Dissent Justice William O. Douglas argued that the exclusionary rule must be used to enforce 4th Amendment rights. Without the exclusion of illegally obtained evidence, he noted, the constitutional protections against unreasonable searches and seizures are practically worthless.

Significance This was the first time that 4th Amendment rights were incorporated by the 14th Amendment and applied to the states, a precedent that has been followed ever since the *Wolf* case. In 1961, in *Mapp* v. *Ohio*, the Court accepted the dissenting position of the *Wolf* case and applied the exclusionary rule to the states, thus overturning the *Wolf* decision.

SEE ALSO

Exclusionary rule; Incorporation doctrine; Mapp v. Ohio; Searches and seizures; Weeks v. United States

Women in the federal judiciary

IN 2000, 20 PERCENT of all federal judges were women. Before 1928, there had never been a female federal judge. In that year, however, Genevieve Cline was appointed to the U.S. Customs Court by President Calvin Coolidge. The first female Supreme Court justice was Sandra Day O'Connor, appointed by President Ronald Reagan in 1981. Ruth Bader Ginsburg, appointed by Bill Clinton in 1993, was the second woman to serve on the Supreme Court.

Woodbury, Levi

ASSOCIATE JUSTICE,
1845–51

☆ Born: Dec. 22, 1789, Francestown, N.H.
☆ Education: Dartmouth College, B.A., 1809; Tapping Reeve Law School, 1810
☆ Previous government service: clerk, New Hampshire Senate, 1816; associate justice, New Hampshire Superior Court, 1817–23; governor of New Hampshire, 1823–24; Speaker, New Hampshire House of Representatives, 1825; U.S. senator from New Hampshire, 1825–31, 1841–45; U.S. secretary of the navy, 1831–34; U.S. secretary of the Treasury, 1834–41
☆ Appointed by President James K. Polk as a recess appointment Sept. 20, 1845; replaced Joseph Story, who died; nominated by Polk Dec. 23, 1845
☆ Supreme Court term: confirmed by the Senate Jan. 3, 1846, by a voice vote; served until Sept. 4, 1851
☆ Died: Sept. 4, 1851, Portsmouth, N.H.

LEVI WOODBURY was a Jacksonian Democrat who served less than six years on the Supreme Court. During his brief term, he tended to side with the majority on the Taney Court. He especially favored the rights and powers of the states in cases regarding conflicts with the federal government. In general, Woodbury's judicial career lacked distinction.

Woods, William B.

ASSOCIATE JUSTICE,
1881–87

☆ Born: Aug. 3, 1824, Newark, Ohio
☆ Education: Western Reserve College, 1841–44; Yale College, B.A., 1845
☆ Previous government service: mayor of Newark, Ohio, 1856; Ohio House of Representatives, 1858–62, Speaker, 1858–60, minority leader, 1860–62; chancellor, Middle Chancery District

of Alabama, 1868–69; judge, U.S. Circuit Court for the Fifth Judicial Circuit, 1869–80
☆ Appointed by President Rutherford B. Hayes Dec. 15, 1880; replaced William Strong, who retired
☆ Supreme Court term: confirmed by the Senate Dec. 21, 1880, by a 39–8 vote; served until May 14, 1887
☆ Died: May 14, 1887, Washington, D.C.

WILLIAM B. WOODS served briefly on the Supreme Court during the 1880s. His main contributions to constitutional law came through his narrow interpretation of the 14th Amendment. For example, he sided with the Court's majority in the *Civil Rights Cases* (1883) to declare unconstitutional the Civil Rights Act of 1875, which was designed to use federal authority to protect black Americans against abuse of their rights by state government.

Writing for the Court in *Presser v. Illinois* (1886), Justice Woods argued that the Bill of Rights restricted only the federal government and could not be applied to the states through the 14th Amendment. This position was not overturned until the second quarter of the 20th century. In general, Justice Woods favored limitations on federal power in favor of state powers and rights.

Worcester v. Georgia

☆ 6 Pet. 515 (1832)
☆ Vote: 5–1
☆ For the Court: Marshall
☆ Dissenting: Baldwin

IN THE EARLY 19th century, the Cherokee people owned a vast area of land in Georgia. They organized a thriving community with a constitution and republican institutions of government. They clearly meant to live as a free and

The Cherokee newspaper published articles in both the Cherokee language and English. Chief Justice John Marshall ruled in Worcester v. Georgia *that the Cherokees were not subject to the laws of Georgia.*

sovereign, or self-governing, people. Georgia state government officials, however, had a different view of Cherokee destiny. They enacted laws that placed Cherokee lands under the control of Georgia county governments.

The Cherokees objected to Georgia's efforts to rule them. They brought suit directly to the U.S. Supreme Court on grounds that they were an independent nation whose rights had been violated by the state of Georgia. Writing for the Court, Chief Justice John Marshall, in *Cherokee Nation* v. *Georgia* (1831), held that the Court had no jurisdiction, under the U.S. Constitution, to deal with this issue because the Cherokees were "a domestic, dependent nation"—not a truly sovereign nation.

In March 1831 the Georgia militia arrested Samuel A. Worcester and thereby reopened the legal issue of Cherokee rights in the United States. Worcester was a white Christian missionary who lived among the Cherokee people. He was charged by the Georgia government with violation of a law prohibiting "all white persons [from] residing within the limits of the Cherokee nation...without a license or permit from his excellency the [Georgia] governor." A Georgia state court found Worcester guilty and sentenced him to four years in the state penitentiary. Worcester appealed to the U.S. Supreme Court.

The Issue Worcester's attorneys claimed that the Georgia law he violated was unconstitutional because it conflicted with U.S.–Cherokee treaties, the contract and commerce clauses of the U.S. Constitution, and the sovereign status of the Cherokee nation. Should the national rights of the Cherokees be recognized? Should the Georgia law at issue in this case be declared void?

Opinion of the Court Chief Justice John Marshall decided against Georgia. He wrote that the Cherokee and other "Indian nations" were "distinct, independent political communities, retaining their original natural rights." This was a dramatic change from the Court's decision one year earlier in *Cherokee Nation* v. *Georgia*. Marshall overturned Worcester's conviction and ordered his release from prison.

Significance President Andrew Jackson and the executive branch of the federal government refused to abide by the Court's decision. Worcester remained in jail and served his four-year sentence. The Georgia government moved against the Cherokee people, who were eventually forced to move west of the Mississippi River.

Chief Justice Marshall's *Worcester* opinion departed from his *Cherokee Nation* opinion. Nevertheless, the *Cherokee Nation* opinion prevailed in subsequent cases, to the disadvantage of the people classified in the 1831 case as "domestic, dependent nations."

FURTHER READING
Perdue, Theda. *The Cherokee.* New York: Chelsea House, 1988.

Yates v. United States

☆ *354 U.S. 298 (1957)*
☆ *Vote: 6–1*
☆ *For the Court: Harlan*
☆ *Dissenting: Clark*

☆ *Not participating: Brennan and Whittaker*

CONGRESS PASSED the Smith Act in 1940 to limit the political activities of radical opponents of the U.S. government, such as the Communist Party of the United States (CPUSA). The Smith Act made it a crime for anyone knowingly to advocate the forcible overthrow of the U.S. government or to organize or participate in any group committed to the purpose of violent revolution against the U.S. government. Oleta O'Connor Yates was one of 14 members of the CPUSA convicted for violating the Smith Act.

The Issue Could the Smith Act be used to prohibit advocacy of violent overthrow of the government merely as an idea (but not as a direct incitement to forcible political revolution)? Was the Smith Act a violation of the 1st Amendment to the Constitution, which guarantees the individual's rights to freedom of speech, press, petition, and assembly? Should the convictions of Yates and her associates be upheld or reversed?

Opinion of the Court The convictions of Yates and her associates were reversed, but the Smith Act was not ruled unconstitutional. Rather, the Court's interpretation of the Smith Act was narrowed to the point of making it virtually unenforceable. Justice John Marshall Harlan emphasized the difference between advocating ideas (abstractions) and advocating immediate illegal action directed toward violent overthrow of the government. Harlan ruled that Yates and her associates were doing merely the former. Yates and the others therefore had been wrongly convicted under an incorrect interpretation of the Smith Act, said Justice Harlan.

Significance The *Yates* opinion took the "teeth" out of the Smith Act. Given the Court's restrictive interpretation of the law, it became very difficult to enforce. After the *Yates* case, there were no more prosecutions carried out to enforce the Smith Act.

SEE ALSO
Freedom of speech and press

Youngstown Sheet & Tube Co. v. Sawyer

☆ *343 U.S. 579 (1952)*
☆ *Vote: 6–3*
☆ *For the Court: Black*
☆ *Concurring: Frankfurter, Douglas, Jackson, Burton, and Clark*
☆ *Dissenting: Vinson, Reed, and Minton*

IN THE SPRING of 1952, the United States was in the midst of the Korean War, and the nation's steelworkers were about to go on strike. Harry Truman and his advisers feared a long strike could bring disaster: U.S. troops in Korea might run short of weapons and ammunition.

The President acted forcefully. On April 8, a few hours before the expected start of the strike, Truman issued Executive Order No. 10340. This order directed Secretary of Commerce Charles Sawyer to take control of the nation's steel mills temporarily and to keep them running. The steel companies accepted the order but moved to fight Truman's action in court.

Taking temporary control of the steel mills was not the only alternative open to Truman. The President had another way to deal with the strike. He chose not to use it.

In 1947 Congress had passed the Taft-Hartley Act. Under this law, the President could get a court order delaying the strike for 80 days. During this "cooling off" period, the steelworkers'

President Harry Truman announces on radio and TV that he has seized the nation's steel mills. The Supreme Court, however, ordered the President to return the mills to their owners.

union and the mill owners would have tried to settle their differences.

Truman disliked the Taft-Hartley Act. He thought it was anti-labor. He had vetoed it in 1947, but Congress had overridden his veto. He had never used the law and would not do so in the steel strike.

Furthermore, Truman believed the blame for the strike did not lie with the steelworkers. The union had already postponed the strike four times in an effort to reach a settlement. Government arbitrators had recommended a compromise, which the union had accepted. The steel companies had rejected those recommendations, even though in 1951 the companies earned their greatest profits in more than 30 years. President Truman believed the steel companies were using the emergency of the Korean War to force the steelworkers to accept low wages. Under such circumstances Truman held the companies, and not the workers, responsible for the crisis in the industry, and he decided to seize the steel mills.

The steel companies quickly challenged Truman's action in the federal district court in Washington, D.C. Within a few days the case went to the Supreme Court.

The Issue President Truman's order was a remarkable assertion of Presidential power. The President was not carrying out or acting under a law passed by Congress. No law authorized a President to seize and operate the steel mills. By his order, President Truman was, in effect, making law—a power reserved to Congress by Article 1 of the Constitution.

Had the President overstepped the constitutional boundary that separated the functions of the legislative and executive branches? Or did the Constitution give Truman powers to protect the nation in times of national emergency?

The steel companies argued that the President's order clearly violated the Constitution. They said neither the Constitution nor existing laws gave him authority to seize private property. In addition, Congress had already set up procedures to handle the strike in the Taft-Hartley Act. Thus, they claimed the President had exceeded his constitutional authority.

The President argued that his authority, as chief executive under Article 2 of the Constitution, gave him power to keep steel production going in times of national emergency. In addition, he argued that his power as commander in chief allowed him to take actions necessary to protect the lives of U.S. troops. This power included ensuring a steady flow of steel to produce weapons.

Opinion of the Court On June 2 the Supreme Court ruled against the President. The Court judged Truman's seizure of the steel mills an unconstitutional exercise of power.

Justice Hugo L. Black, in the majority opinion, said that the President had no power, as either chief executive or commander in chief, to seize private property—even temporarily and during a national emergency. Black said that the power to authorize such an action belonged to Congress, not to the President. Thus, Truman could not seize the steel mills unless Congress passed legislation enabling him to do so. Because Congress had not done so, the seizure was illegal.

Black noted that, in writing the 1947 Taft-Hartley Act, Congress had considered letting Presidents seize factories in the event of strikes but had rejected the idea. Thus, by his executive order Truman had attempted to make his own law. Yet the Constitution, Black said, did not permit him to do so. The Constitution limited the President "to the recommending of laws he thinks wise and the vetoing of laws he thinks bad."

Dissent Three justices, all Truman appointees, issued a strong dissent. They argued that during a grave national crisis, such as the Korean War, the Constitution allowed the President to exercise unusual powers. Chief Justice Fred Vinson wrote, "Those who suggest that this is a case involving extraordinary powers should be mindful that these are extraordinary times." Vinson added that Truman's actions followed the tradition of taking extraordinary actions in times of crisis established by such Presidents as Abraham Lincoln, Grover Cleveland, Woodrow Wilson, and Franklin Roosevelt.

Significance The *Youngstown* decision required the government to return the steel mills to their owners immediately. Truman promptly complied with the Court's ruling even though he strongly disagreed with it. The steel strike began, and it lasted for 53 days. When it ended, the steel companies agreed to a contract within one cent of the settlement recommended by the government arbitrators. Truman never used the Taft-Hartley Act to intervene. The President did claim that in the summer and fall of 1952 the strike caused some shortages of ammunition.

In this decision, the Court clearly established that there are limits on the powers a President can derive from the Constitution, even during a national emergency. For nearly 20 years Presidential power had been growing through a series of crises, including the Great Depression and World War II. The *Youngstown* decision had the effect of slowing this steady growth.

This case shows how strong Presidents can try to expand the powers of the office. It also demonstrates how the Supreme Court can act to preserve the separation of powers inherent in the U.S. constitutional system.

SEE ALSO

Constitutionalism; Separation of powers

FURTHER READING

Donovan, Robert J. "Truman Seizes Steel." *Constitution* 2, no. 3 (Fall 1990): 48–57.
Marcus, Maeva. *Truman and the Steel Seizure Case: The Limits of Presidential Power.* New York: Oxford University Press, 1992.
Westin, Alan F. *The Anatomy of a Constitutional Law Case: Youngstown Sheet & Tube v. Sawyer.* New York; Columbia University Press, 1990.

Zorach v. Clauson

☆ *343 U.S. 306 (1952)*
☆ *Vote: 6–3*
☆ *For the Court: Douglas*
☆ *Dissenting: Black, Frankfurter, and Jackson*

IN 1948 the New York City public schools introduced a "released time" program for religious education, under which students could leave the public schools before the end of the regular school day to attend religious classes of their choosing. During the 1940s and 1950s these programs were widespread. Tessim Zorach, a resident of New York City, complained that the city school system's "released time" program violated the establishment clause of the 1st Amendment.

The Zorach *case decided that a New York law allowing students to be released early from public school in order to attend religious instruction was not in violation of the Constitution.*

The Issue The 1st Amendment of the Constitution prohibits government from enacting laws "respecting an establishment of religion." Does this mean that there must be complete separation of church and state? Or does this establishment clause permit certain kinds of governmental association with religion, as long as the government does not discriminate in its treatment of different religions?

Opinion of the Court Justice William O. Douglas upheld the New York City "released time" program because the religious instruction was not carried out in public school buildings. Rather, public school students could choose to participate, during the official school day, in religious instruction outside the public schools. Douglas emphasized that a "released time" program in Champaign, Illinois, had been declared unconstitutional only because religious instruction was provided in the public school buildings during the school day (*Illinois ex rel. McCollum* v. *Board of Education,* 1948).

Justice Douglas wrote these often-quoted words in support of permissible governmental accommodation of religion:

> We are a religious people whose institutions suppose a Supreme Being. . . . When the state encourages religious instruction or cooperates with religious authorities by adjusting the schedule of public events to sectarian needs, it follows the best of our traditions. For it then respects the religious nature of our people and accommodates the public service to their spiritual needs. To hold that it may not would be to find in the Constitution a requirement that the government show a callous indifference to religious groups. That would be preferring those who believe in no religion over those who do believe.

Dissent Justice Hugo Black emphasized that the location of religious instruction involved in "released time" programs was not relevant. It was the connection between government-supported public schools and the content of the religious instruction that, according to Black and the other dissenters, was not permitted by the 1st Amendment as applied to the states through the 14th Amendment. Black wrote that the resources and authority of the public schools had been unconstitutionally put at the service of private religious groups.

Significance "Released time" programs expanded in the wake of the *Zorach* decision. However, they declined in use and importance in the 1970s and 1980s. The enduring importance of the *Zorach* case is the argument for a constitutional accommodation of government and religion provided by Justice Douglas. In line with this opinion, the Court ruled in *Zobrest* v. *Catalina School District* (1993) that local government funds could be used to pay for a sign-language interpreter to assist a deaf student at a private school operated by the Catholic church.

SEE ALSO

Establishment clause; Religious issues under the Constitution

FURTHER READING

Alley, Robert S. *The Supreme Court on Church and State.* New York: Oxford University Press, 1988.

Zurcher v. The Stanford Daily

☆ *436 U.S. 547 (1978)*
☆ *Vote: 5–3*
☆ *For the Court: White*
☆ *Dissenting: Stewart, Marshall, and Stevens*
☆ *Not participating: Brennan*

IN APRIL 1971 a group of demonstrators seized the administrative offices of Stanford University Hospital. They blocked entrances and would not permit people to move freely through the facility. The Palo Alto city police confronted

the demonstrators and a riot resulted. Several police officers were injured. The *Stanford Daily*, a student newspaper, published a report of the riot that included pictures.

The identities of the rioters could not be determined from the pictures published in the newspaper. The police, however, thought the photographer might have other pictures in his office that could be used to identify some of the rioters. They obtained a warrant and searched the offices of the *Stanford Daily*, but they found no additional pictures. However, while they searched for pictures the police saw confidential papers in the newspaper's files. These papers included information about the management of the newspaper and the personal activities of students.

The *Stanford Daily* brought suit against the police. The student publishers claimed that the police's search of their offices violated their constitutional rights under the 1st, 4th, and 14th Amendments.

The Issue The students argued that a reasonable police search of a newspaper office should be based on a subpoena, not a warrant. A subpoena is an order requiring a person to appear before a court of law. A subpoena issued by a local court would have required representatives of the student newspaper to submit to police, for their examination, any pictures in their possession about the riot. This procedure, the students said, would have eliminated the possibility of police seeing confidential documents in their files not related to the purpose of the search. The city government replied that the warrant was legally obtained and the subsequent search properly conducted.

Was there a violation of the student newspaper's 4th Amendment rights to protection against unreasonable searches? And did the case involve a violation of the 1st Amendment guarantee of a free press?

Opinion of the Court Justice Byron White ruled against the *Stanford Daily*. He referred to the intentions of those who proposed and ratified the federal Bill of Rights: they did not, he wrote, "forbid warrants where the press was involved." Justice White emphasized that the press should not have special privileges with regard to the authorization of search warrants. Further, he contended that requiring a subpoena before the issuance of a search warrant would unduly interfere with effective enforcement of the law.

Dissent Justice Potter Stewart argued that the search without a subpoena was a violation of 1st and 4th Amendment rights because police were able to examine sensitive papers having no relationship to the purpose of the search. This kind of invasion of privacy, wrote Stewart, could intimidate newspaper publishers and thereby interfere with freedom of the press.

Significance The *Zurcher* decision prompted Congress to pass the Privacy Protection Act of 1980. This law prohibits federal government agents from carrying out searches and seizures in newspaper offices on "work-product materials unless the reporter or writer is suspected of committing a crime or there is some life-threatening situation." This federal law does not apply to state or local police, however. Thus the *Zurcher* ruling stands as a legal precedent.

SEE ALSO

Freedom of speech and press; Searches and seizures

APPENDIX 1

TERMS OF THE JUSTICES OF THE U.S. SUPREME COURT

PRESIDENT/JUSTICE		OATH TAKEN		TERM END
George Washington				
John Jay*		19 Oct. 1789	R	29 June 1795
John Rutledge		15 Feb. 1790	R	5 Mar. 1791
William Cushing		2 Feb. 1790	D	13 Sept. 1810
James Wilson		5 Oct. 1789	D	21 Aug. 1798
John Blair, Jr.		2 Feb. 1790	R	25 Oct. 1795
James Iredell		12 May 1790	D	20 Oct. 1799
Thomas Johnson	R	19 Sep. 1791		
		6 Aug. 1792	R	16 Jan. 1793
William Paterson		11 Mar. 1793	D	9 Sept. 1806
John Rutledge*†	R	12 Aug. 1795		15 Dec. 1795
Samuel Chase		4 Feb. 1796	D	19 June 1811
Oliver Ellsworth*		8 Mar. 1796	R	15 Dec. 1800
John Adams				
Bushrod Washington	R	9 Nov. 1798		
		4 Feb. 1799	D	26 Nov. 1829
Alfred Moore		21 Apr. 1800	R	26 Jan. 1804
John Marshall*		4 Feb. 1801	D	6 July 1835
Thomas Jefferson				
William Johnson		8 May 1804	D	4 Aug. 1834
Henry Brockholst Livingston	R	20 Jan. 1807		
		2 Feb. 1807	D	18 Mar. 1823
Thomas Todd		4 May 1807	D	7 Feb. 1826
James Madison				
Joseph Story		3 Feb. 1812	D	10 Sept. 1845
Gabriel Duvall		23 Nov. 1811	R	14 Jan. 1835
James Monroe				
Smith Thompson		10 Feb. 1824	D	18 Dec. 1843
John Quincy Adams				
Robert Trimble		16 June 1826	D	25 Aug. 1828
Andrew Jackson				
John McLean		11 Jan. 1830	D	4 Apr. 1861
Henry Baldwin		18 Jan. 1830	D	21 Apr. 1844
James M. Wayne		14 Jan. 1835	D	5 July 1867
Roger B. Taney*		28 Mar. 1836	D	12 Oct. 1864
Philip P. Barbour		12 May 1836	D	25 Feb. 1841
John Catron		1 May 1837	D	30 May 1865
Martin Van Buren				
John McKinley		9 Jan. 1838	D	19 July 1852
Peter V. Daniel		10 Jan. 1842	D	31 May 1860
John Tyler				
Samuel Nelson		27 Feb. 1845	R	28 Nov. 1872

* See notes, page 384

PRESIDENT/JUSTICE		OATH TAKEN		TERM END
James K. Polk				
Levi Woodbury	R	23 Sept. 1845		
		3 Jan. 1846	D	4 Sept. 1851
Robert C. Grier		10 Aug. 1846	R	31 Jan. 1870
Millard Fillmore				
Benjamin R. Curtis	R	10 Oct. 1851	R	30 Sept. 1857
Franklin Pierce				
John A. Campbell		11 Apr. 1853	R	30 Apr. 1861
James Buchanan				
Nathan Clifford		21 Jan. 1858	D	25 July 1881
Abraham Lincoln				
Noah H. Swayne		27 Jan. 1862	R	24 Jan. 1881
Samuel F. Miller		21 July 1862	D	13 Oct. 1890
David Davis		10 Dec. 1862	R	4 Mar. 1877
Stephen J. Field		20 May 1863	R	1 Dec. 1897
Salmon P. Chase*		15 Dec. 1864	D	7 May 1873
Ulysses S. Grant				
William Strong		14 Mar. 1870	R	14 Dec. 1880
Joseph P. Bradley		23 Mar. 1870	D	22 Jan. 1892
Ward Hunt		9 Jan. 1873	R	27 Jan. 1882
Morrison R. Waite*		4 Mar. 1874	D	23 Mar. 1888
Rutherford B. Hayes				
John Marshall Harlan		10 Dec. 1877	D	14 Oct. 1911
William B. Woods		5 Jan. 1881	D	14 May 1887
James A. Garfield				
Stanley Matthews		17 May 1881	D	22 Mar. 1889
Chester A. Arthur				
Horace Gray		9 Jan. 1882	D	15 Sept. 1902
Samuel Blatchford		3 Apr. 1882	D	7 July 1893
Grover Cleveland				
Lucius Q. C. Lamar		18 Jan. 1888	D	23 Jan. 1893
Melville W. Fuller*		8 Oct. 1888	D	4 July 1910
Benjamin Harrison				
David Brewer		6 Jan. 1890	D	28 Mar. 1910
Henry B. Brown		5 Jan. 1891	R	28 May 1906
George Shiras, Jr.		10 Oct. 1892	R	23 Feb. 1903
Howell E. Jackson		4 Mar. 1893	D	8 Aug. 1895
Grover Cleveland				
Edward D. White		12 Mar. 1894	P	18 Dec. 1910
Rufus W. Peckham		6 Jan. 1896	D	24 Oct. 1909

☆ A P P E N D I X 1 ☆

PRESIDENT/JUSTICE	OATH TAKEN		TERM END
William McKinley			
Joseph McKenna	26 Jan. 1898	R	5 Jan. 1925
Theodore Roosevelt			
Oliver Wendell Holmes, Jr.	8 Dec. 1902	R	12 Jan. 1932
William R. Day	2 Mar. 1903	R	13 Nov. 1922
William H. Moody	17 Dec. 1906	R	20 Nov. 1910
William H. Taft			
Horace H. Lurton	3 Jan. 1910	D	12 July 1914
Charles E. Hughes	10 Oct. 1910	R	10 June 1916
Edward D. White*†	19 Dec. 1910	D	19 May 1921
Willis Van Devanter	3 Jan. 1911	R	2 June 1937
Joseph R. Lamar	3 Jan. 1911	D	2 Jan. 1916
Mahlon Pitney	18 Mar. 1912	R	31 Dec. 1922
Woodrow Wilson			
James C. McReynolds	5 Sept. 1914	R	31 Jan. 1941
Louis D. Brandeis	5 June 1916	R	13 Feb. 1939
John H. Clarke	1 Aug. 1916	R	18 Sept. 1922
Warren G. Harding			
William H. Taft*	11 July 1921	R	3 Feb. 1930
George Sutherland	2 Oct. 1922	R	17 Jan. 1938
Pierce Butler	2 Jan. 1923	D	16 Nov. 1939
Edward T. Sanford	5 Feb. 1923	D	8 Mar. 1930
Calvin Coolidge			
Harlan F. Stone	2 Mar. 1925	P	2 July 1941
Herbert C. Hoover			
Charles E. Hughes*†	24 Feb. 1930	R	1 July 1941
Owen J. Roberts	2 June 1930	R	31 July 1945
Benjamin N. Cardozo	14 Mar. 1932	D	9 July 1938
Franklin D. Roosevelt			
Hugo L. Black	19 Aug. 1937	R	17 Sept. 1971
Stanley F. Reed	31 Jan. 1938	R	25 Feb. 1957
Felix Frankfurter	30 Jan. 1939	R	28 Aug. 1962
William O. Douglas	17 Apr. 1939	R	12 Nov. 1975
Frank Murphy	18 Jan. 1940	D	19 July 1949
Harlan F. Stone*†	3 July 1941	D	22 Apr. 1946
James F. Byrnes	8 July 1941	R	3 Oct. 1942
Robert H. Jackson	11 July 1941	D	9 Oct. 1954
Wiley B. Rutledge	15 Feb. 1943	D	10 Sept. 1949
Harry S. Truman			
Harold H. Burton	1 Oct. 1945	R	13 Oct. 1958
Fred M. Vinson*	24 June 1946	D	8 Sept. 1953
Tom Clark	24 Aug. 1949	R	12 June 1967
Sherman Minton	12 Oct. 1949	R	15 Oct. 1956

PRESIDENT/JUSTICE		OATH TAKEN		TERM END
Dwight D. Eisenhower				
Earl Warren*	R	5 Oct. 1953		
		2 Mar. 1954	R	23 June 1969
John M. Harlan II		28 Mar. 1955	R	23 Sept. 1971
William J. Brennan, Jr.	R	16 Oct. 1956		
		22 Mar. 1957	R	20 July 1990
Charles E. Whittaker		25 Mar. 1957	R	31 Mar. 1962
Potter Stewart	R	14 Oct. 1958		
		15 May 1959	R	3 July 1981
John F. Kennedy				
Byron R. White		16 Apr. 1962	R	28 June 1993
Arthur J. Goldberg		1 Oct. 1962	R	25 July 1965
Lyndon B. Johnson				
Abe Fortas		4 Oct. 1965	R	14 May 1969
Thurgood Marshall		2 Oct. 1967	R	1 Oct. 1991
Richard M. Nixon				
Warren E. Burger*		23 June 1969	R	26 Sept. 1986
Harry A. Blackmun		9 June 1970	R	3 Aug. 1994
Lewis F. Powell, Jr.		7 Jan. 1972	R	26 June 1987
William H. Rehnquist		7 Jan. 1972	P	26 Sept. 1986
Gerald R. Ford				
John Paul Stevens		19 Dec. 1975		
Ronald Reagan				
Sandra Day O'Connor		25 Sept. 1981		
William H. Rehnquist*†		26 Sept. 1986		
Antonin Scalia		26 Sept. 1986		
Anthony M. Kennedy		18 Feb. 1988		
George Bush				
David H. Souter		9 Oct. 1990		
Clarence Thomas		1 Nov. 1991		
Bill Clinton				
Ruth Bader Ginsburg		10 Aug. 1993		
Stephen G. Breyer		3 Aug. 1994		

NOTES

President/Justice column:
Presidents are listed in the shaded lines; the justices whom they appointed are in untinted lines.
* = chief justice
† = nomination for promotion to chief justice only; see prior listing for service as associate justice

Oath Taken column:
R = recess appointment; the justice took office before being confirmed by the Senate; he may have taken a second oath after confirmation

Term End column:
D = died
P = promoted to chief justice (see separate listing for service as chief justice)
R = retirement/resignation

VISITING THE SUPREME COURT BUILDING

The public may visit the Supreme Court Building at 1 First Street, N.E., Washington, D.C., 20543, every week of the year, Monday through Friday, from 9:00 A.M. until 4:30 P.M. except on legal holidays. More than 700,000 people annually visit the Supreme Court Building. Visitors have access only to certain parts of the ground floor and first floor of the Supreme Court Building. The floor plans on this page show the areas open to visitors. Only the rooms with labels in the diagrams are accessible; all others are closed to visitors.

Visitors can see a film about the Court in a room on the ground floor. Staff members of the curator's office also give lectures about the Court and its history. Courtroom lectures are presented daily, every hour on the half hour, from 9:30 A.M. to 3:30 P.M., when the Court is not in session.

The courtroom includes seats for about 300 visitors, which are available on a first come, first seated basis. Demand is usually high. The Court is in session to hear oral arguments in the Court chamber (courtroom) from 10:00 A.M. to noon and from 1:00 to 3:00 P.M. on Monday, Tuesday, and Wednesday, for two-week periods each month, beginning on the first Monday in October until the end of April of each year. A session may also be held on Monday of the third week of the month. From mid-May through June, the courtroom sessions convene at 10:00 A.M. The Court uses these sessions to deliver its opinions on cases heard previously.

The exhibit hall on the ground floor contains portraits and statues of the justices and other displays of documents and memorabilia relating to the work of the Court. The curator prepares two exhibits a year using the Court's collections of photographs, prints, films, manuscripts, and other memorabilia. The curator's office also collects decorative and fine arts.

The kiosk of the Supreme Court Historical Society, on the ground floor next to the exhibit hall, sells books and other materials that provide visitors with additional information about the Supreme Court Building and the operations of the Court.

This floor plan indicates the parts of the Supreme Court Building open to the public.

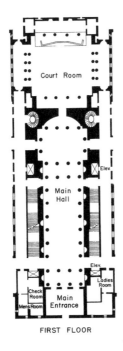

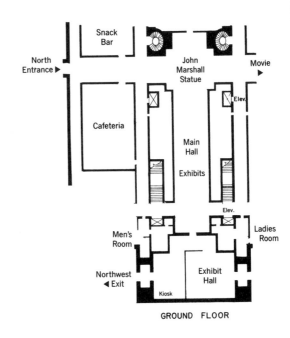

WEB SITES

All web sites listed are up-to-date and working at the time of publication.

American Bar Association

www.abanet.org

Full-text articles on legal issues and research are provided along with other resources for continuing legal education about federal and state courts, judges, and lawyers.

Cornell Legal Information Institute

http://supct.law.cornell.edu/supct

Contains all U.S. Supreme Court opinions since May 1990 and 600 opinions on major cases throughout the Court's history.

Federal Judicial Center

www.fjc.gov

Provides general information about the federal judiciary, including a history of federal courts and a biographical database of federal judges since 1789.

Federal Judiciary

www.uscourts.gov

Provides the latest news about the federal judicial system; answers to frequently asked questions; and information about the structure and functions of the federal courts.

FindLaw

www.findlaw.com

Includes information about the U.S. federal judiciary and the judiciaries of the 50 states. Provides opinions from the Supreme Court and all 13 federal circuits and the appellate courts of the 50 states.

History of the Federal Judiciary

http://air.fjc.gov/history/about_bdy.html

Presents information about the history of the federal courts, the judges who have served since 1789, and landmark judicial legislation from the Judiciary Act of 1789 to the present.

H-LAW

http://h-net.msu.edu/~law

This online discussion list stresses legal and constitutional history. It includes book reviews and links to the American Society for Legal History.

LEXIS-NEXIS

www.lexis-nexis.com

Opinions, briefs, and secondary materials on U.S. Supreme Court cases are provided; daily opinion service provides immediate access to decisions of all U.S. district courts, U.S. Circuit Courts of Appeals, specialized federal courts, and state courts.

Library of Congress: U.S. Judicial Branch Resources

http://lcweb.loc.gov/global/judiciary.html

Links are provided to numerous sites related to the federal judicial branch of government, including those with information about federal laws, judicial opinions, court rules, and law journals.

Oyez, Oyez, Oyez: A U.S. Supreme Court Database of Northwestern University

http://oyez.nwu.edu

Provides access to U.S. Supreme Court cases with texts of opinions and recordings of oral arguments in recent cases; contains biographical data on all Supreme Court justices and links to their opinions.

Supreme Court Historical Society

www.supremecourthistory.org

Provides access to opinions of notable Supreme Court cases and information on the society's programs and publications.

Supreme Court Reporter

www.westgroup.com

Provides reprints of United States Reports, the official record of U.S. Supreme Court decisions, which are published originally by the Superintendent of Documents, the U.S. Government Printing Office.

Supreme Court Reports, Lawyers' Edition

www.lexis.com

Provides reprints of all U.S. Supreme Court decisions, summaries of briefs, and annotations of key ideas and arguments.

Supreme Court of the United States

www.supremecourtus.gov/index.html

This official site of the Court includes information about the history, structure, functions and rules of the federal judiciary; opinions on all cases that have gone before the Court; oral arguments; the Court's docket; and a guide to visiting the Court.

United States Law Week

www.bna.com

Provides reprints of United States Reports, the record of the U.S. Supreme Court's decisions, which are published originally by the Superintendent of Documents, the U.S. Government Printing Office.

WESTLAW

www.westlaw.com

Provides access to opinions, briefs, oral arguments, and secondary materials related to cases of the U.S. Supreme Court.

FURTHER READING

Many entries in this volume include references to books dealing with that specific subject. The following volumes are more general in scope. They provide useful ideas and information for your further study of the Supreme Court and its role in the constitutional history of the United States.

Abraham, Henry J. *The Judicial Process.* New York: Oxford University Press, 1993.

Abraham, Henry J., and Barbara Perry. *Freedom and the Court: Civil Rights and Liberties in the United States.* New York: Oxford University Press, 1998.

Amar, Akhil Reed. *The Bill of Rights: Creation and Reconstruction.* New Haven, Conn.: Yale University Press, 1998.

Anastaplo, George. *The Constitution of 1787: A Commentary.* Baltimore: Johns Hopkins University Press, 1989.

Arbetman, Lee, and Richard L. Roe. *Great Trials in American History.* St. Paul, Minn.: West, 1985.

Bailyn, Bernard, ed. *The Debate on the Constitution: Federalist and Antifederalist Speeches, Articles, and Letters During the Struggle Over Ratification.* 2 vols. New York: Library of America, 1993.

Barnes, Patricia G. *Desk Reference on American Courts.* Washington, D.C.: Congressional Quarterly, 2000.

Baum, Laurence. *The Supreme Court.* 7th ed. Washington, D.C.: Congressional Quarterly, 2001.

Bernstein, Richard B., and Jerome Agel. *Amending America: If We Love the Constitution So Much, Why Do We Keep Trying to Change It?* New York: Random House, 1993.

Biskupic, Joan, and Elder Witt. *Guide to the U.S. Supreme Court.* Washington, D.C.: Congressional Quarterly, 1997.

———. *The Supreme Court and Individual Rights.* Washington, D.C.: Congressional Quarterly, 1997.

———. *The Supreme Court and the Powers of the American Government.* Washington, D.C.: Congressional Quarterly, 1997.

———. *The Supreme Court at Work.* Washington, D.C.: Congressional Quarterly, 1997.

Bowen, Catherine Drinker. *Miracle at Philadelphia: The Story of the Constitutional Convention.* 1966. Reprint. Boston: Little, Brown, 1987.

Burt, Robert A. *The Constitution in Conflict.* Cambridge: Harvard University Press, 1992.

Carp, Robert A., and Ronald Stidham. *Judicial Process in America.* Washington, D.C.: Congressional Quarterly, 1996.

Collier, Christopher, and James Lincoln Collier. *Decision in Philadelphia: The Constitutional Convention of 1787.* New York: Random House, 1986.

Cooper, Phillip J. *Battles on the Bench: Conflict Inside the Supreme Court.* Lawrence: University Press of Kansas, 1999.

Cox, Archibald. *The Court and the Constitution.* Boston: Houghton Mifflin, 1987.

Currie, David P. *The Constitution in the Supreme Court: The First Hundred Years.* Chicago: University of Chicago Press, 1985.

———. *The Constitution in the Supreme Court: The Second Century.* Chicago: University of Chicago Press, 1991.

———. *The Constitution of the United States: A Primer for the People.* Chicago: University of Chicago Press, 1988.

Cushman, Clare, ed. *The Supreme Court Justices.* Washington, D.C.: Congressional Quarterly, 1995.

Epstein, Lee, and Thomas G. Walker. *Constitutional Law for a Changing America.* 4th ed. Washington, D.C.: Congressional Quarterly, 2001.

Epstein, Lee, et al. *The Supreme Court Compendium: Data, Decisions, and Developments.* Washington, D.C.: Congressional Quarterly, 1997.

★ FURTHER READING ★

Franck, Matthew J. *Against the Imperial Judiciary: The Supreme Court versus the Sovereignty of the People.* Lawrence: University Press of Kansas, 1996.

Friedman, Lawrence M. *A History of American Law.* 2nd rev ed. New York: Simon & Schuster, 1986.

Friedman, Leon, and Fred L. Israel, eds. *The Justices of the United States Supreme Court, 1789–1991.* 5 vols. Rev. ed. New York: Chelsea House, 1992.

Friendly, Fred W., and Martha J. H. Elliott. *The Constitution: That Delicate Balance.* New York: Random House, 1984.

Garraty, John A., ed. *Quarrels That Have Shaped the Constitution.* New York: Harper & Row, 1987.

George, Robert P., ed. *Great Cases in Constitutional Law.* Princeton, N.J.: Princeton University Press, 2000.

Greenberg, Ellen. *The Supreme Court Explained.* New York: Norton, 1997.

Guitton, Stephanie, and Peter H. Irons, eds. *May It Please the Court: The Most Significant Oral Arguments Made Before the Supreme Court Since 1955.* New York: New Press, 1994.

Hall, Kermit L. *The Magic Mirror: Law in American History.* New York: Oxford University Press, 1989.

———. *By and for the People: Constitutional Rights in American History.* Arlington, Ill.: Harlan Davidson, 1991.

———. *The Oxford Companion to the Supreme Court of the United States.* New York: Oxford University Press, 1992.

———. *The Oxford Guide to United States Supreme Court Decisions.* New York: Oxford University Press, 2001.

Hall, Kermit L., William M. Wiecek, and Paul Finkelman. *American Legal History: Cases and Materials.* New York: Oxford University Press, 1991.

Harrell, Mary Ann, and Burnett Anderson. *Equal Justice Under Law.* Washington, D.C.: Supreme Court Historical Society, 1982.

Horowitz, Morton J. *The Transformation of American Law, 1780–1860.* New York: Oxford University Press, 1992.

———. *The Transformation of American Law, 1870–1960: The Crisis of Legal Orthodoxy.* New York: Oxford University Press, 1992.

Irons, Peter. *The Courage of Their Convictions. Sixteen Americans Who Fought Their Way to the Supreme Court.* New York: Free Press, 1988.

———. *A People's History of the Supreme Court.* New York: Viking, 1999.

Johnson, Herbert Alan. *American Legal and Constitutional History.* Lanham, Md.: University Press of America, 2001.

Johnson, John W. *Historic U.S. Court Cases, 1690–1990, An Encyclopedia.* New York: Garland, 1992.

Jost, Kenneth. *The Supreme Court A to Z.* 2nd ed. Washington, D.C.: Congressional Quarterly, 1998.

Kahn, Ronald. *The Supreme Court and Constitutional Theory, 1953–1993.* Lawrence: University Press of Kansas, 1995.

Karp, Robert A. *The Federal Courts.* Washington, D.C.: Congressional Quarterly, 2001.

———. *Judicial Process in America.* Washington, D.C.: Congressional Quarterly, 2001.

Kelly, Alfred H., Winfred A. Harbison, and Herman Belz. *The American Constitution: Its Origins and Development.* New York: Norton, 1990.

Ketchum, Ralph. *Framed for Posterity: The Enduring Philosophy of the Constitution.* Lawrence: University Press of Kansas, 1993.

Lazarus, Edward. *Closed Chambers: The Rise, Fall, and Future of the Modern Supreme Court.* New York: Penguin, 1999.

Leuchtenburg, William E. *The Supreme Court Reborn: The Constitutional Revolution in the Age of Roosevelt.* New York: Oxford University Press, 1995.

*The Supreme
Court library*

Levy, Leonard W., Kenneth L. Karst, and Dennis J. Mahoney, editors. *Encyclopedia of the American Constitution.* 4 vols. New York: Macmillan, 1986.

Lively, Donald E. *Landmark Supreme Court Cases.* Westport, Conn.: Greenwood, 1999.

Lutz, Donald S. *The Origins of American Constitutionalism.* Baton Rouge: Louisiana State University Press, 1988.

Marcus, Maeva. *Origins of the Federal Judiciary.* New York: Oxford University Press, 1992.

Mauro, Anthony. *Illustrated Great Decisions of the Supreme Court.* Washington, D.C.: Congressional Quarterly, 2000.

McCloskey, Robert G., and Sanford Levinson, eds. *The American Supreme Court.* 2nd ed. Chicago: University of Chicago Press, 1994.

Meltzer, Milton. *The Bill of Rights: How We Got It and What It Means.* New York: Crowell, 1990.

O'Brien, David M. *Storm Center: The Supreme Court in American Politics.* 5th ed. New York: Norton, 1999.

Peck, Robert S. *We the People: The Constitution in American Life.* New York: Abrams, 1987.

Perry, Barbara A. *The Priestly Tribe: The Supreme Court's Image in the American Mind.* Westport, Conn.: Praeger, 1999.

———. *The Supremes: Essays on the Current Justices of the Supreme Court of the United States.* New York: Peter Lang, 1999.

Perry, H. W., Jr. *Deciding to Decide: Agenda Setting in the United States Supreme Court.* Cambridge: Harvard University Press, 1991.

Ritchie, Donald A. *The U.S. Constitution.* New York: Chelsea House, 1989.

Ryden, David K., ed. *The U.S. Supreme Court and the Electoral Process.* Washington, D.C.: Georgetown University Press, 2000.

Schwartz, Bernard. *Decision: How the Supreme Court Decides Cases.* New York: Oxford University Press, 1996.

———. *The Great Rights of Mankind: A History of the American Bill of Rights.* Madison, Wis.: Madison House, 1992.

———. *A History of the Supreme Court.* New York: Oxford University Press, 1993.

———. *Main Currents in American Legal Thought.* Durham, N.C.: Carolina Academic Press, 1993.

Semonche, John E. *Keeping the Faith: A Cultural History of the U.S. Supreme Court.* Lanham, Md.: Rowman & Littlefield, 2000.

Shapiro, Fred R., ed. *American Legal Quotations.* New York: Oxford University Press, 1993.

Shnayerson, Robert. *The Illustrated History of the Supreme Court of the United States.* New York: Abrams, 1986.

Sunderland, Lane V. *Popular Government and the Supreme Court.* Lawrence: University Press of Kansas, 1996.

Urofsky, Melvin I. *A March of Liberty: A Constitutional History of the United States.* New York: Knopf, 1988.

Wagman, Robert J. *The Supreme Court: A Citizen's Guide.* New York: Pharos Books, 1993.

Wiecek, William M. *Liberty Under Law: The Supreme Court in American Life.* Baltimore: Johns Hopkins University Press, 1988.

Witt, Elder. *Guide to the U.S. Supreme Court.* Washington, D.C.: Congressional Quarterly, 1989.

———. *The Supreme Court and Individual Rights.* Washington, D.C.: Congressional Quarterly, 1988.

———. *The Supreme Court at Work.* Washington, D.C.: Congressional Quarterly, 1990.

Woodward, Bob, and Scott Armstrong. *The Brethren: Inside the Supreme Court.* New York: Simon & Schuster, 1979.

Yalof, David A. *Pursuit of Justices: Presidential Politics and the Selection of Supreme Court Nominees.* Chicago: University of Chicago Press, 1999.

INDEX

Page numbers in *italics* refer to illustrations. Page numbers in **bold** refer to main article entries.

Abington School District v. *Schempp* (1963), 9, **11–12**, 116, 123, 197, 270, 319, 354
abortion rights, **12–14**, 45, 148, 241–42, 269, 285–86, 358–59
Abrams, Jacob, 14
Abrams v. *United States* (1919), **14–16**, 81, 136, 137, 144, 158–59, 294, 299
accused, rights of the, 38–39, 41, 59, 98, 111–13, 141–42, 145–46, 220–21, 279–84, 300–301, 333–34
actual malice, 51, 236
Adair v. *United States* (1908), 86, 140
Adams, John, 71, 114, 173, 204–5, 207–8, 260, 299
Adams, John Quincy, 334
Adamson v. *California* (1947), 44, 135
Adkins v. *Children's Hospital* (1923), 322, 360
Adler v. *Board of Education* (1952), 220
administration of federal courts, 16
administrative assistant to the Chief Justice, 309
Administrative Office of the United States Courts, **16**
admiralty and maritime law, **16–17**
advisory opinions, 17, 188
Aetna Life Insurance Co. v. *Haworth* (1937), 187
affirmative action, **17–19**, 78–79, 118–20, 174–75, 254, 264–66, 348–49
African Americans, 17–19, 20, 53–54, 59, 67–68, 77–79, 101–2, 110, 118–20, 131–32, 218, 352
Agostini v. *Felton* (1997), **20–21**
Agricultural Adjustment Act, *181*
Aguilar v. *Felton* (1985), 20
Allegeyer v. *Louisiana*, 305
Allegheny County v. *American Civil Liberties Union, Greater Pittsburgh Chapter* (1989), 271
amendments to the Constitution, **21–24**, 42, 95, 277–78. See also specific amendments by number
American Bar Association, 24–25
American Bar Association Committee on Federal Judiciary, **24–25**, 28
American Civil Liberties Union (ACLU), **25–26**, 143, 274–75
American Federation of Labor, 229–31
amicus curiae, **26**, 245
anti-Semitism, 49–50, 81, 216
appeal, **26–27**

appellant, **27**
appellate jurisdiction, 184. *See also* jurisdiction
appellee, **27**
appointment of justices, 24–25, **27–29**, 186, 267–69, 301
apportionment, 32–34, 278–79, 357
Aquinas, Thomas, 231
Argersinger v. *Hamlin* (1972), 98
Arthur, Chester, 46
Articles of the Constitution. See Constitution, U.S.
assembly and petition, rights to, **29–32**, 42
associate justices. See justices of the Supreme Court
attainder, bill of, **32**, 280–81

Badger, George, 268
"bad tendency" test, 15, 50
bail, **32**
Bailey v. *Drexel Furniture Co.* (1922), 86
Baker, Charles, 32–34
Baker v. *Carr* (1962), **32–34**, 50–51, 357
Bakke, Allan, 264–66. *See also Regents of the University Of California* v. *Bakke* (1978)
Baldwin, Henry, **34**
Baldwin v. *New York* (1970), 333
Bank of the United States, *213*
Barbour, Philip Pendleton, **34–35**, 114
Bar of the Supreme Court, **35**
Barron, John, 35–36
Barron v. *Baltimore* (1833), **35–36**, 42, 136, 164, 281
Benton v. *Maryland* (1969), **37**, 166, 247, 283
Bethel School District No. 403 v. *Fraser* (1986), **37–38**, 154, 317, 332
Betts v. *Brady* (1942), **38–39**, 108, 133, 142
Bible reading in schools, 11–12, 269–74
Bill of Rights, 22, 36, **39–43**, 44, 48, 95, 110, 111–13, 163–67, 198–200, 261, 279–84, 333–34, 356. *See also* specific amendments by number
birth control, 12–14, 147–48, 153–54, 258
Black, Hugo Lafayette, 39, **43–45**, 64, 107, 108, 109, 110, 115, 122–23, 138, 142, 148, 170, 193, 259, 262, 270, 303, 332, 374–75, 376–77
Black, Jeremiah, 268
Blackmun, Harry A., 12–13, **45–46**, 189, 214, 259, 266, 283, 285–86, 359
Blackstone, William, *88*
Blair, John, Jr., **46**

Blatchford, Samuel, **46–47**
Board Of Education of the Westside Community Schools v. *Mergens* (1990), 320
Bolivia, 336–37
Bond v. *United States* (2000), 298
Bork, Robert, 48, 246, 268–69
Bowers v. *Hardwick* (1986), 177
Boykin v. *Alabama* (1969), 250
Bradford, Edward, 268
Bradley, Joseph, **47**, 80, 119, 306
Bradwell v. *Illinois* (1873), 119
Brandeis, Lewis Dembitz, 15, 28, 30, **47–49**, 63, 81, *108*, 110, 138, 144–45, 186, 216, 226, 242, 258, 305, 360, 367–68
Brandeis brief, 48, **49**, 226
Brandenburg v. *Ohio* (1969), **49–50**, 137, 249, 294, 299, 368
Breaking the Vicious Cycle: Towards Effective Risk and Regulation (Breyer), 52
Brennan, William J., Jr., 33, 45, **50–51**, 62, 154, 170, 175, 186, 210, 236, 245, 266, 327, 340, 344, 349
Brewer, David, **51–52**
Breyer, Stephen G., **52–53**, 223
Bridges v. *California* (1941), 44
brief, **53**
Brown, Henry B., **53–54**, 250
Brown II (1955), 56
Brown v. *Board of Education* (1954), 17, 26, **54–56**, 78, 88, 96–97, 108, 110, 118, 121, 132, 152, 168, 209, 226, 229, 251–52, 254, 257, 300, 302, 323, 352, 356
Buchanan, James, 83
buildings, Supreme Court, 2, **56–59**, *88*, *117*, *199*, 324, 385
Bunting v. *Oregon* (1917), 202
Burch v. *Louisiana* (1979), 334
Burger, Warren E., 25, 28, 38, 45, **58–59**, 70, 124, 197, 217, 238, 264, 266, 283, 317–18, 342
Burr, Aaron, 22–23
Burton, Harold H., **59–60**
Burton v. *Sills* (1968), 49
Bush, George H. W., 283, 309, 329–30
Bush, George W., 179–80, 249
Bush v. *Gore* (2000), 179–80, 249
Butler, Pierce, **60**, 186, 233, 256
Byrnes, James F., **60–61**, 186

Calder v. *Bull* (1798) 70, 157
Calhoun, John, 240
California v. *Acevedo* (1991), 65
California v. *Greenwood* (1988), 297
Campbell, John A., 61, 196

Cantwell v. *Connecticut* (1940), 166, 272

capital punishment, **61–63**

capitol building, *57, 58*

Cardozo, Benjamin N., **63–64**, 187, 216, 246–47, 360

Carr, Joseph Cordell, 32–34

Carroll v. *United States* (1925), **64–65,** 297, 344

Carswell, G. Harrold, 45, 268

Carter, Jimmy, *247*

Carter v. *Carter Coal Co.* (1936), 86

Catron, John, **65**

Certiorari, writ of, **65–66**, 82, 245, 286

chambers, **66**

Champion v. *Ames* (1903), 86

Chandler v. *Miller* (1997), 298

Chaplinski v. *New Hampshire* (1942), 195

Charles River Bridge v. *Warren Bridge* (1837), **66–67**, 324–25

Chase, Salmon P., **67–68**, 70, 328

Chase, Samuel, **68–69**, 161, 162

checks and balances. *See* separation of powers

Cherokee Nation v. *Georgia* (1931), 330, 372

Cherokees, 330, 372

Chicago, Burlington & Quincy Railroad Company v. *Chicago* (1897), 164, 166, 185, 261–62

Chicago Tribune, 232–34

chief justice, 16, **69–71**, 185, 244. *See also* individual chief justices

child labor, 151–52

Chimel v. *California* (1969), 297

Chisholm v. *Georgia* (1793), 22, 46, **71–72**, 170, 173, 277

church and state, separation of. *See* religious issues under the Constitution

Church of Jesus Christ of Latter-Day Saints, 272–73

Church of the Lukumi Babalu Aye v. *City of Hialeah* (1993), 192, 273, 309

Circuit Court Of Appeals, **72–73,** 130–31, 183, 248

The Citadel, 346–47

citation, 73

citizenship, 73–74, 347–48

City of Boerne, Texas v. *Flores* (1997), **75–77**

civil law, 77, 100, 333

civil rights, 17–19, 42, 55–56, **77–79,** 96–97, 112–13, 118–20, 155–56, 174–75, 228, 235–36, 250–52, 307–8, 315–16, 322–23

Civil Rights Act (1875), 79–80, 315–16, 371

Civil Rights Act (1964), 78, 98, 118, 155, 174–75, 264–66, 349

Civil Rights Act (1991), 79, 120, 277–78

Civil Rights Cases (1883), **79–80,** 371

Clark, Ramsay, 81

Clark, Tom, 11, **80–81**, 154, 203

Clarke, John H., 15, **81–82**

class action, 82

clear and present danger test, 15–16, 50, 135–39, 293–94, 299, 368

clerk of the court, **82**, 309

clerks of the justices, **82–83**

Cleveland, Grover, 140, 171, 196, 248

Clifford, Nathan, **83**

Cline, Genevieve, 370

Clinton, Bill, 52, 83–85, 143, 274, 370

Clinton v. *City of New York* (1998), **83–85**

Code of Conduct for United States Judges, 121–22

Cohens v. *Virginia* (1821), **85**, 127, 130, 208, 315

Cole v. *Arkansas* (1947), 166, 282

Collin v. *Smith* (1978), 31

Commentaries on the Law of England (Blackstone), 88

commerce power, **85–88**, 140–41, 151–52, 155–56, 215, 227–28, 229–31, 238–40, 312, 337–38, 338–39

common-law, **88**

The Common Law (Holmes), 158

Communications Decency Act, 274–75

communism, 106–7, 315–16, 367–68, 372–73

concurring opinion, **88–89**, 108, 203, 244, 252, 304

conference, **89–90**

confirmation of justices, 27–29, 267–69, 301

Constitution, U.S., 7, **94–96**. *See also* amendments to the Constitution; Bill of Rights; specific amendments by number

    Article 1, 69, 83–85, 85–87, 90, 95, 125, 132–33, 150, 155, 161–62, 163, 215, 229–31, 238–40, 260–61, 280, 302–4, 312, 339, 374–75

    Article 2, 27–28, 69, 95, 126, 186, 247, 302–4, 374–75

    Article 3, 28, 69–70, 71, 95, 114, 167, 175, 178, 183, 184–85, 186, 206, 208, 281, 294–96, 302–4, 333–34

    Article 5, 277–78

    Article 6, 92, 95, 180, 206, 211

    Article 7, 253

constitutional construction, **90**, 163, 175–76, 212–14, 245–46

constitutional convention, 21–22, 46, 126, 172, 248, 287, 369

constitutional democracy, **90–92**, 95, 128–30, 180–82, 231, 240, 253, 276–77, 302–4, 373–75

constitutional law, **94**, 95, 163–67, 231, 257

contempt power of the courts, **96**

Continental Congress, 17, 172, 287

contract, liberty of, 225–26, 229–31

contract clause, 66–67, **96**, 104, 132–33, 227–28, 260–63

Coolidge, Calvin, 160, 313, 370

Cooper v. *Aaron* (1958), 88, **96–97**, 110, 118

corporal punishment in schools, 319

counsel, right to, 38–39, 42, **98**, 220–21, 254–56, 279–84

Court of Appeals, 27, **99–100**, 130–31, 183–84

court-packing plan, **98–99**, 160, 185, 230, 361

Cox v. *Louisiana* (1965), 44

Cranch, William, 176

criminal law, 74, **100**

Crittenden, John, 268

cruel and unusual punishment, **61–63**, 74, **100–101**, 210

curator, office of the, 310

Curtis, Benjamin R., **101–2**, 295–96

Curtiss-Wright Export Corp., United States v. (1936), 336–37

Cushing, Caleb, 268

Cushing, William, **102**

Dallas, Alexander, 276, 315

Daniel, Peter V., **102–3**

Darby Lumber Co., United States v. (1941), 86, 152, **337–38**

Dartmouth College v. *Woodward* (1819), 66, 96, **103–4**, 208, 261

Data Systems Office, **104**

Davis, David, **104–5**

Day, William R., **105**, 151–52, 359–60

death penalty, **61–63**

decision days, **106**

Decker, Bernard, 31

Declaration of Independence, 93, 116, 199, 231, 281

DeJonge v. *Oregon* (1937), 30, 160, 166

De Lovio v. *Boit* (1815), 17

Democracy in America (Tocqueville), 7

Dennis v. *United States* (1951), **106–7**, 110, 138, 172, 252, 352

direct election of senators, 23

discuss list, **107**

dissenting opinion, **108**, 203, 244, 252, 304

district courts, federal, **126**, 130–31

double jeopardy, 37, **109**, 245–46, 279–84

Douglas, Stephen, 296

Douglas, William O., 39, 62, 107, **109–10**, 131–32, 147, *162*, 176, 187, 258, 270, 370, 376

Douglass, Frederick, 116

draft, military, 342–43

drug testing in schools, 350–52

due process of law, 12–14, 21–22, 23–24, 37, 44, 63, 64, 98, 109, **111–13**, 115, 123, 131, 141–42, 144–45, 145–46, 147–48, 168–69, 188–90, 201–2, 214, 225–26, 227–28, 229–31, 240, 246–47, 254–56, 257–60, 279–84, 285–86, 296–99, 318–19, 321, 331–32, 335, 337, 364–65

Duncan v. *Louisiana* (1968), **113**, 166

Duvall, Gabriel, 103, **113–14**

E. C. Knight Co., United States v. (1895), 305, **338–40**

Education Consolidation and Improvement Act, 221–24

18th Amendment, 23, 242–43

8th Amendment, 32, 63, 73–74, 100–101, 111, 165, 210, 279–84

Eisenhower, Dwight, 45, 50, 59, 97, 153, 356

11th Amendment, 22–23, 46, 72, 85, 277

Ellsberg, Daniel, 237–38

Ellsworth, Oliver, 70, **114**

eminent domain, **115**, 185

Employment Division, Department of Human Resources of Oregon v. *Smith* (1990), 75–76, 273

Engel v. *Vitale* (1962), 12, 26, **115–16**, 121, 123, 197, 270, 319, 354

English Bill of Rights, 29

Enlightenment, 231

Equal Access Act (1984), 361–63

equality under the Constitution, 18, 79–80, **116–21**, 155–56, 174–75, 250–52, 263–64, 264–66, 307–8, 322–23

equal protection of the laws, 18, 23, 53–54, 79–80, **121**, 218, 263–64, 264–66, 278–79, 321, 346–47

Escobedo v. *Illinois* (1964), 145

Espionage Act (1917), 14, 81, 249, 293–94

establishment clause, **11–12**, 20–21, 115–16, **121**, 123, 196–98, 223–24, 269–74, 319–20, 362–63, 375–77

ethics in the judicial branch, 121–22

Everson v. *Board of Education of Ewing Township*, **122–23**, 166, 197, 270

exclusionary rule, 81, **123**, 203–4, 283, 296–99, 340–41, 359–60, 366, 369–70

executive privilege, 59, **124**, 341–42

ex parte, **124**

Ex Parte Milligan (1866), 68, 105, **124–25**, **150**

Ex Parte Vallandigham (1864), 322, 358

Ex Parte Virginia (1880), 316

Ex Parte Yerger (1869), 150

ex post facto law, **125**

ex rel, **126**

Fairfax's Devisee v. *Hunter's Lessee* (1813), 211

Fairy Labor Standards Act, 337–38

Faubus, Orval, 96–97

federal district courts, **126**, 130–31

Federalism, 86–88, 103–4, **126–28**, 132–33, 135, 151–52, 198–200, 240, 311, 312, 324–25, 337–38, 355

The Federalist, 91, 92, 93, 127, **128–30**, 163, 165, 167, 172, 181, 276, 302–4

Federal Judicial Center, 16, 81

federal judicial system, *99*, *126*, 130–31, 183–84

Federal Trade Commission Act (1914), 239

Field, Stephen Johnson, **131–32**, 306

15th Amendment, 23, 78, 117, 160, 307–8, 353

5th Amendment, 35–36, 37, 41, 63, 109, 110, 111–13, 115, 117, 125, 133, 145–46, 147–48, 151–52, 155, 156, 164, 169, 185, 192–94, 220–21, 227–28, 229–31, 242–43, 246–47, 258–59, 261, 279–84, 300–301, 305–6, 321, 335, 337, 359–60

fighting words, 195

1st Amendment, 11, 14–15, 20–21, 26, **29–32**, 37–38, 40–41, 44, 48, 49–50, 50–51, 75–77, 106–7, 110, 115–16, 122–23, 133–34, 144–45, 153–55, 160, 164, 192, 196–98, 216–17, 218–19, 221–24, 232–34, 235–36, 237–38, 241, 257–60, 269–74, 274–75, 290, 293–94, 299, 309, 312, 314, 315–16, 317–18, 319–20, 327–28, 331–32, 342–43, 353–54, 361–63, 367–68, 375–77, 377–78

First Monday in October, 243

Fiske v. *Kansas* (1927), 164, 166, 290

flag burning, 327–28

Fletcher v. *Peck* (1810), 96, 103–4, 127, **132–33**, 208, 261

Ford, Gerald, *91*

Fortas, Abe, 38, 133–34, **133–34**, 142, *167*, 168–69, 187, 189, 268, 317

14th Amendment, 12, 17–19, 23, 26, 30, 33, 37, 39, 42, 44, 48, **54–56**, 63, 64, 73–74, 75–77, 80, 102, 109, 110, 111–13, 115–16, 117, 119, 121, 123, 128, 131, 133, 135, 141–42, 145–46, 147–48, 152, 160, 163–67, 169, 201–2, 203–4, 214, 216, 217, 218, 225–26, 227, 232–34, 241, 246–47, 250–52, 254–56, 258–59, 261, 263–64, 264–66, 272, 278–79, 279–84, 285–86, 288–89, 296, 305–7, 307–8, 311, 312, 315–16, 318–19, 321, 323, 326, 331–32, 335, 342–43, 346–47, 347–48, 353–54, 357, 364–65, 367–68, 369, 371, 377–78

4th Amendment, 41, 65, 94, 95, 110, 123, 147–48, 191, 194–95, 203–4, 234–35, 242–43, 258–59, 260, 279–84, 296–99, 311, 312, 318, 326, 340–41, 343–45, 350–52, 359–60, 366, 369–70, 377–78

Frankfurter, Felix, 33, 113, **134–35**, 137, 143, 176, 187, 218–19, 296, 365, *370*

Fraser, Matthew, 37–38

freedom of association, 153

freedom of speech and press, 14–15, 21–22, 25–26, 37–38, 40–41, 49–50, 106–7, 135–39, 144–45, 153–55, 158–59, 194–95, 216–17, 232–34, 235–36, 293–94, 299, 317–18, 331–32, 342–43, 367–68, 372–73, 377–78. *See also* 1st Amendment; 14th Amendment; seditious libel

free exercise clause, **140**

Fuller, Melville W., 70, **140**, 323, 339

Fulton, Robert, 87, 140–41

Furman v. *Georgia* (1972), 62, 101

gag law, 232–34

Garcia v. *San Antonio Metropolitan Transit Authority* (1985), 86

Garfield, James, 212

Garrison v. *Louisiana* (1964), 299

gay rights, 78

gender discrimination, 263–64. See also affirmative action; women's rights

general welfare clause, 90

Georgia v. *South Carolina* (1990), 184

Georgia v. *Stanton* (1868), 234

Gibbons v. *Ogden* (1824), 87, 127, **140–41**, 238–40

Gideon v. *Wainwright* (1963), 39, 98, 108, 133, **141–42**, 166, 256, 282, 356

Gilbert, Cass, 57

Gilbert v. *Minnesota* (1920), 48

Ginsberg, Ruth Bader, **143–44**, 187, 223, 264, 347, 370

Ginsburg, Douglas, 268

Gitlow v. *New York* (1925), 26, 36, 48, 136, **144–45**, 164–65, 166, 241, 289–90

Gobitis, Minersville School District v., (1940), **218–19**, 314, 365

Goldberg, Arthur J., 52, 133, **145**, 148, 187, 258, 300–301

good faith exception, 123, 204, 283, 298, 340–41, 366

Gore, Albert, 179–80, 249

Goss v. *Lopez* (1975), 318

grand jury, **145–46**

Granger Cases, 227–28

Grant, Ulysses S., 47, 83, 185, 353

Gray, Horace, 82–83, **146**, 348

Green v. *County School Board of New Kent County, Virginia*, (1968), 56

Green v. *United States* (1957), 109

Gregg v. *Georgia* (1976), 62–63, 101

Grier, Robert C., **146–47**

Griffin v. *California* (1965), 356

Griswold v. *Connecticut* (1965), 12, 48, 52–53, 110, **147–48**, 153, 166, 177, 243, 258–60

Grovey v. *Townsend* (1935), 308

gun control, 41, **148–49**

habeas corpus, writ of, 38–39, 125, **150–51**, 218, 280

Hague v. *Congress of Industrial Organizations* (1939), 30, 166

Hamilton, Alexander, 92, 93, 128–30, 163, 167, 173, 181

Hammer v. *Dagenhart* (1918), 86, **151–52**, 337–38

Handgun Control, Inc., *148*

Harding, Warren G., 60, 160, 323

Harlan, John Marshall, 80, 108, 118, **152–53**, 239, 251, 261, 282, 336–37, 339, 373

Harlan, John Marshall, II, 33, 148, **153**, 177, 221, 259, 279, 301

Harriman, Edward J., 238–40

Harrison, Benjamin, 171

Harris v. *McRae* (1980), 13

Hayes, Rutherford B., 152, 212

Haynsworth, Clement, 45, 268

Hazelwood School District v. *Kuhlmeier* (1988), 38, **153–55**, 318, 332

Heart of Atlanta Motel v. *United States* (1964), 17, 78, 80, 86, 118, **155–56**

Hill, Anita, 329–30

Hill, James, 238–40

Hirabayashi v. *United States* (1943), **156–57**, 288, 314

Hispanic Americans in the federal judiciary, 157

Historical Society, Supreme Court, 158

holding company, 238–40

Holmes, Oliver Wendell, Jr., 15, 31, 81, **108**, 144–45, 152, **158–59**, 187, 202, 293–94, 299, 338, 368

Honig v. *Doe* (1988), 319

Hoover, Herbert, 160

Hornblower, William, 268

Hughes, Charles Evans, 30, 70, *108*, **159–60**, 187, 230, 233, 262, 316, 323, 360–61

Hunt, Ward, **160–61**

Hurtado v. *California* (1884), 282

Hylton v. *United States* (1796), 68, 161, 170–71

illegal aliens, 305

Illinois ex rel. McCollum v. *Board of Education* (1948), 126, 376

Illinois v. *Wardlow* (2000), 298

impeachment, **161–62**, 302–4

implied powers, **162–63**, 212–14, 240

income tax, 23, 171, 261

incorporation doctrine, 26, 36, 39, 42–43, 44, 48, 64, 98, 110, 112–13, 133, 135, 144–45, 148–49, **163–67**, 203–4, 214, 216–17, 232–34, 245–46, 254–56, 279–84, 290, 298–99, 300–301, 315–16, 335, 369–70

independent judiciary, 162, 167

in forma pauperis, 167

Ingraham v. *Wright* (1977), 319

injunction, 167–68

In re, 168

In re Gault (1967), 133–34, **168–69**, 189, 214

In re Oliver (1948), 166, 282

In re Winship (1970), **169–70**, 189

Internet, 274–75

Iredell, James, **170–70**

Jackson, Andrew, 34, 65, 103, 114, 215, 216, 240, 315, 324, 372

Jackson, Howell E., 171

Jackson, Robert H., 82, 91, 113, 123, **171–72**, 193–94, 194–95, 219, 272, 364–65

Jacobellis v. *Ohio* (1964), 313

Jaffree, Ishmael, *354*

Japanese Americans, internment of, 156–57, 192–94

Jay, John, *17*, 70, 128–30, **172–73**, 208, 287–88

Jay Treaty, 124, 288

Jefferson, Thomas, 22–23, 40, 69, 91, 114, 129–30, 162, 174, 197, 199, 204–5, 270, 299, 333

Jehovah's Witnesses, 218–19, 272, 314, 364–65

Johnson, Andrew, 68, 102, 185

Johnson, Lyndon, 69, 78, 80, 133–34, *167*, 209, *308*

Johnson, Thomas, 173

Johnson, William, 173–74

Johnson v. *Transportation Agency of Santa Clara County* (1987), 19, 119–20, 174–75

Jones & Laughlin Steel Corp., National Labor Relations Board v. (1937), 86, 98, **229–31**, 262, 292, 340

Jones v. *Clear Creek Independent School District* (1993), 197, 320

judicial activism and judicial restraint, 33–314, 51, 135, **175–78**, 234, 245–46, 302–4, 309, 353

Judicial Conference of the United States, 16

judicial power, 70, 161–62, 175–78, **178–80**, 184–85, 204–7, 209–10, 252–53, 302–4

Judicial Reorganization Bill, 98

judicial restraint. *See* judicial activism and judicial restraint

judicial review, 92–93, 94, 161, 170–71, 175–78, **180–83**, 204–7, 207–9, 209–10, 252–53, 257, 294–96, 303, 311, 355

Judiciary Act (1789), 69, 72, 85, 96, 114, 180, **183**, 187, 204–7, 211, 240–41, 248, 315, 325

Judiciary Act (1801), 185

Judiciary Act (1802), 185

Judiciary Act (1807), 185

Judiciary Act (1869), 72, **183**, 185

Judiciary Act (1891), 73, 183–84

jurisdiction, 65–66, 178–80, **184–85**, 187–88, 209–10, 294–96

jus sanguinis, 348

just compensation, 115, 185

justices of the Supreme Court, **185–87**, 381–84. *See also* individual justices

justiciable questions, **187–88**, 252–53

Justinian I, 77

juvenile justice, 168–69, **188–90**, 214, 279–84, 317–20, 366

Kahn v. *Shevin* (1974), 264

Kaiser Aluminum and Chemical Company, 348–49

Katz v. *United States* (1967), 48, **190–91**, 199, 243, 259–60, 297, 312

Kennedy, Anthony M., 76, 187, **191–92**, 223, 309

Kennedy, John F., 145, 209, 366

Kennedy, Robert, 34

Kidd v. *Pearson* (1888), 86

King, Edward, 268

King, Martin Luther King, 78

Klopfer v. *North Carolina* (1967), 166, 283

Korean War, 373–75

Korematsu v. *United States* (1944), **192–94**, 228, 284, 288, 314

Kovacs v. *Cooper* (1949), 137, 200, 331
Ku Klux Klan, *44, 50,* 294
Kunz v. *New York* (1951), 194–95

labor unions, 229–31
Lamar, Joseph R., 48, **195**
Lamar, Lucius Q. C., **195–96**
Lamb's Chapel v. *Center Moriches Union Free School District* (1993), 320
Lawyer's Edition, 196
Lee v. *Weisman* (1992), 197, 270, 319
Legal Counsel, Office of the, 310
Lemon Test, 21, 196–98, 222–23, 271, 363
Lemon v. *Kurtzman* (1971), **196–98,** 271, 354
Lenin, Vladimir, 14
Leon, United States v. (1984), 123, 204, 267, 283, 298, **340–41,** 366
LEXIS, **198,** 311, 336
libel, 235–36
liberty of contract, 225–26, 229–31
liberty under the Constitution, 7, 42–43, 79–80, 92, 93, 111–13, **198–200,** 276–77
Librarian, Supreme Court, 310
Life of George Washington (Marshall), 207
limited government, 92
Lincoln, Abraham, 68, 93, 105, 125, 217–18, 296, 322, 358
"line-item veto," 83–85
Livingston, Henry Brockholst, 200–201
Lochner v. *New York* (1905), **201–2,** 249, 262
Locke, John, 231
loose construction of the Constitution, 51, 90, 163, 208–9, 314–15
Loving v. *Virginia* (1967), 118
Lurton, Horace H., 202
Lynch v. *Donnelly* (1984), 271
Lynch v. *Household Finance Corporation* (1972), 262

Madison, James, 7, 29–30, 40, 42, 91, *93,* 114, 127, 136, 163, 165, 173, 181–82, 199, 204–7, 248, 273, 276, 302–4
Magna Carta, *111,* 150, 281
majority opinion, 88–89, **203,** 244, 252, 304
Malinski v. *New York* (1945), 113
Malloy v. *Hogan* (1964), 166, 282, 300–301
mandamus, writ of, 205
Mapp v. *Ohio* (1961), 26, 81, 123, 166, **203–4,** 282, 297–98, 340, 356, 366, 370

Marbury v. *Madison* (1803), 69, 161, 171, 176, 179, 181–82, **204–7,** 208, 295, 303
Marshall, John, 28, 34, 36, 42–43, 69, 70, 85, 90, 103–4, 114, 127, 130, 133, 140–41, 161, 163, 174, *178,* 180–82, 201, 204–7, **207–9,** 211, 213–14, 261, 263, 304, 314–15, 324, 330, 333, 355, 358, 372
Marshall, Thurgood, 20, 38, 45, 55–56, 62, 78, 186, 187, **209–10,** *230,* 266, 289, 307–8, 322–23, 329, 344–45
Marshall v. *Barlow's Inc.* (1978), 297
Marshal of the Supreme Court, 310
Marsh v. *Alabama* (1946), 262
Marsh v. *Chambers* (1983), 271
Martin v. *Hunter's Lessee* (1816), 85, **210–11,** 263, 315
Maryland v. *Wilson* (1997), 298
Massachusetts Body of Liberties, 29, 111, 281
Massachusetts Constitution, 29
Matthews, Stanley, 212, 268
McCray v. *United States* (1904), 86
McCulloch v. *Maryland* (1819), 9, 90, 127, 130, 163, 208, **212–14**
McKeiver v. *Pennsylvania* (1971), 189, **214**
McKenna, Joseph, 187, **214–15**
McKinley, John, 215
McKinley, William, 105, 215
McLaurin v. *Board of Regents* (1950), 352
McLean, John, 215–16
McReynolds, James Clark, 48, 65, 81, **216,** 256, 337
Meek v. *Pittenger* (1975), 222
Miami Herald Publishing Co. v. *Tornillo* (1974), 216–17
Michigan v. *Sitz* (1990), 297
Micou, William, 268
Miller, Samuel Freeman, **217–18,** 306
Milliken v. *Bradley* (1974), 300
Minersville School District v. *Gobitis* (1940), **218–19,** 314, 365
Minneapolis and St. Louis Railway Company v. *Bombolis* (1916), 334
Minnesota v. *Dickerson* (1993), 297
minority rights. *See* affirmative action; civil rights; constitutional democracy; equality under the Constitution; liberty under the Constitution
Minor v. *Happersett* (1875), 119
Minton, Sherman, 220
Miranda v. *Arizona* (1966), 26, **220–21,** 282–83, 300–301, 356, 366
Miranda warning, *221*
Missouri Compromise, 294–96
Missouri ex rel. Gaines v. *Canada*

(1938), 118, 160
Mitchell, John, *345*
Mitchell v. *Helms* (2000), 221–24
monopolies, 238–40
Moody, William Henry, **224–25,** 335
Moore, Alfred, 225
Moran v. *Burbine* (1986), 221
Morehead v. *New York ex rel. Tipaldo* (1936), 360
Morgan, J. P., 238–40
Mugler v. *Kansas* (1887), 261–62
Mulford v. *Smith* (1939), 86
Muller v. *Oregon* (1908), 47–48, 49, 202, **225–26**
Munn v. *Illinois* (1877), **227–28,** 262, 353
Murphy, Frank, 39, *178,* 187, 193, **228**
Murphy v. *Waterfront Commission of New York* (1964), 301
Myers v. *United States* (1926), 304, 324

NAACP Legal Defense Fund, 55, 62, 78, 209, 228–29
National Association for the Advancement of Colored People (NAACP), 17, 20, 26, 28, 54, 77–78, 97, 118, 209–10, **228–29,** 307–8, 322–23
National Association for the Advancement of Colored People v. *Alabama ex rel. Patterson* (1958), 153
National Bank, 212–14
National Industrial Recovery Act (NIRA), 291–92
National Labor Relations Act, 229–31, 292
National Labor Relations Board, 229–31
National Labor Relations Board v. *Jones & Laughlin Steel Corp.* (1937), 86, 98, **229–31,** 262, 292, 340
National League of Cities v. *Usery* (1976), 86
National Organization of Women (NOW), 17, 28, *121*
National Rifle Association (NRA), *149*
National Treasury Employees Union v. *Von Raab* (1989), 259
naturalization, 73–74
natural law, 231, **231**
Near v. *Minnesota* (1931), 136, 160, 165, 166, **232–34,** 241, 257
necessary and proper clause, 90. *See also* constitutional construction; implied powers
Nelson, Samuel, 234
New Deal. *See* court-packing plan; National Industrial Recovery Act (NIRA); Roosevelt, Franklin D.

New Jersey Plan, 248
New Jersey v. *T.L.O.* (1985), 38, 154, **234–35**, 297, 318, 366
New York Journal, 136
New York Railroad Company v. *White* (1917), 249
New York Times Co. v. *Sullivan* (1964), 51, 136, 137, **235–36**, 299
New York Times Co. v. *United States* (1971), 233, **237–38**, 357
New York v. *Quarles* (1984), 264, 283
19th Amendment, 23–24
9th Amendment, 42, 110, 147–48, 258
Nixon, Richard, 45, 52, 59, *124*, 146, 267, 283, 341–42, 345–46
Nixon, United States v. (1974), 59, 124, **341–42**
nomination of justices, 24–25, 27–29, 267–69, 301
nonpreferentialist doctrine, 270
Norris v. *Alabama* (1935), 256
Northern Securities Co. v. *United States* (1904), **238–40**
Northwest Ordinance, 111
nullification, **240**

oath of office, 240–41
obiter dictum, **241**
O'Brien, United States v. (1968), 92, **342–43**
O'Connor, Sandra Day, 25, 76, 143, 187, 223–24, **241–42**, *243*, 267, 275, 351–52, 363, 370
Office of the Curator, 310
Office of the Legal Counsel, 310
Ohio Criminal Syndicalism Act, 49–50
Ohio v. *Akron Center for Reproductive Health* (1990), 13
Olmstead v. *United States* (1928), 48, 191, **242–43**, 258–60, 297
Olney, Richard, 47
Omnibus Crime Control and Safe Streets Act, 345–46
opening day, 243–44, 325–26
opinions, 88–89, 108, 203, **244**, 252, 304
oral argument, 244–45
ordered liberty, 93, 199
orders list, 245
Oregon v. *Mitchell* (1970), 277
original intent, **245–46**
original jurisdiction, 184
Osborn v. *Bank of the United States* (1824), 179

Palko v. *Connecticut* (1937), 37, 64, **246–47**
Paraguay, 336–37

pardon power, 247
Parker, John, 268
Parker v. *Gladden* (1966), 166, 282
Paterson, William, 161, **247–48**
Peckham, Rufus W., 201, **248–49**, 262, 268
Pennsylvania Declaration of Rights, 136
Pentagon Papers. *See New York Times Co.* v. *United States* (1971)
per curiam, 244, **249**
peyote, 273
Pierce v. *United States* (1920), 249
Pitney, Mahlon, **249**
Planned Parenthood, *147, 257*
Plessy v. *Ferguson* (1896), 54, 55–56, 108, 118, 132, 152, **250–52**, 257, 300, 302, 323, 347–48, 356
plurality opinion, 88–89, 203, 244, **252**, 304
Poe v. *Ullman* (1961), 153, 258
Pointer v. *Texas* (1965), 166, 282
political questions, 188, **252–53**
Polk, James, 147
Pollock v. *Farmers' Loan and Trust Co.* (1895), 171, 277
polygamy, 272–73
popular sovereignty, 253
Powell, Lewis F., Jr., 89, **254**, 265–66, 283, 289
Powell v. *Alabama* (1932), 142, **254–56**, 282, 322
precedent, 94, 108, 256–57, 277–78
presidential elections, 22–23
Presser v. *Illinois* (1886), 148, 371
prior restraint, 232–34, 237–38, **257**
privacy, right to, 12–13, 42–43, 45, 48, 110, 137–38, 147–48, 153, **257–60**, 285–86, 312–13
Privacy Protection Act (1980), 378
Prize Cases (1863), 147, 358
probable cause, **260**, 269–99, 343–45
procedural due process, 147–48
Prohibition, 23–24, 242–43
property rights, 42–43, **260–63**, 290–91, 305–7
Public Information Office, 310–11
Public Nuisance Abatement Law, 232–34
Publius, 129–30

Quilici v. *Village of Morton Grove* (1983), 149

Railroad Retirement Board v. *Alton Railroad* (1935), 86
Randolph, Edmund, 248

Read, John, 268
Reagan, Ronald, *28, 83,* 241, 283, 327, 370
recusal, 263
Red Lion Broadcasting Co. Inc. v. *Federal Communications Commission* (1969), 217
Reed, Stanley F., **263**, 308
Reed v. *Reed* (1971), 119, 121, 143, **263–64**
Regents of the University of California v. *Bakke* (1978), 18, 89, 119, 254, **264–66**
Rehnquist, William H., 70, 82, 116, 187, 190, 192, 223, **266–67**, 271, 275, 283, 285–86, 327–28, 349, 354, 359
rejection of Supreme Court nominees, 24–25, 27–29, **267–69**, 301
Religious Freedom Restoration Act (RFRA), 75–77
religious issues under the Constitution, **11–12**, 20–21, 42–43, 75–77, 116, 122–23, 191–92, 196–98, 218–19, 221–24, **269–74**, 309, 314, 319–20, 353–54, 361–63, 364–65, 375–77
Reno v. *American Civil Liberties Union,* **274–75**
reporter of decisions, 73, 275–76, 310, 336
republicanism, 128–30, 253, 276–77
reversals of Supreme Court decisions, **277–78**, 302–4
reverse discrimination, 19
Reynolds v. *Sims* (1964), 34, 51, 278–79, 357
Reynolds v. *United States* (1879), 272
rights of the accused, 38–39, 42–43, 59, 98, 99–100, 111–13, 141–42, 145–46, 220–21, **279–84**, 300–301, 333–34
right to bear arms, 148–49
right to reply, 216–17
Roberts, Owen J., 98–99, 193, **284**, 360–61
robing room, 284–85
Robinson v. *California* (1962), 166, 282
Roe v. *Wade* (1973), 12–13, 45, 148, 241–42, 244, 259, 267, 269, **285–86**, 358–59
Roosevelt, Franklin D., 24, 43, 60, 81, 83, 98–99, 110, 134–35, 156–57, 160, 171–72, 185, 216, 220, 228, 229–31, 263, 284, 288, 291–92, 313, 322, 336–37, 350, 361
Roosevelt, Theodore, 105, 158–59, 224
Rule of Four, 286
rule of law, *91,* 92–93
rule of reason, 367
Rules of the Court, 66, 286–87
Rust v. *Sullivan* (1991), 286

Rutledge, John, 70, 187, 268, **287–88**
Rutledge, Wiley B., 82, 123, 219, **288**

Sacco, Nicola, 63
salaries of justices, 187
San Antonio Independent School District v. Rodriguez (1973), 288–89
Sanford, Edward Terry, 144, 241, **289–90**, 367–68
Santa Clara County v. Southern Pacific Railroad Co. (1886), 290–291
Saturday Press, 232–34
Scalia, Antonin, 83, 175, 187, 223, 273, **291**, 330, 347, 351–52
Schall v. Martin (1984), 190
Schechter Poultry Corp. v. United States (1935), **291–92**
Schempp, Abington School District v., (1963), 9, **11–12**, 116, 123, 197, 270, 319, 354
Schenck v. United States (1919), 14, 50, 136, 137, 144, 158–59, **293–94**, 299
Schneiderman v. United States (1943), 178
school financing, 288–89
school prayer, 115–16, 121, 269–74, 353–54, 361–63
Scott, Dred, 294–96
Scottsboro boys, 254–56
Scott v. Sandford (1857), 61, 101–2, 216, 277, **294–96**, 324
searches and seizures, 22, 41, 42–43, 64–65, 123, 190–90, 203–4, 234–35, 242–43, 260, 279–84, **296–99**, 318, 326, 340–41, 343–45, 359–60, 366, 369–70
secession, 68, 240, 328
2nd Amendment, 41, 148–49, 165
Sedition Act (1789), 299
Sedition Act (1918), 14
seditious libel, 136, 293–94, **299,** 367–68
segregation, de facto and de jure, **54–56,** 59, 60, 96–97, 117, 140, 152, 177, 250–52, 254, **300,** 302, 322–23, 352
selective incorporation doctrine, 64, 335
self-incrimination, privilege against, 42–43, **300–301**
Senate Judiciary Committee, 25, 28, 267–69, 301
senators, direct election of, 23
seniority, 301–2
separate but equal doctrine, **54–56,** 59, 60, 117, 132, 140, 152, 250–52, 300, **302,** 322–33, 347–48
Separate Car Law, 250–52
separation of church and state. *See* religious issues under the Constitution

separation of powers, 17, 40, 129, 162–63, 167, 175–78, 180–82, 261, 277, **302–4,** 341–42, 373–75
seriatim opinions, 208, 244, **304**
17th Amendment, 23
7th Amendment, 41, 165, 333–34
Seward, William H., 46
sexual harassment, 329–30
Shaughnessy v. United States (1953), 113
Sherbert v. Verner (1963), 75–76, 273
Sherman Antitrust Act, 238–40, 338–40, 367
Shiras, George, Jr., 305
Shreveport Rate Cases (1914), 86
16th Amendment, 23, 171, 261, 277
6th Amendment, 38–39, 41, 98, 111, 113, 125, 141–42, 145, 169, 214, 279–84, 319, 333–34
Skinner v. Railway Labor Executives Association (1989), 259
Slaughterhouse Cases (1873), 218, 316
slavery, 23, 65, 67–68, 116, 121, 215, 216, 231, 250–52, 294–96, 300, 322, 324, 358
Smith Act, 106–7, 352, 373
Smithsonian Institution, 71
Smith v. Allwright (1944), 77, 118, **307–8**
solicitor general, 308
Souter, David, 21, 223–24, 308–9
South Carolina Exposition and Protest (Calhoun), 240
South Carolina v. Katzenbach (1966), *78, 307,* 308
speech and press, freedom of. *See* freedom of speech and press
Spencer, John, 268
staff of the court, nonjudicial, 275–76, **309–11**
Standard Oil v. United States (1910), 367
standing to sue, 311
The Stanford Daily, Zurcher v., **377–78**
stare decisis, 108, 257, 365. *See also* precedent
state courts, 311
status offenses, 188–90
statute, 311
Stevens, John Paul, 38, 70, 84, 223, 235, 275, **312,** 327–28, 344, 354, 363
Stewart, Potter, 12, 62, 116, 148, 191, 259, 262, **312–13,** 378
Stone, Harlan Fiske, 28, 70, 157, 187, 219, 301, **313–14,** 338, 360
Stone v. Graham (1980), 319
stop and frisk, 326
Story, Joseph, 16, 28, 67, 85, 174, 209, 211, **314–15**

Strauder v. West Virginia (1880), 119, 316
strict construction of the Constitution, 90, 202
strikes, 229–31, 373–75
Stromberg v. California (1931), 26, 136, 160, 165, 166, 241, **315–16,** 332, 342–43
Strong, William, 316
student rights under the Constitution, 38, 42–43, 133–34, **140–42,** 234–35, 317–20, 331–32
substantive due process, 112–13, 147–48, 201–2
Summa Theologica (Aquinas), 231
Supreme Court Building Commission, 57
Supreme Court reporter, 196, **321**
supreme law of the land, 91, 92
suspect classifications, 321
Sutherland, George, 65, 256, **321–22,** 336–37
Swayne, Noah H., 306, *322*
Sweatt v. Painter (1950), 77–78, 118, **322–23,** 352
Swift and Co. v. United States (1905), 86
symbolic speech, 327–28, 331–32

Taft, William Howard, 57, 65, 70, 160, 273, **323–24,** 366–67
Taft Court, *94*
Taft-Hartley Act, 373–75
Taney, Roger Brooke, 61, 67, 70, 102, 114, 150, 187, 262, 268, 294–96, 315, **324–25,** 330
Taylor v. Louisiana (1975), 119
10th Amendment, 42, 67, 151–52, 238–40, **337–38**
terms of the Supreme Court, 187, 325–26, 381–84
Terry v. Ohio (1968), 260, 298, **326**
test cases, 327
Texas v. Johnson (1989), 137, 200, **327–28**
Texas v. White (1869), 68, 127, 240, **328**
3rd Amendment, 41, 110, 165
13th Amendment, 23, 68, 80, 117, 216, 250–52, 296
Thomas, Clarence, 20, 187, 223–24, **329–30,** 347
Thompson, Smith, 330
Thornburgh v. American College of Obstetricians and Gynecologists (1986), 259
time, place, and manner rule, 331
Tinker v. Des Moines Independent Community School District (1969), 38, 44, 133–34, 317, **331–32**

Tocqueville, Alexis de, 7
Todd, Thomas, 333
tort, 333
total incorporation doctrine, 44, 135, 335. *See also* incorporation doctrine
trial by jury, 113, 214, 279–84, **333–34**
Trimble, Robert, **334**
Trop v. *Dulles* (1958), 74, 101
Truman, Harry S., 59–60, 81, 172, 303, 373–75
12th Amendment, 22–23
20th Amendment, 24
21st Amendment, 23–24
22nd Amendment, 24
23rd Amendment, 23–24
24th Amendment, 24
25th Amendment, 24
26th Amendment, 277
27th Amendment, 24
Twining v. *New Jersey* (1908), 164, 224–25, **335**
Two Treatises of Government (Locke), 231

United States Reports, 9, 73, 196, 245, 275, 286, 321, **336**
United States v. *Butler* (1936), 313
United States v. *Cruikshank* (1876), 161
United States v. *Curtiss-Wright Export* Corp. (1936), **336–37**
United States v. *Darby Lumber Co.* (1941), 86, 152, **337–38**
United States v. *E. C. Knight Co.* (1895), 305, **338–40**
United States v. *Eichman* (1990), 327
United States v. *Grimaud*, 195
United States v. *Leon* (1984), 123, 204, 267, 283, 297–98, **340–41,** 366
United States v. *Lopez* (1995), 53
United States v. *Miller* (1939), 149
United States v. *Nixon* (1974), 59, 124, **341–42**
United States v. *O'Brien* (1968), 92, **342–43**
United States v. *Paradise* (1987), 19, 119
United States v. *Reese* (1876), 160
United States v. *Ross* (1982), 65, 95, 200, 297, **343–45**
United States v. *Schwimmer* (1929), 30–31
United States v. *United States District Court* (1972), 345–46
United States v. *Virginia* (1996), 346–47

United States v. *Wong Kim Ark* (1898), 74, 146, **347–48**
United Steelworkers of America v. *Weber* (1979), 19, 119, **348–49**
University of California, 264–66
U.S. District Courts, 130–31

Van Buren, Martin, 103, 215
Van Devanter, Willis, 99, **349–50**
Vanzetti, Bartolomeo, 63
Vernonia School District v. *Acton* (1995), 298, **350–52**
Vietnam War, 44, 134, 233, 237–38, 317, 331–32, 342–43
Vinson, Fred M., 70, 82, 106–7, 138, 194, 252, 323, **352,** 375
Virginia Military Institute (VMI), 346–47
Virginia Plan, 248
Volstead Act, 64–65
voting rights, 23, 32–34, 278–79, 307–8
Voting Rights Act (1965), 78, 308

Wagner Act. *See* National Labor Relations Act
Waite, Morrison R., 70, 160, 227–28, 273, 290, **352–53**
Wallace v. *Jaffree* (1985), 116, 121, 270, 312, 319, **353–54**
wall of separation, 269–74
Ward's Cove Packing Company v. *Atonio* (1989), 79, 277
Ware v. *Hylton* (1796), 68, 102, 175, 180–81, 248, **355**
Warren, Earl, 28, 34, 50, 56, 59, *69,* 70, 74, 97, 101, 110, 128, 134, 176, 221, 279, 283, 326, 343, **355–57**
Warren Court, *186*
Washington, Bushrod, 21, **357–58**
Washington, George, 17, 21, 24, 42, 71, 102, 114, 124, 126, 170, 173, 248, 287, 341, 357, 369
Washington Post, 237–38
Washington v. *Seattle School District* No. 1 (1982), 300
Washington v. *Texas* (1967), 166, 283
Watergate, 52, 146, 341–42
Wayne, James M., 358
Webster, Daniel, 35, 103
Webster v. *Reproductive Health Services* (1989), 13, 203, 286, **358–59**
Weddington, Sarah, 285
Weeks v. *United States* (1914), 123, 204, 243, 297, **359–60,** 370344
Weems v. *United States* (1910), 100–101

West Coast Hotel Co. v. *Parrish* (1937), 98, 112, 128, 202, 262, 291, 340, **360–61**
WESTLAW, 311, 336, **361**
West River Bridge Co. v. *Dix* (1848), 261
Westside Community Board of Education v. *Mergens* (1990), 361–63
West Virginia State Board of Education v. *Barnette* (1943), 91, 172, 176, 219, 272, 314, **364–65**
Wheaton, Henry, 276
White, Byron R., 13, 62, 143, 147–48, 154, 177, 235, 266, 286, 318, 340, 344, **365–66,** 377–78
White, Edward D., 70, 187, 239, 323, **366–67**
Whitney v. *California* (1927), 30, 48–49, 49–50, 138–39, **367–68**
Whittaker, Charles E., 368–69
Wickard v. *Filburn* (1942), 86
Williams, George, 268
Williams v. *Florida* (1970), 334
Wilson, James, 369
Wilson, Woodrow, 14, 48, 159
Wilson v. *Arkansas* (1995), 298
Wolcott, Alexander, 268
Wolf v. *Colorado* (1949), 166, 282, 294, 296, **369–70**
Wolman v. *Walter* (1977), 222
women in the federal judiciary, 370
women's rights, *21, 22, 28,* 119, *121,* 174–75, 263–64
Wong Kim Ark, United States v. (1898), 74, 146, 347–48
Wong Wing v. *United States* (1896), 305
Woodbury, Levi, **371**
Woods, William B., **371**
Wood v. *Georgia* (1962), 146
Worcester v. *Georgia* (1832), 330, **371–72**
worker compensation, 249

Yates v. *United States* (1957), 107, 137, 294, **372–73**
Youngstown Sheet & Tube Company v. *Sawyer* (1952), 303, **373–75**

Zobrest v. *Catalina School District* (1993), 20–21, 198, 272, 377
Zorach v. *Clauson* (1952), 270, **375–77**
Zurcher v. *The Stanford Daily* (1978), **377–78**

John J. Patrick is director of the Social Studies Development Center, professor of education, and director of the ERIC Clearinghouse for Social Studies/Social Science Education at Indiana University. He has also taught history, civics, and government at the secondary level. His many publications include *Founding the Republic, Constitutional Debates on Freedom of Religion, Lessons on the Constitution, Lessons on the Federalist Papers, How to Teach the Bill of Rights, James Madison and The Federalist Papers, Ideas of the Founders on Constitutional Government*, and the textbooks *American Political Behavior* and *History of the American Nation*. Professor Patrick was the chief consultant to the video series *The U.S. Constitution,* produced by the Agency for Instructional Technology, as well as for several other award-winning video series. He has served as a consultant to civic education programs in several post-communist countries, including Estonia, Latvia, Lithuania, and Poland.